Matthew Harris

SAMS

Teach Yourself

Microsoft® Excel 2000 Programming

in 21 Days

SAMS

A Division of Macmillan Computer Publishing
201 West 103rd St., Indianapolis, Indiana, 46290 USA

Sams Teach Yourself Microsoft® Excel 2000 Programming in 21 Days

Copyright © 1999 by Sams Publishing

International Standard Book Number: 0-672-31543-2

Library of Congress Catalog Card Number: 98-88583

Printed in the United States of America

First Printing: May 1999

01   00   99   4   3   2   1

Trademarks

Warning and Disclaimer

EXECUTIVE EDITOR
Chris Denny

ACQUISITIONS EDITOR
Chris Denny

DEVELOPMENT EDITOR
Anthony Amico

MANAGING EDITOR
Jodi Jensen

SENIOR EDITOR
Susan Ross Moore

COPY EDITOR
Heather Urschel

INDEXER
Kevin Kent

PROOFREADERS
Mona Brown
Jill Mazurczyk

TECHNICAL EDITOR
Per Blomqvist

SOFTWARE DEVELOPMENT SPECIALIST
Craig Atkins

INTERIOR DESIGN
Gary Adair

COVER DESIGN
Aren Howell

LAYOUT TECHNICIANS
Ayanna Lacey
Heather Miller
Amy Parker

Contents at a Glance

Contents

About the Author

Matthew Harris, a consultant living in Oakland, California, has been involved with the microcomputer industry since 1980. He has provided programming, technical support, training, and consulting services to the 1990 International AIDS Conference, the University of California at San Francisco, and many private companies, both large and small. A certified hardware technician, Mr. Harris began programming applications for IBM PCs and compatibles in 1983 and has written both commercially distributed applications and in-house applications for many clients. He also has taught classes on using MS-DOS and on programming in BASIC and Pascal. Mr. Harris is the author of *The Disk Compression Book* and the coauthor of *Using FileMaker Pro 2.0 for Windows* (both published by Que Corporation). Mr. Harris is a contributing author to *Using Word for Windows 6, Using Excel 5, Excel Professional Techniques, Using Paradox 4.5 for DOS, Using Paradox for Windows 5.0, The Paradox Developer's Guide, Using MS-DOS 6, Unveiling Windows 95,* and *Using Access 7 for Windows,* all published by Que Corporation. Mr. Harris is also a contributing author to *Database Developer's Guide With VB 4,* published by Sams Books. Mr. Harris can be reached via CompuServe at 74017,766 or through the Internet at 74017.766@compuserve.com.

Dedication

To Roger Jennings, who gave me a chance, way back when.

Acknowledgments

I would like to thank all of the individuals at Sams who worked on this book for their hard work and dedication to quality books. I'd like to give special thanks to Chris Denny for his help, and a big tip of the hat to Susan Moore, Heather Urschel, Tony Amico, and Per Blomqvist for helping me make this the best possible book.

Tell Us What You Think!

As the reader of this book, *you* are our most important critic and commentator. We value your opinion and want to know what we're doing right, what we could do better, what areas you'd like to see us publish in, and any other words of wisdom you're willing to pass our way.

As Associate Publisher for Que Corporation, I welcome your comments. You can fax, email, or write me directly to let me know what you did or didn't like about this book—as well as what we can do to make our books stronger.

Please note that I cannot help you with technical problems related to the topic of this book, and that due to the high volume of mail I receive, I might not be able to reply to every message.

When you write, please be sure to include this book's title and author as well as your name and phone or fax number. I will carefully review your comments and share them with the author and editors who worked on the book.

Fax: 317.581.4770

Email: office_sams@mcp.com

Mail: Robb Linsky, Associate Publisher
          Sams Publishing
          201 West 103rd Street
          Indianapolis, IN 46290 USA

Introduction

What's New in This Book?

While revising this book to cover the change from Excel 8 in Office 97 to Excel 9 in Microsoft Office 2000, I have seized every opportunity to improve and enhance the book:

- Enhancements based on reader feedback from the first through third editions are included throughout the book. As well as expanding various discussions, many tips and notes were added in response to reader comments or queries.

- All chapters and all program code examples are completely revised throughout to include new features of Microsoft Office 2000.

- Day 11, "Creating Your Own Data Types and Object Classes," is a new chapter devoted exclusively to creating custom object classes and data types. This new lesson also explains how to use custom object classes to enhance or alter the performance of VBA's and Excel's built-in objects.

- Day 13, "Managing Files With Visual Basic for Applications," has been expanded to include an explanation of how to use VBA's `Open`, `Write`, and `Read` statements to create and utilize custom data files.

- Day 20, "Working with Other Applications," was revised to describe the new ActiveX features in VBA, and to improve the lesson's discussion of Automation and OLE. Day 20 was also revised to explain how to send keystrokes to an application or use another application's procedures stored in a Dynamic Link Library (DLL). Sending keystrokes and using DLLs enables you to control applications that do not support Automation, or to make use of dialog boxes that can't be controlled with Automation or as ActiveX controls.

- The lesson in Day 21, "Using Event Procedures and Add-Ins," was revised to better explain how to create Excel Add-In programs, and to contain a better discussion of how to design an Excel Add-In program.

Conventions Used in This Book

This book uses different typefaces to differentiate between code and regular English, and also to help you identify important concepts.

Text that you type and text that should appear on your screen is presented in monospace type.

`It will look like this to mimic the way text looks on your screen.`

Placeholders for variables and expressions appear in *monospace italic* font. You should replace the placeholder with the specific value it represents.

This arrow (➥) at the beginning of a line of code means that a single line of code is too long to fit on the printed page. Continue typing all characters after the ➥ as though they were part of the preceding line.

Note

A Note presents interesting pieces of information related to the surrounding discussion.

Tip

A Tip offers advice or teaches an easier way to do something.

Caution

A Caution advises you about potential problems and helps you steer clear of disaster.

NEW TERM New Term icons provide clear definitions of new, essential terms. The term appears in italic.

INPUT The Input icon identifies code that you can type in yourself. It usually appears next to a listing.

OUTPUT The Output icon highlights the output produced by running a program. It usually appears after a listing.

ANALYSIS The Analysis icon alerts you to the author's line-by-line analysis of a program.

Do/Don't boxes offer advice on what to do or not to do in certain situations. They look like this:

Do

DO brush after every meal.

DON'T

DON'T take candy from strangers.

WEEK 1

At a Glance

As you get ready for your first week of learning how to program in Visual Basic for Applications, you need only two things: this book and a copy of Excel 2000. If you don't have Excel 2000, you can still use this book, although its value to you will be somewhat limited. (In a pinch, you can use Excel 95 or Excel 97.) It is difficult to learn a programming language well by just reading a book. The best way to learn Visual Basic for Applications is to actually record and edit macros and to enter and run your own procedures written from scratch as you simultaneously work your way through the lessons in this book. The examples and exercises in this book offer you the hands-on experience you need to master Visual Basic for Applications programming. You'll also gain many skills that you'll be able to apply to VBA programming in Microsoft Access, Microsoft Word, Microsoft Outlook or any other application included in Microsoft Office 2000 (Professional or Standard editions).

This book is arranged so that each day ends with several quiz questions and some exercises. At the end of each lesson, you should be able to answer all the quiz questions and complete all the exercises. Appendix A, "Answers," includes answers to all the quiz questions and solutions to most of the exercises. In the exercise solutions for most of the early lessons, you'll find additional programming explanations and tips related to the specific exercise solution.

1

2

3

4

5

6

7

Make every attempt to complete every exercise; this book uses several of the program solutions for exercises in early chapters as the basis for additional exercises, examples, or explanations in later chapters. For example, Day 2 makes use of a macro that you create while performing Exercise 1 from Day 1.

What's Ahead?

The first week covers basic material that you need to know to get started recording, editing, and writing Visual Basic for Applications (VBA) program code. The lessons in the first week also explain how to create user-defined functions for your Excel worksheets.

In Day 1, "Getting Started," and Day 2, "Writing and Editing Simple Macros," you learn how to record and edit a VBA macro, how to recognize the basic elements of a VBA procedure, and how to get started writing your own VBA macros without recording. These two chapters also introduce you to some of the features of VBA's Object Browser, an important tool for VBA programming. Day 2 also shows you how to make your macros display simple messages onscreen.

In Day 3, "Understanding Data Types, Variables, and Constants," you learn how to use variables to store data temporarily in your VBA macros and procedures. You also learn about the different types of data that VBA can store and manipulate, and how to use constants to simplify the way you include unchanging values in your VBA statements. Day 3 also describes how to get input from your VBA macro's user. In Day 4, "Operators and Expressions," you learn how to incorporate variables and constants into expressions that calculate new values.

Day 5, "Visual Basic and Excel Functions," explains all about the various functions VBA provides. You learn what a function is and how to use function results in your expressions. VBA functions enable you to convert values from one data type to another, to get information about VBA, and to perform mathematical computations and various other tasks. Day 5 also shows you how to utilize the built-in functions of Excel in VBA and, finally, how to use Excel's built-in worksheet functions.

In Day 6, "Creating and Using VBA Function Procedures and Excel User-Defined Functions," you learn how to create your own custom functions for use in your VBA macros and procedures and how to create and use custom functions for your Excel worksheets.

The first week's lessons end with Day 7, "Understanding Objects and Collections." Day 7 teaches you what program objects are and how to recognize and understand various object references that you'll see in the macros you record. This lesson teaches you about object properties and methods and explains how to retrieve or change the values of an object's property or how to use an object's methods.

This is a lot of material to cover in just one week, but if you take the information one chapter a day, you should have no problems.

WEEK 1

DAY 1

Getting Started

Welcome to *Sams Teach Yourself Excel 2000 Programming in 21 Days*. In this lesson for the first day, you learn:

- What macros are and how they are used.
- How Visual Basic for Applications relates to and enhances macros.
- Why you need to add Visual Basic for Applications program commands to recorded macros, and why you should use Visual Basic for Applications to program macros without recording.
- How to record and run a macro.

Macros and Programming Languages

Before you start writing your own macros, you should have a good understanding of what a macro is and how a Visual Basic for Applications (VBA) programmed macro differs from a recorded macro.

What Is a Macro?

Eventually—regardless of the operating system or software applications you use—you'll notice that you execute the same sequences of commands over and over in order to accomplish routine tasks. Rather than repeat the command sequence every time you want to perform a task, you can create a *macro* to make an application execute the sequence of commands on its own. Macros enable you to enter a single command that accomplishes the same task that would otherwise require you to enter several commands manually.

Note

> Recorded command sequences were originally called *macro-commands*; modern usage has shortened the term to the simpler *macro*. (The term *macro* is found as a prefix for several words in the English language; it is derived from the Greek word meaning *enlarged* or *elongated*.) In the context of computers and application software, *macro* is always understood to mean a macro command.

Macros provide benefits other than convenience. Because computers are much better suited to performing repetitive tasks than human beings, recording repeated sequences of commands in a macro increases the accuracy of the work you perform, as well as the speed. After you record the correct series of commands, you can count on the computer to repeat the sequence flawlessly each time it executes the macro. Another benefit from using macros is that a human operator is not usually needed while a macro executes. If the macro is particularly long, or performs operations that require substantial computer processing time (such as database queries and sorts), you are free to leave the computer and do something else, or to switch to a different application and continue working on some other task.

A macro recorder records *all* the user's actions—including mistakes and false starts. When an application program (such as Excel) plays back a macro, it performs each recorded command in the exact sequence you originally performed them. Early macro recorders had a serious drawback: If you recorded a lengthy series of actions that contained a minor mistake, the only way to remove the mistake was to record the macro all over again. Also, if you needed to make a minor change in a long macro, you had to

1

re-record the entire macro. Often, re-recording a long macro simply led to additional mistakes in the new recording. For these reasons, software developers added the capability to edit macros to their macro recorders, so you could more easily correct minor mistakes or make other changes in a macro without re-recording it entirely.

> **Note**
>
> Not every application contains a macro recorder. Microsoft Access, for example, uses a *macro builder* instead of a macro recorder like the one found in Microsoft Excel or Microsoft Word. In Access' macro builder, instead of having the application record actions as you perform them, you select the actions you want the macro to carry out from a predefined list of commands.

A Brief History of Visual Basic for Applications

Visual Basic for Applications (VBA), although still a relatively new product, comes from a background with a history almost as long as that of the entire computer industry. Visual Basic for Applications is a modern dialect of the BASIC programming language that was first developed in the early 1960s. (BASIC is an acronym for Beginner's All-Purpose Symbolic Instruction Code.)

Although, by today's standards, the original BASIC programming language was severely limited, it was easy to learn and understand, and rapidly became very widespread. Versions of BASIC were (and still are) produced for use on all types of computers. Microsoft's GWBASIC (GW stands for Graphics Workshop) was one of the first programming languages available for the computers that evolved into the modern-day personal computer. GWBASIC was supplied with MS-DOS versions prior to Version 5.0. Early PC computers manufactured by IBM even contained a version of BASIC built into the computer's ROM (Read-Only Memory) chips.

Over the years, the original design and specifications for BASIC have been improved. As the technology for programming languages advanced and changed, various software publishers added to the capabilities of the original BASIC. Modern dialects of BASIC usually have many or all the features found in other programming languages of more recent origin, such as Pascal, C, or C++.

In the late 1980s, Microsoft published a tremendously enhanced version of the BASIC language, called QuickBASIC. QuickBASIC incorporated almost all the features found in state-of-the-art software development systems of the day. Microsoft now includes a version of QuickBASIC with DOS Versions 6.0 and higher (but not in Windows 95).

After several versions of QuickBASIC, in 1992 Microsoft introduced Visual Basic for Windows. As with QuickBASIC, Visual Basic for Windows added state-of-the-art features, and was closely integrated with the Windows environment. Visual Basic provides commands for creating and controlling the necessary elements of a Windows program: dialog boxes, menu bars, drop-down lists, command buttons, check boxes, toolbars, and so on. In particular, Visual Basic incorporates the necessary commands to use Object Linking and Embedding (OLE) to communicate or share data with other Windows applications. Current versions of Visual Basic for Windows include support for ActiveX controls and Automation, which provides the means to control other applications from your Visual Basic code. Visual Basic is essentially a new programming language for Windows, with its roots in BASIC.

At the same time BASIC was evolving and improving, so were the macro recorders used in applications programs. Over the years, application macros gradually became more complex and sophisticated in response to users' desires to make macros more flexible in function and easier to maintain. Many macro languages began to include capabilities similar to those usually found only in complete programming languages.

Many applications' macro languages differ greatly from product to product, however. This means you might need to learn several different macro languages; as a result, you might experience a loss in productivity while you learn the new macro language. To eliminate the need to learn a new macro language for each product, Microsoft began to incorporate elements of the BASIC programming language in the macro languages of its products. As an example, the macro language for Microsoft's Word for Windows (prior to Word 97) was known as WordBASIC, whereas the programming language for Microsoft Access 2.0 was known as Access Basic.

To unify the macro languages in its Windows applications, and to integrate those applications' macro languages with Windows' OLE and Automation capabilities, Microsoft has created a special version of the Visual Basic language, called Visual Basic for Applications (abbreviated VBA). Excel 5 was the first released product to include Visual Basic for Applications (VBA). With the release of Microsoft Office 97, VBA was implemented in Microsoft Word, Access, Excel, PowerPoint, and Outlook.

Visual Basic for Applications is essentially the same as Visual Basic for Windows, with some slight, but significant, differences. VBA macro programs are stored in a file format used by the application you wrote the Visual Basic for Applications macro in, rather than individual text files. For example, VBA macro programs created in Excel are stored in an Excel workbook file, VBA programs created in Word are stored in a document file, and VBA programs in Access are stored in an Access database file.

1

To run a Visual Basic for Applications macro program, you must start it by using the application you wrote the macro in. For example, you cannot start an Excel VBA macro from any program other than Excel—although another application could use Automation to cause Excel to execute a particular macro. Although the core features of VBA remain the same in each application, each different application adds special commands and objects (depending on the specific application) to Visual Basic for Applications. For example, VBA in Excel contains many commands that pertain only to worksheets and the tasks that you can perform with a worksheet. Similarly, VBA in Word contains commands that pertain only to manipulating the text in a document, whereas VBA in Access contains commands that pertain only to database manipulation, and so on.

Note

Each application that includes Visual Basic for Applications is called a VBA *host application*. Because each host application (Excel, Word, Access, and so on) adds features to VBA that pertain only to that host application, there are several distinct "flavors" of VBA. When referring to VBA features specific to a particular host application, this book uses the terms *Excel VBA*, *Word VBA*, *Access VBA*, and so on to distinguish the particular implementation of Visual Basic for Applications under discussion. This book uses the single term *VBA* when describing features common to Visual Basic for Applications in all host applications.

By having only one macro programming language in all its products, Microsoft ensures that a great deal of what you learn about Visual Basic for Applications in one application applies to using VBA in another application. In fact, Visual Basic 4 (and higher) also supports VBA, so you can easily convert any programs you write in VBA to a complete Visual Basic program.

Why Learn Visual Basic for Applications?

Because you can use the macro recorder in Excel to record your actions in a macro and then later play them back, it might at first seem unnecessary to learn VBA. Recorded macros alone, however, cannot always fill your needs. A recorded macro can only play back each action you perform, in the same sequence you originally performed the actions, without deviation. You can use Visual Basic for Applications to enhance your recorded macros, greatly increasing their flexibility and power.

Recorded macros are inflexible, so they cannot respond to changed or changing conditions. You can create a macro programmed in VBA, however, that will evaluate various

predetermined conditions and choose a different series of actions based on those conditions. If you execute an Excel macro, for example, that attempts to select a worksheet
named Sales Chart when there is no such worksheet in the current workbook, your
recorded macro will fail to execute correctly, and Excel will display an error message
dialog. By adding VBA programming to this recorded macro, you could make it first test
for the existence of the specified worksheet before selecting it, or even insert and rename
a new worksheet if the desired worksheet does not exist.

Note

> If you have experience with Microsoft Access, using Access' Macro Builder
> might seem a bit like programming, but it isn't. The Access Macro Builder
> only allows you to select actions from a predefined list. The macros you cre-
> ate with the Access Macro Builder have many of the same limitations that
> recorded macros have—they lack the flexibility of VBA's decision-making
> commands and the capability to repeat actions efficiently.

When it comes to repetitive actions within the macro itself, recorded macros are rather
limited. If you want a recorded macro to repeat an action several times, you must manually repeat that action the desired number of times when you record the macro. The
macro then always repeats the action the same number of times, every time you execute
the macro, until you edit the macro or re-record it. In contrast, a macro programmed in
VBA can use predetermined conditions—or input from the macro's user—to repeat an
action for a flexible number of times, or to choose whether the action should be performed at all.

As an example, you might want to record a macro to change the width of several adjacent columns in an Excel worksheet. If you want the macro to change the width of the
first three columns in the worksheet, you must manually repeat the resizing operation for
each of the three columns as you record the macro. The recorded macro only (and
always) changes the width of the first three columns of a worksheet—you cannot use the
same macro to change the width of two columns or four columns. Also, if you changed
the width of the first three columns, your recorded macro only operates on the first three
columns—you cannot use the same macro to change the width of the second through
fourth columns rather than the first through third. By adding Visual Basic for
Applications programming to this recorded macro, you can create a macro that asks you
how many, and which, columns to resize, and even enables you to specify the new column width.

These two examples represent a couple of the simplest tasks that you can perform with
VBA in your macros. There are many circumstances under which you will want to add

decision making and efficient repetition to recorded macros. The only way to get these features is to manually add VBA program statements to your recorded macro.

In addition to enhancing specific recorded macros, you can also use VBA to connect, organize, and control several recorded macros that you use to perform a complex overall task made up of several smaller tasks. For example, you might regularly import data from a database program into an Excel worksheet, format the data for display, generate a chart from the data, and then print the chart and formatted report.

To pull all these individual tasks together to create a single task performed by a single macro, you might first record a separate macro for each of the individual tasks—a macro to import the data, another macro to format the data for display, another macro to create the chart, and yet another macro to print the data. Next, you would organize the recorded macros so that they are executed in the proper sequence by a single macro that you write with VBA.

You can also use Visual Basic for Applications to control the execution of other applications (by using Automation) and to automate the sharing of data between applications (by using OLE), as explained in Day 20, "Working with Other Applications."

Recording A New Macro

Before you can enhance a macro with Visual Basic for Applications, you must first record a macro to enhance. This section shows what you need to know, in general, to record a macro. A later section, "Putting it Together: Recording Your First Macro," takes you through a step-by-step example of recording a macro in Excel 2000.

Typically, recording a macro involves four major steps:

1. *Set up the starting conditions for the macro.* Setting up the starting conditions for a macro means establishing the same conditions in your work environment that you expect to exist at the time you play back the recorded macro.

2. *Start the macro recorder and name the macro.* At the same time you start the macro recorder, you must give your macro a name and select where the recorded macro is to be stored. When starting the macro recorder in Excel 2000, you might optionally choose to assign a shortcut key command to run the macro.

3. *Perform the actions that you want recorded for later use.* You can record into a macro any action that you can perform by using the keyboard or mouse, including executing previously recorded macros. The specific actions that you perform depend on the task that you want to record.

4. *Stop the macro recorder.* When you stop the macro recorder, your actions are no longer recorded and stored in the macro. After you stop the macro recorder, the new recorded macro is immediately available for use.

> **Note**
>
> This book concentrates exclusively on operations in Excel 2000 for two reasons. First, Excel is typically one of the most frequently used applications in the Microsoft Office application suite. (The standard edition of Microsoft Office does not contain Access; only the MS Office Premium edition includes Access.) Second, Excel is one of the two Microsoft Office products that contain a macro recorder (MS Word is the only other Office application with a macro recorder). Using the macro recorder as a springboard to VBA programming makes learning VBA much easier.

The following sections describe the first two general steps for recording a macro in greater detail.

Setting Up a Macro's Starting Conditions

Before recording any macro, you must set up the conditions under which you will later run the macro. (*Running* or *executing* a macro means playing back the recorded instructions in the macro.) Suppose, for example, you want to create a macro that applies a particular font, font size, and font color to any selected cells in an Excel worksheet. The starting conditions for this macro would be an open worksheet with a selected cell or range of cells.

You need to set up starting conditions for a macro before you start the Macro Recorder because the Macro Recorder records *all* the actions you perform. If you start the Macro Recorder and then open a workbook, display a worksheet, and then select cells, those actions become part of the resulting recorded macro. Your completed macro is then overly specific: it always opens the same workbook and formats the same cells on the same worksheet. To create a general-purpose, text-formatting macro that you can use for *any* selected cell or range of cells, you should start the Macro Recorder *after* opening a workbook, selecting a worksheet, and selecting the cells you want to format.

After you have established the starting conditions for your macro, you're ready to start the Macro Recorder.

Starting the Macro Recorder and Selecting Options

To start recording a macro in Excel 2000, choose the Tools, Macro, Record New Macro command. Excel displays the Record Macro dialog. You use the Record Macro dialog to

1

give your new macro a name, and to select where you want Excel to store the new macro. You must specify a name for the macro and a location to store the macro in before you can actually begin recording a macro. Excel's Record Macro dialog also enables you to optionally assign a shortcut key to run the new macro. You will learn more about this option in the specific step-by-step instructions in the next section.

Note
> Macro names must begin with a letter, although they can contain numbers. Macro names cannot include spaces or punctuation characters. In Excel, you may enter a macro name up to 63 characters in length.

Excel's Record Macro dialog contains the following four controls (the actual dialog box is shown in Figure 1.2):

- *Macro Name text box.* The first Record Macro dialog option to fill in is the Macro Name. By default, VBA selects a macro name consisting of the word Macro followed by a number corresponding to the number of macros you've recorded in this work session. You should enter a name for the macro that conveys some meaning about what the macro does. For example, if you record a macro to generate a chart from sales data in a worksheet, you might enter the name **MakeSalesChart** in the Macro Name text box.

- *Shortcut key text box.* Use this text box to optionally assign a shortcut keystroke to execute your new macro. Enter the letter or symbol of the keyboard key you want to use as the shortcut command into this text box. Use this option only if you're certain that you'll use the macro you are about to record with great frequency. All Excel macro shortcut keys are the combination of the keystroke you enter plus the Ctrl key—if you type **a** in the Shortcut key text box, the actual shortcut keystroke is Ctrl+a. If you type **A** as the shortcut key, the resulting shortcut keystroke is Ctrl+Shift+A.

- *Store Macro In drop-down list.* This drop-down list lets you choose where the recorded macro should be stored. The available choices are: Personal Macro Workbook, New Workbook, and This Workbook. If you choose Personal Macro Workbook, Excel stores the new recorded macro in a special workbook, named Personal.xls, that is automatically loaded whenever Excel starts. Use the Personal Macro Workbook choice if you want your new macro to be available at all times. If you choose This Workbook, Excel stores the new recorded macro in the currently active workbook. Use the This Workbook choice if you want your new macro to be available only when the current workbook is open. Choose New Workbook to cause Excel to create a new workbook in which to store the macro—the workbook that was active when you started the macro recorder remains the active workbook; any actions you record are performed in that workbook and not in the new workbook created to store the macro. Regardless of which workbook you choose to store the new recorded macro in, the macro is attached to the workbook as a VBA *module*. Modules are described in more detail in the next lesson.

- *Description text box*. The information in the Description text box isn't directly used by the macro. The Description text box is just a place to keep some notes and comments about what the macro does. When you record a macro, VBA fills in a default description stating the date that the macro was recorded and by which user. (VBA obtains the user name from the User Name text box in the Options dialog; this text box is found on the General tab in Excel. You can display the Options dialog by choosing the Tools, Options command.) Each time you record a macro, you should add comments about what the macro does, and what its purpose is.

Do

DO use a meaningful name for your recorded macro, one that reflects the action the macro carries out. A name such as `MakeSalesChart` or `FormatArialBold12` communicates much more than default names such as `Macro1`.

DO be sure to enter any special prerequisites for the macro in the Description text box, such as whether or not a particular workbook should be open, or whether a particular worksheet or cell must be selected before using the macro.

Putting It Together: Recording Your First Macro

As a specific example, let's assume that you frequently apply a 12-point bold Arial font as the character formatting style for worksheet cells you want to draw attention to, without changing any other part of the cells' formatting. You can't use an Excel named style (accessed through the Format, Style menu command) to apply the desired character formatting because you'd affect *all* the cells' attributes (such as date or currency formatting), not just the character format. Instead, you must set the font attributes manually each time.

Selecting the Arial font, adjusting the font size, and applying the bold attribute to the text involves several mouse or keyboard operations. To reduce the amount of time required to format the text, you decide to record a macro that selects the 12-point bold Arial font and applies that character formatting to whatever cell or range of cells is currently selected.

The remainder of this section takes you step-by-step through the process of recording a new macro to apply the desired font characteristics.

Set Up the Starting Conditions

Because you want this macro to work on any selected cell or range of cells, the starting conditions for this macro are an open workbook with a selected range of cells on the active worksheet. To set up the starting conditions for this specific example in Excel, follow these steps:

1. Start Excel 2000, if it isn't already running.

2. Open any workbook.

3. Select any worksheet.

4. Select any cell on the worksheet. Figure 1.1 shows a sample workbook open with a single cell selected.

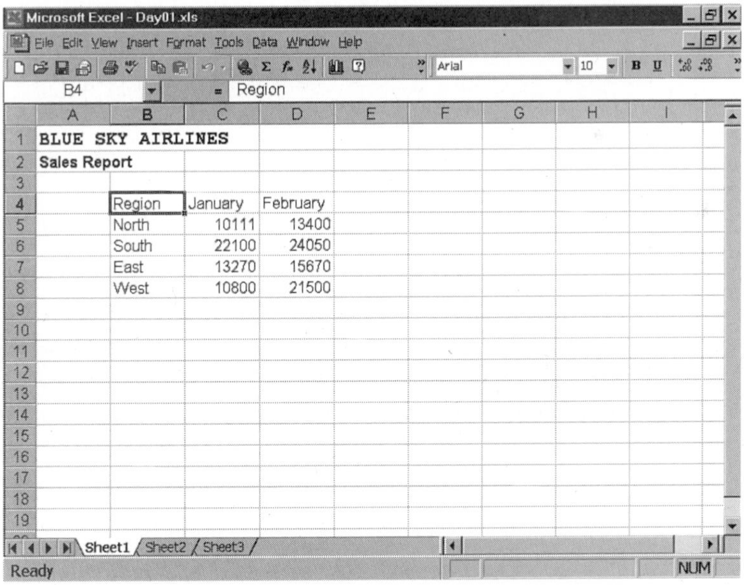

FIGURE 1.1

Set up the starting conditions for the Excel text formatting macro before starting the Macro Recorder.

By selecting a cell in an open worksheet, you have created the necessary starting conditions to record this general-purpose macro for applying character formatting to any selected cell or range of cells in an Excel worksheet.

Name the Macro and Select a Storage Location

Now you are ready to start the Excel Macro Recorder, name the macro, choose a location to store the new macro, and select additional options. Follow these steps:

1. Choose the Tools, Macro, Record New Macro command. Excel displays the Record Macro dialog shown in Figure 1.2.

FIGURE 1.2

The Excel Record Macro dialog.

2. In the Macro Name text box, type **FormatArialBold12** as the name of the macro. This name helps you remember what this macro does.

3. Leave the default description entered in the Description text box, but type the following text as an addition to the existing description: **Format cell text with Arial bold 12-point font**. This additional descriptive comment helps you (and others) determine what the macro's purpose is.

4. Use the Store Macro In drop-down list to select a location in which to store the recorded macro. Because you want this macro to be available in any work session, choose **Personal Macro Workbook**.

5. If you're certain that you'll use the macro you are about to record with great frequency, you might want to assign a shortcut key to run the macro. If so, type the shortcut key that you want to use to run your macro in the Shortcut Key text box of the Record Macro dialog.

6. Click the OK button to start recording your macro.

Figure 1.3 shows the Record Macro dialog filled in for the FormatArialBold12 example macro.

Note

When you select the Personal Macro Workbook as the location in which to store your new macro, Excel stores the macro in a special workbook file named Personal.xls in the startup folder. Excel automatically opens workbook files stored in its startup folder each time you start Excel. Because macros in any open workbook are available for use, storing a macro in the Personal.xls workbook causes it to be available in any Excel work session. When you select Personal Macro Workbook as the storage location for your new macro, Excel creates the Personal.xls workbook file if it doesn't already exist. (If you installed Excel or Microsoft Office 2000 using the default folders, Excel's startup folder is \Program Files\Microsoft Office\Office\Xlstart.)

You might not notice that the Personal.xls workbook is open because, by default, Excel hides the Personal.xls workbook file after creating it. (Refer to Excel's online help for information on hiding and unhiding workbook files.)

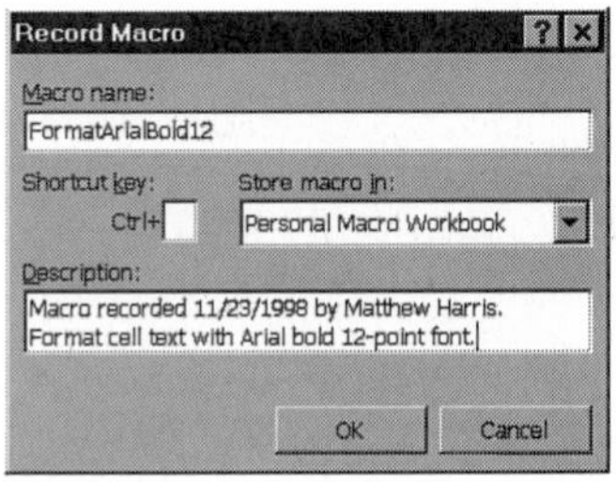

FIGURE 1.3

The completed Record Macro dialog for the sample FormatArialBold12 *macro.*

Do

DO store general-purpose Excel macros in the Personal.xls workbook.

DO store macros that relate specifically to a single workbook in the workbook to which the macro relates.

DO remember that Excel macro shortcut keys are the combination of the keystroke you enter plus the Ctrl key—if you type **a** in the Shortcut Key text box, the actual shortcut keystroke is Ctrl+a. If you type **A** as the shortcut key, the resulting shortcut keystroke is Ctrl+Shift+A.

DON'T

DON'T assign a shortcut key to a macro unless you really do expect to use the macro with great frequency—if you assign shortcut keys to all your Excel macros, you'll quickly run out of unassigned keys.

Record Your Actions

As soon as you click the OK button in the Record Macro dialog, Excel starts the Macro Recorder, displays the Stop Recorder toolbar, and begins recording your actions. Excel's Macro Recorder stores each action you perform in the new macro until you stop the Macro Recorder.

Figure 1.4 shows Excel's Stop Recorder toolbar displayed during a macro recording session. (The macro being recorded in Figure 1.4 is the `FormatArialBold12` example macro.) Notice that the word *Recording* appears in the status bar at the bottom left side of the Excel window to help remind you that Excel is recording all your actions.

FIGURE 1.4

Excel displays the Stop Recorder toolbar and the word Recording *in the status bar while you record a macro.*

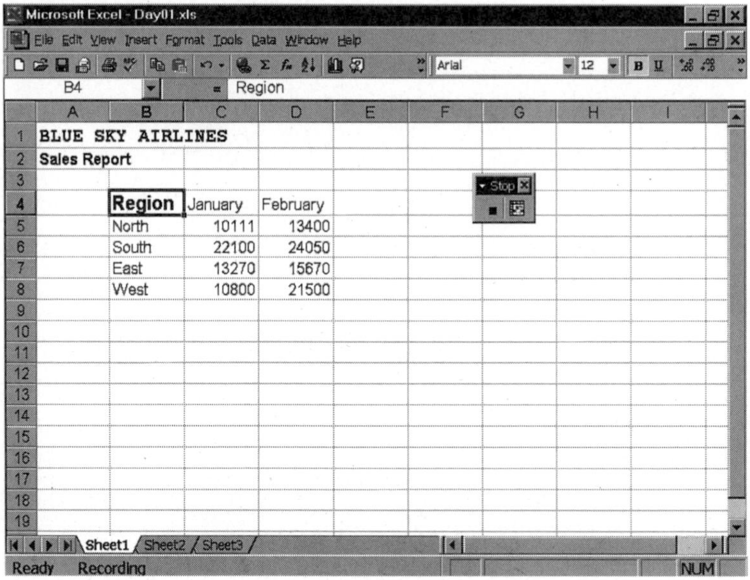

By default, Excel's Stop Recorder toolbar contains two command buttons (refer to Figure 1.4). The left button is the Stop button; click this button to stop the Macro Recorder. The right button is the Relative Reference button. By default, Excel records absolute cell references in your macros. If you start recording with cell B4 selected, for example, and then select the cell to the right of B4—that is, cell C4—your recorded macro also selects cell C4 each and every time it runs.

If you click the Relative Reference button, however, Excel records a relative cell reference each time you select a cell. If the currently selected cell is B4, and you select the cell to its right while recording with relative references, Excel records that you selected a cell 1 column and 0 rows to the right of the current cell. When you run the recorded macro, it selects whatever cell is immediately to the right of the active cell.

The Relative Reference button is a *toggle* button—that is, it turns relative reference recording on and off. When relative reference recording is off, the Relative Reference button has a flat appearance; moving the mouse pointer over the button causes it to change to a raised appearance (the button's "up" position). When relative reference recording is on, the Relative Reference button on the Stop Recorder toolbar has a sunken appearance (it is in its "down" position). Clicking the Relative Reference button alternates between turning relative reference recording on (the button is down) and off (the button is up). You can turn relative reference recording on and off as you want during recording.

To complete the `FormatArialBold12` macro, perform these actions:

1. Choose the Format, Cells command to display the Format Cells dialog.
2. Click the Font tab to display the Font options, if necessary. (Figure 1.5 shows the Format Cells dialog with the Font options displayed.)

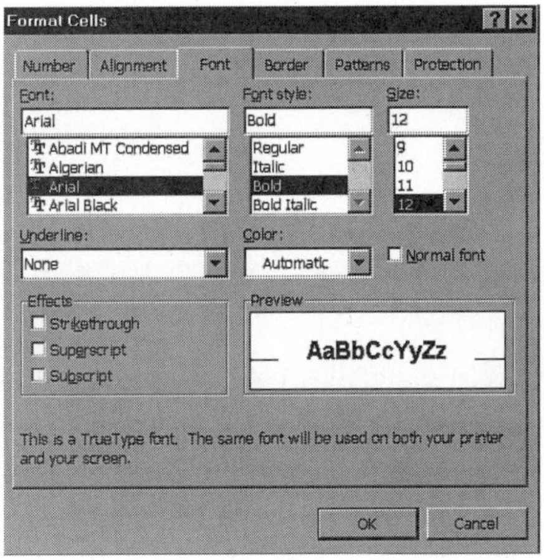

FIGURE 1.5

Excel's Format Cells dialog, showing the Font options filled in for the `FormatArialBold12` *macro.*

3. Select **Arial** in the Font list. (Perform this step even if the Arial font is already selected.)
4. Select **Bold** in the Font Style list.

5. Select **12** in the Size list.

6. Choose OK to close the Format Cells dialog and apply the changes to the selected cell in the worksheet.

> **Tip**
>
> You might also select the font, font size, and font style by using Excel's Formatting toolbar—be sure to select each option, though, even if it is already selected, or Excel won't record the corresponding action.

Stop the Macro Recorder

When you have completed the series of actions that you want to record, you should immediately stop Excel's Macro Recorder. To stop the Macro Recorder, click the Stop Macro button on the Stop Recorder toolbar (or choose the Tools, Macro, Stop Recording command).

For the `FormatArialBold12` example macro, you should stop the Macro Recorder immediately after you choose OK to close the Format Cells dialog. Your new Excel macro is now complete and ready to run. You'll learn how to run your new macro later in this lesson.

Do

DO remember to stop the macro recorder as soon as you complete the series of actions you want to record; the recorder continues to record all your actions until you stop it.

DON'T

DON'T forget that Excel stores the completed macro in the location you chose in the Record Macro dialog.

Macro Source Code

When you record a macro in Excel, the Macro Recorder stores a series of text instructions that describe, in the Visual Basic for Applications programming language, the various actions you perform while the recorder is on. This text description of your commands is called the *source code* for the macro. Later, when you run the macro, VBA reads the recorded instructions in the source code and executes each instruction in sequence, thereby duplicating the actions that you performed when you recorded the macro.

The following lines list the source code produced when you recorded the FormatArialBold12 macro. Notice that the name and the description of the macro that you entered in the Record Macro dialog is included at the beginning of the recorded macro source code.

```
Sub FormatArialBold12()
'
' FormatArialBold12 Macro
' Macro recorded 11/23/1998 by Matthew Harris.  Format cell text with
' Arial bold 12-point font.
'
    With Selection.Font
        .Name = "Arial"
        .FontStyle = "Bold"
        .Size = 12
        .Strikethrough = False
        .Superscript = False
        .Subscript = False
        .OutlineFont = False
        .Shadow = False
        .Underline = xlUnderlineStyleNone
        .ColorIndex = xlAutomatic
    End With
End Sub
```

Don't be dismayed if this source code listing doesn't make a lot of sense to you right now. You can record and execute macros without ever looking at the macro's source code, or even knowing what it does. The next lesson explains the various parts of a macro and also explains how to locate the source code for a particular macro and display it for editing or inspection.

Note

If you performed any actions other than those specified in the preceding numbered steps, your recorded Excel macro will contain additional statements corresponding to your additional actions. If you used Excel's Formatting toolbar to change the font formatting, your macro will be much longer than the one shown here.

Running Macros

After you have recorded a macro, you can run the macro. Running the macro causes Excel to carry out all the instructions recorded in the macro.

In Excel, you run a macro by choosing the Tools, Macro, Macros command. Excel displays the Macro dialog shown in Figure 1.6. Select the macro you want to run in the Macro Name list, and then click the Run button to execute that macro. (Other buttons in the Macro dialog are described in following lessons.)

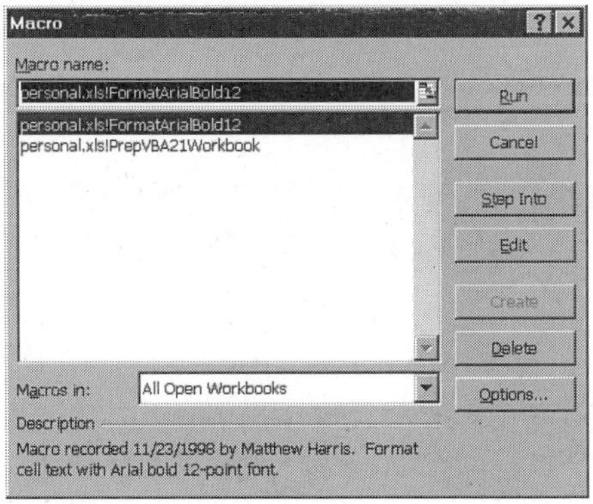

FIGURE 1.6

Use Excel's Macro dialog to select a macro to run. Only the macros available in open workbooks are listed.

For example, to run the `FormatArialBold12` Excel macro you just recorded, first select a cell in a worksheet (preferably one that contains some text, so you can see the changes). Next, choose the Tools, Macro, Macros command to display the Macro dialog, and then select the `PERSONAL.XLS!FormatArialBold12` macro in the Macro Name list. Finally, choose the Run button to execute the `FormatArialBold12` macro. The text in whatever cell was selected when you ran the `FormatArialBold12` macro has its formatting changed to 12-point bold Arial font.

The Macro dialog in Excel lists the macros stored in any workbooks that are currently open, including workbooks that are open but hidden (refer to Fig. 1.6). The name of the workbook that contains the macro is listed in front of the macro name in the Macro Name list if the macro is not in the current workbook (as with the `PERSONAL.XLS!FormatArialBold12` macro). If the macro you want isn't listed, you must open the workbook in which the macro is stored to make the macro available before you open the Macro dialog.

If you assigned a shortcut key in Excel's Record Macro dialog, you can run that specific macro by pressing the assigned shortcut-key combination. As with the macros listed in Excel's Macro dialog, only macros stored in a currently open workbook (it doesn't have to be the active workbook) have their shortcut keys activated.

 Note

> Excel macros are available only if the workbook in which the macro is stored is currently open. The workbook doesn't have to be the active workbook in order for its macros to be available, nor does the workbook have to be visible.

As you might already know, you can also run macros in Excel by assigning them to custom toolbar buttons and by creating custom menu choices for the macros. You can also assign a macro to a button or graphic object placed directly into an Excel worksheet. Day 17, "Menus and Toolbars," describes how to assign a macro to a toolbar button, menu command, or graphic object in a worksheet from a programmer's point of view. Refer to Excel's online help system for more information about using interactive features to assign macros to menus, toolbar buttons, and graphic objects in worksheets.

Summary

Today you learned about the history of the Visual Basic for Applications programming language, and you learned how macro languages gradually became complex enough to be considered programming languages. Microsoft has greatly increased the power and convenience of the macro languages in its products by making Visual Basic the macro-programming language of the Office 2000 products. Adding Visual Basic decision-making and looping structures to recorded macros increases their power. By using Visual Basic for Applications, you can create macro programs to suit a wide variety of needs.

In this lesson, you learned how to record an Excel macro and how to run a macro that you have recorded. These are the most basic skills you need to get started with VBA. Many of the macros that you use your VBA programming skills on will begin with a macro that you recorded. The next lesson teaches you how to edit a recorded macro.

Q&A

Q What is a VBA host application?

A A VBA *host application* is any application that contains Visual Basic for Applications. Microsoft's Word, Excel, Access, Outlook, and Project are all VBA host applications.

Q Do all VBA host applications have a macro recorder?

A No. Microsoft's Access, for example, doesn't have a macro recorder.

Q Is recording a macro the only way to create an Excel macro?

A No. You can also create a macro by writing source code directly in a VBA module. The next lesson describes how to create a macro without recording.

Q When recording an Excel macro, do I have to leave the Stop Recorder toolbar on the screen?

A No. If you want, click the top right corner of the Stop Recorder toolbar to close it, or use the View, Toolbars command to hide the Stop Recorder toolbar. When you are ready to stop recording the macro, use the Tools, Macro, Stop Recording command.

Q Can I give a macro a different name after I have recorded it?

A Yes, although you can only rename a macro by editing the macro source code directly, as described in the next lesson. Renaming a macro, however, might cause some minor problems. If your macro is assigned to menu commands, a shortcut key, or to buttons or graphic objects, these custom controls will still try to run the macro using its old name. If you rename a macro, you will have to reassign each custom control and menu to the new macro name. For this reason, it is much better to spend a little time carefully choosing a macro's name, rather than count on renaming the macro later.

Q Can I assign an Excel macro to shortcut key after I record it?

A Yes. Use Excel's Macro dialog to assign a shortcut key to a macro. Choose the Tools, Macro, Macros command to open the Macro dialog. Next, select the macro you want to assign a shortcut key to in the Macro Name list, and then click the Options button to display Excel's Macro Options dialog. Type the shortcut key you want for your macro, and then click OK. To add an Excel macro to a toolbar, choose the Tools, Customize command to display the Customize dialog. Use the Customize dialog to add a macro to an Excel toolbar

Q Can I assign an Excel macro to a menu or toolbar?

A Yes. To add an Excel macro to a toolbar, choose the Tools, Customize command to display the Customize dialog. Next, use the Toolbars tab of the Customize dialog to display the toolbar to which you want to add the macro, and then drag the macro you want to add to the toolbar from the Commands list in the Macros category of the Commands tab. Day 17 covers customizing menus and toolbars in more detail.

Q If I do assign a macro in Excel to a shortcut key when I record the macro, can I later change or remove the shortcut key after I record the macro?

A Yes. You can change or remove shortcut key assignments in Excel by displaying the Macro Options dialog for the macro whose shortcut key you want to change or remove, and then deleting the entry in the Shortcut Key text box. You can also remove any macro from a toolbar by displaying the Customize dialog (choose the Tools, Customize command) and then dragging the macro off the toolbar.

Workshop

The Workshop section presents Quiz questions to help you cement your new knowledge, and Exercises to give you experience using what you have learned. Try to understand the questions and exercises before moving on to the next lesson. Answers are in Appendix A.

Quiz

1. What were the reasons recorded macros evolved toward programming languages?
2. How does Visual Basic for Applications differ from Visual Basic?
3. List three benefits obtained by adding Visual Basic program elements to a recorded macro.
4. Can you assign an Excel macro to a toolbar when you first record it?
5. Where does Excel store the macros you record?
6. How do you execute a macro in Excel?
7. How do you start the Macro Recorder?
8. Where would you store an Excel macro if you wanted it to be available to any open workbook in any work session?
9. Which macros would you expect to find listed in Excel's Macro dialog?

Exercises

1. Record a new Excel macro as follows:

   Start the macro recorder, setting the options in the Record Macro dialog so that the macro is stored in the Personal Macro Workbook.

   Give the macro the name **NewBook**.

   Record the following actions: Choose the File, New command to create a new workbook, and then use the File, Save As command to save the workbook (use the name **NewWorkbook**). Immediately after saving the file, choose the File, Close command to close the file.

   Stop the macro recorder.

2. Use the Windows Explorer (or just use a window on the desktop) to delete the NewWorkbook.xls file you created when you recorded the macro in Exercise 1. Now run the NewBook macro you just recorded. What happens? (Hint: Use the Explorer or the File, Open command to check the contents of the folder where you saved the new workbook in Exercise 1.)

3. Now run the NewBook macro again. What happens? (Hint: Choose Cancel or End in each dialog that appears.)

DAY 2

Writing and Editing Simple Macros

Now that you know how to record and run a macro, and you understand the benefits of adding VBA programming to your macros, you are ready to learn how to edit existing macros and to create new macros without recording. In today's lesson you learn

- How to use the Visual Basic Editor in Excel to edit or write macros.
- What types of error messages you can expect to see when editing or running a macro, and how to solve the problems that produce those error messages.
- How to enable a macro to display simple messages for the user to read.

Understanding the Visual Basic for Applications Environment

In Day 1, you learned how to record and run macros in Excel. Before you edit or write macros, you need to learn more about where macros are stored. You also need to have a general understanding of the VBA Editor, its menu commands and toolbar buttons, and how they fit into Excel.

> **Note**
>
> This book concentrates exclusively on VBA programming in Excel because this application is one of the most common, and definitely one of the most friendly, VBA programming environments. To learn VBA programming in Microsoft Access, you might want to read Sams' *Access Developer's Guide* by Roger Jennings.

Understanding Modules

You know from Day 1 that Visual Basic for Applications macros are stored as part of the files in which Excel normally keeps its data: Excel macros are stored in Excel's workbook files. Macros are stored in a special part of the workbook file called a *module*. A VBA module contains the macro *source code*, which is the text representation of the instructions in the macro. Each Excel workbook file can contain none, one, or several modules. (The modules stored in a single Excel workbook are collectively referred to as a *project*.) Each Excel module can contain the source code for none, one, or several VBA macros.

> **Note**
>
> In Microsoft Office 2000, all applications that include VBA—such as MS Word, Access, Project, and so on—store their macro source code in modules attached to the application's standard data files. MS Word, for example, stores VBA code in modules that are part of each document or template, and Access stores VBA code in modules that are part of the database file.

Understanding how Excel names the modules it creates will help you locate your recorded macros when you want to view or edit them.

When you record an Excel macro, you can only specify the workbook in which Excel will store the recorded macro—the current workbook, a new workbook, or the Personal.xls workbook. Excel chooses the module in which it stores the recorded macro, and creates that module, if necessary.

When Excel creates the module in which it stores the recorded macro, it gives the module the name *ModuleN*, where *N* is the number of modules created for a particular workbook during the current work session. For example, the first time you store a recorded macro in the personal macro workbook (named Personal.xls), Excel creates a module named Module1 to store the recorded macro. If you continue to record macros in the same work session and store them in the personal macro workbook, Excel continues to store the recorded macros in the same Module1 module until you choose a different workbook to store a recorded macro in. If, later in the same work session, you again choose to store recorded macros in the personal macro workbook, Excel adds another module, named Module2, to the Personal.xls workbook.

If a workbook already contains a module with the same name Excel has chosen for a new module, Excel raises the number in the module name until the name for the new module no longer conflicts with the names of existing modules. For instance, if you start a new Excel work session and then choose to store a recorded macro in the personal macro workbook, Excel initially chooses the name Module1 for the new module. Excel chooses the name Module1 because the new module is the first module created for the Personal.xls workbook in the current work session. If, however, the Personal.xls workbook already contains modules named Module1 and Module2, Excel raises the number in the module name so that there is no conflict with existing names; the new module gets the name Module3.

Note

Excel uses the same rules for choosing the name of a module that you insert manually with the Visual Basic Editor's Insert, Module command as it does when Excel creates a module to store a recorded macro. Inserting modules is described later in this lesson.

Examining the Visual Basic Editor

In order to view the modules stored in a particular workbook—and the macro source code they contain—you must use the Visual Basic Editor. The Visual Basic Editor provides a "workbench" you use to create new modules, view the contents of existing modules, create or edit macro source code, create custom dialog boxes, and all other tasks related to creating and maintaining your Visual Basic for Applications programs. In this book, the Visual Basic Editor is referred to simply as the *VB Editor*.

The VB Editor contains the same features in Excel that are present in all other MS Office 2000 VBA host applications. When you use the VB Editor in Excel, you're really using the same VB Editor available to you in MS Word, MS Access, and other Office applications. The next few paragraphs describe how to start the VB Editor, explain the

purpose of the various windows displayed by the VB Editor, and introduce you to the VB
Editor's menu and toolbar commands.

Starting the VB Editor

To view modules or the VBA source code they contain, you must first start the VB
Editor. To start the VB Editor, use one of the following techniques:

- Choose the Tools, Macro, Visual Basic Editor menu command.
- Press Alt+F11.

Whichever technique you use, Excel will start the VB Editor. Figure 2.1 shows a typical
VB Editor window displayed by Excel. (The source code window occupying the right-
hand side of the figure only appears after you open a specific module to display the
macro source code it contains.)

FIGURE 2.1

*A typical VB Editor
window.*

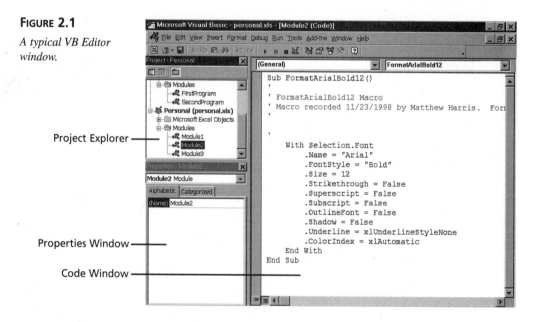

Understanding the VB Editor's Windows

The VB Editor displays three child windows. (A *child* window is any window contained
within another window; the window containing the child windows is called the *parent*
window.) Each of the VB Editor's three child windows displays important information
about your VBA project. (A *project* is the group of modules and other objects stored
in a particular workbook or workbook template.) Each of the VB Editor's windows is

displayed, by default, in the docked positions shown in Figure 2.1. (*Docking* a VB Editor window means dragging the child window to the top, bottom, left, or right edges of the VB Editor parent window; the docked child window is then attached to the edge of the VB Editor window.)

If you want, you can move any of the VB Editor's child windows to a different location onscreen by dragging the window's title bar the same way you would move any window on the Windows desktop. Dragging one of the child windows away from its docked position causes it to become a *floating* window. (Floating windows always remain visible on top of other windows.) You can also resize any of the VB Editor's child windows by dragging the window's borders to increase or decrease the size of the window—again, just like changing the size of any window on the Windows desktop.

The VB Editor's three child windows and their purpose are summarized in the following list (refer to Figure 2.1):

- *Project Explorer*. The Project Explorer window contains a tree diagram of the currently open workbooks and the objects contained in those workbooks (Excel objects, modules, references, forms, and so on). Use the Project Explorer window to navigate through the various modules and other objects in your VBA project.

- *Properties Window*. The Properties Window lists all the properties of the currently selected object. In some cases, as in the Properties Window shown in Figure 2.1, the object's properties consist of only its name. (You learn more about objects and object properties in Day 7, "Understanding Objects and Collections.") The Alphabetic tab of the Properties Window presents a list of the selected object's properties listed alphabetically by property name. The Categorized tab of the Properties Window lists the object's properties sorted by category. Don't worry too much about the contents of the Properties Window right now; you learn more about using the Properties Window as you progress through the lessons in this book.

- *Code Window*. The Code Window is where you view, edit, or create your VBA source code. Use the Code Window to write new macros or edit existing macros.

The Project Explorer window and the Code Window each require a little more explanation than the preceding summary. The next two sections give you more detailed information about the Project Explorer and the Code Window.

The Project Explorer Window

By default, the Project Explorer uses a collapsible folder diagram like the one shown in Figure 2.1 to display the contents of the currently open projects. Click the plus sign (+) in the box to the left of an entry to expand that branch of the tree diagram, or click the minus sign (-) to collapse that branch of the tree diagram.

You select objects in the Project Explorer by clicking the object. The viewing option shown in Figure 2.1 uses folders to group together objects of the same general type—in this case, Excel objects, modules, and references (no references are visible in Figure 2.1). The viewing option shown in Figure 2.2 simply lists all the objects contained in a particular project without grouping them in any way. You change between the two viewing options by clicking the Toggle Folders button.

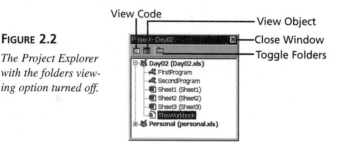

FIGURE 2.2

The Project Explorer with the folders viewing option turned off.

The Project Explorer window contains two other buttons in addition to the Toggle Folders button: View Code and View Object. The View Object button displays the object (such as a workbook or worksheet) corresponding to the selected item in the Project Explorer window. The View Code button displays the contents of a selected module in the Code Window.

> **Note**
>
> When you're working with your macro source code in the Code Window, you might want to close the Project Explorer and the Properties Window to make more room for the Code Window so that you can see more of your code at one time. You can close any of the VB Editor's child windows— Project Explorer, Properties Window, or Code Window—by clicking the Close Window button at the top right corner of the window (refer to Figures 2.2 and 2.3). You can re-display the Project Explorer or the Properties Window by clicking their buttons on the VB Editor's toolbar, or by choosing the View, Project Explorer and View, Properties Window commands.

The Code Window

Figure 2.3 shows a Code Window that has been moved and resized so that it shows more of the macro's source code, and so that the various features of the Code Window are more obvious. (In this case, the Code Window displays Module2 of the Personal.xls workbook file, and shows the source code for the two macros you recorded in Day 1.)

The default view of your VBA source code is the Full Module View shown in Figure 2.3. In Full Module View, all the macro source code in a module is displayed at once in a scrolling text window. Each macro in Full Module View is separated by a thick gray line. The VB Editor also permits you to view the contents of a module in Procedure View. (*Procedure* is another term for macro; you'll learn more about procedures later in this chapter.) The same module shown in Full Module View in Figure 2.3 is shown in Procedure View in Figure 2.4. You select the viewing mode you want by clicking the buttons at the bottom left corner of the Code Window.

FIGURE 2.3

The VB Editor's Code Window in Full Module View.

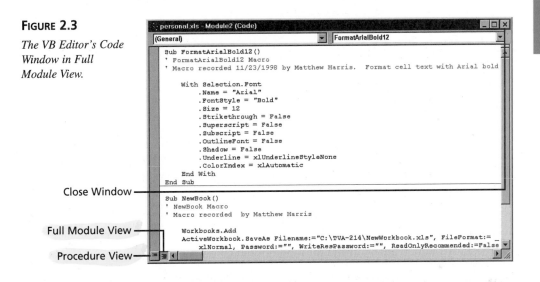

FIGURE 2.4

The same module from Figure 2.3 shown in Procedure View.

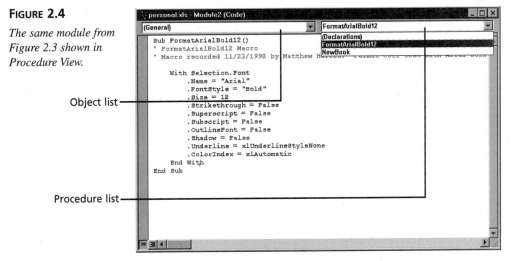

In Figure 2.4, notice that only one macro's source code is visible at a time when the Code Window is in Procedure View. Use the Procedure drop-down list (shown open in Figure 2.4) to view a different macro. In Full Module View, you can also use the Procedure drop-down list to quickly jump to a particular macro.

Use the Object list to select the object whose procedures you want to view or edit. For standard modules—such as the ones in which your recorded macros are stored—the only choice in the Object drop-down list is (General). You'll learn more about the uses of the Object list as you proceed through the lessons in this book.

Now that you know more about the VB Editor's windows, you're ready to learn about the VB Editor's toolbar and menu, which provide the commands that help you manipulate the Project Explorer, Properties Window, and Code Window, and their contents.

Introducing the VB Editor's Menus

This and the following sections give you an overview of the VB Editor's menus and tool-bar. Don't be dismayed if the purpose or meaning of the commands described in the next two sections doesn't make much sense to you right now. Almost all the VBA menu commands described in the following paragraphs are used to carry out activities that you have not yet learned about. Each lesson fully describes the menu commands relevant to the topics in that lesson. Right now, you just need to get acquainted with the available commands. If you're adventurous, go ahead and try some of these commands—just be sure you practice on a workbook that doesn't contain irreplaceable data.

Note

Don't try to memorize all the menu and toolbar commands discussed in this chapter. Most of these commands relate to activities you haven't yet learned about. Instead, use the following description of the VB Editor's menu and toolbar commands to obtain an overview of the VB Editor's capabilities. Each lesson in this book explains the relevant menu and toolbar commands in more detail. You might want to use this section as a reference when you begin working in the VB Editor on more complex tasks.

The File Menu   The File menu, as in all Windows applications, contains commands related to saving and opening files. In the VB Editor, the File menu provides you with the commands you need to save changes to your VBA project and print your VBA macro source code. Table 2.1 summarizes the File menu commands, their shortcut keys, and the purpose of each command.

TABLE 2.1   FILE MENU COMMANDS

Command	Shortcut	Action
Save *\<project\>*	Ctrl+S	Saves the current VBA project to disk, including all modules and forms.
Import File	Ctrl+M	Adds an existing module, form, or class to the current project. You can only import modules, forms, or classes previously saved with the Export File command from another project.
Export File	Ctrl+E	Saves the current module, form, or class in a text file format for importation into another project or for archival purposes.
Remove *\<item\>*		Permanently deletes the currently selected module or form from your VBA project. This command is disabled if no item is selected in the Project Explorer.
Print	Ctrl+P	Prints a module or form for documentation or archival purposes.
Close and Return	Alt+Q	Closes the VB Editor and returns you to the host application from which you opened the VB Editor.

Note   You learn about user-defined forms—which you use to create custom dialog boxes—in Day 16, "Creating Custom Dialog Boxes."

The Edit Menu   The Edit menu contains the commands related to manipulating your macro source code in the Code Window and objects on forms. Table 2.2 summarizes the available Edit menu commands, their shortcut keys, and the action each command performs.

TABLE 2.2   EDIT MENU COMMANDS

Command	Shortcut	Action
Undo	Ctrl+Z	Undoes the most recent command. Not all commands can be undone.
Redo		Redoes the most recent command you have undone.

continues

TABLE 2.2 CONTINUED

Command	Shortcut	Action
Cut	Ctrl+X	Cuts the selected text or object and places it on the Windows Clipboard. The selected text or object is deleted from the module or form after cutting.
Copy	Ctrl+C	Copies the selected text or object and places it on the Windows Clipboard. The selected text or object remains unchanged.
Paste	Ctrl+V	Pastes text or an object from the Windows Clipboard into the current module or form.
Clear	Del	Deletes the selected text or object from the module or form.
Select All	Ctrl+A	Selects all text in a module or all objects on a form.
Find	Ctrl+F	Similar to the Find command in Excel, enables you to locate specific text in a module.
Find Next	F3	Repeats the last Find operation.
Replace	Ctrl+H	Similar to the Replace command in Excel, enables you to locate specific text in a module and replace it with different text.
Indent	Tab	Indents all selected text one tab stop.
Outdent	Shift+Tab	Moves all selected text to the left by one tab stop.
List	Ctrl+J	Opens a drop-down list in the Properties/Methods Code Window showing the properties and methods of the object name you just typed. When the insertion point is in a blank space in the Code Window, this command opens a list of globally available properties and methods.
List Constants	Ctrl+Shift+J	Opens a drop-down list in the Code Window showing valid constants for a property you just typed preceding an equal sign (=).
Quick Info	Ctrl+I	Opens a pop-up help window showing the correct syntax for a procedure, function, or method you just typed in the Code Window.

Command	Shortcut	Action
Parameter Info	Ctrl+Shift+I	Opens a pop-up help window showing the parameters (also called *arguments*) of a procedure, function, or statement you just typed in the Code Window.
Complete Word	Ctrl+Space	Causes the VB Editor to complete the word you are typing as soon as you type enough characters for VBA to recognize which key word you are typing.
Bookmarks		Opens a submenu of choices to place, remove, or jump to bookmarks you have placed in your module. VB Editor bookmarks don't have names.

Note You'll learn more about properties and methods in Day 7, "Understanding Objects and Collections," and Day 19, "Controlling Excel with VBA."

The View Menu   The View menu provides the commands that enable you to select which elements of the VB Editor you view and how you view them. Table 2.3 summarizes the available View menu commands, their shortcut keys, and the action produced by that command.

TABLE 2.3   VIEW MENU COMMANDS

Command	Shortcut	Action
Code	F7	Activates the Code Window to display the VBA source code associated with a selected module or form.
Object	Shift+F7	Displays the object currently selected in the Project Explorer.
Definition	Shift+F2	Displays the VBA source code for a procedure or function under the cursor; displays the Object Browser for objects in a VBA reference.
Last Position	Ctrl+Shift+F2	Jumps to the last position in a module after using the Definition menu command or after editing code.

continues

TABLE 2.3 CONTINUED

Command	Shortcut	Action
Object Browser	F2	Opens the Object Browser, which enables you to determine which macros are currently available. The section "Finding Recorded Macros" later in this lesson describes the Object Browser in more detail. Later lessons describe other features of the Object Browser.
Immediate Window	Ctrl+G	Displays the VBA Debugger's Immediate Window.
Locals Window		Displays the VBA Debugger's Locals Window.
Watch Window		Displays the VBA Debugger's Watch Window.
Call Stack	Ctrl+L	Displays the call stack for the current VBA function or procedure.
Project Explorer	Ctrl+R	Displays the Project Explorer window.
Properties Window	F4	Displays the Properties Window.
Toolbox		Displays the Toolbox toolbar. You use the Toolbox to add controls to custom dialog boxes; you learn about the Toolbox in Day 16.
Tab Order		Displays the Tab Order dialog. You use the Tab Order dialog when creating custom dialog boxes, as described in Day 16.
Toolbars		Displays a submenu that enables you to show or hide the VB Editor's various toolbars or to open the Customize dialog to customize one of the VB Editor's toolbars.
<host application>	Alt+F11	Returns you to the host application from which you started the VB Editor, but leaves the VB Editor open. The specific name of this choice depends on which VBA host application you start the VB Editor from—Excel, in this book.

The Insert Menu The commands on the Insert menu enable you to add various objects—such as modules and forms—to your project. There are no keyboard shortcuts for any of the commands on the Insert menu. Table 2.4 summarizes the actions performed by each of the Insert menu commands.

TABLE 2.4 INSERT MENU COMMANDS

Command	Action
Procedure	Inserts a new **Sub**, **Function**, or **Property** procedure in the current module. (*Procedure* is another name for macro.)
UserForm	Adds a new form (used to create custom dialog boxes) to your project. Custom dialog boxes are discussed in Day 16.
Module	Adds a new module to your project. The VB Editor gives the module a name according to the rules described earlier in this lesson.
Class Module	Adds a new class module to your project. You use class modules to create custom objects in your project.
File	Enables you to insert a text file containing VBA source code into a module.

2

The Format Menu The Format menu's commands are used when you create your own custom dialog boxes and other forms. The Format menu's commands enable you to align objects on the form to each other, adjust the size of a control to fit its contents, and many other useful tasks. The Format menu commands are presented here for completeness; you won't put them to use until you begin to create your own custom dialog boxes as described in Day 16. Table 2.5 summarizes the Format menu commands and their actions; none of the Format menu commands have keyboard shortcuts.

TABLE 2.5 FORMAT MENU COMMANDS

Command	Action
Align	Opens a submenu of commands that enable you to align selected objects on a form to each other. You can align objects to the top, left edge, right edge, bottom, center, or middle of a designated object.
Make Same Size	Opens a submenu of commands that enable you to make selected objects the same size as a designated object.
Size to Fit	Simultaneously changes the width and height of an object to fit its contents.
Size to Grid	Simultaneously changes the width and height of an object to the nearest grid marks. (When designing forms, the VB Editor dis plays a grid on the form to help you position and size objects on the form.)

continues

TABLE 2.5   CONTINUED

Command	Action
Horizontal Spacing	Opens a submenu of commands that enable you to adjust the horizontal spacing of selected objects. You can make the horizon tal spacing even, reduce it, increase it, or remove all horizontal space between the objects.
Vertical Spacing	Opens a submenu of commands that enable you to adjust the vertical spacing of selected objects. You can make the vertical spacing even, reduce it, increase it, or remove all vertical space between the objects.
Center in Form	Opens a submenu of commands that enable you to adjust the position of selected objects to be centered horizontally or vertically on the form.
Arrange Buttons	Opens a submenu of commands that enable you to automatically arrange command buttons on a form in an evenly spaced row across the bottom or right-hand edge of a form.
Group	Binds several selected objects together in a single group so that you can move, resize, cut, or copy the objects as a single unit. Individual objects in a group can still be selected in order to alter their specific properties.
Ungroup	Removes the grouping from objects you have previously bound together with the Group command.
Order	Opens a submenu of commands that enable you to change the top-to-bottom order (called the *z-order*) of overlapping objects on a form. Use the Order command to ensure that, for example, a text box always appears on top of a graphic object on the form.

The Debug Menu

You use the commands on the Debug menu when you are testing or debugging your macros. (*Debugging* is the name given to the process of finding and correcting errors in a program.) You learn how to use the commands on the Debug menu in Day 15, "Debugging and Testing VBA Code," which describes how to find and correct errors in your macro source code. Table 2.6 summarizes the Debug menu commands, their short-cut keys, and the action they perform.

TABLE 2.6 DEBUG MENU COMMANDS

Command	Shortcut	Action
Compile <project>		Compiles the project currently selected in the Project Explorer.
Step Into	F8	Executes your VBA source code one statement at a time.
Step Over	Shift+F8	Similar to the Step Into command, Step Over enables you to execute all the instructions in a macro without pausing at each individual statement.
Step Out	Ctrl+Shift+F8	Executes the remaining statements in a macro without pausing at each individual statement.
Run to Cursor	Ctrl+F8	Executes VBA source code statements from the currently executing statement to the current cursor position.
Add Watch		Enables you to specify variables or expressions containing values you want to inspect as your VBA source code executes.
Edit Watch	Ctrl+W	Enables you to edit the specifications for watched variables and expressions you created previously with the Add Watch command.
Quick Watch	Shift+F9	Displays the current value of a selected expression.
Toggle Breakpoint	F9	Marks (or unmarks) a place in your VBA source code where you want execution to halt.
Clear All Breakpoints	Ctrl+Shift+F9	Removes all the breakpoints in a module.
Set Next Statement	Ctrl+F9	Enables you to alter the normal execution of your code by manually specifying the next line of source code to be executed.
Show Next Statement		Causes the VB Editor to indicate the next line of code that will be executed by highlighting it.

The Debug menu's commands enable you to closely control the execution of a macro, to stop and start the macro at specified points, and to trace the execution of a macro step by step. Each of the debugging commands is described in detail in Day 15.

The Run Menu   The commands on the Run menu enable you to start executing a macro, interrupt or resume a macro's execution, or reset an interrupted macro to its state before execution. You learn how to use some of the commands on the Run menu later in this lesson; the remainder of the Run menu's commands are discussed in Day 15. Table 2.7 summarizes the Run menu's commands, their keyboard shortcuts, and their resulting actions.

TABLE 2.7   RUN MENU COMMANDS

Command	Shortcut	Action
Run Sub/User Form	F5	Causes VBA to run the macro you are currently editing, that is, VBA runs whatever macro that currently contains the text insertion point. If a form is active, VBA runs the form.
Break	Ctrl+Break	Interrupts execution of your VBA source code and causes the VB Editor to enter Break mode. (*Break mode* is used when debugging your VBA code and is the topic of Day 15.)
Reset		Clears all module-level variables and the Call Stack. (Variables are discussed in Day 3; the Call Stack is discussed in Day 15.)
Design Mode		Turns Design mode on and off for a project. In Design mode, no code in your project is being executed and control events aren't processed.

The Tools Menu   The commands on the Tools menu not only enable you to select a macro to execute, but also enable you to gain access to external libraries of macros and additional forms controls (other than those built into VBA). The Tools menu commands also give you access to the VB Editor's Options dialog and the properties for the VBA project currently selected in the Project Explorer. Table 2.8 summarizes the Tools menu commands and their actions. There are no shortcut keys for any of the Tools menu's commands.

TABLE 2.8   TOOLS MENU COMMANDS

Command	Action
References	Displays the References dialog, which enables you to establish references to object libraries, type libraries, or another VBA project. After a reference is established, the objects, methods, properties, procedures, and functions in the reference appear in the Object Browser dialog.
Additional Controls	Displays the Additional Controls dialog, which enables you to customize the Toolbox toolbar so that you can add controls to your forms other than those built in to VBA. The Additional Controls dialog also enables you to add buttons to the Toolbox toolbar that permit you to add insertable objects (such as an Excel worksheet or Word document) to a form.
Macros	Displays the Macro dialog, which enables you to create, edit, exe cute, or delete a macro.
Options	Displays the Options dialog, which enables you to select various options for the VB Editor, such as the number of spaces in a tab stop, when VBA checks the syntax of your statements, and so on. You learn about the settings in the Options dialog as they become relevant to various topics under discussion throughout this book.
<project> Properties	Displays the Project Properties dialog, which enables you to set various properties of your VBA project such as the project name, description, and help file. The Project Properties dialog also per mits you to protect your project so that it can't be edited by any one without the correct password.
Digital Signature	Displays the Digital Signature dialog, which enables you to view the current signature information or to "sign" your VBA project with an existing signature certificate.

Note   The specific additional controls, if any, that you can access through the Tools, Additional Controls command depend on what software you have installed on your computer. Typically, the additional controls that might be available to you are ActiveX controls supplied through a third-party vendor or that are supplied as part of another application.

> **Note**
>
> Digital signatures and certificates—a new feature of VBA in Microsoft Office 2000—enable VBA software developers to secure their applications against the addition of harmful virus programs and enable users to permit only the execution of macros bearing signatures from a trusted source. Digital signatures and certificates are explained in more detail in Day 21, "Using Event Procedures and Add-ins."

Other Menus   There are three additional menus in the VB Editor: the Add-Ins, Window, and Help menus. The Add-Ins menu has only one choice—Add-In Manager. The Add-Ins, Add-In Manager command displays the Add-In Manager dialog box. You use the Add-In Manager to add or remove Visual Basic add-in programs. Like the add-in programs that you use in Excel, VBA in Office 2000 now supports the use of add-in programs to enhance the functionality of the VB Editor. Visual Basic add-in programs are available from third-party software vendors.

The VB Editor's Window and Help menus both contain commands identical to the Window and Help menus found in other Microsoft Windows applications. The commands on the Window menu enable you to select the active window, split the current window, tile the VB Editor's child windows vertically and horizontally, arrange the VB Editor's child windows in a cascading stack, or line up the icons of minimized child windows. This chapter doesn't discuss the Window menu's commands in detail because they are identical to the Window menu commands found in Excel, Word, and other Microsoft applications.

The Help menu's commands are also identical to the Help menu commands found in Excel, Word, and other Microsoft Windows applications. The VB Editor's Help menu enables you to get context-sensitive help through the Microsoft Office Assistant, and to view the VBA online help files for the host application from which you started the VB Editor. If you have a modem and an Internet account, you can use the Help, MSDN on the Web command to connect to a variety of Web pages that contain information about Microsoft products and VBA programming.

The final command on the Help menu is the About Microsoft Visual Basic command. This command displays a dialog containing a copyright notice about Microsoft Visual Basic. The About Microsoft Visual Basic dialog also contains a command button—System Info—that displays information about your computer system, such as which video, sound, and printer drivers are installed, which programs are currently loaded into memory, which programs are registered in the Windows System Registry, and other technical information. You'll learn how to use the About Microsoft Visual Basic dialog to obtain information about OLE and Automation objects in Day 20, "Working with Other Applications."

Introducing the VB Editor's Toolbar

Choosing a command button with a mouse is easier for many users than choosing a menu command. The VB Editor, therefore, provides the most important and frequently used commands as buttons on a toolbar. If you're working extensively within the VB Editor, you might find that using the command buttons on the various VB Editor toolbars speeds up your work.

By default, the VB Editor displays only its Standard toolbar, shown in Figure 2.5. In addition to the Standard toolbar, the VB Editor offers three other toolbars: Edit, Debug, and UserForm. You learn how to use the Debug toolbar in Day 15. You learn how to use the UserForm toolbar in Day 16, "Creating Custom Dialog Boxes."

The VB Editor's Edit toolbar contains several command buttons that are useful when editing text in the Code Window. The Edit toolbar even offers a couple of commands not available on the Standard toolbar. The Standard and Edit toolbars are described later in this section.

You can control which toolbars the VB Editor displays with the View, Toolbars command. Because the VB Editor does not, by default, display the Edit toolbar, you'll need to display it manually. If you or another user hides the VB Editor's Standard toolbar, you might also need to use the View, Toolbars command to display the Standard toolbar. To display or hide any of the VB Editor's toolbars, follow these steps:

1. Choose the View, Toolbars command to display a submenu listing all the VB Editor's toolbars.

2. Click the name of the toolbar you want to display. For example, to display the Edit toolbar, click Edit on the submenu. The VB Editor then displays the selected toolbar.

Tip

You can also display the submenu of available VB Editor toolbars by *right-clicking* (clicking the right mouse button) on any visible toolbar and then choosing the toolbar you want to display from the resulting pop-up menu.

By default, the VB Editor displays the Standard toolbar in its *docked* (fixed) position at the top of the VB Editor window (refer to Figure 2.1 for a full-screen example showing the Standard toolbar in its docked position). You can also display a toolbar in a floating window, called an *undocked* toolbar. When a toolbar is undocked, it appears in a window with borders and a title bar; Figure 2.6 shows an undocked Edit toolbar. You dock and undock toolbars in the VB Editor the same way you dock and undock toolbars in Excel: Drag the toolbar to the location you want and then release the mouse button. (Refer to the VB Editor's online help for more information on displaying, moving, docking, and undocking toolbars.)

The next few paragraphs first describe the commands available on the Standard toolbar, and then describe the additional commands available on the Edit toolbar.

The Standard Toolbar   The VB Editor's Standard toolbar contains 18 buttons. Each button is a shortcut to a menu command. Table 2.9 summarizes the action associated with each of the Standard toolbar's command buttons. As you study Table 2.9, refer to Figure 2.5 to match each command button's name with the icon on the front of the button.

FIGURE 2.5

The VB Editor's Standard toolbar contains buttons for the most important and most commonly used commands.

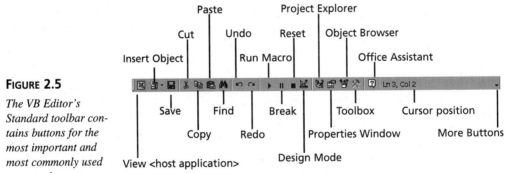

Paste   Project Explorer

Cut   Undo   Reset   Object Browser

Insert Object   Run Macro   Office Assistant

Save   Find   Break   Toolbox   Cursor position

Copy   Redo   Properties Window   More Buttons

View <host application>   Design Mode

> **Note**
>
> You can customize any of the VB Editor's toolbars using the same techniques as customizing a toolbar in Excel 2000. Tables 2.9 and 2.10, along with Figures 2.5 and 2.6, show the VB Editor's Standard and Edit toolbars in their default configuration. If you or another user has customized these toolbars, you might see additional command buttons not described here. Refer to the VB Editor's online help for more information on customizing toolbars.

TABLE 2.9 THE STANDARD TOOLBAR COMMANDS

Button	Action
View *<host application>*	Switches to the VBA host application from which you started the VB Editor. This button's icon changes depending on the specific application from which you started the VB Editor; in Figure 2.5, the VB Editor was started from Excel.
Insert Object	Click the down-arrow to the right of this button to display a list of objects you can insert into the current project: UserForm, Module, Class Module, or Procedure. Same as the Insert menu commands of the same name.
Save	Saves the current project; the same as choosing File, Save.
Cut	Cuts the selected text or object and places it on the Windows Clipboard; the same as the Edit, Cut command.
Copy	Copies selected text or object to the Windows Clipboard; the same as the Edit, Copy command.
Paste	Pastes text or an object from the Windows Clipboard into the Code Window or user form at the cursor position; the same as the Edit, Paste command.
Find	Opens the Find dialog to locate a specific word or phrase in a module; the same as the Edit, Find command.
Undo	Undoes the most recent command, if possible (not all actions can be undone); the same as the Edit, Undo command.
Redo	Redoes the last undone command; the same as the Edit, Redo command.
Run	Executes the current procedure or form; the same as the Run, Sub/UserForm command.
Break	Interrupts the execution of your VBA code; the same as the Run, Break command.
Reset	Resets your VBA code to its initial state; the same as the Run, Reset command.
Design Mode	Causes the VB Editor to enter Design mode; the same as the Run, Design Mode command.
Project Explorer	Displays the Project Explorer window; the same as the View, Project Explorer command.
Properties Window	Displays the Properties Window; the same as the View, Properties Window command.

continues

TABLE 2.9   CONTINUED

Button	Action
Object Browser	Displays the Object Browser dialog; the same as the View, Object Browser command.
Toolbox	Displays the Toolbox toolbar; the same as the View, Toolbox command.
Office Assistant	Displays the Microsoft Office Assistant for context-sensitive help with the task you're currently working on; the same as the Help, Microsoft Visual Basic Help command.
Cursor position	This region of the Standard toolbar isn't actually a command button, and only appears when the cursor is in the Code Window. This area tells you what line of a module the insertion point cursor is on and in what column of the line. In Figure 2.5, the insertion point cursor is on line 3 in column 2.
More Buttons	Click the down-pointing arrow to display a palette of frequently used command buttons that you might want to add to the toolbar.

Note

As with the menu commands, don't let yourself be disturbed if the purpose or meaning for any of the buttons on the VB Editor's toolbars aren't completely clear to you right now. Each lesson fully describes the commands and toolbar buttons that relate to the topics covered in that lesson. This section is only intended to acquaint you with the commands available from the VB Editor's toolbars.

The Edit Toolbar   As you learn more about writing your own VBA code and you work increasingly in the Code Window, you might find that using the Edit toolbar to provide shortcuts for various editing commands saves you time and effort. The VB Editor does not automatically display the Edit toolbar, you must first manually display the Edit toolbar by following the two-step process described at the beginning of this section. Table 2.10 summarizes the default command buttons on the Edit toolbar and each button's action. As you study Table 2.10, refer to Figure 2.6 to match each button's name with the icon on the front of the toolbar button.

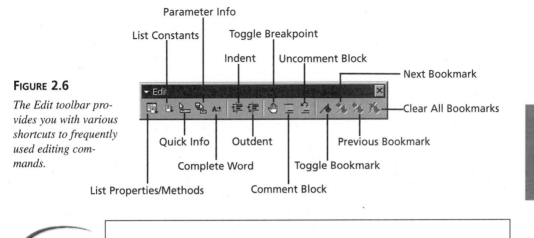

FIGURE 2.6

The Edit toolbar provides you with various shortcuts to frequently used editing commands.

2

Tip

You can dock the Edit toolbar (or any other VB Editor toolbar) by dragging it to the top, bottom, left edge, or right edge of the VB Editor window.

TABLE 2.10   THE EDIT TOOLBAR COMMANDS

Button	Action
List Properties/Methods	Displays a drop-down list of properties and methods belonging to the object you just typed; the same as Edit, List Properties/Methods.
List Constants	Displays a drop-down list of predefined constants; the same as Edit, List Constants.
Quick Info	Displays a pop-up window showing the correct syntax for an object method; the same as Edit, Quick Info.
Parameter Info	Displays a pop-up window showing the parameters (also called *arguments*) of a VBA function or statement; the same as Edit, Parameter Info.
Complete Word	Completes the current VBA keyword as soon as you type enough characters for VBA to identify the word you're typing; the same as Edit, Complete Word.
Indent	Moves selected text to the right by one tab stop; the same as Edit, Indent.
Outdent	Moves selected text to the left by one tab stop; the same as Edit, Outdent.
Toggle Breakpoint	Sets or removes a breakpoint in your VBA source code; the same as Debug, Toggle Breakpoint.

continues

TABLE 2.10   CONTINUED

Button	Action
Comment Block	Changes a selected block of text in the Code Window into comments by adding a comment character at the beginning of each selected line. There is no equivalent menu command. Comments and comment characters are discussed later in this chapter.
Uncomment Block	Removes the comment character from a block of selected text in the Code Window. There is no equivalent menu command.
Toggle Bookmark	Sets or removes a bookmark in your VBA source code; the same as Edit, Bookmarks, Toggle Bookmark.
Next Bookmark	Moves the insertion point in the Code Window to the next bookmark; the same as Edit, Bookmarks, Next Bookmark.
Previous Bookmark	Moves the insertion point in the Code Window to the previous bookmark; the same as Edit, Bookmarks, Previous Bookmark.
Clear All Bookmarks	Removes all the bookmarks in the module; the same as Edit, Bookmarks, Clear All Bookmarks.

Note

Almost all VBA host applications, including MS Excel, MS Word, and now MS Access 2000, use the same VB Editor described in this lesson. In general, you'll find that what you learn about the VB Editor in Excel will apply to any other VBA application in which you program—that's the whole point of using VBA in the first place.

Editing Macros

Before you can edit a macro, you must display the module that contains the macro you want to edit and locate the macro in the module. For example, to edit the Excel FormatArialBold12 macro you recorded in Day 1, you must first display the module in the Personal.xls workbook (where the recorded macro was stored) that contains the FormatArialBold12 macro's source code.

This section first describes how to display a VBA module, shows you a couple of different techniques for finding specific macros, and then acquaints you with the various parts of a recorded macro before explaining how to edit the macro itself.

Displaying a Module

Before you can display and edit a particular macro, you first must display the module containing that macro. To display a module in the VB Editor, follow this procedure:

1. Press Alt+F11 to activate the VB Editor if it isn't already open.
2. Choose the View, Project Explorer command to display the Project Explorer window if it isn't already displayed.
3. Navigate the tree list in the Project Explorer to locate the module you want to display. If the Folders viewing option in the Project Explorer is on, you'll find all of a project's modules in the Modules folder of your project. (Refer to Figure 2.1 or Figure 2.7 for a view of the Project Explorer's folder tree.)
4. Double-click the module you want to display. The VB Editor displays the module in a Code Window.

After you display a module, you can use the Procedure list in the Code Window to display a specific macro in the module. You can also use the technique described in the following section to find a macro without first opening the module containing the macro.

Finding Recorded Macros

You learned at the beginning of this lesson that Excel creates new modules as needed to store the macros that you record. Because of the way Excel inserts and names new modules in a workbook, you can end up with several different modules in a single workbook, all of which have very similar names. As a result, you might sometimes find it difficult to determine which module contains a particular macro. As an example, when you recorded the FormatArialBold12 macro in lesson 1, you stored it in the Personal.xls workbook. If this was the first macro you ever recorded and stored in Personal.xls, Excel stored the FormatArialBold12 macro in a module named Module1. If you then recorded the NewBook macro from Exercise 1.1 in the same Excel working session, Excel also stored it in the Module1 module. If you exited Excel between the time you recorded FormatArialBold12 and the time you recorded NewBook, Excel stored the NewBook macro in a different module (most likely Module2). As you can see, if you want to edit the NewBook macro, you might not be able to tell immediately which module in Personal.xls contains the source code for NewBook without actually looking at all of the modules in the workbook.

Using the Object Browser's Search Feature

Instead of hunting through all the text in all the modules looking for a particular macro that you want to edit, you can use the Object Browser to locate the macro you want to display or edit.

To use the Object Browser to locate and display a macro, follow these steps:

> **Note**
>
> As well as being general steps for locating a macro's source code in Excel, the procedure described here includes the specific information to locate the `FormatArialBold12` macro recorded in Day 1. If you want to follow along with the specific example, start Excel before beginning with step 1 of this process.

1. Press Alt+F11 to open the VB Editor if it isn't already displayed.
2. Choose View, Project Explorer to display the Project Explorer window if it isn't already open (see Figure 2.7).

FIGURE 2.7

Select a project in the Project Explorer before searching for a macro in the Object Browser.

3. In the Project Explorer window, select the VBA Project in which you want to find a macro. For example, to find the `FormatArialBold12` macro you recorded in Day 1, select the Personal.xls workbook in the Project Explorer, as shown in Figure 2.7.

> **Note**
>
> You must select the VBA Project in which you want to find a macro in the Project Explorer window before searching with the Object Browser. Macros in your project only appear in the Object Browser when that project is selected in the Project Explorer.

4. Choose the View, Object Browser command. The VB Editor displays the Object Browser dialog shown in Figure 2.8.

> **Tip**
>
> You can also start the Object Browser by clicking the Object Browser command button on the VB Editor's toolbar.

View Definition

FIGURE 2.8

Use the Object Browser dialog to help locate macros and the modules they are stored in.

Project/Library list

Search Text

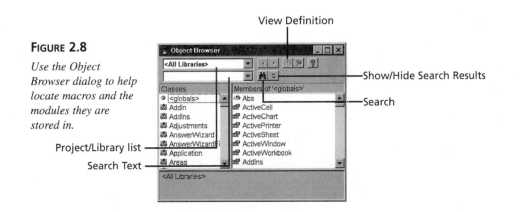

Show/Hide Search Results

Search

5. Make sure that <All Libraries> is selected in the Project/Library drop-down list (refer to Figure 2.8). The Object Browser displays all the available modules and objects in the Classes list.

6. Type the name of the macro you want to find in the Search Text box. For example, to locate the source code for the FormatArialBold12 macro, type **FormatArialBold12** in the Search Text box.

7. Click the Search button in the Object Browser (refer to Figure 2.8). The Object Browser searches through your VBA project (as well as all other currently available object libraries) for the text you entered in the Search Text box.

   After searching, the Object Browser changes its appearance to display the Search Results list, as shown in Figure 2.9. If the Object Browser found macros matching the search text you entered, it displays them in the Search Results list. Otherwise, the Search Results list displays the message No items found.

FIGURE 2.9

The Object Browser after searching for the FormatArialBold12 macro in the Personal.xls VBA project.

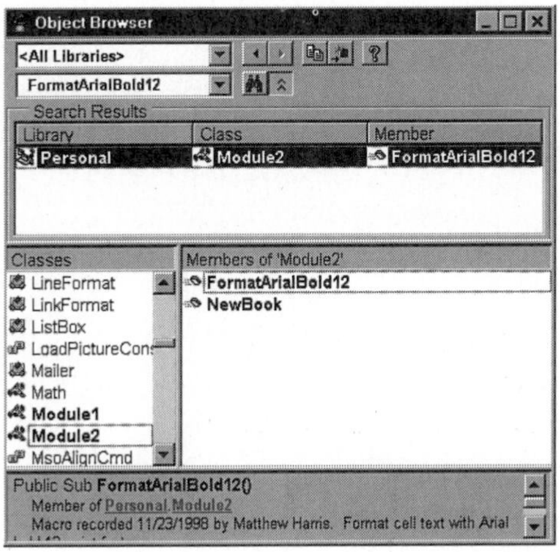

2

8. Click the macro in the Search Results list and then click the View Definition button in the Object Browser (refer to Figure 2.8). The VB Editor opens the Code Window for the module containing the macro and displays the macro's source code.

As soon as you click the View Definition button, the VB Editor opens the Code Window and displays the module that contains the macro you searched for, placing the insertion point near the beginning of the macro's source code.

Listing Project Modules with the Object Browser

If your project doesn't contain many different modules, you might find it easier to locate a macro by following this alternative procedure:

1. Press Alt+F11 to open the VB Editor.

2. Choose View, Project Explorer to display the Project Explorer window if it isn't already open.

3. In the Project Explorer window, select the VBA Project in which you want to find a macro.

4. Choose the View, Object Browser command. The VB Editor displays the Object Browser dialog.

5. Select the name of your project in the Project/Library drop-down list of the Object Browser. Unless you have changed the name of your project, Excel gives it the name VBAProject. You'll learn how to rename a project later in this book.

 Note

> The default name of the VBA project associated with Personal.xls is Personal.

6. Select a module in the Classes list. The Object Browser now displays all the macros in the selected module in the Members of *<object>* list. (The exact title of this list changes depending on the object selected in the Classes list.)

7. Select the macro whose source code you want to view in the Members of *<object>* list.

8. Click the View Definition button in the Object Browser. The VB Editor opens the Code Window for the module containing the macro and displays the macro's source code.

When you select an individual project in the Project/Library drop-down list of the Object Browser, the Classes list contains only those objects that are part of your project—usually one or more modules, the Excel workbook itself, and one or more worksheets. Figure 2.10, for example, shows the Object Browser window with the `Personal` project from the Personal.xls workbook selected in the Project/Library list. Notice that the Classes list in Figure 2.10 contains `ThisWorkbook` (a reference to Personal.xls), two modules, and three worksheets.

FIGURE 2.10

You can also use the Object Browser to view the contents of various objects in your project.

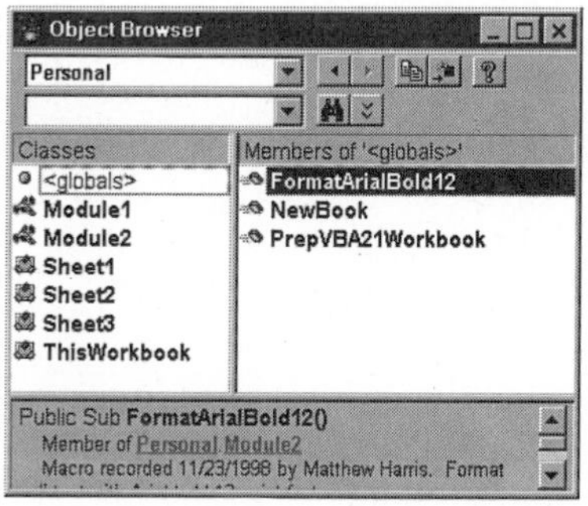

After you display a macro in the Code Window—using any of the techniques described in the preceding section—you can view or edit the macro's source code. Figure 2.11 shows the Code Window displaying the macro source code from the `NewBook` macro recorded as a result of performing Exercise 1.1 in Day 1. In Figure 2.11, the Project Explorer and Properties Window have been closed so that the Code Window could be made as large as possible.

After you display the macro you want to edit, you can use the horizontal and vertical scrollbars to position the macro in the window. You can also use the Edit, Find command to search for a macro name in a module. Using the Edit, Find command to search for text in a module works the same as searching for text in an Excel worksheet. (Refer to the VB Editor's online help for information on the Edit, Find command.)

Do

DO remember you can open any module by double-clicking it in the Project Explorer window.

DO remember that you can also find macros in the Code Window by using the Procedure list and selecting the macro you want to view or edit.

DON'T

DON'T forget that the Project Explorer window only lists projects in open workbooks. If the project file (.xls or .xla) you want isn't listed in the Project Explorer, you must return to Excel and open the desired project file.

DON'T forget that the Object Browser only lists objects contained in (or referenced by) the project you have selected in the Project Explorer window.

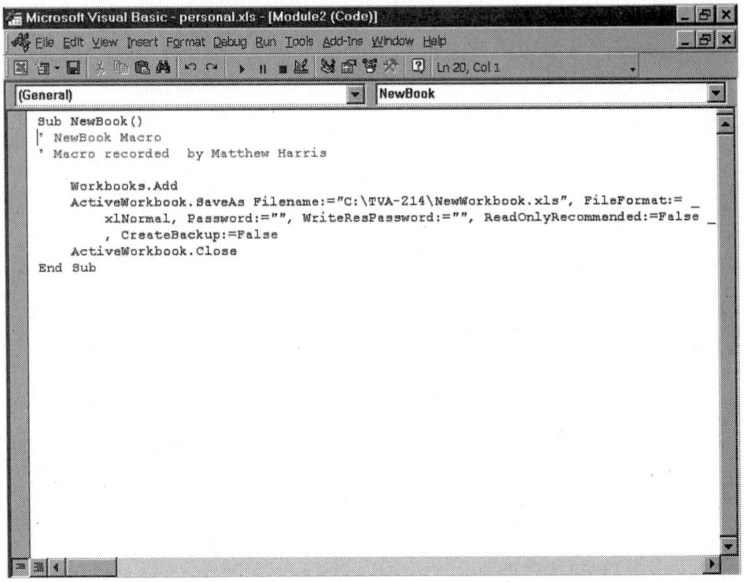

FIGURE 2.11

Viewing macro source code in the Code Window (the Project Explorer and Properties Window have been closed).

```
Sub NewBook()
' NewBook Macro
' Macro recorded  by Matthew Harris

    Workbooks.Add
    ActiveWorkbook.SaveAs Filename:="C:\TVA-214\NewWorkbook.xls", FileFormat:= _
        xlNormal, Password:="", WriteResPassword:="", ReadOnlyRecommended:=False _
        , CreateBackup:=False
    ActiveWorkbook.Close
End Sub
```

Parts of a Recorded Macro

If you examine several recorded macros, you'll notice they all have several features in common. Listing 2.1 shows the source code for the FormatArialBold12 macro you recorded in Day 1. Listing 2.2 shows the source code for the NewBook macro you recorded in Exercise 1.1.

Note

The macro source code in actual modules does not include a number in front of each line; line numbers appear in all of the listings in this book to make it easier to identify and discuss particular lines in the various macro example listings.

LISTING 2.1 THE FormatArialBold12 MACRO

```
 1:   Sub FormatArialBold12()
 2:   ' FormatArialBold12 Macro
 3:   ' Macro recorded 11/23/1998 by Matthew Harris.  Format cell text
 4:   ' with Arial bold 12-point font.
 5:
 6:       With Selection.Font
 7:           .Name = "Arial"
 8:           .FontStyle = "Bold"
 9:           .Size = 12
10:           .Strikethrough = False
11:           .Superscript = False
12:           .Subscript = False
13:           .OutlineFont = False
14:           .Shadow = False
15:           .Underline = xlUnderlineStyleNone
16:           .ColorIndex = xlAutomatic
17:       End With
18:   End Sub
```

LISTING 2.2 THE NewBook MACRO

```
 1:   Sub NewBook()
 2:   ' NewBook Macro
 3:   ' Macro recorded   by Matthew Harris
 4:
 5:       Workbooks.Add
 6:       ActiveWorkbook.SaveAs Filename:= _
 7:           "C:\TVA-214\NewWorkbook.xls", _
 8:           FileFormat:= xlNormal, _
 9:           Password:="", WriteResPassword:="", _
10:           ReadOnlyRecommended:=False, CreateBackup:=False
11:       ActiveWorkbook.Close
12:   End Sub
```

ANALYSIS In both Listing 2.1 and Listing 2.2, line 1 is the beginning of the recorded macro. Every VBA macro begins with the keyword **Sub** followed by the macro name. The line that contains the **Sub** keyword and the macro's name is referred to as the macro *declaration* line, because this is the line that makes the macro's existence known to VBA. The macro name, in turn, is always followed by a pair of empty parentheses; the purpose and use of these parentheses is explained fully in Days 6 and 12. For now, you need only know that the parentheses always appear after the macro name in a recorded macro.

> **Note**
>
> A *keyword* is a word that is part of the VBA programming language, rather than a word—such as a macro name—that the user creates. VBA keywords are printed in bold monospace type in the text of this book, but not in the code listings.

Lines 2 through 4 in Listing 2.1 are comments, as are lines 2 and 3 in Listing 2.2. A *comment* is a line in a VBA macro that does not actually contain instructions that are part of the macro. You use comments to provide documentation within the macro's source code about that macro. Notice that each comment line begins with an apostrophe (`'`) character. VBA treats any text that follows an apostrophe as a comment, starting at the apostrophe to the end of the line.

A recorded macro always begins with comment lines that state the name of the macro and contain the text that you entered in the Description text box of the Record Macro dialog at the time you recorded the macro. The specific number and content of comment lines in a recorded macro depends on the length of the description you entered.

Immediately following the macro's declaration is the *body* of the macro (which might or might not include comment lines). In Listing 2.1, lines 2 through 17 make up the body of the FormatArialBold12 macro; in Listing 2.2, lines 2 through 11 make up the body of the NewBook macro. Each line in the macro's body consists of one or more VBA statements. A VBA *statement* is a series of keywords and other symbols that together make up a single complete instruction to VBA—sort of like a single sentence in the English language. Just as a paragraph is made up of several sentences, so is a VBA macro made up of several statements.

The VBA statements in a recorded macro contain the instructions that perform actions equivalent to the actions you performed as you recorded the macro. For instance, line 7 in Listing 2.1 selects the Arial font, line 9 sets the font size, and so on. In Listing 2.2, line 5 creates a new workbook and line 11 closes the workbook. Each of these statements corresponds to an action you performed when recording the macro.

After the body of the macro comes the line containing the **End Sub** keywords, which tell VBA that it has reached the end of the macro. The macro in Listing 2.1 ends in line 18, and the macro in Listing 2.2 ends in line 12.

When you run a macro, VBA begins with the first line in the body of the macro (the first line after the macro declaration) and executes the instructions in that line sequentially from left to right. VBA then moves to the next line and executes the instructions in that line, and so on until it reaches the end of the macro, signified by the **End Sub** statement.

VBA ignores any comment lines that appear in the body of the macro.

As you have probably already noticed, many of the lines in both recorded macros are indented from the left edge. Each level of indentation helps to visually separate one part of the macro from another. Notice that the entire body of each macro is indented between the **Sub...End Sub** keywords. This helps your eye pick out the body of the macro. At other points (lines 7 through 16 in Listing 2.1) the statements are indented even farther. This second, greater level of indentation helps you identify all the statements enclosed by the **With...End With** keywords. (Days 7 and 11 describe the **With...End With** statement.)

The macro recorder automatically indents the code it produces to make the recorded macro more understandable to a human reader. As you write your own macros, you also should indent your code to help identify various sections of your macro. There is no requirement that you indent lines; the macros in Listings 2.1 and 2.2 would run just as well if all the lines began flush with the left edge of the module. Line indenting is just a formatting convention adopted by good programmers to make their programs easier to understand and maintain.

If you use a color monitor when you view a recorded macro onscreen, you will notice that different parts of the macro's text are displayed with different colors. Comments are displayed with green text, whereas the **Sub**, **End Sub**, and other VBA keywords are displayed with blue text. The remaining text in the macro is displayed in black text to indicate that it contains data and program statements created by the user. VBA color-codes the text onscreen so that you can more easily tell what part of a macro or statement you are looking at.

Editing Macro Text

Editing macro source code in a module uses commands and techniques that you're already familiar with as a Windows or Excel user. Editing text in a module displayed by the Code Window is exactly like editing text in the Windows Notepad or in WordPad. You use the same keyboard, mouse, or Edit menu commands to add, delete, select, cut, copy, or paste text in a module that you use in the Windows Notepad, WordPad, or in MS Word. (Refer to Tables 2.2 and 2.10 for a summary of the editing menu and toolbar commands available in the VB Editor.)

Tip

You can use the Edit, Find command to locate specific words or phrases within a module, or use the Edit, Replace command to replace specific words or phrases.

You can save changes you make in a module by using the VB Editor's File, Save command, or by clicking the Save button on the toolbar. Any changes you make in a module are also saved whenever you save the workbook file containing the module. (Excel will prompt you to save any changes you made to Personal.xls when you exit.)

As an example of how to edit a macro, let's add some comments to the macro you recorded in Exercise 1.1 of the lesson in Day 1.

Refer to Listing 2.2, which shows how the NewBook macro from Exercise 1.1 might look. The macro source code in Listing 2.2 has been reformatted so that its statements will fit inside the margins of this book and so that it is a little more readable. Your macro's source code will appear somewhat different. In particular, lines 6 through 10 of Listing 2.2 occupy fewer lines in the recorded macro (refer to Figure 2.11).

UNDERSTANDING VBA's LINE-CONTINUATION SYMBOL

Take another look at lines 6 through 9 in Listing 2.2. Notice the underscore (_) character at the end of each of these lines. Notice also that there is a space preceding the underscore separating it from the other text on the line. This special combination of a space character followed by an underscore at the end of a line is called the *line-continuation* symbol, and signals to VBA that the next line of the macro is to be joined to the current line to form a single statement.

In Listing 2.2, lines 6 through 10 together are actually a single statement—in this case, the command that saves the workbook and sets several options for the saved workbook. In order to make the macro more readable, the macro recorder divided this single *logical* line into several *physical* lines by using the line-continuation symbol. (The macro source code was then further edited to add more line-continuation symbols.)

Without the line-continuation symbol dividing the single logical line into several shorter physical lines, the line for this statement would extend far beyond the edge of even a maximized module window, requiring you to excessively scroll the window to see the entire statement. Later, when you write your own macros, you can use the line-continuation character yourself to help make your macros more readable.

Notice also that the statements divided by the line-continuation symbol are further indented to help you identify the statements divided over more than one physical line.

To add comments to the NewBook macro, follow these steps:

1. Move the insertion point to the end of line 4 (see Listing 2.2).

2. Press Enter to insert a blank line.

3. Type an apostrophe (')—all comments begin with an apostrophe.

4. Now type the comment, in this case, type this sentence: **Next line creates a new workbook**.

5. Repeat steps 1 and 2 to insert a blank line in front of line 6 (refer to Listing 2.2).

6. Type an apostrophe to mark the line as a comment, and then type this sentence: **Next line saves the workbook**.

Listing 2.3 shows the modified NewBook macro; the added comments are now lines 5 and 7. Unless you reformatted your recorded macro to match Listing 2.2, your edited macro should look similar to the one shown in Figure 2.12.

INPUT **LISTING 2.3** ADDED COMMENTS IN THE NEWBOOK MACRO

```
1:    Sub NewBook()
2:    ' NewBook Macro
3:    ' Macro recorded  by Matthew Harris
4:
5:'Next line creates a new workbook
6:        Workbooks.Add
7:        'Next line saves the workbook
8:        ActiveWorkbook.SaveAs Filename:= _
9:            "C:\TVA-214\NewWorkbook.xls", _
10:           FileFormat:= xlNormal, _
11:           Password:="", WriteResPassword:="", _
12:           ReadOnlyRecommended:=False, CreateBackup:=False
13:        ActiveWorkbook.Close
14:   End Sub
```

As you add the comments to the NewBook macro, notice that when you insert the new line and begin typing, the text you type is black. When you move the insertion point to any other line—whether by pressing Enter, using the arrow keys, or clicking the mouse—the new comment line turns green. This is because VBA examines each new line you type (or existing lines that you alter) whenever the insertion point leaves the line.

VBA examines each new or altered line in the macro to determine whether the line is syntactically correct. (*Syntax* is the name given to the rules for arranging words and symbols in a programming—or human—language.) If the new or changed line does have the correct syntax, VBA then color codes the parts of the line using the color-coding scheme described earlier. If there is a syntax error in the line, VBA color codes the entire line red and displays one of several possible syntax error messages. Syntax error messages are described in more detail later in this lesson.

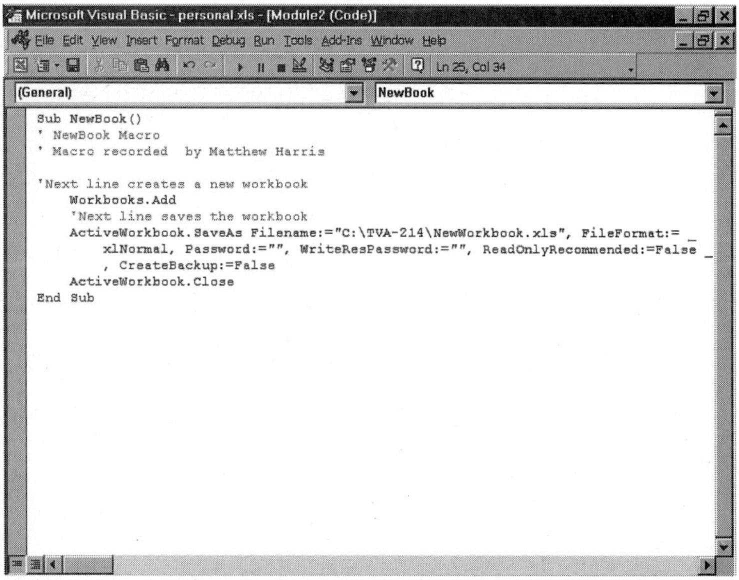

FIGURE 2.12

The edited NewBook macro in the Code Window.

```
Microsoft Visual Basic - personal.xls - [Module2 (Code)]
File  Edit  View  Insert  Format  Debug  Run  Tools  Add-Ins  Window  Help         Ln 25, Col 34
(General)                                          NewBook

     Sub NewBook()
     ' NewBook Macro
     ' Macro recorded  by Matthew Harris

     'Next line creates a new workbook
         Workbooks.Add
         'Next line saves the workbook
         ActiveWorkbook.SaveAs Filename:="C:\TVA-214\NewWorkbook.xls", FileFormat:= _
             xlNormal, Password:="", WriteResPassword:="", ReadOnlyRecommended:=False _
             , CreateBackup:=False
         ActiveWorkbook.Close
     End Sub
```

Do

DO add comments to the body of a macro while it is still fresh in your mind what actions you recorded, especially if you record long macros. Adding comments to recorded macros will make it easier to change the macro later if you need to.

DO add comments that explain the purpose or reason for any changes you make to a recorded macro. Again, these comments make it easier to determine which parts of a macro you edited and what those changes accomplish.

Moving or Copying a Macro from One Module to Another

Before you edit a macro, you might want to make a backup copy of the macro's source code, especially if you plan to make extensive changes in the macro or if the macro is long or performs complex actions. If you make a copy of the macro source code text, you can easily go back to the original recorded version of the macro if your changes don't work out as you anticipated.

To copy a single macro, use the Windows Clipboard by following these steps:

1. Display the macro you want to copy.

2. Select all of the macro's source code text. Make sure you include all of the macro, including the **Sub** and **End Sub** lines and all of the lines between.

3. Use the Edit, Copy command to copy the macro text to the Windows Clipboard.

4. Now display the module you want to copy the macro to.

5. Use the Edit, Paste command to paste the macro text into the module.

You can use the technique just described to copy a macro to the same module, a different module in the same project, or a module in a different project. You can also use this technique to paste macro text into other Windows applications, such as Windows Notepad.

Do

DO make a backup copy of a macro if you are not certain how your changes will work out or if your macro was difficult to record.

DON'T

DON'T make a backup copy of a macro in the same module that contains the original macro. If a module contains two or more macros with the same name, VBA cannot determine which macro to run and displays an error message stating that there is an *ambiguous name* in the module.

Saving and Importing Modules as Text Files

If you want to make a backup copy of an entire module, you can save it as a text file. Saving an entire module as a text file is useful if you want to import the module into another VBA project, create archival copies of your work, or transfer VBA modules to Visual Basic 6. Saving a module as a text file is called *exporting* the module. After you export a module, you can import that module into any VBA or Visual Basic project.

Exporting Modules

To export a module as a text file, follow these steps:

1. Select the module you want to export in the Project Explorer window.

2. Choose the File, Export File command. The VB Editor displays the Export File dialog shown in Figure 2.13. The Export File dialog works essentially the same as any Windows File Save dialog.

FIGURE 2.13

Use the Export File dialog to save an entire module as a text file.

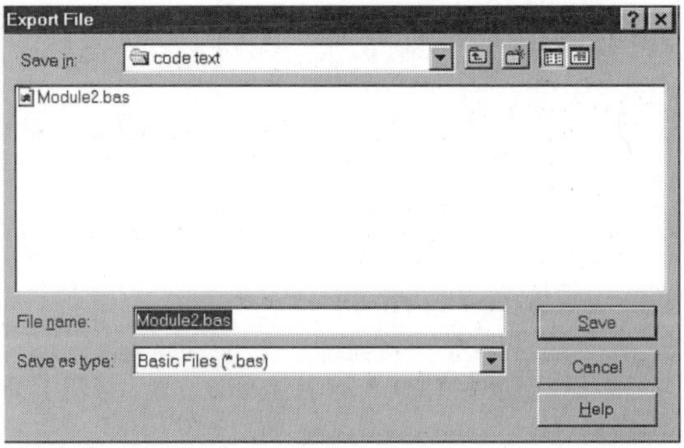

3. Make sure `Basic Files (*.bas)` is selected in the Save As Type list. The .bas extension identifies the file as a VBA or Visual Basic source code file. The information stored in the file is plain text.

4. Use the Save In list to navigate to the disk drive and folder in which you want to save the exported module.

5. Enter the name you want for the exported file in the File Name text box. The VB Editor enters the name of the module for you by default.

6. Click Save to export the file. The VB Editor exports the selected module and closes the Export File dialog.

When you export a module, the VB Editor creates a plain text file containing all the macros in the module. If you want, you can view or edit .bas files created by the VB Editor with Windows Notepad. Figure 2.14 shows the module containing the `NewBook` macro of Listing 2.3 displayed in Windows Notepad after exporting it to a .bas text file. Notice that the text in the .bas file displayed by Notepad in Figure 2.14 contains several lines—each beginning with the word `Attribute`—that are not visible in the module in the Code Window in Figure 2.12. The VB Editor adds these extra lines to the exported .bas file because they contain information that VBA or Visual Basic will need if you later want to import the .bas file into another project.

Importing Modules

You can add any module you have exported as a .bas file to any of your VBA projects. You add a module to your project by *importing* a .bas text file. To import a .bas file, follow these steps:

1. Select the project into which you want to import the .bas file in the Project Explorer window.

FIGURE 2.14

An exported module file displayed in Windows Notepad.

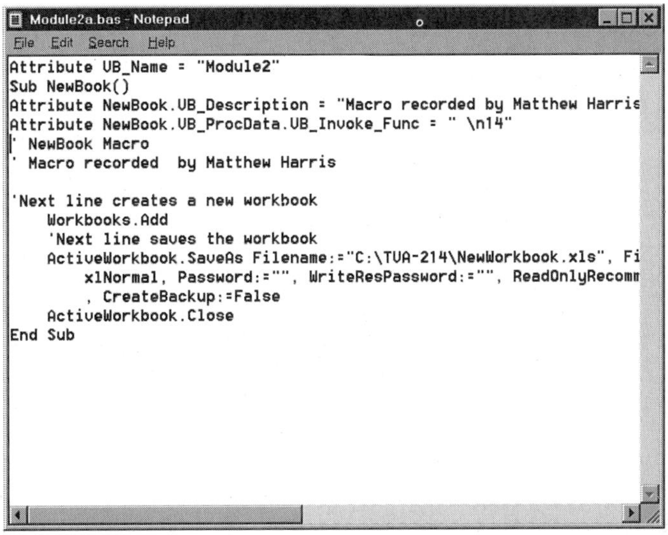

```
Module2a.bas - Notepad
File  Edit  Search  Help
Attribute UB_Name = "Module2"
Sub NewBook()
Attribute NewBook.UB_Description = "Macro recorded by Matthew Harris
Attribute NewBook.UB_ProcData.UB_Invoke_Func = " \n14"
' NewBook Macro
' Macro recorded  by Matthew Harris

'Next line creates a new workbook
    Workbooks.Add
    'Next line saves the workbook
    ActiveWorkbook.SaveAs Filename:="C:\TUA-214\NewWorkbook.xls", Fi
         xlNormal, Password:="", WriteResPassword:="", ReadOnlyRecomm
         , CreateBackup:=False
    ActiveWorkbook.Close
End Sub
```

2. Choose the File, Import File command. The VB Editor displays the Import File dialog. The Import File dialog works essentially the same as any Windows file opening dialog.

3. Use the Look In list to navigate to the disk drive and folder that contains the file you want to import into your project. The file must be one that you created by using the VB Editor to export a module.

4. Make sure `VB Files (*.frm,*.bas,*.cls)` is selected in the Files Of Type list.

5. Double-click the name of the file you want to import. The VB Editor reads the file and adds the module to your project. If your project already contains a module with the same name as the one you import, the VB Editor adds a number at the end of the module name (1, 2, 3, and so on) to create a unique module name.

Do

DO keep in mind as you learn about forms in Day 16, "Creating Custom Dialog Boxes," that you can export and import a text description of any forms you create the same way you export and import modules. Text descriptions of forms are stored in files with a .frm extension. When VBA imports a .frm file, it uses the text description in the file to re-create your form.

DO remember that the .cls file extension is for Class modules, which enable you to create your own customized objects in VBA. Class modules are discussed in Day 11, "Creating Your Own Data Types and Object Classes."

Removing Modules from a Project

Occasionally, you might decide that you no longer need the macros contained in a particular module. You might want to remove a module from a project because the macros it contains have been superseded by newer versions, or because the module contains experimental macros that you no longer need or want. Whatever the reason, you can remove a module from a VBA project by following these steps:

1. Select the module you want to remove from your project in the Project Explorer window of the VB Editor.

2. Choose the File, Remove *<object>* command. The VB Editor displays a message dialog asking if you want to export the module before removing it.

> **Tip**
> You can also remove a module by right-clicking it in the Project Explorer window and choosing Remove from the resulting pop-up menu.

3. Click Yes if you want to export the module before removing it. (Exporting the module as a .bas file is highly recommended unless you're absolutely certain that you'll never want to refer to the macros contained in that module again.) Otherwise, click No to remove the module without exporting it.

4. If you choose to export the module before removing it, the VB Editor displays the Export File dialog described earlier in this section. Complete the Export File dialog as described previously and click Save.

   Whether or not you choose to export the module, the VB Editor now removes the module from your project.

Do
DO be careful when you select the module to remove. You cannot undo removing a module.
DO keep in mind that you can remove other objects, such as forms, from your project the same way you remove modules.
DO export any objects you remove unless you're certain you'll never refer to that object or its contents again.

Writing New Macros and Procedures

To write a macro of your own without using the macro recorder, you can type the macro into an existing module or create a new module to contain the macro.

UNDERSTANDING THE TERMS *Macro* AND *Procedure*

So far, this book has used the term *macro* to refer to both macros you record and macros you write. There is another term, however, that helps distinguish between recorded macros and macros you write yourself. Strictly speaking, the term *macro* applies only to instructions that you record with the macro recorder. Macros you write from scratch are more accurately referred to as *sub procedures*, or just *procedures*. The rest of this book uses the term *macro* to refer to code that you record with the macro recorder and the term *procedure* to refer to VBA code you write yourself.

Inserting and Renaming a Module

If the workbook you want to store a procedure in does not already contain a module, you must insert a module before you can write a VBA procedure in that project. You might also insert a new module if the existing modules are getting full (a module can contain a maximum of about 4,000 lines) or if you just want to create the new VBA procedure in its own module.

If you need (or decide) to write your VBA procedure in a new module, follow these steps to add a module to your project:

1. In the VBA host application (that is, Excel), make sure the document, template, or workbook in which you want to store the procedure is open.

2. Press Alt+F11 to activate the VB Editor.

3. In the Project Explorer, select the project to which you want to add a module.

4. Choose the Insert, Module command (or use the Insert drop-down list on the toolbar). The VB Editor adds a new module to your project and opens a Code Window for the new module.

When the VB Editor inserts a new module, it gives the module a name following the naming rules explained earlier in this chapter; your new module will have the default name Module followed by a number. Whenever you insert a module, you should rename it so that the module has a descriptive name. To rename a module, follow these steps:

1. In the VB Editor, select the module you want to rename.

2. If the Properties Window isn't already visible, choose the View, Properties Window command (or click the Properties button on the toolbar) to display it. Figure 12.15 shows the Properties Window for a module that still has its default name; modules have only one property: their name.

3. In the Name text box in the Properties Window, type the new name for your module. As soon as you move the insertion point out of the Name text box, the VB Editor renames the module.

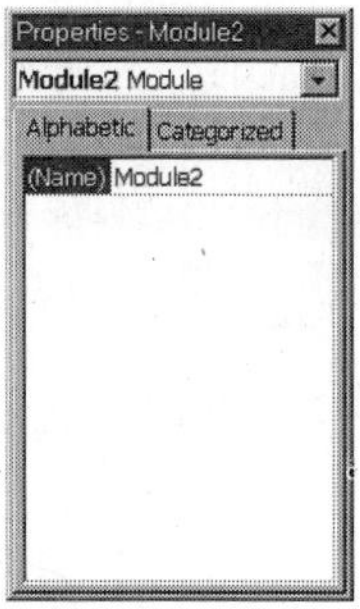

FIGURE 2.15

Change the name of a module by changing its Name *property.*

Do

DO rename a new module immediately after inserting it, and give it a descriptive name so that you can more easily identify the procedures in that module. The VB Editor's default names, such as Module1, don't tell you a lot about the procedures in that module.

Selecting an Existing Module

To write a new procedure in an existing module, you must first open a Code Window for the module in which you want to write the procedure. To open a Code Window for a module, either double-click the module in the Project Explorer, or select the module in the Project Explorer and then choose View, Code.

Writing the Procedure Text

To write the source code text for the procedure—whether you add the procedure to a new or existing module—position the insertion point in the Code Window at the place in the module where you want to type the new procedure.

You can type the new VBA procedure's source code anywhere in a module, as long as you make sure that you insert the new procedure *after* the **End Sub** statement that ends the preceding procedure and *before* the **Sub** statement that begins the next procedure in the module. Many users find it easiest to simply add new procedures at the end of the module.

When you write a procedure, you must specify the procedure's name and include the **Sub** keyword at the beginning of the procedure and the **End Sub** keywords at the end of the procedure. If you omit any of these three elements, the syntax of your procedure won't be correct and VBA will display an error message when you attempt to run the procedure.

The classic first program in any programming language is a program that displays the message *Hello, World!* on the screen. Listing 2.4 shows such a VBA program consisting of a single procedure.

To enter this VBA program yourself, follow these steps:

1. Open any Excel workbook or create a new workbook.
2. Press Alt+F11 to activate the VB Editor.
3. In the Project Explorer, select the document or workbook in which you want to store your first program.
4. Choose Insert, Module to add a new module to your project. The VB Editor adds a new module and opens a Code Window for it.
5. Rename the new module, giving it the name **FirstProgram**.
6. Make sure the insertion point is at the beginning of a blank line in the Code Window and type the text shown in Listing 2.4, pressing Enter at the end of each line to start a new line.

   Type the source code from Listing 2.4 into the module exactly as it appears in the listing, but without the line numbers. (Remember, the line numbers are not part of the procedure and macro listings, the numbers are included in this book only to make it easier to identify and discuss specific parts of the source code.)

The VB Editor contains several features to help you write procedures. First, as soon as you press Enter after typing the **Sub** keyword and the procedure name, the VB Editor automatically adds the **End Sub** keywords for you. This way, you don't have to worry about accidentally forgetting this critical element of your procedure.

Second, the VB Editor includes a feature known as Auto Quick Info. As soon as you type MsgBox and then press the space bar (line 2 of Listing 2.4), a pop-up window appears showing you the complete list of arguments for the built-in VBA procedure or function you just typed: MsgBox, in this case. Figure 2.16 shows the pop-up window with

2

information about the built-in VBA MsgBox procedure's arguments. The argument whose value you are currently expected to type is shown in bold text in the Quick Info pop-up window. (An *argument* is information that a procedure needs to carry out its task; you learn more about arguments later in this lesson and in Day 5, "Visual Basic and Excel Functions.") The Quick Info pop-up window closes if you press Enter to start a new line in the Code Window or use the arrow keys or mouse to move the insertion point away from the current line. (You can also close the Quick Info pop-up window by pressing the Esc key.)

FIGURE 2.16

The Quick Info pop-up window for MsgBox.

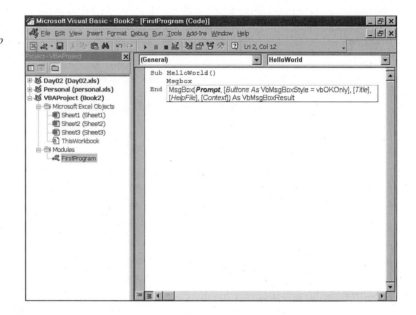

If you find Auto Quick Info distracting, you can turn this feature on and off by using the Tools, Options command in the VB Editor. Refer to the VB Editor's online help for more information about the Options dialog.

INPUT   **LISTING 2.4**   THE HelloWorld PROCEDURE

```
1:  Sub HelloWorld()
2:      MsgBox "Hello, World!"
3:  End Sub
```

ANALYSIS   The first line in Listing 2.4 is the procedure declaration. The *procedure declaration* (also called a *macro declaration*) is the statement that tells VBA about the existence of the procedure and indicates the beginning of the procedure's source code.

Every procedure declaration must begin with the **Sub** keyword followed by a space and then the name of the procedure. In Listing 2.4, the procedure's name is HelloWorld. The final part of the procedure declaration is the pair of empty parentheses. These parentheses are required (you learn about their purpose in Days 6 and 12). If you don't include the parentheses, VBA adds them to the procedure declaration when the insertion point leaves the declaration line.

For a procedure declaration to be syntactically correct, the **Sub** keyword must be the first word on the line and the procedure declaration must be the only VBA statement in the line, although you can add a comment after the declaration.

Note

You can add comments to the end of a line that contains a VBA statement by typing a space, an apostrophe ('), and then the comment itself. Comments formatted this way are called *trailing comments*. The following VBA code fragment shows a trailing comment:

```
ChDir "E:\" 'changes the current directory to E:\
```

The second line in Listing 2.4 forms the body of the procedure and is the only statement in the procedure that does any work. The body of a procedure can consist of none, one, or many statements. The MsgBox statement displays a message in a dialog box onscreen; a later section of this chapter describes the MsgBox statement.

The third and final line of the HelloWorld procedure, **End Sub**, completes the procedure. This line signals to VBA that this is the end of the procedure; VBA stops executing the procedure when it reaches this line. Like the procedure declaration, the **End Sub** statement must be the first two words in the line and must be on a line by itself, although you can add a trailing comment after it. As mentioned previously, the VB Editor automatically adds this line for you after you type the procedure declaration.

Note

Sub procedures are saved whenever the workbook file that contains the procedure is saved.

After you enter the source code for the HelloWorld procedure, run it by using the technique you learned in Day 1:

1. Choose the Tools, Macros command to display the Macros dialog box.
2. Select the HelloWorld procedure in the Macro Name list.
3. Click the Run button.

When VBA executes the HelloWorld procedure from Listing 2.4, it displays the dialog shown in Figure 2.17. Click the OK button to clear the dialog and end the procedure.

FIGURE 2.17

The HelloWorld *proce-dure shown in Listing 2.4 displays its mes-sage in this dialog box.*

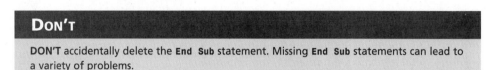

DON'T

DON'T accidentally delete the **End Sub** statement. Missing **End Sub** statements can lead to a variety of problems.

Notice that, even in this short procedure, the body of the procedure is indented to set it off from the procedure declaration and ending. You should always indent your code to make it more readable. Compare Listing 2.4 with the following listing; you can see that even short procedures are more readable when properly indented.

```
1:  Sub HelloWorld()
2:  MsgBox "Hello, World!"
3:  End Sub
```

THE AUTO-INDENT FEATURE

The VBA text editor contains a feature called *auto indenting*, which helps you format your source code with various indentation levels. If auto indenting is turned on, whenever you press Enter to begin a new line, the insertion point in the new line automatically moves to match the indentation level of the line above it. (Press Backspace to return to a previous level of indentation.)

To turn auto indenting on or off, select or clear the Auto Indent check box on the Editor tab of the Options dialog. (Choose the Tools, Options command to open the Options dialog.) Auto indent is on by default.

Running a Procedure While Editing

Whether you are writing a new procedure or editing a recorded macro, you need to run the procedure to test the result of your efforts. You already know how to use the Macros dialog to run a macro or procedure; you can also run a macro or procedure directly from the module while you are editing.

To run a procedure while editing, follow these steps:

1. Make sure the insertion point is positioned somewhere in the procedure you want to run, either in the body of the procedure, in the declaration line of the procedure, or in the **End Sub** statement of the procedure.

2. Choose the Run, Run Sub/UserForm command. VBA executes the entire procedure from beginning to end.

Tip

> You can also run a procedure while editing by positioning the insertion point anywhere in the procedure's source code and clicking the Run Sub/UserForm button on the Visual Basic toolbar or by pressing F5.

For example, to run the HelloWorld procedure, position the insertion point anywhere in the procedure's source code and then choose the Run, Run Sub/UserForm command.

If the insertion point isn't inside a procedure's source code when you use the Run, Run Sub/UserForm command or press the Run Sub/UserForm toolbar button, VBA can't tell which procedure you want to run and displays the Macros dialog instead.

Displaying Messages to a Procedure's User

Listing 2.4 includes the VBA MsgBox statement, which you can use to make your procedures display a message onscreen. Messages or other information that a procedure displays onscreen, sends to a printer, or writes to a disk file are called *output*. The MsgBox statement is the simplest form of onscreen output you can include in your VBA procedures.

The MsgBox statement is like a procedure that is built-in to VBA. The line in the HelloWorld procedure that contains the MsgBox statement causes VBA to run, or *call*, that built-in procedure. Here's the MsgBox statement from Listing 2.4 again:

MsgBox "Hello, World!"

The quoted text on the line after the procedure name MsgBox is the text of the message to be displayed by MsgBox. VBA passes this additional information to the MsgBox procedure for its use. Additional information passed on for use by a procedure that your source code calls is referred to as an *argument* for that procedure. The text "Hello, World!" is the argument for the MsgBox procedure. (Days 6 and 12 describe how to write your own procedures that use arguments.) The double quotation marks (") in the "Hello World!" argument indicate that the text enclosed in quotation marks is data in the procedure, rather than instructions that VBA is supposed to carry out.

Refer again to Figure 2.17, and notice that the title bar of the dialog displayed by the MsgBox statement contains the words *Microsoft Excel*. By default, a dialog displayed by MsgBox has a title indicating the host application that is running the VBA procedure: Microsoft Excel, in this case.

You can change the title of the dialog that MsgBox displays. Listing 2.5 shows the HelloWorld procedure from Listing 2.4 with the MsgBox statement altered so that the dialog shown in Figure 2.18 appears. Compare Figure 2.18 with Figure 2.17, and notice that the title of the MsgBox dialog is now *Greeting Box*.

INPUT **LISTING 2.5** DISPLAYING A CUSTOMIZED TITLE BAR WITH MsgBox

```
1:  Sub HelloWorld()
2:      MsgBox "Hello, World!", , "Greeting Box"
3:  End Sub
```

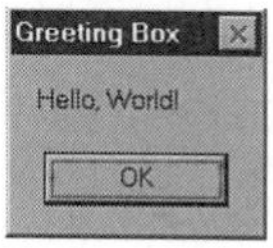

FIGURE 2.18

The MsgBox statement in Listing 2.5 displays this dialog. Notice that the title of this dialog is different from the one shown in Figure 2.17.

ANALYSIS The MsgBox statement (line 2 of Listing 2.5) in the procedure now looks somewhat different from its previous form, although it still performs the same purpose in the procedure: to display a message to the procedure's user. In Listing 2.5, the MsgBox statement now contains three arguments after it; each argument is separated from the others with a comma.

The first argument of the MsgBox statement is the same as it was in Listing 2.4, and is the text to be displayed by MsgBox (shown in the Quick Info pop-up window as the Prompt argument). Because this variation of the MsgBox statement has more than one argument, the first argument is followed by a comma; *argument lists* in VBA procedures are separated by commas, just as items in a list in the English language are separated by commas.

As soon as you typed the comma separating the first argument from the second argument, you probably noticed that the Quick Info pop-up window changed: The Buttons argument in the Quick Info window becomes bold and the Prompt argument returns to a normal text style. At the same time, a drop-down list appears in the module; this drop-down list contains all of the legitimate values for the `Buttons` argument. The drop-down list that appears is the result of the VB Editor's Auto Data Tips feature. Auto Data Tips works in a fashion similar to Auto Quick Info, but displays lists of permissible values for procedure arguments and other elements in your VBA code.

The second argument of the `MsgBox` statement is optional; this example omits the optional second argument. Because the optional argument is left out, a single space character is shown in the argument list as a placeholder. This blank space indicates to VBA that the optional argument in the list is missing. A comma follows the placeholding space character to separate it from the next argument in the list. (If you do not type the space character between the two commas, VBA adds it for you, but you do have to type both commas yourself.)

The optional second argument in the `MsgBox` statement is the `Buttons` argument. The `Buttons` argument appears in the Quick Info pop-up window enclosed in square brackets to indicate that it is an optional argument. The `Buttons` argument specifies how many and what type of command buttons appear in the dialog displayed by `MsgBox`. When you omit the optional second argument (as in this example), the dialog that `MsgBox` displays contains only one button: the OK button. (You'll learn more about the `Buttons` optional argument in Days 5 and 8.)

The third and final argument in the `MsgBox` statement specifies the title for the dialog (refer to Figure 2.18). As soon as you type the comma that separates the second and third arguments in the `MsgBox` statement's argument list, the Quick Info pop-up window indicates that the argument value you are expected to type now is for the `Title` argument.

Like the first argument, the text for the dialog's title bar is enclosed in quotation marks (`"`). VBA always recognizes quoted text as data rather than text that contains program instructions. If you omit the quotation marks for either the `MsgBox` message text or the text for the dialog's title bar, VBA displays an error message. Because the third argument is also the last argument, no comma after the third argument is needed.

Understanding Error Messages While Writing, Editing, or Running a Procedure

As you write or edit your procedures, you might make various mistakes as you create or alter the statements in your procedures. VBA can detect many of these errors as you write or edit the source code, and detects other errors as you run the procedure.

Syntax Errors

Syntax is the name given to the specific order of words and symbols that makes up a valid VBA statement. Some of the most common error messages you encounter when writing or editing VBA procedures are *syntax errors*. Syntax error messages inform you of problems in a VBA statement such as missing commas, missing quotation marks, missing arguments, and so on.

Whenever you write a new line of code or change an existing line of code, VBA parses the line when the insertion point leaves the new or changed line. (*Parsing* is the name given to the process of breaking a VBA statement into its component parts and determining which parts of the line are keywords, variables, or data; the process is similar to parsing a sentence in English to determine its component parts, such as nouns, verbs, adjectives, and so on.) After VBA successfully parses a line of code, it then compiles that line of code. (*Compiling* in VBA means preparing the source code in a form that VBA can directly execute without having to parse the code again.)

When VBA successfully parses and compiles a line of code in a procedure without finding any errors, it color-codes the various parts of the line. VBA keywords are shown in blue, comments are shown in green, and data or other statements are shown in black text. If, however, VBA detects a syntax error in the line during the parsing or compilation process, VBA color-codes the entire line in red and displays a dialog containing an error message.

Examine the following code fragment, which shows an incorrectly written MsgBox statement:

```
MsgBox "Hello, World!", , Greeting Box
```

In this example, the quotation marks required around the text specifying the title of the dialog were accidentally omitted. As a result, VBA cannot determine that the two words in the last argument are data; instead, VBA assumes that the word Greeting is a variable name. (A *variable* is a way of naming a memory location used to store data. Variables are described in the next chapter.)

Because VBA assumes the third argument is a variable named Greeting, it expects a comma or the end of the argument list for the MsgBox procedure. Instead, VBA finds a space character followed by what appears to be another variable name. VBA colors the entire line red to indicate that it contains an error, highlights the word or symbol at the place in the line where VBA determines the error exists, and then displays the error dialog shown in Figure 2.19. You can see the highlighted word Box in the source code where VBA detected the error.

FIGURE 2.19

VBA displays error messages about syntax errors as you type or change each line.

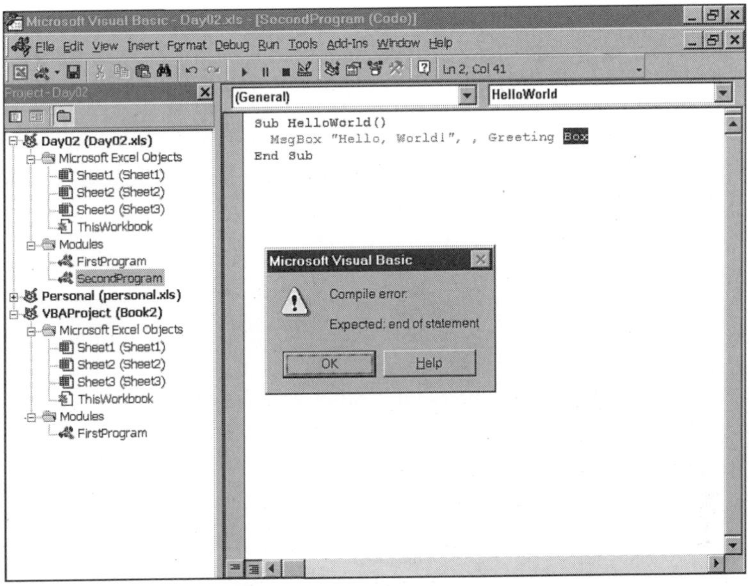

If you receive a compile or syntax error message like this, click the Help button to access VBA's online help system and get more information about the specific syntax error encountered. To clear the error dialog, click the OK button.

After you clear the error dialog from the screen, try to fix the syntax error. You can move the insertion point from the line after clearing the syntax error dialog, but the line remains colored red to indicate that it contains an error. VBA won't parse or compile the line containing the syntax error again until you run the procedure or until you again edit that line. VBA only parses lines in a procedure when you move the insertion point away from the line immediately after making changes or when you run the procedure.

Tip

You can turn the syntax checking feature on and off. Although it is highly recommended that you leave the syntax checking turned on (it can save you a great deal of time and frustration later), you can disable syntax checking by selecting the Tools, Options command to display the Options dialog box. To disable syntax checking, select the Editor tab (if necessary) to display the Editor options and clear the Auto Syntax Check check box. Choose OK when you finish setting the Editor options.

Disabling syntax checking merely disables the syntax error message dialogs. VBA still parses each new or edited line as you move the insertion point away from that line, and color codes lines with syntax errors red. VBA will always report on syntax errors when it compiles your source code.

When VBA is executing a procedure and encounters a line containing a syntax error, it stops executing the procedure, displays the module containing the procedure that has the syntax error, selects the specific line in the module where it detected the error, and then displays another compile error dialog.

The error dialog that VBA displays for a syntax error it encounters while executing a procedure usually contains much less detail about the specific error than the error dialog that VBA displays when it first detects the syntax error after you write or change the line. For this reason—and to avoid problems caused when a procedure's execution is unexpectedly terminated—you should always attempt to correct syntax errors the first time VBA detects them.

VBA is capable of detecting a large variety of syntax errors, informing you of missing commas, missing quote marks, and others. Not every syntax error message is so explicit, however. In some cases, VBA can't always tell you what's wrong with the syntax of a particular statement, only that there is a syntax error.

> **Tip**
>
> If you need help resolving syntax errors with a specific VBA keyword or built-in procedure (such as MsgBox), position the insertion point over the keyword or procedure name and press F1. VBA displays the online help for that keyword or procedure (if there is any).

Runtime Errors

It is possible for you to create a syntactically correct VBA statement that still doesn't execute properly. Errors that only show up when you actually run the procedure are called *runtime* errors. There are many different types of runtime errors. Runtime errors are usually caused by missing procedure arguments, arguments of the wrong data type, missing keywords, attempts to access non-existent disk drives or directory folders, or errors in logic.

Study the following VBA statement, which again contains an improperly formed MsgBox statement:

```
MsgBox "Hello, World!", "Greeting Box"
```

In this example, VBA finds nothing wrong with the syntax of the MsgBox statement: The data text is properly enclosed in quotation marks and the argument list is correctly separated with commas. (Because all arguments except the first argument for MsgBox are optional, VBA accepts two arguments for MsgBox as correct syntax.) When VBA attempts to execute the statement in this line, however, it displays the error dialog shown in Figure 2.20.

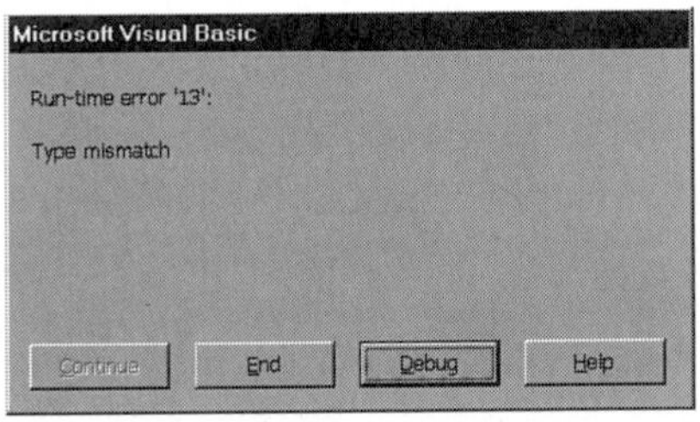

FIGURE 2.20

VBA detects some errors only when the procedure is running, and consequently displays a runtime error dialog.

This dialog informs you that an error occurred while VBA was running the procedure and displays a message describing the error. In this case, the specific error is a *type mismatch*. If you look again at the `MsgBox` statement above, you'll notice that the placeholding comma for the optional `Buttons` argument of `MsgBox` is missing (compare this to line 2 of Listing 2.5).

When VBA parses this statement, it compiles the quoted text `"Greeting Box"` as the second argument of `MsgBox`, instead of as the third argument, because of the missing placeholding comma. Because the command button argument must be a number, not text, VBA complains that the type of the data passed to the `MsgBox` procedure does not match the type of data expected for that argument. (Data types are explained in more detail in the next chapter.)

The error dialog box for runtime errors contains several command buttons. The following list summarizes each of these buttons:

- Continue—Choose this command button to continue the procedure. Some runtime errors allow you to continue running the procedure; for most runtime errors, however, this command button is disabled.

- End—Choose this command button to end the procedure.

- Debug—Choose this command button to enter Break mode and use the VB Editor's debugging features to help track down and solve the problem that caused the runtime error. Debugging is described in Day 15.

- Help—This command accesses the VBA online help system and displays the help topic describing the precise runtime error that has occurred. Use this button to get more information if it is not clear to you what the runtime error message means.

If you don't understand why the use of a particular VBA keyword or procedure causes a runtime error, you can get help with that specific keyword or procedure by positioning the insertion point over that word and pressing F1. VBA displays the online help topic for that keyword or procedure, if available.

Printing Your Source Code

At some point in time, you'll probably want to print some of your VBA source code. You might want to print a procedure for archival or documentation purposes, to show to a colleague, or to study. (Studying the macros produced by the Macro Recorder is a good way to help yourself learn VBA.)

When you print your VBA source code, you can choose to print all the modules in your project at once or to print only the currently selected module. You can't select individual procedures for printing.

To print your source code, follow these steps:

1. In the Project Explorer, select the module or project you want to print. If you want to print only selected text in a module, display the module and select the text you want printed.

2. Choose the File, Print command. The VB Editor displays the Print dialog (see Figure 2.21).

FIGURE 2.21

You can specify a variety of printing options in the Print dialog.

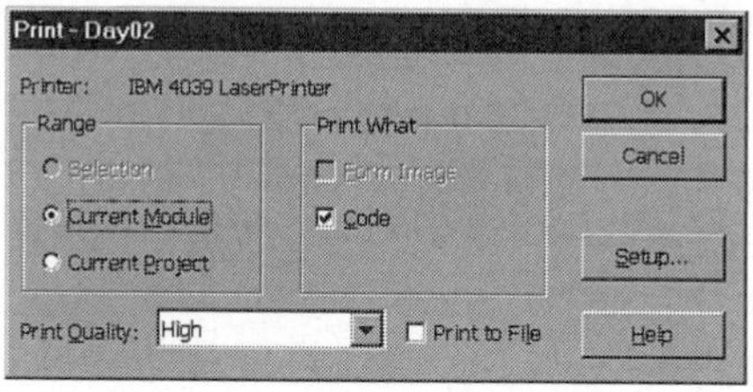

3. In the Range group of controls, select whether to print the current text selection, the selected module, or the entire project.

4. In the Print What group of controls, make sure that the Code check box is selected (in order to print your source code); if your project contains forms, select the Form Image check box to print a picture of your form.

5. Select any other printing options you want the same way you do when printing in Excel.

6. Click the OK button to print your source code.

When you print a project or module, you cannot preview the printed module, and the printed output from the module is always formatted the same way (except for page orientation, which you can control by clicking the Setup button in the Print dialog).

Summary

In today's lesson, you were introduced to the VB Editor's menu and toolbar commands before you learned how to locate, display, and edit a macro. You also learned how to make copies of individual macros and how to export entire modules as text files.

Next, you learned how to get started writing your own procedures without recording. You then learned how to make your procedures display messages for the procedure's user, followed by a discussion and explanation of the syntax and runtime errors you are likely to encounter as you write, edit, and run your procedures. Finally, you learned how to make a printed copy of your module sheets.

2

Q&A

Q I don't like the colors that the VB Editor uses to color-code the different parts of the VBA source code. Can I change the colors used?

A Yes, you can change the colors that the VB Editor uses to identify different parts of your source code. Choose the Tools, Options command to display the Options dialog and select the Editor Format tab, if necessary, to bring the formatting options to the front. Select the item whose color you want to change in the Code Colors list and select the color for the text in the Foreground and Background drop-down list boxes. Usually, you should select only the foreground color and leave the background color set to **Automatic**. When you are satisfied with your changes, choose OK.

Q I don't like the display font for the source code in my modules. Is there any way to change the display font and point size?

A Yes, you can change the display font and size used in the modules. Like the color options, the font and point size options are found on the Editor Format tab of the Options dialog. Select the display font in the Font drop-down list and choose the point size in the Size drop-down list. A sample of the text appears in the lower-right area of the Editor Format tab.

Q Do I have to indent code the same way the recorder does?

A No, you don't have to indent code the same way the recorder does; in fact, you don't have to indent your code at all.

There is nothing in VBA that requires you to indent your code; indenting code is merely a formatting convention used to make the code more readable for human beings. If you prefer a different indenting style, go ahead and use that style. It is highly recommended, however, that you do indent your code in some fashion in order to make it easier to understand.

Q When should I insert a new module to write a procedure?

A Insert a new module for a procedure whenever you want to start a new category of procedures or if a module is getting full—a module can contain up to 4,000 lines of code, approximately.

Q How can I select the font and formatting used when I print a module?

A Although you can use the Printer Setup dialog (accessed through the Setup button in the Print dialog) to alter the printing orientation (Portrait or Landscape), you cannot change the font or formatting used to print a module. Modules always print in the same font used onscreen, and with only the formatting that you put in the module by indenting your code, leaving blank lines, and so on. If, for some reason, you must change the font or print formatting of a procedure or module, use the Edit, Copy command to copy the text from the module to the Windows Clipboard, and then paste the text into a word processor (such as Windows WordPad, Microsoft Word, and so on) and use the word processor's features to change fonts and formatting in the module.

Workshop

The Workshop section presents Quiz questions to help you cement your new knowledge and Exercises to give you experience using what you have learned. Answers are in Appendix A.

Quiz

1. What is a VBA *module*?
2. What is the purpose of adding comments to a recorded macro? Should you use comments in procedures that you write yourself?
3. What is a VBA *keyword*?
4. What are the required parts of a procedure?
5. What is a *procedure declaration*?
6. What is the *body* of a procedure and where is it found?
7. What important tool does the VB Editor provide to help you locate specific macros?
8. Why is recorded VBA source code indented? Why should you indent your source code?
9. What is the purpose of the MsgBox procedure?
10. What is an *argument*? What is an *argument list*?

11. What is the *line-continuation symbol* and what is it used for?

12. What action does VBA perform whenever you move the insertion point to another line after editing or typing a line of VBA code?

13. What is a *syntax* error?

14. What is a *runtime* error?

Exercises

1. Start Excel 2000, activate the VB Editor, and then insert a new module in the Personal.xls workbook. Rename the module so that it has the name ProgramHelp. Now type the following program listing (omitting the line numbers):

```
1:  Sub ExcelVBAHelp()
2:  ' This procedure opens the Excel VBA Help
3:  ' reference at the object model topic
4:  '
5:      Application.Help "VBAXL9.CHM"
6:  End Sub
```

When you finish entering the procedure, run it. You should see the Visual Basic Reference online help file for Excel opened to the Excel Object Model topic.

2. Write a procedure to display the message I am a Visual Basic message in a dialog with a single button and the title VBA Message.

3. **BUG BUSTER:** Find the error in the following procedure (enter the procedure in a module and run it to help find the error):

```
1:  Sub Broken()
2:      MsgBox Yet Another Message
3:  End Sub
```

2

DAY 3

Understanding Data Types, Variables, and Constants

In this lesson, you learn about the types of data that VBA can manipulate, and how to add temporary data storage to your VBA procedures. In this lesson, you learn

- What a data type is, and what data types are inherent to VBA.
- What a variable is, and how to create and use variables in your procedures.
- What a constant is, and how to create and use constants in your procedures.
- How to get input from your procedure's user and store that input in a variable—an important first step in adding interactive decision-making to your programs.

Examining Visual Basic Data Types

Before you learn about variables, you should understand how VBA stores different kinds of information. VBA stores data in a way that distinguishes between numbers, dates, and text. *Data type* is the term that refers to the specific kinds of data that VBA can store and manipulate, such as text and numbers.

> **Note**
>
> The information in this chapter applies to VBA in any host application that implements VBA: Excel 2000, Word 2000, Access 2000, and so on. In fact, the information in this chapter is also applicable to Visual Basic. What you learn about data types, variables, and constants in this chapter is true in any "flavor" of Visual Basic you end up programming in.

Table 3.1 summarizes VBA's data types, shows how much memory each type consumes, briefly describes the data type, and gives the range of values that the data type can store. For data types that store numbers, the range of possible values indicates the largest and smallest number that VBA can store using that data type. For non-numeric data types, the value range indicates the upper and lower limits of values that VBA can store using those types.

> **Note**
>
> A *byte* is the typical unit used to measure computer memory and disk storage. A byte consists of eight *bits* (binary digits). Typically, a single alphabetic character requires a single byte of storage.

TABLE 3.1 VISUAL BASIC DATA TYPES

Type Name	Size in Bytes	Description and Value Range
Array	As required by the type and number of array elements	Each array element's range is the same as the base type. The number of elements in an array has no fixed limit.
Byte	1 (8 bits)	Stores positive numbers from 0 to 255.
Boolean	2 (16 bits)	Stores logical values; can contain only the values **True** or **False**.
Currency	8 (64 bits)	-922,337,203,685,477.5808 to 922,337,203,685,477.5807

Type Name	Size in Bytes	Description and Value Range
Date	8 (64 bits)	Stores a combination of date and time information. Dates can range from January 1, 0100 to December 31, 9999. Times can range from 00:00:00 to 23:59:59.
Double	8 (64 bits)	Negative numbers: from $-1.79769313486232 \times 10^{308}$ to $-4.94065645841247 \times 10^{-324}$. Positive numbers: from $4.94065645841247 \times 10^{-324}$ to $1.79769313486232 \times 10^{308}$.
Integer	2 (16 bits)	Whole numbers from -32,768 to 32,767.
Long	4 (32 bits)	Whole numbers from -2,147,483,648 to 2,147,483,647.
Object	4 (32 bits)	Used to access any object recognized by VBA. Stores the memory address of the object.
Single	4 (32 bits)	Negative numbers: from -3.402823×10^{38} to $-1.401298 \times 10^{-45}$. Positive numbers: from 1.401298×10^{-45} to 3.402823×10^{38}.
String	1 byte per character	Used to store text. Can contain 0 characters up to approximately 2 billion characters. In Windows 3.1, string length is a maximum of 65,535 (64KB) characters.
Variant	16 bytes, plus 1 byte per character	The Variant type can store any other data type. The range for Variants depends on the data actually stored: If text, the range is that of a string type; if numeric, the range is that of a Double type.

Later in this section, each data type listed in Table 3.1 (except **Object** and **Array** types) is described in more detail. The **Object** and **Array** types are described in their own separate lessons. Arrays are the topic of Day 14, "Arrays," and objects are the topic of Day 7, "Understanding Objects and Collections."

You can convert most of the data types listed in Table 3.1 to another data type. The next lesson shows how VBA automatically converts data and briefly describes how to manually convert data types. This lesson focuses on the different data types themselves: their qualities, their limits, and their uses.

SCIENTIFIC NOTATION

In Table 3.1, you might see a way of representing numbers—called *scientific notation*—that is unfamiliar to you. Scientific notation is used to represent very large and very small numbers in a compact format. In scientific notation, values are represented without leading or trailing zeros, and there is only one digit to the left of the decimal. The number is multiplied by 10 raised to some power (the *exponent*) to show where the decimal point actually lies. Scientific notation is compact and readable compared to a number in standard notation with 300 zeroes after it.

Keep in mind that a negative exponent results in a smaller number; a positive exponent results in a larger number. You cannot use superscript characters in source code, so VBA uses a variation of scientific notation devised especially for computers. In VBA's scientific notation, use the letter *E* followed by the exponent, instead of writing *×10*. The following table gives examples of numbers in VBA scientific notation and standard notation.

-1.23E2	-123
-1.23E-2	-0.0123
2.5E10	25,000,000,000
7E9	7,000,000,000
2.5E-10	0.00000000025
1.7E1	17
1.7E0	1.7

Dates

VBA uses the **Date** data type to store dates and times. **Date** type data uses 8 bytes of memory for every date/time combination stored.

Note

As you work with VBA **Date** type information, be aware that VBA's **Date** types aren't the same as the date types used in Excel worksheets or Access databases, although they have many similarities.

Usually, you need not be concerned with how VBA stores **Date** type information: You simply display, store, or otherwise manipulate a date; VBA automatically handles all the details of converting the serial date number into year, month, day, and time information for you.

When VBA displays dates (by using MsgBox, for example), the date displays in the short date format that your computer system uses. Similarly, VBA displays the time information stored with a **Date** using the 12- or 24-hour time format for your computer.

3

Tip

In Windows and Windows NT, you can change the date and time formats for your computer by choosing the Regional Settings icon in the Control Panel.

VBA's **Date** data type is a *serial date*. (Serial dates store a date as a number of days from a given starting date, instead of keeping track of months and years separately.) The base date for VBA's **Date** type is December 30, 1899. VBA uses negative numbers to represent dates before 12/30/1899 and positive numbers to represent dates after that. The number *0* represents the date 12/30/1899, itself. In this scheme, January 1, 1900 is represented by the number *2* (1/1/1900 is 2 days after 12/30/1899); the number *-2*, however, is the date 12/28/1899 (two days before 12/30/1899).

Note

Excel and other VBA host applications, such as MS Access, have their own serial date data types. Excel for Windows, for example, uses serial date numbers, but uses a different base date: January 1, 1900. (You can also set Excel for compatibility with the Macintosh date system, which uses serial dates from January 1, 1904.)

VBA always uses the same base date for its **Date** type serial dates, regardless of the host application's date scheme—VBA always uses 12/30/1899 as the base date.

In a serial date number, the whole part of the number (digits to the left of the decimal) is the total number of days from the base date. Optionally, a VBA serial date can have digits to the right of the decimal that indicate the time of day as a fraction of a day. One hour is 1/24 of a day, approximately 0.0416. Similarly, one minute is 1/1,440 of a day, and a second is 1/86,400 of a day.

You can subtract dates from each other or add or subtract numbers to a date to change its value. For instance, if you want to determine the number of days between two dates, simply subtract the earlier date from the later date. VBA knows, because the values are **Date** type values, that the intent of the computation is to obtain the difference, in days, between the two dates. Similarly, if you want to find out the date 60 days from a given date, just add 60 to the date—VBA computes a date 60 days later.

VBA provides several built-in procedures (described in Day 5) to extract separately the year, month, day, hours, minutes, and seconds stored by a **Date** type.

Numbers

VBA has six different numeric data types: **Byte**, **Integer**, **Long**, **Single**, **Double**, and **Currency**. A numeric data type stores numbers using various formats depending on the specific numeric type. Numeric data types provide a compact and efficient way to store numbers. The numeric data type that occupies the most memory (and has the greatest range of possible values) takes up no more than 8 bytes of memory to store numbers that can have as many as 300 digits. The following paragraphs describe each of the numeric types in more detail.

Byte, Integer, and Long Integer Data

An *integer* is a whole number with no fractional part. The numbers *1*, *3,768*, and *12* are all integers; the numbers *1.5*, *3.14*, and *17.2* are not integers. (The number *1.0* is not an integer, even though the fractional part is zero—integers never contain a decimal point, even if the decimal fraction is zero.)

VBA provides three different integer data types: **Byte**, **Integer**, and **Long** integer. The **Byte** data type is the smallest of VBA's three integer data types, and can only store numbers from 0 to 255. The **Byte** data type uses only one byte of storage (255 is as high as you can count with only 8 bits). You cannot store negative numbers in a **Byte** data type. Typically, **Byte** data types are used to store binary data (graphics files, sound files, and so on).

The **Integer** data type requires 2 bytes of memory to store a number; the range of numbers you can store as an **Integer** data type is from -32,768 up to 32,767. Because the range for an **Integer** data type is fairly limited, VBA provides another, larger integer type: the **Long** *integer*. A **Long** integer (referred to simply as a **Long**) uses 4 bytes of memory to store a number and has a value range from -2,147,483,648 to 2,147,483,647.

Byte, **Integer**, and **Long** integer data types have a couple of advantages over other numeric data types: Integers require less memory to store a number than VBA's other numeric data types, and mathematical and comparison operations on **Byte**, **Integer**, or **Long** data type numbers are faster than those for floating-point numeric types. **Byte**, **Integer**, and **Long** data types have many uses. Most frequently, you use integer data types for cumulative counting operations because of their compact size and faster speed in arithmetic operations. Use a **Byte**, **Integer**, or **Long** type for numbers that do not have a fractional part.

VBA automatically converts **Byte**, **Integer**, and **Long** data types into text when you display them using procedures such as MsgBox. The next lesson contains more information about VBA's automatic data type conversions.

Floating-Point Numbers

Floating-point numbers can have any number of digits before or after the decimal point (within the range limits of the specific data type). Floating-point numbers get their name from the fact that the decimal point "floats" from one position to another depending on whether the value stored is large or small. The numbers *11.0123*, *-1107.1*, *0.0125*, and *435.67876* are all floating-point numbers. Floating-point numbers are also sometimes called *real* numbers. Use floating-point data types any time you need to store a number that has a fractional part.

VBA has two different floating-point data types: **Single** and **Double**. The **Single** data type requires 4 bytes of memory, and can store negative numbers from -3.402823×10^{38} to $-1.401298 \times 10^{-45}$ and positive numbers from 1.401298×10^{-45} to 3.402823×10^{38}. Numbers stored using the **Single** data type are called *single-precision* numbers. The **Double** data type requires 8 bytes of memory, and can store negative numbers from $-1.79769313486232 \times 10^{308}$ to $-4.94065645841247 \times 10^{-324}$ and positive numbers from $4.94065645841247 \times 10^{-324}$ to $1.79769313486232 \times 10^{308}$. Numbers stored using the **Double** data type are called *double-precision* numbers. (You can store the value *0* in any of VBA's numeric data types.)

Although single- and double-precision numbers have greater ranges than other numeric data types, they have a couple of minor disadvantages. Operations performed on floating-point numbers are somewhat slower than similar operations on other numeric data types. Also, numbers stored as floating-point data types can be subject to small rounding errors. Like the integer data types, VBA automatically converts **Single** and **Double** values into text when you display them with procedures such as MsgBox. If a floating-point number is very large or very small, VBA displays the number in scientific notation.

The Currency Data Type

VBA's **Currency** data type is a *fixed-point* number, that is, the decimal point always occurs in the same place—there are always four places to the right of the decimal point. Use the **Currency** data type to store numbers when accuracy is extremely important, as is true with money calculations.

The **Currency** data type requires 8 bytes of memory, and can store numbers from -922,337,203,685,477.5808 to 922,337,203,685,477.5807. Mathematical operations on **Currency** data type numbers have little or no rounding errors and are therefore somewhat more accurate than floating-point numbers. Rounding errors with **Currency** type numbers typically occur only when you multiply or divide **Currency** type numbers by values with a different numeric type. Like all the other numeric data types, VBA automatically converts **Currency** values into text when you display them.

3

Text Strings

Any text data stored in a VBA program is called a *string*; strings in VBA are stored using the `String` data type. Strings get their names because text data is commonly regarded as a string of characters. A string can contain any kind of text character: letters of the alphabet, digits, punctuation, or various symbols. Strings in VBA code are always enclosed in double quotation marks ("). `"Fred and Wilma"`, `"3.14"`, `"Robert Silverberg"`, and `"16,000.00"` are all strings. There are two categories of string: variable-length strings, which grow or shrink in size as the string they store changes size, and fixed-length strings, which always remain the same size. All strings in VBA are variable-length strings unless you specify a fixed length, as described later in this chapter.

`String` data types play an important role in most VBA programs. Most user input (in dialogs, worksheet cells, and so on) is string data. Also, because you can only display text onscreen, all other data types must be converted to string data before you can display them. Many of VBA's built-in procedures—such as `MsgBox`—use string data in all or some of their arguments.

VBA provides several operators to *concatenate* (connect together) and compare strings; VBA also has several built-in procedures to help you extract substrings from larger strings, search for characters or words in a string, change the case of letters in a string, and so on. The next lesson describes VBA's string operators, and Day 5 describes VBA's string manipulation procedures.

Logical Values

Typically, a VBA program makes decisions by testing whether various conditions are true or false. To simplify testing various conditions, and to provide a means of storing the results of such tests, VBA provides a logical data type. Logical values of True and False are referred to as *Boolean* values. (The name comes from a mathematician named Boole who developed a system of logical mathematics.) The VBA logical data type is also called the `Boolean` data type.

VBA's `Boolean` data type requires 2 bytes of memory and can have one of two values: `True` or `False`. If you display a `Boolean` data type onscreen, VBA automatically converts it to a string containing either the word *True* or the word *False*. `Boolean` values are produced as the result of a comparison operation. (A *comparison operation* is when you compare one thing to another, such as comparing two numbers to see which is greater or comparing two strings to see which is alphabetically lower.) Tomorrow's lesson describes VBA's various comparison operations.

Variant Data

The **Variant** data type is a special data type that can store any of the data types listed in Table 3.1, including **Object** and **Array** types. VBA uses the **Variant** data type for all variables unless you explicitly declare the data type for the variable, as described later in this chapter.

Variant data types take on the characteristics of the particular data type they are currently storing. If a **Variant** data type contains string data, for example, the **Variant** takes on the characteristics of a **String** data type. If a **Variant** data type contains numeric data, the **Variant** takes on the characteristics of a numeric data type—usually a **Double**, although **Variant** types can also have the characteristics of **Integer**, **Long**, **Single**, or **Currency** types.

A **Variant** data type uses the most compact representation possible for the data it contains. If VBA stores a whole number in a **Variant**, the number is handled as an **Integer** or as a **Long**, depending on its size. For instance, VBA treats the number 15 in a **Variant** type as an **Integer**; it would treat the number 1,000,000 in a **Variant** type as a **Long**.

VBA stores most floating-point numbers in a **Variant** as the **Double** data type. VBA includes the **Variant** data type so that you don't always have to be concerned with specifying the data types of variables you use in your code. Any variable for which you do not specifically declare the data type becomes a **Variant** data type.

Although **Variant** data types are convenient and relieve you of some work when writing your procedures, they do require more memory than any other data type except for large strings and arrays. (**Array** types are described fully in Day 14.) Also, mathematical and comparison operations on **Variant** data types are slower than similar operations performed on any other data type. In general, you should avoid using **Variant** variables—relying on **Variant** variable data types can lead you to sloppy programming habits and make it difficult to find and eliminate bugs in your programs.

Understanding Variables

Variables are important because they provide a computer program with a way to temporarily store and manipulate data. This section gives you an understanding of what a variable is and how to create them.

What Is a Variable?

A *variable* is a name given by you, the programmer, to an area of the computer's memory used to store data of any type. Think of a variable as a pigeon-hole in which you can put any single item of data and save it for later use. The variable's name is the identifying label for that pigeon-hole. The contents of the pigeon-hole (the *value* of the variable) can change, but the name of the variable remains the same. VBA variables can store any of the data types listed in Table 3.1.

In some senses, a variable is like a named worksheet cell. In Excel, you can give a name to a cell in a worksheet and then refer to that worksheet cell by its name so that you don't have to use—or even remember—the cell's actual row and column address each time you want to refer to the data or formula in that worksheet cell.

In the same way, a VBA variable is a name that refers to a specific memory location in your computer so that you don't have to worry about the actual memory address of the stored data: You use the variable name to refer to whatever data is stored in that memory location. VBA handles all the details of finding specific memory locations in your computer for you. You never have to worry about the specific address of a variable's data, just use the variable name to refer to the stored data.

You use variables in VBA statements the same way you use variables in algebraic equations. The variable represents a numeric quantity, text, date, or other information that is not known precisely at the time you write the statement, but will be present and available when VBA executes the statement.

Whenever a variable name appears in a VBA statement, VBA inserts into the statement the actual value currently stored in the memory location referred to by the variable. In the following example, if the variable AnyNum contains the number 2, the entire statement evaluates to the number 4:

```
AnyNum + 2
```

When VBA executes the preceding statement, it substitutes the number 2 (stored in the variable named AnyNum) into the statement, adds it to the number 2 that is written directly into the statement, and comes up with the result: 4. If the variable AnyNum contains the number 4 instead, the same statement (AnyNum + 2) evaluates to 6.

As another, more complex example of how you use variables, examine the following formula, which computes what percentage one number is of another number (you might recall this formula, or one like it, from your high-school mathematics courses):

```
Percent = (Part ÷ Whole) × 100
```

In this sample statement, the variables named Part and Whole represent two different numbers. The formula in this statement computes what percentage Part is of the Whole; the variable named Percent stores the result of the computation. When VBA executes this statement, it retrieves whatever numbers are stored in the memory locations referred to by Part and Whole and inserts them into the statement before performing any computations.

If the variable Part contains the number 5 and Whole contains the number 20, VBA substitutes these values when it executes the statement to create the following interim statement (VBA stores such interim statements internally and discards them when it has finished executing the statement; you will never see the interim statements that VBA constructs):

```
Percent = (5 ÷ 20) × 100
```

Next, VBA performs the computation and stores the result in the memory location referred to by the Percent variable: 5 divided by 20 is 0.25, and 0.25 multiplied by 100 is 25; therefore, the value that VBA ends up storing in the Percent variable is the number 25. Any number previously stored in the Percent variable is replaced by this new value.

Note

> VBA doesn't really use the division (÷) and multiplication (×) symbols shown in the sample formulas in this section because you can't type these symbols at the keyboard. Instead, VBA uses the slash (/) and the asterisk (*) to indicate division and multiplication. Day 4 describes all of VBA's arithmetic operation symbols and their meanings. This chapter uses the standard division (÷) and multiplication (×) symbols so that you can focus on the discussions of variables and their use without worrying about what unfamiliar symbols might mean.

Choosing Variable Names

With only a few restrictions, you can choose any name you want for a variable. This section first explains VBA's rules and limitations for variable names and then gives you some guidelines for naming your variables.

> **UNDERSTANDING IDENTIFIERS**
>
> An *identifier* is a name you give to the elements that you create in your procedures and modules, such as variables. The term identifier comes from the fact that the names you create identify specific memory locations (in the case of a variable name), groups of instructions (in the case of a macro or procedure name), or other program elements.
>
> The same rules and guidelines explained in this section for choosing a variable name also apply to choosing other identifier names. Later lessons refer you to these rules for creating identifiers.

A variable name must follow these rules:

- The variable name must begin with a letter of the alphabet.
- After the first letter, the variable name can consist of any combination of digit, letter, or underscore (_) characters.
- Variable names cannot contain spaces, a period (.), or any of the symbols VBA uses to indicate mathematical or comparison operations (=, +, -, and so on).
- Variable names cannot exceed 255 characters in length.
- A variable's name cannot duplicate certain VBA keywords. If you choose variable names that duplicate these keywords—called *restricted keywords*—VBA displays one of several possible syntax error messages.
- A variable's name must be unique within its *scope*, that is, the variable name must be unique within the procedure or module in which you declare the variable. If you inadvertently give two variables the same name in the same procedure, or you give a variable a name that is the same as a procedure name in the same module, VBA displays an error message when you run the procedure.

Some examples of valid variable names are:

```
MyVar
PayDate
New_Item
Percent
Whole
Part
Line12
```

The following examples are *not* valid variable names:

```
New Item       'Not valid because it contains a space character
5thDimension   'Does not begin with a letter
Dim            'duplicates a VBA restricted keyword
Week/Day       'Contains an invalid character: VBA interprets
               'the slash character as a division operation
```

Names for variables are not *case sensitive,* that is, the capitalization of the variable name does not matter. The variable names MyVar and myvar are the same as far as VBA is concerned. In fact, VBA regularizes the capitalization of variable names in your code based on the capitalization you used the last time you typed the variable name. For example, if you type the variable name MyVar and then later type the variable name as myvar, VBA changes the previous MyVar to myvar.

When you choose names for variables, try to make the name as descriptive as possible; choose names like PcntProfit rather than X or Y. A good name for a variable that stores a value representing a temperature in degrees Celsius, for example, is CelsiusTemp or, possibly, DegreesC. In the percentage formula example in the preceding section, the variable names Part and Whole were chosen to reflect the purpose and use of the numbers they store.

3

Do

DO remember that although capitalization of variable names (or other identifiers) does not matter to VBA, adding capitalization can make your code much easier for a human being to read and understand.

DO remember to take advantage of the underscore (_); you can use the underscore as a substitute for a space character to make your variable names (and other identifiers) more readable. The second and third identifiers in the following are much more readable than the first due to the addition of capital letters and underscores:

```
verylongidentifiername
VeryLongIdentifierName
Very_Long_Identifier_Name
```

Creating Variables

The simplest way to create a variable is to just use the variable in a VBA statement. VBA creates a variable and reserves memory for the variable's storage location the first time the variable appears in a VBA statement, usually a statement that stores a data value in the variable.

Storing a data value in a variable is called *assigning the variable* or *making an assignment.* You make an assignment to a variable by using the assignment operator, which is represented by the equals sign (=). The following line is an example of assigning a value to a variable:

```
MyVar = 15
```

This statement stores the numeric value 15 in the memory location specified by the variable name MyVar. If this is the first statement in a procedure to use this variable, VBA creates the variable, reserves a memory location to store the variable's data, and then stores the number 15 in the new memory location specified by the variable name.

If the MyVar variable already exists, VBA simply stores the number 15 in the memory location referred to by MyVar. The new value replaces whatever was previously stored in MyVar and the previous contents of MyVar are lost.

Creating a variable by just using it in a statement is called an *implicit variable declaration*. By using the variable in a statement, you are implicitly telling (declaring to) VBA that you want to create that variable. All variables that VBA creates with an implicit variable declaration have the **Variant** data type. Implicit variable declaration is also known less formally as *on-the-fly* variable declaration.

Implicit variable declaration is convenient, but it has potential problems. One such problem occurs when you have a variable named MyValue, for example, and later misspell its name as MValue. Depending on exactly where the misspelled variable name occurs in your code, VBA might produce a runtime error or simply create a new variable. If VBA does create a new variable, you might end up with subtle problems in your code that are very difficult to find.

Implicit variable declaration also causes problems if you write an assignment statement mistakenly believing that you are implicitly declaring a new variable when you are really using a previously created variable. In this case, you inadvertently destroy the previously stored value. This kind of problem usually does not result in a runtime error, but instead tends to result in other problems of which the cause is difficult to locate.

For these reasons and others, VBA provides a way for you to make *explicit* variable declarations. Declaring variables explicitly provides these advantages:

- Explicit declaration speeds up the execution of your code. VBA creates all the variables declared explicitly in a module or procedure before it executes the procedure's code. The speed of your code's execution increases by the amount of time otherwise required to analyze and create an implicitly declared variable.

- Explicit declaration helps avoid errors due to misspelling a variable name, as described in the preceding paragraphs.

- Explicit variable declarations make your code easier to read and understand. By seeing all the variable declarations at the beginning of a module or procedure, a human reader can more easily determine which variables are used in that module or procedure.

- Explicitly declaring a variable helps regularize the variable name's capitalization. If you declare a variable explicitly, VBA always changes the capitalization of the variable name in a VBA statement to match the capitalization of the variable name in the variable declaration instead of using the capitalization from the last time you typed the variable name. For example, if you explicitly declare a variable capitalized as `MyValue` and then later type the variable name as `myvalue`, VBA changes `myvalue` to match the capitalization in the explicit declaration: `MyValue`.

Note

Although **Variant** data types can store **Date** type data, a **Variant** might not correctly store a date obtained from Excel. For example, VBA won't recognize a date from an Excel worksheet cell as a date unless the Excel date is formatted with one of Excel's date formats. A **Date** type, however, will correctly store the Excel date from the worksheet cell regardless of its formatting. Conversely, when you insert a date value from VBA into an Excel worksheet cell, the date information is not correctly interpreted if it comes from a **Variant** data type instead of a **Date** type. For these reasons, you should always explicitly declare variables you use for dates as a **Date** data type. (Specifying the data type of a variable is explained later in this chapter.)

SYNTAX

To explicitly declare a variable, use VBA's **Dim** statement with the following syntax:

```
Dim name
```

name is any valid variable identifier. For example:

```
Dim PcntProfit
```

The statement above tells VBA to create a variable named `PcntProfit`. (The **Dim** keyword, by the way, is an abbreviation of the word *dimension*.) All variables that you create with this form of the **Dim** keyword are **Variant** type variables. (You learn how to create variables with specific data types later in this lesson.)

Note

Whenever VBA creates a new variable, it *initializes* the variable: strings are set to contain no characters, numbers are set to 0, **Boolean** variables are initialized to **False**, and dates are initialized to December 30, 1899.

If you want, you can declare several variables on the same line, separating each variable name with a comma, as shown in the following syntax example:

SYNTAX

```
Dim name1, name2, nameN
```

name1, *name2*, and *nameN* are any valid VBA variable names. You can list as many variable names as you desire. The following `Dim` statement declares three different variables
(`PcntProfit`, `Gross_Income`, and `Total_Costs`):

```
Dim PcntProfit, Gross_Income, Total_Costs
```

You can only declare a variable once in a particular procedure or module. As long as the
`Dim` statement comes before any statements that actually use the variable, you can place
the `Dim` statement anywhere in a procedure. The best programming practice, however,
gathers all explicit variable declarations into a single area at the beginning of a procedure.

Listing 3.1 shows the `HelloWorld` procedure from yesterday's lesson modified to explicitly declare a variable named `HelloMsg`, which it uses to store the text the `MsgBox` statement will display. (The `HelloWorld` procedure in Listing 3.1 displays the dialog shown
in Figure 3.1.)

INPUT   **LISTING 3.1**   THE *HelloWorld* PROCEDURE WITH AN EXPLICIT VARIABLE
DECLARATION

```
1:  Sub HelloWorld()
2:      Dim HelloMsg     'stores text for the MsgBox message
3:      HelloMsg = "Hello, World!"
4:      MsgBox HelloMsg, , "Greeting Box"
5:  End Sub
```

ANALYSIS   The `Dim` statement appears in line 2 of Listing 3.1. When VBA executes this
statement, it creates the variable `HelloMsg` and reserves memory storage space
for it. (The `HelloMsg` variable is a **Variant** type; unless you specify the variable's type as
described later in this lesson, VBA always creates **Variant** type variables.) Line 2
includes a trailing comment that indicates the purpose of the variable.

Line 3 of Listing 3.1 makes an assignment to the `HelloMsg` variable; this line stores the
string "`Hello, World!`" in the memory location referred to by the `HelloMsg` variable.
Next, line 4 uses the `HelloMsg` variable as one of the arguments for the `MsgBox` procedure. When VBA executes line 4, it retrieves the string stored in `HelloMsg` and passes
that string to `MsgBox` as its first argument. `MsgBox` displays the same message dialog
as before, but `MsgBox` now gets its first argument from a variable, and that variable contains the same string information that was previously written directly into the `MsgBox`
statement.

FIGURE 3.1

The HelloWorld *procedure displays this message dialog.*

Do

DO add comments explaining how a procedure uses a particular variable, even if the variable has a properly descriptive name. Comments increase the readability of your procedures (and make it easier to change them later if you need to).

DO always manually initialize a variable by making an assignment to it before using that variable in other operations.

DON'T

DON'T assume that just because VBA initializes a newly created variable, the new variable contains any particular value.

Scope: Determining Which Variables Are Available

The term *scope* refers to the area of a VBA procedure or module in which a given variable, procedure, or other identifier is accessible. This section discusses the two basic scope levels: procedure-level and module-level. Variables, procedures, and identifiers that are available only inside a procedure have procedure-level scope, and those that are available to all procedures in a module have module-level scope.

Procedure-Level Scope

A variable declared inside a procedure is available only inside that procedure. The HelloMsg variable shown in line 2 of Listing 3.1, for example, is only available in the HelloWorld procedure; no other procedure can access that variable. In fact, the HelloMsg variable really exists only while VBA is actually executing the HelloWorld procedure. The HelloMsg variable is therefore said to have *procedure-level* scope.

Although it might not seem so at first, VBA restricts the availability of variables through its scope rules to help simplify things for you, the programmer. Because a variable with procedure-level scope is not available to any procedure except the procedure in which you declare the variable, you don't have to worry quite so much about duplicate variable names.

The rules for choosing variable names tell you that a variable's name must be unique within its scope. For variables with procedure-level scope, this means that you cannot declare two variables with the same name in the same procedure. (Obviously, neither VBA nor a human being can tell which variable you intend to use if they both have the same name.)

Because procedure-level scope restricts a variable's availability to the procedure in which you declare the variable, however, you can safely use the same variable name in *different* procedures. Look at Listing 3.2, which shows two complete procedures. (HelloWorld in this listing displays the same dialog shown previously in Figure 3.1.)

INPUT   **LISTING 3.2**   PROCEDURE-LEVEL SCOPE

```
1:  Sub HelloWorld()
2:      Dim HelloMsg    'stores text for the MsgBox message
3:      HelloMsg = "Hello, World!"
4:      MsgBox HelloMsg, , "Greeting Box"
5:  End Sub
6:
7:  Sub HelloDave()
8:      Dim HelloMsg    'stores text for the MsgBox message
9:      HelloMsg = "Hello, Dave!"
10:     MsgBox HelloMsg, , "Another Message Box"
11: End Sub
```

ANALYSIS   Lines 1 through 5 contain the same HelloWorld procedure from Listing 3.1, which works exactly the same. A second procedure, HelloDave, has been added to the module and begins on line 7 of Listing 3.2. The HelloDave procedure works exactly the same as the HelloWorld procedure, it just displays a different text message and title in its dialog. Figure 3.2 shows the message dialog displayed by the HelloDave procedure.

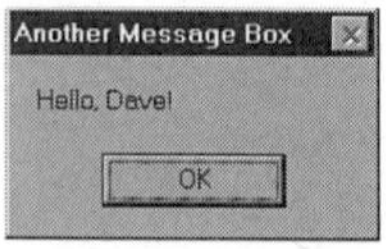

FIGURE 3.2

The HelloDave *proce-dure in Listing 3.2 displays this message dialog.*

Notice in lines 2 and 8 that both procedures use the **Dim** statement to declare variables named HelloMsg. This is reasonable because the variable name HelloMsg is a good, descriptive name for the variable's contents and purpose in both procedures.

Because the HelloMsg variables are declared inside separate procedures and have procedure-level scope, there is no ambiguity about which variable VBA should use. In the HelloWorld procedure, VBA uses the HelloMsg variable declared locally in that procedure (line 2 of the listing). In the HelloDave procedure, VBA uses the HelloMsg variable declared locally in that procedure (line 8).

Module-Level Scope

Sometimes you'll want to have several procedures access the same variable. Usually it's more efficient to compute a value once, store it in a variable, and then use that variable in several procedures than it is to compute the same value over and over again.

For example, you might write several procedures, all of which need to use a value for the gross sales income for your company. One procedure might use the figure for gross sales to compute the percent of profit earned, another procedure might use the gross sales figure to compute gross profits, yet another procedure would use the gross sales figure to compute net profits, and so on.

If you declare a Sales variable to store the computed figure for gross sales inside a procedure, the Sales variable has procedure-level scope and no other procedure can access the value stored in Sales. This means that your procedures for computing percent profit, gross profit, and net profit each must compute the value for gross sales themselves. Obviously, computing the gross sales figure repeatedly is wasted time and effort.

Instead, it would be more efficient to create a procedure that computes only the figure for gross sales and stores that figure in a variable named Sales, which is available to all the other procedures. This way, you compute the value for Sales only once: When the percent profit procedure needs this value, it uses the value stored in the Sales variable; the separate procedures for computing gross profit and net profit also would use the previously computed figure stored in the Sales variable.

VBA enables you to declare variables that several procedures can access at once. When a variable is available to all the procedures in a module, the variable is said to have *module-level* scope. VBA limits the scope of a module-level variable to the module in which you declare the variable. (VBA does provide ways you can force a variable to have even greater scope; Day 10, "Advanced Techniques for Using Data Types and Variables," describes those techniques.)

To make a variable available to all the procedures in a particular module, place the Dim statement for that variable at the beginning of the module, before any procedure declarations. Listing 3.3 shows an entire module that contains two simple procedures and a single module-level variable declaration. The `HelloWorld` procedure in Listing 3.3 displays the message dialog already shown in Figure 3.1, and the `HelloDave` procedure displays the same message dialog shown in Figure 3.2.

> **Note**
>
> The area at the beginning of a module, before any procedure declarations, is referred to as the *declaration* area of the module because this is where you place module-level variable declarations and other directives to VBA that affect the entire module. You can easily jump to the declaration area of any module by choosing (`Declarations`) in the Procedure list of the Code Window.

INPUT **LISTING 3.3** MODULE-LEVEL VARIABLE SCOPE

```
1:  Dim HelloMsg    'used by all procedures in this module
2:
3:  Sub HelloWorld()
4:      HelloMsg = "Hello, World!"
5:      MsgBox HelloMsg, , "Greeting Box"
6:  End Sub
7:
8:  Sub HelloDave()
9:      HelloMsg = "Hello, Dave!"
10:     MsgBox HelloMsg, , "Another Message Box"
11: End Sub
```

ANALYSIS In this listing, lines 3 through 6 contain the `HelloWorld` procedure and lines 8 through 11 contain the `HelloDave` procedure. Notice that neither of these procedures contains any **Dim** statements. Instead, line 1 uses a **Dim** statement to declare a module-level variable named `HelloMsg`.

Because line 1 declares the `HelloMsg` variable at a module-level, it is available to all the procedures in the same module. In lines 4 and 5 of the `HelloWorld` procedure, VBA uses the module-level `HelloMsg` variable. Similarly, in lines 9 and 10 of the `HelloDave` procedure, VBA uses the same module-level `HelloMsg` variable.

Using Variables with the Same Name at Different Scope Levels

A variable name must be unique within its scope. Just as you cannot declare two variables with the same name in the same procedure, you cannot declare two module-level variables with the same name in the same module for the same reasons.

You can, however, safely have variables with the same name at *different* scope levels. When variables have the same name but different scope, VBA uses the variable with the most *local* scope. You've already partially seen how this works in Listing 3.2, which shows two different procedures, each of which declares its own variable but uses the same name for the variable. You saw that because the variables have procedure-level scope, each procedure can use only its own *local* variable. Listing 3.4 shows an entire module containing three procedures, all of which use variables with the same names.

INPUT   **LISTING 3.4**   COMBINED MODULE-LEVEL AND PROCEDURE-LEVEL SCOPE

```
1:  Dim HelloMsg     'used by all procedures in this module
2:                   'that do not have their own HelloMsg variable
3:  Sub HelloWorld()
4:       HelloMsg = "Hello, World!"
5:       MsgBox HelloMsg, , "Greeting Box"
6:  End Sub
7:
8:  Sub HelloDave()
9:       HelloMsg = "Hello, Dave!"
10:      MsgBox HelloMsg, , "Another Message Box"
11: End Sub
12:
13: Sub AnotherMessage()
14:      Dim HelloMsg     'local declaration: this procedure uses this
15:                       'variable
16:      HelloMsg = "Yet Another Message"
17:      MsgBox HelloMsg, , "Yet Another Message Box"
18: End Sub
```

ANALYSIS   Listing 3.4 shows three different procedures. You've already seen the first two procedures in Listing 3.3. The third procedure, AnotherMessage, begins in line 13 and ends in line 18. The AnotherMessage procedure works the same as the preceding procedures, displaying a message in a dialog by using a MsgBox statement.

Notice that line 1 of the listing declares a module-level variable, HelloMsg. Line 14, in the AnotherMessage procedure, also declares a variable named HelloMsg. When VBA executes the HelloWorld procedure, it uses the HelloMsg variable declared in line 1. HelloWorld has no variables declared locally, there is no possible ambiguity, and therefore VBA uses the module-level variable. Similarly, when VBA executes the HelloDave procedure, it also uses the HelloMsg variable declared in line 1.

The `AnotherMessage` procedure, however, contains its own `HelloMsg` variable declaration (line 14). When VBA executes lines 16 and 17, therefore, it resolves any ambiguity about which `HelloMsg` variable to use by using the most local variable: the `HelloMsg` variable declared at procedure level in line 14 of the `AnotherMessage` procedure.

The module-level `HelloMsg` variable declared in line 1 is not accessible to the `AnotherMessage` procedure.

> **Note**   Procedure-level variables are frequently referred to as *local* variables because their declarations are local to the currently executing procedure.

Persistence: Determining How Long Variables Retain Their Value

Persistence is the term used to refer to the length of time that any given variable retains the value assigned to it. Values assigned to variables persist only as long as the variable is active within its scope.

When you declare a variable inside a procedure, that variable exists only while VBA is executing the procedure containing that particular variable. When VBA executes a procedure, it reserves memory space for all the variables declared locally in that procedure, whether the variables are declared explicitly or implicitly. When VBA stops executing that particular procedure, VBA returns the memory used by the procedure's local variables to the general pool of available computer memory and the procedure's local variables cease to exist.

For instance, when VBA begins executing the `HelloWorld` procedure in Listing 3.1, it reserves memory space for the `HelloMsg` variable. When VBA finishes executing `HelloWorld`, it returns the memory reserved for the `HelloMsg` variable to the general pool of available memory, essentially destroying whatever value was stored in `HelloMsg`.

Procedure-level variables are created each time a procedure begins to execute and are destroyed whenever the procedure stops executing. Stated in more technical terms, a local variable is undefined (or *out of context*) until the procedure that declares it begins to execute. When the procedure that declares the variable stops executing, the variable is once again undefined.

Variables that you declare at the module level persist for as long as VBA is executing a procedure in that module. When VBA executes a procedure, it actually looks through the entire module that contains the procedure it is executing and creates any module-level variables. As long as VBA is executing a procedure in that module, the values stored in the module-level variables are retained.

Requiring Explicit Variable Declaration

Although implicit variable declaration (declaring variables by just using them) is convenient, it does have some inherent problems. As long as you can declare variables implicitly, you run the risk of inadvertently creating a new variable when you really intend to use an existing variable, or of using an existing variable when you really intend to create a new one. Both of these mistakes lead to bugs in your code that are very difficult to track down. (A *bug* is any defect in your code that prevents it from executing correctly or that results in erroneous computations.)

Earlier you learned how to use the **Dim** statement to declare variables and help reduce the problems associated with implicit declaration. Using **Dim** alone to declare variables won't always help you detect or prevent the subtle errors related to implicit variable declaration as long as VBA enables you to declare variables implicitly.

To help you detect errors associated with implicit variable declaration at all times, VBA provides the **Option Explicit** command. When you use **Option Explicit**, VBA requires you to declare all variables with a **Dim** statement before you use them. The **Option Explicit** command essentially prohibits implicit variable declaration anywhere in a module that contains the **Option Explicit** command.

To require explicit declaration for all variables in a module, add the **Option Explicit** command to the declarations area of the module, that is, at the beginning of the module before any variable or procedure declarations. Listing 3.5 shows the same module from Listing 3.3, but with the **Option Explicit** command added.

INPUT   **LISTING 3.5**   THE *Option Explicit* MODULE COMMAND

```
1:  Option Explicit   'require all variables in module be declared
2:                     'explicitly
3:  Dim HelloMsg     'used by all procedures in this module
4:
5:  Sub HelloWorld()
6:      HelloMsg = "Hello, World!"
7:      MsgBox HelloMsg, , "Greeting Box"
8:  End Sub
9:
10:  Sub HelloDave()
11:      HelloMsg = "Hello, Dave!"
12:      MsgBox HelloMsg, , "Another Message Box"
13: End Sub
```

3

ANALYSIS Except for line 1, the procedures in this module work exactly the same as described for Listing 3.3.

Line 1 of the module in Listing 3.5 contains the **Option Explicit** command. Because of this command, all the variables in this module must be declared with the **Dim** statement. If you add an implicit variable declaration to this module, VBA displays a runtime error message stating that the variable is undeclared.

Note

> Commands such as **Option Explicit** are called *compiler directives*. Compiler directives don't actually cause VBA to perform an action, but instead tell VBA how it should operate. The VBA compiler is the part of VBA that reads your source code and compiles it into the machine instructions that your computer needs to carry out the specified task. A compiler directive simply instructs VBA about specific rules that you want VBA to follow when it compiles your source code.

The **Option Explicit** command affects only the module in which it appears. If the project that contains this module also contains other modules, the other modules are unaffected by the **Option Explicit** command in line 1. You must include the **Option Explicit** command in each module for which you want to require explicit variable declarations.

Do

DO use the **Option Explicit** command in your modules. Requiring yourself to declare variables explicitly helps reduce your opportunities to make a mistake, and consequently helps you write bug-free code.

Specifying the Data Type of a Variable

All variables in VBA, whether implicitly or explicitly declared, are of the **Variant** data type unless you specify the variable's data type in the statement that declares the variable. So far, you've seen examples of variables declared both implicitly and explicitly. In all of these examples, the variables were *untyped*, that is, their data types were not specified. All of these variables were therefore of the **Variant** type because untyped variables in VBA are always **Variant** data types.

> **Tip**
>
> Because including `Option Explicit` in all your modules is so helpful, the VB Editor provides a way to automatically include `Option Explicit` in every new module you create. To make the VB Editor add the `Option Explicit` command to each new module, select the Require Variable Declaration option in the Editor tab of the VB Editor's Options dialog. To set the Require Variable Declaration option, follow these steps:
>
> 1. Choose the Tools, Options command. The VB Editor displays the Options dialog.
> 2. Click the Editor tab to display the editing options, if necessary.
> 3. Select the Require Variable Declaration check box.
> 4. Choose OK. The VB Editor closes the Options dialog.
>
> Now, each time you—or the Macro Recorder—insert a new module into a project, the VB Editor automatically adds the `Option Explicit` command at the beginning of the module.
>
> Selecting the Require Variable Declaration option in the Options dialog only affects new modules; if you want to require explicit variable declaration in an existing module, you must add `Option Explicit` by editing the module yourself. Requiring variable declaration affects all applications that use the VB Editor; if you start the VB Editor from Excel and set the Require Variable Declaration option, new modules in MS Word, MS Access, or another VBA host application will also require explicit variable declaration.

Declaring *typed* variables (variables whose data type you specify) offers several advantages:

- Typed variables make your program code faster. Because you tell VBA the type of the variable when you declare it, your program speed is increased by the amount of time VBA would otherwise spend analyzing a **Variant** type variable to determine its specific type.

- Typed variables make your program code more efficient. **Variant** variables can take up much more memory than variables of specific types. A typed variable uses up only as much memory as required by that specific type. Using typed variables can greatly reduce the amount of memory that your VBA program requires; in some cases, using typed variables can make the difference between whether your procedure has enough memory to work or not.

- Typed variables make your program code easier to read and understand.
- Programs that use typed variables help you prevent bugs. Typed variables help reveal certain kinds of programmer error—such as incompatible mixes of data types—because VBA displays runtime errors that would not occur if the variables were untyped.

There are other reasons why you might want to declare typed variables. For example, although **Variant** data types can store dates, a **Variant** variable might not correctly store a date from Excel. VBA variables explicitly declared with the **Date** type do not have this problem.

You declare a variable's type in the same statement you use to declare the variable. You can declare a typed variable either when you declare the variable implicitly, or when you declare the variable explicitly with **Dim**. When you declare **String** type variables, you can also specify a particular length for the string.

Using **Dim** to Declare Typed Variables

To declare a variable and its type with the **Dim** statement, add the keyword **As** after the variable name and then type the name of the data type that you want the variable to have. The general syntax to use the **Dim** statement to declare a typed variable is

```
Dim varname As type
```

varname represents any valid VBA variable name and *type* represents any one of VBA's data type names. (Table 3.1 lists the names of all of VBA's data types.)

The following lines show examples of the correct syntax for typed variable declarations:

```
Dim PcntProfit As Single
Dim Gross_Sales As Currency
Dim PayDay As Date
Dim Message As String
Dim Counter As Integer
```

If you want, you can also declare several typed variables with a single **Dim** statement, as shown in the following line; separate each variable and type declaration from the next with a comma (,):

```
Dim PcntProfit As Single, Gross_Sales As Currency, Message As String
```

▲ **SYNTAX** ▼

Do

DO declare the data type for each variable individually when you declare several typed variables in a single `Dim` statement. If you omit the data type, VBA creates a variable with a `Variant` data type. In the following line, for example, `NetValue` has the `Variant` data type:

```
Dim NetValue, PcntProfit As Single
```

DO declare each variable on a separate line. Declaring each variable on a separate line makes it easier to determine what variables you have declared and what each variable's data type is.

Using Type-definition Characters to Declare Typed Variables

You can also specify the type of a variable when you declare the variable implicitly by adding a special symbol—called a *type-definition character*—to the end of the variable's name. Table 3.2 lists VBA's type-definition characters and the types they indicate.

TABLE 3.2 TYPE-DEFINITION CHARACTERS

Definition Character	Type
!	`Single`
@	`Currency`
#	`Double`
$	`String`
%	`Integer`
&	`Long`

Notice that there are only six type-definition characters; there are no type-definition characters for **Byte**, **Boolean**, **Date**, **Object**, or **Array** data types. Type-definition characters can only appear at the end of a variable name.

Note

Type-definition characters are a historic legacy in VBA. In early dialects of BASIC, type-definition characters were the *only* way to specify a variable's data type. Although you should know what the type-definition characters are and how they are used, there is seldom much need to use them; using the `Dim` statement with the `As` keyword is much easier and clearer. Most VBA programmers do not use type-definition characters.

Listing 3.6 shows yet another variation of the HelloWorld procedure from Day 2.

INPUT   **LISTING 3.6**   EXPLICIT AND IMPLICIT TYPE DECLARATION

```
1:  Sub HelloWorld()
2:      Dim HelloMsg As String
3:      HelloMsg = "Hello, World!"
4:      Title$ = "Greeting Box"
5:      MsgBox HelloMsg, , Title$
6:  End Sub
```

> **Note**
>
> If you enter Listing 3.6 in a module that contains the **Option Explicit** direc-
> tive, you will receive a runtime error when you try to execute the procedure.
> Line 4 of Listing 3.6 contains an implicit variable declaration, which is pro-
> hibited by the **Option Explicit** directive. To execute the procedure in
> Listing 3.6, enter it in a module that does not contain the **Option Explicit**
> directive.

ANALYSIS   This version of HelloWorld works much the same as previous versions. Line 1 contains the procedure declaration. In line 2, a **Dim** statement explicitly declares the HelloMsg variable. Because the **Dim** statement includes the **As** keyword and the type name **String**, the HelloMsg variable has the **String** data type. Line 3 assigns text for the message to the HelloMsg string variable.

Line 4 implicitly declares the Title$ variable at the same time it assigns text for the message dialog title to the variable. Because the Title$ variable name ends with the type-definition character for a string, this variable also has the **String** data type. Finally, line 5 uses the MsgBox statement to display the message dialog; in this statement, both the text for the message and the dialog's title bar come from variables: HelloMsg and Title$, respectively.

If either line 3 or line 4 tried to assign numeric or date type data to the HelloMsg or the Title$ variables, VBA would display a type-mismatch runtime error and halt the execu-tion of the procedure.

After you add a type-definition character to a variable, you must include the type-definition character each time you use the variable name. If the type-definition character were left out of the Title$ variable name in line 5 (where Title$ is used for the first time after its implicit typed declaration), VBA would display a runtime error and stop executing the procedure.

> **Tip**
>
> You can also use type-definition characters in `Dim` statements to specify the data type of a variable. The following two `Dim` statements have the same effect—to declare a variable named `Count` with the `Integer` data type:
>
> `Dim Count As Integer`
>
> `Dim Count%`
>
> (If you put both of these lines in the same procedure, VBA produces a run-time error complaining that there is a duplicate variable declaration.)

> **Note**
>
> After you declare a typed variable, whether you declare the variable explicitly or implicitly and no matter how you specify the type, the variable retains that same data type for as long as it exists. You cannot re-declare a variable or re-specify its data type.

3

Using `Dim` to Declare Fixed-Length String Variables

Whether you declare **String** data type variables by using `Dim` or the **$** type-definition character, the string variables you create are all, by default, variable-length strings.

Variable-length string variables change size depending on the size of the string stored by the variable. For some purposes, you'll want to use a *fixed-length* string. Fixed-length strings always have the same size. Fixed-length strings are useful if you want to ensure that the text stored in the string variable always contains the same number of characters.

You can use fixed-length strings to help line up information into columns for display, for example, or to ensure that string data stored in a particular variable never exceeds a certain length. There is only one way to declare a fixed-length string variable: You must use the `Dim` statement. The following line demonstrates the general syntax to create a fixed-length string:

▼ **SYNTAX**

`Dim varname As String * N`

varname is any valid variable name and *N* is any number from 1 up to the maximum string length of approximately 2 billion characters (formerly 65,000 (64KB) characters in Windows 3.1).

The following statement is an example of a fixed-length string declaration:

▼ `Dim LastName As String * 30`

▲ An asterisk (*) followed by a number after the **String** keyword tells VBA to create the string variable as a fixed-length string with a specified length (in this case, 30 characters).

Understanding Constants

A *constant* is a value in your VBA program that does not change. The procedure examples presented so far use string constants such as "Hello World!" and "Greeting Box". Constants like this are referred to as *literal constants* because you write the literal value directly into your code.

You can also write literal numeric and date constants into your VBA source code; examples of numeric literal constants include the numbers 36, 3.14, and 212. Examples of literal date constants include the dates #12/31/96# or #October 28, 1997# (you learn more about writing date constants later in this lesson). If you examine most recorded macros, you'll find other examples of literal constants (frequently, literal string constants). You can only change constants by editing the VBA source code.

You use constants, such as the string constants in the HelloWorld procedure, to provide data that does not change in a procedure—the opposite of a variable, which you use to provide data that does change. You can use constants as arguments for procedures or in mathematical and comparison operations.

Constants do not have to be literal constants; VBA enables you to create *named constants* (also called *symbolic constants*). A named constant, like a variable, has a name that you give to it; that name represents a specific, unchanging value. Also like a variable, VBA substitutes the specific value referred to by the constant's name into a statement at the point in the statement where VBA encounters the named constant. Unlike a variable, however, the value of a named constant never changes; like a literal constant, the only way to change the value associated with a named constant is to edit the VBA source code.

Use named constants to improve the readability and understandability of your procedures. For example, a procedure that performs geometric calculations is much easier to read and understand if you use a named constant, Pi, instead of the literal constant 3.14.

You also use named constants to make it easier to update and maintain your procedures and programs. For instance, if you have a VBA program that computes a tax liability for your company, it's possible that the tax rate might change sometime in the future. If you put the tax rate in your program as a literal constant, you might have difficulty updating your program to use the new tax rate—you'll have to search through the entire program and change every occurrence of the tax rate value. If, instead, you use a named constant for the tax rate, you only have to change the value for the tax rate in one location—the statement that declares the named constant—to update your program to use the new tax rate.

In general, you should use named constants instead of literal constants for values that you use repeatedly in a procedure or module or for values that are difficult to remember or whose meaning is not immediately clear.

Creating Named Constants

To choose the name for a constant, observe the same rules and guidelines that you follow to choose a variable name. (Refer to the section "Creating Variables" earlier in this lesson for an explanation of the rules for choosing identifier names.)

Like a variable, you must declare a named constant before you can use it. Unlike a variable, however, you must always declare named constants explicitly by using the **Const** keyword. The next line shows the general syntax to declare a named constant:

```
Const name = value
```

name represents any valid identifier and *value* represents any data value: numeric, string, or date. The next few lines show several named constant declarations:

```
Const BoilingPoint = 212
Const SalesTax = 8.25
Const Greeting = "Hello"
```

Each constant declaration begins with the **Const** keyword and is followed by the constant's name, an equals sign (=), and the value assigned to the constant.

If you want, you can declare several constants with the same **Const** statement by separating each constant declaration and value assignment with a comma (,). The following line has the same effect as the three separate lines shown above:

```
Const BoilingPoint = 212, SalesTax = 8.25, Greeting = "Hello"
```

You can specify a literal value for a named constant, include previously defined constants, or use any of VBA's mathematical or comparison operations as part of the constant declaration with the following restrictions: You cannot concatenate strings, use variables, or use the **Is** operator in a constant declaration. (String concatenation, mathematical and logical operators, and the **Is** operator are described in the next lesson.)

The following constant declarations, for example, show both the use of a previously defined constant and the use of a mathematical operator in the constant declaration:

```
Const BoilingPoint = 212
Const DangerZone = BoilingPoint + 50
```

▼ SYNTAX

3

Constant Scope

Like variables, you can declare named constants inside your procedures or in the declarations area at the beginning of a module. A constant declared inside a procedure has procedure-level scope and a constant declared in the declarations area of a module has module-level scope. Named constants follow the same scope rules as variables do in all respects.

Because one of the major purposes for using a named constant is to avoid repeating or duplicating literal constant values throughout your procedures, you'll usually want to have your named constants available to all procedures in a module. Therefore, you should usually place constant declarations at the module level so that they have the greatest scope.

Whenever VBA encounters a named constant in a statement, it inserts the value associated with the constant into the statement. Examine Listing 3.7, which shows an entire module. This procedure calculates the area of a circle and stores the value in a variable.

INPUT   **LISTING 3.7**   USING CONSTANTS: COMPUTING THE AREA OF A CIRCLE

```
1:  Const Pi = 3.14
2:  Dim CircleArea As Single
3:
4:  Sub Calc_CircleArea()
5:      Dim Radius As Single
6:      Radius = 5
7:      CircleArea = Pi * (Radius * Radius)
8:      MsgBox CircleArea, ,"Area of a Circle"
9:  End Sub
```

ANALYSIS   Line 1 in Listing 3.7 declares a module-level constant, Pi, which represents an approximation of the number π. Line 7 of the listing contains a statement that computes the area of a circle; when VBA executes this statement, it inserts the value 3.14 at the location occupied by the constant name Pi. When VBA executes the Calc_CircleArea procedure, the MsgBox statement in line 8 displays the number 78.5. Notice that the CircleArea variable is declared at the module level so that the value computed in the Calc_CircleArea procedure is available to other procedures in the same module.

Writing Literal Constants

Even if you never use a literal constant in your VBA code—an unlikely event—you must still write literal constants when you declare named constants. There are a few rules you must observe when you write literal constants; the following paragraphs describe the rules for writing **String** constants, numeric constants, **Date** constants, and **Boolean** constants.

String Constants

To write literal string constants in your VBA code, follow these rules:

- String constants must be enclosed in double quote marks ("). The following example is not legal because it doesn't have quotation marks:

```
This is not a valid string constant.
```

- A blank string constant (called a *null string* or an *empty string*) is indicated by two quotation marks together with nothing between them: "".

- A string constant must be all on the same line. You cannot use the line-continuation symbol to continue a literal string constant to another line. Neither of the following examples are valid because they split the string constant across more than one line:

```
"This is not a
valid string constant"
"Neither is this a _
valid string constant"
```

If you included any of the examples from the preceding list in a procedure, VBA would display a runtime error and stop executing the procedure. The following example is a valid string constant:

```
"This string constant is valid."
```

Numeric Constants

These rules apply to literal numeric constants; a numeric constant can contain any of VBA's numeric types.

- Numeric constants must consist only of the number characters 0 through 9.

- A numeric constant can optionally begin with a minus sign (-) and can contain a decimal point.

- You can use scientific notation for numeric constants.

No other symbols or characters are allowed in a numeric constant. The following examples are valid numeric constants:

```
12
-14.3
6.6E2
```

- Do not use dollar signs or whole-number separators in numeric constants. The following are not valid numeric constants:

```
$656        'not valid: contains a dollar sign
6,560       'not valid: contains a whole-number separator
```

Date Constants

VBA recognizes date constants in any one of several different formats; you must enclose all date constants, however, in pound signs (#). The following lines show some of the date constant formats that VBA recognizes:

```
#2-5-98 21:17#
#February 5, 1998 9:17pm#
#Mar-31-98#
#15 April 1998#
```

No matter which of the preceding formats you write the literal data constant in, VBA reformats the date constant (when you move the insertion point away from the line after writing the constant) to conform to one of the following two formats, depending on whether or not the date constant also contains time information:

```
#2/5/98 9:17:00 PM#
#2/5/98#
```

If you omit the pound signs (#) when you write a literal date constant, VBA cannot correctly interpret the date constant as a date. Instead, VBA tries to evaluate the date information as variable names, numeric constants, and mathematical operators. For example, VBA attempts to interpret the following date—which is missing the pound signs—as a mathematical expression involving division:

```
3/15/99
```

Don't enclose literal date constants in quotation marks, either, or VBA will interpret the date as a string constant instead of a date constant. For example, VBA interprets the following line as a string constant, not a date:

```
"3/15/99"
```

Boolean Constants

There are only two valid Boolean constants: **True** and **False**. Your VBA program statements must always use the keywords **True** and **False** to express the desired Boolean value as a constant. When you write the keywords in your macros, remember to spell the word out in full and don't use quotation marks.

Specifying the Data Type of a Constant

When you declare a named constant or write a literal constant, VBA considers the value represented by the constant to have the data type most consistent with the expression assigned to the constant. For example, VBA treats a constant containing a string as a **String** data type when determining whether the constant is appropriately combined with other data values.

Occasionally, you might want to specify the data type of a constant. Declaring a specific data type for a constant can improve the accuracy of a calculation: By declaring a constant with a **Double** data type, for example, VBA computes the result of mathematical operations involving that constant by using the greater range of the **Double** data type. You might also want to specify that a constant be an **Integer**, **Long**, **Currency**, or other type to ensure that the results of mathematical operations that use that constant have a particular type. (As you will learn in the next lesson, VBA determines the data type for the result of a computation based on the data type of the values in the computation.)

You can use **Byte**, **Boolean**, **Integer**, **Long**, **Single**, **Double**, **Currency**, **Date**, or **String** data types for constants (but not **Object** or **Array** types). Declaring a type for a constant is similar to declaring the type for a variable, except that the declaration begins with the keyword **Const**. The general syntax for declaring a typed constant is as follows:

▼ **SYNTAX**

```
Const name As type = value
```

In this syntax sample, *name* is any valid constant name, *type* is the name of any one of VBA's data types, and *value* is the value you want to assign to the constant. The following line illustrates a valid constant declaration with a specific type:

```
Const Pi As Double = 3.14
```

▲ This example declares the constant Pi as a **Double** data type with the value 3.14.

Understanding Intrinsic Constants

VBA provides several *intrinsic constants* (also referred to as *predefined constants*). An intrinsic constant is a named constant that has already been defined for you. In addition to the constants that VBA predefines, the VBA host application also predefines several constants for use with that host application. For example, Excel 2000 contains several intrinsic constants for use with Excel workbooks, charts, and so on. Similarly, MS Word contains several intrinsic constants for use with Word documents and templates, and MS Access contains intrinsic constants related to various database activities and properties.

Intrinsic constants defined by VBA all begin with the letters vb to indicate that they are defined by Visual Basic for Applications (or Visual Basic). As an example, the constants vbOKOnly, vbOKCancel, and vbAbortRetryIgnore are all defined by VBA. Excel intrinsic constants all begin with the letters xl so that you know they are defined by Excel; some of Excel's intrinsic constants include xlChart, xlCountrySetting, and xlWorksheet. Intrinsic constants from other VBA host applications use similar two-letter abbreviations to indicate which application contains the constant. For example, MS Word intrinsic constants all begin with the letters wd.

Intrinsic constants make it easier to use some of VBA's built-in procedures, such as the MsgBox statement you've already seen and the InputBox statement you learn about later in this lesson. Although none of the MsgBox examples have used it so far, you might recall from earlier discussions that MsgBox has an optional argument that specifies the number of buttons in the dialog; typically, you use VBA's intrinsic constants for the buttons argument in MsgBox. (Day 8, "Making Decisions in Visual Basic," describes how to use the buttons argument for MsgBox.)

Similarly, the intrinsic constants defined by Excel make it easier to use the various properties and methods that belong to objects in Excel. (You learn more about properties and methods in Day 7.)

Note

Use intrinsic constants defined by VBA, Excel, or another VBA host application the same way you use constants that you declare yourself. Specific intrinsic constants are described throughout this book in the chapters that cover the topics that those intrinsic constants relate to.

Using the Object Browser to Find Available Intrinsic Constants

To see a complete list of intrinsic constants available, whether defined by VBA or the host application, use the Object Browser and follow these steps:

1. Press Alt+F11 to activate the VB Editor.
2. Choose the View, Object Browser command (or click the Object Browser button on the toolbar). The VB Editor displays the Object Browser dialog. Figure 3.3 shows the Object Browser dialog with the list of VBA constants displayed.

Tip

You can also open the Object Browser dialog by pressing F2.

After you open the Object Browser dialog, follow these additional steps to view the VBA intrinsic constants:

1. Select VBA in the Project/Library drop-down list of the Object Browser dialog.

2. Select Constants in the Classes list.

3. To get more information about a particular intrinsic constant, select the constant in the Members Of 'Constants' list.

   After you select a constant in the Members Of 'Constants' list, the selected constant name appears at the bottom of the Object Browser dialog. For more information about the selected constant, click the Object Browser's Help button (the button with a question mark on it).

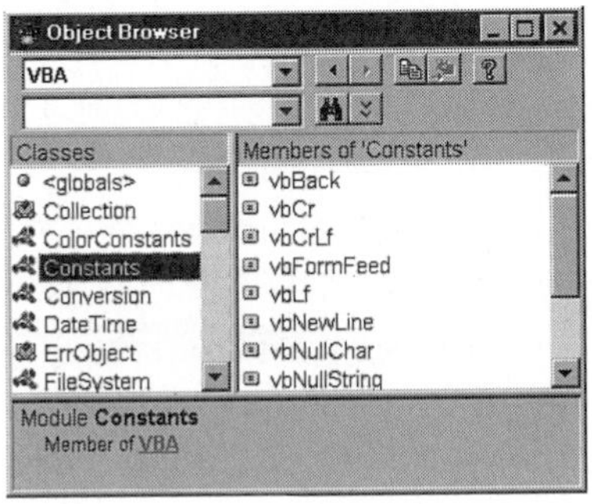

FIGURE 3.3

Use the Object Browser to view lists of constants defined by VBA, Excel, or another VBA host application.

3

> **Note**
>
> The VBA intrinsic constants are the same in all VBA host applications. Intrinsic constants for a specific application, such as Excel, are only available when you work with VBA in that application. For example, you won't find the Excel xlWorksheet constant listed in the Object Browser in MS Word; the xlWorksheet constant is only available when you use VBA in Excel.

If there is online help available for the item selected in the Classes list, the Object Browser's Help button (the one with a question mark on it at the top right of the Object Browser dialog) is enabled, as shown in Figure 3.3. Click this button to access the help topic for the selected item. Not all objects in the Object Browser have additional help available.

To view a list of intrinsic constants defined by a VBA host application, follow the same procedure just described, but choose the host application's library in the Project/Library drop-down list instead of VBA. For example, to view Excel's intrinsic constants, select Excel in the Project/Library drop-down list. You can only view intrinsic constants for the

VBA host application from which you started the VB Editor unless you create a reference to another host application's library as described in Day 12, "Creating Libraries and Whole Programs: Modular Programming Techniques."

Getting Data from Your Procedure's User

In Day 2, you learned how to make your procedures display messages by using VBA's MsgBox statement; several examples in this chapter have also used MsgBox. Earlier in this lesson, you learned how to create variables and constants. Now you're ready to learn how to use these elements together to get information from your procedure's user.

Obtaining data, storing it in a variable, and displaying the results of actions performed on or as a result of the user's entered data are the essential elements required to write interactive procedures. (An *interactive* procedure is one that exchanges information with its user, that is, the procedure interacts with its user by displaying messages and receiving input.) Interactive procedures are often more useful than macros created exclusively by recording. By getting information from the user, an interactive procedure can perform the same operations using different data.

Data entered by a user is called *input*. To get input from your procedure's user, use the InputBox function. (A *function* is a special type of VBA procedure that returns a value.) The InputBox function displays a dialog that contains text that prompts the user to input some value and a text box to enter the value in. The dialog that InputBox displays also contains OK and Cancel command buttons.

When you use InputBox, you supply the string used to prompt the user for input. Optionally, you might also supply a string argument that InputBox uses as the title of the dialog it displays.

The syntax for the InputBox function is

▼ SYNTAX

```
stringvar = InputBox (Prompt[, Title])
```

stringvar represents any variable that can store a string (either a **String** type variable or a **Variant** type). The *Prompt* argument represents any string value (literal, constant, or variable). InputBox displays this string as the prompt in the dialog; you must always supply the *Prompt* argument, it is a *required argument*.

The *Title* argument is an optional second argument for InputBox. (All optional elements in the syntax lines are enclosed in square brackets.) *Title* also represents any string value, literal, constant, or variable. InputBox displays the text in this string in the title bar of the dialog. If you omit the *Title* argument, VBA displays the word Input in

▲ the title bar of the InputBox dialog.

Listing 3.8 shows an entire module containing a single procedure, a module-level constant declaration, and a module-level variable declaration. This procedure, like the one in Listing 3.7, computes the area of a circle. Unlike the procedure in Listing 3.7, which always computes the area of a circle with a radius of 5 units, this procedure gets the radius of the circle from the procedure's user.

INPUT   **LISTING 3.8**   GETTING INPUT WITH THE *InputBox* STATEMENT

```
1:  Const Pi As Single = 3.14     'an approximation of the value pi.
2:  Dim CircleArea As Single      'stores the computed area of a circle
3:
4:  Sub Calc_CircleArea()
5:      Const BoxTitle = "Area of a Circle"
6:      Dim Radius As Single, Temp As String
7:      Temp = InputBox("Enter circle radius", BoxTitle)
8:      Radius = CSng(Temp)      — Convert string to single precision
9:      CircleArea = Pi * (Radius * Radius)
10:     MsgBox CircleArea, , BoxTitle
11: End Sub
```

ANALYSIS   Line 1 of Listing 3.8 declares the module-level constant `Pi`. Line 2 declares the module-level variable `CircleArea`. These items are declared at the module level so that they are available throughout the module—other procedures in the same module might need access to the value for π, and another procedure might need to use the value for the circle's area once it has been calculated.

Line 4 contains the actual procedure declaration; as before, this procedure is named `Calc_CircleArea`. Line 5 declares a procedure-level constant, `BoxTitle`; this constant is only available locally within the `Calc_CircleArea` procedure. `BoxTitle` was declared locally in this procedure because it is unlikely this constant will be used in any other procedure; its purpose—to supply fixed text for the title bars of all dialogs displayed by `Calc_CircleArea`—is rather specific to `Calc_CircleArea`. Line 6 declares all the variables used locally in this procedure (`Radius` and `Temp`) and also specifies the data types for those variables.

Pay close attention to line 7 of Listing 3.8. This statement calls the `InputBox` function. `InputBox` displays its first argument as text in the dialog, prompting the user to enter a value of some kind. In this statement, `InputBox` displays the text `Enter circle radius` to let the procedure's users know what value they are expected to enter. `InputBox` displays the second argument as the title of the dialog. Here, the string value represented by the constant `BoxTitle` is used for the `InputBox` dialog title.

Do

DO try to make the prompt text for the InputBox function as clear and descriptive as possible regarding the type of value you expect your procedure's user to type in.

When the InputBox statement in line 7 executes, it displays the dialog shown in Figure 3.4. The user types a number into the text box and chooses either the OK or Cancel command buttons to close the dialog, as with any other Windows dialog.

FIGURE 3.4

This is the input dialog displayed by the InputBox *function in line 7 of Listing 3.8.*

ANALYSIS Whenever you call a function, you must somehow use the value returned by the function. (The value returned by a function is called the *function result.*) Frequently, you use a function result by assigning it to a variable, as shown in line 7 with the InputBox function, which has its result assigned to the Temp variable. (Days 5 and 6 discuss functions in more detail.)

The function result of InputBox is always a string (this is why the Temp variable was declared as a **String**). Refer again to Figure 3.4. If the user chooses the OK command button, InputBox returns whatever the user typed into the text box as the function result. If the user chooses the Cancel command button (or presses Esc or uses the Close button in the dialog), InputBox returns an empty string as the function result.

Because the Temp variable was explicitly declared as a **String** type, the string value must be converted to a numeric value before you can use it in mathematical computations. Line 8 of Listing 3.8 does exactly that by using VBA's built-in **CSng** function to convert the user's input to a **Single** type number. **CSng** is one of several data conversion functions described in more detail in Day 5.

Finally, line 9 computes the area of the circle and assigns the result to CircleArea. Line 10 uses MsgBox to display the computed area. Notice that the MsgBox statement in line 10 uses the same BoxTitle constant to specify the title for the MsgBox dialog as was used in line 7 for InputBox.

This is an ideal use for a constant: Using a constant for the title bar ensures that all the title bars in this particular procedure are the same, and avoids the need to type the entire title more than once. Incidentally, the amount of computer memory that VBA would need to store the literal constants for duplicate title bar strings is also saved.

Summary

Today you learned about the different types of data that VBA can manipulate and store. You learned that a variable is a named memory storage location used to temporarily store information that a procedure is working with. You also learned how to name and declare variables and how to specify a variable's data type. This chapter explained the scope rules that determine a variable's availability and how long VBA retains the values stored in a variable. You learned about literal constants and the rules governing writing literal constants of different types. You also learned what a named constant is, how to declare named constants, and how to specify a constant's type. Finally, you learned how to use VBA's InputBox function to obtain input from a procedure's user.

Q&A

Q Do I have to declare the data types of variables or named constants?

A No, you don't have to specify a data type when you declare a variable or a constant. If you don't specify a data type when you declare a variable, VBA creates a **Variant** type variable. If you don't specify a data type when you declare a constant, VBA chooses the most compatible data type for the value represented by the constant. It is often a good idea to declare the type of both variables and constants, however. If for no other reason, declaring the data type of a variable helps you think through exactly what you expect to use the variable for.

Q How do I know which data type to use when I declare a variable?

A Choose the data type for a variable based on the kind of information you want to store in that variable. If the variable will store text information, use the **String** data type; if the variable will hold numbers representing dollar or other money values, use the **Currency** type, and so on. If you know that numeric values stored in a particular variable will not exceed certain ranges, choose the smallest numeric data type that has a range equivalent to, or only slightly greater than, the range of values you expect to store in the variable in order to conserve computer memory.

This last suggestion also helps you detect possible errors in your program. If you declare a variable as an **Integer** data type because you do not expect it to store values outside the **Integer** range, and then later get number overflow errors when your procedure runs, the error messages might indicate a bug in the procedure. (*Overflow* occurs when a number is too large to be stored in the data type used for it.)

Q When and where should I declare variables?

A You should develop the habit of declaring all of your variables all of the time by using the **Option Explicit** command to require variable declaration as described earlier in this chapter. (All of the examples in this book from this point on use only explicitly declared variables.) Declaring all variables explicitly is good programming technique. By declaring your variables ahead of time, you not only get the benefits described earlier in the chapter, but you force yourself into doing a little planning ahead, which can save you a great deal of time and frustration later on.

Declare variables at the beginning of the procedure or module that you want to use that variable in. Unless you specifically want a variable to be available throughout a module, you should declare all of your variables locally within a procedure instead of at module level.

Q If the function result from InputBox is always a String data type, does that mean I can't get other data types from my procedure's user?

A Yes, and no. It is true that the function result of InputBox is always a **String**. However, VBA provides a variety of ways to translate data from one data type to another, such as the **CSng** function used in Listing 3.8. Usually, you can convert the strings returned by InputBox into any other data type except **Object** and **Array**, depending on the specific contents of the returned string. By converting the returned strings, you can use InputBox to obtain dates, currency values, and integer or floating-point numeric values.

Workshop

The Workshop section presents Quiz questions to help you cement your new knowledge and Exercises to give you experience using what you have learned. Answers are in Appendix A.

Quiz

1. How many numeric data types are there in VBA?
2. What is the difference between the **Integer** and **Single** data types? **Integer** and **Long**?
3. What is a type-definition character?
4. What does it mean to declare a variable implicitly? What about explicitly?
5. What rules does VBA impose on identifier names? What other guidelines should you follow when choosing an identifier name?
6. What are the advantages of explicitly declaring a variable?
7. What are the advantages of specifying the type of a variable, whether it is declared explicitly or implicitly?
8. Why should you use named constants in your procedures?
9. What is the purpose of the InputBox function?
10. Which of the InputBox arguments described in this lesson is required?
11. What data type is always returned by the InputBox function?

Exercises

1. Based on the stated use for a data item, decide whether the item is a variable or a constant and then choose names and write typed declarations for each of the following (where possible, write the typed declaration both with and without using type-definition characters):
   ```
   (a) a computed count of columns in a worksheet
   (b) the computed total sales, in dollars, of the East
       Coast division of a company
   (c) the projected number of respondents from a
       marketing survey
   (d) the computed surface area of a cylinder
   (e) the multiplier to convert inches to centimeters
   (f) the computed profit, expressed as a percentage,
       for the first quarter of the year
   (g) the self-employment tax rate
   ```

2. From scratch, write a procedure named EchoThis that uses InputBox to get a sentence (or a word) from the user and then display the user's input with MsgBox.

3. In the Personal.xls workbook, record a macro named OpenSheet3 that performs the following actions: open any existing workbook file and select a worksheet named *Sheet3* (use a different sheet name, if necessary). Stop the recorder. Now edit the macro so that it uses InputBox to ask the user for a filename and opens the workbook file whose name the user typed in. (HINTS: First examine the recorded macro statements to determine which statement opens the workbook file. Insert your InputBox statement ahead of the file-opening statement. Assign the result from InputBox to a variable, and then substitute that variable for the literal constant filename that was recorded in the macro.)

   Run the edited macro to test it. Be sure you enter a valid filename when you test your macro.

4. Modify the Excel NewBook macro you recorded in Exercise 1 of Day 1 so that it uses InputBox to get from the user the filename for the new workbook that the macro creates and saves.

DAY 4

Operators and Expressions

By now, you know how to record and edit macros, how to write simple procedures of your own, and how to create and use constants and variables. Now you are ready to learn how to combine variables and constants together to create new values. In this lesson, you learn

- What an expression is and how to construct expressions.
- What the various arithmetic, comparison, string, and logical operators are, how they work, and how to use them in expressions.
- About data type compatibility in expressions and how VBA can sometimes automatically convert data into compatible types.
- How VBA determines the data type of an expression and how to override VBA's type determination.
- How VBA determines the order of operations performed in complex expressions and how to alter the evaluation order.

As you read this particular lesson, don't try to memorize all the facts in this chapter. If you can answer all the quiz questions and perform the exercises at the end of today's lesson, you'll have mastered the most important aspects of the information presented here. As you continue with later lessons in this book, and with your VBA programming in general, refer back to this chapter to brush up on specific details.

Understanding Operators and Expressions

An *expression* is a value or group of values that expresses a single quantity. Every expression *evaluates to* (results in) a single quantity or value. The expression 2+2, for example, evaluates to 4. Expressions are made up of any one or more of the following building blocks:

Constants (literal or named)

Variables (of any data type)

Operators

Arrays

Array elements

Functions

All expressions result in a single value that has one of the data types you learned about in Day 3. Expressions also can evaluate to one of the special values `Empty` or `Null`. VBA provides the keywords `Empty` and `Null` to indicate special conditions in a variable or expression. The `Empty` value represents an uninitialized `Variant` type variable or the result of an expression that contains an uninitialized `Variant` type variable. The `Null` value represents an expression that contains invalid data. Day 10, "Advanced Techniques for Using Data Types and Variables," describes the `Empty` and `Null` keywords and the values they represent in more detail.

Some examples of expressions include the following:

Expression	Description
5	Contains one value and evaluates to the number 5.
"5"	Contains one value and evaluates to the single-character string 5.
"To" & "day"	Contains two string values and one operator; evaluates to the single string *Today*.

`c * (p/100)`	Results in a number obtained by multiplying the contents of variable c by the value obtained after dividing the contents of variable p by the constant 100.
`CStr(1200)`	Uses a VBA function and evaluates to the function result; in this case, a single string value of 1200 (**CStr** converts numbers to equivalent strings).
`MyValue <= 7`	Evaluates to a logical value; in this case indicating whether the contents of variable MyValue are less than or equal to the constant number value 7.

In the preceding examples, notice that the number 5 is *not* the same as the alphanumeric character "5"; the first is a numeric data type (specifically, an **Integer**) and the second is a **String** data type (even though it contains only one character).

You use *operators* to combine, compare, or otherwise manipulate specific values within an expression. Operators get their name because they are the symbols that indicate specific mathematical or other operations to be carried out on various values in an expression. When you use an operator in an expression, the data items—whether variables or constants—that the operator acts on are called the *operands*; most operators require two operands. In the expression 2+1, for example, the numbers 2 and 1 are the operands of the addition operator (+). An expression can contain none, one, or several operators.

You use expressions to perform calculations and compare values and to supply values as arguments for VBA's various functions and procedures. All expressions evaluate to a single value with a specific data type. In VBA, an expression is sort of like a sentence in English. All of your VBA statements contain one or more expressions—every example you've seen in this book so far contains at least one expression.

All Visual Basic expressions evaluate to a value that has one of Visual Basic's data types. The following list summarizes the different types of VBA expressions:

- A *date expression* is any expression that evaluates to a **Date** type value. Date expressions can include date constants, variables that contain dates or numbers, numeric constants, dates returned by functions, and arithmetic operators.

- A *numeric expression* is any expression that evaluates to a number of any type: **Byte**, **Integer**, **Long**, **Single**, **Double**, or **Currency**. Numeric expressions can include variables that contain numbers, numeric constants, functions that return numbers, and arithmetic operators. Numeric expressions can also include string expressions that VBA can convert to a number. (If all the characters in a string are digits, VBA can convert the string to a numeric value; for example, VBA can convert the string "36" to the number 36.)

- A *string expression* is any expression that evaluates to a **String** type value. String expressions can include variables that contain strings, string constants, functions that return strings, or string concatenation operators. String expressions can also include numeric expressions that VBA can convert to a string.

- A *logical expression* is any expression that evaluates to a **Boolean** type value: **True** or **False**. Logical expressions can consist of variables that contain Boolean values, Boolean constants, functions that return Boolean values, comparison operators, or logical operators.

- An *object expression* is any expression that evaluates to a reference to a specific object. Objects and object expressions are described in Day 7, "Understanding Objects and Collections."

Data Type Compatibility

Not all data types are compatible with each other; you cannot combine incompatible data types in the same expression. For example, it makes no sense to arithmetically add the string `"fruit fly"` to the number 12—the expression is not meaningful, and VBA cannot evaluate it.

Many data types are compatible with each other, however. For example, you can combine different numeric data types in the same expression; VBA automatically handles the necessary data type conversions among the different numeric types. VBA can also sometimes automatically convert other data types so that all the types in an expression are compatible, although it cannot always do so. **String** and **Date** types, for example, are compatible with numeric types only under specific conditions, which are described later in this chapter.

Keeping track of, and knowing, the data type of an expression is fairly important because expressions that contain incompatible data types cause VBA to produce a *type-mismatch* runtime error when your procedure executes. When VBA encounters an expression containing different data types, it first tries to resolve any data type difference by converting values in the expression into compatible data types. If VBA cannot successfully resolve the type differences by converting data types, it displays the type-mismatch runtime error and your procedure stops executing.

If you assign the result of an expression to a variable, and the variable type is incompatible with the type of the expression result, VBA also displays a type-mismatch error.

Similarly, using the result of an expression as an argument for a function or procedure also results in a type-mismatch error if the argument data type and the expression result have incompatible data types.

The following expression, for example, is not valid because it attempts to combine a string with a number:

```
"128" + 256
```

If your procedure contains an expression like this, VBA generates a type-mismatch run-time error and your procedure stops executing.

Either of the following modifications to the previous expression are valid, although the two expressions produce very different results:

```
"128" + "256"    'Evaluates to the string "128256"
128 + 256        'Evaluates to the number 384
```

VBA provides a variety of functions for converting information of one data type to another, such as strings to numbers, numbers into strings, and so on (in the preceding lesson, you saw the **CSng** function used to convert a **String** to a **Single** numeric type). VBA's data conversion functions are described in more detail in Day 5, "Visual Basic and Excel Functions."

Visual Basic's Automatic Data Conversions

VBA uses various different rules to automatically convert data into compatible types. VBA chooses the data conversion rules it applies to a particular expression based on the specific data types and operators used in an expression.

VBA can perform automatic data type conversions most readily when an expression contains **Variant** type variables because the data type of a **Variant** is not fixed. When an expression contains literal constants, typed variables, or typed constants, VBA applies stricter data type conversion rules because the data type of these items is fixed. (Remember, a *typed variable* or a *typed constant* is one for which you have explicitly declared the data type with either the **As** keyword or a type-definition character, as described in the preceding lesson.)

When an expression contains elements which have fixed data types, VBA tries to convert the other data types in the expression to be compatible with the fixed data type; the data type of the expression result will also have the data type of the fixed data types in the expression.

The following expressions illustrate how the data types and operator affect the data type conversions that VBA makes, and how VBA determines the expression result type:

Expression	Description and Result Type
Num + Str	Produces type mismatch when Num is a declared numeric type and Str is a declared **String** type.
	Performs string concatenation when Num is a **Variant** and Str is a declared **String** type; result is a **String** type.
	Performs arithmetic addition when Num is a declared numeric type and Str is a **Variant**, or when both Num and Str are **Variant** type; result is a numeric type.
Num + "3"	Always performs arithmetic addition, whether Num is a declared numeric type, or a **Variant** type containing a number; result is a numeric type.
	Performs string concatenation if Num is a **Variant** containing string data.
3 + Str	Performs arithmetic addition if Str is a **String** or **Variant** containing text that VBA can convert to a number; the result is a numeric type.
	Produces type mismatch if Str contains text that VBA can not convert to a number.
Num & Str	Always performs string concatenation, regardless of the variable types; result is a **String** type.
	This expression never produces a type-mismatch error.

Pay special attention to the last item in the preceding list. This expression uses the string concatenation operator (&), which joins two strings together. Because you can use this operator *only* with strings, VBA converts the data types in the expression to strings, regardless of their original data type and whether any variables in the expression have specific types. (String concatenation is described in more detail later in this chapter.) As each operator is described in the later sections of this chapter, any special data conversion rules that VBA applies for that specific operator are also described.

You might notice that most of the expressions in the preceding list produce a type-mismatch error only when both of the operands in the expression have specific and different types. You might also notice that the expressions do not produce type-mismatch errors when one of the operands is a **Variant** type variable. As mentioned before, VBA can most readily perform automatic data type conversions on **Variant** data types. Do not, however, use **Variant** data types merely to avoid type-mismatch errors.

TAKING ADVANTAGE OF TYPE-MISMATCH ERRORS

Type-mismatch errors aren't necessarily a tragedy; in fact, type-mismatch errors can be of great use to you. In Day 3, you were told that one of the reasons for declaring the specific data type of a variable is to help locate certain kinds of programmer errors. Mixing data types in a single expression might not always be what you intend, especially because mixing data types in a single expression might not always produce a desirable result.

Suppose, in the expression 3 + Str, you intend to concatenate the character 3 with a string stored in the variable Str, but accidentally omit the quotation marks around the digit character 3. Instead of a string constant, you have mistakenly included a numeric constant in the expression. This expression never performs string concatenation, which is what you actually desired. If the Str variable is specifically declared as having the **String** type, however, VBA generates a type-mismatch error when it evaluates this expression, revealing your mistake so that you can correct it.

Numeric Type Conversions

VBA usually converts all numeric data types to the greatest precision type in the expression and then gives the expression's result that type. For example, if an expression contains numeric values with **Integer** and **Single** types, the expression result is **Single**—the greatest precision type in the expression.

> **Note**
>
> *Precision* refers to the number of significant digits that a numeric data type can store. *Significant digits* means the digits in a number that are most important to representing the numeric value. Numbers written in scientific notation (explained in a sidebar in Day 3) include only the significant digits, excluding leading or trailing zeroes.

If you assign the result of a numeric expression to a variable that has a lower precision than the expression's actual result type, VBA rounds the expression result until its precision matches the expected type. For example, if you assign a numeric expression that results in a **Double** type number to an **Integer** type variable, VBA rounds the double-precision number until it is an **Integer**. The following code fragment illustrates this:

```
Dim Num As Integer
Num = 1 + 1.51    'Stores the integer 3 in Num
```

In the preceding line, the actual expression result is a **Double** type number: 2.51. VBA rounds this number to 3 so that it is compatible with the **Integer** data type of the variable that stores the expression result.

String and Number Conversions

If VBA converts a number to a string, VBA creates a string containing all the digits of the number and the decimal (if the number has one). The number 412.72, for example, converts to the string "412.72". If the number is very large or very small, VBA might create a string representation of the number in scientific notation: the number 0.0000000003937, for example, converts to the string "3.937E-11".

VBA can convert a string to a number only if the string contains the character representation of a number in either decimal format or scientific notation. The strings "98.6", "12", "-16.7", and "1.2E10" all represent numbers, and VBA can convert them to numbers. The strings "1,024", "$74.50", and "Fred and Ethel" cannot be converted to numbers because they contain non-numeric characters.

Boolean Conversions

When VBA converts **Boolean** type values to numbers, the value **True** converts to -1 and the value **False** converts to 0. When VBA converts a number to a **Boolean** type, zero converts to **False** and any other value converts to **True**. When VBA converts **Boolean** type values to strings, VBA uses the string "True" for **True** and "False" for **False**. VBA cannot convert string expressions to a **Boolean** type; it can only convert numeric expressions into **Boolean** values. When you use **Boolean** type values in arithmetic expressions, VBA always converts them to numbers, even if all other parts of the expression are also **Boolean** variables or constants.

Date Conversions

When VBA converts a **Date** data type to a number, the resulting numeric value is a **Double** type number that contains the number of days from December 30, 1899 (a negative number represents a date earlier than 12/30/1899). The number's decimal portion (if any) expresses the time of day as a fraction of a day; 0 is midnight and 0.5 is noon. VBA's conversion of numeric data types into **Date** data types is simply the inverse of the **Date** to number conversion just described.

> **Note**
>
> If an expression results in a value outside the range of the data type for that expression, VBA displays a numeric overflow or underflow error message at runtime and your procedure stops executing. (*Overflow* occurs when a number is too large for its data type; *underflow* occurs when a number is too small.)
>
> If the expression contains a literal constant, you can occasionally solve this problem by using a type-definition character with the literal constant to force the expression to evaluate to a numeric type with a greater range. For example, in an expression such as the following (where the variable Num is declared as an **Integer**), VBA treats the expression result as an **Integer** because all the operands in the expression have the **Integer** type:
>
> ```
> Num * 2      'this expression result is of Integer type
> ```
>
> If Num contains a value large enough that multiplying it by two produces a number greater than 32,767, VBA displays an overflow runtime error message and stops executing your procedure. The next expression, however, uses a type-definition character to alter the data type of the constant operand in the expression (remember, **&** is the type-definition character for a **Long** integer):
>
> ```
> Num * 2&     'this expression result is of the Long type
> ```
>
> Because VBA always assigns a data type to the expression result that is the same as the data type in the expression with the greatest range, this second expression has a **Long** result.

4

The Assignment Operator (=)

The preceding lesson briefly acquainted you with the assignment operator (=). You use the assignment operator to assign an expression result to a variable or to assign the value stored in one variable to another variable. The assignment operator stores whatever value is represented by an expression or variable on the right side of the assignment operator (=) in the memory location referred to by the variable on the left side of the operator.

> **Note**
>
> The assignment operator (=) does *not* fulfill the same function you might be accustomed to from working with algebraic equations. In algebra, the equal sign (=) indicates quantities that are equal to each other, and you solve an equation to find the numbers that will make the equality statement true—the action represented by the equal sign (=) in an algebraic equation is actually a test for equality (described later in this lesson), not an assignment operation. The assignment operation always indicates that a value is to be stored in a specified memory location, which is indicated by the variable at the left side of the assignment operator.

The assignment operation has two different syntax forms, both of which are equally acceptable and accomplish the same purpose. The first form of the assignment operation uses the keyword **Let** and has the following general syntax:

```
Let varname = expression
```

varname represents any VBA variable and *expression* represents any VBA expression. This syntax is the original form of the assignment operation used in the earliest versions of the BASIC programming language. The following VBA statement is an example of a **Let** assignment statement:

```
Let X = Y      'assigns value represented by Y to the variable X
```

The second form for assignment operations is much more common in VBA programming, and is the form used throughout this book. The general syntax of this more common form of the assignment statement is

```
varname = expression
```

varname represents any variable and *expression* represents any expression. The following statements are examples of this simpler, more common assignment statement (the first line assigns the contents of Y to X; the second line assigns to MyVar the result of adding 12 to the contents of YourVar):

```
X = Y
MyVar = 12 + YourVar
```

▲

In both forms of the assignment statement, the variable on the left side of the assignment operator (=) receives and stores the value that results from evaluating the expression on the right side of the assignment operator. When VBA executes an assignment statement, it first evaluates the expression on the right side of the assignment operator (=) and then stores the expression result in the variable whose name appears at the left side of the assignment operator.

Always keep in mind that VBA evaluates the expression on the right side of the assignment operator *before* storing any data in the variable on the left side of the assignment operator (=). This is an important concept. In many procedures, you will find assignment statements similar to these:

```
Count = Count + 1
GrossTotal = GrossTotal + SubTotal
```

You might use assignment statements like these if you keep a running count of something or if you compute a grand total by adding together several subtotal figures. It might not be immediately obvious to you what value ends up stored in the variable in a statement like this or whether VBA can even execute these statements.

Statements like these work because VBA computes the expression result on the right side of the assignment operator (=) first, and then assigns the value to the variable on the left of the assignment operator. For example, assume that the variable Count contains the value 9 at the time VBA executes the following statement:

```
Count = Count + 1
```

First, VBA evaluates the expression on the right side of the assignment operator. To evaluate the expression, VBA retrieves the current value—9—stored in the Count variable and adds 1 to it, resulting in the number 10. Next, VBA assigns this new value to the Count variable, completing the assignment operation. When VBA has finished executing this assignment statement, Count contains the numeric value 10 (the previous contents of Count, if any, are replaced by this new value).

Rather than reading an assignment statement as *x equals y*, many programmers learn to read assignment statements as *x gets y* or *let x be equal to y*. These last two ways of reading assignment statements reflect the action of the assignment operation more clearly; if you develop the mental habit of reading assignment statements this way, you will find it easier to understand the program statements that you encounter in recorded macros, examples in this book, or other VBA source code that you might want to read and understand.

You will see and use the shorter form of the assignment operation much more often than the longer form, mostly because the short form involves less typing. The long form of the assignment operation, with the keyword **Let**, is often recommended for beginning programmers because it helps distinguish the assignment operation from the equality comparison operation—both of which use the same symbol to indicate the desired operation.

Although the two operations use the same symbol, do not confuse the assignment operator with the equal sign (=) used to test for equality. The following two statements are *not* the same. The first statement assigns the value 5 to the variable MyVal; the second statement is a logical expression that evaluates as either **True** or **False** depending on whether MyVal already contains the number 5:

```
MyVal = 5      'assigns the number 5 to MyVal
(MyVal = 5)    'compares contents of MyVal to the number 5
```

Notice that the second line in the preceding example is not actually a complete VBA statement (although it is a complete expression) because the result of the logical expression is not used in any way; a line like this in one of your procedures would produce a syntax error. To make a syntactically valid VBA statement, the statement must use the expression result in some fashion: assign it to a variable, use it as a function or procedure argument, and so on.

When you assign an expression result to a variable with a specific data type, the expression result must have a data type compatible with the variable receiving the assignment. In many cases, VBA can convert the data type of an expression result to a type compatible with the variable receiving the assignment, if the expression result and variable do not already have compatible types. **Variant** type variables, by their nature, can receive assignments of any data type; the **Variant** takes on the data type of the expression result assigned to it.

Do

DO remember that you can assign any numeric variable or expression to any other numeric type variable or to a **Variant** type variable. If you assign a numeric expression to a typed variable with a lower precision or range (such as assigning a **Double** to a **Long** type), VBA rounds the value to match the precision of the variable receiving the assignment.

DON'T

DON'T forget that, if you assign a **Variant** variable containing a number to a **String** type variable, VBA automatically converts the number to a string. (Typed numeric variables or numeric constants assigned to a **String** type variable produce a type-mismatch error.)

Arithmetic Operators

VBA can perform all the standard arithmetic operations: addition, subtraction, multiplication, and division. VBA also has a mathematical operator to raise numbers to a specified power and provides additional special math operators for integer and modulo division. Table 4.1 summarizes VBA's arithmetic operators. (In the table, N is any valid VBA numeric expression.)

TABLE 4.1 ARITHMETIC OPERATORS

Operator	Syntax	Name/Description
+	N1 + N2	Adds N1 to N2.
-	N1 - N2	Subtracts N2 from N1.
	-N1	Unary minus (a negative number).
*	N1 * N2	Multiplies N1 by N2.
/	N1 / N2	Divides N1 by N2.

Operator	Syntax	Name/Description
\	N1 \ N2	Integer division. Divides N1 by N2, discarding any fractional part so that the result is an integer.
Mod	N1 Mod N2	Modulo division. Divides N1 by N2, returning only the remainder of the division operation.
^	N1 ^ N2	Exponentiation. Raises N1 to the N2 power.

The following sections describe each of these operators in detail.

Addition (+)

The addition operator (+) performs simple addition. Both operands must be numeric expressions or strings that VBA can convert to a number. You can also use the addition operator to perform arithmetic with **Date** data types. The following sample expressions illustrate the correct syntax for the addition operator:

```
MyVal + 1          'adds 1 to the contents of MyVal
MyVal + YourVal    'adds the contents of MyVal and YourVal
```

The data type of an addition expression's result usually is the same as the most precise data type in the expression. If an expression contains both **Integer** and **Long** data types, for example, the result of that expression is a **Long** data type. There are some exceptions to this rule, however, particularly if the expression includes **Variant** type variables. The following list summarizes these exceptions:

- The data type result of adding a **Single** and a **Long** is a **Double**.

- If you add a **Date** data type to any other data type, the expression always results in a **Date** type.

- If you assign the result of an addition expression to a **Variant** variable that currently has an **Integer** type, and if the expression result is greater than (overflows) the range of values for the **Integer** type, VBA converts the result to a **Long**. After assignment, the **Variant** variable also has the **Long** data type.

- If you assign the result of an addition expression to a **Variant** variable that currently has a **Long**, **Single**, or **Date** type, and if the expression result overflows the range of the numeric type, VBA converts the result to a **Double**. After assignment, the **Variant** variable also has the **Double** data type.

- If either operand in the addition expression is **Null** or evaluates to **Null**, the addition expression also results in **Null**. (**Null** is a special value that you can assign only to **Variant** type variables to indicate that they do not contain valid data. **Null** is described in more detail in Day 10.)

> **Note**
>
> The order of precision for VBA's numeric data types from least precise to most precise is **Byte**, **Integer**, **Long**, **Single**, **Double**, and **Currency**.

Some additional examples of valid addition expressions are

```
Now + 1              'expression result is Date type
PcntProfit + 0.5     '
#1/1/99# + 60        'adds 60 days to the literal date 1/1/99
```

In the first example in the preceding code, Now is a VBA function that returns a **Date** value corresponding to the current date and time (according to your computer's clock).

Subtraction (-)

The subtraction operator (-) fulfills two different purposes. You use the subtraction operator either to subtract one number from another or to indicate the unary minus.

A *unary minus* is the minus sign you place in front of a number to indicate that it is a negative number. In VBA, you can also place the minus sign in front of a variable or other expression to indicate that the value of the variable or expression should be negated. Placing the unary minus in front of a variable or expression is the same as multiplying that number by -1. The following expressions illustrate the unary minus:

```
-1               'a negative literal constant
-MyVal           'negates whatever number is stored in MyVal
-(MyVal + 10)    'negates the result of adding 10 to MyVal
```

The last two expressions in the preceding example show how you can use the unary minus to negate a numeric variable's value or the result of an expression. If MyVal contains the number 5, the result of the second expression above is -5 and the result of the third expression is -15.

The next few sample expressions illustrate the subtraction operator used to perform subtraction:

```
Now - 60         'expression result is a Date type
40 - MyVal       'the difference between 40 and MyVal
GrSales - Costs  'the difference between GrSales and Costs
```

Both operands in a subtraction expression must be numeric variables or expressions or a string expression that VBA can convert to a number. You can also use the subtraction operator to perform arithmetic with dates. The data type of a subtraction expression's result usually is the same as the most precise data type in the expression.

VBA follows the same rules for determining the data type of a subtraction expression's result as it does for expressions that use the addition operator, with the following additional rules:

- If one of the operands in the subtraction expression is a **Date** type, the data type of the expression result is **Date**.

- If both operands in the subtraction expression are **Date** types, the data type of the expression result is **Double**.

Note

> Although you can concatenate (join) two strings together with the (+) operator, you cannot use the (-) operator to divide or split apart a string. Instead, you must use VBA's Mid, Left, or Right functions to split strings apart. These functions are described in the next lesson.

Multiplication (*)

The multiplication operator (*) multiplies two numbers together; the result of a multiplication expression is the product of the two operands. Both operands in a multiplication expression must be numeric expressions or strings that VBA can convert to a number. The following sample expressions illustrate the correct syntax for the multiplication operator:

```
4 * 10              'multiplies 4 by 10; result is 40
NumVal * 2          'result is product of NumVal and 2
NumVal * OtherVal   'result is product of NumVal and OtherVal
```

The data type of a multiplication expression's result usually is the same as the most precise data type in the expression. VBA follows the same rules for determining the data type of a multiplication expression's result as it does for expressions that use the addition operator. In multiplication expressions, all **Variant** variables that contain **Date** type values are converted to numeric values.

Division (/)

This division operator (/) is sometimes referred to as the *floating-point* or *real number* division operator to help distinguish it from the integer division operator described in the next section. The floating-point division operator performs standard arithmetic division on its operands. In division expressions, the first operand is divided by the second operand; the expression result is the quotient. Both operands in a floating-point division expression must be numeric expressions or strings that VBA can convert to a number.

The following expressions illustrate the use of the division operator:

```
9 / 3            'Divides 9 by 3
NumVal / 17      'Divides the value in the NumVal variable by 17
Minutes / 60     'Divides the value in the Minutes variable by 60
```

If either operand in a floating-point division expression has the value **Null**, the expression result is also **Null**. The data type result of a floating-point division operation is usually **Double**, with the following exception: If both of the operands in the division expression have the **Integer** or **Single** type, the floating-point division expression result is **Single** unless the expression result overflows (or underflows) the value range for a **Single**. If the result overflows the range for a **Single**, VBA converts the result to a **Double** data type.

> **Note**
>
> Dividing any number by zero results in a runtime error. The rules of mathematics state that it isn't possible to divide a number by zero. Because of this mathematical rule, VBA always generates a runtime error when it encounters a statement that attempts to divide a number by zero.

Integer Division (\)

Integer division is essentially the same as floating-point division, except that expressions that use the integer division operator (\) always result in a whole number with no fractional part. Both operands in an integer division expression must be numeric expressions or strings that VBA can convert to a number. The following sample expressions illustrate the correct syntax for the integer division operator:

```
4 \ 2.5          'Divides 4 by 2.5; returns the value 1
6 \ NumVal       'Divides 6 by contents of NumVal
MyVal \ NumVal   'Divides MyVal by NumVal
```

In integer division, VBA rounds each operand (if necessary) to an **Integer** or **Long** number before performing the division operation. For example, in the integer division expression 19.5 \ 2, VBA rounds the value 19.5 to 20 before carrying out the division operation; the result of this expression is 10.

VBA discards any fractional remainder resulting from an integer division expression result. For example, the floating-point division expression 18 / 5 evaluates to 3.6, but the integer division expression 18 \ 5 evaluates to 3. Notice that VBA does not round the integer division quotient, it simply truncates the result so that it is a whole number.

The data type result of an integer division expression is either an **Integer** or a **Long**; VBA uses the smallest data type that will accommodate the expression result. If either operand in an integer division expression is **Null**, the expression result is also **Null**.

Modulo Division (Mod)

Modulo division is the complement of integer division. In modulo division, the expression returns only the remainder of the division operation as an integer. Both operands in a modulo division expression must be numeric expressions or strings that VBA can convert to a number. The following sample expressions illustrate the modulo division operator:

```
4 Mod 2              'returns the value 0
5.4 Mod 3            'returns the value 2
6 Mod NumVal         'if NumVal contains 5, returns 1
MyVal Mod NumVal     'Divide MyVal by NumVal, return remainder
```

In modulo division, VBA rounds each operand (if necessary) to an **Integer** or **Long** number before performing the division operation, just like integer division. For example, in the second sample expression preceding, VBA rounds the number 5.4 to 5 before performing the division operation; 3 goes into 5 once, with 2 as a remainder—the expression therefore returns 2 as the expression result.

The data type result of a modulo division expression is either an **Integer** or a **Long**; VBA uses the smallest data type that accommodates the expression result. If either operand in a modulo division expression is **Null**, the expression result is also **Null**.

Exponentiation (^)

The exponentiation operator (^) raises a number to a specified power. Exponentiation says how many times a number should be multiplied by itself; for example, 2^3 is the same as 2×2×2. To write 2^3 as a VBA statement, use the following expression:

```
2 ^ 3
```

Both operands in an exponentiation expression must be numeric expressions or strings that VBA can convert to a number. The operand to the left of the exponentiation operator can be a negative number only if the operand on the right side of the exponentiation operator is an integer. If either operand is **Null**, the expression result is also **Null**; otherwise, the data type result of an exponentiation expression is a **Double** data type.

Comparison Operators

Comparison operators are also sometimes referred to as *relational* operators. Most often, you use comparison operations to establish the criterion for making a decision, or to formulate a description of the conditions under which a group of commands are to be repeated (looping). (Day 8, "Making Decisions in Visual Basic," describes VBA's decision-making statements; Day 9, "Repeating Actions in Visual Basic: Loops," describes VBA's looping statements.)

The result of any comparison operation is a **Boolean** type value: **True** or **False**. You use comparison operators to compare literal, constant, or variable values of any similar type.

Table 4.2 lists all the comparison operators available in VBA and describes their function (in the table, E represents any valid VBA expression).

TABLE 4.2 COMPARISON OPERATORS

Operator	Syntax	Name/Description
=	E1 = E2	Equal to. True if E1 is equal to E2, false otherwise.
<	E1 < E2	Less than. True if E1 is less than E2, false otherwise.
<=	E1 <= E2	Less than or equal to. True if E1 is less than or equal to E2, false otherwise.
>	E1 > E2	Greater than. True if E1 is greater than E2, false otherwise.
>=	E1 >= E2	Greater than or equal to. True if E1 is greater than or equal to E2, false otherwise.
<>	E1 <> E2	Not equal to. True if E1 is not equal to E2, false otherwise.
Is	E1 Is E2	Is. Both operands must be **Object** type values. True if E1 refers to the same object as E2, false otherwise.
Like	E1 Like E2	Like. Both operands must be **String** type values. True if E1 matches the pattern contained in E2.

If both operands in a comparison expression have the same data type, VBA performs a straightforward comparison for that data type. If both operands are strings, for example, VBA makes a string comparison; if both operands are dates, VBA makes a date comparison, and so on.

The following sample expressions illustrate the use of and syntax for various comparison operators:

```
MyVal = 2           'evaluates to True if MyVal contains 2
4 <> 5              'evaluates to True: 4 does not equal 5
NumVal < 17         'True if NumVal is less than 17
"Sam" < "Joe"       'False; "Joe" is alphabetically less than "Sam"
"Fred" < "Freddy"   'True; "Fred" is shorter than "Freddy"
Now > #5/30/1999#   'True if Now is greater than May 30, 1999
```

The first three sample expressions provide examples of numeric comparison, the next two examples are string comparisons, and the final sample expression is a date comparison.

Note

Remember that VBA date values can include time information. When you compare date values, VBA actually compares the date *and* time information. For this reason, even if the month, day, and year of two dates are the same, they might not be equal to each other if the time portion of the date value is different. For example, the date #1/1/97# is less than the date #1/1/97 9:00:00 AM#. In the first date, no time value is supplied and VBA assumes that the time is 00:00:00. Even though the year, month, and day is the same in the second date, it has a later time, and is therefore greater than the first date.

To compare only the year, month, and day part of a **Date** type value, you can use VBA's **CInt** or **CLng** functions to convert the serial date value to an **Integer** or **Long** number. Converting a serial date to a whole number isolates the year, month, and day information; you can then directly compare these numbers to compare the dates that they represent. (VBA's serial date numbers were described in Day 3; data type conversion functions are described in Day 5.)

In numeric comparison expressions, the specific type of a numeric value in the expression is not important. However, if you compare values with different data types—such as comparing an **Integer** to a **String** or a **Variant** to some other type—you might receive type-mismatch errors or results other than those you expect.

If both operands in a comparison expression have definite types (either because they are constants or typed variables) and those types are not compatible, VBA displays a type-mismatch error. The following expressions, for example, produce type-mismatch errors because they attempt to compare incompatible data types:

```
1 > "zero"
NumVal% <= StrVal$
```

If one or both of the operands in a comparison expression is a **Variant** type variable, VBA will try to convert the **Variant** data to a compatible type, if necessary. If a data conversion is necessary and VBA can't convert the **Variant** to a compatible type, it displays a runtime error message.

Because you cannot always easily tell whether VBA will perform a numeric comparison or a string comparison when you mix numeric and string values in a comparison expression, you should always use one of VBA's type conversion functions (such as **CStr**) to explicitly convert values to numbers or strings so that both operands in a comparison expression have the same data type. (Conversion functions are described in the next lesson.)

String Comparisons

Comparing strings is a little more complicated than comparing numbers. In VBA, a string is equal to another string only when both strings contain exactly the same characters in exactly the same order and are exactly the same length.

Examine the following expressions:

```
"abc" = "abc"      'True: both strings are the same
"abc" = "abc "     'False: the strings are not the same
```

In the first expression, the strings are equal to each other: both strings contain the same characters in the same order and are the same length. In the second expression, the strings are not equal to each other: the string on the right-hand side of the operator has an additional space character at the end of the string. VBA does *not* ignore leading or trailing space characters when it compares strings.

When VBA compares strings with relational operators, it compares each string from left to right, character by character. In essence, VBA sorts the two strings alphabetically. VBA considers whichever string comes first in alphabetical order to be the "lesser" string. If two strings are different lengths but are otherwise identical, the shorter of the two strings is the "lesser" string. The next few sample expressions help illustrate how string comparisons work:

```
"abc" < "abc "     'True: the string on the left is shorter
"abcd" > "abc"     'True: the string on the left is longer
"aaa" < "aab"      'True: 1st string is less than the 2nd string
"aab" < "abb"      'True
"abb" < "abc"      'True
```

Binary and Text String Comparison

So far, the string comparison expressions shown include only strings consisting of lower-case characters. VBA offers two different ways to deal with comparing characters of different cases. The first technique that VBA uses to compare strings is called a *binary* compare, and is the default comparison technique.

To understand how binary comparison works, you need to remember that all information in your computer must be stored as a number. To store text, your computer uses a scheme in which each character that your computer can display has a unique number. The letters *a* through *z* all have unique consecutive numbers, as do the letters *A* through *Z*. Typically, the uppercase letters *A* through *Z* have lower numbers than the lowercase letters *a* through *z*. The number corresponding to a particular letter or other character is called the *character code* for that character.

> **Tip**
>
> Pay attention when you compare fixed- and variable-length strings. Remember that a fixed-length string always contains the same number of characters, and that a variable-length string increases or decreases in size depending on the size of the string stored in it. Examine the following VBA code fragment:
>
> ```
> Dim FixLen As String * 10, VarLen As String
> FixLen = "test"
> VarLen = "test"
> MsgBox (FixLen = VarLen)     'displays False
> ```
>
> Because FixLen is *always* 10 characters in length, it is longer than VarLen, which is only four characters long. VBA considers FixLen to be greater than VarLen. To avoid this type of problem with both fixed- and variable-length strings, use the Trim function to remove leading and trailing blanks from a string, as shown in the following example (the Trim function is described more fully in the next chapter):
>
> ```
> Dim FixLen As String * 10, VarLen As String
> FixLen = "test"
> VarLen = "test"
> MsgBox (Trim(FixLen) = VarLen)     'displays True
> ```

4

When VBA performs a binary comparison of string information, it uses the actual binary number equivalent for each character as it compares each pair of characters. Because the uppercase letters have lower binary numbers, uppercase letters alphabetize before lower-case letters. In other words, when VBA performs a binary string comparison, the string "AAA" is less than the string "aaa".

The second type of comparison that VBA offers is called *text* comparison. In a text comparison, VBA does not use the binary number equivalent for each character; instead, VBA considers uppercase letters to be equivalent to lowercase letters. In a text comparison, the string "AAA" is equal to the string "aaa". The next two sample expressions help illustrate the difference between binary and text string comparisons:

```
"Fred" = "fred"     'False in a binary comparison,
                    'True in a text comparison
"Fred" < "fred"     'True in a binary comparison,
                    'False in a text comparison
```

Choosing the String Comparison Technique

SYNTAX

To control whether VBA uses binary or text comparison, use the **Option Compare** directive:

```
Option Compare [Text ¦ Binary]
```

▼ To specify binary string comparisons, use the **Binary** keyword; to specify text comparisons, use the **Text** keyword. The **Option Compare** directive must appear on a line by itself at the module level, that is, in the declarations area of the module:

▲ ```
Option Compare Text
```

You can only use the **Option Compare** directives at the module level, and they affect only the comparisons made by procedures in that particular module. Typically, you place the **Option Compare** directive in the declarations area of your module before any variable or procedure declarations. If neither **Option Compare** command is present, VBA uses binary comparisons.

## The **Like** Operator

The **Like** operator gives you the ability to perform a special type of string comparison operation. You can only use the **Like** operator with strings.

The **Like** operator tests a string to determine whether it matches a specified pattern. You can use the **Like** operator to perform searches through text data to find all the words or phrases that match a particular pattern; a search of this type is often referred to as a *fuzzy search*.

**▼ SYNTAX**

The general syntax for the **Like** operator is

```
StrExpr1 Like StrExpr2
```

StrExpr1 represents any valid VBA string expression. *StrExpr2* represents a string expression specially constructed to specify a pattern that the **Like** operator compares to *StrExpr1*.

The **Like** expression evaluates **True** if the first operand (*StrExpr1*) matches the pattern in the second operand (*StrExpr2*); otherwise, the expression evaluates to **False**. Both operands in the expression must be string expressions or VBA displays a type-mismatch error.

▲

You specify the pattern to compare a string to by using various special characters. The following expression is **True** when AnyStr contains strings such as "Fred", "Ferdinand", "Food", "Fraud", and so on:

```
AnyStr Like "F*d"
```

The next expression evaluates **True** when AnyStr contains strings such as "cut", "cot", "cat", and so on:

```
AnyStr Like "c?t"
```
```

VBA expects the operand to the right of the **Like** operator to contain a string expression that specifies a pattern. Table 4.3 summarizes the techniques and symbols for constructing matching patterns for the **Like** operator.

TABLE 4.3 PATTERN-MATCHING CHARACTERS FOR THE Like OPERATOR

Pattern Character(s)	Matches Up With
#	Any single digit, 0 through 9.
*	Any number of characters in any combination or no characters.
?	Any single character.
[list]	list is a list of specific characters. Matches any single character in list.
[!list]	list is a list of specific characters. Matches any single character *not* in list.

Use the last two pattern character specifications in Table 4.3 to list individual characters that you want to match or not match. The following expressions show how to use the square brackets with a character list.

This expression is **True** if AnyStr contains "big" or "bid", and **False** if it contains "bit" or "bin":

AnyStr Like "bi°"

The next expression is **True** if AnyStr contains "big", "bid", or "bin", and **False** if it contains "bit":

AnyStr Like "bi[!t]"

The following expression is **True** if AnyStr contains "bin" or "bit", and **False** if AnyStr contains "bid" or "big":

AnyStr Like "bi[!dg]"

You can also use the square brackets to specify a range of characters to match or not match:

AnyStr Like "bi[a-f]"
AnyStr Like "bi[!a-f]"

The first example above is **True** whenever AnyStr contains one of the strings "bia", "bib", "bic", "bid", "bie", or "bif" and **False** otherwise. The second example expression is the inverse of the first, and is **False** whenever AnyStr contains one of the strings "bia", "bib", "bic", "bid", "bie", or "bif". The second expression is **True** for any string that contains the first two letters bi and does *not* end with the letters a through f.

4

When you specify a range of characters, you must specify the range from lowest to highest character. For example, the range pattern [a-f] is valid, but [f-a] is not. VBA ignores pairs of square brackets with nothing inside ([]).

Because the left bracket ([), question mark (?), number sign (#), and asterisk (*) characters have special meanings in the pattern string, you must enclose them inside square brackets if you want to make them part of the pattern to match. For example, if you want to find out if a string ends with a question mark, you would use the following expression (which is **True** if AnyStr contains any number or combination of characters ending with a question mark):

```
AnyStr Like "*[?]"
```

The right bracket (]) and exclamation mark (!) characters also have special meanings in the pattern string; to match these characters, make sure that they are *outside* the square brackets of a character list. For example, to determine whether a string ends with an exclamation mark, you use the following expression (which is **True** if AnyStr contains any number or combination of characters ending with an exclamation mark):

```
AnyStr Like "*!"
```

To match a hyphen character in the pattern string, place the hyphen at the beginning or end of a character list inside the square brackets. Placing the hyphen in any other location specifies a range of characters. The next expression shows how to match a hyphen character (this expression is **True** if AnyStr contains "big-headed", "pig-headed", "plug-ugly", "tag-along", and so on):

```
AnyStr Like "*g[-]*"      'True
```

The results of string comparisons that use the **Like** operator are also affected by the **Option Compare** setting. If the comparison option is set for binary string comparisons, the **Like** operator distinguishes between upper- and lowercase letters. If the comparison option is set for text comparison, the **Like** operator is not case sensitive.

Whether or not VBA is currently using binary or text comparison also affects what characters the **Like** operator includes in various ranges that you might specify. If, for example, you have specified the range [e-i] and the comparison option is set for binary comparison, only the characters *e, f, g, h,* and *i* match the specified range. If the comparison option is set for text comparison, however, the range includes several more characters: *E, e, È, è, É, é, Ê, ê, Ë, ë, F, f, G, g, H, h,* and *I, i* are all included in the range [e-i] when the **Option Compare Text** option is on. Notice that the characters *Ì, ì, Í, í, Î, î, Ï,* and *ï* are not included in the range; the specified range ended with the letter i, and accented characters are higher in the alphabetic sort order than unaccented characters.

Note

If you only want to find out whether a string is part of another string, use the VBA Instr function instead of the **Like** comparison operator. For example, if you simply want to determine whether the string *big* is part of the string *bigger*, use the Instr function. Day 5 describes VBA functions.

The Is Operator

VBA has one final comparison operator: the **Is** operator. You can only use the **Is** operator to compare **Object** type expressions. Expressions that include the **Is** operator always result in a **Boolean** value.

The **Is** operator expression evaluates to **True** when both object expressions refer to the same object; it evaluates to **False** otherwise. VBA provides the **Is** operator because none of the other comparison operators are meaningful when used with **Object** type expressions. Object expressions are really memory addresses that refer to a specific object in your host application (Excel, Word, Access, or some other application that implements VBA). Day 7 explains objects more fully.

Logical Operators

Most often, you use VBA's logical operators to combine the results of individual comparison expressions in order to build up complex criteria for making a decision within your procedure or for establishing the conditions under which a group of statements will repeat.

You can use any valid expression that has a **Boolean** result as the operands for a logical operator or a number that VBA can convert to a **Boolean** value. VBA considers 0 to be equivalent to the **Boolean** value **False**, and any other numeric value equivalent to the **Boolean** value **True**.

Usually, the result of a logical operation is a **Boolean** type value, although some logical operations might result in the special value **Null** if one or more of the operands are **Null**. Because VBA treats the special value **Empty** as 0, VBA treats operands in logical expressions that contain **Empty** as if they contain the **Boolean** value **False**.

Table 4.4 lists the logical operators available in VBA, along with their syntax and a brief description of how the operator works. (In the table, E represents any valid expression with a **Boolean** result, such as a comparison operation.)

TABLE 4.4 LOGICAL OPERATORS

Operator	Syntax	Name/Description
And	E1 And E2	Conjunction. True if both *E1* and *E2* are true; false otherwise.
Or	E1 Or E2	Disjunction. True if either or both *E1* or *E2* is true; false otherwise.
Not	Not E1	Negation. True if *E1* is false, false if *E1* is true.
Xor	E1 Xor E2	Exclusion. True if *E1* is true or *E2* is true, but not both; false otherwise.
Eqv	E1 Eqv E2	Equivalence. True if *E1* is the same value as *E2*; false otherwise.
Imp	E1 Imp E2	Implication. False whenever *E1* is true and *E2* is false; true otherwise.

Note

The VBA logical operators **And**, **Not**, and **Or** are similar to the AND, NOT, and OR worksheet functions built into Excel. Excel does not, however, have equivalent functions for the VBA **Eqv**, **Imp**, or **Xor** operators.

Understanding Truth Tables

The following sections describe each of VBA's logical operators in more detail. First, however, it is important that you know how to read a Boolean truth table. A *truth table* is a table that shows all the possible combinations of values for a particular type of logical expression and their results.

Most truth tables have three columns: The first column is for the value of the first operand, the second column is for the value of the second operand, and the last column always contains the value of the expression result. Each row in the table is for a particular combination of values. Examine the following line from the **And** operator's truth table:

```
    False              True            False
```

In this line, the first operand is **False**, the second operand is **True**, and the result of the **And** operation when the operands have the given values is **False**. This line in the truth table says that the result of the expression **False And True** is **False**.

And

The **And** operator performs a logical conjunction. The result of the **And** operation is **True** only when both of its operands are true; otherwise it is **False**.

▼ SYNTAX

The **And** operator has the following general syntax:

Operand1 And *Operand2*

Operand1 and *Operand2* are any valid VBA logical expressions. (A *logical expression* is any VBA expression that results in a **Boolean** type value: **True** or **False**.) The following truth table shows the results of the **And** operation.

Operand1	Operand2	*Expression Result*
True	True	True
True	False	False
False	True	False
False	False	False

▲

Use the **And** operator to find out whether two different conditions are true at the same time. For example, you would use the **And** operator in an expression like the following:

```
(Gross_Sales < 50000) And (Net_Profit < 10000)
```

The preceding expression evaluates **True** if both the value contained in `Gross_Sales` is less than 50,000 *and* the value contained in `Net_Profit` is less than 10,000.

Notice that the two operands in this expression are comparison expressions; notice also the parentheses around the expressions that make up the **And** operator's operands. Parentheses tell VBA to evaluate the expression inside the parentheses *before* evaluating other parts of the expression. Also, the parentheses help make the expression more readable for a human being by grouping together the related parts of the expression. Parentheses used to group parts of an expression into a sub-expression are a common feature in expressions of all types: numeric, string, date, and comparison, as well as logical expressions.

Or

The **Or** operator performs a logical disjunction, more frequently referred to as an *inclusive or*. The result of the **Or** operation is **True** whenever either or both operands is **True**; otherwise the result is **False**.

SYNTAX

The **Or** operator has the following general syntax:

Operand1 Or *Operand2*

Operand1 and *Operand2* are any valid VBA logical expressions. The following truth table shows the results of the **Or** operation.

Operand1	Operand2	Expression Result
True	True	True
True	False	True
False	True	True
False	False	False

Use the **Or** operator to find out whether one or the other of two different conditions is true. For example, you would use the **Or** operator in an expression like the following:

(Gross_Sales < 50000) Or (Net_Profit < 10000)

The preceding statement evaluates **True** if either the value contained in Gross_Sales is less than 50,000 *or* the value contained in Net_Profit is less than 10,000.

Not

The **Not** operator performs logical negation; it inverts whatever value it is used with. The **Not** operator uses only one operand, and results in **True** whenever the operand is false or **False** whenever the operand is **True**.

SYNTAX

The **Not** operator has the following general syntax:

Not *Operand1*

Operand1 is any valid VBA logical expression. The following truth table shows the results of the **Not** operation.

Operand1	Expression Result
True	False
False	True

Xor

The **Xor** operator performs a logical exclusion, and is more frequently referred to as an *exclusive or*. The result of the **Xor** operation is **True** when either—but not both—operand is true; otherwise, the result is **False**.

SYNTAX ▼

The **Xor** operator has the following general syntax:

Operand1 Xor *Operand2*

Operand1 and *Operand2* are any valid VBA logical expressions. The following truth table shows the results of the **Xor** operation.

Operand1	Operand2	Expression Result
True	True	False
True	False	True
False	True	True
False	False	False

Eqv

The **Eqv** operator performs a logical equivalence operation; using the **Eqv** operator is similar to a test for equality. The result of the **Eqv** operation is **True** whenever both operands are the same; otherwise, the result is **False**.

SYNTAX ▼

The **Eqv** operator has the following general syntax:

Operand1 Eqv *Operand2*

Operand1 and *Operand2* are any valid VBA logical expressions. The following truth table shows the results of the **Eqv** operation.

Operand1	Operand2	Expression Result
True	True	True
True	False	False
False	True	False
False	False	True

If either operand expression in an **Eqv** operation expression is **Null**, the expression result is also **Null**.

Imp

The **Imp** operator performs a logical implication. The **Imp** operator tests the relationship between two logical values when the truth of one value implies the truth of another value; as a result, the **Imp** operation produces the value **True** only when the second operand does not contradict the first operand. The **Imp** operator has the following syntax:

4

SYNTAX

Operand1 `Imp` *Operand2*

Operand1 and *Operand2* are any valid VBA logical expressions. The following truth table shows the results of the **Imp** operation.

Operand1	*Operand2*	*Expression Result*
True	True	True
True	False	False
False	True	True
False	False	True

If P and Q are variables containing logical values, the results of the two following expressions are equivalent:

```
P Imp Q
Not (P And (Not Q))
```

These expressions are equivalent because logical implication says that if one condition exists, a second condition must also exist. The result of a logical implication can be true even when the first condition is false, as long as the second condition is true. However, the result of logical implication cannot be true if the first condition is true and the second condition is false. The effects of logical implication are not nearly as intuitive or easy to understand as the other logical operators; fortunately, use of the logical implication operator is rarely necessary.

String Concatenation Operators

VBA lets you join strings together to form larger strings. Joining one string to another is called *concatenating* the strings. String concatenation is extremely useful and generally quite straightforward, although there are a few issues you need to be aware of.

Using String Concatenation

One of the most frequent uses for string concatenation is to assemble strings from various sources within your procedure to create customized messages for display. Listing 4.1 shows an Excel VBA procedure that asks the user for a workbook filename, opens that workbook, and then selects a particular worksheet for the user (in this case, a worksheet named Sales Report).

INPUT **LISTING 4.1** STRING CONCATENATION

```
 1:  Sub Open2DataEntry()
 2:  ' String Concatenation Demonstration
 3:
 4:      Const BoxTitle = "Data Entry Setup"
 5:      Const ShtName = "Sales Report"
 6:
 7:      Dim FName As String
 8:
 9:      'get the workbook name from user
10:      FName = InputBox("Enter the name of workbook to open:", _
11:                      BoxTitle)
12:
13:      'open the workbook
14:      Workbooks.Open FileName:=FName
15:
16:      'select the worksheet
17:      ActiveWorkbook.Sheets(ShtName).Select
18:
19:      'report to user
20:      MsgBox "Workbook " & FName & " opened, " & ShtName & _
21:              " selected.", , _
22:              BoxTitle & " Complete"
23:  End Sub
```

4

ANALYSIS Line 1 contains the procedure declaration. Line 4 declares a string constant that is used to supply the title bar for the various dialogs this procedure displays. Line 5 declares a string constant that is used to specify the name of the worksheet to select. Line 7 declares a variable to store the workbook name that the user enters. Lines 10 and 11 contain a single statement that uses the InputBox function to obtain a filename from the procedure's user. Line 14 opens the workbook file using the workbook filename obtained from the user in line 10. Line 17 selects the Sales Report worksheet.

(The instruction to open a workbook file in line 14 was copied from a recorded macro; the literal string in the original recorded macro was replaced with the FName variable so that different filenames could be supplied to this command depending on the user's input. The instruction in line 17 to select the Sales Report worksheet was constructed in the same way.)

In lines 20 through 22, notice how the MsgBox statement uses concatenated strings to assemble a message for the user and to assemble a new title bar for the MsgBox dialog. (The MsgBox statement in lines 20 through 22 is one VBA statement—notice the line continuation symbol at the end of lines 20 and 21.)

The string expression in lines 20 and 21 for the MsgBox procedure's first argument combines literal strings with the string in the FName variable and with the string indicated by the ShtName constant to form a single text string that VBA passes to MsgBox. The string concatenation expression in line 22 constructs the MsgBox procedure's second argument specifying the dialog's title. The string expression in line 22 combines the string indicated by the constant BoxTitle with a literal string constant.

If you execute this procedure and enter the name **VBA_Sample.xls** when the procedure prompts you to enter a filename, the MsgBox statement in lines 20 through 22 displays the dialog shown in Figure 4.1. (This example assumes that you actually have a workbook named VBA_Sample.xls in the current folder; otherwise, VBA displays a runtime error. If you experiment with this listing, make sure you enter a valid workbook name; you might need to type the complete path to the workbook you want to open.)

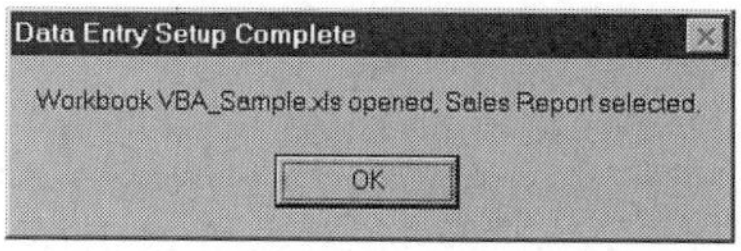

FIGURE 4.1

The MsgBox *statement in lines 20 through 22 of Listing 4.1 displays this dialog if you enter the filename VBA_Sample.xls.*

Data Entry Setup Complete

Workbook VBA_Sample.xls opened, Sales Report selected.

OK

String Concatenation Operators

VBA provides two different operators for string concatenation; the following paragraphs describe each of these concatenation operators and their preferred usage.

The Preferred Concatenation Operator: (&)

You can only use the ampersand (&) operator to concatenate strings; this operator has no other purpose or function in VBA. All the examples in this book use the ampersand operator for string concatenation. The ampersand is the preferred string concatenation operator because it leaves no doubt as to what operation you intend. The general syntax for the ampersand operator is

Operand1 & *Operand2*

Operand1 and *Operand2* represent any valid string or numeric expression. If one or both of the operands is a numeric expression, VBA converts the number to a string before performing the concatenation operation. The data type result of string concatenation is always a **String** data type. If an operand in a string concatenation expression is **Null** or **Empty**, VBA treats that operand as a zero-length string (that is, a string that does not contain any characters). Listing 4.1, in the preceding section, contains several examples of the & operator.

▼ SYNTAX

▲

> **Note**
>
> If you don't separate the & operator from the variable name in front of it with at least one space, VBA assumes that you want to use the ampersand (&) as a **Long** type-definition character instead of as a string concatenation operator. This situation has varying results: In some cases, VBA converts the variable or expression result to a **Long** data type number; in other cases VBA displays a runtime or syntax error of some kind. If you declare all your variables with specific types (as is good programming practice), VBA will display an error message.

The Addition Operator Used for String Concatenation: (+)

You can also use the plus (+) operator to concatenate strings. The + operator has syntax and operand requirements the same as those for the & operator, with one major exception. The + operator for string concatenation is a historic inheritance from the original versions of the BASIC programming language. These early versions of BASIC did not make a great distinction between string concatenation and addition. In VBA, however, the primary purpose of the plus (+) operator is for arithmetic addition. Whenever VBA encounters an expression that uses the + operator, it first tries to perform arithmetic addition. VBA only performs string concatenation with the + operator if one of the operands is a string expression and cannot be converted to a number or if both operands are strings.

Do

DO use the & operator for string concatenation to avoid ambiguity about the operation you intend and to ensure that VBA performs string concatenation.

DON'T

DON'T use the + operator for string concatenation, because expressions that use the + operator can be ambiguous to both VBA and a human reader.

Understanding Operator Precedence and Complex Expression Evaluation

A *complex expression* is simply any expression built from two or more other expressions. Just as you build complete sentences in English by assembling words and phrases together, you create complex expressions in VBA by assembling various simpler expressions.

Many of the expressions that you write will be complex expressions, especially when you write the expressions that determine decision-making or looping control in your procedures or if you need to write expressions that represent various mathematical formulas.

To learn how VBA evaluates complex expressions, study the following expression, which is the VBA implementation of the formula for computing the volume of a sphere (`Radius` is a variable containing the radius of the sphere; `Pi` is a named constant):

```
(4 / 3) * Pi * Radius ^ 3
```

Notice that this expression contains four operators acting on five different values. Because each operator requires two operands, you might wonder how VBA evaluates this expression, which has an odd number of operands in it. The answer is fairly simple: VBA groups values in the expression operator by operator, performs the indicated operation, and substitutes the resulting value into the expression. You might recall this process (called *reducing the terms of an expression*) from your high-school or college mathematics courses.

VBA uses standard *operator precedence* rules to determine which operations in the expression to evaluate first. VBA always evaluates expressions enclosed in parentheses first. In the preceding expression for computing the volume of a sphere, VBA evaluates the expression `4 / 3` first because it is enclosed in parentheses. After performing the division operation, VBA substitutes the resulting value—`1.333333`—into the expression. The interim expression that VBA computes internally, shown in the following, now has three operators and four different values:

```
1.333333 * Pi * Radius ^ 3
```

Next, VBA performs the exponentiation operation: `Radius ^ 3`. VBA performs the exponentiation operation now because the exponentiation operator has the highest priority of the remaining operators in the expression according to VBA's rules of operator precedence. As VBA performs the exponentiation operation, it retrieves whatever value is stored in `Radius` and raises it to the third power. VBA then substitutes that value into the expression. If `Radius` contains the number 2, the resulting value of the expression `Radius ^ 3` is 8 (2 raised to the third power). The interim expression that VBA computes internally, shown in the following, now has two operators and three different values:

```
1.333333 * Pi * 8
```

Finally, VBA performs the two multiplication operations in the expression. The multiplication operators, as you might guess, have the same priority level in VBA's operator precedence rules. There are no remaining parentheses in the expression, either. In this situation, VBA determines which operation to perform first by performing the operations in order from left to right.

The leftmost multiplication operation is the expression `1.333333 * Pi`. VBA therefore performs this multiplication operation first. If the constant `Pi` contains the value 3.14, the result of this multiplication operation is `4.186665`. The interim expression that VBA computes internally, shown in the following, now has one operator and two different values:

`4.186665 * 8`

There is only one operation left to perform. VBA performs the final multiplication operation—`4.186665 * 8`—and obtains the number `33.493324`.

VBA has now evaluated the expression to a single value and returns that value as the expression's result.

The preceding analysis of how VBA evaluates a complex expression illustrates VBA's rules for determining the *evaluation order* of an expression, which are summarized as follows:

- Parts of an expression enclosed in parentheses are always evaluated first. If the expression enclosed in parentheses is another complex expression, VBA applies these same rules to the expression within the parentheses.
- Specific operations are performed depending on the operator's precedence. The precedence of VBA's various operators is shown in Table 4.5.
- When operators have equal precedence, they are evaluated in order from left to right.

Do

DO use parentheses to override VBA's normal order of evaluation whenever necessary—VBA always evaluates expressions enclosed in parentheses first.

DO group values in an expression with parentheses any time you are uncertain how VBA will evaluate the expression or any time the evaluation order of an expression is not immediately obvious.

DO remember that grouping expressions with parentheses is an important way to make your procedures more readable and easier to understand.

VBA evaluates expressions in this general order:

- Arithmetic operators, first.
- String concatenation operators, second.
- Comparison operators, third.
- Logical operators, last.

Table 4.5 lists the exact operator precedence that VBA uses. Read the operator precedence from the top of the table to the bottom. Operators are listed from highest precedence to lowest precedence. Operators listed in the same row of the table have equal precedence. Operators with equal precedence are evaluated in order from left to right as they appear in the expression.

TABLE 4.5 OPERATOR PRECEDENCE FROM HIGHEST TO LOWEST

Operator	Comments
^	Exponentiation, highest priority.
-	Unary minus.
*, /	Multiplication and division have equal precedence; they are evaluated as they are encountered from left to right.
\	
Mod	
+, -	Addition and subtraction have equal precedence; they are evaluated as they are encountered from left to right.
&	All string concatenation is performed after any arithmetic operations in the expression and before any comparison or logical operations.
<, <=, >, >=, =, <>, Is, Like	All comparison operators have equal precedence, and they are evaluated as they are encountered from left to right. Use parentheses to group comparison operators in expressions.
Not	
And	
Or	
Xor	
Eqv	
Imp	

Summary

In this lesson, you learned what expressions and operators are and you learned how to use operators. You learned about each of VBA's arithmetic, string, comparison, and logical operators in detail.

Today's lesson explained why knowing the data type of an expression result is important, and the rules that VBA uses to determine the data type of an expression result for each operator and operand type involved. You learned how data type compatibilities can affect the results of an expression, and you also learned that VBA can often automatically convert values into compatible data types.

Finally, you learned how VBA evaluates complex expressions and the rules that VBA uses to determine which operations in a complex expression to perform first.

Q&A

Q Do I need to memorize all the data type and data conversion rules that VBA uses when it evaluates expressions?

A No, you don't need to memorize this information. It is important, however, that you have a basic understanding of what these rules are and how VBA applies them, even if you don't memorize all the fine details. This knowledge helps you write programs that are bug-free. By knowing how VBA evaluates expressions and determines expression results, you can control the numeric precision of expression results and therefore increase the accuracy of your program's computations. This knowledge also helps you identify the source of various different program errors that you might experience.

Q I'm not sure that I understand how to use the logical or comparison operators.

A You don't usually use logical and comparison operators in expressions in the same way that you use arithmetic or string concatenation operators. With arithmetic or string operators, you typically assign the expression result to a variable or use it as a procedure or function argument. More typically, however, you use the results of expressions with logical and comparison operators to determine the existence or absence of a certain condition, such as whether a particular count has exceeded a preset value or whether the user entered a particular response to a prompt. Logical and comparison expressions are essential components of the decision-making and looping commands described in Days 8 and 9.

4

Q How do I know which string concatenation operator to use?

A Always use the ampersand (**&**) operator for string concatenation. VBA provides the plus (+) operator for string concatenation in order to make it easier to translate programs from other dialects of the BASIC programming language into VBA, if necessary.

Workshop

The Workshop section presents Quiz questions to help you cement your new knowledge and Exercises to give you experience using what you have learned. Answers are in Appendix A.

Quiz

1. What is an expression? An expression result?
2. How many different values can an expression contain? How are the values in an expression connected together?
3. Can a single value, such as a literal constant or a variable, be considered an expression?
4. What can you use the result of an expression for? Must you use the result of an expression?
5. What are the two uses of the equal sign (=) as an operator?
6. What is the difference between the / operator and the \ operator?
7. If NumVal and StrVal are both **Variant** type variables, and NumVal contains 17 and StrVal contains "23", what is the result of each the following expressions?

   (a) NumVal < 5

   (b) NumVal + StrVal

   (c) NumVal & StrVal

   (d) NumVal - (5 + (6 * 2))

   (e) StrVal & "Skidoo"

Exercises

1. Add parentheses to each of the following expressions so that they produce the indicated result:

Expression	Result
(a) 3 * 5 - 7	-6
(b) 4.7 + 26 / 10	3.07
(c) 312 / 47 + 16 - 2	5.114754
(d) 17 - 5 - 44 / 2 ^ 2	100

2. Write, from scratch, a procedure named ThreeWords that uses three different InputBox statements to get three words from the user. Assemble the three words into a single string (with spaces between each word) and then display the assembled string onscreen with a MsgBox statement. In your procedure, declare a named string constant for the string "Input: ". Use this string constant and the string concatenation operator to alter the title of each of the three dialogs displayed by the InputBox statement so that the title of the first dialog is "Input: First Word", the title of the second dialog is "Input: Second Word", and the title of the third dialog is "Input: Third Word".

4

DAY 5

Visual Basic and Excel Functions

You've already used one of VBA's built-in functions: InputBox. Now that you know all about expressions, you're ready to learn how to incorporate functions into your expressions. Today you learn

- What a function is and how to use functions in expressions.
- How to use the Object Browser to determine what functions are available.
- How to save typing time and programming effort by using the Object Browser to insert VBA functions and their argument lists into your code.
- How to utilize the most important VBA functions to convert data from one type to another or to manipulate strings.

Understanding Functions

A *function* is a built-in formula that operates on expressions and generates values. A function always *returns* a value, which VBA inserts into your program at the point where the function name occurs. VBA functions fall into several groups according to the type of operation or calculation they perform. You use functions to provide values in an expression and to perform tasks such as the following:

- Converting text strings to other data types.

- Getting information about text strings.

- Converting other data types to text strings.

- Formatting numbers or other data types for display.

- Manipulating or generating date values.

- Performing trigonometric, logarithmic, statistical, financial, and other calculations.

- Getting information about files, disk drives, or the environment in which VBA is currently running.

This chapter summarizes each of the different categories of functions and describes in detail the most important VBA functions and their uses. Later lessons describe other functions summarized in this chapter as they become relevant to the topics of those lessons. Also, as you will learn in the next lesson, you can create your own functions for use in your VBA procedures.

In the examples and text so far, you have encountered examples of both VBA procedures and VBA functions. Don't let yourself get confused between the terms *function* and *procedure*. Generally, a procedure carries out a specific task (or group of tasks), just as a particular menu command in Excel carries out a specific task. A function, on the other hand, usually operates on one or more values and provides a specific value in return, such as a formula in an Excel worksheet cell.

Using Functions in Assignments and Expressions

To use a function, simply type the function name in a VBA statement—along with any arguments the function requires—at the point in the statement where you want to use the function result. (Putting a function name in a VBA statement to invoke a function is referred to as *calling* the function.) The following statements show typical uses of functions:

```
Tomorrow = Now + 1
AnyStr = CStr(AnyValue)
```

In the first statement, the Now function obtains the date and time from your computer system's clock and returns that information as a **Date** type value. When VBA executes this statement, it inserts the date value returned by the Now function into the expression at the point occupied by the Now keyword. VBA then evaluates the expression, adding one to the date returned by Now, and assigning that result to the variable Tomorrow. If today is August 8, 1999, after the execution of this statement, the date value stored in Tomorrow is August 9, 1999.

The second statement uses the **CStr** function, which converts its argument into a **String** data type and then returns that string. When VBA executes this statement, it passes the value stored in the AnyValue variable to the **CStr** function. **CStr** converts the value into a string and returns that string as the function result. For instance, if AnyValue contains the number 12, **CStr** returns the string "12". VBA then inserts the string returned by **CStr** into the expression at the point occupied by the **CStr** keyword. In this case, the function result is the only value in the expression, so VBA simply assigns the string value returned by **CStr** to the variable AnyStr.

The next statement is another example of the way you typically use functions:

```
MsgBox TypeName(AnyVar)
```

This statement uses the VBA TypeName function, which returns a string containing the name of the data type of its argument. When VBA executes this statement, it first calls the TypeName function, passing whatever value is stored in the AnyVar variable to the TypeName function. TypeName determines what data type was passed to it and returns a string stating the name of the data type. VBA then inserts the string returned by TypeName into the statement at the point occupied by the TypeName function name. Because the TypeName function name is placed in the statement as the argument to the MsgBox procedure, VBA passes the result of the TypeName function as an argument to MsgBox. If the variable AnyVar is a **Variant** type variable, TypeName returns the string "Variant", and the MsgBox procedure displays the word Variant onscreen.

These three examples illustrate some important facts about functions:

- You can use a function result as part of an expression.
- You can assign a function result to a variable.
- You can use a function result to supply a value in another procedure's or function's argument list.
- Functions have their argument lists enclosed in parentheses.

Essentially, you can use a function to supply a value anywhere in any VBA statement where you can legitimately use a constant or variable value. Listing 5.1 shows a complete procedure to further demonstrate how you use functions in expressions.

LISTING 5.1   USING FUNCTIONS

```
 1:   Sub FuncDemo()
 2:       Dim vDate
 3:       Dim tDate As Date
 4:       vDate = CStr(Now)
 5:       tDate = Time
 6:       MsgBox "Today's date: " & vDate
 7:       MsgBox "The current time: " & tDate
 8:       MsgBox "The variable vDate is type: " & TypeName(vDate)
 9:       MsgBox "The variable tDate is type: " & TypeName(tDate)
10:   End Sub
```

ANALYSIS   Line 1 contains the procedure declaration for the FuncDemo procedure. Lines 2 and 3 declare variables for FuncDemo to use. Line 2 declares the variable vDate; this variable is a **Variant** type because the variable declaration does not specify a data type. Line 3 declares the variable tDate; this variable is a **Date** type.

Line 4 is the first statement in FuncDemo that performs any work. When VBA executes line 4, it first calls the Now function, which returns the current date and time from your computer system's clock as a **Date** type value. VBA then inserts the result from the Now function into the statement. Because the Now function appears in the statement as the argument to the **CStr** function, VBA passes the Now function's result to the **CStr** function—**CStr** returns the string equivalent of whatever argument is passed to it. In this case, the argument is a **Date** type value (the Now function result), so **CStr** returns a string containing the current date and time. If today is February 6, 1999 and the time is 1:05 p.m. and 5 seconds, the **CStr** function in line 4 returns the string 2/6/99 1:05:05 PM. To complete the execution of the statement in line 4, VBA assigns the result of the **CStr** function to the vDate variable.

When VBA executes the statement in line 5, it first calls the Time function, which returns the time of day from your computer system's clock as a **Date** type value. If the current time is 3:54 p.m., the Time function in line 5 returns the value 3:54:00 PM as a **Date** data type. VBA then assigns the **Date** value returned by the Time function to the tDate variable.

Line 6 uses MsgBox to display a literal string concatenated with the value stored in the vDate variable. Notice the use of the ampersand (**&**) string concatenation operator. When VBA executes this statement, it first concatenates the literal string with the string contained in the vDate variable (remember, line 4 stored the current date and time in the vDate variable by using the **CStr** function to convert the date returned by the Now function into a string). Next, VBA passes the single string resulting from the string concatenation expression as the argument to the MsgBox procedure. If today is February 6, 1999 and the time is 1:05 p.m. and 5 seconds, the MsgBox statement in line 6 displays the dialog shown in Figure 5.1.

FIGURE 5.1

The MsgBox *statement in line 6 of Listing 5.1 displays this dialog showing the current date and time (according to your computer's clock).*

Line 7 also uses MsgBox. When VBA executes this statement, it first evaluates the expression that supplies the argument to MsgBox. This time, the string expression consists of a literal string concatenated with a **Date** type value. Because the expression contains the string concatenation operator (**&**), VBA correctly assumes that the intent of this expression is to produce a **String** type value. VBA therefore automatically converts the value in tDate into a string and then performs the specified concatenation operation. Next, VBA passes the string resulting from the concatenation expression as the argument to MsgBox. If the current time is 3:55 p.m. exactly, the MsgBox procedure in line 7 displays a dialog similar to the one shown in Figure 5.1, but containing the message The current time: 3:55:00 PM onscreen.

Lines 8 and 9 also use MsgBox. This time, each line displays a message stating the data type of a variable. When VBA executes line 8, it first calls the TypeName function. The argument for the TypeName function is the vDate variable. TypeName analyzes the contents of the vDate variable and returns a string that contains the name of the data type of the information stored by vDate. The vDate variable contains string data, so the TypeName function returns a string containing the word String. VBA next inserts the string returned by TypeName into the expression that forms the argument for the MsgBox procedure. Now, VBA finishes evaluating the expression by concatenating the literal string with the string returned by TypeName. The MsgBox procedure in line 8 then displays the dialog box shown in Figure 5.2.

FIGURE 5.2

The MsgBox *statement in line 8 of Listing 5.1 displays this dialog, revealing the data type of the data stored in the* vDate *variable.*

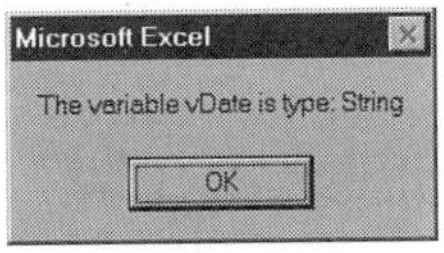

5

VBA executes line 9 similarly. Because tDate is a **Date** type variable, the TypeName function returns a string containing the word Date. The MsgBox statement in line 9 therefore displays the message The variable tDate is type: Date.

Do

DO remember that the TypeName function reports on the type of data *stored* by a variable, not the type of the variable itself. Line 8 of Listing 5.1 correctly reports that the data stored in the variable is a string, which is correct; TypeName can't help you determine whether the variable type is a string (in this case it's a **Variant** type containing a string).

DON'T

DON'T forget to include the parentheses around a function's argument list (see the section "Ignoring a Function's Result" later in this chapter).

Understanding Function Arguments and Function Results

As you've seen in the examples so far, and in Listing 5.1, some functions require one or more arguments, others do not. Functions that don't require arguments usually just retrieve a value that is not otherwise available. As an example, the Time function, which returns the current time from your computer's clock, does not require any arguments. To use a function that does not use any arguments, just type the function name into your program, as shown in the following statement:

```
TimeNow = Time
```

Other functions require that you supply one or more values for them to act on. The Sqr function, for example, returns the square root of a number; in order for Sqr to calculate a square root, you must supply a number for Sqr to act on, as shown in the next statement:

```
Root = Sqr(AnyNum)
```

You supply values to a function through the function's argument list. Enclose the argument list in parentheses and, if there is more than one argument, separate each argument in the list with a comma, as you learned to do in Day 2 with the MsgBox procedure.

The data type of a value returned by a function depends on the specific function. Most functions return **Variant** type data values, although other functions return specific data types such as **String**, **Double**, and **Integer**. VBA often can automatically convert a function's result to a data type compatible with other values in the expression that contains the function, just like VBA converts data types in variable assignments and expression evaluation. All the data type compatibility rules you learned in Day 4 that apply to **Variant** and typed variables and constants also apply to the values returned by functions.

Ignoring a Function's Result

Normally, you must use the value returned by a function in some way—either by including the function result in an expression or an argument list or by assigning it to a variable. In some cases, however, you might want to ignore the result returned by a function.

Day 2 mentioned that VBA's MsgBox procedure has an optional second argument that enables you to specify how many command buttons appear in the message dialog. You can use the command button argument in the MsgBox procedure to display a message that asks the user a question and enables the user to respond to your question by choosing a command button in the message dialog.

If you use this optional command button argument for MsgBox, you must be able to obtain a value from MsgBox that indicates which button the user chose. In fact, the MsgBox procedure is really a function; most of the time you use the MsgBox function, however, you ignore its result.

All the examples and procedure listings in this book so far have omitted the command-button argument from the MsgBox statements. When you omit the command-button argument, MsgBox displays a dialog that contains only one button. Because the MsgBox dialog, as used so far, contained only one button, it didn't matter what the result of the MsgBox function was, so all the MsgBox statements thus far have ignored the MsgBox function's result, using MsgBox statements similar to the following (which simply consists of the MsgBox function name followed by its argument list):

```
MsgBox AnyText, , AnyTitle
```

VBA provides several intrinsic constants for specifying the buttons in the MsgBox dialog (Day 8, "Making Decisions in Visual Basic for Applications," describes these constants in more detail). One of these constants, vbYesNo, indicates to MsgBox that it should include a Yes button and a No button in the dialog that it displays. The following statement produces the dialog shown in Figure 5.3:

```
MsgBox "Do you see two buttons?", vbYesNo, "Button Demonstration"
```

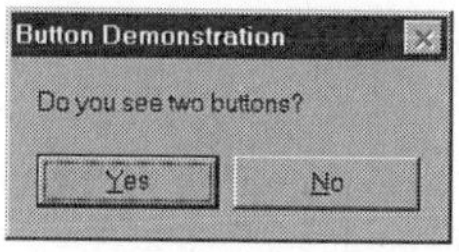

FIGURE 5.3

A MsgBox *dialog
showing the result of
including the buttons
argument.*

There's only one problem with this statement: The result of the user's choice is *not*
returned in any way; this statement still ignores the MsgBox function result.

To retrieve the MsgBox function result, you must change this statement in two ways: You
must add parentheses around the argument list, and you must alter the statement so that it
uses the function result in some way. Typically, you assign the MsgBox function result to
a variable so that you can later test the function result in another statement to determine
which button your procedure's user actually chose. The next line shows the MsgBox statement altered so that it returns a value (notice the line-continuation symbol—this is a single VBA statement):

```
Response = MsgBox ("Do you see two buttons?", vbYesNo, _
                   "Button Demonstration")
```

When VBA executes this statement, it displays the same dialog shown in Figure 5.3.
When the user chooses either the Yes button or the No button, VBA closes the dialog and
stores a number representing the chosen button in the Response variable.

Notice that the first MsgBox statement, which ignores the MsgBox function result, does not
have any parentheses around the argument list, and that the second MsgBox statement,
which uses the MsgBox function result, *does* have parentheses around the argument list.

These two MsgBox statements illustrate an important fact about functions: By omitting
the parentheses around the function's argument list, you tell VBA that you want to ignore
the function's result. When you omit the parentheses around the argument list, VBA
treats the function call as if it were a call to a procedure and does not return the function
result.

If you look again at the function examples earlier in this chapter and at the functions
used in Listing 5.1, you'll notice that all the statements that call a VBA function include
parentheses around the function's argument list, even when the argument list contains
only one argument. Functions that do not have arguments do not require parentheses
when you call them.

You can't ignore the result of every VBA function, nor would you necessarily want to.
Ignoring the result of a function is only useful with functions (such as MsgBox) that carry
out some task as part of producing their return value. You ignore the function result when

you want the function to carry out its task, but you don't care about the result of that task. The MsgBox function, as an example, carries out the task of displaying a message onscreen in a dialog box as part of the task involved in returning a choice from the user. MsgBox is also useful if all you want to do is just display a message; in this case, you use the function to display a message, but ignore its result. (Day 8 explains how to use MsgBox to enable your program's user to make choices affecting the execution of your program.)

If you try to ignore the result of a function that has no arguments (such as the Now function) or any other function whose result cannot be ignored, VBA displays one of several possible runtime errors depending on the specific function, although you usually receive a type-mismatch or syntax error. Typically, VBA prevents you from ignoring the result of any function whose name is a VBA keyword (such as **CStr** and other conversion functions) and those functions whose only purpose is to provide some returned value, such as the mathematical functions.

Using a Function's Named Arguments

You learned in Day 2 that you must list a procedure's arguments in a specific order. Similarly, you must also list a function's arguments in a specific order. Functions that use more than one argument depend on the position of a value in the argument list to determine which argument that value represents. For instance, you've learned that for MsgBox the first argument is the message to display, the second argument is the number and type of buttons for the dialog, and the third argument is the title of the dialog.

Even though the second MsgBox argument specifying the command buttons for the dialog is optional, and has been omitted in almost all of the examples and exercises so far, you still must include placeholding commas for the second argument in the argument list. As you saw in Day 2, omitting the placeholding commas for the second argument causes a type-mismatch error.

As you might have discovered by now, it's often easy to inadvertently omit placeholding commas or to transpose argument values in functions that have optional arguments or have several arguments, despite the help offered by the Auto Quick Info feature of the VB Editor. When you omit or transpose arguments in a function's argument list, you might get type-mismatch errors or, worse, no error at all. Sometimes, transposing values (such as row and column coordinates) in a function's argument list does not produce any type of runtime error; your program simply produces the wrong answer and you can't figure out why.

To help prevent programmer errors, and to make it easier to use functions that have optional arguments, VBA provides an alternative to listing the values in an argument list

5

in a specific order. You can also pass argument values to a function by using the function's *named arguments*. The following lines show two MsgBox statements that have
exactly the same effect: The first statement uses the standard method of listing arguments
and the second statement uses the named argument method of listing arguments (both
statements ignore the MsgBox function result):

```
MsgBox AnyMsg, , AnyTitle
MsgBox Prompt:=AnyMsg, Title:=AnyTitle
```

The second statement uses named arguments for the message (or prompt) that MsgBox
displays and for the title argument that specifies the title for the message dialog by
assigning a value to each named argument. The argument name for the MsgBox title,
 for example, is Title; the expression Title:=AnyTitle assigns the contents of the
variable AnyTitle as the argument value, which VBA passes to MsgBox to be used as
the dialog's title.

Similarly, the argument name for the MsgBox prompt text is Prompt, and the expression
Prompt:=AnyMsg assigns the contents of the variable AnyMsg as the argument value,
which VBA passes to MsgBox to be used as the text displayed by the message dialog.

> **Note**
>
> The symbol that assigns a value to a named argument (:=) is not exactly the
> same as the regular assignment operator (=). If you omit the colon (:) when
> you assign a value to a named argument, VBA does not necessarily detect a
> syntax error, but is unable to interpret the statement correctly. When VBA
> executes the statement, it displays one of several possible runtime errors,
> frequently a type-mismatch error.

When you use named arguments, you don't have to include placeholding commas for
optional arguments. Notice, in the second statement above, that there is no placeholder
comma between the arguments for the prompt and title, as there is in the first statement.
In fact, named arguments don't have to appear in any particular order. In the second
statement, you could list the Title argument before the Prompt argument:

```
MsgBox Title:=AnyTitle, prompt:=AnyMsg
```

MsgBox still uses the value assigned to the Title argument as the dialog title. When you
use named arguments, VBA uses the name of the argument to determine what value that
argument represents.

The `InputBox` function also has named arguments, as do all of the VBA functions. The following statement shows an `InputBox` statement that uses named arguments:

```
User_Input = InputBox(Prompt:=AnyText, Title:=AnyTitle)
```

Notice that this statement includes parentheses around the argument list. You must always include parentheses around the argument list when you use a function's result, whether or not you use named arguments when you call the function.

Do

DO remember that VBA uses the name of the argument to determine what value that argument represents.

DO include parentheses around a function's argument list whenever you use the function's result.

Note

You cannot mix named arguments with a standard argument list in the same function call. You must either use named arguments or a standard argument list for each individual function call, although you do not have to use the same method of listing arguments in every function call.

To determine the names of a function's arguments, use the Auto Quick Info pop-up window that appears as you type the function's name. (Auto Quick Info was described in Day 2.) Alternatively, use the Object Browser to paste the function's name and complete named argument list into your program code as described in the section "Using the Object Browser to Insert Function Calls," later in this chapter. To get more information on any function's purpose and full details about its arguments, search VBA's online help for the particular function name.

Using Visual Basic for Application's Functions

VBA's various built-in functions fall into several different categories based on the general purpose of the functions in that category (such as mathematical, data conversion, date and time, interaction, string, and disk information). The next few sections discuss each function category and include a table listing the functions and summarizing their actions.

5

Unfortunately, discussing every VBA function in detail is beyond the capacity of this book. Fortunately, though, most of the VBA functions—such as the mathematical functions—are fairly self-explanatory and don't require much discussion. Other functions, such as some of the data type conversion and string-handling functions, are discussed in more detail. VBA's string manipulation functions are of sufficient importance that a separate section of this lesson has been devoted to explaining their use.

> **Tip**
>
> To get more information about a specific function, type the function name, highlight it, and then press F1. VBA displays the online reference with that particular function as the current topic.

Mathematical Functions

VBA provides a standard selection of mathematical functions. Use these functions in expressions or to provide arguments for other functions in any of the ways already described. Table 5.1 summarizes the mathematical functions available in VBA. In the table, N stands for any valid numeric expression; all function arguments are required unless otherwise noted.

TABLE 5.1 VBA's MATHEMATICAL FUNCTIONS

Function(Arguments)	Returns/Action
Abs(N)	Returns the absolute value of N.
Atn(N)	Returns the Arctangent of N as an angle in radians.
Cos(N)	The Cosine of the angle N, where N is an angle measured in radians.
Exp(N)	Returns the constant *e* raised to the power N. (*e* is the base of natural logarithms, and is approximately equal to 2.718282.)
Fix(N)	Returns the integer part of N. Fix does *not* round the number, it discards any fractional portion. If N is negative, Fix returns the nearest negative integer greater than or equal to N.
Int(N)	Returns the integer part of N. Int does *not* round the number, it discards any fractional part. If N is negative, Int returns the nearest negative integer less than or equal to N.
Log(N)	Returns the natural logarithm of N.
Rnd(N)	Returns a random number; argument is optional. Rnd is used to provide a random factor in programs that simulate some real-world event, such as stock market simulations. Use the Rnd function only after initializing VBA's random number generator with the Randomize statement.

Function(Arguments)	Returns/Action
Round(N, P)	Returns the result of rounding a number, N, to the number of decimal places indicated by P. If you omit P, Round returns the result of rounding N to a whole number.
Sgn(N)	Returns the sign of a number: -1 if N is negative, 1 if N is positive, 0 if N is 0.
Sin(N)	Returns the Sine of an angle; N is an angle measured in radians.
Sqr(N)	Returns the square root of N. VBA displays a runtime error if N is negative. (By mathematical definition, negative numbers cannot have a square root.)
Tan(N)	Returns the Tangent of an angle; N is an angle measured in radians.

Do

DO keep in mind that the Fix and Int functions *truncate* integers, that is, they discard the fractional portion of the number without rounding. The only difference between the Fix and Int functions is how they handle negative numbers.

DO use the **CInt** function (described in the next section of this lesson) if you want to *round* numbers to the nearest integer.

DO use the Round function to round a number with a specific number of decimal places, such as rounding 2.534 to 2.53.

DON'T

DON'T forget that you can derive additional trigonometric functions from the basic VBA math functions, if you need them. For example, if you need to compute the Cotangent of an angle, you can use the formula 1/Tan(x) to find the Cotangent. For a list of common derived math functions and their formulas, search the VBA online help for the topic "Derived Math Functions." As you learn in Day 6, "Creating and Using VBA Function Procedures and Excel User-Defined Functions," you can then write your own functions to create the derived math functions.

5

Data Conversion Functions

Visual Basic provides several functions to convert one data type into another. Use these data conversion functions to resolve type-mismatch errors and to maintain explicit control over the data types in your expressions.

For example, if you receive a type-mismatch error for a particular expression, you might be able to convert values in the expression to types that are compatible with each other by using one of the conversion functions. As another example, you might want to keep the result of an expression within the range of a **Single** numeric type (most numeric expressions result in a **Double**); in this case, you would use the **CSng** function to convert the expression result to a **Single** type number, as shown in this statement:

```
AnySingle = CSng(412/14)
```

Table 5.2 summarizes VBA's conversion functions. In the table, N stands for any numeric expression, S stands for any string expression, and E stands for an expression of any type. Each function's arguments are required unless otherwise noted.

TABLE 5.2   DATA CONVERSION FUNCTIONS

Function(Arguments)	Returns/Action
Asc(S)	Returns the character code number corresponding to the first letter of the string S. The letter A, for example, has the character code 65.
Chr(N)	Returns a string containing the character that corresponds to the character code N, which must be a number between 0 and 255, inclusive. The character code 65, for example, returns the letter A.
Format(E, S)	Returns a string containing the value represented by E, formatted according to instructions contained in S. You can use Format to convert numbers such as 1000 to strings like $1,000.00.
Hex(N)	Returns a string containing the hexadecimal representation of N.
Oct(N)	Returns a string containing the octal representation of N.
RGB(N, N, N)	Returns a **Long** integer representing an RGB color value. N in each argument must be an integer between 0 and 255, inclusive. From left to right, the arguments are the values for red, green, and blue.
Str(N)	Returns the string equivalent of the numeric expression N.
Val(S)	Returns a numeric value corresponding to the number represented by the string S. S must contain only digits and a single decimal point, otherwise VBA cannot convert the number. If VBA can't convert the string in S, the Val function returns 0.
CBool(N)	Returns the **Boolean** equivalent of the numeric expression N.
CByte(E)	Returns a numeric value of type **Byte** (0 through 255); E can be any valid numeric expression or a string expression that can be converted to a number.

Function(Arguments)	Returns/Action
CCur(E)	Returns a numeric value of type **Currency**; E can be any valid numeric expression or a string expression that can be converted to a number.
CDate(E)	Returns a **Date** type value. E can be any valid expression (either a string or number) that represents a date within the range 1/1/100 through 12/31/9999, inclusive.
CDbl(E)	Returns a numeric value of type **Double**; E can be any valid numeric expression or a string expression that can be converted to a number.
CInt(E)	Returns a numeric value of type **Integer**; E can be any valid numeric expression or a string expression that can be converted to a number.
CLng(E)	Returns a numeric value of type **Long**; E can be any valid numeric expression or a string expression that can be converted to a number.
CSng(E)	Returns a numeric value of type **Single**; E can be any valid numeric expression or a string expression that can be converted to a number.
CStr(E)	Returns a **String** type value; E can be any valid numeric or string expression.
CVar(E)	Returns a **Variant** type value; E can be any valid numeric or string expression.

The most frequent conversion functions you'll use are the functions (grouped together at the end of Table 5.2) that begin with the letter C—which stands for *convert*—followed by an abbreviation of a type name: **CStr**, **CSng**, **CDbl**, and so on (these functions are printed in bold monospace type because they are VBA keywords).

Note

Using typed variables and type conversion functions requires you, the programmer, to be aware of when VBA converts data types in your code from one type to another. As you learned in Day 4, relying exclusively on VBA's automatic type conversion rules might not produce the results you want or expect because some operators—such as the plus sign (+)—behave differently depending on the data type of the values in the expression. Using typed variables and type conversion functions helps you avoid or locate subtle errors resulting from data type conversions you did not anticipate.

5

Date and Time Functions

Use VBA's date and time functions to obtain the current date or time, break a date value into its component parts, or to convert strings and numbers to **Date** type values.

Table 5.3 summarizes VBA's date and time functions and their effects. In the table, N is any valid numeric expression and D is any valid date expression (including **Date** type values, numbers, or strings that VBA can convert to a date). All function arguments are required, unless otherwise noted.

TABLE 5.3 DATE AND TIME FUNCTIONS

Function(Arguments)	Returns/Action
Date	Returns the current date from your computer system's clock. (You can also use this function as a procedure to set your computer system's clock. Refer to VBA's online help for details.)
Time	Returns the current time from your computer system's clock as a **Date** value. (You can also use this function as a procedure to set your computer system's clock. Refer to VBA's online help for details.)
Now	Returns the current date and time from your computer system's clock.
Year(D)	Returns an integer containing the year part of the date expression. The year is returned as a number between 100 and 9999.
Month(D)	Returns an integer containing the month part of the date expression. The month is returned as a number between 1 and 12, inclusive.
Day(D)	Returns an integer containing the day part of the date expression. The day is returned as a number between 1 and 31, inclusive.
Weekday(D)	Returns an integer containing the day of the week for the date in the date expression. The weekday is returned as a number between 1 and 7, inclusive; 1 is Sunday, 2 is Monday, and so on.
Hour(D)	Returns an integer containing the hour part of the time contained in the date expression. The hour is returned as a number between 0 and 23, inclusive. If the date expression does not contain a value for the time, Hour returns 0.
Minute(D)	Returns an integer containing the minutes part of the time contained in the date expression. The minutes are returned as a number between 0 and 59, inclusive. If the date expression does not contain a value for the time, Minute returns 0.

Function(Arguments)	Returns/Action
Second(D)	Returns an integer containing the seconds part of the time contained in the date expression. The seconds are returned as a number between 0 and 59, inclusive. If the date expression does not contain a value for the time, Second returns 0.
DateSerial(N, N, N)	Returns a serial date value for a specified date. From left to right, the arguments represent the year, month, and day. The year argument must be a whole number between 100 and 9999, month must be between 1 and 12, and day must be between 1 and 31 (all ranges are inclusive).
TimeSerial(N, N, N)	Returns a serial time value for a specified time. From left to right, the arguments represent the hours, minutes, and seconds. The hour argument must be a whole number between 0 and 23, minutes and seconds must both be numbers between 0 and 59 (all ranges are inclusive).
DateValue(E)	Returns a **Date** value equivalent to the date specified by E, which must be any string, number, or constant representing a date.
TimeValue(E)	Returns a **Date** value containing the time specified by E, which must be any string, number, or constant representing a time.
Timer	Returns a number representing the number of seconds since midnight according to your computer system's clock.

User Interaction Functions

You're already acquainted with VBA's interactive functions for exchanging input and output with your procedure's user: InputBox and MsgBox. These are the only user interaction functions in VBA, although the Interaction class in the Object Browser does list several functions and procedures in addition to InputBox and MsgBox. The other interaction functions enable you to interact with the Windows operating system or with other applications. For example, you can use the other interaction functions and procedures to retrieve or add Windows Registry settings, to send keystrokes to another application, or to utilize Automation features to control another application's objects. These are all fairly advanced programming tasks. You'll learn more about controlling other applications with VBA's other interaction functions in Day 20, "Working with Other Applications." This lesson concentrates only on the user interaction functions, InputBox and MsgBox.

InputBox

Both MsgBox and InputBox have several optional arguments that have not yet been described. The complete general syntax for the InputBox function is

InputBox(*Prompt* [, *Title, Default, XPos, YPos, HelpFile, Context*])

Prompt is any string expression. The *Prompt* argument is the only required argument for InputBox, all the other arguments are optional. The square brackets in the argument list of the syntax example indicate that the remaining arguments are optional.

You're already familiar with the *Prompt* and *Title* arguments: The first is a string used to tell the user what information you expect them to enter; the second is a string used as the title for the input dialog.

The *Default* argument is also any string expression; use the *Default* argument to provide a default value for the user's input. The following statement, for example, asks the user to enter a filename and suggests the name NEWFILE. The dialog produced by this statement, showing the default value, is shown in Figure 5.4.

▲
```
User_Input = InputBox("Enter a file name: ", _
                      "Make a File", "NEWFILE")
```

FIGURE 5.4

Use the optional arguments for InputBox *to specify a default value for the user's input.*

As you might have noticed, the InputBox dialog displays in the center of the screen. You might want the dialog to display in another position onscreen, especially if you have other dialogs open that you want to remain visible. Staggering input dialogs as they're opened helps your procedure's user keep track of where she is in a particular sequence of dialogs.

The *XPos* and *YPos* arguments can be any numeric expression. These arguments enable you to specify where in the active window the input dialog appears. *XPos* and *YPos* provide the coordinates for the top left corner of the dialog box. *XPos* is the horizontal distance from the left edge of the window; *YPos* is the vertical distance from the top of the window. Both distances are measured in *twips*: one twip equals 1/20 of a point (a point is a measurement of printing type size). Because a point is 1/72 of an inch, a twip is therefore approximately equal to 0.0007 inches.

> **Caution**
>
> Be careful if you specify the position of the InputBox dialog. It is possible for you to specify positions for the XPos and YPos arguments so large that the dialog does not appear onscreen at all because its position is beyond the right or bottom edge of the window. Although the dialog is not visible, it *is* active, so none of the controls you can see onscreen will work until you respond to the "invisible" dialog.

The last two optional arguments for the InputBox function are the *HelpFile* and *Context* arguments. *HelpFile* is a string expression that contains the name of a Windows help file, which is usually a help file that you create using the Windows Help File compiler. *Context* is a numeric expression specifying the topic in the help file that pertains to the dialog you are displaying, for example, 0 is usually the table of contents for a help file.

If you specify either *HelpFile* or *Context*, you must specify both. Whenever you specify a help file for an input dialog, VBA automatically adds a Help command button to the dialog. (VBA does not include the Windows Help Compiler; if you want to create your own custom help files, you must obtain the Windows Help Compiler separately from Microsoft or use a third-party help authoring tool such as Blue Sky software's RoboHelp or WexTech's Doc-to-Help.)

To use named arguments for InputBox, just use the argument names given in the syntax example above: Prompt, Title, Default, XPos, YPos, HelpFile, and Context. The following statement produces the same dialog shown in Figure 5.4, but uses named arguments:

```
User_Input = InputBox(prompt:="Enter a file name: ", _
                      Title:="Make a File", Default:="NEWFILE")
```

MsgBox

The complete argument list for the MsgBox function is similar to that for InputBox:

▼ SYNTAX

MsgBox(*Prompt* [, *Buttons*, *Title*, *HelpFile*, *Context*])

The only required argument for MsgBox is the *Prompt* argument, which can be any string expression; all other arguments are optional. The *Title*, *HelpFile*, and *Context* arguments in MsgBox have the same purpose and requirements as their counterparts in the InputBox function. Notice that MsgBox does not have arguments for the dialog's position; the MsgBox dialog always displays near the center of the window. Notice also that MsgBox

▼ has a *Buttons* argument instead of a *Default* argument.

5

▼ In MsgBox, the *Buttons* argument is a numeric expression that specifies how many and
what kind of buttons appear in the MsgBox dialog. The *Buttons* argument also specifies
the default button in the dialog and whether the dialog contains the standard Windows
Critical, Information, Exclamation, or Question icons for cautionary and user-query messages. The following statement, for example, displays the dialog shown in Figure 5.5:

```
User_Input = MsgBox("Choose a button", vbYesNo, "Button Test")
```

This statement uses the vbYesNo constant, which is one of the intrinsic constants that
VBA provides expressly for use with MsgBox. Using these VBA constants, and using the
▲ value returned by the MsgBox function, is described in Day 8.

FIGURE 5.5

The MsgBox *function
provides options to
specify how many and
what kinds of com-
mand buttons appear
in the dialog.*

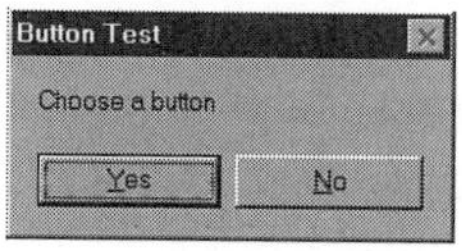

Do

DO use the named arguments for InputBox and MsgBox to make using their various arguments simpler and to make your VBA statements easier for a human being to read and
understand.

DO use the line-continuation symbol to put each named argument on a separate line
whenever your statements begin to get excessively long:

```
User_Input = MsgBox(Prompt:="Choose a button", _
                    Buttons:=vbYesNo, _
                    Title:="Button Test")
```

This statement is easy for a human being to read and understand; many of the examples
later in this book use formatting like this to make them more understandable.

String Functions

You use VBA's string functions to find strings inside other strings, to compare strings to
each other, and to copy selected portions of strings. You'll use VBA's string functions
frequently because string data is so important—you'll encounter string data in every
VBA application, whether in Excel or another VBA host application. Often, you'll need
to manipulate string data obtained as user input with InputBox. Other times, string data
will appear in your VBA code as filenames for Excel workbooks, Word documents,
Access databases, and other types of data stored in disk files.

String data is also important in Excel as worksheet names, named ranges of data, and so on. This section summarizes the available VBA string functions; a later section gives more detail on how to use the most important and useful string functions.

In Table 5.4, N is any valid numeric expression and S is any valid string expression. Unless otherwise noted, all function arguments are required.

TABLE 5.4 STRING FUNCTIONS

Function(Arguments)	Returns/Action
Filter(A1, S1, B1, N1)	Returns a subset array of strings from A1 (an array of strings to be filtered). B1 and N1 are optional. If B1 is **True** or omitted, the returned array includes strings from A1 that match S1. If B1 is **False**, the returned array includes strings from A1 that do not match S1. N1 specifies whether to perform a case-sensitive search; if N1 is omitted, Filter uses the current **Option Compare** setting.
InStr(N1, S1, S2, N2)	Returns the position of S2 in S1. N1 is the starting position for the search; N2 specifies whether to perform a case-sensitive search. N1 and N2 are optional. If N2 is omitted, the search uses the current setting of **Option Compare**. If N2 is included, you must also include N1.
Join(A1, S1)	Returns a **String** assembled from the strings in the array A1. S1 is optional, and indicates the delimiting character inserted between the assembled strings. If S1 is omitted, Join connects the strings with a space character.
LCase(S)	Returns a **String** type containing a copy of S with all uppercase characters converted to lowercase characters.
Left(S, N)	Returns a **String**; copies N characters from S, beginning with the leftmost character of S.
Len(S)	Returns the number of characters in S, including leading or trailing spaces.
LTrim(S)	Returns a copy of the string S after removing any space characters from the left side of the string (leading spaces).
Mid(S, N1, N2)	Returns a **String**; copies N2 characters from S beginning with the character position in S specified by N1. N2 is optional; if you omit N2, Mid returns all the characters in string S from position N1 to the end of the string.

continues

TABLE 5.4   CONTINUED

Function(Arguments)	Returns/Action
Replace(S1, S2, S3, N1, N2, N3)	Returns a **String** copied from S1, with each occurrence of S2 replaced by S3. N1, N2, and N3 are all optional. N1 indicates at what point in S1 the character replacement should begin. N2 indicates how many times the replacement should be made. N3 specifies whether to perform a case-sensitive search; if N3 is omitted, Replace uses the current **Option Compare** setting.
Right(N, S)	Returns a **String**; copies N characters from S beginning with the rightmost character of S. For example, Right("outright", 5) returns the string "right".
RTrim(S)	Returns a copy of the string S after removing any space characters from the right side of the string (trailing spaces).
Space(N)	Returns a string of spaces N characters long.
Split(S1, S2, N1, N2)	Returns an array of strings created by dividing S1 into smaller strings. The optional S2 argument is a single-character string indicating where S1 should be divided; if S2 is omitted, Split divides S1 at each space character. N1 and N2 are optional. N1 specifies an upper limit to the number of splits to be made, and N2 specifies whether to perform a case-sensitive search.
StrComp(S1, S2, N)	Compares S1 to S2 and returns a number indicating the comparison result: -1 if S1 < S2, 0 if S1 = S2, 1 if S1 > S2. N is optional; it indicates whether to make a case-sensitive comparison. If N is omitted, strings are compared using the current **Option Compare** setting.
StrConv(S, N)	Returns a **String** converted to a new form, depending on the numeric code specified by N. VBA provides intrinsic constants for use with StrConv; the most useful are vbProperCase (converts the string so that each letter starting a word is capitalized), vbLowerCase (converts the string to all lowercase letters), and vbUpperCase (converts the string to all uppercase letters).
String(N, S)	Returns a **String** N characters long of the character specified by the first character in S. For example, String(5, "x") returns the string xxxxx.
StrReverse(S1)	Returns a **String** type that is a copy of S1 with the order of characters in the string reversed. For example, StrReverse("Fred") returns "derf."

Function(Arguments)	Returns/Action
Trim(S)	Returns a copy of the string S after removing both leading and trailing space characters from the string.
UCase(S)	Returns S with all lowercase characters converted to upper case characters.

Several of the data type conversion functions listed in Table 5.2 are also related to string manipulation—Chr, Format, and **CStr**, in particular. The sections "Using Functions to Manipulate Strings" and "Formatting Data Values" later in this chapter contain more information on using string data in VBA.

Disk, Directory Information, and Other Functions

Occasionally, your programs might need to obtain information about a disk drive, locate a particular file, or make a list of files. VBA provides several different disk and directory information functions to help you accomplish these tasks. Day 12, "Creating Libraries and Whole Programs: Modular Programming Techniques," gives information on managing files and disk directories from your VBA programs.

VBA provides several other functions not mentioned in this chapter. These additional functions enable you to communicate with other applications, get information about run-time errors, get information about arrays, and manipulate various objects in Excel. Later lessons discuss these other functions as they become relevant.

Using Excel's Functions

5

In addition to the functions built in to Visual Basic for Applications, Excel has a wide variety of functions that perform mathematical, logical, financial, and statistical operations on data in worksheets. Excel makes many, but not all, of these functions available to VBA.

Note

Other VBA host applications, such as Word 2000 or Access 2000, also make some or all of their functions available to VBA. The information in this section about using host application functions in VBA applies to all VBA host applications. (Remember, the *host application* is the application in which you are developing your VBA procedures, such as Excel 2000.)

The functions that Excel or another host application makes available to VBA are not part of VBA, they are part of the host application. The Excel worksheet functions, for example, aren't part of the VBA programming language, they are part of the Excel host application. Not every VBA host application contains functions that you can use in VBA. The functions available to VBA in one host application might not be available in another host application. If you intend to write VBA procedures that can run in any host application, don't use functions from a host application because they might not be available in every application. For instance, if you want to write a procedure that you can use in either Word, Excel, Access, or Microsoft Project, don't use Excel functions in your VBA statements.

To use a function that belongs to a host application, you access the function in VBA through the `Application` program object. The `Application` object in VBA represents the host application and all its resources. (Objects are explained in more detail in Day 7, "Understanding Objects and Collections"; using Excel objects is explained in Day 19, "Controlling Excel with VBA.")

Note

> Although many of Excel's mathematical functions duplicate VBA's mathematical functions, Excel contains many more specialized statistical and financial functions than VBA. If you're programming Excel operations in VBA, you'll probably want or need to use many of the worksheet functions that are part of Excel. As you'll learn in Day 19, you can use Automation features to utilize Excel worksheet functions in VBA applications other than Excel.

As an example, the following statement uses the Excel `Max` function, which returns the largest number in its argument list:

```
MsgBox Application.Max(4, 1, 3, 2)      'Displays 4
```

In this statement, notice that the word `Application` is followed by a period (`.`) and then the name of the function, `Max`, without any spaces. The period—called a *dot separator*—indicates that the statement refers to the `Max` function, which is part of the `Application` object. When you use a host application's functions in your VBA statements, you must include the `Application` keyword and the dot separator in front of each function's name. For example, to use any of Excel's worksheet functions in your VBA statements, you must include the `Application` keyword and the dot separator (`.`) in front of every Excel function name.

> **Note**
>
> You cannot ignore the result of an Excel function. You must always include the parentheses in a call to an Excel function, and you must always use the function result in some way, either as a value in an expression, an argument for another function or procedure, or in an assignment statement.

If you're an experienced Excel worksheet user, you might have already noticed that Excel has many functions that have the same names as some of the functions listed in Tables 5.1 through 5.4.

Because you must always specify the Application keyword when you use a host application function, there is never any ambiguity for either VBA or for a human reader as to which function (VBA or Excel) your statement refers to. As an example, the following code fragment shows two statements:

```
Rslt = Log(AnyNum)
Rslt = Application.Log(AnyNum)
```

The first statement calls the VBA Log function; the second statement calls Excel's Log function. To use the VBA version of a function, just use the function name by itself; to use the host application's version of a function, include the Application keyword.

> **Caution**
>
> Excel (or other host application) functions that have the same name as VBA functions do not necessarily carry out the same tasks or produce the same results. For example, the Excel LOG function is different from the VBA Log function, and they return different answers: the Excel LN function is the one that matches the effects of VBA's Log function. Carefully review the action and result of an Excel function before using it in place of a VBA function—otherwise, your procedures might produce erroneous results.

Not every Excel function is available to VBA. As an example, some Excel functions that duplicate VBA functions are unavailable because there is no point in making them available. Specifically, the Excel functions Date, Year, Month, Day, Hour, Minute, and Second all duplicate VBA's Date, Year, Month, Day, Hour, Minute, and Second functions in both behavior and purpose. None of these Excel functions are available to VBA. Occasionally, some host application functions are not available to VBA, whether or not they duplicate VBA functions.

5

If you are uncertain whether a particular Excel function is available to VBA, use the Object Browser (as described in the next section of this chapter) to see if the Members list includes the function you want when `Application` is selected in the Classes list and `Excel` is selected in the Library/Project list. If the function you want is not listed, it is not available to VBA.

To find out what functions Excel (or any other application) has available, and to find out what the uses and purposes of those functions are, use the online help system and search for the word *functions*.

Using the Object Browser to Insert Function Calls

The combined number of functions available to you through VBA and Excel is substantial: There are literally several hundreds of functions available in Excel VBA.

Obviously, it is difficult (if not impossible) to memorize the purpose, use, and arguments for this many different functions. Most people end up memorizing the names and arguments of only those functions that they use frequently, and then rely on a general knowledge of available functions to help them locate a specific function for a specific purpose.

You can use the Object Browser to help you locate available functions and determine what their argument lists and named arguments are. The Object Browser is an important tool that also enables you to access any online help available for specific functions, and to paste a "template" for the function call into your procedure's source code, including all of the function's named arguments.

Viewing and Inserting Visual Basic's Functions

To insert a function call into your VBA source code, you start the Object Browser the same way you have already learned: Choose the View, Object Browser command or click the Object Browser button on the VB Editor's toolbar. Whichever technique you use to start the Object Browser, VBA displays the Object Browser window shown in Figure 5.6.

Note

> The Object Browser window lists *all* of the procedures, constants, and commands available, not just functions. As a result, you will see many more items listed in the Object Browser than just the functions described in this chapter. Many of the items you see listed are described in later lessons.

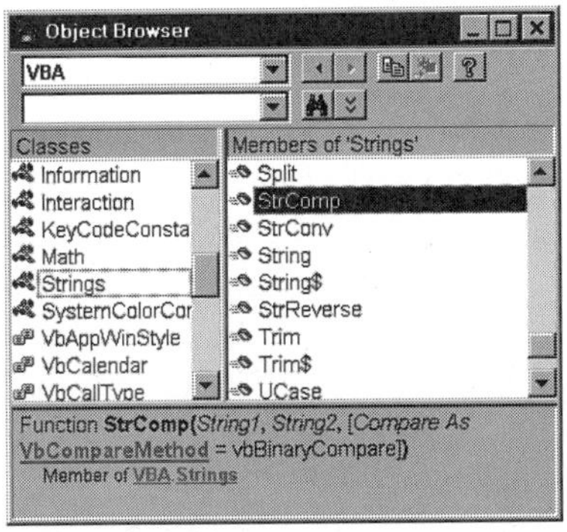

FIGURE 5.6

Use the Object Browser to determine which functions are available, and to insert a function call with all its named arguments into your code.

You've already learned how to use the Object Browser to view the intrinsic constants that VBA provides; viewing the available functions is very similar. To view the available VBA functions, follow these steps:

1. Select VBA in the Project/Library drop-down list box at the top of the Object Browser window.

   The Classes list now shows the various categories of objects, functions, procedures, and constants defined by VBA.

2. Select the function category in which you are interested (Constants, Conversion, DateTime, FileSystem, Information, Interaction, Math, or Strings) in the Classes list. Figure 5.6 shows the Strings category selected.

3. Select the specific function you want to use—or want to get more information about—in the Members of *<class>* list. Figure 5.6 shows the **StrComp** function selected.

At the bottom of the Object Browser window in Figure 5.6, notice that the **StrComp** function name and complete argument list appear. Each name that appears in the argument list is the name to use for the function's named arguments. The Object Browser always uses this area of the dialog to show you the correct argument syntax and named arguments for whatever function you select in the Members of *<class>* list.

Notice that the syntax information area at the bottom of the Object Browser also indicates the data type of the function's arguments. The StrComp function shown in Figure 5.6, for example, has an optional argument—Compare—that is of the data type VbCompareMethod. (VbCompareMethod is a custom data type; you learn about custom data types in Day 10.) If no data type is specified for a function's argument, the function argument is a **Variant** data type.

5

Refer again to Figure 5.6 and notice the command button with a question mark on it at the upper right of the Object Browser window. When this button is enabled, there is online help available for the item selected in the Classes or Members of <*class*> lists. Click this button to view whatever help is available for the selected item. The online help for VBA functions describes any limitations on the range or data type of the function arguments, explains which arguments are optional, and explains how to interpret the function's return values.

Tip

> The window at the bottom of the Object Browser—where a function's syntax and argument list appears—often contains hotspot words in bold, green, underlined text (refer to Figures 5.6 and 5.7). Clicking one of these hotspot words causes the Object Browser to display that particular library or class. For example, in Figure 5.6, the selected StrComp function's optional Compare argument's data type (VbCompareMethod) is displayed in bold, green, underlined text. Clicking the VbCompareMethod hotspot causes the Object Browser to display the VbCompareMethod class of intrinsic constants; the Members of VbCompareMethod list then shows all the intrinsic constants defined in the VbCompareMethod class module.

To paste the function name and the function's complete argument list into your program source code, follow these steps:

1. Position the insertion point in your module at the place where you want to use the function's result.

2. Open the Object Browser window and select the function that you want to paste into your source code in the Members of <*class*> list, as described above.

3. Click the Copy button in the Object Browser. The Object Browser copies the selected function name to the Windows Clipboard.

4. Close the Object Browser and press Ctrl+V to paste the function name into the Code Window.

Do

DO keep in mind that you can paste the entire argument list for a function by selecting text in the bottom part of the Object Browser window, clicking the Object Browser's Copy button to copy the selected text to the Windows Clipboard, and then pasting it into your module.

DO remember to add any assignment expressions, variables, or other elements to make the pasted function and argument list into a syntactically valid statement.

Viewing and Inserting Excel's Functions

To use the Object Browser to view the functions that a VBA host application makes available to VBA, or to paste a host application function into your source code, follow these steps:

1. Open the Object Browser window.

2. Select Excel in the Project/Library drop-down list at the top of the Object Browser window.

   The Classes list now shows the various categories of functions, procedures, constants, and other program objects defined by Excel, as shown in Figure 5.7.

3. In the Classes list, select the category of function you're interested in. For example, to view available worksheet functions, select WorksheetFunction in the Classes list, as shown in Figure 5.7.

4. Select the specific function you want to use—or want to get more information about—in the Members of *<class>* list. Figure 5.7 shows the Excel Sum function selected.

Note

Because you can only access Excel's functions in VBA through the Application object—the repository of all of Excel's resources—you must select Excel in the Project/Library list to display Excel's functions (see Figure 5.7). The Object Browser then lists all the functions, commands, and other resources that Excel makes available through the Application object.

Tip

The Application object, in general, is the repository of any VBA host application's resources. You can use the Object Browser to view the functions and objects made available by any VBA host application, if you select the specific application library in the Project/Library list of the Object Browser. The Object Browser then lists all of the functions, commands, and other resources that the host application makes available through the Application object.

5

FIGURE 5.7

*You can also use the
Object Browser to view
and insert functions
from Excel.*

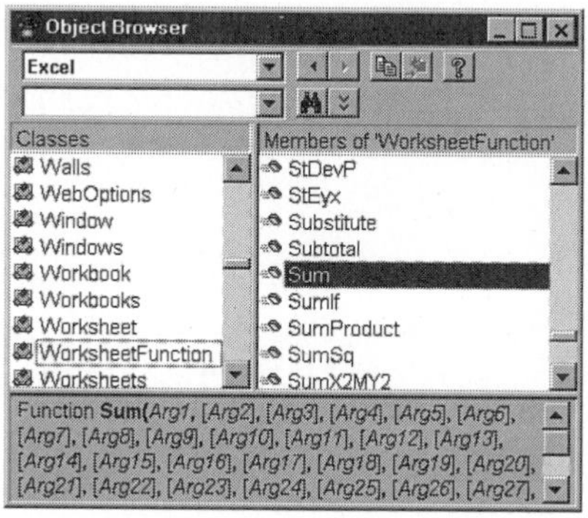

Do

DO remember that a particular host application's library is only available if you start the VB Editor from that particular host application. For example, you can only list the Excel library in the Object Browser window if you start the VB Editor from Excel. In Day 12 you learn how to create additional library references for your VBA projects.

DO remember that you can only access a host application's functions when you include the Application keyword and the dot separator (.) in front of the function name.

DO add the Application keyword and the dot separator (.) whenever you use the Object Browser to paste a host application function into your source code.

Using Functions to Manipulate Strings

Manipulating string data is an important part of many programs, especially programs that interact with a human user. Interactive programs need to manipulate string data for two reasons: to formulate messages you want to display to the user, and because the user's input (via InputBox) comes into your program as string data.

The more effectively you can manipulate string data, the more likely you are to be able to display attractive, coherent messages for your program's user. Also, the greater your skill in string manipulation, the more likely you will be able to successfully analyze the strings that your program's user enters.

VBA provides many different functions as tools to help you manipulate string data. VBA's string functions were summarized in Table 5.4, earlier in this chapter. This and the next section describe how to use the most important string functions and some of the data conversion functions to perform both simple and complex operations on string data in your programs.

Removing Extraneous Space Characters

Occasionally, string data in your program ends up containing extraneous space characters either at the end of the string or at the beginning of the string. These leading and trailing spaces occur for different reasons.

One of the most common sources of leading or trailing space characters occurs when you use the InputBox function to obtain input from the user. InputBox returns *all* the text a user types, including any extra space characters. If the user types extra spaces before or after the actual input value, the InputBox function returns those extra spaces as part of its return string.

Another common source of leading or trailing spaces in string data occurs when you use the contents of a fixed-length string variable. A fixed-length string always has the same length, and VBA pads the data assigned to the string variable (usually with trailing spaces) to fill out the declared string length, if necessary. As a result, whenever you use a fixed-length string there is a good chance it will contain trailing spaces.

Extraneous leading or trailing spaces in a string can cause a variety of difficulties, some only cosmetic, others more serious. When you assemble strings for display, the extra space characters can cause large gaps in your text, resulting in an unattractive and hard-to-read display. In other cases, extraneous leading and trailing spaces can affect string comparisons, the reported length of the string, and several other factors. These effects can cause the string value to be unusable in some other expression, or they might just cause your procedure to produce erroneous results. Either way, you can have a potentially serious problem.

VBA provides a trio of functions specifically for the purpose of removing—that is, trimming—unwanted leading and trailing spaces from a string. The first function, RTrim, removes space characters from the right side of the string (trailing spaces). The second function, LTrim, removes space characters from the left side of the string (leading spaces). The third function, Trim, removes both leading and trailing spaces from the string.

These string-trimming functions do not actually change the string: You pass the string you want trimmed as a function argument and the function returns a *copy* of the string with the extra spaces removed. The procedure in Listing 5.2 demonstrates the use of the string-trimming functions.

5

 LISTING 5.2 DEMONSTRATION OF RTrim, LTrim, AND Trim FUNCTIONS

```
1:  Sub TrimDemo()
2:      Dim ExSpace As String
3:      ExSpace = "    mad dog    "
4:      MsgBox "{" & ExSpace & "}"
5:      MsgBox "{" & RTrim(ExSpace) & "}"
6:      MsgBox "{" & LTrim(ExSpace) & "}"
7:      MsgBox "{" & Trim(ExSpace) & "}"
8:  End Sub
```

ANALYSIS Line 1 contains the procedure declaration for TrimDemo, line 2 declares a string variable, and line 3 assigns a string with both leading and trailing spaces (four each) to the ExSpace variable. Line 4 uses MsgBox to display the unaltered ExSpace string. The string expression for the MsgBox argument concatenates a pair of curly braces around the ExSpace string to help show whether there are leading or trailing spaces in the string. When VBA executes this MsgBox statement, it displays the dialog shown in Figure 5.8.

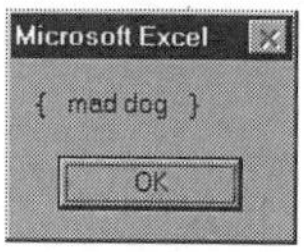

FIGURE 5.8

The procedure in Listing 5.2 displays this dialog to show that the string stored in ExSpace has leading and trailing spaces in it.

Lines 5 through 7 of Listing 5.2 each use one of the three string-trimming functions to remove leading and trailing spaces from the ExSpace string; each line uses MsgBox to display the result of the string-trimming function. Keep in mind that the contents of the string variable ExSpace don't change: The string-trimming functions return a copy of the string in ExSpace with the extraneous characters removed.

Do

DO remember that when you compare strings with VBA's comparison operators, VBA considers the longer string to be greater than the other string, provided the two strings are otherwise identical.

DO use the Trim function to remove leading and trailing spaces from strings before you compare them. By using the Trim function, you ensure that the string comparison is not affected by leading or trailing spaces that aren't usually significant to a human being, but are significant to your computer.

Determining the Length of a String

Frequently, you will need to know the length of a string (that is, how many characters are in the string), especially when you are formatting messages for the user or when formatting string data that your procedure inserts into an Excel worksheet. VBA provides the Len function to enable you to obtain the length of a string. The general syntax for the Len function is

```
Len(String)
```

String represents any valid VBA string expression. The following statement shows the Len function used in an assignment statement:

```
StrLen = Len("Alison")      'returns 6
```

Again, fixed-length strings are a special case. Because a fixed-length string is always the same length, the Len function always returns the declared length of the string. For example, if you declare FirstName as a string variable 20 characters in length, the Len function always returns 20 as the length of the string in FirstName, even if the name stored in the variable is *Sam*, which is only three characters long; the rest of the 20-character length is all space characters.

Usually, when you use the Len function, your intent is to find out how many characters are in the string *excluding* any leading or trailing spaces. Continuing with the FirstName example, if you want to know the actual length of the name stored in the variable, use a statement similar to the following:

```
NameLen = Len(Trim(FirstName))
```

In this statement, the Trim function removes any leading or trailing spaces from the string in the variable and the Len function reports the length of the trimmed string. If FirstName contains *Sam*, NameLen would end up with the value 3.

Comparing and Searching Strings

Day 4 showed you how to compare strings using comparison operators and explained the effects of the **Option Compare Binary** and **Option Compare Text** settings.

VBA also provides a couple of functions to help you compare strings. The first function, **StrComp**, simply compares two different strings. In some circumstances, you might want to use **StrComp** instead of the comparison operators (=, <, or >) to compare strings because **StrComp** enables you to specify whether to perform a binary or text comparison, overriding the module-level **Option Compare** setting for just that particular comparison.

For example, you might decide that you want most of your string comparisons to ignore the case (upper or lower) of the characters when comparing strings; consequently, you add the **Option Compare Text** statement to your module. You might then want to perform a specific string comparison that *is* case sensitive; you then use VBA's **StrComp** function and specify a case-sensitive comparison.

Using the StrComp Function

The general syntax for the **StrComp** function is

StrComp(*String1*, *String2* [, *Compare*])

String1 and *String2* represent any two string expressions you want to compare. The optional *Compare* argument can be any one of the following intrinsic constants:

- vbBinaryCompare to compare the two strings with a binary (case sensitive) comparison.
- vbTextCompare to compare the two strings with a text (not case sensitive) comparison.
- vbDatabaseCompare is only meaningful in Microsoft Access; it causes the string comparison to use whatever comparison method has been set for the current database. If you use vbDatabaseCompare in any flavor of VBA other than Access VBA, you'll receive a runtime error stating that there has been an invalid procedure argument.

If you omit the *Compare* argument, **StrComp** uses the current **Option Compare** setting. When **StrComp** executes, it compares the two strings using the specified comparison method and returns one of the following values:

- -1 if *String1* is less than *String2*
- 0 if *String1* and *String2* are equal to each other
- 1 if *String1* is greater than *String2*

The procedure in Listing 5.3 demonstrates the **StrComp** function.

INPUT **LISTING 5.3** DEMONSTRATION OF **StrComp** FUNCTION

```
1:  Sub Demo_StrComp()
2:      Const Dflt = "Suggested"
3:      Dim UserStr As String
4:      UserStr = InputBox(Prompt:="Enter some text:", _
5:                         Title:="String Comparison", _
6:                         Default:=Dflt)
7:      MsgBox StrComp(UserStr, Dflt, vbTextCompare)
8:  End Sub
```

ANALYSIS Line 1 contains the procedure declaration for Demo_StrComp. Line 2 declares a constant, Dflt, for use as the default prompt in a later InputBox statement. Line 3 declares a string variable, UserStr, to hold the result of the InputBox function. Lines 4 through 6 are a single statement that calls the InputBox function to obtain a string from the user. The InputBox function call uses named arguments and specifies the prompt, dialog title, and suggested default value for the InputBox dialog. The statement assigns the result of the InputBox function to the UserStr variable.

Line 7 contains the **StrComp** function call; the statement uses MsgBox to simply display the **StrComp** function's returned value directly onscreen. The **StrComp** function call in line 7 uses all the possible arguments for **StrComp**. This statement passes the UserStr variable and the Dflt constant to **StrComp** for comparison. Line 7 also specifies that **StrComp** should perform a text comparison (the vbTextCompare intrinsic constant indicates a text comparison). This procedure reveals whether the user accepted the suggested default value for the InputBox function, or if the user entered a string lesser or greater than the string in the suggested default.

Do

DO consider creating module-level constant declarations for the **StrComp** function's return values—this is an ideal use for named constants.

Using the InStr Function

VBA's other string comparison function, InStr, helps you determine whether one string contains another string. This function is useful in a number of circumstances. For example, use InStr if you want to determine whether a string the user entered contains a particular word. As another example, use InStr if you want to determine whether a string contains characters that would prevent it from being converted to a number.

SYNTAX

The general syntax for the InStr function is

```
InStr([Start, ] String1, String2 [, Compare])
```

String1 and String2 are any valid string expressions. InStr searches String1 to see if it contains String2. The optional Start argument is any numeric expression; this argument, if supplied, tells InStr at what character position in String1 the search should begin. The optional Compare argument specifies whether InStr should use binary or text comparison while searching for String2 in String1. The permissible values for the InStr function's Compare argument are the same intrinsic constants used by the **StrComp** function: vbBinaryCompare, vbTextCompare, and vbDatabaseCompare.

5

▼   InStr returns a number indicating the character position in *String1* where *String2* was found; if InStr does not find *String2* within *String1*, InStr returns 0. If either *String1* or *String2* is **Null**, InStr returns **Null**.

▲   Listing 5.4 demonstrates the use of InStr.

INPUT   **LISTING 5.4**   DEMONSTRATION OF InStr FUNCTION

```
1:  Sub Demo_InStr()
2:      Const Dflt = "Suggested"
3:      Dim UserStr As String
4:      UserStr = InputBox(Prompt:="Enter some text:", _
5:                         Title:="String Searching", _
6:                         Default:=Dflt)
7:      MsgBox InStr(1, UserStr, Dflt, vbTextCompare)
8:  End Sub
```

ANALYSIS   Line 1 contains the procedure declaration for Demo_InStr. Lines 2 and 3 declare a string constant and string variable for use with the InputBox function. Lines 4 through 6 contain a single statement that calls the InputBox function to obtain a string from the user and stores that string in the UserStr variable.

Line 7 contains the InStr function call; the function's returned value is simply displayed onscreen (line 8). The InStr function call in line 7 uses all the possible arguments for InStr. In this statement, InStr searches to see whether the string in UserStr contains the string indicated by the Dflt constant and uses a text comparison. Because this call to InStr includes the optional comparison argument, the statement also includes the starting position for the search. InStr begins searching for the Dflt string in the first character position of UserStr.

If UserStr contains the string Suggested text, InStr returns 1. If UserStr contains the string This text was Suggested, InStr returns 15. If UserStr contains the string This is some text, InStr returns 0. Finally, the InStr function result is passed as the argument to MsgBox (still in line 7), which displays the result of the call to InStr.

Breaking a String into Smaller Parts

In many procedures, you will need to break a string into its component parts. For example, you might need to analyze a string that the user enters to determine whether it contains more than one word and, if it does, separate out the individual words that the user entered. You'll see samples of this type of string manipulation in later lessons and example code listings.

The Left Function

VBA provides three functions to help you extract *substrings* from larger strings. (A substring is any string that is—or can be—part of a larger string.) The first of VBA's substring functions is the Left function, which returns a copy of a specified portion of a string. The general syntax for the Left function is

Left(*string, length*)

string represents any valid string expression and *length* is any numeric expression. The Left function returns a copy of *string*, beginning with the first character in *string* and continuing for the number of characters specified by *length*. If *length* is a number greater than the actual length of *string*, Left returns the entire *string*.

In the following statement, Left copies the first 17 characters of the string OldStr and returns those characters as a string; this statement assigns the function result of Left to the variable NewStr. If OldStr contains the string The quick red fox jumps over the lazy brown dog, NewStr contains The quick red fox after VBA executes this statement.

   NewStr = Left(OldStr, 17)

The Right Function

The next VBA substring function is the Right function. The general syntax for the Right function is

Right(*string, length*)

string represents any valid string expression and *length* is any numeric expression. The Right function returns a copy of *string*, beginning with the *last* character in the string and continuing *from right to left* for the number of characters specified by *length*. If *length* is a number greater than the actual length of *string*, Right returns the entire *string*. The Right function always copies characters from the end of the string, working back toward the beginning of the string without reversing the order of the characters.

In the following statement, the Right function returns the last four characters of the string stored in OldStr. If the OldStr variable contains the string hairball, this statement stores the string ball in NewStr.

NewStr = Right(OldStr, 4)

The Mid Function

You might want to extract a substring from somewhere in the middle of a string, rather than from the left or right end of the string. Such a situation might occur if you are extracting individual words from a line of text. To extract a substring from the middle of another string, VBA provides the Mid function. The Mid function has the following general syntax:

▼ SYNTAX

```
Mid(string, start [, length])
```

string represents any string expression and *start* and *length* represent any numeric expression. The Mid function returns a copy of *string*, beginning at the character position in *string* specified by *start*. The optional *length* argument specifies how many characters Mid copies from *string*. If you omit *length* (or *length* is greater than the remaining length of *string*), Mid copies all of the remaining characters in *string* from the position indicated by *start* to the end of *string*. If *start* contains a number greater than the actual length of *string*, Mid returns an empty string.

The following statement shows an example of the Mid function:

```
NewStr = Mid(OldStr, 3, 4)
```

In the preceding statement, if OldStr contains the string unknowingly, this statement stores the string know in NewStr.

▲

> **Note**
>
> VBA does have one other function you can use to divide a string into smaller parts: the Split function. The Split function returns an array of strings; Split creates the array by dividing a source string wherever a delimiter character you specify (typically a space character) occurs. This chapter does not discuss the Split function in more detail because you have not yet learned about arrays. Arrays are covered in Day 14.

Using String Characters You Cannot Type at the Keyboard

Sometimes you need to include a character in a string for which there is no key on the keyboard, such as a Greek letter, the symbol for Yen, or the copyright symbol.

You might also need to include a character in a string that already has some special meaning to VBA, such as the quotation mark symbol ("). You can't include characters such as the quotation mark (") directly in a string because VBA always assumes that this character starts or ends a string. The following statement, for example, will not execute without producing a runtime or syntax error:

```
MsgBox "This "cannot" work"
```

Although this statement might be intended to display the string This "cannot" work onscreen, VBA can't execute it. Because the quotation mark (") tells VBA that a literal string is either beginning or ending, VBA parses the MsgBox argument above into three pieces: a string (This), a variable name (cannot), and another string (work).

To include characters that you cannot type at the keyboard or that have special meanings to VBA in a string, you use the VBA Chr function. The Chr function has the following general syntax:

▼ SYNTAX

Chr(*charcode*)

charcode represents any numeric expression that is a valid code for the character set used by your computer. *charcode* must be a number between 0 and 255. As you might remember from the discussion about binary and text string comparison, your computer stores letters internally as numbers and uses a scheme where every character has its own unique number. The Chr function takes the code for a particular character as its argument and then returns a string containing just the character specified by the numeric code passed to Chr.

To see a list of the character codes that VBA recognizes and their corresponding characters, open the VBA online help system and look in the Contents tab under the heading *Miscellaneous*, or search for the topic *character sets*. Looking up the character code for the quote mark (") reveals that it has code 34. By using the Chr function to supply the quote mark, the following statement displays the message: This "will" work:

▲ MsgBox "This " & Chr(34) & "will" & Chr(34) & " work"

After you use the Chr function to get the desired character as a string, you can use the string concatenation operator (**&**) to assemble that character into a string. The following statement, for example, adds the copyright symbol to the beginning of the literal string and displays the result onscreen (see Figure 5.9):

MsgBox Chr(169) & "1999, The Walkabout Group"

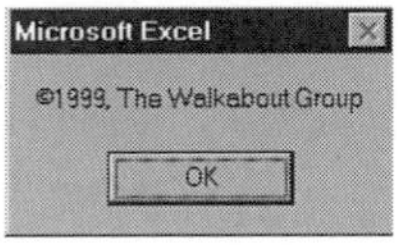

FIGURE 5.9

Use the Chr function to add characters you can't type at the keyboard.

You can also control how messages that you display are formatted by adding special characters to the string. One of the characters you can produce with the Chr function is the carriage-return character (character code 13). This is the character that your computer generates when you press the Enter key on your keyboard, and—when used in text—indicates the start of a new line. As shown in Figure 5.10, the following statement uses Chr to add a carriage-return character to a concatenated string so that the resulting dialog contains two lines of text (this is a single statement, notice the line continuation symbol at the end of the first line):

```
MsgBox "This is the first line" & Chr(13) & _
       "This is the second line"
```

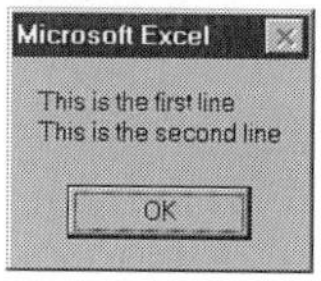

FIGURE 5.10

Use the Chr function to add characters to strings that affect how text is formatted when displayed or printed.

Because the characters to start a new line are so important in formatting messages and other string data that your VBA procedures manipulate, VBA provides you with several intrinsic constants for these characters so that you don't have to use the Chr function:

- vbCr is the carriage-return character (character code 13). This constant is the equivalent of the expression Chr(13). Including vbCr in a string causes VBA—and most Windows applications—to start a new line when displaying the string. In some cases, such as when you send a string to a printer, the carriage-return character merely causes the insertion point to move to the beginning of the current line without advancing to the next line.

- vbLf is the line-feed character (character code 10). This constant is the equivalent of the expression Chr(10). Including vbLf in a string also causes VBA and most Windows applications to start a new line when displaying the string. In some cases, such as sending a string to a printer, the line-feed character merely causes the insertion point to advance to the next line without returning to the left edge of the print region.

- vbCrLf is the carriage-return/line-feed character pair and is equivalent to the expression Chr(13) & Chr(10). When used in strings displayed by VBA, vbCrLf causes VBA to start a new line when displaying the string. For some purposes, such as sending text to a printer or for DOS-format text files, you need to use vbCrLf to both advance the insertion point to a new line and move the insertion point to the left edge of the print region.

- `vbNewLine` represents whatever character(s) is used to produce a new line for the computer software platform that your VBA procedure is executing in. Use the `vbNewLine` constant in procedures that you expect to execute in either Windows or Macintosh versions of MS Excel.

- `vbTab` is the tab character (character code 9). This is the character produced when you press the Tab key on your keyboard. The `vbTab` constant is the equivalent of the expression `Chr(9)`. You can include tab characters in strings to help align data in columns.

The following example produces the same dialog shown in Figure 5.10, but uses the `vbCr` constant instead of the `Chr` function to add the carriage-return character to the string:

```
MsgBox "This is the first line" & vbCr & _
       "This is the second line"
```

Do

DO declare module-level constants for the character code numbers you use frequently. Using module-level constants helps make your programs more readable and easier to maintain. For example, a module that makes frequent use of the copyright symbol might contain the following module-level declaration:

```
Const CRightSym As Integer = 169     'copyright symbol
```

The copyright example already given would then appear as follows (and would produce the same dialog already shown in Figure 5.9):

```
MsgBox Chr(CRightSym) & "1999, The Walkabout Group"
```

5

Formatting Data Values

Although VBA can automatically convert any data type into a string for display with `MsgBox` or for insertion into an Excel worksheet cell, VBA's choice of data format might not always be what you desire.

When VBA converts a number into a string, it does not add thousands separators, dollar signs, or other numeric formatting to the string. In addition, if the number is very large or very small, VBA produces a string showing the number in scientific notation. For example, VBA converts the number 3145.25 into the string 3145.25. If this number represents a dollar amount, you might prefer to convert it to a string containing a dollar sign and a thousands separator: $3,145.25.

Similarly, when VBA converts dates and times into strings, it always uses the short date and time format used by your computer's operating system and always displays both the date and time. You might prefer to use a different date or time format or to display only the date or only the time.

You can use the Format function to obtain almost any data format you want when converting numbers or dates into strings—you can even use Format to format string data according to a particular pattern. You might also want or need to create custom display formats if you have some special format in which you want data to appear.

> **Tip**
>
> VBA's Format function is identical to Excel's Format function, and uses the same data-formatting placeholders as Excel.

To use the Format function, you can either specify a predefined format (called a *named format*) or create an image of the specific format you want by using combinations of a special group of characters called *placeholders*. Use an image you create with placeholder characters if none of the named formats meet your requirements. As an example of both techniques of using the Format function, the following two MsgBox statements each display the same dialog (shown in Figure 5.11): The first statement uses a named format and the second statement uses an image with placeholders:

```
MsgBox Format(#2/27/76#, "Long Date")
MsgBox Format(#2/27/76#, "dddd, mmmm dd, yyyy")
```

FIGURE 5.11

Using the Format function to alter the string format of a date value.

Table 5.5 lists the named formats available to you and explains their effect.

TABLE 5.5   NAMED FORMATS FOR USE WITH THE Format FUNCTION

Named Format	Effect
General Date	Formats both the date and time information in a serial date number using the short date and short time format settings for your computer. Same as VBA's default conversion of serial dates into strings.
Long Date	Formats only the date portion of a serial date using the long date settings for your computer.

Named Format	Effect
Medium Date	Formats only the date portion of a serial date using the medium date settings for your computer.
Short Date	Formats only the date portion of a serial date using the short date settings for your computer.
Long Time	Formats only the time portion of a serial date using the long time settings for your computer.
Medium Time	Formats only the time portion of a serial date using the medium time settings for your computer.
Short Time	Formats only the time portion of a serial date using the short time settings for your computer.
General Number	Formats a number into a string without any special characters. Same as VBA's default conversion of numbers into strings.
Currency	Formats a number with a currency symbol, thousands separator, and only two decimal places. The currency symbol and decimal separator is determined by the Windows local settings.
Fixed	Formats a number so that there is always at least one digit before the decimal separator and at least two digits after the decimal separator.
Standard	Formats a number with a thousands separator, at least one digit in front of the decimal separator, and at least two digits after the decimal separator.
Percent	Formats the number as a percentage by multiplying it by 100 and adding the percent symbol. For example, 0.21 is returned as 21% when formatted as a percent.
Scientific	Formats the number in standard scientific notation. (Day 3 contains a sidebar explaining scientific notation.)
Yes/No	Causes the Format function to return the string Yes if the number being formatted is non-zero; returns the string No for any zero value. You'll use this named format most frequently with **Boolean** type values.
True/False	Causes the Format function to return the string True if the number being formatted is non-zero; returns the string False for any zero value. This named format is most useful with **Boolean** values.
On/Off	Causes the Format function to return the string On if the number being formatted is non-zero; returns the string Off for any zero value. Used most frequently to format **Boolean** values.

5

> **Note**
>
> You can change the long, medium, and short date and time formats for your computer through the Windows Control Panel. You can also change the symbols used for the thousands separator and the decimal separator in the Windows Control Panel.

If you want to create custom formats for numbers, dates, or times, you can assemble a string containing placeholder characters to specify the formatting image that you want the Format function to use when converting values into a string. Table 5.6 lists the custom placeholder symbols used to create format images for use with the Format function. Except as noted, the example numeric value that Table 5.6 uses is 1234.5. Bold type distinguishes the placeholders that you type from the surrounding text. The resulting string is shown in monospace type.

TABLE 5.6   PLACEHOLDERS FOR CREATING CUSTOM FORMATS

Placeholder	Effect
0	Digit placeholder—displays a digit if one exists in the position or a zero if not. You can use the 0 placeholder to display leading zeros for whole numbers and trailing zeros in decimal fractions. **00000.000** displays 01234.500.
#	Digit placeholder—displays a digit if one exists in the position, otherwise nothing. The # placeholder is equivalent to 0, except that leading and trailing zeros aren't displayed. **#####.###** displays 1234.5. *(is no digits is too or too places*
$	Displays a dollar sign in the position. **$###,###.00** displays $1,234.50.
.	Decimal placeholder—displays a decimal point at the indicated position in a string of 0 and # placeholders. **##.##** displays 1234.5.
%	Percent placeholder—multiplies the value by 100 and adds a percent sign in the position shown with 0 and # placeholders. **#0.00%** displays 0.12345 as 12.35% (12.345 is rounded to 12.35).
, (comma)	Thousands separator—adds commas as thousands separators in strings of 0 and # placeholders. **###,###,###.00** displays 1,234.50.
E— e—	Displays values in scientific notation with the sign of exponent for negative values only. **#.####E—00** displays 1.2345E03. 0.12345 is displayed as 1.2345E—01.
E+ e+	Displays values in scientific notation with the sign of exponent for positive and negative values. **#.####E+00** displays 1.2345E+03.
/	Separates the day, month, and year to format date values. **mm/dd/yy** displays 06/06/97. You can substitute hyphens to display 06-06-97.

Placeholder	Effect
m	Specifies how to display months for dates. **m** displays 1, **mm** displays 01, **mmm** displays Jan, and **mmmm** displays January.
d	Specifies how to display days for dates. **d** displays 1, **dd** displays 01, **ddd** displays Mon, and **dddd** displays Monday.
y	Displays the day of the year as a number from 1 to 366.
yy	Specifies how to display years for dates. **yy** displays 97 and **yyyy** displays 1997.
q	Displays the quarter of the year as a number from 1 to 4.
w	Displays the day of the week as a number (1 is Sunday).
ww	Displays the week of the year as a number from 1 to 54.
: (colon)	Separates hours, minutes, and seconds in format time values. **hh:mm:ss** displays 02:02:02.
h	Specifies how to display hours for time. **h** displays 2 and **hh** displays 02.
n	Minutes placeholder for time. **n** displays 1 and **nn** displays 01. **hhnn "hours"** displays 1600 hours.
s	Seconds placeholder for time. **s** displays 1 and **ss** displays 01.
AM/PM	Displays time in 12-hour time with AM or PM appended. **h:nn AM/PM** displays 4:00 PM. Alternative formats include am/pm, A/P, and a/p.
@	Character placeholder—displays a space if there is no corresponding character in the string being formatted. **@@@@** displays the string Hi with two leading spaces. (The default fill order is from right to left.)
&	Character placeholder—displays the corresponding character, or nothing. **&&&&** displays the string Hi without any extra spaces.
>	Displays all characters as uppercase.
<	Displays all characters as lowercase.
!	Forces the Format function's string result to be filled from left to right; otherwise the string is filled from right to left. **!@@@@** displays the string Hi with two trailing spaces.

When you use the Format function to format strings and numbers, you can create additional sections in the format image to vary the display format according to the value being formatted. The sections of a format image are separated by semicolons (;). As an example, the following image contains two sections and formats negative numbers differently from positive numbers:

```
$###,###,##0.00;$(###,###,##0.00)
```

The preceding image formats the number 1234567.89 as $1,234,567.89 and formats -1234567.89 as $(1,234,567.89).

You can have up to two sections in a format image for formatting a string. If the format image contains only one section, the format image applies to all formatted strings. If the format image contains two sections, the first section applies to string data and the second section applies to **Null** values and zero-length strings (that is, strings that don't contain any characters, represented by ""). Consider the following statement, which displays the result of the Format function used with a two-part format image for strings:

```
MsgBox Format(strData, "(@@@)-@@@-@@@@;no phone number")
```

The preceding statement displays (510)-555-1212 in the resulting message dialog if strData contains "5105551212". If strData contains a zero-length string (""), the preceding statement displays no phone number in the message dialog.

You can have up to four different sections in a format image used to format numeric values. The first section is used for positive numbers, the second section is used for negative numbers, the third section is used for zero values, and the fourth section is used for **Null** values. The following format image contains four sections:

```
"$###,###,##0.00;$(###,###,##0.00);0.00;Null value"
```

The preceding format image formats negative numbers with parentheses, specifies that zero values should always be shown as 0.00, and returns a text message if the value being formatted is **Null**. The preceding image formats the number 1234567.89 as the string $1,234,567.89. The number -1234567.89 is formatted into the string $(1,234,567.89). A value of 0 is formatted into the string 0.00 whereas a **Null** value would be formatted into the string Null value.

Summary

In this lesson you learned what a function is and how to use functions in expressions. You also learned how to ignore the result of a function, and, more important, how to use a function's named arguments to simplify using optional arguments. Next, you reviewed the various categories of functions available in VBA.

You also learned how to access the functions that Excel makes available to VBA. You learned how to use the Object Browser to determine exactly which functions are available, and to insert the function name and its named arguments into your source code. This lesson concluded by showing you how important effective string manipulation can be. You learned the essentials of using VBA's string manipulation functions and how to format data values into strings for display.

Q&A

Q In the Tables of VBA functions, I noticed that there are two different functions that convert numbers to strings: `Str` and `CStr`. Which one should I use?

A Usually, you should use the **CStr** function. The **CStr** function uses the international settings in your computer system (accessed through the Regional Settings icon in the Windows Control Panel) to determine which symbol your computer uses to indicate the decimal place in a number. If you change the nationality settings for your computer system—and therefore change the decimal separator character—the **CStr** function will still correctly convert numbers to strings. The `Str` function, on the other hand, assumes that the number decimal separator character is a period (.) and always uses that character. `Str` is provided mostly for backward compatibility with older dialects of BASIC.

Q I also noticed in the Tables of VBA functions that there is more than one function to convert strings to numbers: `Val`, `CInt`, `CLng`, `CSng`, `CDbl`, and `CCur`. Which one should I use?

A The situation with `Val` and the other functions that convert strings to numbers is similar to that with `Str` and **CStr**. The `Val` function assumes that the decimal number separator is a period (.), whereas the other functions use whatever number separator is specified by the international settings for your computer system. In general, you should use the **CInt**, **CLng**, **CSng**, **CDbl**, and **CCur** functions instead of `Val`. Both `Str` and `Val` are included in VBA to maintain compatibility with early versions of the BASIC programming language; the **CStr**, **CInt**, **CLng**, **CSng**, **CDbl**, and **CCur** functions are newer and more effective additions to the language.

Q I'm not sure I understand how named arguments differ from a standard argument list.

A A standard argument list simply contains the values to be passed to the function, separated by commas and arranged in a specific order. VBA determines which value to use for each argument based on its position in the argument list. With named arguments, you use the specific name of an argument to identify the value for that argument. When you use named arguments, you do not have to list them in any particular order.

Q I'm not sure I understand how to use the `HelpFile` and `Context` arguments in the `InputBox` and `MsgBox` functions.

A Unless you purchase the Windows Help Compiler from Microsoft (or some third-party help development tool), it is unlikely that these arguments will be of any use to you. The `HelpFile` argument specifies the name of a file that you have previously prepared by using the Windows Help Compiler. The `Context` argument specifies

5

the specific help topic that you want displayed when the user chooses the Help button. When the user chooses the Help button, VBA activates the Windows Help program—the same program used by every Windows application to display its online help files—and displays the help topic specified by the context number. To get some idea of how this works, enter the following procedure in an Excel module (without the line numbers) and run it:

```
1:  Sub Demo_HelpButton()
2:    Dim msgText As String
3:    msgText = "Help button gets VB Help Contents"
4:    MsgBox Prompt:=msgText, _
5:           Title:="Help Button Demonstration", _
6:           Buttons:= vbMsgBoxHelpButton, _
6:           HelpFile:="VBAXL9.CHM", _
7:           Context:=0
8:  End Sub
```

If you choose the Help button in the dialog displayed by the preceding procedure, you will see the Microsoft Excel Objects hierarchy diagram in the Excel VBA online help. VBA's online help is stored in the file Vbaxl9.chm and the context 0 is the table of contents.

Q All the information about the Format function is a little intimidating. Do I really need to memorize all that?

A No, you don't have to memorize all the options for the Format function. It is important that you know about the availability of the Format function, and that you understand the basics of how you can use the Format function to customize VBA's conversion of numbers and dates into strings.

Workshop

Answers are in Appendix A.

Quiz

1. List three tasks that you would typically use a function to help you perform.

2. Where in a VBA statement can you use the value returned by a function?

3. How do you tell VBA that you want to ignore a function's result? Can you ignore the result of every VBA function?

4. What is the difference between the functions provided by VBA and the functions provided by Excel?

5. What is the VBA keyword that you must use in order to access an Excel function?

6. Is it possible to ignore the result of an Excel function?

7. What use is the Object Browser to you?

8. Why is manipulating string data important?

Exercises

1. Add the data conversion functions to the following statements so that no type mismatch errors occur and the expression has the stated value (HINT: write a procedure that uses a MsgBox statement to display the result of each expression, and remember that the **String** data type is designated by $, **Integer** by %, **Currency** by @, and **Single** by !):

   ```
   (a) Sum$ = 12 + 15       'Sum$ should contain "27"
   (b) Num% = "47" + "52"  'Num% should contain 99
   (c) Num@ = 12.98 * "16"    'Num@ should contain 207.68
   (d) Root! = Sqr(User_Input$)'If User_Input$ contains "4",
                               'then Root! should contain 2.
   ```

2. Write a procedure that obtains three numbers from the user and then displays the smallest of the numbers entered. Use the Excel MIN function to determine the smallest number. In your procedure, use the named arguments for InputBox and MsgBox.

3. Write a procedure that obtains a word or phrase from the user and then displays the first three characters of the user's input, the last four characters of the user's input, and the four characters after the first two characters of the input string.

4. Write a procedure that obtains a string from the user and then displays the result of searching the entire string for the letter "L". (In this exercise, just display the numeric result of the InStr function.)

5

DAY 6

Creating and Using VBA Function Procedures and Excel User-Defined Functions

On Day 5, you learned what a function is and how to use the built-in functions of both VBA and Excel (or other VBA host applications). In this lesson, you learn how to create your own customized VBA functions. This lesson also shows you how to create customized functions for use in Excel worksheets. Today, you'll learn

- How to create function procedures with named arguments, optional arguments, and specific data type results, and how to ensure that your function procedures are usable by Excel.

- How to use your custom function procedures in your VBA procedures or from Excel.

- Tips and requirements for designing functions in general, and specifically functions for use in Excel worksheets.
- What a recursive function is and what benefits and problems are associated with recursive functions.

Understanding Function Procedures and User-Defined Functions

Before you start writing your own customized functions, you need to become acquainted with the terminology and concepts used to discuss the functions that you write in VBA. Although there is really only one way to create custom functions in VBA, you can—by observing certain guidelines and restrictions—create a specific variety of customized functions suitable for use by Excel (or another VBA host application).

A *function procedure* is a special kind of VBA procedure that returns a result. Your function procedures—just like the built-in VBA functions—can have optional arguments or use named arguments. You can use your function procedures to supply values in expressions and assignments or as arguments to other functions and procedures. You write the program statements that determine the arguments the function uses, the actions the function performs, and the value that the function returns.

You can even use function procedures that you create in your Excel worksheets, much the same way you use Excel's built-in worksheet functions. For Excel to use your function procedures, the code in the function procedure must adhere to certain guidelines and restrictions, however.

Note

In Excel, you can use VBA functions to expand the collection of built-in worksheet functions. Other VBA host applications, such as Access, also permit you to use functions you create with VBA to expand and enhance its built-in collection of functions. In all VBA host applications, you can use a VBA function to supply a value for a control on a form, such as a text box. (You'll learn about forms in Day 16, "Creating Custom Dialog Boxes.")

From Excel's point of view, the VBA function procedures that it uses are *user-defined functions*. This term distinguishes the function procedures you write from the built-in Excel functions. Although all user-defined functions are also function procedures, not all function procedures meet the requirements for a user-defined function.

Function procedure is the most general term for functions you create; the term *user-defined function* describes a specific type of function procedure, one that Excel can use. You cannot use function procedures that do not meet the requirements for a user-defined function in an Excel worksheet formula; you can only use those functions in statements in your own procedures.

Usually, you create function procedures to perform computations, get information, or to format data, just like the built-in VBA functions. For example, you might have an Excel VBA program that analyzes energy consumption data. In this program, you might have several places where you need to convert natural gas consumption measured in therms to measurements in BTUs. Instead of typing the formula for converting therms to BTUs in your program every place that you use that formula—which increases the chance that you'll make a typing mistake that results in an erroneous computation somewhere—you can write a function procedure that accepts a value in therms as an argument and returns a value in BTU as the function result.

Similarly, formulas to convert feet to centimeters, pounds to kilograms, Fahrenheit to Celsius, or that compute profit margins, commissions, discounts, and so on are all possible uses for function procedures.

You can also replace long, complicated worksheet formulas with a single user-defined function. It is usually easier to use and remember a single user-defined function name than a complex formula. As an example, you might have a worksheet with a range named Sales and a range named Costs, each of which contains the sales figures and costs for a particular quarter of the year. You might then enter a formula in the worksheet, similar to the following, that computes the percent profit using the named ranges in the worksheet:

```
=((SUM(Sales) -SUM(Costs))/SUM(Costs))*100
```

A formula of this length is fairly tedious to enter, and this formula is actually quite simple compared to some of the formulas that many Excel users use. The more often you use this formula, the more likely you are to make a typing mistake when you enter it. Also, it is not necessarily obvious what this formula does when you first see it. You can eliminate these problems by creating a VBA user-defined function for Excel. For example, you might create a function named Calc_PcntProfit that receives the range names as arguments and returns the result of the formula's computation as the function result. A user-defined function like this is easier to use and remember than the longer Excel formula.

6

Creating Function Procedures

You cannot use the Macro Recorder to record a function procedure, although you can edit a recorded macro and turn it into a function procedure. Most of the time, though, you create your function procedures by writing the function procedure directly into a VBA module.

Writing a Function Procedure

Function procedures are very similar to the VBA procedures you already know how to write. The main difference between a function procedure and other procedures—apart from the fact that functions return a value and procedures do not—is that you enclose a function procedure with the keywords **Function** and **End Function** instead of the **Sub** and **End Sub** keywords you are already familiar with.

▼ SYNTAX

The general syntax for a function procedure is

```
Function name([arglist])
    'VBA Statements
    [name = expression]
End Function
```

Every function procedure begins with the restricted keyword **Function** followed by the name of the function procedure. *name* represents the name you choose for the function procedure. Function names must follow the same rules as any other identifier name in VBA: They must begin with a letter, cannot contain spaces or any of the arithmetic, logical, or relational operator symbols, and cannot duplicate any of VBA's restricted keywords.

After the function's name comes the function's argument list, which is enclosed in parentheses. In the syntax sample, *arglist* represents the argument list for your function procedure. *arglist* is optional; you don't have to write functions that use arguments, although you probably will want to. If you do include the argument list, separate each argument name with a comma (,).

The optional syntax element *name* = *expression* represents the *function assignment*, which tells VBA what value the function should return. Although this part of a function is, technically, optional, you should always include a function assignment statement in your function procedures. Finally, the function declaration ends with the keywords **End**

▲ **Function**.

Note

Even if a function has no arguments—such as VBA's Now, Date, or Time functions—you must include parentheses for the argument list in the function declaration. For instance, you might write a function procedure that returns the name of the file containing the current workbook so that you can insert the filename into a worksheet cell. A function like this doesn't need arguments because it doesn't require any outside information to do its job. Such a function would have a declaration like this:

```
Function ThisBookName()
```

Usually, a function's purpose is to perform some computation or other manipulation of specific data and to return the result of that manipulation. As you already know, you pass information to VBA's built-in functions by specifying values in the function's argument list. When you declare a function procedure, you list a name for each argument you intend to pass to your function, separating each argument name in the list with a comma. Argument names must follow the naming conventions that apply to any VBA identifier.

The names that you provide in the argument list are like variables: they refer to whatever value you provide at the time your function is called, whether your function is called by a VBA statement or by Excel. Whenever the argument name appears in a statement inside the function, VBA behaves as if the argument name is a variable containing the value provided in the argument list in the statement that called your function.

Note

Argument names have the same scope as variables declared locally within the function procedure, that is, argument variables are not accessible outside the function procedure's argument list in which they are declared.

Look again at the previous syntax sample, at the line containing the statement *name* = *expression*. This line represents the *function assignment*. *name* is the function's name and *expression* is any expression that produces the value you want the function to return. The function assignment tells VBA what value the function will return. Notice that the function assignment uses the function procedure's name as if it were a variable and assigns a value to it. Function procedures can have none, one, or several different function assignment statements.

6

The first function example you'll study helps manipulate strings. As you might remember from Day 5, the Len function reports the length of a string including any leading or trailing spaces. If you want to find the length of a string *excluding* leading and trailing spaces, you could use *nested* function calls (one function call inside another) like this:

```
StrLen = Len(Trim(AnyStr))
```

In the preceding statement, the Trim function first trims any leading and trailing spaces from the string stored in the variable AnyStr; the result from the Trim function provides the argument for the Len function so that the string length returned by Len excludes leading and trailing spaces.

This type of operation is a good candidate for a function procedure. Using a single call to your custom function procedure is simpler and easier than repeatedly writing the nested function call shown above. Listing 6.1 shows just such a simple function procedure, SLen, which returns the length of a string excluding leading or trailing spaces.

INPUT   **LISTING 6.1**   A SIMPLE FUNCTION PROCEDURE: SLen

```
1:   Function SLen(tStr)
2:        SLen = Len(Trim(tStr))
3:   End Function
```

ANALYSIS   Line 1 contains the function declaration for SLen. The line begins with the required **Function** keyword followed by the function name. Following the function name is the opening parenthesis, which tells VBA that this is the start of the function's argument list. Next is the argument name tStr. The argument name tells VBA that one argument must be passed to the function procedure when it is called. Finally, line 1 ends with the closing parenthesis, which ends the function's argument list.

Note
> When you press Enter after typing the **Function** keyword, the function name, and the function's argument list, the VB Editor automatically fills in the **End Function** keywords, just like when you type the **Sub** keyword to create a procedure.

Line 2 of the SLen function is the line that does all the function's work, and contains the function assignment for SLen. When VBA evaluates the expression Len(Trim(tStr)), it takes the string received through the tStr argument and passes it to the VBA Trim function to remove any leading or trailing spaces. The result of the Trim function is, in turn, used as the argument for the Len function. VBA then assigns the result of the Len function to the function name, SLen. SLen then returns the length of the argument string, excluding any leading or trailing spaces.

When VBA evaluates the expression Len(Trim(tStr)) and assigns the expression's result to the SLen function name in line 2, VBA is performing the *function assignment*. The function assignment tells VBA what value the function should return.

Finally, line 3 ends the function procedure with the keywords **End Function**. After VBA executes this line, execution returns to whatever procedure statement called the SLen function, and VBA inserts the SLen function result into that statement at the point where the SLen function name occurs.

Do

DO make sure that you include a function assignment statement in your function procedures. There is no point in writing a function procedure that does not return a result.

DO remember that VBA doesn't generate any error messages if you forget to include a function assignment statement in your function procedure; you must make sure you include the function assignment yourself.

To use the SLen function, you would use a statement similar to the following, which displays the result of SLen for the string "   mad dog   ":

```
MsgBox SLen("    mad dog    ")
```

In this statement, the argument string has four leading and four trailing spaces, and the length of the string (as reported by VBA's Len function) is 15. The SLen function reports the length of the string without its leading and trailing spaces; the preceding statement displays the number 7.

Creating User-Defined Functions for Excel

Function procedures that follow certain restrictions on their activities are called user-defined functions (abbreviated UDF), and are the only function procedures that Excel can use in a worksheet cell's formula.

All restrictions on user-defined functions stem from one basic restriction: A UDF cannot alter Excel's environment in any way. This means that a user-defined function cannot select, insert, delete, or format any data in any worksheet, chart sheet, or other sheet. A UDF also cannot add, delete, or rename sheets or workbooks, nor can it change screen views, and so on. For example, you cannot use a function procedure as a user-defined function in Excel if it selects cells or changes the current worksheet in any way.

6

In addition, a UDF cannot set object properties or use object methods because, in most cases, setting object properties or using object methods results in changes to Excel's environment (objects, methods, and properties are described in the next lesson). A user-defined function can, however, retrieve object property values and execute any object methods that do not change Excel's environment.

Usually, a user-defined function should only make calculations or perform manipulations based on data received through its argument list or retrieved from Excel. You could use the SLen function shown in Listing 6.1 as a user-defined function, it meets all of the requirements.

> **Note**
>
> Neither VBA nor Excel displays an error message if you use a function procedure that does not actually meet the restrictions for user-defined functions as a UDF. Instead, your function is just unable to return a result. For example, if you try to insert a value in an Excel worksheet cell by using a function procedure that violates the rules for user-defined functions, the cell displays the Excel #VALUE! error message, which indicates only that the function or formula for that cell is unable to return a valid result.

Declaring a Data Type for a Function's Result

Unless you specify otherwise, the result that your function procedure returns has the **Variant** data type. As you learned in Day 3, values stored or handled as **Variant** data types take up more memory than any other data type and require more time to handle.

You can specify the data type of a function result for the same reasons you specify the data type of variables and constants: to speed up the execution of your code, to use memory more efficiently, to make your code easier to understand, and to help catch programmer errors by forcing an awareness of when VBA converts data from one type to another. Consider declaring a specific data type result for all the function procedures that you write.

To specify the data type of a function's return value, simply add the keyword **As** and the desired data type name to the end of the function declaration line.

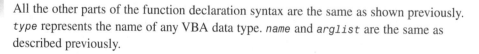

Including the function type declaration, the general syntax for a function declaration is

```
Function name([arglist]) [As type]
```

All the other parts of the function declaration syntax are the same as shown previously. *type* represents the name of any VBA data type. *name* and *arglist* are the same as described previously.

VBA prohibits you from assigning an incompatible data type to the function's result in any function procedure that has a declared data type for its result. If, for example, you mistakenly write a function assignment statement so that you assign, say, an **Integer** to the result of a function with a declared **String** type result, VBA displays a type-mismatch error.

If you assign a data type that is not the same as the declared return type for the function procedure but is otherwise compatible, VBA converts the value to the type specified for the function when it returns the function result. For example, if you assign a **Double** data type to a function whose result you declared as a **Long**, VBA does not produce any errors, it just converts the **Double** to a **Long** type when it returns the function result.

Declaring the data type of a function result has one other effect: If the function procedure ends without executing a function assignment statement, VBA returns a zero-length string for **String** type functions and 0 for function procedures that return a numeric data type. (An untyped function procedure that ends without executing a function assignment statement returns a **Variant** type result containing the special value **Empty**.)

Listing 6.2 shows the SLen function modified so that it always returns a value of the **Long** data type.

INPUT   **LISTING 6.2**   SPECIFYING THE DATA TYPE OF THE SLen FUNCTION RESULT

```
1:  Function SLen(tStr) As Long
2:  'returns length of tStr, excluding leading/trailing spaces
3:      SLen = Len(Trim(tStr))
4:  End Function
```

ANALYSIS   Line 1 contains the function declaration for SLen. This function has the same name and argument list as the function in Listing 6.1, but this time the data type of the function's result is also declared. After the closing parenthesis that ends the function's argument list, the **As** keyword appears followed by the **Long** type name. This tells VBA that the SLen function should always return a result with the **Long** data type.

The **Long** data type was chosen as the data type for the SLen function result for two reasons. First, because the length of a string is always a whole number—you can never have a fractional part of a character. Second, because an **Integer** type does not have enough range to hold the maximum possible string length—the largest positive number an **Integer** data type can represent is 32,767, but strings can be up to approximately 2 billion characters in length. The **Long** data type, therefore, is the smallest data type that still accommodates the entire possible range of values that the function might return.

Line 2 is a comment line stating the purpose and action of the function procedure.

6

Line 3 works exactly the same as line 2 in Listing 6.1. Because this version of SLen has a data type specified for its return value, VBA would display a type-mismatch error if you assigned, say, a string value to SLen in line 3, instead of a numeric value.

Without the typed function result, if you did assign a **String** type value instead of a numeric value to the function result, VBA would accept the string in the function assignment to SLen and SLen would return that string value as its result. If you then used the SLen result in an arithmetic expression, the arithmetic expression might result in an erroneous computation or a runtime error of some kind. Tracing errors caused by function return values of an unexpected data type can be difficult because the error can propagate through several function or procedure calls before producing a noticeable error. Declaring the data type of a function's result helps you prevent and detect the source of such errors.

Do

DO choose a data type for the result of your function procedures that requires the least amount of memory, but still accommodates the full range of possible values that the function might return. For general-purpose numeric or mathematical functions, a **Double** type for the function result is fairly typical.

DO consider how you intend to use the function when you choose the data type for the function's result; the intended use of a function procedure can affect your choice for the function's data type. For example, if you intend to use your function procedure solely to perform some type of financial computation, you should declare a **Currency** type for the function result.

DO include a line or two of comments for each function or other procedure that you write in order to document your VBA code and to help you if you later need to modify the code. (Although the purpose and operation of a function you write today might seem obvious, it might not seem so obvious three months from now.)

Declaring Data Types for a Function's Arguments

Unless you specify otherwise, VBA passes all of a function procedure's arguments into the function procedure as **Variant** data types. Like a function procedure's result, you can also declare specific data types for each argument in the function procedure's argument list.

You use arguments with specific data types for the same (by now) familiar reasons that you use for typing variables or function results. Typing arguments for a function procedure also helps you (or the function's user) enter arguments of the correct type, and in the correct order, when the function is called.

To declare specific data types for a function procedure's arguments, simply use the **As** keyword followed by the desired data type name, after the argument name in the argument list. Listing 6.3 shows the SLen function modified to accept only **String** type data in the tStr argument.

INPUT   **LISTING 6.3**   SPECIFYING THE DATA TYPE OF THE SLen FUNCTION ARGUMENT

```
1:  Function SLen(tStr As String) As Long
2:  'returns length of tStr, excluding leading/trailing spaces
3:      SLen = Len(Trim(tStr))
4:  End Function
```

ANALYSIS   Except for the function procedure declaration in line 1, Listing 6.3 is identical to Listing 6.2. Now that the argument's data type is declared, VBA only allows values of the **String** data type to appear as the argument when the SLen function is called. Calling SLen with any other data type value—even a **Variant**—as an argument produces a type-mismatch error (specifically, an *argument type mismatch*).

Creating Optional Arguments

Usually, all the arguments you list in a function procedure's argument list must be supplied each time you call the function; these arguments are *required* arguments. You've already learned about optional function arguments from working with VBA's InputBox and MsgBox functions. You can create optional arguments for your own function procedures, as well.

Use optional arguments to control how a function performs its task. For example, one of the optional arguments for the MsgBox function controls how many command buttons appear in the dialog that MsgBox displays. The FlipCase function shown in Listing 6.4 uses an optional argument to control how many characters the function operates on.

When you include optional arguments in an argument list, you must list all the required arguments first; after the first optional argument, all succeeding arguments in the argument list must also be optional. You can even specify a data type and default value for optional function arguments.

To create an optional argument, insert the VBA **Optional** keyword in front of the argument's name in the argument list of the function procedure declaration, as shown in line 1 of Listing 6.4.

6

LISTING 6.4 THE FlipCase FUNCTION: OPTIONAL ARGUMENTS

```
 1:  Function FlipCase(tStr As String, Optional nChar) As String
 2:  'reverses the case - upper to lower, lower to upper - of
 3:  'the first nChar characters in tStr. If nChar is omitted,
 4:  'flips the case of all characters in tStr
 5:
 6:      Dim k As Long     'loop counter
 7:      Dim TestC As String * 1
 8:
 9:      If IsMissing(nChar) Then
10:         nChar = Len(tStr)
11:      End If
12:
13:      For k = 1 To nChar
14:        TestC = Mid(tStr, k, 1)
15:        If (StrComp(TestC, "A", vbBinaryCompare) >= 0) And _
16:           (StrComp(TestC, "Z", vbBinaryCompare) <= 0) Then
17:          Mid(tStr, k, 1) = LCase(TestC)
18:        ElseIf (StrComp(TestC, "a", vbBinaryCompare) >= 0) And _
19:               (StrComp(TestC, "z", vbBinaryCompare) <= 0) Then
20:          Mid(tStr, k, 1) = UCase(TestC)
21:        End If
22:      Next k
23:      FlipCase = tStr
24:  End Function
```

ANALYSIS Line 1 contains the function declaration for FlipCase, which has two arguments in its argument list. The first argument, tStr, has the specific **String** type declared for it. When FlipCase is called, the first argument is required and must be a string. A comma separates the two arguments in the list; the second argument is prefaced with the **Optional** keyword, which tells VBA that this argument can be omitted when the FlipCase function is called. (If the FlipCase function has more than the two arguments shown, any additional arguments in the list after the nChar argument would have to be optional, as well.) No data type is declared for the optional nChar argument; by default, the nChar optional argument is therefore a **Variant** data type. (Remember, any untyped variable, function, or argument automatically becomes a **Variant** type.)

Finally, the FlipCase function declaration ends by specifying that the data type returned by FlipCase must always be a **String** type.

The FlipCase function is more complex than any of the previous examples of either procedures or functions, and includes a couple of program structures that you have not seen before: one for decision-making and one for repeating a group of actions. Although each of these structures is described in detail in later lessons, the next few paragraphs describe the essentials behind the operation of the FlipCase function procedure.

Lines 2 through 4 simply contain the function procedure's documenting comments. Lines 6 and 7 contain the declarations for the variables used by FlipCase.

Lines 9 through 11 illustrate a typical use of an important built-in VBA function: IsMissing. The IsMissing function exists solely to determine whether a **Variant** optional argument was included in a function procedure's call; it returns **True** only if the **Variant** optional argument was *not* included. (You learn how VBA deals with omitted optional arguments with a declared data type in the next section of this lesson.)

Lines 9 through 11 use an **If...Then** decision structure (described in detail in Day 8, "Making Decisions in Visual Basic") to alter the value of nChar depending on whether the argument was included in the function call. If nChar is missing, it is assigned a value equal the length of the string in the tStr argument. In this way, FlipCase controls how many characters are affected by its manipulations—only a few, or the entire string.

Lines 13 through 22 carry out the actual work of the FlipCase function and consist of two different control structures, one nested inside the other. The outermost control structure is a **For...Next** loop, which begins in line 13. (**For...Next** loops are described in detail in Day 9, "Repeating Actions in Visual Basic: Loops.") A **For...Next** loop causes the statements it encloses to be repeated a set number of times. In this case, the statements enclosed by the **For...Next** loop are repeated the number of times specified by nChar.

The first statement inside the **For...Next** loop (line 14) uses the VBA Mid function to copy one character from tStr and store it in the TestC variable. (The variable k contains the current count of times through the **For...Next** loop, so the first time through the loop the first character of tStr is copied, the second time through the loop the second character of tStr is copied, and so on.) The character is copied to the TestC variable so that the Mid function only has to be called once, therefore saving some execution time. Using the TestC variable to hold the character being tested also helps make the program code easier to read.

After copying the character to be tested, line 15 uses another **If...Then** structure to determine whether the character in TestC is an uppercase letter. Notice the line-continuation character at the end of line 15. The logical expression in lines 15 and 16 is **True** if the character is greater than or equal to "A" and is less than or equal to "Z", that is, if the character is in the range of uppercase letters. The expression uses the VBA **StrComp** function to ensure that the comparisons are always binary comparisons, rather than text comparisons. Using the **StrComp** function ensures that this function will always work as expected, regardless of the **Option Compare** setting.

If the character in TestC is an uppercase letter, line 17 executes. Line 17 uses the VBA **Mid** procedure, which replaces one or more characters in a string. The **Mid** procedure

6

statement in line 16 replaces the character in tStr that was originally copied into TestC with its lowercase equivalent, which is obtained by using the LCase function.

> **Note**
>
> Don't be confused by the Mid *function* and the **Mid** *procedure*, both of which are used in Listing 6.4. The Mid function returns a string from the middle of another string; the **Mid** procedure is used to replace one or more characters in a string with a different string. The FlipCase function uses the Mid function to return a specified character from the string being manipulated. Later in the FlipCase function, the **Mid** procedure is used to replace a character in the string with its upper- or lowercase equivalent. The name of the Mid function is printed in a plain monospace font in this book because, when used as a function name, it is not a reserved word of the VBA programming language; if you want, you could write your own function named Mid. The name of the **Mid** procedure is printed in bold monospace font in this book because, when used as a procedure, it *is* a reserved word of the VBA programming language. The VB Editor color-codes the **Mid** procedure's name blue on your screen and prohibits you from creating your own procedure named **Mid**.

If the character in TestC is not an uppercase letter, execution passes to line 18, where TestC is again tested, this time to see if it is a lowercase letter. The logical expression establishes whether the character in TestC is in the range of lowercase letters. Again, the **StrComp** function is used in the expression to ensure that the string comparisons are binary comparisons, regardless of the **Option Compare** setting. (If a text comparison were made instead of a binary comparison, the FlipCase function wouldn't work because it would be unable to distinguish between upper- and lowercase letters!)

If the character in TestC is a lowercase letter, line 20 executes. Line 20 also uses the **Mid** procedure to replace the character in tStr that was originally copied into TestC with its uppercase equivalent, which is obtained by using VBA's UCase function.

Notice that, if the character in TestC is neither an uppercase nor a lowercase letter, the function makes no alteration in tStr—if the character isn't an uppercase or lowercase letter, it must be a digit or punctuation character and no case conversion is needed (or even possible).

Line 22 is the end of the **For...Next** loop; when the **For...Next** loop has executed the specified number of times (equivalent to the value specified by nChar), execution passes to line 23, which contains the function assignment statement. The function has completed its work and returns the altered value in tStr as the function result.

Specifying an Optional Argument's Data Type

In Listing 6.4, the optional nChar argument of the FlipCase function is a **Variant** data type; because no data type is specified for the nChar argument, VBA makes it a **Variant** by default. In some cases, you want a function's argument to be a **Variant** data type. Most of the time, however, you should declare a specific data type for an optional function argument. You declare an optional argument's data type for the same reasons you declare a required argument's data type: to help yourself and others use your functions correctly, and to help you locate statements that pass incorrect values to the function.

You declare an optional argument's data type the same way you declare a required argument's data type—with the **As** keyword. The following code fragment shows the FlipCase function declaration altered to declare the optional nChar argument as a **Long** data type:

```
Function FlipCase(tStr As String, Optional nChar As Long) As String
```

Listing 6.6 shows the FlipCase function procedure modified to use an optional argument with a declared data type.

Specifying a Default Value for Optional Arguments

When you declare an optional function argument, VBA reserves space for that argument. Because optional arguments might or might not be present at the time your function is called, you can tell VBA to assign a default value to the optional argument. VBA uses the default value whenever your function is called without that particular optional argument included. You assign a default value to an optional argument by using the equal sign (=) and supplying a constant value, much the same way you declare a named constant:

```
Function FlipCase(tStr As String, Optional nChar As Long = 0) As String
```

The preceding code fragment declares the FlipCase function. The FlipCase declaration indicates that the tStr argument is of type **String** and is required. The nChar argument is optional, is of type **Long**, and—if not included when the function is called—has the default value of 0. Listing 6.6 shows the FlipCase function modified to use an optional argument with a declared type and a default value.

6

Note

The IsMissing function only works with optional arguments of the **Variant** data type. For all other optional argument data types, VBA initializes the argument value as it would for any new variable (strings are zero-length and numeric types are 0), and IsMissing always returns **False**. To detect a missing typed optional argument, test for 0 or a zero-length string, as shown in Listing 6.6.

Understanding and Controlling How VBA Passes Arguments

Now that you know how to create function procedures with typed arguments and optional arguments, you're ready to take a closer look at the mechanisms VBA uses to actually pass argument data to a function procedure. Next, you learn how to control which mechanism VBA uses and when to choose one mechanism over another.

Understanding Arguments Passed by Reference and by Value

There are two ways that VBA passes information into a function procedure: *by reference* and *by value*. By default, VBA passes all arguments by reference. When VBA passes data through a function argument by reference, it really just passes a memory address that refers to the original data specified in the function's argument list at the time the function was called. This means that, if your function alters the values in any of its argument variables, the original data passed to the function through that argument variable is also changed.

When VBA passes an argument by value, however, VBA makes a *copy* of the original data and passes that copy to the function. If your function changes the value in an argument passed by value, only the copy of the data changes; the original data does not change. Passing by reference allows the original data passed through a function argument to be changed by the function; passing by value does not allow the original data value to be changed.

To better understand the difference between passing argument values by reference and by value, consider this analogy: A colleague tells you that there is a sales proposal in a basket on her desk and asks you to read the proposal and write your comments in the margins. When you carry out the requested task, you get her proposal from the basket on the desk and write your comments directly on it; when you are done, you leave the altered proposal in the same basket you found it in. Your colleague passed the data (the sales proposal) to you *by reference*. You received a reference to the location of the data and changed that data.

If, on the other hand, your colleague gave you a photocopy of the sales proposal and asked you to write your comments on the photocopy, she would have passed the data to you *by value*. You received a copy of the actual data (its value), changed that data, and returned the changed copy. Your colleague's original sales proposal remains unchanged and unaffected by the transaction.

Because passing by reference enables a function to change the original data value of its arguments, arguments passed by reference might have undesirable side effects. Listing 6.5 shows a procedure designed to test the `FlipCase` function in Listing 6.4.

INPUT **LISTING 6.5** TEST PROCEDURE TO DEMONSTRATE FlipCase FUNCTION'S SIDE
EFFECTS

```
 1:  Sub Test_FlipCase()
 2:      Dim UserIn As String, Num As Long
 3:      UserIn = InputBox(prompt:="Enter some text:", _
 4:                        Title:="FlipCase Test")
 5:      Num = 5
 6:      MsgBox FlipCase(UserIn, Num)
 7:      MsgBox UserIn
 8:      MsgBox FlipCase(UserIn)
 9:      MsgBox UserIn
10:  End Sub
```

ANALYSIS Line 2 of this procedure declares some variables. Line 3 uses the InputBox function to ask the user to enter some text. Line 5 sets the variable Num to 5. Line 6 tests the FlipCase function with its optional argument (a numeric variable arbitrarily assigned a value of 5) and uses MsgBox to display the FlipCase function result. Line 7 displays the original value—the string stored in UserIn—passed to FlipCase. Line 8 tests the FlipCase function without its optional argument; line 9 again displays the contents of the UserIn variable.

If you enter both Listings 6.4 and 6.5, run the Test_FlipCase procedure, and then enter the string *FlipCase* as the test string, you might notice some peculiar results. In line 6 of Listing 6.5, VBA executes the first call to the FlipCase function. As expected, the function returns the string *fLIPcase*: a copy of the string stored in UserIn with the case of the first five characters reversed (see Figure 6.1). Line 7, however, displays the original string input by the user, and it too has changed to *fLIPcase* (line 7 displays a dialog identical to the one in Figure 6.1). If you look again at Listing 6.4 (lines 17 and 20), you can see that the FlipCase function directly alters the string argument tStr. Because tStr is passed by reference (VBA, by default, passes all arguments by reference), any changes to tStr are really changes to the original data in the UserIn variable in the Test_FlipCase procedure.

6

FIGURE 6.1

*Both lines 6 and 7 in
Listing 6.5 produce
this dialog showing
that the* FlipCase
*function has modified
the contents of the
argument variable
passed to it.*

You can see the same thing happen again when lines 8 and 9 in Listing 6.5 execute: The function correctly returns the string *FlipCASE* as its result, but now the original string the user entered is also changed to *FlipCASE*.

Specifying Whether to Pass an Argument by Reference or by Value

Clearly, side effects caused by a function altering values in arguments passed by reference are not necessary, and, in most cases, are highly undesirable. Side effects can cause serious problems elsewhere in your programs. Tracking down problems caused by side effects is often very difficult because there is seldom an immediately obvious cause for a variable's change in value. (*Side effect* is a general term used to refer to any alteration in a variable's value, or in the environment of an executing program, that is not explicitly programmed.)

To prevent side effects like this, the function needs to work with a copy of the argument value instead of the original data. You could, of course, declare a local variable in the function procedure and copy the arguments into that local variable. Copying argument values into local function variables, however, is usually not desirable: The additional variables increase the memory required by the function and the amount of work that you, the programmer, must perform. The extra variables can also clutter up your program code, making it more difficult to understand and troubleshoot.

An easier and more desirable way to ensure that a function works only with copies of an argument value, rather than the original argument value, is to tell VBA that the argument should be passed by value rather than by reference. (Remember, passing by value gives the function a *copy* of the argument value; passing by reference gives the function access to the *original* data in the argument.)

To specify whether VBA passes an argument by value or by reference, use the **ByVal** and **ByRef** keywords in front of the argument for which you want to specify the passing method. As you might expect from their names, **ByVal** causes VBA to pass the argument by value, and **ByRef** causes VBA to pass the argument by reference.

The following line shows the function declaration for the FlipCase function modified so that the tStr argument is passed by value and the nChar argument is passed by reference:

```
Function FlipCase(ByVal tStr As String, Optional ByRef nChar) As String
```

The nChar argument can be safely passed by reference because it is modified by the FlipCase function only when it is not present as an argument. If the **ByRef** keyword for the nChar argument is omitted from the declaration above, nChar is still passed by reference because VBA, by default, passes all arguments by reference.

Listing 6.6 shows the `FlipCase` function modified to utilize a typed optional argument and to pass the `tStr` argument by value in order to avoid any side effects.

INPUT

LISTING 6.6   USING TYPED OPTIONAL ARGUMENTS AND PASSING ARGUMENTS BY VALUE

```
 1:  Function FlipCase(ByVal tStr As String, _
 2:                    Optional ByRef nChar As Long = 0) As String
 3:  'reverses the case - upper to lower, lower to upper - of
 4:  'the first nChar characters in tStr. If nChar is omitted,
 5:  'flips the case of all characters in tStr
 6:
 7:      Dim k As Long      'loop counter
 8:      Dim TestC As String * 1
 9:
10:      If (nChar = 0) Then
11:         nChar = Len(tStr)
12:      End If
13:
14:      For k = 1 To nChar
15:         TestC = Mid(tStr, k, 1)
16:         If (StrComp(TestC, "A", vbBinaryCompare) >= 0) And _
17:            (StrComp(TestC, "Z", vbBinaryCompare) <= 0) Then
18:           Mid(tStr, k, 1) = LCase(TestC)
19:         ElseIf (StrComp(TestC, "a", vbBinaryCompare) >= 0) And _
20:            (StrComp(TestC, "z", vbBinaryCompare) <= 0) Then
21:           Mid(tStr, k, 1) = UCase(TestC)
22:         End If
23:      Next k
24:      'FlipCase = tStr
25:  End Function
```

ANALYSIS   Listing 6.6 shows another version of the `FlipCase` function, which works exactly the same as explained in Listing 6.4, with the exceptions of lines 1 and 2 (the function declaration) and line 10.

The `FlipCase` function declaration in lines 1 and 2 (notice the line-continuation character at the end of line 1) indicates that the first argument, `tStr`, is to be passed by value, is required, and must be a **String** data type. The second function argument is optional, is passed by reference, is a **Long** data type, and—if omitted—has a default value of 0. As before, the function returns a **String** type result.

Line 10 needed to be modified to accommodate the fact that the `IsMissing` function only works for **Variant** optional arguments: `IsMissing` always returns **False** for optional arguments with a type other than **Variant**, whether or not the argument was included in the actual function call. To detect a missing `nChar` argument, it is therefore necessary to test for the presence of the default value, 0. (This is also the same value that VBA would

6

have initialized the nChar argument to, even if no default value had been specified.) Line 10 in Listing 6.6 therefore tests to see if nChar is equal to 0; if it is, it's reasonable to assume that the nChar argument was omitted. Line 11 then assigns the length of tStr as the value for nChar, and the function executes as described for Listing 6.4.

If you change the FlipCase function in Listing 6.4 to match the FlipCase function shown in Listing 6.6 and then run the Test_FlipCase procedure again, you can see that the original string entered by the user is no longer affected by the FlipCase function. This is the result of adding the **ByVal** keyword to the tStr argument.

Do

DO check carefully each time you write a function procedure to make sure that it does not alter its arguments.

DO add the **ByVal** keyword to each argument that your function procedure modifies.

DO go ahead and declare an argument with the **ByVal** keyword to pass it by value if you have doubts as to whether that particular argument should be passed by reference or by value; the memory and speed penalties of passing by value are not that great. Also, passing an argument by value is still more efficient, and makes for cleaner code, than making your own copy of the argument value in a local variable.

Don't

DON'T declare arguments by value (**ByVal**) unless your function procedure modifies that argument, because passing arguments by value can use more memory and require more time to execute than passing arguments by reference—passing an argument by value causes VBA to make a copy of the data for the argument.

Using Function Procedures in Visual Basic for Applications

You use your own function procedures in VBA statements just as you do any of VBA's built-in functions; all the same rules and conventions explained in Day 5 for using built-in functions apply to using your own function procedures. Lines 6 and 8 of Listing 6.5 show typical calls to a function procedure.

Remember, you must include the parentheses around the argument list when you call a function unless you intend to ignore the function's result. (Like VBA's built-in functions, you can also ignore the result of your own function procedures, although you'll seldom need or want to.)

If you want to use named arguments when you use your own function procedures, just use the names from the argument list in your function procedure's declaration. For example, to use a named argument in a call to the SLen function (Listing 6.3), use a statement similar to the following (AnyStr and MyString are string variables):

```
AnyStr = SLen(tStr:=MyString)
```

To use named arguments in a call to the FlipCase function in Listing 6.4 or Listing 6.6, use a statement similar to this next one (AnyStr and UserIn are string variables; AnyNum is an integer variable):

```
AnyStr = FlipCase(tStr:=UserIn, nChar:=AnyNum)
```

If you have trouble remembering all the named arguments for one of your own functions, make sure that you have the Auto Quick Info feature turned on. If the Auto Quick Info feature is on, the VB Editor displays a pop-up window listing the named arguments of your function, just as it does for VBA's built-in functions. Figure 6.2 shows a Code Window where the user is in the process of typing a function call to the FlipCase function of Listing 6.6; notice the pop-up window displaying the function's name, its named arguments, and the function's return type. You can turn the Auto Quick Info feature on or off by choosing Tools, Options to display the Options dialog; next, click the Editor tab to display the VB Editor's options and then set or clear the Auto Quick Info check box.

FIGURE 6.2

The Auto Quick Info feature displays a pop-up window showing the argument list for your own functions, as well as VBA's built-in functions.(FC)

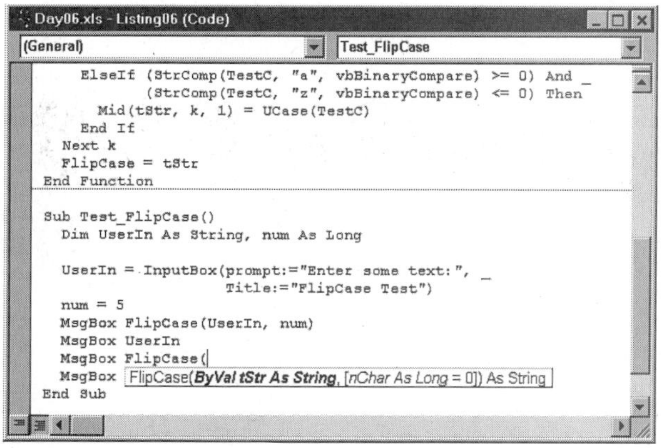

Using the Object Browser to Find Your Function Procedures

If you can't remember which module you stored a particular function in, you can use the Object Browser to see which of your function procedures are currently available and to quickly display the VBA source code for your function.

To use the Object Browser with your own functions, start the Object Browser as you have already learned to do: Choose the View, Object Browser command or click the Object Browser button on the VB Editor's toolbar to display the Object Browser window.

You already know how to use the Object Browser to display the available VBA or Excel host application functions. The Project/Library drop-down list displays all the currently open application files, as well as the always-present VBA choice. To display the custom functions (and other procedures) in a particular VBA project, follow these steps:

1. Select the project's name in the Project/Library drop-down list. Figure 6.3 shows the Object Browser window with the Day06 project selected in the Project/Library list. (In Figure 6.3, notice that the Project Explorer window shows that the Day06 project is stored in the Day06.xls workbook file; the Project Explorer always indicates the filename in which a project is stored in parentheses after the project's name.)

   After you select a project in the Project/Library list box, the Classes list contains a list of all the modules and other objects in the selected project.

FIGURE 6.3

Use the Object Browser to locate your VBA functions and procedures and to display the source code for a function or procedure.

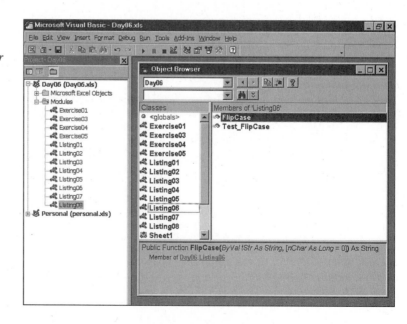

2. Select a module in the Classes list. Figure 6.3 shows the module called `Listing06` selected.

   After you select a module in the Classes list, the Members of *<class>* list contains a list of all procedures and functions declared in the selected module.

3. Select the function or procedure whose source code you want to view in the Members of *<class>* list. When you select one of your own functions or procedures, the Object Browser's Show button is enabled.

4. Click the Show button to display the function or procedure's source code. The VB Editor opens the appropriate module and positions the insertion point in the first line after the function or procedure declaration.

Tip

You can also copy text from the Object Browser for your own functions and procedures to the Windows Clipboard the same way you do for VBA's built-in functions. Day 5 explained how to copy text from the Object Browser to the Windows Clipboard.

Do

DO remember that the Show button in the Object Browser is only enabled if the source code for a selected function or other procedure is available.

DO remember that you can only execute a function by using it in a VBA statement, by calling it from the host application (such as using the function in an Excel worksheet), or by using the function in an expression in the Immediate window of the VB Editor. (Using the Immediate window is described in Day 15, "Debugging and Testing VBA Code.")

DON'T

DON'T try to use the Macro dialog (opened by choosing the Tools, Macros command) to execute a function procedure. VBA expects function procedures, by their nature, to return a value and assumes that there is no point in executing the function by itself. VBA therefore does not list function procedures in the Macro Name list in the Macro dialog.

6

Entering a Function Procedure Description with the Object Browser

Refer again to Figure 6.3: The `FlipCase` function from Listing 6.6 is selected in the Members of *<class>* list. Notice that—just like the built-in VBA and host application functions—the function name and all of its arguments are displayed near the bottom of the Object Browser window (underneath the Classes and Members lists). Unlike VBA's built-in functions, however, no description of the function's purpose appears. You can use the Object Browser to add a description to each of your functions or procedures.

Adding a description to a function or procedure is often useful. For example, the description you enter for a function by using the Object Browser appears not only in the Object Browser, but also in Excel's Function Wizard. Providing a description for your function procedure can therefore assist someone trying to use your function in a worksheet cell formula.

To enter a description for your function procedure, follow these steps:

1. Select your function procedure in the Object Browser, as already described.

2. Right-click the function to which you want to add a description and choose Properties from the resulting pop-up menu. The VB Editor displays the Member Options dialog shown in Figure 6.4.

3. Enter a description for the function (or procedure) in the Description text box. Figure 6.4 shows a description of the FlipCase function already entered in the Description text box.

4. Click OK. The Object Browser closes the Member Options dialog and returns you to the Object Browser.

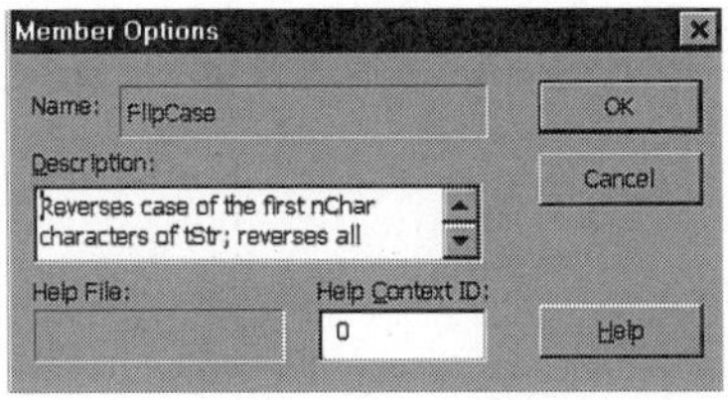

FIGURE 6.4

Enter a helpful description for your functions and procedures in the Member Options dialog.

Figure 6.5 shows how the Object Browser window appears after adding the description shown in Figure 6.4. Notice that the display of the function name and its arguments at the bottom of the Object Browser window now includes the new description for the FlipCase function

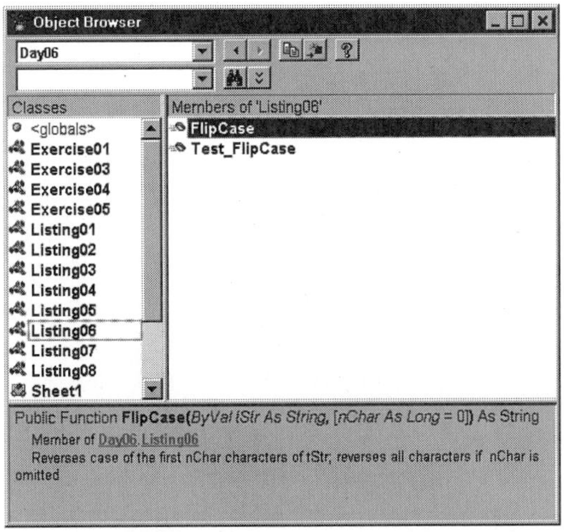

FIGURE 6.5

The description you add in the Member Options dialog displays in the Object Browser window.

Using User-Defined Functions in Excel Worksheets

To use a user-defined function in Excel, enter the function name and its arguments as a formula in a worksheet cell the same way you would enter any of Excel's built-in functions. VBA even makes your user-defined functions available through Excel 2000's Function Palette. (Remember, a user-defined function is just a function procedure that meets certain requirements for use by the VBA host application—Excel, in this case.)

If you can't remember the user-defined function's name or its arguments, you can usually find user-defined functions listed under the User-Defined category in Excel's Paste Function dialog. (You display Excel's Paste Function dialog by clicking the Paste Function button on the toolbar, choosing Insert, Function from the menu, or by selecting More Functions in the drop-down list of the Function Palette.)

Figure 6.6 shows the Paste Function dialog with User Defined selected in the Function Category list and the FlipCase function selected in the Function Name list. (Refer to your Excel documentation or online help for complete information on using the Function Wizard.) The module name appears in front of the function name in Figure 6.6 because the project contains more than one module that stores functions that have the same name. Usually, you won't have this situation, and only the function name will appear in the Function Name list of the Paste Function dialog. Notice that the FlipCase function name, along with any description that you entered for that user-defined function (as described in the preceding section of this chapter), is displayed at the bottom of the Paste Function dialog.

6

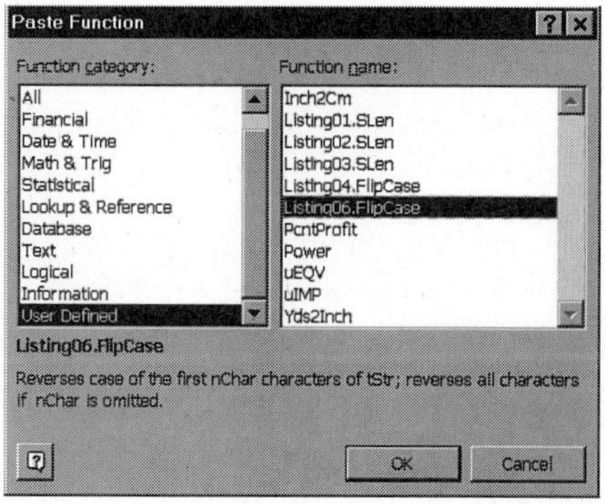

FIGURE 6.6

Using Excel's Paste Function dialog to enter a user-defined function in a worksheet cell.

Paste your VBA functions from the Paste Function dialog as you would for any of Excel's built-in functions, filling in values for the function arguments as necessary.

Do

DO use the Object Browser to enter a description for your user-defined functions, especially if you intend to develop special-purpose functions in VBA and distribute them for use by other Excel users.

Tip

If you use a user-defined function in a worksheet cell, and the displayed result of the function is the Excel #VALUE! error value, carefully double-check the code in your function procedure to make sure that it does not violate any of the rules for user-defined functions. Neither Excel nor VBA prohibit you from using a function procedure that violates the rules for user-defined functions in a worksheet cell. Because your function procedure violates the user-defined function rules, however, VBA does not execute the function; instead, it returns the Excel #VALUE! error value to the cell.

Designing Function Procedures

Whenever you write a function procedure, always keep in mind that the purpose of a function is to return a value of some kind. Keep your function procedures simple and to the point. Usually, a function should only contain the program code necessary to perform the desired computation or data manipulation; a function should never carry out actions not directly related to producing its return value.

Consider writing a function any time you find yourself using the same mathematical formula more than two or three times. As the examples in this chapter show, function procedures are also useful for manipulating data other than numbers. Consider writing a function any time you find yourself using the same expression or group of expressions more than two or three times.

Although the expression for a calculation might be quite simple, you should still write a function procedure if you use the expression frequently. By writing a function procedure, you eliminate any chance that you'll make a typing mistake when you enter the expression, and you also give the expression a meaningful name. For instance, you might find that you frequently enter a date expression—such as Now + 30—that computes a due date for an invoice based on the date the invoice is issued. By writing a function named InvoiceDue that returns the invoice's due date, you not only ensure that the calculation is performed the same way every time it is needed, you also make your program code self-documenting.

Although you can ignore the result of a function procedure, you should write your function procedures so that ignoring their result is meaningless. This is another way of saying that your functions should not perform actions beyond those absolutely necessary to produce the desired return result.

Do

DO consider VBA functions such as **StrComp**, Mid, the data conversion functions **CStr** and **CDbl**, and so on, as guiding examples of how a function procedure should perform. Each function performs a single task and returns a single result without altering the original data contained in any arguments passed to it.

Don't

DON'T consider the VBA MsgBox function as a guiding example for writing functions. The MsgBox function fulfills truly unique needs in VBA; as a result, it performs much more work, with many more options, than functions typically should.

6

Although you might be tempted to use arguments passed by reference to create a function that returns more than one result—by using the function's returned value and one or more modified arguments to get results—*don't* do this. A function should *never* change the original data in the arguments passed to it. As discussed later in Day 12, "Creating

Libraries and Whole Programs: Modular Programming Techniques," there are legitimate circumstances under which you will want to—and should—modify values in arguments passed by reference; in those circumstances, you should use a procedure, not a function. Make sure that your functions do not alter arguments passed by reference; use the **ByVal** keyword to pass arguments by value whenever necessary.

Many of the functions that you write will turn out to have uses in programs or worksheets other than the one for which you originally write the function procedure. The SLen and FlipCase functions used in this chapter, for example, are very general-purpose functions; they are likely to be useful in a number of different expressions in several different procedures.

Because any function procedure in any currently open project document is available to any other currently open document in the same application, you can gather general-purpose functions together into a single project. By gathering general-purpose function procedures together into a single project, you create a *library* of functions. For example, you might put all of your general-purpose Excel function procedures in a workbook file named MyFunctions.xls. Creating libraries of functions and procedures is described in Day 12.

Do

DO double-check every function you write to make sure that the function contains a function assignment. That is, be certain that your function will return a result other than the default empty **Variant**, zero-length **String**, or zero numeric value.

DO avoid side effects by being certain that you include the **ByVal** keyword for every argument that the function procedure modifies.

DO make sure that your function's program code adheres to all the restrictions for user-defined functions explained at the beginning of this chapter if you expect to use your function in Excel worksheet cells.

Designing Functions for Excel

When you write function procedures for use as a user-defined function in Excel worksheets, there are a few facts you should be aware of above and beyond the general requirements for user-defined functions:

- User-defined functions that you intend to use in Excel cannot have names that resemble either A1 or R1C1 style cell reference notations.

- Any string (text) data returned from VBA to Excel cannot be greater than 255 characters in length. If your UDF returns a string greater than 255 characters in length to an Excel worksheet cell, Excel truncates the string to the maximum length of 255 characters before inserting it into the worksheet cell.

- If you write a user-defined function for Excel that returns a date value, make certain that you specify the data type of the function's result as a **Date** type. Excel only applies a date format to a function result in a worksheet cell if it has the VBA **Date** data type. (Excel converts the VBA **Date** type to an Excel date automatically.)

One final concern exists regarding user-defined functions for Excel, and centers around what point in time Excel actually calls the user-defined function (UDF) in order to calculate or recalculate the worksheet cell formula of which the UDF is a part.

By default, Excel calls a UDF to recalculate the worksheet cell formula whenever the values used for the function's arguments change, much the same way Excel determines when to recalculate any worksheet formula. You can, however, set up a UDF so that Excel recalculates it whenever Excel recalculates *any* cell in the worksheet.

You should mark a UDF as *volatile* when its argument values don't come from other worksheet cell values. For example, assume you have a UDF named PcntProfit that computes a percentage profit. This UDF might have two arguments, one to specify the worksheet cell that contains the total income figure and another to specify the worksheet cell that contains the total cost. Because the PcntProfit function's arguments specify cell coordinates, changing the *contents* of the cell doesn't change the PcntProfit function's argument value. If you edit the contents of either the total cost or total income cells, Excel will not recalculate PcntProfit; the PcntProfit function might then display erroneous results. If you mark this UDF as volatile, however, it will always display the correct value because Excel will recalculate it whenever you change any cell on the worksheet.

A user-defined function that recalculates whenever Excel changes any cell in the worksheet is called a *volatile* function. To mark a UDF as a volatile function, add the following statement to the function immediately after the function declaration:

```
Application.Volatile
```

This VBA statement that marks a UDF as a volatile function is really a type of procedure (called a *method*) that belongs to Excel. Because the method belongs to Excel, you must specify the Application object when you use the Volatile method, just like you must specify the Application object when you use an Excel function in a VBA statement. Listing 6.7 shows a volatile function, named PcntProfit, that returns a number representing the percent of profit earned given gross sales and net costs.

6

INPUT   **LISTING 6.7**   A VOLATILE USER-DEFINED FUNCTION IN EXCEL

```
1:  Function PcntProfit(grSales As Currency, _
2:                      netCosts As Currency) As Currency
3:      Application.Volatile
4:      PcntProfit = ((grSales - netCosts) / netCosts) * 100
5:  End Function
```

ANALYSIS   Lines 1 and 2 contain the function declaration for PcntProfit. (Notice the line-continuation symbol at the end of line 1; this declaration was put on two lines to make it more readable.) PcntProfit has two arguments, grSales and netCosts; both arguments are required. Each argument has its data type declared as the **Currency** type. Because no argument passing method is specified, both arguments are passed by reference—the default passing method. The PcntProfit function declaration ends by specifying that the function's result is always a **Currency** data type. The **Currency** type was selected for both the function arguments and the function's result because this function is intended primarily for use with values representing money.

Line 3 contains the Application.Volatile statement; as required, it is the first statement in the function after the function declaration. The Application.Volatile statement "registers" the user-defined function with Excel so that Excel calls the function to recalculate the worksheet cell formula in which the function appears whenever Excel recalculates *any* cell in the worksheet.

Do

DO use the Application.Volatile method only when necessary. Making all your worksheet functions volatile can result in unnecessary recalculation, which increases the overall time required to recalculate a worksheet.

Understanding Recursion

Before ending this lesson on writing your own function procedures, there is one final concept that is important for you to understand, although it is not directly a part of creating VBA function procedures.

A *recursive* function or procedure is one that calls itself. In almost all cases, recursion is a mistake on the part of the programmer that results in outright program *crashes*, or failures—the most common symptom of a recursion problem is an out-of-memory or out-of-stack-space error. (A *stack* is a temporary working area of your computer's memory.

VBA uses the stack memory area to hold interim expression results, copies of function arguments passed by value, function procedure results, and any other time it needs temporary working space. If your procedures use lots of memory while they are working, they can use up their temporary work space.)

Analyzing a Recursive Function's Operation

Listing 6.8 shows a function, named Power, that returns the power of a number given the number and the power to raise it to.

INPUT   **LISTING 6.8**   THE POWER FUNCTION: A RECURSIVE EXAMPLE

```
1:  Function Power(num As Double, pwr As Integer) As Double
2:  'recursively raises num to the power specified by pwr
3:      If pwr = 0 Then
4:          Power = 1                           'ends recursion
5:      Else
6:          Power = num * Power(num, pwr - 1)   'recursion
7:      End If
8:  End Function
```

Line 1 contains the Power function declaration. Power has two required arguments, num and pwr, and returns a **Double** type result.

Look closely at line 6 and notice that this line of the function calls itself. The Power function works by taking advantage of the fact that a number raised to a power n is the same as that number multiplied by itself to the $n-1$ power. For example, 2^3 is the same as $2 \times 2^{3-1}$ or 2×2^2.

To understand how the Power function works, assume that you initially call the function with the following statement to display the result of raising 2 to the third power:

```
MsgBox Power(2, 3)
```

At this point, in the first call, the num argument contains 2 and the pwr argument contains 3. Line 3 starts an **If...Then** statement, which determines whether it is time to stop the recursion. This line tests to see whether or not pwr is equal to 0. In this call, pwr is equal to 3, so execution skips to line 6.

Line 6 makes the function assignment; the expression assigned to the Power function result says that the function result is equal to num multiplied by the result of calling the Power function again, this time passing pwr minus 1 as the second argument.

6

If you substitute the literal interim values for this example into the expression, the call to the Power function in line 6 at this point is

```
Power(2, 3-1)
```

In this the second call to the Power function, num is still 2, but the pwr argument is now 2 (3-1=2) instead of 3. Again, line 3 tests the value of the pwr argument to see if it is equal to 0; it is not, so VBA again executes the function assignment in line 6. The expression in the function assignment calls the Power function again, once again passing pwr minus 1 as the second argument.

If you again substitute the literal interim values for this example into the expression in line 6, the call to the Power function at this point is

```
Power(2, 2-1)
```

Once again, in this third call to the Power function, num is still 2, but pwr is now 1 (2-1=1). Yet again, line 3 tests the value of the pwr argument to see if it is equal to 0; again, it is not, so the function assignment in line 6 is executed a third time, resulting in a fourth call to the Power function.

In the fourth call to the Power function, pwr is 0 (1-1=0); when line 3 tests the value of the pwr argument to see if it is equal to 0, the comparison is finally true and VBA executes line 4 of the Power function, ending the recursion. Line 4 is another function assignment statement, this time simply assigning the number 1 as the function result. (Any number raised to the 0 power is 1.)

In the first through third calls to the Power function, Power has not yet returned any results because VBA cannot completely evaluate the expression in the function assignment statement (line 6) until the series of recursive calls halts in the fourth call to Power. Now that the Power function actually returns a result, the recursive process ends and each separate call to the Power function returns its result.

The fourth call to Power returns the number 1 into the expression in line 6 of the third call to the Power function. Substituting literal interim values from the example, this expression is now equal to 2×1. The result returned by the third call to the Power function is therefore 2.

VBA, in turn, returns this value—2—to the function assignment expression in the second call to the Power function so that (substituting literal interim values) this expression is now equal to 2×2. The second call to the Power function therefore returns 4 to the function assignment expression of the first call to the Power function.

Substituting literal values again, the expression from the first call to Power is now equal to 2×4. Finally, the original, first call to the Power function returns the value 8, which is the correct result of raising 2 to the third power. The following list summarizes the function returns from each successive call to Power:

1	4th call
2×1=2	3rd call
2×2=4	2nd call
2×4=8	1st call

Incidentally, you don't really need to write a Power function; the VBA exponentiation operator (^) has the same effect. The Power function was chosen to illustrate recursion because it provides one of the simplest and easiest to understand examples of how recursion works.

 Note

> The Power function has one flaw: It won't work if you try to use it to raise a number to some negative power. If you pass a negative power value to the Power function, it will recurse infinitely, that is, it will never stop calling itself. (The value of the pwr argument is already less than 0; subtracting one just keeps making the negative number larger, so it will never be equal to 0.) If you feel adventurous, you can demonstrate for yourself the results of infinite recursion by calling Power with a negative value as the pwr argument.

Avoiding Accidental Recursion and Other Recursion Problems

Now that you understand a bit about how a recursive function procedure works, you are ready to understand the drawbacks of recursive routines and how recursion is usually the result of a programmer mistake.

One of the most obvious drawbacks of recursive functions and procedures is that they are often difficult to understand. Another drawback of recursive functions and procedures is that they can use up a lot of memory: Each time a recursive function calls itself, VBA passes all its arguments again and memory space is reserved for the function result. The amount of memory used by a series of recursive function calls can be significant depending on the size of the arguments (in bytes) and the size of the function return (in bytes).

6

Almost any task you can perform with a recursive function you can also perform with a looping structure without the extra memory penalty; it is also often easier to understand a looping structure rather than a function that accomplishes its job through recursion. (Looping structures are described in Day 9.)

Inadvertent recursion is a fairly common programmer error, especially for beginning programmers. As you begin writing functions, it is easy to get confused when you write the function assignment statement and inadvertently create a statement that calls the function recursively, instead of assigning the function result. Because you tell VBA what value to return as the function result with a function assignment, it is also easy to forget that the function name is *not* a variable, and to attempt to treat the function name like a variable name. Such attempts usually result in accidental recursive calls.

If you accidentally create a recursive function procedure, it is unlikely that the recursion will ever end because recursive functions must be carefully constructed so that there is some condition that terminates the recursive calls. If a function does not test for some condition to explicitly end the recursion—like the Power function does—the recursive function calls continue until VBA runs out of memory, at which time a runtime error occurs.

Typically, when you execute a function that contains an inadvertent recursive call, your computer will seem to stop working for several seconds before VBA displays the out-of-memory runtime error.

Summary

In today's lesson, you learned how to create your own function procedures, and you learned about the special restrictions on function procedures you intend to use with Excel or another host application. You learned how to declare a specific data type for a function's result, how to declare data types for a function's arguments, and how to create functions with optional arguments. This lesson taught you the difference between arguments passed by reference and arguments passed by value, and how to control which method VBA uses for specific arguments in your functions.

You also learned how to use your function procedures in VBA statements and in Excel worksheets. You learned how to use the Object Browser to add a description to a function, and received some tips and guidelines on designing function procedures for use in VBA, and for use in Excel.

Finally, you learned what a recursive function is and saw an example of a recursive function procedure. You learned that recursion is a difficult programming technique, and you received some pointers on avoiding accidental recursion.

Q&A

Q I can't find my function procedure in the Object Browser.

A You might be looking at the wrong module. Use the Object Browser's search feature (described in Day 2) to search for a specific function name. You might also try selecting a different module in the Classes list of the Object Browser. If you still can't find the function, it might be in a different project. Try selecting a different project in the Project/Library drop-down list, or try selecting All Libraries in the Project/Library drop-down list. If you still can't find the function you are looking for, it might be in a project that isn't currently open. Remember that the Object Browser only lists modules and functions in open projects.

The Object Browser lists functions and procedures whether or not the project containing the function is hidden—as long as a file is open, the Object Browser lists it.

Q There is no description for my function procedure in Excel's Paste Function dialog.

A If there is no description for your function procedure in the Excel Paste Function dialog, it just means that you did not enter a description for that function procedure by using the Object Browser. To have a description of your function procedure appear in the Function Wizard, follow the instructions at the end of the section "Using Function Procedures in Visual Basic for Applications," in this chapter.

Q Do I really have to understand how recursion works? It seems sort of mysterious to me.

A It is important that you understand what recursion is and what a recursive function call looks like so that you can avoid or recognize an accidental recursive function call. It is not essential, however, that you be able to write recursive functions right now, or ever. Recursion is a subtle programming technique; there are very few tasks that cannot be accomplished more obviously or easily some other way.

Q I've written a function, but I'm not certain that it is returning the correct result. How can I verify its operation?

A Always test your functions before you rely on them. To test a function, write a procedure to call the function and display its result. Your test procedure should call the function with test values in the arguments for which you have manually calculated the correct answer. Next, call the function with argument values at the extreme limits of the range the function will accept. For example, if your function has an argument with a **Single** data type, test the function with the smallest and largest possible numbers the **Single** data type can hold.

If both of these tests produce the correct answer without any runtime error messages, your function is probably working just fine.

6

Refer to the procedure in Listing 6.5 for an example of a procedure that tests a function. Notice that this testing procedure not only displays the value of the function result, but also displays the original arguments after each function call to check whether or not the function arguments have been inadvertently modified. Notice also that the procedure tests the function both with and without its optional argument. If your function has optional arguments, be sure to test its behavior for every possible combination of present or missing arguments.

Q **I understand what the `FlipCase` function does, but I'm not sure I understand exactly how the `For...Next` and `If...Then` structures work.**

A As you might have gathered by now, it is difficult to get much work done without making some kind of a decision in your program code. If you understand the general flow of the function's operation, and, in particular, the function assignment statements, you're doing just fine. Any questions you have about the `For...Next` and `If...Then` structures should be answered in Days 8 and 9.

Workshop

Answers are in Appendix A.

Quiz

1. What distinguishes a function procedure from any other procedure you write?

2. Explain the difference between a function procedure and a user-defined function.

3. What are the rules that a user-defined function must observe?

4. What is a function assignment? Can a function procedure contain more than one function assignment?

5. What is recursion?

6. When would you use recursion?

7. When would you use the `IsMissing` function?

8. Does the `IsMissing` function work for optional arguments with a data type other than **Variant**?

9. Why is the **StrComp** function used in the `FlipCase` function?

10. When (and why) should you pass function arguments by value?

11. If you want to find a particular function procedure, would you use the Tools, Macro command, or the View, Object Browser command? Why?

Exercises

1. As mentioned in the previous lesson, Excel does not have built-in functions for the **Xor**, **Eqv**, or **Imp** operators in VBA (although it does have built-in function equivalents for the **And**, **Or**, and **Not** operators). The following listing shows an example of a function procedure that provides an equivalent to the VBA **Xor** operator, and can be used in an Excel worksheet:

```
1: Function uXOR(L1 As Boolean, L2 As Boolean) As Boolean
2:     uXOR = L1 Xor L2
3: End Function
```

   The function is named uXOR for "user Xor"—remember, you cannot give your functions names that duplicate VBA restricted keywords such as **Xor**.

   Write two functions, one named uEQV and the other named uIMP, to provide equivalents that Excel can use for the VBA **Eqv** and **Imp** operators, respectively.

2. Use the Object Browser to add a description to the function procedures you just created in Exercise 1.

3. Write a function, named Yds2Inch, to convert yards to inches, and also write a procedure to test the function. Yds2Inch should accept a single argument, which is assumed to be a measurement in yards, and return a value in inches. (**HINT:** Because there are 36 inches in a yard, multiply the number of yards by 36 to determine the number of inches.)

4. Write another function, this time named Inch2Cm, to convert inches to centimeters, and also write a procedure to test this function. Inch2Cm should accept a single argument, which is assumed to be a measurement in inches, and return a value in centimeters. (**HINT:** Multiply inches by 2.54 to get a measurement in centimeters.)

5. Write a procedure that uses the InputBox function to get a number representing a measurement in yards from the user and then prints the equivalent value in centimeters—use the two functions Yds2Inch and Inch2Cm from Exercises 3 and 4 to convert the yards to centimeters.

6

DAY 7

Understanding Objects and Collections

Day 1 described how Visual Basic for Applications evolved, in part, from the original macro languages found in Microsoft Excel, Word, and other applications. VBA performs as a macro language, giving you control over a host application by enabling you to manipulate the host application's objects. In today's lesson, you learn

- What an object is and what object properties and methods are.
- To understand the **Object** data type and how to use object variables in expressions.
- How to use object methods and properties in your VBA code.
- What a collection of objects is and how objects can contain other objects.
- How to use object collections and containers.
- How to use the Object Browser with objects, methods, and properties.

Understanding Objects

In the mid 1980s, a new concept in computer programming known as *object-oriented programming* (OOP) was developed. Object-oriented programming has become increasingly popular over the years; the Windows desktop, in fact, embodies many object-oriented principles. The central idea behind object-oriented programming is that a software application—like the real world around you—should consist of distinct objects, each of which has its own specific qualities and behaviors.

An object-oriented application organizes data and program code into cohesive objects that make it easier to design, organize, and work with complex data structures and actions performed on or with that data. Each object in the software application contains program code and data bound together to form a single item. Most applications contain many different types of objects.

VBA gives you access to its host application's objects and to objects in other applications. (Day 20, "Working with Other Applications," describes how to use VBA to access and control objects in other applications.) To use VBA to gain procedural control over the host application, you manipulate the host application's objects in your VBA code. (Performing an action under *procedural control* means that you control the action from a VBA procedure you write.) You can even create your own objects with VBA by using class modules. (You'll learn about class modules in Day 11, "Creating Your Own Data Types and Object Classes.")

In Excel, workbooks, worksheets, data ranges, charts, graphic objects, dialogs, and Excel itself are all objects. In Day 19, "Controlling Excel with VBA," you learn more about using Excel's objects; today's lesson concentrates on giving you a general understanding of what objects are and how you use them.

Note

> What you learn in this lesson will help you work with VBA in applications other than Excel. All VBA host applications—such as MS Word, MS Access, and Microsoft Project—have objects accessible to VBA in the same way that Excel's objects are. Objects in other VBA host applications exist for the same reasons and purposes as objects in Excel. The specific objects in a VBA host application, however, vary depending on the application. The objects in Access, for example, all pertain to databases and database manipulation, whereas the objects in Excel pertain to worksheets, workbooks, and so on.

Object Properties

Just like objects in the real world, VBA objects have various inherent qualities, or *properties*. A portable heater, for example, has properties such as how many watts of heat it puts out, how many cubic feet of air per minute the fan circulates, and what its current thermostat setting is. The heater also has properties such as its weight, color, length, height, and so on. Similarly, objects in Excel also have properties that dictate their appearance and behavior: An Excel worksheet has the property of being visible or not, rows in a worksheet or table have a height property, columns have a width property, and so on.

Properties govern the appearance and behavior of an object. To change an object's appearance or behavior, you change its properties. To change the behavior of a portable heater, for example, you change its thermostat setting; to change its appearance, you might paint it a different color, thereby changing its color property. In Excel, you might change the behavior of a worksheet by changing the calculation property from automatic to manual, or change the worksheet's appearance by specifying a new color for the text or graphics in the sheet.

To find out about the current appearance and behavior of an object, you examine its properties. To find out the heat output of a heater, you read the heater's wattage from the nameplate on the heater. Similarly, you find out the disk, folder, and name of an Excel workbook by examining the workbook's `FullName` property.

Some of an object's properties you can change, others you cannot. With a portable heater, you can change the current thermostat setting—the heater's "thermostat" property—to determine when the heater will start or stop, but you cannot change the heater's wattage, its "heat output" property. Similarly, you can change some of a VBA object's properties, but not others. For example, in an Excel workbook, you can change the name of the workbook's author by changing the `Author` property, but you cannot change the workbook's `Name` property (the `Name` property of a workbook contains the workbook's disk filename and can't be changed without creating a new disk file or renaming the workbook file outside of Excel).

Some objects have properties with the same or similar names: The `Application`, `Workbook`, and `Worksheet` objects in Excel all have a `Name` property, for example. Don't get confused: Each object keeps the data for its own properties separate from other objects. Figure 7.1 shows a schematic representation of two Excel worksheet objects detailing their properties and their methods. Notice that each worksheet object stores the data for its properties within the worksheet itself, along with the user data. (*User data*

7

just means any data that an object stores that comes directly from the user, such as the data contained in a worksheet's cells.) Although Figure 7.1 shows Excel worksheets, the same situation pertains to all other VBA host applications; each object stores its own property data.

FIGURE **7.1**

Each object stores its own property information, but objects of the same type (such as the worksheets shown here) share their method code.

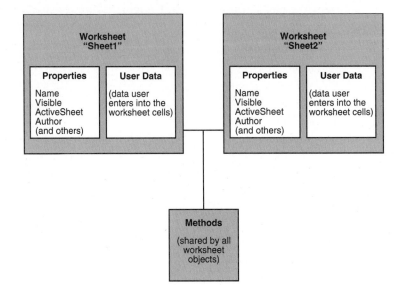

Object Methods

Objects in the real world almost always have some type of inherent behavior or action that they perform. A videocassette recorder (VCR), for example, has a built-in capability to record television programs onto magnetic tape. You could say that the VCR has a *method* of recording video onto tape. VBA's objects also have inherent behaviors or capabilities, called *methods*. An Excel workbook object, for example, has the built-in capability to add a new worksheet to itself, thus, it has a *method* for adding worksheets (called, in fact, Add).

Methods change the values of an object's properties; methods also perform actions on or with data stored by the object. Methods are much like the VBA procedures you are already familiar with, but they are attached to an object; you must access an object's methods through the object.

One of the reasons object-oriented programming has become a popular design technique is because it enables software designers to create more efficient programs by sharing executable code more easily. Instead of keeping a separate copy of the code for each method for each object, VBA objects of the same type (such as the worksheet objects shown in Figure 7.1) share their method code.

Although objects of the same type do share the code for their methods, a method is considered part of the object: When you access a particular method for a specific object, the method acts only on the object through which you access the method.

When you change the temperature setting of an oven, you don't need to know exactly how the oven regulates its temperature, you only need to know how to change the oven's thermostat property to set the desired temperature. When you use a VCR to record a television show, you don't worry about exactly how the VCR goes about recording the video images onto the tape; in fact, the details of a VCR's recording method might be a complete mystery to you. All you need to know to make the VCR record a show on tape is what settings you make to the VCR's controls to start the recording process. After you start the VCR's recording method, the VCR's internal mechanisms take over and the VCR records the show onto tape without requiring any further knowledge or attention from you.

In the same way, you don't have to worry about how Excel or VBA object methods operate, nor do you have to worry about how an object stores or manipulates the user's data. All you need to know is how to specify a particular object and how to specify the particular method you want to use (or the particular property you want to retrieve or change). The built-in code for the VBA object handles all the details for you, without further knowledge or attention from you.

Object Classes

Program objects are grouped into hierarchical *classes*, or families, of objects, just like objects in the real world around you. All objects in the same class have the same (or similar) properties and methods. Each class of object can contain one or more subclasses. Objects that belong to a particular class of objects are called *members* of that class.

To better understand how objects are organized in a class hierarchy, study Figure 7.2, which shows a diagram of how you might classify various types of space heaters. The basic class—space heater—appears at the top of the class hierarchy. Figure 7.2 shows three *subclasses* of space heater: gas-burning, oil-burning, and electrically powered space heaters. Gas-burning space heaters are further divided into two additional subclasses: those that burn natural gas and those that burn liquid propane gas. Similarly, electric space heaters are also divided into two additional subclasses: those that run on AC current and those that run on DC current. There are no subclasses for oil-burning space

7

heaters, because almost all oil-burning space heaters use kerosene. Gas-burning heaters, oil-burning heaters, and electric heaters are all *members* of the class of space heaters. In turn, AC-powered and DC-powered heaters are members of the class of electric heaters. (You can probably see now where the Object Browser's terminology for the Class and Members of <*class*> lists comes from.)

FIGURE 7.2

A hypothetical object class hierarchy for space heaters.

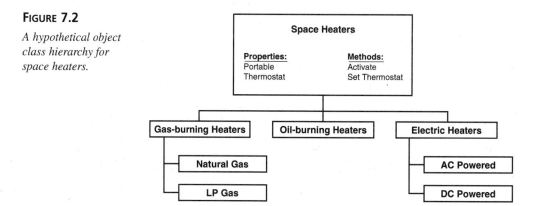

The box at the top of Figure 7.2 also lists a couple of hypothetical properties and methods that are common to the general class of space heaters. The `Portable` property indicates whether the heater is portable and the `Thermostat` property is the current thermostat setting. If you could manipulate a space heater with VBA code, you would retrieve the heater's `Portable` property to find out whether the heater is portable. Similarly, you would retrieve the `Thermostat` property to determine the heater's current thermostat setting. The hypothetical `Activate` method of the class of space heaters represents whatever action you take to turn the heater on. If a space heater could be programmed with VBA, you would execute the `Activate` method to turn the heater on. The `SetThermostat` method corresponds to whatever action you take to set a heater's thermostat; again, if you could program a space heater with VBA, you would execute the heater's `SetThermostat` property (and provide a value for the new setting) to change the heater's thermostat setting.

Because each of the subclasses of heaters shown in Figure 7.2 belongs to the general class of space heaters, each of the heater subclasses *inherits* the properties and methods of the class above it in the hierarchy. For example, a DC-powered electrical heater has the `Portable`, `Thermostat`, `Activate`, and `SetThermostat` properties and methods in common with the general class of space heaters. Furthermore, each additional subclass can add its own properties or methods to the basic class. For example, electric space heaters might also have `Wattage` and `Amps` properties to indicate how much electricity they consume.

A class provides a definition for an object's properties and methods. When you or the host application actually create an object for you to work with, it is called an *instance* of the object. For example, if you go to the hardware store and buy a portable electric heater, you have in your possession a specific instance of a heater belonging to the class of electric heaters.

Excel belongs to a general class of objects: VBA host applications. When you start Excel on your computer, you create an instance of Excel. If your computer has enough memory resources, you can start Excel more than once; each time you start Excel you create another instance of Excel on your computer. Each time you create or open a workbook in Excel, you are creating an instance of a `Workbook` object.

VBA enables you to create your own object classes by inserting a class module into your project. Your class module contains all the property and method definitions for your object; you can then create instances of your custom object. You'll learn more about creating customized classes in Day 11.

Using Objects

VBA program statements that use objects typically perform one or more of the following actions:

- Examine the current condition or status of an object by retrieving the value stored in a particular property.
- Change the condition or status of an object by setting the value stored in a particular property.
- Use one of the object's methods to cause the object to carry out one of the object's built-in tasks.

As an example, you might determine the name of the currently active worksheet in Excel by retrieving the string stored in the worksheet's `Name` property. (A worksheet's `Name` property contains the name of the worksheet as shown on the sheet's tab.) To change the name of a worksheet, you assign a new string to that worksheet's `Name` property. To add a worksheet to a workbook, you use the workbook's `Add` method.

To use an object's properties or methods, you must specify the object whose properties or methods you want to use at the same time you specify the specific property or method to use.

7

In your VBA statements, use the general syntax shown below to specify an object property or method:

```
Object.identifier
```

▼ *Object* is any valid reference to an object. You create object references by setting a variable to refer to an object or by using object methods or properties that return an object reference. *Identifier* is any valid property or method name; VBA displays a runtime error message if you attempt to use properties or methods that are not actually part of the specified object. The first example below is a reference to a worksheet's Name property; the second example is a reference to a workbook's Activate method (both use an object variable to supply the object reference):

```
aSheet.Name
aBook.Activate
```
▲

In the syntax, and in both examples, notice that a period (.) separates the object reference from the property or method name. In a sense, this *dot separator* also connects the object reference to the property or method identifier. Because you access a property or a method through the object, you have to specify the object reference and the property or method identifier together. The dot separator tells VBA where the object reference ends and where the property or method identifier begins. At the same time, the dot separator connects the object reference and the property or method name to form a single identifier in the VBA statement.

You must remember to include the dot separator or else VBA won't be able to interpret your program instructions correctly. In the next two examples, the dot separator has been omitted:

```
aSheetName
aSheet Name
```

In the first line above, the object reference (a variable named aSheet) is not separated from the property identifier (Name) at all. VBA interprets this as a single variable or procedure identifier. Unless you actually have a variable or procedure named aSheetName, VBA either displays a runtime error or creates a new variable, depending on whether you have specified **Option Explicit** in the module.

In the second of the preceding examples, the object reference is not connected to the property identifier at all. In this case, VBA interprets the statement as a call to a procedure named aSheet with a single argument in a variable named Name, and might produce one of several possible syntax or runtime errors.

Table 7.1 lists some of the more important objects (from a VBA programmer's point of view) in Excel. The table shows the object's name and a brief description of the object. (Keep in mind that Excel contains many more objects than the few listed in Table 7.1.)

TABLE 7.1 COMMON EXCEL OBJECTS

Object	Description
Application	Excel (the host application) itself.
Chart	A chart in a workbook.
Font	This object contains the font and style attributes for text displayed in a worksheet.
Name	A defined name for a range of worksheet cells.
Range	A range of cells (one or more) or a named range in a worksheet.
Window	Any window in Excel; windows are used to display worksheets, charts, and so on.
Workbook	Any open workbook.
Worksheet	Any worksheet in a workbook.

Using Object Properties

You can use object properties in only two ways: You can *get* the value of the property, or you can *set* the value of a property. As mentioned earlier in today's lesson, not all of an object's properties are changeable. Object properties you cannot change are referred to as *read-only* properties; properties you can set are called *read-write* properties.

Typically, properties contain numeric, string, or **Boolean** data type values, although some properties can return **Object** or other data types.

You specify a property with this general syntax:

Object.property

Object represents any valid VBA object reference and *property* represents any valid property name for the referenced object.

You retrieve or refer to the values in object properties by using the properties in expressions the same way you use any other variable or constant value. You can assign a property's value to a variable, use object properties in expressions, as arguments to functions and procedures, or as arguments for an object's methods.

7

To assign the value in an object property to a variable, use the following general syntax:

```
Variable = Object.Property
```

Variable is any variable of a type compatible with the object property, *Object* is any valid object reference, and *Property* is any valid property name for the referenced object. In the following example, the string stored in the Name property of the Excel worksheet referenced by the object variable aSheet is assigned to the AnyStr variable:

```
AnyStr = aSheet.Name
```

You can also use an object property directly in an expression or as an argument to a function or procedure. The next few lines are all legitimate uses of an object's property (in each line, aSheet is an object variable set to refer to an Excel worksheet):

```
MsgBox aSheet.Name
AnyStr = "This sheet is named: " & aSheet.Name
MsgBox LCase(aSheet.Name)
```

Almost every object in VBA has a property that contains its name. The following statement uses MsgBox to display the FullName property of an Excel workbook object; the FullName property contains the disk, folder path, and filename of a workbook:

```
MsgBox aBook.FullName
```

In the preceding example, aBook is a variable set to refer to an open workbook object. If aBook refers to a workbook named Sales.xls in the My Documents disk folder, for instance, the message dialog from the preceding statement displays C:\My Documents\SALES.XLS.

To set an object property, simply assign the new value to the property by using the following basic syntax:

```
Object.Property = Expression
```

Object is any valid object reference, *Property* is any property of the referenced object, and *Expression* is any VBA expression that evaluates to a data type compatible with the property. The following line, for example, changes the name of the worksheet referenced by the object variable aSheet by assigning a value to the Name property of the sheet:

```
aSheet.Name = "First Quarter"
```

This next example changes the text displayed in the status bar at the bottom left corner of the application window by assigning a string to the StatusBar property of the Application object (the Application object is VBA's host application, Excel in this case):

 `Application.StatusBar = "Generating 3rd Quarter Summary Report"`

Do

DO use the `Application.StatusBar` property in your procedures to display messages about actions your procedure performs, especially if some of those actions take a long time (such as sorting a long list, querying a remote database, or updating OLE links). By adding a status bar message or prompt, you let the user know that your procedure is still working. Use a statement like the following:

```
Application.StatusBar = "Message about current actions"
```

DON'T

DON'T forget to return control of the status bar when working in Excel. In Excel, you must set the `Application.StatusBar` property to **False** when your procedure is done, otherwise Excel continues to display the status bar message you set. Use a statement like the following to clear your status bar message and return control of the status bar to Excel:

```
Application.StatusBar = False
```

Table 7.2 lists some of the most common or useful object properties in Excel VBA. The table shows the property's name, a brief description of the property's data type and meaning, and commonly used objects that have this property.

TABLE 7.2 COMMON AND USEFUL EXCEL OBJECT PROPERTIES

Property	Type/Meaning	Found in These Objects
ActiveCell	Object: the active cell in the worksheet.	Application, Window
ActiveChart	Object: the active chart.	Application, Window, Workbook
ActiveSheet	Object: the active sheet.	Application, Window, Workbook
Count	Integer: the number of objects in a collection.	All collection objects
Formula	String: the formula for a worksheet cell.	Range
Index	Integer: the number of the object in a collection.	Worksheet
Name	String: name of the object.	Application, Workbook, others

continues

7

TABLE 7.2 CONTINUED

Property	Type/Meaning	Found in These Objects
Path	String: the disk drive and directory the object is stored in.	AddIn, Application, Workbook
Saved	Boolean: whether the workbook was saved since it last changed.	Workbook
Selection	Object: the current selection.	Application, Window
StatusBar	String: status bar message.	Application
ThisWorkBook	Object: workbook from which current procedure is executing.	Application
Type	Integer: a number indicating the type of the object.	Window, Worksheet, Chart
Visible	Boolean: whether Excel displays the object.	Application, Worksheet, Range, others
Value	(varies): the actual value displayed in a cell.	Range

Using Object Methods

You use an object's methods in your VBA statements just as you would any of VBA's built-in procedures.

The basic syntax to use an object method is

```
Object.Method
```

For object methods that have required or optional arguments, use this syntax:

```
Object.Method Argument1, Argument2, Argument3...
```

In both syntax lines, *Object* represents any valid VBA object reference and *Method* represents the name of any method belonging to the referenced object. In the second syntax line, *Argument1*, *Argument2*, and so on represent the arguments in the method's argument list. Just like the arguments for any VBA procedure call, you must list the method's arguments in order, separating each argument in the list with a comma and including placeholding commas for omitted optional arguments. A method can have none, one, or several arguments in its argument list; a method's arguments can be required or optional.

As an example, Excel workbooks have an `Activate` method that makes the workbook the current workbook and activates the first sheet in the workbook. If you set a variable, aBook, to refer to a workbook object, the following statement activates that workbook (later sections in today's lesson describe how to set a variable to refer to an object):

```
aBook.Activate
```

Although the `Activate` method has no arguments, many object methods do have one or more arguments. The next example uses the `SaveAs` method of an Excel workbook object; the example uses the one required argument for the `SaveAs` method and one of several optional arguments for the method.

```
ActiveWorkbook.SaveAs Filename:="C:\VBA21\NEWFILE.xls",
➥FileFormat:=xlNormal
```

Many objects have methods that return values in the same way that a function returns a value. To use the value returned by a method, you must place parentheses around the method's argument list and include the method call in an assignment statement or other expression, just like using a function. You can also ignore the result returned by a method the same way you can ignore the result of a function. To ignore a method's result (if it has one), call the method without parentheses around the argument list as you would for a method that does not return a result.

As an example, the Excel `Address` method (which belongs to the `Range` object) returns the address of a range of cells in a worksheet as a string. The next example shows a VBA statement that uses the `Address` method (myRange is an object variable that references a range of cells on a worksheet):

```
MsgBox myRange.Address
```

If the variable myRange in the preceding line refers to the first cell in the worksheet, the `MsgBox` statement in the preceding example line displays the string $A$1.

Although the example just given shows the `Address` method without any arguments, the `Address` method does have several optional arguments. These optional arguments specify the style of the worksheet cell address that the method returns and whether the returned cell coordinates are absolute or relative. The next example shows the `Address` method used with its third optional argument (which specifies the style of the cell coordinates returned):

```
MsgBox myRange.Address(, , xlR1C1)
```

In the preceding statement, notice that you must include placeholding commas for omitted optional arguments in the argument list of the method, just like any other procedure

7

or function. Because the reference style argument is the third argument, two place-holding commas precede it in the argument list. xlR1C1 is an intrinsic Excel constant that indicates that the worksheet cell coordinates use the R1C1 notation style; if the myRange object variable refers to the cell in the second row and the third column, the example above displays the string R2C3.

Methods also have named arguments, just like other VBA procedures and functions. You can rewrite the last example using named arguments to appear as follows:

```
MsgBox myRange.Address(ReferenceStyle:=xlR1C1)
```

Use named arguments with methods to simplify both writing and reading your VBA code. The next two examples each show a statement that uses the SaveAs method of an Excel workbook object (this method does not return a result) to save the workbook under a new name (the object variable aBook refers to a workbook):

```
aBook.SaveAs "NEWNAME.XLS", xlNormal, , , , True
aBook.SaveAs FileName:="NEWNAME.XLS", _
             FileFormat:=xlNormal, _
             CreateBackup:=True
```

Both of these statements use only three of six optional arguments for the SaveAs method. The first statement uses a standard argument list, the second statement uses named arguments. You can tell how much easier it is to understand the purpose and action of the second statement than the first. (Notice the line continuation symbols and indentation used in the second statement to also help make the line more readable.)

Note

If you don't see much difference between a method and a procedure, you're not confused or missing anything. There is really only one difference between an object method and any other VBA procedure (built-in or user-written): A method belongs to a specific object, and you can only use the method by accessing it through that object. You can frequently recognize calls to methods in VBA code by the fact that the method is attached to an object reference with a dot separator, as shown in the examples in this section.

As you can see from the example statements in this section, using object methods in your VBA code is just like using any VBA procedure or method, except that you must specify the object to which the method belongs. Today's lesson only shows you the general rules and guidelines for using objects, methods, and properties. Day 19 describes many of the methods and properties used as examples in this lesson in more detail.

Later sections of this lesson teach you how to use the Object Browser to get more information on the objects, methods, and properties available in VBA.

Table 7.3 lists some of the most common or useful methods belonging to Excel objects. The table shows the method's name, a brief description of the method's purpose, and some of the commonly used objects that have this method.

TABLE 7.3 COMMON AND USEFUL EXCEL OBJECT METHODS

Method	Purpose	Found in These Objects
Activate	Activates the object.	Window, Workbook, Worksheet, Range, others
Address	Returns the cell coordinates of the specified object.	Range
Calculate	Calculates open workbooks, a worksheet, or a range.	Application, Range, Worksheet
Cells	Returns a Range object.	Application, Range, Worksheet
Charts	Returns a collection of chart sheets.	Application, Workbook
Clear	Clears the data stored in the specified object.	Range
Close	Closes the specified object.	Window, Workbook, Workbooks
Justify	Justifies the text stored in the specified object.	Range
Run	Executes a specified procedure or function.	Application, Range
Save	Saves the workbook file.	Application, Workbook
SaveAs	Saves the specified object in another file.	Workbook, Worksheet
Select	Selects the specified object.	Range, Sheets, Worksheets
SendKeys	Sends keystrokes to dialog boxes in host application.	Application
Sheets	Returns a collection of all sheets in a workbook.	Application, Workbook
Volatile	Registers a function as volatile (see Day 6).	Application
Workbooks	Returns a collection of workbooks.	Application
Worksheets	Returns a collection of worksheets.	Application, Workbook

7

Declaring Object Variables

You might recall from the lesson in Day 3 on data types that, in addition to the **Byte**, **Integer**, **Long**, **Single**, **Double**, and **String** data types, VBA also has an **Object** data type. Variables or expressions of the **Object** data type refer to a VBA object or an object belonging to the host application, such as Excel's Workbook, Worksheet, and Range objects.

As with VBA's other data types, you can declare variables in your modules, procedures, and functions with the specific **Object** type, as shown in the following statement:

```
Dim myObject As Object
```

You can set the variable myObject created by the preceding **Dim** statement to contain a reference to any VBA or host application's object. If you intend to use an **Object** type variable for certain specific kinds of objects, you can also declare an object variable for that specific kind of object:

```
Dim aBook As Workbook
```

You can only use the aBook object variable created by this second **Dim** statement to store references to Workbook objects; if you attempt to set the aBook variable to refer to a Range or Worksheet object, VBA displays a type-mismatch error.

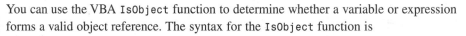

You can use the VBA IsObject function to determine whether a variable or expression forms a valid object reference. The syntax for the IsObject function is

```
IsObject(Object)
```

Object represents the variable or expression that you want to test; IsObject returns **True** if *Object* is a valid object reference, **False** otherwise. You can also use the VBA TypeName function to determine the object type of a variable; Day 10 describes how to use the TypeName function.

Using Objects in Expressions and Assignments

An *object expression* is any VBA expression that specifies a particular object. All object expressions must evaluate to a single object reference; you use object expressions for the sole purpose of creating references to specific objects in your VBA programs.

An object expression can consist of object variables, specific object references, or an object method or property that returns an object. All the following examples are valid object expressions (using Excel objects):

Application	The object's name: refers to the application object, Excel.

`Application.ActiveSheet`	An object property that returns an object reference: the active sheet.
`Application.Workbooks`	An object method that returns a collection of objects: all open workbooks.
`aBook`	An object variable: initialized in a **Set** statement, refers to an object.

You cannot use **Object** type variables or object expressions in arithmetic, logical, or comparison operations. An object reference—whether created with an object expression or stored in an object variable—is really just a memory address that indicates the location in your computer's memory where the referenced object is stored. Because the object reference is really a memory address, arithmetic, logical, and comparison operations are not meaningful. For example, adding together the street address of the building you are sitting in right now with the address of the building next door will not necessarily produce another valid address on your street—so it is with object references.

Before you can use an object variable to refer to an object, you must set that variable to contain a reference to the desired object. Assigning an object reference to an object variable is not the same as making other variable assignments; to assign an object reference to an object variable, use the **Set** keyword.

The **Set** keyword has this general syntax:

```
Set Var = Object
```

Var is any object variable or **Variant** type variable. *Object* is any valid object reference; it can be another object variable or an object expression. If *Var* is a variable declared with a specific object type (such as `Range` or `Workbook`), it must be of a type compatible with the object referenced by *Object*.

The following program fragment matches the variable and object types correctly (using Excel objects):

```
Dim aSheet As Worksheet
Set aSheet = Application.ActiveSheet
```

The next VBA program fragment, however, results in a type-mismatch error because the `ActiveSheet` property returns a `Worksheet` object, not a `Workbook` object:

```
Dim aBook As Workbook
Set aBook = Application.ActiveSheet
```

7

To specify a particular object in an expression, or to set an object variable to refer to that object, use methods and properties that return objects, such as the ActiveWorkbook and ActiveSheet properties of the Application object or the Cells method of the Worksheet object.

Although the standard comparison operators (<, <=, >, >=, <>, =) are not meaningful when used with objects, VBA does provide one comparison operator designed exclusively for use with object expressions and variables: the **Is** operator.

The **Is** operator has the following syntax:

Object1 Is *Object2*

Object1 and *Object2* are any valid object references. Use the **Is** operator to determine whether two object references indicate the same object. The result of the **Is** comparison operation is **True** if the object references are the same, **False** otherwise.

Listing 7.1 shows a VBA procedure that makes a backup copy of the active workbook. You might use a procedure like this if you want to provide an easy way for a user to save a copy of the active workbook under a different name without changing the filename of the active workbook in memory the way the File, Save As command (and the Workbook object's SaveAs method) does.

INPUT **LISTING 7.1** THE Backup_ActiveBook PROCEDURE

```
 1:  Sub Backup_ActiveBook()
 2:  'Creates backup copy of active workbook under new filename
 3:  'using the SaveCopyAs method. New name has "(backup)" appended
 4:
 5:     Dim FName As String
 6:     Dim OldComment As String
 7:
 8:                         'preserve original file comments
 9:     OldComment = ActiveWorkbook.Comments
10:
11:     'Add new comments for the backup copy
12:     ActiveWorkbook.Comments = "Backup copy of " & _
13:                          ActiveWorkbook.Name & _
14:                          ", made by backup procedure."
15:
16:     'Make backup filename from original filename
17:     FName = Left(ActiveWorkbook.Name, _
18:                  InStr(ActiveWorkbook.Name, ".")) & _
19:                  "(backup).xls"
20:
21:     ActiveWorkbook.SaveCopyAs FileName:=FName
22:     ActiveWorkbook.Comments = OldComment     'restore comments
23:  End Sub
```

ANALYSIS This procedure uses a couple of different Excel objects, properties, and methods. The `ActiveWorkbook` object reference used throughout the `Backup_ActiveBook` procedure (lines 9, 12, 13, 17, 18, 21, and 22) is a property of the Excel `Application` object that returns an object reference to the currently active workbook. (As you learn in the next section, you can usually omit the object reference for properties and methods of the `Application` object.)

Line 1 contains the procedure declaration for `Backup_ActiveBook`. Lines 2 and 3 are comments describing the purpose and action of the `Backup_ActiveBook` procedure.

Lines 5 and 6 of the procedure declare the `FName` and `OldComment` variables, respectively; both variables are strings. Line 9 copies the string in the `Comments` property of the `ActiveWorkbook` object to the `OldComment` variable. Next, lines 12 through 14 (notice the line continuation symbol at the end of lines 12 and 13) set a new value for the `Comments` property of the `ActiveWorkbook` object. The `Comments` property of a workbook object contains the comment text you enter in the Properties dialog that Excel displays whenever you save a workbook for the first time or through the File, Properties command.

Lines 17 through 19 form a single VBA statement; notice the line-continuation symbol at the end of lines 17 and 18 indicating that these three lines are a single VBA statement. This statement uses the `Left` and `InStr` functions to help create a new filename for the backup copy of the active workbook. The `InStr` function returns the position of the filename separator (`.`) in the `Name` property of the `ActiveWorkbook` object. (The `Name` property of a workbook contains the workbook's filename.)

The result of the `InStr` function (line 18) determines how many characters the `Left` function copies from the `Name` property of the `ActiveWorkbook`. Because the `InStr` function returns the position of the filename separator (`.`), `Left` returns the workbook's filename up to and including the separator, but does not copy the *XLS* extension. Instead, the string *(backup).xls* is concatenated to the filename string. If the `ActiveWorkbook.Name` property contains *Day07.xls*, for example, this expression evaluates to *Day07.(backup).xls*. The assignment operator in line 17 stores this new filename in the `FName` variable.

Now, line 21 uses the `ActiveWorkbook.SaveCopyAs` method to save the active workbook under a new filename in the current drive and directory; the name of the active workbook file in memory remains the same.

Finally, line 22 restores the original contents of the `ActiveWorkbook.Comments` property; the active workbook file is now in exactly the same condition it was before this procedure started. The new copy of the workbook on disk is exactly the same as the workbook in memory, except that the comments in the Properties sheet for the workbook indicate that the new file is a backup copy and gives the original workbook's filename.

7

> **Note**
>
> The `Backup_ActiveBook` procedure in Listing 7.1 saves the copy of the workbook on the current disk drive in the current folder, which might be a different drive or folder than the one from which the workbook was loaded. The `Name` property returns only the name of the workbook, excluding disk drive and folder information. Later, you'll learn how to get the full disk and folder information from a workbook.

Referring to Objects by Using `With...End With`

As you can see from Listing 7.1, your procedures are likely to refer to the same object frequently, with several statements in a row all referring to objects or methods that belong to the same object. Every statement in Listing 7.1 from line 9 to line 22 uses a property or method of the object referenced by `ActiveWorkbook`. VBA provides a special structure, the **`With...End With`** structure, that enables you to refer to properties or methods that belong to the same object without specifying the entire object reference each time.

The general syntax of the **`With...End With`** structure is

```
With Object
' statements that use properties and methods of Object
End With
```

`Object` is any valid object reference. Listing 7.2 shows the `Backup_ActiveBook` procedure again, this time using the **`With...End With`** structure.

INPUT

LISTING 7.2   ADDING ***With...End With*** TO THE `Backup_ActiveBook` PROCEDURE

```
 1:   Sub Backup_ActiveBook()
 2:   'Creates backup copy of active workbook under new filename
 3:   'using the SaveCopyAs method. New name has "(backup)" appended
 4:
 5:      Dim FName As String
 6:      Dim OldComment As String
 7:
 8:    With ActiveWorkbook
 9:                       'preserve original file comments
10:      OldComment = .Comments
11:
12:      'Add new comments for the backup copy
13:      .Comments = "Backup copy of " & .Name & _
14:                   ", made by backup procedure."
```

```
15:
16:        'Make backup filename from original filename
17:        FName = Left(.Name, InStr(.Name, ".")) & "(backup).xls"
18:
19:        .SaveCopyAs FileName:=FName
20:        .Comments = OldComment      'restore comments
21:     End With
22:  End Sub
```

ANALYSIS This version of the `Backup_ActiveBook` procedure operates in exactly the same way as the version shown in Listing 7.1. The version shown in Listing 7.2, however, incorporates the **With...End With** structure. Line 8 starts with the keyword **With** followed by the `ActiveWorkbook` object reference, therefore beginning the entire **With** statement.

Line 10 assigns the contents of the `ActiveWorkbook.Comments` property to the `OldComment` string variable. Notice that this time, only the dot separator (`.`) is included in front of the `Comments` property. Because this statement occurs inside the **With** `ActiveWorkbook` statement, VBA knows that the object reference for the `.Comments` property is the `ActiveWorkbook` as long as the dot separator appears in front of the `Comments` property name.

Lines 13 and 14 are a single VBA statement that assigns a new value to the `.Comments` property. Line 17 assembles a new filename, as in Listing 7.1, and stores it in `FName`. In line 17, notice that the statement uses the `.Name` property the same way as the `.Comments` property. Because these statements are inside the **With...End With** statement and they include the dot separator in front of the property name, VBA knows that the reference for the `.Name` property is the `ActiveWorkbook` object.

Line 19 uses the `.SaveCopyAs` method to save the backup copy, and line 20 restores the original comment to the `.Comments` property. In each of these lines, because the line is inside a **With** statement that specifies the `ActiveWorkbook` object, VBA knows that the correct object reference for each property or method preceded by a dot separator (`.`) is the `ActiveWorkbook` object.

Finally, line 21 completes the **With** statement with the **End With** keywords.

You can see that Listing 7.2 obviously required less typing than Listing 7.1; it is also easier to read and understand. Simplify your code by using the **With...End With** structure whenever you have several program statements together that use properties or methods from the same object reference.

7

Do

DO remember that using **With...End With** will speed the execution of your procedures: VBA only has to find the referenced object once, at the beginning of the **With** statement; your procedure is therefore speeded up by the amount of time required to resolve the object reference for each property or method inside the **With** statement.

DO remember to preserve any data you want to change only temporarily. The Backup_ActiveBook procedure, for example, alters the Comments property of the active workbook. The procedure therefore uses a variable to preserve the original comments *before* making the change and then restores the original comment.

Don't

DON'T get input from the user unless you really need to or really want to. The Backup_ActiveBook procedure might have been written with an InputBox statement to get the filename instead of assembling the filename automatically. In this case, generating the filename automatically ensures that the backup files created by this procedure are easily identifiable, and the user is saved the extra work of entering the filename. By generating the new filename within the procedure, you also eliminate any potential problems caused by a user entering an invalid filename.

Working with Object Collections and Object Containers

An object *collection* is a group of related objects, such as all the worksheets in a workbook or all the characters in a paragraph. An object in a collection is called an *element* of that collection.

A collection is, itself, an object; collections have their own properties and methods. Every collection, for example, has a Count property that returns the number of elements in the collection. If the active workbook has 16 worksheets in it, the following expression evaluates to the number 16:

collection object

```
Application.ActiveWorkbook.Worksheets.Count
```

In the preceding expression, Worksheets is the collection of all worksheets in a workbook, ActiveWorkbook is a property of the Excel Application object that returns the active workbook, and Count is the property of the Worksheets collection that returns the total number of worksheets in the collection.

This sample expression also helps illustrate how objects contain other objects. A *container* object is any object that contains one or more other objects. In the example, `Application` contains the object referenced by `ActiveWorkbook`, which in turn contains the collection object `Worksheets`. All the container object references are joined together with a dot separator (`.`) to form a single object expression.

Many objects contain other objects of differing types: A workbook contains `Module`, `Chart`, and `Worksheet` objects; a worksheet, in turn, might contain `DrawingObjects`, `ChartObjects`, or `OLEObjects`. Figure 7.3 shows a partial tree diagram of Excel objects showing how objects contain other objects. The hierarchy of objects and containers illustrated in Figure 7.3 is called the *object model*.

FIGURE 7.3

Excel's `Application` *object contains object collections, such as* `Workbooks`, *which contain yet other objects, such as individual worksheets.*

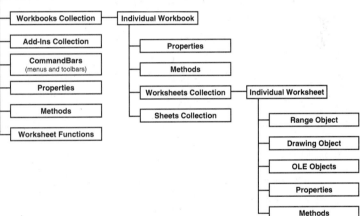

You can see from Figure 7.3 that the `Application` object is the outermost container; the `Application` object contains all other objects. The `Application` object contains collections that, in turn, contain other collections. You can see that the Excel `Application` object contains the `Workbooks` and `AddIns` collections: `Workbooks` is the collection of all open workbooks and `AddIns` is the collection of all installed add-in applications. The Excel `Workbooks` collection, in turn, contains the `Worksheets` and `Sheets` collections. The `Worksheets` collection contains individual worksheets.

Note

Figure 7.3 shows only a partial diagram of the relationships between various objects and their containers. Excel provides many more objects and collections than those shown in the diagram.

7

Figure 7.3 gives you an idea of how to specify complex object references. To make it clear to VBA which object you want to refer to, you might need to specify the object's container. To refer to a particular sheet in an Excel workbook, for example, you might need to include a reference to the workbook that contains the worksheet:

```
Workbooks("Sales.xls").Worksheets("Sales Report")
```

The preceding object expression uses the Excel Workbooks collection to refer to the Sales.xls workbook, and then uses the Worksheets collection contained in the Sales.xls workbook object to refer to a specific sheet. (How to indicate single items in a collection is described a little later in this lesson.) The following sample expression shows an even more complex object reference:

```
Application.Workbooks("Sales.xls").Worksheets("Sales Report").Range("A1")
```

The object expression in the preceding line refers to the cell A1 on the Sales Report sheet of the Sales.xls workbook. As you can see from these two examples, specifying a complete object reference through all of an object's containers can be quite tedious. Fortunately, VBA enables you to omit the Application object reference for almost all objects that the Application object contains. If you omit the Application object reference, VBA assumes that you mean the host application—Excel—and supplies the reference for you. The following object expression, therefore, refers to the same object as the preceding expression (cell A1 on the Sales Report sheet of Sales.xls):

```
Workbooks("Sales.xls").Worksheets("Sales Report").Range("A1")
```

You only have to specify the Application object when a reference might otherwise be ambiguous or when using built-in Excel worksheet functions, as described in Day 5.

If you omit the Excel Workbooks object reference, VBA usually—but not always—assumes that you mean the current active workbook. The next object expression is equivalent to the one just shown, provided the Sales.xls workbook is the active workbook:

```
Worksheets("Sales Report").Range("A1")
```

If Sales.xls is the active workbook and Sales Report is the active sheet, this next object expression is also equivalent to the one just shown:

```
Range("A1")
```

In many of your procedures, however, you cannot be certain that any particular workbook or worksheet is active at the time your procedure executes, so you'll probably need to specify at least some of the containers for the object you want to refer to.

Tip

> Remember to use methods and properties that return objects (such as `ActiveWorkbook`) to make object container references shorter. Using the `With...End With` statement is an ideal way to avoid writing lengthy object references more than once or twice in a procedure.

It is possible for the same object to be an element in more than one collection. For example, an Excel `Worksheet` object is an element of both the `Worksheets` collection and the `Sheets` collection. `Worksheets` is a collection of all the worksheets in a workbook; `Sheets` is a collection of all sheets in a workbook, including worksheets and chart sheets. Because the `Sheets` collection contains all sheets in a workbook and `Worksheets` contains all worksheets, any worksheet belongs to both collections. Similarly, a particular Excel `Range` object, which refers to a range of cells in a worksheet, might be contained by a `Worksheet` object and also contained in a `Column` or `Row` object.

All these objects in containers and collections might be a little confusing to you, especially those objects that are contained in more than one object or collection at the same time. Although it might seem that objects in VBA can be in two places at once, this really isn't true. To better understand container objects and collections, you must keep in mind that program objects are not really a physical thing contained in another physical thing. Instead, remember that an object that contains another object really just has a memory address that refers to the contained object. Containers refer to the objects they "contain" through their memory addresses. Just as many different people might have your mailing address without you being physically present in their homes, any particular program object can be referred to by several other objects through its address.

Note

> If you ever need to refer to an object's container, just use the object's `Parent` property. All objects have a `Parent` property, which returns an object reference to the object's container. The following object expression, for example, refers to the Excel `Application` object, which contains the `Workbooks` collection:
>
> `Workbooks.Parent`

Table 7.4 lists some of the most frequently used object collections in Excel. The table shows the collection's name and a brief description of the collection's purpose.

7

TABLE 7.4 COMMON EXCEL COLLECTIONS

Collection	Purpose
Charts	The collection of all chart sheets in a workbook.
ChartObjects	The collection of all chart objects in a worksheet.
Windows	The collection of all windows in the application, whether or not the window is onscreen.
Workbooks	The collection of all workbooks currently open in the application.
Worksheets	The collection of all worksheets in a workbook.

Adding to Collections

Most of the time, you work with elements that already exist in a collection. Occasionally, you might want or need to add an element to a collection. In Excel, you'll probably want to create a new workbook or add a new worksheet to a workbook; to do so, you'll need to add a new element to the appropriate object collection.

Every collection has an Add method, which adds a new element to the collection. Many of the Add methods have one or more arguments that enable you to specify various initial values or conditions for the new object's properties. The following statement shows the Add method of the Workbooks collection used to create a new Excel workbook:

```
Workbooks.Add
```

This statement creates a new workbook and makes it the active workbook. Day 19 gives you more information about adding elements to collections in Excel.

Referring to Specific Objects in a Collection or Container

To specify a single element of a collection, use the following general syntax:

```
Collection(Index)
```

Technically, this syntax specifying a single object in a collection is known as an *object accessor*. Collection is any valid object expression that refers to a collection. Index can be either a string or an integer designating the specific element you want. When the Index argument is a string, the string must contain the text name of the object. In Excel, for example, you can use the name of a worksheet as shown on the sheet's tab, the name of a named range in a worksheet, the filename of a workbook, the name of a toolbar button or menu command, and so on as an *Index* for the appropriate collection. For example, to refer to a worksheet named *July Data* in the active workbook, you would use the following statement:

```
Worksheets("July Data")
```

When the *Index* argument is an integer, it is the number of the element in the collection. Each element in a collection is numbered in the order it was added to the collection. For this reason, there is no easy way to determine the index number for any given collection element.

Usually, you should use a text name to refer to an element in a collection; this not only makes certain which element you want to refer to, but also makes your code easier to read. `Worksheets("July Data")` is much easier to understand than `Worksheets(5)`. (Many objects do have an `Index` property that returns the index number of the object in their collection, but you still have to be able to refer to the element in the collection before you can retrieve the `Index` property.)

If you want to refer to all the elements in a collection, don't include any index. The following statement, for example, closes *all* of the visible, open workbooks in Excel:

```
Workbooks.Close
```

Do

DO keep in mind that the methods and properties in the `Application` object belong to Excel, not to VBA. As you work in various VBA host applications, some of the methods and properties in the `Application` object might vary depending on the specific host application: Excel, Word, Access, and so on.

Don't

DON'T forget that the `Application` object provides many useful methods and properties, as well as providing a container for Excel's (or another host application's) objects. For example, remember that you access Excel's worksheet functions—such as SUM, MIN, MAX, and so on—through the `Application` object, as explained in Day 5.

7

Note

The `Application` object can contain methods with names that duplicate the names of VBA procedures or functions. When using a host application method that duplicates a VBA procedure or function name, you must specify the `Application` object, otherwise VBA assumes that you want to use the VBA procedure or function.

The Excel `Application` object, for example, contains an `InputBox` method. Excel's `InputBox` method isn't the same as VBA's `InputBox` function: The Excel `Application.InputBox` method has one more argument than the VBA `InputBox` method; this extra argument enables you to restrict the type of data (numeric, date, text) that the user enters in the dialog. To use Excel's `InputBox` method, you must specify the `Application` object:

`Application.InputBox`

Otherwise, VBA assumes you want to use the VBA `InputBox` function.

Using the Object Browser with Objects, Methods, and Properties

You have already learned how to use the Object Browser to locate and get help on VBA and host application functions, procedures, and constants (Day 5). Using the Object Browser with objects, methods, and properties is very similar; in fact, the Object Browser's primary purpose—as its name suggests—is to enable you to browse through all the objects available in VBA and the host application, along with their various methods and properties.

You already know how to start the Object Browser: Click the Object Browser button on the Visual Basic toolbar, or choose the View, Object Browser command to display the Object Browser window shown in Figure 7.4.

Tip

You can also start the Object Browser by pressing F2 whenever the VB Editor is active.

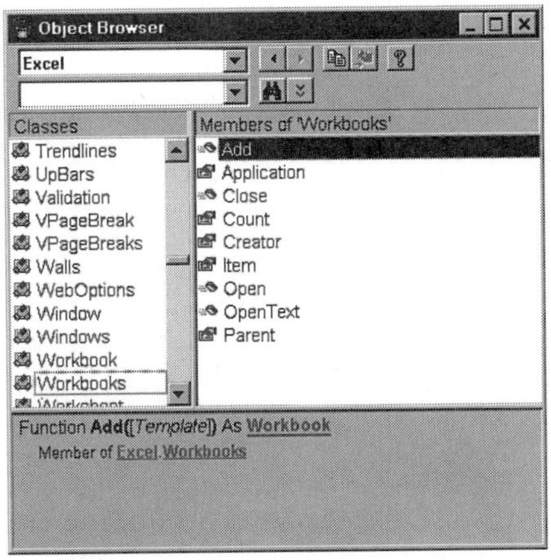

FIGURE 7.4

Use the Object Browser to determine what objects are available and what properties and methods belong to a particular object.

To view a list of the available Excel objects, and to view a list of properties and methods for a particular object, follow these steps:

1. Open the Object Browser window.

2. Select Excel in the Project/Library drop-down list at the top of the Object Browser window. Figure 7.4 shows the Excel library already selected in the Project/Library drop-down list.

   After you select the Excel library in the Project/Library drop-down list, the Classes list contains all the Excel objects available to VBA.

3. In the Classes list, select the object whose methods and properties you are interested in. Figure 7.4 shows the Workbooks collection object selected in the Classes list.

4. To get more information about the object you have selected in the Classes list, click the question mark (**?**) button (in the upper right of the Object Browser window) to access the VBA online help system.

Note

You can only get help for an object selected in the Classes list if the object is selected *without* a selection in the Members of *<class>* list. (Selecting an object in the Classes list clears any selection from the Members of *<class>* list.)

After you select an object in the Classes list, the Members of *<class>* list in the Object Browser window displays all the methods and properties for the selected object.

7

5. In the Members of *<class>* list, select the particular method or property you are interested in. The Object Browser now displays the method or property name at the bottom of the window; if you select a method that has arguments, the Object Browser also lists all of the method's arguments. Figure 7.4 shows the Add method of the Workbooks collection selected.

Note

The Object Browser distinguishes methods and properties from each other in the Members of *<class>* list by displaying special icons at the left of each item in the list. Properties are indicated by an icon of a hand pointing at an index card, and methods are indicated by an icon that looks like a flying green brick (see Figure 7.4). A small blue ball (not visible in Figure 7.4) indicates that the property or method is globally available.

6. Click the question mark (?) button in the Object Browser window to access the VBA online help system for detailed information on the method or property selected in the Members of *<class>* list.

Do

DO remember to supply the object reference and dot separator (.) for each method or property that you use in your VBA code.

DO omit the parentheses from a method's argument list if the method does not return a result or if you choose to ignore the result that the method returns.

DO use the Object Browser to become familiar with the various objects, methods, and properties available to you and to speed up writing your program code.

DON'T

DON'T feel compelled to use all of a method's arguments if you don't need them. Simply ignore any optional arguments.

Summary

In today's lesson, you learned that an object is a set of data and code bound together into a single unit. You learned that object properties store data about the condition and status of an object, and that object methods are special procedures and functions that provide the inherent behaviors and actions that an object has. You also learned that objects are grouped into hierarchies of classes and subclasses.

You learned how to use objects in your VBA code, and you learned the basic syntax for specifying an object's method or property. You learned how to declare variables of the `Object` data type, and you learned that you must use the VBA `Set` command to assign an object reference to an object variable. You also learned how to use the `With...End With` statement structure when several program statements refer to the same object in order to make it easier to write and read your program code.

Next, you learned what a collection of objects is and how objects can contain other objects; you also learned how to specify a particular object by forming complex object references through an object's containers, and how to specify a particular object in a collection.

Finally, you saw how to use the Object Browser to view available objects, methods, and properties. You also saw how to access the VBA online help through the Object Browser for detailed information about objects, methods, and properties.

Q&A

Q I'm trying to write a VBA procedure that changes the way the active worksheet gets displayed, but I don't know which object is the correct one to reference, and if I did know which object to reference, I still don't know which property to change or whether there is a method to do what I want!

A If you're not sure what objects or methods you should use to accomplish a particular task, use the Macro Recorder to record the task (or a similar one) and then examine the recorded code to see which objects, properties, and methods it uses. You can then edit or copy the recorded statements to use in your procedure. You can also use the objects, properties, and methods you see in the recorded statements as the basis for doing research in the online help system or with the Object Browser.

Recording code with the Macro Recorder and then editing it to streamline or generalize its operation is a good programming technique for an environment like VBA and is a technique that works well in Excel.

7

Q **Why should I declare a specific object type, such as `Range` or `Workbook`, instead of the more general `Object` type?**

A Declaring a specific object type helps you track programmer errors. If you make a mistake and set the object variable reference incorrectly, having a more specific object type might pinpoint the error for you because VBA is likely to produce a type-mismatch error. Otherwise, you can have trouble tracking down such errors.

Q **Does VBA create a new object when I declare an object variable and then use the `Set` command to assign an object to that variable?**

A When you declare an object variable and subsequently set it to refer to an object, you are *not* creating a new object; you create a new *reference* to the object. You can have several object variables that all reference the same object, if you want.

You use object variables to give meaningful shorthand names to the objects that your program manipulates. For instance, your code is easier to understand if it contains references such as `DataSheet` rather than `Workbooks("Ch07.xls").Worksheets("DataSheet")`.

Q **If VBA understands the `Application` object reference tacitly, why should I ever specify the `Application` object in an object reference?**

A Although the `Application` object is optional for many object references, it is required for others. Usually, you must specify the `Application` object when there is a possibility of some ambiguity about which object you want to reference. For example, to use Excel's worksheet functions, you must specify the `Application` object, as you learned in Day 5 and as shown in the following sample lines:

```
AnyVar = Application.Sum(Range("A1:A12"))
AnyVar = Application.Max(Range("A1:A12"))
AnyVar = Application.Min(Range("A1:A12"))
```

Each of the lines above uses a built-in Excel worksheet function (SUM, MAX, MIN) and assigns the result of the Excel function to a variable, `AnyVar`. To avoid any possible ambiguity between Excel's built-in functions, VBA's built-in functions, and functions you might have written yourself with the same names, VBA requires you to specify the `Application` object.

Q **Does the index string to specify a particular element in a collection always have to be a quoted literal string?**

A No. The index string can be a string variable or any string expression that evaluates to a valid name for an element in the collection.

Q How do I figure out how to create the object reference for an object that I want to use?

A Create object references from the outermost container object to the innermost container, ending with the specific method or property you want:

```
Application.Container1.Container2.ThingYouWant
```

The `Application` object is always the outermost container. Remember that the `Application` object, and other objects, have properties and methods that return references to objects; use the Excel `Application` object's `ActiveWorkbook`, `ActiveSheet`, and `ActiveWindow` properties to refer to the currently active workbook, sheet, or window, for example.

Also, you can use an object's `Parent` property to determine that object's container. As an example, you might want to determine whether the container for the current `Window` object—a worksheet with several charts, perhaps—has data displayed in more than one window. To determine which workbook contains the current active window, use the `ActiveWindow` property of the `Application` object to reference the active window and then use the `Parent` property of the active window to reference the workbook containing that window. The following line, for example, uses the `MsgBox` statement to display the name of the workbook that contains the active window:

```
MsgBox ActiveWindow.Parent.Name
```

This next line again uses `MsgBox`, this time to display the count of windows that the parent workbook of the active window contains

```
MsgBox ActiveWindow.Parent.Windows.Count
```

In general, you should create object references by working from the known toward the unknown. Both of the preceding sample lines begin by referencing a property of the `Application` object (the `Application` object is always available, and therefore always "known"). Next, each statement uses a property of the `Window` object (`Parent`) to reference the object's container.

Workshop

Answers are in Appendix A.

7

Quiz

1. What is the main idea behind object-oriented programming?

2. In an object-oriented application, what is an object?

3. What is a property? What do you use object properties for?

4. Are all of an object's properties changeable?

5. If you change, say, the Name property of an object, does your change affect the Name property of other objects?

6. What is a method? What do you use object methods for?

7. Name three actions typically performed by VBA code that uses objects, properties, and methods.

8. What is the basic syntax required to use a property or method of an object?

9. What is the purpose of the dot separator (.) in an object reference?

10. What is an object expression, and what do you use object expressions for?

11. How do you create object references?

12. What is a collection of objects? What is an element in a collection?

Exercises

1. **BUG BUSTER:** The following procedure uses the Excel Workbooks collection's Add method to create a new workbook and then fills in the new workbook's summary information with a combination of information obtained from the user in a series of InputBox statements and with information obtained from the Application object's OrganizationName property. (The summary information is the same information you can fill in manually by choosing the File, Properties command. The OrganizationName property of the Application object contains the organization name entered when you installed Excel.)

   This procedure has a flaw in it, however, and does not correctly carry out its job. If **Option Explicit** is set in the module containing this procedure, VBA displays a runtime error message stating that there are undefined variables. If **Option Explicit** is not set, the procedure executes without errors, but does not change the summary information of the new workbook.

   Rewrite this procedure so that it works correctly.

```
1:  Sub NewBook()
2:  'Creates new workbook, and fills in the summary information
3:  'for the new workbook with some information from the user,
4:  'and some information from the Application object.
5:
```

```
 6:    Const nbTitle = "New Book"
 7:
 8:    Workbooks.Add      'adds workbook to Workbooks collection
 9:    With ActiveWorkbook
10:      Title = InputBox(prompt:= _
11:                       "Enter a title for this workbook:", _
12:                       Title:=nbTitle)
13:      Subject = InputBox(prompt:= _
14:                       "Enter the subject of this workbook:", _
15:                       Title:=nbTitle)
16:      Author = Application.OrganizationName
17:      Keywords = ""
18:      Comments = InputBox(prompt:= _
19:                      "Enter a comment regarding this workbook:", _
20:                      Title:=nbTitle)
21:    End With
22: End Sub
```

2. Rewrite the following procedure (which displays information about the Excel
   `Application` object's operating environment and user) to use a **With...End With**
   statement.

```
 1:  Sub Show_SystemInfo()
 2:  'uses various properties of the host application to display
 3:  'information about your computer system
 4:
 5:    MsgBox "Host Application: " & vbCR & _
 6:          Application.Name & " v" & Application.Version & _
 7:          ", Build " & Application.Build & vbCR & vbCR & _
 8:          "Library Path: " & Application.LibraryPath & _
 9:          vbCR & vbCR & "User: " & Application.UserName & vbCR & _
10:          "          " & Application.OrganizationName
11:
12:    MsgBox "Operating System:" & _
13:          Application.OperatingSystem & vbCR & vbCR & _
14:          "Mouse is Available: " & _
15:          Application.MouseAvailable & vbCR & vbCR & _
16:          "Total Memory: " & Application.MemoryTotal & _
17:          vbCR & "Used Memory: " & Application.MemoryUsed & _
18:          vbCR & "Free Memory: " & Application.MemoryFree
19: End Sub
```

3. **BUG BUSTER:** Excel has an `InputBox` function that is slightly different from the
   VBA `InputBox` function. The Excel `InputBox` function has one more argument
   than the VBA `InputBox` function: a `Type` argument that enables you to specify the
   type of data that the user can enter into the `InputBox`. A value of 1 in the `Type`
   argument causes Excel to restrict the user's input to some valid number; Excel displays an error message if the user enters any text that contains characters other than
   the digits 0 through 9 or a single decimal point (.).

7

The GetNumber function in the following listing is intended to return a number obtained from the user. It uses the Excel InputBox function with the Type argument to restrict the user's input to a number. The Test_GetNumber procedure simply uses VBA's MsgBox to display the result of the GetNumber function so that you can test the GetNumber function's operation.

The GetNumber function has a flaw in it, however. When you try to use this function, VBA displays an error message stating that a named argument is not found. Alter the GetNumber function so that it performs correctly.

```
1:  Function GetNumber()
2:  'uses the application's InputBox function to return
3:  'a number obtained from the user.
4:
5:    GetNumber = InputBox(Prompt:="Enter a number:", _
6:                             Type:=1)
7:  End Function
8:
9:
10: Sub Test_GetNumber()
11:     MsgBox GetNumber
12: End Sub
```

4. When you use the Insert, Worksheet command in Excel to insert a worksheet, Excel gives the worksheet a name like *Sheet3* or *Sheet8*, depending on how many sheets you have inserted in the current working session. If you want the worksheet to have a different name, you must manually rename it by double-clicking the worksheet's tab or by choosing the Format, Sheet, Rename command.

It might be more convenient for you to insert a worksheet and give it the desired name in a single operation. In this exercise, you write a general-purpose procedure that inserts a worksheet into the active workbook and gives the new worksheet a new name at the same time. You should write this procedure from scratch in a module in the Personal.xls workbook. Name your procedure SheetInsert, and make sure that it performs the following actions:

(a) Use a variable to preserve an object reference to whatever sheet is active at the start of the procedure.

(b) Use VBA's InputBox function to obtain a new name from the user and store this name in a string variable.

(c) Use the Add method of the Worksheets collection to add a worksheet to the active workbook.

(d) Assign the sheet name obtained from the user to the Name property of the new worksheet.

(e) Use the `Select` method and the object reference you preserved at the start of the procedure to restore the worksheet that was originally active at the time the procedure started.

HINTS: Remember that the `ActiveSheet` property of the `Application` object returns an object reference to the active worksheet; also remember that when you use the `Add` method to insert a sheet, Excel inserts the new sheet and then makes it the active sheet. Try recording a macro that does the same job and studying the objects and methods that appear in the recorded macro.

7

WEEK 1

In Review: A Basic Workbook Creation Utility

After finishing your first week of learning how to program with VBA, you should feel comfortable using Excel's Macro Recorder to record and run a macro. You should now know how to start the VB Editor and how to use the Object Browser to locate your recorded macros. You should also feel comfortable using the Visual Basic Editor to edit recorded macros and procedures and to write your own procedures and functions from scratch.

The following listing contains an entire Excel VBA module and pulls together many of the topics from the previous week.

1

2

3

4

5

6

7

INPUT   **LISTING R1.1**   A NEW WORKBOOK CREATION UTILITY FOR EXCEL

```
 1:   Option Explicit
 2:
 3:   Sub NewBook()
 4:   'Creates a new workbook, then saves it with a name obtained
 5:   'from the user. This procedure was created by editing a
 6:   'recorded macro.
 7:     Const nfTitle = "Creating New Workbook File"
 8:     Const nfPrompt1 = "Enter the "        '1st part of prompt
 9:                                           '2nd part of prompt
10:     Const nfPrompt2 = " for this new workbook." & vbCr & _
11:                       "(Press Esc or choose Cancel to skip.)"
12:
13:     Dim FName As String                  'file name from user
14:
15:     'display message in Excel's status bar
16:     Application.StatusBar = "Creating New Workbook " & _
17:                       "File: NewBook Procedure"
18:
19:     Workbooks.Add     'Add method creates new workbook
20:
21:     With ActiveWorkbook          'now get summary information
22:
23:        'get the title information from user
24:        .Title = InputBox(prompt:=nfPrompt1 & "title" & _
25:                          nfPrompt2, Title:=nfTitle)
26:
27:        'get the subject information from user
28:        .Subject = InputBox(prompt:=nfPrompt1 & "subject" & _
29:                          nfPrompt2, Title:=nfTitle)
30:
31:        'get author information from user, suggest logon
32:        'user name (in UserName property of Application object)
33:        'as the default value for the author information
34:        .Author = InputBox(prompt:=nfPrompt1 & "author" & _
35:                          nfPrompt2, Title:=nfTitle, _
36:                          Default:=Application.UserName)
37:
38:        'get the list of keywords from user
39:        .Keywords = InputBox(prompt:=nfPrompt1 & "keywords" & _
40:                          nfPrompt2, Title:=nfTitle)
41:
42:        'get comments from user
43:        .Comments = InputBox(prompt:=nfPrompt1 & "comments" & _
44:                          nfPrompt2, Title:=nfTitle)
45:     End With
46:
47:        'Now get new file name from user by calling GetBookName
48:        'function. Call to GetBookName doesn't use nfPrompt2
49:        'string, because it's not appropriate to skip entering a
50:        'file name. Instead, call to GetBookName uses a prompt
```

```
51:        'suggesting the user store the new file in the My Documents
52:        'folder, with a name of NewWorkbook.
53:     FName = GetBookName(lPrompt:=nfPrompt1 & "File Name " & _
54:            "for this workbook." & vbCr & _
55:            "You MUST enter a file name." & vbCr & _
56:            "Include the disk drive and directory name, " & _
57:            "if you want to store this workbook someplace " & _
58:            "other than the current drive and directory.", _
59:                    lTitle:=nfTitle, _
60:                    lDflt:="C:\My Documents\NewWorkbook.xls")
61:
62:     'Now, save the new workbook file:
63:     ActiveWorkbook.SaveAs FileName:=FName, _
64:                        FileFormat:=xlNormal, _
65:                        ReadOnlyRecommended:=False, _
66:                        CreateBackup:=False
67:     'return control of status bar to Excel
68:     Application.StatusBar = False
69: End Sub      'NewFile
70:
71:
72:  Function GetBookName(lDflt As String, _
73:                    Optional lPrompt, _
74:                    Optional lTitle) As String
75:  'Gets workbook name, and returns it as a string. The
76:  'function has a required argument for the default file
77:  'name used in the input dialog box, and has two optional
78:  'arguments used for the prompt string and title used in the
79:  'input dialog box. If the title is not supplied when this
80:  'function is called, no title appears in input dialog box.
81:
82:      'check to see if a prompt string was included
83:    If IsMissing(lPrompt) Then
84:      'if no prompt string, then set one.
85:      lPrompt = "Enter a workbook name:"
86:    End If
87:
88:      'use InputBox to get the file name.
89:    GetBookName = InputBox(prompt:=lPrompt, _
90:                        Title:=lTitle, _
91:                        Default:=lDflt)
92:  End Function     'GetBookName
93:
94:
95:  Sub Test_GetBookName()
96:  'This procedure tests the GetBookName function
97:    MsgBox GetBookName("default only")
98:    MsgBox GetBookName(lPrompt:="Some prompt", _
99:                    lDflt:="default")
100:   MsgBox GetBookName(lDflt:="default", _
101:                    lTitle:="title")
102: End Sub
```

After completing the quiz and exercises in Days 1 and 2, you should be able to record the macro on which the NewBook procedure is based and then edit the NewBook macro to add the interactive features not found in the recorded macro. You should also feel comfortable entering the GetBookName function and the Test_GetBookName procedure.

The procedure and function listings here contain more comments than many of the other procedure and function examples you have seen so far. These comments are typical of real-world VBA programs, and provide enough information that any VBA programmer can easily read and understand the purpose and actions performed by the NewBook proce-dure and the GetBookName function. In particular, notice the comments at the beginning of each procedure and function declaration. The comments at the beginning of each pro-cedure or function describe the purpose of the procedure or function; the comments for the GetBookName function also describe the function's arguments and return result.

Line 1 of this listing contains the module-level **Option Explicit** command, which tells Visual Basic that all the variables used in this module must be explicitly declared with a **Dim** statement.

Line 3 contains the procedure declaration for the NewBook procedure. This procedure is based on the macro you recorded in Exercise 1 of Day 1, but has had several features added to it that cannot be incorporated into a procedure by recording alone. Lines 4, 5, and 6 contain comments about what the NewBook procedure does and its origins. (The original recorded macro, you might recall, created a new workbook and saved it with the name NewFile.xls.) The NewBook procedure creates a new workbook, gets the work-book's summary information from the user, gets a filename from the user, and then saves the workbook file, leaving the new file open as the active workbook.

Lines 7 through 11 declare constants for use within the NewFile procedure. The nfTitle constant contains a string used as a title for all the dialogs the NewBook procedure dis-plays. The nfPrompt1 constant contains a string used to form the first part of the prompt text displayed by every InputBox dialog that NewBook displays. The nfPrompt2 constant contains a string used to form the second part of the prompt text displayed by almost every InputBox dialog in the NewBook procedure. For cosmetic reasons, the nfPrompt2 constant contains a carriage-return character to start a new line in the dialog's text. Notice that this constant is assembled by concatenating two strings with the intrinsic VBA constant vbCr. The easiest way to include a carriage-return character in a string is to use one of the VBA intrinsic constants (vbCr, vbCrLf, vbNewLine) or to use the Chr function to provide the character equivalent of the carriage-return numeric code. Using a Visual Basic function such as Chr is not allowed in constant declarations, but you can concatenate strings or add numbers using literal or other constant values in a constant declaration.

Line 13 declares the only variable that NewBook uses. The FName variable stores the file-name obtained from the procedure's user.

Line 16 begins the actual work that the NewBook procedure performs. This line, as explained in the comment in line 15, sets the Excel status bar to display the message Creating New Workbook File: NewBook Procedure. The Excel status bar message is changed so that the procedure's user has some additional information about what activity is occurring.

Line 19 uses the Workbooks collection's Add method to create a new workbook. This line comes from the original recorded macro, and a comment describing its action has been added. Remember, one of the best ways to find out which objects and methods to use to carry out a particular task in VBA is to record that task, or one that is similar, and then edit or copy the resulting macro code. When line 19 executes, Excel creates a new work-book and makes it the active workbook.

Line 21 starts a **With...End With** statement in which the summary information for the new workbook is entered by the procedure's user. This **With...End With** statement was added to the original recorded macro. Remember that ActiveWorkbook is a property of the Application object that returns the current active workbook; in this case, the new workbook created in line 19.

Also added to the original recorded macro are the workbook's summary information properties (Title, Subject, Author, Keywords, and Comments). Each of these workbook properties is set by obtaining the information from the procedure's user with an InputBox statement. (This is the information that displays in the workbook's Summary tab in the Properties dialog that you can display with the File, Properties command.)

Notice that, whenever one of the workbook summary information properties—Title, Subject, Author, Keywords, or Comments— is used inside the **With...End With** state-ment, it is preceded by a dot separator (.). The dot separator is required to enable VBA to make the appropriate association between the specific property and the object it belongs to, as explained in Day 7. The NewBook procedure won't work correctly if the dot separators are omitted.

Line 24 uses the InputBox function to get a string from the user and then assigns that string to the Title property of the active workbook. Notice that the InputBox function call uses named arguments. The prompt argument is a string assembled by concatenating the nfPrompt1 constant, a literal string, and the nfPrompt2 string variable. The title of the dialog displayed by InputBox is supplied by the nfTitle string constant.

Line 28 similarly obtains a string from the user for the workbook's Subject property. Notice that this call to InputBox also uses named arguments, and that the prompt string is assembled the same way as for the Title property, except that a different literal string is used in the string expression for the dialog's prompt. By using a combination of constants, literal strings, and string variables, the programmer was able to provide specific, customized messages for each InputBox prompt without typing the entire string each time; this technique also uses less memory, requires less code, and is clearer and easier to read than typing out the entire prompt string each time it is used in a statement.

Lines 31 through 33 are comments about the action performed in line 34. Line 34 also uses InputBox to get a string from the user; in this case, however, the InputBox function call includes an argument to specify the default value in the InputBox dialog. The default value argument passed to InputBox comes from the UserName property of the Application object, which contains the user name you entered when you logged on to Windows. If your Windows installation doesn't require you to logon, the UserName property contains the user name you entered when you installed Excel.

Lines 39 and 43 get the keywords and subject summary information using the same techniques as lines 24 and 28. Line 45 signals the end of the **With...End With** statement.

Lines 47 through 52 are comments explaining what the next action in the procedure is and explaining why the nfPrompt2 variable is not used in the prompt for obtaining the new workbook name from the user.

Line 53 calls the GetBookName function and assigns its result to the FName variable. The GetBookName function is a special function written for the general-purpose task of obtaining a workbook filename from the user. You can use the GetBookName function from any of your procedures or macros in which you need to get a workbook filename from the user, whether you intend to open, create, or close that workbook. The operation of the GetBookName function is described in more detail later in this section. Line 53 calls GetBookName and passes arguments for the InputBox prompt and title message and for a suggested default workbook name. '

Line 63 uses the SaveAs method of a workbook object (specified by ActiveWorkbook) to save the workbook. This command also appeared in the original recorded macro. In the original macro, the filename specified for the file copy was a literal string. For this version of the NewBook procedure, the SaveAs statement was edited so that the Filename:= named argument uses whatever string is stored in the FName variable as the name of the saved workbook. The statement was reformatted to be more easily readable. Also, a couple of the named arguments from the original, recorded statement were removed; they were optional arguments and had zero-length strings assigned to them. The Macro

Recorder often records object method arguments that are not really required; often, if you see named arguments in recorded macros that pass empty strings, you can safely delete those named arguments.

Finally, line 68 restores control of the status bar to Excel. This line is fairly important; without this line, Excel continues to display the status bar message specified in line 16 until you actually exit from Excel or until another procedure changes the status bar message.

The NewBook procedure ends in line 69 of the listing with the **End Sub** keywords. The remaining code in this listing defines other functions or procedures in the module. You might recall that the original recorded macro closed the workbook file after creating and saving it. Because a user is most likely to want to begin working immediately with a workbook that they create, the recorded instruction that closed the workbook file was removed from this version of the NewBook procedure.

Line 72 begins the function declaration for the GetBookName function. This function has three arguments and returns a string value. The first argument, lDflt is required; the remaining two arguments, lPrompt and lTitle, are optional. Notice that the function declaration has been divided over several different lines in the module by using the line-continuation symbol. The function declaration was split up like this so that it is easier to see what the various function arguments and their options are. Lines 75 through 80 are comments that explain the behavior and purpose of the GetBookName function.

Line 83 of the listing begins the actual code for the GetBookName function. This line uses the **If...Then** structure (very briefly introduced in this week) and the IsMissing function to determine whether a prompt argument was included when GetBookName was called. If a prompt was not included, line 85 assigns a sort of generic prompt suitable for the task that this function carries out.

Line 89 is the heart of the GetBookName function: It contains the function assignment statement to specify the function's return value and uses the InputBox function to get that value at the same time. Notice that the GetBookName function arguments are simply passed on as arguments to the InputBox function.

The GetBookName function was written for use with the NewBook procedure for a couple of different reasons. First, getting a workbook name is likely to be a frequent activity in many different procedures. Second, using a function to obtain the workbook name makes it possible to concentrate all the relevant code in a single location, without repeating that code over and over again in every procedure that needs to get a workbook name. If you ever decide to alter how various procedures obtain filenames from the user—say, by validating the filename in some way—you only have to modify the GetBookName function to have the changes applied in all procedures that use GetBookName to get workbook names from the user.

Line 92 contains the keywords **End Function** to end the GetBookName function definition.

Finally, lines 95 through 102 define a procedure named Test_GetBookName that tests the GetBookName function. Before relying on the GetBookName function to behave correctly in the NewBook procedure, Test_GetBookName was used to test GetBookName. Notice that Test_GetBookName tests all the possible combinations of required and optional arguments for GetBookName, and simply displays the result of the GetBookName function. If the GetBookName function were slightly more complex, this procedure should also have used variables and displayed the original argument values to ensure that GetBookName did not alter its arguments. In this case, the function is short enough that you can easily see it does not alter its arguments—except for lPrompt, which only gets modified if it is missing in the first place.

WEEK 2

At a Glance

You've finished your first week of learning how to program in Visual Basic for Applications. By now, you should feel comfortable entering, editing, and using procedures and functions in your modules, whether you record a macro and then edit it, or whether you write a procedure or function from scratch.

What's Ahead?

The second week, like the first, covers a lot of material. You'll learn about many of the key features of Visual Basic for Applications.

In Day 8, "Making Decisions in Visual Basic," you learn how to use VBA's decision-making structures: `If...Then` and `Select Case`. In Day 9, "Repeating Actions in Visual Basic: Loops," you learn how to add efficient repetition to your procedures by using VBA's looping structures.

In Day 10, "Advanced Techniques for Using Data Types and Variables," you learn more about VBA's scope rules and how to increase or limit the scope of variables, procedures, and functions. In Day 11, "Creating Your Own Data Types and Object Classes," you learn how to create your own custom data types with the `Type` keyword. Day 11 also teaches you how to use class modules to create your own object classes; you can use custom object classes to create new objects for use in Excel or to enhance or alter the behavior of built-in Excel objects.

In Day 12, "Creating Libraries and Whole Programs: Modular Programming Techniques," you learn how to create libraries of VBA procedures and functions. Day 12 also gets you started writing programs that consist of several procedures and functions working together, and shows you how to add argument lists to your procedures.

In Day 13, "Managing Files with Visual Basic for Applications," you learn how to use VBA's file management functions and statements to get information about files, create or remove disk folders, and copy or delete files. Day 13 also shows you how to use custom data files with VBA's **Open**, **Write**, and **Read** statements. Day 14, "Arrays," shows you how to create and sort arrays.

The material in this second week builds on what you learned in the first week. Be sure to answer all the quiz questions at the end of each day and be sure you try to complete each of the exercises. The best way to make the new material that you learn a real part of your everyday knowledge is to put that knowledge to work. You must write programs in order to learn how to program.

By the end of the first week, you learned to write simple VBA functions and procedures to carry out a single task. By the time you finish the second week, you should be able to write complex programs that can perform just about any job. Like the first week, the second week covers a lot of material, but if you take the information one chapter a day, you shouldn't have any problems.

DAY 8

Making Decisions in Visual Basic for Applications

Today, you learn how to write procedures or functions that alter their behavior based on various conditions. You learn

- What decision-making and branching commands are and how they work.
- How to construct logical statements to determine which branch of code your procedure should execute.
- How to make simple decisions in a function or procedure with the `If...Then` decision-making structure.
- How to make more complex decisions by nesting `If...Then` structures.
- How to make decisions involving many choices at once with the `Select...Case` structure.
- How to unconditionally change the execution of your code with a `GoTo` statement.
- Why and how to end a procedure, function, or an entire program early.
- How to use the `Buttons` argument in `MsgBox` to let your procedure's user make simple choices.

Understanding VBA's Decision-Making Commands

Up to this point, you've written procedures and functions that VBA executes in a completely linear fashion, much the same way that VBA executes a recorded macro: VBA begins executing statements starting with the first statement after the procedure's or function's declaration line. VBA continues to execute each statement, line by line, until it reaches the **End Sub** or **End Function** statement that marks the end of that procedure's or function's definition, or until a runtime error occurs. The *flow* of VBA's execution goes straight through, from beginning to end, without alteration.

Procedures and functions like this, although capable of carrying out fairly sophisticated tasks, lack the capability to make decisions that result in performing different actions under different circumstances. You'll encounter many situations where you need or want your procedures or functions to perform different actions under different circumstances. For example, if you write a procedure that gets the name of a workbook from the user and then opens that workbook, you might consider it desirable to have your procedure offer to create the workbook if it doesn't already exist. In a situation like this, your procedure would use VBA's decision-making statements to offer the user the chance to create the workbook. Your procedure would then use VBA's decision-making commands again to evaluate the user's choice and either create the workbook or end the procedure's execution.

You will frequently use decision-making commands to evaluate specific items of data and then choose different actions based on that single data item. For example, you might write a procedure that checks a column in a worksheet to make sure that all of the numbers entered in that column are between 1 and 10. Your procedure might then examine each column entry separately and execute some special action whenever it encounters a column entry outside the specified range.

Decisions do not always involve reacting to problems. If you want your procedure's user to make some kind of a choice about what your procedure should do next, you might use the InputBox function to get text input from the user, or use the MsgBox function to let the user make a choice by clicking a command button in the message dialog. (Using MsgBox to let your procedure's user make choices is described at the end of this chapter.) After you get the user's choice, your procedure must be able to execute a course of action corresponding to that choice.

Your procedures, of course, can't really "make a decision" the same way that a human being can. Your procedures can, however, choose predefined courses of action based on simple conditions and make relatively complex decisions by combining smaller decisions.

8

When you use VBA's decision-making statements, you define a condition or set of conditions under which VBA executes one or another *branch* of your procedure's code. Because decision-making statements affect the top-to-bottom flow of execution in your program, they are often referred to as *flow control* or *program control* statements, but are known more technically as *conditional* and *unconditional branching* statements.

A *conditional branching statement* is a decision-making structure that chooses one or another branch of the procedure's code based on some predefined condition or group of conditions. An *unconditional branching statement* is a statement that simply alters the flow of the procedure's execution without depending on any specific condition. You'll use conditional branching with much greater frequency than you'll use unconditional branching.

A conditional branching statement—such as `If...Then`—typically consists of the following elements:

- A logical expression that specifies the conditions under which a particular series of VBA statements should be executed.
- VBA keywords that mark the beginning and end of the VBA statements that are to be conditionally executed.

When VBA encounters a conditional branching statement such as `If...Then` it first evaluates the logical expression that describes the conditions under which a particular action should be performed. If the logical expression is `True`, the predefined conditions are fulfilled and VBA executes the designated statements.

When VBA encounters an unconditional branching statement—the `GoTo`—it immediately begins executing the statements indicated by the branching command.

You specify the criteria on which VBA makes decisions in conditional branching statements by constructing a logical expression that describes the condition under which you want VBA to execute a particular series of statements. You use VBA's various comparison and logical operators (described in Day 4) to construct the logical expressions in your branching statements.

Making Simple Choices

VBA's simplest decision-making statements are the `If...Then` and `If...Then...Else` statements. The `If...Then` statement gives VBA the capability to choose a single alternative branch of a procedure's execution. The closely related `If...Then...Else` statement gives VBA the capability to choose between two alternative branches of a procedure's execution based on whether the specified condition is true.

Choosing a Single Branch Using If...Then

You've already seen examples of the **If...Then** statement used to test whether or not a function's optional arguments were included when the function was called. The **If...Then** statement chooses a single alternative branch of execution in your procedure or function code.

The **If...Then** statement has two different syntax forms. The simplest form is the single-line **If...Then** statement:

    If *condition* Then *statements*

condition is any logical expression and *statements* can be none, one, or many VBA statements; all the statements must be on the same line, however. When VBA executes a statement like this, it first evaluates the logical expression represented by *condition*; if this logical expression evaluates to **True**, VBA executes the statement or statements after the **Then** keyword up to the end of the line. VBA then resumes execution with the first statement after the line that contains the **If...Then** statement.

If the logical expression represented by *condition* is **False**, VBA immediately executes the first statement in the line following the line that contains the **If...Then** statement, without executing the alternate branch at all. The following procedure fragment shows a typical single-line **If...Then** statement:

▲   ` If temperature > 100 then MsgBox "Too hot!" `

PLACING SEVERAL STATEMENTS ON THE SAME LINE

You can include multiple VBA statements on a single line by separating each statement with a colon (:), as shown in the following example:

    statement1 : *statement2* : *statementN*

In this line, *statement1*, *statement2*, and *statementN* each represent any single, valid VBA statement. You can include as many statements on a single line as you want, up to the maximum line length limit for a module.

Lines with many statements in them can be difficult to read and understand, however. In general, you should only place a single statement on each line.

Listing 8.1 shows a slightly modified version of the GetBookName function shown previously in the "Week 1 in Review" listings.

INPUT   **LISTING 8.1**   THE GetBookName FUNCTION

```
1:  Function GetBookName(lDflt As String, _
2:                      Optional Prmpt, _
3:                      Optional lTitle) As String
4:
5:      'check for prompt string included in the argument list
6:      If IsMissing(Prmpt) Then Prmpt = "Enter a workbook name:"
7:
8:      'use InputBox to get the filename.
9:      GetBookName = InputBox(prompt:=Prmpt, _
10:                            Title:=lTitle, _
11:                            default:=lDflt)
12: End Function    'GetBookName
```

ANALYSIS   This function works exactly as described in the "Week 1 in Review" section. Line 1 contains the function declaration, which specifies one required argument and two optional arguments for the function and also specifies the function's result as a **String**.

Pay close attention to line 6, which contains a single-line **If...Then** statement. When VBA executes line 6, it first evaluates the condition expression IsMissing(Prmpt). The IsMissing function returns **True** if the Prmpt argument is missing from the argument list at the time the GetBookName function is called. If IsMissing returns **True**, VBA executes the statement Prmpt = "Enter a workbook name:", which assigns a default string to the Prmpt argument variable. If IsMissing returns **False**, VBA does *not* execute the statement after the **Then** keyword and the contents of the Prmpt argument variable remain unaltered.

In this way, the GetBookName function provides a default value for its own Prmpt argument whenever the Prmpt optional argument is omitted. The assignment to the Prmpt argument variable occurs only when the IsMissing function returns **True**.

Finally, line 9 of GetBookName uses the InputBox function to obtain the return value of the function.

▼ SYNTAX   The second form of the **If...Then** statement is called a *block* **If** statement. In the block **If...Then** statement, the condition and statements are written on separate lines, as shown in the following general syntax:

```
If condition Then
    statements
End If
```

▼ *condition*, like the single-line **If...Then** statement, represents the logical expression defining the condition under which VBA should execute the alternate statements. *statements* represents none, one, or several VBA statements; the statements can be on a single line or on several lines. Finally, the keywords **End If** signal VBA that the end of the alternate branch of statements has been reached. The **End If** keywords must appear on a line by themselves, although you can include a trailing comment on that line.

Just like the single-line **If...Then** statement, VBA first evaluates the logical expression represented by *condition*. If this expression is **True**, VBA executes the statements in the alternate branch starting with the first statement on the line after the line containing the **If...Then** keywords. VBA continues executing statements in the alternate branch until it reaches the **End If** keywords. VBA then continues executing statements starting with the first statement after the **End If**.

If the logical expression represented by *condition* evaluates to **False**, VBA does not execute any of the statements in the alternate branch; instead VBA immediately con-
▲ tinues executing statements beginning with the first statement after the **End If**.

You've already seen a couple of examples of the block **If...Then** statement in previous lessons. The following lines show a typical block **If...Then** statement:

```
If temperature > 100 Then
    MsgBox "Too hot!"
End If
```

In the preceding statement, if the value stored in the temperature variable is greater than 100, VBA executes the MsgBox statement to display the message *Too hot!*. If the value stored in the temperature variable is 100 or less, VBA executes the first statement that appears after the **End If** keywords. Remember, the **End If** keywords must appear on a line by themselves.

Do

DO use a single-line **If...Then** statement when the logical expression for the condition is not very long and there are only one or two statements in the alternate program branch.

DO use the block **If...Then** statement if the logical expression is long or if there are many statements in the alternate program branch. The block **If** form is usually much easier to read and understand.

8

DON'T

DON'T forget that the **End If** keywords terminating a block **If** must appear on a line by themselves.

Choosing Between Branches Using `If...Then...Else`

The `If...Then` statement allows you to specify only a single alternate branch of statements in your procedure. Frequently, however, you will need or want to choose between one of two different alternate statement branches depending on a specific condition. VBA provides the `If...Then...Else` and `If...Then...ElseIf` statements for just that purpose.

▼ SYNTAX

Like `If...Then`, VBA's `If...Then...Else` statement has two forms: a single-line form and a block form. The general syntax for the single-line `If...Then...Else` statement is

```
If Condition Then Statements Else ElseStatements
```

`Condition` represents any valid logical expression. `Statements` and `ElseStatements` each represent any one or more VBA statements. Like the single-line `If...Then` statement, all the statements and keywords of the single-line `If...Then...Else` must appear on the same line.

When VBA executes the single-line `If...Then...Else` statement, it first evaluates the logical expression represented by `Condition`; if this expression evaluates as **True**, VBA executes the statements between the keywords **Then** and **Else** (represented by `Statements`) and resumes execution with the first statement following the line that contains the `If...Then...Else`.

If the logical expression represented by `Condition` evaluates to **False**, VBA executes the statements after the **Else** keyword up to the end of the line (represented by `ElseStatements`) and continues execution with the first statement after the line that

▲ contains the `If...Then...Else`.

The following line shows a typical example of a single-line `If...Then...Else` statement:

```
If temperature > 100 Then MsgBox "Hot!" Else MsgBox "Less Hot!"
```

In this example, if the value in the `temperature` variable is greater than 100, the condition expression is **True** and VBA executes the `MsgBox` statement to display the message *Hot!* onscreen. If `temperature` contains a number that is 100 or less, the condition is **False** and VBA executes the `MsgBox` statement after the **Else** keyword to display the message *Less Hot!* onscreen.

As you can tell from this simple single-line **If...Then...Else** example, the single-line form might not be easy for a human being to read. Also, because all elements of a single-line **If...Then...Else** statement must appear on the same line, the size and number of statements you can include in the alternate execution branches are limited by the amount of space available in the line.

▼SYNTAX

The block **If...Then...Else** statement is easier to read and understand, and, because you can place statements on different lines within the block **If...Then...Else** statement, there is no limit on the size or number of statements you can include in the alternate branches. The general syntax of the block **If...Then...Else** statement is

```
If Condition Then
     Statements
Else
     ElseStatements
End If
```

Condition represents any valid logical expression; *Statements* and *ElseStatements* each represent none, one, or several VBA statements. When VBA executes a block **If...Then...Else** statement, it first evaluates the logical expression represented by *Condition*. If the expression evaluates to **True**, VBA executes all the statements (represented by *Statements*) between the **Then** keyword and the **Else** keyword. VBA then resumes execution with the first statement that appears after the **End If** keywords, which signal the end of the block **If...Then...Else** statement.

If the logical expression represented by *Condition* evaluates to **False**, VBA executes all the statements (represented by *ElseStatements*) between the **Else** keyword and the **End If** keywords. VBA then continues execution with the first statement that appears after the **End If** keywords. Like the block **If...Then** statement, the **End If** keywords must appear on a line by themselves, although you can add a trailing comment to that line.

▲

The **If...Then...Else** statement chooses one or the other branch, but never both at the same time. The following example shows a typical block **If...Then...Else** statement:

```
If temperature > 100 Then
     MsgBox "Hot!"
Else
     MsgBox "Less Hot!"
End If
```

This example contains the same statement shown for the single-line **If...Then...Else**, but using the block form instead. When VBA executes this statement, it first evaluates the logical expression `temperature > 100`. If `temperature` contains a value greater than 100—the logical expression is **True**—VBA executes the `MsgBox "Hot!"` statement and then executes the first statement after the **End If** keywords. If the number stored in the temperature variable is 100 or less, the logical condition expression is **False** and VBA executes the MsgBox "Less Hot!" statement; VBA then continues execution with the first statement after the **End If** keywords.

Listing 8.2 shows another version of the GetBookName function with a block **If...Then...Else** statement added to it.

LISTING 8.2   THE BLOCK **If...Then...Else** STATEMENT

```
 1: Function GetBookName(ByVal lDflt As String, _
 2:                       Optional Prmpt, _
 3:                       Optional lTitle) As String
 4:
 5:     'was a prompt string included in the argument list?
 6:     If IsMissing(Prmpt) Then Prmpt = "Enter a workbook name:"
 7:
 8:     'if default name is not an empty string, convert it to
 9:     'all uppercase letters, otherwise assign a name to it.
10:     If lDflt <> "" Then
11:        lDflt = UCase(lDflt)
12:     Else
13:        lDflt = "NEWFILE.XLS"
14:     End If
15:
16:     'use InputBox to get the filename.
17:     GetBookName = InputBox(prompt:=Prmpt, _
18:                            Title:=lTitle, _
19:                            default:=lDflt)
20: End Function
21:
22:
23: Sub Test_GetBookName()
24: 'This procedure tests the GetBookName function
25:    MsgBox GetBookName("")
26:    MsgBox GetBookName("default only")
27:    MsgBox GetBookName(Prmpt:="A prompt", lDflt:="default")
28:    MsgBox GetBookName(lDflt:="default", lTitle:="title")
29: End Sub
```

This version of GetBookName operates exactly like the version shown previously in Listing 8.1, with the exception of the added **If...Then...Else** statement in lines 10 through 14.

The first line in this function that VBA executes is line 6, which uses a single-line **If...Then** statement to test whether the optional Prmpt argument was supplied when the function was called. If the Prmpt argument is missing, VBA executes the assignment statement at the end of line 6 to assign a default value to the Prmpt argument variable.

The next line VBA executes is line 10, which begins a block `If...Then...Else` statement. When VBA executes this line, it first evaluates the logical expression `lDflt <> ""`. This expression evaluates to `True` if the value contained in the `lDflt` argument variable is *not* an empty (zero-length) string—although the `lDflt` argument is required, it is possible for you to call the `GetBookName` function with an empty string passed as the `lDflt` argument.

If the `lDflt` argument does not contain an empty string, VBA executes the `lDflt = UCase(lDflt)` statement, which uses the `UCase` function to convert the string in the `lDflt` argument to all uppercase letters. VBA continues executing statements starting with line 17, the first statement after the `End If` keywords of the `If...Then...Else` statement.

If the `lDflt` argument *does* contain an empty string, VBA executes the `Else` branch of the `If...Then...Else` statement, consequently executing the `lDflt = "NEWFILE.XLS"` statement, which simply assigns a string to the `lDflt` argument variable. VBA continues executing statements starting with line 17, the first statement after the `End If` keywords of the `If...Then...Else` statement.

Line 17 assigns the result of the `InputBox` function as the `GetBookName` function result.

Note

> Notice that the function declaration (line 1) for this version of the `GetBookName` now passes the `lDflt` argument by value because the added `If...Then...Else` statement in lines 10 through 14 alters the `lDflt` argument variable. The `ByVal` keyword was added so that the source of the `lDflt` argument is not permanently changed outside of the `GetBookName` function. (Remember, passing by value provides your function with a copy of the argument data, as explained in Day 6.)

Finally, lines 23 through 29 of Listing 8.2 contain a procedure used to test the behavior of the `GetBookName` function. Now, whenever you call the `GetBookName` function, it always displays the suggested default workbook name in capital letters, and if an empty string for the default book name is passed to the function, the function supplies its own default name: `NEWFILE.XLS`.

ANALYSIS You will see many more examples of `If...Then` and `If...Then...Else` statements throughout the remaining lessons in this book.

Making Complex Choices

So far, you have seen how to construct branching statements that choose a single alternate branch of procedure execution or choose between one of two alternate branches of procedure execution. Frequently, however, you will need or want to make more complex choices in your procedures, choosing between three, four, or more different alternate branches.

Nested If...Then Statements

For more complex decision-making requirements, you can place an **If...Then** or **If...Then...Else** statement inside another **If...Then** or **If...Then...Else** statement, which is called *nesting* statements. (*Nesting* means placing one type of flow control structure inside another.)

Although you can nest the single-line forms of **If...Then** and **If...Then...Else** statements, such statements are quite difficult for a human reader to understand. When you nest **If...Then** and **If...Then...Else** statements, use the block forms of these statements for clarity.

Listing 8.3 shows a simple procedure to illustrate how nested **If...Then...Else** statements work. The EvalTemperature procedure gets a number from the user and then evaluates that number.

 Note

> The example in Listing 8.3, for simplicity, nests only one **If...Then...Else** statement inside another. You can nest as many **If...Then...Else** statements inside each other as you want.

INPUT **LISTING 8.3** NESTED **If...Then...Else** STATEMENTS

```
1:  Sub EvalTemperature()
2:
3:      Dim temperature
4:
5:      temperature = Application.InputBox( _
6:                          prompt:="Enter the temperature:", _
7:                          Title:="EvalTemp Procedure", _
8:                          Type:=1)
9:
10:     If temperature > 100 Then
11:         MsgBox "Too hot!"
```

continues

LISTING 8.3 CONTINUED

```
12:   Else
13:     If temperature > 50 Then
14:       MsgBox "Stay cool!"
15:     Else
16:       MsgBox "Too cold!"
17:     End If
18:   End If
19: End Sub
```

ANALYSIS Line 3 of the procedure declares the `temperature` variable to store input obtained from the user. Line 5 uses the Excel `Application` object's version of the `InputBox` function, and includes the `Type:=1` optional argument to specify that only a numeric value may be entered in the input dialog. VBA displays an error message if the user enters a non-numeric value, and waits until the user does enter a numeric value or chooses Cancel in the input dialog. (The `Type:=` argument is not available in VBA's `InputBox` function.)

Pay close attention to lines 10 through 18 in this listing. When VBA executes line 10, it first evaluates the logical expression `temperature > 100`. If the value stored in the `temperature` variable is greater than 100, VBA executes line 11, displaying the message *Too hot!* onscreen, and continues execution with the first statement after the **End If** keywords in line 18—in this case, the end of the procedure.

If the value in the `temperature` variable is 100 or less, however, the condition for the **If** statement beginning in line 10 is **False** and VBA executes the **Else** branch beginning in line 13.

Line 13 starts another **If...Then...Else** statement, which is nested inside the **If...Then...Else** statement that begins in line 10. This second **If...Then...Else** statement in line 13 is the *inner* statement of the nested **If...Then...Else** statements because it is contained completely inside the *outer* statement that begins in line 10.

If the logical expression `temperature > 50` evaluates to **True** (the value in the `temperature` variable is greater than 50), VBA executes the `MsgBox` statement in line 14, which displays the message *Stay cool!* onscreen. VBA then continues execution with the first line after the **End If** statement in line 17—in this case, the end of the outer **If...Then...Else** statement.

If the value in the `temperature` variable is 50 or less, however, the logical expression in the inner **If...Then...Else** statement in line 13 evaluates to **False** and VBA executes the **Else** branch of the inner **If...Then...Else** statement in line 16, which displays the message *Too cold!* onscreen. VBA then continues execution with the first line after the **End If** statement in line 17.

8

The **If...Then** keywords in line 10, the **Else** keyword in line 12, and the **End If** keywords in line 18 are all part of the outer **If...Then...Else** statement. The **If...Then** keywords in line 13, the **Else** keyword in line 15, and the **End If** keywords in line 17 are all part of the inner, nested **If...Then...Else** statement.

Notice how the statements and keywords that are part of the nested **If...Then...Else** statement are indented from the keywords and statements that form the outer **If...Then...Else** statement. This indentation helps you more easily identify which keywords and statements belong to the inner and outer nested **If...Then...Else** statements; the inner **If...Then...Else** statement is indented farther from the left edge than the outer statement.

Like other indentation, there is nothing in VBA that forces you to indent your code, but you should always indent nested **If...Then...Else** statements to make your code easier to read, understand, and maintain.

Do

DO use varying levels of indentation in your source code to make your code more readable and easier to understand, especially when nesting **If...Then...Else** statements.

DON'T

DON'T write code that looks like this:

```
If temperature > 100 Then
MsgBox "Too hot!"
Else
If temperature > 50 Then
MsgBox "Stay cool!"
Else
MsgBox "Too cold!"
End If
End If
```

Although VBA will execute these statements in exactly the same way as lines 10 through 18 in Listing 8.3, you can see that it is almost impossible to tell which statements and keywords form the inner and outer nested **If...Then...Else** statements.

Using If...Then...ElseIf

VBA provides a shorthand version of the **If...Then...Else** statement to provide a more concise equivalent for the kind of nested **If...Then...Else** statements shown in Listing 8.3. This shorthand variation is the **If...Then...ElseIf** statement.

▼ SYNTAX

The general syntax for the **If...Then...ElseIf** statement is

```
If Condition1 Then
        Statements
ElseIf Condition2
        ElseIfStatements
[Else
        ElseStatements]
End If
```

Condition1 and *Condition2* each represent any valid logical expression; *Statements*, *ElseIfStatements*, and *ElseStatements* each represent none, one, or several VBA statements.

When VBA executes an **If...Then...ElseIf** statement, it first evaluates the logical expression represented by *Condition1*. If the expression evaluates to **True**, VBA executes all the statements (represented by *Statements*) between the **Then** keyword and the **ElseIf** keyword. VBA then resumes execution with the first statement that appears after the **End If** keywords, which signal the end of the **If...Then...ElseIf** statement.

If the *Condition1* logical expression evaluates to **False**, VBA evaluates the logical expression represented by *Condition2*. If the *Condition2* expression evaluates to **True**, VBA executes all the statements (represented by *ElseIfStatements*) between the **ElseIf** keyword and the **End If** (or optional **Else**) keywords. VBA then continues execution with the first statement that appears after the **End If** keywords. The **End If** keywords must appear on a line by themselves.

If the *Condition2* logical expression evaluates to **False**, VBA skips the *ElseIfStatements* and continues execution with the first statement after the **End If** keywords. You can optionally include an **Else** clause in the **If...Then...ElseIf** statement. If the *Condition1* logical expression *and* the *Condition2* logical expressions are **False** and there is an **Else** clause, VBA executes the statements represented by *ElseStatements*. After executing the *ElseStatements*, VBA continues execution with the first statement after the **End If** keywords.

The following example shows lines 10 through 18 of Listing 8.3 rewritten to use the **If...Then...ElseIf** statement:

```
If temperature > 100 Then
    MsgBox "Too hot!"
```

```
ElseIf temperature > 50 Then
     MsgBox "Stay cool!"
Else
     MsgBox "Too cold!"
End If
```

The preceding **If...Then...ElseIf** statement behaves exactly the same as the nested **If...Then...Else** statements in lines 10 through 18 of Listing 8.3, with the same results—this form is just more compact.

If you want, you can include more than one **ElseIf** clause in an **If...Then...ElseIf** statement as long as all the **ElseIf** clauses come before the **Else** clause. VBA only executes the statements in an **ElseIf** clause if the logical expression in that clause is true.

Using the **If...Then...ElseIf** statement is a matter of personal preference. Many programmers feel that their code is more understandable and maintainable by using nested **If...Then...Else** statements instead of the **If...Then...ElseIf** statement. Originally, **If...Then...ElseIf** was added to BASIC to provide a functionality similar to the **Select...Case** statement described in the next section; it remains in VBA in order to make it easier to translate existing BASIC programs into VBA. When you need to make very many choices, the **Select Case** statement is superior to either nested **If...Then...Else** statements or the more compact **If...Then...ElseIf** statement.

Using the **Select Case** Statement

The example of nested **If...Then...Else** statements in Listing 8.3—and the **If...Then...ElseIf** statements explained previously—easily make a three-way decision, but what if you need to choose between 5, 8, or 10 different courses of action? What if several possible conditions all lead to the same branching choice?

To choose among several possible branches of procedure execution, you can nest **If...Then...Else** statements many levels deep, but following the course of the decision branches becomes progressively more difficult for the human reader. Alternatively, you could add additional **ElseIf** clauses to an **If...Then...ElseIf** statement, with one **ElseIf** clause for each conditional branch. The **If...Then...ElseIf** statement has a similar problem, however: When there are many **ElseIf** clauses, the **If...Then...ElseIf** statement becomes difficult to read and follow.

> ## Do
>
> **DO** use a **Select Case** statement if you need to choose among more than three or four possible branches of execution.

> ## DON'T
>
> **DON'T** nest **If...Then...Else** statements too deeply; they can be almost impossible for a human reader to follow.

Fortunately, VBA offers a conditional branching statement for use when you must choose among a large number of different branches: the **Select Case** statement. **Select Case** operates much the same as multiple independent **If** statements, but it is a bit easier to follow. You use the **Select Case** keywords with multiple **Case** statements, where each **Case** statement tests for the occurrence of a different condition. Only one of the **Case** branches will be executed. A **Case** branch can contain none, one, or several VBA statements.

The **Select Case** statement has the following general syntax:

```
Select Case TestExpression
     Case ExpressionList1
          statements1
     Case ExpressionList2
          statements2

     .
     .
     .

     Case ExpressionListN
          statementsN
     [Case Else
          ElseStatements]
End Select
```

TestExpression is any numeric or string expression, usually a single variable. *ExpressionList1*, *ExpressionList2*, and *ExpressionListN* each represent a list of logical expressions. Each expression in the list must be separated by a comma. *statements1*, *statements2*, *statementsN*, and *ElseStatements* each represent none, one, or several VBA statements. You can include as few or as many **Case** *ExpressionList* clauses in a **Select Case** statement as you want.

When VBA executes a **Select Case** statement, it first evaluates the *TestExpression* and then compares the result of that expression to each of the expressions listed in each *ExpressionList*. If the value represented by *TestExpression* matches an expression in the *ExpressionList* for one of the **Case** clauses, VBA executes the statements for that

8

clause. If the *TestExpression* value matches more than one **Case** clause, VBA only executes the statements in the first matching **Case** clause. *TestExpression* is frequently just a single variable name or a mathematical or numeric expression, rather than a logical expression. The expressions in the *ExpressionList* are typically logical expressions.

When VBA finishes executing the statements in the first matching **Case** clause, it continues execution with the first statement after the **End Select** keywords, which mark the end of the **Select Case** statement.

If the *TestExpression* value does *not* match any of the **Case** clauses and the optional **Case Else** clause is present, VBA executes the statements represented by *ElseStatements* before continuing on to the statement after the **Select Case** statement.

In the separate **Case** clauses, the *ExpressionList* can consist of one or more expressions separated by a comma. *ExpressionList* has the following general syntax:

```
expression1, expression2, expressionN
```

Expressions in *ExpressionList* can be any numeric string or logical expression. The expressions in *ExpressionList* can also specify a range of values by using the **To** operator:

```
expression1 To expression2
```

For example, to specify a range of numbers from 1 to 10 in a **Case** *ExpressionList* clause, you use the following expression:

```
Case 1 To 10
```

To select branches based on whether *TestExpression* is greater than, less than, equal to, or some other relational comparison, use the following general syntax:

```
Is ComparisonOperator expression
```

In the preceding line, *ComparisonOperator* is any of VBA's relational operators except for the **Is** and **Like** operators; *expression* is any VBA expression. To execute the statements in a **Case** branch when the *TestExpression* is greater than 10, for example, you would use the following expression:

```
Case Is > 10
```

 Note

> The **Is** keyword used in **Select Case** statements is *not* the same as the **Is** comparison operator; you cannot use the **Is** comparison operator or the **Like** operator in a **Select Case** statement.

Listing 8.4 shows an example of a **Select Case** statement.

```
 1:  Sub EvalTemperature()
 2:
 3:    Dim temperature
 4:
 5:    temperature = Application.InputBox( _
 6:                        prompt:="Enter the temperature:", _
 7:                        Title:="EvalTemp Procedure", _
 8:                        Type:=1)
 9:
10:    Select Case temperature
11:      Case Is > 100
12:        MsgBox "Too hot!"
13:      Case 75 To 100
14:        MsgBox "Stay cool!"
15:      Case 50 To 74
16:        MsgBox "Okay."
17:      Case Is > 32
18:        MsgBox "Pretty cold."
19:      Case Else
20:        MsgBox "Freezing and below!"
21:    End Select
22: End Sub
```

ANALYSIS   The EvalTemperature procedure in this listing works essentially the same as the procedure in Listing 8.3. Like the procedure in Listing 8.3, line 5 gets a number from the user.

Lines 10 through 21 contain a **Select Case** statement. Line 10 contains the start of the **Select Case** statement. The test expression in line 10 consists of a single variable: the temperature variable. As you know, the result of an expression containing a single variable is the value stored in the variable. VBA therefore compares whatever value is stored in the temperature variable to the conditions specified in each **Case** branch of the **Select Case** statement.

First, VBA checks to see whether the value in the temperature variable matches the condition specified in the first **Case** clause (line 11). This **Case** condition contains the expression **Is > 100**. If the value in temperature is greater than 100, the MsgBox statement in line 12 executes, displaying the message *Too hot!* onscreen. The condition in this case branch is equivalent to the following **If** statement:

```
If temperature > 100 then MsgBox "Too hot!"
```

When VBA finishes executing the statement in line 12, it continues execution with the first statement in the procedure after line 21, which contains the **End Select** keywords that mark the end of the **Select Case** statement.

If the value in the temperature variable is 100 or less, VBA skips to the next **Case** condition in line 13. This **Case** condition uses the **To** operator to specify a range of numbers. If the value in temperature is any number from 75 to 100, VBA executes the MsgBox statement in line 14 and continues execution with the first statement after the **End Select** keywords in line 21.

If the value in the temperature variable is not in the range of 75 to 100, VBA skips to the next **Case** condition in line 15, which also tests to see whether the value in temperature falls within a particular range: this time the range of numbers from 50 to 74. If the test expression (temperature) matches the condition, VBA executes line 16 and continues with the statements after the **End Select** statement; otherwise, VBA again skips to the next **Case** condition. VBA behaves the same way for the remaining **Case** condition in line 17.

Finally, if the value in the temperature variable does not match any of the **Case** conditions, VBA executes the **Case Else** branch of the **Select Case** statement.

If the user enters the number 8 in response to the Application.InputBox statement in line 5, VBA executes the **Select Case** statement in lines 10 through 21 by first evaluating the test expression, which—because it contains only the variable temperature—evaluates to the number 8.

When VBA evaluates the **Case** condition in line 11, the condition is not true; 8 is not greater than 100. VBA goes on to the **Case** condition in line 13; again the condition is not true (8 is not in the range 75 to 100). VBA skips to the **Case** condition in line 15. The number 8 is not in the range 50 to 74, either, so VBA again skips to the next **Case** condition, this time in line 17. This condition is not true either (8 is not greater than 32).

VBA has now tested the result of the test expression against all of the specified conditions in the **Select Case** statement and has not found a match for any of them. VBA therefore executes the **Case Else** branch of the **Select Case** statement in line 19, resulting in the message dialog shown in Figure 8.1. When VBA has finished executing the **Case Else** branch, execution continues with the first statement after the **End Select** statement in line 21—the end of the procedure, in this case.

FIGURE 8.1

If you enter the number 8 in the input dialog in Listing 8.4, VBA displays this message dialog.

Note

If the user enters a number greater than 74 but less than 75, VBA ends up executing the fourth **Case Else** branch (line 17 of Listing 8.4). A number such as 74.5, for example, does not match any of the specified conditions in any of the first three **Case** branches in the **Select Case** statement in Listing 8.4. Entering the value of 74.5 for the temperature causes the *Pretty cold* message to display, which is obviously incorrect. The range in line 15 of Listing 8.4 should really have been 50 To 75 so that there is no gap in the ranges. Because VBA executes only the first matching **Case** condition, numbers with a value of 75 are still handled by the first **Case** branch starting in line 13. A number such as 74.5, however, would now be handled correctly by the **Case** branch starting in line 15.

Do

DO use a **Select Case** statement if you need to choose among more than three or four different courses of action.

DO use a **Select Case** statement if you need to choose the same course of action when several different conditions are true. The following **Case** clause, for example, will have its associated statements executed whenever the test expression evaluates to one of the numbers 2, 4, 6, or 8.

```
Case 2, 4, 6, 8
```

Don't

DON'T forget to carefully construct your ranges and various other **Case** conditions to avoid gaps in value ranges such as the one noted for Listing 8.4.

Unconditional Branching

An unconditional branching statement *always* changes the flow of statement execution in a VBA procedure or function. VBA does not test any conditions (hence the term *unconditional*), it simply switches execution to a specified location.

8

VBA has only one unconditional branching statement: **GoTo**. There are very few reasons to use the **GoTo** statement; in fact, procedures that use many **GoTo** statements tend to be very difficult to understand. In almost every circumstance where you might use a **GoTo** statement, you can use one of the **If** statements, a **Select Case** statement, or one of the looping structures you learn about in the next lesson to accomplish the same purpose with greater ease and clarity.

The **GoTo** statement is a holdover from early versions of the BASIC programming language, which didn't have the sophisticated **Select Case** decision-making statement described in this chapter or the powerful looping structures described in the next chapter. Programmers in early versions of BASIC used **GoTo** to simulate the effects of the more sophisticated VBA statements. In VBA, you should use the **GoTo** statement as little as possible.

You should take the time to understand how the **GoTo** statement works as an unconditional branching statement, mostly to help you understand how the error-handling **GoTo** operates, but also because you will occasionally see this command used by other programmers.

Do

DO try to use some other structure, such as a **Select Case** statement or one of the looping structures described in the next lesson, instead of a **GoTo** statement.

Don't

DON'T use a **GoTo** statement except as part of an **On Error GoTo** statement (described in Day 18, "Error Handling").

SYNTAX

The **GoTo** statement has the following general syntax:

```
GoTo line
```

line represents any valid line label or line number in the same procedure or function that contains the **GoTo** statement. When VBA executes a **GoTo** statement, it immediately shifts procedure execution to the line specified by *line*.

A *line label* is a special type of identifier that identifies a particular line by name. Line labels have the following general syntax:

name:

name represents any valid VBA identifier. A line label can begin in any column on a line as long as it is the first non-blank character on the line. A *line number* is essentially the same as a line label, but is just a number, not an identifier. Using line numbers in VBA procedures is extremely unusual; you should always use a line label, instead.

Listing 8.5 shows a procedure that employs one of the most common legitimate uses for a **GoTo** statement in a VBA procedure: The procedure uses the **GoTo** statement to skip to the end of the procedure when the user chooses the Cancel command button in an input dialog.

INPUT   **LISTING 8.5**   **THE GoTo STATEMENT**

```
1:  Sub MakeSalesRpt_Chart()
2:  'This procedure asks for a sheet name containing source
3:  'data, then asks for a range of cells containing the data
4:  'to chart. Next, the procedure asks for a sheet name to put
5:  'the pie chart on. The procedure then creates the chart,
6:  'and uses the ChartWizard method to make a pie chart.
7:
8:     Const sTitle = "Make Sales Report Chart"
9:
10:    Dim SrcShtName As String
11:    Dim SourceRng As String
12:    Dim DestShtName As String
13:
14:       'get source sheet name
15:    SrcShtName = InputBox(prompt:= _
16:                 "Enter the name of the sheet " & _
17:                 "containing the data to graph:", _
18:                       Title:=sTitle)
19:    'check to see if user entered name or chose Cancel
20:    If Len(Trim(SrcShtName)) = 0 Then
21:      MsgBox "Data sheet name not entered -ending procedure"
22:      GoTo GiveUp
23:    End If
24:     'select source sheet so user can refer to it
25:    Sheets(SrcShtName).Select
26:
27:     'get source range
28:    SourceRng = InputBox(prompt:= _
29:                 "Enter the range of the data to graph " & _
30:                 "using R1C1 notation:", _
31:                       Title:=sTitle)
32:      'check to see if user entered range or chose Cancel
```

8

```
33:    If Len(Trim(SourceRng)) = 0 Then
34:      MsgBox "Source range not entered - ending procedure"
35:      GoTo GiveUp
36:    End If
37:
38:      'get destination sheet name
39:    DestShtName = InputBox(prompt:="Enter the name of " & _
40:                      "the sheet to contain the graph:", _
41:                          Title:=sTitle)
42:      'check to see if user chose Cancel
43:    If Len(Trim(DestShtName)) = 0 Then
44:      MsgBox "Chart destination sheet name not entered" & _
45:            " - ending procedure"
46:      GoTo GiveUp
47:    End If
48:
49:      'select the destination sheet and create chart
50:    Sheets(DestShtName).Select
51:    ActiveSheet.ChartObjects.Add(96, 37.5, 234, 111).Select
52:
53:      'use ChartWizard Method to create chart.
54:    With Sheets(SrcShtName)
55:      ActiveChart.ChartWizard Source:=.Range(SourceRng), _
56:                              Gallery:=xlPie, _
57:                              Format:=7, _
58:                              PlotBy:=xlColumns, _
59:                              CategoryLabels:=1, _
60:                              SeriesLabels:=1, _
61:                              HasLegend:=1, _
62:                              Title:="Sales Report"
63:    End With
64: GiveUp:
65:    'end of the procedure - canceling user input jumps here
66: End Sub
```

> **Note**
> If you want to type this listing in and experiment with it, make sure that you use R1C1 notation such as C5:D8. Also make sure that the data you select is suitable for graphing with a pie chart.

ANALYSIS   The `MakeSalesRpt_Chart` procedure is an edited version of a recorded Excel macro. First, a macro to create a pie chart was recorded. The recorded macro was then copied to another module and edited. The macro's name was changed to `MakeSalesRpt_Chart`, and various constant and variable declarations were added. Next, VBA statements to get input from the user and to evaluate the user's input were added to the procedure.

Lines 10 through 12 each declare a string variable. SrcShtName holds the name of the worksheet that contains the data to graph, SourceRng holds the name or description of the range of data to graph, and DestShtName holds the name of the worksheet on which the procedure will put the resulting graph.

Line 15 starts the actual work of the MakeSalesRpt_Chart procedure. This line uses the InputBox function to get the name of the worksheet that contains the source data. The result of the InputBox function is assigned to the SrcShtName variable.

Line 20 starts a block **If...Then** statement. In the logical expression, the Trim function first trims any leading or trailing spaces from the string in SrcShtName and the Len function returns the length of the trimmed string. If the length of the trimmed string is 0, the user either did not enter a name in the input dialog or chose the Cancel command button—the InputBox function returns an empty string if the user presses Esc or chooses Cancel.

In either case, there is no point in continuing the procedure. The MsgBox statement in line 21 displays a message explaining that the procedure will now end. Line 22 contains a **GoTo** statement. When VBA executes this line, it immediately shifts execution to the line containing the line label GiveUp:, skipping over any statements between the line that contains the **GoTo** and the line that contains the specified line label. VBA then continues execution with the statement on the line following the line label. In this case, the GiveUp: label is in line 64, just before the **End Sub** statement.

Line 25 uses the **Select** method of the Sheets collection to select the worksheet named by SrcShtName so that the user can see the data source sheet while entering the coordinates of the range of data to graph.

Next, line 28 uses InputBox to get the coordinates of the range of data to graph from the user and assigns the user's entry to the SourceRng variable. As with the name of the source worksheet, line 33 tests to see whether the string obtained for the range of data to graph contains anything other than blank space or the empty string returned when the user chooses the Cancel command button in the input dialog.

Again, if the SourceRng variable does not contain any data, there is no point in continuing the procedure. When the string length comparison expression in line 33 is **True**, VBA executes lines 34 and 35. Line 34 displays a message to the user that the procedure will now end, and line 35 causes VBA to skip to the GiveUp: line label.

Line 39 gets the name of the sheet that will contain the finished pie chart and assigns it to the DestShtName variable. Once again, in line 43 an **If...Then** statement tests to see whether the user entered a string or chose Cancel. Again, if the string entered by the user is empty or all blank space, there is no point in continuing the procedure; VBA executes the alternate statements in the **If...Then** statement. Again, VBA is directed to skip to the GiveUp: label at the end of the procedure.

VBA only gets to execute line 50 if the procedure's user actually enters all three requested values. In line 50, the Select method of the Sheets collection is used to select the worksheet that will contain the finished pie chart. Line 51 uses the Add method of the ChartObjects collection of the active sheet to create and select the new chart object. Lines 50 and 51 were obtained from a recorded macro.

Line 55 uses the ChartWizard method of the active sheet object to set the specifications for the chart object created in line 51. Although the line from the recorded macro was reformatted and a **With...End With** statement was added (line 54) to make this method call more readable, it is essentially unchanged from the line in the original recorded macro. The programmer added only the SrcShtName and SourceRng variables and removed only a couple of named arguments that were assigned empty strings.

> **Tip**
>
> You can usually safely remove named arguments that are assigned empty strings from any recorded statement because empty strings are also the standard default value for most omitted optional arguments.

Finally, line 64 contains the GiveUp: line label. This line is the line to which all the **GoTo** statements in this procedure pass execution. Because line 64 is the last statement in the procedure before the end of the procedure in line 66, all the **GoTo** statements have the effect of ending the procedure early. As you will learn in the next section, there is an even easier way to accomplish the same task.

Ending Procedures, Functions, and Entire Programs Early

As you can see from the procedure in Listing 8.5, there are circumstances—such as a user canceling an input dialog or the absence of some expected data—in which there is no point in continuing the execution of your procedure or function. If you have written an entire program that contains procedures that call other functions and procedures (as described in Day 12, "Creating Libraries and Whole Programs: Modular Programming Techniques"), you might even decide there are circumstances in which your entire program should stop running, such as a missing worksheet, allowing a user to cancel the program, and so on.

VBA provides the **Exit** and **End** statements to enable you to either terminate a procedure or function or halt your entire program.

Using the Exit Statement

To make a single procedure or function stop executing, you use one of two available forms for the VBA **Exit** statement, depending on whether you want to terminate a function or a procedure.

SYNTAX

The **Exit** statement has the following two syntax forms:

```
Exit Sub
Exit Function
```

Exit Sub and **Exit Function** both work exactly the same way and have the same effects; you use **Exit Sub** to end a procedure and **Exit Function** to end a function.

Listing 8.6 shows the same MakeSalesRpt_Chart procedure from Listing 8.5, but uses the **Exit Sub** statements to end the procedure early.

INPUT   **LISTING 8.6**   ENDING A PROCEDURE EARLY WITH **Exit Sub**

```
 1:  Sub MakeSalesRpt_Chart()
 2:  'This procedure asks for a sheet name containing source
 3:  'data, then asks for a range of cells containing the data
 4:  'to chart. Next, procedure asks for a sheet name to put
 5:  'the pie chart on. The procedure then creates the chart,
 6:  'and uses the ChartWizard method to make a pie chart.
 7:
 8:     Const sTitle = "Make Sales Report Chart"
 9:
10:     Dim SrcShtName As String
11:     Dim SourceRng As String
12:     Dim DestShtName As String
13:
14:      'get source sheet name
15:     SrcShtName = InputBox(prompt:= _
16:                  "Enter the name of the sheet " & _
17:                  "containing the data to graph:", _
18:                         Title:=sTitle)
19:      'check to see if user entered name or chose Cancel
20:     If Len(Trim(SrcShtName)) = 0 Then
21:       MsgBox "Data sheet name not entered -ending procedure"
22:        Exit Sub
23:     End If
24:      'select source sheet so user can refer to it
25:     Sheets(SrcShtName).Select
26:
27:      'get source range
28:     SourceRng = InputBox(prompt:= _
29:                  "Enter the range of the data to graph " & _
30:                  "using R1C1 notation:", _
31:                         Title:=sTitle)
32:      'check to see if user entered range or chose Cancel
```

```
33:    If Len(Trim(SourceRng)) = 0 Then
34:      MsgBox "Source range not entered - ending procedure"
35:      Exit Sub
36:    End If
37:
38:      'get destination sheet name
39:    DestShtName = InputBox(prompt:="Enter the name of " & _
40:                        "the sheet to contain the graph:", _
41:                           Title:=sTitle)
42:    'check to see if user chose Cancel
43:    If Len(Trim(DestShtName)) = 0 Then
44:      MsgBox "Chart destination sheet name not entered" & _
45:          " - ending procedure"
46:      Exit Sub
47:    End If
48:
49:      'select the destination sheet and create chart
50:    Sheets(DestShtName).Select
51:    ActiveSheet.ChartObjects.Add(96, 37.5, 234, 111).Select
52:
53:      'use ChartWizard Method to create chart.
54:    With Sheets(SrcShtName)
55:      ActiveChart.ChartWizard Source:=.Range(SourceRng), _
56:                          Gallery:=xlPie, _
57:                          Format:=7, _
58:                          PlotBy:=xlColumns, _
59:                          CategoryLabels:=1, _
60:                          SeriesLabels:=1, _
61:                          HasLegend:=1, _
62:                          Title:="Sales Report"
63:    End With
64: End Sub
```

ANALYSIS This version of the MakeSalesRpt_Chart procedure works the same as the procedure shown in Listing 8.5, except that this version uses the **Exit Sub** statement to end the procedure early rather than the **GoTo** and line label arrangement.

Notice lines 22, 35, and 46. Each of these lines contains an **Exit Sub** statement. Like the procedure shown in Listing 8.5, the **If...Then** statements cause VBA to execute the statements in lines 22, 35, and 46 whenever the user enters a blank string, chooses the Cancel command button, or presses Esc in any of the three input dialogs.

Each **Exit Sub** statement causes VBA to immediately stop executing statements in the procedure. After executing the **Exit Sub** statements, VBA stops executing the current procedure and returns to execution in whatever procedure or function called the procedure containing the **Exit Sub** statement.

> **Note**
>
> If you use an **Exit Sub** or **Exit Function** statement in a procedure or function called by another VBA procedure or function, that function continues to execute. The **Exit Sub** and **Exit Function** statements only stop execution of the current procedure or function.

Do

DO use an **Exit Sub** or **Exit Function** statement instead of a **GoTo** to end a procedure or function early. The **Exit Sub** statement makes it more obvious that your procedure will stop executing—and therefore makes your procedure easier to write, read, and understand.

Using the End Statement

You're now familiar with the **End Sub** and **End Function** keywords used to signal to VBA that it has reached the end of a procedure or function. These keyword phrases tell VBA to stop executing statements in the current procedure or function and to resume execution in the procedure or function that called the current procedure or function. If the current procedure was not called by another procedure, VBA ceases all statement execution.

For example, consider Listing R1.1 in the "Week 1 In Review" section of this book. The NewBook procedure gets a workbook name from the user by calling a function named GetBookName. When VBA executes the NewBook procedure and encounters the statement in NewBook that calls the GetBookName function, VBA passes the function's arguments and then begins executing statements in the GetBookName function. VBA executes statements in GetBookName until it reaches either the **End Function** statement at the end of the function definition or until it executes an **Exit Function** statement. In either case, VBA stops executing the code in the GetBookName function and returns the function result to the NewBook procedure.

After VBA returns from the GetBookName function call, it finishes evaluating whatever expression uses the function result and continues executing the statements in the NewBook procedure, beginning with the statement after the one that called the GetBookName function.

As it is, the NewBook procedure continues to execute even if the user cancels the input dialog displayed by the GetBookName function. Obviously, if the user cancels entering a workbook name, there is no point in continuing the NewBook procedure—without a workbook name there isn't any work for the NewBook procedure to perform.

In this situation, it would be nice if you could write the GetBookName function so that if the user cancels the input dialog displayed by GetBookName, the entire process of creating a new workbook is also canceled. As shown in the examples in Listing 8.6, you can use a combination of **If...Then** statements and the **Exit Function** statement to detect when the user cancels an input operation and to end the function immediately, if that happens.

If you just end the GetBookName function early, however, VBA simply returns to the NewBook procedure and continues to execute it, which is not what you desire. Instead, you must completely end VBA's execution of your program. (A program can be a single procedure or hundreds of procedures and functions working together.)

SYNTAX ▲

To completely end VBA's execution of your program, use the **End** keyword on a line all by itself:

End

When VBA executes the preceding statement, it stops all execution of procedure and function statements. Any variables in existence cease to exist and their values are lost.

Listing 8.7 shows the GetBookName function rewritten so that it completely ends whatever program VBA is executing if the user cancels the input dialog.

INPUT   **LISTING 8.7**   ENDING PROGRAM EXECUTION WITH **End**

```
1:  Function GetBookName(ByVal lDflt As String, _
2:                    Optional Prmpt, _
3:                    Optional lTitle) As String
4:
5:        'was prompt string included in argument list?
6:     If IsMissing(Prmpt) Then Prmpt = "Enter a workbook name:"
7:
8:     'if default name is not an empty string, convert it to
9:     'all upper-case letters, otherwise assign a name to it.
10:    If lDflt <> "" Then
11:       lDflt = UCase(lDflt)
12:    Else
13:       lDflt = "NEWFILE.XLS"
14:    End If
15:
16:       'use InputBox to get the filename.
17:    GetBookName = InputBox(prompt:=Prmpt, _
18:                        Title:=lTitle, _
19:                        default:=lDflt)
20:
```

continues

LISTING 8.7 CONTINUED

```
21:     'check: did user cancel operation?
22:     If Len(Trim(GetBookName)) = 0 Then
23:         MsgBox prompt:="Program Canceled", Title:=lTitle
24:         End   'cancel entire program
25:     End If
26: End Function
27:
28:
29: Sub Test_GetBookName()
30: 'This procedure tests the GetBookName function
31:
32:     MsgBox GetBookName(lDflt:="", lTitle:="Cancel Test")
33: End Sub
```

ANALYSIS This version of the GetBookName function is the same—and works exactly the same way—as the function described in Listing 8.2. Only lines 21 through 25 were added to this function to give it the capability to end the entire program if the user cancels the input dialog in line 17.

Line 17 uses the InputBox function to obtain a string from the user; the string returned by InputBox is assigned to the GetBookName function result. If the user presses the Esc key or chooses the Cancel button, InputBox returns an empty (zero-length) string.

Line 22 is the start of a block **If...Then** statement. The test condition for the **If...Then** statement uses the Trim and Len functions to get the length of the string stored in the function's result, excluding any blank spaces. If the length of the string returned by InputBox is zero, the user either entered a blank string as the workbook name, chose the Cancel command button in the input dialog, or pressed the Esc key.

If InputBox returns an empty string, VBA executes line 23, which uses MsgBox to display a message onscreen stating that the program has been canceled. Next, VBA executes the **End** statement in line 24. When VBA executes this line, it ceases all execution—it does *not* return to the procedure that called the GetBookName function. No additional statements are executed in any procedure or function.

Lines 29 through 33 are a simple procedure to test the GetBookName function. When VBA executes the test procedure, it begins executing GetBookName when it is called in line 32 of the test procedure. If the user cancels the input dialog in the GetBookName function, VBA executes the **End** statement in GetBookName and stops *all* execution—VBA does not even finish executing the MsgBox statement in line 32 of the test procedure!

8

Do

DO write any of your procedures or functions that use the **End** statement so that they will display some message or notification to the user explaining what is about to happen and why before the statement that actually contains the **End** statement. If you don't, your procedure's users might be completely mystified as to why the procedure or program they were using suddenly stopped working. If you end the program because of some user action—such as canceling an input dialog—without an explanation, your procedure's user might never figure out why the procedure ends; in fact, users are prone to consider such things to be a defect in your procedure.

Don't

DON'T forget to close workbooks or do other "housekeeping" before your procedure executes an **End** statement so that your program's user doesn't have to clean up things such as half-finished charts or deal with workbooks that have unsaved data when your program ends.

Using MsgBox to Let Users Make Choices

By now, you should be quite comfortable using the MsgBox statement to display messages to the user in titled dialog boxes. You can also use the VBA MsgBox procedure as a function to get choices from the user in response to messages or questions that your procedure displays by including the optional Buttons argument. For many simple choices, using the MsgBox function to get a response from the user is much easier than getting text input from the user with an InputBox function and then analyzing that text to determine what choice the user made.

When you include the Buttons argument—and the necessary parentheses for a function call—the MsgBox statement operates like a function and displays a message dialog that can contain a variety of command buttons. MsgBox returns a numeric result indicating which command button the user chose. You specify the number and type of command buttons displayed in the MsgBox dialog through the Buttons argument.

Listing 8.8 shows a simple procedure that demonstrates the use of the Buttons argument.

INPUT **LISTING 8.8** USING MsgBox AND THE Buttons ARGUMENT TO GET USER INPUT

```
 1:  Sub Demo_MsgBoxFunction()
 2:  'This procedure demonstrates the MsgBox used as a function
 3:
 4:    Const mTitle = "MsgBox Button Demonstration"
 5:    Dim Resp As Integer
 6:
 7:    Resp = MsgBox(prompt:="Choose a button.", _
 8:                  Title:=mTitle, _
 9:                  Buttons:=vbYesNoCancel + vbQuestion)
10:    Select Case Resp
11:      Case Is = vbYes
12:        MsgBox prompt:="You chose the 'Yes' button.", _
13:               Title:=mTitle, _
14:               Buttons:=vbInformation
15:      Case Is = vbNo
16:        MsgBox prompt:="You chose the 'No' button.", _
17:               Title:=mTitle, _
18:               Buttons:=vbInformation
19:      Case Is = vbCancel
20:        MsgBox prompt:="You chose the 'Cancel' button.", _
21:               Title:=mTitle, _
22:               Buttons:=vbCritical
23:    End Select
24: End Sub
```

ANALYSIS The Demo_MsgBoxFunction procedure just demonstrates how to use the MsgBox statement as a function, the effects of various Buttons arguments, and how to evaluate the value that the MsgBox function returns.

Line 1 contains the procedure declaration and line 2 contains a comment briefly describing the purpose of this procedure. Line 4 declares a constant for use as the title of the MsgBox dialog and line 5 declares an Integer type variable, Resp, to hold the result returned by the MsgBox function.

Line 7 contains the call to the MsgBox function and assigns the MsgBox result to the Resp variable. Notice that the MsgBox function call spans three lines, 7, 8, and 9, using the line-continuation symbol.

Notice that the MsgBox function call in lines 7 through 9 observes all the requirements for using a function: The argument list is enclosed in parentheses and the result of the function is used—assigned to a variable, in this case.

The argument list for the MsgBox function call starting in line 7 contains the familiar named arguments: prompt:=, to specify the text displayed in the message dialog, and Title:=, to specify the title of the message dialog. The function call also contains the new Buttons:= argument.

The Buttons argument passes the sum of two of VBA's intrinsic constants; you combine values for the Buttons argument by adding together the intrinsic constants. VBA defines several constants explicitly for use with the Buttons argument in MsgBox. (A list of the Buttons arguments for MsgBox is on the inside back cover of this book.)

The Buttons argument for MsgBox enables you to specify the number and type of buttons and whether the message dialog contains one of Windows's icons to indicate a Warning message, Query message, Information message, or Critical Warning message. You can also use the Buttons argument to specify which of the displayed buttons (button 1, 2, 3, or 4) is the default button in the message dialog. You can only specify one button style, one icon, and one default button option at a time.

In line 9 (part of the MsgBox function call beginning in line 7), the vbYesNoCancel constant specifies that the MsgBox dialog should contain three command buttons: a Yes button, a No button, and a Cancel button. The vbQuestion constant specifies that the message dialog should contain the Windows' Query message icon.

When VBA executes the MsgBox function call in lines 7 through 9, it displays the dialog shown in Figure 8.2. This dialog remains onscreen until the user chooses one of the command buttons or presses the Esc key. (Pressing the Esc key in a MsgBox dialog, like pressing Esc in any Windows dialog, is the same as choosing Cancel.)

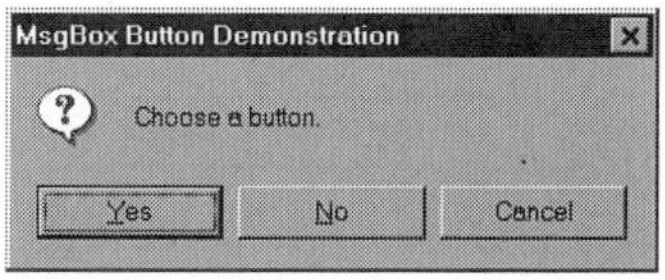

FIGURE 8.2

The MsgBox *function call in line 7 of Listing 8.8 displays this dialog. Notice the Yes, No, and Cancel command buttons and the Windows Query message icon—all specified by the* Buttons *argument.*

MsgBox Button Demonstration

(?) Choose a button.

[Yes]   [No]   [Cancel]

As soon as the user chooses a command button in the message dialog, VBA returns a numeric value corresponding to the user's choice. In line 7, the result of the MsgBox function is assigned to the Resp variable. VBA uses different values depending on which command button the user chose. VBA uses one value to indicate the Yes button, another value to indicate the No button, and yet another value for the Cancel button. The MsgBox function can also display dialogs with Abort, Retry, and Ignore buttons in various combinations. Because each button has its own specific return value, VBA provides several intrinsic constants to represent the possible return values of the MsgBox function. The inside back cover of this book contains a list of the VBA constant values that MsgBox can return.

Line 10 begins a **Select Case** statement that evaluates the value returned by the MsgBox function in line 7, which is stored in the Resp variable. The test expression for the **Select Case** statement is the Resp variable itself, so VBA compares the value in the Resp variable to see whether it matches any of the **Case** conditions in the **Select Case** statement.

Line 11 contains the first **Case** condition. It tests to see whether the Resp variable is equal to the predefined constant vbYes. This constant represents the value returned by MsgBox when the user chooses the Yes command button (see Figure 8.3).

If the **Case** condition in line 11 is **True**, that is, if the user did choose the Yes command button, VBA executes the corresponding statements for this **Case** branch starting in line 12. Lines 12 through 14 contain a single MsgBox statement. This time, the MsgBox statement is in its more familiar form as a procedure call, but still uses the optional Buttons argument (line 14). When VBA executes this statement, it displays the dialog shown in Figure 8.3.

The Buttons argument in line 14 uses the vbInformation constant to specify that the Windows's Information icon should be included in the message dialog. Because no value specifying the number of buttons was included, the message dialog contains the usual single OK command button. Notice that this call to MsgBox does not include parentheses; VBA therefore ignores the function's result. (You learned about ignoring a function's result in Day 5.)

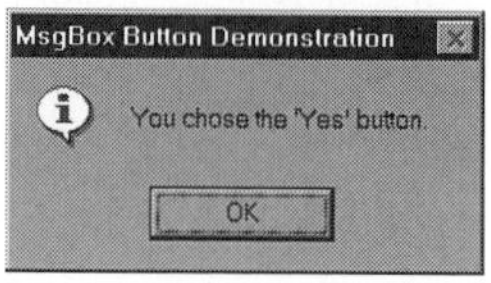

FIGURE 8.3

VBA displays this dialog if the user chose the Yes command button. Notice the Windows Information message icon.

If the user chose the No button, the **Case** condition in line 15—which tests to see whether the result in Resp is equal to the intrinsic vbNo constant—is **True**, and VBA executes the corresponding MsgBox statement in lines 16 through 18. This statement displays a message dialog similar to the one shown in Figure 8.3, except that it announces that the user chose the No button. Once again, the Buttons argument was included in order to include the Windows' Information message icon in the message dialog.

If the user chose the Cancel button, the **Case** condition in line 19—which tests to see whether the result in Resp is equal to the intrinsic vbCancel constant— is **True**, and VBA executes the corresponding MsgBox statement in lines 20 through 22. When VBA executes this statement, it displays the dialog shown in Figure 8.4.

FIGURE 8.4

VBA displays this dialog if the user chose the Cancel command button. Notice the Windows Critical Warning message icon.

The Buttons argument in line 22 uses the vbCritical constant to specify that the Windows' Critical Warning icon should be included in the message dialog. Because no value specifying the number of buttons was included, the message dialog contains the usual single OK command button.

Finally, the **Select Case** statement ends in line 23 and line 24 is the end of the Demo_MsgBoxFunction procedure.

You'll see many more examples of the MsgBox function used to obtain a choice from the user throughout the rest of this book.

There is one remaining item that you can specify with the Buttons argument for MsgBox that was not included in Listing 8.8: You can specify whether the first, second, third, or fourth command buttons in MsgBox dialogs are the initial default command buttons.

As you have seen so far, MsgBox usually makes the first command button in its dialog the default button. Refer to Figure 8.2 and notice that the Yes button is marked as the initial default command button. If, after VBA displays the dialog in Figure 8.2, the user just presses the Enter key, VBA behaves as if the user chose the Yes button.

Do

DO use the VBA intrinsic constants for the `Buttons` argument in `MsgBox` and for the `MsgBox` return values. Using the intrinsic constant names makes your code easy to write, read, and understand.

DO remember that to combine values in the `Buttons` argument of `MsgBox`, you add the values together with the addition operator (+).

DO remember that you can view all the available intrinsic constants related to `MsgBox` in the Object Browser. To view the intrinsic constants for the `Buttons` argument, select VBA in the Project/Library list of the Object Browser and then select VbMsgBoxStyle in the Classes list; the Members Of list will display the intrinsic constants for the `Buttons` argument's values. If you select VbMsgBoxResult in the Classes list, the Members Of list displays the intrinsic constants for the `MsgBox` function's return value.

DON'T

DON'T try to specify more than one set of buttons, more than one icon, or more than one default button at one time. For example, using the expression `vbYesNoCancel + vbAbortRetryIgnore` as the `Buttons` argument value will *not* produce a dialog with six buttons in it. The results of trying to specify more than one set of buttons, more than one icon, or more than one default button at one time can be unpredictable, and certainly will not have the desired effect.

DON'T use literal numeric values for either the `Buttons` argument in `MsgBox` or the `MsgBox` return value. Using the literal numeric values makes your code difficult to read and understand.

You might prefer that the default button be some button other than the first one listed in the message dialog. For example, if you use `MsgBox` to ask the user to confirm deleting a worksheet in a workbook, you might prefer that the default command button be the No button instead of the Yes button—because a deleted worksheet cannot be recovered, it makes sense to help the user avoid inadvertently confirming a deletion if they just keep pressing the Enter key. (Almost everyone has had the experience of accidentally making a choice they didn't really want just because they hit the Enter key one time too many.)

To change the default command button, add one of the VBA intrinsic constants—`vbDefaultButton1`, `vbDefaultButton2`, `vbDefaultButton3`, or `vbDefaultButton4`—to the `Buttons` argument. The following procedure fragment shows the `MsgBox` statement from lines 7 through 9 of Listing 8.8 modified so that the default command button in the message dialog is the No button:

```
Resp = MsgBox(prompt:="Choose a button.", _
              Title:=mTitle, _
              Buttons:=vbYesNoCancel + vbQuestion + _
                       vbDefaultButton2)
```

When VBA executes the preceding statement, it displays the dialog shown in Figure 8.5. This dialog is identical to the one shown previously in Figure 8.2, except that the addition of the vbDefaultButton2 value in the Buttons argument causes the second button—in this case the No button—to become the initial default command button.

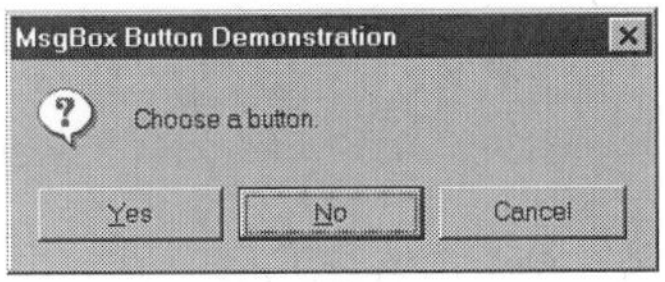

FIGURE 8.5

Compare this dialog to the one shown in Figure 8.2. Notice that the No button is now the default command button as a result of adding vbDefaultButton2 *to the* Buttons *argument.*

Summary

In today's lesson, you learned how VBA's decision-making commands work, and about a few of the many circumstances under which you will want your procedures to make decisions and choose an alternate series of actions. You also learned the difference between conditional branching statements and unconditional branching statements.

You learned how to use the **If...Then** statement to make simple, single branch choices, and how to use the **If...Then...Else** statement to make choices between two different branches of procedure statements. You then learned how to nest **If...Then...Else** statements inside each other to make more complex decisions involving more than two alternate branches, and how to use the **If...Then...ElseIf** statement to simplify some nested **If...Then...Else** statements.

Next, you learned how to use the **Select Case** statement to choose one of several possible branches of execution; you learned that the **Select Case** statement is a powerful alternative to using nested **If...Then...Else** statements. You also learned about unconditional branching with VBA's **GoTo** statement, and you learned that the **GoTo** statement has very limited uses in contemporary VBA programming.

You learned when and how to use **Exit Function** and **Exit Sub** statements to end a procedure or function's execution early, as well as when and how to use the **End** statement to end an entire program's execution. This chapter also explained the specific differences between using one of the **Exit** statements and using the **End** statement.

Finally, this chapter taught you how to use the optional Buttons argument with MsgBox to specify the type and number of command buttons in the message dialog, and to specify which (if any) Windows message icon to include in the message dialog. You also learned how to use MsgBox as a function to return the user's choices.

Day 9, "Repeating Actions in Visual Basic: Loops," teaches you how to use VBA's looping commands to repeat actions.

Q&A

Q **I'm not sure I understand exactly when I should use the** If...Then...ElseIf **statement.**

A The **If...Then...ElseIf** statement is most useful when you need to choose among three or four different branches depending on various conditions. The **If...Then...ElseIf** statement is really an alternative to the **Select Case** statement, and both statements have much the same effect: They enable you to choose one of several different branches. If you don't feel comfortable using the **If...Then...ElseIf** statement, simply use the **Select Case** statement instead.

Q **I'm not sure I understand how to write the logical test expressions for the various** If...Then **statements.**

A Usually, you specify a condition for a branching statement by constructing a logical expression that evaluates to **True** when the desired condition for executing a particular procedure branch is also true and evaluates to **False** when the desired condition is not true.

Most of the time, you can figure out how to write the correct logical expression by just carefully stating the condition in English and then substituting VBA comparison or logical operators for parts of the English sentence. For example, if you want a particular branch of your procedure to execute whenever the value in a variable named NetIncome drops below 10,000, you can state the situation in English, first: *when* NetIncome *is less than 10,000.* From this English statement, you can see that you are comparing NetIncome to the constant value 10,000, and that the comparison operator is the less than comparison (<). With this information, you can construct the following expression:

```
NetIncome < 10000
```

This logical expression is **True** whenever NetIncome drops below (is less than) 10,000. You can construct more complex logical statements the same way. Suppose you want a particular branch of your procedure executed whenever the value in NetIncome drops below 10,000 or whenever the percent profit (PcntProfit) drops below 15 percent. Carefully state the situation in English, first: *when* NetIncome *is less than 10,000; or when* PcntProfit *is less than 15*. In this English statement, you can see that two smaller expressions are connected together by the word *or*. Write the smaller expressions first.

The first expression (NetIncome < 10000) has already been determined. The second expression compares PcntProfit to 15 and uses the less than operator (<) again. With this information, you can construct the second part of the logical expression:

```
PcntProfit < 15
```

Now connect the two smaller expressions with the logical operator corresponding to the English word that connected the expressions—**Or**—as in the following expression (you must include parentheses around the smaller parts of the expression, or the expression will not produce the results you expect):

```
(NetIncome < 10000) Or (PcntProfit < 15)
```

Q One of the examples in this chapter used the Excel Application.InputBox function instead of VBA's InputBox statement to restrict the user's input to a number. How do I find out more about using the Excel Application.InputBox function?

A You can find out more about the Application.InputBox function, or any other object, property, or method that you see in recorded macros or examples in this book, by using the Object Browser as described in Day 5. To get more information about the Excel Application.InputBox function specifically, open the Object Browser window and select Excel in the Project/Library drop-down list, select Application in the Classes list, and then select InputBox in the Members of 'Application' list. Finally, select the **?** button at the upper right of the Object Browser window.

Q I understand how the GoTo statement works, but I'm not sure when or why to use the GoTo statement.

A Except in relation to the special error-handling **GoTo** statements described in Day 18, you really should never have to use the **GoTo** statement. This chapter makes sure you know about the **GoTo** statement so that you will be more ready to understand the error-handling **GoTo** statements described in Day 18, and so that you will be able to understand source code written by other programmers that uses the **GoTo**

statement. You should always try to use conditional branching commands and looping commands to structure your code, instead of using a **GoTo** statement. If you need to end a procedure or program early, use the **Exit** or **End** statements in preference to a **GoTo** statement.

Workshop

Answers are in Appendix A.

Quiz

1. What is a conditional branching statement? An unconditional branching statement?

2. How do you specify the condition that VBA uses to determine whether to execute a particular program branch?

3. What are VBA's conditional branching statements?

4. What are VBA's unconditional branching statements?

5. What is the term used to describe the situation when you enclose one **If...Then** or **If...Then...Else** statement inside another?

6. How many **ElseIf** clauses can an **If...Then...ElseIf** statement contain? Can an **If...Then...ElseIf** statement also include an **Else** clause? If you can include an **Else** clause in an **If...Then...ElseIf** statement, where would you place it and how many can you include?

7. How many **Case** clauses can you include in a **Select Case** statement? How do you specify a branch of statements for VBA to execute if none of the **Case** clauses in a **Select Case** statement are met? Where does that specification go inside the **Select Case** statement?

8. When and why would you use a **Select Case** statement instead of several nested **If...Then...Else** statements?

9. What do you use the **Exit Sub** statement for? What about **Exit Function**?

10. What effect does the **End** keyword on a line by itself have?

11. What purpose does the Buttons argument for MsgBox serve? What tools does VBA provide to help you specify values for the Buttons argument?

12. When you use MsgBox as a function, what does its result value represent? What tools does VBA provide to help you interpret this result?

Exercises

This chapter has only two exercises. Although Exercise 8.1 is fairly simple, Exercise 8.2 is fairly complex, and contains the same amount of work usually spread over two or three exercises. Don't be discouraged by this exercise's apparent complexity; it is really fairly simple. Rather than trying to write the entire procedure for Exercise 8.2 all at once, first write a procedure that just accomplishes the first task in the list. When that procedure works okay, add the code to accomplish the second task in the list, and so on. If you get stumped, take a look at the answer in Appendix A.

1. **BUG BUSTER:** The `Select Case` statement in the following procedure is supposed to display a message dialog stating whether the number stored in the Num variable is less than 0, between 0 and 10, between 10 and 20, or none of these. As it is, however, this `Select Case` statement erroneously reports that numbers such as 10.01 and 0.7 are greater than 20. Correct this `Select Case` statement.

```
1:  Sub Case_Demo()
2:
3:      Dim sNum As String
4:      Dim Num As Double
5:
6:      sNum = InputBox("enter a number:")
7:      Num = CDbl(sNum)
8:
9:      Select Case Num
10:         Case Is < 0
11:             MsgBox "Num is less than 0"
12:         Case 1 To 10
13:             MsgBox "Num is between 0 and 10"
14:         Case 11 To 20
15:             MsgBox "Num is between 10 and 20"
16:         Case Else
17:             MsgBox "Num is greater than 20"
18:     End Select
19: End Sub
```

2. The digits on a telephone dial (or number pad) are each associated with a specific group of alphabetic letters. Write a procedure that asks the user for a letter of the alphabet and then displays the corresponding telephone digit for that letter.

   The digits and their corresponding letters are

   ```
   2 = ABC
   3 = DEF
   4 = GHI
   5 = JKL
   6 = MNO
   7 = PRS
   8 = TUV
   9 = WXY
   ```

There is no digit corresponding to either Q or Z.

Your procedure should perform each of the following actions:

- Use the `InputBox` function to ask the user to enter a single letter of the alphabet.

- Use the `Len` function in a logical expression to determine whether the user canceled the input dialog. If so, your procedure should display a message stating that its operation was canceled and then terminate the procedure's execution. Your message dialog should include the Windows exclamation mark (!) warning icon. (HINT: Use an **If...Then** statement to make this test and choose the alternate branch. Add the `vbExclamation` constant in the `Buttons` argument of the `MsgBox` statement to display the exclamation point icon.)

- Use the `Len` function in a logical expression to determine whether the user did, in fact, enter a single character. If the length of the string the user entered is greater than 1, display a message stating that the user entered a string that was too long and then terminate the procedure's execution. This message dialog also should contain the Windows Exclamation warning message icon.

- Evaluate the user's input and display the digit corresponding to the letter the user entered. If the user entered a letter or other character that does not have a digit equivalent, your procedure should display a message stating that fact. (HINT: To simplify the comparisons you have to make, convert the user's input to uppercase with the `UCase` function and use the **Select Case** statement to evaluate the user's input.)

- When your message dialog displays the telephone digit equivalent to the letter entered by the user, the message dialog should repeat the user's letter as part of its message and also include the Windows Information icon. (HINT: Add the `vbInformation` constant to the `MsgBox` statement.)

Most of the work that this procedure does is to check the user's input. As you will learn in Day 10, "Advanced Techniques for Using Data Types and Variables," validating the information that the user enters can avoid many different errors and problems in your VBA procedures.

DAY **9**

Repeating Actions in Visual Basic: Loops

Now that you know how to choose different courses of action based on prede-termined conditions, you are ready to learn how to make your VBA procedures repeat actions either a predetermined number of times or while a particular con-dition does or does not exist. In today's lesson, you learn

- What looping commands do, and to understand the difference between loops that repeat a definite number of times and loops that repeat an indefinite number of times.

- When and how to use VBA's **For** loop structures to repeat actions a fixed number of times.

- When and how to use VBA's **Do** loop statement to repeat actions a flexi-ble number of times.

- To understand and use the four different configurations of the **Do** loop statement.

- How and under what circumstances to end a loop before it has finished executing.

- How to use nested loops.

Understanding Looping Commands

One of the drawbacks of recorded macros is their inability to repeat actions unless you record the desired action repeatedly. VBA provides several powerful and versatile structures that enable you to repeat actions easily and to control closely the manner in which VBA repeats those actions.

Program structures that cause one or more statements to execute repeatedly are called *looping* structures because the flow of the procedure's statement execution *loops* through the same statements repeatedly. Each time VBA finishes one complete cycle of executing all the statements enclosed by the looping structure is called an *iteration* of the loop.

Some looping structures are constructed so that they will always execute a set number of times. Loop structures that always execute a set number of times are called *fixed iteration* loops. Other types of looping structures repeat a flexible number of times depending on some set of conditions. Because the number of times these flexible looping structures repeat is indefinite, they are called *indefinite loops*.

In both fixed and indefinite looping structures, there is some expression that determines how many times the loop repeats. This expression is called the *loop determinant*, or the *loop invariant*. In a fixed loop structure, the loop determinant is almost always a numeric expression. In an indefinite loop structure, the loop determinant is typically a logical expression that describes the conditions under which the loop may continue repeating or stop repeating. You construct and use logical expressions for indefinite loop determinants the same way you construct and use logical expressions in VBA's conditional branching (decision-making) statements.

There are two basic ways that you can construct an indefinite loop. You can construct the loop so that VBA tests the loop's determinant condition *before* it executes the loop. If the condition for repeating the loop is not true, VBA skips over the statements in the loop altogether. You can also construct the loop so that VBA tests the loop's determinant condition *after* it executes the statements in the loop.

Figure 9.1 shows how VBA executes a loop that tests the determinant condition before executing the statements inside the loop. At the top of the loop, VBA tests the determinant condition (represented by the diamond-shaped box). If the conditions for executing the loop are met, VBA executes the statements inside the loop. After executing the last statement inside the loop, VBA returns to the top of the loop and evaluates the loop's determinant condition again. If the conditions for executing the loop are still met, VBA repeats the statements inside the loop and again returns to the top of the loop to test the determinant. As soon as the conditions for executing the loop are no longer met, VBA stops executing the loop and begins executing any statements after the loop.

Notice that, if the conditions for executing the loop are *not* met the first time VBA tests the loop determinant condition, VBA does not execute the statements inside the loop at all; instead, VBA skips over the body of the loop. (The *body* of a loop is the block of VBA statements enclosed by the beginning and ending of the loop.)

FIGURE 9.1

The flow of VBA's statement execution for a loop that tests its determinant condition before executing statements inside the loop.

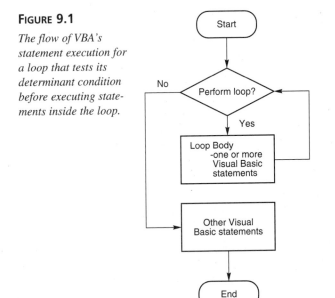

9

Figure 9.2 shows how VBA executes a loop that tests its determinant condition *after* executing the statements in the loop body. VBA first executes all statements in the loop body. When it reaches the end of the loop body, VBA evaluates the loop's determinant condition (represented by the diamond-shaped box). If conditions for executing the loop are met, VBA returns to the top of the loop and repeats the instructions in the body of the loop. At the end of the loop, VBA again tests the loop's determinant condition. As soon as the conditions for executing the loop are no longer met, VBA stops executing the loop and begins executing any statements after the loop.

Notice that, in this scenario, VBA always executes the statements in this loop at least once.

FIGURE 9.2

The flow of VBA's statement execution for a loop that tests its determinant condition after executing statements inside the loop.

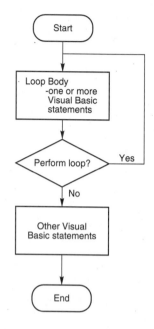

You can also construct an indefinite loop so that it does not have a determinant condition at all. Loops that do not have a determinant condition repeat forever, and are called *infinite loops*. An infinite loop never ends; most infinite loops are the result of a programmer's error, although there are a few uses for an infinite loop.

The following sections in today's lesson explain the specific details of constructing fixed and indefinite loops, and how to construct loops that test determinant conditions before or after executing the loop body. The following sections also explain the circumstances under which you might use each type of loop.

Fixed Repetition: The For Loops

The simplest looping structure is the fixed loop. VBA provides two different fixed loop structures: **For...Next** and **For Each...Next**. Both fixed loop structures are called **For** loops because they always execute *for* a specified number of times.

Using the For...Next Loop

The first of VBA's **For** loops is the **For...Next** loop. Use the **For...Next** loop when you want to repeat an action or series of actions a set number of times.

SYNTAX

The **For...Next** loop has the following general syntax:

```
For counter = start To end [Step StepSize]
      statements
Next [counter]
```

counter represents any VBA numeric variable, usually an **Integer** or **Long** data type. *start* represents any numeric expression, and specifies the starting value for the *counter* variable. *end* is also a numeric expression that specifies the ending value for the counter variable.

9

By default, VBA *increments* (adds to) the *counter* variable by 1 each time it executes the statements in the loop. You can specify a different increment value by including the optional **Step** keyword. If you include the **Step** keyword, you must then specify the amount to increment the *counter* variable. In the preceding syntax sample, *StepSize* represents any numeric expression, and specifies the amount to increment the *counter* variable.

statements represents none, one, or many VBA statements. These statements make up the body of the **For** loop; VBA executes each of these statements each time it executes the loop.

The **Next** keyword signals to VBA that it has reached the end of the loop; the optional *counter* after the **Next** keyword must be the same *counter* variable you specified after the **For** keyword at the beginning of the loop structure. Include the optional *counter* variable after the **Next** keyword to improve the readability of your program code (especially with nested **For...Next** loops).

When VBA executes a **For...Next** loop, it first assigns the value represented by *start* to the *counter* variable. VBA then executes all the statements represented by *statements* until it reaches the **Next** keyword. The **Next** keyword signals to VBA that it has reached the end of the loop's body. VBA then increments the *counter* variable by *StepSize* if the **Step** optional keyword is included. If **Step** is not specified, VBA increments the *counter* variable by 1. VBA now returns to the top of the loop and compares the current value of the *counter* variable to the value represented by *end*. If *counter* is less than or equal to *end*, VBA executes the loop again. If *counter* is greater than *end*, VBA continues execution with the first statement after the **Next** keyword.

Using For...Next with a Count That Goes Up

Listing 9.1 shows a simple demonstration of the **For...Next** loop. This procedure obtains two numbers from the user, adds together every whole number in the range specified by the two numbers, and then displays the resulting sum onscreen. If you run this procedure and enter the numbers 4 and 8, for example, the procedure adds together the numbers 4, 5, 6, 7, and 8 and displays the number *30*.

INPUT   **LISTING 9.1**   A DEMONSTRATION OF THE **For...Next** LOOP, COUNTING UP

```
 1:  Sub Demo_ForNext()
 2:
 3:      Dim k As Integer
 4:      Dim uStart As String
 5:      Dim uEnd As String
 6:      Dim uSum As Long
 7:
 8:      uStart = InputBox("Enter an integer number:")
 9:      uEnd = InputBox("Enter another integer number:")
10:
11:      uSum = 0
12:      For k = CInt(uStart) To CInt(uEnd)
13:          uSum = uSum + k
14:      Next k
15:
16:      MsgBox "The sum of the numbers from " & uStart & _
17:              " to " & uEnd & " is: " & uSum
18:  End Sub
```

ANALYSIS   Lines 3 through 6 declare several variables for this procedure to use. The k variable is used as the **For...Next** loop's counter variable; the other variables are used to hold the starting and stopping values obtained from the user and to hold the sum of numbers.

Line 8 uses InputBox to get a number from the user and stores that number in uStart. Line 9 also uses InputBox to get a number from the user, this time storing it in uEnd. (This procedure assumes the first number entered is smaller than the second number entered.)

Line 11 sets the uSum variable to 0; no processing of the user's input has taken place yet, so the sum must be zero.

Finally, line 12 starts the **For...Next** loop. When VBA executes this line, it first executes the **CInt** function calls, which convert the user's string input into **Integer** numbers, and then inserts the resulting integer values into the statement.

VBA assigns the integer equivalent of the value stored in uStart to the counting variable, k. If you enter the number 4 in the first input dialog, the k counting variable receives the value 4 at the start of the loop.

Next, still in line 12, VBA compares the value in k to the integer equivalent of the number stored in uEnd. If k is less than or equal to the value in uEnd, VBA executes the body of the loop. If you enter the number 8 in response to the second input dialog, VBA compares 4 to 8; 4 is indeed less than 8, so VBA executes the statement in line 13.

This loop has only one statement in its body: the addition and assignment expression in line 13. This line adds the current value of k to the current contents of the uSum variable and then assigns the result of that addition to uSum. The first time through the loop, k is equal to 4 and uSum contains 0; after VBA finishes executing this statement, the value stored in uSum is the result of adding 0 + 4, so uSum ends up containing the number 4.

Now VBA encounters the **Next** statement in line 14. This statement signals the end of the **For** loop's body; VBA increments the counter variable and returns to the top of the loop. At this point, the counter variable, k, still contains the number 4. The **Step** option was not specified in this **For...Next** loop, so VBA uses the default increment step and adds 1 to the contents of k. The counting variable now contains the number 5.

VBA returns to the top of the loop in line 12 and compares the value in the counter variable, k, to the number represented by the contents of the uEnd variable. k currently contains 5, which is still less than 8, so VBA again executes the statement in line 13. After executing the statement in line 13, the uSum variable contains the value 9: the result of adding 4 (the previous contents of uSum) to 5 (the current counter value).

Again, VBA encounters the **Next** statement in line 14, increments the counter variable k, and returns to the top of the loop to compare the value in the counter variable to the ending value. The following table lists the values of the counter variable, k, and the uSum variable for each repetition of the loop:

Loop	Value of k	Value of uSum
0	0	0 (loop has not started)
1	4	4
2	5	9
3	6	15
4	7	22
5	8	30

The fifth time VBA executes the loop, k contains the value 8. After VBA increments the loop counter in line 14, k has the value 9. When VBA returns to the top of the loop, the value in the counter variable is no longer less than or equal to the specified ending value of 8. At last, the value in the loop counter exceeds the value specified for the ending count, and VBA stops executing the loop.

Now that the loop has ended, VBA continues execution with the MsgBox statement in line 16, which displays the two numbers that you entered and the sum of all integers in that range.

9

You'll see many other examples of **For...Next** loops throughout this book. You will frequently use **For...Next** loops with arrays (covered in Day 14, "Arrays").

Note

If the first value the user enters (in uStart) is larger than the second value the user enters (in uEnd), the **For...Next** loop does not execute at all: the starting value for the loop counter exceeds the ending value before the loop ever executes. When this happens, VBA does not execute the loop at all. For example, if you enter 8 first and then enter 4, the loop does not execute; VBA skips over the statements in the loop and execution moves from line 12 to line 16.

Do

DO use an **Integer** or **Long** data type variable for the counter in **For...Next** loops. Using an **Integer** or **Long** data type saves memory and speeds up the execution of your loop.

DO specify the counter variable after the **Next** statement. Although placing the counter variable after the **Next** statement is optional, it greatly improves the readability of your program code. Also, VBA does not have to spend time determining which counter variable belongs with that **Next** statement, so your loops execute faster.

DO take advantage of the fact that you can count from any number up to any other number, if you want.

Using For...Next with a Count That Goes Down

You don't always have to write **For...Next** loops that count up. Sometimes it's easier or more useful to write a **For** loop that counts down. To make a **For...Next** loop count down, use the **Step** keyword and a negative number for the step value.

Listing 9.2 shows the same procedure from Listing 9.1, but it has been modified to include a **For...Next** loop that counts down from a higher starting value to a lower ending value. Like the procedure in Listing 9.1, this procedure gets two numbers from the user, adds together every whole number in the range specified by the two numbers, and then displays the resulting sum onscreen. If you run this procedure and enter the numbers 8 and 4, for example, the procedure adds together the numbers 8, 7, 6, 5, and 4 and displays the number 30.

INPUT   **LISTING 9.2**   MAKING A **For...Next** LOOP THAT COUNTS DOWN

```
 1:  Sub Demo_ForNextDown()
 2:
 3:      Dim k As Integer
 4:      Dim uStart As Integer
 5:      Dim uEnd As Integer
 6:      Dim uSum As Long
 7:
 8:      uStart = CInt(InputBox("Enter an integer number:"))
 9:      uEnd = CInt(InputBox("Enter another integer number:"))
10:
11:      uSum = 0
12:      For k = uStart To uEnd Step -1      'loop counts down
13:          uSum = uSum + k
14:      Next k
15:
16:      MsgBox "The sum of the numbers from " & uStart & _
17:              " to " & uEnd & " is: " & uSum
18:  End Sub
```

ANALYSIS   Line 8 is different from the corresponding line in Listing 9.1. When VBA executes this statement, it first calls InputBox to get a number from the user. After the user enters a number, VBA calls the **CInt** function and converts the **String** result of the InputBox function to an **Integer** type value. VBA stores the result of the **CInt** function (an integer number with the value corresponding to the string entered by the user) in the uStart variable.

Similarly, line 9 also uses InputBox to get a value from the user, calls the **CInt** function to convert the string entered by the user to an integer, and assigns the resulting integer to the uEnd variable. This procedure does not perform any checking of the user's input: It assumes that the first number entered is *larger* than the second number entered.

The **CInt** function was used directly in the statements that obtain input from the user in order to speed up the **For...Next** loop: In the procedure in Listing 9.1, VBA has to execute the **CInt** function each time it evaluates the loop's determinant condition (line 12 of Listing 9.1), which slows the loop down. In Listing 9.2, the strings entered by the user in the two InputBox statements have already been converted to numbers; the loop that starts in line 12 of Listing 9.2 therefore executes that much faster.

Line 12 of Listing 9.2 starts the **For...Next** loop. When VBA executes this line, it assigns the value stored in uStart to the counting variable, k. If you enter the number 8 in the first input dialog, the k counting variable receives the value 8 at the start of the loop.

Line 12 includes the **Step** keyword, so VBA also checks the *step value*—the amount by which VBA will increment the loop counter. In this loop, the step value is a negative number: -1. Because the step value is a negative number, VBA makes this loop count down rather than up. VBA *decrements* (subtracts from) the loop counter instead of incrementing it.

Because VBA is counting down, it checks to see whether the value of the loop counter is greater than or equal to the specified ending value instead of checking whether the loop counter is less than or equal to the ending value.

Still in line 12, VBA now compares the value in k to the number stored in uEnd. If k is greater than or equal to the value in uEnd, VBA executes the body of the loop. If you enter the number 4 in response to the second input dialog, VBA compares 8 to 4; 8 is greater than 4, so VBA executes the statement in line 13.

The statement in line 13 adds the current value of k to the current contents of the uSum variable and then assigns the result of that addition to uSum. The first time through the loop, k is equal to 8 and uSum contains 0, so after VBA finishes executing this statement, the value stored in uSum is 8, that is, 0 + 8.

VBA encounters the **Next** statement in line 14. The **Step** option was specified in this **For...Next** loop, so VBA uses the specified step value and subtracts 1 from the contents of k. The counting variable now contains the number 7.

VBA returns to the top of the loop in line 12 and compares the value in the counter variable, k, to the number in the uEnd variable. k currently contains 7, which is still greater than 4, so VBA again executes the statement in line 13. After executing the statement in line 13, the uSum variable contains the value 15, that is, 8 + 7.

Again, VBA encounters the **Next** statement in line 14, decrements the counter variable k, and returns to the top of the loop. The following table lists the values of the counter variable, k, and the uSum variable for each repetition of the loop:

Loop	*Value of* k	*Value of* uSum
0	0	0 (loop has not started)
1	8	8
2	7	15
3	6	21
4	5	26
5	4	30

The fifth time VBA executes the loop, k contains the value 4. After VBA decrements the loop counter in line 14, k has the value 3. VBA then returns to the top of the loop and compares the value in k to the value in uEnd. The value in the counter variable is no longer greater than or equal to the ending value, so VBA stops executing the loop.

Now that the loop has ended, VBA continues execution with the MsgBox statement in line 16, which displays the two numbers that you entered and the sum of all integers in that range.

9

Note

> If the first value the user enters is smaller than the second value, the For...Next loop does not execute at all for essentially the same reason that the loop in Listing 9.1 does not execute if the starting value is larger than the ending value. In Listing 9.2, for example, if you enter 4 first and then enter 8, the loop will not execute: VBA skips over the statements in the loop and execution moves from line 12 to line 16.

Do

DO use the Step keyword and a negative number to make VBA count down in a For...Next loop.

DO remember that when a For...Next loop counts *down,* it executes for as long as the counter variable is *greater than* or equal to the ending value, and that when it counts *up,* it executes for as long as the counter variable is *less than* or equal to the ending value.

DO remember that you can specify any numeric value as the Step value in a For...Next loop. You can write For...Next loops that increment or decrement the counter variable by 0.1, 2, 5.1 or any decimal number.

Putting the For...Next Loop to Work

The example procedures in Listings 9.1 and 9.2 show how the For...Next loop operates with various options, but they don't actually accomplish a particularly useful task. Typically, you use For...Next loops when you want to perform an action a fixed number of times or to perform operations on (or with) a fixed number of items.

You might use a For...Next loop to examine all the characters in a string, to apply the same font and character formatting to the first three columns in a worksheet, or some similar task involving a fixed number of items.

Listing 9.3 shows a **For...Next** loop that is used to repeat actions on every character in a string. The PCase function in Listing 9.3 returns a copy of its string argument with the first letter of each word capitalized and all other letters in lowercase characters. For example, if you pass either of the strings *LEAPING LIZARDS* or *leaping lizards* to the PCase function, it returns the string *Leaping Lizards*. Listing 9.3 also includes a procedure to test the PCase function.

INPUT

LISTING 9.3   USING **For...Next** TO PERFORM AN ACTION WITH EVERY CHARACTER IN A STRING

```
1:  Function PCase(iStr As String) As String
2:  'returns a copy of the string in the iStr argument with
3:  'the first letter of each word capitalized -- Proper Case
4:
5:    Dim oStr As String
6:    Dim k As Long
7:              'start output string with first letter
8:    oStr = UCase(Left(iStr, 1))
9:     'was prev char a space? if so, current char starts word
10:   For k = 2 To Len(iStr)
11:     If Mid(iStr, k - 1, 1) = " " Then
12:       oStr = oStr & UCase(Mid(iStr, k, 1))
13:     Else              'if not, force to lower case
14:       oStr = oStr & LCase(Mid(iStr, k, 1))
15:     End If
16:   Next k
17:
18:   PCase = oStr      'assign function result
19: End Function
20:
21:
22: Sub test_PCase()
23: 'this procedure tests the PCase function
24:
25:    Dim uStr As String
26:
27:    uStr = InputBox("Enter a string containing several " & _
28:                    "words separated by spaces:")
29:    MsgBox "You Entered: " & uStr & Chr(13) & _
30:           "PCase result: " & PCase(uStr)
31: End Sub
```

ANALYSIS

Line 1 contains the PCase function declaration; this function has a single required argument (passed by reference) and the function's result is declared as a **String** type. Line 5 declares a string variable, oStr, to hold the modified copy of the iStr argument as it is assembled. Line 6 declares a **Long** type variable, k, for use as the loop counter variable. (VBA strings can be as large as two billion characters—the limit of a **Long** integer—so this procedure uses a **Long** type loop counter to accommodate the maximum possible string size.)

In line 8, the Left function copies the first character from the iStr argument and the UCase function converts that character to its uppercase equivalent (if any); the result is then assigned to the oStr variable. Because the first letter in the iStr argument is also the start of a word, line 8 just converts the copy of that letter and stores it in oStr.

Line 10 begins the **For...Next** loop. The first time through this loop, VBA assigns the starting value 2 to the loop counter, k. The loop starts with the second character in iStr because the first character was already handled in line 8. The ending value for the counter variable in the **For** loop is obtained by using the Len function to return the length of the string stored in iStr. This **For...Next** loop will execute starting from a count of 2 up to the number of characters in iStr, executing the loop body once for each remaining character in iStr.

Line 11 begins the body of the **For...Next** loop: This loop contains a single **If...Then...Else** statement in its body. Line 11 is also the beginning of the **If...Then...Else** statement that forms the body of the loop.

The PCase function is used to capitalize the first letter of each word; it therefore has to be able to tell when a new word starts. The usual definition of a word—as far as most computer programs are concerned—is any group of characters separated from other characters in a string by a space. For the PCase function to identify the first letter of a word, it checks to see whether the character immediately preceding it is a space.

Line 11 uses the Mid function to return one character from iStr. The starting position from which Mid copies the character is specified as k-1, and the number of characters to copy is specified as 1. The first time through the loop, k has the value 2, indicating the second character in iStr, so the Mid function in line 11 returns the first character of the string in iStr (2-1). The logical expression in the **If...Then...Else** statement tests whether the character returned by the Mid function is a space character.

If the character preceding the current character in iStr (specified by k) is a space, the character indicated by the value in k must be the beginning of a word in the string. When the logical expression in line 11 is **True**, VBA executes line 12, which again uses Mid to copy a single character from iStr. This time, Mid copies one character starting at position k in iStr; the result of the Mid function is passed to the UCase function, which converts it to uppercase. The result of the UCase function is concatenated to the end of the string already in oStr and the result is stored in oStr. As the loop executes, oStr gradually gets longer and longer as each individual character from iStr is evaluated and copied to oStr. At the end of the loop, oStr will have the same length as iStr.

If the character preceding the current character in iStr (specified by k) is *not* a space, the character indicated by the value in k must be somewhere in the middle of a word in iStr. When the logical expression in line 11 is **False**, VBA executes line 14, which again uses Mid to copy a single character from iStr. Mid copies one character starting at position k in iStr; the result of the Mid function is passed to the LCase function, which converts it to lowercase (characters in the middle of a word should be lowercase). The result of the LCase function is concatenated to the end of the string already in oStr and the result is stored in oStr.

Whether or not VBA executes line 12 or line 14, the next line it executes is line 16, which contains the **Next** statement. At this point, VBA increments the loop counter, k, by one (no **Step** value was specified) and returns to the top of the loop in line 10. If k is still less than or equal to the length of the string in iStr, VBA executes the loop body again.

When the loop has finished executing, all the characters in iStr have been evaluated and VBA then executes line 18, which assigns the function's return value. The value in oStr is assigned to the function result and the function ends in line 19, returning its result.

Lines 22 through 31 contain a simple procedure to test the PCase function. Line 27 uses the InputBox function to get a string from the user. Line 29 uses the MsgBox function to display the string the user entered, and includes a call to the PCase function, displaying its result when passed the user's string. If you enter the string leaping lizards, the MsgBox statement in lines 29 and 30 displays the dialog shown in Figure 9.3.

FIGURE 9.3

The test_PCase *function displays this dialog if you enter the string* leaping lizards.

This type of manipulation—evaluating every character in a string, every column in a row, every row in a worksheet, and so on—is an ideal use for the **For...Next** loop.

Note

You don't really need to write a PCase function for use in your VBA procedures. The PCase function is used in this chapter because it is an easy-to-understand example of string manipulation using a **For** loop. VBA includes a function, StrConv, that performs the same task, plus a variety of other tasks. You can use the StrConv function to convert strings to all uppercase, all lowercase, proper case, and to convert strings to or from Unicode. (Unicode is the International Standards Organization scheme for character coding.) To learn more about the StrConv function, refer to the VBA online help system.

Do

DO allow VBA to handle incrementing or decrementing the loop counter "naturally," making your For...Next loops easier to understand and write.

DON'T

DON'T change the value of a For...Next loop counter variable inside the body of the loop. Although you can assign a new value to the loop counter variable inside the loop, altering the loop counter's value might cause your For...Next loop to execute too many or too few times, leading to subtle bugs in your procedures.

Using the For Each...Next Loop

The second For loop is the For Each...Next loop. Unlike the For...Next loop, the For Each...Next loop does not use a loop counter. Instead, For Each...Next loops execute for as many times as there are elements in a specified group, such as a collection of objects or an array. (You learned about collections of objects in Day 7; Day 14 describes arrays.) In other words, the For Each...Next loop executes once *for each* item in a group.

▼ SYNTAX

The For Each...Next loop has the following general syntax:

```
For Each element In group
      statements
Next [element]
```

element is a variable used to iterate through all the items in the specified group. *group* is either a collection object or an array. If *group* is a collection object, *element* must be a **Variant** type variable, an **Object** type variable, or a specific object type, such as Range, Worksheet, Cell, Chart, and so on. If *group* is an array, *element* must be a **Variant** type variable. *statements* represents none, one, or several VBA statements making up the body of the loop.

The For Each...Next loop has fewer options than the For...Next loop. Counting up or counting down is not relevant to a For Each...Next loop; the For Each...Next loop always executes as many times as there are elements in the specified group.

▲

Listing 9.4 shows a function named SheetExists, which uses the For Each...Next loop to determine whether a particular sheet exists in an Excel workbook.

9

LISTING 9.4 USING **For Each...Next**

```
 1: Function SheetExists(sName As String) As Boolean
 2: 'Returns True if sName sheet exists in the active workbook
 3:
 4:    Dim aSheet As Object
 5:
 6:    SheetExists = False   'assume sheet won't be found
 7:
 8:      'cycle through all sheets, compare each sheet's name to
 9:      'sName, as a text comparison.
10:    For Each aSheet In ActiveWorkbook.Sheets
11:      If (StrComp(aSheet.Name, sName, 1) = 0) Then
12:        SheetExists = True    'sheet names match, return true
13:      End If
14:    Next aSheet
15: End Function
16:
17:
18: Sub Test_SheetExists()
19: 'tests the SheetExists function
20:
21:    Dim uStr As String
22:
23:    uStr = InputBox("Enter the name of a sheet in the " & _
24:                    "current workbook:")
25:    If SheetExists(uStr) Then
26:      MsgBox "Sheet '" & uStr & _
27:             "' DOES exist in the current workbook."
28:    Else
29:      MsgBox "Sheet '" & uStr & _
30:             "' does NOT exist in the current workbook."
31:    End If
32: End Sub
```

ANALYSIS This function has one required argument, sName, which contains a string representing the name of the sheet being searched for. SheetExists returns a **Boolean**
type value: **True** if the sheet named by sName exists in the current workbook, **False** otherwise. You might use a function like this in one of your procedures to ensure that a
worksheet or chart sheet exists before your procedure attempts to select that sheet; if
your procedure tries to select a sheet that does not exist, VBA displays a runtime error
message and stops executing your program. A function like SheetExists enables you to
write your procedures so that they can detect and avoid possible errors that might occur,
such as when a user enters a nonexistent worksheet name.

Line 4 declares the aSheet object variable for use in the **For Each...Next** loop. Line 6 assigns the value **False** to the SheetExists function result. This statement assumes that the sheet named in sName will *not* be found. Assuming failure simplifies the decision-making task in the remaining portion of this function. Now, the function only has to detect if the sheet is found and assign **True** to the function result.

Line 10 starts the **For Each...Next** loop using the aSheet object variable as the element variable for the loop. The specified group is the ActiveWorkbook.Sheets collection. ActiveWorkbook is a property of the Application object, and returns an object reference to the current active workbook. Sheets is a workbook method that returns the collection of all sheets in the workbook, including worksheets and chart sheets.

Line 10 tells VBA to execute the statements in the loop body for as many times as there are sheets in the active workbook, that is, to repeat the actions once for each object in the Sheets collection. As VBA begins the **For Each...Next** loop, it assigns aSheet to refer to the first object in the Sheets collection, whatever that sheet happens to be.

Line 11 starts the body of the loop, which consists of a single **If...Then** statement. When VBA executes line 11, it first calls **StrComp** to compare the string in sName to the string stored in the Name property of the sheet currently referenced by aSheet. This call to **StrComp** specifies that the comparison should be a text comparison, and therefore unaffected by any differences in capitalization between the string in sName and the string in the sheet's Name property. Line 11 uses **StrComp** to compare the strings, rather than a simple relational operator, to ensure that the string comparison is always a text comparison regardless of the **Option Compare** settings.

If the string in sName matches the string in the sheet's Name property, VBA executes line 12, which assigns the value **True** to the function's result.

Whether or not the string in sName matches the string in the sheet's Name property, VBA next executes line 14, which contains the **Next** keyword ending the **For Each...Next** loop. VBA now returns to the top of the loop in line 10 and checks to see whether all the elements in the group have been used. If not, VBA assigns the next element in the Sheets collection to the aSheet object variable and executes the loop again. If the active workbook contains 10 sheets, for example, the **For Each...Next** loop executes 10 times; if the active workbook contains four sheets, the loop executes four times.

When VBA finishes executing the loop for all the elements in the ActiveWorkbook.Sheets collection, it continues execution with line 15, which ends the SheetExists function and returns the function result. If, at any time during the execution of the **For Each...Next** loop, the string in sName matched the string in one of the sheets' Name properties, SheetExists returns **True**, indicating that the sheet specified by sName

9

does exist in the active workbook; otherwise, the function returns **False**, indicating that the sheet does not exist.

Lines 18 through 29 declare a procedure, Test_SheetExists, to test the SheetExists function. Line 23 of the test procedure uses InputBox to get a sheet name from the user, and lines 25 through 31 contain an **If...Then...Else** statement that calls the SheetExists function, evaluates its result, and then displays a message dialog stating whether the sheet name entered by the user does in fact exist in the current workbook.

When VBA executes line 25, it calls the SheetExists function, passing the string entered by the user (uStr) as the argument to SheetExists. If the user entered a valid sheet name, SheetExists returns **True** and VBA executes line 26 to display a message to that effect. If the user entered an invalid sheet name, SheetExists returns **False** and VBA executes line 29, displaying a message that the sheet does not exist.

You will see many more examples of the **For Each...Next** loop throughout the rest of this book, particularly in Day 14, where you learn how to use **For Each...Next** with arrays.

Do

DO make sure that the **For Each** element variable is of a type compatible with the specified group. For example, if you specify a collection of worksheets, the element variable should be a **Variant**, a generic **Object** type, or a Worksheet object type.

DO use the trick of assuming a particular outcome of a test to simplify the decision-making process for that test, as shown in the SheetExists function in line 6.

DO use the **StrComp** function to compare strings when you want to ensure that a string comparison is either a binary or text comparison, and that the comparison is unaffected by the **Option Compare** settings.

Flexible Repetition: The Do Loops

VBA provides you with an extremely powerful looping statement to create indefinite looping structures in your procedures and functions. Essentially, you construct all of VBA's indefinite loops with a single indefinite looping statement: the **Do** statement. The **Do** statement has so many options and is so flexible that, in effect, it provides you with four different loop constructions in two basic categories.

The two basic categories of **Do** loop constructions are loops that test the determinant condition *before* executing the body of the loop, and loops that test the determinant condition *after* executing the body of the loop. Later sections in this chapter describe when and how to use these two categories of looping structure and their specific syntax.

There are two basic ways to control how many times an indefinite loop executes, regardless of whether VBA tests the loop's determinant condition before or after it executes the body of the loop:

- *Count-controlled loops.* In a count-controlled loop, the body of the loop executes while a particular count is above or below some specified limit; it is similar to a **For...Next** loop, except that you, the programmer, are responsible for initializing the counting variable and incrementing or decrementing the count. You might write a count-controlled loop using the **Do** statement if the counting step is irregular, or if there is no way to determine the ending limit until after the loop has started executing. For example, you might want to pace through the first 16 rows of a worksheet, sometimes advancing a single row at a time and other times advancing two rows at time. Because the number of rows to advance (that is, the step for the count) changes, you cannot use a **For...Next** loop; you must use a **Do** loop instead.

- *Event-controlled loops.* In an event-controlled loop, the determinant condition becomes true or false based on some event or action that occurs within the loop. For example, you might write a loop that executes indefinitely until the user enters a particular value in an input dialog. The user's input of that particular value is the event that ends the loop. As another example, you might perform operations on the cells in a worksheet until you reach an empty cell; reaching the empty cell is the event that ends the loop.

Understanding How VBA Tests the Loop Determinant

You specify the determinant condition for an indefinite loop with a logical expression in the same way you construct logical expressions for use with **If...Then** statements.

VBA provides two different ways of testing the determinant condition for a loop. You can construct a loop so that it executes for as long as the loop's determinant condition is **True** and stops executing when the determinant condition becomes **False**. You can also construct a loop so that it executes for as long as the loop's determinant condition is **False** and stops executing when the determinant condition becomes **True**.

To make a loop execute as long as its determinant condition is **True**, use the optional **While** keyword in the **Do** loop statement. VBA then executes the loop *while* the condition is **True** and stops executing the loop as soon as the determinant condition becomes **False**.

Suppose you want to write a procedure that helps a user enter data into a worksheet. For a data entry procedure, you usually want the procedure to repeat whatever statements get information from the user while there is still more data to enter and to stop repeating those statements when there is no more data. You might, therefore, write a **Do** loop that repeatedly gets data from the user and continues to execute for as long as the user enters non-blank strings and then stops as soon as the user enters a blank string. You would write the determinant condition for this loop so that the logical expression is **True**—and so the loop continues to execute—as long as the user's input is *not* an empty string. If the user's input is stored in a variable named uStr, the logical expression for the loop determinant could be either of the following:

```
uStr <> ""
Len(Trim(uStr)) <> 0
```

Both of the preceding logical expressions are **True** when the string in uStr is not zero-length (or all spaces, as in the second example).

To make a loop execute as long as its determinant condition is **False**, use the optional **Until** keyword in the **Do** loop statement. VBA then executes the loop *until* the condition is **True**, that is, the loop continues to execute as long as the condition is **False** and stops executing as soon as the determinant condition becomes **True**.

For example, you might want to write a procedure that advances column by column across a worksheet applying a particular text and character formatting to column headings and stopping at the first blank column. You can write a **Do** loop that repeats the statements to format a column heading until a blank cell is encountered. You would write the determinant condition for this loop so that the logical expression is **False** as long as the current cell is not blank and is **True** whenever the current cell is blank. Using the ActiveCell property of the Application object to return the current active cell, and using the Value property to obtain the cell's contents, your logical expression for the determinant could be either of the following:

```
ActiveCell.Value = ""
Len(Trim(ActiveCell.Value)) = 0
```

Both expressions evaluate **True** when the current cell is empty.

Whether you use the **While** or **Until** keywords depends mostly on how you think about the conditions that determine whether the loop should execute, and on how easily you can construct a logical expression for the loop's determinant condition:

- Use **While** if you want the loop to continue executing as long as the specified condition is **True**.
- Use **Until** when you want the loop to continue executing as long as the specified condition is **False**.

You can always write the same loop structure either way, depending on how you formulate your logical expression; the loop structure you choose is largely a matter of personal preference.

The following sections describe in detail how to use the specific options of the **Do** statement.

> **Caution**
>
> Be careful, as you construct your **Do** loops, to choose a determinant condition that will, at some point, really cause the loop to stop executing. The most common error that programmers make when constructing indefinite loops is making a mistake in formulating the loop's determinant condition, resulting in a loop that never stops executing because the determinant condition never becomes **False** (or **True**, in an **Until** loop). Loops that never stop executing are called *infinite* loops because they execute infinitely.
>
> If you end up with an infinite loop in one of your procedures, that procedure will never end and your computer system might appear to have crashed or locked up. If the apparent computer system crash is the result of an infinite loop, you can interrupt your procedure as described in the sidebar in this section.
>
> If you suspect that your computer has locked up due to an infinite loop in one of your procedures, try to interrupt the procedure by pressing the Esc key (see sidebar). *Only reboot your computer as a last resort*; rebooting your computer can cause loss of data in programs that are active at the time you reboot the computer.

How to Interrupt an Executing Procedure

Because one of the most common problems you'll encounter while working with indefinite loop structures is inadvertently creating an infinite loop, it is important that you know how to interrupt VBA when it is executing your procedures. Use the same technique to interrupt recorded macros or to interrupt the execution of procedures and functions you have written from scratch.

To interrupt VBA's execution, press the Esc key or press the Ctrl+Break key combination. VBA finishes executing the current statement, suspends any further statement execution, and displays the runtime error dialog shown in Figure 9.4. The command buttons in this runtime error dialog are the same as those in any other runtime error dialog (originally described in Day 2), and have the same effects, summarized following:

- *Continue.* Resumes VBA's execution of program statements. Usually, you should *not* make this choice after interrupting an infinite loop because it will just start the infinite loop again.
- *End.* Ends the program. All variables and their contents are lost. This is the command button you should usually choose after interrupting an infinite loop.

- *Debug.* Activates VBA's break mode so that you can examine the contents of variables and pace through the execution of your loop to determine why it isn't stopping. Using the VBA break mode and program debugging is the topic of Day 15, "Debugging and Testing VBA Code."

- *Help. Activates* VBA's online help system to display information about why code execution has been interrupted. The Help button isn't very useful if you interrupt code execution by pressing Esc or Ctrl+Break: The help topic merely states that code execution has halted as a result of pressing Esc or Ctrl+Break and gives instructions on how to enter break mode or end code execution.

You cannot interrupt VBA while it is displaying a dialog box; you must close any input, message, or other dialogs before you can interrupt a procedure—fortunately, the Esc key also closes open dialogs.

Depending on your exact loop and the statements it contains, VBA might not respond to a single Esc or Ctrl+Break keystroke. In fact, you usually must press and hold down the Esc key to interrupt an executing procedure. If you do hold down the Esc key, you can inadvertently close the runtime error dialog (see Figure 9.4). As a result, the error dialog might flash on the screen too quickly for you to read it. If this does happen to you, don't worry; you'll probably have a good idea of which loop was stuck based on how far your procedure got before it broke down, and the typical choice for this runtime error dialog is to choose the End command button, which is the equivalent of the Esc key, anyway.

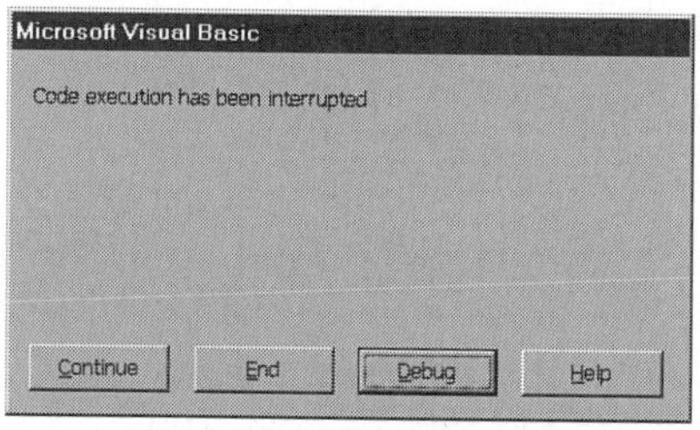

FIGURE 9.4

VBA displays this dialog when you press Esc or Ctrl+Break to interrupt an executing procedure or macro.

Microsoft Visual Basic

Code execution has been interrupted

Continue   End   Debug   Help

Using Loops That Test Conditions Before Execution

To have VBA test the loop determinant condition before executing the body of the loop, you simply place the logical expression for the loop determinant at the beginning of the block of statements that make up the body of the loop. The following sections describe how to use the **While** and **Until** keywords to build loops that test their conditions before executing the loop body.

Building Loops with Do While

The first loop construction that tests its determinant condition before executing the loop is the **Do While**.

9

SYNTAX

The general syntax of the **Do While** statement is

```
Do While condition
    statements
Loop
```

condition represents the logical expression for the loop's determinant. *statements* represents none, one, or several statements that make up the body of the loop. VBA executes all statements in the body of the loop each time it executes the loop. The **Loop** keyword after *statements* indicates the end of the loop's body, and also indicates the point at which VBA returns to the top of the loop to check the determinant condition.

The **Do While** statement has the *condition* expression at the top of the loop, so VBA checks the determinant condition before executing the loop. Because this form uses the **While** keyword, VBA executes the loop as long as the logical expression represented by *condition* is **True**.

When VBA executes a **Do While** loop, it first tests the logical expression represented by *condition*; if it is **True**, VBA executes the statements represented by *statements*. When VBA reaches the **Loop** keyword, it returns to the top of the loop and again checks to see whether the *condition* logical expression is **True**. If *condition* is **True**, VBA executes the loop again; if it is **False**, VBA continues execution with whatever statements appear after the **Loop** keyword.

Notice that if the logical expression represented by *condition* is **False** the first time VBA executes the **Do While** statement, VBA simply skips the loop without executing it at all.

Listing 9.5 shows a simple example of a **Do While** loop that repeatedly gets a number from the user, stopping only after the user has entered 10 odd numbers.

INPUT   **LISTING 9.5**   DEMONSTRATING THE **Do While** LOOP

```
 1:  Sub Count_OddNums()
 2:  'counts the odd numbers entered by the user, and stops
 3:  'executing when a total of 10 odd numbers has been entered
 4:
 5:      Const ocTitle = "Odd Number Count"
 6:
 7:      Dim OddCount As Integer    'holds count of odd numbers
 8:      Dim OddStr As String       'string to display odd nums
 9:      Dim Num                    'Variant to hold user input
10:
11:      OddStr = ""
12:      OddCount = 0    'initialize the loop counter
```

continues

LISTING 9.5   CONTINUED

```
13:     Do While OddCount < 10
14:         Num = InputBox("Enter a number:", ocTitle)
15:         If (Num Mod 2) <> 0 Then
16:             OddCount = OddCount + 1
17:             OddStr = OddStr & Num & " "
18:         End If
19:     Loop
20:
21:     MsgBox prompt:="You entered the following odd " & _
22:                    "numbers:" & Chr(13) & OddStr, _
23:             Title:=ocTitle
24: End Sub
```

ANALYSIS   Count_OddNums simply demonstrates how you go about constructing a **Do While** loop. The loop in this procedure executes while the user has entered less than 10 odd numbers (an *odd* number is any number that you cannot divide evenly by 2). At first, it might seem that you could accomplish this task with a **For...Next** loop, but that is not really possible. Although the loop in this procedure is a count-controlled loop, the counter that controls the loop's execution is not necessarily incremented every time the loop executes. If the user enters an even number, the loop does not increment the count of odd numbers. The only way to create a count-controlled loop that increments the counter variable at irregular intervals is with some variety of the **Do** statement.

Line 7 declares an **Integer** type variable, OddCount, to hold the count of odd numbers. Line 8 declares a **String** type variable, OddStr, to hold a string assembled from all the odd numbers the user enters while the loop is executing. Line 9 declares a **Variant** type variable, Num, to hold the user's input. This procedure uses a **Variant** type variable for the user's input to avoid having to explicitly convert the string from the InputBox function into a number.

Line 11 initializes the OddStr variable by assigning an empty string to it. Line 12 contains a very important assignment statement related to the loop's execution. Line 12 initializes the OddCount variable to 0, ensuring that the loop beginning in line 13 does start execution. (*Never* assume that a variable contains any particular value unless you assign that value to the variable in one of your program statements.)

Line 13 starts the **Do** loop. This statement has the **While** keyword and loop determinant condition at the top of the loop, so VBA will execute this loop while the logical expression for the loop's determinant condition is **True**, and VBA will also test the determinant condition before executing the loop. The first time VBA evaluates this statement, the value stored in the OddCount variable is 0, so the expression OddCount < 10 is **True** and VBA begins executing the loop starting with line 14.

Line 14 is the first statement in the body of the loop; it uses InputBox to get a number from the user and stores the user's input in the Num variable.

Line 15 is an **If...Then** statement that evaluates the number entered by the user. When VBA evaluates the expression (Num Mod 2) <> 0, it first performs the modulo division inside the parentheses. (Remember, VBA evaluates the portions of an expression enclosed in parentheses first.) The **Mod** division operator, as you might recall from Day 4, returns the remainder of a division operation. After performing the **Mod** division, VBA performs the indicated relational operation. If the result of the **Mod** division is not equal to 0, the expression is **True**; if the result of the **Mod** division operation is equal to 0, the expression is **False**. An odd number is a number that cannot be divided evenly by 2; therefore, if there is a remainder after dividing Num by 2, Num must contain an odd number.

If Num is an odd number, VBA executes the statements in lines 16 and 17. Line 16 increments the counter variable for the loop by adding one to the current value of OddCount and then assigning the result of that addition to OddCount. The statement in line 17 concatenates the string equivalent of the odd number to the end of the string in the OddStr variable. (The loop assembles this string so that the user's input can be displayed when the loop is finished executing.)

When VBA executes line 19, the **Loop** keyword tells VBA that it has reached the end of the loop's body and that it should go back to the top of the loop. VBA returns to line 13 and again evaluates the logical expression for the loop's determinant condition. If OddCount is still less than 10, VBA executes the body of the loop again, gets another number from the user, evaluates it to see whether it is an odd number, and increments the OddCount variable, as necessary.

As soon as the user has entered 10 odd numbers, however, the value in the OddCount variable is also 10, and the logical expression of the loop's determinant condition is no longer **True**. VBA then skips over the body of the loop and continues execution with the first statement after the line that contains the **Loop** keyword: line 21, in this case.

The statement in line 21 displays a message to the user that includes the OddStr string variable to show the odd numbers entered by the user.

As you study this **Do While** loop, notice that the loop can actually execute many more than 10 times. For example, if you run this procedure and enter all the whole numbers from 1 to 20, the loop executes 20 times, although only 10 odd numbers are entered.

Building Loops with Do Until

The **Do While** variation of the **Do** statement is only one way to construct a **Do** statement that tests its determinant condition before executing the body of the loop. You can also use the **Do Until** form of the **Do** statement to build a **Do** loop that tests its determinant condition before executing the body of the loop.

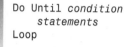

The general syntax of the **Do Until** statement is

```
Do Until condition
    statements
Loop
```

condition represents the logical expression for the loop's determinant and *statements* represents the VBA statements that make up the body of the loop. The **Loop** keyword after *statements* indicates the end of the loop's body, and also indicates the point at which VBA returns to the top of the loop to check the determinant condition.

The **Do Until** statement has the *condition* expression at the top of the loop, so VBA tests the loop's determinant condition before executing the loop. Because this form includes the **Until** keyword, VBA executes the loop as long as the logical expression represented by *condition* is **False**.

When VBA executes a **Do Until** loop, it first tests the logical expression represented by *condition*; if it is **False**, VBA executes the statements represented by *statements*. When VBA reaches the **Loop** keyword, it returns to the top of the loop and again checks to see whether the *condition* logical expression is **False**. If *condition* is **False**, VBA executes the loop again; if it is **True**, VBA continues execution with whatever statements appear after the **Loop** keyword.

▲ If *condition* is **True** the first time VBA executes the **Do Until** statement, VBA skips the loop without executing it at all.

Listing 9.6 shows a simple example of a **Do Until** loop that repeatedly gets a number from the user, stopping when the user enters an even number greater than 10.

INPUT   **LISTING 9.6**   DEMONSTRATING THE **Do Until** LOOP

```
1:    Sub Stop_AtEvenNums()
2:    'receives numbers from the user until the user enters an
3:    'even number greater than 10, and then stops executing.
4:
5:        Const evTitle = "Stop At Even Numbers"
6:
7:        Dim EvenFlag As Boolean
8:        Dim Num                      'Variant to hold user's input
```

```
9:
10:    EvenFlag = False   'initialize loop's control "flag"
11:    Do Until EvenFlag = True
12:      Num = InputBox("Enter a number:", evTitle)
13:      If ((Num Mod 2) = 0) Then
14:        If Num > 10 Then
15:          MsgBox prompt:="You entered an even number " & _
16:                     "greater than 10 - the loop ends.", _
17:                Title:=evTitle
18:          EvenFlag = True
19:        Else
20:          MsgBox prompt:="You entered an even number " & _
21:                     "less than (or equal) 10 - the loop " & _
22:                     "continues.", _
23:                Title:=evTitle
24:        End If
25:      Else
26:        MsgBox prompt:="You entered an odd number.", _
27:                Title:=evTitle
28:      End If
29:    Loop
30:
31:    MsgBox prompt:="The loop has ended.", Title:=evTitle
32:  End Sub
```

ANALYSIS Stop_AtEvenNums demonstrates how to construct a **Do Until** loop. The loop in this procedure executes until the user enters an even number greater than 10. The loop in this procedure also demonstrates an event-controlled loop. The event that ends the loop's execution is the user's entry of an even number.

Line 7 declares a **Boolean** type variable, EvenFlag. This **Boolean** variable is used as a "flag" to signal whether the loop in the procedure should continue executing. Flag-controlled loops are a special variety of event-controlled loop. In this flag-controlled loop—because the loop uses the **Until** keyword—a *raised* flag (one with the value **True**) indicates that the loop should stop executing. In a loop that uses the **While** keyword, you would usually construct the loop so that it continues to execute when the flag value is **True**.

Line 8 declares a **Variant** type variable, Num, to store the user's input. Because the value is stored in a **Variant** type variable, VBA handles the string to number conversion automatically.

Line 10 initializes the EvenFlag variable to **False**. This initialization statement is very important to the loop that begins in line 11. By assigning the value **False** to the EvenFlag variable, this statement ensures that the loop in line 11 will actually start.

The first time VBA evaluates the statement in line 11, the value stored in the EvenFlag variable is **False**, so the expression for the loop determinant—which contains only the EvenFlag variable—is also **False**, and VBA begins executing the body of the loop starting with line 12.

Line 12 uses InputBox to obtain a number from the user and stores it in the Num variable. Next, the **If...Then...Else** statement in line 13 tests the number the user entered. First, VBA evaluates the expression (Num Mod 2) = 0—notice that this expression is *not* the same as the expression used in Listing 9.5 to test for an odd number. This time, the result of the **Mod** division is tested to see whether it is equal to 0. If there is no remainder after dividing Num by 2, Num must be an even number.

If Num is an even number, VBA continues execution with line 14, which begins a nested **If...Then...Else** statement. The **If...Then...Else** statement in line 14 tests the value stored in Num to see whether that value is greater than 10. If Num is greater than 10, VBA executes line 15, which uses the MsgBox statement to display a message stating that the user's number is even and that it is greater than 10.

Line 18 is also very important in this loop. This line sets the EvenFlag variable **True**. After VBA executes this statement, the loop determinant condition is **True** and the loop stops executing the next time VBA evaluates the loop determinant expression. Notice that VBA only executes this statement in line 18 when the value in Num is both even *and* greater than 10.

If the value in Num is not greater than 10, VBA executes the **Else** clause starting in line 19, which consists of the single MsgBox statement in line 20. Line 20 displays a message stating that the user's number was even, but less than 10. No change is made to the EvenFlag variable, so the loop continues executing.

If the value in Num is not an even number, VBA executes the **Else** clause in line 25, which contains a single MsgBox statement in line 26 that displays a message stating the user's number was odd.

No matter which branch of the nested **If...Then...Else** statements ends up being executed, VBA continues execution with the **Loop** statement in line 29. The **Loop** keyword signals the end of the loop and VBA returns to the top of the loop in line 11.

VBA again checks the expression for the loop determinant. If the EvenFlag variable is still **False**, VBA executes the loop again. If the user enters an even number greater than 10, causing the statement in line 18 to execute, EvenFlag is **True** and VBA does not execute the loop but continues execution with line 31. Line 31 contains a MsgBox statement that displays a message stating the loop has ended.

Using Loops That Test Conditions After Execution

To have VBA test the loop determinant condition after executing the body of the loop, you simply place the logical expression for the loop determinant at the end of the block of statements that make up the body of the loop after the **Loop** keyword that signals the end of the loop. The following sections describe how to use the **While** and **Until** keywords to build loops that test their conditions after executing the loop body.

Building Loops with `Do...Loop While`

The first loop construction that tests its determinant condition after executing the loop body is the **Do...Loop While**.

The general syntax of the **Do...Loop While** statement is

```
Do
    statements
Loop While condition
```

statements represents none, one, or several VBA statements making up the body of the loop. The **Loop** keyword after *statements* indicates the end of the loop's body and also indicates the point at which VBA returns to the top of the loop. *condition* represents the logical expression for the loop's determinant.

In this syntax form, the **Do...Loop While** statement has the *condition* expression at the bottom of the loop, so VBA checks the determinant condition after executing the loop. Because this form of the **Do** statement uses the **While** keyword, VBA executes the loop as long as the logical expression represented by *condition* is **True**.

When VBA executes a **Do...Loop While** statement, it first executes the statements represented by *statements*. When VBA reaches the **Loop While** keywords, it tests the logical expression represented by *condition*; if the logical expression is **True**, VBA returns to the top of the loop and again executes the body of the loop. When VBA again reaches the **Loop While** keywords at the bottom of the loop, it checks to see whether the *condition* logical expression is still **True**. If *condition* is **True**, VBA executes the loop again; if it is **False**, VBA continues execution with whatever statements appear after the line containing the **Loop** keyword.

▲ Notice that regardless of the value of the logical expression represented by *condition*, this loop always executes at least once.

The GetInput procedure in Listing 9.7 is a prototypical form of a data-entry procedure that uses a **Do...Loop While** loop construction to get input from the user until the user enters the word *exit*, indicating that data entry is complete.

9

```
 1: Sub GetInput()
 2: 'demonstrates Do...Loop While structure. Loops repeatedly
 3: 'while user's input does not equal the word "exit"
 4:
 5:    Const iTitle = "Data Entry"
 6:
 7:    Dim uStr As String
 8:
 9:    Do
10:       uStr = InputBox(prompt:="Enter a string " & _
11:                               "('exit' to end):", _
12:                       Title:=iTitle, _
13:                       default:="exit")
14:       'statements to process or validate user's input, or to
15:       'store user's input in worksheet cell, etc. go here.
16:       MsgBox prompt:="You entered: " & uStr, Title:=iTitle
17:    Loop While uStr <> "exit"
18:
19:       MsgBox prompt:="Data entry completed.", _
20:              Title:=iTitle, Buttons:=vbExclamation
21: End Sub
```

ANALYSIS   The `GetInput` procedure loops indefinitely, continuing for as long as the user does *not* enter the word *exit*. You might use a procedure like this to help a user perform data entry for one of your worksheets. The `Do` loop in the `GetInput` procedure is a variety of event-controlled loop that is often referred to as a *sentinel-controlled* loop. Sentinel-controlled loops get their name from the fact that they watch for a particular value—called the *sentinel* value—to appear. In this procedure, the loop's sentinel value is a string containing the single word *exit*.

Line 9 begins the `Do` loop statement in this procedure. Because the `Do` keyword appears on the line by itself, it merely indicates to VBA the beginning of the loop's body. There is no additional keyword (**While** or **Until**) and no logical expression for the loop's determinant condition in this line, so VBA simply continues execution with the first statement in the loop's body in line 10.

Line 10 uses `InputBox` to obtain a string from the user. In this procedure, the user is simply prompted to enter a string. Notice that the prompt string for `InputBox` includes instructions on how to end the data entry loop. This `InputBox` statement also suggests the word *exit* as the default value for the user's input.

The comments in lines 14 and 15 represent any additional processing of the user's input that you might want to include: storing the data in a worksheet cell or mailmerge field, adding it to an array, ensuring that the data is numeric, non-numeric, or any other data validation or processing. Line 16 contains a `MsgBox` statement that simply echoes the user's input.

Line 17 contains the **Loop** keyword that indicates the end of the loop's body. This line also contains the **While** keyword and the logical expression for the loop's determinant condition. When VBA executes this statement, it evaluates the logical expression for the loop determinant. Because this loop uses the **While** keyword, VBA continues to execute the loop as long as the logical expression for the loop's determinant condition is **True**. If the string entered by the user in line 10 does not contain the single word *exit*, the expression `uStr <> "exit"` is **True** and VBA returns to the top of the loop and repeats the body of the loop.

If the user did enter the word *exit* (either by accepting the suggested default for the `InputBox` function call in line 10 or by actually typing the word), the expression `uStr <> "exit"` is **False** and VBA continues execution with line 19, ending the loop.

Lines 19 and 20 contain a `MsgBox` statement that displays a message stating that the data entry is complete. Notice that this `MsgBox` statement uses the `Buttons` argument to display the Windows' Exclamation icon in the message dialog. Line 21 contains the **End Sub** statement that ends the procedure.

Do

DO make sure that your `InputBox` prompts give your procedure's user enough information about what kind of information you expect her to enter and how to end or cancel (if possible) the task that your procedure carries out.

Building Loops with `Do...Loop Until`

You can also use the `Do...Loop Until` form of the `Do` statement to build a `Do` loop that tests its determinant condition after executing the body of the loop.

▼ SYNTAX

The general syntax of the `Do...Loop Until` statement is

```
Do
    statements
Loop Until condition
```

statements represents the VBA statements that make up the body of the loop. *condition* represents the logical expression for the loop's determinant.

▼   The **Do...Loop Until** statement has the *condition* expression at the bottom of the loop, so VBA checks the determinant condition after executing the loop. Because this form of the **Do** statement uses the **Until** keyword, VBA executes the loop as long as the logical expression represented by *condition* is **False**.

When VBA executes a **Do...Loop Until** statement, it first executes the statements represented by *statements*. When VBA reaches the **Loop** keyword, it tests the logical expression represented by *condition*; if the logical expression is **False**, VBA returns to the top of the loop and again executes the body of the loop. When VBA reaches the **Loop** keyword at the bottom of the loop, it again checks to see whether the *condition* logical expression is **False**. If *condition* is **False**, VBA executes the loop again; if it is **True**, VBA continues execution with whatever statements appear after the line containing the **Loop** keyword.

▲   Notice that this loop always executes at least once, regardless of the value of the logical expression represented by *condition*.

Listing 9.8 shows another version of the prototypical data-entry loop shown in Listing 9.7. The GetInput procedure in Listing 9.8 uses a **Do...Loop Until** loop construction to get input from the user until the user cancels the input dialog or enters a blank string. Apart from using a different loop construction, GetInput in Listing 9.8 is also slightly more sophisticated than the version shown in Listing 9.7. GetInput in Listing 9.8 asks the user to confirm that she wants to end the data-entry process before it actually ends the loop.

INPUT   **LISTING 9.8**   A SMARTER VERSION OF *GetInput* USING A **Do...Loop Until** LOOP

```
1:   Sub GetInput()
2:   'demonstrates Do...Loop Until structure. Loops repeatedly
3:   'until user cancels input dialog box or enters blank string
4:
5:     Const iTitle = "Data Entry"
6:
7:     Dim uStr As String
8:     Dim Check As Integer
9:
10:    Do
11:      uStr = InputBox(prompt:="Enter a string " & _
12:                            "(Cancel to end):", _
13:                         Title:=iTitle)
14:      If uStr = "" Then    'confirm ending data entry
15:        Check = MsgBox(prompt:="End data entry?", _
16:                    Title:=iTitle, _
17:                    Buttons:=vbYesNo + vbQuestion + _
```

```
18:                                    vbDefaultButton2)
19:        If Check = vbNo Then uStr = "x"
20:     Else
21:        'statements to process or validate user input, or to
22:        'store user input in worksheet cell, etc. go here
23:        MsgBox prompt:="You entered: " & uStr, Title:=iTitle
24:     End If
25:   Loop Until uStr = ""
26:
27:     MsgBox prompt:="Data entry completed.", _
28:            Title:=iTitle, Buttons:=vbExclamation
29: End Sub
```

ANALYSIS Line 10 begins the **Do** loop statement in this procedure. Because the **Do** keyword appears on the line by itself, it merely indicates to VBA the beginning of the loop's body. There is no additional keyword (**While** or **Until**) and no logical expression for the loop's determinant condition in this line, so VBA simply continues execution with the first statement in the loop's body in line 11, which uses InputBox to obtain a string from the procedure's user.

Line 14 begins an **If...Then...Else** statement to evaluate the user's input. If the string the user entered (stored in uStr) is empty (""), the user either canceled the input dialog or entered a blank string. This **If...Then...Else** statement ensures that the user really wants to end the data-entry process.

If uStr is empty, VBA executes the statements in lines 15 through 19. Line 15 starts a MsgBox function call that displays a Yes/No message asking the user whether data entry should end. Notice that this MsgBox function call uses the Buttons argument to specify that the message dialog contains two buttons—Yes and No—and specifies that the second button (the No button) is the default. Notice also that the vbQuestion constant is also added to the Buttons argument so that the message dialog displays the Windows Query icon.

Line 19 contains an **If...Then** statement that evaluates the user's choice from the MsgBox function call in line 15. If the user chooses the No button in the message dialog, signifying that the data-entry process should continue, this statement assigns the single letter x to the uStr variable. This statement is necessary to keep the loop running because the loop stops executing whenever the uStr variable contains an empty string; this statement ensures that the uStr variable does *not* contain an empty string so that VBA continues to execute the loop.

9

If the uStr variable is not empty when VBA performs the comparison for the
If...Then...Else statement in line 14, VBA executes the **Else** clause in lines 20
through 23. This procedure, like Listing 9.7, just shows you how to set up a loop for a
data entry process without actually doing anything with the data the user enters.

Line 25 contains the **Loop** keyword, which indicates the end of the loop's body. This line
also contains the **Until** keyword and the logical expression for the loop's determinant
condition. When VBA executes this statement, it evaluates the logical expression for the
loop determinant. Because this loop uses the **Until** keyword, VBA continues to execute
the loop as long as the logical expression for the loop's determinant condition is **False**.
If the string entered by the user in line 14 is *not* empty (""), the expression uStr = "" is
False; VBA returns to the top of the loop and executes the body of the loop again.

If the user did enter an empty string or canceled the input dialog and also confirmed that
data entry should end, the expression uStr = "" is **True** and VBA ends the loop, continuing execution with line 27. Notice that if the user did *not* confirm ending the data entry,
uStr contains the single character *x*, and VBA does continue executing the loop because
uStr is not empty.

Do

DO use a **Do...Loop While** or **Do...Loop Until** loop construction if you want VBA to
always execute the statements in the body of the loop at least once, no matter what.

DO consider including statements to confirm the cancellation of interactive looping
processes, as shown in Listing 9.8.

Ending Loops Early

Many of the reasons why you might end a loop early are similar to the reasons you might
end a procedure or entire program early: A user cancels an input dialog, an expected
value does not appear, and so on. There are additional reasons for ending a loop early,
however, besides detecting some particular error. In some cases, you might want to terminate a loop early—particularly **For...Next** and **For Each...Next** loops—because its
task is completed and additional looping is simply a waste of time.

VBA provides two statements that enable you to terminate a loop early. The particular
statement that you use depends on the type of loop that you want to end:

- Use the **Exit For** statement to end either a **For...Next** or a **For Each...Next**
  loop early. Usually, you end **For** loops early because the specific goal of the loop
  is accomplished and you don't want VBA to waste time executing the loop
  unnecessarily.

- Use the **Exit Do** statement to end any of VBA's **Do** loops early. Usually, you end **Do** loops early because of some situation that not only makes continuing the loop unnecessary, but also might affect the way VBA evaluates the logical expression for the loop's determinant condition.

With the exception that you use **Exit For** to end a **For** loop early and you use **Exit Do** to end a **Do** loop early, both statements are essentially the same.

Listing 9.9 shows the same SheetExists function from Listing 9.4, but it has been modified to include the **Exit For** statement.

INPUT **LISTING 9.9** USING **Exit For** TO END A LOOP EARLY

```
1: Function SheetExists(sName As String) As Boolean
2: 'Returns True if sName sheet exists in active workbook
3:
4:    Dim aSheet As Object
5:
6:    SheetExists = False   'assume sheet won't be found
7:
8:      'cycle through all sheets, compare each sheet's
9:      'name to sName, as a text comparison.
10:   For Each aSheet In ActiveWorkbook.Sheets
11:     If (StrComp(aSheet.Name, sName, 1) = 0) Then
12:       SheetExists = True   'sheet names match, return true
13:       Exit For             'no point in continuing loop
14:     End If
15:   Next aSheet
16: End Function
17:
18:
19: Sub Test_SheetExists()
20: 'tests the SheetExists function
21:
22:    Dim uStr As String
23:
24:    uStr = InputBox("Enter the name of a sheet in the " & _
25:                    "current workbook:")
26:    If SheetExists(uStr) Then
27:      MsgBox "Sheet '" & uStr & _
28:             "' DOES exist in the current workbook."
29:    Else
30:      MsgBox "Sheet '" & uStr & _
31:             "' does NOT exist in the current workbook."
32:    End If
33: End Sub
```

9

ANALYSIS This version of SheetExists works exactly the same as the function shown in Listing 9.4, except that this version uses the **Exit For** statement to end the **For Each...Next** loop in the function early.

Notice line 13 in Listing 9.9. This line, which contains the **Exit For** statement, is the only line that is different in this version of the SheetExists function.

Line 10 starts the **For Each...Next** loop using the aSheet object variable as the element variable for the loop. The specified group is the ActiveWorkbook.Sheets collection object. Line 10 tells VBA to execute the statements in the loop body for as many times as there are sheets in the active workbook, that is, to repeat the actions once for each object in the Sheets collection.

If the string in sName matches the string in the sheet's Name property, VBA executes line 12, which assigns the value **True** to the function's result.

The next statement that VBA executes is in line 13, the added **Exit For** statement. When VBA executes this statement, it immediately ends the **For Each...Next** loop and continues execution with the first statement after the **Next** keyword—line 16, in this case, which ends the SheetExists function.

Because the purpose of SheetExists is to simply return **True** whenever it finds a sheet with the specified name in the active workbook, there is no point in continuing the **For Each...Next** loop after the first matching name is found, especially because Excel ensures that every sheet in a workbook has a unique name. As soon as a match between sName and a sheet's Name property is found, any additional executions of the statements inside the loop is just wasted processing time. By exiting a loop early in circumstances like this, you can speed up VBA's execution of your programs. Although the saved time in a function like SheetExists might be measured in milliseconds, the cumulative total of time saved in a complex program can be significant.

VBA executes line 15, which contains the **Next** keyword ending the **For Each...Next** loop, only if the string in sName does not match the string in the sheet's Name property. VBA now returns to the top of the loop in line 10 and checks to see whether all the elements in the specified group have been used. If not, VBA assigns the next element in the Sheets collection to the aSheet object variable and executes the loop again.

In the SheetExists function in Listing 9.4, the **For Each...Next** loop always executed a number of times corresponding to the number of sheets in the active workbook. If the active workbook contained 10 sheets, for example, the **For Each...Next** loop executed 10 times; if the active workbook contained four sheets, the loop executed 4 times.

In this version, however, the number of times the **For Each...Next** loop executes might be fewer than the number of sheets in the active workbook, although it will never execute more times than there are sheets in the active workbook. If the active workbook contains 10 sheets, for example, and sName matches the Name property of the second sheet in the workbook, VBA only executes the **For Each...Next** loop twice. If sName matches the Name property of the 8th sheet in the workbook, VBA executes the **For Each...Next** loop 8 times. VBA only ends up executing this loop all 10 times if it does not find a match or if the matching sheet is also the 10th sheet in the workbook. Potentially, then, using the **Exit For** statement to end the loop early saves the time required to execute the loop as many as 9 times and as few as 1 time.

Many of the loops you write might execute hundreds of times; you can see that strategically ending a loop's execution early can save a lot of unnecessary processing.

In Listing 9.9, lines 19 through 33 declare a procedure, Test_SheetExists, to test the SheetExists function. This test procedure is identical to the test procedure in Listing 9.4.

Do

DO use an **Exit For** statement to end a **For Each...Next** or **For...Next** loop early if additional looping becomes unnecessary.

DON'T

DON'T use a **GoTo** statement to jump out of an executing loop. Using **GoTo** statements makes your code difficult to read and understand.

DON'T use the **Exit Do** statement to end a **Do** loop unless absolutely necessary, that is, if you can't figure out any other way to end the loop.

Nesting Loops

You can enclose loops inside of other loops similar to the way you can enclose **If...Then** statements inside each other. Enclosing one looping structure inside another is referred to as *nesting* loops. You can nest looping structures of any type (mixed **For** and **Do** loops) to any level.

There are a few things you need to keep in mind when you nest loops, however. The following list summarizes points to watch for when you enclose one looping structure inside another:

- When you nest **For...Next** loops, each loop must have its own unique counter variable.

- When you nest **For Each...Next** loops, each loop must have its own unique element variable.

- If you use an **Exit For** or **Exit Do** statement in a nested loop, only the currently executing loop ends; VBA continues executing the next higher-level loop.

Nesting For Loops

Listing 9.10 shows a simple procedure that uses nested **For...Next** loops. The FormatHeading procedure is intended for use in Excel, and applies a 12-point bold Arial font to the first three rows of the first six columns of the current active worksheet. The outer loop in the procedure counts down the rows and the inner loop counts across the columns.

INPUT   **LISTING 9.10**   NESTED **For...Next** LOOPS

```
 1:  Sub FormatHeading()
 2:  'This procedure applies 12-point bold Arial font to
 3:  'first 3 rows and first 6 columns of active worksheet
 4:
 5:     Dim Rnum As Integer, Cnum As Integer
 6:
 7:     For Rnum = 1 To 3
 8:        For Cnum = 1 To 6
 9:           Cells(Rnum, Cnum).Select
10:           With Selection.Font
11:              .Name = "Arial"
12:              .FontStyle = "Bold"
13:              .Size = 12
14:              .Strikethrough = False
15:              .Superscript = False
16:              .Subscript = False
17:              .OutlineFont = False
18:              .Shadow = False
19:              .Underline = xlNone
20:              .ColorIndex = xlAutomatic
21:           End With
22:        Next Cnum
23:     Next Rnum
24:  End Sub
```

ANALYSIS You might use a procedure such as FormatHeading to apply a uniform font, font style, and point size to the cells of a worksheet that you use for both the worksheet's heading and for the column headings. FormatHeading uses two **For...Next** loops, one nested inside the other, to apply the 12-point bold Arial font.

The outer **For...Next** loop counts from 1 to 3, and the procedure uses the outer loop's counter variable to supply a row coordinate each time VBA executes the loop. Therefore, the outer loop counts three rows from the top of the worksheet down.

The inner **For...Next** loop counts from 1 to 6, and the procedure uses the inner loop's counter variable to supply a column coordinate each time VBA executes the loop. Therefore, the inner loop counts six columns from left to right across the worksheet.

As FormatHeading executes, it starts in the first row and the first column. As the inner loop's count increases, the procedure formats each column in the first row, moving across the worksheet from left to right. When the inner loop finishes executing, the first six columns in the first row are formatted. The outer **For...Next** loop then increments its counter variable, advances to the next row, and again executes. Because VBA also executes the inner **For...Next** loop again (it is part of the outer loop's body), the first six columns of the second row are formatted. The same thing happens again for the third row. The outer **For** loop only executes three times, so the FormatHeading procedure ends after the third execution of the outer loop.

The outer **For...Next** loop begins in line 7. Rnum is the counter variable for this loop. The outer **For** loop stops executing as soon as Rnum is greater than 3, that is, after the loop executes three times.

The inner **For...Next** loop begins in line 8. Cnum is the counter variable for this loop. The inner **For** loop stops after it has executed six times.

Line 9 uses the Cells method of the Excel Application object to return a Range object specified by using Rnum and Cnum as row and column coordinates. The statement also uses the Select method of the Range object to select the specified cell on the active worksheet. The Cells statement was copied from a recorded macro that contained only two actions: Selecting a cell and applying the desired formatting. The cell selection statement was copied into this procedure and the literal values from the recorded statement were replaced with the Rnum and Cnum variables.

Line 10 begins a **With** statement. Selection is a property of the Application object that returns the current selection. In this case, the current selection is the single cell selected by the statement in line 9. The Selection.Font object contains all the font settings for the current selection. The statements inside the **With** statement in lines 11 through 20 all

9

change properties of the Font object so that the selection has the desired bold Arial font at 12 points. These statements, like the statement in line 9, were copied from a recorded macro.

Line 22 contains the **Next** statement that marks the end of the body of the inner loop. Notice how including the counter variable name after the **Next** keyword, along with proper indentation, helps you tell the difference between the inner and outer loops. When VBA executes the statement in line 22, it increments the Cnum loop counter and goes back to the top of the inner loop in line 8. In line 8, VBA checks the new value of the loop counter variable against the ending value and executes the loop again, if necessary.

When the inner **For...Next** loop (lines 8 through 22) finishes executing, VBA executes line 23. This line contains the **Next** statement that marks the end of the outer loop's body. When VBA executes the statement in line 23, it increments the Rnum loop counter and goes back to the top of the outer loop in line 7. In line 7, VBA checks the new value of the Rnum loop counter against the ending value and executes the loop again, if necessary.

When the outer **For...Next** loop (lines 7 through 23) finishes executing, VBA executes line 24, which ends the procedure.

> **Tip**
>
> You can also nest **For Each...Next** loops the same way you nest **For...Next** loops; use a technique similar to that shown in Listing 9.10.

Nesting Do Loops

Listing 9.11 shows a procedure that uses nested **Do** loops to help a user perform the data entry needed to generate an invoice. The outer loop in the MakeInvoices procedure gets invoice numbers from the user until there are no more invoices to enter or until the user cancels the input dialog. The inner loop in the MakeInvoices procedure gets line-item numbers for the invoice until there are no more line-items to enter or the user cancels the input dialog. As you study this procedure, keep in mind that it is just a skeleton. In reality, you would probably need to collect much more information than this procedure does. This demonstration procedure was kept as simple as possible to make it easier for you to understand how the nested loops are constructed and how they interact.

INPUT   **LISTING 9.11**   NESTED DO LOOPS

```
1:  Sub MakeInvoices()
2:  'provides data entry for invoices and line items on each
3:  'invoice. Outer loop gets info about a single invoice,
4:  'inner loop gets info about line-items in the invoice.
```

```
 5:
 6:     Const miTitle = "Invoice Data Entry "
 7:
 8:     Dim InvcNum As String * 5      'the invoice number
 9:     Dim ItemNum As String * 16     'line item stock ID number
10:     Dim ItemDone As Boolean        'done getting line items
11:     Dim InvcDone As Boolean        'done getting invoices
12:
13:     InvcDone = False   'make sure loop starts
14:     Do Until InvcDone        'loop for getting invoices
15:
16:           'ask for an invoice number
17:         InvcNum = InputBox(prompt:="Enter Invoice Number:", _
18:                        Title:=miTitle)
19:         If Trim(InvcNum) = "" Then       'invoice entry canceled
20:           MsgBox prompt:="Invoice Entry Canceled.", _
21:                 Title:=miTitle, Buttons:=vbExclamation
22:           InvcDone = True      'done getting invoices
23:           ItemDone = True      'no point in getting line items
24:         Else
25:           ItemDone = False     'prepare line item loop
26:         End If
27:
28:
29:         Do Until ItemDone           'loop to get line items
30:             'ask for a line item number
31:           ItemNum = InputBox(prompt:="Enter line #:", _
32:               Title:=miTitle & "- Line Items for " & InvcNum)
33:           If Trim(ItemNum) = "" Then       'line item canceled
34:             MsgBox prompt:="Line Item entry for Invoice #" & _
35:                          InvcNum & " ended.", _
36:                   Title:=miTitle
37:             ItemDone = True      'done getting line items
38:           Else
39:             'statements to store entered data, get more info
40:             'about the line item, and so on would go here.
41:             MsgBox prompt:="You entered line item #" & _
42:                        ItemNum & " on Invoice #" & InvcNum, _
43:                 Title:=miTitle & "- Line Items for " & InvcNum
44:           End If
45:         Loop   'ending line item entry loop
46:     Loop   'ending invoice entry loop
47:
48:     MsgBox prompt:="Invoice Entry complete", Title:=miTitle
49: End Sub
```

ANALYSIS The MakeInvoices procedure uses the outer **Do** loop to get invoice numbers. When the user enters an invoice number, the inner **Do** loop starts and repeatedly gets line-item numbers from the user. The user signals that there are no more line-item numbers to enter by entering a blank string or by canceling the input dialog. (To keep this procedure fairly simple, no confirmation screening was added to any of the input dialog cancellations.)

When the user signals that there are no more line-items to enter, the inner **Do** loop stops executing and the outer **Do** loop resumes. The outer **Do** loop repeats, asking the user for another invoice number (the procedure assumes that the user has more than one invoice to enter).

Lines 8 through 11 declare several variables. InvcNum is for the invoice number and ItemNum is for the line-item number. Notice that both of these strings are fixed-length strings. ItemDone and InvcDone are **Boolean** variables used to control the execution of the line-item and invoice **Do** loops, respectively.

Line 13 initializes the InvcDone variable as **False** to ensure that the loop will actually start executing. Line 14 starts the outer **Do** loop. The logical expression for the loop determinant is the single **Boolean** variable InvcDone. This **Do** statement uses the **Until** keyword, so VBA checks this loop determinant's condition before executing the body of the loop and continues executing the loop for as long as InvcDone is **False**.

The statement in line 17 uses the InputBox function to get an invoice number from the user and assigns the InputBox result to the InvcNum variable. Lines 19 through 26 contain an **If...Then...Else** statement that evaluates the user's input in InvcNum.

In line 19, if InvcNum contains a blank string, VBA executes the statements in lines 20 through 23, which display a message to the user that invoice entry will end and set *both* of the loop controlling flags to **True**, signifying that both line-item *and* invoice entry is complete. If InvcNum is not blank, VBA executes line 25, which sets the ItemDone flag to **False**, signifying that line-item entry should be performed.

Whichever branch of the **If...Then...Else** statement was chosen in line 19, VBA next executes line 29, which is the start of the inner **Do** loop. This loop is constructed much the same as the outer loop; it just uses a different flag variable. The inner, nested **Do** loop that starts in line 29 has its determinant condition tested before VBA executes the body of the loop, and the loop will execute for as long as ItemDone is **False**.

If the invoice entry is finished (lines 20 through 23 were executed), ItemDone is **True** and the inner loop starting in line 29 does *not* execute; instead, VBA skips over the body of the inner loop and executes line 46, which marks the end of the outer **Do** loop. VBA returns to the top of the outer loop in line 14 and checks the determinant condition;

InvcDone is also **True**, so the outer loop ends as well.

If line 25 executed as a result of the **If...Then...Else** statement in line 19, ItemDone is **False** and the inner **Do** loop in line 29 *does* begin to execute.

Line 31 uses the InputBox function to get a line-item number from the user and assigns it to the ItemNum variable. Lines 33 through 44 contain an **If...Then...Else** statement that evaluates the user's input in ItemNum.

In line 33, if ItemNum contains a blank string, VBA executes the statements in lines 34 through 37, which display a message to the user that line-item entry will end and set the ItemDone flag to **True**, signifying that line-item entry is complete. If ItemNum is not blank, VBA executes the statements in lines 39 through 43. These statements merely display a message dialog that echoes the user's input. If this procedure were really used to get data entry, this is where the statements that stored the data or performed additional evaluation on the data would appear.

Whichever branch of the **If...Then...Else** statement was chosen in line 33, VBA next executes line 45, which is the end of the inner **Do** loop. VBA returns to the top of the inner loop in line 29 and checks the determinant condition of the loop again. If ItemDone is still **False**, VBA executes the loop again.

If ItemDone is **True**, VBA continues execution with the statement in line 46, which ends the outer **Do** loop. VBA returns to the top of the outer loop in line 14 and checks the loop's determinant condition again. If InvcDone is still **False**, VBA executes the outer loop again.

If InvcDone is **True**, VBA continues execution with line 48, which displays a message stating that the entry process is complete. Line 49 is the end of the MakeInvoices procedure.

Summary

In this lesson, you learned some of the different terminology used to describe different kinds of loops and the various parts of a loop. You learned what a loop determinant is, and you learned the difference between a fixed and indefinite loop. You also learned how loops that test their determinant condition before executing the body of the loop are different from loops that test their determinant condition after executing the body of the loop.

First, you learned how to construct fixed loops with the **For...Next** and **For Each...Next** statements. You learned about the options for the **For...Next** loop, and you learned how to construct **For...Next** loops both with counts that go up and counts that go down. You also learned how to use the **For Each...Next** loop to perform operations involving all of the elements in a particular group.

Next, you learned how to construct indefinite loops using the **Do** loop statement. This chapter showed you how VBA tests **Do** loop determinant conditions, how to use the **Do** statement to construct loops that test their determinant before execution, and to construct loops that test their determinant after execution. You learned about the four different ways to construct **Do** loops: `Do While`, `Do Until`, `Do...Loop While`, and `Do...Loop Until`.

This chapter also described some of the reasons why you might want or need to end a loop early, and showed you how to use the `Exit For` and `Exit Do` statements to end `For` and **Do** loops. Finally, this chapter showed you how to nest loops and gave you some examples of typical uses for nested `For...Next` loops and nested **Do** loops.

Q&A

Q I'm not sure if I should use a `For` loop or a `Do` loop.

A Deciding whether to use a **For** loop or a **Do** loop is pretty straightforward. If you want the loop to repeat a set number of times whenever it executes, and you can easily use constants or a mathematical expression to define the upper and lower limits for the loop's counting, use a **For** loop. If you're not sure how many times the loop might need to execute, or you cannot easily use constants or numeric expressions to set a lower and upper limit for the loop's count, you should use a **Do** loop.

Q I think I understand how the fixed loop statements work, but I'm not sure whether I should use a `For...Next` loop or a `For Each...Next` loop.

A Use a **For...Next** loop when you can control the loop's execution by counting the number of times it executes. Use a **For Each...Next** loop to operate on all the elements in a collection, such as all the sheets in a workbook.

Q I'm pretty sure I should use a `Do` loop for a particular task, but how can I tell whether I've picked the right one of the four `Do` loop variations?

A Choosing the "right" loop structure is mostly a matter of choosing the loop structure that is the easiest for you to set up and involves the simplest logical expressions for the loop determinant conditions. Usually, carefully stating the looping conditions in English will give you a good idea of which **Do** loop variation you should use.

In English, try to express the looping operation you want to perform in one of the following sentence forms, and your loop will practically write itself:

- From the first (or second or third, and so on) up to the *n*th thing, do... (A **For...Next** loop.)
- From the *n*th thing down to the first (or second or third, and so on), do... (A **For...Next** loop with a negative **Step** value.)
- For the number of times specified by... (Another **For...Next** loop.)
- For every (or for each) item in the... (A **For Each...Next** loop.)
- While some condition exists, do... (A **Do While** loop.)
- Do this task at least once and, while these conditions exist, repeat it... (A **Do...Loop While** loop.)
- Until these conditions come into existence, do... (A **Do Until** loop.)
- Do this task at least once, repeating it until these conditions come into existence... (A **Do...Loop Until** loop.)

When you compose your English sentence to help you determine the correct looping structure, avoid sentences like "For as long as there is input, prompt the user for more input." By using a phrase like *For as long as* you might end up confusing yourself. In this example, you're really looking for an English sentence "While there is input, prompt the user for more input." This last sentence is very clear, and you can easily see that you would need to write a **Do While** loop statement to put this thought into action.

You could also express the same thought as "Prompt the user for input until there is no more input." Phrased this way, you might write a **Do...Loop Until** statement—either approach can work equally well, and both accomplish the same purpose. The only difference between the two is which is easier for *you* to phrase and understand.

Workshop

Answers are in Appendix A.

Quiz

1. What is the difference between a fixed loop and an indefinite loop?
2. Can you change the number of times a **For...Next** loop executes?
3. In a **Do** loop, how does VBA tell whether to test the determinant condition before or after executing the body of the loop?

4. In a **Do** loop, how does VBA tell whether to continue executing the loop while the determinant condition is **True** or to continue executing the loop until the determinant condition is **True**?

5. What is a count-controlled **Do** loop? When would you use a count-controlled **Do** loop?

6. What is an event-controlled **Do** loop?

7. What is a flag-controlled **Do** loop?

Exercises

1. **BUG BUSTER:** The following procedure is supposed to repeatedly get a number from the user and stop executing when the user enters the word *exit*. This procedure uses the Excel `Application.InputBox` function to get input from the user. The procedure uses the Excel `Application.InputBox` function instead of the VBA `InputBox` function because of the optional `Type` argument in Excel's `Application.InputBox` function that enables you to specify that the user's input must be numeric.

As written, the loop in this procedure has a fatal flaw: It will never stop executing. Find the problem with this loop and correct it. (HINT: The problem lies with the manner in which the loop's determinant condition is defined.)

Note

If you enter this procedure and execute it before you correct its problem, be prepared to use the Esc key to interrupt the procedure's execution, as described in the sidebar earlier in this chapter.

```
1:  Sub GetNumber()
2:  'loops indefinitely, getting numeric input from user
3:
4:    Dim iNum
5:
6:    Do
7:      iNum = Application.InputBox(prompt:="Enter number:", _
8:                                  Type:=1)
9:    Loop Until iNum = "exit"
10:
11:    MsgBox "Number entry ended."
12: End Sub
```

2. Write a procedure that gets three words from the user, assembles them into a single string, and then displays that string. Your procedure should include the following features:

   - Use a **For...Next** loop to repeat the input statement that requests the user to input a word.
   - Include statements to screen the user's input and stop the loop if the user enters a blank string or cancels the input dialog.
   - Use no more than two string variables to get and assemble the three words.

3. Modify the procedure you wrote for the previous exercise so that it will loop indefinitely, collecting words from the user until the user enters a period (.) by itself. (HINT: Replace the **For** loop with a **Do** loop.)

4. Write a function named IsBookOpen that returns **True** if a particular workbook is open and **False** if it is not. Model your function on the SheetExists function shown earlier in this chapter. For your function, use the Workbooks collection—this collection contains all the currently open Excel workbooks. The name of the workbook is stored in the workbook's Name property, just like a worksheet's name. For a workbook, however, the string stored in the Name property is the workbook's filename on disk. For example, the personal macro workbook's Name property contains the string *PERSONAL.XLS*.

   As part of this exercise, write a procedure to test the IsBookOpen function.

5. Write a function named SVal that receives a **String** type argument and returns a **Double** type result that contains the numeric equivalent of the value in its argument. Your function should remove all the non-digit characters (except the decimal point) from the argument string and then use the VBA Val function to convert the string to a number.

   For example, if the argument contains the string *$1,000.00,* your function should first convert the string to *1000.00* so that it can be converted to a number and then pass the new string to the Val function to convert it into a number.

   As part of this exercise, write a procedure to test the SVal function.

DAY 10

Advanced Techniques for Using Data Types and Variables

This chapter expands your knowledge of variable scope and persistence, and shows you how to use VBA's functions to get information about the data type stored in a variable. Today, you learn

- How to get information about the data type stored in a **Variant** or other type of variable, and how to get information about the data type of an expression's result.

- How to determine whether a **Variant** or **Object** type variable has ever been assigned a value.

- How to use data type information functions combined with looping structures and **If** statements to validate the input that your procedure obtains from the user (or other sources).

- How to alter the persistence of variables to retain the value that the variable stores between function or procedure calls.

Getting Information About Variables and Expressions

There are many different circumstances in which you'll find it useful to get more information about a variable or expression in your VBA code. This section starts out by describing a few of these circumstances, and then discusses the VBA information functions you can use to get more information about a variable or an expression.

One situation in which you might need to get more information about a variable occurs when your functions and procedures have arguments with a **Variant** data type (usually an optional argument). As you know, a **Variant** can contain any data type. So, your function might expect a numeric type in a particular argument, but—because the argument is a **Variant**—VBA allows you to pass a **String**, **Date**, or other data type when you actually call the function. To avoid runtime errors in your function, you might need to use VBA's data type information functions to determine what data type was actually passed to your function and attempt to convert it—or display an error message—before your function uses the value.

> **Note**
>
> One reason you might use a **Variant** optional argument in a function or procedure is to make use of the IsMissing function: The IsMissing function only works if the argument being tested is a **Variant**. If you do use a **Variant** optional argument, you need to check to ensure that the argument's value is of the correct data type.

You might want to use VBA's information functions to get more information about a variable's data type to find out exactly what an object variable or object expression refers to. For example, if you are unsure whether an object reference in Excel refers to a Workbook or to a Worksheet object, you can use the TypeName function to find out; the TypeName function returns a string containing the object's specific name: *Workbook* for a Workbook object, *Range* for a Range object, and so on.

Yet another situation in which VBA's data type information functions become useful is when you use the InputBox function to get input from your procedure's user. The data type information functions can help you ensure that your procedure's user does actually enter the information your procedure asked for. The section "Validating User Input" later in this chapter describes how to validate user input in more detail.

Table 10.1 summarizes VBA's data information functions. Some of these functions just give you general information about the type of data an expression represents, others give you more detailed information. The following sections of this chapter describe these data type information functions and their uses in more detail.

In Table 10.1, V represents any single variable name and E represents any valid VBA expression. All function arguments shown in Table 10.1 are required unless otherwise noted.

TABLE 10.1 DATA TYPE INFORMATION FUNCTIONS

Function	Purpose/Meaning
IsArray(V)	Returns **True** if V is an array variable; **False** otherwise. (Day 14 describes VBA's **Array** data type.)
IsDate(E)	Returns **True** if E is a valid **Date** expression; **False** otherwise. E can be either a **Date** value or a string expression representing a date.
IsEmpty(E)	Returns **True** if expression E is empty; **False** otherwise. E can be a numeric or string expression, but is usually a **Variant** type variable (a **Variant** with no value). Always returns **False** if E contains more than one variable.
IsError(E)	Returns **True** if E is a **Variant** variable storing a numeric expression representing one of VBA's error codes (or a user-defined error code); returns **False** otherwise.
IsMissing(V)	Returns **True** if the optional argument variable V is a **Variant** data type and was *not* included in the argument list of a function or procedure. IsMissing returns **False** otherwise. (Day 6 describes how to use the IsMissing function.)
IsNull(E)	Returns **True** if the expression E contains the special **Null** value (which indicates that the variable does not contain valid data), **False** otherwise. E can be any numeric or string expression; if any variable in the expression is **Null**, the entire expression evaluates to **Null**.
IsNumeric(E)	E can be any numeric or string expression. Returns **True** if E is a numeric data type (**Byte, Integer, Long, Single, Double** or **Currency**) or a string that VBA can convert to a number; returns **False** otherwise. IsNumeric always returns **False** if E is a **Date** expression. If E is **Empty**, IsNumeric returns **True**.
IsObject(E)	Returns **True** if the expression E refers to a valid Automation object; **False** otherwise. Some, but not all, Automation objects are also VBA or host application objects; Day 20 describes Automation and OLE objects. (*Automation* was known formerly as *OLE Automation*.)

continues

TABLE 10.1   CONTINUED

Function	Purpose/Meaning
TypeName(E)	Returns a string containing the name of the data type of expression E. E can be any expression or variable except a user-defined type.
VarType(V)	Returns a number indicating the data type of variable V. V can be any variable except a user-defined type.

Using Visual Basic for Application's Data Information Functions

VBA provides several functions that enable you to test whether a variable or expression contains a particular type of data and that give you a general idea of the variable's status. Each of these functions has a single argument and returns a **Boolean** value (**True** or **False**).

You can use these functions to get information about variables or expressions, including argument variables. These general information functions are IsArray, IsDate, IsError, IsMissing, IsNumeric, IsObject, IsEmpty, and IsNull. Notice that each of these function names begins with the word *Is*, letting you know that the function tests the type and status of a variable or expression. Refer to Table 10.1 for a summary of each function's action and what arguments it takes.

Using these testing functions is really quite straightforward. Because these functions return a **Boolean** result, you'll find yourself using them frequently in **If...Then** statements and in logical expressions that define a **Do** loop's determinant condition.

Each of the following sample lines shows the general syntax for these functions:

```
IsArray(varname)
IsDate(expression)
IsError(expression)
IsMissing(argname)
IsNumeric(expression)
IsObject(expression)
```

varname represents any variable name, *expression* represents any VBA numeric, date, or string expression, and *argname* represents any argument variable name in the argument of one of your function procedures.

You have already learned how to use the IsMissing function (in Day 6), so this chapter does not describe the IsMissing function. This chapter does not describe the IsArray function in detail, either, because you have not yet learned about the **Array** data type. You use the IsArray function to determine whether a particular variable is an array. (An array is similar to a collection of objects; Day 14, "Arrays," explains in more detail what an **Array** is and how to use one.)

Because the IsEmpty and IsNull functions are so closely related to VBA's special **Empty** and **Null** values, these two functions are described in the later section of this chapter that describes the use and purpose of the **Empty** and **Null** values.

You use the remaining three functions—IsDate, IsNumeric, and IsObject—in similar ways and for similar purposes. Listing 10.1 shows the FlipCase function from Day 6. This version of FlipCase not only uses the IsMissing function to determine whether the optional argument is present, but also uses the IsNumeric function to determine whether the argument contains the correct type of data.

INPUT   **LISTING 10.1**   VERIFYING AN OPTIONAL ARGUMENT'S DATA TYPE

```
 1: Function FlipCase(ByVal tStr As String, _
 2:                 Optional ByVal nChar) As String
 3: 'Reverses case of the first nChar characters in tStr.
 4: 'If nChar omitted, flips the case of all chars in tStr
 5:   Dim k As Long                    'loop counter
 6:   Dim TestC As String * 1          'string for testing
 7:
 8:      'if nChar is missing, or is not numeric...
 9:   If IsMissing(nChar) Or (Not IsNumeric(nChar)) Then
10:     nChar = Len(tStr)      'nChar gets entire tStr length,
11:   End If                   'thus avoiding a runtime error
12:
13:   For k = 1 To nChar
14:     TestC = Mid(tStr, k, 1)
15:     If (StrComp(TestC, "A", 0) >= 0) And _
16:       (StrComp(TestC, "Z", 0) <= 0) Then
17:       Mid(tStr, k, 1) = LCase(TestC)
18:     ElseIf (StrComp(TestC, "a", 0) >= 0) And _
19:            (StrComp(TestC, "z", 0) <= 0) Then
20:       Mid(tStr, k, 1) = UCase(TestC)
21:     End If
22:   Next k
23:   FlipCase = tStr
24: End Function
```

10

ANALYSIS The FlipCase function in Listing 10.1 operates essentially the same way as the versions shown in Day 6. The major difference in this version is the addition of the IsNumeric function to the **If...Then** statement in line 9. This **If...Then** statement now checks not only whether the nChar argument was included when the function was called, but also checks to see whether the value contained in nChar is numeric. The following paragraphs give a line-by-line explanation of FlipCase. Some of the details of FlipCase's operation that were explained in Day 6 are not repeated here.

As before, FlipCase takes two arguments. The first argument, tStr, is required and is passed by value. The second argument, nChar, is optional, has the **Variant** data type (by default), and is also passed by value. The **ByVal** keyword was added to the nChar argument for this version of FlipCase because this version might modify nChar. Passing by value protects the source of the argument's data from being altered when the argument variable is altered within the function.

Lines 9 through 11 contain an **If...Then** statement that adjusts the value in nChar, if necessary. The first part of the logical expression in the **If...Then** statement, IsMissing(nChar), is **True** if the nChar argument is missing. The second part of the logical expression (Not IsNumeric(nChar)) is **True** whenever the value in nChar is non-numeric or can't be converted to a number. (Remember, the **Not** logical operator inverts the value of a logical expression; if IsNumeric returns **False**, meaning that nChar contains non-numeric data, the expression Not IsNumeric is **True**.)

Because the logical expressions in line 9 are connected with the **Or** logical operator, the entire logical expression is **True** whenever *either* of the two sub-expressions is **True**. As a result, VBA executes the statement in line 10 whenever nChar is missing or whenever nChar contains non-numeric data. The statement in line 10 simply sets nChar to be equal to the length of the string in tStr.

Setting nChar to the length of the string in tStr whenever nChar starts out containing non-numeric data avoids a runtime error in line 13, which uses nChar to establish the ending count for the **For...Next** loop. For example, without the additional testing in line 9, if the statement that calls FlipCase passes the string *five*—which VBA cannot convert to a number—as the value for nChar, a type mismatch error occurs in line 13 when VBA tries to convert the string *five* to a number for use as the ending count of the loop. By including the IsNumeric test and reassigning a numeric value to nChar, there is no longer a possibility that a runtime error will occur in line 13; the test for missing or non-numeric data in lines 9 through 11 ensures that nChar will always have a numeric value by the time it gets used in line 13.

The **For** loop in lines 13 through 22 works as described in Day 6: Each character of the string in tStr is examined individually and converted to either upper- or lowercase, as appropriate. Finally, line 23 assigns the function's result.

Do

DO use the data information functions to ensure that optional **Variant** arguments contain the correct data types, and then convert or alter the data in the argument to the expected type if you want to avoid potential runtime errors in your functions and procedures.

Don't

DON'T assume that the statement that calls your function will always pass the right type of data to your function's optional **Variant** arguments, especially if you write user-defined functions for use by other users.

10

The short procedure in Listing 10.2 shows another typical use of VBA's data information functions. The InvoiceDate procedure in Listing 10.2 uses the IsDate function to control a **Do...Loop Until** structure, forcing the loop to repeat until the user enters a valid date expression in the input dialog.

INPUT **LISTING 10.2** VERIFYING THE DATA TYPE OF A USER'S INPUT

```
 1:  Sub InvoiceDate()
 2:  'repeats indefinitely, until the user enters a valid date.
 3:
 4:    Dim uDate As Variant
 5:
 6:    Do
 7:      uDate = InputBox(prompt:="Enter the invoice date: ", _
 8:                       Title:="Invoice Date")
 9:    Loop Until IsDate(uDate)
10:    MsgBox "You entered the date: " & _
11:           Format(uDate, "long date")
12: End Sub
```

ANALYSIS In a practical application, the InvoiceDate procedure might be part of a larger procedure or might actually be written as a function that gets a date from the user and returns that date as the function's result.

Line 4 declares a variable, uDate, to hold the user's input. Notice that this variable is declared as a **Variant**, primarily to make any subsequent data type conversions a little easier.

Line 6 begins a **Do...Loop Until** statement. Because the determinant condition is at the end of the loop, VBA tests the loop determinant condition after executing the body of the loop. After reading the **Do** statement that starts the loop, VBA immediately moves on to execute the statement in line 7, which is the first—and only—statement in the loop's body.

The InputBox statement in lines 7 and 8 prompts the user to enter a date (the date of a hypothetical invoice) and stores the string entered by the user in the uDate variable. For simplicity, this procedure does not contain any statements to handle the possibility that the user canceled the input dialog.

Line 9 marks the end of the loop and contains the loop's determinant condition. After VBA executes the body of the loop, it evaluates the logical expression in line 9. Because this loop uses the **Until** keyword, VBA will execute the loop until this logical expression becomes **True**. The logical expression contains the single call to the IsDate function. If the string the user entered represents a valid date, that is, the string contains information that VBA can convert to a **Date** type value, IsDate returns **True** and VBA stops executing the loop. Otherwise, IsDate returns **False** and VBA executes the **Do** loop again.

For example, if you enter the string *Dec. 12, 1939*, the IsDate function returns **True** because VBA can convert this string to a **Date** type value. Similarly, if you enter strings such as *4/1/95* or *5-12-98*, the IsDate function also returns **True**, ending the loop. If you enter a string like *December twelfth, 1939*, however, IsDate returns **False** because VBA cannot convert this string to a date and the loop executes again. The IsDate function will also return **False** for an invalid date, such as *February 30, 1998,* or *December 0, 1999.*

Finally, line 10 uses a MsgBox statement to display the date that the user entered.

Do

DO use the VBA information functions to help you verify that a user enters the kind of data you expect.

DO use any of the VBA data information functions in ways similar to those just shown in Listing 10.1 and 10.2 for IsNumeric and IsDate.

> **DON'T**
>
> **DON'T** use the *Is* information functions if you need specific information about the data type in a variable, use the TypeName or VarType functions (described in the next section) instead.

Determining the Specific Data Type of a Variable or Expression

VBA provides two functions—TypeName and VarType—especially for the purpose of determining what type of data a variable contains or for determining the data type of an expression. TypeName and VarType give you more specific detail than the other data type information functions.

In general, you use the TypeName and VarType functions for the same reasons and purposes you use the more general information functions (IsNumeric, IsDate, and so on) described in the preceding section. You might use one of these two functions if you need to know specifically whether an expression or variable contains an **Integer** or a **Double** data type instead of just knowing that it is a numeric variable, or if you need to know the specific type of object that an object variable refers to, such as a Range, Workbook, Worksheet, or other object.

You might also use the TypeName function if you're not sure how an expression will evaluate. For example, you can set up an expression just like the one you want to use in your procedure and use a MsgBox statement and the TypeName function to display the name of the data type for the expression's result. For instance, if you're uncertain whether an expression such as tNum + tStr results in a numeric or string data type when one variable contains a string and the other contains a number, you might use a test procedure such as the one shown in Listing 10.3 to display the data type of the expression's result.

LISTING 10.3   USING A TEST PROCEDURE TO DISPLAY THE DATA TYPE OF AN EXPRESSION RESULT

`INPUT`

```
1:  Sub Find_Type()
2:    Dim tNum As Variant
3:    Dim tStr As Variant
4:
5:    tNum = 5
6:    tStr = "2"
7:    MsgBox TypeName(tNum + tStr)
8:  End Sub
```

ANALYSIS Listing 10.3 is very simple. Lines 2 and 3 declare a couple of variables, and lines 5 and 6 assign a numeric value to tNum and a string value that represents a number to tStr. (If you try to add the numeric and string constants together directly, VBA displays a type-mismatch error.) Line 7 contains a MsgBox statement that displays the result of the TypeName function. In this statement, TypeName's result is a string containing the name of the data type to which the expression tNum + tStr evaluates.

If you enter and run this procedure, the resulting message dialog displays the word *Double*, indicating that the result of this expression is a **Double** type. This is a much more specific bit of information than you could obtain by using the IsNumeric function: With TypeName, you can determine not only that the value is numeric, but also what its specific numeric type is.

The next two sections describe the TypeName and VarType functions and their return values in detail.

Understanding the TypeName Function's Results

The TypeName function, as its name suggests, returns a string that contains the name of the data type for the variable or expression passed as its argument.

The general syntax of the TypeName function is

TypeName(*varname*)

varname represents any VBA variable name or expression. Table 10.2 summarizes the possible strings that TypeName returns depending on the specific data type of *varname*.

TABLE 10.2 RETURN VALUES FOR THE TypeName FUNCTION

Return String	Meaning
objecttype	An Automation object whose type is *objecttype*. For example, TypeName returns *Workbook* for a Workbook object and *Worksheet* for a Worksheet object. (Some, but not all, VBA and host application objects—such as Worksheet, Workbook, and Range—are Automation objects.)
Boolean	A **Boolean** type.
Byte	A **Byte** type.
Currency	A **Currency** type.
Date	A **Date** type.
Double	A **Double** floating-point type.
Empty	An uninitialized **Variant** type.

Return String	Meaning
Error	A **Variant** that contains one of VBA's or a user-defined error code. (Day 18 describes how to use error codes and handle various VBA errors.)
Integer	An **Integer** type.
Long	A **Long** integer type.
Nothing	An uninitialized **Object** type variable, that is, an **Object** type variable that does not refer to an object.
Null	A **Variant** that contains the special value **Null**, indicating that the variable or expression does not contain valid information.
Object	An object that does not support Automation.
Single	A **Single** floating-point type.
String	A **String**.
Unknown	An Automation object with an unknown type, usually an object that belongs to an application other than VBA's host application. (Day 20 describes how to use Automation and OLE in VBA to manipulate objects belonging to other applications.)

10

When you use the TypeName function, it returns one of the strings shown in Table 10.2. A few of the strings that TypeName returns require some additional explanation.

First, when you use the TypeName function to return the type of an object variable or object expression, TypeName returns a string with the specific object's name, if the object is an Automation object. (*Automation* was formerly known as *OLE Automation*; you can also control many OLE objects with your VBA code.) TypeName returns the generic string *Object* only if the object variable or expression references an object that does not support Automation. Sometimes, TypeName cannot determine the specific type of an Automation object; when this happens, TypeName returns the string *Unknown*. This last case usually occurs for Automation objects that are not part of VBA, but that you created by following the techniques described on Day 20.

Second, if the variable you test with TypeName is an array, TypeName adds a pair of empty parentheses to its return string. For example, an array of **Long** integers causes TypeName to return the string *Long()*. The *()* at the end of the data type name tells you that the variable you tested with TypeName is an array.

Usually, as in the demonstration procedure in Listing 10.4, you will use TypeName with a single variable as the argument, rather than a complex expression.

LISTING 10.4 A DEMONSTRATION OF THE RESULTS THAT TypeName RETURNS UNDER DIFFERENT CIRCUMSTANCES

```
 1:  Sub Demo_TypeName()
 2:     Dim aVariant As Variant
 3:     Dim anObject As Object
 4:     Dim anArray() As Integer
 5:
 6:     MsgBox TypeName(aVariant)     'uninitialized variant variable
 7:     MsgBox TypeName(anObject)     'uninitialized object variable
 8:     MsgBox TypeName(anArray)      'an array of integers
 9:
10:     Set anObject = ActiveWorkbook
11:     MsgBox TypeName(anObject)     'OLE Automation object: Workbook
12:     Set anObject = ActiveSheet
13:     MsgBox TypeName(anObject)     'OLE Automation object: depends on
14:                                   'active sheet: "Chart", "Worksheet",
16:                                   'etc.
15:  End Sub
```

ANALYSIS The Demo_TypeName procedure just puts the TypeName function through some of its paces. Line 1 contains the procedure declaration and lines 2 through 4 declare some variables. Notice that aVariant is a **Variant** type variable and anObject is a generic **Object** type variable. The anArray() variable declared in line 4 is an **Array** type variable: The parentheses after the variable name indicate that it is an array. This array's elements are of type **Integer**. (Arrays contain several elements, sort of like a collection object; although you don't learn about arrays in detail until Day 14, showing the TypeName results for an array here is a useful part of this demonstration.)

Line 6 uses MsgBox to display the string returned by TypeName. The argument for TypeName in this statement is the **Variant** type variable, aVariant. This variable has not yet had any value assigned to it, so TypeName reports that it is empty and the message dialog displays the word *Empty*.

Line 7 also uses MsgBox to display the string returned by TypeName. In this statement, the argument for TypeName is the **Object** type variable, anObject. This **Object** variable has not yet been used in a **Set** statement to make it refer to a particular object; as a result, anObject does not refer to any object. TypeName indicates this fact by returning the string "Nothing." The message dialog displayed by line 7, therefore, contains the word *Nothing*.

Line 8, like the preceding two lines, displays the result of the TypeName function. In this statement, the argument for the TypeName function is the array variable, anArray. The message dialog displayed by this line contains the string *Integer()*. TypeName is reporting that the basic data type of this variable is the **Integer** type, but that the variable is also an array of integers. TypeName adds the parentheses after the data type name to tell you that the variable is an array.

Line 10 contains a **Set** statement that sets the anObject object variable to refer to the current active workbook. Line 11 contains another statement that uses MsgBox to display the result of the TypeName function. In this case, the argument to TypeName is an **Object** type variable set to refer to a specific object. As a result, TypeName returns a string that contains the name of the specific object type that the variable references. Here, anObject was set to refer to a Workbook object, so TypeName returns the string *Workbook*. (Most of the objects accessible to you in VBA are Automation objects.)

Next, line 12 again contains a **Set** statement, this time setting the object variable, anObject, to refer to the current sheet in the active workbook. Again, line 13 displays the result of the TypeName function. The actual string that TypeName returns in this statement depends on the type of sheet active at the time you run this procedure. If you run this procedure while the current sheet is a worksheet, TypeName returns the string *Worksheet*.

The TypeName function has many practical uses. Listing 10.5 shows the Excel FormatArialBold12 procedure that you recorded in Day 1 modified to perform a more complex task. This version of the FormatArialBold12 procedure has one optional argument, which specifies the range of Excel worksheet cells to be formatted. (You'll learn about procedures that have arguments in detail in Day 12, "Creating Libraries and Whole Programs: Modular Programming Techniques.") If the optional argument is omitted, this version of FormatArialBold12 formats the current selection displayed in the active window.

Using the TypeName function, the FormatArialBold12 procedure has been modified so that it simply exits if the object passed to the procedure isn't a range of cells on a worksheet, thus preventing a runtime error if you accidentally call this procedure with an improper object reference.

INPUT **LISTING 10.5** USING THE TypeName FUNCTION TO PREVENT A RUNTIME ERROR

```
1:    Sub FormatArialBold12(Optional ByVal objRange)
2:    'applies 12-point Arial bold font to the object objRange,
3:    'provided the objRange object is actually a worksheet range
4:    'If the optional objRange object isn't passed, then this
5:    'procedure formats the current selection displayed in the
6:    'active window; if the optional objRange argument is
7:    'included, but isn't a Range object, then this procedure
8:    'exits without doing anything.
```

continues

LISTING 10.5 CONTINUED

```
 9:
10:     If IsMissing(objRange) Then
11:        Set objRange = ActiveWindow.RangeSelection
12:     Else
13:        If TypeName(objRange) <> "Range" Then
14:           Exit Sub
15:        End If
16:     End If
17:
18:     With objRange.Font
19:        .Name = "Arial"
20:        .FontStyle = "Bold"
21:        .Size = 12
22:        .Strikethrough = False
23:        .Superscript = False
24:        .Subscript = False
25:        .OutlineFont = False
26:        .Shadow = False
27:        .Underline = xlNone
28:        .ColorIndex = xlAutomatic
29:     End With
30:  End Sub
31:
32:  Sub Test_FormatArialBold12()
33:     FormatArialBold12
34:     FormatArialBold12 objRange:=ActiveSheet.Cells(2, 2)
35:     FormatArialBold12 objRange:=ActiveSheet
36:  End Sub
```

ANALYSIS Line 1 contains the procedure declaration; like functions, you can declare procedures with both required and optional arguments. (You'll learn more about declaring and using procedure arguments in Day 12.) This version of the FormatArialBold12 procedure has one optional argument, objRange, which is passed by value. Lines 2 through 8 are comments explaining the purpose and operation of the FormatArialBold12 procedure.

Lines 10 through 16 are the important lines in this version of FormatArialBold12. Line 10 begins an **If...Then** statement that uses the IsMissing function to test whether the optional objRange argument was included. If the objRange argument was omitted, line 11 is executed. Line 11 uses the **Set** keyword to assign an object reference to the objRange argument variable. ActiveWindow is a property of the Excel Application object, which returns a reference to the active window. RangeSelection is a property of the Window object, which returns a reference to the active selection in the worksheet displayed by that window. The expression ActiveWindow.RangeSelection, therefore, returns an object reference to the current selection in the currently active window of Excel.

If the objRange argument is included in the call to the FormatArialBold12 procedure, VBA executes the **Else** branch (lines 12 through 16), which contains a nested **If...Then** statement. The inner **If** statement (which starts in line 13) uses the TypeName function to test whether the specific object reference in the objRange argument variable is an Excel Range object. (Excel Range objects represent one or more worksheet cells.) If the objRange argument contains a reference to an object other than an Excel Range object, the expression TypeName(objRange) <> "Range" is **True** and VBA executes line 14, which exits the procedure. By exiting the procedure, a runtime error is avoided in line 18, where the objRange variable is used.

If, however, the object reference in the objRange argument variable is a Range object, the TypeName function returns the string *Range*, the expression in line 13 is **False**, and VBA continues execution with line 18.

Line 18 starts a **With** statement. Font is a property of the Range object, which returns an object reference to the font settings of the range's contents. Lines 19 through 28 set various font properties for the range. The FormatArialBold12 procedure ends in line 30.

Lines 32 through 36 of Listing 10.5 show a testing procedure for the FormatArialBold12 procedure. Line 33 calls FormatArialBold12 with no arguments to format whatever cells are currently selected on the worksheet displayed by the active window. Line 34 calls the FormatArialBold12 procedure again, this time passing a specific range of cells: Cells is a property of the Excel Worksheet object that returns either all the cells on a worksheet or a specific cell indicated by its row and column coordinates. (You'll learn more about the Cells property in Day 19, "Controlling Excel with VBA.") The call to FormatArialBold12 in line 34 causes FormatArialBold12 to format the cell in the second column of the second row of the active sheet. Finally, line 35 calls the FormatArialBold12 procedure and deliberately passes an incorrect object reference (ActiveSheet is a property of the Excel Application object that returns a reference to the currently active sheet).

10

Do

DO use the TypeName function—and VBA's other data type information functions—to help you write code that anticipates and avoids possible runtime errors, especially if you intend to distribute your procedures to other users.

Understanding the VarType Function's Results

The VarType function is similar to the TypeName function; you use both functions for the same purposes and in essentially the same way. The VarType function, however, returns a numeric code to indicate the data type of its argument instead of the string returned by TypeName. Also, the use of VarType is slightly more restricted than TypeName.

SYNTAX

The general syntax of the VarType function is

VarType(*varname*)

varname represents any VBA variable name. Notice that, unlike TypeName, the *varname* argument must always be a single variable name. Table 10.3 summarizes the numeric codes that VarType returns depending on the specific data type of *varname*.

TABLE 10.3 RETURN VALUES FOR THE VarType FUNCTION

VBA Constant	Value	Meaning
vbEmpty	0	Uninitialized **Variant** type.
vbNull	1	**Variant** that does not contain valid data.
vbInteger	2	**Integer** type.
vbLong	3	**Long** integer type.
vbSingle	4	**Single** floating-point type.
vbDouble	5	**Double** floating-point type.
vbCurrency	6	**Currency** type.
vbDate	7	**Date** type.
vbString	8	**String** type.
vbObject	9	**Object** type, usually an Automation object. (Use the TypeName function to find the specific object type.)
vbError	10	A **Variant** containing a VBA or user-defined error code. (Day 18 describes VBA's error codes.)
vbBoolean	11	**Boolean** type.

VBA Constant	Value	Meaning
vbVariant	12	**Variant** type. VarType only returns this value combined with vbArray to indicate an array of **Variant**s.
vbDataObject	13	A data access object; usually an OLE object. (You learn about OLE objects on Day 20.)
vbDecimal	14	A Decimal type floating-point number. Decimal type numbers can only be stored in a **Variant** variable. The Decimal floating-point numbers are used internally by VBA; you cannot declare variables with a Decimal type.
vbByte	17	**Byte** type.
vbArray	8192	**Array** type. VarType always combines this value (by arithmetic addition) with one of the other type codes listed in this table to indicate the specific type of the array's elements. VarType never returns the vbArray type code alone.

When you use the VarType function, it returns one of the number values shown in Table 10.3. A few of the codes that VarType returns require some additional explanation.

First, when you use VarType to return the type of an object variable, notice that VarType can only tell you whether the variable is an **Object** type that supports Automation or an **Object** type that does not support Automation. Also, if you use VarType on an uninitialized **Object** type variable, VBA displays a runtime error complaining that the object variable is not set. If you need to find out the specific type of an object, or you need to find out whether an object variable has ever been set to refer to an object, use the TypeName function instead.

Second, if the variable you test with VarType is an array, VarType arithmetically adds the code for an **Array** type to the code for the data type of the elements in the array. For example, an array of **Long** integers causes VarType to return the value *8195*, which is equal to 8192 (the code for an **Array** type) plus 3 (the code for a **Long** integer type). Therefore, any code value greater than 8192 tells you that the variable you tested with VarType is an array. (Day 13, "Managing Files with Visual Basic for Applications," contains a sidebar explaining how to use logical operators to make bit-wise comparisons to determine which attributes a file has; you can use a similar technique to isolate the values contained in the number returned by the VarType function.)

> **Do**
>
> **DO** use the VBA constant names shown in Table 10.3 to refer to the various codes that `VarType` returns. Using VBA's predefined constant names makes your code more readable and easier to debug.

Understanding the Special `Empty` and `Null` Values

VBA provides two special values, indicated by the keywords `Empty` and `Null`, to represent uninitialized, absent, or invalid data. The two values have similar meanings, but different purposes.

The `Empty` Value

VBA uses the `Empty` value to indicate a `Variant` variable that has never had a value assigned to it. When VBA creates a new `Variant` type variable, it automatically assigns it the `Empty` value. The `Variant` variable keeps the `Empty` value until you assign some other value to the `Variant` variable.

The `Empty` value does not cause runtime or type mismatch errors if it ends up being included in an expression. When VBA encounters a `Variant` variable containing the `Empty` value in a numeric expression or otherwise used as a number, VBA treats the `Empty` value as if it is zero (0). When VBA encounters a `Variant` variable containing the `Empty` value in a string expression, VBA treats `Empty` as if it is a zero-length string (`""`).

You can also directly assign the `Empty` value to a `Variant` variable if you want to indicate that the variable does not contain any data. To assign the `Empty` value to a variable, use a statement such as the following (where V is any `Variant` type variable):

```
V = Empty
```

Because VBA treats `Empty` as if it were 0 or a zero-length empty string (`""`) depending on the context of the expression, you can't use relational operators to find out whether a `Variant` variable contains the special `Empty` value or really contains 0 or an empty string. For this reason, VBA includes the `IsEmpty` function.

The general syntax of the `IsEmpty` function is

```
IsEmpty(expression)
```

In the preceding syntax sample, *expression* represents any VBA `Variant` type variable or expression. `IsEmpty` returns `True` if *expression* is a single `Variant` type variable containing the special `Empty` value; `False` otherwise. Usually, you use the `IsEmpty` function with only a single variable name as the argument. Although you can pass a complex expression as the *expression* argument, `IsEmpty` always returns `False` if *expression* contains more than one variable.

You can also use the `TypeName` or `VarType` functions to find out whether a particular **Variant** variable contains the **Empty** value.

The **Null** Value

VBA provides the **Null** value to indicate a **Variant** type variable that does not contain any valid data. Unlike the **Empty** value, VBA does not assign the **Null** value to variables. The only way a variable can have the **Null** value is if you directly assign **Null** to that variable or if you assign the result of an expression that contains a **Null** value to that variable.

The **Null** value does not cause runtime or type mismatch errors if it ends up being included in an expression. When VBA encounters a **Variant** variable containing the **Null** value in an expression, the entire expression results in **Null**. (This behavior is described by saying that the **Null** value *propagates*—that is, spreads—through expressions.)

VBA includes the **Null** value to help make it easier for you to deal with database information and to program database type applications. Many database applications—such as Microsoft Access—use the **Null** value to indicate missing or invalid data in the database. For example, you might have a procedure that helps perform data entry for a worksheet database in Excel. You might assign the **Null** value to a variable in your database program to indicate, for instance, that an invoice number has not yet been entered or that an invalid invoice number was entered.

You can also use the **Null** value to indicate whether the value returned by a function is valid. For example, if you write a function that uses `InputBox` to get a value from a user and the user cancels the input dialog, you might want your function to return **Null** to indicate that its operation was canceled and that it is not returning any valid data.

To assign the **Null** value to a variable, use a statement such as the following (where V is any **Variant** type variable):

```
V = Null
```

VBA includes the `IsNull` function to let you determine whether a **Variant** type variable contains the special **Null** value. You cannot use VBA's relational operators to determine whether a variable contains **Null**.

The general syntax of the `IsNull` function is

▼ SYNTAX

```
IsNull(expression)
```

In the preceding syntax sample, *expression* represents any VBA **Variant** type variable or expression. The `IsNull` function returns **True** if *expression* is a single **Variant** type variable that contains **Null**; **False** otherwise. If *expression* contains more than one variable and any one of the variables contains **Null**, the entire expression evaluates to **Null** and `IsNull` returns **True**.

10

> **DON'T**
>
> **DON'T** confuse `Empty` and `Null`. VBA assigns `Empty` to indicate that the `Variant` variable has not yet been assigned a value (initialized). `Null`, on the other hand, requires you to deliberately assign the value to some variable to indicate invalid data.

> **Do**
>
> **DO** use the `IsEmpty` and `IsNull` functions to test for the `Empty` and `Null` values in a variable. Standard comparison operators will not work for detecting either of these values.

Defensive Programming: Preventing Errors Before They Happen

Defensive programming is just one of many names given to various programming techniques intended to reduce bugs and problems with your programs. The goal of defensive programming is to avoid runtime errors and other failures in your procedures by anticipating and preventing errors before they happen.

You have already seen several examples of defensive programming techniques in each of the chapters in this second week of learning VBA. Decision-making structures, loops, and VBA's data type information functions are all essential tools to start making your procedures and programs "bulletproof," that is, immune to unwanted runtime errors caused by invalid, missing, or erroneous data values.

Following these defensive programming practices is especially important if you expect to distribute your functions or procedures to other users. For example, you might be responsible for setting up Microsoft Excel on computers for less experienced users. If so, you might end up writing or recording several macros to help less-experienced users perform routine tasks, such as adding data to certain spreadsheets, generating reports, creating certain business documents, and so on.

If this is your situation, your procedures and programs will get the best reception from their users if your procedures run without runtime errors. A procedure that fails in the middle of a complex task can leave a less-experienced user at a loss as to what to do next.

At the least, a procedure for use by inexperienced users should anticipate a runtime error and terminate its own execution more gracefully than VBA's runtime error dialog. For example, it is much better for a procedure to display a clear-cut message about why it can't carry out its task and then end its own execution than it is for a user to receive VBA's occasionally obscure runtime error messages.

Even if you expect no one else to use your procedures except yourself, you should still practice defensive programming. If a procedure that performs some relatively complex task—such as data-entry in a worksheet or creating and printing a report—fails due to a runtime error, you might find it difficult or annoying to recover from the partially completed task.

Checking Arguments and Other Internal Values

One defensive programming technique is to validate values that come from outside the function or procedure, such as a function's arguments. A related defensive programming technique is to ensure that the environment in which a procedure executes is actually the environment in which you intend it to execute.

10

Listings 10.1 and 10.5 (earlier in this chapter) both show examples of this kind of defensive programming in action. Both the FlipCase function and the FormatArialBold12 procedure contain code that checks the status of various internal conditions and prevents certain predictable errors from occurring.

The FlipCase function, for instance, has code that ensures that the optional nChar argument has the expected numeric type value. The same section of code also ensures that if the nChar optional argument is missing, FlipCase provides a substitute value. Adding this extra code prevents a runtime error from occurring in the rest of the function's code where the expected value from nChar actually gets used.

As another example, the FormatArialBold12 procedure has code that ensures that the optional objRange argument contains a reference to an object that can actually be formatted and prevents a runtime error from occurring later when the procedure actually attempts to change the Font object's properties.

You can ensure that your procedures and functions run smoothly, without interruptions from runtime errors, by adding similar internal value and environment checking code to your procedures and functions.

Validating User Input

When one of your procedures is working correctly, you can count on your computer and VBA to carry out the instructions in your procedure exactly the same way each time you run the procedure. You cannot count on a human being to behave the same way, however.

If your procedure or function gets input from a user—whether that user is yourself or someone else—you can't count on a human being to always perform the same way or to enter data without occasionally making mistakes. Even if you write absolutely error-free VBA code, an incorrect value entered by your procedure's user can end up producing a runtime error due to type mismatches or other problems.

For example, suppose you write a procedure that asks the user to enter a date value as a string. Suppose, also, that you want to save the user some typing, so you write your procedure so that it expects the user to enter only the month and day and then concatenates a string containing the current year to the end of whatever string the user enters. If the user doesn't know—or ignores—the fact that the procedure adds the current year and enters the complete date *10/29/99*, your procedure still adds the current year (*/99*, for instance) to the date string the user entered, resulting in the string *10/29/99/99*, which is not a valid date expression. If your procedure tries to convert this value to a date, VBA displays a runtime error and stops executing your procedure.

As another example, if you write a procedure that needs to get a numeric value from a user and the user enters a non-numeric string, you'll probably end up with a type-mismatch runtime error at the point in your procedure where one of your VBA statements tries to use the non-numeric value from the user as a number.

For procedures that you use yourself, you can often prevent problems like this just by making sure that your input dialog prompt text clearly states what kind of value to enter. For procedures that another person will use, you should add code to your procedure that analyzes the user's input to ensure that it matches what your procedure expects, in addition to including clear and explicit prompt text. In the example of getting a date string, you might add code to your procedure that evaluates the string entered by the user and only adds the year to the string if the user omits it.

You should also be sure to handle obvious issues, such as what happens if a user cancels an input dialog. Many of the listings in Days 8 and 9 show **If...Then** and loop structures that evaluate the user's input, handling dialog cancellations and blank strings appropriately. Listing 10.2 shows a rudimentary data entry loop that ensures that the value entered in the input dialog is, in fact, the expected **Date** data type—or a string that VBA can convert to a **Date**.

Do

DO evaluate a user's input to ensure that the user's value is really what the procedure needs. You should construct a loop to repeatedly get data from the user until the user enters a value of the expected type or range.

Don't

DON'T frustrate your procedure's users: If you refuse their input, display a message that tells the users why the data they entered is not acceptable.

Listing 10.6 shows a function, GetInteger, that gets an **Integer** type value from the user. This function clearly prompts the user for the type of information desired and then carefully evaluates the string that the user types in to determine whether the user actually entered an **Integer** value. If the user enters non-numeric data, a floating-point number, or a number outside the range for an **Integer** data type, the function displays a message stating the problem and then repeats the request for an integer.

INPUT **LISTING 10.6** CHECKING USER INPUT TO ENSURE VALID DATA VALUES

```
1:   Function GetInteger() As Variant
2:   'asks user for an integer value, and makes sure that the
3:   'entered value is really an integer
4:
5:     Const iTitle = "Get Integer"
6:     Const IntMax = 32767    'largest positive num for integer
7:     Const IntMin = -32768   'largest negative num for integer
8:
9:     Dim uNum As Variant
10:    Dim Okint As Boolean
11:
12:    OKint = False     'make sure loop starts
13:    Do Until OKint
14:      uNum = InputBox(prompt:="Enter an integer value: ", _
15:                  Title:=iTitle)
16:      If IsNumeric(uNum) Then      'value is at least numeric
17:        uNum = CDbl(uNum)           'convert to Double
18:        If ((uNum >= IntMin) And (uNum <= IntMax)) Then
19:          If (uNum - Int(uNum)) = 0 Then      'no fractions
20:            uNum = CInt(uNum)                'final conversion
21:            OKint = True                'it is an okay integer
22:          Else                      'user entered floating point
```

continues

LISTING 10.6   CONTINUED

```
23:              MsgBox prompt:="Enter a number without " & _
24:                        "a decimal, only!", _
25:                   Title:=iTitle, Buttons:=vbExclamation
26:          End If
27:        Else          'user entered out-of-range number
28:          MsgBox prompt:="You must enter a number " & _
29:            "between " & IntMin & " and " & IntMax & ".", _
30:                Title:=iTitle, Buttons:=vbExclamation
31:        End If
32:      Else              'user entered non-numeric string
33:        If uNum = "" Then    'check to see if user canceled
34:          uNum = MsgBox(prompt:="Cancel Integer entry?", _
35:                        Title:=iTitle, _
36:                      Buttons:=vbYesNo + vbQuestion)
37:          If uNum = vbYes Then    'user canceled
38:            GetInteger = Null       'assign Null to result
39:            Exit Function          'end function
40:          End If
41:        Else
42:          MsgBox prompt:="You must enter a number!", _
43:                 Title:=iTitle, _
44:                 Buttons:=vbExclamation
45:        End If
46:      End If
47:    Loop
48:    GetInteger = uNum
49: End Function
50:
51:
52: Sub Test_GetInteger()
53:    Dim iNum As Variant
54:
55:    iNum = GetInteger
56:    If IsNull(iNum) Then
57:      MsgBox "Integer Entry was canceled"
58:    Else
59:      MsgBox "You entered: " & iNum
60:    End If
61: End Sub
```

ANALYSIS   This function is fairly straightforward, although it might seem complex when you first look at it. This function gets input from the user and then applies the following tests to the user input:

- Is the data numeric?

- If it is numeric, does the value fall within the range of permitted values for an **Integer** type number?

- If it is numeric and within the range of an **Integer**, is the data a whole number without a fractional part?

Only if the value entered by the user passes all three of these tests does the function return the user's value. If the value entered by the user fails any of these tests, the function displays a message telling the user what's wrong with the data entered and loops to get another value from the user. GetInteger also checks to see whether the user canceled the dialog, confirms the cancellation, and returns **Null** if the user does cancel the input operation.

Line 1 contains the GetInteger function declaration. Notice that the function's return data type is a **Variant**, rather than an **Integer**. GetInteger returns a **Variant** data type so that it is able to return a **Null** type value in case the user cancels the input dialog.

Lines 5 through 7 declare several constants. iTitle supplies a title for all the dialogs that this function displays. IntMax is the maximum value that an **Integer** data type can contain and IntMin is the minimum value that an **Integer** data type can contain.

Line 9 declares the uNum variable, which is used to hold the user's input. Notice that this variable is a **Variant** type, which makes the evaluation and processing of this variable somewhat easier. Line 10 declares a **Boolean** type variable, OKint. OKint is used as a flag to control the execution of the loop that displays the input dialog and evaluates the user's input.

Line 12 assigns **False** to the OKint variable so that the loop in line 13 will start to execute.

Line 13 is the start of a **Do Until** loop. The body of this loop contains all the statements from line 14 through line 46. This loop executes until OKint becomes **True**.

The first statement in the loop body is in line 14; this statement uses the InputBox function to prompt the user to enter an integer value and then assigns the user's input to uNum.

Line 16 contains an **If...Then...Else** statement that checks whether the user's input is at least numeric. If the string in uNum is *not* numeric, VBA executes the **Else** clause for this statement in lines 32 through 46. In this **Else** clause, line 33 contains a nested **If...Then...Else** statement that checks whether the string in uNum is empty. If uNum is empty, line 34 uses MsgBox to ask the user whether the data entry should be canceled. If the user answers "Yes," line 38 assigns the **Null** value to the GetInteger function result and line 39 ends the function. This way, you can test the function's result to determine whether the data-entry was canceled; if the GetInteger result is **Null**, the user canceled the data entry.

10

If uNum is not empty, VBA executes the **Else** clause for the nested **If** statement in lines 41 through 45. These lines use MsgBox to display a message to the user that she must enter a numeric value, and execution then passes to line 47, which marks the end of the loop body. (Remember, this branch of the code only executes if the user entered a non-numeric value.)

If, in line 16, the value in uNum is numeric, VBA continues execution with line 17. This statement converts the user's string to a **Double** type number and stores the result back into uNum. (uNum is a **Variant** type, so it can contain any data type.) Converting the user's input to a **Double** type number makes the remaining tests somewhat easier; it is now possible to make simple arithmetic comparisons instead of complex string analysis.

Line 18 begins a nested **If...Then...Else** statement that checks to see whether the value in uNum falls within the range of permissible values for an **Integer** data type. The expression ((uNum >= IntMin) And (uNum <= IntMax)) is **True** whenever uNum falls between –32768 and 32767, inclusive.

If the value in uNum is not within the range of acceptable values for an **Integer**, VBA executes the **Else** clause in lines 28 through 31. These lines simply display a message dialog stating that the user must enter a number in the specified range. VBA then continues execution with line 47, which indicates the end of the loop body.

If, in line 18, the value in uNum is within the permissible range for an **Integer**, VBA continues execution with line 19, which contains yet another nested **If...Then...Else** statement.

In line 19, the **If...Then...Else** statement uses the expression (uNum - Int(uNum)) = 0 to determine which branch of code to execute. This expression subtracts the integer equivalent (returned by VBA's Int function) of the **Double** type number in uNum from uNum itself. If the difference between the two is 0, the number in uNum has no fractional part. (This expression uses the Int function instead of **CInt** because **CInt** *rounds* numbers before converting them to integers, whereas Int *truncates*, or discards, the fractional part.)

If the expression in line 19 is **False**, the user entered a floating-point number, so VBA executes the nested **Else** clause in lines 22 through 26. These lines simply display a message dialog to the user stating that she must enter a number with no decimal point. Execution then continues with line 47, marking the end of the loop's body.

If the expression in line 19 is **True**, the value the user entered is indeed an integer. VBA continues execution with line 20, which uses **CInt** to convert uNum to an **Integer**. This conversion is required so that the **Variant** data type returned by GetInteger has the **Integer** type; otherwise, it will have a **Double** type.

Line 21 assigns **True** to OKint, indicating that the user successfully entered an integer value, thus ending the loop. VBA only executes this line when the user's value passes all three tests. If the user's value fails any of the tests, GetInteger displays the appropriate message and repeats the entry loop.

When the user does enter an integer, the loop stops executing and VBA executes line 48, which assigns the GetInteger function result, and the function ends.

Lines 52 through 61 contain a procedure to test the GetInteger function. Line 55 calls GetInteger and assigns its return value to the iNum variable declared in line 53. Notice the **If...Then...Else** statement in lines 56 through 60. This statement uses the IsNull function to determine whether the value returned by GetInteger and stored in iNum is **Null**. If it is **Null**, the user canceled the input dialog in the GetInteger function and the function result does not contain any valid data.

10

Do

DO make your programming task easier by writing a list of all the conditions that you want to test for like the list at the beginning of the Analysis section for Listing 10.6. Writing a list like this before you start programming can help you avoid false starts, wasted effort, and possibly a great deal of frustration.

DO consider writing your own data type information functions to expand on the data type information functions that VBA provides, especially if you find yourself writing code to check whether a number is an **Integer**, **Double**, and so on. For example, if you find yourself writing many procedures or functions that check to make sure a value is, say, an **Integer**, you might find it useful to write an IsInteger function with a **Boolean** result to save yourself from writing the same value-testing code over and over again.

Validating Other Input

Your procedures can obtain data from other sources besides input entered into a dialog by a user. Your procedures are also likely to use data values obtained from worksheet cells or from external data files.

Usually, you should apply some or all of the same kinds of data validation to any data your procedure obtains from any source. For instance, if your procedure obtains data from a worksheet cell, you should apply the same data checking routines as you would apply to data obtained directly from the user through an input dialog. Use the same defensive programming techniques to validate data from other sources as those just described for validating a user's direct input.

Preserving Variables Between Function and Procedure Calls

In Day 3, you learned about variable *persistence*, or how long a variable retains the value you assign to it. You learned that procedure-level variables retain their values only for as long as the procedure in which you declare the variable continues to execute.

There are, however, some circumstances under which you want a variable to retain its value. For example, you might want a procedure that creates charts to number each chart that it creates sequentially, even if the procedure only creates one chart at a time, by retaining a sequential count within the chart creating procedure. As another example, you might want to write a procedure that gets a worksheet name from the user and retains the last worksheet name the user entered to suggest it as a default for the next time you call the procedure to get a worksheet name.

You can override VBA's normal variable persistence rules by adding the **Static** keyword to the variable's declaration or by adding the **Static** keyword to the function or procedure declaration. By adding the **Static** keyword, you tell VBA not to dispose of the variable's contents, but to retain the variable and its stored data indefinitely. Static variables persist from the time they are created until you either close the project (an Excel workbook) in which the variables are declared or you end the current host application work session.

The general syntax for using the **Static** keyword to create a single static variable is

```
Static varname [As vartype]
```

varname represents any valid VBA variable name and *vartype* represents any of VBA's data types: **Byte**, **Integer**, **Long**, **Single**, **Double**, **Currency**, **String**, or **Date**. Essentially, the syntax for creating a single static variable, including the optional **As** keyword, is the same as using **Dim** to declare a variable. By using the **Static** keyword instead of **Dim**, you tell VBA to create a variable that retains its value indefinitely. You can declare individual static variables only at the procedure level.

You can make all the variables in a function or procedure static by placing the **Static** keyword at the beginning of the procedure or function declaration, as shown in the following general syntax samples:

```
Static Function name([arglist]) [As vartype]
Static Sub name()
```

name represents any valid VBA identifier for a function or procedure name, *arglist* represents any valid argument list definition for the function, and *vartype* represents the function result's data type.

▼ If you declare an entire function or procedure with the **Static** keyword, all the variables declared within the function or procedure retain their values in between calls to that par-

▲ ticular function or procedure.

Listing 10.7 shows the MakeSalesRpt_Chart procedure from Day 8, which has been modified to use static variables. This version of MakeSalesRpt_Chart retains the values that the user enters for the source worksheet and the data range to be graphed the first time the procedure is executed during a particular work session and suggests these values the next time the procedure is executed. MakeSalesRpt_Chart also keeps a running count of the charts generated and adds this number to the chart name for each chart the procedure creates.

INPUT   **LISTING 10.7**   USING **Static** VARIABLES

```
 1:  Sub MakeSalesRpt_Chart()
 2:  'asks for a sheet name that contains source data, and then
 3:  'asks for a range of cells containing data to chart. Next,
 4:  'asks for a sheet name to put the pie chart on. Procedure
 5:  'then creates chart in a fixed location, and uses the
 6:  'ChartWizard method to make a pie chart.
 7:  'This procedure uses Static variables, so subsequent runs
 8:  'suggest the last used source sheet name and range.
 9:
10:     Const sTitle = "Make Sales Report Chart"
11:
12:     Static SrcShtName As String
13:     Static SourceRng As String
14:     Static ChartCount As Variant
15:     Dim DestShtName As String
16:
17:         'get source sheet name
18:     SrcShtName = InputBox(prompt:="Enter the name of " & _
19:             "the sheet containing the data to graph:", _
20:                        Title:=sTitle, _
21:                        default:=SrcShtName)
22:
23:         'check to see if user entered name or chose Cancel
24:     If Len(Trim(SrcShtName)) = 0 Then
25:         MsgBox "Data source not entered - ending procedure"
26:         Exit Sub
27:     End If
28:         'select source sheet so user can refer to it
29:     Sheets(SrcShtName).Select
30:
31:         'get source range
32:     SourceRng = InputBox(prompt:="Enter the range of " & _
```

continues

10

LISTING 10.7　CONTINUED

```
33:                           "data to graph using R1C1 notation:", _
34:                               Title:=sTitle, _
35:                               default:=SourceRng)
36:
37:        'check to see if user entered range or chose Cancel
38:        If Len(Trim(SourceRng)) = 0 Then
39:          MsgBox "Source range not entered - ending procedure"
40:          Exit Sub
41:        End If
42:
43:        'get destination sheet name
44:        DestShtName = InputBox(prompt:="Enter the name of " & _
45:                     "the sheet that will contain the graph:", _
46:                               Title:=sTitle)
47:
48:        'did user enter destination name or choose Cancel?
49:        If Len(Trim(DestShtName)) = 0 Then
50:          MsgBox "Chart sheet not entered - ending procedure"
51:          Exit Sub
52:        End If
53:
54:
55:        'select the destination sheet and create chart
56:        Sheets(DestShtName).Select
57:        ActiveSheet.ChartObjects.Add(96, 37.5, 234, 111).Select
58:
59:        'set up the chart count
60:        If IsEmpty(ChartCount) Then
61:          ChartCount = 1
62:        Else
63:          ChartCount = ChartCount + 1
64:        End If
65:
66:        'use ChartWizard Method to create chart.
67:        With Sheets(SrcShtName)
68:          ActiveChart.ChartWizard Source:=.Range(SourceRng), _
69:                              Gallery:=xlPie, _
70:                              Format:=7, _
71:                              PlotBy:=xlColumns, _
72:                              CategoryLabels:=1, _
73:                              SeriesLabels:=1, _
74:                              HasLegend:=1, _
75:                              Title:="Sales Report" & ChartCount
76:        End With
77: End Sub
```

ANALYSIS   Lines 12 through 15 declare the variables that this procedure uses. SrcShtName, SourceRng, and ChartCount are all declared as **Static** variables, so they will keep their value in between calls to MakeSalesRpt_Chart. The DestShtName variable is not declared as a static variable, so its value is lost as soon as MakeSalesRpt_Chart stops executing. The ChartCount variable is a new addition to this procedure and is used to supply a running count of the number of charts that this procedure creates in the current Excel work session. Declaring ChartCount as a **Static Variant** type variable makes it possible to use the IsEmpty function to determine whether this procedure has been executed previously during the current Excel work session.

Lines 18 through 21 get the name of the worksheet that contains the data to be charted. Notice that the InputBox function in these lines now uses the Default argument and passes the SrcShtName variable as the suggested default. The first time MakeSalesRpt_Chart executes in the current Excel work session, these statements display the dialog shown in Figure 10.1. Notice that the text box in this input dialog is blank.

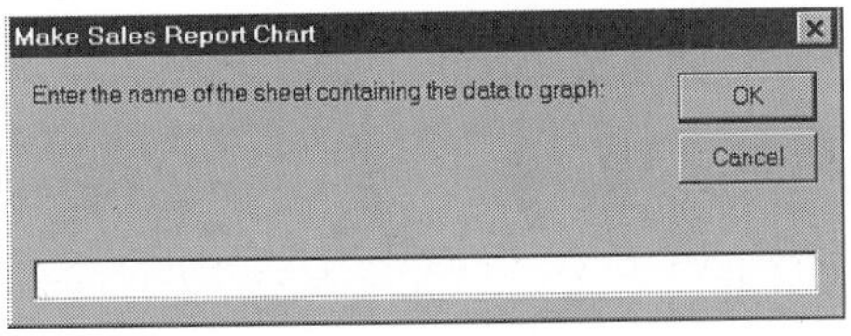

10

FIGURE 10.1

MakeSalesRpt_Chart *displays this dialog to get the data source worksheet name from the user the first time she executes this procedure in a particular work session.*

Make Sales Report Chart

Enter the name of the sheet containing the data to graph: OK   Cancel

Lines 24 through 27 evaluate the user's input, checking to see whether the user canceled the input dialog. If the user canceled the input dialog, VBA executes the statements in lines 25 and 26, displaying a message that input was canceled and ending the procedure.

Line 29 selects the worksheet that the user named so that the user can see the data sheet when asked to enter the range for the data to chart.

Lines 32 through 35 get the data range to be charted. Notice that this InputBox function also includes the Default argument and passes the SourceRng variable as the suggested default value. The first time MakeSalesRpt_Chart executes during the current Excel work session, these statements display the dialog shown in Figure 10.2. Notice that the text box in this input dialog is also blank.

FIGURE 10.2

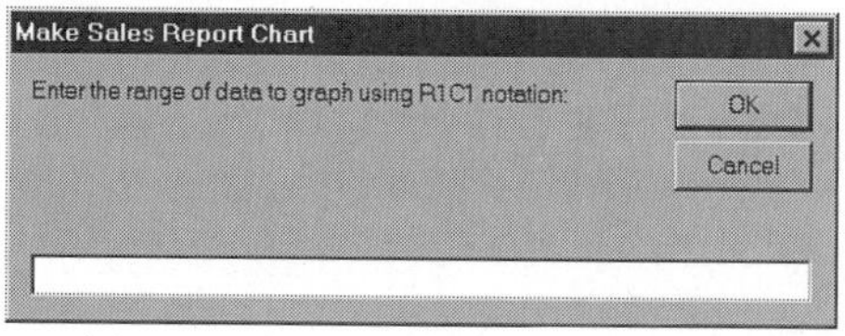

MakeSalesRpt_Chart *displays this dialog to get the range of data to chart from the user the first time she executes this procedure in a particular work session.*

Lines 37 through 41 check to see whether the user canceled the range input dialog, displaying a message and ending the procedure if the user did cancel.

Lines 44 through 46 get the name of the worksheet on which the completed chart should be placed. Notice that this InputBox function call does not suggest a default sheet name for the chart's destination, and that the DestShtName variable is the only variable in this procedure that is not static. DestShtName was not declared static because it is unlikely that you will want to place the new chart on top of the last chart you created. These statements display the dialog shown in Figure 10.3. Notice that this text box, too, is blank.

FIGURE 10.3

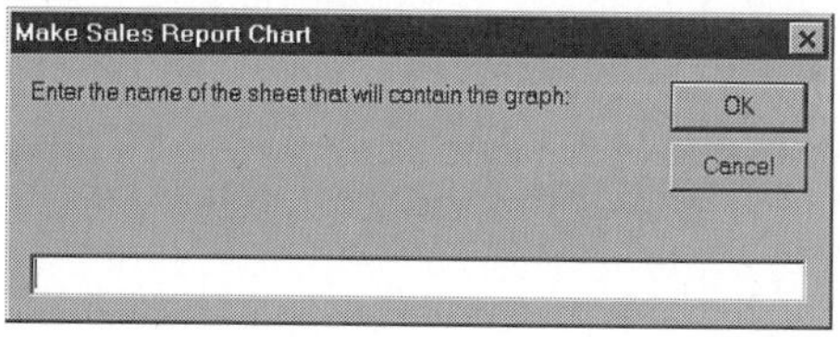

MakeSalesRpt_Chart *displays this dialog to get the name of the worksheet in which to place the completed chart.*

Once again, lines 49 through 52 check to see whether the user canceled the operation. Now, lines 56 and 57 select the destination sheet and create the new chart object.

Lines 60 through 64 are also new to this version of MakeSalesRpt_Chart. This If...Then...Else statement checks to see whether the ChartCount variable is **Empty**; remember, a **Variant** type variable that has never had a value assigned to it contains the special **Empty** value. If ChartCount is empty, this is the first time in the current work session that the procedure has executed, and the statement in line 61 assigns the value 1 to ChartCount. If ChartCount is not **Empty**, this procedure has been executed at least once before in this work session, and the statement in line 63 increments ChartCount by 1. This If...Then...Else statement works only because ChartCount is a static variable and retains its value in between calls to MakeSalesRpt_Chart. If ChartCount is not declared with the **Static** keyword, it would be **Empty** every time this procedure executes because VBA would create it anew each time the procedure started execution and would destroy it each time the procedure completed execution. Because it is static, however, ChartCount effectively keeps a running total of the number of charts created by this procedure in this work session.

Finally, lines 67 through 75 use the ChartWizard method to create the chart using the specified data range from the specified worksheet. Figure 10.4 shows a sample chart created with the MakeSalesRpt_Chart procedure. Notice that the chart title in Figure 10.4—Sales Report1—ends with the number 1. This is the result of concatenating the ChartCount value with the chart name in line 75.

FIGURE 10.4

An example of a pie chart created by the MakeSalesRpt_Chart procedure. Notice the number 1 at the end of the chart title.

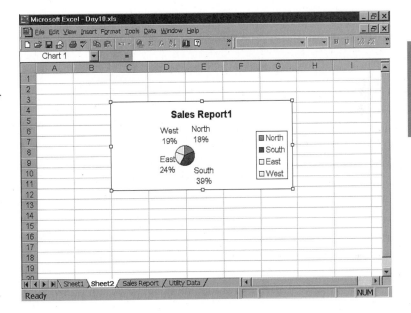

Now, if you execute MakeSalesRpt_Chart a second time in the same work session, the procedure behaves exactly the same as just described, but the contents of some of the dialogs it displays are different.

In lines 18 through 21, when MakeSalesRpt_Chart asks for the source data sheet name, it displays the dialog shown in Figure 10.5 (assuming that Sales Report was the worksheet name you entered last time you executed MakeSalesRpt_Chart). Because the SrcShtName variable is static, it retained its value between the first and second time the MakeSalesRpt_Chart was executed. Because the InputBox statement in lines 18 through 21 uses SrcShtName as the suggested input default, the MakeSalesRpt_Chart procedure is able to suggest the name of the last source worksheet as the source worksheet for this time.

FIGURE 10.5

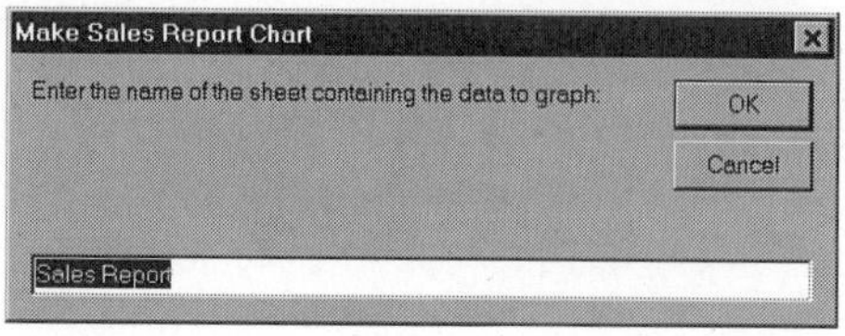

MakeSalesRpt_Chart
*displays this dialog
suggesting the last
source worksheet you
used each additional
time you execute this
procedure in a partic-
ular work session.*

Similarly, when MakeSalesRpt_Chart asks for the source data range in lines 32 through 35, it displays the dialog shown in Figure 10.6 (assuming that B4:D8 was the range you entered last time you executed MakeSalesRpt_Chart).

FIGURE 10.6

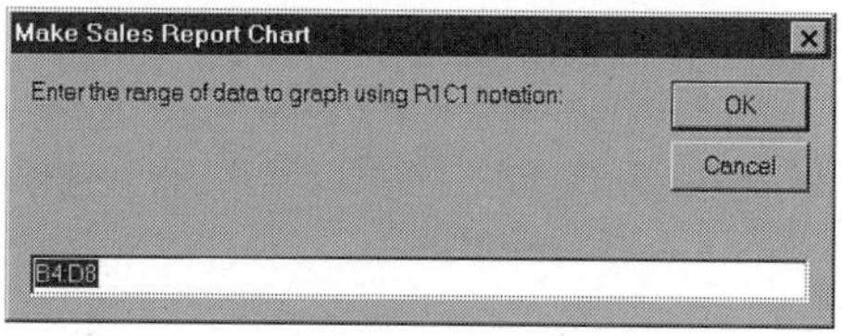

MakeSalesRpt_Chart
*displays this dialog
suggesting the last
range you used each
additional time you
execute this procedure
in a particular work
session.*

When MakeSalesRpt_Chart asks for the destination worksheet in lines 44 through 46, it displays the same dialog shown previously in Figure 10.3.

Finally, when MakeSalesRpt_Chart finishes creating its second chart, assuming you again charted the same data, the chart appears like the one shown in Figure 10.7. Notice that the chart title in Figure 10.7—Sales Report2—ends with the number 2. This is the result of concatenating the ChartCount (which increases by 1 each time you execute MakeSalesRpt_Chart) with the chart name in line 75.

You'll see additional examples of static variables in listings throughout the rest of this book.

FIGURE 10.7

MakeSalesRpt_Chart
*created this pie chart
the second time it was
used to chart data.
Notice the number 2 at
the end of the chart
title.*

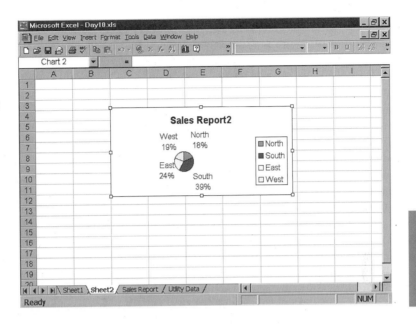

Summary

Today you learned how to use VBA's data type information functions to get more information about the type of data stored in **Variant** variables. In particular, you learned how to interpret the results of the TypeName and VarType functions and the differences between these functions. You also learned about VBA's special **Empty** and **Null** values, their differences, and their uses. In particular, you learned that VBA automatically assigns the **Empty** value to a **Variant** type variable to indicate that the variable has not yet been assigned a value.

Next, you learned how to combine VBA's type information functions, decision-making statements, and looping structures to help avoid runtime errors by ensuring that the data values your functions and procedures use internally have the correct or expected values, and by ensuring that data values your functions and procedures obtain from a user or some other source also have the correct or expected values.

This chapter also showed you why and how to declare variables that retain their values between calls to a function or procedure by declaring them with the **Static** keyword.

Q&A

Q Why is it so important to check internal data values? I'm writing the code, so I know what values will be passed when I call a function.

A The main reason you should check internal data values is to guard against human error. No one can really remember everything about the functions or procedures that they write, especially if you want to use a function that you wrote several days, weeks, or months ago. Adding the internal value-checking code can save you a great deal of frustration later on, especially if you make sure that your procedure or function makes an explicit complaint about what is wrong with its data values.

Frequently, your own error messages will be more clear than the runtime or compile errors that VBA displays. Also, if VBA displays a runtime error that results from an incompatible value passed as an optional function argument, the point at which VBA detects the error can be far away in your code from the actual source of the error.

Finally, it is much better to have your procedures shut down in an orderly fashion when your own code detects some potential error than to have to clean up a mess that might remain when a procedure fails unexpectedly with a runtime error.

Q Why is it necessary to spend so much programming effort screening the values that a user enters in an input dialog?

A The amount of effort you spend adding program instructions to validate a user's data input depends greatly on who you expect to be the primary user of the procedures and functions that you write. If you want to distribute your procedures or functions to other users, you should really spend the extra effort to make sure that your procedures and functions validate the data that the user enters. You'll only frustrate or confuse users if your procedures simply repeat input dialogs without any statement as to why or if your procedures crash with runtime errors.

Even if you are the only person who uses your procedures, you should at least include some rudimentary data validation to guard against having to clean up after a procedure that fails part way through its task with a runtime error.

Workshop

Answers are in Appendix A.

Quiz

1. What is the purpose of the VBA information functions that begin with the word Is?

2. What are the three VBA data type information functions that you are most likely to use on a regular basis?

3. Which of the VBA data type information functions give you the most specific information about the variable you are checking?

4. If you want to find out the specific type of an object reference, which data type information function should you use?

5. What does the IsMissing function tell you?

6. When the TypeName function returns the strings "Nothing" or "Unknown", what does that mean?

7. What does the **Empty** value signify? Does VBA ever assign this value to a variable?

8. What does the **Null** value signify? Does VBA ever assign this value to a variable?

9. What is *defensive programming*?

10. What is the purpose and effect of the **Static** keyword?

11. How do you use the **Static** keyword?

Exercises

1. Write a function named IsMasterCard that returns **True** if the string in the argument represents a valid MasterCard credit card number or **False** if the number is not a valid MasterCard number. Your function should have a single required string argument.

   A valid MasterCard credit card number always begins with the digit *5* and consists of four groups of four digits, with each digit group separated by a hyphen: 5234-5678-9012-3456. For this exercise, assume that the separating dashes are a required part of the credit card number. (HINT: Use the following logical expression with the **Like** operator (described in Day 4) to determine whether the function's argument is or is not a valid MasterCard credit card number: StrVal Like 5###-####-####-#### where StrVal is the string that contains the MasterCard number. This expression is **True** if StrVal matches the pattern specified after the **Like** operator.)

2. Write a procedure that gets a MasterCard number from the user. Your procedure should loop indefinitely until the user enters a valid MasterCard number. Use the IsMasterCard function you wrote in Exercise 1, preceding, to validate the user's input. Make sure that your procedure permits the user to cancel the entry operation and confirms the cancellation. Also, make sure that your procedure displays a message to the user stating *why* the loop is repeating.

DAY 11

Creating Your Own Data Types and Object Classes

This chapter teaches you how to create your own custom data types for specialized data-storage purposes and how to use your custom data types in your VBA code. This lesson also shows you how to create your own object classes in VBA. Creating custom object classes is essential to expanding the capabilities of Excel's built-in objects, and will help you understand how to create custom dialog boxes (creating custom dialog boxes is covered in Day 16). Today, you learn

- How to create custom data types.
- How to use a custom data type to fulfill special needs or to make it easier to manipulate groups of data values as a single unit.
- How to use class modules to create your own customized program objects.
- How to use your customized object classes in your VBA code.

Creating Your Own Data Types

VBA enables you to create additional data types, called *user-defined types*, that you can use in your procedures and functions. A user-defined type lets you bind together several related pieces of information into a single unit. You can then pass that single unit as an argument to a function or return that unit as a function result.

You create and use user-defined data types to simplify some programming tasks and to reduce the overall number of variables in your program. User-defined data types make it easier for you to store and manipulate complex groups of data.

For example, if you want to write a procedure (or several procedures and functions) that help you create invoices and enter each invoice's line-item information, you might end up declaring several different variables to store all the information your procedure needs to collect. You might need a variable for the invoice number, a variable for the customer name, a variable for the billing address, another variable for the shipping address, another variable for the invoice total, yet another variable for the invoice date, and so on—and this partial list doesn't even begin to include variables that store the invoice's line items.

As you can see, you might quickly end up with a large number of variables. Keeping track of so many variables is inconvenient, at best, and sometimes gets downright confusing. By creating a user-defined data type for your invoice information, you can consolidate all of these different data elements into a single data type and then declare and use a single variable to hold all the invoice information, referring only to the elements in the variable that you need at any one time.

In a sense, you can think of a user-defined type as being a sort of suitcase in which you can pack different types of data. You can handle the suitcase as if it is a single unit, passing it back and forth as a single item. You only worry about the specific contents of the suitcase when you need to access or store some particular item inside the suitcase.

Defining a User-Defined Data Type

Before you can declare and use any variables with a user-defined type, you must first define the type. You construct your user-defined types from the fundamental VBA data types you learned about in Day 3: **Byte**, **Integer**, **Long**, **Single**, **Double**, **Currency**, **Date**, **Boolean**, and **Variant**. You can also include arrays in your user-defined types and include previously defined user-defined data types.

▼ SYNTAX

To define a user-defined data type, use the **Type** statement in the declarations area of a module. The **Type** statement has the following general syntax:

```
Type VarName
    ElementName As type
    [ElementName As type]
    [ElementName As type]
...
End Type
```

Both *VarName* and *ElementName* represent any valid VBA identifier. *type* represents any VBA data type name or any previously defined user-defined type name. More specifically, *VarName* is the name for the new data type you are defining. *ElementName* is the name of a data element in the user-defined type. A user-defined type can contain one or more elements. You must specify the data type of each element in your user-defined type by following *ElementName* with the **As** keyword and the name of the specific data type for that element. An element's type can be any of VBA's inherent data types, an array, or a previously defined user-defined data type.

VBA allows the **Type** statement to appear only at the module level. You must place all of your user-defined type definitions in the definition area at the beginning of the module before any procedure or function declarations and before any variable declarations that use that user-defined type.

> **Tip**
>
> You can quickly jump to the declarations area of any module that is open in the VBA Editor by selecting (Declarations) in the Procedure drop-down list of the Module window.

11

For example, you might define a user-defined type for a mailing address:

```
Type MailingData
    Street As String
    City As String
    State As String *2
    Zip As String * 5
End Type
```

This type definition creates a user-defined type named MailingData, which contains four elements: Street (the street name and number), City (the city's name), State (a two-letter state abbreviation), and Zip (a five-digit ZIP code).

As another example, to declare a user-defined type to hold invoice information, you might use the following definition:

```
Type InvoiceHeading
    Number As Integer
    DateIssued As Date
    Customer As String
    ShipAddress As MailingData
    BillAddress As MailingData
    Total As Currency
End Type
```

The preceding type definition creates a user-defined type named InvoiceHeading, which contains six elements: Number (the invoice number), DateIssued (the invoice date), Customer (the customer name), ShipAddress (the shipping address), BillAddress (the billing address), and Total (the total of the invoice).

Notice that the BillAddress and ShipAddress elements have the previously defined user-defined MailingData type. These two elements, therefore, also contain all the same elements as the MailingData type. In a sense, the InvoiceHeading data type is a suitcase that contains other suitcases: the BillAddress and ShipAddress elements.

Each user-defined data type requires as much computer memory to store as the combined memory storage used by its elements. For example, a user-defined type that has four elements, each of which is an **Integer**, requires a total of 8 bytes of computer memory to store. Each **Integer** type element requires 2 bytes (the size of an **Integer**), and there are four elements, so the combined total storage is 8 bytes.

Note

> You cannot use the TypeName, VarType, or any other VBA data type information functions with variables of user-defined types, although you can use the information functions with any individual elements of a user-defined type.

Declaring Variables That Have a User-Defined Type

You declare a variable with a user-defined type the same way you declare any other variable in your procedures and functions, as long as you declare the variable explicitly. Obviously, you cannot implicitly declare a variable with a user-defined type because VBA has no way of knowing which user-defined type you want the variable to have.

Use the **Dim** or **Static** keywords to declare a variable with a user-defined type. You can declare variables that have a user-defined type at either a procedure level or at a module level. The following two statements each declare a variable with a user-defined type. The first statement declares a variable with the InvoiceHeading type, and the second statement declares a variable with the MailingData type.

```
Dim Invoice As InvoiceHeading
Dim Address As MailingData
```

Using Variables with User-Defined Types

You use variables that have user-defined types much the same way that you use other types of VBA variables. One of the few areas in which variables with user-defined types differ from other types of variables is when you need to refer to a particular element in a user-defined variable.

You are already familiar with the dot separator (.) used in object references. You know that the dot separator both joins and separates two different identifiers so that VBA can tell when you want to refer to an object, property, or method that belongs to another object.

VBA also uses the dot separator to create references to the elements in a variable with a user-defined type. For example, if you declare a variable named Address that has the user-defined type MailingData—as defined in the examples in the preceding sections of this lesson—you would refer to the City element of the variable with the following expression:

```
Address.City
```

Similarly, if you have variables named MyAddress and YourAddress, both declared with the user-defined type MailingData, you would refer to the Zip elements with the following expressions:

```
MyAddress.Zip
YourAddress.Zip
```

In all three of the preceding expressions, the dot (.) between the two names tells VBA that the two names together form a single identifier. VBA, therefore, first refers to the memory location referred to by the variable name and then uses the element name to refer to the specific information stored in that element of the variable.

Look again at the user-defined type definition for the example of an invoice header information:

```
Type InvoiceHeading
    Number As Integer
    DateIssued As Date
    Customer As String
    ShipAddress As MailingData
    BillAddress As MailingData
    Total As Currency
End Type
```

11

Notice again that the `ShipAddress` and `BillAddress` elements in the `InvoiceHeading` user-defined type are declared as having the previously defined user-defined type `MailingData`. If you have a variable, `Invoice`, that has the user-defined type `InvoiceHeading`, and you want to refer to the `City` element of the shipping address, use an expression like this:

```
Invoice.ShipAddress.City
```

When VBA evaluates this expression, it first references the data stored in the `Invoice` variable. The first dot separator lets VBA know that you want to refer to the `ShipAddress` element in the `Invoice` variable; the second dot separator lets VBA know that, in turn, you want to refer to the `City` element of the `ShipAddress` element. Just like with object references, the dot separator (`.`) connects the separate names into a single identifier while also letting VBA—and you—know what the individual references are.

If you have two variables with the same user-defined type, you can directly assign one variable to the other, as shown in the following statement:

```
MyAddress = YourAddress
```

Assuming both variables in the preceding assignment statement have the user-defined type `MailingData`, VBA copies all the information in each of the individual elements in `YourAddress` and stores them in the corresponding elements in `MyAddress`.

You cannot, however, assign a user-defined variable to another user-defined variable if they do not have the same type. For example, you could not assign the contents of a variable with the `MailingData` type to a variable with the `InvoiceHeading` type.

To assign values from or to individual elements in a user-defined type, you must specify an element in the user-defined type explicitly. For example, to assign a value to the `City` element of the variable `MyAddress` (assuming `MyAddress` has the user-defined type `MailingData`), you use the following statement:

```
MyAddress.City = "Oaktown"
```

In the preceding statement, VBA stores the string *Oaktown* in the `City` element of the `MyAddress` variable. Data that you assign to an element in a variable with a user-defined type must be compatible with the data type of that element.

To retrieve the information stored in a particular element of a user-defined type variable and assign it to another variable, use a statement like this:

```
AnyStr = MyAddress.City
```

In this statement, VBA retrieves whatever string is stored in the `City` element of the `MyAddress` variable and stores it in the variable `AnyStr`.

You can use elements from a variable with a user-defined type in any expression or as arguments for procedures and functions where the data type of the specific element is compatible with that expression or argument type. You can even declare functions that return a result that has a user-defined type. (Listing 11.1 shows an example of such a function.)

DON'T

DON'T try to assign a variable with a user-defined type to a `Variant` type variable; VBA will display a type-mismatch error if you do.

In Day 7, you learned how to use the `With` statement in object references to save yourself some typing and to make your VBA code easier to read. You learned to use the `With` statement whenever you want to refer to several properties or methods of the same object at once. You can also use the `With` statement to simplify references to elements of a user-defined type variable. The following code fragment shows how you can use the `With` statement:

```
With MyAddress
    .Street = "123 American Lane, Suite 24"
    .City = "Oaktown"
    .State = "CA"
    .Zip = "94609"
End With
```

When VBA executes the preceding statements, it first encounters the `With` keyword followed by the variable name. VBA then knows that it should reference data stored in the `MyAddress` variable. Notice that each element of the `MyAddress` variable that appears in the assignment statements has a dot separator (`.`) in front of it. When VBA executes these statements, it internally supplies the `MyAddress` variable reference for the missing reference (indicated by the dot separator) in each statement. As with object references and the `With` statement, you must include the dot separator. The `End With` keywords signal the end of the `With` statement.

Now you are ready to see a user-defined type put into action. Listing 11.1 shows the listing for an entire VBA module. This module contains a definition for a user-defined type and also a single procedure and function declaration. The `UtilityBill` user-defined type is set up to store all the relevant information for a single month's utility bill. It has elements (sometimes called *fields*) to store the billing date, the total cost of the bill, the number of therms used in that month (a *therm* is a unit used to measure natural gas consumption), and another element to store the number of kilowatt-hours used (abbreviated KWH, used to measure consumption of electricity).

11

The `Enter_UtilityCosts` procedure controls data entry and storage for the monthly utility bill figures; the `Get_UtilityItem` function handles the task of getting the individual values for a single utility bill from the user. Altogether, this module contains a single, simple program to handle the data entry of utility bills. You might use a program like this if you need to enter and analyze your company's (or your own) energy costs and consumption.

INPUT   **LISTING 11.1**   DEFINING, CREATING, AND USING USER-DEFINED TYPES

```
 1:  Option Explicit
 2:
 3:  Const BillTitle = "Utility Bill Data Entry"
 4:
 5:  Type UtilityBill
 6:      BillDate As Variant
 7:      Cost As Currency
 8:      Therms As Integer
 9:      Kwh As Integer
10:  End Type
11:
12:
13:  Sub Enter_UtilityCosts()
14:  'this proc enters utility bill information. It calls the
15:  'Get_UtilityItem function to get data for a single utility
16:  'bill, and then transfers the data to a worksheet, looping
17:  'until there is no more data.
18:      Dim Bill As UtilityBill
19:      Dim Done As Boolean
20:      Dim RNum As Integer
21:
22:      Worksheets("Utility Data").Select
23:
24:      RNum = 0
25:      Done = False
26:      Do Until Done
27:          Bill = Get_UtilityItem
28:          If IsNull(Bill.BillDate) Then
29:              Done = True
30:          Else
31:              RNum = RNum + 1
32:              With Bill
33:                  Cells(RNum, 1).Value = .BillDate
34:                  Cells(RNum, 2).Value = .Cost
35:                  Cells(RNum, 3).Value = .Therms
36:                  Cells(RNum, 4).Value = .Kwh
37:              End With
38:          End If
39:      Loop
```

```
40:      MsgBox prompt:="Data entry complete. " & RNum & _
41:             " records entered.", Title:=BillTitle
42: End Sub
43:
44:
45: Function Get_UtilityItem() As UtilityBill
46: 'gets all the data for a single utility bill, and
47: 'returns it in a utility bill user type.
48:
49:      Dim Item As UtilityBill
50:      Dim Tmp As Variant
51:
52:      With Item
53:         Do          'get the date of the bill
54:            Tmp = InputBox(prompt:="Enter the date of " & _
55:                       "the bill:", Title:=BillTitle)
56:            If Tmp = "" Then         'did user cancel?
57:               Tmp = MsgBox(prompt:="End data entry?", _
58:                       Title:=BillTitle, _
59:                       Buttons:=vbQuestion + vbYesNo)
60:               If Tmp = vbYes Then        'return null date
61:                  .BillDate = Null
62:                  Get_UtilityItem = Item
63:                  Exit Function
64:               End If
65:            End If
66:         Loop Until IsDate(Tmp)
67:         .BillDate = CDate(Tmp)     'fill billing date field
68:
69:         Do               'get the cost
70:            Tmp = InputBox(prompt:="Enter the total " & _
71:                       "cost of the bill:", Title:=BillTitle)
72:            If Tmp = "" Then        'not allowed to cancel
73:               MsgBox prompt:="You must enter the cost!", _
74:                       Title:=BillTitle, Buttons:=vbExclamation
75:            End If
76:         Loop Until IsNumeric(Tmp)
77:         .Cost = CCur(Tmp)          'store cost in cost field
78:
79:         Do               'get therms
80:            Tmp = InputBox(prompt:="Enter the total " & _
81:                       "Therms on this bill:", Title:=BillTitle)
82:            If Tmp = "" Then
83:               MsgBox prompt:="You must enter Therms!", _
84:                       Title:=BillTitle, Buttons:=vbExclamation
85:            End If
86:         Loop Until IsNumeric(Tmp)
87:         .Therms = CInt(Tmp)            'fill therms field
88:
```

continues

LISTING 11.1 CONTINUED

```
 89:       Do              'get KWH
 90:           Tmp = InputBox(prompt:="Enter the total KWH " & _
 91:                          "on this bill:", Title:=BillTitle)
 92:         If Tmp = "" Then
 93:             MsgBox prompt:="You must enter the KWH!", _
 94:                    Title:=BillTitle, Buttons:=vbExclamation
 95:         End If
 96:       Loop Until IsNumeric(Tmp)
 97:       .Kwh = CInt(Tmp)              'store KWH in Kwh field
 98:     End With
 99:     Get_UtilityItem = Item      'return filled UtilityBill
100: End Function
```

ANALYSIS Lines 1 through 12 of this listing represent the module's declarations area. Line 1 contains the **Option Explicit** directive, which tells VBA that all variables in this module must be declared explicitly. Line 3 declares a module-level string constant to supply the text for the titles of all the dialogs that the procedures or functions in this module display.

Lines 5 through 10 contain a user-defined type definition. The name of this user-defined type is UtilityBill, and it contains the following elements: BillDate (a **Variant** type element), Cost (a **Currency** type element), Therms (an **Integer** type element), and Kwh (another **Integer** type element). The BillDate element's type was chosen to be a **Variant** type, rather than a **Date** type, so that it is possible to set the BillDate value to **Null**, indicating that there is no valid data stored in a variable that has the UtilityBill type. The **End Type** keywords in line 10 signal the end of the user-defined type definition for UtilityBill.

Lines 13 through 42 contain the Enter_UtilityCosts procedure. Line 13 contains the procedure declaration, and lines 14 through 17 contain comments about what the procedure does.

Lines 18 through 20 declare the variables that the Enter_UtilityCosts procedure uses. The Bill variable has the UtilityBill user-defined type. Done is a **Boolean** variable used to control a loop's execution and RNum is an **Integer** variable used to keep track of which row in a worksheet the utility bill information should be stored in.

Line 22 uses the Select method of the Worksheets collection to select a worksheet named Utility Data. This is the worksheet that will store the utility bill data that this procedure collects.

> **Note**
>
> Your workbook must contain a worksheet named Utility Data in order for the program in Listing 11.1 to work correctly.

Lines 24 through 39 perform the real work of the Enter_UtilityCosts procedure. Line 24 sets the RNum variable to 0 because no data has been entered yet. Line 25 sets the Done variable to **False** so that the loop in lines 26 through 39 will start to execute.

Line 26 starts a **Do Until** loop that executes until the Done variable is **True**. (The Enter_UtilityCosts procedure uses a loop because it assumes that the user might have more than one utility bill to enter; by using a flag-controlled **Do** loop, this procedure is able to gather information for an indefinite number of utility bills.)

Pay special attention to line 27. This line contains a single assignment expression that assigns the result of the Get_UtilityItem function directly to the Bill variable. The Get_UtilityItem function's result (line 45) is declared as having the UtilityBill user-defined type, as does the Bill variable. (The details of the Get_UtilityItem function's operation are described a little later in this analysis.)

Lines 28 through 30 contain an **If...Then...Else** statement that chooses which branch of code to execute based on whether the BillDate element of the UtilityBill item returned by the Get_UtilityItem function contains the **Null** value. If the BillDate element of Bill contains **Null**, VBA executes line 29, which simply assigns **True** to the Done variable, signaling that it is time for the loop to end.

If the BillDate element of Bill is not **Null**, VBA executes the statements in lines 31 through 37. The statement in line 31 increments the value of RNum by one, advancing to the next row in the worksheet. Line 32 starts a **With** statement for the Bill variable to make the next few statements easier to write and read.

Lines 33 through 36 each store one element from the Bill variable into a single cell in the worksheet. Each statement uses the Cells method of the Application object to return a reference to a cell on the active worksheet. The arguments for the Cells method are, first, the row coordinate, and, second, the column coordinate. Line 33 stores the contents of the BillDate element in the first column of the row indicated by RNum. Line 34 stores the contents of the Cost element in the second column of the row indicated by RNum; similarly, line 35 stores the contents of the Therms element in the third column, and line 36 stores the contents of the Kwh element in the fourth column of the worksheet. Line 37 contains the **End With** keywords, indicating the end of the **With** statement.

11

Line 39 contains the **Loop** keyword that marks the end of the loop. When VBA executes this line, it returns to the top of the loop and checks the determinant condition before executing the loop body again. When the loop is complete, VBA executes line 40, which uses MsgBox to display a message to the user that the data entry operation is finished and reports how many items were entered based on the row count stored in RNum.

Line 42 contains the **End Sub** keywords, which mark the end of the Enter_UtilityCosts procedure.

Now, take a look at how the Get_UtilityItem function works. Lines 45 through 100 contain the Get_UtilityItem function's definition.

Line 45 contains the function's declaration. The Get_UtilityItem function has no arguments, but notice its return value type: This function returns the user-defined type UtilityBill.

Although this function might seem long, its operation is fairly simple. Lines 49 and 50 declare the variables that this function uses. Item has the user-defined UtilityBill type and is used to hold the data that this function gets from the user until the function is ready to return its result. The Tmp variable has a **Variant** type and is used to temporarily hold the data obtained from the user with the InputBox function.

Line 52 starts a **With** statement that encloses almost the entire body of the function because so many of the statements in this function refer to elements of the Item variable.

Lines 53 through 66 contain a **Do...Loop Until** statement that loops repeatedly until the user enters a valid date value. Line 54 assigns the result of a call to the InputBox function to the Tmp variable. Lines 56 through 65 contain a couple of nested **If...Then** statements that evaluate the user's input from line 54.

If the user enters a blank string for the date or cancels the input dialog, VBA executes lines 57 through 64. Line 57 is just a little bit tricky. To avoid declaring more variables than absolutely necessary, this statement makes the Tmp variable do a little double-duty work. At the point when VBA executes this statement, the value stored in Tmp has already been evaluated (line 56) and is no longer needed. It is, therefore, safe to use the Tmp variable again to hold the value returned by the MsgBox function in line 57. This MsgBox function asks the user whether the data entry should end and uses the Buttons argument to include Yes and No command buttons in the message dialog, along with the Windows Query icon.

Line 60 contains another **If...Then** statement to evaluate the user's response to the message dialog displayed by line 57. If the user answers *yes* to ending the data entry, VBA executes lines 61 through 63. Line 61 assigns the **Null** value to the BillDate element of the `Item` variable (remember, this portion of the function's code is inside a **With** statement). By assigning the **Null** value to the `BillDate` element, this function makes it possible to determine whether its result contains any valid data. Line 62 then assigns the function's result and line 63 exits the function.

If the user does not enter a blank string or cancel the input dialog, or if the user answers *No* to ending the data entry, VBA continues execution with line 66, which contains the end of the **Do** loop along with the loop's determinant condition. If the user input in `Tmp` is not a valid date value or a value that VBA can convert to a date, VBA executes this loop again.

To keep this example function shorter and less complex, it does not include any code to let the user know why the loop is repeating. If you really want to write a program like this and give it to other people to use, you should include code—as shown in previous examples—that tells the user why the loop is repeating (they didn't enter a valid date).

As soon as the user enters a valid date, VBA executes line 67, which converts the string stored in `Tmp` (obtained from the user) to a **Date** and stores it in the `BillDate` element of the `Item` variable. (Again, remember that the statements in this portion of the function are enclosed by a **With** statement.)

Next, lines 69 through 76 contain a **Do...Loop Until** loop that repeats until the user enters a numeric value for the utility bill's cost. Notice that, in lines 72 through 75, if the user cancels this input dialog or enters a blank string, the function refuses to allow a cancellation of data entry at this point and simply displays a message insisting that the user must enter the cost.

As soon as the user enters a numeric value, VBA executes line 77, which converts the string entered by the user and stored in `Tmp` into a **Currency** type value and stores it in the `Cost` element of the `Item` variable.

Now, lines 79 through 86 get the value for the therms. Again, this loop refuses to permit the user to cancel the data entry operation at this point and insists that the user enter a value for the therms. As soon as the user enters a numeric value, the loop stops executing and VBA executes line 87, which converts the string entered by the user to an **Integer** type value and stores it in the `Therms` element of the `Item` variable.

Finally, lines 89 through 96 get the value for the kilowatt-hours used, and line 97 converts the string entered by the user to an **Integer** type value and stores it in the `Kwh` element of the `Item` variable.

Now that the function has obtained data for all the elements in the `Item` variable from the user, the **With** statement ends in line 98 with the **End With** keywords.

11

Line 99 assigns the Item variable to the function's result and the Get_UtilityItem function ends, returning its result.

If you tried to collect all of this data without using a user-defined type, you would have to declare and keep track of four separate variables. You would have either had to include all the code for getting the various data values from the user in the Enter_UtilityCosts procedure, which would make that procedure very long and probably rather difficult to understand because it would then contain five nested loop structures, or write four separate functions for obtaining each different value. By putting all four of the data values together in a single user-defined type, you can use a single function to get and return all the data at once, greatly simplifying the Enter_UtilityCosts procedure.

The Get_UtilityItem function is also slightly less complex than it might be otherwise because the code in that function concentrates on getting the data values only and does not have to deal with storing the data or recognizing when it is necessary to end data entry altogether; it just has to make sure that it gets the correct values in the correct elements of the user-defined type.

Do

DO use user-defined types to simplify obtaining, storing, and manipulating groups of related data.

DO remember that all your user-defined type definitions must appear at the module level in the declarations area of the module.

DO remember that variables and constants declared at the module level have module-level scope and are available to all the procedures or functions in that module.

DO remember that you can always use the CDate function to convert a value into a VBA Date type.

Don't

DON'T forget to include the dot separator (.) in front of the element names of a variable that has a user-defined type.

DON'T forget that Excel might not store date values from your VBA variables correctly unless your variable has the explicit Date type.

Creating Your Own Program Objects

As mentioned earlier in this book, you can create your own object classes in VBA. There are basically three different techniques you can use to create a customized object class:

- *Add code in a module attached to an Excel application object, such as a workbook or worksheet.* Use this technique if you want to create a template object that extends the capabilities of the original object. For example, you might want to create a worksheet that starts a data entry program whenever you activate that worksheet. To do so, you could write the necessary VBA code in the worksheet's module, thus creating a new type of worksheet object with customized properties and methods that you have written. You'll learn more about creating this type of customized object class in Day 19, "Controlling Excel with VBA."

- *Add code in a module attached to a VBA Form object.* As explained in Day 16, "Creating Custom Dialog Boxes," you use VBA forms to create dialog boxes for your programs. By adding VBA code to a form object, you create a customized form object with properties and methods that you define: You can base an entire VBA application on one or more customized form objects.

- *Add a class module to your project, and define the object's methods and properties in the class module.* Create new object classes with a class module whenever you want or need a special object that isn't based on an existing Excel application object such as a workbook.

Creating customized object classes based on workbooks and worksheets is discussed in Day 19, and using VBA forms is discussed in Day 16. This lesson describes how to create new object classes by adding a class module to your project. The following sections first give you an understanding of what a class module is, describe the essential principles behind designing an object class, and conclude by showing you how to add a class module and presenting an example of a user-defined object class.

Note

Creating new object classes is an advanced programming topic. Because you should understand at least the rudiments of programming class modules, this book covers the basics of how to create a new object class with a class module. A fully detailed discussion of all the design principles and programming techniques for creating new object classes is, unfortunately, beyond the scope of this book.

Understanding Class Modules

A *class module* is a special variation of the standard module you have been using in this book so far. Each class module in a project represents a separate object class; the class module contains the variables and VBA code that define the object class. You can only define an object class in a class module; each class module can define only one object class.

To create a new object class, you first add a class module to your project and then write the VBA code that defines the class's properties and methods (as described later in this lesson). In a sense, a class module fulfills the same purpose as the **Type** keyword in a user-defined data type: It provides a means for you to present your new object definition to VBA.

You don't execute the code in your class module the same way you execute code in standard modules. Instead, you declare an object variable that has a data type corresponding to your custom class and utilize that object's methods and properties in code stored in a standard module, just like an object that is part of Excel (or another VBA host application). Utilizing your custom object class is somewhat like using a user-defined data type: You declare a variable with the appropriate type and then use it in your VBA program statements.

Each class module can contain variables to store the object's internal data, special procedures to retrieve or set the object's properties, and procedures and functions that make up the object's methods. The next section discusses the basic principles behind designing an object class.

Designing an Object Class

Before you even add a class module to your project, you should carefully work out your object's design. The following list summarizes the most important requirements for designing an object class:

- All the information that pertains to the object must be stored within the object itself. Usually, you declare several module-level variables in the class module to hold information that represents the object. You can also use one or more **Static** variables within the object's method code to preserve data that helps describe the object.

- All the code needed to manipulate the object's data, or to affect the object's behavior, must also be part of the object itself. This means that you will write procedures in the class module, and these procedures become the object's methods.

- All the code needed to generate values based on the object's data must be part of the object. This means that you will write functions in the class module, and these functions also become the object's methods.

These object design requirements all stem from the basic concept of object-oriented programming: A program object should be a complete, discrete object, just like the objects in the real world around you. A program object should always be *encapsulated*, that is, the object's data and all the code that defines the object's various behaviors is bound together into a single item.

Do

DO supply any external data needed by your object's methods as an argument to that method.

DON'T

DON'T write method code that references variables outside your object's class module. Doing so means that your object's data isn't properly encapsulated.

DON'T attempt to write procedures or functions in a standard module that attempt to alter or manipulate the internal data variables of your object. Apart from the fact that VBA won't permit you to access those variables, only the object's own methods and property procedures should alter the object's internal data values.

11

When you design an object class, follow this basic procedure:

1. Decide what data is needed to completely represent your object. This is usually more easily said than done. In this step, you need to attempt to identify the essential pieces of information that completely identify an object. For example, the essential information needed to describe a circle is the location of its center point and its radius. All other information about the circle—its diameter, its circumference, its area, and the location of any point on the circle's circumference—can be derived from these two pieces of information. If your circle object also represents a graphic object that might be drawn onscreen, your circle object might also include information about the weight of the line that draws the circle, the circle's color, the color (if any) that the circle is filled in with, and other information related to the circle's physical appearance.

2. After you identify the essential information that describes the object you want to create, you need to divide your list of data items into two categories. First, identify those data values that you might need or want to set or retrieve; these will become your object's properties. Second, identify those data values that—although essential to creating the object's identity—don't need to be set or retrieved by code that isn't part of the object. Although you need to declare variables for all the object's essential data items, you only need to write property procedures for those data values that need to be set or retrieved by code external to the object.

3. Decide which of your object's properties should be read/write and which properties should be read-only. Any property that has a value that will be necessary or appropriate for you to change will be a read/write property. Any property that you'll need to retrieve but won't need to change will be a read-only property. For example, if you're creating an abstract representation of a circle, you need to be able to both set and retrieve the coordinates of the circle's center point and the length of the circle's radius. You would, therefore, need to create three read/write properties: The X and Y coordinates of the circle's center point and the length of the circle's radius.

4. List all the actions that you want your object to be able to carry out on or with its own data. In this step, you are defining the behavior that you want your object to have. Each action in your list will be a method of your object. You will write a **Sub** procedure for each method in your list that carries out an action. If one of the methods in your list computes and returns a value, you will write a **Function** procedure to return the value.

> **Tip**
>
> If you have experience with database design, you might notice a similarity between the first stages of designing an object class and the early stages of designing a database record: In both cases, the goal is to determine what the minimum amount of information is that is required to create a unique identity for a particular object.

Day 7 used the example of different types of space heaters to help explain how objects can be grouped into classes. This section continues that example by creating an abstract representation of an electric space heater as an example of designing, creating, and using a user-defined object class.

To keep things simple, consider that the essential information required to describe any particular electric heater is really only three pieces of information: Whether the heater is currently turned on, what the heater's current thermostat setting is, and what the heater's wattage is. The object must, therefore, store these three pieces of information internally. If any of your object's methods display dialog boxes (as the electric heater object does), you might find it useful to declare constants to help provide uniform titles in your object's dialogs. Table 11.1 lists all the data that the electric heater object needs to maintain internally. Each of the variables is prefaced with the letters *eh* to indicate that it is internal to the electric heater object.

TABLE 11.1 THE ELECTRIC HEATER OBJECT'S INTERNAL DATA

Name	Type	Description
ehActive	**Boolean** variable	Indicates whether the heater is currently on or off.
ehThermostat	**Single** variable	The current thermostat setting, stored as a decimal fraction representing a percentage of full on (1 is 100 percent on).
ehTitle	**String** constant	A constant used to supply the title for any input or message dialogs displayed by this object.
ehWattage	**Integer** variable	The heater's wattage.

In order to get information about the heater's status, you need to be able to retrieve the values indicating whether the heater is on, the heater's wattage, and the heater's current thermostat setting. All three of these items therefore need to be defined as properties of the heater object.

In addition to retrieving the value that indicates whether the heater is on or off, you also need to change this value if you want to turn the heater on (or off). The property that indicates the on/off status of the heater should therefore be a read/write property.

Similarly, you need to set the heater's wattage as well as merely retrieve it; thus, the wattage property is also a read/write property. It was decided that one of the heater's behaviors should be the capability to get a new thermostat setting from the user; as a result, the current thermostat setting is a read-only property. Table 11.2 lists the electric heater object's properties and indicates whether the property is to be defined as a read/write property or as a read-only property.

11

TABLE 11.2 THE ELECTRIC HEATER OBJECT'S PROPERTIES

Property	Data Type	Read/Write	Description
Active	**Boolean**	Read/Write	If **True**, indicates that the heater is on; **False** indicates that the heater is off. Set this property **True** to turn the heater on; **False** to turn it off.
Setting	**Single**	Read-Only	This property returns the current thermostat setting as a percentage (0–100) of maximum.
Watts	**Integer**	Read/Write	This property returns or sets the heater's wattage.

Finally, the electric heater object needs a few basic behaviors. First, it should be able to obtain a new thermostat setting from the user. Second, it should be able to return a number indicating the number of kilowatt-hours that the heater consumes while it is in operation. Third, the heater should be able to display a message dialog displaying information about the heater's current status. Table 11.3 lists the electric heater's methods and indicates whether the method is to be written as a **Sub** procedure or as a **Function**.

TABLE 11.3 THE ELECTRIC HEATER OBJECT'S METHODS

Method	Code As	Description
SetThermostat	**Sub**	Sets thermostat by prompting the user for a number from 1 to 100.
EnergyUsed	**Function**	Returns a **Single** indicating the heater's energy consumption in kilowatt-hours based on the current wattage and thermostat setting.
Show	**Sub**	Displays information about the heater: wattage, whether on or off, thermostat setting, energy consumption.

Note

The electric heater object example isn't as frivolous as it might seem at first. Many businesses use programs constructed with objects like this to model energy costs, heating and ventilating needs, and other factors. Objects like this are also used in various simulation programs. The electric heater object

> presented here has been kept deliberately simple. In a practical application, the electric heater object might contain a method that, given the cost of a kilowatt-hour of electricity, reports the cost of operating the heater for an hour at its current thermostat setting. As another example, a fully developed electric heater object might also contain a method that would report the number of BTU being given off by the heater with its current wattage and thermostat setting, and so on.

Now that some design criteria for an electric heater object have been defined, the next section shows you how to create the actual object class definition.

Creating a User-Defined Class

To actually create a custom object class, you follow this basic four-step process:

1. Add a class module to your project and rename the class module so that it has the name you want for your new object class. For example, the class module for the electric heater object is named ElectricHeater.

2. Declare the object's internal data variables in the declarations area of the class module.

3. Write the object's property procedures. You must write a **Property Get** procedure for each property you intend to read from, and you must write a **Property Let** procedure for each property you want to be able to set. The **Get** property procedure enables you to read a property's value and the **Let** property procedure enables you to set a property's value.

4. Write the object's method definitions. The object's method definitions appear in the class module as **Sub** and **Function** procedures.

The next two sections show you how to create a class module and how to add the necessary variable, procedure, and function declarations needed to define an object's properties and methods.

Inserting and Renaming a Class Module

To insert and rename a class module, follow these steps:

1. In the VB Editor, choose Insert, Class Module. The VB Editor adds a new class module to the project and gives it a default name of Class1 (if there is already a class module with that name in the project, the VB Editor uses Class2, Class3, and so on). As when adding a·standard module, the VB Editor opens the new class module in a Code Window, ready for you to type in your VBA code.

11

2. Choose the View, Properties Window command—or click the Properties Window toolbar button—to display the Properties Window (if it isn't already displayed).

3. In the Name text box of the Properties Window, type the new name for your object class. Figure 11.1 shows the Properties Window for the ElectricHeater class from Listing 11.2 (presented in the next section of this lesson).

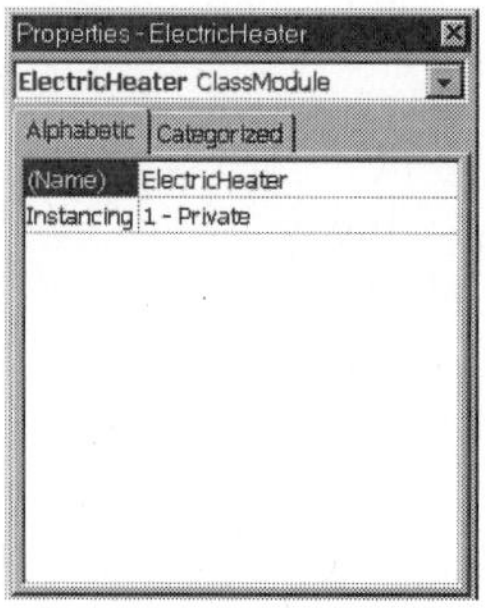

FIGURE 11.1

Renaming a class module.

> **Note**
>
> It is very important that you rename your class module and that you choose the class module name carefully. The name you give to the class module is the name of your new object class, and is the name you must use for the object type in all your VBA code that references your new class object. Names for class modules must conform to the same identifier name rules that you learned to follow when creating names for variables, procedures, and functions.

After you add the class module and give it a name, you're ready to add the variables, constants, procedures, and functions that will make up your new object's method and property definitions.

> **Note**
>
> When renaming a class module, you should you leave the Instancing property set to Private (refer to Figure 11.1). When the Instancing property is set to Private, your custom class is available only in the workbook that contains the object's defining class module. The only other available choice for the Instancing property is PublicNoCreate; setting your class module to have the PublicNoCreate property will make your custom object class available to other Excel workbooks, but you won't be able to create a new instance of your custom object class. Although using the Private setting for the Instancing property restricts the scope of your custom object class to the workbook containing the class module, the Private setting enables you

> to create as many instances of your custom object as you want. (Public and private scope are explained in Day 12, "Creating Libraries and Whole Programs: Modular Programming Techniques.")

Writing the Class Property and Method Definitions

Writing an object's method definitions is the same as writing any procedure or function in VBA, and uses the same syntax that you have already learned for writing functions and procedures. Each function or procedure that you write in a class module becomes available as one of the class's methods. (As explained in Day 12, you can use the **Private** keyword to prevent a procedure or function in a class module from being available outside the module.)

Writing an object's property definitions is essentially the same as writing the standard functions and procedures that you've become accustomed to, but it requires a special syntax: **Property Get** procedures enable you to retrieve an object's property value, and **Property Let** procedures enable you to assign a value to an object's property.

▼ SYNTAX

A **Property Get** procedure has this general syntax:

```
Property Get name([arglist]) [As TypeName]
    [statements]
    name = expression
    [statements]
End Property
```

11

The **Property** keyword indicates that this is an object's property procedure, whereas the **Get** keyword indicates that this property procedure will return a property value, much like a standard VBA function procedure. In the syntax example, *name* is the name of the property procedure and is also the name of the property you want to retrieve. Property names must follow the same identifier naming rules as variables and other procedure or function names.

The optional *arglist* represents the argument list for the property procedure. *arglist* has the same syntax that you learned for function arguments in Day 6. (You'll learn more about procedure arguments in Day 12.) *TypeName* represents any VBA or user-defined data type and specifies the data type returned by the **Property Get** procedure. *statements* represents none, one, or many VBA statements.

The *name = expression* statement is like a function's assignment statement: *name* is the name of the **Property Get** procedure and *expression* represents the value that you want to return as the property's value. The **End Property** keywords indicate the end of the property procedure's code. Listing 11.2 contains several examples of **Property Get**

▲ procedures.

Writing a **Property Get** procedure creates a readable property for your object. If you write only a **Property Get** procedure for an object's property, you are essentially creating a read-only property for that object. Usually, you write **Property Get** procedures in pairs with **Property Let** procedures or—if the property is an object reference—a **Property Set** procedure. Creating a **Property Let** or **Property Set** procedure enables you to set an object property's value.

A **Property Let** procedure has this general syntax:

```
Property Let name([arglist,] value)
    [statements]
End Property
```

The **Property** keyword here also indicates that this is an object's property procedure, and the **Let** keyword indicates that this property procedure will assign a value to a property. In the syntax example, *name* is the name of the property procedure and is also the name of the property you want to assign a value to. The optional *arglist* represents the argument list for the property procedure.

The *value* argument is a required part of a **Property Let** procedure. *value* represents the new value to be assigned to the property and can be any of VBA's data types except an object reference. *statements* represents none, one, or many VBA program statements. Typically, the statements in a **Property Let** procedure evaluate the *value* argument and then store it in a module-level variable in the class module. Listing 11.2 contains examples of **Property Let** procedures.

If your object has properties that refer to other objects, you might want to assign an object reference to a property. To assign object references to a property, you must use a **Property Set** procedure instead of a **Property Let** statement.

A **Property Set** procedure has this general syntax:

```
Property Set name([arglist,] reference)
    [statements]
End Property
```

The syntax of the **Property Set** procedure is identical to **Property Let** procedure, with one exception: A **Property Set** procedure requires a *reference* argument instead of a *value* argument. *Reference* represents a valid reference to an Excel object, VBA object, user-defined object, or an Automation object from another VBA host application.

> **Note**
>
> You might want to end the execution of a property procedure early for many of the same reasons you might want to end a function's or procedure's execution early. You can also use the `Exit` keyword to end a property procedure's execution early. Use the `Exit Property` statement (on a line by itself) to end a property procedure's execution early.

Listing 11.2 shows an entire module that contains all the code needed to implement the `ElectricHeater` class object with the properties, methods, and internal data described in Tables 11.1 through 11.3.

INPUT **LISTING 11.2** DEFINING A NEW OBJECT CLASS IN A CLASS MODULE

```
 1:  Option Explicit
 2:
 3:  Const ehTitle = "Electric Heater"
 4:
 5:  Dim ehWattage As Integer      'heater's wattage
 6:  Dim ehThermostat As Single    'Thermostat setting
 7:  Dim ehActive As Boolean       'whether heater is on or off
 8:
 9:  Property Get Active() As Boolean
10:      Active = ehActive
11:  End Property
12:
13:  Property Let Active(Status As Boolean)
14:      ehActive = Status
15:      If Status Then Me.SetThermostat
16:  End Property
17:
18:  Property Get Setting() As Single
19:      Setting = ehThermostat * 100
20:  End Property
21:
22:  Property Get Watts() As Integer
23:      Watts = ehWattage
24:  End Property
25:
26:  Property Let Watts(W As Integer)
27:      ehWattage = W
28:  End Property
29:
30:  Sub SetThermostat()
31:  'sets the heater's thermostat with a value obtained from user
32:
```

11

continues

LISTING 11.2   CONTINUED

```
33:     Const strErrMsg = "Please enter a number between 0 and 100"
34:
35:     Dim Temp As Variant
36:     Dim fGoodValue As Boolean
37:
38:     Do
39:       Temp = InputBox(prompt:="Enter Thermostat Setting:", _
40:                       Title:=ehTitle, _
41:                       Default:=(ehThermostat * 100))
42:       If Len(Trim(Temp)) = 0 Then Exit Sub
43:       If Not IsNumeric(Temp) Then
44:         MsgBox prompt:=strErrMsg, Title:=ehTitle, _
45:               Buttons:=vbExclamation
46:       Else
47:         Temp = Int(Temp)
48:         If (Temp < 0) Or (Temp > 100) Then
49:           MsgBox prompt:=strErrMsg, Title:=ehTitle, _
50:                 Buttons:=vbExclamation
51:         Else
52:           Temp = CSng(Temp / 100)
53:           fGoodValue = True
54:         End If
55:       End If
56:     Loop Until fGoodValue
57:
58:     ehThermostat = Temp
59:
60:   End Sub
61:
62:   Function EnergyUsed() As Single
63:   'returns the heater's energy consumption in kilowatt-hours,
64:   'based on the current wattage and thermostat setting
65:
66:     If Not Me.Active Then
67:       EnergyUsed = 0
68:     Else
69:       EnergyUsed = CSng((ehWattage * ehThermostat) / 1000)
70:     End If
71:   End Function
72:
73:   Sub Show()
74:   'displays information about this instance of the heater:
75:   'wattage, whether on or off, thermostat setting, and
76:   'energy consumption
77:
78:     Dim strMsg As String
79:
80:     With Me
```

```
81:     strMsg = "The heater is "
82:     If .Active Then
83:       strMsg = strMsg & "ON"
84:     Else
85:       strMsg = strMsg & "OFF"
86:     End If
87:
88:     strMsg = strMsg & "." & vbCr & vbCr
89:     strMsg = strMsg & "Watts: " & .Watts & vbCr
90:     strMsg = strMsg & "Thermostat: " & .Setting & "%" & vbCr
91:     strMsg = strMsg & "Energy Consumed: " & .EnergyUsed & " KWH"
92:
93:     MsgBox prompt:=strMsg, Title:=ehTitle, Buttons:=vbInformation
94:   End With
95: End Sub
```

ANALYSIS Lines 1 through 7 of Listing 11.2 represent the declarations area of the class module. Line 1 contains the **Option Explicit** directive, which tells VBA that all variables in the module must be explicitly declared. Line 3 declares the ehTitle string constant, which is used to supply the text for the title of any dialogs displayed by this object's methods. Lines 5 through 7 declare the variables used to store the object's internal data. Refer to Table 11.1 for an explanation of the purpose of these variables.

Note

> All custom object classes, by default, have a scope private to the workbook that contains the object's defining class module. This means that your custom object class is not available to procedures or functions in a workbook other than the workbook containing the custom object's class module. To use a custom object class in more than one workbook, you must duplicate the class module in each workbook in which you want to use that object class. (*Scope*, as you might recall from Day 3, refers to the availability of a variable or object; public and private scope are explained fully in Day 12.)

Because the constant and variables declared in lines 3 through 7 appear in the declarations area of the class module, that is, at the module level, they are available to all procedures and functions in the module. Although these constants and variables will appear in the Object Browser, they are private to the class module and are not available to procedures or functions in other modules. (You learn about private module variables in detail in Day 12.)

11

Refer to Table 11.2, which lists the desired properties for the ElectricHeater object and indicates whether the property should be read-only or read/write. The first property in the table is the Active property, which is read/write. To create this property, it is necessary to write a **Property Get** procedure to retrieve the property value and a **Property Let** procedure to assign a value to the property.

Lines 9 through 16 contain the property procedures needed to define the Active property. Compare line 9 with line 13. Line 9 contains the declaration of the **Property Get** procedure for the Active property, whereas line 13 contains the declaration for its **Property Let** procedure. Notice that both procedures are named Active; this is required in order to create both the "read" portion and the "write" portion of the read/write property. Because the Active property is a **Boolean** property (refer to Table 11.2), the **Property Get** Active procedure in line 9 returns a **Boolean** data type. In the **Property Let** Active procedure (line 13), the Status argument is the required argument by which the new property value is passed into the procedure; the Status argument is a **Boolean** type because it must match the return data type of the corresponding **Property Get** Active procedure.

The **Property Get** Active procedure merely returns the current value of ehActive (line 10), which is the internal variable that stores the heater's current operating status: **True** if the heater is on, **False** if the heater is off. The **Property Let** Active procedure first assigns the new value in the Status argument to the ehActive variable in line 14. Next, line 15 checks to see whether the heater is being turned on (that is, Status is **True**). If so, the object's own SetThermostat method is called. This has the effect of ensuring that a new thermostat setting is obtained whenever the heater is turned on.

Notice the use of the **Me** keyword in line 15. The **Me** keyword returns a reference to the current instance of an object; use the **Me** keyword whenever you want to refer to an object's own properties or methods within code that is, itself, part of the object. When VBA executes a statement containing the **Me** keyword, it calls the referenced property or method code from within the current object.

Now look at lines 18 through 20, which contain the **Property Get** Setting procedure. The Setting property is a read-only property, so only a **Get** procedure is needed. The Setting property is intended to return a value indicating what percent of maximum the heater's thermostat is currently set to. The ehThermostat variable stores a **Single** decimal number representing this percentage: 1 corresponds to 100 percent, 0.5 is 50 percent, 0.1 is 10 percent, and so on. Line 19 therefore multiplies ehThermostat by 100 and returns the result as the value of the Setting property. Notice that the **Property Get** Setting procedure's result is declared as a **Single**.

Lines 22 through 28 contain the **Property Get** Watts and **Property Let** Watts procedures; this pair of property procedures creates the read/write Watts property. Compare the procedure definitions (lines 22 and 26, respectively) and notice that both procedures have the same name and that where the **Get** procedure returns a value of **Integer** type, the **Let** procedure has an argument of the **Integer** type—the procedures are correctly matched in name and data type to create the Watts read/write property with an **Integer** value. The **Property Get** Watts procedure simply returns whatever value is currently stored in the ehWattage variable, whereas the **Property Let** Watts procedure simply stores the new wattage value in ehWattage.

Lines 30 through 60 contain the SetThermostat procedure; this procedure creates the SetThermostat method of the ElectricHeater object (refer to Table 11.3). The SetThermostat method loops until the user enters a number between 0 and 100 as a new value for the heater's thermostat setting. When a value in the correct range has been obtained from the user, it is divided by 100 to create a **Single** decimal number and then stored in the ehThermostat variable.

Lines 62 through 71 contain the EnergyUsed function, which creates the EnergyUsed method of the ElectricHeater object. The EnergyUsed method is intended to return a number indicating the kilowatt-hours that the heater is currently consuming, and is therefore written as a function so that it can return a result. The EnergyUsed method first checks to see whether the heater is actually on. Notice the use of the **Me**.Active expression in line 66, which uses the value returned by the object's own Active property to determine whether the heater is actually on. If the heater isn't on, the EnergyUsed method simply returns 0 (line 67). Otherwise, line 69 computes the kilowatt-hours that the heater is currently consuming and returns that value as the method's result.

Finally, lines 73 through 95 contain the Show method. The Show method displays a message box that contains information about the object's current status: whether the heater is on or off, the current wattage, thermostat setting, and energy used. Notice the **With Me** statement that begins in line 80; notice also that all the information displayed by the Show method is obtained by calling the ElectricHeater object's own properties and methods.

Do

DO ensure that the names of your **Property Get** and **Property Let** procedures match exactly; it takes both to create a read/write property.

DO ensure that the value returned by a **Property Get** procedure has the same data type as the value passed to a **Property Let** procedure; the data types between the two procedures must match or VBA displays a compile error.

DO use the **Me** keyword whenever you need to refer to an object's methods within the object's own method code.

> ## DON'T
>
> **DON'T** forget that you create a read-only property by writing only the **Property Get** procedure for that property. If you want, you can create a write-only property by writing only a **Property Let** procedure.

As you add properties and methods to your object class, they will be listed in the Object Browser. Figure 11.2 shows the Object Browser with the `ElectricHeater` class selected in the Classes list and the `Setting` method selected in the Members of 'ElectricHeater' list.

FIGURE 11.2

Your class modules appear in the Classes list of the Object Browser, and your object's methods and properties appear in the Members of <class> list.

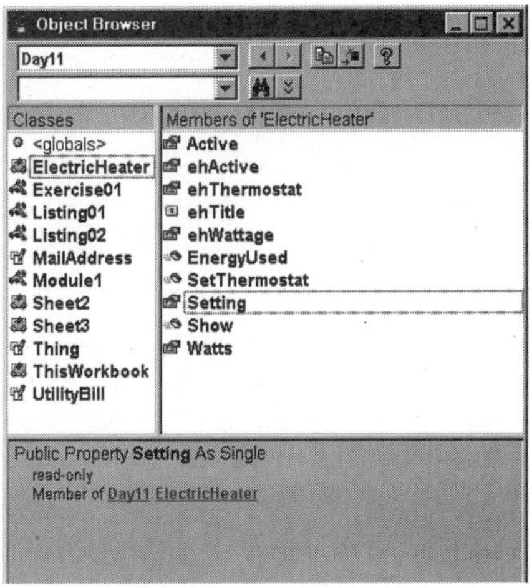

Using a User-Defined Class

You use your custom class objects in much the same way that you use objects that are part of Excel or any VBA host application, with one exception. Before you can use your custom object class, you must create a new instance of the object with the **New** keyword. (An *instance*, you might recall from Day 7, is a specific occurrence of an object.)

SYNTAX

You can use the **New** keyword either as part of a **Dim** statement or as part of a **Set** statement:

```
Dim objvar As New ClassName
Set objvar = New ClassName
```

In the first syntax form, *objvar* is any valid VBA identifier and *ClassName* is the name of the class you want to create a new object instance from. *ClassName* represents the name of a user-defined object class; this is the same as the class module's name. The following statement, for example, creates a new instance of the `ElectricHeater` class:

▼ `Dim objHeater As New ElectricHeater`

When VBA executes the preceding statement, it creates a new instance of the
ElectricHeater object and initializes the objHeater variable to reference that instance.

In the second syntax form, *objvar* represents an object variable that has already been
declared. *Objvar* can be a **Variant** variable, a generic **Object** variable, or an object variable declared with a specific class type. *ClassName* represents the name of a user-defined
object class; this is the same as the class module's name. As an example, the first statement below declares an object variable and the second statement creates a new instance
of the ElectricHeater class:

```
Dim objHeater As Object
Set objHeater = New ElectricHeater
```

When VBA executes the first statement preceding, it creates a generic **Object** variable.
When VBA executes the second statement preceding, it creates a new instance of the
ElectricHeater object and assigns the objHeater variable to reference that new
▲ instance.

Listing 11.3 shows a simple procedure that exercises the properties and methods of the
ElectricHeater object class. The Test_Heater procedure creates a new instance of the
ElectricHeater object, assigns values to its properties, and utilizes its methods.

> **Note**
>
> You must enter the Test_Heater procedure in a standard module in the
> same workbook that contains the ElectricHeater class module from Listing
> 11.2. Listing 11.3 won't work if you enter it into the same class module as
> the code that defines the ElectricHeater class.

INPUT   **LISTING 11.3**   USING A USER-DEFINED CLASS OBJECT

```
1:    Option Explicit
2:
3:    Sub Test_Heater()
4:
5:        Dim objHeater As ElectricHeater
6:
7:        Set objHeater = New ElectricHeater
8:
9:        objHeater.Watts = InputBox(prompt:="Enter heater wattage:")
10:       objHeater.Show
11:
12:       With objHeater
13:          .Active = True    'turns the heater on
```

continues

LISTING 11.3   CONTINUED

```
14:        MsgBox "Heater is currently using " & .EnergyUsed & " KWH"
15:
16:        .Show
17:        .Active = False   'turns heater off
18:        .Show
19:
20:        .Active = True    'turn heater on
21:        .Show
22:
23:        .SetThermostat
24:        .Show
25:
26:        .SetThermostat
27:        .Show
28:
29:        .Active = False
30:        .Show
31:    End With
32:  End Sub
```

ANALYSIS   Line 5 of Listing 11.3 declares the objHeater variable, specifying that it has the
ElectricHeater data type. Line 7 uses a **Set** statement with the **New** keyword to
create a new instance of the ElectricHeater object class and assigns a reference to the
new object instance to the objHeater variable.

Line 9 uses the Watts method of the ElectricHeater object to set the heater's wattage;
the value is obtained from the user by using InputBox. Line 10 calls the ElectricHeater
object's Show method to display the heater's current status. In both lines 9 and 10, notice
the use of the dot separator (.) with the objHeater variable to reference the object's
methods and properties, just like using the object methods and properties of objects built
in to Excel or another VBA host application.

Line 12 begins a **With** statement. Line 13 sets the heater on. Line 14 uses the
EnergyUsed method in a MsgBox statement to display the kilowatt-hours that the heater is
currently consuming. Line 16 invokes the ElectricHeater's Show method again, and line
17 turns the heater off by setting the Active property to **False**. Line 23 uses the
SetThermostat method to get a new thermostat setting from the user.

Do
DO use the dot separator (.) to refer to the properties and methods of a user-defined class the same way you would for any built-in VBA object.
DO use the `With` statement to simplify references to a user-defined object's properties and methods the same way you would for any built-in VBA object.

Summary

Today you learned why and how to define your own customized data types. You learned how to create a user-defined type definition, how to declare variables that have a user-defined type, and how to access individual elements in a variable that has a user-defined type. You also saw an example of how to put user-defined data types to work for you.

Extending the topic of user-defined data types to user-defined objects, this chapter showed you how to define your own object classes. You learned how to add a class module to your project, the basic techniques for designing an object class, and how to define the class's properties and methods. Finally, you learned how to use your object class in your VBA code.

Q&A

Q Why can't I store a user-defined type variable directly into an Excel worksheet cell or into another variable?

A You can only assign the contents of a variable with a user-defined type to another variable if they both have the same user-defined type. You can't assign a user-defined type variable directly to a worksheet cell or other variable because your user-defined type is an aggregate of several different data values. Your user-defined type makes it more convenient for you to store and pass several data items, but you must refer to specific elements of the variable in order to store those elements in a worksheet cell or a another variable.

Q I think I understand how to create a new object class, but why should I create a new object class?

A The primary advantage of creating a custom object class is that the data and the methods used to manipulate that data are encapsulated. As an example, assume that you have a series of procedures that creates a sales chart based on data in an Excel worksheet. By rewriting these procedures to create a sales chart object, you can make it easier to utilize your VBA code to create a chart. Custom class objects are useful for any group of data that you can model as an object with specific properties and methods.

11

Q **If my custom object class is available only in the workbook that contains the class's defining class module, how can I use my custom object class in more than one workbook?**

A To use a user-defined object class in more than one workbook, you must copy the class module into each workbook in which you want to use that object class. The easiest way to copy a class module from one workbook to another is to first export the class module as a text file by using the VB Editor's File, Export File command. You can then easily add the entire class module to another workbook by using the VB Editor's File, Import File command.

Workshop

Answers are in Appendix A.

Quiz

1. What is a user-defined type?
2. What VBA keyword starts a user-defined type definition?
3. Where do you place a user-defined type definition?
4. How do you create a user-defined class?
5. How do you define the properties of a class?
6. Specifically, what must you do in order to create a read/write property for a user-defined object?
7. How do you define the methods of a class?
8. Why should you immediately rename any new class module?
9. Can you access an object defined in a class module from another workbook?
10. Can you use the Object Browser to view the available methods and properties of a user-defined object?

Exercises

1. Declare a user-defined data type that will hold all the information necessary for a mailing list. Your user-defined type should include elements for the following information: first name, last name, company name, street address, city, state, and ZIP code.

2. Write both a function that gets data for the mailing list user-defined type you created in Exercise 1, preceding, and a procedure that calls that function and stores the data in a worksheet. Your function's result should be a user-defined type. (HINT: Copy the portions of the `Enter_UtilityCosts` procedure in Listing 11.1 that select a worksheet and store the data in the worksheet.)

DAY 12

Creating Libraries and Whole Programs: Modular Programming Techniques

Today's lesson teaches you how to organize your procedures and functions when they are stored in several different modules. This chapter also teaches you how to get started writing programs that consist of several different procedures working together to complete a complex job. In today's lesson, you learn

- How to use modules to organize commonly used procedures and functions into libraries of procedures so that those procedures or functions are available all the time.

- How to use the **Public** and **Private** keywords to increase or limit the availability of variables, constants, functions, and procedures in your modules.

- How to get started designing and creating large-scale programs using several different procedures, functions, and modules working together to complete a single task.

- How to use argument lists so that your procedures can receive information from and return information to the procedures that call them.

Using Modules More Effectively

You already know that you store your procedure and function source code in a module. In the first and second lessons in this book, you learned how the Macro Recorder in Excel chooses which module to store a recorded macro in, and you learned how to add new modules to VBA projects stored in Excel workbooks. This section teaches you how to use modules to organize your commonly used procedures and functions and how to make them available for use in every Excel work session.

You can use modules to organize your recorded macros and procedures and to make it easier to keep track of many different macros. Many users organize procedures into various categories based on the procedure's task or purpose and then store each category in its own module, sometimes in its own workbook.

For instance, you might decide that you want some or all of your worksheets to have a standardized look, and therefore choose certain fonts, font styles, and point sizes as standards for titles, column and row headings, and so on. You might then end up recording or writing several different macros or procedures—such as the FormatArialBold12 macro you recorded in Day 1—that apply the specific font styles or other formatting for the various standards you decide on.

For procedures that you use frequently and want to have available in all (or most) of your workbooks, you probably don't want to copy all the modules into each and every workbook that uses those procedures. Apart from simply being a lot of work, duplicating frequently used procedures in every workbook that uses them can cause a lot of confusion and unnecessarily increases the size of your workbooks, both in terms of the amount of disk storage that they require and in terms of the amount of memory that they require.

Also, if you decide to change a frequently used procedure that you have duplicated in several different workbooks, you must edit and test each and every copy of the procedure, or at least copy the altered procedure into all the workbooks that use it. Going through such complex copying and editing tasks only increases the probability that something will go wrong and that your results will be less than satisfactory.

Creating an Excel template does not solve the duplication problem. When you create a new workbook based on an Excel template, Excel *copies* any modules in the template to the new workbook file, leading to the same problems with duplicate procedures just described.

Instead, the best way to make commonly used procedures and functions available is to create a *library* of procedures and functions. A library of VBA procedures and functions works much like a public library filled with books and magazines: Any time you (or one of your procedures) needs to use a particular function or procedure stored in the library, VBA looks up the necessary code in the library and executes it.

When describing Excel's Personal macro workbook (stored in Personal.xls), Day 1 mentioned that you can run any procedure from the Macro dialog as long as the workbook in which you stored it is open. You can see this for yourself by looking at the list of procedures in the Macro dialog; notice that the Macro Name list always shows all the procedures in the currently open workbooks. (The Macro dialog lists procedures without arguments only and never lists functions.) Figure 12.1 is a diagram showing how all the procedures in the modules of all open workbooks are available to all other open workbooks.

FIGURE 12.1

Procedures in any open workbook are available to all other open workbooks in the same instance of Excel.

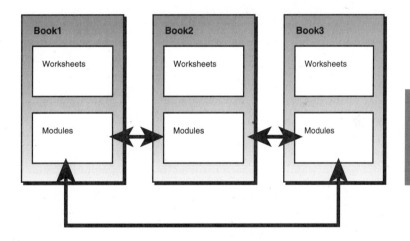

12

When VBA executes a procedure or function, it first searches the current module for the requested procedure or function. If VBA does not find the procedure or function in the current module, it then searches the other modules in the current project (if any). If VBA still cannot find the requested procedure or function, it then searches through any referenced workbooks to find the procedure or function. (Creating and using references to workbooks is described later in this section.)

Note

Although Excel's Macro dialog makes procedures in any open workbook available to any other workbook (that is, you can execute the procedure as a macro), you cannot use procedures or functions in VBA code if the procedure or function is stored in a workbook other than the workbook in which you are currently writing code. To make the procedures and functions of another workbook available to the workbook in which you are writing code, you must establish a reference to the external project, as described later in this lesson.

As an example, although the ExcelVBAHelp procedure (which is stored in the Personal.xls workbook) can be run from any open workbook by using the Macro dialog, you can't call the ExcelVBAHelp procedure from VBA code in any workbook other than Personal.xls unless you have established a reference to Personal.xls (as described later in this lesson).

This behind-the-scenes look-up process that VBA performs is the key to how libraries of procedures and functions work. In order to make a commonly used procedure available to any Excel workbook, all you have to do is make sure that the procedure is stored in a workbook that will be among the workbooks that VBA searches, either an open workbook or a workbook for which you have established a reference.

Do

DO establish a reference to workbooks if you intend to use procedures or functions stored in those workbooks in VBA code in your current workbook.

DO remember that the Macro dialog lists only procedures without arguments.

DON'T

DON'T duplicate procedures and functions in multiple workbooks. Instead, create a library workbook that holds one copy that can be used by all other workbooks.

Creating an Excel Library Workbook

To create a general- or special-purpose library of functions and procedures in Excel, simply create a workbook that contains only VBA modules. Although it doesn't really matter if the workbook contains worksheets as well as modules, there is no point in including worksheets or charts in a VBA library workbook. Because they aren't used, the worksheets or charts in a VBA library workbook just consume disk space and computer memory unnecessarily. The Personal.xls workbook described in the first lesson is one example of a library workbook.

As an example of creating a library of procedures and functions, assume that you have recorded or written several different macros and procedures to help you create and format Excel charts. To create a library of chart-making and formatting procedures, you might create an Excel workbook named ChartTools.xls and then move all your chart-related procedures into that workbook's modules. You have created a library of chart-making and formatting procedures. The only remaining thing for you to do is to make your library of procedures available during your Excel work sessions.

Although it isn't required by VBA, most users further group related procedures together within a library workbook. For example, in the ChartTools.xls library workbook, if you have several procedures that help you create and format pie charts, you might group all of them together in a single module named PieCharts. Similarly, if you also have several procedures that help you create and format bar charts, you might group all those procedures together in another module named BarCharts, also in the ChartTools.xls workbook.

By grouping all your chart-related procedures together in a single workbook and further dividing them into specific categories within the library workbook, you not only make it possible to have your library of procedures available at all times, but you also make it easier to find a particular procedure if you ever need to modify it, and you also make it easier to share your library workbook—or selected portions of it—with other users.

12

Do

DO gather general-purpose functions (such as the `FlipCase` and `SLen` functions given as examples in earlier chapters) together into a single library workbook so that you can use them in all of your procedures.

DO consider using the Personal.xls workbook to store all your general-purpose procedures and functions.

Making Library Procedures and Functions Available

To make an Excel library of your VBA procedures available, you must load the workbook so that its modules are available to other currently open workbooks. The next few sections explain how to load an Excel workbook in order to make available the functions and procedures they contain.

You can make Excel library workbooks available by using the File, Open command; any open workbook's procedures are available to any other open workbook in the same instance of Excel. This technique has two drawbacks. First, you must manually make the library available. This might not be a problem if the library contains procedures that you don't use on a daily basis, but the usual goal of creating a library in the first place is to avoid having to perform any special action to make the library's contents available. Having to explicitly open the library workbook will probably be inconvenient in the case of most general-purpose libraries.

The second drawback to the technique of loading a library by opening the workbook is the fact that this only makes the procedures in the library available, and only those procedures without arguments, at that. Although you can execute any procedure in the library workbook by using the Macro dialog, you still can't use the functions stored in the library—except in an Excel worksheet formula.

Excel provides you with a means of overcoming both of these drawbacks. You can automatically load a library file in Excel by placing the library in Excel's startup folder. Although this will make the procedures in the library available to you through the Macro dialog, it still won't permit you to utilize any of the procedures or functions from the library in any VBA code that isn't part of the same library project. To overcome this difficulty, Excel enables you to create a reference to the library. The next few paragraphs describe how to automatically load libraries and how to create references to libraries.

> **Tip**
>
> You can use the techniques described here to make procedures and functions in any Excel workbook available, even if you haven't formally organized those procedures into a library.

Using the Startup Folder to Load a Library

The easiest way to make your library projects available in every Excel work session is to put your library workbooks in Excel's startup folder or in the alternate startup folder. Whenever you start Excel, it opens any files that are in the startup or alternate startup folders. As mentioned before, when your Excel library workbook is open, all the procedures stored in it become available in the Macro dialog.

Use the Windows Desktop to move or copy your library file to the startup or alternate startup folder, or use Excel's File, Save As command to save a copy of the library file in the startup or alternate startup folder.

> **Tip**
>
> You can also make Excel automatically load a workbook on startup by placing a Windows shortcut in the Excel startup folder.

Excel's startup folder is named X1start. The specific location of the X1start subfolder varies depending on which version of Microsoft Office you have and whether it was installed using the default folders. The name and location of Excel's startup folder is established at the time you install Excel and cannot be changed.

The best way to determine the precise name of Excel's startup folder is to utilize the StartupPath property of Excel's Application object. The StartupPath property contains the full path of Excel's startup folder. You can easily use the Application.StartupPath property to display the full path of Excel's startup folder. Enter the following procedure listing and then execute it; the resulting message dialog displays the full folder path, including the drive letter, for Excel's startup folder (see Listing 12.1).

INPUT   LISTING 12.1   USING VBA TO DISPLAY THE EXCEL STARTUP FOLDER

```
1:    Sub ShowStartupPath()
2:        MsgBox Application.StartupPath
3:    End Sub
```

ANALYSIS   Line 2 of the listing uses the MsgBox procedure to display the StartupPath property of the Application object. If you used the suggested defaults when you installed Excel with Microsoft Office 2000, this procedure displays the dialog shown in Figure 12.2 for Excel.

12

FIGURE 12.2

The StartupPath *property contains the full folder path to Excel's startup directory.*

Microsoft Excel
C:\WINDOWS\Application Data\Microsoft\Excel\XLSTART
OK

Excel's use of an alternate startup folder is optional. For Excel to use an alternate startup folder, you must use the Tools, Options command to enter the name and full folder path for the alternate startup folder. Unlike the startup folder, you can change the alternate startup folder at any time—although Excel only looks in the alternate startup folder when it first starts a new work session.

To set the alternate startup folder from the Excel menus, follow these steps:

1. Choose the Tools, Options command. Excel displays the Options dialog.

2. Click the General tab, if necessary, to bring the General options to the front of the dialog box. Figure 12.3 shows the open Options dialog with the General tab showing.

3. Enter the full folder pathname, including the disk drive letter, in the Alternate Startup File Location text box. If you want, you can use UNC (Universal Naming Convention) folder names to set the alternate startup file location to a folder accessible over the network.

4. Click OK; Excel closes the Options dialog and changes the alternate startup directory.

   The next time you start Excel, it uses the folder path you just entered as the alternate startup folder.

FIGURE 12.3

Use the General sheet in the Options dialog to enter the name and path for Excel's alternate startup folder.

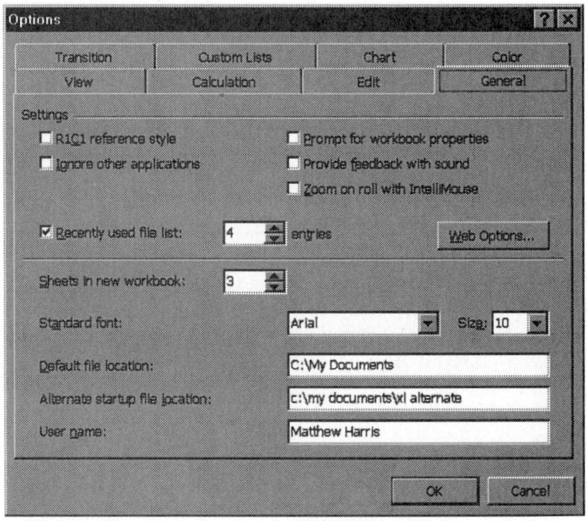

Use the `AltStartupPath` property of the Excel `Application` object to find out what Excel's current alternate startup folder is or to set a new alternate startup folder. Enter the following procedure listing in an Excel module and then execute it; the resulting message dialog displays the full path, including the drive letter, for Excel's alternate startup directory.

INPUT   **LISTING 12.2**   USING VBA TO DISPLAY EXCEL'S ALTERNATE STARTUP FOLDER

```
1:    Sub ShowAlternateStartPath()
2:        MsgBox Application.AltStartupPath
3:    End Sub
```

ANALYSIS   Line 2 of the listing uses the MsgBox procedure to display the AltStartupPath property of the Application object. If you entered the alternate startup file location shown in Figure 12.3, this procedure displays the dialog shown in Figure 12.4.

FIGURE 12.4

The AltStartupPath *property of the Excel* Application *object contains the full folder path to the Excel alternate startup folder.*

Microsoft Excel

C:\MY DOCUMENTS\XL ALTERNATE

OK

If the AltStartupPath property returns a zero-length string, Excel is not currently using the alternate startup folder option. Although the StartupPath property is a read-only property (you can retrieve its value, but you can't change it), the AltStartupPath property is a read/write property (you can both retrieve or change its value).

To change Excel's alternate startup folder from within a VBA procedure, simply assign a string containing the new alternate startup folder name to the AltStartupPath property. Be sure to include the drive letter and full path, just as if you were entering the alternate startup folder in the Options dialog. Listing 12.3 shows how to change the alternate startup folder with a VBA statement. (As is the case when you change the alternate startup folder with the Options dialog, Excel won't actually use the new alternate startup folder name until you restart Excel.)

INPUT   **LISTING 12.3**   CHANGING THE EXCEL ALTERNATE STARTUP FOLDER WITH VBA

```
1:    Sub ChangeAlternateStartPath()
2:        Application.AltStartupPath = "C:\My Documents\AltStart"
3:    End Sub
```

ANALYSIS   In Listing 12.3, substitute any string variable or constant containing the name and path of the alternate startup folder that you want for the quoted string in line 2.

12

Do

DO use Excel's Window, Hide command to hide your library workbooks to reduce clutter in your work environment and to help avoid making inadvertent changes in your library workbook. Excel will still open the hidden workbook in the startup or alternate startup folder. (Refer to your Excel documentation for more information on hiding and unhiding workbook files.)

DO use the Excel Tools, Protection, Protect Workbook command to protect your library workbook against inadvertent changes. If you plan to distribute your library workbook to other users, you might also want to use the password option of this command to prevent others from making changes in your library workbook. (Refer to Excel's online help system for more information on protecting workbooks.)

DO remember that Excel opens all workbooks in *both* the startup folder and the alternate startup folder.

Apart from the fact that loading a library workbook on startup still doesn't provide access to the library's procedures and functions for your VBA code, using a library loaded on startup has other drawbacks. Because the library file is always open, it therefore always consumes a certain amount of computer memory. Also, the amount of time that Excel requires to initially load itself into memory increases proportionally for each workbook in its startup folder. You can avoid these two difficulties by creating a reference (described in the next section) to make your library workbooks available instead of placing the library workbook in Excel's startup folders.

Using References to Access Library Procedures and Functions

Another way to make Excel automatically open a library workbook is to create a *reference* from one workbook to another. Creating a reference to a library workbook provides several advantages. First, whenever you open a workbook that contains a reference to another workbook, Excel will automatically open the referenced workbook if it is not already open. Second, unlike workbooks loaded from a startup folder, referenced workbooks are only opened if needed, thereby saving a certain amount of loading time and computer memory.

Most important, creating a reference to another workbook makes the procedures and functions of that workbook available for use in VBA code, not just in the Macro dialog.

Note

You can only reference VBA projects created by the same host application from which you create the reference. For example, from an Excel VBA project, you can only establish references to other Excel VBA projects.

To create a reference in a VBA project, follow these steps:

1. Open the workbook to which you want to add the new reference and then start the VB Editor.

2. Make sure that the project you want to add the reference to is selected in the Project Explorer and choose the Tools, References command. The VB Editor displays the References dialog shown in Figure 12.5.

   The Available References list in the References dialog includes all open VBA projects.

3. Select the check box to the left of the workbook in the Available References list to create a reference to that workbook.

4. If the project you want to establish a reference to is not listed in the Available References list, click the Browse button. VBA displays the Add Reference dialog, which looks and works just like a standard File Open dialog.

5. Use the Files of Type list in the Add Reference dialog to select the type of project to which you want to establish a reference: To reference a workbook, select Microsoft Excel Files.

6. Select the project file that you want to reference in the Add Reference dialog and click Open; VBA closes the Add Reference dialog and displays the selected project in the Available References list with its check box selected.

FIGURE 12.5

Use the VB Editor's References dialog to establish references from one VBA project to another.

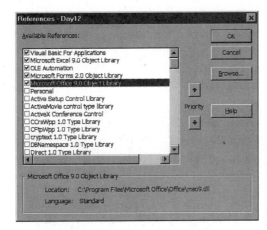

7. After you select all the references you want for the current project, click OK to close the References dialog. The VB Editor stores the new reference information in the current project and Excel opens the referenced workbook if it is not already open.

Now, whenever the workbook containing the reference is opened, Excel will automatically ensure that the referenced workbook is also opened.

In addition, the procedures and functions in the referenced library project are now available to your VBA code, not just in the Macro dialog.

To remove a reference that you have established for a particular project, perform the same steps just given for creating a reference, but clear the check box for the reference that you want to remove instead of selecting it.

> **Caution**
>
> Don't clear the check boxes for the Visual Basic For Applications reference, the Office Object Library, or the Excel Object Library reference, or your project will be unable to access those resources, such as Excel's Workbook, Worksheet, and Application objects and VBA's built-in functions such as CInt, Len, MsgBox, and so on.

After you establish a reference, whenever you call a procedure from the referenced project, VBA reads the referenced function or procedure from the referenced project.

When you create a reference to a workbook, the referenced workbook is opened for viewing and editing in both Excel and in the VB Editor. Whenever you open a workbook that has a reference to another workbook, the referenced workbook's modules and objects appear in the VB Editor's Project Explorer window, and the referenced workbook's worksheets will be visible in Excel. If you want, you can display or edit the VBA code in the referenced workbook's modules, unless those modules have been protected.

As with library workbooks that are loaded from a startup folder, you'll probably want to hide or protect the workbook to avoid cluttering your workspace and to prevent other users from casually altering your workbook. To prevent other users from editing your library workbook's VBA code, you must password-protect your modules as described in Day 21 in the section titled "Creating an Add-In Application." Procedures and functions in a referenced workbook that is password-protected will appear in the Object Browser, but the referenced modules cannot be displayed or edited.

Using a reference to provide access to your library workbooks does have one drawback: You must create each reference individually for each VBA project. If you have five workbooks, for example, and you want all of them to reference the same library workbook, you must go through the process of creating a reference five times, once for each workbook that references the library.

Note

For any open project that contains references, the Object Browser lists the procedures and functions available in the referenced project. You can use the Object Browser to look up the functions or procedures in the referenced project or to show the source code for the procedures and functions in the referenced project, just as you would for any other project's procedures or functions—regardless of whether the library workbook's code is locked for viewing (that is, cannot be displayed).

As usual, the Macro dialog will display procedures from the referenced workbook, as for any other open workbook.

Tip

You can create a reference to a library workbook in an Excel template. Every workbook you create based on that template will then include the reference to the library workbook. (Refer to Excel's online help system for more information on creating Excel templates.)

Do

DO remember that each individual workbook must have its own separate reference to the library workbook in order to access it.

DO hide a referenced library workbook to avoid cluttering up your workspace, and consider protecting your workbook if you intend to distribute your referenced library workbook to other users.

DO protect the code in your referenced library workbook and lock it against viewing (as described in Day 21) if you intend to distribute your library workbooks to other users.

12

Advanced Scope Rules for Cross-Module Programming

Now that you're learning how to share the code in your modules with other projects by creating libraries of VBA code, you are ready to learn how VBA applies its scope rules across modules. (Writing programs that have their source code distributed through more than one module is often referred to as *cross-module* programming because the program crosses through several modules.) This knowledge of VBA's scope rules for multiple modules will also help you use and understand the large-scale programming techniques described in the next section of this chapter.

With programs that use procedures in more than one module, the scope rules are only slightly more complex than the scope rules you learned in Day 3. Also, VBA provides you with a couple of different ways to increase or limit the scope of your constants, variables, procedures, functions, and user-defined types among various different modules.

Understanding Private and Public Scope

All the scope rules you learned in Day 3 for single modules still apply in situations involving multiple modules. Local variables and constants—that is, variables and constants declared at the procedure level—are available only within the procedure or function in which you declare them. Variables and constants that you declare at the module level are available to all procedures or functions within that same module.

Although variables and constants that you declare at the module level are available to any procedure and function in that module, they are *not* available to procedures and functions in a *different* module. The scope of module-level variables and constants is limited to the module in which you declare those variables or constants.

In VBA, items such as variables and constants whose scope is limited to a single module have *private* scope because their use is private within the particular module that contains their declaration statements. All variables or constants that you declare at the module level in the declarations area of a module (by using a **Dim** statement) have private scope, which means they are limited to the module in which they are declared.

In VBA, items that are available to all modules of all projects have *public* scope because they are publicly available to all modules in all projects. All procedures, functions, or user-defined type definitions in a module have public scope and are available to all modules in all projects.

Incidentally, items with public scope are sometimes referred to as *global* variables because they are available globally, that is, throughout the entire "world" of your program. You might also hear programmers with experience in programming languages other than VBA refer to variables and constants with module-level scope as global variables because they are globally available within their particular module. To avoid confusion, VBA (and this book) uses the term *private* to refer to items with a module-level scope and *public* to refer to items that have a scope extending across several modules.

The following list summarizes VBA's three different scope levels:

- *Local scope:* Variables and constants declared within a procedure or function. Items with local scope are available only within the particular procedure or function in which you declare them.

- *Private scope:* Variables and constants declared at the module level. Items with private scope are available to any procedure or function in the *same* module in which you declare the variables or constants, but are not available outside that module.

- *Public scope:* Procedures, functions, and user-defined types. Items with public scope are available throughout the module in which you declare them, to any other module in the same project, or to other projects—provided the project containing the module in which you declare the procedures, functions, or user-defined types has a reference created for it.

Do

DO remember that when variables, constants, functions, or procedures have the same name but different scope, VBA uses the variable, constant, function, or procedure with the more local scope.

DO remember that variables, constants, functions, or procedures at the same scope level cannot have the same name. For example, you cannot have a module-level variable that has the same name as a function, procedure, or user-defined type in the same module.

DO try to use unique names for all your variables, constants, functions, procedures, and user-defined types to avoid confusion and ambiguities that lead to subtle defects in your programs.

Don't

DON'T forget that you must create a reference to a library project before you can use its procedures and functions in your VBA code. Only after you've created a reference to the library project do the public and private scope rules described in this section apply; until you create the reference, none of the procedures, functions, variables, or constants in the library project are visible to your current VBA project.

12

Overriding Visual Basic for Application's Scope Rules

Sometimes you might want to limit or increase the availability of a particular variable, constant, procedure, function, or user-defined type, or even the contents of an entire module. VBA provides you with two different keywords—**Public** and **Private**—and a module-level compiler directive that enable you to change the scope of various items.

 Note   Remember that a *project* is the collective name for all the VBA modules and objects stored in a particular workbook.

Making Entire Modules Private to a Single Project

Occasionally, you might want to make sure that the procedures, functions, and user-defined types in a particular module are *not* available to any project other than the project in which you declare those items.

As an example, assume you have two different Excel workbooks. One workbook contains data about gross sales and another workbook contains budget data for your department. In both workbooks, you might have a group of procedures that you use to create quarterly reports from the data in that workbook. Your procedures might have names such as FirstQuarterReport, SecondQuarterReport, and so on. If you have both the sales and budget workbooks open, and you want to generate a sales report for the first quarter of the year, you might execute the FirstQuarterReport procedure to generate the report for you. If, however, you inadvertently execute the FirstQuarterReport procedure for the budget workbook instead of the sales workbook, your procedure might fail or you won't get the report you were expecting.

To avoid accidentally executing a procedure with the same name in the wrong project, you can make the entire contents of a module *private* so that the procedures in that module cannot be used by any project except the project that contains that particular module.

As another example, suppose you have written some procedures or functions that you intend to call only from other procedures or functions and should not be executed by themselves. By making the module private, you can reduce the possibility that you might accidentally execute one of these procedures or functions. Making a module private is, essentially, the reverse of creating a library: Instead of ensuring that the procedures and functions are universally available, you ensure that the procedure and functions in that module can be used only from that particular project.

SYNTAX

To make a module private, use the **Option Private Module** statement in the module with this syntax:

```
Option Private Module
```

The **Option Private Module** statement restricts the availability of all procedures, functions, user-defined types, and any module-level variables or constants declared in that module to the particular project that contains the module. You must place the **Option Private Module** statement on a line by itself in the declarations area of the module, before any variable, constant, procedure, function, or user-defined type definitions.

To help you understand the effects of the **Option Private Module** statement, Figure 12.6 shows Excel's Macro dialog. Notice that several procedures, named Proc1, Proc2,

Proc3, and Proc4, appear in the Macro Name list and are all contained in the Day12a.xls workbook. Because the Macro Name list includes the workbook name in front of the procedure name, you can tell that the Day12a.xls workbook containing these procedures is not the current workbook. The Day12a.xls workbook module that contains these procedure declarations does *not* include the **Option Private Module** statement, so the procedures are available to any other workbooks.

FIGURE 12.6

Normally, all the procedures in a module in an open Excel workbook are available to any other workbook through the Macro dialog.

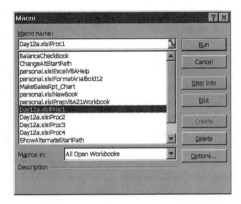

Now, look at Figure 12.7, which also shows Excel's Macro dialog. The **Option Private Module** statement was added to the Day12a.xls workbook module that contains the declarations for Proc1, Proc2, Proc3, and Proc4. Because the module containing these procedures is now private to the Day12a.xls workbook, they no longer appear in the Macro Name list of the Macro dialog.

12

FIGURE 12.7

Adding the **Option Private Module** *directive to a module restricts the availability of procedures and functions in that module to the project that contains that particular module.*

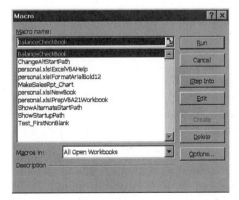

> **Note**
>
> Using the `Option Private Module` statement in a module only restricts the availability of procedures and functions to the single project that contains the module in which you declare those functions and procedures. Because procedures and functions, by default, have public scope, they are still available to other modules in the same project.

Using the `Private` Keyword to Limit Scope to a Single Module

The `Private` keyword restricts the scope level of a particular variable, constant, function, procedure, or user-defined type. Use the `Private` keyword if you have individual procedures, functions, or user-defined types in a module that you don't want to be available to other modules.

The `Private` keyword makes a VBA program item have private scope, overriding whatever scope level VBA would normally assign to that item. Use the `Private` keyword to reduce the scope level of items—such as procedures and functions—that otherwise would have a public scope level.

For instance, you might have a function that gets some data value from a user, such as the data-entry functions in the previous lesson. If the data-entry function is specific to a particular project or task—as is the `Get_UtilityItem` function in Listing 11.1—you might not want this function to be publicly available. By adding the `Private` keyword to the function's declaration, you can change its scope so that it is only available within the module in which you declare it. The next few paragraphs show you the general syntax for using the `Private` keyword in variable, constant, procedure, function, and user-defined type declarations.

To declare a private variable, use the following general syntax:

```
Private VarName [As TypeName]
```

VarName represents any valid VBA variable name. *TypeName* represents any valid VBA data type name or any user-defined data type name. Notice that this is exactly the same syntax you would use in a `Dim` statement, it just substitutes the `Private` keyword for `Dim`. You can only make `Private` variable declarations at the module level.

To declare a private constant, use this general syntax:

```
Private Const ConstName [As TypeName] = expression
```

ConstName represents any valid VBA constant name, *TypeName* represents any valid VBA data type name or any user-defined data type name, and *expression* represents any

▼   VBA expression. This is exactly the same syntax you use in a plain **Const** declaration statement. You can only make **Private** constant declarations at the module level.

To make a function or procedure private to the module in which you declare it, just add the **Private** keyword to the function or procedure declaration, as shown in the following:

```
Private Function name([arglist]) [As TypeName]
Private Sub name([arglist])
```

name represents any valid VBA function name, *TypeName* represents any valid VBA data type name or any user-defined data type name, and *arglist* represents the function's or procedure's argument list. Notice that, except for the addition of the **Private** keyword, this is exactly the same syntax you would use for any function or procedure declaration. (A later section in this chapter describes procedures that use arguments.)

You can also restrict the availability of a user-defined type to a single module by adding the **Private** keyword to the first line of the type definition:

```
Private Type VarName
```

▲   *VarName* represents any valid VBA identifier that you choose as the name for your user-defined type.

Do

DO remember that you can only use the **Private** keyword at the module level; you cannot use it to change the scope of local variables or constants.

12

Using the `Public` Keyword to Increase Scope to All Modules

The **Public** keyword increases the scope level of a particular variable, constant, function, procedure, or user-defined type, making it available to all modules in all projects. Use the **Public** keyword if you have individual variables or constants that you want to make available to other modules in the same or another project.

The **Public** keyword makes a VBA program item have public scope, overriding whatever scope level VBA would normally assign to that item. Use the **Public** keyword to raise the scope level of items—such as variables and constants—that otherwise would have a private scope level.

For instance, you might recall that the section "Using String Characters You Cannot Type at the Keyboard" in Day 5 suggested using constants to supply commonly used character codes for use with the Chr function. That section gave examples such as the CRightSym constant for the copyright symbol (code 169), and suggested that you declare such constants at the module level so that they would be available to all the procedures and functions in that module.

Constants like this, however, are useful in *all* your modules. In fact, constant declarations such as CRightSym are the kind of constant declarations that you would like to put in a library project and make universally available to all of your VBA procedures and functions. Constants declared at the module-level, however, have a private scope: They are available throughout the module in which you declare them, but are not available in other modules. By adding the **Public** keyword to the constant's declaration, you can change its scope so that it *is* available outside the module in which you declare it. The next few paragraphs show you the general syntax for using the **Public** keyword in variable, constant, procedure, function, and user-defined type declarations.

> **Note**
>
> VBA doesn't permit you to declare **Public** fixed-length string variables in a class module, but you can declare other **Public** variables and constants in a class module.

To declare a public variable, use the following general syntax:

```
Public VarName [As TypeName]
```

VarName represents any valid identifier and *TypeName* represents any valid data type name. This is the same syntax you use in a **Dim** statement, but using the **Public** keyword instead of **Dim**. You can only make **Public** variable declarations at the module level.

To declare a public constant, use this general syntax:

```
Public Const ConstName [As TypeName] = expression
```

ConstName represents any valid identifier, *TypeName* represents any valid data type name, and *expression* represents any expression. This is the same syntax you use in a plain **Const** declaration statement, with only the **Public** keyword added. You can only make **Public** constant declarations at the module level.

To declare a public function or procedure, just add the **Public** keyword to the function or procedure declaration:

```
Public Function name([arglist]) [As TypeName]
Public Sub name([arglist])
```

▼ *name* represents any valid identifier, *TypeName* represents any valid data type, and *arglist* represents the function's or procedure's argument list. Except for the addition of the **Public** keyword, this is exactly the same syntax you would use for any function or procedure declaration.

Similarly, you can also add the **Public** keyword to a user-defined type definition (*VarName* represents any valid identifier):

▲ `Public Type VarName`

Do

DO use the **Public** keyword at the module level only; you cannot use it to change the scope of local variables or constants.

DON'T

DON'T forget that even if you add the **Option Private Module** statement to a module, the public scope items in that module remain available to other modules in the same project, but not outside that project.

If you add the **Option Private Module** statement to a module so that the entire module is private to its project, you can still make module-level variables and constants in the private module available to other modules in the same project. To make variables and constants in a private module available to other modules in the same project, declare them with the **Public** keyword as shown previously.

The **Option Private Module** statement restricts the availability of public scope items in that module to the project that contains the module. The **Public** keyword makes a variable or constant available outside of its module, so the combined effect is to make the variable or constant available to all the modules of that one project only.

Understanding and Avoiding Circular References

A *circular reference* occurs when an item—such as a constant—is defined by another item—such as another constant—which is defined by the first item. To better understand the concept of a circular reference, consider the following two English sentences:

Fast means *quick*.

Quick means *fast*.

12

In the first sentence, the word *fast* is defined as meaning *quick*; in the second sentence, *quick* is defined as meaning *fast*. No real definition of either word is given; the two definitions simply refer to each other without supplying any additional information. This is a circular reference, also referred to as a *circular dependency*.

In VBA, you end up with circular references if your module contains constant declarations like the following:

```
Const A = B
Const B = A
```

In a single module, you probably won't make a mistake like this; the two statements are obviously wrong. If you do create a circular reference like this in a single module, VBA can tell that no real value is specified for the constant and displays an error message stating that an expression is required for the first constant declaration.

When you declare **Public** constants, however, the likelihood increases that you will accidentally create a circular reference between two public constants in two different modules. If one module contains this declaration:

```
Public Const A = B
```

And another module contains this constant declaration:

```
Public Const B = A
```

VBA then displays an error message stating that there are circular dependencies between modules.

Do

DO put all your public constant declarations in a single module; by gathering your public constants into a single module, you make it easier to check all of the constant definitions at once.

Don't

DON'T create circular references. To avoid circular references, you just have to be careful with your constant declarations.

Understanding and Using Module Qualifiers

Occasionally, you might want to access a private variable, constant, procedure, or function in some other module, but you don't want to make the item public or there is some reason you cannot make the item public. You can still access private variables, constants, procedures, and functions in a module by specifying the particular module that contains the item you want access to. You specify the module by adding the module's name—called a *module qualifier*—to the name of the variable, constant, procedure, or function you want to use in that module.

Another reason to use a module qualifier is to avoid any ambiguity when you must refer to public variables, constants, procedures, or functions whose names duplicate the name of some other item that has public scope in a different module. As you know, identifiers must be unique within their scope level, so VBA prevents you from creating variables, constants, functions, procedures, or user-defined types whose names duplicate each other in the *same* module. When you work with several modules at the same time, however, it is possible that public identifiers in one module might duplicate a public identifier in another module. Specifying the precise module that contains the item you want with a module qualifier resolves any ambiguity in this situation.

> **Note**
>
> To use module qualifiers, you must have established a reference (as described earlier in this chapter) to the project whose procedures you are using if they are not in the same project as the calling procedure.

12

SYNTAX

The general syntax for adding a module qualifier is

```
ModuleName.Identifier
```

`ModuleName` represents the name of the module as it appears in the Project Explorer. Notice the dot separator (`.`) after the module name. Like object references and references to elements in a user-defined type, the dot separator joins the two identifiers together into a single reference. `Identifier` is any VBA variable, constant, procedure, or function declared in the module indicated by `ModuleName` that has module-level scope.

You might also need to include the project name as part of the module qualifier, particularly if you have two different projects that have modules whose names duplicate each other. To include the project name in the module qualifier, you add the project name to the module name using the dot separator (`.`):

```
ProjectName.ModuleName.Identifier
```

▼   In this syntax form, *ProjectName* represents any VBA project name, as shown in the
Project Explorer window.

Going back to the ChartTools.xls library workbook example described earlier in this
chapter, if ChartTools.xls contains modules named *PieCharts* and *BarCharts*, and each of
these modules contains a procedure named MkSalesChart, you could use the following
module qualifiers to refer to the specific procedure in each module:

```
PieCharts.MkSalesChart
BarCharts.MkSalesChart
ChartTools.PieCharts.MkSalesChart
ChartTools.BarCharts.MkSalesChart
```

The first line refers to the MkSalesChart procedure in the *PieCharts* module; the second
line refers to the MkSalesChart procedure in the *BarCharts* module. The third and fourth
lines refer to the same procedures in the same modules as the first and second lines, but
▲   also include the project's name.

> **Note**
>
> Excel versions 5 and 7 permitted you to create module names that contained
> spaces. VBA 5.x—which is the version of VBA included in Excel 97 or high-
> er—generally does not permit you to create module or other object names
> that violate VBA's identifier naming rules. If you're working in Excel 7 or
> Excel 5, you might encounter module names that contain spaces or other-
> wise violate VBA's identifier naming rules. In this case, you must enclose the
> module name in square brackets as shown in the following (in this case, the
> square brackets are actually part of the syntax; you *must* include them):
>
> [*Module Name*].*Identifier*
>
> In the preceding syntax sample, notice that the dot separator (.) still
> appears between the module qualifier and the identifier.

Understanding Structured Programming Techniques

As you increasingly automate your work with VBA, you might realize at some point
that, for some tasks, you're just executing several macros one right after the other.
Usually, this is the point at which most people decide to organize the procedures related
to a particular series of tasks into a single, cohesive program. This section is intended to
help you design and create large-scale programs that consist of several procedures all
working together, whether you sit down to write that program all at once or you decide
to reorganize and join together existing procedures.

Understanding Procedures that Call Other Procedures

In the examples in the last lesson, you might have noticed that some of the functions and procedures seemed rather long; you might even have found the longer function or procedure examples a little difficult to follow all at once. From these examples—which actually carry out pretty simple jobs—you can easily imagine how a single procedure to perform a complex task might quickly become overwhelmingly long and convoluted; so long, in fact, that creating, understanding, and maintaining such a procedure becomes almost impossible.

The solution to this problem is to divide the VBA code that performs a task into several different procedures that are called by another procedure. By dividing the task into smaller steps and writing a separate procedure for each step, you make your procedures easier to write, debug, and update. To carry out all the steps to complete the task, you write another procedure that executes each of the smaller procedures in the correct order.

As an example, say you want to write a procedure that uses data in one of your Excel workbooks to compute quarterly profit and loss statements, create some charts showing sales and costs for each quarter, and then print the report. You could write a single procedure that goes through all the steps needed to compute the various totals, create the charts, and print the reports. A single procedure to perform all the steps necessary for this job might be several hundred lines in length, contain many nested **If...Then** statements and looping structures, and will surely be so complex that its creation and maintenance might seem an absolute nightmare.

Writing several procedures that work together, however, makes this programming task manageable. By dividing the overall job into its component parts and creating a procedure to carry out that single part of the overall job, you keep individual procedures at a level of complexity that remains comprehensible. This technique of dividing a large job into smaller jobs to make the overall task easier to program is often referred to as the *divide-and-conquer* approach to programming.

12

Applying the divide-and-conquer technique to the example of computing quarterly profit and loss statements, you might write several separate procedures: a single procedure that computes gross income, a procedure that computes gross expenses, a procedure that computes net income, another procedure that creates the necessary charts, and yet another procedure that prints the report.

Figure 12.8 shows how your separate procedures relate to various parts of the overall job. Notice that each part of the overall task has a corresponding procedure.

FIGURE 12.8

*Make large program-
ming tasks easier by
writing small proce-
dures to carry out sin-
gle steps of a task.*

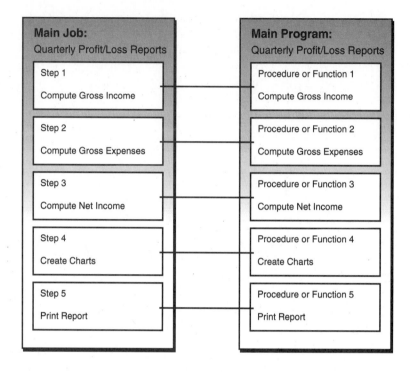

You might wonder what the benefit of writing several different procedures is, because
you probably don't want to have to execute each procedure separately. To join all your
separate procedures together into a single program (the Main Program box in Figure
12.8), you simply write a procedure that calls all the other procedures or functions in the
correct order.

You already know how to call a function from a procedure; calling procedures from
another procedure is very much the same. If the procedures you write for steps 1 through
5 in Figure 12.8 are named `CompGrossIncome`, `CompGrossExpenses`, `CompNetIncome`,
`CreateCharts`, and `PrintReport`, the main procedure that executes all these procedures
might look like this:

```
Sub QuarterlyReport()
    CompGrossIncome
    CompGrossExpenses
    CompNetIncome
    CreateCharts
    PrintReport
End Sub
```

As you can see, this procedure doesn't perform any work except to call, in the correct sequence, the procedures that carry out the necessary steps to complete the quarterly report. The QuarterlyReport procedure is short and simple; you can easily read this procedure and determine, in general, what tasks it performs. The specific details of each task are contained in the individual procedures called by the QuarterlyReport procedure.

Another benefit of dividing a large task into smaller pieces and writing a separate procedure for each piece of the task is that you make it possible to reuse some of the VBA code that you write. For example, if you also generate annual profit and loss reports, you'll probably find that you can use the same procedures you wrote to compute gross income, gross expenses, and net income for the quarterly report when you compute the same figures for an annual report just by changing the data that the procedures work with from quarterly to annual figures.

Being able to reuse code is one of the greatest benefits of a structured programming language such as VBA. If you include all the code for a single task in a single procedure, you must write that code again for any other task that might use the same or similar VBA code. By separating common activities into individual procedures, you make it possible to have several different programs use the same procedures, eliminating any necessity to program the same task more than once.

Later in this chapter, you'll learn how to use procedure arguments to exchange data values among different procedures, making your procedures even more flexible and powerful.

Top-Down Design and Step-Wise Refinement

12

One of the most accepted computer program design strategies is referred to as *top-down* design. When you design a program using a top-down approach, you start out by designing the most general part of the process you want to program—the "top"—and then proceed to more and more specific details of the process, working your way "down."

To apply top-down design techniques to your programs, follow this general process:

- Begin by outlining, in the most general terms, the tasks that your program will perform.
- Choose a procedure name for each step in your top-level general outline. If your top-level general outline has five steps in it, you should choose five different procedure names.

- For each individual step in your top-level outline, create a more specific outline for all the tasks necessary to carry out that one step. After completing this second-level outline, choose procedure names to correspond to each step in this outline.

- For each individual step in your second-level outline, create a more specific outline of the tasks necessary to carry out that one step. Continue making successively more specific outlines for each sub-task until you reach a level of simplicity where you can easily write the VBA code to carry out that task in a single, short procedure or function.

This process of successive outlining is also known as *step-wise refinement,* because you gradually refine each step into its component parts, successively reducing complex actions into their more easily understood component parts.

One of the benefits of top-down design and step-wise refinement is that it helps you focus your efforts for greatest effect. If you're stumped about exactly how to write the code for a particular sub-task, don't worry about it. Assign a procedure name to the task, pretend you have a friend who'll show up later and tell you how to write the code for that part, and continue with your outlining process.

Frequently, by the time you finish outlining the other tasks in your program, it will become clear to you how to perform the task you were unsure of. Even it hasn't, you have still isolated your area of uncertainty down to a very few procedures and you know where to concentrate your research or experimentation efforts. This is another way to apply the divide-and-conquer approach to computer programming.

Following this top-down design approach will also help you determine whether you really have all the data necessary to carry out a particular task, as well as helping you decide what kind of variables and constants you might need to declare and what kinds of user-defined types you might need.

To use a top-down design approach for the quarterly profit and loss reporting example used in the preceding section, you might start out with the following English-language outline:

(A) Compute gross income

(B) Compute gross expenses

(C) Compute net income

(D) Create charts

(E) Print report, including charts

This outline describes the entire task you want your program to perform in very general terms. The main procedure of your program will correspond to this top-level outline and will consist of several statements that simply call the appropriate procedures in the correct order.

Now outline, in more detail, each separate task from the top-level outline. The second-level outline for step (A), computing the gross income, might look like the following:

(A.1)   Total the sales figures for the Western region.

(A.2)   Total the sales figures for the Eastern region.

(A.3)   Total the sales figures for the Southern region.

(A.4)   Add together the subtotals for the Western, Eastern, and Southern regions.

Looking at this second-level outline for the process of computing the gross sales, you can see that you need at least three different variables here, one for each regional sales subtotal. You can also see that the first three steps might require additional refinement, but that you can accomplish the fourth step with a simple arithmetic expression after you compute the various subtotals. Therefore, you need to write procedures for the first three steps, but not for the fourth step, because it is simple enough that you can directly write the VBA statements for that step.

Now, working with step (A.1) from the second-level outline, you might produce this third-level outline:

(A.1.a) Select the worksheet that contains the sales figures for the Western region.

(A.1.b) Add together all the numbers in column B of the worksheet (this column contains the figures for the weekly sales totals as submitted by the regional manager).

(A.1.c) Store the subtotal just computed in the variable for the Western regional sales total.

In this third-level outline, you can see that each of the three steps are simple enough that you can easily write the VBA code statements to carry out each step. In fact, each step in this outline corresponds to only one or two VBA statements. This particular level does not need any additional refinement; you have just outlined the steps for a single procedure.

12

When you make the third-level outline for step (A.2), you might end up with the following third-level outline:

(A.2.a)   Select the worksheet that contains the sales figures for the Eastern region.

(A.2.b)   Add together all the numbers in column B of the worksheet (this column contains the figures for the weekly sales totals as submitted by the regional manager).

(A.2.c)   Store the subtotal just computed in the variable for the Eastern regional sales total.

Notice that, except for the worksheet that contains the source data and the variable that stores the regional subtotal, this outline is identical to the third-level outline for step (A.1). This situation tells you that you should use the same procedure to carry out both steps and just tell the procedure which worksheet to select and which variable to store the subtotal in. Because a function can return a result, you might even decide that it is more appropriate to write a function to carry out the task of computing a regional sales subtotal and then create a function that takes the worksheet name for the source data as an argument and returns the subtotal as its result.

This example only carries the outline process down three levels and only fully outlines a couple of steps. There is no fixed rule about how many outline levels to create, just keep refining each outline to a lower and lower level until you reach the point where each step in your outline roughly corresponds to between one and four VBA statements.

Do

DO write short procedures that perform a single, simple task. As a rule of thumb, you shouldn't let your procedures get much longer than 20 or 30 lines—about one or two screens full. If your procedure gets much longer than that, you're probably trying to make it do too much work.

DO avoid long procedures that perform many different tasks. The longer and more complex a single procedure gets, the more likely you are to make a programming mistake or to have difficulty updating the procedure. Also, if you have very long procedures, it is likely that you are duplicating much more of your VBA code than is necessary.

Don't

DON'T forget the KISS principle—"Keep It Sweet and Simple"—when you write your procedures and functions.

Using Modules to Organize Your Programming Projects

Usually, you should put all the code for a single program in a single workbook, with the exception of any general-purpose procedures or functions that you keep in a library workbook. Use different modules in your project to help organize your program's code. Another reason for keeping all the VBA source code for a single program in a single workbook is that, by starting out with all the code in a single workbook, you make it easier to convert your program to an add-in program, as described in Day 21, "Using Event Procedures and Add-Ins."

With large projects, distribute the source code into several different modules, where each module contains the program source code to carry out specific tasks within the larger program. For example, it will be easier for you to develop and understand a VBA program that imports data into a worksheet, formats and charts the data, and then prints the chart and a report if you divide the program into several modules. One module, for example, might contain the procedures and functions that import the data, another module might contain the procedures and functions that format and chart the data, and so on.

Within a single module, you should organize your source code by following a few conventions, which the VB Editor is designed to help you do. First, place all your **Option** directives in the declarations area at the very beginning of the module, before any other VBA statements. VBA's **Option** directives include **Option Explicit**, **Option Compare**, **Option Private Module**, and so on. Second, place all your user-defined type definitions after the **Option** statements, but before any variable, constant, procedure, or function declarations. Next, declare all your module-level or public variables and constants and then declare all your functions and procedures.

The following code template, which does not contain any actual VBA code, shows how you should organize the code within individual modules:

```
'Declarations Area:
        'Option statements: Option Explicit, Option Compare, and so on
        'User-defined type definitions
        'Module-level variable and constant declarations

'Procedure and function declarations.
```

12

Using Procedure Arguments to Communicate Data Between Procedures

Just as you can create functions that receive data values passed in an argument list, you can also create procedures that receive data values passed as arguments. Essentially, creating argument lists for both procedures and functions is the same. The next few sections describe when and why you should create procedures with argument lists and how to specify and use an argument list for a procedure.

Understanding When and Why You Should Use Argument Lists with Your Procedures

There are two main reasons to use an argument list in your procedures:

- An argument list is a convenient, efficient, and trouble-free way to pass information to a procedure that needs the information to complete its task. By using arguments to supply values to a procedure, you can make your procedures more flexible and more powerful.

- An argument list is also a convenient, efficient, and trouble-free way to *return* data from a procedure. To return data from a procedure, use an argument passed by reference; just like in a function, when a procedure changes the value of an argument passed by reference, the original data value changes.

In the section on top-down program design, you saw a case history of using top-down design and step-wise refinement to outline your program. You saw that the outlining process revealed how the steps for computing the sales subtotal for a single region were identical, except for the name of a worksheet containing figures to be totaled and the name of a variable to hold the total. Because the code for computing each regional subtotal is so similar, you should use the same procedure to compute all the regional subtotals.

To use the same procedure to compute the subtotal for each region, you must somehow be able to tell the procedure what worksheet to select and what variable to store the subtotal in. You can do both by passing arguments to the procedure: one argument for the worksheet name and another argument—passed by reference—for the variable to store the regional subtotal in. You then write the procedure so that it computes a subtotal for whatever worksheet name you pass to it and stores the subtotal in whatever variable you pass to it. By adding arguments to the procedure, you make it possible to use the same procedure to compute the regional sales subtotal for any of the sales regions, depending on the worksheet name you pass to it. In fact, you could use this same procedure to compute a subtotal for *any* worksheet you name.

Passing information to a procedure through its argument list also reduces the number of module-level or public variables that you need to declare. This is really quite helpful: It can reduce the amount of memory that your program needs and definitely eliminates a potential source of errors and confusion. The greater the number of module-level or public variables in your program, the greater is the chance that you will inadvertently use the wrong variable, leading to various side effects and subtle bugs. Use argument lists to make information available to a procedure instead of a module-level variable.

Specifying a Procedure's Argument List

You specify argument lists for procedures exactly the same way you specify argument lists for functions. You already know that you must include parentheses after the procedure name in every procedure declaration; by now, you've probably realized that the empty parentheses indicate to VBA that the procedure has no arguments.

The full syntax for a procedure declaration is

```
Sub name([arglist])
    statements
End Sub
```

▼ SYNTAX

name represents the procedure name, *arglist* represents the procedure's optional argument list, and *statements* represents the VBA statements that make up the body of the procedure. The argument list can consist of one or more arguments, with each argument in the list separated by a comma. A single argument in the list has this general syntax:

```
[Optional] [ByVal ¦ ByRef] varname [As typename]
```

Just like a function, the **Optional** keyword indicates that the argument is optional. You can include either the **ByVal** keyword or the **ByRef** keyword, but not both. The **ByVal** keyword tells VBA to pass the argument by value and the **ByRef** keyword tells VBA to pass the argument by reference. (You learned the difference between arguments passed by value and by reference in Day 6.) *varname* represents the argument name; it can be any valid VBA identifier. The final part of the argument syntax is the **As** keyword followed by *typename*, which represents any valid VBA or user-defined data type. Unless

▲ you specify the argument's data type, VBA passes the argument as a **Variant** data type.

12

Do

DO list all of a procedure's required arguments first, with all optional arguments at the end of the argument list (VBA requires you to do this).

DO use the IsMissing function to test for the presence or absence of optional **Variant** arguments within the procedure, just as you do in a function with optional arguments.

Do

DO remember that you cannot use the `IsMissing` function to determine whether an optional argument with a data-type other than **Variant** is missing (the `IsMissing` function only works with optional arguments of the **Variant** type).

DO remember that you can set a default value for an optional argument in a procedure declaration the same way you can in a function declaration.

DO remember that VBA, by default, passes arguments by reference. If you omit either the **ByRef** or **ByVal** keywords, VBA passes the argument by reference.

DO remember that argument names have the same scope as variables declared locally within the procedure, that is, argument variables are not accessible outside the procedure in whose argument list you declare them.

DO check carefully each time you write a procedure to make sure it alters only the arguments you intend it to.

Using Procedures That Have Arguments

Although creating an argument list for a procedure is exactly like creating an argument list for a function, calling a procedure with arguments is slightly different. When you pass arguments to a procedure, you do not include any parentheses around the argument list, even though you must enclose the argument list in parentheses when you declare the procedure.

To call a procedure and pass arguments to it, just type the procedure's name, a space, and then list each argument value in the argument list, separating each value with a comma. You can also use named arguments when you specify the values in the procedure's argument list: Just use the name of the argument as it appears in the argument list of the procedure's declaration.

Assume that you have a procedure named `CompGrossIncome` that has the following declaration:

```
Sub CompGrossIncome( SheetName As String, sTotal As Currency)
```

This declaration tells VBA that `CompGrossIncome` has two required arguments. The first argument, `SheetName`, is a string; the second argument, `sTotal`, is a **Currency** type value. VBA passes both arguments by reference because the **ByVal** keyword is not present.

To call the `CompGrossIncome` procedure and specify values for its argument list, you could use either of the following statements:

```
CompGrossIncome "Eastern", GrSales
```

```
CompGrossIncome SheetName:="Eastern", sTotal:=GrSales
```

The first line just lists the values for the arguments in the correct order, separating each value in the argument list with a comma. The second line uses named arguments to specify the values in the procedure's argument list, also separating each argument with a comma.

If you try to pass arguments to a procedure that you did not declare with an argument list, VBA displays a syntax error stating that the procedure has the wrong number of arguments. If your procedure has required arguments (any argument declared without the **Optional** keyword is required) and you leave one or more of them out, VBA displays the same "wrong number of arguments" syntax error message.

Note
> The Macro dialog does *not* list procedures that have required arguments because there is no way for you to supply the argument values. You can only execute procedures that have required arguments by calling the procedure in a VBA program statement. The Macro dialog only lists procedures without arguments, although it will list a procedure if *all* of its arguments are optional.

Listing 12.4 shows two different procedures. The MakeSalesRpt_Chart procedure in Listing 12.4 is similar to the MakeSalesRpt_Chart procedure used as an example in previous lessons. The new feature in this listing is the fact that MakeSalesRpt_Chart now calls the Make_LabeledPieChart procedure to create the actual chart, instead of creating the chart itself.

12

INPUT

LISTING 12.4 USING A PROCEDURE'S ARGUMENTS TO SEND INFORMATION TO THE PROCEDURE

```
1:  Sub Make_LabeledPieChart(srcSheet As String, _
2:                           sRng As String, _
3:                           destSheet As String, _
4:                           chTitle As String)
5:  'creates labeled pie chart in a fixed location, on the
6:  'worksheet named by destSheet, then uses ChartWizard method to
7:  'plot data from the range named by sRng on the sheet named by
8:  'srcSheet. New pie chart gets title specified by chTitle.
9:
10:     'select the destination sheet and create chart
11:     Sheets(destSheet).Select
12:     ActiveSheet.ChartObjects.Add(96, 37.5, 234, 111).Select
13:     'use ChartWizard Method to create chart.
14:     With Sheets(srcSheet)
15:       ActiveChart.ChartWizard Source:=.Range(sRng), _
```

continues

LISTING 12.4   CONTINUED

```
16:                                    Gallery:=xlPie, _
17:                                    Format:=7, _
18:                                    PlotBy:=xlColumns, _
19:                                    CategoryLabels:=1, _
20:                                    SeriesLabels:=1, _
21:                                    HasLegend:=1, _
22:                                    Title:=chTitle
23:    End With
24: End Sub
25:
26: Sub MakeSalesRpt_Chart()
27: 'Asks for a sheet name containing source data, and then
28: 'asks for a range of cells containing the data to chart.
29: 'Next, this procedure asks for a sheet name to put the pie
30: 'chart on. This procedure then calls Make_LabeledPieChart
31: 'procedure to make a pie chart.
32:    Const sTitle = "Make Sales Report Chart"
33:
34:    Static SrcShtName As String
35:    Static SourceRng As String
36:    Dim DestShtName As String
37:
38:     'get source sheet name
39:    SrcShtName = InputBox(prompt:="Enter the name of " & _
40:               "the sheet containing the data to graph:", _
41:                        Title:=sTitle, _
42:                        default:=SrcShtName)
43:
44:     'check to see if user entered name or chose Cancel
45:    If Len(Trim(SrcShtName)) = 0 Then
46:      MsgBox "Data source not entered - ending procedure"
47:      Exit Sub
48:    End If
49:        'select source sheet so user can refer to it
50:    Sheets(SrcShtName).Select
51:
52:     'get source range
53:    SourceRng = InputBox(prompt:="Enter the range of " & _
54:               "the data to graph using R1C1 notation:", _
55:                        Title:=sTitle, _
56:                        default:=SourceRng)
57:
58:     'check to see if user entered range or chose Cancel
59:    If Len(Trim(SourceRng)) = 0 Then
60:      MsgBox "Source range not entered - ending procedure"
61:      Exit Sub
62:    End If
63:
```

```
64:     'get destination sheet name
65:     DestShtName = InputBox(prompt:="Enter the name of " & _
66:                 "the sheet that will contain the graph:", _
67:                         Title:=sTitle)
68:
69:     'did user enter destination name or choose Cancel
70:     If Len(Trim(DestShtName)) = 0 Then
71:       MsgBox "Destination not entered - ending procedure"
72:       Exit Sub
73:     End If
74:
75:     'use Make_LabeledPieChart procedure to create chart.
76:     Make_LabeledPieChart srcSheet:=SrcShtName, _
77:                   sRng:=SourceRng, _
78:                   destSheet:=DestShtName, _
79:                   chTitle:="Sales Report"
80: End Sub
```

ANALYSIS Lines 1 through 24 contain the definition for the Make_LabeledPieChart procedure. This procedure makes a labeled pie chart using the source data sheet,
source data range, destination worksheet, and chart title passed to the procedure as arguments. Because the procedure receives all the information it needs to make the chart
through its argument list, you can use this procedure to create a pie chart from data in
any range of any worksheet and place the chart on any worksheet.

The Make_LabeledPieChart procedure's declaration and argument list are in lines 1
through 4. Notice the line-continuation symbol at the end of lines 1, 2, and 3: Lines 1
through 4 are a single procedure declaration. The argument list was divided over several
physical lines in order to make it easier to read.

Make_LabeledPieChart has four different arguments, all of which are required and all of
which are strings. The srcSheet argument contains the name of the worksheet that has
the source data to be charted; the sRng argument contains a string specifying the range of
data from the source worksheet to chart; the destSheet argument contains the name of
the worksheet on which the procedure places the resulting chart; and chTitle is a string
containing the title for the new chart.

Line 11 selects the destination sheet for the chart using the Sheets collection and the
destSheet argument variable to specify the destination sheet. Line 12 then creates the
chart object on the destination sheet in a fixed location and selects the new chart object.

Line 14 begins a **With** statement for the worksheet object specified by srcSheet. Lines
15 through 22 are a single VBA statement that uses Excel's ChartWizard method to create the desired pie chart. In line 15, notice that the source range argument, sRng, is used

12

to specify the data source for the chart. The worksheet of the source range is specified by the **With** statement in line 14. In line 22, notice that the chTitle argument is used to supply the title for the pie chart.

The Make_LabeledPieChart procedure gets all the information it needs to carry out its task through its argument list. As long as you want a labeled pie chart with this format, you can use this procedure to chart data from any source and insert the pie chart in any worksheet (provided the source and destination are in the same workbook). This is a classic example of a short, simple procedure that does one task well.

Lines 26 through 80 contain the definition for the MakeSalesRpt_Chart procedure. This procedure has no arguments. The MakeSalesRpt_Chart procedure carries out the task of getting a source worksheet name, data range, and destination worksheet name from the user.

Lines 39 through 42 get the worksheet name for the data source from the user, and lines 45 through 48 check to see whether the user canceled the input dialog. If the user canceled the input dialog the procedure ends; otherwise, it continues on to line 50, which selects the named source data sheet.

Lines 53 through 56 get the source range from the user, and lines 58 through 62 again check to see whether the user canceled the input dialog. Lines 64 through 73 get the destination sheet name and test again to see whether the user canceled the operation by entering a blank string or canceling the input dialog.

Finally, lines 76 through 79 call the Make_LabeledPieChart procedure to actually create the new pie chart.

The advantage of creating the Make_LabeledPieChart procedure is that you gain a general-purpose procedure that can create a pie chart in a particular format for any source and destination. The procedure is short, simple, and easy to understand. You can use it to create similar charts for sales, expenses, net profit, and so on.

The example in Listing 12.4 only used the procedure's arguments to send information to a procedure. Listing 12.5 shows a procedure that uses its arguments, passed by reference, to return values to the procedure that called it. Listing 12.5 also shows two different procedures. The first procedure, FirstNonBlankCell, searches the first 10 columns of the first 16 rows of a worksheet. It returns in its arguments the row and column coordinates of the first non-blank cell that it finds. The second procedure simply helps you test the FirstNonBlankCell procedure.

LISTING 12.5   USING A PROCEDURE'S ARGUMENTS TO RETURN VALUES FROM THE
PROCEDURE

```
 1: Sub FirstNonBlankCell(nRow As Long, nCol As Long)
 2: 'Loops through first 16 rows and 10 columns of the active
 3: 'worksheet, looking for a non-blank cell. Returns the row
 4: 'and column coordinates in nRow and nCol. If no non-blank
 5: 'cell found in the first 16 rows and 10 columns,
 6: 'returns 0 in both coordinates.
 7:    Dim Rcount As Integer
 8:    Dim Ccount As Integer
 9:
10:    nRow = 0        'assume a non-blank cell is not found
11:    nCol = 0
12:
13:      'if active sheet is not a worksheet, then stop now
14:    If TypeName(ActiveSheet) <> "Worksheet" Then Exit Sub
15:
16:    For Rcount = 1 To 16
17:      For Ccount = 1 To 10
18:        If Not IsEmpty(Cells(Rcount, Ccount).Value) Then
19:          nRow = Rcount
20:          nCol = Ccount
21:          Exit Sub
22:        End If
23:      Next Ccount
24:    Next Rcount
25: End Sub
26:
27:
28: Sub Test_FirstNonBlank()
29:
30:    Dim Rows As Long
31:    Dim Cols As Long
32:    Dim OldSheet As Object
33:    Static sName As String
34:
35:    Set OldSheet = ActiveSheet
36:
37:    sName = InputBox("Enter a worksheet name:")
38:    Worksheets(sName).Select
39:    FirstNonBlankCell nRow:=Rows, nCol:=Cols
40:
41:    If Rows = 0 Then
42:      MsgBox "No non-blank cells were found."
43:    Else
44:      MsgBox "The first non-blank cell is in row " & _
45:              Rows & ", column " & Cols
46:    End If
47:    OldSheet.Select
48: End Sub
```

12

ANALYSIS Lines 1 through 25 contain the definition for the `FirstNonBlankCell` procedure. The procedure has two required arguments, both of which are **Long** type numbers and both of which are passed by reference. The first argument, `nRow`, represents a row coordinate, and the second argument, `nCol`, represents a column coordinate. Because VBA passes these two arguments by reference (the default passing method in VBA), any time the `FirstNonBlankCell` procedure changes these argument values, the original data value is changed. The `FirstNonBlankCell` procedure uses the argument variables to pass values back to the procedure that called it.

Because 0 is not a legitimate value for a row or column coordinate in Excel, `FirstNonBlankCell` signals that it was unable to find a non-blank cell by setting the `nRow` and `nCol` values to 0.

This procedure must loop through rows and columns of a worksheet, so it needs to have a couple of loop counting variables, one for rows and one for columns. Lines 7 and 8 declare the loop counting variables—`Rcount` for rows and `Ccount` for columns—for the `FirstNonBlankCell` procedure.

Lines 10 and 11 each assign 0 to the `nRow` and `nCol` argument variables. Assuming that the procedure will fail to find a non-blank cell simplifies the remaining tests that this procedure must make. The procedure now only has to determine whether it finds a non-blank cell without testing for blank cells.

Line 14 uses the `TypeName` function in a single-line **If...Then** statement to ensure that the current sheet is actually a worksheet and to prevent a runtime error from occurring later in the procedure. If the active sheet is not a worksheet, there are no cells to examine and the `FirstNonBlankCell` procedure should end immediately (**Exit Sub**). Because values indicating failure to locate a non-blank cell were already assigned to the argument variables in lines 10 and 11, no additional assignment or processing is necessary—the procedure simply exits.

Lines 16 through 24 contain a **For...Next** loop that paces through the first 16 rows of the worksheet. The upper limit of 16 was arbitrarily chosen because 16 rows roughly corresponds to the maximum number of rows that you can see in a full-window display of a worksheet (for most computer systems).

The first line in the body of the **For...Next** loop that counts through the rows (line 17) starts a nested **For...Next** loop (the nested loop occupies lines 17 through 23). The inner loop paces through the first 10 columns of a worksheet. The upper limit of 10 columns was arbitrarily chosen because 10 columns roughly corresponds to the maximum number of columns that you can see in a full-window display of a worksheet.

The body of the inner **For...Next** loop is a single **If...Then** statement that uses the IsEmpty function to test whether the worksheet cell specified by the current row and column count is empty. If the cell is not empty, lines 19 and 20 assign the current row and column counts to the nRow and nCol argument variables respectively. Line 21 then exits the FirstNonBlankCell procedure. At this point, the values of nRow and nCol reflect the location of the first non-blank cell and whatever procedure called FirstNonBlankCell now has those values available to it.

Lines 28 through 48 contain a simple procedure, Test_FirstNonBlank, that you can use to test the FirstNonBlankCell procedure. Line 28 contains the procedure definition and lines 30 through 33 declare some variables for Test_FirstNonBlank. The first two variables, Rows and Cols, are used as the argument for FirstNonBlankCell. The OldSheet object variable is used, for convenience, to save and restore whatever sheet was active at the time you executed Test_FirstNonBlank. Finally, the static sName variable is used to hold the name of the worksheet you want FirstNonBlankCell to check. sName is declared as a static variable for convenience in successive testing runs.

Line 35 saves a reference to whatever sheet is active at the time you execute Test_FirstNonBlank. Line 37 uses the InputBox function to get the name of the worksheet you want to test FirstNonBlankCell on and line 38 selects that sheet.

Line 39 calls the FirstNonBlankCell cell procedure, passing the Rows and Cols variables as the procedure's arguments. Notice that the Test_FirstNonBlank procedure has *not* assigned any value to either of these variables. When VBA executes this statement, it calls the FirstNonBlankCell procedure, which executes as described in the first few paragraphs of this analysis. When the FirstNonBlankCell procedure has finished executing, VBA continues execution with line 41 of the Test_FirstNonBlank procedure.

Line 41 begins an **If...Then...Else** statement that evaluates the value in the Rows variable. If the Rows variable contains 0, the FirstNonBlankCell procedure did not find any non-blank cells and VBA executes line 42, which displays a message dialog stating that no non-blank cells were found.

If, however, the Rows variable contains a number other than 0, the FirstNonBlankCell procedure *did* locate a non-blank cell, and the non-blank cell's row and column coordinates are now stored in the Rows and Cols variables. VBA then executes the statement in line 44, which displays a message dialog reporting the row and column number of the non-blank cell.

Once again, notice that the Test_FirstNonBlank procedure does not contain any assignment statements to either the Rows or Cols variables. The values for these variables are assigned in the FirstNonBlankCell procedure; because the FirstNonBlankCell

12

procedure's arguments are passed by reference, any changes to those arguments are reflected in the original source of the argument value specified when you call the procedure. The `FirstNonBlankCell` procedure uses its arguments to return values to the procedure that called it.

The advantage of using arguments passed by reference in a procedure to return values, rather than a function, is that you can use the `ByRef` arguments in a procedure to return more than one value at a time.

Do

DO use `ByRef` arguments in a procedure's argument list to return values from a procedure *only* when you need to return more than one value at a time. (Remember, if you omit the `ByRef` or `ByVal` keyword, VBA's default method of passing arguments is by reference.)

DO use a function to return a single value.

DO remember that you can use the Object Browser to find or show your procedures in exactly the same way you do for your function procedures. You can also use the Object Browser's options to specify comments for your procedures as you do for your functions. Using the Object Browser was described in Day 6.

Don't

DON'T use `ByRef` arguments in a function to return values other than the function result. Functions should always return a *single* value and should *never* modify their arguments.

Summary

In this chapter you learned how to organize your commonly used procedures into a library and how to make that library available to other projects. You learned how to make library projects available by placing them in Excel's startup directory so that the library project is opened automatically every time you start Excel. You also learned how to create references from one project to another.

You learned how VBA determines the scope of variables, constants, procedures, functions, and user-defined types when your program uses code in different modules, and you learned the difference between local scope, private scope, and public scope. You also learned how to increase or limit the scope of variables, constants, procedures, functions, and user-defined types by adding the **Public** or **Private** keywords to their declarations. You then learned how to use module qualifiers to refer to specific items in specific modules and workbooks. You learned that you can only use module qualifiers to refer to items in workbooks to which there is a reference.

Next, this chapter showed you how to use the most prevalent techniques—top-down design combined with a process of step-wise refinement—to design large-scale programs. You learned how your procedures can call other procedures, and you learned how to use several different modules to organize the various procedures and functions that make up your programs.

This chapter showed you how to create and use argument lists with your procedures. You learned when and why to use arguments with your procedures, and you learned how to specify an argument list for your procedures. Finally, you saw examples of how to use procedure arguments to both send information to a procedure, and to return values from a procedure.

Q&A

Q Do I have to create a library workbook?

A No, you don't have to create a library workbook. Using a library workbook, however, can reduce the number of times you end up writing the same code over and over again. Also, if you attach procedures to toolbar buttons and menu choices, as described in Day 17, you need to make sure that the procedures for those menus and toolbar buttons are always available. The best way to do this is to put those procedures in a library project. In general, the benefits of creating a library project more than make up for the amount of work and care needed to create the library project.

Q When you talk about the scope level of user-defined types, I'm a little confused. Do you mean the scope of variables with user-defined types, or do you mean the definition of a user-defined type?

A The scope of a user-defined type refers to the scope level at which the user-defined type *definition* is available. You can only declare variables with a particular user-defined type if the user-defined type definition is available at the scope level in which you declare the variable. If you declare a user-defined type definition with the `Private` keyword, the user-defined type is only available within the module in which you declare it. This means that you can only declare variables with that user-defined type in the same module in which the type definition appears. If you want to declare variables with the user-defined type in another module, you must allow the user-defined type definition to remain public so that it is available outside its own module.

12

Q **I'm a little confused. If the scope of a module-level variable is already limited to the module in which I declared it, what effect does using the `Private` keyword (instead of `Dim`) have?**

A You're right, this is a little confusing. There is absolutely no difference between using the **Private** keyword and the **Dim** keyword to declare a module-level variable. In both cases, the scope of the variable is limited to the module in which it is declared. The only reason you might use the **Private** keyword to declare a module-level variable is to reinforce the distinction between variables private to that module and any variables in the same module that you declare with the **Public** keyword.

Q **I also don't understand the effect of adding the `Public` keyword to a procedure, function, or user-defined type definition, because they naturally have public scope. Why should I use the `Public` keyword to declare a procedure, function, or user-defined type?**

A There is absolutely no difference in the scope of a procedure, function, or user-defined type declared with or without the **Public** keyword. You use the **Public** keyword to reinforce the distinction between any public procedures and functions and any procedures or functions declared with the **Private** keyword in the same module.

Q **When I use procedure arguments, do I have to send information, or only return information?**

A Although the two examples of procedures with argument lists in this chapter show one procedure whose arguments are only used to supply information and another procedure whose arguments are only used to return values, you don't have to restrict yourself to doing only one or the other. For example, you could easily modify the `FirstNonBlankCell` procedure in Listing 12.5 so that it receives the name of the worksheet to test as one of its arguments. The procedure then might have the following declaration:

```
FirstNonBlankCell(ByVal SheetName As String, _
                  ByRef nRow As Long, _
                  ByRef nCol As Long)
```

The `SheetName` argument supplies information to the procedure (the name of the worksheet to test) and the other two arguments return values, as before. One thing you should *not* do, however, is use the same argument to *both* send information and then to return information—making an argument perform double-duty like that is kind of sneaky, which is why it might seem tempting, but it is also quite confusing and can lead to obscure problems with your programs.

Workshop

Answers are in Appendix A.

Quiz

1. How does VBA search for a particular procedure?

2. Do you use the Object Browser or Macro dialog to see a list of available functions?

3. How do you create a library project?

4. What are two ways to make the procedures in a library project available in the Macro dialog?

5. How do you make the procedures and functions in a library project available for use in the VBA code in another project?

6. What `Application` object property returns the name of Excel's startup folder? Can you change the name of the startup folder with this property?

7. What `Application` object property returns the name of Excel's alternate startup folder? Can you change the name of the alternate startup folder with this property?

8. How do you create a reference to another project?

9. What is *private scope*? *Public scope*?

10. What is the effect of the **Option Private Module** statement?

11. What is the effect of using the **Private** keyword? The **Public** keyword?

12. Can you use the **Public** and **Private** keywords to change the scope of a local variable?

13. What are the two main reasons you should create an argument list for a procedure?

14. Does the Macro dialog list procedures that have arguments? What about the Object Browser?

15. If you want to use a procedure's argument to return a value, would you pass that argument by reference or by value?

Exercises

1. The following listing represents an entire module. Add the **Public** or **Private** keywords to each of the declarations in the module so that every item that normally has private scope has public scope, and every item that normally has public scope has private scope. Then, add the necessary statements so that none of the items in this module can be used in any project except the one that contains this module.

12

(For simplicity, the actual code in the function procedures and bodies in this listing has been omitted.)

```
 1:        Option Explicit
 2:
 3:        Type InvoiceHeader
 4:             CustomerName As String
 5:             CustomerNumber As Integer
 6:             InvoiceNumber As Long
 7:             InvoiceDate As Date
 8:        End Type
 9:
10:        Dim Spinning As Boolean
11:        Dim CurrentInvoice As Long
12:        Dim InvoiceList() As InvoiceHeader
13:
14:
15:        Sub FetchInvoice()
16:            ' procedure body
17:        End Sub
18:
19:
20:        Sub ShutDown()
21:            ' procedure body
22:        End Sub
23:
24:
25:        Sub LocateInvoiceBody()
26:            ' procedure body
27:        End Sub
28:
29:
30:        Sub DisplayLineItems()
31:            ' procedure body
32:        End Sub
33:
34:        Function InvoiceTotal() As Currency
35:            ' procedure body
36:        End Function
```

2. Write a top-down design for a program to balance your checkbook. Your design should incorporate these features:

- The program should start by requiring you to enter the starting balance for your checking account.

- The program should enable you to enter transactions until there is no more data to enter. Enter credits (deposits) as positive numbers and debits (checks or withdrawals) as negative numbers.

- When receiving the amount of a transaction, your program should check to make sure that the entry is numeric and display appropriate error messages.
- After entering each transaction, the program should display the amount of the transaction, whether the transaction is a credit or debit, and the new balance. If the balance of the account drops below $100, the program should display a warning message.

3. Write the VBA program from the design you created in Exercise 2.

12

DAY 13

Managing Files with Visual Basic for Applications

At some point, you'll probably want your procedures to be able to copy or delete a workbook or other file. You'll also probably want to rename a file or find a particular file on the disk. Visual Basic for Applications provides you with a variety of statements, functions, and methods to carry out common file management tasks. Today, you learn

- How to understand file attributes and how to retrieve information about a file's attributes or change a file's attributes.
- How to get information about a file, such as the file's length or the date and time that the file was last changed.
- How to create or remove disk folders (directories).
- How to copy, move, rename, or delete disk files.

- How to find out what the current folder and disk drive is and how to change the current drive and folder.

- How to search a disk folder for all files that match a particular file specification (such as `*.XLS`).

- How to make your Excel VBA procedures display the same File Open and File Save As dialogs that Excel itself uses to select or enter filenames interactively.

Understanding File Management

This section first describes what file management is and discusses some of the typical activities you might perform as part of your file management tasks. This section then gives you an overview of Visual Basic for Applications' file management functions, statements, and methods.

What Is File Management?

File management is the term used to describe the actions you perform with files stored on your disk drives. File management includes actions such as copying files to make a backup, deleting unused files to make more disk space available, moving files from one disk or folder to another, and creating or deleting disk directories. File management also includes activities such as viewing a list of files in a folder to find out the size of a file or the date and time that the file was last modified.

> **Note**
>
> The Windows Desktop and help system uses the term *folder* to refer to what experienced Windows or DOS users know as *directories*. This book uses the term *folder* for consistency with current terminology; in some cases, this book will also use the term *directory*.

You probably perform file management tasks every day, although you might not use that term to describe what you do. Any time you use the Windows Desktop, Explorer, or DOS commands to copy, delete, or rename files, get a listing of files currently stored in a folder, or create or remove a disk subfolder, you are performing file management tasks. VBA enables you to perform the most common file management tasks under the control of a procedure or function that you write.

Reviewing Visual Basic for Applications' File Management Capabilities

Table 13.1 summarizes VBA's file management functions, statements, and methods. The first column in the table shows the VBA keyword and the second column in the table indicates whether the keyword is for a function, statement, or object method. Finally, the third column of Table 13.1 contains a brief description of the purpose of each function, statement, or method.

TABLE 13.1 FILE MANAGEMENT FUNCTIONS, METHODS, AND STATEMENTS

Name	Category	Purpose
ChDir	Statement	Changes the current directory (folder).
ChDrive	Statement	Changes the current disk drive.
CurDir	Function	Returns the current directory (folder) path as a string.
Dir	Function	Returns the name of a directory or file that matches a particular filename (including wildcards) passed as a string argument. Use to find one or more files on a disk.
FileCopy	Statement	Copies a file.
FileDateTime	Function	Returns a **Date** type value containing the date and time the file was last changed.
FileLen	Function	Returns the length of a file, in bytes.
GetAttr	Function	Returns a number representing the combined attributes of a file or disk directory, such as System, Hidden, and so on.
GetOpenFileName	Method	Displays Excel's Open File dialog and returns the filename selected by the user. Not available in Word.
GetSaveAsFileName	Method	Displays Excel's Save As dialog and returns the filename selected by the user. Not available in Word.
Kill	Statement	Deletes files from the disk drive.
MkDir	Statement	Creates a disk directory (folder).
Name	Statement	Renames or moves a file.
RmDir	Statement	Deletes a disk directory (folder).
SetAttr	Statement	Sets a file's attributes.

13

You might notice that Table 13.1 does not list any of the arguments for any of the items in the table. Several of these functions, statements, and methods have fairly complex argument lists and options. Beginning with the next section of this chapter, each VBA file management function, statement, or method in Table 13.1 is described in full, with all of its arguments and options.

The file management statements, functions, and object methods that VBA provides divide roughly into six different areas of functionality:

- Getting or changing a file's attributes.
- Retrieving or locating filenames.
- Getting or changing the current disk drive and folder or creating or removing disk folders.
- Copying and deleting files.
- Renaming or moving files.
- Getting information about files, such as the file length and the date and time the file was last modified.

Subsequent sections in this chapter each describe one of these areas of functionality and describe all the VBA statements that relate to that type of file management activity.

Working with File Attributes

Before proceeding with a detailed discussion of VBA's file management functions, statements, and object methods, you should understand what file attributes are and what they mean. This section starts out by explaining file attributes, and then describes the VBA function to retrieve a file's attribute information and the VBA statement for changing a file's attributes.

Understanding File Attributes

Every file stored on any Windows 95/98 (or earlier DOS version) disk has *attributes*, regardless of the specific type of disk drive (hard disk, floppy disk, RAM drive, ZIP drive, Syquest drive, and so on). Windows and DOS use a file's attributes to determine what file management activities are permitted for that file. For example, Windows (or DOS) prohibits you—and any application programs—from deleting, modifying, or renaming files that have a read-only attribute.

Windows creates a file's attribute information when you, or an application program running on your computer, create the file. In a sense, a file's attributes are like object properties: A file's attributes give the file certain characteristics depending on the specific attributes that it has. File attributes are part of the file information that Windows stores on your disk drive. Windows stores the file attribute information for a particular file along with the file's name, size, and date and time information.

Windows automatically updates and maintains a file's attribute information for you. Most of the time, you'll never be aware of a file's attributes, and usually there is no reason for you to need to know what a file's attributes are. In some cases, though, being able to understand and use a file's attributes is very important. In particular, you need to understand file attributes and their meanings to get the full benefit from VBA's Dir function.

Windows (and DOS) uses a total of seven different file attributes to specify different characteristics for a file. Each of the separate file attributes can be combined with other attributes, except the Volume Label attribute. For example, a file could have the Hidden, System, Directory, Archive, and Read-Only file attributes all at once. The following list gives the name of each file attribute and describes its meaning.

- *Archive.* The Archive attribute indicates whether a file has changed since the last time you backed it up with a backup program such as Windows' BACKUP or a third-party backup program such as Fastback!, BackIt, Norton Backup, or others.

  If a file has the Archive attribute, it means that the file needs to be backed up. If a file does *not* have the Archive attribute, the file has *not* changed since the last time it was backed up.

- *Directory.* If a file has the Directory attribute, it means that the file is actually a disk directory or subdirectory (a *folder* in Windows terminology). A disk directory is really a file that contains information about other files; when you create a directory, Windows creates the special directory file and gives it the Directory attribute. The Directory attribute lets Windows know that this file contains information about other files and prevents the directory from being renamed, copied, or deleted like a regular data file.

- *Hidden.* If a file has the Hidden attribute, Windows "hides" the file by omitting it from most directory displays—although Windows does have a viewing option that displays the names of hidden files.

- *Normal.* The Normal file attribute is really the absence of any special file attributes. A so-called Normal (also sometimes called *general*) file attribute just means that the file does not have any of the other file attributes, except possibly the Archive attribute to indicate whether the file needs to be backed up.

- *Read-Only.* The Read-Only attribute means that you can read from the file but you cannot change the file. Windows prohibits you from changing, deleting, or renaming a file that has the Read-Only attribute.

13

- *System.* The System attribute tells Windows that the file is part of your computer's operating system. Like Read-Only files, Windows prohibits you from changing a file that has the System attribute. Also, if you create a startup disk with the DOS SYS command (or with the Windows Control Panel), any files that have the System attribute are transferred to the new startup disk.

- *Volume Label.* The Volume Label informs Windows that this file is a disk's volume label. (A *volume label* is the name you give to a hard disk or floppy disk when you format the disk, use the DOS LABEL command, or change the Label property on the disk's properties sheet.) Volume Labels aren't really a complete file, they are just filename entries in the disk's root directory with the Volume Label file attribute. A disk can have only one volume label at a time.

DON'T

DON'T confuse opening an Excel workbook in read-only mode with the Read-Only file attribute. Excel's read-only mode for workbooks affects whether Excel permits you to alter the file. The Read-Only file attribute is maintained at the operating-system level of your computer's operation. A file with the Read-Only attribute cannot be changed or modified by any application, nor can it be deleted. If you open a workbook in Excel that has the Read-Only attribute set, Excel opens the workbook in read-only mode and prohibits you from making changes to the Read-Only workbook.

Windows represents each different file attribute with a unique code number and stores the number with the file's name and size information. If a file has more than one attribute, Windows adds the code numbers for each attribute together and stores their sum. The next section describes how you can retrieve and interpret the code number for a file's attributes.

Table 13.2 lists all the file attribute codes that Windows uses and the intrinsic VBA constants for those attribute codes. As with all other numeric codes for which VBA defines a constant, you should use the VBA constant for the code number instead of the code number itself.

TABLE 13.2 VISUAL BASIC FOR APPLICATIONS' FILE ATTRIBUTE CONSTANTS

VBA Constant	Decimal Value	Binary Value	Meaning
vbNormal	0	00000000	Normal
vbReadOnly	1	00000001	Read-Only

vbHidden	2	00000010	Hidden
vbSystem	4	00000100	System
vbVolume	8	00001000	Volume Label
vbDirectory	16	00010000	Disk directory or subdirectory
vbArchive	32	00100000	Archive. If set, indicates that file has changed since the last backup.

Getting a File's Attributes

To find out what attributes a particular file has, use VBA's GetAttr function.

The GetAttr function has the following general syntax:

GetAttr(*pathname*)

pathname is any VBA string expression that represents a valid filename. *pathname* can include the drive letter and full folder path; if you don't include the drive letter, GetAttr searches for the specified file in the current disk drive; if you don't include the folder path, GetAttr searches in the current folder.

▲ GetAttr returns a number that contains the sum of all the numeric codes for a file's attributes.

Listing 13.1 shows an example that uses the GetAttr function and also demonstrates how to interpret the function's result.

INPUT **LISTING 13.1** USING THE GetAttr FUNCTION AND INTERPRETING ITS RESULT

```
 1:  Sub ShowFileAttr(fName As String)
 2:  'displays a message box showing the file
 3:  'attributes of the filename in the fName argument.
 4:
 5:    Dim fAttr As Integer
 6:    Dim mStr As String
 7:
 8:    fAttr = GetAttr(fName)
 9:    mStr = UCase(fName)
10:    mStr = mStr & " has these attributes: " & vbCr
11:    If (fAttr And vbReadOnly) Then _
12:               mStr = mStr & "Read-Only" & vbCr
13:    If (fAttr And vbHidden) Then _
14:               mStr = mStr & "Hidden" & vbCr
```

continues

13

LISTING 13.1   CONTINUED

```
15:     If (fAttr And vbSystem) Then _
16:                 mStr = mStr & "System" & vbCr
17:     If (fAttr And vbVolume) Then _
18:                 mStr = mStr & "Volume" & vbCr
19:     If (fAttr And vbDirectory) Then _
20:                 mStr = mStr & "Directory" & vbCr
21:     If (fAttr And vbArchive) Then _
22:                 mStr = mStr & "Archive" & vbCr
23:     MsgBox mStr
24: End Sub
25:
26: Sub ListFileAttr()
27:
28:     Dim strPath As String
29:
30:     ShowFileAttr fName:="c:\io.sys"
31:     ShowFileAttr fName:="c:\msdos.sys"
32:
33:     strPath = Application.StartupPath
34:     ShowFileAttr fName:=strPath
35:
36:     strPath = strPath & "\Personal.xls"
37:     ShowFileAttr fName:=strPath
38: End Sub
```

ANALYSIS   Listing 13.1 contains two different procedures. The first procedure, ShowFileAttr, occupies lines 1 through 24, and the second procedure, ListFileAttr, occupies lines 26 through 38. ListFileAttr simply calls ShowFileAttr several times, passing a different filename each time.

Line 1 contains the procedure declaration for ShowFileAttr; this procedure has a single, required argument named fName with a **String** data type. Line 5 declares an **Integer** type variable, fAttr, to store the value returned by the GetAttr function. Line 6 declares a **String** type variable, mStr, to store the message that this procedure assembles.

When VBA executes the statement in line 8, it calls GetAttr, passing whatever string is in the fName argument variable as the argument for GetAttr and storing the function result in the fAttr variable. If the string in fName does not contain a valid filename, VBA displays a runtime error with the message "path not found."

Lines 9 and 10 put together the first part of the message that this procedure displays. Line 9 uses the UCase function to convert the filename in fName to uppercase, just for cosmetic reasons.

Lines 11 through 22 contain a series of **If...Then** statements that evaluate the number stored in **fAttr**, which contains the sum of all the code numbers for the file's attributes. Notice that these **If...Then** statements are *not* nested. Instead, the value in **fAttr** is tested six different times, once for each possible attribute value. Remember, the attribute value that Windows stores with the file is the sum of all the code numbers for each of the file attributes that the file has. If the file attribute that a particular **If...Then** statement tests for is present, a string containing the appropriate attribute name gets added to the message string stored in **mStr**.

BIT-WISE COMPARISONS

It might not seem clear to you how the logical expressions in lines 11 through 22 in Listing 13.1 work. These expressions work because, when you use a logical operator (**And**, **Or**, **Xor**, **Not**, and so on) with numeric values, VBA operates on the individual *bits* that make up the numbers.

Look again at Table 13.2 and notice that the actual values of the attribute code numbers are not sequential. Look closely at the Binary Value column and notice that each file attribute number forms a unique pattern of ones and zeros. Each file attribute number is an even power of two, so that when you write the number using binary digits, as shown in Table 13.2, the file attribute code number is either just 1 or a 1 with only zeroes after it.

When VBA makes a bit-wise comparison, it compares the binary digits in each number. Depending on the specific logical operator, VBA performs an **And**, **Or**, **Xor**, **Not**, or **Imp** comparison on each pair of bits from the two numbers it is comparing. If the result of the comparison is **True**, VBA places a 1 in the corresponding digit for its answer; it places a 0 if the comparison is **False**. Because an **And** logical operation is **True** whenever both of its arguments are **True**, the result of the expression 1 **And** 1 is **True**.

The expressions in Listing 13.1 work by performing a logical **And** on the **fAttr** variable's contents and one of the VBA file attribute constants, thus making a bit-wise comparison between the two numbers. If the file has the Hidden and Read-Only attributes, for example, the value in **fAttr** is 3 (the sum of 1+2; refer to Table 13.2). Written in binary notation, the number 3 is 11. The binary value for the Read-Only attribute is 01 and the binary value for the Hidden attribute is 10. The result of the expression 11 **And** 01 is **True**, indicating that the Read-Only attribute is present.

13

The **MsgBox** statement in line 23 displays the message string that the previous statements assembled, and line 24 is the end of the **ShowFileAttr** procedure.

Line 26 contains the declaration for the **ListFileAttr** procedure, which simply calls the **ShowFileAttr** procedure several times, passing it different filenames. Line 30 causes **ShowFileAttr** to display the file attributes for the IO.SYS file. This file is part of the

Windows operating system and is always located in the root directory of your startup disk. Because the IO.SYS file is part of the Windows operating system, it has the System file attribute; in addition, it has a Read-Only attribute to prevent you from accidentally deleting this important file, and it also has the Hidden attribute so that it does not usually appear in Windows' desktop file windows or in the Explorer's directory listings. When VBA executes line 30, it displays the dialog shown in Figure 13.1.

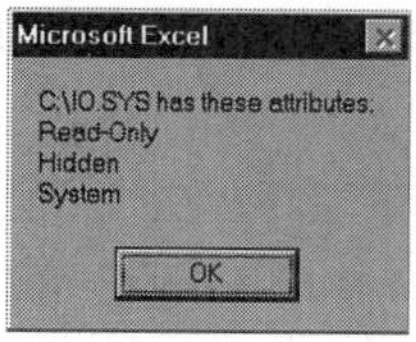

FIGURE 13.1

The ShowFileAttr *procedure displays this dialog for the IO.SYS system file on your Windows startup disk.*

```
Microsoft Excel                    ⊠
   C:\IO.SYS has these attributes.
   Read-Only
   Hidden
   System

        [      OK      ]
```

The ShowFileAttr procedure displays a similar dialog for the C:\MSDOS.SYS file. Notice that line 29 specifies a folder name (the Excel startup folder) rather than an actual filename. When this line executes, a dialog stating that it has the Directory attribute appears. (Remember, *folder* and *directory* are the same thing.) The final dialog, depending on whether you have recently backed up the Personal.xls file, either displays the Archive attribute or no attributes.

Note

There is no test in the ShowFileAttr procedure for the Normal file attribute because the Normal file attribute is merely the absence of any other file attributes.

Do

DO declare all variables that you use to store file attribute codes as Integer type variables. A file attribute code number will never exceed the permissible range of an Integer.

DON'T

DON'T forget that file attribute codes are always handled as a single number containing the sum of all the individual code numbers for the file's attributes.

Changing a File's Attributes

Occasionally, you might want to change a file's attributes. For example, you might want to change a template workbook's file attributes to include the Read-Only attribute to make sure that you can't accidentally delete that workbook template.

You can use the SetAttr statement to change a file's attributes. SetAttr fulfills the same purpose as the File, Properties command (available on any Windows folder-viewing window or by right-clicking a file's icon) or the DOS ATTRIB command.

The SetAttr statement has the following general syntax:

SYNTAX

SetAttr pathname, attributes

pathname represents any string expression containing a valid Windows file specification (a filename and, optionally, the full folder path and a drive letter). attributes represents a numeric expression. The numeric expression for attributes must be a number between 1 and 255, and must consist of one of the file attribute code numbers or a sum of file attribute code numbers.

Listing 13.2 shows an example of how you might use the SetAttr statement.

INPUT **LISTING 13.2**   USING THE SetAttr STATEMENT TO CHANGE A FILE'S ATTRIBUTES

```
 1:    Sub DelProtectFile(fName As String)
 2:    'sets Read-only attribute for file named in fName
 3:
 4:       Dim fAttr As Integer
 5:
 6:       fAttr = GetAttr(fName)
 7:
 8:           'don't set the attribute if it's already set
 9:       If Not CBool((fAttr And vbReadOnly)) Then
10:         SetAttr fName, fAttr + vbReadOnly
11:       End If
12:
13:       MsgBox prompt:="Read-only file attribute for " & _
14:                     fName & " set.", _
15:             Title:="Delete Protection"
16:    End Sub
17:
18:
19:    Sub Test_DelProtectFile()
20:       Dim iName As String
21:
22:       iName = Application.GetOpenFilename
23:       DelProtectFile iName
24:       ShowFileAttr iName
25:    End Sub
```

13

ANALYSIS The DelProtectFile procedure protects files from accidental deletion or alteration by giving the file the Read-Only file attribute without affecting the file's other attributes. DelProtectFile has a single required **String** type argument named fName, which is used to pass a filename to the procedure. Line 4 declares the fAttr variable; the procedure uses this variable to store a number for the file's attributes.

Line 6 uses GetAttr to retrieve the file attributes from the file specified by fName. Lines 9 through 11 contain an **If** statement that executes the SetAttr statement only if the file does not already have the Read-Only attribute. Line 10 contains the actual call to SetAttr. Notice that the old file attributes are arithmetically added to the vbReadOnly constant to specify the file's new attributes. This way, the file's original attributes are preserved.

Finally, lines 13 through 15 contain a MsgBox statement that displays a message notifying the user that the file has the Read-Only attribute set.

The Test_DelProtectFile procedure simply exercises the DelProtectFile procedure. Line 22 uses Excel's GetOpenFileName method (described in the next section) to get a filename from you. Line 23 then calls the DelProtectFile procedure to set the file's attributes to include the Read-Only attribute. Finally, line 24 calls the ShowFileAttr procedure (shown in Listing 13.1) to display a message dialog verifying the file's new attributes.

Do

DO keep in mind that, when you set a file's attributes, the file then has *only* the attributes you set. To add to a file's attributes without changing its existing attributes, you must retrieve its current attributes first, add the new attribute, and then set the file attributes.

DON'T

DON'T try to give a file the Directory (vbDirectory) or Volume Label (vbVolume) attributes with SetAttr, or VBA displays a runtime error.

DON'T add file attribute codes to an existing file attribute code number without ensuring that the attribute code does *not* already contain the attribute code you want to add. Otherwise, you might end up giving the file an attribute other than the ones you expected.

Tip

Use the **Or** operator to add a new file attribute to an existing set of file attributes. Using the **Or** operator to combine file attributes in a bit-wise operation avoids any possible problems that might occur when using arithmetic addition to combine new attributes with existing attributes. The result of the expression 0 **Or** 1 is 1; the result of the expression 1 **Or** 1 is also 1. Because of this, you can combine a new file attribute with an existing file attribute number by using an expression similar to OldAttr **Or** vbArchive. If the Archive attribute is not set in OldAttr, it will be set as a result of the **Or** operation. If the Archive attribute is already set, it will remain unchanged.

Getting or Finding Filenames

This section first shows you how to use VBA's Dir function to search a disk folder for one or more files that match a particular filename. Next you learn how to use VBA to include Excel's own File Open and File Save As dialogs in your procedures. You can use Excel's built-in File Open and File Save As dialogs to enable your procedure's user to easily and accurately supply filenames to your procedures.

Using the Dir Function to Find Files

Occasionally, you might need to search a disk directory to see whether it contains one or more files that match a particular filename specification, such as \My Documents*.xls. To search a disk directory, use VBA's Dir function. The Dir function fulfills for VBA the same purposes as the file list in a Windows folder window or the DOS DIR command: It gives you an opportunity to see what files are stored in a particular folder and to see what other folders are present.

The Dir function has the following general syntax:

▼ SYNTAX

```
Dir(pathname[, attributes])
```

pathname represents any **String** expression that results in a valid filename. The filename can contain a drive letter and the full folder path. The filename can also include wildcard file characters. The optional *attributes* argument is a number representing the attributes of the files you want to search for. If you include the *attributes* argument, Dir searches for files that have those attributes. If you omit the *attributes* argument, Dir searches for normal files, that is, any file except those with Hidden, Volume Label, Directory, or System file attributes.

▼ When you call the Dir function with the *pathname* argument, it returns a string containing the name of the first file it finds that matches the filename in the *pathname* argument.

13

▼ If your filename contains wildcards (* or ?), to find *all* the files in a directory that match your filename you must use the Dir function in two stages. First, you call Dir with the *pathname* argument to get the *first* matching file, and then you call Dir repeatedly *without* arguments until Dir returns an empty string. As soon as Dir returns an empty string, there are no more files that match your filename. If you call Dir again without specifying

▲ a filename, VBA generates a runtime error.

Listing 13.3 shows an example of Dir used to locate only one file.

INPUT   LISTING 13.3   FINDING A SINGLE FILE USING Dir

```
 1:    Function IsDiskFile(fName As String) As Boolean
 2:    'return True if fName is found on disk, False otherwise
 3:
 4:      If (Dir(fName) <> "") Then
 5:        IsDiskFile = True
 6:      Else
 7:        IsDiskFile = False
 8:      End If
 9:    End Function
10:
11:
12:    Sub Test_IsDiskFile()
13:      Dim iName As String
14:
15:      iName = InputBox(prompt:="Enter a filename:", _
16:                       Title:="Testing IsDiskFile")
17:      MsgBox iName & " exists: " & IsDiskFile(iName)
18:    End Sub
```

ANALYSIS   Lines 1 through 9 contain the IsDiskFile function, which has a single required **String** type argument, fName. IsDiskFile returns a **Boolean** result: **True** if the filename in fName exists on the disk drive, **False** if it does not.

The operation of the IsDiskFile function is quite simple. Line 4 contains an **If...Then...Else** statement that—as part of its logical expression—calls the Dir function, passing the contents of fName as the filename to search for. No argument for attributes is specified in this call to Dir, so it will find any file *except* ones that have Hidden, System, Directory, or Volume Label attributes.

Because the purpose of the IsDiskFile function is merely to determine whether a particular file does or does not exist, the return result of the Dir function is not used except to compare it to an empty string. If the `Dir` function result is *not* an empty string, `Dir` finds the specified file and VBA executes line 5, which assigns the function result **True**. If the `Dir` function result is an empty string, no matching file was found and VBA executes line 7, which assigns **False** to the function result.

Lines 12 through 18 declare a procedure to test the `IsDiskFile` function. This test procedure uses the `InputBox` function to get a filename from the user and then calls the `IsDiskFile` function as part of a `MsgBox` statement, which displays a message stating whether the filename entered by the user exists.

Notice that if you call the `IsDiskFile` function with a filename that includes single (?) or multiple (*) wildcard characters, the function returns **True** if there is at least one file that matches the wildcard specification. (Refer to your Windows online help for complete information on wildcard characters in filenames.)

> **Note**
>
> When searching for filenames, you can use one of two wildcard characters: a question mark (?) or an asterisk (*). These wildcard characters fulfill a purpose similar to the one you learned for the regular expression search characters of the **Like** operator in Day 4. The question mark (?) represents any single character in a filename and the asterisk (*) represents any number of any characters in a filename. Consider the following two examples:
>
> ```
> Book?.xls
> Book*.xls
> ```
>
> The first example will produce a match for any file named "Book" followed by any single character and having the .xls extension, such as Book1.xls, Book2.xls, Booky.xls, and so on. The second example will produce a match for any file named "Book" followed by any number of characters and having the .xls extension, such as BookEnd.xls, BookList.xls, Book Schedule.xls, and so on.

You can also use the `Dir` function to find all the files in a folder that match a particular filename. This feature of the `Dir` function is most useful when your filename contains wildcard characters. You might use the `Dir` function this way if you want to find all the template files in a particular folder.

Listing 13.4 shows an example of how you use the `Dir` function to locate more than one file.

13

LISTING 13.4 FINDING SEVERAL FILES USING Dir

```
 1:  Sub ShowFiles()
 2:  'displays the names and attributes of all files in
 3:  'the specified directory
 4:
 5:     Dim sAttr As Integer
 6:     Dim fName As String
 7:     Dim pName As String
 8:     Dim fCount As Integer
 9:
10:     pName = InputBox("enter a directory to search in:")
11:     If Trim(pName) = "" Then Exit Sub
12:     If Right(pName, 1) <> "\" Then pName = pName & "\"
13:
14:     sAttr = vbDirectory + vbArchive + vbReadOnly + _
15:             vbHidden + vbSystem
16:
17:       'get the first file name and attributes
18:     fName = Dir(pName & "*.*", sAttr)
19:     If (fName <> "") And _
20:         ((fName <> ".") And (fName <> "..")) Then
21:       ShowFileAttr pName & fName
22:       fCount = 1
23:     End If
24:
25:     Do While (fName <> "")
26:       fName = Dir()
27:       If (fName <> "") And _
28:         ((fName <> ".") And (fName <> "..")) Then
29:         ShowFileAttr pName & fName
30:         fCount = fCount + 1
31:       End If
32:     Loop
33:
34:     MsgBox fCount & " files found."
35:  End Sub
```

The ShowFiles procedure asks the user to enter a folder (directory) name and then uses the Dir function to find all the files in that directory. Lines 5 through 8 declare several variables. The sAttr variable is used to hold a file attribute number, fName is used to temporarily store the names of the files returned by Dir, and pName is used to store the name of the directory path that this procedure searches. The fCount variable is used to hold a count of all the files found.

Line 10 calls the InputBox function to get a directory name from the user. Line 11 checks to make sure that the user did not cancel the dialog; if the dialog is canceled, the procedure simply ends. Line 12 checks to make sure that the directory path the user entered ends with the path separator character (\) and adds it to the end of the directory path stored in pName, if it is missing.

Line 14 sets up the sAttr variable to contain the attributes for the files that Dir will search for. Notice that sAttr is set up to contain all the possible file attributes except the Volume Label attribute.

Line 18 makes the first call to the Dir function, using the directory path in pName, and adds to it the file specification *.* (which will find all files), and also passes sAttr to specify which file attributes to search for. By specifying all the file attributes (except Volume Label), Dir will find any file in the specified directory, including any subdirectories in that directory. The Dir function result is assigned to fName.

Lines 19 through 23 contain an **If...Then** statement that evaluates the string returned by Dir and stored in fName. Notice that the logical expression for this **If** statement is actually split over two lines: 19 and 20. The first part of the expression tests to see whether fName is empty. The second part of the expression (line 20) checks to make sure that fName does not contain either a string consisting of a single period (.) or a string consisting of two periods (..). These special strings are used by the Windows file system to indicate the current directory (.) and the parent directory of the current directory (..). Although these special filenames are technically directories, and the Dir function will report their existence with the kind of attribute and wildcard specification used in this example, they don't actually exist on the disk, and any attempt to get their file attributes with GetAttr results in a runtime error.

If fName is not empty and does not contain the special directory entries (. or ..), VBA executes line 21, which calls the ShowFileAttr procedure from Listing 13.1 to display a message box showing the filename and its actual attributes. VBA then executes line 22, which starts the count of found files by assigning 1 to fCount.

Now that the first matching file has been found, you must use the second-stage format of the Dir function to find the remaining files in the directory. Lines 25 through 32 contain a **Do** loop that executes for as long as fName does not contain an empty string. If at least one matching file was found in the Dir function call in line 18, this loop will execute at least once.

Pay special attention to line 26. This statement calls the Dir function again without any arguments. When you call Dir like this, VBA assumes that you want to find more files matching the specification for the pathname and attributes arguments you used the last time you called Dir. The Dir function returns the next file in the directory that matches the previous filename and attribute specifications. If there are no more files, Dir returns an empty string.

13

Lines 27 through 31 contain an `If...Then` statement identical to the one in lines 19 through 23. If the string in `fName` is not empty and does not contain the special directory entries (. and ..), VBA executes line 29 to call the `ShowFileAttr` procedure and line 30 to increment the count of found files.

When all the matching files in the directory have been found, `Dir` returns an empty string and the loop stops executing. Line 34 displays a message dialog indicating how many matching files were found.

Do

DO remember that VBA in Excel (or any host application designed for Windows 95 or higher) recognizes and can use Windows long filenames.

Using Excel's Built-In Dialogs to Get Filenames

Excel's `Application` object has two methods—`GetOpenFilename` and `GetSaveAsFilename`—that you can use in your Excel VBA code to simplify the task of obtaining a filename from the user. The next two sections describe how to use these two methods in your procedures.

Using the `GetOpenFilename` Method

Many of the examples earlier in this book use the `InputBox` function to get filenames from a procedure's user. Although getting a filename with `InputBox` works okay, it doesn't have the advantages of using a file-oriented dialog such as Excel's File Open dialog box, which actually lets you see what files are on the disk and lets you look at file lists from different disk drives and directories.

You can use Excel's `GetOpenFilename` method in your Excel VBA code to display a dialog that both looks and behaves the same as the dialog that Excel displays when you choose the File, Open command. The `GetOpenFilename` method returns a string that contains the filename selected by the user, including the drive letter and complete folder path. If the user cancels the dialog, `GetOpenFilename` returns the **Boolean** value **False** as its result.

The Excel `GetOpenFilename` method has this general syntax:

object.GetOpenFilename(*fileFilter*, *filterIndex*, *title*, *multiSelect*)

object must be a reference to the Excel `Application` object. Although the *object* reference to the Excel `Application` object is required, all the `GetOpenFilename` arguments are optional. *fileFilter* represents any valid **String** expression, specially formatted to

▼ specify the file filters listed in the Files of Type drop-down list box in the File Open dialog. If you omit the *fileFilter* argument, the file filter for the Files of Type drop-down list is All Files (*.*).

filterIndex represents any numeric expression and indicates which file filter VBA should use as the default for the Files of Type drop-down list. If you omit this argument or specify a number greater than the actual number of file filters, the first file filter becomes the default. *title* represents any **String** expression and is the title VBA displays in the File Open dialog. If you omit *title*, VBA displays the dialog with the usual *Open* title.

Finally, *multiSelect* represents any **Boolean** expression or value. If *multiSelect* is **True**, the File Open dialog enables the user to select multiple file names. When *multiSelect* is **True**, GetOpenFilename returns an array containing the names of all the selected files; you'll learn about arrays in tomorrow's lesson (Day 14).

To specify the file filter string, format a string as follows:

```
"FilterName1,filespec1,FilterName2,filespec2,FilterNameN,filespecN"
```

FilterName represents the text that you want VBA to display in the Files of Type drop-down list box. *filespec* represents the file specification that Windows 95/98 uses to restrict the files listed in the File Open dialog. You can list as many file filters as you want.

The following line shows a sample file filter string:

```
"XL 9 Templates (*.xlt),*.xlt,Workbooks (*.xls),*.xls"
```

The preceding filter string causes the two choices Xl 9 Templates (*.xlt) and Workbooks (*.xls) to appear in the Files of Type drop-down list box. When you select Xl 9 Templates (*.xlt) in the Files of Type list box, the file specification *.xlt appears in the Name text box and the file list contains only files that match the *.xlt file
▲ specification.

Listing 13.5 shows an example that uses the GetOpenFilename method.

| INPUT | **LISTING 13.5** USING GetOpenFilename TO GET A FILENAME FROM YOUR PROCEDURE'S USER |

```
1:  Sub Open2DataEntry()
2:  'opens a specified workbook to the Sales Report
3:  'worksheet.
4:
5:     Const iTitle = "Data Entry Setup"
```

continues

LISTING 13.5 CONTINUED

```
 6:     Const ShtName = "Data Entry"
 7:
 8:     Const FilterList = _
 9:     "Templates (*.xlt),*.xlt,Workbooks (*.xls),*.xls"
10:
11:     Dim fName As String
12:
13:     With Application
14:     fName = .GetOpenFilename(Title:=iTitle, _
15:                             filefilter:=FilterList, _
16:                             filterindex:=2)
17:     End With
18:     If fName = "False" Then
19:       MsgBox prompt:="Operation Canceled", _
20:             Title:=iTitle
21:       Exit Sub
22:     End If
23:
24:     Workbooks.Open Filename:=fName
25:     ActiveWorkbook.Sheets(ShtName).Select
26:     MsgBox prompt:="Workbook " & fName & _
27:                    " opened, " & ShtName & _
28:                    " selected.", _
29:             Title:=iTitle & " Complete"
30: End Sub
```

ANALYSIS The Open2DataEntry procedure opens a workbook selected by its user and then selects a worksheet named Data Entry in the open workbook. (This procedure assumes that any workbooks it opens will have a worksheet named Data Entry.) This procedure declares a couple of constants in lines 5 and 6. The iTitle constant is used to supply titles for dialogs that this procedure displays and ShtName supplies the name for the worksheet.

Lines 8 and 9 require a close look. Notice the line-continuation symbol at the end of line 8. These two lines together are a single constant declaration. The FilterList constant supplies the string for the file filters in the later call to the GetOpenFilename method.

Line 11 declares the fName variable to hold the filename obtained from the user. Lines 14 through 16 contain a single statement that calls the GetOpenFilename method and assigns its result to fName. Notice the dot separator in front of the GetOpenFilename method name, and notice that this statement is inside a **With** Application statement. Whenever you use the GetOpenFilename method, you must specify the Application object reference for the method.

When VBA executes this statement, it displays the dialog shown in Figure 13.2. Figure 13.2 shows the Files of Type list box open so that you can see the effect of the `fileFilter` argument. Notice that the dialog in the figure is identical to the Excel File Open dialog, except for the dialog's title and the contents of the Files of Type list box. Because the `filterIndex` argument (line 16) is set to 2, the `Workbooks (*.xls)` filter is the default filter rather than `Templates (*.xlt)`.

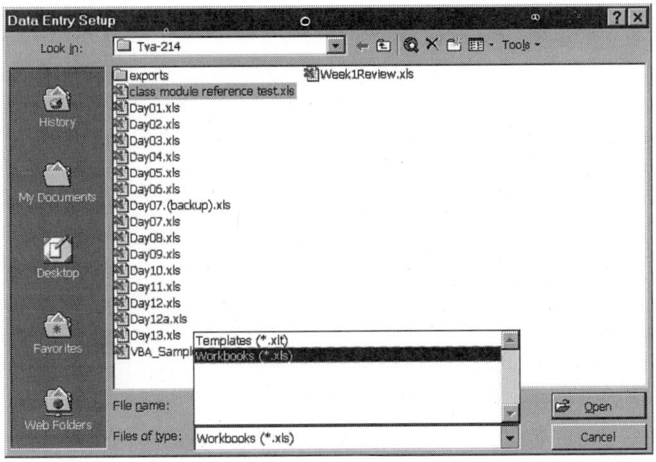

FIGURE 13.2

The OpenDataEntry *procedure uses the* GetOpenFilename *method to display this dialog. Notice the file filters in the Files of Type list.*

You select a name in the dialog just as you would in Excel's File Open dialog. When you choose Open, the `GetOpenFilename` method returns a string containing the filename, drive letter, and full folder path (the `multiSelect` argument wasn't used, so you can select only one filename). If you choose Cancel, `GetOpenFilename` returns the **Boolean** value **False**. Because, in this case, `fName` is a **String** variable, VBA automatically converts **False** to the string *False*.

Note

The `GetOpenFilename` method restricts the files listed in the Files of Type list box to ones that match the file types you specify with the `fileFilter` argument. For example, if you specify a file filter of `"Workbooks,*.xls"`, the `GetOpenFilename` dialog will display *only* workbook files. In the `Open2DataEntry` procedure in Listing 13.5, the user's choices are restricted to Excel template and workbook files only; the user is unable to select any other type of file in the dialog displayed by this procedure.

13

ANALYSIS Lines 18 through 22 contain an **If** statement that checks to see whether you canceled the GetOpenFilename dialog. If so, the MsgBox statement in lines 19 and 20 displays a message that the operation is canceled and VBA exits the procedure.

Line 24 opens the workbook you selected, and line 25 selects the Data Entry sheet. If you want to test this procedure, make sure the workbook you select has a worksheet named Data Entry in it or change the constant declaration in line 6 to match the name of a worksheet in one of your workbooks. Finally, lines 26 through 29 contain a MsgBox statement reporting a successful completion of the procedure's task.

Do

DO remember that GetOpenFilename returns a string when you select a filename and the **Boolean** value **False** when you cancel the dialog. If you assign the GetOpenFilename result to a **Variant** type variable, you'll need to test for **False** instead of the string *False*.

DO remember that GetOpenFilename returns an array of strings if you use a value of **True** for the optional multiSelect argument, even if the user only selects one file. Arrays are the topic of the lesson in Day 14.

DO remember that omitting the fileFilter argument causes the dialog displayed by GetOpenFilename to list files of all types.

DON'T

DON'T be confused if you see an additional argument, buttonText, listed for the GetOpenFilename method in the Object Browser or the online help. In Windows, GetOpenFilename ignores the buttonText argument; this argument is provided to maintain compatibility with Excel for the Macintosh.

DON'T forget that the file types from which the user can select are restricted by the fileFilter argument. To enable a user to select any type of file, you must include the *.* file type in the fileFilter argument.

Using the GetSaveAsFilename Method

You can also use Excel's GetSaveAsFilename method to display a dialog that looks and behaves the same as the dialog box that Excel displays when you choose the File, Save As command. The GetSaveAsFilename method also returns a string that contains the filename the user selects, including the drive letter and complete directory path. If the user cancels the dialog, GetSaveAsFilename returns the **Boolean** value **False**.

▼ SYNTAX

The `GetSaveAsFilename` method has this general syntax:

object`.GetSaveAsFilename(`*initialFilename*`, `*fileFilter*`, `*filterIndex*`, `*title*`)`

The `GetSaveAsFilename` method has almost exactly the same arguments and syntax as the `GetOpenFilename` method. *object* is a reference to the `Application` object, *fileFilter* is a **String** expression formatted to specify the file filters listed in the Save as Type drop-down list, *filterIndex* is a numeric expression indicating which file filter VBA should use as the default, and *title* is a **String** expression for the dialog's title bar. If you omit *title*, VBA displays the dialog with the usual *Save As* title.

The `GetSaveAsFilename` method has one more argument, *initialFilename*, which represents any valid filename. If you specify this optional argument, the filename you specify for *initialFilename* appears in the File Name text box when the Save As dialog first displays.

You specify file filter strings for `GetSaveAsFilename` the same way you format them for `GetOpenFilename`.

Listing 13.6 shows an example that uses the `GetSaveAsFilename` method.

INPUT

LISTING 13.6 USING `GetSaveAsFilename` TO GET A FILENAME FROM YOUR PROCEDURE'S USER

```
1:    Sub Convert2Template()
2:    'saves the current workbook as a template file.
3:
4:        Const FilterList = "Templates (*.xlt),*.xlt"
5:        Const iTitle = "Convert WorkBook to Template"
6:        Static sName As String
7:        Static TCount As Variant
8:        Dim iName As String
9:
10:       If IsEmpty(TCount) Then
11:          TCount = 1
12:       Else
13:          TCount = TCount + 1
14:       End If
15:
16:       sName = "Template" & CStr(TCount) & ".xlt"
17:       With Application
18:          iName = .GetSaveAsFilename(InitialFilename:=sName, _
19:                                     FileFilter:=FilterList, _
20:                                     Title:=iTitle)
21:       End With
22:
23:       If iName = "False" Then
24:          MsgBox prompt:="Conversion to Template Canceled.", _
```

13

continues

LISTING 13.6 CONTINUED

```
25:                Title:=iTitle
26:     Else
27:        ActiveWorkbook.SaveAs filename:=iName, _
28:                          FileFormat:=xlTemplate
29:     End If
30:  End Sub
```

ANALYSIS The Convert2Template procedure saves the current workbook as an Excel template file and uses the GetSaveAsFilename method to obtain the name for the new template file. Line 4 declares a constant for the file filter; line 5 declares a constant to supply the titles for the dialogs that this procedure displays.

Lines 6 and 7 declare some **Static** variables. sName is used to supply a suggested name for the new template file and TCount is used to number the default template names. Line 8 declares iName as a **String** type variable to hold the filename you select.

Lines 10 through 16 set up the template file counter and assemble the suggested template filename. Lines 18 through 20 contain a single statement that calls the GetSaveAsFilename method and assigns its result to iName. Notice the dot separator (.) in front of the GetSaveAsFilename method name, and notice also that this statement is inside a **With** Application statement. You must always specify the Application object (or a reference to it) when you call the GetSaveAsFilename method.

When VBA executes the statement in line 18, it displays the dialog shown in Figure 13.3. Notice that the dialog in the figure is exactly the same as Excel's Save As dialog, except for the dialog title and the contents of the Save as Type list.

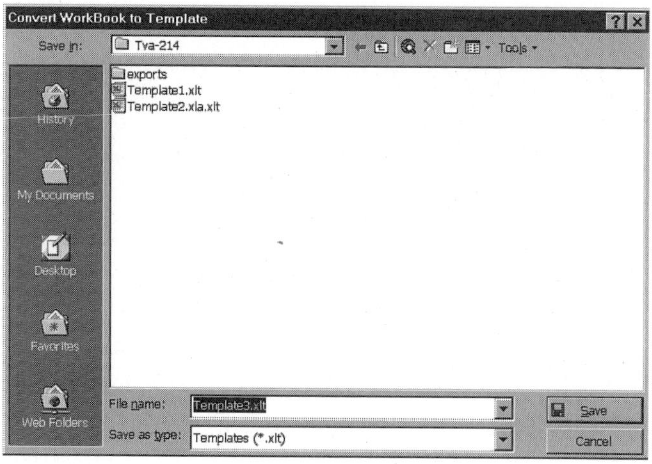

FIGURE 13.3

The Convert2Template *procedure uses the* GetSaveAsFilename *method to display this dialog.*

> **Note**
>
> The `fileFilter` argument for the `GetSaveAsFilename` method restricts not only the files listed in the dialog, but also ensures that the filename entered by the user ends up with the three-letter file type extension specified by the current choice in the Save as Type drop-down list.
>
> Unless the user types the correct three-letter file type extension as part of the file name she enters, the `GetSaveAsFilename` method *always* adds the three-letter extension for the file type specified in the Save as Type list.
>
> Look again at Figure 13.3 and notice the file named `Template2.xla.xlt`. This file was saved previously with the `Convert2Template` procedure. At that time, the user entered the filename `Template2.xla` in the File Name text box. Because Windows long filenames permit more than one period in a filename, and because the `.xla` file type extension did not match any of the file types specified in the `fileFilter` argument, the `GetSaveAsFilename` method added the `.xlt` file type extension (the current selection in the Save as Type list) to the filename before creating the file.
>
> You must include the `*.*` file type in the `fileFilter` argument to enable users to enter any file type extension.

Line 23 starts an **If...Then...Else** statement that evaluates whether the user canceled the `GetSaveAsFilename` dialog. If the user chose the Cancel button (or pressed Esc), the statement in line 24 executes, displaying a message dialog informing the user that the conversion to a template has been canceled. If the user didn't cancel the `GetSaveAsFilename` dialog, the statement in line 27 calls the `SaveAs` method, saving the active workbook as an Excel template file. (You'll learn more about the `SaveAs` method in Day 19, "Controlling Excel with VBA.")

Do

DO keep in mind that both `GetOpenFilename` and `GetSaveAsFilename` can change the current disk drive and folder. You might want to use the `CurDir` function to get the current drive and folder and store it in a variable so that you can switch back to the current disk drive and folder with `ChDrive` and `ChDir`. (These other functions and statements are described later in this chapter.)

DO use the `fileFilter` argument to ensure that your procedure's user can only enter filenames of particular types—that way you can ensure that your procedure only creates files with the specified types. For example, you might want to write all your Excel VBA procedures so that they are only capable of creating files with one of the file types known to Excel.

13

Working with Disk Drives and Folders

This section shows you how to use VBA's functions and statements to retrieve the current disk drive and folder, how to change the current drive or folder, and how to create or remove subfolders. Remember, the *current drive* is the drive that Excel uses when you don't otherwise indicate a specific drive letter. Similarly, the *current folder* is the disk folder Excel uses if you don't specify a particular folder.

Getting the Current Folder Path and Drive Letter

Retrieving the current disk drive and folder path is quite simple. You get both pieces of information by using the CurDir function. CurDir returns a string that contains the full pathname for the current folder, including the drive letter. (CurDir gets its name as an abbreviation of *current directory*; remember that a folder and a directory are the same thing.)

CurDir has this general syntax:

CurDir[(*drive*)]

drive represents any **String** expression and tells CurDir which disk drive's current folder you want. If you omit the *drive* argument, CurDir returns the current folder of the current disk drive. Usually, *drive* contains only a single letter; if you pass a string with more than one character in it, CurDir uses the first character in the string as the drive letter.

▲ Listing 13.7 shows an example of the CurDir function.

INPUT **LISTING 13.7** USING THE CurDir FUNCTION TO OBTAIN THE CURRENT DIRECTORY AND DRIVE

```
 1:   Sub ShowCurDriveDir()
 2:   'displays current drive and directory
 3:
 4:      Dim DirName As String
 5:      Dim DirLetter As String
 6:
 7:      DirName = CurDir()
 8:      DirLetter = Left(DirName, 1)
 9:      MsgBox "The current drive is: " & DirLetter
10:      MsgBox "The current directory is: " & DirName
11:
12:      DirName = CurDir("A")
13:      MsgBox "The current directory of drive A is: " & _
14:              DirName
15:   End Sub
```

ANALYSIS This procedure just demonstrates how the CurDir function works. Lines 4 and 5 declare some variables for the procedure. DirName holds the result from the CurDir function and DirLetter holds the drive letter extracted from the CurDir function's result.

Line 7 calls the CurDir function with no arguments so that it returns the current folder of the current disk drive and assigns its result to DirName. Line 8 uses the Left function to copy the first letter from DirName and assigns it to DirLetter. Because CurDir returns the entire folder path, including the drive letter, the first character of the CurDir function result is always the drive letter. Lines 9 and 10 each display a message dialog; the message displayed by line 9 states the current drive letter, and the message displayed by line 10 states the current folder of that drive.

Next, line 12 calls the CurDir function again, this time passing the single letter A as an argument. The argument tells CurDir to report the current folder of the disk in drive A:. (If you don't have a disk in your drive A: when you execute this procedure, you might get a runtime error.) Finally, line 13 displays a message dialog showing the current folder of drive A:.

Changing the Current Folder

If you want your VBA procedure to change the current folder to a different folder, use the ChDir statement. If you have experience using DOS, you'll recognize that VBA's ChDir fulfills the same purpose as the DOS CHDIR and CD commands. (The name ChDir is an abbreviation of *change directory*.)

SYNTAX

The ChDir statement has the following general syntax:

ChDir *path*

path represents any **String** expression that results in a valid folder pathname. *path* can optionally contain a drive letter. If you do include a drive letter in the *path* argument, ChDir changes the current folder of the drive specified in *path* without changing the current drive. (To change the current drive, use the ChDrive statement described next.)

▲ Listing 13.8 shows an example using the ChDir statement.

INPUT **LISTING 13.8** USING ChDir

```
1:  Sub Demo_ChDir()
2:  'demonstrates the ChDir statement
3:
4:    Dim oldDir As String
5:
```

13

continues

LISTING 13.8   CONTINUED

```
6:     MsgBox "Current directory: " & CurDir()
7:     oldDir = CurDir()
8:     ChDir "\my documents"
9:     MsgBox "New directory: " & CurDir()
10:    ChDir oldDir
11:    MsgBox "Current directory: " & CurDir()
12:  End Sub
```

ANALYSIS   This procedure demonstrates the operation of the ChDir statement. Line 4 declares a **String** variable, oldDir, to store the current folder before it is changed. Line 6 uses MsgBox to display the current folder, and line 7 stores the current folder (returned by CurDir) in the oldDir variable.

Line 8 uses the ChDir statement to change the current folder to the \My Documents folder. (This procedure assumes that the \My Documents folder is not the current folder and that it is on the same disk drive as the current folder; if you enter this procedure, you might want to choose your own folder name for this line.) Next, line 9 displays a message dialog displaying the new current folder. Line 10 again uses the ChDir statement, this time to restore the original folder. Finally, line 11 displays another message dialog to confirm that the current folder is back to the original folder.

Do

DO save the current folder name in a variable so that you can restore that folder as the current folder.

DON'T

DON'T forget that the GetOpenFilename and GetSaveAsFilename methods can result in changes to the current drive or folder. You might want to save the current folder name in a string variable and then use ChDir and ChDrive to restore the original drive and folder.

Changing the Current Disk Drive

To change the current disk drive, you must use the ChDrive statement. (ChDrive is an abbreviation for *change drive*.)

SYNTAX

The ChDrive statement has the following general syntax:

ChDrive *drive*

drive is any **String** expression that represents a disk drive letter. If *drive* contains more than one character, ChDrive uses only the first character in the string for the drive letter. If you specify an empty string for the *drive* argument, the current drive doesn't change. If you specify a character other than one of the letters A through Z, VBA displays a runtime error. VBA also displays a runtime error if you specify a drive letter for a drive that does not actually exist on your computer system—although you can use drive letters of disks connected to your computer through a network.

▲ Listing 13.9 demonstrates the use of the ChDrive statement.

INPUT **LISTING 13.9** USING ChDrive TO CHANGE THE CURRENT DISK DRIVE

```
1:    Sub Demo_ChDrive()
2:        Dim oldDir As String
3:
4:        oldDir = CurDir()
5:        MsgBox "The current directory is: " & oldDir
6:        ChDrive "A"
7:        MsgBox "The new drive and directory: " & CurDir()
8:        ChDrive oldDir
9:        ChDir oldDir
10:       MsgBox "The current directory is: " & CurDir()
11:   End Sub
```

ANALYSIS Line 2 declares a **String** variable, oldDir, to store the current folder. Line 4 calls the CurDir function and assigns its result to oldDir. Line 5 displays a message dialog showing the current disk drive and folder as returned by CurDir (and now stored in oldDir).

Line 6 uses the ChDrive statement to change the current disk drive to A:. (Make certain that there is a disk in drive A: before you run this procedure.) Line 7 displays another message dialog to confirm that the new current disk drive is drive A:.

Next, line 8 uses the ChDrive statement to restore the original disk drive as the current disk drive. Because CurDir always includes the drive letter in its return string, oldDir is used as the argument for ChDrive. ChDrive uses only the first letter of the string, which is the old current drive letter, and therefore restores the original disk drive as the current disk drive. To make certain that the original folder is also restored, line 9 uses the ChDir statement to restore the original folder as the current folder. Finally, line 10 displays another message dialog to confirm that the current drive and folder are now restored.

13

Creating Disk Folders

Occasionally, you might want one of your procedures to create a new disk subfolder to store new workbook files in or for some other reason. To create a disk folder, use the MkDir statement. The MkDir statement fulfills the same purpose as the DOS MKDIR or MD commands, or the Windows File, New, Folder command. (MkDir is an abbreviation of *make directory*.)

▼ SYNTAX

The MkDir statement has the following general syntax:

MkDir *path*

path represents any **String** expression that results in a valid folder pathname. *path* can optionally contain a drive letter. If you don't include a drive letter in the *path* argument, MkDir creates a new folder on the current disk drive. If *path* specifies a folder that already exists or includes invalid filename characters, VBA displays a runtime error. If you try to create a subfolder in a folder that does not exist, VBA also displays a runtime error. Using MkDir does not change the current drive or folder.

▲   Listing 13.10 shows an example using the MkDir statement.

INPUT   **LISTING 13.10**   USING MkDir TO CREATE A NEW DISK DIRECTORY

```
1:    Sub Demo_MkDir()
2:    'demonstrates the MkDir statement
3:
4:       Dim newDir As String
6:
7:       newDir = "A:\test1"
8:       MkDir newDir
9:       ChDir newDir
10:      MsgBox "The current directory of A: is: " & _
11:              CurDir("A")
12:   End Sub
```

ANALYSIS   Line 4 declares the newDir **String** type variable to hold the new folder name. Line 7 assigns the string A:\test1 to newDir, and then line 8 uses the MkDir statement to create the new folder (make sure you have a disk in drive A: when you run this procedure, or VBA displays a runtime error). After creating the new folder, line 9 changes the current folder on drive A: to the newly created folder, and the statement in lines 10 and 11 uses MsgBox to display the current folder of drive A:, verifying the creation of the new folder.

Removing Disk Folders

As well as creating new folders, you might occasionally want one of your procedures to remove a disk subfolder. To remove a disk folder, use the RmDir statement. The RmDir statement fulfills the same purpose as the DOS RMDIR or RD commands; in Windows, you use the File, Delete command to delete both files and folders. (RmDir is an abbreviation for *remove directory*.)

▼ SYNTAX

The RmDir statement has the following general syntax:

RmDir *path*

path represents any **String** expression that results in a valid folder pathname. *path* can optionally contain a drive letter. If you don't include a drive letter in the *path* argument, RmDir removes the folder on the current disk drive. If *path* specifies a folder that does not already exist or that includes invalid filename characters, VBA displays a runtime error.

▲ Listing 13.11 shows an example using the RmDir statement.

INPUT **LISTING 13.11** USING RmDir TO REMOVE A FOLDER

```
1:  Sub Demo_RmDir()
2:  'demonstrates the RmDir statement
3:
4:      Dim delDir As String
5:
6:      delDir = "A:\TEST1"
7:      If CurDir("A") = delDir Then ChDir "A:\"
8:      RmDir delDir
9:  End Sub
```

ANALYSIS Line 4 declares a **String** type variable, delDir, to hold the name of the folder to remove. Line 6 assigns the folder name A:\TEST1 to delDir (this procedure assumes that you ran the procedure in Listing 13.10 to create the Test1 folder on drive A:). Line 7 calls the CurDir function to determine the current folder for drive A:. If the current folder of drive A: is the same as the folder to be removed, line 7 calls the ChDir function to change the current folder of drive A: to the root folder. You cannot remove a disk folder if it is the current folder or is not empty.

Next, line 8 uses the RmDir statement to remove the Test1 subfolder from the disk in drive A:.

13

Do

DO use the `Dir` function to determine whether a folder is empty before using `RmDir`, and use the `Kill` statement (described later in this chapter) to remove files from the folder. Use `RmDir` to remove any subfolders from the folder you want to remove.

DO use the `CurDir` function to check whether the folder you want to remove is the current folder.

Don't

DON'T try to remove a folder that contains files or other folders, or VBA will display a runtime error.

DON'T try to remove a folder if it is the current folder, or VBA will display a runtime error.

Copying and Deleting Files

Copying and deleting files are, perhaps, the two most common file management activities that most people perform. This section describes how you can copy or delete files under the control of your VBA procedures.

Copying a File

To copy a file, use the `FileCopy` statement. This VBA statement is equivalent to the DOS `COPY` command or the Windows File, Copy command.

The `FileCopy` statement has the following general syntax:

```
FileCopy source, destination
```

Both *source* and *destination* are **String** expressions that result in valid filenames. They can optionally include the full folder path and drive letter. If you try to copy a file onto itself, VBA displays a runtime error. VBA also displays a runtime error if you try to copy a file and there is not enough disk space to hold the copied file.

INPUT   **LISTING 13.12**   A PROCEDURE THAT USES THE `FileCopy` STATEMENT

```
1:    Sub CopyFiles()
2:    'copies a file selected by the user to a new name, drive
3:    'or directory selected by the user.
4:
```

```
5:      Dim sName As String
6:      Dim dName As String
7:
8:      Do
9:        With Application
10:         sName = .GetOpenFilename(Title:= _
11:                              "File Copy - Source")
12:         If sName = "False" Then Exit Sub
13:         dName = .GetSaveAsFilename(Title:= _
14:                              "File Copy - Destination")
15:         If dName = "False" Then Exit Sub
16:       End With
17:       FileCopy source:=sName, destination:=dName
18:     Loop
19:   End Sub
```

ANALYSIS This procedure enables the user to select a file to copy and then to select the drive, folder, and filename to copy the file to. Lines 5 and 6 declare two **String** type variables to hold the source filename and the destination filename. Line 8 begins an infinite Do loop (a loop with no determinant condition). The loop in lines 8 through 18 executes until the user cancels one of the two file dialogs. Line 9 starts a **With Application** statement. Lines 10 and 11 contain a single statement that calls the GetOpenFilename method to display the file open dialog and assigns the filename (the method's result) to the sName variable.

Line 12 checks to see whether the user canceled the file opening dialog. If so, the procedure exits. Otherwise, VBA continues and executes the statement in lines 13 and 14, which uses the GetSaveAsFilename method to let the user select a filename, disk drive, and folder for the copied file. Line 15 checks to see whether the user canceled the file dialog. If so, the procedure exits. Otherwise, VBA continues on to execute the FileCopy statement in line 17.

When VBA executes the FileCopy statement in line 17, it copies the file (whose name is stored in sName) to the new name, drive, and folder stored in dName. After copying the file, the Do loop repeats.

13

Do

DO determine whether an open file has read-only status by checking the value in the Workbook object's ReadOnly property. If the ReadOnly property is **True**, it has read-only status.

Deleting a File

To delete a file, you use the dramatically named `Kill` statement. The `Kill` statement fulfills the same purpose as the DOS `DEL` command or the Windows File, Delete command.

The general syntax of the `Kill` statement is

```
Kill pathname
```

pathname is any **String** expression that results in a valid filename specification. *pathname* can include the drive letter, full folder path, and wildcard characters (* and ?). If *pathname* includes wildcard characters, `Kill` deletes *all* files that match the specification in *pathname*.

▲ Listing 13.13 shows an example of the `Kill` statement in action.

INPUT **LISTING 13.13** USING `Kill` TO DELETE FILES

```
 1:  Sub DelFiles()
 2:  'deletes files until user cancels file dialog box.
 3:
 4:     Dim fName As String
 5:     Dim Ans As Integer
 6:
 7:     Do
 8:        With Application
 9:          fName = .GetOpenFilename(Title:="Delete File")
10:        End With
11:        If fName = "False" Then Exit Sub
12:        Ans = MsgBox(prompt:="Delete " & fName & "?", _
13:                     Title:="Delete File", _
14:                     Buttons:=vbQuestion + vbYesNo)
15:        If Ans = vbYes Then
16:           Kill fName
17:        End If
18:     Loop
19:  End Sub
```

ANALYSIS This procedure uses the GetOpenFilename method to let the user select a file-name, confirms the deletion, deletes the file, and then repeats. Line 4 declares a **String** type variable to store the filename, and line 5 declares an **Integer** type variable to store the user's response to the confirmation message dialog.

Line 7 starts an infinite **Do** loop, which executes until the user cancels the file dialog. Line 8 begins a **With** statement. Line 9 calls the GetOpenFilename method and assigns its result to fName. Line 11 checks to see whether the user canceled the file dialog and exits the procedure if the user canceled. Next, lines 12 through 14 contain a single MsgBox statement that asks the user to confirm deleting the selected file. If the user confirms the deletion, VBA executes the Kill statement in line 16, which deletes the file.

Do
DO check a file's attributes before attempting to delete it. If you try to delete a file that has any of the Hidden, System, or Read-Only file attributes, VBA displays a runtime error. Use the GetAttr function to retrieve a file's attributes, and the SetAttr statement to change them, if you want to be able to delete files with the Hidden, System, or Read-Only file attributes.

DON'T
DON'T try to delete an open workbook, or VBA displays a runtime error.

Renaming or Moving Files

Occasionally, you might need to change the name of an existing file or you might want to move the file to another folder on the same disk drive. To rename a file or to move it to another folder, use the Name statement.

SYNTAX

The Name statement has the following general syntax:

```
Name oldpathname As newpathname
```

oldpathname and *newpathname* are **String** expressions that result in valid filenames. Both can optionally include the full folder path, including the drive letter. If you do include the drive letter, however, both *oldpathname* and *newpathname* must include the same drive letter, or VBA displays a runtime error. The filename in *newpathname* cannot refer to a file that already exists, or VBA displays a runtime error. If *oldpathname* and

13

▼ *newpathname* refer to different folders, VBA moves the file to the new folder and changes its name, if necessary.

▲ Listing 13.14 shows a procedure that uses the Name statement to rename files.

LISTING 13.14 USING Name TO RENAME OR MOVE FILES

```
 1:  Sub RenameOrMoveFile()
 2:  'renames or moves a disk file
 3:
 4:      Const iTitle = "Rename Or Move - "
 5:      Dim oldName As String
 6:      Dim newName As String
 7:      Dim oldDir As String
 8:
 9:      oldDir = CurDir()
10:      With Application
11:        oldName = .GetOpenFilename(Title:=iTitle & "Source")
12:        If oldName = "False" Then Exit Sub
13:
14:        newName = .GetSaveAsFilename(InitialFilename:=oldName, _
15:                                     Title:=iTitle & "New Name")
16:        If newName = "False" Then Exit Sub
17:      End With
18:
19:      If Left(oldName, 1) = Left(newName, 1) Then
20:        Name oldName As newName
21:      Else
22:        FileCopy oldName, newName
23:        Kill oldName
24:      End If
25:
26:      ChDrive oldDir
27:      ChDir oldDir
28:  End Sub
```

ANALYSIS This procedure renames or moves a file. The procedure's user selects the file-name, folder, and disk drive for both the original file and for the file's new name and/or location. Line 4 declares a string constant to supply the titles for dialogs displayed by this procedure. Lines 5 through 7 declare the variables that this procedure uses. oldName is used to hold the file's old name, newName is for the file's new name, and oldDir is used to hold the name of the current drive and folder at the time this procedure starts and to restore it when the procedure is complete.

Line 9 calls the CurDir function and stores its result in oldDir. Line 10 begins a **With** statement for the Application object. Line 11 uses the GetOpenFilename method to let the user select a file to rename or move. Line 12 uses an **If** statement to check whether the user canceled the GetOpenFilename dialog; if so, the procedure exits.

Next, line 14 calls the GetSaveAsFilename method to let the user select the new filename, drive, and folder. Notice that this call to GetSaveAsFilename uses the InitialFilename argument to fill in the suggested new filename. Line 16 checks to see whether the user canceled this dialog and exits the procedure if she did.

Line 19 starts an **If...Then...Else** statement that evaluates whether the user selected a different drive to move the file to. The logical expression for the **If** statement in line 19 uses the Left function to return the first letter of both the oldName and the newName strings. If the two letters are the same, the user is renaming or moving the file on the same disk drive and VBA executes the Name statement in line 20 to rename the file. If the folder paths in oldName and newName are different, Name moves the file to the new folder.

If the first letter of oldName and newName is different, the user elected to move the file to a different disk drive. You cannot use Name to move files to another disk drive, so this procedure uses FileCopy to copy the file to the other disk drive and then uses Kill to delete the original file.

Finally, the ChDrive and ChDir statements restore the original disk drive and folder that were current when this procedure started. (Remember, the GetOpenFilename and GetSaveAsFilename methods might change the current drive and folder.)

Do

DO move a file from one disk to another by copying the file with FileCopy and then delete the source file with Kill, as shown in Listing 13.14.

Don't

DON'T confuse the Name *statement* with the Name *property* that many objects have. The Name statement renames files, the Name property of an object stores that object's name.

DON'T try to move a file from one disk to another by using the Name statement.

DON'T try to rename an open file. If you do, VBA displays a runtime error. You must close open files before renaming them.

13

Getting Information about Files

Sometimes, knowing the size of a file or the date and time that a file was last modified is important. If you have a procedure that backs up your workbook files, for example, you might want to write the procedure so that it checks to make sure that it is not replacing a more recent file with an older version.

Getting a File's Time and Date Stamp

Any time you, or one of your application programs such as Excel, changes a disk file, the Windows file system records the date and time—according to your computer's clock—with the file so that you can tell when a file was last modified. To make this information available in your VBA procedures, use the `FileDateTime` function. This function returns the date and time information from the file as a VBA **Date** type value.

▼ SYNTAX

The general syntax for the `FileDateTime` function is

```
FileDateTime(pathname)
```

pathname is any **String** expression that results in a valid filename specification. *pathname* can optionally include the drive letter and full folder path, but cannot contain wild-card characters (* or ?).

▲ Listing 13.15, in the next section, shows an example using the `FileDateTime` function.

Getting the Length of a File

To find out how big a file is, use the `FileLen` function. `FileLen` returns the length of a file in bytes.

▼ SYNTAX

The `FileLen` function has the following syntax:

```
FileLen(pathname)
```

pathname is any **String** expression that results in a valid filename specification. *pathname* can optionally include the drive letter and full folder path, but cannot contain wild-card characters. If *pathname* specifies an open file, `FileLen` returns the size of the file the last time it was saved to disk.

▲ Listing 13.15 shows an example using the `FileLen` function.

INPUT **LISTING 13.15** USING THE `FileDateTime` AND `FileLen` FUNCTIONS

```
1:  Sub ShowFileDateSize(fName As String)
2:  'displays the size and date a file was last changed.
3:
```

```
 4:        Dim msg1 As String
 5:        Dim msg2 As String
 6:        Dim fDate As Date
 7:        Dim fLen As Long
 8:
 9:        fDate = FileDateTime(fName)
10:        fLen = FileLen(fName)
11:        msg1 = "Size: " & Format(fLen, "###,###,###") & _
12:               " bytes."
13:        msg2 = "Last modified: " & _
14:               Format(fDate, "long date") & _
15:               " at " & Format(fDate, "long time")
16:        MsgBox Title:="File Date and Size", _
17:               prompt:=fName & Chr(13) & _
18:               msg1 & Chr(13) & msg2
19:     End Sub
20:
21:     Sub Test_ShowFileDateSize()
22:        Dim sName As String
23:
24:        Do
25:           With Application
26:              sName = .GetOpenFilename(Title:="File Date/Size")
27:           End With
28:           If sName <> "False" Then ShowFileDateSize sName
29:        Loop Until sName = "False"
30:     End Sub
```

ANALYSIS   The ShowFileDateSize procedure uses the FileLen and the FileDateTime functions to display a message dialog showing the current size of a file and the date and time that the file was last modified. ShowFileDateSize has a single **String** type argument, fName, that is used to tell ShowFileDateSize which file's information to display.

Lines 4 through 7 declare several variables for this procedure. The first two variables, msg1 and msg2, are used to assemble the message text that this procedure displays. fDate and fLen are used to store the date and time information and the file size information, respectively. Notice that fLen is a **Long** data type, because a file's length can run into millions of bytes.

Line 9 calls the FileDateTime function, using fName to specify the filename argument, and stores the function's result in fDate. Next, line 10 calls the FileLen function, also using fName to specify the filename argument, and stores this function's result in fLen.

Next, lines 11 and 12 contain a single statement that assembles the first part of the message that this procedure displays and stores it in msg1. Lines 13 through 15 contain a single statement that assembles the second part of the message that this procedure displays

13

and stores it in msg2. Finally, the MsgBox statement in lines 16 through 18 displays the file's name, the size of the file, and the date and time the file was last modified.

Lines 21 through 30 contain a procedure that tests the ShowFileDateSize procedure. This procedure uses the GetOpenFilename method to let you select a file and then calls the ShowFileDateSize procedure. The ShowFileDateSize procedure produces a dialog similar to the one shown in Figure 13.4.

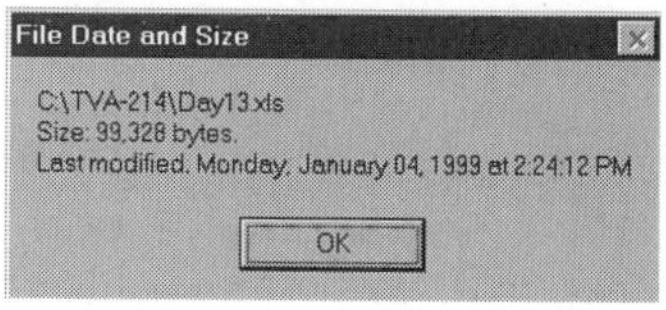

FIGURE 13.4

The ShowFileDateSize *procedure uses the* FileLen *and* FileDateTime *functions to gather information about a file's size and when it was last modified.*

File Date and Size

C:\TVA-214\Day13.xls
Size: 99,328 bytes.
Last modified: Monday, January 04, 1999 at 2:24:12 PM

OK

Summary

In today's lesson, you learned how to use VBA's built-in functions and statements to perform all the file management tasks available in VBA. You also learned how to use the GetOpenFilename and GetSaveAsFilename methods to display Excel's File Open and File Save As dialog boxes from your own procedures.

You learned how to search a folder for a single filename or several filenames. You learned how to find out what the current disk drive and folder are, and how to change the current folder or drive. This chapter taught you how to use VBA to create or remove disk folders, and how to copy, rename, move, or delete a file. Finally, this chapter showed you how to get the date and time that a file was last modified, and how to retrieve the file's length.

Q&A

Q How can I find out how much free space there is on a disk before I copy a file to it so that I don't get a runtime error if the disk is full?

A Unfortunately, VBA does not provide any way to find out how much free space is on a disk drive. If you want to avoid runtime errors when copying files (or using any of VBA's disk or other statements), use the error-handling features described in Day 18.

Q In the Object Browser and online help, I notice that Excel has another file-related method, `FindFile`. What does this method do and how do I use it?

A The `FindFile` method opens the same dialog as the Excel File, Open command. When the user selects a filename, Excel opens that file. The `FindFile` method has no arguments; it returns **True** if a file was successfully opened or **False** if the user canceled the dialog. You can't control the `FindFile` dialog from your procedure; it works the same as if you opened it by choosing the Excel File, Open command. Because you can't control the `FindFile` dialog from your procedure, the `FindFile` method's usefulness is fairly limited.

You can use the `FindFile` dialog to enable your procedure's user to search for, preview, and open workbooks, but you can't get any information about what files the user searches for or previews. As soon as the user either cancels the `FindFile` dialog or opens a workbook, your procedure continues execution. To use the `FindFile` method in a procedure, call it with a statement like the following (you must specify the `Application` object reference):

```
Application.FindFile
```

Workshop

Answers are in Appendix A.

Quiz

1. What are the seven different attributes that a disk file can have?
2. When a file has more than one attribute, how are the attributes combined into a single number?
3. Which function do you use to get a file's attributes? What is the function's result?
4. Can you use `SetAttr` to give a file the Directory or Volume Label attributes?
5. What do the `GetOpenFilename` and `GetSaveAsFilename` methods do?
6. How do you use the `Dir` function to find more than one file in a folder?
7. How do you find out the current disk drive and folder?
8. Which VBA statement would you use to copy a file?
9. Which VBA statement would you use to move a file from one folder to another on the same disk drive? Can you use the same statement to move a file to a different disk drive?

13

Exercises

1. **BUG BUSTER:** The following two code fragments each produce a runtime error. Can you spot what's wrong? (Assume that fName is a **String** variable.)

   (A)

   ```
   fName = GetOpenFilename
   ```

   (B)

   ```
   With Application
       fName = GetSaveAsFilename
   End With
   ```

2. **BUG BUSTER:** The following statement will produce a runtime error. Why?

   ```
   Name "C:\EXAMPLES\SALES.XLS" As "A:\SALES.XLS"
   ```

3. Using the IsDiskFile function in Listing 13.3 as a model, write a **Boolean** function named IsDiskFolder that returns **True** if a specified disk folder exists and **False** if it does not.

4. Write a procedure that uses the InputBox function to get a folder name from the user and then changes the current folder to the folder entered by the user. Use the IsDiskFolder function you wrote in Exercise 3 to test whether the folder exists before you try making it the current folder. If the folder does not exist, your procedure should ask whether to create it. Be sure to handle the situation correctly if the user cancels the input dialog.

DAY 14

Arrays

This chapter teaches you about arrays. Arrays are a common and practical way of storing many different pieces of related data. Arrays are useful in creating sorted or unsorted lists of data, storing tables of information, and for many other tasks. You can access information stored in an array in any order. In today's lesson, you learn what an array is and how to

- Declare arrays using the **Dim** statement.
- Use arrays in your VBA procedures.
- Get information about an array with the IsArray, LBound, and UBound functions.
- Perform operations on every element in an array using the **For...Each** loop structure.
- Redimension arrays using the **ReDim** statement.
- Clear and remove arrays using the **Erase** statement.
- Pass arrays as arguments to procedures or functions.
- Sort an array into a particular order.
- Search the elements in an array to find a particular item in the array.

Understanding Arrays

An *array* is a collection of variables that share the same name and basic data type. Like the user-defined data types that you learned about in Day 11, "Creating Your Own Data Types and Object Classes," an array is a convenient way of storing several related data items together in a single container for greater programming convenience and efficiency. Unlike user-defined data types, however, every data item stored in an array must have the same data type; for example, if you create an array to store **Integer** data types, all data items stored in that array must be **Integer** numbers.

Arrays are typically used to represent lists or tables of information where all of the entries in the list or table are the same type of data, that is, the list contains only **Double** numbers, **Strings**, **Currency** values, and so on. An array enables you to store and manipulate many data items through a single variable. In addition to reducing the total number of different variable names you must keep track of, another primary advantage of using arrays is that you can use loops to easily process the various elements of arrays. By combining arrays and looping structures (typically **For...Next** or **For...Each**), you can write a few statements that process a large amount of data. Performing the same tasks using separate variables might require hundreds of statements.

Understanding Single-Dimensional Arrays

The least complex array is simply a list of data items; this kind of array is called a *simple* or *single-dimensional* array. Single-dimensional arrays get their name from the fact that a list of data is like a line drawn on a sheet of paper; the list has only one dimension— length—and is therefore single-dimensional (or one-dimensional).

Figure 14.1 shows a diagram of a single-dimensional array. Each data item stored in an array is called an *element* of the array. The array in Figure 14.1 has 10 elements in it; each element stores a **Double** type number. Notice that the elements in the array are numbered from 0 to 9, for a total of 10 elements. (This kind of numbering system is common in computer programming, and is called *zero-based* numbering.)

To access data stored in a particular array element, you specify the name of the array followed by the number—called the *subscript* or *index*—of the element whose contents you want to retrieve or alter. The subscript must always be enclosed in parentheses. For example, if the array in Figure 14.1 is named NumArray, the following statement assigns the number 55.4 to the variable AnyNum:

```
AnyNum = NumArray(7)
```

FIGURE **14.1**

A single-dimensional numeric array; single-dimensional arrays are essentially just lists of data of the same type.

FIGURE **14.1**

A single-dimensional numeric array; single-dimensional arrays are essentially just lists of data of the same type.

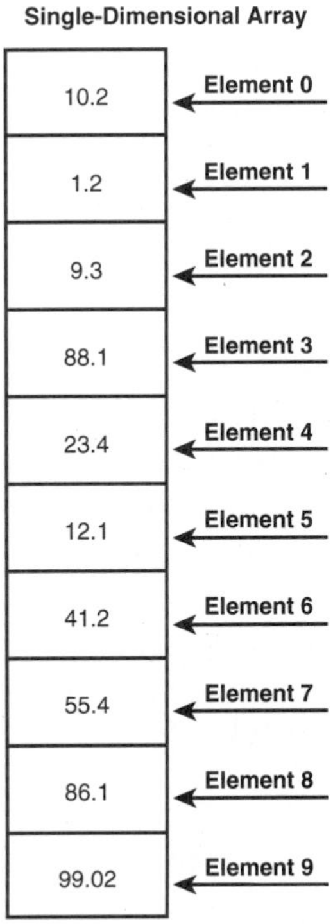

In this statement, the number 7 is the array subscript; notice that it is enclosed by parentheses and is *not* separated with any spaces from the array's name. Because element numbering starts with 0, the element that this statement references is actually the eighth element of NumArray.

Look at Figure 14.1 again and notice that the array element numbered 7 contains the value 55.4. When VBA executes the preceding statement, it retrieves the value 55.4 from the specified array element and stores that value in the AnyNum variable, just like any other variable assignment.

You also use a subscript whenever you want to store data in a particular array element. The next statement, for example, stores the number 12 in the eighth element of the array shown in Figure 14.1:

```
NumArray(7) = 12
```

14

When VBA executes this statement, it puts the value 12 into the specified array element, replacing the previous contents of that element—again, just like any other variable assignment. You can use an array element in any VBA expression the same way you would use any constant or variable value in an expression.

Mostly, you'll use single-dimensional arrays to represent lists of data values.

Understanding Multi-Dimensional Arrays

Single-dimensional arrays work well when you need to represent simple lists of data. Frequently, however, you'll need to represent tables of information in your programs, with the data organized in a row and column format—sort of like the cells in an Excel worksheet. To do so, you need to use a *multi-dimensional* array.

Figure 14.2 shows a diagram of the most common form of multi-dimensional array: a two-dimensional array. Multi-dimensional arrays get their name because they have more than one dimension: length (the number of rows in the array), width (the number of columns in the array), and even other dimensions, as you'll see later in this section.

FIGURE 14.2

A two-dimensional numeric array; two-dimensional arrays are typically used to represent tables of data in a row and column format.

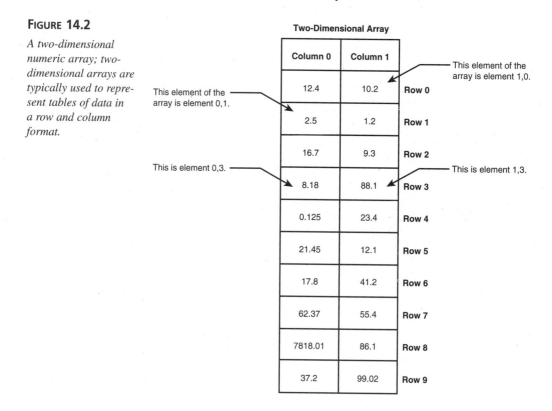

The two-dimensional array in Figure 14.2 has two columns (numbered 0 and 1) and 10 rows (numbered 0 through 9) for a total of 20 elements. Like single-dimensional arrays, you access elements in a multi-dimensional array by *subscripting* the array, that is, you use the numbers of the column and row to specify a particular element in the array. Subscripting a two-dimensional array is a lot like specifying a cell in an Excel worksheet; the first dimension of the array corresponds to the worksheet's columns and the second dimension of the array corresponds to the worksheet's rows.

If the array in Figure 14.2 is named `NumTable`, the following statement assigns the value `10.2` (from the first row in the second column of the array) to the variable `AnyNum`:

```
AnyNum = NumTable(1, 0)
```

Similarly, the following statement stores the value `2.5` in the second row of the first column of the array:

```
NumTable(0, 1) = 2.5
```

In both of the preceding statements, notice that the subscripts to the array are enclosed in parentheses and that the column and row coordinates are separated by commas.

Arrays can have more than two-dimensions. Figure 14.3 shows a three-dimensional array; this array has length, width, and height (so to speak). You can think of the elements in a three-dimensional array as being like a bunch of boxes stacked so many boxes wide, so many boxes deep, and so many boxes high. Another way to think of a three-dimensional array is as a series of pages in a book, with each page containing a table with the same number of rows and columns. Figure 14.3 shows an array with three "pages" (numbered 0 through 2); each page contains a table with two columns and 10 rows. The subscripts for each array element are written into the element boxes in the figure.

You can also create arrays with more than three dimensions; in fact, VBA enables you to create arrays with up to 60 dimensions. Working with arrays that have four or more dimensions quickly becomes rather mind-boggling; fortunately, you'll probably never have to. Mostly, you'll use single- and two-dimensional arrays in your programming. You'll seldom need to use arrays more complex than a list or table of data, so don't worry too much about arrays with more than two dimensions—although you might occasionally use a three-dimensional array, the need for such complex arrays is small.

14

FIGURE 14.3

A three-dimensional array used to represent pages of tables.

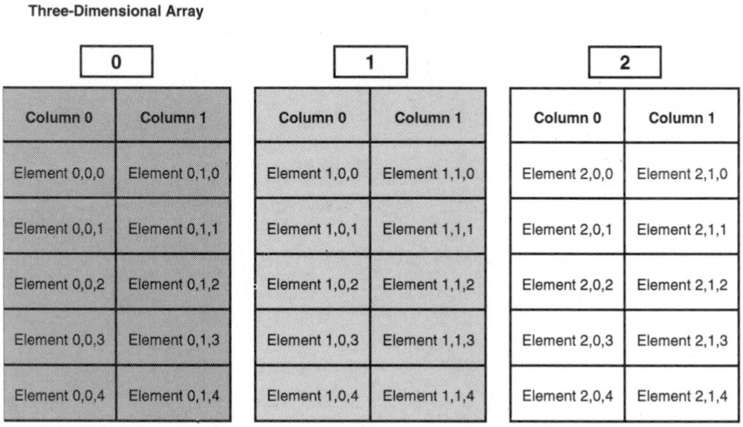

Three-Dimensional Array

	0			1			2	
Column 0	**Column 1**		**Column 0**	**Column 1**		**Column 0**	**Column 1**	
Element 0,0,0	Element 0,1,0		Element 1,0,0	Element 1,1,0		Element 2,0,0	Element 2,1,0	
Element 0,0,1	Element 0,1,1		Element 1,0,1	Element 1,1,1		Element 2,0,1	Element 2,1,1	
Element 0,0,2	Element 0,1,2		Element 1,0,2	Element 1,1,2		Element 2,0,2	Element 2,1,2	
Element 0,0,3	Element 0,1,3		Element 1,0,3	Element 1,1,3		Element 2,0,3	Element 2,1,3	
Element 0,0,4	Element 0,1,4		Element 1,0,4	Element 1,1,4		Element 2,0,4	Element 2,1,4	

Do

DO remember to include the parentheses around an array's subscript.

DO remember to separate the subscripts for a multi-dimensional array with commas.

DO use integer numbers (whole numbers without a decimal fraction) for an array's subscripts.

DON'T

DON'T separate the array's subscript value from the array's name: type both the array name, the parentheses, and the subscript value as one word in your VBA code.

Static and Dynamic Arrays

As you'll learn in the next section of this lesson, you usually specify the number of elements in an array at the time you declare the array. The array declaration tells VBA how large the array's various dimensions are. After you declare the array, VBA allocates enough memory for all the array's elements. For the array in Figure 14.1, VBA would allocate enough memory for 10 integers; for the array in Figure 14.2, VBA would allocate enough memory for 20 integers; and so on.

> **Note**
>
> Array variables are subject to the same scope and persistence rules as any other variable. Variable scope and persistence was explained in Day 3, "Understanding Data Types, Variables, and Constants," and Day 11.

VBA keeps memory for all of the elements in the array reserved for as long as the array variable exists. Arrays like this are called *static* arrays because the number of elements in the array doesn't change.

Choosing the size of an array can be difficult if you're not sure how much data is going to go into an array or if the amount of data collected for an array varies greatly. If you sometimes have 100 values to store, and other times only have 10 values, you're potentially wasting the space required to store 90 values (the difference between the largest number of values and the smallest number).

For situations like this, VBA supports a special type of array called a *dynamic* array. Dynamic arrays get their name because you can change the number of elements in the array as your VBA program executes. A dynamic array (combined with the right programming) can grow or shrink to accommodate exactly the required number of elements without wasting any space. To change the size of a dynamic array, use the **ReDim** statement described later in this lesson.

Now that you're acquainted with how arrays store data, you're ready to learn how to declare and use arrays, as described in the rest of this lesson.

The `Option Base` Statement

So far, you've seen arrays with zero-based numbering. In zero-based numbering, the subscript for the first element in any dimension of an array is 0; an array with 10 elements therefore has subscripts 0 through 9. Obviously, zero-based numbering can be confusing because the subscript 0 really indicates the first element in an array, the subscript 5 really indicates the sixth element of the array, and so on.

It would be much more convenient if an array's elements were numbered starting with 1 instead of 0. If an array's subscript numbering started at 1, the subscript 1 would indicate the first element of the array, the subscript 5 would indicate the fifth element, and so on.

Fortunately, VBA does enable you to specify the starting number for an array's elements. You can either specify the low number for an array's subscripts when you declare the array (described later in this lesson), or you can use the **Option Base** compiler directive to specify whether you want array subscript numbering to start at 0 or 1.

14

The general syntax for the **Option Base** compiler directive is

```
Option Base 0 ¦ 1
```

The **Option Base** statement enables you to specify 0 or 1 as the default starting number for array subscripts. If you don't use the **Option Base** statement, VBA starts array subscript numbering at 0 (the default). You must place the **Option Base** statement in the declarations area of a module before any variable, constant, or procedure declarations. You can't place the **Option Base** statement inside a procedure.

The next two statements show examples of the **Option Base** compiler directive:

```
Option Base 0    ' the default setting
Option Base 1    ' array subscripts start with 1
```

> **Note**
>
> You can only have a single **Option Base** statement in a module; the **Option Base** statement affects all the arrays declared in a module, whether they are local to a procedure or declared at the module level.

Declaring Arrays

By now, you're familiar with the **Dim** statement used to declare variables. As you might expect, you also use the **Dim** statement to declare arrays. In fact, you might recall that the **Dim** keyword is an abbreviation for *dimension*. In the original BASIC programming language, the **Dim** keyword was used exclusively for *dimensioning* arrays, hence the abbreviation. Modern VBA has extended the **Dim** keyword for use with all variables, however. You can declare both single- and multi-dimensional arrays with **Dim**.

The general syntax for declaring an array with the **Dim** statement is

```
Dim VarName([Subscripts])[As Type]
```

VarName represents any name for the array that meets VBA's rules for identifier names. The *Subscripts* clause represents the dimension(s) of the array. You can declare arrays with up to 60 dimensions. For a single-dimensional array, include one *Subscripts* clause; for a two-dimensional array, include two *Subscripts* clauses (separated by a comma), and so on for as many dimensions as you want your array to have. Each *Subscripts* clause adds a new dimension to the array.

Note   You can also declare static and dynamic arrays using the **Public, Private,**
and **Static** keywords, just as you would any other variable—and with the
same affects on the array's scope and persistence. Use the array declaration
syntax shown here and simply substitute the **Public, Private,** or **Static** keywords for the **Dim** keyword, as desired.

The *Subscripts* clause has this syntax:

```
[lower To] upper [,[lower To] upper] . . .
```

lower specifies the lower range of valid subscripts for the array. *upper* specifies the
upper limit for the array's subscripts. Notice that only the *upper* limit is required; the
lower **To** portion of the *Subscripts* clause is optional. If you specify only the *upper*
limit, VBA numbers the array's elements depending on the **Option Base** setting. If
Option Base 1 is in effect, VBA numbers the elements in the array from 1 to *upper*;
otherwise VBA numbers the array elements from 0 to *upper*.

Including the *lower* **To** portion of the *Subscripts* clause can help make your code easier to understand and can help reveal programmer mistakes so that you can write more
reliable programs. Including the *lower* **To** portion of the *Subscripts* clause also enables
you to specify a starting subscript for an array other than 0 or 1. For example, you might
want to create an array with elements numbered 5 through 10 or -5 through 0, depending
on the specific job you're trying to accomplish.

Like standard variable declarations, you can declare a specific data type for an array by
including the **As** *type* clause in the declaration. Every element in the array will have the
data type you specify. *type* represents any valid VBA data type: **Currency, Double,**
String, and so on. You can also declare arrays of a user-defined data type. If you omit
type, all the elements in the array have the **Variant** type. VBA initializes the elements of
numeric arrays with zeros and the elements of string arrays with empty strings.

Notice that the *Subscripts* clause is optional. To create a dynamic array, omit the
Subscripts clause altogether (you must include the parentheses in the array declaration,
whether or not you specify *Subscripts*).

The following examples are all valid array declarations:

```
Dim January(1 To 31) As String
Dim January(31) As String    'assumes Option Base 1
Dim MailingList() As MailData    'dynamic array of user-defined type
```

14

```
▼   Dim Grab_Bag()    'dynamic array of Variants
    Dim LookupTable(2, 10)    'assumes Option Base 1
    Dim HexMultiplication(0 To 15, 0 To 15) As String
    Dim LookupBook(1 To 3, 1 To 2, 1 To 10)
```

In these examples, notice that, if **Option Base** 1 is selected, the first two statements declare identical arrays: both are single-dimensional and both have 31 elements subscripted 1 through 31. The third array declaration (for `MailingList`) has a user-defined type as the data type of the array's elements. (User-defined data types were described in Day 11.) Both the third and fourth array declarations omit the subscripts from the declaration; they are dynamic arrays. The fifth and sixth examples declare two-dimensional
▲   arrays, and the final example declaration declares a three-dimensional array.

Do

DO remember that including the *Subscripts* clause in an array declaration creates a static array with a fixed number of elements.

DO remember that omitting the *Subscripts* clause in an array declaration creates a dynamic array.

DO keep in mind that the **Option Base** setting can affect the total number of elements in an array. Consider the following declaration:

```
Dim NumArray(10)
```

If **Option Base** is 1, this array's elements are subscripted with the numbers 1 through 10, for a total of 10 elements. If, however, there is no **Option Base** statement, or **Option Base** is set to 0, this array's elements are subscripted with the numbers 0 through 10, for a total of *11* elements.

Using Arrays

After you declare an array, using it in your VBA code is straightforward. As explained at the beginning of this lesson, to access an element of an array you state the name of the array followed by a subscript value enclosed in parentheses.

SYNTAX

The general syntax for accessing an array element is

```
arrayName(validIndex1, [validIndex2]...)
```

arrayName represents the name of an array. *validIndex1* represents a valid subscript value for the first dimension of the array. *validIndex2* represents a valid subscript value for the second dimension of the array, if there is one. You must supply a subscript value for every dimension in the array every time you access an element in the array. For a
▼   two-dimensional array, for example, you must always specify two subscripts. A valid

subscript is any VBA variable or expression that results in an integer number that falls within the range of the array's declared dimensions. For example, a valid subscript value for a single-dimensional array declared with subscripts from 1 to 10 could be any VBA expression that results in an integer number from 1 to 10. Using a subscript lower or higher than the range for a particular dimension in an array causes VBA to display a run-time error.

The following code fragment shows a typical array declaration and usage:

```
Dim Factorial(0 To 30) As Double
Dim I As Integer
Factorial(0) = 1
For I = 1 To 30
    Factorial(I) = I * Factorial(I - 1)
Next I
```

Listing 14.1 shows the DemoStaticArray procedure, which declares and uses a numeric array to gather and subsequently process a group of numbers. As you study Listing 14.1, notice that it contains an entire module, including the compiler directives, module-level constant declarations, and two complete procedures.

When you execute the DemoStaticArray procedure, it first prompts you to enter a number specifying how many numbers the procedure should collect for processing. (DemoStaticArray requires you to enter a number between 3 and 15). Next, DemoStaticArray prompts you to enter the specified number of numeric values, storing each value you enter in an element of the array. After you enter all the values, DemoStaticArray displays the values you entered on a worksheet. (The worksheet display is for reference only; all data entry and data processing is based on the contents of the array.) Finally, DemoStaticArray asks you to specify a range of array elements (such as the first through fifteenth numbers in the list, or the second through eighth numbers in the list) for which DemoStaticArray will calculate the sum and average. DemoStaticArray first asks you for the low limit of the range, and then asks for the high limit of the range. After getting the range, DemoStaticArray adds together all the numbers in the range and displays both their sum and average.

INPUT **LISTING 14.1** THE DemoStaticArray PROCEDURE DECLARES AND USES A STATIC NUMERIC ARRAY

```
1:    Option Explicit
2:    Option Base 1
3:
4:    'Listing 14.1. The DemoStaticArray procedure, which declares
5:    '  and uses a static numeric array.
```

continues

14

LISTING 14.1   CONTINUED

```
6:
7:     'maximum array elements
8:     Const ARRAY_MAX As Integer = 15
9:
10:    'minimum numbers to be entered
11:    Const ARRAY_MIN As Integer = 3
12:
13:    Sub DemoStaticArray()
14:       'declare single-dimensional array
15:       Dim NumArray(ARRAY_MAX) As Double
16:       Dim aSum As Double       'for sum of numbers
17:       Dim Count As Integer     'loop counter
18:       Dim NumCnt As Integer    'for count of numbers
19:       Dim cLow As Integer      'low limit for sum
20:       Dim cHigh As Integer     'high limit for sum
21:       Dim mStr As String       'message string
22:       Dim pStr As String       'prompt string
23:       Dim tRsp As String       'for input box responses
24:       Dim oldSheet As String   'original sheet name
25:
26:       'preserve original sheet name
27:       oldSheet = ActiveWorkbook.ActiveSheet.Name
28:
29:       'select a new sheet
30:       ActiveWorkbook.Sheets("Sheet1").Select
31:
32:       'clear the worksheet cells for later display
33:       'of the array's contents
34:       For Count = 1 To (ARRAY_MAX + 2)
35:          Cells(Count, 1).Value = ""
36:          Cells(Count, 2).Value = ""
37:       Next Count
38:
39:       'prompt for number of values to be entered;
40:       'requires a minimum of ARRAY_MIN numbers
41:       Do
42:          pStr = "Type the number of values to enter (" & _
43:                 ARRAY_MIN & " To" & _
44:                 Str(ARRAY_MAX) & ") "
45:          tRsp = InputBox(prompt:=pStr, _
46:                          Title:="Integer Input", _
47:                          Default:=ARRAY_MAX)
48:          If Len(Trim(tRsp)) = 0 Then
49:             CancelDemo cMsg:="Array sizing canceled.", _
50:                        rSheet:=oldSheet
51:          Else
52:             NumCnt = CInt(tRsp)
53:          End If
54:
```

Cells(row, column)

```
55:     If (NumCnt < ARRAY_MIN) Or (NumCnt > ARRAY_MAX) Then
56:        MsgBox "Please enter a number between " & _
57:              ARRAY_MIN & " and " & ARRAY_MAX
58:     End If
59: Loop Until (NumCnt >= ARRAY_MIN) And (NumCnt <= ARRAY_MAX)
60:
61: 'enter values into the array
62: For Count = 1 To NumCnt
63:   pStr = "Enter value number " & Count
64:
65:   'get a value
66:   tRsp = InputBox(prompt:=pStr, _
67:                   Title:="Numeric Input", _
68:                   Default:=Count)
69:   'check for cancellation
70:   If Len(Trim(tRsp)) = 0 Then
71:     CancelDemo cMsg:="Data entry canceled", _
72:                rSheet:=oldSheet
73:   Else
74:     'store each value in a member of array NumArray
75:     NumArray(Count) = CDbl(tRsp)
76:   End If
77: Next Count
78:
79: 'display the elements of NumArray on the worksheet
80: For Count = 1 To NumCnt
81:   Cells(Count, 1).Value = "Value(" & Count & ")"
82:   Cells(Count, 2).Value = NumArray(Count)
83: Next Count
84:
85: 'query repetitively for the range of elements in the
86: 'array for which to calculate the sum and average
87: Do
88:   'get the low subscript of the elements to add
89:   Do
90:     tRsp = InputBox(prompt:="Enter subscript for " & _
91:                     "the low end of range to add:", _
92:                     Title:="Integer Input", _
93:                     Default:="1")
94:     If Len(Trim(tRsp)) = 0 Then
95:       cLow = 0
96:     Else
97:       cLow = CInt(tRsp)
98:     End If
99:
100:    If (cLow < 1) Or (cLow >= NumCnt) Then
101:      MsgBox prompt:="You must enter a number " & _
102:                     "between 1 and " & (NumCnt - 1)
103:    End If
```

continues

14

LISTING 14.1   CONTINUED

```
104:     Loop Until (cLow >= 1) And (cLow < NumCnt)
105:
106:     'get the high subscript of the elements to add
107:     Do
108:       tRsp = InputBox(prompt:="Enter subscript for " & _
109:                          "the high end of range to add:", _
110:                        Title:="Integer Input", _
111:                        Default:=NumCnt)
112:       If Len(Trim(tRsp)) = 0 Then
113:         cHigh = 0
114:       Else
115:         cHigh = CInt(tRsp)
116:       End If
117:
118:       If (cHigh <= cLow) Or (cHigh > NumCnt) Then
119:         MsgBox prompt:="You must enter a number " & _
120:                        "between " & (cLow + 1) & _
121:                        " and " & NumCnt
122:       End If
123:     Loop Until (cHigh > cLow) And (cHigh <= NumCnt)
124:
125:     'add the elements of NumArray together, starting from
126:     'NumArray(cLow) to NumArray(cHigh)
127:
128:     'initialize the sum to 0, then loop through array
129:     'to compute the sum for the specified range
130:     aSum = 0
131:     For Count = cLow To cHigh
132:       aSum = aSum + NumArray(Count)
133:     Next Count
134:
135:     'display the results of the sum and average
136:     mStr = "Sum of NumArray(" & cLow & ") to NumArray(" & _
137:            cHigh & ") = " & aSum & vbCr
138:     mStr = mStr & "Mean of NumArray(" & cLow & _
139:            ") to NumArray(" & cHigh & ") = " & _
140:            (aSum / (cHigh - cLow + 1)) & _
141:            vbCr & vbCr & "Add another set of values?"
142:     Count = MsgBox(prompt:=mStr, _
143:                    Buttons:=vbInformation + vbYesNo, _
144:                    Title:="Output")
145:   Loop Until Count = vbNo
146:
147:   'restore original sheet
148:   ActiveWorkbook.Sheets(oldSheet).Select
149: End Sub
150:
```

```
151: Sub CancelDemo(cMsg As String, rSheet As String)
152: 'displays the prompt specified by cMsg, makes the sheet
153: 'specified by rSheet the current sheet, and ends program
154:   MsgBox prompt:=cMsg, Title:="Static Array Demo"
155:   ActiveWorkbook.Sheets(rSheet).Select
156:   End  'ends entire program
157: End Sub
```

ANALYSIS The DemoStaticArray procedure demonstrates typical techniques for declaring a static array, filling the array with data, and then processing the data in the array. The DemoStaticArray procedure also demonstrates several of the programming practices mentioned in preceding lessons.

Listing 14.1 contains a couple of compiler directives and a couple of module-level constant declarations. Line 2 is the **Option Base** 1 compiler directive, which tells VBA to use 1 as the starting number for elements of all arrays declared in this module. Line 8 declares a constant specifying the maximum size for an array; line 11 specifies another constant specifying the minimum number of elements for an array. (By using constants to specify things such as the minimum and maximum dimensions for an array, you make it easier to change the code that handles an array if you later want to change the size of the array.)

Line 13 contains the DemoStaticArray function declaration. Line 15 declares a single-dimensional static array that will have ARRAY_MAX elements, all of which will have the **Double** data type. Because of the **Option Base** 1 directive, the array's elements will be numbered 1 through ARRAY_MAX (whatever the value of the ARRAY_MAX constant is). Lines 16 through 24 declare several other variables that the DemoStaticArray procedure uses: loop counters, high and low subscript values, prompt strings, message strings, and so on.

Because this procedure will change the active sheet, line 27 stores the name of the current sheet in the oldSheet variable so that this procedure can later restore the sheet that was current at the time the procedure started executing.

Line 30 uses the Select method of the Sheets property to change the active sheet to a worksheet named "Sheet1". The **For...Next** loop in lines 34 through 37 clears the cells in the worksheet in which the procedure will later display the contents of the array's elements. Notice that the loop's ending value is calculated by using the ARRAY_MAX constant plus 2 (to clear an extra two rows on the worksheet). By using the constant value to set the ending limit of the loop, all you have to do to increase the maximum size of the array is change the ARRAY_MAX constant declaration—you don't have to fix all of the **For...Next** loops in the procedure or program.

14

Now the procedure's real work gets started. Lines 41 through 59 contain a **Do...Until** loop that gets a number from the user for how many array elements to fill. Lines 42 through 44 assemble a prompt string for the input dialog displayed by lines 45 through 47. Notice that the InputBox statement suggests the maximum size of the array as the number of elements to be filled. Lines 48 through 53 evaluate the user's input (stored in tRsp) to make sure that the user hasn't canceled the input dialog. If the dialog was canceled, the CancelDemo procedure is called with appropriate arguments. (The CancelDemo procedure is in lines 151 through 157 of the listing.) If the input dialog wasn't canceled, the string in tRsp is converted to an **Integer** type number (**CInt**) and is stored in the NumCnt variable.

Next, lines 55 through 58 evaluate the value in NumCnt to make sure that it meets or exceeds the minimum size of the array and is not greater than the maximum size of the array. Finally, the loop ends in line 59; the loop only ends if the user has entered a number that is between the minimum and maximum number of elements.

Line 62 starts a **For...Next** loop that prompts you for a numeric value and then stores that value in an element of the array. The loop executes for the number of times entered in NumCnt. Line 63 assembles a prompt string for the input dialog displayed by lines 66 through 68. Notice that the default value for this input dialog is the current value of the loop counter; if you want, you can simply press Enter or click OK to enter a number in each of the input dialogs displayed by this loop. The **If** statement that begins in line 70 checks to see whether the user has canceled the data entry; if so, the CancelDemo procedure is again called, ending the entire program. Otherwise, the statement in line 75 converts the user's input into a **Double** number (**CDbl**) and stores it in the array element referenced by the current value of the loop counter. The first time this loop executes, it stores the value entered by the user in element 1, the second time the loop executes, it stores the value in element 2, and so on. The **For...Next** loop ends in line 77.

Note

Notice that the For...Next loops in the DemoStaticArray procedure all use the same loop-counting variable: Count. You can do this because none of the loops are nested inside of each other and only one loop at a time executes, so they can all share the same loop counter variable, thereby reducing the total number of variables that your program needs to use.

Lines 80 through 83 contain another **For...Next** loop counter that simply displays the contents of the array's elements on the worksheet selected earlier in the procedure. This display is just to help you see what's going on as the procedure executes; you could omit these statements without affecting the operation of the DemoStaticArray procedure.

Lines 87 through 145 are a **Do...Until** loop that first prompts for the lower and upper limits of a range of array elements to process and then adds together all the array elements and computes their average.

Line 89 begins a nested **Do...Until** loop that asks the user for the lower limit of array elements to process. Notice that this loop doesn't permit the user to cancel it; instead, it simply requires the user to enter a number somewhere between the first element in the array and one element less than the number of data items in the array. (It's necessary to prohibit the user from selecting the last element in the array as the lower limit, otherwise the upper limit has to be beyond the end of the array.)

Line 107 begins another nested **Do...Until** loop, this time to get the upper limit of array elements to process. Notice that this loop also doesn't permit the user to cancel it, and simply requires the user to enter a number somewhere between the lower limit already chosen and the maximum number of filled elements in the array (represented by NumCnt). The loop ends in line 123.

Line 130 makes sure that the aSum variable starts out initialized at 0, and then the **For...Next** loop in lines 131 through 133 computes the sum by looping through all the array elements (from the low number to the high number) and successively adding their contents to the aSum variable.

Lines 136 through 141 assemble message text showing the low and high limits the user entered, the sum of all of the elements in the range, and the average (mean) of the elements in the range. Notice that the average is calculated on-the-fly in line 140 as the message text is being assembled. The MsgBox function call in line 142 displays the just assembled message and asks the user whether to process another range of elements in the array. The Buttons argument in line 143 causes the MsgBox statement to display the Information icon and to display Yes and No buttons in the dialog. The return value from the MsgBox statement is stored in the Count variable—a somewhat sneaky use of the Count variable, but it eliminates a variable from the procedure.

Figure 14.4 shows a sample session with the DemoStaticArray procedure displaying the MsgBox statement from line 142.

Finally, line 145 evaluates the contents of Count as the determinant condition for the loop: If the user chose Yes in the message dialog displayed by line 142, VBA executes the loop again (going back to line 89); otherwise, the loop ends. Finally, line 148 restores the sheet that was active when the DemoStaticArray procedure was called and the procedure ends in line 149.

14

FIGURE 14.4

A sample output display from the DemoStaticArray *procedure in Excel.*

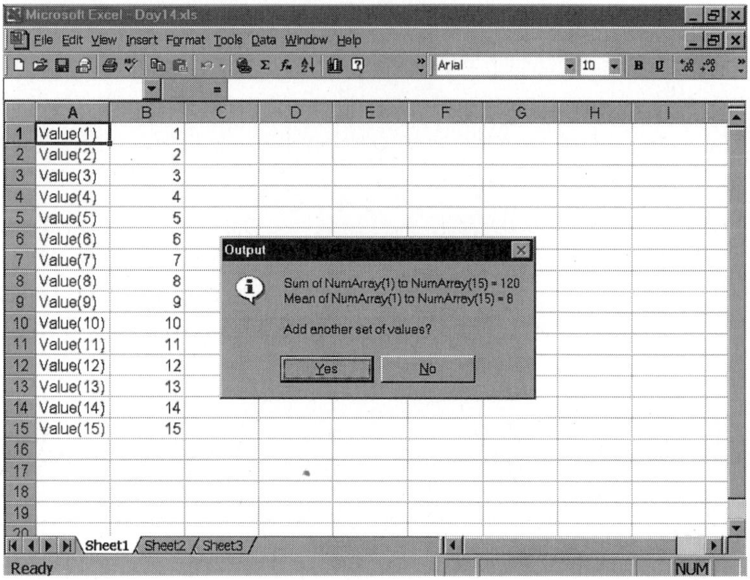

The CancelDemo procedure (lines 151 through 157) deserves just a few words of explanation. The CancelDemo procedure was written to help keep the DemoStaticArray procedure from getting too long, and to provide a generic method of canceling the entire procedure. There are two different places where the DemoStaticArray procedure permits the user to cancel data input and thereby cancel the entire program. Both cancellation points require a message letting the user know that the operation was canceled and the "housekeeping" chore of restoring the sheet that was originally active at the time DemoStaticArray began executing. To avoid duplicating code, the CancelDemo procedure was written: CancelDemo receives an argument for the message to display (so that the cancellation message can be specific) and an argument for the sheet to restore.

Do

DO use constants to specify the maximum and minimum sizes of arrays—doing so makes it much easier to make changes in your code that processes arrays. In Listing 14.1, for example, if you want to change the maximum size of the array to 20 elements, you only have to change the ARRAY_MAX constant declaration. Because all the array handling code uses that constant, you won't have to worry about the change affecting how For...Next loops operate on the array.

Using ReDim with Dynamic Arrays

As mentioned earlier in this lesson, there might be circumstances in which you don't know exactly how many elements you'll need in an array. The demonstration program in Listing 14.1 rather arbitrarily assumes that there will never be more than 15 numbers to process, although it does let you process less than 15 numbers.

If, in the procedure in Listing 14.1, you choose to process fewer than 15 numbers, any unused array elements are still taking up memory (because the array is declared as a static array with 15 elements, it will always have 15 elements). Having unused array elements wastes memory and uses up computer resources that might be needed by other procedures or programs. Another problem with the procedure in Listing 14.1 is that it won't enable you to process more than 15 numbers.

Using a dynamic array instead of a static array solves both problems. By using a dynamic array, you can create an array that is as small or as large as you need. You create dynamic arrays with the **Dim** statement and then establish their size with the **ReDim** statement as your procedure executes.

The general syntax for the **ReDim** statement is

```
ReDim [Preserve] varname(subscripts) [As type] _
                 [,varname(subscripts)[As type]] . . .
```

The optional keyword **Preserve**, as its name suggests, causes VBA to preserve the data in an existing array when you change the array's size with **ReDim**. *varname* represents the name of the array. *subscripts* represents the dimensions of the array. (The syntax for the *subscripts* clause in the **ReDim** statement is the same as for the **Dim** statement.) *type* represents any VBA or user-defined data type. You need to use a separate **As** *type* clause for each array you define. In the case of a **Variant**-type array, the *type* describes the type of each element of the array, but does not change the **Variant** to some other type.

The following are all valid examples of dynamic array declarations and possible **ReDim** statements used with those dynamic arrays:

```
Dim aMonth() As String    'declares dynamic array aMonth
ReDim aMonth(1 To 30)     'resizes array to 30 elements
ReDim aMonth(1 To 31)     'resizes array to 31 elements
ReDim Preserve aMonth(1 To 31) 'resizes array to 31 elements, keeping
contents
Dim LookupTable() As Integer  'declares dynamic array
ReDim LookupTable(3, 15)      'resizes array in two dimensions
ReDim LookupTable(4, 20)      'resizes two-dimensional array
ReDim Preserve LookupTable(4, 25)  'can only resize last dimension
Dim Grab_Bag As Variant       'declares Variant type variable
ReDim Grab_Bag(20) As Integer  'creates array of 20 integers in Variant
```

▲ SYNTAX

14

▼ The preceding examples illustrate some important points about dynamic arrays. First, you can only resize the last dimension of a multi-dimensional array when you use the **Preserve** keyword. Second, you can use **ReDim** to create a typed array inside a **Variant** type variable. Because **Variant** type variables can hold data of *any* type, you can use a **Variant** type variable to store a dynamic array! (Using a **Variant** type variable to store a dynamic array makes it possible to **ReDim** the array *and* change the data type of the

▲ array.)

Typically, you'll use the **ReDim** statement to size or resize a dynamic array that you've previously declared using the **Dim**, **Private**, **Public**, or **Static** statements. You can use the **ReDim** statement to modify the number of elements and dimensions in a dynamic array as many times as you want. You cannot, however, use the **ReDim** statement to change the data type of an array—unless the array is contained in a **Variant** type variable or the array's elements themselves are **Variants**. If the dynamic array is stored in a **Variant** type variable, you can change the data type by using the **As** *type* clause in the **ReDim** statement.

Note

> Attempting to use **ReDim** on a static array (an array whose dimensions you explicitly define in a **Dim**, **Public**, **Private**, or **Static** declaration) causes VBA to display a runtime error.

Tip

> VBA in any of the Microsoft Office 2000 (or later) host applications permits you to assign the entire contents of an array into a dynamic array by using an assignment statement similar to the following:
>
> DynArray( ) = AnyArray( )
>
> After VBA executes this statement, the dynamic array to the left of the assignment operator (=) contains a copy of the array at the right-hand side of the assignment operator. If necessary, VBA redimensions the dynamic array to match the size of the array assigned to it. If the dynamic array receiving the assignment has a declared data type, then the array assigned to it must have a compatible data type.

Listing 14.2 demonstrates the use of a dynamic array. The DemoDynamicArray procedure in Listing 14.2 performs exactly the same job as the procedure in Listing 14.1, but uses a dynamic array to enable as many or as few numbers to be entered and processed as the user wants without wasted memory.

LISTING 14.2 THE DemoDynamicArray PROCEDURE DECLARES AND USES A DYNAMIC ARRAY

INPUT

```
 1:   Option Explicit
 2:   Option Base 1
 3:
 4:   'minimum numbers to be entered
 5:   Const ARRAY_MIN As Integer = 3
 6:
 7:   Sub DemoDynamicArray()
 8:     Dim NumArray() As Double    'declare dynamic array
 9:     Dim Array_Size As Long      'for array size
10:     Dim aSum As Double          'for sum of numbers
11:     Dim Count As Long           'loop counter
12:     Dim cLow As Long            'low limit for sum
13:     Dim cHigh As Long           'high limit for sum
14:     Dim mStr As String          'message string
15:     Dim pStr As String          'prompt string
16:     Dim tRsp As String          'for input box responses
17:     Dim oldSheet As String      'original sheet name
18:
19:     'preserve original sheet name
20:     oldSheet = ActiveWorkbook.ActiveSheet.Name
21:
22:     'select a new sheet
23:     ActiveWorkbook.Sheets("Sheet1").Select
24:
25:     'prompt for number of values to be entered;
26:     'requires a minimum of ARRAY_MIN numbers
27:     pStr = "Type the number of values to enter (" & _
28:               ARRAY_MIN & " is the minimum):"
29:     Do
30:       tRsp = InputBox(prompt:=pStr, _
31:                       Title:="Specify Array Size", _
32:                       Default:=ARRAY_MIN)
33:       If Len(Trim(tRsp)) = 0 Then
34:         CancelDemo cMsg:="Array sizing canceled.", _
35:                    rSheet:=oldSheet
36:       Else
37:         Array_Size = CInt(tRsp)
38:       End If
39:
40:       If (Array_Size < ARRAY_MIN) Then
41:         MsgBox "Please enter a number greater than " & _
42:               (ARRAY_MIN - 1) & "."
43:       End If
44:     Loop Until (Array_Size >= ARRAY_MIN)
45:
46:     'size the dynamic array
```

continues

14

LISTING 14.2   CONTINUED

```
47:     ReDim NumArray(Array_Size)
48:
49:     'clear worksheet cells for display of array contents
50:     ClearDisplay Rows:=(Array_Size + 2), Cols:=2
51:
52:     'enter values into the array
53:     For Count = 1 To Array_Size
54:       pStr = "Enter value number " & Count
55:       'get a value
56:       tRsp = InputBox(prompt:=pStr, _
57:                       Title:="Numeric Input", _
58:                       Default:=Count)
59:       'check for cancellation
60:       If Len(Trim(tRsp)) = 0 Then
61:         CancelDemo cMsg:="Data entry canceled", _
62:                    rSheet:=oldSheet
63:       Else
64:         'store each value in a member of array NumArray
65:         NumArray(Count) = CDbl(tRsp)
66:       End If
67:     Next Count
68:
69:     'display the array's contents on the worksheet
70:     DisplayArray Rows:=Array_Size, ArrayVal:=NumArray
71:
72:     'query repetitively for the range of elements in the
73:     'array for which to calculate the sum and average
74:     Do
75:       'get the low subscript of the elements to add
76:       Do
77:         tRsp = InputBox(prompt:="Enter subscript for " & _
78:                         "the low end of range to add:", _
79:                         Title:="Integer Input", _
80:                         Default:="1")
81:         If Len(Trim(tRsp)) = 0 Then
82:           cLow = 0
83:         Else
84:           cLow = CInt(tRsp)
85:         End If
86:
87:         If (cLow < 1) Or (cLow >= Array_Size) Then
88:           RangeErrorMsg mLow:=1, mHigh:=Array_Size - 1
89:         End If
90:       Loop Until (cLow >= 1) And (cLow < Array_Size)
91:
92:       'get the high subscript of the elements to add
93:       Do
94:         tRsp = InputBox(prompt:="Enter subscript for " & _
95:                         "the high end of range to add:", _
```

```
 96:                          Title:="Integer Input", _
 97:                          Default:=Array_Size)
 98:         If Len(Trim(tRsp)) = 0 Then
 99:           cHigh = 0
100:         Else
101:           cHigh = CInt(tRsp)
102:         End If
103:
104:         If (cHigh <= cLow) Or (cHigh > Array_Size) Then
105:           RangeErrorMsg mLow:=cLow + 1, mHigh:=Array_Size
106:         End If
107:       Loop Until (cHigh >= cLow) And (cHigh <= Array_Size)
108:
109:       'add the elements of NumArray together, starting from
110:       'NumArray(cLow) to NumArray(cHigh)
111:
112:       'initialize the sum to 0, then loop through array
113:       'to compute the sum for the specified range
114:       aSum = 0
115:       For Count = cLow To cHigh
116:         aSum = aSum + NumArray(Count)
117:       Next Count
118:
119:       'display the results of the sum and average
120:       mStr = "Sum of NumArray(" & cLow & ") to NumArray(" & _
121:             cHigh & ") = " & aSum & vbCr
122:       mStr = mStr & "Mean of NumArray(" & cLow & _
123:             ") to NumArray(" & cHigh & ") = " & _
124:             (aSum / (cHigh - cLow + 1)) & _
125:             vbCr & vbCr & "Add another set of values?"
126:       Count = MsgBox(prompt:=mStr, _
127:                      Buttons:=vbInformation + vbYesNo, _
128:                      Title:="Output")
129:     Loop Until Count = vbNo
130:
131:     'restore original sheet
132:     ActiveWorkbook.Sheets(oldSheet).Select
133: End Sub
134:
135: Sub RangeErrorMsg(mLow As Long, mHigh As Long)
136:   MsgBox prompt:="You must enter a number " & _
137:                  "between " & mLow & " and " & _
138:                  mHigh, _
139:          Title:="Dynamic Array Demo"
140: End Sub
141:
142: Sub CancelDemo(cMsg As String, rSheet As String)
143: 'displays the prompt specified by cMsg, makes the sheet
144: 'specified by rSheet the current sheet, and ends program
```

14

continues

LISTING 14.2   CONTINUED

```
145:    MsgBox prompt:=cMsg, Title:="Dynamic Array Demo"
146:    ActiveWorkbook.Sheets(rSheet).Select
147:    End   'ends entire program
148: End Sub
149:
150: Sub ClearDisplay(Rows As Long, Cols As Long)
151: 'clears the worksheet cells used by DemoDynamicArray
152:    Dim rCount As Long
153:    Dim cCount As Long
154:
155:    For rCount = 1 To Rows
156:      For cCount = 1 To Cols
157:        Cells(rCount, cCount).Value = ""
158:        Cells(rCount, cCount).Value = ""
159:      Next cCount
160:    Next rCount
161: End Sub
162:
163: Sub DisplayArray(Rows As Long, ArrayVal As Variant)
164: 'display the elements of the array passed in ArrayVal
165:    Dim rCount As Long
166:
167:    For rCount = 1 To Rows
168:      Cells(rCount, 1).Value = "Value(" & rCount & ")"
169:      Cells(rCount, 2).Value = ArrayVal(rCount)
170:    Next rCount
171: End Sub
```

ANALYSIS   The DemoDynamicArray procedure is very similar to the DemoStaticArray procedure from Listing 14.1, but has some important differences. This analysis will focus on the important similarities and differences between the two procedures.

First of all, line 2 of Listing 14.2 contains the **Option Base** 1 directive so that all arrays in this module will start numbering their elements at 1. Notice that there is only a constant declaration for the minimum size of the array (line 5), but no constant specifying the maximum size of the array. In this procedure, the user specifies the maximum size of the array.

Line 8 declares the dynamic array NumArray. VBA knows this is a dynamic array because the parentheses in the array declaration are empty. The **As** clause specifies that all the elements in the dynamic array are **Double** numbers. Lines 9 through 17 declare the variables that the DemoDynamicArray procedure uses while it is working. Notice that line 9 declares the Array_Size variable: This variable will hold the size of the array as entered by the user; it replaces the ARRAY_MAX constant from Listing 14.1. Notice also that the NumCnt variable is no longer used; because the DemoDynamicArray procedure simply creates an array of the desired size, there is no longer any need to separately keep track of how many elements in the array have valid data as compared to the maximum size of the array. In DemoDynamicArray the array never has unused elements in it.

Lines 20 through 23 perform the same housekeeping chores—preserving the currently active sheet and selecting the working sheet—as were performed in Listing 14.1.

In the DemoDynamicArray procedure, there's no point in doing anything until the desired size of the array has been obtained from the user, so lines 29 through 44 contain a **Do...Until** loop that asks the user to enter the total number of values to be entered into the array. This loop repeats until the user has entered a number greater than or equal to the minimum array size of three elements. Notice that the user's input is used to initialize the Array_Size variable.

Line 47 is the crucial statement in this procedure. This line uses the **ReDim** statement to establish the size of NumArray. This statement creates a single-dimensional array with Array_Size elements in it. If the user enters 3 in the input dialog, NumArray ends up with three elements; if the user enters 20 in the input dialog, NumArray ends up with 20 elements, and so on.

Line 50 calls the ClearDisplay procedure (which occupies lines 150 through 161 and is explained later in this analysis). This procedure is new in this listing, and clears the worksheet prior to displaying the array's contents.

Note

The ClearDisplay and DisplayArray procedures were created to remove code not directly related to array processing from the DemoDynamicArray procedure. The DemoDynamicArray procedure no longer contains any code to display the array's contents or manipulate the display area. Making this change in the DemoDynamicArray procedure brings it into greater compliance with the program design rules discussed in Day 12, "Creating Libraries and Whole Programs: Modular Programming Techniques," and accomplishes two goals: First, it shortens the array-handling procedure, making it a bit easier to follow. Second, it isolates the display-oriented code outside the array-handling procedure. With an appropriate replacement for the ClearDisplay and DisplayArray procedures, the DemoDynamicArray procedure can now be used in any VBA project, whether or not that project is in Excel. Use similar design techniques if you want to create procedures that you can use in any version of VBA.

14

Lines 53 through 67 prompt the user for values to enter into the array's elements, just like the corresponding data-entry loop in Listing 14.1. Next, line 70 calls the DisplayArray procedure to display the array's contents on the worksheet, passing the size of the array and the array itself as arguments. The DisplayArray procedure also is new to this listing; it occupies lines 163 through 171 and is explained later in this analysis.

Finally, lines 74 through 129 ask the user for the upper and lower limits of the array elements for which the procedure will compute the sum and average. This loop, and the statements it contains, works the same way as in Listing 14.1. Notice, however, that the Array_Size variable is used in place of the ARRAY_MAX constant that was used in Listing 14.1. Also, the nested **Do** loops call another procedure, RangeErrorMsg, to display error messages, instead of displaying their error messages themselves.

The RangeErrorMsg procedure occupies lines 135 through 140 of Listing 14.2. The RangErrorMsg procedure—like the ClearDisplay and DisplayArray procedures—was added to shorten the DemoDynamicArray procedure and to make your programming efforts more efficient. Although the savings in this short program isn't significant, a longer program might realize a substantial reduction in length and complexity by using a shorter, general-purpose procedure to carry out the task of displaying certain related kinds of error messages.

The CancelDemo procedure in lines 142 through 148 works the same as the corresponding procedure in Listing 14.1.

The ClearDisplay procedure is declared in line 150. ClearDisplay has two required arguments: the number of rows to be cleared and the number of columns to be cleared. ClearDisplay uses two counting variables (lines 152 and 153) and a pair of nested **For...Next** loops to clear each cell in the specified rows and columns.

The DisplayArray procedure is declared in line 163. DisplayArray has two required arguments: the number of rows in the array and a **Variant** to contain the actual array. A **Variant** argument is used to make it possible to pass an array as a procedure argument; you'll learn more about arrays as function and procedure arguments later in this lesson. DisplayArray uses a single counting variable and displays the contents of the array on the worksheet, as already described in Listing 14.1.

Figure 14.5 shows a sample session with the DemoDynamicArray procedure. In the figure, notice that the list of data items extends beyond the bottom edge of the visible portion of the worksheet—the user in this session selected an array with 20 elements in it.

FIGURE 14.5

A sample session with the DemoDynamicArray *procedure.*

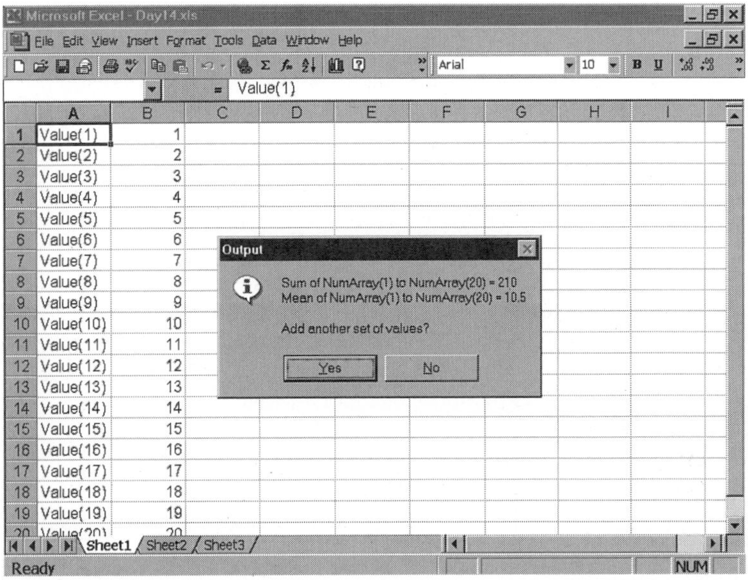

Do

DO remember that you create dynamic arrays in a **Dim**, **Public**, **Private**, or **Static** declaration by using only empty parentheses.

DO remember that you can only use **ReDim Preserve** to change the size of the *last* dimension of a multi-dimensional array. You can change all the dimensions of a multi-dimensional array with the **ReDim** keyword alone, however.

DO isolate application-specific code in separate procedures whenever possible so that you can easily adapt general-purpose procedures to any variety of VBA: Excel VBA, Word VBA, Access VBA, and so on.

DON'T

DON'T forget that you can't change the data type of an array with **ReDim** unless the array is contained in a **Variant** type variable or is a **Variant** array.

14

The LBound and UBound Functions

To keep track of the sizes of both static and dynamic arrays, you might find yourself using one or a pair of variables to store the minimum and maximum subscripts for an array, as shown in Listings 14.1 and 14.2. Unfortunately, if you rely on keeping track of the upper and lower limits of an array's subscripts with your own variables, you're taking on all the responsibility of keeping those variables up-to-date and accurate. If you don't, your procedure won't work correctly; you'll end up processing fewer elements than the array actually contains, or you'll get runtime errors from trying to access an array with subscripts beyond the actual size of the array. Such program bugs can be difficult to track down.

Fortunately, VBA includes a couple of functions that relieve you of the burden of manually keeping track of the upper and lower limits of an array yourself: the LBound and UBound functions. These functions return the lower and upper boundary subscript values of a static or dynamic array.

The general syntax for the LBound and UBound functions is

```
LBound(arrayName [, dimension])

UBound(arrayName [, dimension])
```

The LBound function returns the first subscript of the array represented by *arrayName*. The UBound function returns the highest subscript of the array represented by *arrayName*. You can use these two functions with either static or dynamic arrays. *dimension* represents an integer number specifying the dimension of the array for which you want to obtain the lower or upper boundary. If you omit *dimension*, VBA returns the boundary for the first dimension of the array.

The following code fragments are examples of using the LBound and UBound functions:

```
Dim S(3 To 9) As String
For I = LBound(S) To UBound(S)
  S(I) = String(10, 65 + I)
Next I

Dim Data10Year(1 To 365, 1990 To 1999)
For DayNum = LBound(Data10Year, 1) To UBound(Data10Year, 1)
  For YearNum = LBound(Data10Year, 2) To UBound(Data10Year, 2)
    Matrix(DayNum, YearNum) = Rnd
  Next YearNum
Next DayNum
```

▼ In the second example, notice that the LBound and UBound functions use the optional *dimension* argument. The outer **For...Next** loop executes for as many elements as there are in the first dimension of the Data10Year array, whereas the inner **For...Next** loop executes for as many times as there are elements in the second dimension of the
▲ Data10Year array.

There are some cases when the information returned by the UBound function won't necessarily be very useful to you. Frequently, you might not completely fill an array with valid data (like the array in Listing 14.1), or you might need to perform some processing on the array before it is completely filled. Usually, you'll start storing data in the first element of an array and gradually use elements with higher and higher subscripts. Often, the subscript of the last element in the array that contains meaningful data is less than the highest subscript in the array (as reported by the UBound function). In such a situation, you must use a separate variable to keep track of the *highest working index* of an array. You can also think of the highest working index as the *current working index* of the array. (An array's subscript and index are the same thing.)

To illustrate this point, Figure 14.6 shows a sample array named WordList, which is partway through a data-entry process. The first six elements of the array contain meaningful data (the list of words that has been entered so far), whereas the last four elements contain empty strings. Notice that the current, or highest, working index of the array is the sixth element. If you need to manipulate the list in some way before data entry is complete, you need a variable (as suggested in the figure) to keep track of the current working index.

FIGURE 14.6

A partially filled array. Notice that the variable Curindex *stores the current working index of the* WordList *array. Only elements between the lower boundary of the array and the current working index contain meaningful data.*

WordList Array

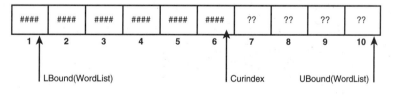

14

Using Erase to Clear or Remove Arrays

VBA provides a special statement—**Erase**—that enables you to perform one of two tasks, depending on whether you're manipulating a static or dynamic array. For static arrays, **Erase** enables you to clear all of the array's elements, essentially re-initializing the array to the same condition it had when VBA created it in memory. For dynamic arrays, **Erase** enables you to completely remove the array and its contents from your computer's memory.

After you fill an array's elements, the data in the array remains (whether the array is static or dynamic) until you either assign new values to the array's elements or until VBA disposes of the array. (Arrays follow the same scope and persistence rules as any other variable in VBA, as explained in Day 3 and Day 12.)

In some circumstances, you might want to clear all the values in the array—setting numeric values to 0, string values to empty strings, and so on. Generally, you'd write a **For...Next** or **For...Each** loop to set all of the elements in an array to a particular value. The following code fragments show both a **For...Next** and a **For...Each** loop used to initialize all of the values in a numeric array to **0**:

```
For k = LBound(NumArray) To UBound(NumArray)
  NumArray(k) = 0
Next k

For Each Num In NumArray
  Num = 0
Next Num
```

The first code fragment uses a **For...Next** loop and the LBound and UBound functions to loop through all of the elements in the array; the second code fragment uses **For...Each** to loop through every element in the array, also setting each element to **0**. Although these loops are quite short, you can accomplish the same task for a static array even more efficiently with a single **Erase** statement:

```
Erase NumArray
```

Arrays tend to consume relatively large quantities of memory: An array of 20 elements, for example, consumes as much memory as 20 separate variables of the same data type. Because arrays require so much memory, you should clear dynamic arrays from memory whenever they're not actually in use. (Static arrays cannot be removed from memory until VBA automatically disposes of the array.)

Just like any other locally declared variable, VBA removes arrays declared locally in a procedure from memory whenever the procedure stops executing. Arrays declared at the module level, however, remain in existence as long as any procedure in that module is executing. If you have a large program, you might want (or need) to reclaim the memory used by module-level dynamic arrays. The **Erase** statement enables you to do just that.

▼ SYNTAX

The general syntax for the **Erase** statement is

```
Erase array1 [, array2, ...]
```

array1 and *array2* represent any valid VBA array name. You can list as many arrays in the **Erase** statement as you want, separating each array name with a comma.

The Erase statement removes dynamic arrays from memory, freeing up the memory formerly in use by that array. If you **Erase** a dynamic array, you must re-create the array with a **ReDim** statement before you can use that particular dynamic array again. If you try to access elements in a dynamic array that you've used the **Erase** statement on without redimensioning it, VBA displays a runtime error.

The **Erase** statement's behavior for static arrays is slightly more complex and depends on the specific data type of the array's elements. The following table summarizes the effect of the **Erase** statement on static arrays of various types (the **Empty** and **Nothing** values were discussed in Day 11).

Static Array Type	Effect of Erase Statement
Any numeric type	Sets array elements to 0.
Any string type	Sets array elements to zero-length string (" "); sets fixed-length strings as all space characters.
Variant	Sets array elements to **Empty**.
Object	Sets array elements to **Nothing**.
Any user-defined type	Sets each variable in the user-defined type individually: numeric types set to 0, **String** to zero-length, **Variant** to **Empty**, Object to **Nothing**.

You can place the **Erase** statement anywhere in your code that it's needed. The following code fragment shows an example of the **Erase** statement in use:

```
Dim NumArray(1 To 10) As Single   'declares static array
Dim k as Variant                  'multi-purpose loop counter

'fill an array with the squares of its subscripts
For k = LBound(NumArray) To UBound(NumArray)
  NumArray(k) = k * k
Next k

'display the squares
For k = LBound(NumArray) To UBound(NumArray)
  MsgBox "The square of " & k & " is " & NumArray(k)
Next k
```

14

```
▼   're-initialize the array
    Erase NumArray

    For k = LBound(NumArray) To UBound(NumArray)
      MsgBox NumArray(k)     'displays zero
▲   Next k
```

Do

DO remember that **Erase** does *not* remove static arrays from memory, it only re-initializes the array's elements.

DO remember that **Erase** *does* remove a dynamic array from memory, destroying the contents of the array.

DON'T

DON'T forget that you can use the **For Each** looping structure to process all the elements in an array.

Using Arrays as Arguments to Procedures and Functions

VBA enables you to pass arrays as arguments to your procedures and functions. This capability can be very useful; because you don't have to specify the size of the array that is passed as an argument, you can write general-purpose array processing procedures or functions. For example, you could write a function that receives a numeric array as an argument and returns the average of all the numbers in the array as the function's result. As another example, you could write a procedure that receives an array as an argument passed by reference and sorts that array (you'll learn about sorting arrays later in today's lesson). In both of these examples, you can write the procedure or function to operate on an array of any size: 5 elements, 10 elements, 100 elements, and so on.

The general syntax to declare array arguments in a procedure or function is the same as you already learned for any procedure or function arguments (described in Day 6, "Creating and Using VBA Function Procedures and Excel User-Defined Functions," and Day 11):

```
[ByVal ¦ ByRef] arrayname() As type
```

▼ Like the procedure and function arguments you already learned about, the **ByVal** keyword tells VBA to pass the array argument by value; the **ByRef** keyword tells VBA to pass the array argument by reference. As usual, if you omit **ByVal** and **ByRef**, VBA passes the array argument by reference.

arrayname() represents the array argument; you can use any valid VBA identifier as the name of the array argument. You must always include the empty parentheses after the *arrayname*; the parentheses tell VBA that this argument is an array. *type* represents any valid VBA or user-defined data type.

The following code fragments show how to include arrays as arguments to procedures and functions:

```
Sub ShowText(Lines(), NumLines As Integer)
  'receives a Variant type array passed by reference
...
End Sub

Sub SortList(ByRef List() As String, NumLines As Integer)
  'receives a String type array passed by reference
...
End Sub

Function ComputeAve(Numbers() As Double) As Double
...'receives a Double type array passed by reference
End Function
```

▲

Do

DO remember that passing arguments by value (with the **ByVal** keyword) causes VBA to pass a *copy* of the data to the function or procedure.

DO remember that VBA in any Microsoft Office 2000 (or higher) host application enables you to create functions that return an array as the function's result.

DON'T

DON'T pass arrays by value unless you absolutely must; passing large arrays by value can quickly exhaust your computer's memory resources, resulting in out-of-memory runtime errors.

14

Sorting Arrays

Apart from numerical or other computations involving data stored in an array, the two array manipulations you'll perform most often are sorting and searching an array. *Sorting* an array simply refers to the process of arranging the values in the array elements in either ascending or descending order. In an array sorted in ascending order, for example, the first element of the array contains the data with the lowest value, the second element of the array contains the data with the next highest value, and so on—the last element in the array holds the data with the greatest value. An array sorted in descending order has the highest value in the first element and the lowest value in the last element of the array.

You usually sort an array if you need to process or display the data in the array in a particular order, or if you need to search for a particular data value in the array. Searching for specific data values stored in an array is usually much faster and efficient if the array has been sorted.

Over the years, computer scientists have spent a lot of effort developing various techniques for sorting arrays of data in an attempt to increase the speed and efficiency of the sorting process. There is now a large number of sorting techniques available; each technique has various advantages and disadvantages. Unfortunately, there are far too many sorting techniques for this book to cover; many authors have written entire books on the subject of sorting arrays. Fortunately, there are a couple of sorting techniques that are both easy to understand and relatively easy to program.

Listing 14.3 shows a procedure that uses the *bubble-sort* technique to sort an array. The bubble-sort technique is one of the simplest sorting techniques. The bubble-sort works by comparing adjacent elements in the array and exchanging their positions, as necessary. The bubble-sort gets its name because it causes the elements in the array to slowly move (or "bubble") upward to their final location in the sorted array.

The following code outline—or pseudo-code—shows how the bubble-sort technique works for an ascending sort:

```
Given an array named Nums:
1:  Loop from 1st Nums element up to next-to-last Nums element, with
    counter I
1A:   Loop from Nums element after element indexed by the outer loop
      counter
           up to last Nums element, with counter J
1B:      If Nums(I) > Nums(J), then exchange contents of Nums(I) and
         Nums(J)
```

The above pseudo-code can be further refined into the following VBA statements:

```
'Given an array Nums with subscripts from 1 to N.
For I = LBound(Nums) To (UBound(Nums) - 1)
  For J = (I + 1) To UBound(Nums)
    If Nums(I) > Nums(J) Then
      tmp = Nums(I)
      Nums(I) = Nums(J)
      Nums(J) = tmp
    End If
  Next J
Next I
```

To create a descending sort order, simply change the greater-than comparison operator (>) to a less-than comparison operator (<): The bubble-sort will then arrange the array in descending order.

Note

Code outlines like the one in this section, and those described in Day 12, are often called *pseudo-code* because the English statements in the code outline only approximate the computer language statements that you'll have to write. Writing the pseudo-code for a complex process is a good design tool; it can help you more easily determine exactly how the actual program statements should be written to accomplish the task you want.

Listing 14.3 contains the DemoBubbleSort procedure, which uses an Excel worksheet to graphically demonstrate how the bubble-sort operation works. The DemoBubbleSort procedure doesn't require any user input; it uses the Rnd function to fill an array with random numbers and then sorts the array. As the DemoBubbleSort procedure executes, you'll see it display pointers indicating the array elements being compared and exchanged. As you watch this procedure execute, keep in mind that the display on the worksheet is only for effect; the sorting is taking place in the array.

14

INPUT

LISTING 14.3 THE DemoBubbleSort PROCEDURE VISUALLY DEMONSTRATES THE BUBBLE-SORT TECHNIQUE FOR SORTING ARRAYS

```
1:   Option Explicit
2:   Option Base 1
3:
4:   'declare constants
5:   Const ARRAY_MAX As Integer = 10
6:   Const DELAY_TIME As Single = 1
7:   Const FORMATSTR As String = "####"
8:   Const COMPSTR1 As String = "<---- compare this element"
9:   Const COMPSTR2 As String = "<---- with this element"
10:  Const COMPSTR3 As String = "<---- swap this element"
11:
12:  Sub DemoBubbleSort()
13:
14:     Dim IntArr(ARRAY_MAX) As Integer
15:     Dim I As Integer
16:     Dim J As Integer
17:     Dim oldSheet
18:
19:     'reseed random number generator
20:     Randomize Timer
21:
22:     'assign random numbers to the elements of array IntArr
23:     For I = 1 To ARRAY_MAX
24:        IntArr(I) = Int(Rnd * 1000)
25:     Next I
26:
27:     'preserve current sheet, switch to new sheet
28:     oldSheet = ActiveSheet.Name
29:     Sheets("Sheet1").Select
30:
31:     'display the array elements
32:     DisplayArray ArrayVal:=IntArr
33:
34:     'start sorting the array
35:     For I = 1 To ARRAY_MAX - 1
36:       For J = I + 1 To ARRAY_MAX
37:          'display arrows that indicate the
38:          'elements being compared
39:          ShowCompare COMPSTR1, I, COMPSTR2, J
40:
41:          If IntArr(I) > IntArr(J) Then
42:            Beep 'sound the speaker
43:            'indicate that compared elements
44:            'will be swapped
45:            ShowCompare COMPSTR3, I, COMPSTR2, J
46:            'swap elements at index I and J
47:            Swap IntArr(I), IntArr(J)
48:            'display the new positions of the
```

```
49:              'swapped elements
50:              DisplaySwapped Row1:=I, Row2:=J, ArrayVal:=IntArr
51:          End If
52:       Next J
53:    Next I
54:    MsgBox prompt:="Array is now sorted!", _
55:           Buttons:=vbInformation, _
56:           Title:="Bubble-Sort Information"
57:    'restore original sheet
58:    Sheets(oldSheet).Select
59: End Sub
60:       '
61: Sub Swap(I1 As Integer, I2 As Integer)
62:    Dim Temp As Integer
63:    Temp = I1
64:    I1 = I2
65:    I2 = Temp
66: End Sub
67:
68: Sub WaitAWhile(ByVal Interval As Single)
69:    Dim TheTime As Date
70:    TheTime = Timer
71:    Do
72:    Loop Until (Timer - TheTime) >= Interval
73: End Sub
74:
75: Sub ShowCompare(S1 As String, I1 As Integer, _
76:                 S2 As String, I2 As Integer)
77:    Cells(I1, 2).Value = S1
78:    Cells(I2, 2).Value = S2
79:    WaitAWhile DELAY_TIME
80:    Cells(I1, 2).Value = ""
81:    Cells(I2, 2).Value = ""
82: End Sub
83:
84: Sub DisplayArray(ArrayVal() As Integer)
85:    Dim k As Integer
86:
87:    For k = 1 To UBound(ArrayVal)
88:      Cells(k, 1).Value = Format(ArrayVal(k), FORMATSTR)
89:    Next k
90: End Sub
91:
92: Sub DisplaySwapped(Row1 As Integer, _
93:                    Row2 As Integer, _
94:                    ArrayVal() As Integer)
95:
96:    Cells(Row1, 1).Value = ArrayVal(Row1)
97:    Cells(Row2, 1).Value = ArrayVal(Row2)
98: End Sub
```

14

ANALYSIS Figure 14.7 shows a sample run with the DemoBubbleSort procedure comparing the data in the first and tenth elements of the array (displayed in cells A1 and A10 of the worksheet).

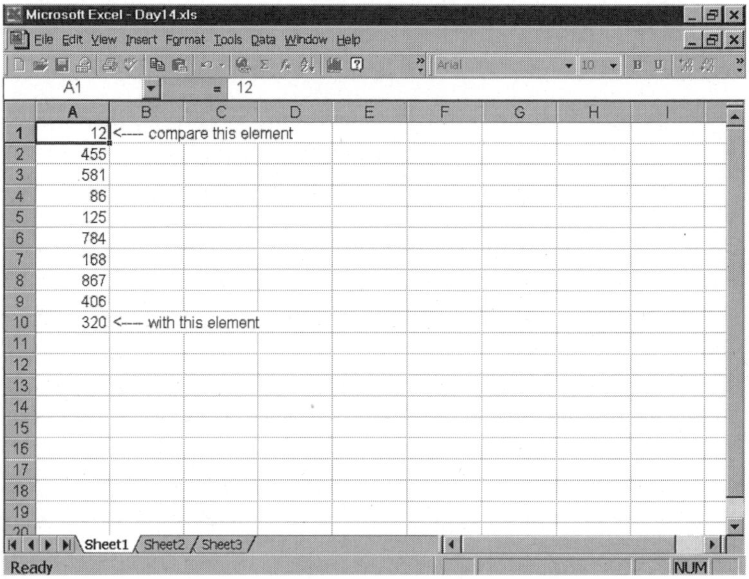

FIGURE 14.7

A sample run of the DemoBubbleSort procedure in Listing 14.3.

Notice that Listing 14.3 contains a complete module, with a total of six different procedures. Notice also that line 2 contains the **Option Base** 1 statement so that VBA will start array subscript numbering at 1 for all arrays in this module.

Lines 5 through 10 contain several module-level constants used to establish the maximum size of the array, the length of the delay, and various strings used to form messages displayed by the procedure.

The DemoBubbleSort procedure itself occupies lines 12 through 59. The procedure's code begins with several variable declarations (lines 14 through 17). Line 14 declares the static array that will later be sorted, I and J are loop counter variables, and oldSheet is a string variable to hold the name of the current worksheet.

Line 20 uses the Randomize statement to initialize VBA's random number generator, and the **For** loop in lines 23 through 25 uses the Rnd function to fill the array with random numbers. (The Rnd function was mentioned in Day 5. Rnd returns a random number as its result; before using the Rnd function, however, you must initialize VBA's random number generator with the Randomize statement.)

Lines 28 and 29 preserve the current sheet's name (for later restoration) and select a worksheet on which to display the progress of the sorting process. Line 32 calls the DisplayArray procedure to display the unsorted array's contents on the worksheet.

The real work of the DemoBubbleSort procedure begins on line 35. The nested **For** loops (the outer loop begins in line 35, the inner loop on line 36) result in every element of the array being compared with every other element of the array.

Line 39 calls the ShowCompare procedure to display markers on the worksheet showing which elements of the array are currently being compared. Line 41 makes the actual comparison test between the array elements; if the array element specified by the outer loop counter is greater than the array element specified by the inner loop counter, the two values need to be swapped.

Note

> To change the bubble-sort from an ascending sort to a descending sort, change the comparison operator in line 41 of Listing 14.3 to a less-than (<) comparison; the array will now be sorted in descending order.

If the values in the array elements are out of order, the Beep statement in line 42 gives you an audible alert that a swap is taking place and the ShowCompare procedure is called again, this time to indicate which elements are being swapped. Beep makes Windows play the default system beep sound (for computers with sound cards) or makes your computer's speaker sound a tone (for computers without sound cards). Line 47 calls the Swap procedure, which actually exchanges the array elements. Line 50 calls the DisplaySwapped procedure, which updates the display of the array's values on the worksheet. The inner **For** loop ends in line 52 and the outer **For** loop ends in line 53.

Lines 54 through 56 simply display a message to let you know that the sorting operation is complete; line 58 restores the sheet that was current when the DemoBubbleSort procedure began executing.

Lines 61 through 66 contain the Swap procedure. Notice that this procedure's arguments are passed by reference (the VBA default) so that any changes that Swap makes to its argument's values are reflected in the original argument variables. Swap just exchanges the contents of its two argument variables; the Temp variable is used to temporarily hold one of the values being exchanged.

Lines 68 through 73 contain the WaitAWhile procedure. This procedure waits for a set period of time by recording the system timer value when the procedure starts and then

14

looping until the difference between the old timer value and the current timer value exceeds the specified interval. (Your computer system's timer records the number of seconds that have elapsed since midnight—the VBA Timer function returns the computer system's timer value.)

Lines 75 through 82 contain the ShowCompare procedure. This procedure simply displays its string arguments on the current worksheet at the specified row coordinates, calls the WaitAWhile procedure, and then clears the message strings from the worksheet.

Lines 84 through 90 contain the DisplayArray procedure. Like the corresponding procedure from Listing 14.2, this procedure simply displays the contents of the array on the active worksheet.

Lines 92 through 98 contain the DisplaySwapped procedure. This procedure updates the position of any array elements that have been swapped during the array's sorting process.

You should enter the DemoBubbleSort procedure and then run it a few times to get a feel for how the bubble-sort works. Notice that each element in the array is successively compared to the remaining higher elements, gradually moving the high values to the end of the array. If the screen messages are too brief for you, increase the amount of time that the messages remain onscreen by increasing the value of the DELAY_TIME constant.

Now that you have a good feel for how the bubble-sort works, take a look at Listing 14.4. Listing 14.4 does essentially the same things as Listing 14.3, but all the cosmetic code has been removed from the procedures and the bubble-sort code itself has been moved into a couple of general-purpose sorting procedures with array arguments. One procedure provides a general-purpose ascending bubble-sort and the other procedure provides a general-purpose descending bubble-sort. The Sorter procedure in Listing 14.4 is a practical implementation of the bubble-sort technique, executing the sorting process at its maximum speed.

INPUT

LISTING 14.4 THE Sorter PROCEDURE SORTS AN ARRAY USING THE BUBBLE-SORT METHOD AND A COUPLE OF GENERAL-PURPOSE SORTING PROCEDURES

```
1:   Option Explicit
2:   Option Base 1
3:
4:   Private Const FORMATSTR As String = "####"
5:   Private Const ARRAY_MAX As Integer = 10
6:
7:   Sub Sorter()
8:     'declare constants
9:     Const iTitle As String = "Sorter Information"
10:
11:    'declare variables
```

```
12:    Dim IntArr(ARRAY_MAX) As Integer
13:    Dim Count As Integer
14:    Dim oldSheet As String
15:
16:    'reseed random number generator
17:    Randomize Timer
18:
19:    'assign random numbers to the elements of array IntArr
20:    For Count = 1 To ARRAY_MAX
21:      IntArr(Count) = Int(Rnd * 1000)
22:    Next Count
23:
24:    'preserve current sheet, switch to new sheet
25:    oldSheet = ActiveSheet.Name
26:    Sheets("Sheet1").Select
27:
28:    'display the array elements
29:    DisplayArray IntArr
30:
31:    MsgBox prompt:="Ready to start sorting.", _
32:           Buttons:=vbInformation, _
33:           Title:=iTitle
34:
35:    'sort the array in ascending order
36:    BubbleSortAscending IntArr
37:
38:    'display the sorted array elements
39:    DisplayArray IntArr()
40:
41:    MsgBox prompt:="Array now sorted in ascending order", _
42:           Buttons:=vbInformation, _
43:           Title:=iTitle
44:
45:    'sort the array in descending order
46:    BubbleSortDescending IntArr
47:
48:    'display the sorted array elements
49:    DisplayArray IntArr
50:
51:    MsgBox prompt:="Array now sorted in descending order", _
52:           Buttons:=vbInformation, _
53:           Title:=iTitle
54:
55:    'restore worksheet
56:    Sheets(oldSheet).Select
57: End Sub
58:
59: Sub BubbleSortAscending(AnyArray() As Integer)
60:    Dim I As Integer, J As Integer
```

14

continues

LISTING **14.4**   CONTINUED

```
61:
62:      'sorts any integer array in ascending order
63:      For I = LBound(AnyArray) To UBound(AnyArray) - 1
64:        For J = I + 1 To UBound(AnyArray)
65:          If AnyArray(I) > AnyArray(J) Then
66:            Swap AnyArray(I), AnyArray(J)
67:          End If
68:        Next J
69:      Next I
70:    End Sub
71:
72:    Sub BubbleSortDescending(AnyArray() As Integer)
73:      Dim I As Integer, J As Integer
74:
75:      'sorts any integer array in descending order
76:      For I = LBound(AnyArray) To UBound(AnyArray) - 1
77:        For J = I + 1 To UBound(AnyArray)
78:          If AnyArray(I) < AnyArray(J) Then
79:            Swap AnyArray(I), AnyArray(J)
80:          End If
81:        Next J
82:      Next I
83:    End Sub
84:
85:    Sub Swap(I1 As Integer, I2 As Integer)
86:      Dim temp As Integer
87:      temp = I1
88:      I1 = I2
89:      I2 = temp
90:    End Sub
91:
92:    Sub DisplayArray(AnyArray() As Integer)
93:      Dim k As Integer
94:
95:      For k = LBound(AnyArray) To UBound(AnyArray)
96:        Cells(k, 1).Value = Format(AnyArray(k), FORMATSTR)
97:      Next k
98:    End Sub
```

ANALYSIS   The Sorter procedure in Listing 14.4 is an improved, no-frills version of the sorting procedure in Listing 14.3. This new version uses the procedures BubbleSortAscending and BubbleSortDescending to sort the array in either ascending or descending order, respectively. Each of these procedures has a single array argument, AnyArray, which is passed by reference. Consequently, when either BubbleSortAscending or BubbleSortDescending sorts the elements of the array argument passed to them, they are sorting the original array.

Note

> Both the `BubbleSortAscending` and `BubbleSortDescending` procedures
> assume that the entire array is filled with valid data to be sorted. If you
> want to sort only a portion of the array, you must modify the sorting proce-
> dures to use a second argument specifying the maximum number of ele-
> ments to sort and then modify the loops to use that argument as the maxi-
> mum count.

Notice that the `Sorter` procedure calls the `DisplayArray` procedure (which also has an array argument) to display the sorted array on the worksheet.

Searching Arrays

Frequently, you'll need to search an array to see whether it contains a particular value. There are two basic techniques for searching arrays: a linear search and a binary search.

In a *linear* search, you simply start at the beginning of the array and examine each element in turn until you find an element that contains the value you're searching for. There are several variations on the basic linear search method. Use a linear search on an unsorted array or if you need to find all occurrences of a particular value in the array.

For sorted arrays, the binary search method is much faster and more efficient. In a *binary* search, you successively divide the array in half (hence the name "binary") and search only the half of the array that is likely to contain the value you're looking for. Binary searching only works on sorted arrays.

The next two sections of this lesson look at each searching technique in more detail.

Using Linear Searches

The basic linear search method is completely straightforward. Suppose you have an array that contains 10 unsorted integers and has subscripts from 1 to 10. To perform a linear search on this array, you simply start with element 1, testing to see whether it contains the value you're looking for. If it does, the search is over; if it doesn't, you continue with the second element and test it for a match with the value you're searching for. The search continues until you either locate the desired value or you run out of array elements to test. The pseudo-code for a linear search might look like this:

```
1:  Set a Not-Found Boolean flag to True.
2:  Set a variable, I, to the starting array subscript.
3:  Do the next step while these two conditions are true:
        I is less than or equal to the upper boundary of the array
        the Not-Found flag remains True
```

14

3A: If the element referenced by I is not equal to the value being
sought then:
        increment the subscript variable, I
        otherwise, set the Not-Found flag to false

The Not-Found **Boolean** flag indicates whether the linear search is successful. If the
search is successful, the matching value in the array will be found in the array element
subscripted by the value in the variable I.

Listing 14.5 shows the LinearSearch procedure, which visually demonstrates how a linear search on an array works. The LinearSearch procedure creates an array, fills the
array with random numbers, and then searches the array for a number specified by the
user.

LISTING 14.5   THE LinearSearch PROCEDURE PERFORMS A VISUAL
INPUT   DEMONSTRATION OF THE LINEAR SEARCH IN AN ARRAY

```
1:   Option Explicit
2:   Option Base 1
3:
4:   Private Const SHORT_DELAY = 1
5:
6:   Sub LinearSearch()
7:     'declare constants
8:     Const ARRAY_MAX As Integer = 10
9:     Const iTitle = "Linear Search"
10:
11:    'declare variables
12:    Dim IntArr(ARRAY_MAX) As Integer
13:    Dim I As Integer
14:    Dim NotFound As Boolean
15:    Dim oldSheet As String
16:    Dim SrchFor As Variant
17:    Dim Rsp As Integer
18:    Dim pStr As String
19:
20:    'preserve the current sheet, select worksheet
21:    oldSheet = ActiveSheet.Name
22:    Sheets("Sheet1").Select
23:
24:    Randomize Timer  'seed the random number generator
25:
26:    For I = 1 To ARRAY_MAX   'assign random values to array
27:      IntArr(I) = Int(Rnd * 1000)
28:    Next I
29:
30:    DisplayArray IntArr    'display the array elements
31:
```

```
32:     'get a value to search for from user, until the user
33:     'doesn't want to search anymore
34:     Do
35:       SrchFor = Application.InputBox( _
36:                 prompt:="Enter a number to search for:", _
37:                 Title:=iTitle & " Input", _
38:                 Type:=1)
39:       SrchFor = CInt(SrchFor) 'convert value to integer
40:
41:       'start searching
42:       I = 1
43:       NotFound = True
44:       Do
45:         'display "?=?" near searched entry
46:         ShowSearch Row:=I, Num:=SrchFor
47:
48:         'no match found?
49:         If IntArr(I) <> SrchFor Then  'increment search index
50:           I = I + 1
51:         Else    'set not-found flag to FALSE
52:           NotFound = False
53:         End If
54:       Loop Until I > ARRAY_MAX Or NotFound = False
55:
56:       If NotFound Then     'display no-match found message
57:         pStr = "No match for " & SrchFor
58:       Else  'display found-match message
59:         pStr = "Found " & SrchFor & " at IntArr(" & I & ")"
60:       End If
61:
62:       pStr = pStr & Chr(13) & Chr(13) & _
63:             "Search for another number?"
64:       Rsp = MsgBox(prompt:=pStr, _
65:                   Title:=iTitle, Buttons:=vbYesNo)
66:     Loop Until Rsp = vbNo
67:
68:     Sheets(oldSheet).Select  'restore original sheet
69:  End Sub
70:
71:  Sub WaitAWhile(Interval As Single)
72:     Dim TheTime As Date
73:     TheTime = Timer
74:     Do
75:     Loop Until (Timer - TheTime) >= Interval
76:  End Sub
77:
78:  Sub DisplayArray(AnyArray() As Integer)
79:     Dim k As Integer
80:
```

14

continues

LISTING 14.5   CONTINUED

```
81:    For k = LBound(AnyArray) To UBound(AnyArray)
82:       Cells(k, 1).Value = AnyArray(k)
83:    Next k
84: End Sub
85:
86: Sub ShowSearch(Row As Integer, Num As Variant)
87: 'indicate row being tested
88:
89:    Cells(Row, 2).Value = "?=? " & Num
90:    WaitAWhile SHORT_DELAY
91:    Cells(Row, 2).Value = ""
92: End Sub
```

 Figure 14.8 shows the result of a sample session with the LinearSearch procedure after successfully searching for the value 219.

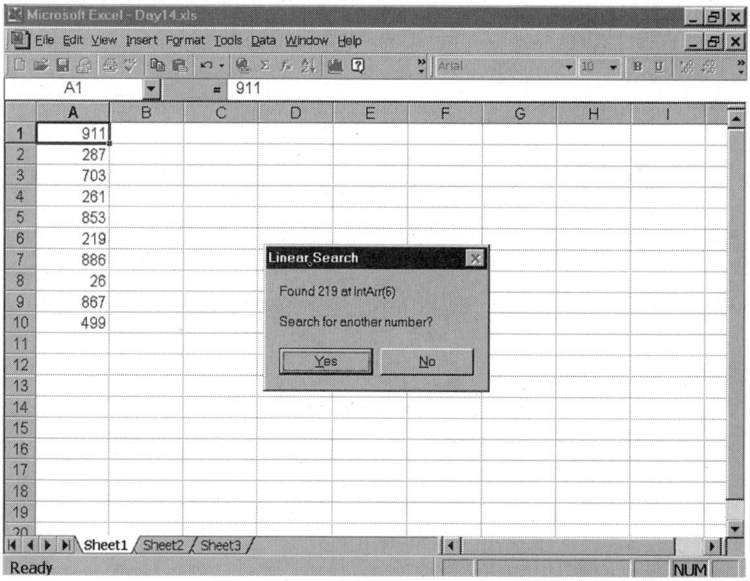

FIGURE 14.8

*The result of a suc-
cessful search with
the* LinearSearch
procedure.

	A	B	C	D	E	F	G	H	I
1	911								
2	287								
3	703								
4	261								
5	853								
6	219								
7	886								
8	26								
9	867								
10	499								

Linear Search

Found 219 at IntArr(6)

Search for another number?

[Yes]   [No]

Line 4 declares a module-level constant used to specify a delay value. The LinearSearch
procedure begins in line 6. Lines 8 and 9 declare a couple of constants used by the
LinearSearch procedure. Notice the ARRAY_MAX constant in line 8. Lines 12 through 18
declare the variables that this procedure uses. Notice the IntArr declaration in line 12.

Lines 21 through 30 set up the procedure's task: The current sheet name is preserved, a worksheet is selected, the array is filled with random numbers, and the contents of the array are displayed on the worksheet by calling the DisplayArray procedure in lines 78 through 84.

Line 34 starts a **Do...Until** loop; this loop executes until the user indicates that she no longer wants to search the array for a number. Line 35 uses the Excel InputBox function to get a number from the user (the Excel InputBox function was used in order to ensure that the user does enter a number—line 39 converts the user's number to an integer).

The actual work of the search begins in lines 42 and 43, which set up the starting conditions for the **Do...Until** loop that starts in line 44. This **Do** loop executes until either a match is found or the subscript counter exceeds the maximum size of the array.

Line 46 calls the ShowSearch procedure (lines 86 through 92), which displays a symbol on the worksheet so that you can see which array element is currently being tested.

Lines 49 through 53 perform the actual search test: The **If...Then...Else** statement tests to see whether the current array element matches the value being searched for. If it does not match, the subscript variable is incremented by 1 and the loop continues; otherwise, the NotFound flag is set **False**.

Line 54 ends the loop, testing to see whether the NotFound flag is **False** or if the subscript variable (I) exceeds the maximum size of the array. If either condition is true, the loop ends.

The **If...Then...Else** statement in lines 56 through 60 checks to see whether a match was found and assembles an appropriate message. Finally, lines 62 through 65 complete the message string and display it in a MsgBox dialog that also asks the user if she wants to search for another number. If the user chooses Yes, the loop starting in line 34 executes again. Otherwise, line 68 restores the original sheet and LinearSearch ends.

Lines 71 through 76 contain the WaitAWhile procedure you're already familiar with from Listing 14.3. Lines 78 through 84 contain the familiar DisplayArray procedure, and lines 86 through 92 contain the ShowSearch procedure.

Using Binary Searches

For sorted arrays, the binary search method is regarded by most programmers as the best general-purpose method for searching. Rather than searching the ordered array sequentially, the binary search takes advantage of the array's sorted order. Because the array is sorted, it is safe to assume that if an element in the middle of the array is greater than the value being searched for, the sought after value can be found in the first half of the array.

14

On the other hand, if the element in the middle of the array is less than the value you're searching for, the sought after value can be found in the second half of the array. After determining which half of the array the sought after value is in, the binary search then takes that half of the array and divides *it* in half. The binary search repeats this halving of the array until it either finds a match for the sought after value or runs out of pieces of the array to search in.

To better understand the binary search, suppose you're looking for the name Harris in a 1,000-page phone book. Using the binary search method, you start by opening the phone book to page 500 (half of 1,000). You see the name Maynard at the top of the page. Because Harris comes before Maynard, you know that the name you're looking for must be in the first half of the phone book. Now you have 500 pages to search in. Next, you open the phone book to page 250 (half of 500) and find the name Fogarty at the top of the page. Harris comes after Fogarty, so you now know that the name you're looking for is in the second half of the first 500 pages of the phone book. You now only have to search in pages 250 through 500. Next, you select the halfway point between 250 and 500, which is page 375. You can proceed with narrowing down the range of pages you're looking at until you either find the name Harris or you determine that there is no page in the phone book with that name on it.

The pseudo-code for a binary search looks like this:

```
1:   Set the low interval limit (called Low), to 1.
2:   Set the high interval limit (called High) to upper boundary of the
     array.
3:   Do the next steps until one of these two conditions is true:
         the element indexed by median of Low and High equals the sought
         value
         Low has become greater than High
3A:  Set a half-way point (called Median) as the median value of Lo and
     High.
3B:  If the sought value is less than the value subscripted by Median
     then
        set High to be the Median - 1
     otherwise, set Low to be the Median + 1
```

When the binary search is complete, you can determine whether it was successful by comparing the value of the array element subscripted by the contents of the median variable with the value being searched for. If they are equal, the search was successful; if they aren't, the search was unsuccessful. Figure 14.9 illustrates the steps of a binary search.

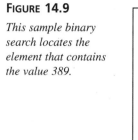

FIGURE 14.9

*This sample binary
search locates the
element that contains
the value 389.*

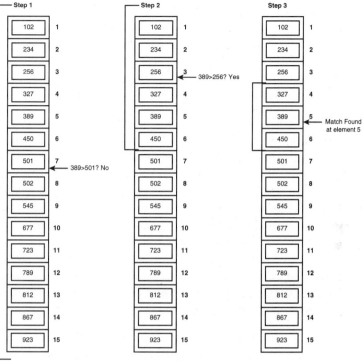

The BinarySearch procedure in Listing 14.6 visually demonstrates how a binary search works. The procedure creates an integer array, fills the array with random numbers, sorts the array, and then displays the array's contents on a worksheet. The procedure then asks the user for a number to search for.

LISTING 14.6 THE BinarySearch PROCEDURE CREATES A VISUAL
INPUT DEMONSTRATION OF A BINARY SEARCH ON AN ARRAY

```
 1:    Option Explicit
 2:    Option Base 1
 3:
 4:    Private Const ARRAY_MAX As Integer = 10
 5:    Private Const SHORT_DELAY = 1
 6:
 7:    Sub BinarySearch()
 8:
 9:       Const iTitle = "Binary Search"
10:
```

continues

14

LISTING 14.6   CONTINUED

```
11:      'declare variables
12:      Dim IntArr(ARRAY_MAX) As Integer
13:      Dim I As Integer
14:      Dim Hi As Integer
15:      Dim Lo As Integer
16:      Dim Median As Integer
17:      Dim oldSheet As String
18:      Dim SrchFor As Variant
19:      Dim Rsp As Integer
20:      Dim pStr As String
21:
22:      'preserve the current sheet, select worksheet
23:      oldSheet = ActiveSheet.Name
24:      Sheets("Sheet1").Select
25:
26:      Randomize Timer  'seed the random number generator
27:
28:      For I = 1 To ARRAY_MAX  'assign random values to array
29:        IntArr(I) = Int(Rnd * 1000)
30:      Next I
31:
32:      BubbleSort IntArr  'sort array IntArr1
33:
34:      DisplayArray IntArr 'display the elements of array
35:
36:      'get a value to search for from user, until the user
37:      'doesn't want to search anymore
38:      Do
39:        SrchFor = Application.InputBox( _
40:                 prompt:="Enter a number to search for:", _
41:                 Title:=iTitle & " Input", _
42:                 Type:=1)
43:        SrchFor = CInt(SrchFor) 'convert value to integer
44:
45:        'start searching
46:        Lo = LBound(IntArr)
47:        Hi = UBound(IntArr)
48:        Do
49:          Median = (Lo + Hi) \ 2  'integer division
50:          'display "?=?" near searched entry
51:          ShowSearch Row:=Median, Num:=SrchFor
52:
53:          If SrchFor < IntArr(Median) Then
54:            Hi = Median - 1
55:          Else
56:            Lo = Median + 1
57:          End If
58:        Loop Until (SrchFor = IntArr(Median)) Or (Lo > Hi)
59:
```

```
 60:          'found match
 61:          If SrchFor = IntArr(Median) Then   'found-match message
 62:            pStr = "Found " & SrchFor & " at IntArr(" & _
 63:                   Median & ")"
 64:          Else  'display no-match found message
 65:            pStr = "No match for " & SrchFor
 66:          End If
 67:
 68:          pStr = pStr & Chr(13) & Chr(13) & _
 69:                 "Search for another number?"
 70:          Rsp = MsgBox(prompt:=pStr, _
 71:                       Title:=iTitle, Buttons:=vbYesNo)
 72:       Loop Until Rsp = vbNo
 73:
 74:       Sheets(oldSheet).Select   'restore original sheet
 75:    End Sub
 76:
 77:    Sub WaitAWhile(Interval As Single)
 78:       Dim TheTime As Double
 79:       TheTime = Timer
 80:       Do
 81:       Loop Until (Timer - TheTime) >= Interval
 82:     End Sub
 83:
 84:    Sub BubbleSort(AnyArray() As Integer)
 85:    'sorts any integer array in ascending order
 86:       Dim I As Integer, J As Integer
 87:       For I = LBound(AnyArray) To UBound(AnyArray) - 1
 88:         For J = I + 1 To UBound(AnyArray)
 89:           If AnyArray(I) > AnyArray(J) Then
 90:             Swap AnyArray(I), AnyArray(J)
 91:           End If
 92:         Next J
 93:       Next I
 94:    End Sub
 95:
 96:    Sub Swap(I1 As Integer, I2 As Integer)
 97:       Dim temp As Integer
 98:       temp = I1
 99:       I1 = I2
100:       I2 = temp
101:    End Sub
102:
103:   Sub DisplayArray(AnyArray() As Integer)
104:      Dim k As Integer
105:
106:      For k = LBound(AnyArray) To UBound(AnyArray)
107:        Cells(k, 1).Value = AnyArray(k)
108:      Next k
109:   End Sub
```

14

continues

LISTING 14.6   CONTINUED

```
110:
111: Sub ShowSearch(Row As Integer, Num As Variant)
112: 'indicate row being tested
113:
114:    Cells(Row, 2).Value = "?=? " & Num
115:    WaitAWhile SHORT_DELAY
116:    Cells(Row, 2).Value = ""
117: End Sub
```

 Figure 14.10 shows the result of a sample session with the BinarySearch procedure after successfully searching for the value 583.

FIGURE 14.10

The BinarySearch *pro-
cedure after searching
for the value 583.*

	A	B	C	D	E	F	G	H	I
1	9								
2	61								
3	164								
4	186								
5	262								
6	473								
7	583								
8	649								
9	738								
10	944								

Binary Search

Found 583 at IntArr(7)

Search for another number?

Yes   No

Lines 4 and 5 declare private module-level constants, and lines 9 through 20 declare the
various constants and variables used in the BinarySearch procedure. Lines 23 through
30 perform the same housekeeping tasks as before.

After the array has been filled with random numbers, however, line 32 calls the
BubbleSort procedure (lines 84 through 94 in Listing 14.6) to sort the array in ascending
order. (This is the same bubble-sorting routine that you're already familiar with, but sorts
in an ascending order only.) After sorting the array, line 34 calls the DisplayArray procedure to display the contents of the sorted array on the worksheet.

Line 38 begins a `Do...Until` loop that, as before, executes until the user no longer wants to search for numbers in the array. Lines 39 through 43 use Excel's `InputBox` function to get a number from the user and convert it to an integer.

Line 46 begins the actual binary search process. Lines 46 and 47 set up the starting conditions for the `Do...Until` loop that starts in line 48. The `Lo` variable is the lower boundary of the array segment currently being searched; `Hi` is the upper boundary of the array segment. When the loop first starts, the upper and lower boundaries are set equal to the array's actual physical boundaries. The `Do` loop starting in line 48 executes until either a match is found or the low boundary of the array segment currently being searched ends up higher than the upper boundary of the array segment.

Line 49 sets the `Median` variable to point to an element halfway between the current upper and lower boundaries of the array segment currently being searched. Notice the use of the integer division operator (\) in this statement.

Line 51 calls the `ShowSearch` procedure (lines 111 through 117) to display a marker on the worksheet so that you can see which array element is currently being tested. Lines 53 through 57 actually perform a matching test. If the value being searched for is less than the value of the array element specified by `Median`, the upper boundary of the array segment currently being searched (`Hi`) is set as being one less than the current `Median`; otherwise, the lower boundary is raised to be one more than the current `Median`.

Lines 61 through 66 check to see whether a match was found and assemble an appropriate message string. Notice that determining whether a match was found simply involves checking to see if the array element referenced by `Median` matches the sought after value (`SrchFor`).

Lines 68 through 71 complete the message string and use a `MsgBox` dialog to ask the user whether to search for another number in the array.

The remainder of this module contains several procedures that you're already familiar with from listings earlier in this lesson: Lines 77 through 82 contain the `WaitAWhile` procedure, lines 84 through 94 contain the `BubbleSort` procedure (this one performs an ascending sort only), lines 96 through 101 contain the `Swap` procedure used by `BubbleSort`, lines 103 through 109 contain the `DisplayArray` procedure, and lines 111 through 117 contain the `ShowSearch` procedure.

Do
DO use a linear search anytime you aren't certain whether the array you're searching is sorted.

14

> **DON'T**
>
> **DON'T** use a binary search on an unsorted array; it won't work, and you'll get erroneous results from the search.
>
> **DON'T** use a linear search when you know the array is sorted. Although the linear search will produce the correct result, binary searches are much faster and more efficient.

Summary

This chapter introduced you to arrays—the simplest and perhaps most useful data structure in many programming languages. You learned that an array is a collection of variables that share the same name. You also learned that you access individual elements in an array through an integer subscript or index value.

This chapter showed you how to use the **Option Base** directive to control whether VBA starts numbering array elements with 0 or 1. Next, you learned how to declare static and dynamic arrays with the **Dim** statement, and you learned how to use **ReDim** to change the size and dimensions of a dynamic array. Then you learned how to use the **Erase** statement to re-initialize a static array, or to remove a dynamic array from memory. You also learned how to use the LBound and UBound functions to determine the upper and lower boundaries of an array.

Finally, you learned how to sort an array by using the classic bubble-sort technique, and you then learned reliable methods for searching both sorted and unsorted arrays.

Q&A

Q Why does VBA use zero-based numbering for arrays? It seems an awkward and difficult numbering system.

A VBA, and most other programming languages, use zero-based numbering for array subscripts because of the way arrays are stored in memory. When VBA creates an array, it simply reserves a single, contiguous block of memory large enough to accommodate all of an array's elements. When you subscript the array, you're really telling VBA how far into the contiguous block of memory the data you want is stored—the array's subscript is translated into an offset value for the memory address. The first element of an array, therefore, is at offset 0, the second element is at offset 1, the third element at offset 2, and so on.

Q Which `Option Base` **statement should I use?**

A Use whichever **Option Base** statement makes you most comfortable. For many people, it's easiest to deal with arrays whose subscripts start with 1, so you'll probably want to include **Option Base** 1 in your modules. If you feel comfortable with zero-based array numbering, use **Option Base** 0 (or just omit the **Option Base** directive). Even if you do use the default zero-based numbering, you might want to add the **Option Base** 0 directive to your modules to explicitly indicate which numbering scheme you're using in that module.

Q **Are there any side effects for not using** `Option Base` **1?**

A Only if you consistently think of array subscripts beginning at 1. If you don't use **Option Base** 1, but write all your code using 1 as the beginning subscript, you're wasting the array element at subscript 0. Also, if you sometimes use 1 as the beginning array subscript and other times use the `LBound` function to obtain the lowest array index, you might end up with bugs in your programs that are difficult to track down.

Q **Can I alter the data types of the array elements in a** `ReDim` **statement?**

A You can only alter an array's data type if you created the array in a **Variant** variable with the **ReDim** statement in the first place; otherwise, VBA does *not* permit you to change the data type of an array's elements. The following code fragment shows how to use **ReDim** to create an array in a **Variant** variable.

```
Dim aList As Variant
ReDim aList(10) As Integer  'integer array inside Variant
ReDim aList(5)  'still an integer array
ReDim aList(10) As String  'now it's a String array in Variant
```

Q **Can I alter the data type of a dynamic array in a** `ReDim` **statement after I erase it with an** `Erase` **statement?**

A No. When you declare a dynamic array, VBA assigns a specific data type to the array's elements—**Variant**, by default, if you don't use the **As** clause to specify a data type. Although the **Erase** statement reclaims any memory used by the dynamic array, VBA does *not* destroy the array. VBA retains information about the array's name and data type in its internal table of variables and their corresponding memory addresses, although there is no memory allocated to the array. Consequently, whenever you **ReDim** the array, VBA still knows what data type the elements of the array should be and prohibits you from changing it. This behavior actually supports good programming practice, discouraging you from using the same array to store different types of data.

14

Workshop

Answers to quiz questions and exercises are in Appendix A.

Quiz

1. How many array elements are in the following declarations?

```
Option Base 1
Dim Lookup(10, 3, 5) As Integer
Dim Cube(3, 3, 3) As Double
```

2. Study the following multi-dimensional array declaration:

```
Option Base 1
Dim A(1980 To 1990, 10, 5 To 9)
```

For the array declaration just shown, what are the values returned by the following function calls:

```
(A)   LBound(A, 1)
(B)   LBound(A, 2)
(C)   LBound(A, 3)
(D)   UBound(A, 1)
(E)   UBound(A, 2)
(F)   UBound(A, 3)
```

3. **BUG BUSTER:** What is wrong with the following set of statements?

```
1:    Option Base 1
2:    Dim X(10, 20) As Double
3:
4:    For I = 1 To 10
5:      For J = 1 To 20
6:        X(I, J) = Int(Rnd * 1000)
7:      Next J
8:    Next I
9:
10:   ReDim X(5, 10) As Single
11:
12:   For I = 1 To 5
13:     For J = 1 To 10
14:       X(I, J) = Int(Rnd * 1000)
15:     Next J
16:   Next I
```

4. Will inserting an **Erase** X statement before the **ReDim** statement (line 10) in the preceding program fix the problem?

5. Can you use an array element anywhere in a VBA statement where you could use a simple variable?

6. Will a linear search work correctly on a sorted array? An unsorted array?

7. Why should you use a binary search on a sorted array? Can you use a binary search on an unsorted array?

Exercises

1. Modify the Sorter procedure from Listing 14.4 to create another procedure, named Sorter2. The new procedure should declare a two-dimensional array, fill it with random numbers, and then sort the two-dimensional array. The Sorter2 procedure's array should have five columns and 15 rows. When sorting the array, Sorter2 should then sort the array based on the values in the second column. Keep in mind that your sorting process will need to swap entire rows, not just the elements in the 2nd column of the array.

2. Given the following code fragment, what values are stored in the array A?

```
Dim A(1 To 9) As Long
Dim I As Integer
A(LBound(A)) = 2
For I = LBound(A) + 1 To UBound(A)
    A(I) = 2 * A(I - 1) - 1
Next I
```

3. **BUG BUSTER:** What is wrong with the following statements?

```
1:  Dim ProjIncome(1995 To 1999) As Double
2:  Dim I As Integer
3:  ProjIncome(1995) = 1000
4:  For I = 1995 To 2000
5:      ProjIncome(I) = 1.1 * ProjectIncome(I - 1)
6:  Next I
```

4. **BUG BUSTER:** What is wrong with the following statements?

```
1:  Option Base 1
2:  Dim X(100) As Double
3:  Dim I As Integer
4:  For I = 1 To 100
5:      X(I) = I * I
6:  Next I
7:  For I = 1 To 100
8:      Cells(I, 1).Value = X(I)
9:  Next I
10: ReDim X(10) As Integer
11: For I = 1 To 10
12:     X(I) = I * I
13: Next I
14: For I = 1 To 10
15:     Cells(I, 1).Value = X(I)
16: Next I
```

14

5. **BUG BUSTER:** What is wrong with these statements?

```
1:  Option Base 2
2:  Dim A(9) As Long
3:  Dim I As Integer
4:  A(LBound(A)) = 2
5:  For I = LBound(A) + 1 To UBound(A)
6:    A(I) = 2 * A(I - 1) - 1
7:  Next I
```

6. **BUG BUSTER:** What is the error in the following statements?

```
1:  Option Base 1
2:  Dim A(9) As Long
3:  Option Base 0
4:  Dim B(9) As Long
5:  Dim I As Integer
6:  A(LBound(A)) = 2
7:  For I = LBound(A) + 1 To UBound(A)
8:    A(I) = 2 * A(I - 1) - 1
9:    B(I) = 2 * A(I - 1)
10: Next I
```

7. **BUG BUSTER:** What is the error in the following statements?

```
1:  Dim A(9) As Long
2:  Option Base 0
3:  Dim B(9) As Long
4:  Dim I As Integer
5:  A(LBound(A)) = 2
6:  For I = LBound(A) + 1 To UBound(A)
7:    A(I) = 2 * A(I - 1) - 1
9:    B(I) = 2 * A(I - 1)
10: Next I
```

WEEK 2

In Review: Enhancing the Workbook Creation Utility

You've finished your second week of learning how to program in Visual Basic for Applications. By now you should feel relatively comfortable with VBA. You have covered all the core concepts in Visual Basic for Applications.

The following listings contain several complete VBA modules for Excel that pull together many of the VBA programming elements and concepts from the previous week.

The modules in this section together make up a single Excel VBA program that enables a user to create a new workbook file and give it a name in a single operation, without duplicating the names of any workbooks that might already be open or on the disk in the same folder. The program also enables the user to optionally specify the number and names of the worksheets in the workbook.

This program was designed using the top-down and step-wise refinement techniques described in Day 12. The pseudo-code below shows the major design outline for this program:

```
1.  Get a workbook filename from the user.
2.  Make sure the workbook doesn't already exist.
       a.  If the workbook is already open, offer to
           make it the active workbook.
       b.  If the workbook isn't open, but exists in
           the current folder, offer to open the
           workbook.
```

3. Create the new workbook, using the standard Excel workbook defaults
4. Get summary information for the new workbook.
    a. Require the user to enter the author information.
    b. Require the user to enter the title of the workbook.
    c. All other summary information is optional.
5. Ask user if she/he wants to adjust the number of worksheets in the workbook
    a. Get the number of worksheets from user, requiring at least 1 worksheet, and don't allow user to cancel
    b. Create or eliminate sheets from the workbook until it contains the user's specified number of worksheets
6. Ask user if she/he wants to change the default names of the worksheets in the workbook.
    a. Get worksheet names from user for as many worksheets as are in the workbook; ensure that names are unique
    b. Ask user whether to sort the worksheet names alphabetically.
        b.1 If so, sort the array of worksheet names.
    c. Rename all worksheets in the workbook, using array of worksheet names previously obtained from user.
7. Save the new workbook, but leave it open as the current workbook, with the first sheet selected.

As you study the following listings, pay attention to how each task is handled by its own procedure or function, and how various procedures call several different functions or procedures to accomplish their own tasks. Notice also that the source code has been divided into three different modules: one module for the main program, another module to hold the supporting procedures and functions highly specific to the main task, and a third module to hold the more generic functions used by the program.

INPUT   **LISTING R2.1**   THE OpenNewBook PROGRAM'S MAIN MODULE AND PROCEDURE

```
 1:    Option Explicit
 2:
 3:    Type SmryInfo    'same data as summary info properties page
 4:       Title As String
 5:       Subject As String
 6:       Author As String
 7:       Keywords As String
 8:       Comments As String
 9:    End Type
10:
11:    Sub OpenNewBook()
12:    'Creates a new workbook, ensuring that the chosen workbook
13:    'is not already open, and does not already exist in the
14:    'current disk folder. Optionally allows user to select the
15:    'number of worksheets and modules, and allows user to give
16:    'them specific names when creating the workbook.
17:
18:       Const nfTitle = "Open New Workbook"
```

```
19:
20:     Dim fName As String          'filename, including path
21:     Dim BName As String           'filename, without path
22:     Dim OKName As Boolean
23:     Dim Smry As SmryInfo            'book's summary info
24:     Dim Ans As Integer             'answers from MsgBox
25:     Dim mPrompt As String           'prompt for MsgBox
26:     Dim nBook As Workbook        'object for new workbook
27:
28:     'display status bar message
29:     Application.StatusBar = "Creating New Workbook..."
30:
31:     BName = "New Workbook"          'get new filename from user
32:     OKName = False
33:     Do
34:       fName = GetBookName(Dflt:=BName, Title:=nfTitle & _
35:                     " - Select Save As Name for New Workbook")
36:       If fName = "False" Then EndNewBook      'user canceled
37:
38:       BName = FullName2BookName(fName)
39:       If IsBookOpen(BName) Then
40:         mPrompt = BName & " is already open. " & _
41:                   "Would you like to switch to it?"
42:         Ans = MsgBox(Prompt:=mPrompt, Title:=nfTitle, _
43:                     Buttons:=vbQuestion + vbYesNo)
44:         If Ans = vbYes Then
45:           Workbooks(BName).Activate
46:           EndNewBook
47:         End If
48:       ElseIf IsDiskFile(fName) Then
49:         mPrompt = fName & vbCr & _
50:                   " already exists. Would you like to open it?"
51:         Ans = MsgBox(Prompt:=mPrompt, Title:=nfTitle, _
52:                     Buttons:=vbQuestion + vbYesNo)
53:         If Ans = vbYes Then
54:           Workbooks.Open fName
55:           EndNewBook
56:         End If
57:       Else
58:         OKName = True   'book is neither open nor exists
59:       End If
60:     Loop Until OKName
61:
62:     'create new workbook with one worksheet
63:     Set nBook = Workbooks.Add(xlWorksheet)
64:
65:     'get summary information
66:     GetSmryInfo Info:=Smry, Title:=nfTitle
67:     With nBook     'fill in summary information
```

continues

```
68:       .Title = Smry.Title
69:       .Subject = Smry.Subject
70:       .Author = Smry.Author
71:       .Keywords = Smry.Keywords
72:       .Comments = Smry.Comments
73:    End With
74:
75:    mPrompt = "Adjust number of worksheets in workbook?" & _
76:              vbCr & "Workbook currently has " & _
77:              nBook.Worksheets.Count & " worksheets."
78:    Ans = MsgBox(Prompt:=mPrompt, Title:=nfTitle, _
79:              Buttons:=vbQuestion + vbYesNo)
80:    If Ans = vbYes Then 'set up new worksheets
81:       NewBook_Worksheets nBook, nfTitle
82:    End If
83:
84:    'Finally, save the new workbook file
85:    nBook.SaveAs fileName:=fName, _
86:              FileFormat:=xlNormal, _
87:              ReadOnlyRecommended:=False, _
88:              CreateBackup:=False
89:    nBook.Activate
90:    nBook.Sheets(1).Activate
91:    EndNewBook 'do housekeeping
92: End Sub
```

ANALYSIS Listing R2.1 is the first module of the program and contains only one procedure, OpenNewBook. This procedure is a more fully developed version of the NewBook procedure from last week's review, and incorporates almost all the VBA features that you've learned in the past week.

Notice the user-defined data type (Day 11) declared in lines 3 through 9. OpenNewBook uses this user-defined type to pass the summary information back and forth between this procedure and the procedure that actually gets the information from the user. A **Do** loop (Day 9) starts in line 33 and repeats until the filename chosen by the user does not duplicate the name of a workbook that is already open or already exists on the disk in the current folder.

The OpenNewBook procedure calls many other procedures and functions that help it do its work. These other procedures avoid duplication of code and make it possible for the OpenNewBook procedure to operate in a flexible and efficient manner. All of the procedures and functions that OpenNewBook calls are in the second and third modules (Listing R2.2 and Listing R2.3).

Line 34 of `OpenNewBook` calls the `GetBookName` function to get the workbook filename from the user. Line 38 calls the `FullName2BookName` function to get just the workbook name out of the filename selected by the user. (The filename returned by `GetBookName` contains the full folder path, including the drive letter.)

Lines 39 through 59 contain several nested **If...Then...Else** statements that test to ensure that the workbook filename selected by the user doesn't duplicate the name of a workbook that is already open or the name of a workbook that is already stored on the disk. In the process of testing whether the workbook already exists, `OpenNewBook` calls the functions `IsBookOpen` and `IsDiskFile` (both of these are in the third module).

Line 63 uses the `Add` method of the `Workbooks` collection to create a new workbook containing only one worksheet; the statement in line 63 also sets an object variable (Day 7) to refer to the newly created workbook. The original statement for the `Add` method was taken from a recorded macro. The `Add` method was then researched in the online help system, which revealed that the `Add` method returns an object reference to the newly created workbook object and has an optional argument to specify that the new workbook should contain only a single worksheet. If an object method returns a result, you can use that method in your VBA code like a function—just remember to include the parentheses, and to use the result in an expression somehow.

Note

> Several of the statements in all three modules shown here were created by copying statements from recorded macros. The methods from the recorded macro statements were then researched in the online help system to find out about additional options for those methods. You can use this technique to help develop your own VBA code.

Line 66 calls the `GetSmryInfo` procedure, which uses a procedure argument passed by reference (Day 12) to return the summary information for the new workbook to `OpenNewBook`.

Lines 75 through 82 carry out the task of asking the user whether to adjust the number of worksheets in the workbook. If the user does choose to adjust the number of workbooks, the statement in line 81 calls the `NewBook_Worksheets` procedure. `NewBook_Worksheets` carries out the task of getting the desired number of worksheets from the user, optionally allowing the user to rename the worksheets and alphabetically sort their names.

Finally, lines 85 through 88 save the new workbook, and lines 89 and 90 ensure that the new workbook is the active workbook, with its first worksheet selected.

The next listing shows another complete module that contains all of the procedures
called directly by OpenNewBook. (All three modules must be in the same workbook for
OpenNewBook to operate correctly.)

LISTING R2.2   THE OpenNewBook PROGRAM'S SUPPORTING PROCEDURES
MODULE

```
1:    Option Private Module
2:    Option Explicit
3:
4:    Public Const STREQUAL As Integer = 0 'StrComp: equality
5:    Public Const STRLESS As Integer = -1 'StrComp: less than
6:    Public Const STRGREAT As Integer = 1 'StrComp: greater than
7:
8:    Sub EndNewBook()
9:    'ends OpenNewBook program, after cleaning up
10:     Application.StatusBar = False
11:     End
12:   End Sub
13:
14:
15:   Sub GetSmryInfo(ByRef Info As SmryInfo, _
16:                   ByVal Title As String)
17:   'returns workbook summary information
18:     Title = Title & " Summary Information"
19:     With Info       'get summary information
20:       .Author = GetSmryItem(Item:="author", Title:=Title, _
21:                             Dflt:=Application.UserName, _
22:                             Required:=True)
23:       .Title = GetSmryItem(Item:="title", Title:=Title, _
24:                             Required:=True)
25:       .Subject = GetSmryItem(Item:="subject", Title:=Title)
26:       .Keywords = GetSmryItem(Item:="keywords", Title:=Title)
27:       .Comments = GetSmryItem(Item:="comments", Title:=Title)
28:     End With
29:   End Sub
30:
31:
32:   Function GetSmryItem(Item As String, _
33:                        Optional ByVal Title, _
34:                        Optional Dflt, _
35:                        Optional Required) As String
36:   'gets file summary info for specified Item
37:
38:     Const Prmpt1 = "Enter the "
39:     Dim Prmpt2 As String        '2nd part of prompt
40:     Dim tStr As String
41:
42:     If IsMissing(Title) Then Title = UCase(Item)
```

```
43:    If IsMissing(Required) Or _
44:        VarType(Required) <> vbBoolean Then
45:      Required = False
46:      Title = Title & " - Optional Entry"
47:    Else
48:      Title = Title & " - Required Entry"
49:    End If
50:
51:    Prmpt2 = " for this workbook."
52:    If Not Required Then
53:      Prmpt2 = Prmpt2 & vbCr & _
54:              "(Press Esc or choose Cancel to skip.)"
55:    End If
56:
57:    Do
58:      tStr = InputBox(Prompt:=Prmpt1 & Item & Prmpt2, _
59:                    Title:=Title, Default:=Dflt)
60:      If Required And (Trim(tStr) = "") Then
61:        MsgBox Prompt:="You must enter the " & Item & "!", _
62:              Title:=Title & " - ERROR", _
63:              Buttons:=vbExclamation
64:      End If
65:    Loop Until (Not Required) Or (Trim(tStr) <> "")
66:    GetSmryItem = tStr
67:  End Function
68:
69:
70:  Sub NewBook_Worksheets(ByRef Book As Workbook, _
71:                        ByVal Title As String)
72:  'Get and set number of worksheets for the new workbook
73:
74:    Dim shtNames() As String      'array for workbook names
75:    Dim numSheets As Integer  'number of worksheets from user
76:    Dim Ans As Integer        'MsgBox answers
77:    Dim k As Integer          'loop counter
78:    Dim Sht As Worksheet
79:    Dim Sht2 As Worksheet
80:
81:    Title = Title & " - Select Worksheets"
82:
83:    Do    'get desired number of worksheets
84:      numSheets = GetInteger(Prompt:="Enter number of " & _
85:                        "worksheets for this workbook:", _
86:                        Title:=Title, Default:=1)
87:      If numSheets < 1 Then
88:        MsgBox Prompt:="You must have at least one " & _
89:                      "worksheet in a workbook!", _
90:              Title:=Title, _
91:              Buttons:=vbExclamation
```

continues

LISTING R2.2   CONTINUED

```
 92:        End If
 93:    Loop Until numSheets >= 1
 94:
 95:    Ans = MsgBox(Title:=Title, _
 96:                Buttons:=vbQuestion + vbYesNo, _
 97:                Prompt:="Change default worksheet names?")
 98:    If Ans = vbNo Then   'just add sheets
 99:       For k = (Book.Worksheets.Count + 1) To numSheets
100:          Set Sht = Book.Worksheets(Book.Worksheets.Count)
101:          Set Sht2 = Book.Worksheets.Add
102:          Sht2.Move after:=Sht
103:       Next k
104:       Exit Sub 'no more work to do
105:    End If
106:
107:    ReDim shtNames(1 To numSheets)   'size the array of names
108:    For k = 1 To numSheets
109:       shtNames(k) = "Sheet" & k    'make default names
110:    Next k
111:
112:    'get names of worksheets from user
113:    Get_NameList Book:=Book, List:=shtNames, _
114:                Prompt:="Enter a worksheet name:", _
115:                Title:=Title
116:    Ans = MsgBox(Title:=Title, _
117:                Buttons:=vbQuestion + vbYesNo, _
118:              Prompt:="Sort worksheet names alphabetically?")
119:    If Ans = vbYes Then BubbleSortStrings shtNames
120:
121:    'create the worksheets with names
122:    With Book
123:       'start by just renaming the first sheet
124:       .Worksheets(1).Name = shtNames(1)
125:       For k = 2 To numSheets
126:          Set Sht = .Worksheets(.Worksheets.Count)
127:          Set Sht2 = .Worksheets.Add
128:          Sht2.Move after:=Sht
129:          Sht2.Name = shtNames(k)
130:       Next k
131:    End With
132: End Sub
133:
134:
135: Sub Get_NameList(Book As Workbook, _
136:                  List() As String, _
137:                  Prompt As String, _
138:                  Title As String)
139: 'gets a list of worksheet names as strings
```

```
140:   Dim k As Long, tStr As String, GoodName As Boolean
141:
142:   For k = LBound(List) To UBound(List)
143:     Do 'ask for a unique name
144:       tStr = InputBox(Prompt:=Prompt, _
145:                       Title:=Title, _
146:                       Default:=List(k))
147:       If Trim(tStr) = "" Then
148:         Exit Sub  'user canceled, no more work
149:       Else
150:         If StrComp(tStr, List(k), vbTextCompare) = STREQUAL Then
151:           GoodName = True
152:         Else
153:           If InListSoFar(List, tStr, k - 1) Or _
154:             SheetExists(Book, tStr) Then
155:             MsgBox Prompt:="Use a different name. " & _
156:                    "This name already exists; " & _
157:                    "sheet names must be unique.", _
158:                    Title:="Sheet Name Error", _
159:                    Buttons:=vbExclamation
160:             GoodName = False
161:           Else
162:             GoodName = True
163:             List(k) = tStr
164:           End If
165:         End If
166:       End If
167:     Loop Until GoodName
168:   Next k
169: End Sub
170:
171: Sub BubbleSortStrings(Arr() As String)
172: 'sorts any string array in ascending order
173:   Dim I As Integer, J As Integer
174:   For I = LBound(Arr) To UBound(Arr) - 1
175:     For J = I + 1 To UBound(Arr)
176:       If StrComp(Arr(I), Arr(J), vbBinaryCompare) = STRGREAT Then
177:         Swap Arr(I), Arr(J)
178:       End If
179:     Next J
180:   Next I
181: End Sub
182:
183:
184: Sub Swap(T1 As Variant, T2 As Variant)
185:   Dim tmp As Variant
186:   tmp = T1: T1 = T2: T2 = tmp
187: End Sub
```

ANALYSIS   All of the functions and procedures in this second module must be called by another procedure or function: Almost all of them are intended to be called only by the OpenNewBook procedure. Notice the **Option Private Module** compiler directive (Day 12) in line 1. This directive means that none of the procedures or functions in this module are available outside of the workbook that contains this module.

The module begins with several constant declarations at the module level (lines 4 through 6). These constants need to be available to all the modules in the program, so they have been declared with the **Public** keyword (Day 12). The **Public** keyword makes the constants available outside of this module, whereas the **Option Private Module** directive limits their scope to the workbook that contains this module, only. These constants are used to represent the StrComp function's results, thus making the VBA code that uses StrComp easier to understand.

Lines 8 through 12 contain the EndNewBook procedure. The EndNewBook procedure simply makes sure that Excel gets back control of its status bar and then uses the **End** statement to stop program execution. A procedure like this is useful because there are several places in OpenNewBook where the procedure should stop. Because the OpenNewBook procedure does use Excel's StatusBar property to display a status message while it is running, the two statements to restore the status bar control to Excel and to exit the sub procedure were repeated several times. By using the EndNewBook procedure, the OpenNewBook procedure is made shorter and easier to understand. If, in the future, you modify OpenNewBook so that it changes other parts of Excel's environment (like whether Excel updates the screen), you can add any other "housekeeping" chores to the EndNewBook procedure.

Lines 15 through 29 contain the GetSmryInfo procedure. Notice that this procedure not only has arguments, but uses the Info argument to return data to the procedure that called it (Day 12). The Info argument has the user-defined SmryInfo data type; this procedure fills all of the elements in the Info argument variable. Notice also, that GetSmryInfo calls a function, GetSmryItem, to obtain the values for the specific elements.

Lines 32 through 67 contain the GetSmryItem function, which returns a single string value. GetSmryItem has several arguments; most of them are optional. The Item argument is the name of the summary information item that GetSmryItem is asking the user for. The optional Dflt argument is a string suggesting the contents of the particular summary information item being obtained. The optional Required argument is used to determine whether GetSmryItem should require the user to enter the requested information, or if it's acceptable to skip entering it. Notice how the GetSmryItem function checks for missing optional arguments and optional arguments with the correct data type and sets appropriate default values for missing or bad optional arguments.

Lines 70 through 132 contain the NewBook_Worksheets procedure. This procedure has two arguments: one for an object reference to the workbook being created and another argument for a title to be displayed by this procedure's message dialogs. The procedure declares several variables; notice the dynamic array (Day 14) declared in line 74 and the object variables (Day 7) declared in lines 78 and 79.

The NewBook_Worksheets procedure starts out with a **Do** loop that asks the user for the number of worksheets to put in the workbook until the entered number is at least 1. Notice that this procedure calls a general-purpose function, GetInteger, to get an integer number. (GetInteger is in the third module.) The statements in lines 95 through 98 check to see whether the user wants to change the default worksheet names. If not, the **For** loop in lines 99 through 103 creates the needed number of new worksheets, moving each new worksheet to the end of the workbook. Line 104 exits from the NewBook_Worksheets procedure because there is no further work to be done.

If the user does want to change the default worksheet names, lines 107 through 110 dimension the shtNames dynamic array so that it is large enough to hold all of the needed worksheet names and then fill the array with faked default worksheet names. Next, lines 113 through 115 call the Get_NameList procedure to fill the shtNames array with worksheet names from the user. The Get_NameList procedure uses an argument passed by reference to return values in the shtNames array. Lines 117 through 119 ask the user whether to sort the list of worksheet names alphabetically and call the BubbleSortStrings procedure to sort the shtNames array.

Finally, lines 122 through 131 create and rename the new worksheets in the workbook. Because the workbook was created with a single worksheet in it, line 124 simply renames that worksheet, and the **For** loop (line 125) creates and names only the additionally required worksheets.

Lines 135 through 169 contain the Get_NameList procedure. This procedure generically fills a list (passed by reference as a string array argument) with sheet names, ensuring that no sheet name entered into the list duplicates an existing sheet name in the workbook or any sheet name entered into the list so far. In order to know which workbook to check for duplicate names, Get_NameList takes an object reference to a workbook as a required argument, along with arguments for the string array, a prompt to display, and a title for its message dialogs.

The Get_NameList procedure uses the LBound and UBound functions so that it can work with any string array. This procedure uses the StrComp procedure in order to ensure that strings are always compared as text (that is, without regard to capitalization). Get_NameList calls the InListSoFar and SheetExists functions to help determine whether the user has entered a unique sheet name. This procedure loops until either all the elements in the array have been processed or the user cancels one of the input dialogs.

Lines 171 through 181 contain the BubbleSortStrings procedure. This procedure is exactly the same as the bubble-sort procedures you saw in Day 14, but it has been modified to alphabetically sort strings instead of numbers. Notice that line 176 uses the StrComp function to compare the strings. This way, the string comparison is controlled and is not affected by the **Option Compare** settings—this procedure will always make a case-sensitive alphabetic comparison of strings, which is what it is supposed to do.

Finally, lines 184 through 187 contain the Swap procedure used by BubbleSortStrings. Notice that this version of Swap has been modified to use **Variant** type variables: It can swap the values of any data type. The advantage of changing the Swap procedure this way is that it can now be used by *any* bubble-sort procedure, whether the bubble-sort is sorting strings or numbers.

The third and final module that makes up this complete program is a group of supporting functions.

INPUT   **LISTING R2.3**   THE OpenNewBook PROGRAM'S SUPPORTING FUNCTIONS MODULE

```
1:   Option Private Module
2:   Option Explicit
3:
4:   Function GetBookName(Dflt As String, _
5:                        Optional Title) As String
6:   'gets a workbook file name, returns "False" if canceled
7:     Dim Fltr As String, tName As String
8:
9:     If IsMissing(Title) Then    'was Title in argument list?
10:      Title = "Enter Workbook Name"
11:    End If
12:
13:    Fltr = "Excel Workbooks,*.xls"  'allow only workbooks
14:    With Application
15:      tName = .GetSaveAsFilename(InitialFilename:=Dflt, _
16:                                 FileFilter:=Fltr, _
17:                                 Title:=Title)
18:    End With
19:    GetBookName = tName     'return filename
20:  End Function
21:
22:
23:  Function FullName2BookName(fileName As String) As String
24:  'returns workbook filename from a filename with full path
25:    Dim tName As String, k As Long
26:
```

```
27:     tName = ReverseStr(fileName)     'reverse the filename
28:     k = InStr(tName, "\")          'find the first backslash
29:
30:     If k = 0 Then  'copy everything in front of backslash
31:       FullName2BookName = fileName
32:     Else
33:       tName = Left(tName, k - 1)
34:     End If
35:
36:     'reverse it again, and return result
37:     FullName2BookName = ReverseStr(tName)
38: End Function
39:
40:
41: Function IsBookOpen(ByVal BName As String) As Boolean
42: 'returns True if book is open
43:     Dim aBook As Object
44:
45:     IsBookOpen = False    'assume failure
46:     BName = Trim(BName)
47:     For Each aBook In Workbooks
48:       If StrComp(aBook.Name, BName, vbTextCompare) = STREQUAL Then
49:         IsBookOpen = True
50:         Exit For
51:       End If
52:     Next aBook
53: End Function
54:
55:
56: Function IsDiskFile(fName As String) As Boolean
57: 'return True if fName is found on disk, False otherwise
58:     If (Dir(fName) <> "") Then
59:       IsDiskFile = True
60:     Else
61:       IsDiskFile = False
62:     End If
63: End Function
64:
65:
66: Function InListSoFar(List() As String, _
67:                      SrchFor As String, _
68:                      Limit As Long) As Boolean
69: 'performs linear search of List for SrchFor
70:     Dim k As Long
71:
72:     InListSoFar = False 'assume failure
73:     For k = LBound(List) To Limit
74:       If StrComp(List(k), SrchFor, vbTextCompare) = STREQUAL Then
75:         InListSoFar = True
```

continues

LISTING R2.3 CONTINUED

```
76:       Exit Function
77:     End If
78:   Next k
79: End Function
80:
81:
82: Function SheetExists(Book As Workbook, _
83:                      ShtName As String) As Boolean
84: 'returns true if sheet exists in specified book.
85:   Dim Sht As Object
86:
87:   SheetExists = False 'assume failure
88:   For Each Sht In Book.Sheets
89:     If StrComp(Sht.Name, ShtName, vbTextCompare) = STREQUAL Then
90:       SheetExists = True
91:       Exit Function
92:     End If
93:   Next Sht
94: End Function
95:
96:
97: Function GetInteger(Prompt As String, _
98:                     Optional Title, _
99:                     Optional Default) As Long
100: 'returns an integer number
101:   Dim tRsp As Variant
102:
103:   If IsMissing(Title) Or VarType(Title) <> vbString Then
104:     Title = "Integer Input"
105:   End If
106:   If IsMissing(Default) Or _
107:     (Not IsNumeric(Default)) Then
108:     Default = ""
109:   Else
110:     Default = CLng(Default)
111:   End If
112:
113:   Do  'get input until numeric, no cancel
114:     tRsp = InputBox(Prompt:=Prompt, _
115:                     Title:=Title, _
116:                     Default:=Default)
117:     If (Not IsNumeric(tRsp)) Or _
118:        (Len(Trim(tRsp)) = 0) Then _
119:       MsgBox Prompt:="You must enter an integer!", _
120:              Title:=Title, Buttons:=vbExclamation
121:   Loop Until IsNumeric(tRsp) And (Len(Trim(tRsp)) > 0)
122:   GetInteger = CLng(tRsp)   'assign function result
123: End Function
```

```
124:
125:
126: Function ReverseStr(Str As String) As String
127: 'reverses the order of characters in the Str argument
128:   Dim k As Long, tStr As String
129:
130:   tStr = ""
131:   For k = 1 To Len(Str)
132:     tStr = Mid(Str, k, 1) & tStr
133:   Next k
134:   ReverseStr = tStr
135: End Function
```

ANALYSIS This module contains the supporting functions used by procedures in both Listing R2.1 and Listing R2.2. The functions in this module are more general-purpose than the procedures and functions in Listing R2.2, and were segregated into a third module to make it easier to later copy them into another workbook that might need similar support functions or to put these functions into a library workbook.

Notice that this module, like Listing R2.2, contains the **Option Private Module** compiler directive, making all the procedures and functions in this module private to the workbook that contains them.

Lines 4 through 20 contain the GetBookName function. This version of the GetBookName function is similar to the one from the week 1 review, but it has been greatly enhanced. This version of GetBookName has different arguments than the previous version. Instead of using InputBox, this version uses the GetSaveAsFilename method (Day 13) to get the filename from the user in line 15. Because the specified filter string includes only the .xls extension, GetSaveAsFilename does not permit the user to select a filename for a file type other than an Excel workbook. Notice that GetBookName returns the string "False" if the user cancels the file selection.

Lines 23 through 38 contain the FullName2BookName function. This function returns just the filename part of a string that contains a full file path specification (a full path specification includes the drive letter and complete folder path—like the strings returned by the GetSaveAsFilename method described in Day 13).

Notice that FullName2BookName calls yet another function, ReverseStr, to help it accomplish its task. In a full folder path, the filename is the part after the last backslash (\) in the path. Because all of VBA's string searching functions only search from left to right, it's difficult to find the *last* occurrence of a particular character, so

FullName2BookName works by reversing the full path name and then copying all the characters up to the *first* backslash. For example, if the folder path is C:\Budget\June.xls, FullName2BookName reverses it to slx.enuJ\tegduB\:C, copies slx.enuJ from it, and then reverses it again to get June.xls.

Lines 41 through 53 contain the IsBookOpen function, which returns a **Boolean** result indicating whether the workbook specified in its argument is open. This function uses a **For Each...Next** loop (Day 9) to check all of the currently open workbooks in the Workbooks collection.

Lines 56 through 63 contain the IsDiskFile function, which returns a **Boolean** value indicating whether there is a file on the disk matching the drive, folder, and filename in the fName argument. Notice the call to the Dir function in line 58. IsDiskFile is identical to the function of the same name described in Day 13.

Lines 66 through 79 contain the InListSoFar function, which returns a **Boolean** result depending on whether the value in the SrchFor argument is found in the List array up to the element specified by Limit. InListSoFar performs a simple linear search on the array (Day 14). (InListSoFar uses a linear search, instead of the more efficient binary search, because the array isn't sorted at this point and binary searches only work on sorted arrays.)

Lines 82 through 94 contain the SheetExists function, which also returns a **Boolean** value, this time depending on whether the worksheet specified by ShtName exists in the workbook specified by Book.

Lines 97 through 123 contain the GetInteger function, which returns a **Long** integer number. This function has a required argument for a prompt string to be displayed by the InputBox dialog and two optional arguments for the dialog title and default input value. Notice the code in lines 103 through 111 that checks for the presence of the optional arguments and assigns reasonable default values if the optional arguments are missing or of the wrong type. Line 113 starts a **Do** loop that repeats until the user enters a numeric value; the user isn't allowed to cancel the input dialog. As soon as the user enters a numeric value, the user's number is converted to a **Long** integer (discarding any decimal fraction) and returned as the GetInteger function result.

Finally, lines 126 through 135 contain the ReverseStr function. This function simply returns a copy of the string passed as its argument, with the order of its characters reversed. Notice that line 128 declares two variables in a single **Dim** statement. Line 131 starts a **For...Next** loop (Day 9) that loops for as many times as there are characters in the Str argument string, assembling them in reverse order.

This program uses almost all of what you've learned in your first two weeks of VBA programming. As you can see, much of what you learned in the second week makes it easier (and possible) to create powerful and flexible programs by using several procedures and functions that work together. In the coming week, you'll continue to build on what you have learned so far.

WEEK 3

15

16

17

18

19

20

21

At a Glance

You have finished your second week of learning how to program in Visual Basic for Applications. By now, you should feel comfortable using Visual Basic for Applications; you've covered all the core features of the language. Now you're ready to learn about some of VBA's advanced features.

What's Ahead?

Now that you have a firm grasp of the core features of the VBA programming language, you have all the resources necessary to take advantage of VBA's advanced features. In this third week, you learn how to make your VBA programs perform as if they are part of Excel, and how to give your programs a polished, professional appearance and behavior.

In Day 15, "Debugging and Testing VBA Code," you learn how to use the debugging features of the VB Editor to examine your program's operation and to find and correct errors in your programs. The VB Editor's debugging tools enable you to closely examine how your procedures and programs execute, and make it possible for you to locate or trace various problems that would otherwise be almost impossible to find.

In Day 16, "Creating Custom Dialog Boxes," you learn how to create and use custom dialogs for your programs. Day 17, "Menus and Toolbars," teaches you how to use VBA's menu and toolbar statements to create and manage Excel's menus and toolbars under the control of your procedures.

Day 18, "Error Handling," teaches you how to use VBA's error-handling capabilities so that your programs and procedures can handle runtime errors gracefully and professionally without crashing. Day 19, "Controlling Excel with VBA," gives you additional information about controlling Excel's objects through your VBA procedures and programs. In Day 20, "Working with Other Applications," you learn how to use program objects from other Windows applications, such as controlling Word from Excel and vice versa. Day 20 also shows you how to use functions and procedures in DLL files and how to control other applications by sending keystrokes.

Finally, Day 21, "Using Event Procedures and Add-Ins," describes how to use procedures that execute automatically whenever you open or close a workbook or document, and how to specify a particular procedure to be executed whenever a particular event occurs. Day 21 concludes with an explanation of how you can convert your own programs into an Excel add-in program.

Appendix A contains all the Quiz answers and solutions to most of the Exercises in each chapter.

DAY 15

Debugging and Testing VBA Code

Bugs are errors in your code that cause your programs to produce erroneous results or prevent them from executing altogether. Today's lesson teaches you about VBA's debugging tools. The VB Editor provides several powerful features to help you track down and correct the sources of bugs in your procedures and functions. In this lesson, you'll learn about

- The basic types of bugs you're likely to encounter as you develop your procedures and functions.

- Using breakpoints and the VB Editor's break mode to suspend the execution of your program code and to control and monitor the execution of your code.

- Working with watch variables and expressions to monitor the values that your code produces as it executes.

- Using the Step Into and Step Over commands to see your code execute line by line and procedure by procedure.

- Tracing the order of procedure calls.
- Using the Immediate Window to view special debugging output from your program or to test the results of various expressions as your program executes.

Today's lesson starts by discussing the basic techniques for *debugging* (that is, locating and eliminating bugs) and then presents examples of using those techniques.

Basic Types of Program Bugs

In computer programming, Murphy's Law ("If anything can go wrong, it will") is especially applicable. Just about any aspect of a program can go wrong. Every computer programmer, regardless of experience or computer language, must spend a certain amount of time tracking down errors and defects in her code. Such defects and errors typically result in programs that stop executing suddenly (they *crash*) or produce erroneous results. Any defect or error in a computer program is called a *bug*.

You'll encounter four basic types of bugs as you program in VBA:

- *Syntax errors* are the result of typing errors, such as misspelling a VBA keyword, a variable, or procedure name. Syntax errors usually occur as you write your code. As you learned in Day 2, "Writing and Editing Simple Macros," the VB Editor can detect most syntax errors as you edit or type each line in your program. (VBA checks syntax when you move the insertion point away from a newly edited or typed line.) Other syntax errors can occasionally show up as compile errors.

- *Compile errors* are the result of statements that VBA cannot correctly compile, and can occur when you attempt to run a VBA procedure. If VBA detects any problems with your code during compilation, it displays an error message and does not execute any code. For example, if you have **Option Explicit** in a module and you use a variable without first declaring it in a **Dim** statement, VBA moves the insertion point to the point where it detected the undeclared variable and displays a compile error.

- *Runtime errors* are the result of expressions or statements that VBA cannot evaluate or execute, such as invalid operations, invalid procedure and function arguments, or illegal mathematical operations. Runtime errors occur as your program code executes. Typical examples of causes of runtime errors are expressions that result in mathematical underflow or overflow, type mismatches in assignment expressions or procedure arguments, attempting to open nonexistent files, or attempting to divide by zero.

- *Logical errors* are the result of a programmer's error in reasoning. Erroneous results are the typical symptoms of logical errors in a program: Your procedures or functions might produce numerical results that are incorrect, a task might be performed incorrectly or incompletely, or your procedure might even perform the wrong task. Some, but not all, logical errors will also result in a runtime error, depending on the specific results of the reasoning flaw.

15

THE VBA COMPILER

When VBA executes any code in a newly created or edited module, it *compiles* the code in that module. As VBA compiles a module, it reads through all the source code in the module. During compilation, VBA builds its internal tables of variables and constants and ensures that all of the decision-making and looping structures, as well as procedure and function declarations, are correctly formed. VBA also checks all procedure and function calls to make sure that the correct number and type of required arguments are provided. This compilation process is an essential step in VBA's preparation to execute your code. It is also during the compilation step that VBA processes the compiler directives (such as `Option Explicit`, `Option Compare`, and `Option Base`) and ensures that all the code in the module meets any restrictions established by the compiler directives.

Generally, VBA compiles your code only once, the first time you execute a procedure after writing or editing it. When you save the project, the compiled code is saved along with your source code. Each successive time you execute that procedure, VBA uses the pre-compiled code in order to save the time it takes to compile the code. VBA compiles your source code again whenever you add to a module or edit existing code in a module.

Tip

You can force VBA to compile your code at any time by choosing the Debug, Compile *<project>* command. VBA compiles all the code in the entire project. You can save a certain amount of debugging time by compiling your code and resolving all the compiler's errors before you try to run your code.

Using the Break Mode

In order to debug your VBA code, you'll frequently need to see exactly how VBA is executing your program statements and what values are stored in various variables at particular moments in your program's execution. For example, you might have a bug in a procedure that sorts an array, resulting in the array remaining unsorted. It will be a lot easier to find the bug in your sorting procedure if you can tell which branches of `If...Then` statements are being executed, check to make sure that `Do` loops execute correctly, or inspect the values stored in variables *as your sorting procedure executes.*

The VB Editor's *break mode* gives you the ability to interact more intimately with your VBA code than when you simply execute one of your programs. When you execute a procedure, your code executes from start to finish at the greatest speed that VBA is capable of; you can't see exactly which parts of your code are executing at any given moment, nor can you tell what value a variable holds at any particular moment. In break mode, however, you gain the ability to execute your code (or parts of it) one line or procedure at a time—sort of like executing your programs in slow motion. Executing your programs one statement at a time is called *single-stepping* through your program.

VBA provides five different ways to activate the VB Editor's break mode:

- Click the Debug button in a runtime error dialog box.
- Set one or more breakpoints.
- Use the **Stop** statement in your code.
- Use the Debug, Step Into command (or press F8).
- Press Esc or Ctrl+Break to interrupt VBA code execution.

Each of these different techniques for activating the VB Editor's break mode is described in the following sections of this lesson.

In addition to the debugging commands available through the Debug menu, the VB Editor provides a Debug toolbar that contains buttons for the most frequently used debugging commands. Figure 15.1 shows the VB Editor's Debug toolbar in its floating window. Use this figure to help identify the Debug toolbar buttons for the commands discussed in the remainder of this lesson.

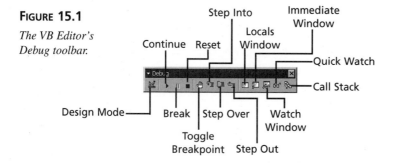

FIGURE 15.1

The VB Editor's Debug toolbar.

Note The VB Editor does not display the Debug toolbar automatically. To display the Debug toolbar, choose the View, Toolbars, Debug menu command. (A check mark appears to the left of the Debug choice on the menu if the toolbar is already displayed.) You can dock the Debug toolbar the same as any other toolbar, or customize it the same way you would customize a toolbar in Excel.

Entering Break Mode from an Error Dialog

Whenever a runtime error occurs while one of your VBA procedures or functions is executing, VBA displays an error dialog like the one shown in Figure 15.2 (the specific error message will vary depending on the actual runtime error that occurred). This error dialog displays the runtime error number, a brief explanation of the nature of the error, and several command buttons. In Figure 15.2, for example, the runtime error is number 11 and is described briefly as `Division by zero`.

FIGURE 15.2

A typical runtime error dialog.

Runtime error dialogs contain the following command buttons:

- Continue—Continues execution of interrupted VBA code. The Continue command button is usually disabled when a runtime error occurs, as shown in Figure 15.2.
- End—Ends all VBA code execution and terminates break mode.
- Debug—Displays the VBA statement that caused the runtime error, opening the appropriate project and module if necessary. VBA remains in break mode, ready for you to inspect variable values, the chain of procedures that led up to the currently executing procedure, and other related debugging activities. Use the Debug command button to quickly jump to the statement that contains the problem.
- Help—Displays the online help topic for the particular runtime error.

To enter break mode from a runtime error message dialog, simply click the Debug button. The VB Editor opens a Code Window to display the statement that caused the runtime error, as shown in Figure 15.3. Notice that the currently executing statement is indicated by a yellow highlight and a yellow arrow in the margin to the left of the Code Window. (In Figure 15.3, the Project Explorer and Properties Window have been closed so that the maximized Code Window will fill the entire available display space; this makes more of your source code visible at one time. Also, the Debug toolbar has been displayed.)

FIGURE 15.3

A typical Code Window in break mode.

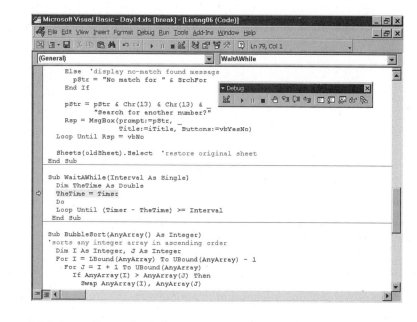

Setting and Using Breakpoints

To locate the cause of both runtime and logical bugs, you'll almost always need to single-step through the statements in your program. Single-stepping through your program's statements enables you to either see exactly which code executes before and as a runtime error occurs or lets you observe the operation of a group of statements that don't seem to be working correctly.

Single-stepping through all the statements in a procedure or a program can be fairly time-consuming and tedious. You'll seldom want or need to single-step through *all* of the statements in your program. Fortunately, the VB Editor enables you to execute most of your code at full speed, entering break mode only when certain, specific statements in your code execute. (Remember, you must be in break mode before you can single-step through your code.)

15

A *breakpoint* is a line in your code that you have specially marked; when VBA encounters a breakpoint, it switches from normal code execution to break mode. By using breakpoints, you can execute most of your program at full speed, entering break mode only when VBA reaches the particular statements that you're interested in examining closely. After it is set, a breakpoint remains in effect until you either remove it or close the project that contains the module in which you set the breakpoint.

You can set a breakpoint on any line in your source code that contains an executable statement. Usually, you'll set breakpoints slightly ahead of the statements that you know or suspect are causing problems. To set a breakpoint, follow these steps:

1. Display the VBA module and procedure containing the statements you want to single-step through.

2. In the Code Window, place the insertion point on the line where you want VBA to switch from normal execution to break mode. This line will become the new breakpoint, and must contain an executable VBA statement.

3. Choose the Debug, Toggle Breakpoint command to insert the breakpoint. VBA color-codes the line in the Code Window to indicate that it is selected as a breakpoint, as shown in Figure 15.4: the breakpoint line is highlighted in dark red and a dark red dot appears next to the line in the Code Window's left margin.

Tip

You can also press F9 or use the Toggle Breakpoint button on the VB Editor's Debug toolbar to set a breakpoint. You can also set a breakpoint by clicking in the left margin of the code window at the line where you want to set the breakpoint.

Note

To remove a breakpoint, perform the same steps as for adding a breakpoint: If you use the Toggle Breakpoint command on a line that already has a breakpoint set, VBA removes the breakpoint. To clear all the breakpoints in a module, choose the Debug, Clear All Breakpoints command or press Ctrl+Shift+F9.

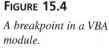

FIGURE 15.4

A breakpoint in a VBA module.

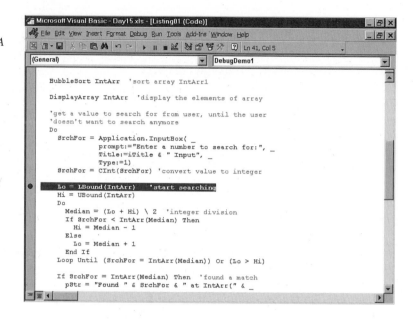

Using the Stop Statement

Breakpoints set with the Toggle Breakpoint command only remain in effect for the current work session. Sometimes, and particularly for complex programs, your debugging efforts might extend over several work sessions. As a result, you might want to set a more-or-less permanent breakpoint. VBA provides the **Stop** keyword for exactly that purpose.

Whenever VBA encounters the **Stop** statement, it stops executing your code, displays the module and procedure containing the currently executing statement, and enters break mode. When you use the **Stop** statement, you create a *hard-coded breakpoint*, that is, the breakpoint becomes an actual part of your VBA code. The only way to remove the breakpoint created by the **Stop** statement is to remove the **Stop** statement from your source code.

Typically, you'll insert the **Stop** statement in your code whenever you need a persistent breakpoint; when you finish debugging your program, edit your source code to remove the **Stop** statement.

Do

DO keep in mind that breakpoints set with the Toggle Breakpoint command only remain in effect for the current work session.

DO use the `Stop` statement to create a breakpoint that remains permanently in your code.

Don't

DON'T forget to remove `Stop` statements when you are finished developing your procedures and functions.

Entering Break Mode Using the Step Into Command

You already know that you can execute a procedure directly from its source code by using the Run, Run Macro command or by clicking the Run Macro button on the VB Editor's toolbar.

Similarly, you can start executing any procedure in break mode. Simply place the insertion point inside the procedure you want to execute in break mode and choose the Debug, Step Into command. (You can also press F8 or click the Step Into command button on the Debug toolbar.) VBA enters break mode and makes the procedure declaration the current executing statement. As mentioned before, the current executing statement is indicated in the Code Window during break mode by a yellow highlight and margin arrow as shown previously in Figure 15.3.

Entering Break Mode by Interrupting Code Execution

As you've already learned, VBA enables you to interrupt code execution by pressing the Esc key (or by pressing the Ctrl+Break key combination). When you interrupt code execution, VBA displays an error dialog; this dialog indicates that code execution was interrupted and offers you the same choices as VBA's runtime error dialog: Continue, End, Debug, and Help. To work with your code in break mode, choose the Debug command button; VBA enters break mode and displays the statement that was executing at the time you interrupted the procedure.

Ending Break Mode

Often, you might single-step through part of your code and then want the rest of your program to execute at full speed. The rest of the time, you'll probably want to end both the break mode and execution of your code so that you can make changes in your source code to correct the problems you've identified while using break mode.

To end break mode and continue executing your program at full speed, choose the Run, Continue command. VBA ends break mode and continues executing your code at full speed until VBA encounters the normal end of your program. If VBA encounters a breakpoint or a **Stop** statement before it reaches the end of your program, VBA will again enter break mode. (You can also end break mode and continue program execution by pressing F5 or by clicking the Continue toolbar button.)

To end break mode and also end all program execution, choose the Run, Reset command. VBA ends break mode and halts all code execution; all variables lose their values and all procedures are removed from memory. (You can also end break mode and halt program execution by clicking the Reset button on the VBA toolbar.)

Do
DO remember that the Continue command replaces the Run command on the Run menu when you are in break mode. Also, the Continue toolbar button replaces the Run toolbar button when in break mode.
DO remember that you might not always be able to continue code execution—either single-stepping or normally—if you enter break mode from a runtime error dialog. Usually, an error serious enough to produce a runtime error prevents VBA from being able to execute any more statements in your program.

Using the Step Into Command

Now that you understand how to enter and end break mode, you're ready to learn how to use the Step Into command to single-step through your code while in break mode. Stepping into statements enables you to thoroughly examine the execution of a procedure, function, or of an entire program in order to debug it.

When you use the Step Into command to single-step through your source code, VBA steps *into* every procedure or function call that it encounters so that you end up single-stepping each and every statement that VBA executes. The single-stepping process with the Step Into command enables you to follow the execution of every statement in the main procedure and every statement in every function or procedure called directly or indirectly by the main routine.

15

Before using the Step Into command, you need some code to single-step through. Listing 15.1 contains a slightly shortened version of the `BinarySearch` procedure (and its supporting procedures) from Day 14 "Arrays." (This version of `BinarySearch` doesn't animate the search process; it only displays the array's contents so that the user can see what values should be found in the array.) The procedures in Listing 15.1 are for you to have some code to work with while learning about the debugging commands.

INPUT   **LISTING 15.1**   SOME CODE TO DEMONSTRATE VBA DEBUGGING

```
1:   Option Explicit
2:   Option Base 1
3:
4:   Private Const ARRAY_MAX As Integer = 10
5:
6:   Sub DebugDemo1()
7:     Const iTitle = "Binary Search"
8:
9:     Dim IntArr(ARRAY_MAX) As Integer
10:    Dim I As Integer
11:    Dim Hi As Integer
12:    Dim Lo As Integer
13:    Dim Median As Integer
14:    Dim oldSheet As String
15:    Dim SrchFor As Variant
16:    Dim Rsp As Integer
17:    Dim pStr As String
18:
19:    oldSheet = ActiveSheet.Name   'preserve current sheet
20:    Sheets("Sheet1").Select       'select new worksheet
21:
22:    Randomize Timer   'seed the random number generator
23:    For I = 1 To ARRAY_MAX  'assign random values to array
24:      IntArr(I) = Int(Rnd * 1000)
25:    Next I
26:
27:    BubbleSort IntArr   'sort array IntArr1
28:
29:    DisplayArray IntArr  'display the elements of array
30:
31:    'get a value to search for from user, until the user
32:    'doesn't want to search anymore
33:    Do
34:      SrchFor = Application.InputBox( _
35:              prompt:="Enter a number to search for:", _
36:              Title:=iTitle & " Input", _
37:              Type:=1)
38:      SrchFor = CInt(SrchFor) 'convert value to integer
39:
```

continues

LISTING 15.1 CONTINUED

```
40:       Lo = LBound(IntArr)     'start searching
41:       Hi = UBound(IntArr)
42:       Do
43:         Median = (Lo + Hi) \ 2  'integer division
44:         If SrchFor < IntArr(Median) Then
45:            Hi = Median - 1
46:         Else
47:            Lo = Median + 1
48:         End If
49:       Loop Until (SrchFor = IntArr(Median)) Or (Lo > Hi)
50:
51:       If SrchFor = IntArr(Median) Then   'found a match
52:         pStr = "Found " & SrchFor & " at IntArr(" & _
53:                 Median & ")"
54:       Else  'display no-match found message
55:         pStr = "No match for " & SrchFor
56:       End If
57:
58:       pStr = pStr & Chr(13) & Chr(13) & _
59:                "Search for another number?"
60:       Rsp = MsgBox(prompt:=pStr, _
61:                    Title:=iTitle, Buttons:=vbYesNo)
62:     Loop Until Rsp = vbNo
63:     Sheets(oldSheet).Select   'restore original sheet
64:  End Sub
65:
66:  Sub BubbleSort(xArray() As Integer)
67:  'sorts integer array in ascending order
68:     Dim I As Integer, J As Integer
69:     For I = LBound(xArray) To UBound(xArray) - 1
70:       For J = I + 1 To UBound(xArray)
71:         If xArray(I) > xArray(J) Then _
72:            Swap xArray(I), xArray(J)
73:       Next J
74:     Next I
75:  End Sub
76:
77:  Sub Swap(I1 As Integer, I2 As Integer)
78:     Dim temp As Integer
79:     temp = I1: I1 = I2: I2 = temp
80:  End Sub
81:
82:  Sub DisplayArray(AnyArray() As Integer)
83:     Dim k As Integer
84:
85:     For k = LBound(AnyArray) To UBound(AnyArray)
86:        Cells(k, 1).Value = AnyArray(k)
87:     Next k
88:  End Sub
```

ANALYSIS The module in Listing 15.1 is essentially the same as the module presented in Listing 14.6—some of the code statements and comments have been reformatted to take up less vertical space, and the search animation has been removed, but the functionality of the procedures in the module is unchanged. The DebugDemo1 procedure works exactly the same as the BinarySearch procedure from Listing 14.6: It creates an array, fills it with random numbers, sorts the array, and then searches the array for values entered by the user. The DisplayArray, BubbleSort, and Swap procedures all work the same as described for Listing 14.6.

The only differences between Listing 15.1 and Listing 14.6 are in how some of the VBA statements are formatted. Notice the colon (:) characters in line 79. The colon separates VBA statements on the same line—sort of the opposite of the line-continuation symbol. The colon (:) character tells VBA that there is more than one logical statement on the same physical line. Also notice the line-continuation character in line 71; using this line-continuation character makes this **If...Then** statement a single-line **If...Then**, eliminating the need for an **End If** statement.

After you enter Listing 15.1, you're ready to use the Step Into command. To practice using the Step Into command (and setting a breakpoint), follow these steps:

1. Move the insertion point to line 27 (the statement that calls the BubbleSort procedure) and choose the Debug, Toggle Breakpoint command to set a breakpoint (or click the Toggle Breakpoint button on the Debug toolbar). VBA highlights the line in your source code to indicate that you have set a breakpoint there. (Setting breakpoints was described in the preceding section of this lesson.)

2. Now run the DebugDemo1 procedure. VBA executes the code in the DebugDemo1 procedure until it reaches the statement where you've set the breakpoint and then switches to break mode. You'll see a Code Window similar to the one shown in Figure 15.5. At this point, VBA is ready to execute the procedure call to the BubbleSort procedure.

3. Choose the Debug, Step Into command (or press F8, or click the Step Into button on the Debug toolbar). VBA executes the statement that calls the BubbleSort procedure, stepping into the BubbleSort procedure's code.

   After choosing the Step Into command, the Code Window displays the procedure declaration for the BubbleSort procedure; VBA is now ready to start executing the statements in that procedure. (In the Code Window, VBA indicates the statement it will execute next with a yellow highlight and a yellow arrow in the left margin, as shown in Figure 15.6.)

FIGURE 15.5

The VB Editor displays this Code Window when it halts at the breakpoint set in line 27 of Listing 15.1.

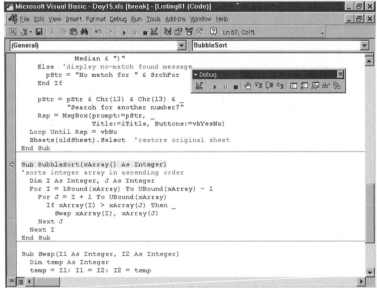

FIGURE 15.6

When single-stepping in break mode, VBA indicates the current statement in the Code Window with an arrow and by highlighting the text.

```
            Median & ")"
      Else  'display no-match found message
        pStr = "No match for " & SrchFor
      End If

      pStr = pStr & Chr(13) & Chr(13) & _
             "Search for another number?"
      Rsp = MsgBox(prompt:=pStr, _
                   Title:=iTitle, Buttons:=vbYesNo)
    Loop Until Rsp = vbNo
    Sheets(oldSheet).Select  'restore original sheet
End Sub

Sub BubbleSort(xArray() As Integer)
'sorts integer array in ascending order
  Dim I As Integer, J As Integer
  For I = LBound(xArray) To UBound(xArray) - 1
    For J = I + 1 To UBound(xArray)
      If xArray(I) > xArray(J) Then _
        Swap xArray(I), xArray(J)
    Next J
  Next I
End Sub

Sub Swap(I1 As Integer, I2 As Integer)
  Dim temp As Integer
  temp = I1: I1 = I2: I2 = temp
```

4. Continue using the Debug, Step Into command to execute statements. VBA executes a single statement each time you issue the Step Into command. As you continue to single-step through Listing 15.1 with the Step Into command, notice that when you reach the call to the Swap procedure in line 72, the Step Into command also single-steps through the statements of the Swap procedure.

15

> **Tip**
>
> The easiest and most practical way to single-step through your code with the Step Into command is to use one of the command shortcuts—either press F8 to issue the Step Into command or click the Step Into command button on the VB Editor's Debug toolbar.

If you continue using the Step Into command to step through all of the statements in both BubbleSort and Swap, you'll follow VBA's code execution until you eventually return to the main procedure. After stepping through all the statements in BubbleSort, VBA execution returns to line 29. If you issue the Step Into command again, you can step into the execution of the DisplayArray procedure called in line 29.

When you're tired of single-stepping through the code in Listing 15.1, you can end all code execution by choosing the Run, Reset command or by clicking the Reset command button on the VB Editor's toolbar.

If you want to finish executing the code in Listing 15.1 at normal speed, choose the Run, Continue command or click the Continue command button on the VB Editor's toolbar.

Using the Step Over Command

As you can see from the preceding exercise, stepping into every procedure call in your code can be quite tedious—it might not always be useful to you, either. For example, if you're stepping through the BubbleSort procedure because you suspect it has a bug in it, but you're confident that the Swap procedure is working fine, you won't want (and don't need) to step through all of the instructions in the Swap procedure every time you step through the BubbleSort procedure.

Fortunately, the VBA Debugger provides the Step Over command, which complements the action of the Step Into command. When you use the Step Over debugging command on a statement that calls a procedure or user-defined function, VBA doesn't step into that procedure's code; instead, it executes the called procedure's code at normal speed and resumes single-stepping with the first statement *after* the procedure call. Stepping over procedure calls helps you focus on debugging the statements in the current procedure without wasting time stepping through the statements in subsidiary procedures that you already know work correctly.

To get some practice using the Step Over command, follow these steps:

1. If you have not already set a breakpoint in line 27 of Listing 15.1, do so now.

2. Execute the DebugDemo1 procedure. As in the previous exercise, VBA executes DebugDemo1 until it reaches the statement containing the breakpoint, and it then enters break mode and displays a Code Window similar to the one already shown in Figure 15.5.

3. Choose the Debug, Step Over command (you can also press Shift+F8 or use the Step Over command button on the Debug toolbar).

   As soon as you choose the Step Over command, VBA executes the statement that calls the BubbleSort procedure, executing the entire BubbleSort procedure (including any procedures called by BubbleSort) at normal execution speed *without* single-stepping through any of the statements in the BubbleSort procedure's code at all. VBA resumes single-stepping with the first statement in DebugDemo1 after the one that called the BubbleSort procedure: line 29 of Listing 15.1.

4. Continue using the Debug, Step Over command to execute statements. VBA executes a single statement each time you issue the Step Over command, except when the statement calls one of your procedures or functions. As you continue to single-step through Listing 15.1 with the Step Over command, notice that when you reach the call to the DisplayArray procedure in line 29, the Step Over command causes VBA to execute the DisplayArray procedure *without* single-stepping through any of its statements; the Step Over command "steps over" the statements in the called procedure.

Tip

> The easiest and most practical way to use the Step Over command is with one of its shortcuts: either press Shift+F8 to issue the Step Over command or click the Step Over command button on the Debug toolbar.

When you're tired of stepping through the code in Listing 15.1 with the Step Over command, you can resume full speed code execution by choosing the Run, Continue command or by clicking the Continue command button on the VB Editor's toolbar. To stop all code execution, choose the Run, Reset command or click the Reset command button on the VB Editor's toolbar.

Using the Step Out and Run To Cursor Commands

Occasionally, you'll find yourself stepping through a procedure when you don't really want to. You might have accidentally used the Step Into command when you meant to use the Step Over command. You might realize that a procedure you're stepping through really is working correctly and you want to quickly get back to single-stepping through the procedure that called the one you're currently stepping through. The VB Editor provides the Step Out command to help you avoid wasting time stepping through procedures unnecessarily.

When you use the Debug, Step Out command (or one of its shortcuts: Ctrl+Shift+F8 or the Step Out command button on the Debug toolbar), VBA executes the remainder of the current procedure or function at full speed and returns to break mode at the first statement after the one that called the currently executing procedure. For example, if you are single-stepping through the `BubbleSort` procedure of Listing 15.1 and you use the Step Out command, VBA executes the remainder of the `BubbleSort` procedure (and any procedures called by it) at full speed, re-entering break mode at line 29: the first statement after the one that called `BubbleSort`.

You might occasionally want to single-step through a procedure's code, but don't want to step through every iteration of a loop—especially because some loops can execute hundreds of times. The VB Editor provides you with the Run To Cursor command to help you skip large loops or other blocks of statements that you already know work correctly to help you avoid wasting time while single-stepping through your code.

To use the Run To Cursor command, position the insertion point in any statement that will be executed after the current statement. Next, choose the Debug, Run To Cursor command (or press Ctrl+F8). VBA executes at full speed all statements from the current statement (indicated by the arrow in the left margin of the Code Window) to the current position of the cursor and then re-enters break mode.

Understanding and Using Watched Variables

Single-stepping through your code alone won't provide all the clues you need to find and eliminate bugs in your programs. By single-stepping through your code, you might be able to tell, for example, that VBA is executing the wrong branch of an `If...Then...Else` statement. In this situation, there's clearly something wrong with the value produced by the logical expression in the `If` statement. But how can you tell whether there is something wrong with the expression you've written, or whether the problem is due to an incorrect value in one of the variables used in the expression?

A *watched* variable enables you to inspect the contents of a variable while your code is executing. By using a watched variable, the Watch Window, and break mode, you can monitor the values generated by your program as it executes. For example, when trying to find out what's wrong with the logical expression of an **If...Then...Else** statement, you would watch the values of any variables in the logical expression and you might also watch the value of the logical expression itself. By watching those variables and the expression result, you'll be able to tell why the **If...Then...Else** statement doesn't have the expected results.

Typically, you watch variables or expressions whose values are associated with logical or runtime errors. You'll probably want to watch all the variables in any expression that produces a runtime error—division by zero, for example—in order to determine which variable(s) is responsible for the runtime error and at which point in your program it acquires the offending value. Such information is invaluable in detecting and correcting bugs in your programs. The VB Editor uses the Watch Window to enable you to monitor the contents of a variable or the values produced by an expression.

> **Note**
>
> The VB Editor doesn't display the Watch Window automatically. You must manually display the Watch Window by choosing the View, Watch Window command or by clicking the Watch Window button on the Debug toolbar.

Figure 15.7 shows the Watch Window with several watched variables and one watched expression listed. Notice that the Watch Window lists the name of expression, the value currently resulting from the expression, the type of the expression, and the context of the expression. The expression itself can be either a single variable name or any expression from your code. (By default, the Watch Window appears in a docked position at the bottom of the VB Editor's window.)

In Figure 15.7, the first four items listed in the Watch Window are single variables; the last item is an expression. In the case of a single variable, the Value column displays the value currently stored in the variable; for expressions, the Value column displays what the expression's result is when evaluated using current variable values. If a listed watched variable is outside of its current scope, the Value column displays <out of context>. For array elements with invalid subscript values, the Value column of the Watch Window displays <subscript out of range>.

FIGURE 15.7

The Watch Window with several watched variables and expressions.

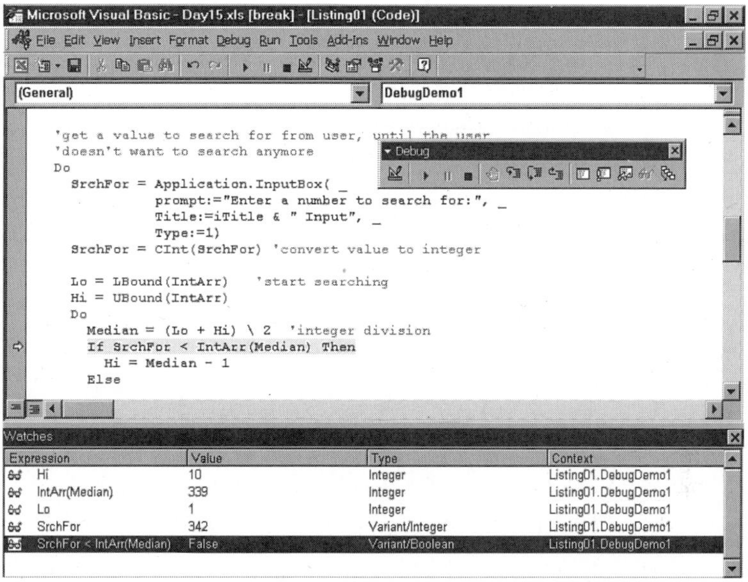

The Type column of the Watch Window tells you what data type the watched expression has. For **Variant** variables—such as the SrchFor variable that appears in Figure 15.7—the Type column tells you what specific data type the **Variant** stores. In Figure 15.7, the SrchFor variable is a **Variant** currently storing an **Integer**.

The Context column of the Watch Window tells you which module and procedure the watched variable or expression is in. All of the watched variables in the Watch Window in Figure 15.7 are in the same module and from the same procedure.

Note

Watch expressions only remain in effect for the current work session.

Adding a Watch Expression

Before you can watch a variable or expression, you must add it to the Watch Window. You can add any variable or expression from your source code to the list in the Watch Window by following these steps:

1. In the Code Window, select the text containing the variable or expression you want to add to the Watch Window. For a single variable name, just place the insertion point somewhere inside the variable name.

2. Choose the Debug, Add Watch command. VBA displays the Add Watch dialog shown in Figure 15.8.

3. Fill in the dialog options (described next) and choose OK. VBA closes the Add Watch dialog and adds the selected variable or expression to the Watch Window.

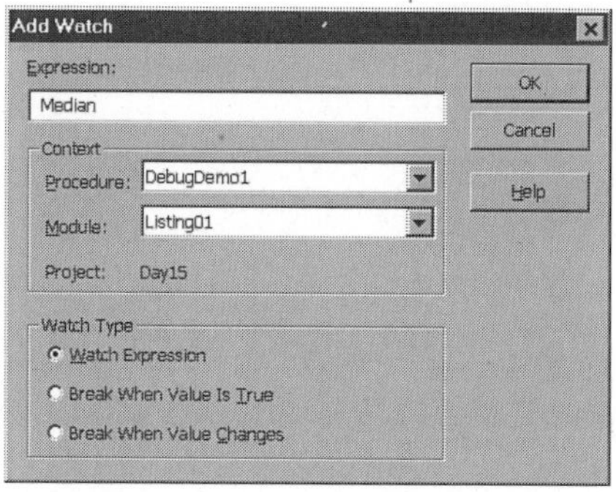

FIGURE 15.8

An Add Watch dialog showing the variable Median *being entered as a watched variable.*

The Add Watch dialog enables you to specify the following options for the new watch expression:

- The Expression edit box enables you to enter the variable or expression that you want to watch. If you've selected text in your source code before opening the Add Watch dialog, the selected text is filled in as the default. You must enter a valid variable name or VBA expression.

- The Context group box contains the Procedure and Module drop-down list boxes. By default, VBA uses the current module and procedure. You can specify a watch variable or expression in a different module or procedure by selecting the desired module in the Module drop-down list and the desired procedure in the Procedure drop-down list.

- The Watch Type group box contains three option buttons: Watch Expression, Break When Value Is True, and Break When Value Changes. You use these options to give the VB Editor special instructions about how you want to handle this watched variable or expression. If you select Watch Expression, VBA simply adds the variable or expression to the Watch Window. If you select Break When Value Is True, VBA enters break mode whenever the variable or expression you're watching evaluates to **True**. The Break When Value Changes option tells VBA to enter break mode whenever the value of the watched variable or expression changes.

Use the last two options in the Watch Type group box (Break When Value Is True and Break When Value Changes) to reduce the amount of time that you spend single-stepping through your code. For example, you might be trying to track down the source of a divide-by-zero runtime error—one of the variables in your division expression ends up with the value zero, causing the runtime error. To eliminate this bug, you need to find the point in your program where that variable is assigned the value 0—or find out whether any value is ever assigned to the variable. To make this process faster, watch the suspected variable with the Break When Value Changes option. You could then execute your code at full speed, entering break mode and viewing the Watch Window only when the value in the suspected variable changes.

To get some practice setting and using watched variables, follow these steps:

1. Clear all the breakpoints from Listing 15.1 by choosing the Debug, Clear All Breakpoints command.

2. Set a breakpoint in line 40 of Listing 15.1. (Setting breakpoints was described earlier in this lesson.)

3. Execute the DebugDemo1 procedure. VBA executes the procedure until it reaches the breakpoint. VBA then enters break mode and displays the Code Window.

4. Choose View, Watch Window or click the Watch Window button on the Debug toolbar to display the Watch Window, if the Watch Window is not already visible.

5. Choose the Debug, Add Watch command. VBA displays the Add Watch dialog, already shown in Figure 15.8.

6. Enter the variable name Lo in the Expression edit box and choose OK. VBA closes the Add Watch dialog and adds the Lo variable to the Watch Window.

7. Repeat steps 5 and 6 to add the variables Hi and Median to the Watch pane and again to add the expression IntArr(Median).

8. Use the Step Over command (described in the preceding section of this lesson) to single step through the **Do** loop in lines 42 through 49. Notice the changes in the Watch Window's display of the watched variables.

Figure 15.7 shows a Watch Window similar to the one you set up when you followed the preceding instructions. If you want, keep single-stepping through subsequent repetitions of the **Do** loop, noticing how the variable values in the Watch Window change as the code in the loop executes.

Editing a Watch Expression

Occasionally, you might want to edit a watched expression. You might just want to change the name of a variable to another similarly named variable to avoid adding a completely new watch variable, or for some other reason. VBA enables you to edit the expressions in the Watch Window.

To edit a watched expression, follow these steps:

1. Choose the View, Watch Window command to display the Watch Window, if it isn't already open.
2. In the Watch Window, select the watch expression you want to edit.
3. Choose the Debug, Edit Watch command. This command invokes the Edit Watch dialog, which is essentially identical to the Add Watch dialog already shown in Figure 15.8.
4. Make whatever changes you want in the watched expression's name, context, or watch type.
5. Choose OK to close the Edit Watch dialog. VBA updates the edited watch expression in the Watch Window.

Deleting a Watch Expression

As you work with watched variables and expressions, you'll find that your list in the Watch Window tends to grow. At some point, you'll probably realize that you don't really need all the watch expressions that you have set, and you'll want to delete some of them from the Watch Window. You can delete a watch expression in one of two ways:

- Select the watch expression you want to delete in the Watch Window and press the Del key. VBA deletes the selected watch expression from the Watch Window without confirmation.

- Select the watch expression you want to delete and then choose the Debug, Edit Watch command. VBA displays the Edit Watch dialog. Choose the Delete command button in the Edit Watch dialog. VBA deletes the selected watch expression from the Watch pane.

Using Quick Watch

As you have just learned, the Add Watch and Edit Watch dialogs make it possible for you to set special options for watched variables, such as whether to enter break mode when a variable's value changes. In most cases, however, you'll probably only want to add the variable to the Watch Window without setting any special options. The VB Editor therefore provides the Quick Watch feature as a faster alternative to using the Add Watch dialog when you don't need or want to set special watch options. (You can always set or change options for watched variables and expressions by using the Edit Watch dialog described earlier in this lesson.)

To use the Quick Watch dialog, follow these steps:

1. In the Code Window, place the insertion point inside the variable you want to view or select the expression you want to view.

2. Choose the Debug, Quick Watch command (you can also press Shift+F9 or click the Quick Watch command button on the Debug toolbar). VBA displays the Quick Watch dialog. Figure 15.9 shows a sample Quick Watch dialog.

3. If you want to add this variable or expression to the Watch Window, click the Add button in the Quick Watch dialog. VBA adds the variable or expression to the Watch Window as a standard watch expression, with the context shown in the Quick Watch dialog.

4. To close the Quick Watch dialog *without* adding the selected variable or expression to the Watch Window, choose the Cancel button.

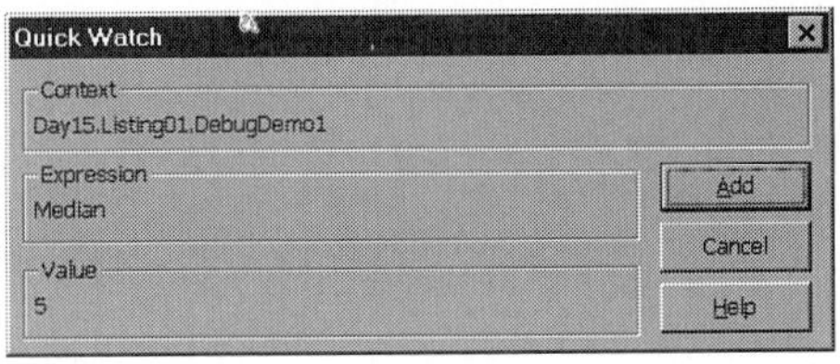

FIGURE 15.9

A Quick Watch dialog showing the current context and value for the Median *variable.*

Using Data Tips

Sometimes, you might just want to take a peek at the value of a variable without adding it to the Watch Window. For example, you might want to get a glance at the current value of a loop counter as you're single-stepping through your code without actually creating a watch for the loop counter.

You can take a quick peek at variable values by using the Auto Data Tips feature. Whenever you are in break mode, you can view the contents of a variable or expression by holding the mouse pointer over the item whose value you want to view. After about half a second, VBA displays a pop-up window showing the current value of that variable. Figure 15.10 shows Listing 15.1 being executed in break mode. The mouse pointer (the I-beam shape) was held over the UBound(IntArr) expression; the pop-up window showing the expression's value appears below the expression.

FIGURE 15.10

Use Auto Data Tips to view an expression's value.

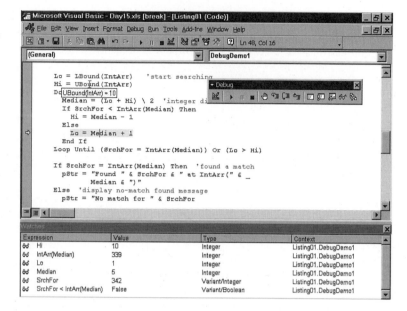

The Auto Data Tips feature is on by default. If Auto Data Tips don't appear, select the Tools, Options command in the VB Editor to display the Options dialog box. Next, click the Editor tab to display the VB Editor's editing options sheet. Make sure that the Auto Data Tips check box is selected. (You can turn Auto Data Tips off by clearing the check box.)

Using the Locals Window

The Locals Window, although not actually part of the Watch Window or the system of setting up watched variables and expressions, performs a related function. The Locals Window displays all the variables local to (or with active scope in) the procedure or function that is currently being executed. Figure 15.11, for example, shows all the local variables of the BubbleSort procedure of Listing 15.1.

The Locals Window displays three columns: Expression (the name of the variable or object), Value (the current contents of the variable or object property), and the Type (the data or object type of the expression). Notice the boxes to the left of the Listing01 and xArray entries in the Locals Window of Figure 15.11. Like the boxes you're used to in other Windows expandable tree lists, these indicate an expanded (if the box contains a minus sign) or expandable (if the box contains a plus sign) entry in the Locals Window. Clicking the plus sign opens a tree diagram of the object's properties and values; clicking the minus sign collapses and hides the tree diagram. In Figure 15.11, for example, the

Listing01 entry displays a list of all module-level variables and constants. Clicking the symbol at the left of the xArray entry displays a list of all elements of the array and the value of each element array. Use the Locals Window to inspect the value and structure of variables and objects in the currently executing procedure, function, or module.

FIGURE 15.11

Use the Locals Window to inspect the value of expressions and objects in the currently executing function, procedure, or module.

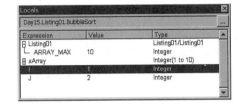

Tracing Procedure Calls

Frequently, you'll need to determine the exact *chain*, or sequence, of procedure calls leading up to a particular statement that generates errors. The chain of procedure calls can be significant because, often, the exact sequence of procedure calls plays an important role in determining the source of an error. For example, you might find a statement that results in a divide-by-zero error, but you don't know why one of the variables in the statement contains a zero. Knowing the exact chain of procedure calls can help you determine, for example, that a procedure was called with an optional argument missing or simply with a bad value in a required argument.

VBA enables you to view the chain of procedure calls through the Call Stack dialog. To view the chain of procedure calls, choose the View, Call Stack command, click the Call Stack command button on the Debug toolbar, or press Ctrl+L. The VB Editor displays the Call Stack dialog shown in Figure 15.12 (the exact chain of procedure calls will vary depending on what code is actually executing at the time you open the Call Stack dialog). As Figure 15.12 shows, the Call Stack dialog lists the sequence of procedure and function calls leading up to the currently executing procedure or function. The currently executing procedure or function is at the top of the list, and each successive list item indicates the procedure or function that called the procedure or function above it in the list.

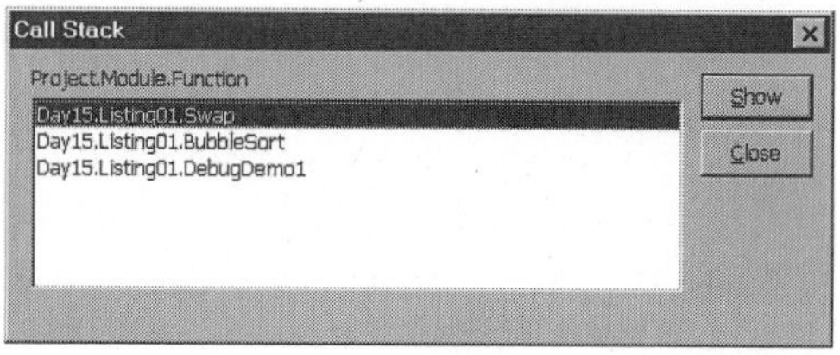

FIGURE 15.12

A Call Stack dialog showing the chain of procedure calls for the Swap *procedure in Listing 15.1.*

To reproduce the Call Stack dialog shown in Figure 15.12, follow these steps:

1. Choose the Debug, Clear All Breakpoints command to remove all breakpoints from Listing 15.1.

2. Set a breakpoint in line 79 of Listing 15.1 (inside the Swap procedure).

3. Execute the DebugDemo1 procedure. VBA executes the procedure until it reaches the breakpoint in line 79, where it enters break mode.

4. Choose the View, Call Stack command, press Ctrl+L, or click the Call Stack button on the Debug toolbar to display the Call Stack dialog already shown in Figure 15.12. The list in the Call Stack dialog shows all the procedure calls leading up to the Swap procedure: Swap was called by BubbleSort, which in turn was called by DebugDemo1.

Notice that the Call Stack dialog contains two command buttons: Show and Close. The Close button simply closes the Call Stack dialog. The Show button, however, performs a very useful function.

Use the Show button in the Call Stack dialog to see the statement that contains the call to a particular procedure. You can use the Show button to help backtrack the argument values passed to a particular procedure. Assume, for example, that you're trying to resolve a divide-by-zero runtime error and you determine that the offending value has been passed into the current procedure as one of the procedure's arguments. Open the Call Stack dialog, select the name of the procedure that called the current procedure, and then choose the Show command button. VBA closes the Call Stack dialog and displays the statement that called the current procedure in the Code Window. You can use the Show button and the Call Stack dialog to work back through the entire chain of procedure calls.

Using the Immediate Window

Sometimes, even the combination of single-stepping, watched expressions, and tracing procedure calls won't be enough to help you track down a bug in your code. The VB Editor offers one final tool to help you locate defects in your code.

The VB Editor's Immediate Window is a free-form editor that enables you to inspect the values in variables, inspect the values of expressions, perform on-the-fly computations, alter the values of variables, and test the results of a function—all while your VBA code's execution is suspended in break mode. To view or use the Immediate Window, choose View, Immediate Window, press Ctrl+G, or click the Immediate Window button on the Debug toolbar; VBA displays the Immediate Window.

You use **Print** commands (or the shorthand **?** for **Print**) to display information in the Immediate Window. You use the **Print** command in the Immediate Window along with a list of variables or expressions. As soon as you type a **Print** command and press Enter, VBA evaluates the expressions you listed with the **Print** command and displays their results on the line below the **Print** command. Figure 15.13 shows a sample session using the Immediate Window.

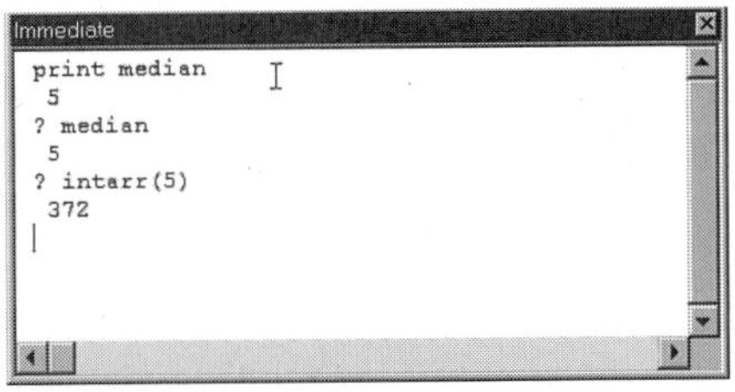

FIGURE 15.13

A session with the Immediate Window showing the output of some Print *commands.*

```
Immediate
print median    I
 5
? median
 5
? intarr(5)
 372
|
```

Using the Debug.Print Statement

The debugging services provided by the VB Editor are embodied by the **Debug** object. The VBA **Debug** object has only one method: the **Print** method. You use the **Debug.Print** method to display information in the Immediate Window as your code executes. To use the **Debug.Print** method, you write VBA statements that call the **Debug.Print** method.

Usually, you use the **Debug.Print** method in combination with the **Stop** statement you learned about earlier in this lesson. Combining these two elements enables you to run your programs at full speed, but still generate debugging information similar to the information you can get by watching variables or expressions. Typically, you add one or more statements calling the **Debug.Print** method and displaying the value of certain variables or expressions on the Immediate Window. Although the Immediate Window is not visible when VBA executes your code normally, VBA will enter break mode whenever it encounters a **Stop** statement, making the Immediate Window available. The Immediate Window then enables you to view any output generated by the **Debug.Print** statements in your code. By using this technique, you can save a lot of debugging time by avoiding single-stepping through code. After you view the information in the Immediate Window, you can resume execution of your program at normal speed.

Listing 15.2 contains the DebugDemo2 procedure and module.

LISTING 15.2 THE DebugDemo2 PROCEDURE ILLUSTRATING THE USE OF `Debug.Print`

```
1:   Option Explicit
2:   Option Base 1
3:
4:   Private Const ARRAY_MAX As Integer = 10
5:
6:   Sub DebugDemo2()
7:     Const iTitle = "Binary Search"
8:
9:     Dim IntArr(ARRAY_MAX) As Integer
10:    Dim I As Integer
11:    Dim Hi As Integer
12:    Dim Lo As Integer
13:    Dim Median As Integer
14:    Dim oldSheet As String
15:    Dim SrchFor As Variant
16:    Dim Rsp As Integer
17:    Dim pStr As String
18:
19:    oldSheet = ActiveSheet.Name   'preserve current sheet
20:    Sheets("Sheet1").Select       'select new worksheet
21:
22:    Randomize Timer  'seed the random number generator
23:    For I = 1 To ARRAY_MAX  'assign random values to array
24:      IntArr(I) = Int(Rnd * 1000)
25:    Next I
26:
27:    BubbleSort IntArr  'sort array IntArr1
28:
29:    DisplayArray IntArr  'display the elements of array
30:
31:    'get a value to search for from user, until the user
32:    'doesn't want to search anymore
33:    Do
34:      SrchFor = Application.InputBox( _
35:               prompt:="Enter a number to search for:", _
36:               Title:=iTitle & " Input", _
37:               Type:=1)
38:      SrchFor = CInt(SrchFor) 'convert value to integer
39:
40:      Lo = LBound(IntArr)    'start searching
41:      Hi = UBound(IntArr)
42:
43:      'display a table heading in Immediate Window
44:      Debug.Print "IntArr(Median) SrchFor", "Lo", "Hi", _
45:               "Median"
46:
47:      Do
```

```
48:            Median = (Lo + Hi) \ 2   'integer division
49:
50:            'display table row in Immediate Window
51:            Debug.Print IntArr(Median), SrchFor, Lo, Hi, Median
52:
53:            If SrchFor < IntArr(Median) Then
54:               Hi = Median - 1
55:            Else
56:               Lo = Median + 1
57:            End If
58:        Loop Until (SrchFor = IntArr(Median)) Or (Lo > Hi)
59:
60:        Stop 'enter break mode
61:
62:        If SrchFor = IntArr(Median) Then   'found a match
63:           pStr = "Found " & SrchFor & " at IntArr(" & _
64:                  Median & ")"
65:        Else   'display no-match found message
66:           pStr = "No match for " & SrchFor
67:        End If
68:
69:        pStr = pStr & Chr(13) & Chr(13) & _
70:                 "Search for another number?"
71:        Rsp = MsgBox(prompt:=pStr, _
72:                     Title:=iTitle, Buttons:=vbYesNo)
73:     Loop Until Rsp = vbNo
74:     Sheets(oldSheet).Select   'restore original sheet
75: End Sub
76:
77: Sub BubbleSort(xArray() As Integer)
78: 'sorts integer array in ascending order
79:    Dim I As Integer, J As Integer
80:    For I = LBound(xArray) To UBound(xArray) - 1
81:      For J = I + 1 To UBound(xArray)
82:        If xArray(I) > xArray(J) Then _
83:            Swap xArray(I), xArray(J)
84:      Next J
85:    Next I
86: End Sub
87:
88: Sub Swap(I1 As Integer, I2 As Integer)
89:    Dim temp As Integer
90:    temp = I1: I1 = I2: I2 = temp
91: End Sub
92:
93: Sub DisplayArray(AnyArray() As Integer)
94:    Dim k As Integer
95:
96:    For k = LBound(AnyArray) To UBound(AnyArray)
97:      Cells(k, 1).Value = AnyArray(k)
98:    Next k
99: End Sub
```

ANALYSIS This listing is identical to Listing 15.1, but has had some **Debug.Print** statements and a **Stop** statement added to it. The **Debug.Print** statement in line 44 was added to create a heading for subsequent values displayed in the Immediate Window. The **Debug.Print** statement in line 51 was added to display the values of the Median, Hi, Lo, and SrchFor variables, and the IntArr array element subscripted by Median. Finally, the **Stop** statement in line 60 was added to cause VBA to enter break mode and enable you to see the values displayed by the **Debug.Print** statements. Figure 15.14 shows the Immediate Window after a sample session with DebugDemo2 completed a single search.

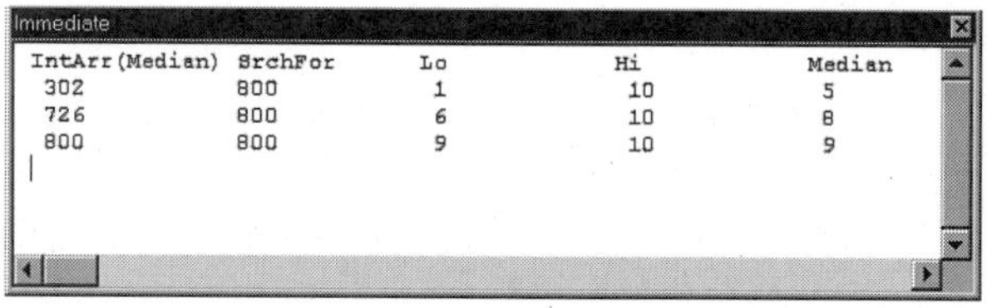

FIGURE 15.14

The Immediate Window showing the output of the **Debug.Print** *statements in Listing 15.2.*

```
Immediate
IntArr(Median)  SrchFor      Lo          Hi         Median
  302            800           1          10           5
  726            800           6          10           8
  800            800           9          10           9
```

When you execute DebugDemo2, VBA executes the procedure at normal speed until it encounters the **Stop** statement in line 60. VBA then enters break mode. You might need to press Ctrl+G to display the Immediate Window. The exact list of values you see printed will depend on the actual list of random numbers that DebugDemo2 generates and the number you entered to search for.

After reviewing the contents of the Immediate Window, continue executing the DebugDemo2 procedure by pressing F5 or clicking the Continue command button on the VB Editor's toolbar. Each time you search for a number in the list, the DebugDemo2 procedure will enter break mode at the **Stop** statement and you'll see a new set of output values in the Immediate Window (these values are generated by the **Do** loop in lines 47 through 58).

Summary

This lesson discussed the various debugging features offered by VBA. You learned that there are four basic types of errors you'll encounter: syntax, compile, runtime, and logical. You also learned the typical causes for these types of errors.

In this lesson, you learned what VBA's break mode is and how to use the break mode in combination with the Step Into, Step Over, Step Out, and Run To Cursor commands to suspend your code's execution and then step through your VBA code one statement or procedure at a time. You learned about VBA's Watch Window, Locals Window, and Immediate Window.

This lesson taught you how to set and clear breakpoints, and showed you how to use them. You were shown how to watch particular variables or expressions in the Watch Window, and how to add, edit, or delete watched variables. You also learned how to use the **Stop** statement as a hard-coded breakpoint.

Next, you learned how and why to trace the chain of calling procedures by using the Call Stack dialog, and, finally, you learned how to use the Immediate Window. As part of learning how to use the Immediate Window, you also learned how to use the **Debug.Print** method in your VBA code to display information on the Immediate Window while your code is executing.

Q&A

Q **Isn't there some way I can turn Debug.Print statements on or off so that I don't have to edit my entire program or procedure again once it's working correctly?**

A No, not directly. There is, however, an indirect way to turn **Debug.Print** statements on and off: You can use special compiler directives to perform what is known as *conditional compilation*. With conditional compilation, you can control what code the VBA compiler actually compiles. Conditional compiler directives work much like the VBA constant declaration and **If** statements you're already familiar with, but are prefaced with a pound sign (#) to differentiate them from regular VBA code.

Use the **#Const** compiler directive to declare a flag to indicate what code you want compiled. Then use the **#If...Then...#Else** compiler directive to control what code is compiled. The following code fragment demonstrates how to use this technique:

```
#Const DEBUGGING = True
#If DEBUGGING Then
  Debug.Print "Debugging is on."
#End If
```

If the DEBUGGING constant defined in the **#Const** declaration is **False**, the **Debug.Print** statement not only won't execute, it won't even be compiled. Whatever the value of the DEBUGGING constant, it only occupies memory during the code compilation—it isn't part of your VBA code and never consumes resources while your code is actually executing.

You can also set conditional compilation constants by entering them in the Conditional Compilation Arguments text box on the General tab of the Project Properties window. Display the Project Properties window by selecting the project in the Project Explorer and then choosing the Tools, *<project>* Properties command. When entering conditional compilation constants in the Project Properties window, you can only enter integer values for the conditional compiler constants. To set the value for the DEBUGGING constant in the preceding example, you would enter **DEBUGGING = 1** into the Conditional Compilation Arguments text box to indicate that DEBUGGING is **True**; use 0 to indicate a value of **False**.

Q Is there a statement that counteracts the Stop **statement?**

A No. To resume program execution, you must use the Run, Continue command. You can, however, use conditional compilation (as described in the preceding Q&A item) to conditionally compile **Stop** statements in your code.

Workshop

Answers are in Appendix A.

Quiz

1. Where do you place a breakpoint in a procedure or function?
2. How can multiple breakpoints help you debug a program?
3. Does VBA enable you to watch the values of an entire array?
4. How can you experiment with calling a function without writing VBA code to call that function?
5. What command do you use to reset single-stepping a procedure in order to rerun it?

Exercises

1. Change line 58 of Listing 15.2 from the following:

   ```
   58:        Loop Until (SrchFor = IntArr(Median)) Or (Lo > Hi)
   ```

   To the following (the > operator has been changed to >=):

   ```
   58:        Loop Until (SrchFor = IntArr(Median)) Or (Lo >= Hi)
   ```

   Run the modified procedure and examine the values generated by the **Debug.Print** statement. What kind of effect does replacing the > operator with >= have on the procedure's operation?

2. Change the following **If** statement in Listing 15.2

```
53:          If SrchFor < IntArr(Median) Then
54:             Hi = Median - 1
55:          Else
56:             Lo = Median + 1
57:          End If
```

to this:

```
53:          If SrchFor < IntArr(Median) Then
54:             Hi = Median
55:          Else
56:             Lo = Median
57:          End If
```

Run the modified procedure and examine the values generated by the **Debug.Print** statement. What effect does this modification have? Does the procedure still work correctly?

3. **BUG BUSTER:** What is the error in this loop?

```
1:  Dim I As Integer
2:  Dim S As String
3:  Dim FindChar As String * 1
4:  Dim ReplChar As String * 1
5:
6:  S = "Hello World!! How are you?"
7:  FindChar = "!"
8:  ReplChar = " "
9:  I = 1
10:
11: Do While I < Len(S)
12:    If Mid(S, I, 1) = FindChar Then
13:       Mid(S, I, 1) = ReplChar
14:    End If
15: Loop
```

4. **BUG BUSTER:** Where is the error in the following statements? What category of errors does it belong to?

```
1:  I = 55
2:
3:  If I < 10 And I > 100 Then
4:     Debug.Print "I = ", I
5:  End If
6:  Debug.Print "Hello!"
```

5. **BUG BUSTER:** Where is the error in the following statements? How can you fix it?

```
1:  Dim S As String
2:  Dim SubStr As String
3:  Dim I As Integer
```

```
4:
5:  S = "The rain in Spain stays mainly in the plain"
6:  SubStr = "ain"
7:  I = InStr(S, SubStr)
8:  Do While I > 0
9:    Debug.Print "Match at "; I
10:   I = InStr(I, S, SubStr)
11: Loop
```

DAY 16

Creating Custom Dialog Boxes

So far, you've learned to use the dialogs that VBA predefines for you: the MsgBox procedure and function and the InputBox function. Although MsgBox and InputBox give your programs the flexibility that only interactive programs can have, they are fairly limited. As you develop more complex programs, you'll want to display dialogs that enable your program's user to select more than one option at a time, to select items from a list, or to input several values at the same time—just like the dialogs that Excel and other Windows applications display. Frequently, you'll want to use dialogs customized specifically for your program, rather than the built-in dialogs that belong to Excel.

Fortunately, VBA enables you to create and use custom dialogs in your programs and procedures by adding a UserForm object to your project. By using VBA user forms, you can create custom dialogs to display data or get values from your program's user in a specific manner that meets your program's needs. For example, you can display a dialog to show a list of various date formats and enable the user to select only one date format from the list.

Custom dialogs enable your program to interact with its user in a sophisticated way and provide a versatile form of data input and output. This lesson gets you started with creating and managing VBA user forms as custom dialogs. Today, you'll learn how to

- Insert a new UserForm into a project.
- Add controls to the UserForm.
- Set the tab order of controls in the UserForm.
- Attach code to the UserForm's controls.
- Set the UserForm's control properties.
- Invoke controls on the UserForm.

Understanding User Forms

You create a custom dialog in VBA by adding a UserForm object to your project. A UserForm object is a blank dialog box; it has a title bar and a Close button, but no other controls on it. You create a customized dialog by adding controls to a UserForm object (usually referred to simply as a *form*). Each UserForm object has inherent properties, methods, and events that it inherits from the class of UserForm objects. Each UserForm object also incorporates a class module in which you add your own methods and properties or write the event-handling code for the form.

EVENTS AND EVENT PROCEDURES

An *event* is something that happens to a dialog box or to a control in the dialog. Typical examples of events include clicking a command button, option button, or check box. Other examples of events include changing the contents of an edit box or a selection in a list. Mouse clicks, key presses, and actions internal to your computer all *trigger*—that is, cause—events. (Another way of saying an event has been triggered is to say that the event *fires*.)

Objects such as forms and controls all *expose*—that is, make available—certain events. You can write your own VBA procedures to respond to events, such procedures are called *event procedures*. In some cases, such as clicking a command button, your event procedure will provide the only action that is carried out in response to that event. In other cases, such as terminating a dialog by clicking the Close button in its title bar, your event procedure only adds to the action that is carried out in response to the event.

Event procedures must all be written in the class module that is part of the UserForm whose events you want to respond to, although your event procedures can call other procedures or functions in a standard module or a referenced library. Event procedures always have a name in the form *ObjectName_EventName*, where *ObjectName* is the name of the form or control and *EventName* is the name of the event you want to handle. By using this naming format, VBA is able to match the correct procedure with the specific event. You'll see several examples of event procedures throughout the rest of this lesson.

When you create a new UserForm object in your project, you create a new subclass of UserForm object. Any procedures or functions that you write in the General section of the form's inherent class module become additional methods for that particular object subclass. You can also create new properties for the form by adding **Property Get** and **Property Let** procedures to its class module. You add code to a form object's inherent class module using the same programming techniques for class modules that you learned about in Day 11. You can create instances of your UserForm subclass with the **Dim** statement and the **New** keyword just as you learned to do with other custom classes in Day 11.

Most of the time, however, you'll control a form object by utilizing the standard methods and properties of the UserForm class and by writing event-handling procedures for your specific form and its controls.

Table 16.1 lists the most common UserForm methods that you'll want to use and summarizes their purpose. Every UserForm you add to your project will have these methods available. Later in this lesson you'll see examples of most of these methods in use.

TABLE 16.1 COMMONLY USED METHODS FOR UserForm OBJECTS

Method	Purpose
Copy	Copies the selected text in a control to the Windows Clipboard.
Cut	Cuts the selected text in a control and places it on the Windows Clipboard.
Hide	Hides the UserForm without unloading it from memory, retaining the values of the form's controls and any variables declared in the form's class module.
Paste	Pastes the contents of the Windows Clipboard into the current control.
PrintForm	Prints an image of the form, including any data entered in the form's controls, using the default Windows printer.
Repaint	Forces the form's image onscreen to be repainted. Use this method if you want to repaint the form without waiting for the normal repaint period.
Show	Makes the form visible onscreen. If the form isn't already loaded into memory, this method first loads the form.

You can set a form object's properties either under programmatic control or in the Properties Window of the VB Editor. Not all of a form's properties are available for alteration in both circumstances. Some properties can only be set in the Properties Window. You'll learn more about setting form and control properties with the Properties Window later in this lesson. You set a form's properties in your VBA code the same way you set any other object's properties: by assigning a new value to the property. Table 16.2 lists the `UserForm` properties that you are most likely to want or need to refer to or alter.

TABLE 16.2 COMMONLY USED PROPERTIES OF `UserForm` OBJECTS

Property	Description
ActiveControl	Returns an object reference to the control on the form that currently has the focus. Read-only.
BackColor	A **Long** integer representing a specific color for the background of the form. The easiest way to set this property is to use the Properties Window to select the color you want; if needed, you can copy the color number from the Properties Window into your code.
Caption	The text that is displayed as the form's title bar. Read/write.
Controls	Returns the collection of all controls on the form. Read-only.
Cycle	Determines whether pressing the Tab key causes the focus to cycle through all controls in all group frames and each page of multi-page controls or only through the current frame or page. Can contain one of the two intrinsic constants `fmCycleAllForms` or `fmCycleCurrentForm`. Read/write.
Enabled	Contains a **Boolean** value indicating whether the form is enabled. If **False**, none of the controls on the form are available. Read/write.
Font	Returns a reference to a `Font` object through which you can select the form's or control's font characteristics.
ForeColor	Same as the `BackColor` property, but establishes the color used for the foreground—usually text—of the form object.

Most of the code that you write in the class module of a form will be event-handling code. Table 16.3 lists the events for which you are most likely to want to write an event-handling procedure. You'll see several examples of event-handling procedures in the code examples later in this lesson.

TABLE 16.3 COMMONLY USED EVENTS OF `UserForm` OBJECTS

Event	Description
Activate	Triggered whenever the form becomes the active window. Use this event to update the contents of a dialog's controls to reflect any changes that occurred while the form window was inactive.
Click	Triggered whenever the surface of the form (any part not occupied by a control) is clicked with the mouse.

Event	Description
DblClick	Triggered whenever the surface of the form (any part not occupied by a control) is double-clicked with the mouse.
Deactivate	Triggered whenever the form ceases to be the active window.
Initialize	Triggered whenever the form is first loaded into memory either as a result of a Load statement or the Show method. Use this event to initialize the form's controls or appearance.
Terminate	Triggered whenever the form is unloaded from memory. Use this event to perform any special housekeeping tasks that might be needed before the form's variables are discarded.

In addition to the methods, properties, and events that the UserForm object provides inherently, VBA provides two statements that are especially useful with form objects: Load and Unload. You can use these statements to either load a form into memory or to remove a form from memory.

SYNTAX

The general syntax for the Load and Unload statements is

Load *Object*

Unload *Object*

▲ In the preceding syntax, *Object* represents any valid reference to a UserForm object.

The Load statement loads the UserForm into memory and triggers the form's Initialize method, but it does not make the form visible onscreen. After the form is loaded, you can use VBA code to manipulate the form object. The Unload statement removes the UserForm from memory, disposing of any variables in the form. After the form has been unloaded, it is no longer available for manipulation by your VBA code.

Now that you know about the basic components of a custom dialog box, you're ready to learn more about the controls that turn a form into a working dialog.

Understanding Controls

A UserForm object can contain controls just like those you find in other dialogs displayed by Excel or other Windows applications. *Controls* are the elements of a dialog box that enable a user to interact with your program. These elements include option buttons, text boxes, scrollbars, command buttons, and so on. This section acquaints you with the standard controls included in VBA that you can add to your forms.

Note

> Many third-party software publishers have made packages of advanced controls available. You can add custom controls (known as ActiveX and Automation objects) to the Toolbox toolbar by first creating a reference from your project to the library containing the custom controls and then adding those controls to the Toolbox.

Each control is an object with specific properties, methods, and events. Like the form that contains them, you can set control properties either under programmatic control or through the Properties Window of the VB Editor. You assign or retrieve a control's property values in VBA code the same way you would for any other object. You'll learn more about using the Properties Window to set control properties later in this lesson.

Table 16.4 lists the standard controls included with Excel VBA and summarizes the purpose of each control. As you'll see from the table, Excel VBA's standard controls include almost all the controls that you see in other Windows applications. (Some other VBA host applications provide additional controls; these additional controls are made available through control libraries supplied with that host application.)

TABLE 16.4 THE STANDARD CONTROLS INCLUDED WITH EXCEL VBA

Control	Purpose
Label	Provides caption labels for controls that don't have their own inherent captions. Use this control to put static text on a user form.
TextBox	A free-form text editing box for data entry; can be either single-line or multi-line.
ComboBox	This control combines an edit box with a list box. Use a combo list-edit box to suggest values for the user to choose from. You can permit the user to enter a value that isn't already in the list, or restrict a user's choices to only those that appear in the combo box.
ListBox	Displays a list of values that the user selects from. You can set list boxes to enable the user to select only a single value or to select multiple values.
CheckBox	A standard check box (a square box; when selected, it contains a check mark). Use check boxes for user selections that are on/off, true/false, and so on. Use check boxes for option selections that are *not* mutually exclusive.

Control	Purpose
OptionButton	A standard option button (a round box; when selected, it is filled with a black dot). Use option buttons for user selections that are not only on/off or true/false, but are also mutually exclusive.
ToggleButton	Use toggle buttons to indicate on/off or true/false settings. Toggle buttons fulfill the same purpose as check boxes, but display the setting as a button in either an "up" or "down" position.
Frame	Visually and logically groups other controls (especially check boxes, option buttons, and toggle buttons). Use a frame to visually group together related controls.
CommandButton	A command button. Use command buttons for actions such as Cancel, Save, OK, and so on. When a user clicks the command button, a VBA procedure attached to the control is executed.
TabStrip	A tab strip control consists of a client area in which you place other controls (such as text boxes, check boxes, and so on) and a strip of tab buttons. Use the tab strip control to create tabbed dialogs that display the same data in different categories.
MultiPage	A multipage control consists of several pages that you can select among by clicking the tab on a page. Use the multipage control to create tabbed dialogs such as the one that appears when you select the Tools, Options command. Use a multipage control when you use different controls to display different data.
RefEdit	A special text box control used to obtain worksheet ranges. Clicking the RefEdit control's inherent command button causes the form to collapse to a size no larger than the control itself, and enables the user to select worksheets and ranges on a worksheet. Clicking the control's button a second time restores the form.
ScrollBar	Scrollbar controls enable you to select a linear value, similar to a spin button control.
SpinButton	Spin button controls are a special variety of text box. You typically use spinner boxes to enter numeric, date, or other sequential values that fall within a specified range. Clicking the up-arrow on the spinner control increases the value in the box, clicking the down-arrow decreases the value in the box.
Image	The image control enables you to display a graphic image on a user form. Use an image control to display graphic images in any of these formats: *.bmp, *.cur, *.gif, *.ico, *.jpg, or *.wmf. You can crop, size, or zoom a graphic to fit the image control, but you can't use an image control to edit the graphic. You can, however, have a specific VBA procedure execute as a result of the user clicking the image control.

16

You manipulate controls primarily through their properties and with event-handling procedures that you create for each control. Table 16.5 lists the most common control properties that you'll need to work with in your VBA code: the properties that let you change the control's label, retrieve the state of the control (that is, find out what selections the user made), and so on.

Note

> Listing all the properties, methods, and events for forms and all the standard controls is, unfortunately, beyond the scope of this book—among the form object and all the standard controls there are literally hundreds of properties, methods, and events. This chapter shows you the most common methods, events, and properties that you'll need to use. Refer to the VBA online help for additional information about specific controls. In particular, use the Object Browser to display help on objects in the MSForms library— this is the library that supplies the UserForm and control objects. After finishing this book, you might also want to read Sams' *Database Developer's Guide with Visual Basic 6*.

TABLE 16.5 COMMONLY USED PROPERTIES OF STANDARD CONTROLS

Property	Applies To	Description
Accelerator	CheckBox, Tab, CommandButton, Label, Page, OptionButton, ToggleButton	Contains the character used as the control's accelerator key. Pressing Alt+ the accelerator key selects the control.
BackColor	All controls	A number representing a specific color for the background of the control.
Caption	Checkbox, CommandButton, Frame, Label, OptionButton, Page, Tab, ToggleButton, UserForm	For a label, the text displayed by the control; for other controls, the label that appears on the face of the button or tab, or that appears next to the frame, check box, or option button.
Cancel	CommandButton	Sets the command button as the dialog's Cancel button; pressing this button or pressing Esc dismisses the dialog. Only one command button on the form can have this property.

Property	Applies To	Description
ControlTipText	All controls	Sets the text that is displayed as a ControlTip (also called ToolTip) when the mouse pointer hovers over the control.
Default	CommandButton	Sets the command button as the default button. When the user presses the Enter key in the dialog, the button behaves as if it has been clicked with the mouse.
Enabled	All controls	Stores a **Boolean** value to determine whether the control is enabled. If Enabled is **False**, it is still displayed in the dialog but cannot receive the focus.
ForeColor	All controls	Same as BackColor, but sets the color for the control's foreground—usually the control's text.
List	ComboBox, ListBox	A **Variant** array (either single- or multi-dimensional) that represents the list contained by the control. Use the index number in Value as a subscript in the List collection to retrieve the text for the selected list item. Use the control's AddItem and RemoveItem methods to add or remove items in the list.
Max	ScrollBar, SpinButton	A **Long** specifying the maximum value of a spin button, or the value when the scrollbar is all the way at the bottom (for a vertical scrollbar) or the right (for a horizontal scrollbar).
Min	ScrollBar, SpinButton	A **Long** specifying the minimum value of a spin button, or the value when the scrollbar is all the way at the top (for a vertical scrollbar) or the left (for a horizontal scrollbar).

16

continues

TABLE 16.5 CONTINUED

Property	Applies To	Description
Name	All controls	Contains the name of the control. You can only set this property in the Properties Window.
RowSource	ComboBox, ListBox	Specifies the source that provides the object's list; in Excel VBA, RowSource is usually a worksheet range.
Selected	ListBox	Returns an array of **Boolean** values for lists that permit multiple selection; each element in the array contains one element corresponding to each item in the list. If an element in the Selected array is **True**, the corresponding list item is selected.
TabIndex	All controls	A number indicating the control's position in the tab order (0 through the number of controls on the form).
TabStop	All controls	A **Boolean** value indicating whether the control can be selected by pressing the Tab key; if TabStop is **False**, you can still click on a control to give it the focus.
Value	All controls	The value of the control's current setting: the text in a text box, whether a check box or option button is selected, an index to the selected item in a list, or a number indicating the current position of a scrollbar or spin button.
Visible	All controls	A **Boolean** value indicating whether the control is visible.

Table 16.6 lists the control events for which you will most likely want to write your own event-handling procedures. Every control you add to your form will have these events available. In particular, you'll use the Click event with command buttons and the AfterUpdate or Change events to validate data or update other controls.

TABLE 16.6   COMMONLY USED EVENTS OF CONTROL OBJECTS

Event	Description
AfterUpdate	Triggered after a particular control's value has been updated.
BeforeUpdate	Triggered after a particular control's value has changed, but before the control is updated.
Change	Triggered whenever the control's value changes.
Click	Triggered whenever the control is clicked with the mouse. Use this event to make a command button carry out an action.
DblClick	Triggered whenever the control is double-clicked with the mouse. Use this event to display additional forms—such as a larger size editing box—when "drilling-down" in a form.
Enter	Triggered whenever a control receives the focus.
Exit	Triggered whenever a control loses the focus.

After you learn the general steps for creating a custom dialog with a form, later sections in this lesson present and explain examples of most of the controls listed in Table 16.4 and several of the properties and events listed in Tables 16.5 and 16.6. The example listings in this lesson also demonstrate how you can make some of the controls change their behavior or otherwise respond to specific events.

Using Forms to Create Custom Dialog Boxes

Creating a custom dialog is a fairly straightforward process. You don't have to write any VBA code to create the dialog box, itself. Instead, you use the VB Editor to graphically create the dialog in a UserForm object. Essentially, you just draw the custom dialog on the form. You can create only one dialog on each form.

To create a custom VBA dialog box, follow these basic steps:

1. Add a UserForm to your project for the new dialog box.
2. Use the Toolbox toolbar to place controls on the form.
3. Use the Properties Window to set the properties of the form and its controls.
4. Adjust the tab order of the form's controls.
5. Add VBA code to the form's class module to handle form and control events to make the form's controls carry out the actions you desire.
6. Write the VBA code in a standard module to display the UserForm dialog and retrieve values from the dialog's controls.

The next few parts of this section show you how to interactively create a form, how to place controls on the form, and how adjust the controls' tab order and properties. The last section of this lesson shows you how to write event-handling procedures and how to use the custom dialog in your code.

Adding a New User Form Object

The first step in creating a custom dialog is to add a new UserForm to your project. The UserForm object contains the dialog box that you draw, as well as provides the workspace in which you draw the dialog box. Because UserForm objects are stored in the UserForms collection of your project, UserForm objects are part of the project.

To add a new UserForm, use the VB Editor's Insert, UserForm command. The VB Editor adds a new UserForm to the current project and gives it a default name—UserFormN—using the same numbering system as for modules. The VB Editor displays the new UserForm in *design mode*, as shown in Figure 16.1. (In design mode, you can add or delete controls on the form, set form or control properties, and otherwise manipulate the appearance of the form interactively. When a form is displayed and in use as part of an executing VBA program, the form is in *run mode*.)

Figure 16.1 shows a newly created user form. Notice the heavy border around the form, indicating that the form is selected. Notice also the dot grid visible on the surface of the form and the Toolbox toolbar to the lower right of the blank form. The dot grid helps you align and size controls on the form and appears only when the form is displayed in design mode. The Toolbox toolbar is the palette from which you select the controls to add to the form, and usually only appears when the form, or one of the controls on the form, is selected.

Do

DO remember that you rename a UserForm object the same way you rename a standard or class module: Display the object's Properties Window by selecting the object in the Project Explorer and then clicking the Properties button on the VB Editor's toolbar. Next, edit the object's Name property in the Properties Window to change the object's name.

DO give your forms descriptive names so that you can easily tell what that form is for.

Don't

DON'T leave a new form with its default name, such as UserForm1 or UserForm2. Instead, rename the new form as soon as you create it.

FIGURE 16.1

A new UserForm *in design mode; notice the dot grid on the form and the presence of the Toolbox.*

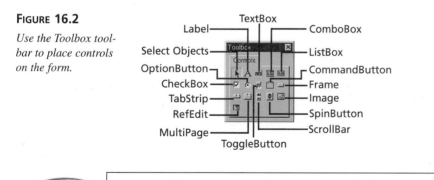

Using the Toolbox Toolbar

Whenever the VB Editor displays a form in design mode, it also displays the Toolbox toolbar. Figure 16.2 shows the Toolbox toolbar in its floating window. The command buttons in the Toolbox activate various tools that enable you to insert controls on the form.

FIGURE 16.2

Use the Toolbox toolbar to place controls on the form.

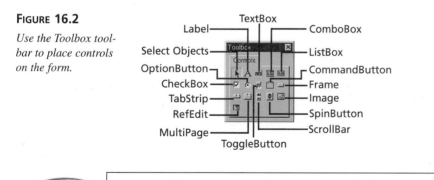

Tip

If the Toolbox toolbar display has been turned off by using the View, Toolbox command (or by clicking the Toolbox button on the VB Editor toolbar), the VB Editor might not display the Toolbox when you display a form in design mode. If the Toolbox doesn't appear when a form is in design mode and selected, use the View, Toolbox command or the Toolbox button on the VB Editor toolbar to display the Toolbox.

16

Note

The Toolbox, like all toolbars, is customizable. If you or another user installed additional controls from third-party vendors or otherwise customized the Toolbox, it might appear differently than the one shown in Figure 16.2. Figure 16.2 shows only the standard controls provided with Excel VBA.

To use the buttons in the Toolbox to insert controls on your form, follow these steps:

1. Click the command button in the Toolbox that corresponds to the control you want to add to the form. The mouse pointer will change to a crosshair pointer when it is over the surface of the form.

2. Position the crosshair over the form where you want the top left corner of the new control to be.

3. Click and hold down the left mouse button.

4. Drag down and to the right until the control is the size you want and then release the mouse button. The VB Editor inserts the control onto the form and the mouse pointer returns to the arrow shape.

Tip

You can resize the form itself by clicking on its title bar to select it and then dragging one of the sizing handles to increase or decrease the size of the form. *Sizing handles* are the small squares that appear at the corners and sides of a graphic object (along with the thick gray border) when that object is selected.

The following list summarizes the general purpose of each type of control you can add from the Toolbox (refer to Figure 16.2); use this list as a guideline in choosing the appropriate control to suit your needs.

- *Label*. Creates a Label control. Use labels to insert text onto the form, such as captions for controls that don't already have their own instructions and tips for using the form, and so on. Also use labels to display information such as the current value of a spin button or scrollbar control. You can change the text in a Label control with VBA code, but your form's user cannot edit the label text. Use Label controls for text that won't change or that you don't want the user to edit.

- *TextBox*. Creates a TextBox control. Use text boxes to obtain or display data that can be represented as text, such as names and addresses, dollar amounts, dates, and so on. Also use text boxes to display information such as the current value of a spin button or scrollbar, and to provide an alternate means of setting the spin button's or scrollbar's value. Text boxes can display single or multiple lines of text. If necessary, text box controls will "grow" a vertical scrollbar to scroll through multiple lines of text.

- *Frame*. Creates a Frame control. Frame controls don't really do anything on their own, but they can contain other controls, usually option buttons, check boxes, or toggle buttons. Use a frame to show the user which controls in a dialog are related to each other or to set a particular group of controls off from other dialog controls. You can prevent the user from tabbing into or out of a frame's group of controls by setting the form's Cycle property to fmCycleCurrentForm. To place other controls inside a frame, you must place the Frame control on the form first and then place the controls that should be inside the Frame.

- *CommandButton*. Creates a CommandButton control. Use command buttons to carry out actions such as when the button is clicked. Actions might or might not include closing or hiding the form, updating data, validating data in the form's controls, and so on.

- *CheckBox*. Creates a CheckBox control. Check boxes include a label as part of the control object. Use check boxes to select true/false, on/off, yes/no values that are *not* mutually exclusive; for example, you can search text for a case-sensitive match and whether you search for whole words only, so you'd use check boxes for selecting these search options.

- *OptionButton*. Creates an OptionButton control. Use option buttons to select true/false, on/off, yes/no values that *are* mutually exclusive; for example, you can't search both forward and backward at the same time, so you'd use an option button for selecting the search direction. You typically place both CheckBox and OptionButton controls inside a Frame control.

- *ToggleButton*. Creates a ToggleButton control. Use toggle buttons to select true/false, on/off, yes/no values. Toggle buttons fulfill the same purpose as check boxes, but display the setting as a button in either an "up" or "down" position. Use toggle buttons for choices that are not mutually exclusive.

- *ListBox*. Creates a ListBox control. Use list boxes when you want to display a list of items and enable the user to select one or more items from the list, without being able to add new items to the list. Use the list box's MultiSelect property to set whether the user can select more than one item in the list. Use list boxes to display lists of things such as workbook names, sheet names, range names, months in the year, and so on.

16

- *ComboBox*. Creates a `ComboBox` control, which combines an edit box with a list box. Use a combo box to create drop-down lists and whenever you want to suggest values for the user to choose from. Combo box lists can be set to permit users to enter a value other than one that appears on the list or restrict the user's choice to only values that appear in the list by setting the `Style` property. Combo boxes can only be used to select one item at a time.

- *TabStrip*. Creates a `TabStrip` control. Tab strip controls have a single client area in which you can place other controls, sort of like a `Frame` control. When you select a new tab, the client area does not change. Instead, you use the `Change` event to update the controls in the tab strip's client area with your own code. Use tab strip controls to create tabbed dialogs where the information on each page of the dialog is displayed in the same controls, but in different categories. For example, if you want to create a form to display a summary of quarterly sales information, you might use a tab strip control with five tabs: one tab for each quarter of the year and a fifth for a year-end summary. Each tab would display the same information: gross sales, gross profit, and so on for a different quarter.

- *MultiPage*. Creates a `MultiPage` control. `MultiPage` controls have multiple client areas in which you can place other controls. When you select a new tab, the entire client area changes to display a different group of controls. Use `MultiPage` controls to create tabbed dialogs where the information on each page of the dialog is displayed in different controls. The Options dialog of Excel is an example of a `MultiPage` control.

- *ScrollBar*. Creates a `ScrollBar` control. Use scrollbars to manually create scrolling controls on a form or to supply sequential numeric values.

- *SpinButton*. Creates a `SpinButton` control. Use spin buttons (also called *spinners*) to supply sequential numeric values in a dialog. Usually, you combine a spin button with a label control to display the spin button's value. You might also want to combine a spin button control with a text box to provide an alternate method of entering a value. When combining a spin button control with a label or text box, you must write the code that keeps the two controls synchronized. Examples later in this lesson show how to synchronize a label or text box control with a spin button.

- *Image*. Creates an `Image` control. Use image controls to display graphics on a form, such as logos, photographs, and so on. The image control exposes events similar to other controls, so you can use an image control to respond to mouse clicks. Image controls can't be edited, so an image control can't receive the focus.

- *RefEdit*. Creates a `RefEdit` control. A `RefEdit` control displays a text box with a button attached to its right edge. Clicking the `RefEdit` control's attached button collapses the entire form to an object no larger than the `RefEdit` text box. When the form is collapsed to the `RefEdit` text box, the user can select worksheets in the workbook and select ranges on a worksheet. Clicking the `RefEdit` control's command button again restores the form to its previous size. Use `RefEdit` controls when you want to enable a user to reveal as much as possible of the screen underlying your form and to make it easier for a user to enter worksheet ranges that you request.

16

Note

When a form is displayed onscreen in design mode, you can test its appearance and behavior by using the Run, Run Sub/UserForm command. The VB Editor then displays the form in run mode, with all of its controls active. Keep in mind, however, that any code utilized by the form that is not stored in the form's class module might not be initialized. Running the form only initializes the code stored in the form's class module; variables in standard modules won't necessarily be initialized. As a result, some of the code related to the form might fail with various runtime errors when you run it unless the form is completely self-contained.

Adding Controls to a Form

When you create a new form, the VB Editor presents you with a completely blank form (refer to Figure 16.1). You add controls to a form by displaying the form and then graphically drawing the controls on the form using the various tools from the Toolbox.

Tip

In general, every form should contain OK and Cancel command buttons or their functional equivalent. The OK button is the button that accepts the dialog's settings and initiates the primary action of the dialog, whereas the Cancel button enables a user to close a dialog without carrying out any action. Usually, the first two controls you should add to a form are command buttons to serve as the OK and Cancel buttons.

Command buttons have a special property—`Cancel`—that designates the Cancel command button (whether or not the command button is actually labeled "Cancel"). Only one command button on a form can have the `Cancel` property set to **True**; setting this property for one command button sets the `Cancel` property for all other command buttons on the form to **False**. If your form contains a command button with the `Cancel` property set, pressing the Esc key has the same effect as clicking that command button.

To add a control to a form, use the Toolbox as described in the preceding section of this lesson. As an example of adding a specific control to a form, add a command button to a new form by following these steps:

1. Choose the Insert, UserForm command. The VB Editor adds a new form, displaying it in design mode, and also displays the Toolbox, as already shown in Figure 16.1.

2. Click the CommandButton tool in the Toolbox. The Toolbox button changes to its "down" position (it has a sunken appearance) to indicate the tool you have selected.

3. Move the mouse pointer over the form; the mouse cursor changes to a crosshair with a symbol of the selected tool attached to it.

4. Position the crosshair where you want the top left corner of the command button to be.

5. Click and drag the mouse cursor down and to the right to draw the command button control. The VB Editor displays a box outline showing the size of the command button while you drag the mouse cursor.

6. Release the mouse button when the command button is the size you want. The VB Editor creates the command button control and inserts it into the form. Figure 16.3 shows a new form as it appears immediately after drawing the command button.

FIGURE 16.3

A UserForm *immediately after adding a* CommandButton *control.*

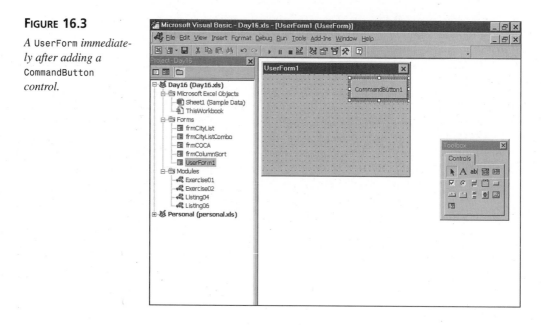

Note

As you draw the command button in this example, you might notice that the top left corner of the command button—as well as the outline of the command button itself—jumps to align itself with the grid pattern on the form. This action—called *snap to grid*—helps you align controls and text on the form. You can turn snap to grid on or off, adjust the size of the grid, or hide the grid by changing settings in the Options dialog of the VB Editor. Choose Tools, Options and click the General tab to display the Form Grid Settings. Select or clear the options you want. Increasing the width or height of grid units spaces the grid points further apart, decreasing the width or height spaces the grid points closer together.

All form controls must have a unique name; you use this name to refer to the control in your VBA code, as explained later in this lesson. Whenever you add a control to a form, VBA gives the new control a default name consisting of the control's type name followed by a number. VBA ensures that the control has a unique name by including the number in the control's name—the number in the name is higher than any other control number. If the command button control you added in the preceding steps is the first command button you added to the form, it receives the name CommandButton1, for example. The next command button you add will be CommandButton2, and so on. If you add a text box control next, it will be named TextBox1.

You can—and should—give controls a more meaningful name by editing the control's Name property in the Properties Window, as described later in this lesson.

Do

DO give your controls meaningful names that help you remember what they are for. A name such as txtFirstName tells you a lot more about what a control does than a name such as TextBox10.

DO remember that control names must follow VBA's standard rules for identifier names: They must begin with an alphabetic character and cannot contain spaces or punctuation.

DO use a prefix for control names, such as txt for text boxes, opt for option buttons, btn for command buttons, and so on. Doing so will help you identify the precise type of control as you use it in your VBA code.

DO remember that each control in a form must have a unique name.

Note

Unfortunately, covering all details of adding and editing each and every control type is beyond the scope of this book. After you are familiar with the basic techniques of adding and editing controls on a form, you can use the online help system to get more information on specific controls and their properties.

Editing Form Controls

After you draw a control on a form, you can resize it, move it, copy it, delete it, change its formatting (font size, style, typeface), or alter its properties (such as the control's name, caption, and so on). You'll need to edit or move form controls as you fine-tune the design and appearance of your dialog; for example, you might decide that a text box is too small or too large for the values that will be entered into it, so you want to change its size. As another example, you'll certainly want to edit the caption of any command button, option button, or check box that you place on the form because the VB Editor gives new command buttons a caption that is the same as the control's default name—you probably don't need a command button labeled "CommandButton7."

Tip

You open an existing form for editing by double-clicking it in the Project Explorer. Alternatively, you can select the form you want to edit in the Project Explorer and then click the Show Object button.

Selecting Controls

To edit a control, you must first select it by clicking on it. Selected controls have a gray border with sizing handles, as shown for the command button that appears in Figure 16.3. To select several controls at once, hold down the Shift key while you click on the controls you want to select. Selecting multiple controls at the same time is useful if you want to make a formatting change that affects all of the controls on the form, such as changing the font size, style, or typeface. Selecting multiple controls is also useful if you want to move several controls at the same time.

Tip

You can semi-permanently group several controls together by using the Format, Group command. When the controls are grouped, they behave as a single object when you select, move, copy, or otherwise edit them. The controls remain grouped until you use the Format, Ungroup command on the selected group.

Moving a Control

To move a control to a new location in the form, first select the control. Next, position the mouse pointer over any part of the gray outline around the selected control *except* one of the sizing handles. Now, click and drag the control to its new position.

Changing a Control's Size

To change the size of a control, first select it. Next, move the mouse pointer over one of the sizing handles (the square boxes that appear at the corners and at the center of the sides of the gray border around the selected object). When the pointer is over a sizing handle, the pointer changes to a double-headed arrow indicating the direction in which you can now resize the selected control. Now, click and drag the sizing handle; the VB Editor displays an outline showing you the new size of the control. When the control is the desired size, release the mouse button; the VB Editor redraws the control to the new size.

Copying, Pasting, and Deleting Controls

One of the easiest ways to create several similar controls—such as several check box or command button controls—is to first create one control, copy it, and then paste the copied control into the form as many times as needed. To copy a form control, simply select it and then use the Edit, Copy command (or press Ctrl+C).

After you copy a control, you can paste it into the same or a different form by using the Edit, Paste command (or press Ctrl+V). After you paste the control, move it to its desired location.

You might occasionally want to delete a control from the form. You might have placed a control you later decide you don't really need, you might have accidentally made too many copies of a control, or for some other reason. To delete a control, select the control and then press the Delete key. The VB Editor deletes the selected control(s).

Editing or Formatting a Control's Caption

To edit the caption text on a control such as a command button, option button, or check box, just click over the text. The VB Editor places the insertion point into the caption text. You can now edit the text using any of the standard Windows text editing commands you're already familiar with. To change the typeface, style, or font size of a control's text, you must display the control's Properties Window and alter the Font property. (Using the Properties Window with controls is described later in this lesson.) You might need to resize label, check box, option box, command button, or other objects to display the entire caption that you type.

16

Tip

To edit the text in the form's title bar, edit the form's Caption property in the Properties Window. Use the form's Font property to format the form's title bar text.

Note

Some controls, such as text boxes, list boxes, and combo boxes, don't have an inherent caption (more properly called a *label*). Use the Label tool to place Label controls in the form near controls that don't have their own inherent labels.

Controlling the Tab Order

When your form is active, it will behave like other Windows dialog boxes. Your dialog's user can move forward from control to control with the Tab key, and backward through the dialog's controls by pressing Shift+Tab. The order in which the controls become active in response to the user pressing Tab or Shift+Tab is called the *tab order* of the controls. Usually, you want the controls' tab order to be (approximately) left-to-right and top-to-bottom; in general, you should make sure that the tab order provides a logical movement sequence through the controls in the dialog.

The VB Editor assigns a default tab order to each control as you add it to the form. The default tab order therefore corresponds to the order in which you place the controls on the form. Frequently, by the time you place all the controls on the form and move them around until you're satisfied with their appearance, the default tab order no longer provides a logical sequence of movement through the dialog's controls.

To change the tab order of the controls in a form, follow these steps:

1. Choose the View, Tab Order command; the VB Editor displays the Tab Order dialog shown in Figure 16.4. The Tab Order list displays all the controls in the form in their current tab order. (Figure 16.4 shows the Tab Order dialog for the Make Regional Sales Chart dialog used in the first example program later in this chapter.)

2. In the Tab Order list, select the control whose position in the tab order you want to change.

Note

Although label controls do appear in the Tab Order dialog and you can change their position in the tab order, VBA doesn't actually make a label control active; label controls are intended only to display text.

FIGURE 16.4

Use the Tab Order dialog to change the tab order of controls in your form.

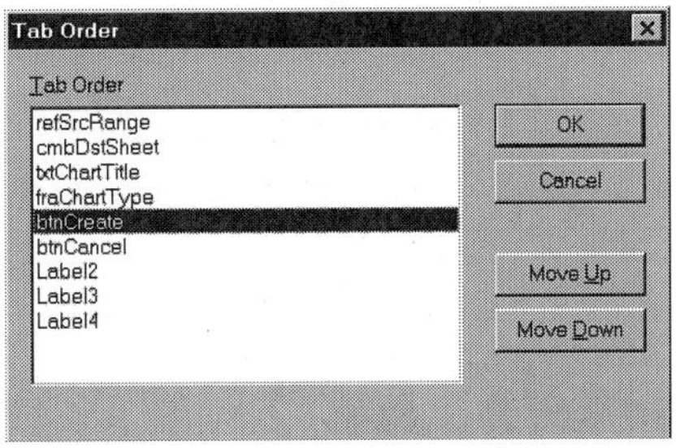

16

3. Use the Move Up or Move Down buttons to change the selected control's position in the tab order. Click the Move Up button to move the control up in the list (that is, earlier in the tab order) or the Move Down button to move the control lower in the list (that is, later in the tab order).

4. Repeat steps 2 and 3 for each control until you are satisfied with the tab order of controls on the form.

5. Choose the OK button in the Tab Order dialog to confirm your changes and close the Tab Order dialog.

Do

DO remember to check the tab order of your controls on your form to ensure that it provides a logical movement sequence through the controls in your form.

Setting Form and Control Properties in Design Mode

Each form and each control on a form has its own set of properties, just like any other VBA or host application object. There are several form and control properties that it is both easier and more practical to set while the form is displayed in design mode, rather than through your VBA code. Properties that you set for a form or control while in design mode become the new default properties for that form or control.

For example, although you can set a control's font, background color, and foreground color with VBA code, you don't usually need to alter these properties while your program is running. Instead, it's much easier to set these properties the way you want at design time. You can also give default values to controls in your form by setting the control's `Value` property. For example, to create a check box on a form that is selected by default, you would set the check box's `Value` property to **True** while in design mode. Every time the form is loaded into memory at runtime, that check box will then be selected.

Similarly, you can also populate list controls at design time by setting the list control's RowSource property. In Excel, you can bind a list to a range of worksheet cells with the RowSource property and bind a text box to a worksheet cell by setting the ControlSource property. Because you want control formatting and default value properties to be more or less permanent for a control, it's most practical to set these (and other) properties in design mode.

> **Tip**
>
> You can also create a default value for a text box by typing the value directly into the text box control on the form. Then, whenever you display the form, the text box will display the default text that you typed.

In design mode, you set a form's or a control's properties by using the Properties Window. The Properties Window lists all of the object's properties that you can set while in design mode. The specific properties that appear in the Properties Window vary depending on the specific control you have selected. Figure 16.5 shows a Properties Window for the btnCreate command button on the frmSalesChart form used in examples later in this lesson.

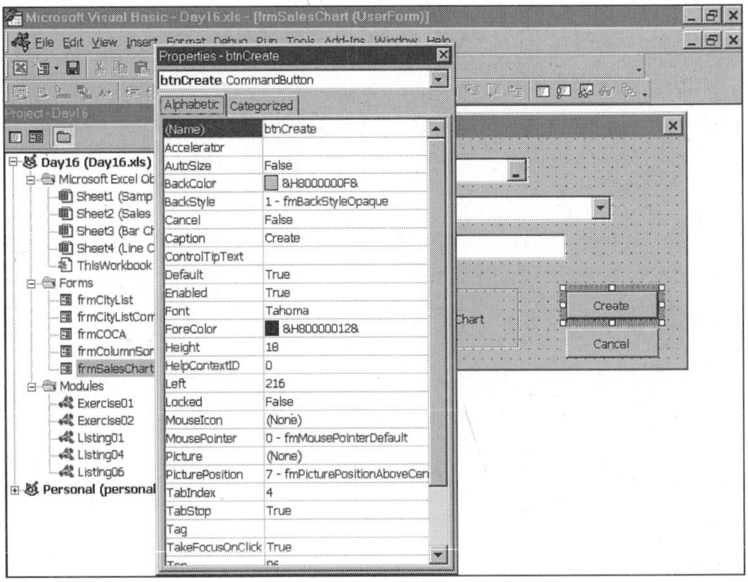

FIGURE 16.5

The Properties Window for a command button showing the Alphabetic listing of properties.

The Properties Window has two pages. The first page, shown in Figure 16.5, is an alphabetic listing of all the object's properties. The second page, shown in Figure 16.6, is a categorized listing of the object's properties. Figure 16.6 shows the same Properties Window in Figure 16.5 with the Categorized list of properties showing. Notice the different categories in bold print in the Properties Window: Appearance, Behavior, Font, and so on. You can collapse or expand the list of properties in a particular category by clicking the box at the left of each category heading.

FIGURE 16.6

The Properties Window for a command button showing the Categorized listing of properties.

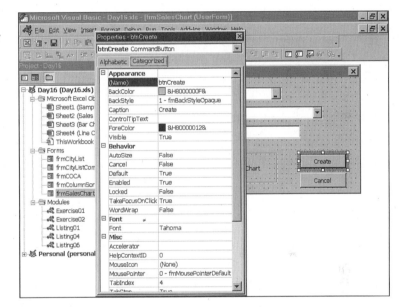

To set a form or control property, click in the text box corresponding to the property you want to change. For most properties, a drop-down list button appears. Click the list button and select the property value you want from the list. Other properties (such as the Name and Caption properties) permit you to enter any text value you want. A few properties display an ellipsis (...) button when you select that property. Clicking the ellipsis button opens additional dialogs to help you set that property.

To change a form's or control's properties, follow these steps:

1. Select the control whose properties you want to modify. To select the form, click anywhere on the surface of the form other than on a space occupied by a control.

2. Choose the View, Properties Window command to display the Properties Window. (Alternatively, click the Properties button on the VB Editor toolbar or press F4.)

3. Fill in the property values you want for the selected control. Refer to Table 16.5 for a list of frequently used properties and their purposes.

4. Click the Close button in the upper-right corner of the Properties Window to close it.

> **Tip**
>
> The Properties Window can be docked like a toolbar or you can use it as a floating window, as shown in Figures 16.5 and 16.6. Dock or undock the Properties Window as you would any toolbar.

Do
DO make sure that your form contains at least one command button with the Cancel property set to **True**; this will enable your dialog to respond to the Esc key.

Displaying User Forms with VBA

VBA uses the graphical form design you create—along with the form and control property settings—to get all the information needed to display the dialog box: the size of the dialog, the controls on it, and so on. As a result, VBA enables you to display the dialog form with a single statement.

To display a custom dialog, you use the UserForm object's Show method:

FormName.Show

In the preceding syntax example, *FormName* represents any user form object in the current project. *FormName* is the name of the form as it appears in the Project Explorer. For example, if you have a form named frmSalesChart, you would display it onscreen with the following statement:

▲ frmSalesChart.Show

If the form is not currently loaded in memory, the Show method loads the form and displays it. If the form is already loaded, the Show method simply displays it. Either way, the Show method displays the form and then gives it the focus. The form remains onscreen until either the UserForm object's Hide method is executed or the form is unloaded with an Unload statement. The form remains loaded in memory until either the instance of the form goes out of scope—that is, the procedure that created this instance of the form object stops executing—or until the form is unloaded with an Unload statement.

Although code in the form's class module will execute when invoked as a result of events in the dialog, the overall execution of your program is suspended until your dialog form is closed or hidden. By default, all VBA forms are *application modal*, which means that you cannot perform any other action in the application until the dialog form has been closed or hidden.

> **Note**
>
> When VBA executes the Show method to display a dialog form, execution in the procedure containing the call to the Show method is suspended until the displayed form is closed by the user. VBA will, however, execute the code for any event procedures in the form's class module. (Writing event procedures is described in the next section.)

16

Using VBA with Controls on a Form

Displaying a dialog box alone usually isn't enough to accomplish your purpose. In almost every case, you'll need to sample the state of the dialog's controls to find out what data or choices the user made. For example, if you use a dialog to get information from a user about which columns and rows in a worksheet should be sorted, you need to be able to find out what values the user entered after the dialog has been closed and before you actually start the sorting operation.

In other cases, you might want to dynamically change the captions of the command buttons (or other controls) in the dialog, dynamically update a label or text box associated with a spinner control, or dynamically validate data entered into the dialog. For example, suppose you have a dialog that is used for data entry in an accounting program you're developing. You might want to validate an account code or department name entered into a text box as soon as the user enters the data.

For the first task, you need to be able to access and manipulate the dialog's controls after the dialog has been closed (but not unloaded from memory). For the second task, you need to be able to create procedures to respond to events in the dialog's controls so that your procedure is automatically executed by the control itself. Creating event procedures is also how you make a command button carry out an action.

The next sections show you how to create an event procedure and how to access the controls in a dialog form.

Writing Event Procedures and Other Form Code

As you work with your dialog forms and their controls, you'll find there are many instances when clicking a control or modifying its data requires the control (or some other part of your program) to respond promptly. VBA enables you to define *event procedures* to respond to specific events. If you do create an event procedure for a particular control's event, that procedure is executed whenever that particular event occurs.

Every UserForm object you add to your project becomes a new class of object in your project. Every UserForm object has an inherent class module in which you must write your event procedures and other code related to your dialog form. Before getting started writing code in your form, however, you should become acquainted with how a form's class module is utilized.

As you already know, the first part of any module is the General area. The General area contains the declarations area. You place all compiler directives at the start of the declarations area, followed by all module-level declarations for variables, constants, and user-defined types. After the declarations area, the remainder of the class module's General area contains **Property Get** or **Property Let** procedures and any additional procedure or function declarations. As you can see, you can create custom properties for your form and you can add special methods to your form with additional procedure and function declarations, just like any other class module.

So far, this explanation has covered elements of the class module that you are already familiar with. In a form's class module, however, the remainder of the class module contains a section for every object on the form, including the form itself. This is the area in which you write event procedures for the form and the controls.

Figure 16.7 shows the Code Window displaying the class module for a form named frmSalesChart. (This form is used in the first example in this lesson.) In Figure 16.7, the Object list in the Code Window is dropped down. Notice that the Object list contains a list of all the control objects on the form, listed by name. (A control's name is the content of its Name property.) You select the object for which you want to write an event procedure in the Object list.

Figure 16.8 shows the same code window, but in this figure, the Procedure list is dropped down. Notice that the btnCreate control is selected in the Object list; the Procedure list shows all the events that this control object supports. To display the VBA code for a particular event, select the event in the Procedure list. The Code Window displays the event procedure (if you have already written one) for that event. If you haven't yet written an event procedure, the Code Window displays a procedure declaration with the appropriate name for this object and event. In Figures 16.7 and 16.8, the `btnOK_Click` procedure is visible in the Code Window; this is the event procedure that handles the click event for the `btnCreate` control object, which is a command button.

FIGURE 16.7

Select a form object for which you want to write an event procedure in the Object list.

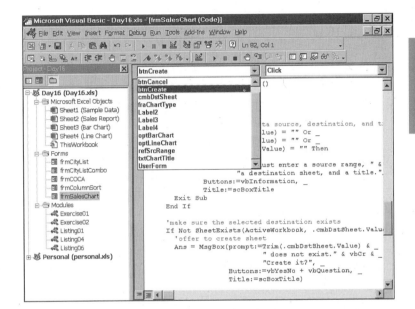

FIGURE 16.8

Select an object's event in the Procedure list to create or edit the event-handling procedure.

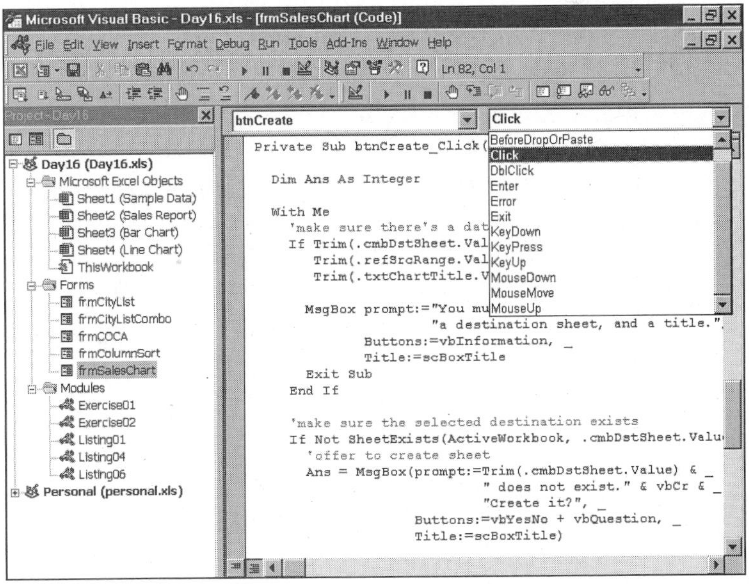

> **Caution**
>
> VBA relies on event procedures having a specific name that enables VBA to match the procedure to a particular object and event. If you edit the name of an event procedure so that it is no longer in the form *ObjectName_EventName*, VBA loses the procedure's association to a particular object and event. The procedure remains in the module, but becomes visible in the General part of the form's module.

To write an event procedure (or other code) for a form or a control, follow these steps:

1. In the Project Explorer, select the UserForm object that contains the control for which you want to write an event procedure.

2. Click the View Code button or choose the View, Code command to display the form's class module in a Code Window.

3. Select the control you want to create an event procedure for in the Object list of the Code Window (refer to Figure 16.7).

4. Select the event that you want to handle in the Procedure list of the Code Window (refer to Figure 16.8).

As soon as you select the event for which you want to write a procedure, the VB Editor does one of two things: If the selected control already has a procedure for that event, the VB Editor displays it in the Code Window. If the control does *not* have a procedure for that event, the VB Editor creates a new event procedure declaration and positions the insertion point in the procedure body, ready for you to begin writing new code. If you want to remove an event procedure, simply delete it from the form's module.

Do

DO rename controls *before* creating an event procedure for the control. VBA will not rename the event procedures if you change the name of a control—you must manually rename each event procedure that you create for a control whose name you change.

DO remember that you select the UserForm object in the Code Window's Object list to gain access to the form's event procedures.

DO try to make your form objects as self-contained as possible. Apply all the class module programming rules and design guidelines that you learned in Day 11 to create your form objects.

DO remember that the code in a form's class module can call procedures or functions stored in standard modules.

Do

DO remember that closing a form with its `Hide` method leaves the form in memory with all its variables intact. Unloading a form terminates that instance of the form, and all its internal values are lost.

DO make sure that you hide a form rather than unload it if you want to refer to the values of the dialog's controls with code in a standard module.

DO keep in mind that all event procedures must be declared **Private** to the form's class module.

Putting It Together: A Self-Contained Dialog

This first example uses a form to create a dialog box that utilizes a text box, labels, a frame, option buttons, a `RefEdit` control, and a couple of command buttons. Figure 16.9 shows, in design mode, the dialog you need to create to use with the code in Listings 16.1 and 16.2. Figure 16.10 shows the same dialog form at runtime.

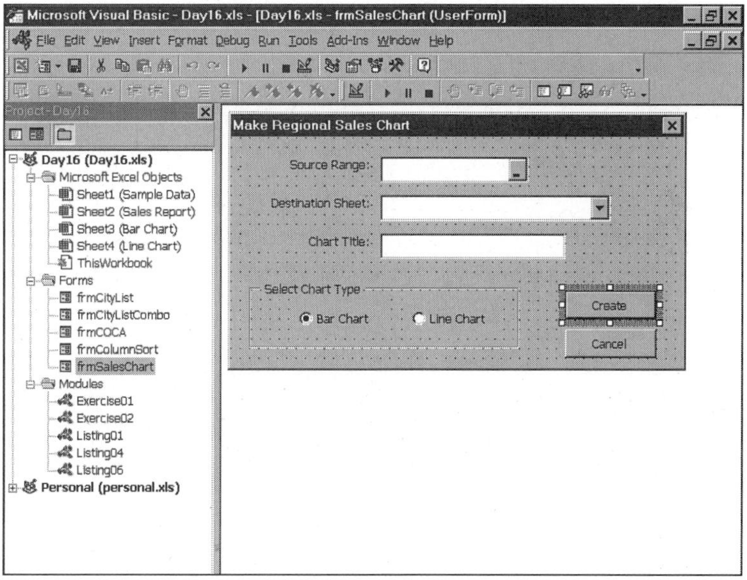

FIGURE 16.9

The Make Sales Chart dialog form in design mode.

FIGURE 16.10

The Make Sales Chart dialog at runtime.

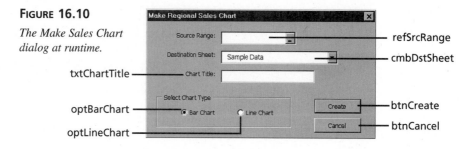

Many Excel users work with similar sets of data on a routine basis, frequently creating charts or graphs of the data they work with. If you're like many other Excel users, you've probably found one or two chart formats that you prefer over others for viewing particular sets of data, such as monthly or quarterly sales figures, and so on. For example, you might have found that a particular style of bar chart or line chart is the most meaningful way for you (or your company's financial manager) to look at data from a quarterly sales report.

In a case like this, although you chart a different set of data each time, you might find that you repeatedly invoke the Chart Wizard and make the same option choices in the Chart Wizard each time you create a new chart. Going through all the choices and options in the Chart Wizard to repeatedly create what is, essentially, the same chart is unnecessarily time-consuming and tedious. You can speed up your work by creating a VBA procedure to create the desired charts for you. As you have probably already discovered, however, entering data ranges into an `InputBox` dialog is difficult and error-prone; you can't see the underlying worksheet that contains your chart's source data, which increases the likelihood that you (or your procedure's user) will enter an incorrect or incomplete range and have to perform the task over again.

You can make the process of creating predefined charts easier and faster by creating a custom dialog in which you enter the chart's source range and where the chart should be created, and then use the form's event procedures to automatically insert a correctly formatted chart into the workbook. If you use a `RefEdit` control for the user to enter the chart's source data, you make it possible for a user to view worksheets and select a range of data for the new chart *while your custom dialog is onscreen*. The `RefEdit` control will automatically fill in the range reference as the user selects the range from a worksheet.

The custom dialog shown in Figure 16.10, along with the code in Listing 16.1, creates a custom dialog that enables a user to select a range of data to be charted, a destination for the resulting chart, a title for the chart, and one of two predefined chart formats. Clicking the Create button in the dialog actually inserts the new chart.

Before you can get started with the code in Listing 16.1, you must create a form and draw the dialog into whose class module you will enter the code from Listing 16.1. To get started with this demonstration dialog, follow these steps:

1. Create a new workbook in Excel.

2. Display the VB Editor and use the Insert, UserForm command to add a form to your project.

3. Use the Properties Window to change the form's Name property to frmSalesChart and its Caption property to Make Regional Sales Chart.

4. Using the techniques described earlier in this lesson, add controls to the form and edit their captions so that your form looks like the one shown in Figure 16.9. Remember that you have to add labels separately for text boxes.

Note

When adding controls to the frmSalesChart form shown in Figures 16.9 and 16.10, add the Frame control *before* you add the option buttons inside the frame; if you don't add the controls in this order, the controls won't be inside the frame.

5. Now, set the Name property for the controls on the form so that each control has the name indicated in Figure 16.10. Be careful when you complete this step: Make sure that the control's new name is exactly as shown in Figure 16.10, otherwise the code from Listing 16.1 will not work correctly.

6. Use the Properties Window to set the following properties: Set the optBarChart control's Value property to **True** (this causes the optBarChart option to be selected when the dialog is first opened), and set the btnCancel control's Cancel property to **True** (this causes a press of the Esc key while the dialog is open to have the same effect as clicking the btnCancel button).

7. Select the frmSalesChart form in the Project Explorer and click the View Code button to display the form's class module in the Code Window.

8. Enter the code from Listing 16.1 into the frmSalesChart form's class module.

The frmSalesChart dialog is a completely self-contained object. When the dialog is displayed onscreen, you enter the range for the chart's source data (using R1C1 notation) in the first text box (the RefEdit control), select a worksheet on which to create the chart in the combo box list, enter a title for the chart in the third text box, and finally select a bar chart or line chart in the options group.

To enter a source range into the refSrcRange control, a user can either type the range
specification directly into the text box of the control or select the range from the worksheet. To select the source range directly from a worksheet, the user clicks the button at
the right edge of the refSrcRange control. Clicking this button collapses the dialog to the
size of the refSrcRange control, as shown in Figure 16.11. When the dialog is collapsed
to the refSrcRange control, it is possible for the user to select worksheets in the current
workbook and to select a range on a worksheet. As the user selects the range—by dragging the mouse—the selected range coordinates, in R1C1 notation, are automatically
entered into the refSrcRange control. Figure 16.11 shows the result of selecting a range
on a worksheet, with the range as it appears in the refSrcRange control after making the
selection.

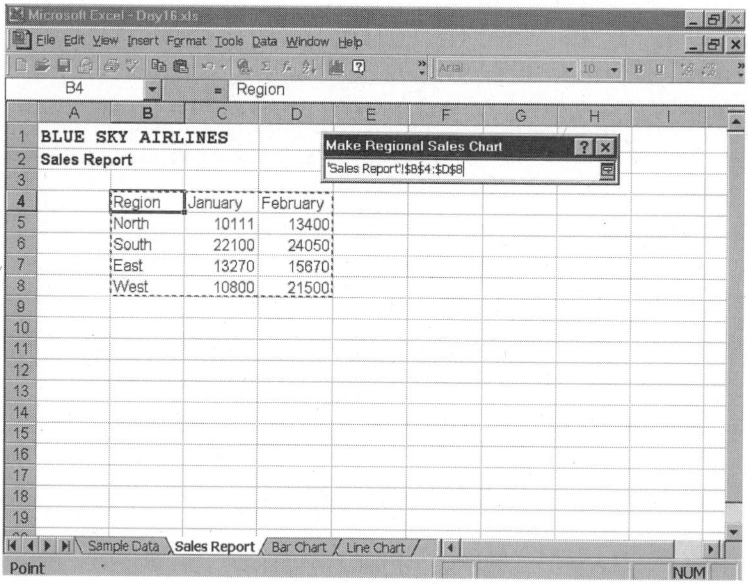

FIGURE 16.11

The RefEdit *control
enables you to select
data ranges on a work-
sheet while a dialog
box is still active.*

In Figure 16.11, notice that the button on the refSrcRange control has changed to show
an arrow and box image. Clicking the button again causes the dialog to expand back to
its original appearance, as shown in Figure 16.12 (which shows the dialog with all
controls filled in).

FIGURE 16.12

The frmSalesChart
dialog with all options
filled in.

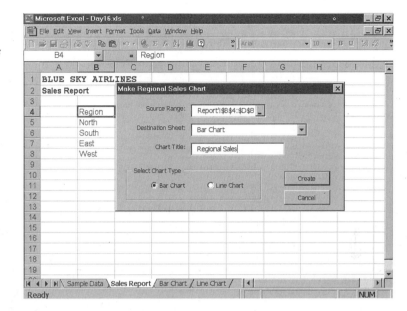

16

To select a worksheet as the destination for the new chart, use the cmbDstSheet combo box control. As explained in the analysis of Listing 16.1, the cmbDstSheet list is *populated*—that is, its list is filled with entries—whenever the form is activated. The cmbDstSheet control's list is populated with a list of all worksheets that exist in the workbook. The cmbDstSheet combo box control is configured with its default properties, so it acts as a true combo box: A user can select an item from the list or freely enter text into the control's text box.

A user selects the worksheet to contain the new chart by selecting an existing worksheet from the cmbDstSheet control's drop-down list or by entering a new worksheet name. As explained in the analysis, if the user types in a name for a worksheet that isn't already in the list, the frmSalesChart dialog will offer to create the new worksheet.

The txtChartTitle control in the frmSalesChart dialog is a standard text box; the user can freely enter any text as a title for the new chart.

To select one of two predefined chart styles, the user clicks one of the option button controls, either optBarChart or optLineChart. Option buttons are used for this selection because the choices are mutually exclusive: You can't create both a bar chart and a line chart at the same time, so a user must select one, but not both. Because these two option button controls are inside a Frame control, the optBarChart control is automatically cleared when optLineChart is clicked and optLineChart is cleared whenever optBarChart is clicked.

Finally, to create the new chart, the user clicks the btnCreate command button control. The btnCreate_Click event procedure for the btnCreate control carries out the task of validating the user's entries in the dialog and then creates the specified chart. To cancel the chart creation process, the user can click the btnCancel command button, press Esc, or click the frmSalesChart dialog's Close button. Canceling the dialog causes no action to take place except to hide the dialog from view.

INPUT   **LISTING 16.1**   THE frmSalesChart FORM'S CLASS MODULE

```
1:  Option Explicit
2:
3:  Const scBoxTitle = "Make Sales Chart"
4:
5:  Private Function SheetExists(Book As Workbook, _
6:                              ShtName As String) As Boolean
7:  'returns true if sheet exists in specified book.
8:    Dim Sht As Object
9:
10:   SheetExists = False 'assume failure
11:   For Each Sht In Book.Sheets
12:     If StrComp(Sht.Name, ShtName, vbTextCompare) = 0 Then
13:       SheetExists = True
14:       Exit Function
15:     End If
16:   Next Sht
17: End Function
18:
19: Private Sub MakeLineChart()
20: 'creates a line chart in a fixed location, on a worksheet
21: 'selected by the user in the cmbDestSheet combo box.
22: 'The chart is plotted using the range specified by refSrcRange
23: 'control.
24:
25:   Dim lChart As Object
26:
27:   'create and select chart on destination sheet
28:   With Sheets(Trim(Me.cmbDstSheet.Value)).ChartObjects
29:     Set lChart = .Add(96, 37.5, 234, 111)
30:   End With
31:
32:   With lChart.Chart
33:     .ChartType = xlLine
34:     .SetSourceData Source:=Range(Me.refSrcRange.Value), _
35:                    PlotBy:=xlColumns
```

```
36:         .HasTitle = True
37:         .ChartTitle.Characters.Text = Me.txtChartTitle
38:         .ApplyDataLabels Type:=xlDataLabelsShowNone, LegendKey:=False
39:         .HasDataTable = False
40:         .Axes(xlCategory, xlPrimary).HasTitle = False
41:         .Axes(xlValue, xlPrimary).HasTitle = False
42:     End With
43:
44:     With lChart.Chart.Axes(xlCategory)
45:         .HasMajorGridlines = False
46:         .HasMinorGridlines = False
47:     End With
48:
49:     With lChart.Chart.Axes(xlValue)
50:         .HasMajorGridlines = True
51:         .HasMinorGridlines = False
52:     End With
53: End Sub
54:
55: Private Sub MakeBarChart()
56: 'creates a bar chart in a fixed location, on a worksheet
57: 'selected by the user in the cmbDestSheet combo box.
58: 'The chart is plotted using the range specified by refSrcRange
59: 'control.
60:
61:     Dim bChart As Object
62:
63:     'create and select chart on destination sheet
64:     With Sheets(Trim(Me.cmbDstSheet.Value)).ChartObjects
65:         Set bChart = .Add(96, 37.5, 234, 111)
66:     End With
67:
68:     With bChart.Chart
69:         .ChartType = xlBarClustered
70:         .SetSourceData Source:=Range(Me.refSrcRange), _
71:                     PlotBy:=xlColumns
72:         .HasTitle = True
73:         .ChartTitle.Characters.Text = Me.txtChartTitle
74:         .Axes(xlCategory, xlPrimary).HasTitle = False
75:         .Axes(xlValue, xlPrimary).HasTitle = False
76:         .ApplyDataLabels Type:=xlDataLabelsShowNone, _
77:                     LegendKey:=False
78:     End With
79: End Sub
80:
81: Private Sub btnCancel_Click()
82:     Me.Hide
83: End Sub
84:
```

continues

LISTING **16.1**   CONTINUED

```
 85:   Private Sub btnCreate_Click()
 86:
 87:      Dim Ans As Integer
 88:
 89:      With Me
 90:        'make sure there's a data source, destination, and title
 91:        If Trim(.cmbDstSheet.Value) = "" Or _
 92:           Trim(.refSrcRange.Value) = "" Or _
 93:           Trim(.txtChartTitle.Value) = "" Then
 94:
 95:          MsgBox prompt:="You must enter a source range, " & _
 96:                      "a destination sheet, and a title.", _
 97:                Buttons:=vbInformation, _
 98:                Title:=scBoxTitle
 99:          Exit Sub
100:        End If
101:
102:        'make sure the selected destination exists
103:        If Not SheetExists(ActiveWorkbook, .cmbDstSheet.Value) Then
104:          'offer to create sheet
105:          Ans = MsgBox(prompt:=Trim(.cmbDstSheet.Value) & _
106:                         " does not exist." & vbCr & _
107:                         "Create it?", _
108:                Buttons:=vbYesNo + vbQuestion, _
109:                Title:=scBoxTitle)
110:          If Ans = vbYes Then
111:            Worksheets.Add.Name = .cmbDstSheet.Value
112:          Else
113:            Exit Sub
114:          End If
115:        End If
116:
117:        'now make the desired chart
118:        If .optBarChart Then
119:          MakeBarChart
120:        Else
121:          MakeLineChart
122:        End If
123:
124:        'hide the form
125:        .Hide
126:
127:        'display the sheet with new chart
128:        Sheets(.cmbDstSheet.Value).Select
129:      End With
130: End Sub
131:
```

```
132: Private Sub UserForm_Activate()
133: 'fills in the cmbDstSheet combo box, and sets a default
134:
135:    Dim aSheet As Worksheet
136:
137:    With Me.cmbDstSheet
138:       .Clear
139:       For Each aSheet In ActiveWorkbook.Worksheets
140:          .AddItem aSheet.Name
141:       Next aSheet
142:       .Value = .List(0)
143:    End With
144: End Sub
```

ANALYSIS Lines 1 through 79 represent the General area of the `frmSalesChart` form's class module. Line 1 is the usual **Option Explicit** compiler directive and line 3 contains a title constant used for the two `MsgBox` dialogs that `frmSalesChart` can display.

Still in the General area of the `frmSalesChart` form's class module, lines 10 through 17 contain the `SheetExists` function, lines 19 through 53 contain the `MakeLineChart` procedure, and lines 55 through 79 contain the `MakeBarChart` procedure. The `SheetExists` function verifies the existence of a worksheet in a specified workbook (you have already seen an explanation of how the `SheetExists` function works in the Week 2 Review).

The `MakeLineChart` procedure creates a predefined line chart, whereas the `MakeBarChart` procedure creates a predefined bar chart. Both procedures are called by the form's event procedures, and both `MakeLineChart` and `MakeBarChart` use values from the `frmSalesChart` form's controls as they carry out their tasks. Notice that `SheetExists`, `MakeLineChart`, and `MakeBarChart` all use the **Private** keyword in their declarations; these procedures and functions are available only within the `frmSalesChart` form's class module.

Lines 81 through the remainder of Listing 16.1 contain the event procedures for the form's controls and event procedures for the form itself. Lines 81 through 83 contain the `btnCancel_Click` procedure. This is the procedure that is invoked whenever the user clicks the `btnCancel` command button on the form. The `btnCancel_Click` procedure contains only one statement and calls the form's own `Hide` method to remove the form from the screen. Hiding the form leaves it in memory, and therefore retains the values of the form's controls.

Lines 85 through 128 contain the `btnCreate_Click` event procedure. This procedure executes whenever the user clicks the `btnCreate` command button on the form. (Although the button's `Caption` property, displayed on the face of the button, is also "Create," it is the button's `Name` property that you must use to refer to the control in VBA code; the `Name` and `Caption` properties do not have to be the same.)

In the `btnCreate_Click` procedure, line 87 declares an **Integer** variable to hold the response of a `MsgBox` function call that might occur later in this procedure. Line 89 starts a **With Me** statement to make referring to the form's controls a bit simpler in the following code.

The `frmSalesChart` form can't carry out its task unless it has all of the requested information: a data source to be charted, a destination to place the new chart, a title for the chart, and what type of chart to prepare.

Line 91 of the `btnCreate_Click` procedure therefore starts an **If** statement whose logical expression tests three different conditions; if any one of these three conditions is true, the chart cannot be completed. If the `cmbDstSheet` control's `Value` property contains an empty string, no destination worksheet has been selected. Similarly, if the `Value` property of either the `refSrcRange` or `txtChartTitle` controls is an empty string, those options haven't been set, either. Notice that each of these expressions is joined by the **Or** operator so that if any one of them is true, the entire expression is true.

If any one of the required entries is missing, lines 95 through 98 use `MsgBox` to display a message to the user stating why the chart won't be created; line 99 exits from the `btnCreate_Click` procedure. The dialog remains onscreen, ready for the user to supply the missing entries.

If all required information is supplied, lines 103 through 113 contain an **If** statement that uses the `SheetExists` function to determine whether the value entered into the `cmbDstSheet` combo box is the name of a worksheet that currently exists in the workbook. Remember, a combo box's drop-down list merely contains suggested entries; the user can still enter any text into the combo box. If the worksheet specified by the `cmbDstSheet.Value` property doesn't already exist, lines 105 through 109 use `MsgBox` to notify the user of that fact and to offer to create the worksheet. Lines 110 through 115 evaluate the user's response; if the user answers Yes, line 111 simultaneously adds and names the new worksheet, otherwise line 113 exits the `btnCreate_Click` procedure.

Next, lines 118 through 122 evaluate the status of the `optBarChart` option button control. Because there are only two chart options, it is safe to assume that `optLineChart` has been chosen any time that `optBarChart` has not been chosen. If `optBarChart` is **True** (that is, selected), line 119 calls the `MakeBarChart` procedure; otherwise, line 121 is executed to call the `MakeLineChart` procedure.

> **Note**
>
> When `OptionButton` controls are placed inside a `Frame` control, the `Frame` control ensures that only one option button in the frame is selected at any one time. In the `frmSalesChart` form, selecting the `optLineChart` option button causes the `optBarChart` option button to become deselected (and the other way around) because the two option buttons are contained in a `Frame` object.

16

Finally, line 125 calls the form's `Hide` method to remove the form from the screen (without unloading it from memory); line 128 selects the destination worksheet, making it the active worksheet so that the user can see the newly created chart.

Lines 132 through 144 contain the `UserForm_Activate` procedure. This procedure executes whenever the `Activate` event occurs: `Activate` occurs whenever the form becomes active. The `UserForm_Activate` procedure first calls the `Clear` method for the `cmbDstSheet` combo box control (line 138) so that subsequent additions are the only items that appear in the list. Lines 139 through 141 use a **For Each** loop to add the name of every worksheet that currently exists in the workbook to the `cmbDstSheet` control's list by calling the control's `AddItem` method in line 140. Finally, line 142 sets a default value for the `cmbDstSheet` control's list selection by assigning the first list element (combo box and other list control lists are zero-based arrays) to the control's `Value` property.

Listing 16.2 shows a procedure that displays the `frmSalesChart` dialog form. Enter Listing 16.2 in a standard module in the same workbook in which you created the `frmSalesChart` dialog.

INPUT   **LISTING 16.2**   A PROCEDURE TO DISPLAY THE `frmSalesChart` DIALOG

```
1:   Sub InsertSalesChart()
2:      frmSalesChart.Show
3:   End Sub
```

ANALYSIS   Listing 16.2 contains only one procedure, which contains only one statement. This statement calls the `Show` method of the `frmSalesChart` form to display the dialog form onscreen. If this is the first time in the current work session that the `InsertSalesChart` procedure has been called, VBA loads the `frmSalesChart` dialog into memory as part of the task of displaying the dialog onscreen. The first time the dialog appears, it looks as shown previously in Figure 16.10.

Each subsequent time you execute the `InsertSalesChart` procedure, the values you last selected for the data source, destination, title, and chart type are retained. Because the dialog form is hidden but not unloaded, it retains the last entries made in its text boxes and other controls.

If you close the project that contains the `frmInsertFigure`, use the Reset command, or perform some other action that unloads the form, the form's controls revert to their default status and the dialog will again appear as shown in Figure 16.10.

The next section contains an example of a dialog form that uses code external to the form's class module and uses a different mix of controls.

Do

DO use the `Me` keyword within a form's class module to refer to the properties and methods of that same instance of the form.

DO keep in mind that the same form programming techniques apply to all variations of VBA, not just Excel.

Putting It Together: A Dialog That Uses Code in a Standard Module

The preceding example showed a self-contained form. Your forms can also use code in standard modules, as shown in the next example. This example uses a dialog form to sort columns on a worksheet.

The `frmColumnSort` form provides a simple dialog to get information about which rows and columns to sort and which column to use as the basis for sorting the rows. The `frmColumnSort` dialog form utilizes text boxes, command buttons, a spin button control, and check box control.

Before you can use the `frmColumnSort` dialog, you need to create the form and a worksheet with some data in it. To get started with this second demonstration procedure, follow these steps:

1. Open or create an Excel workbook and rename a worksheet in the workbook so that it is named **Sample Data**.

2. Enter the following data in the first three columns and the first five rows of the Sample Data worksheet:

   1   222   1

   3   123   3

4   34   5

5   11   4

22   2   2

3. Start the VB Editor and add a UserForm object.

4. Change the UserForm object's Name property to frmColumnSort and its Caption property to Column Sorting.

5. Using the techniques described earlier in this lesson, add controls to the form and edit their captions so that your form looks like the one shown in Figure 16.13. Remember that you have to add labels separately for text boxes.

FIGURE 16.13

The Column Sorting dialog's controls and their names.

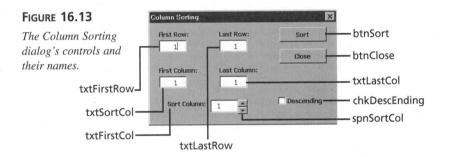

6. Now, set the Name property for the controls on the form so that each control has the name indicated in Figure 16.13. Be careful when you complete this step: Make sure that the control's new name is exactly as shown in Figure 16.13, otherwise the code from Listing 16.3 will not work correctly.

7. Open the form's class module and enter the code from Listing 16.3.

The frmColumnSort dialog gets five numbers from the user all at once. The first four numbers are obtained through text box controls and define a range of columns and rows. The fifth number is obtained through a combination of a spin button control with a dynamically updated text box and specifies a column on which to base a sorting operation. Finally, the Descending check box indicates whether the sort operation should be performed in ascending or descending order.

After the user clicks the Sort button, the frmColumnSort dialog sorts the block of rows in the selected order using the specified sort column to determine the sorted order of the rows. The frmColumnSort dialog calls a bubble-sort procedure stored in a standard module in order to carry out the sorting process. The sorting procedures are presented in Listing 16.4 later in this section.

The frmColumnSort dialog has one important difference in its behavior from the frmSalesChart dialog shown in the preceding example. The frmColumnSort dialog remains onscreen even after performing its primary action; it is a "floating" dialog. The user must click the Close button or press Esc to close this dialog.

INPUT **LISTING 16.3** THE frmColumnSort FORM'S CLASS MODULE

```
 1:   Option Explicit
 2:
 3:   Private Function ValidateSelf() As Boolean
 4:   'validates the contents of the dialogs controls
 5:
 6:     With Me
 7:       'ensure that all values are numeric
 8:       If (Not IsNumeric(.txtFirstCol)) Or _
 9:         (Not IsNumeric(.txtFirstRow)) Or _
10:         (Not IsNumeric(.txtLastCol)) Or _
11:         (Not IsNumeric(.txtFirstCol)) Then
12:         MsgBox Title:=.Caption, _
13:               prompt:="All text box entries must be numbers.", _
14:               Buttons:=vbExclamation
15:         ValidateSelf = False
16:         Exit Function
17:       End If
18:
19:       'ensure that 1st row and column are less than first
20:       If (.txtFirstRow > .txtLastRow) Or _
21:         (.txtFirstCol > .txtLastCol) Then
22:         MsgBox Title:=.Caption, _
23:               prompt:="First row and column must be less than " & _
24:                       "last row and column.", _
25:               Buttons:=vbExclamation
26:         ValidateSelf = False
27:         Exit Function
28:       End If
29:
30:       'ensure that sorting column is within specified range
31:       If (.spnSortCol.Value < .txtFirstCol) Or _
32:         (.spnSortCol.Value > .txtLastCol) Then
33:         MsgBox Title:=.Caption, _
34:               prompt:="Sort column is out of range!", _
35:               Buttons:=vbCritical
36:         ValidateSelf = False
37:         Exit Function
38:       End If
39:
40:       ValidateSelf = True   'if we get this far, data is ok
41:     End With
42:   End Function
```

```
43:
44:  Private Sub btnClose_Click()
45:     Me.Hide
46:  End Sub
47:
48:  Private Sub btnSort_Click()
49:  'carry out the sorting operation
50:
51:      'validate internal data
52:      If Not ValidateSelf Then Exit Sub
53:
54:      With Me
55:        If .chkDescending Then
56:          'sort descending
57:          SortRowsDown FirstRow:=CInt(.txtFirstRow), _
58:                       LastRow:=CInt(.txtLastRow), _
59:                       FirstCol:=CInt(.txtFirstCol), _
60:                       LastCol:=CInt(.txtLastCol), _
61:                       SCol:=.spnSortCol.Value
62:        Else
63:          'sort ascending
64:          SortRowsUp FirstRow:=CInt(.txtFirstRow), _
65:                     LastRow:=CInt(.txtLastRow), _
66:                     FirstCol:=CInt(.txtFirstCol), _
67:                     LastCol:=CInt(.txtLastCol), _
68:                     SCol:=.spnSortCol.Value
69:        End If
70:      End With
71:  End Sub
72:
73:  Private Sub spnSortCol_Change()
74:  'updates the associated label
75:      With Me
76:         .txtSortCol = .spnSortCol.Value
77:      End With
78:  End Sub
79:
80:  Private Sub txtSortCol_Change()
81:  'updates the associated spin control
82:
83:      With Me
84:         'validate numeric entry
85:         If IsNumeric(.txtSortCol) Then
86:           If (CLng(.txtSortCol) < 1) Then
87:             .spnSortCol.Value = 1
88:             .txtSortCol = 1
89:           Else
90:             If (CLng(.txtSortCol) > 99) Then
91:               .spnSortCol.Value = 99
92:               .txtSortCol = 99
```

continues

LISTING 16.3   CONTINUED

```
93:           Else
94:              .spnSortCol.Value = CLng(.txtSortCol)
95:           End If
96:         End If
97:       End If
98:     End With
99: End Sub
100:
101: Private Sub UserForm_Initialize()
102: 'set up the start value for the scrollbar and its label
103:    With Me
104:       .spnSortCol = 1
105:       .txtSortCol = 1
106:       .txtFirstRow = 1
107:       .txtFirstCol = 1
108:       .txtLastRow = 1
109:       .txtLastCol = 1
110:       .chkDescending = False
111:    End With
112: End Sub
```

ANALYSIS   Listing 16.3 contains the entire class module for the frmColumnSort form. Lines 1 through 42 represent the General section of the module. Line 1 contains the **Option Explicit** compiler directive.

Lines 3 through 42 contain a private function, ValidateSelf. The ValidateSelf function returns a **Boolean** result indicating whether the values entered into the dialog's controls are valid. Lines 8 through 17 ensure that the all the values entered in the text boxes are numeric. If they are not all numeric values, an error message is displayed using MsgBox, the function result is set to **False**, and the function exits. Lines 20 through 28 ensure that the starting value for the row and column range is actually less than the values for the ending range. If not, an error message is displayed, the function result is set to **False**, and the function exits. Finally, lines 31 through 38 ensure that the value selected for the column to sort on actually lies within the established range of columns. If not, an error message is displayed, the function result is set to **False**, and the function exits. Only if all tests are successfully completed does line 40 execute; this line sets the function result to **True**, and the ValidateSelf function ends in line 42.

The remainder of Listing 16.3 contains the event procedures for the controls on the frmColumnSort form. Lines 44 through 46 contain the btnClose_Click procedure. This procedure is executed whenever the btnClose command button is clicked. This procedure contains only one statement, which calls the form's Hide method to close the dialog box.

Lines 48 through 71 contain the btnSort_Click event procedure. This procedure executes whenever the btnSort command button is clicked. Line 52 calls the ValidateSelf function to make sure that the dialog's controls contain legitimate values before attempting to carry out the sorting operation. If not, the procedure simply exits. If all the control values are okay, line 55 checks the value of the chkDescending check box control. If this control is selected, its Value property is **True**, indicating that a descending sort should be performed. If the chkDescending check box is selected, lines 57 through 61 execute; these lines contain a single statement that calls the SortRowsDown procedure. SortRowsDown is *not* contained in the form's class module. SortRowsDown is stored in a standard module, shown in Listing 16.4. If the chkDescending check box isn't selected, lines 64 through 68 execute; this single statement calls the SortRowsUp procedure, which is also stored in a standard module (and shown in Listing 16.4).

Notice that the btnSort_Click procedure does *not* contain any statements to close the dialog: There is no call to the form's Hide method. As a result, after the btnSort_Click procedure has finished executing, the dialog remains onscreen with the worksheet visible in the background, as shown in Figure 16.14. To close the dialog, the user must press the Esc key or click the btnClose command button..

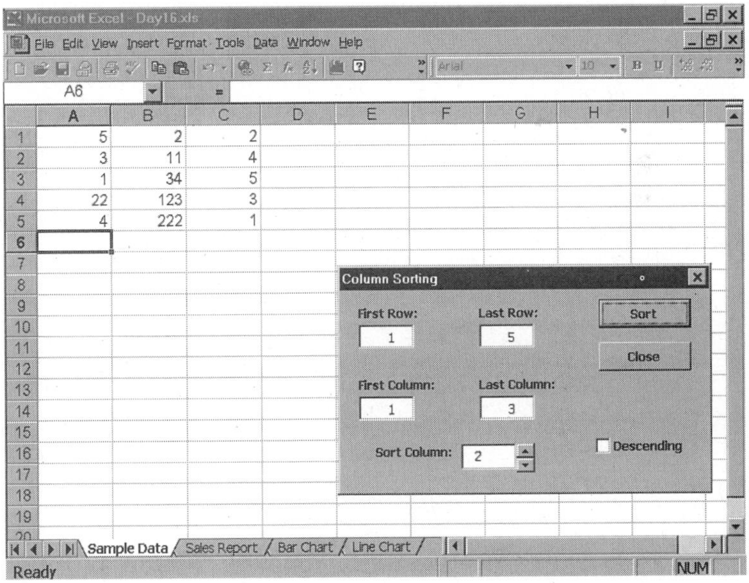

FIGURE 16.14

The frmColumnSort form remains onscreen unless explicitly closed by clicking the Close command button

Lines 73 through 78 contain the spnSortCol_Change event procedure. This procedure executes whenever the spnSortCol spin button control's value changes. This procedure also contains only one statement. Line 76 merely changes the Value property of the txtSortCol text box control to reflect the spin button's current value. The spnSortCol_Change event procedure is one-half the code that keeps this spin button synchronized with its associated text box. Whenever the spin control is clicked, its new value is reflected in the text box.

Lines 80 through 99 contain the txtSortCol_Change event procedure. This procedure executes whenever the value in the txtSortCol text box changes. This event procedure is the other half of the code that keeps the values in txtSortCol and spnSortCol synchronized. Because any text—numbers or letters—can be entered in the txtSortCol text box, the value in txtSortCol must be validated before the spnSortCol control is changed.

First, line 85 tests to ensure that the new value is really a number. If so, line 86 tests whether the new txtSortCol value is less than 1 (there are no columns in a worksheet numbered lower than 1). Notice that the **CLng** function is used to ensure that txtSortCol value is converted into a long integer in case the user entered a number with a decimal fraction. If the txtSortCol value is less than the minimum, the value for both the spin button and the text box are set to be the minimum. Line 90 begins a test to determine whether the txtSortCol value is greater than the maximum of 99; if so, the txtSortCol and spnSortCol controls have both their values set to the maximum. Finally, if the txtSortCol value is not greater than the maximum nor less than the minimum, line 94 sets the spnSortCol control to have the integer numeric equivalent of the value in txtSortCol.

Lines 101 through 112 contain the UserForm_Initialize event procedure. This event procedure is for the form itself, rather than a control on the form, and is executed whenever the form is loaded into memory (that is, initialized). An initialization event procedure is needed for this form because the spin button control must be immediately synchronized with the associated text box value, before the dialog is shown. For completeness, this procedure also establishes starting values for all the form's controls.

Listing 16.4 shows a procedure that displays the frmColumnSort dialog form and also contains the sorting procedures used by the frmColumnSort form's event procedures. The sorting procedures are stored in a standard module because they are general-purpose procedures that can be used by any program to sort blocks of rows and columns. Including the sorting routines as part of the form's code would probably result in an unnecessary duplication of code in your program overall. In a real-world application, general-purpose sorting procedures such as SortRowsUp and SortRowsDown would be stored in a library project. Enter Listing 16.4 in a standard module in the same project in which you created the frmColumnSort dialog.

16

LISTING 16.4 THE STANDARD MODULE CONTAINING CODE REFERENCED BY THE
INPUT frmColumnSort FORM'S CODE

```
1:   Option Explicit
2:
3:   Sub DemoSortDialog()
4:
5:       Const DataSheet = "Sample Data"
6:
7:       Dim aDialog As Object
8:       Dim oldSheet As String
9:
10:      Worksheets(DataSheet).Activate   'select data sheet
11:
12:      Set aDialog = New frmColumnSort   'create a new instance
13:      aDialog.Show                      'show the dialog
14:      Unload aDialog                    'unload the dialog
15:      Set aDialog = Nothing             'dispose the instance
16:  End Sub
17:
18:  Sub SortRowsUp(ByVal FirstRow As Integer, _
19:                    ByVal LastRow As Integer, _
20:                    ByVal FirstCol As Integer, _
21:                    ByVal LastCol As Integer, _
22:                    ByVal SCol As Integer)
23:      Dim I As Integer
24:      Dim J As Integer
25:      Dim k As Integer
26:      Dim Temp As Variant
27:
28:      For I = FirstRow To LastRow - 1
29:        For J = I To LastRow
30:          If Cells(I, SCol).Value > Cells(J, SCol).Value Then
31:            ' swap columns
32:            For k = FirstCol To LastCol
33:              Temp = Cells(I, k).Value
34:              Cells(I, k).Value = Cells(J, k).Value
35:              Cells(J, k).Value = Temp
36:            Next k
37:          End If
38:        Next J
39:      Next I
40:  End Sub
41:
42:  Sub SortRowsDown(ByVal FirstRow As Integer, _
43:                    ByVal LastRow As Integer, _
44:                    ByVal FirstCol As Integer, _
45:                    ByVal LastCol As Integer, _
46:                    ByVal SCol As Integer)
```

continues

```
47:    Dim I As Integer
48:    Dim J As Integer
49:    Dim k As Integer
50:    Dim Temp As Variant
51:
52:    ' start sorting the rows
53:    For I = FirstRow To LastRow - 1
54:      For J = I To LastRow
55:        If Cells(I, SCol).Value < Cells(J, SCol).Value Then
56:          ' swap columns
57:          For k = FirstCol To LastCol
58:            Temp = Cells(I, k).Value
59:            Cells(I, k).Value = Cells(J, k).Value
60:            Cells(J, k).Value = Temp
61:          Next k
62:        End If
63:      Next J
64:    Next I
65:  End Sub
```

ANALYSIS Listing 16.4 starts out with the DemoSortDialog procedure, which displays the frmColumnSort form. DemoSortDialog uses an alternate technique for creating an instance of a UserForm object. Notice the **Object** variable declaration in line 7: The aDialog variable is used to store a reference to an instance of the frmColumnSort form.

First, line 10 of DemoSortDialog activates the worksheet containing the sample data that will be sorted. (You could, in fact, use any worksheet with rows and columns of numeric data.) Next, line 12 creates a new instance of the frmColumnSort object. Line 13 calls the form's Show method to load the new instance of the form into memory and display it onscreen. As long as the form is open onscreen, the execution of the DemoSortDialog procedure is suspended. When the user closes the dialog, execution of DemoSortDialog resumes with line 14, which unloads the form from memory. Finally, line 15 removes the new instance of the frmColumnSort form by setting the aDialog variable to **Nothing**.

Lines 18 through 40 contain the SortRowsUp procedure. This procedure works essentially the same as the bubble-sort procedures for arrays that were presented in Day 14. The SortRowsUp procedure, however, sorts a range of worksheet cells directly from the worksheet without using an array. Finally, lines 42 through 65 contain the SortRowsDown procedure. Again, this procedure works the same as the bubble-sort procedures you're already familiar with, but sorts the worksheet cells in descending order.

It might seem like a lot of work to create the dialogs in the examples in this and the preceding section of this lesson, but it is really worth the effort to create the dialogs and see how the event procedures work.

Do

DO use the `Initialization` or `Activate` events of a form to set up any starting conditions internal to the form.

DO call procedures stored in a standard module from your form's code to avoid duplication of general-purpose procedures. For example, the `frmSalesChart` dialog presented in Listing 16.1 could be improved by removing the `SheetExists` function to a library workbook.

DO give label controls meaningful names if you need to refer to the label in your form's code—you might want to synchronize a label control with a spin button, for example.

DO remember that it is up to you to update the associated text boxes or labels of spin button and scrollbar controls because these controls don't have inherent captions.

DO use event procedures for the `Change`, `BeforeUpdate`, or `AfterUpdate` events to validate data or to synchronize controls with each other.

DO use the control synchronization techniques shown in Listing 16.3 with any combination of controls. You can dynamically update labels, captions, text boxes, lists, and other controls with VBA code in response to a change in the control's value.

Don't

DON'T forget that you can also use an event procedure to update a control's own caption.

Using List Controls

The final example in this lesson doesn't really accomplish any particular task, it demonstrates how you can use a list control and populate the list with VBA code. In this example, the dialog shows a `List` control containing the names of various cities. The dialog also contains OK and Cancel command buttons and a label control at the bottom of the dialog to echo the current list selection. When you select an item in the list, the label control is updated to display the new selection; when you close the dialog by clicking the OK command button, the procedure displays the chosen list item in a `MsgBox` dialog.

Listing 16.5 contains the form's class module, and Figure 16.15 shows the dialog form you need to create for this example. After you create the new form and rename its controls, enter the code from Listing 16.5 into the form's class module.

FIGURE 16.15

This dialog displays the choice from the list in the label control under the list.

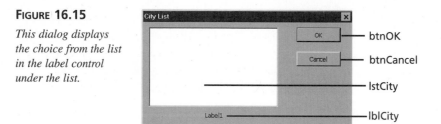

INPUT   **LISTING 16.5**   THE frmCityList FORM'S CLASS MODULE

```
 1:    Option Explicit
 2:
 3:    Dim fCancel As Boolean
 4:
 5:    Property Get Canceled() As Boolean
 6:       Canceled = fCancel
 7:    End Property
 8:
 9:    Private Sub btnCancel_Click()
10:       fCancel = True 'cancel button was clicked
11:       Me.Hide
12:    End Sub
13:
14:    Private Sub btnOK_Click()
15:       fCancel = False   'dialog was confirmed
16:       Me.Hide
17:    End Sub
18:
19:    Private Sub lstCity_Change()
20:       'update the label
21:       With Me
22:          .lblCity.Caption = .lstCity.Value
23:       End With
24:    End Sub
```

ANALYSIS   Listing 16.5 contains the entire class module for the frmCityList form. This form doesn't contain many controls, so its class module is fairly simple, but it does demonstrate some additional important aspects of using custom forms in your VBA code.

Lines 1 through 7 represent the General section of the class module. Notice the variable declaration in line 3; the fCancel variable is a **Boolean** variable used to indicate whether the dialog was closed by clicking the Cancel command button. Because this is a class module, fCancel is not available to any code that is not part of the class module.

Lines 5 through 7 declare a **Property Get** procedure, which creates a read-only property—Canceled—for this class module. (The property is read-only because there is no corresponding **Let** procedure to set its value.) The Canceled property enables your code outside the form to determine whether the dialog was closed by cancellation. The Canceled property simply returns the current value of the fCancel variable.

Lines 9 through 24 of Listing 16.5 contain the event procedures for the form's controls. Lines 9 through 12 contain the btnCancel_Click procedure, which executes whenever the btnCancel command button is clicked. Line 10 sets fCancel to **True** to store the fact that the dialog was closed by clicking the Cancel button; line 11 uses the form's Hide method to close the dialog without unloading it from memory.

Lines 14 through 17 contain the btnOK_Click procedure, which executes whenever the btnOK command button is clicked. Line 15 sets fCancel to **False** to indicate that the dialog was *not* canceled, and line 16 closes the dialog by calling the form's Hide method.

Finally, lines 19 through 24 contain the lstCity_Change procedure, which executes whenever the value of the lstCity list box changes, that is, whenever the user makes a new selection in the list or when the ListIndex property of the list has a new value assigned to it. The statement in line 22 simply assigns the list's current value to the lblCity label control in order to echo the current list selection.

To see how the frmCityList form works, you need to enter the code from Listing 16.6, which contains the DemoListBox procedure to populate the list and exercise the form.

INPUT   **LISTING 16.6**   A STANDARD MODULE TO EXERCISE THE frmCityList FORM

```
1:   Option Explicit
2:
3:   Sub DemoListBox()
4:   'exercises the frmCityList form
5:
6:     Dim aDlg As Object
7:
8:     Set aDlg = New frmCityList   'create new instance
9:     Load aDlg                    'load it into memory
10:
11:    'populate the list from outside the form
12:    With aDlg
13:       .lstCity.Clear    'removes all list entries
14:       .lstCity.AddItem "Paris"      'insert data
15:       .lstCity.AddItem "London"
16:       .lstCity.AddItem "Tokyo"
17:       .lstCity.AddItem "Rome"
18:       .lstCity.AddItem "Madrid"
```

continues

16

LISTING 16.6   CONTINUED

```
19:        .lstCity.AddItem "Bern"
20:        .lstCity.AddItem "Washington"
21:        .lstCity.AddItem "Cairo"
22:        .lstCity.AddItem "Mexico City"
23:        .lstCity.AddItem "Dublin"
24:        .lstCity.AddItem "Warsaw"
25:        .lstCity.AddItem "Vienna"
26:        .lstCity.ListIndex = 0  'establish starting selection
27:    End With
28:
29:    aDlg.Show  'display the dialog
30:
31:    If aDlg.Canceled Then
32:      MsgBox prompt:="City selection was canceled.", _
33:              Title:="List Box Demo", _
34:              Buttons:=vbExclamation
35:    Else
36:      MsgBox prompt:="You chose: " & aDlg.lstCity.Value, _
37:              Title:="List Box Demo", _
38:              Buttons:=vbInformation
39:    End If
40:
41:    Unload aDlg
42:    Set aDlg = Nothing
43:  End Sub
```

Listing 16.6 contains a single procedure, DemoListBox. Line 6 declares an object variable to use for the instance of the frmCityList form that this procedure creates and manipulates. Line 8 actually creates a new instance of frmCityList and line 9 uses the Load statement to load the form into memory without displaying it. The loaded form, although not onscreen, can now be manipulated by your VBA code.

Lines 12 through 27 contain a **With** aDlg statement to manipulate the dialog form. Line 13 calls the Clear method of the list box control to remove any existing list entries. By completely removing all items from the list, this statement helps ensure that the list's contents will be precisely known, that is, the list won't contain any items that this procedure didn't put there.

Lines 14 through 25 each call the list box control's AddItem method to add a new item to the list. These statements each add one item to the list; the list box displays the list items in the order in which they were added to the list. Finally, line 26 sets the list box control's ListIndex property to 0, which is the first item in the list (lists in list box and combo box controls are essentially an array with zero-based numbering). Assigning a value to the ListIndex property triggers the list box's Change event; when the dialog is first displayed onscreen, it will therefore have the first list item selected as the default.

Line 29 actually displays the form onscreen; the form appears as shown in Figure 16.16. As you select items in the list, the label at the bottom of the list changes to reflect the new selection. Notice that the list box control automatically supplies its own scrollbar if the list is longer than will fit in the control on the form.

FIGURE 16.16

The DemoListBox *procedure in Listing 16.6 populates the City List's list box control with this list.*

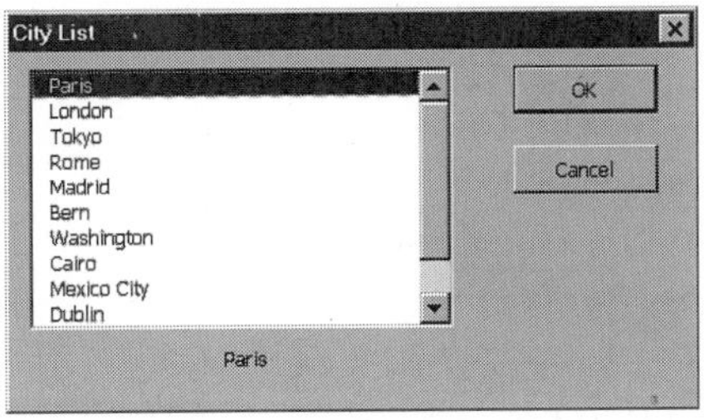

When the user closes the form—either by clicking the OK button or the Cancel button—execution resumes in DemoListBox with line 31. Line 31 starts an **If** statement that tests the value of the frmCityList form's custom Canceled property (lines 5 through 7 of Listing 16.5). If this property is **True**, the dialog was canceled and lines 32 through 34 display a message to that effect. If the Canceled property is **False**, however, frmCityList was closed by clicking the OK command button, so lines 36 through 38 display a message showing the choice that the user made in the list.

Finally, line 41 unloads the form from memory and line 42 disposes of the form instance by setting the aDlg object variable to **Nothing**.

Do

DO keep in mind that you can fill a list by adding items from an array or by linking the list box control to a range of cells in an Excel worksheet—each cell's value becomes an item in the list.

DO keep in mind that the Value property of a list control contains the currently selected item in the list; the ListIndex property stores the currently selected item's index in the array of list items stored in the list's List collection.

DO remember that managing a combo box control is essentially the same as managing a list box control.

Summary

In today's lesson, you learned the basic skills required to work with UserForm objects in VBA in order to create customized dialogs for your programs and procedures. You learned how to create, use, and manage forms and their controls. You learned that you create custom dialogs by drawing them visually on a form. You learned about the basic features of VBA's standard form controls, and how to manipulate them with your VBA code. In particular, you learned how to create event procedures for command buttons and other form controls in the form's class module, and how to use event procedures to update a dialog's controls while the dialog box is still displayed.

Q&A

Q How do I create a drop-down list that restricts the user to only choices from the list?

A Place a ComboBox control on your form where you want to create the drop-down list. Use the Properties Window to set the ComboBox control's Style property to fmStyleDropDownList. The combo box control will now behave like a true drop-down list: The user will be restricted to entries from the list only. Use the AddItem and RemoveItem methods to add or remove elements from the control's list.

Q How do I decide whether to use the Initialization event or the Activate event to set up starting conditions in a form?

A Use the Initialization event when you only need to set up some initial condition once. For example, use the Initialization event to set default values in a dialog's controls or to ensure that related controls—such as a text box and a spin button—are initially synchronized. Use the Activate event when you need to validate or refresh a dialog's controls each time it is activated. For example, the frmSalesChart dialog displays a list of worksheets in the workbook. This list must be updated each time the dialog is activated, because new worksheets might have been created since the time the dialog was loaded into memory.

Q My dialog box never closes; what's wrong with it?

A Any command button on your dialog that should close the dialog box must contain a call to the form's Hide method to close the dialog. If you want your dialog to close after the user presses the Esc key, be certain you have set the Cancel property of one (and only one) of your dialog's command buttons to **True**, and that the command button's Click event procedure contains a call to the Hide method. Otherwise, your dialog form won't respond to the Esc key at all.

Q How can I specify where my dialog form appears onscreen?

A You can control where your form appears onscreen by setting the form's `Top`, `Left`, and `StartupPosition` properties. The `StartupPosition` property controls how VBA displays the dialog when it is first shown: You can choose `Manual`, `CenterOwner`, `CenterScreen`, or `Windows Default` as settings for the `StartupPosition` property. If `StartupPosition` is set to `Manual`, the form is displayed with its top left corner at the position specified by the `Top` and `Left` properties. The `CenterOwner` setting (the default) causes the form to be displayed at the center of the window that owns the form—usually the host application window. `CenterScreen` causes the form to be displayed at the center of the entire display screen, and `Windows Default` causes the form to be displayed at the location where the Windows operating system would display the next window it opens.

Q How can I disable a control in a form?

A You can disable a control by assigning **False** to the `Enabled` property of that control. To enable the control again, assign **True** to the `Enabled` property.

Q How can I hide a control?

A You can hide a control by assigning **False** to the `Visible` property of that control. To show the control, assign **True** to the `Visible` property.

Q How can I make a text box control display multiple lines?

A You can make a text box show multiple lines by assigning **True** to its `MultiLine` property or by setting the `MultiLine` property to **True** in the Properties Window in design mode. Text boxes with the `MultiLine` property set to **True** automatically supply their own scrollbar when the text in the text box exceeds the available display area of the text. You'll generally also want to set the `WordWrap` property to **True** if you set the `MultiLine` property: Setting `WordWrap` to **True** causes the text in a text box to automatically wrap onto additional lines of text to accommodate the current width of the text box control.

Q How can I add and delete items from list box and combo box lists?

A You can add and delete items using the `AddItem` and `RemoveItem` methods. The `AddItem` method has two arguments: The first is a string expression indicating the value to be added to the list and the second is number indicating where in the list the item should be added. If you omit the second argument, `AddItem` adds the item at the end of the list. The `RemoveItem` method takes only one argument: a numeric expression indicating which row in the list to remove.

Q How do I obtain the number of items in a list box or combo box?

A Use the `ListCount` property of the list box or combo box control to find out how many items are in the list.

16

Workshop

Answers are in Appendix A.

Quiz

1. What is meant by *design mode*?

2. What does the Show method do?

3. What does the Hide method do?

4. Can you access or manipulate a form's methods or properties before the form is loaded into memory?

5. What is the effect of the Load statement? The Unload statement?

6. Name two ways you can create an instance of a particular form.

7. What is an *event procedure*?

8. How do you create an event procedure?

9. Can you create custom properties and methods for your form? If so, how?

10. What is meant by *tab order*?

11. What code would you write if you wanted to manipulate the controls in a form before displaying the form onscreen?

12. Does creating a new UserForm object create a new class of object?

Exercises

1. Modify the DemoListBox procedure, along with the frmCityList form, to create a DemoComboBox procedure and frmCityListCombo form, respectively. The new procedure and form should work exactly as shown for Listing 16.5 and Listing 16.6, but using a ComboBox control with a drop-down list instead of a list box. Figure 16.17 shows how the frmCityListCombo form might appear when completed.

2. Create a self-contained form named frmCOCA (COCA stands for Common Command-Oriented Calculator) that has text boxes to get two operands from the user and a drop-down list from which to select a mathematical operator from the user. Include a Calculate command button that performs the specified operation on the two operands and displays the result. Make the COCA form a floating dialog box, as demonstrated in Listing 16.3. (HINT: All of the code for this example can be contained in the form's class module.) Figure 16.18 shows what the frmCOCA form might look like at runtime.

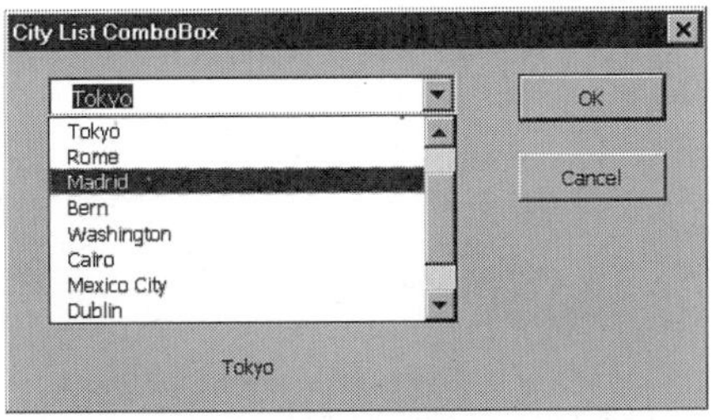

FIGURE 16.17

Create this form for your DemoComboBox procedure.

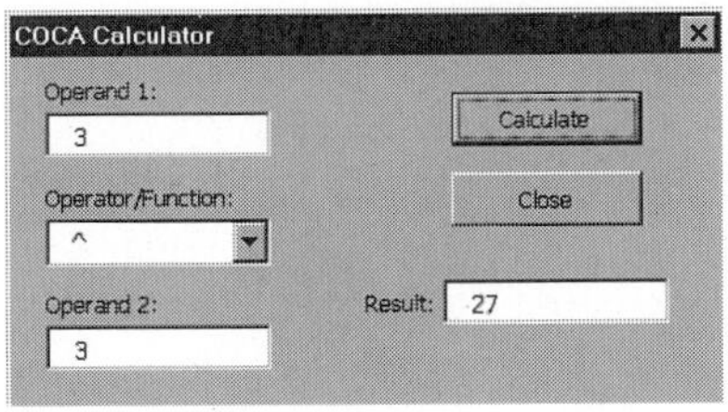

FIGURE 16.18

The COCA calculator should use a floating dialog similar to this one.

16

You should make the COCA calculator capable of handling all of the following operations: + (add), - (subtract), * (multiply), / (divide), ^ (exponentiation), and Sqr (square root). Display the operands in a drop-down list so that only these operands can be entered. (HINT: Set the Style property of the ComboBox control to fmStyleDropDownList to create a drop-down list.)

Make sure you prevent division by zero and attempts to find the square root of a negative number. (HINT: Use a **Select Case** statement to evaluate the operator that the user enters; include a **Case** clause for each operator containing statements that perform the requested operation on the operands.)

Day 17

Menus and Toolbars

Now that you know how to create custom dialog boxes using VBA forms, you're ready to learn about another VBA feature that enables you to create complete, professional programs: menus and toolbars. Visual Basic for Applications makes it possible for you to customize existing menus and toolbars in Excel by adding new commands and submenus, or to create your own complete menus and toolbars. By creating your own menus and toolbars or customizing an existing menu or toolbar, you can add sophisticated extensions to the standard Excel (or other host application) user interface; you can also create complete menu and toolbar systems for your own applications. Today, you'll learn

- What a command bar object is, what a command bar control is, and what properties and methods these objects make available.
- How to add commands or submenus to Excel's predefined command bars—both menus and toolbars.
- How to use command bar and command bar control objects to create and manage customized menus, submenus, and menu commands.
- How to use command bar and command bar control objects to create and manage customized toolbars, toolbar buttons, and how to include text boxes and drop-down lists on your toolbars.

Understanding Command Bars

Excel enables you to create new menus and toolbars or to add new commands to existing menus and toolbars. Before getting into the specifics of how you create (or modify) a new menu or toolbar, you need to understand a bit about the underlying objects that Microsoft Office (versions 97 and higher) uses to implement menus and toolbars. This basic understanding will make it easier for you to understand the detailed instructions for creating menus and toolbars that appear later in this lesson.

As an Excel user, you're already familiar with the built-in menus and toolbars that make it possible for you to issue commands and initiate actions in Excel. The menus and toolbars that an application displays (combined with the various dialog boxes in the application) make up an application's *user interface*, that is, the system through which a user interacts with the application.

From a user's perspective, there is a definite difference between the interface provided by a menu and the interface provided by a toolbar; menus and toolbars have their own distinct appearance and behavior. A menu—also called a *menu bar*—always appears across the top of the application window, underneath the application window's title bar. The choices on a menu bar consist of words representing categories of commands; clicking one of these menu choices displays a list of menu items and/or additional menus (called *submenus*). Menu items represent a command or option; clicking a menu item causes the application to carry out the corresponding action or select the appropriate option.

In contrast, a toolbar can appear in a floating window or docked at the top, bottom, left, or right edge of the application window. Toolbars typically contain buttons; clicking a toolbar button causes the application to carry out a specific command. Toolbars can also contain user interface controls other than buttons: drop-down lists, text boxes, pop-up menus, and others.

At first glance, it would seem that menu bars and toolbars are different objects altogether. Indeed, in Microsoft Excel 7 (and earlier), menu bars and toolbars were represented by two separate object hierarchies: one group of objects for menu bars, menu items, and submenus, and another group of objects for toolbars and toolbar buttons.

Note

The VBA menu bar and toolbar objects prior to Microsoft Office 97 aren't covered in this book. Instead, this book focuses on the current command bar objects used in Office 2000, and were introduced in Office 97. VBA in Office 97 and Office 2000 still supports the older menu bar and toolbar objects for backward compatibility, however. If you have—or obtain—existing VBA code that creates menus or toolbars using the older objects, that VBA code should execute correctly in Office 2000 applications. Code that you write, however, should always use the current command bar objects described in this lesson.

On closer examination, however, menu bars and toolbars have many features in common. For example, both menu bars and toolbars provide a location (the "bar") that can contain interface controls such as menu items, command buttons, and so on. As another example, a menu item carries out the same function as a toolbar button: clicking either a menu item or a toolbar button causes the application to carry out some action. Because of their similarities, it is possible to regard menu bars and toolbars as different types of the same object: a *command bar* object.

All the Microsoft Office 2000 applications (including Excel) implement menu bars and toolbars as different subtypes of a single class of object: the CommandBar object. This consolidation has a primary benefit for VBA programmers: It greatly reduces the number of objects, properties, and methods you need to learn about. In order to create menus and toolbars in VBA under Excel 7 (or earlier), you had to learn how to use 10 different objects and collections and over 23 different properties and methods. By consolidating the functionality of both menu bars and toolbars into a single CommandBar object, the number of objects you need to learn about is almost cut in half.

Command Bar Types

A CommandBar object can be one of three types: a menu bar, a pop-up menu, or a toolbar. Command bars of the menu bar type appear onscreen as a menu bar; they can only appear across the top of the application window, immediately under the application window's title bar. Command bars of the toolbar type (also called *normal* command bars) appear onscreen as a toolbar. Command bars of the pop-up menu type are used to create submenus on a menu bar or pop-up menus on a toolbar.

The type of a command bar is determined by the value stored in the command bar's Type property; you can only set the type of a command bar at the time you create the command bar. The Type property stores a numeric value indicating the type of command bar. In your VBA code, you represent the type of a command bar by using the intrinsic constants listed in Table 17.1. (You can view these intrinsic constants in the Object Browser by selecting Office in the Project/Library drop-down list and then selecting MsoBarType in the Classes list.) As with other intrinsic constants, there is no need for you to be concerned with the actual numeric value represented by the constant; you only need to be concerned with the constant's meaning.

TABLE 17.1 THE MsoBarType INTRINSIC CONSTANTS

Constant Name	Command Bar Type
msoBarTypeMenuBar	Menu bar. This type indicates that the command bar functions as a menu bar, with a menu bar's features and limitations.
msoBarTypeNormal	Toolbar. This type indicates that the command bar functions as a toolbar, with all of a toolbar's features and limitations.
msoBarTypePopup	Pop-up command bar. This type indicates a command bar placed as a control on another command bar; this type of command bar is used primarily to create submenus on a menu bar.

Now that you know about the basic types of command bar, you're ready to learn about the component parts of a command bar, as explained in the next section.

The Parts of a Command Bar

Although you're probably already familiar with the various parts of both menus and toolbars (as they appear onscreen), you need to understand how command bar and control objects work together to form the menus and toolbars you see onscreen. The following sections first describe the components of a menu bar type command bar and then describe the basic components of a toolbar type command bar.

Command Bars as Menu Bars

Figure 17.1 shows the expanded Insert menu from Excel's Worksheet menu bar. (Excel displays the Worksheet menu bar whenever the active window contains a worksheet.) When a CommandBar object has its Type property set to msoBarTypeMenuBar, the command bar object appears as a menu bar. The menu bar type of command bar extends across the top of the application's window (underneath the window's title bar) and lists the first-level menu choices currently available. Each word on the menu bar represents a menu. When you click the menu name on the menu bar, that menu is displayed.

FIGURE 17.1

The expanded Insert menu of Excel's Worksheet menu bar showing the essential elements of a menu bar type command bar.

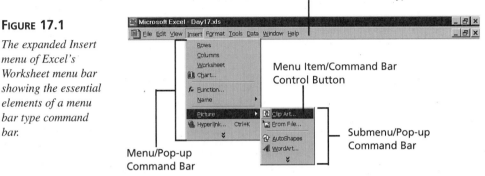

Menu Bar/Command Bar of Menu Bar type

Menu Item/Command Bar Control Button

Submenu/Pop-up Command Bar

Menu/Pop-up Command Bar

`CommandBar` objects are containers; a `CommandBar` object can contain none, one, or several command bar controls. *Command bar controls* are the buttons, submenus, drop-down lists, and so on that appear on a command bar. A command bar's collection of controls can contain other `CommandBar` objects.

Look closely at Figure 17.1 and notice that each first-level menu choice (such as Insert) is a pop-up type command bar object. These pop-up command bars, contained in the menu bar, create the actual menu. The menu lists a series of commands or additional menus that the user can choose from. The commands listed on a menu are typically referred to as *menu items*. In Figure 17.1, the Function and Worksheet choices are both menu items on the Insert menu. Each menu item is a command bar control, specifically, a `CommandBarControl` object. (You'll learn more about the different types of command bar controls later in this lesson.)

From an end user's point of view, additional menus contained in another menu—like the Insert menu contains the Name and Picture menus in Figure 17.1—are called *submenus*. Each submenu is another pop-up type `CommandBar` object, as shown in Figure 17.1.

Note

As you already know, menu choices that lead to other menus are designated by a right-facing arrowhead at the right of the menu choice. Menu choices that lead to dialog boxes are designated by an ellipsis (...) at the right of the menu choice. Choices without either symbol at the right immediately carry out the indicated command. For example, the Name and Picture choices in Figure 17.1 lead to additional menus, whereas the Function choice leads to a dialog. The Worksheet choice is a command that will be carried out immediately when clicked.

When you create and display your custom menus, VBA will automatically add the arrow that indicates a submenu; *you*, however, must remember to provide the ellipsis to indicate that your custom command leads to a dialog.

Command Bars as Toolbars

Figure 17.2 shows Excel's Formatting toolbar in its undocked window. As you study Figure 17.2, compare the command bar and control objects with those shown in Figure 17.1. When a CommandBar object has its Type property set to msoBarTypeNormal, the command bar object appears as a toolbar. The toolbar can be docked, undocked, or customized in the same way as any other toolbar in Excel.

FIGURE 17.2

Excel's Formatting toolbar shown in an undocked window.

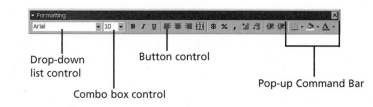

Drop-down list control

Button control

Combo box control

Pop-up Command Bar

Just like menu bar type command bars, CommandBar objects used as toolbars can contain none, one, or several command bar controls. Unlike menus, a toolbar is more likely to contain controls such as combo boxes, drop-down lists, text boxes, and pop-up menus. Also like menu bar type command bars, a toolbar command bar's collection of controls can contain other CommandBar objects. In Figure 17.2, notice that the Formatting toolbar contains a variety of command bar controls, including a pop-up type command bar (used to display a palette of font colors).

Now that you have some idea of the object structure of a command bar, you're ready to learn about some of the specific types of CommandBarControl objects available to you.

Types of Command Bar Controls

As you learned in the preceding sections of this lesson, CommandBar objects can contain none, one, or several CommandBarControl objects. Each CommandBarControl object represents a pop-up menu, command button, drop-down list, or some other command bar control.

The type of a CommandBarControl object is determined by the value stored in the control's Type property; you can only set the type of a command bar control at the time you create the control. The Type property stores a numeric value indicating the specific type of the CommandBarControl object (button, pop-up menu, drop-down list, and so on). In your VBA code, you represent the type of command bar control by using the intrinsic constants listed in Table 17.2. (You can view these intrinsic constants in the Object Browser by selecting Office in the Project/Library drop-down list and then selecting MsoControlType in the Classes list.)

TABLE 17.2 FREQUENTLY USED CommandBarControl OBJECTS

Control Type Constant	Control Object	Purpose
msoControlButton	CommandBarButton	Creates a menu item command on a menu-type command bar. Creates a command button on a toolbar command bar.
msoControlComboBox	CommandBarComboBox	Creates a combo box list control on a toolbar command bar. Not used on menu-type command bars.
msoControlDropdown	CommandBarComboBox	Creates a drop-down list control on a toolbar command bar. Not used on menu-type command bars.
msoControlEdit	CommandBarComboBox	Creates an edit box control on a toolbar command bar. Not used on menu-type command bars.
msoControlPopup	CommandBarPopup	Creates a submenu on a menu-type command bar. Creates a drop-down menu on a toolbar command bar.

17

Depending on the specific control type you select at the time you create a command bar control, the actual CommandBarControl object will end up being one of three different control subclasses: CommandBarPopup, CommandBarComboBox, or CommandBarButton. In Table 17.2, notice that the CommandBarComboBox object implements three of the command bar control types: the combo box list, the drop-down list, and the edit box.

A combo box control enables a user to either enter a value by typing or by selecting a value from a list. The main difference between a combo box and a drop-down list is that a drop-down list limits a user's selection to a value in the list. Similarly, the main difference between a combo box and an edit box is that an edit box doesn't display a list from which to choose a value, although it does enable a user to type in any value. Essentially, edit boxes and drop-down lists each represent a subset of features found in a combo box. The designers of Office therefore reduced the number of control objects needed by using the CommandBarComboBox object to implement all three controls; the specific behavior of the CommandBarComboBox control is dictated by the contents of its Type property.

You'll learn the specifics of using VBA code to create and manipulate command bar controls in later sections of this chapter.

> **Note**
>
> If you check the available MsoControlType constants in the Object Browser, you'll find many more command bar control type constants listed than you see in Table 17.2. Table 17.2 only lists those MsoControlType constants you're most likely to use. Many of the MsoControlType constants listed in the Object Browser represent complex forms of the pop-up menu control used to display color palettes, graphics, and so on. You'll seldom need to use these more complex controls. If you do need to use one of these controls, it's likely that there is a built-in command bar control that you can use. (Built-in command bars and command bar controls are described later in this lesson.)

Command Bar Object Methods and Properties

VBA makes it possible for you to customize the built-in command bars in Excel and to create your own command bars. Before learning how to create your own custom command bar objects or how to modify a built-in command bar, you need to learn more about the specific objects, properties, and methods that you will manipulate with your VBA code. The following sections give you an overview of the various objects, properties, and methods you use to create command bars.

The CommandBars Collection Object

The CommandBars collection object is used to contain none, one, or several command bars. (You learned about object collections in Day 7, "Understanding Objects and Collections.") Table 17.3 lists the CommandBars collection's properties, and Table 17.4 lists the CommandBars collection's methods.

TABLE 17.3 THE CommandBars COLLECTION'S PROPERTIES

Property	Type/Description
ActionControl	Read-only. Returns a reference to the CommandBarControl whose OnAction property is set to the currently executing procedure. Returns **Nothing** if the currently executing procedure was not initiated by a command bar control.
ActiveMenuBar	Read-only. Returns a reference to the CommandBar object that is the active menu bar in the VBA host application.
Count	Read-only, **Long**. Returns a number indicating the number of items in the CommandBars collection.

Property	Type/Description
DisplayKeysInTooltips	Read-write, **Boolean**. If **True**, indicates that shortcut keys should be displayed in the ScreenTips of each command bar control. The DisplayTooltips property must also be set **True**.
DisplayTooltips	Read-write, **Boolean**. If **True**, indicates that command bar control ScreenTips should be displayed. Setting this property immediately affects all the command bars in all Office applications running at that time, and in any Office application opened subsequently, until the property is set again.
LargeButtons	Read-write, **Boolean**. If **True**, indicates that large toolbar buttons should be displayed.
MenuAnimationStyle	Read-write, **Long**. Returns or sets the way a specified command bar is animated. Can be one of the following msoMenuAnimation types: msoMenuAnimationNone, msoMenuAnimationRandom, msoMenuAnimationUnfold, or msoMenuAnimationSlide.

17

In Table 17.3, notice that many of the CommandBars collection's properties correspond to viewing options you can set interactively by using the Customize dialog as described later in this lesson. (The Customize dialog is used to set options for an application's command bars or to interactively create and customize command bars. You can access the Customize dialog by choosing the View, Toolbars, Customize menu command in Excel.) Table 17.4 lists the CommandBars collection's methods.

TABLE 17.4 THE CommandBars COLLECTION'S METHODS

Property	Description
Add	Adds a new command bar to the CommandBars collection.
FindControl	Returns a reference to a specified CommandBarControl object.
ReleaseFocus	Releases the user interface focus from all command bars. Use the SetFocus method of an individual control to give it the focus.

Each of the methods listed in Table 17.4 is described in greater detail later in this lesson.

Most VBA applications contain many different command bars. The individual command bars in an application—whether custom command bars you create or command bars built into the application—are contained in the `Application` object's `CommandBars` collection. You access the application's `CommandBars` collection through the `Application` object's `CommandBars` property.

To return an object reference to the `CommandBars` collection for Excel, use the following syntax:

```
ObjectExpression.CommandBars
```

In the preceding syntax example, *ObjectExpression* represents any valid expression resulting in a reference to an `Application` object. Most of the listings in this lesson contain examples of VBA code that references the `CommandBars` collection.

The `CommandBar` Object

The `CommandBar` object represents a single command bar. You'll need to manipulate `CommandBar` objects not only as menu bars and toolbars, but also as submenus and pop-up menus. Table 17.5 lists the `CommandBar` object's properties, and Table 17.6 lists the `CommandBar` object's methods.

TABLE 17.5 THE `CommandBar` OBJECT'S PROPERTIES

Property	Description
BuiltIn	Read-only, **Boolean**. **True** if the specified command bar is built into the VBA host application.
Controls	Read-only. Returns a `CommandBarControls` collection representing all the controls on the command bar (or the controls on a command bar that is part of a pop-up menu control).
Enabled	Read-write, **Boolean**. **True** if the command bar is enabled. For toolbar command bars, the toolbar appears in the list of available toolbars if this property is **True**.
Height	Read-write, **Long**. Returns or sets the height of a command bar in pixels. If the command bar is docked or protected from resizing, changing this property causes an error.
Index	Read-only, **Long**. Returns the index number of the command bar in the `CommandBars` collection.
Left	Read-write, **Long**. Returns or sets the distance, in pixels, of the command bar's left edge from the left edge of the screen. For a docked toolbar, returns the distance from the left side of the docking area.

Property	Description
Name	Read-write, **String**. Returns or sets the name of the command bar. If the command bar is built in, the Name property returns its U.S. English name. Use the NameLocal property to return the command bar's name, taking into account the local (that is, language) version of the command bar's name.
NameLocal	Read-write, **String**. Returns the name of a built-in command bar as it is displayed in the language version of the VBA host application. Changing the LocalName property for a custom command bar changes the Name property, and the other way around.
Position	Read-write, **Long**. Returns or sets the position of the specified command bar. Use the MsoBarPosition class of intrinsic constants to specify the Position value: msoBarLeft, msoBarTop, msoBarRight, msoBarBottom, msoBarFloating, msoBarPopup, or msoBarMenu. (The msoBarMenu position constant indicates that the command bar is displayed as a menu bar.)
Protection	Read-write, **Long**. Returns or sets the way a command bar is protected from user customization. Can be one of—or a sum of—the MsoBarProtection intrinsic constants: msoBarNoProtection (the default), msoBarNoCustomize, msoBarNoResize, msoBarNoMove, msoBarNoChangeVisible, msoBarNoChangeDock, msoBarNoVerticalDock, msoBarNoHorizontalDock.
RowIndex	Read-write, **Long**. Returns or sets the docking order of a command bar in relation to other command bars in the same docking area. Can be an integer greater than zero, or either of the following MsoBarRow constants: msoBarRowFirst or msoBarRowLast. Command bars with a lower RowIndex are docked first. If more than one command bar has the same RowIndex, the command bar most recently assigned will be displayed first.
Top	Read-write, **Long**. Returns or sets the distance, in pixels, from the top edge of the command bar to the top edge of the screen. For docked toolbars, Top returns or sets the distance from the toolbar to the top of the docking area.
Type	Read-only, **Long**. Returns the type of the command bar; Table 17.1 lists the different types of command bar. The value for this property can only be established when a CommandBar object is created, as described later in this lesson.
Visible	Read-write, **Boolean**. **True** if the command bar is visible. By default, this property is **False** for newly created custom command bars. The Enabled property of a command bar must be set to **True** before the visible property is set to **True**.
Width	Read-write, **Long**. Returns or sets the width, in pixels, of the command bar.

17

> **Note**
>
> To conserve space, the tables in this lesson showing various command bar and control object properties omit those properties common to almost every other object in VBA—properties such as `Application` (which returns a reference to the application to which the object belongs) and `Parent` (which returns a reference to the object's container). Use the Object Browser to view all of an object's properties.

A few of the properties listed in Table 17.5 require some additional explanation. For built-in command bars, the `Name` property contains the command bar's United States English name, whereas the `NameLocal` property contains the command bar's name as given in the language appropriate for the local language version of Microsoft Office. For custom command bars (that is, command bars you create), the `Name` and `NameLocal` properties always contain identical values: a string containing the name you have given your custom command bar.

The `Protection` property enables you to limit the actions that users can perform with a command bar that you create. You can prevent users from customizing, resizing, or moving your command bar. You can also limit the docking options for your command bar: You can prevent users from changing the docking position of your command bar at all or merely prevent your command bar from being docked in a horizontal or vertical position. In particular, you might want to prevent users from docking your command bar vertically (at the left or right edge of the application window) if it contains list or pop-up controls because these controls aren't displayed on vertically docked command bars. To assign values to the `Protection` property of a command bar, use the constants listed for the `Protection` property in Table 17.5. You can assign more than one type of command bar protection by adding the `MsoBarProtection` constants together in the desired combination. Listings later in this lesson show examples of using the `Protection` property.

Table 17.6 lists the `CommandBar` object's methods and briefly describes each one.

TABLE 17.6   THE `CommandBar` OBJECT'S METHODS

Property	Description
Delete	Deletes the specified command bar from the `CommandBars` collection.
FindControl	Returns a reference to a specified `CommandBarControl` object that matches criteria you specify. Use the `FindControl` method to locate a control based on the values of the `CommandBarControl` object's `Type`, `Id`, `Tag`, and `Visible` properties. Optionally, the `FindControl` method will also search all the submenus or pop-up controls on the command bar for the specified command bar control.

Property	Description
Reset	Causes a built-in command bar to reset itself to its original configuration, removing all custom controls and restoring any deleted built-in command bar controls.
ShowPopup	Displays a command bar as a shortcut menu. By default, the shortcut menu is displayed at the current mouse pointer location, although you can optionally specify the location where the shortcut menu is displayed. The ShowPopup method will generate a runtime error unless the command bar's Position property is set to msoBarPopup.

Each of the methods listed in Table 17.6 is described more fully later in this lesson. Before continuing with a discussion of the control objects you can add to a command bar, you need to know just a bit more about the features of Excel's built-in command bars and where Excel stores customized command bars.

Understanding Built-In and Custom Command Bars

VBA enables you to create code that will display, modify, or otherwise manipulate command bars. You will manipulate either command bars that are inherent to Excel or command bars that you create yourself. The next two sections explain the important characteristics of custom and built-in command bars. This section concludes with a sample listing showing you how to list all the command bars built into Excel.

Note Because of space limitations, this lesson does not describe how to use the Customize dialog (accessed through the View, Toolbars, Customize command) to interactively create command bars. Instead, this lesson concentrates on using VBA code to create customized command bars.

Custom Command Bars

Command bars that you create—either interactively or with VBA code—are referred to as *custom* command bars, and you can create custom command bars in Excel VBA. The actual object components that you use to create a custom command bar and its controls are provided through the Office VBA library. (Select Office in the Object Browser's Projects/Libraries list.)

17

With a custom command bar, you can give your VBA programs the same kind of professional user interface used by Excel and other Microsoft Office applications. VBA's `CommandBar` and `CommandBarControl` objects enable you to create your own completely customized menu and toolbar system. Creating a custom menu or toolbar system involves two basic steps:

1. Create a command bar object.
2. Add controls to the command bar.

The sections in the second half of this lesson show you how to write the VBA code needed to create new command bars and how to add controls to the command bar. The next few paragraphs explain where Excel stores the custom command bars that you create.

In Excel, custom command bars are always stored, by default, with the Excel workspace. This means that your custom command bars are available at all times in all workbooks. Specifically, command bars stored in the Excel workspace are stored in a file named *UserName*9.xlb, where *UserName* represents the name that the user entered when logging on to Windows. If the current user did not log on to Windows, command bars in the workspace are saved in the Excel9.xlb file. This storage system has one limitation: Command bars created and saved in the Excel workspace for one user might not be available to other users if they log on with a different user name.

Alternatively, you can attach a command bar from the workspace to a specific Excel workbook. When you attach a command bar to a workbook, a copy of the command bar is stored in the workbook. Whenever that workbook is open, any command bars stored in it are available. Because the workbook contains a complete copy of any attached command bars, you can safely delete the command bar from the Excel workspace. Attaching a custom command bar to an Excel workbook has another advantage: It makes it easier to distribute your custom command bars to other users. If your custom command bar is attached to a workbook, you can distribute your custom command bar and its related VBA code simply by giving users a copy of the workbook containing the command bar and its code modules.

You attach a command bar to a workbook by using the Attach command button in Excel's Customize dialog. (Display the Customize dialog by choosing the View, Toolbars, Customize command.)

Do

DO remember that there is no way you can use VBA code to attach a custom command bar to an Excel workbook.

DO use VBA code to create temporary command bars (as described later in this lesson) to avoid cluttering up a user's .xlb file with custom toolbars.

Built-In Command Bars

Command bars that are inherent to a particular application are referred to as *built-in* command bars. Excel has several different built-in command bars. The built-in command bars include all the menus, toolbars, and shortcut menus that are inherent to Excel. You can customize any of Excel's built-in command bars either interactively (by using the Customize dialog) or by manipulating the command bar with your VBA code.

You can always determine whether a particular command bar is built in to an application by checking the CommandBar object's BuiltIn property; this property always returns **True** for built-in command bars and **False** for command bars you create.

The total number of built-in command bars in an application such as Excel can be fairly large (Excel has more than 80 built-in command bars). This is due, in part, to the fact that most applications display different menu bars depending on the application's current operating mode. Excel, for example, displays different menu bars depending on the type of data displayed in the active window: one menu bar when a worksheet is displayed, a different menu bar for chart sheets, and yet another menu bar when there are no visible workbooks open. Each of these different menu configurations is actually a separate CommandBar object.

Listing Available Built-In Command Bars

When working with command bars, you use the command bar's name (as contained in the Name property) to retrieve a reference to a specific command bar from the CommandBars collection. (Accessing specific command bars in the CommandBars collection is explained later in this lesson.) For command bars you create yourself, you probably already know the name of the command bar; you might not, however, know the correct name for a particular built-in command bar you want to manipulate.

Because of the relatively large number of built-in command bars in Excel, the online help system doesn't list the names of the built-in command bars. One way to find out what command bars are available (and their names) is to look at the list of command bars that appears in the Customize dialog. (You display the Customize dialog by choosing the View, Toolbars, Customize command.)

17

You can also use VBA to create a list of all the built-in Excel command bars (or any VBA host application). The ListBuiltInCommandBars procedure in Listing 17.1 performs the task of listing all of Excel's built-in command bars and provides a basic example of using CommandBar object properties and the CommandBars collection.

LISTING 17.1   THE ListBuiltInCommandBars PROCEDURE CREATES A LIST OF EXCEL'S BUILT-IN COMMAND BARS

INPUT

```
1:  Sub ListBuiltInCommandBars()
2:  'creates an Excel worksheet listing all built-in command bars
3:
4:      Dim CmdBar As CommandBar
5:      Dim RCount As Long
6:
7:      'display information in an Excel worksheet
8:      ActiveWorkbook.Sheets("sheet1").Activate
9:      ActiveSheet.Cells(1, 1).Value = "Command Bars"
10:
11:     RCount = 2
12:     For Each CmdBar In Application.CommandBars
13:       Application.StatusBar = "Listing " & CmdBar.Name
14:       ActiveSheet.Cells(RCount, 1).Value = CmdBar.Name
15:       If CmdBar.BuiltIn Then
16:         ActiveSheet.Cells(RCount, 1).Value = CmdBar.Name
17:         RCount = RCount + 1
18:       End If
19:     Next CmdBar
20:
21:     Application.StatusBar = False
22:  End Sub
```

ANALYSIS   Line 4 of Listing 17.1 declares CmdBar as an object variable with the specific CommandBar object type. Line 5 declares the RCount variable to keep track of the current row in the list this procedure generates.

Line 8 activates a worksheet named "Sheet1" in the active workbook. Line 9 enters a heading for the resulting list of command bars.

Line 11 initializes RCount to 2 to indicate that the next list item should be displayed in the second row of the worksheet. Lines 12 through 19 contain a **For...Each** loop to examine all the command bars in the application's CommandBars collection. The CmdBar object variable is used as the loop variable.

Because building the list of command bars might take a few seconds, line 13 uses the Excel status bar to display a message indicating which command bar is currently being processed so that the user will know that the procedure is still working.

Line 15 contains an `If...Then` statement that checks to see whether the command bar currently being examined (referenced by the `CmdBar` loop variable) is built in. If the command bar's `BuiltIn` property is **True**, the command bar is built in, and lines 16 and 17 are executed. Line 16 displays the command bar's name, obtained from its `Name` property, on the worksheet; line 17 increments the `RCount` variable. Finally, line 21 clears Excel's status bar.

Figure 17.3 shows an Excel worksheet after executing the `ListBuiltInCommandBars` procedure. Notice that the list of command bars includes menu bars (such as Worksheet menu bar and Chart menu bar) as well as toolbars (such as Standard and Formatting).

FIGURE 17.3

An Excel worksheet after executing the `ListBuiltInCommandBars` *procedure.*

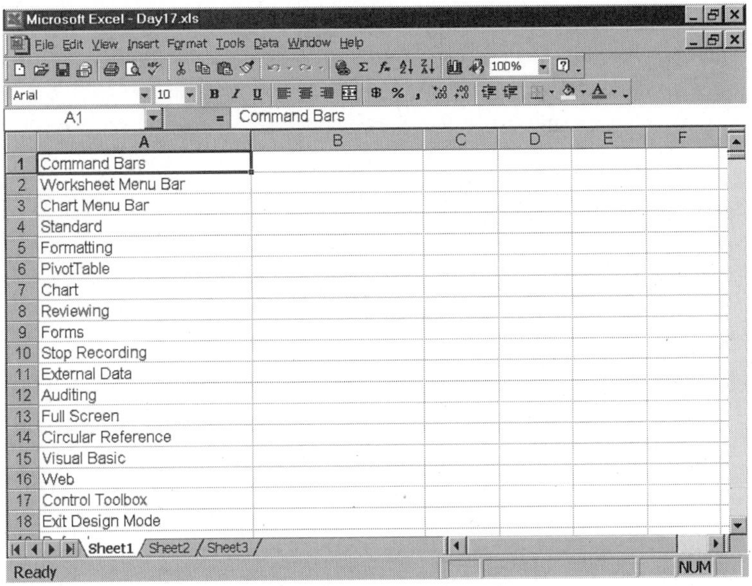

Command Bar Control Objects, Methods, and Properties

Now that you have a firm understanding of the command bar object and collection, you're ready to learn more specific details about the objects you use to place menu choices, command buttons, and other controls on a built-in or custom command bar. The following sections give you an overview of the various objects, properties, and methods you use to create controls on a command bar.

The `CommandBarControls` Collection

A `CommandBarControls` object is the collection of all the controls on a particular command bar. You access a command bar's collection of controls through the `CommandBar` object's `Controls` property. Listings later in this lesson show how to use the `Controls` property to return a `CommandBarControls` object.

The `CommandBarControls` collection is very simple; essentially, it is merely a repository for the command bar's control objects. The only significant property of the `CommandBarControls` collection is the `Count` property. This read-only property returns a **Long** type value indicating the number of controls in the collection (and, therefore, the number of controls on the command bar).

The `CommandBarControls` collection has only one method: the `Add` method. The `CommandBarControls.Add` method adds a new control to a command bar. Using the `CommandBarControls.Add` method is discussed in detail later in this lesson.

The `CommandBarControl` Object

The `CommandBarControl` object represents a single command bar control. You'll need to manipulate `CommandBarControl` objects as choices on menus and buttons on toolbars. Table 17.7 lists the `CommandBarControl` object's properties; Table 17.8 lists the `CommandBarControl` object's methods.

TABLE 17.7   THE `CommandBarControl` OBJECT'S PROPERTIES

Property	Description
BeginGroup	Read-write, **Boolean**. If this property is **True**, the command bar control starts a group of controls on the command bar; a separator bar is displayed in front of the control.
BuiltIn	Read-only, **Boolean**. If this property is **True**, the control is built-in to Excel. If the command bar control is a custom control or a built-in control whose OnAction property has been set, the BuiltIn property is **False**.
Caption	Read-write, **String**. Contains the caption text for the specified control. You use the control name stored in the Caption property to refer to a specific control in the CommandBarControls collection. The caption for a control is displayed as its default ScreenTip.
DescriptionText	Read-write, **String**. Contains the description for the command bar control. The description is displayed in Excel's status bar whenever the user positions the pointer over the control.
Enabled	Read-write, **Boolean**. Set this property **True** to enable the command bar control, **False** to disable it.

Property	Description
Height	Read-write, **Long**. Returns or sets the height of the control in pixels.
HelpContextID	Read-write, **Long**. Contains the context ID number for the help topic attached to the control. The HelpFile property must also be set in order to use this property.
HelpFile	Read-write, **String**. Contains the help filename for the Help topic attached to the command bar control; must be used in conjunction with the HelpContextID property.
Id	Read-only, **Long**. Returns the ID number of the control. Use the Id property to reference specific built-in command bar controls; a control's ID number determines the built-in action for that control. If the control is a custom control, the Id property always returns 1.
Left	Read-only, **Long**. Returns the distance in pixels from the left edge of the control to the left edge of the screen.
OLEUsage	Read-write, **Long**. Enables you to specify how a command bar control is represented when one Office application is merged with another Office application. Unless both applications support command bars, normal OLE menu merging is used, which is controlled by the OLEMenuGroup property. (Refer to the VBA online help for more information on this property.)
OnAction	Read-write, **String**. Contains the name of the VBA procedure to be executed whenever the control is clicked or its value is changed.
Parameter	Read-write, **String**. Some built-in controls use this property to modify their default behavior if the VBA host application is able to use the value. For custom controls, you can use this property to pass information to the control's OnAction procedure or to hold information about the control.
Priority	Read-write, **Long**. Returns or sets the priority of the command bar control. The Priority value determines whether the control can be dropped from a docked toolbar if the toolbar controls don't fit in a single row. Permissible values are from 0 to 7. A Priority value of 1 means the control will never be dropped; 0 enables VBA to automatically determine the control's priority. For any other value, controls with the greatest value are dropped first.
Tag	Read-write, **String**. Contains information about the command bar control, such as information about the control or information that uniquely identifies the control.
TooltipText	Read-write, **String**. Contains the text displayed in the control's ScreenTip. If the TooltipText property contains an empty string, the value of the Caption property is used as the ScreenTip.

continues

17

TABLE 17.7 CONTINUED

Property	Description
Top	Read-only, **Long**. Returns or sets the distance, in pixels, from the top edge of the command bar control to the top edge of the screen.
Type	Read-only, **Long**. Returns the type of command bar control. This property's value can only be set at the time the control is created. Table 17.2 lists the most frequently used control type constants.
Visible	Read-write, **Boolean**. **True** if the command bar control is visible.
Width	Read-write, **Long**. Returns or sets the width, in pixels, of the command bar control.

You'll see examples of almost all the properties listed in Table 17.7 used in listings later in this lesson. Table 17.8 lists the methods belonging to the generic CommandBarControl object.

TABLE 17.8 THE CommandBarControl OBJECT'S METHODS

Method	Description
Copy	Copies the command bar control to another command bar.
Delete	Deletes the command bar control.
Execute	Causes the command associated with a built-in control to be carried out. For custom controls, this method executes the VBA procedure specified by the control's OnAction property.
Move	Moves the command bar control to another command bar.
Reset	Resets a built-in control; this method restores the actions originally performed by the built-in control and resets the control's properties to their initial values.
SetFocus	Moves the keyboard focus to the control so that it can receive keyboard input. The specific keyboard input a control can receive depends on the control's type. If the control's Enable property is **False**, this method will generate a runtime error.

The basic CommandBarControl object has several subclasses, such as CommandBarComboBox, CommandBarButton, and CommandBarPopup. There are actually several more command bar control subclasses, but, unfortunately, there isn't room in this book to describe all the available command bar controls. Instead, this lesson concentrates on giving you a firm understanding of the most commonly used command bar controls.

The next few paragraphs describe the properties and methods of the three most commonly used command bar control subclasses. Only those properties and methods specific to the control subclasses are listed. Each of the following subclasses also has all the properties and methods listed for the generic `CommandBarControl` object in Table 17.8.

The `CommandBarButton` Control Object

The `CommandBarButton` control object is probably the most frequently used command bar control. The `CommandBarButton` control provides buttons on toolbar-type command bars and menu items on menu-type command bars. Table 17.9 lists the `CommandBarButton` object's properties and methods.

TABLE 17.9   PROPERTIES AND METHODS OF THE `CommandBarButton` OBJECT

Property/Method	Description
BuiltInFace	Read-write, **Boolean**. This property is **True** if the control's face (that is, the graphic displayed by the control) is its built-in face. You can only assign **True** to this property, which resets the face to the built-in one.
CopyFace	Method. Copies the face of the control button to the Windows Clipboard.
FaceId	Read-write, **Long**. Used to set or retrieve the ID number for the button face currently assigned to the button control. The `FaceId` property dictates the appearance of a control button, but not the action it carries out. The `Id` property of the control object determines the action performed by the button. The `FaceId` value for a button with a custom face is 0.
PasteFace	Method. Pastes the contents of the Windows Clipboard onto the control button object.
ShortcutText	Read-write, **String**. Contains the shortcut key text displayed next to the button control when that button appears on a menu, submenu, or shortcut menu. The button control's `OnAction` property must be set before you can set the `ShortcutText` property.
State	Read-write, **Long**. Determines the appearance of the button. `State` can contain one of these `MsoButtonState` constants: `msoButtonUp`, `msoButtonDown`, `msoButtonMixed`.
Style	Read-write, **Long**. Determines the way the button control is displayed. `Style` can contain one of these `MsoButtonStyle` constants: `msoButtonAutomatic`, `msoButtonIcon`, `msoButtonCaption`, `msoButtonIconandCaption`.

The `CommandBarPopup` Control Object

The `CommandBarPopup` control object is probably the second most frequently used command bar control. The `CommandBarPopup` control provides menus and submenus on menu-type command bars and pop-up menus on toolbar-type command bars.

The `CommandBarPopup` control has only one special property: the `CommandBar` property. Each `CommandBarPopup` control contains a command bar object you can reference through the `CommandBar` property. The command bar object attached to the `CommandBarPopup` control provides the repository for the pop-up menu's commands and submenus.

The `CommandBarComboBox` Control Object

The third most frequently used command bar control—the `CommandBarComboBox` control—really provides three different controls: a combo box list control, a drop-down list control, and an edit box control. You specify the specific subtype of the `CommandBarComboBox` at the time you create the control. Table 17.10 lists the properties and methods unique to the `CommandBarComboBox` control.

TABLE 17.10 PROPERTIES AND METHODS OF THE `CommandBarComboBox` OBJECT

Property/Method	Description
AddItem	Method. Adds a list item to the combo box (or drop-down) list control. This method generates a runtime error if it is executed for a built-in combo box control or an edit box control.
Clear	Method. Removes all list items from the combo box or drop-down list control.
DropDownLines	Read-write, **Long**. Returns or sets the number of lines in the combo box or drop-down list control. If set to 0, the number of lines in the drop-down list is determined by the number of items in the list. The control must be either a drop-down or combo box list; this property generates a runtime error if executed for a built-in control or for an edit box control.
DropDownWidth	Read-write, **Long**. Returns or sets the width of the list, in pixels. If set to -1, the width of the list is determined by the length of the longest entry in the list. If set to 0, the width of the list is the same as the width of the control.
List	Read-write, **String**. Returns or sets the value of a list item in the combo box control. This property is read-only for built-in controls.
ListCount	Read-only, **Long**. Returns the number of list items in the combo box control.
ListHeaderCount	Read-write, **Long**. Returns or sets the number of list items in the combo box control that appear above the separator line. A value of -1 indicates that there's no separator line in the combo box control.

Property/Method	Description
ListIndex	Read-write, **Long**. Returns or sets the index number of the selected item in the list portion of the combo box control. If nothing is selected in the list, this property returns zero. Setting the ListIndex property causes the control to select the given item and execute the appropriate action in the application.
RemoveItem	Method. Removes a list item from the combo box or drop-down control.
Text	Read-write, **String**. Returns or sets the text in the display or edit portion of a combo box or edit box control.

The listings later in this lesson show examples of using the basic properties and methods for all the command bar control objects described in Tables 17.7, 17.8, 17.9, and 17.10. The next section of this chapter discusses the command bar controls that are built in to Excel.

Built-In Command Bar Controls

Just as Excel contains built-in command bars, Excel also contains built-in command bar controls. These built-in command bar controls carry out predefined tasks, such as saving the active workbook, displaying a Save As dialog, and so on. Excel contains several thousand built-in command bar controls.

Although you can create custom controls and write all the code needed to carry out the desired action for the control, you can frequently save a lot of time and effort by using a built-in command bar control on your custom toolbar or menu. Often, the task you want to perform is one that has already been programmed and is embodied in one of the application's built-in command bar controls, including toolbar buttons, pop-up menus, font-selection drop-down lists, and so on.

Each built-in command bar control is identified by a specific numeric code. You specify which built-in control you want to use by assigning an ID number corresponding to that built-in control to a CommandBarControl object's Id property.

You can always determine whether a particular command bar control is built in to an application by checking the CommandBarControl object's BuiltIn property; this property always returns **True** for built-in controls and **False** for custom controls.

17

The total number of built-in command bar controls in an application such as Excel is
usually quite large—usually a little over 3,000 different controls. Because of the large
number of built-in command bar controls in Excel, the online help system doesn't list the
ID numbers corresponding to the various built-in controls. You can use VBA code to create a list of all of Excel's built-in command bar controls. The
`ListAllCommandBarControls` procedure in Listing 17.2 performs the task of listing all of
Excel's built-in command bar controls and provides a basic example of using
`CommandBarControl` object properties and the `CommandBarControls` collection.

INPUT   **LISTING 17.2**   CREATING A LIST OF BUILT-IN COMMAND BAR CONTROLS

```
1:   Sub ListAllCommandBarControls()
2:   'creates an Excel worksheet listing all
3:   'built-in command bar controls, their names,
4:   'and their ID numbers
5:
6:      Const MaxItems = 4000
7:
8:      Dim CmdBar As CommandBar
9:      Dim aBtn As Object
10:     Dim IDCount As Long
11:
12:     Set CmdBar = CommandBars.Add(Name:="Temporary", _
13:                                  Position:=msoBarFloating, _
14:                                  MenuBar:=False, _
15:                                  temporary:=True)
16:     On Error Resume Next
17:     For IDCount = 1 To MaxItems
18:       Application.StatusBar = "Adding ID " & IDCount
19:       CmdBar.Controls.Add ID:=IDCount
20:     Next IDCount
21:
22:     On Error GoTo 0
23:
24:     'display information in an Excel worksheet
25:     ActiveWorkbook.Sheets("sheet2").Activate
26:     With ActiveSheet
27:       .Cells(1, 1).Value = "ID"
28:       .Cells(1, 2).Value = "Caption"
29:     End With
30:
31:     IDCount = 1
32:     For Each aBtn In CmdBar.Controls
33:       Application.StatusBar = "Listing ID " & IDCount
34:       With ActiveSheet
35:         .Cells(IDCount + 1, 1).Value = aBtn.ID
36:         .Cells(IDCount + 1, 2).Value = aBtn.Caption
37:       End With
```

```
38:        IDCount = IDCount + 1
39:    Next aBtn
40:
41:    CmdBar.Delete
42:
43:    Application.StatusBar = False
44: End Sub
```

ANALYSIS Essentially, the `ListAllCommandBarControls` procedure works by adding built-in control IDs to a temporary command bar object up to an arbitrary limit, which is established by the `MaxItems` constant declared in line 11. `MaxItems` is set at 4000 because experience has shown that Excel contains between 3,000 and 4,000 built-in command bar controls. If you ever execute this procedure and get exactly 4,000 built-in controls, you should raise the `MaxItems` constant to a higher number.

Lines 8 through 10 declare several variables used in the `ListAllCommandBarControls` procedure. `CmdBar` is used to store a reference to a temporary command bar object and `aBtn` is used to store references to various command bar control objects. `IDCount` is used as a loop-counting variable.

Lines 12 through 15 contain a single statement that calls the `Add` method of the application's `CommandBars` collection. This statement creates a new command bar object named "Temporary," which is positioned as an undocked toolbar. The new command bar is temporary, which means it won't be saved automatically by Excel.

Line 16 installs an error-handling trap. In this case, error handling consists of merely continuing with the next statement after the statement that caused the error. This is one of the few cases where this type of error handling is appropriate: It enables this procedure to continue executing even if an invalid control ID is generated.

Note

Listings 17.2 and 17.3 use VBA's **On Error** statement to install error-handling traps that cause the procedure to continue executing even if a runtime error occurs. This aspect of the VBA language has not yet been covered in this book. The error-handling code in Listings 17.2 and 17.3 is essential to their operation, however. Day 18, "Error Handling," covers VBA's error-handling features in detail. For Listings 17.2 and 17.3, you only need to know that the **On Error** statements cause VBA to continue execution with the statement immediately after the statement that caused the runtime error, without halting or displaying a runtime-error dialog.

Lines 17 through 20 contain a **For...Next** loop that creates MaxItems new command bar controls. Each new command bar control is assigned an ID value corresponding to the current loop counter. Line 18 updates the application's status bar so that the user knows the procedure is still working, even if building the command bar takes awhile. Line 19 uses the Add method of the CommandBarControls collection returned by the Controls property of the command bar object referenced by CmdBar to add a new control to the command bar. The new control's Id property is set to equal the current loop counter value by using the ID argument of the Add method.

Line 22 removes the error-handling trap installed previously in line 16.

Lines 25 through 29 select a sheet in the workbook and enter a heading for the list of built-in command bar controls. Lines 32 through 39 contain a **For Each** loop that iterates through all the controls in the command bar referenced by CmdBar. The code inside the loop inserts the control's ID number and caption into the list.

Finally, line 41 uses the Delete method of the command bar referenced by CmdBar to remove that command bar from the application's CommandBars collection. Figure 17.4 shows an Excel worksheet after executing the ListAllCommandBarControls procedure.

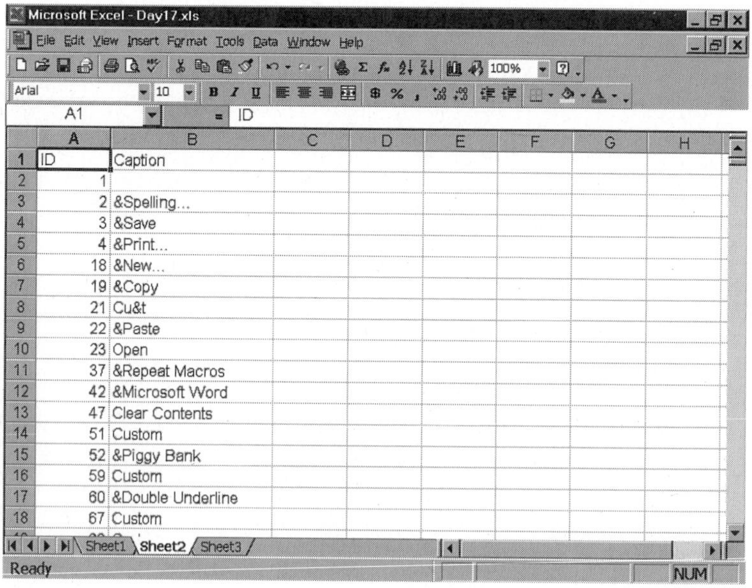

FIGURE 17.4

Excel displays this worksheet after executing the ListAll-CommandBarControls *procedure.*

Do

DO remember that the `Controls` property returns the collection of controls on a command bar.

DO use the application's `StatusBar` property to display progress messages that enable your procedure's users to determine that your procedure is still executing—especially when your procedure performs lengthy tasks.

Command Bar Control Faces

A control's *face* is the graphic image that appears on the face of the control when it is displayed onscreen. A control's `FaceId` property contains a numeric value indicating which control face that control is using. You can choose the control's face from a predefined group of control faces defined by the Office VBA library.

In order to assign a face to a command bar control, you must first know what face ID number corresponds to the face you want. The available face ID numbers and their corresponding graphic images aren't listed in the VBA online help. Instead, you can write a VBA procedure to create toolbars that contain button controls to display all the available faces. Listing 17.3 contains just such a procedure.

INPUT **LISTING 17.3** DISPLAYING ALL THE AVAILABLE CONTROL FACES

```
1:   Option Explicit
2:
3:   Sub DisplayAllFaceIDs()
4:   'creates several toolbars to display all the available button faces
5:   'each toolbar contains 250 button faces.
6:
7:     Const MaxFaces = 250
8:     Dim fDone As Boolean
9:     Dim IDStart As Long
10:    Dim IDEnd As Long
11:    Dim CmdBar As CommandBar
12:    Dim k As Long
13:    Dim aBtn As CommandBarButton
14:    Dim tLeft As Long
15:    Dim tTop As Long
16:
17:    On Error Resume Next
18:
19:    IDStart = 0
20:    IDEnd = MaxFaces - 1
21:    tLeft = 50
```

continues

LISTING 17.3 CONTINUED

```
22:     tTop = 100
23:     fDone = False
24:     Do
25:       Set CmdBar = CommandBars.Add(Position:=msoBarFloating, _
26:                                   MenuBar:=False, _
27:                                   temporary:=False)
28:     With CmdBar
29:       .Left = tLeft
30:       .Top = tTop
31:       .Visible = True
32:       For k = IDStart To IDEnd
33:         Application.StatusBar = "Adding Face: " & k
34:         Set aBtn = .Controls.Add(Type:=msoControlButton, _
35:                                 temporary:=False)
36:         aBtn.FaceId = k
37:         If Err.Number = 0 Then
38:           aBtn.TooltipText = "Face ID: " & k
39:         Else
40:           fDone = True
41:           IDEnd = k - 1
42:           aBtn.Delete
43:           Exit For
44:         End If
45:       Next k
46:     End With
47:
48:     CmdBar.Name = "Faces " & IDStart & " to " & IDEnd
49:     CmdBar.Width = 600
50:
51:     If Not fDone Then
52:       IDStart = IDEnd + 1
53:       IDEnd = IDStart + (MaxFaces - 1)
54:       tLeft = tLeft + 10
55:       tTop = tTop + 20
56:     End If
57:     Loop Until fDone
58:
59:     Application.StatusBar = False
60:   End Sub
```

ANALYSIS The DisplayAllFaceIDs procedure works by creating a series of custom command bars (each with a maximum of 250 buttons) and assigning sequential face ID values to the buttons until an error occurs. When an error occurs in assigning a face ID value to a command button, there are no more valid face ID values left and the procedure ends.

> **Note**
>
> The `DisplayAllFaceIDs` procedure may require several minutes to finish its task, even on a fast computer. Watch Excel's status bar to check the progress of the `DisplayAllFaceIDs` procedure; it updates the status bar each time it adds a new face ID to a custom command bar.

Line 7 declares the `MaxFaces` constant, which limits the maximum number of faces on the command bars that `DisplayAllFaceIDs` creates. Lines 8 through 15 declare the variables used by the `DisplayAllFaceIDs` procedure. `fDone` is a **Boolean** variable used as a flag to control the execution of the **Do** loop in lines 24 through 57. `IDStart` and `IDEnd` are used to store the starting and ending face ID values for each command bar. `CmdBar` and `aBtn` are object variables used to temporarily store references to the new command bars and command bar controls that `DisplayAllFaceIDs` creates. `tLeft` and `tTop` are used to store values for the location of the upper-left corner of each new command bar; `k` is used as a loop-counting variable.

Line 17 installs an error-handling trap that causes the procedure to continue executing with the next VBA statement, even if a runtime error occurs. Lines 19 through 23 initialize the `DisplayAllFaceIDs` procedure's variables: `IDStart` is set to 0 (for the very first face ID) and `IDEnd` is set to one less than the maximum number of faces for a command bar. (Face ID numbers start at 0, so the range 0 through 249 represents the first 250 face ID numbers.) The `tLeft` and `tTop` variables are set to 50 and 100 pixels, respectively. These two variables supply the coordinates for the top left corner of each command bar displayed by `DisplayAllFaceIDs`; the first command bar is displayed with its top left corner 50 pixels from the left edge of the screen and 100 pixels from the top edge of the screen. The `fDone` flag variable is assigned **False**, because the loop hasn't finished creating all the face ID command bars.

Line 24 begins a **Do** loop that creates a command bar and then fills that command bar with 250 control buttons. Each control button on the command bar is assigned a sequential face ID so that the end result of this loop is a series of command bars that, altogether, contain control buttons containing all the available face IDs.

Lines 25 through 27 contain a single statement that uses the `Add` method of the application's `CommandBars` collection to add a new command bar. The position of the new command bar is set to be an undocked toolbar, the new command bar is *not* a menu bar (which means it appears as a standard toolbar), and the new command bar is *not* temporary (which means that the toolbars created by `DisplayAllFaceIDs` will be automatically stored in the Excel workspace). The `Add` method returns an object reference to the newly created command bar, which is assigned to the `CmdBar` variable.

Line 28 begins a **With** statement that contains statements to finish initializing the new command bar. Lines 29 and 30 set the coordinates for the command bar's top left corner by assigning values to the `.Left` and `.Top` properties of the command bar. Line 31 ensures that the new command bar is visible by assigning **True** to the command bar's `.Visible` property.

Lines 32 through 45 contain a **For...Next** loop that populates the command bar with control buttons and assigns a sequential face ID number to each control button. The **For** loop counts up from the current value of `IDStart` to the current value of `IDEnd`. The first time this **For** loop executes, it counts from 0 to 249; the second time this loop executes, it counts from 250 to 499, and so on.

Line 33 updates Excel's status bar to let the user know that the procedure is working (the process of building each command bar takes several seconds, even on a fast computer).

Lines 34 and 35 contain a single statement that uses the `Add` method of the `CommandBarControls` collection returned by the `Controls` property of the `CmdBar` command bar object to create a new command bar control. The `Type:=msoControlButton` argument causes the new command bar control to be created as a `CommandBarButton` control. The `Temporary` argument of the `Add` method is set to **False** so that this command bar control will be saved on the command bar at the end of the current work session. The `Add` method of the `CommandBarControls` collection returns an object reference to the newly created command bar control; this reference is assigned to the `aBtn` object variable.

Line 36 assigns the current value of the **For** loop counter (k) to the `.FaceId` property of the new control button object, referenced by `aBtn`. The first command bar created by this procedure will therefore contain buttons with face IDs from 0 to 249; the second command bar will contain buttons with face IDs from 250 to 499, and so on.

Any attempt to assign an invalid face ID number to the `FaceId` property results in a runtime error. When all the valid face ID numbers have been used, therefore, a runtime error will occur in line 36. Line 37 uses the `Err` object (covered in Day 18) to determine whether a runtime error has occurred. (The error-handling statement in line 17 prevents this procedure from halting when a runtime error occurs.)

If a runtime error has *not* occurred, the statement in line 38 is executed, which assigns a value to the control button's `TooltipText` property so that the face ID number will be displayed in the control button's ScreenTip. (The ScreenTip is the legend that appears when you hover the mouse pointer over a command bar control; the Display ScreenTips option in the Customize dialog must be selected in order for ScreenTips to be displayed.)

If a runtime error *has* occurred, the statements in lines 40 through 43 are executed. These statements first set the fDone flag variable to **True** so that the **Do** loop will end, adjust the value of the IDEnd variable, delete the last command bar button created, and then exit the **For** loop.

Line 48 uses the command bar's Name property to give the command bar a name that indicates which button face IDs are on that command bar. Line 49 sets the command bar's Width property to 600 pixels; this value was arrived at after some trial and error to determine that this width allowed a command bar with 25 buttons in a row and 10 rows of buttons for a total of 250 buttons.

Lines 51 through 56 increment the IDStart, IDEnd, tLeft, and tTop variables only if the fDone flag variable is **False**. The IDStart and IDEnd variables are incremented so that the next time the **Do** loop executes, it will populate the new command bar with the next block of 250 command buttons. The tLeft and tTop variables are incremented so that each subsequent command bar will be displayed slightly lower and to the right of the last command bar.

Figure 17.5 shows an Excel workbook as it appears immediately after executing the DisplayAllFaceIDs procedure. Each command bar created by the DisplayAllFaceIDs procedure contains 250 command buttons, except for the last one (visible on top of the other command bars). The error-handling code and tests in the DisplayAllFaceIDs procedure stops filling the final command bar when all the valid face ID numbers have been used.

FIGURE 17.5

The DisplayAllFaceIDs *procedure creates these command bars, displaying all of the available button faces.*

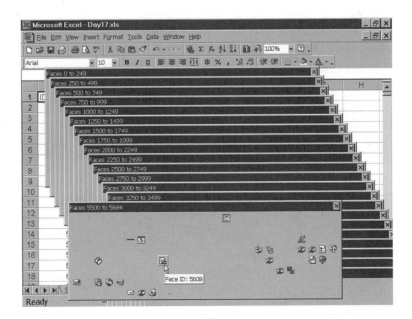

As you might notice in Figure 17.5, many of the button face IDs are blank; these are face IDs that correspond to pop-up menu choices that don't display a graphic next to the menu choice. You might also notice that many of the button face IDs contain identical graphic images. The first 1,000 face ID numbers represent the most interesting and useful button faces.

To see the face ID number that corresponds to a particular control button's image, hover the mouse pointer over that button and read the face ID number from the button's ScreenTip. Figure 17.5 shows a visible ScreenTip.

Do

DO remember that the text displayed for a command bar control's ScreenTip is obtained from the control's `TooltipText` property.

DO remember that ScreenTips are only displayed if the Show ScreenTips on Toolbars check box is selected on the Options tab of the Customize dialog. (Display the Customize dialog by choosing View, Toolbars, Customize.)

DON'T

DON'T forget that many of the button face ID numbers have identical graphic images or are blank. In general, you'll find the first 1,000 or so face IDs to be the most interesting and useful.

Managing Custom and Built-In Command Bars

If you're creating an entire add-in application, you need to know how to create your own custom command bars for use as either menus or toolbars and how to display or remove them. This section shows you how to use command bar objects and methods to create, display, and remove a custom command bar, and how to restore a built-in command bar to its default condition. A code example tying all of these elements together appears at the end of this lesson.

Tip

In general, you should create your own custom command bars instead of modifying built-in command bars. Although you can always restore a built-in command bar to its default condition, it might have already been customized, and the command bar defaults won't really restore the toolbar to the condition that a particular user is used to seeing.

Adding a New Command Bar

The first step in creating a customized menu and toolbar system is to add a new command bar object to the application's collection of command bars. To do this, use the Add method of the CommandBars collection.

▼ SYNTAX

The general syntax for creating a new command bar is

```
CommandBars.Add([Name,] [Position,] [MenuBar,] [Temporary])
```

All of the arguments for the Add method are optional. *Name* represents any valid string expression and specifies the name you want to assign to the new command bar. You use this name to access the new command bar. *Position* represents a numeric expression that results in a valid position number for the new command bar. *Position* can be any of the constants listed in Table 17.11.

MenuBar is a **Boolean** expression indicating whether the new command bar is to be used as a menu bar. If *MenuBar* is **True**, the new command bar is initialized so that it displays onscreen as a menu bar; if it is **False**, the new command bar is displayed as a toolbar. *Temporary* is also a **Boolean** expression, in this case indicating whether the new command bar is temporary. If *Temporary* is **True**, this command bar will *not* be saved at the end of the current work session; otherwise, the new command bar is automatically saved in the Excel workspace.

The Add method creates an empty command bar and adds it to the CommandBars collection; by default, the new command bar is automatically visible. Both Listings 17.2 (lines 17 through 20) and 17.3 (lines 25 through 27) contain examples of using the Add method ▲ to create new command bars.

17

Do

DO delete command bars as soon as you're done with them.

DO add controls to a custom command bar before making it visible. Displaying a blank menu or toolbar isn't very useful.

DON'T

DON'T forget to use the ActiveMenuBar property of the CommandBars collection to determine which menu bar is currently active.

Hiding, Displaying, and Positioning a Command Bar

You can use your VBA code to display or hide either built-in command bars or your custom command bars. The `Visible` property of a command bar controls whether that command bar is displayed onscreen. You can also test the `Visible` property's current value to determine whether the command bar is already displayed onscreen.

You can also specify the position of a command bar by using the `Position` property and one of several intrinsic constant values to specify the command bar's position: floating, or one of several docked positions. Table 17.11 lists the constants for the `Position` property and explains their effect on the command bar's position. (You can display these constants in the Object Browser by selecting Office in the Projects/Libraries list and then selecting `MsoBarPosition` in the Classes list.)

TABLE 17.11 `MsoBarPosition` CONSTANTS FOR A COMMAND BAR'S POSITION PROPERTY

Constant	Effect
msoBarBottom	Docks command bar horizontally at the bottom of the application window.
msoBarFloating	Places command bar in a floating toolbar window.
msoBarLeft	Docks command bar vertically at the left edge of the application window.
msoBarMenuBar	Displays the command bar as a menu bar across the top of the application window.
msoBarPopup	Displays the command bar as a pop-up menu.
msoBarRight	Docks command bar vertically at the right edge of the application window.
msoBarTop	Docks the command bar horizontally at the top of the application window.

Note

A newly created command bar is completely blank. Usually, you'll add controls to a command bar before displaying it. When you display a menu bar type of command bar, it becomes the only menu system available to an interactive user—only the menus on your menu bar will be available. If you display a blank menu bar, then, the user will be unable to carry out any actions! Every menu bar type of command bar that you create should have a command that removes your custom menu and restores the application's original menu bar.

Listing 17.4 demonstrates using the `Visible` and `Position` properties by hiding and displaying the Visual Basic toolbar in all its docked positions and in a floating toolbar window.

LISTING 17.4 THE `DemoToolbarPosition` PROCEDURE CHANGES THE
VISIBILITY AND POSITION OF THE VISUAL BASIC TOOLBAR

`INPUT`

```
 1:   Option Explicit
 2:
 3:   Private Const DELAY1 As Integer = 2
 4:
 5:   Sub DemoToolbarPosition()
 6:
 7:      Const dTitle = "Demo Toolbar Positioning"
 8:
 9:      Dim oldVisible As Boolean
10:      Dim oldPosition As Integer
11:      Dim tBar As CommandBar
12:
13:      MsgBox prompt:="About to change the Visual Basic " & _
14:                     "toolbar settings", _
15:            Buttons:=vbInformation, Title:=dTitle
16:
17:      Set tBar = CommandBars("Visual Basic")
18:      oldVisible = tBar.Visible      'preserve current settings
19:      oldPosition = tBar.Position
20:
21:      If tBar.Visible Then
22:        MsgBox prompt:="VB toolbar will be hidden.", _
23:               Buttons:=vbInformation, Title:=dTitle
24:      Else
25:        MsgBox prompt:="VB toolbar will be displayed.", _
26:               Buttons:=vbInformation, Title:=dTitle
27:      End If
28:
29:      tBar.Visible = Not tBar.Visible  'invert Visible property
30:
31:      'let user know what's going to happen
32:      MsgBox prompt:="The Visual Basic toolbar will be " & _
33:                     "shown floating, and then top, bottom " & _
34:                     "left and right docked, with a brief " & _
35:                     "delay between position changes.", _
36:            Buttons:=vbInformation, Title:=dTitle
37:
38:      tBar.Position = msoBarFloating   'show the toolbar floating
39:      tBar.Visible = True         'force visibility
40:      Wait DELAY1
41:
42:      tBar.Position = msoBarTop    'show toolbar at top dock
43:      Wait DELAY1
44:
45:      tBar.Position = msoBarBottom    'show toolbar at bottom dock
46:      Wait DELAY1
47:
48:      tBar.Position = msoBarLeft      'show toolbar at left dock
```

17

continues

LISTING 17.4 CONTINUED

```
49:     Wait DELAY1
50:
51:     tBar.Position = msoBarRight      'show toolbar at right dock
52:     Wait DELAY1
53:
54:     'restore old toolbar settings.
55:     MsgBox prompt:="Restoring original toolbar settings.", _
56:             Buttons:=vbInformation, Title:=dTitle
57:     tBar.Visible = oldVisible
58:     tBar.Position = oldPosition
59:  End Sub
60:
61:
62:  Sub Wait(Delay As Integer)
63:     Dim TheTime As Single
64:     TheTime = Timer
65:     Do
66:        DoEvents
67:     Loop Until (Timer - TheTime) >= Delay
68:  End Sub
```

ANALYSIS   The DemoToolbarPosition procedure (lines 5 through 59 of Listing 17.4) is really quite simple: It just exercises the use of the Visible and Position properties of the CommandBar object. Lines 13 through 15 display a message dialog informing the user that changes will be made to the Visual Basic toolbar settings.

Line 17 uses the CommandBars property of the Application object to set the tBar object variable to refer to the Visual Basic toolbar. (The Application object reference is understood by default because CommandBars is a global property of the Application object.) The CommandBars property returns a collection of command bars; like any other collection, you specify an individual element of the CommandBars collection by specifying the name of the particular command bar you want to reference. Line 17 therefore assigns a reference to the Visual Basic toolbar to the tBar variable. An object variable is used to refer to the toolbar in order to save a lot of typing and to keep the VBA code shorter and more concise.

Lines 18 and 19 preserve the Visual Basic toolbar's current values for the Visible and Position properties so that they can be restored later.

Lines 21 through 27 use an **If...Then...Else** statement to test the value of the command bar's Visible property. If the command bar is currently visible onscreen, lines 22 and 23 use a message dialog to tell the user that the command bar will now be hidden; otherwise, lines 25 and 26 display a message telling the user that the command bar will now be displayed.

Line 29 simply uses the Not logical operator to invert the current value of the Visible property and assigns the inverted value as the new value of the Visible property. If the command bar is displayed onscreen, line 29 has the effect of hiding it; if the command bar is not displayed, line 29 causes it to become visible onscreen.

Lines 32 through 36 contain a single MsgBox statement that informs the user about what the DemoToolbarPosition procedure will do next.

Line 38 assigns the msoBarFloating constant to the command bar's Position property, causing the command bar to be displayed in a floating toolbar window. Because it's not known for certain whether the toolbar is actually displayed at this point, line 39 forces the toolbar to appear onscreen by assigning True to the Visible property. Line 40 calls the Wait procedure to delay for an amount of time specified by the DELAY1 constant—about 2 seconds, in this case.

Next, line 42 changes the command bar's position so that it is docked at the top of the application window and again delays for about 2 seconds. Now, line 45 changes the command bar's docked position to the bottom of the application window, again delaying for about 2 seconds so that you can see the change onscreen. Similarly, lines 48 and 51 change the command bar's docked position to the left and right of the application window, respectively.

Finally, lines 55 through 58 display a message dialog letting the user know that the Visual Basic toolbar's original settings will now be restored and then assign the preserved values to the toolbar's Visible and Position properties.

Lines 62 through 68 contain the Wait procedure. This procedure accepts a value as the number of seconds to wait. The Wait procedure simply loops until the current system timer value exceeds the timer value that existed at the time the Wait procedure was called by the amount specified in the Delay argument.

Notice the DoEvents statement in line 66 of the Wait procedure. This statement is important because it ensures that Excel has a chance to perform tasks such as updating the screen display while the loop in the Wait procedure executes. Without the DoEvents statement in the Wait procedure, Excel won't be able to display the command bar in its new positions onscreen.

17

Do

DO preserve a command bar's original Position and Visible properties before changing them so that you can restore those settings later.

DO avoid runtime errors in your VBA code by checking the value stored in the Protection property to see whether a particular docking position is permitted. Alternatively, you can also manually check to see whether a particular toolbar can be docked in a particular position.

DON'T

DON'T assume that all command bars (whether built-in or custom) can be docked in all the docking positions. Some command bars are too long to be docked in the left or right docking positions and have their `Protection` property set to prevent them from being docked in these positions. If you attempt to dock a protected toolbar in any of the prohibited locations, VBA generates a runtime error.

Deleting a Command Bar

A command bar, and its accompanying controls, does take up a certain amount of memory. In order to recover the memory resources used by your custom command bar, you should delete any command bars that your program no longer needs. To delete a command bar, use the command bar's `Delete` method.

Note

A custom command bar isn't like a VBA variable—it doesn't go away when your VBA procedure stops running. When you create a new command bar, it remains in Excel's `CommandBars` collection for the remainder of the current work session unless you delete it. In fact, the command bar will be automatically stored in the Excel workspace unless you create the command bar as a temporary command bar (by setting the `Temporary` argument of the `Add` method to **True** at the time you create the command bar).

SYNTAX

The general syntax for deleting a command bar is

`CommandBarObject.Delete`

`CommandBarObject` is any valid object reference to a `CommandBar` object. When VBA executes the `Delete` method, the command bar is removed and any memory used by that command bar is returned to the general pool of available memory. You cannot delete built-in command bars: VBA ignores an attempt to delete a built-in command bar without generating a runtime error. The following sample procedure shows an example of using the `Delete` method:

```
Sub DeleteCustomCommandBars()
  Dim tBar As CommandBar
  For Each tBar in CommandBars
    If Not tBar.BuiltIn Then
      tBar.Delete
    End If
  Next tBar
End Sub
```

▼   The preceding sample procedure deletes all the custom command bars in the applica-
▲   tion's `CommandBars` collection, leaving the built-in command bars unaffected.

Resetting a Built-In Command Bar

If you have edited or modified a built-in command bar, you might want to remove your
custom commands or menus from the command bar at some point. Instead of writing all
the VBA statements to undo any changes you might have made, you can use the `Reset`
method of the `CommandBar` object to return the built-in command bar to its original,
default state.

The general syntax for restoring a built-in command bar is

`CommandBarObject`.Reset

`CommandBarObject` represents any valid object reference to a command bar object. When
the `Reset` method executes, the referenced command bar is restored to its default configuration—*all* custom controls are removed from the command bar, no matter when or
how they were created. The following sample procedure shows an example of the `Reset`
method:

```
Sub ResetWorkSheetMenuBar()
  ' reset the built-in worksheet menu
  CommandBars("Worksheet Menu Bar").Reset
  ' reactivate the worksheet menu
  CommandBars("Worksheet Menu Bar").Visible = True
End Sub
```

Excel's `CommandBars` collection is used to return a reference to the Worksheet Menu Bar,
▲   which is reset and then made visible.

> **Caution**
>
> If you use the `Reset` method on a command bar that has been customized
> with the Customize dialog or by some other VBA program, you might
> remove commands that you don't intend to. Exercise caution when using
> the `Reset` method.

Managing Command Bar Controls

In order to make a custom command bar useful, you have to create and manage the controls that it contains. This section shows you how to create, display, or remove controls
on a menu- or toolbar-type command bar, whether it's a custom command bar or a built-
in command bar. If you add custom controls, you also need to specify the event procedure that you want executed when the control is clicked. In some cases, you might also
want to add a custom control to one of the application's built-in command bars.

To create, manipulate, and manage command bar controls, you need to perform some or all of the following operations:

- Add a control to a command bar.
- Give the new control a name.
- Specify or change an action to be carried out when the control is clicked.
- Set the status bar hint text for a control.
- Enable and disable a control.
- Delete a control.
- Check a control on a menu-type command bar. (*Checking* a control means placing a check mark to the left of the menu item or displaying the menu item's accompanying button in a "down" position.)

The next sections show you how to carry out each of these command bar control management tasks.

Adding Controls to a Command Bar

To add command bar controls to a custom or built-in command bar, use the `Add` method of the `CommandBarControls` collection. A command bar's `Controls` property returns the `CommandBarControls` collection belonging to that command bar.

To add a control to a command bar, use this general syntax:

```
CommandBar.Controls.Add([Type,] [Id,] [Parameter,] [Before,] [Temporary])
```

CommandBar represents any valid object reference to a `CommandBar` object. All of the `Add` method's arguments are optional. The *Type* argument is a numeric expression representing the type of control you want to create. The most commonly used values for the *Type* argument are listed in Table 17.2.

The *Id* argument is a numeric expression representing the ID number of a built-in control. Use the procedure shown in Listing 17.2 to create a list of available built-in controls and their ID numbers. If you omit the *Id* argument, the `Add` method assumes you're creating a custom control and adds a blank control to the command bar.

The *Parameter* argument represents any expression that you want to use to initialize the control's `Parameter` property.

The *Before* argument is any numeric expression and specifies which control on the command bar the new control should be inserted in front of. If you omit this argument, the `Add` method inserts the new control at the end of the command bar.

▼ Finally, the *Temporary* argument is a **Boolean** expression indicating whether the control is a temporary addition to the command bar. If *Temporary* is **True**, the new control is *not* saved with the command bar object; otherwise, the control is automatically saved with the command bar (assuming the command bar itself is saved) at the end of the current work session. Listings 17.2 and 17.3 contain examples of the Add method used to create

▲ new command bar controls.

Do

DO create submenus on a menu-type command bar by specifying msoControlPopup for the Type argument of the Add method.

DO conform to the user-interface design standards for Windows programs by incorporating certain standard menus in every custom menu bar you create. You should always include a File menu, for example, and usually an Edit menu, as well.

Don'T

DON'T forget that you should immediately set the Caption, FaceId, and OnAction properties of a newly created command bar control so that the control will have a name, a graphic image for its face, and an event procedure to carry out an action when the control is clicked.

Naming or Renaming a Command Bar Control

Initially, when you create a new custom command bar control, it has no name. (Built-in command bar controls that you add to a custom command bar already have a name.) A control's name is stored in its Caption property. You should always immediately give a new custom control a name by assigning a value to its Caption property immediately after you create the control.

Occasionally, you might also find cases where you need to change a control's name (usually for controls on menu-type command bars) after you initially give the control a name. The most common example of this circumstance occurs when a command bar is used to display a list of recently opened files, such as Excel's File menu, which provides menu commands to quickly re-open any of the last few workbooks that you opened. To make this part of the menu work, the names of the menu controls must be periodically changed as additional files are opened.

17

Assigning or changing the name of a command bar control is simple: just assign a new value to the control's `Caption` property. The following code fragment demonstrates the use of the `Caption` property to rename a control (these statements change the control's name from Initialize to Init):

```
CommandBars("MyCustomMenu").Controls("&Initialize").Caption = "&Init"
```

Tip

To create a hot key for command bar controls that appear as menu items, include the ampersand (&) character in front of the letter you want to define as the hot key. For example, to make the letter F the hot key in the menu name `File`, you would assign the following string to the control's `Caption` argument:

`&File`

Now, this control is displayed as "<u>F</u>ile" on the menu. If it is a first-level menu choice, the user can press Alt+F to open the <u>F</u>ile menu; otherwise, the user merely presses the F key to activate this control.

Do

DO remember that a control's `Caption` is displayed as the name of a menu choice on menu-type command bars.

DO ensure that each menu or submenu's controls have unique hot-key letters, if you choose to assign hot keys to your custom controls.

Specifying a Control's Event Procedure

You make command bar controls carry out a specific action in much the same way you make a custom dialog button carry out a specific action: by attaching a VBA procedure to the command bar control as an event procedure. Whenever the control is clicked or updated, VBA executes the specified event procedure.

You specify the event procedure for a command bar control by assigning a string to the control's `OnAction` property. The string stored in the `OnAction` property names the specific VBA procedure that you want executed as the control's event procedure. You can assign a value to the `OnAction` property at any time.

SYNTAX

To assign an event procedure to a command bar control, use this general syntax:

`object.OnAction = procName`

`object` represents any valid reference to a `CommandBarControl` object. `procName` is any valid string expression and specifies the event procedure to be executed when the specified control is clicked.

Note

If you assign a value to the `OnAction` property of a built-in command bar control, the event procedure you specify will override the control's built-in action.

Deleting Command Bar Controls

17

You might want to remove controls from a command bar for a variety of reasons. For example, you might want to remove the built-in Format control from the application's menu bar to prevent users from reformatting a worksheet. As another example, you might want to remove a control from one of your custom command bars. Whatever the reason, you can delete controls from both custom and built-in command bars. When a control is no longer needed or valid, you can use the `Delete` method to remove it from the command bar.

SYNTAX

To delete a control, use the `CommandBarControl` object's `Delete` method with the following syntax:

`ControlObject.Delete`

`ControlObject` is any valid reference to a `CommandBarControl` object. When VBA executes the `Delete` method, the specified control is deleted from the command bar. The following code fragment, for example, deletes a control with a `Caption` of "Calculate" from a command bar named "MyCustomMenu":

`CommandBars("MyCustomMenu").Controls("Calculate").Delete`

Enabling or Disabling a Command Bar Control

There are many times when you might want to make a particular command bar control unavailable. For example, you might have written a program that adds a to-do list manager to Excel with a custom Print command that prints the to-do list. If the to-do list is empty, you might want to disable the Print command because there is nothing to print. In this case, you could delete the Print control from the command bar (whether a toolbar or a menu), but this might confuse users of your program; they might not understand why various menu choices or toolbar buttons appear and disappear.

A better technique than deleting a control is to disable it. If you disable the control for your custom Print command, the control is still displayed as part of the menu or toolbar, but it is grayed to show that the command is currently unavailable. Almost every Windows user is familiar with the appearance of a disabled menu choice or toolbar button and will understand that the choice is temporarily unavailable.

To enable or disable command bar controls, simply change the control's `Enabled` property. The `Enabled` property stores a **Boolean** value; if `Enabled` is **True**, the control is enabled. If `Enabled` is **False**, the control is disabled. You can also use the `Enabled` property to determine whether a particular custom or built-in control is currently enabled or disabled.

The following code fragment shows an example of using the `Enabled` property:

```
CommandBars("MyCustomMenu").Controls("Calculate").Enabled = False
```

> **Note**
>
> The `Enabled` property is **True**, by default, for any new command bar controls you create.

Controlling the State of a Command Bar Control

Some types of command bar controls just turn a particular program feature on or off, that is, they are *toggle* commands. For example, the Formula Bar command on Excel's View menu turns the display of the formula bar on and off. When the formula bar is displayed, a check mark appears to the left of the Formula Bar command, indicating that the feature is on. When the formula bar is not displayed, there is no check mark next to the Formula Bar command.

As another example of a toggle control on a command bar, the Web Toolbar button on Excel's Standard toolbar turns the display of the Web toolbar on and off. Whenever the Web toolbar is displayed, the Web Toolbar button is shown in a "down" position to indicate that this feature is currently on. When the Web toolbar isn't visible, the Web Toolbar button is shown in an "up" position to indicate that this feature is currently off.

At some point, you'll probably end up creating your own toggle commands. To display or remove a check mark next to a menu control or to alter the way a control button is displayed, you use the control's `State` property. Each `CommandBarButton` object has a `State` property. This property stores a numeric value indicating the current state of the control. The `State` property can contain any of the `MsoButtonState` constants: `msoButtonUp`, `msoButtonDown`, or `msoButtonMixed`. By default, the `State` property contains `msoButtonUp` when you create a new control. You can also use the `State` property to determine a control's current status.

If a `CommandBarButton` control appears on a menu-type command bar and does not have a specific face ID assigned to it, changing the `State` property to `msoButtonDown` causes a check mark to appear to the left of the menu control. For `CommandBarButton` controls on a toolbar-type command bar or a control on a menu-type command bar that has a face ID assigned to it, setting the `State` property to `msoButtonDown` causes the control's button graphic to appear in a "down" state.

Note

> You can't change the `State` property of built-in controls; the control's built-in behavior governs its `State` control. You can, however, disable built-in controls by setting their `Enabled` property to **False**.

17

Finding Specific Controls

Sometimes you need to locate either a custom or built-in control whose name you don't know exactly. The `CommandBars` collection object provides a method—`FindControl`—that enables you to locate a specific control based on the control's type, ID, visibility, or the value of the control's `Tag` property. Use the `FindControl` method to locate built-in or custom controls.

▼ SYNTAX

The `FindControl` method has the following syntax:

`CommandBarObject.FindControl([Type,] [Id,] [Tag,] [Visible,] [Recursive])`

`CommandBarObject` represents any valid reference to a single `CommandBar` object or to a `CommandBars` collection object. All of the `FindControl` method's arguments are optional. The `FindControl` method returns an object reference to the first control it finds that matches the search criteria you specify. You specify search criteria with the `FindControl` method's arguments. If no matching control is found, the `FindControl` method returns the special object value **Nothing**. If more than one matching control is found, a reference to the first matching control is returned.

`Type` is a numeric expression representing the type of control you are searching for. `Type` can be any one of the `MsoControlType` constants. (You can view a complete list of `MsoControlType` constants in the Object Browser by selecting Office in the Projects/Libraries list and then selecting `MsoControlType` in the Classes list.)

▼

▼ *Id* is a numeric expression representing the control's ID number. This argument is most useful when searching for a built-in command bar control. Because all custom controls have an ID number of 1, using the *Id* argument when searching for custom controls usually isn't useful.

The *Tag* argument represents any value you want to search for. The FindControl method searches for controls whose Tag property contains the same value you specify for the *Tag* argument.

The *Visible* argument is a **Boolean** expression indicating whether you want to restrict the search to only those controls that are currently visible. Finally, the *Recursive* argument is also a **Boolean** expression; setting the *Recursive* argument to **True** indicates that you want to search any command bars contained within the command bar you are searching, that is, search the menus and submenus contained in a command bar.

The following code fragment demonstrates the use of the FindControl method:

```
Set aCtrl = CommandBars("Standard").FindControl(Type:=msoControlCustom, _
                                                 Visible:=True, _
                                                 Recursive:=True)
```

The preceding statement uses the FindControl method to find the first visible custom control on the application's Standard toolbar, searching all submenus and pop-up menus on the Standard toolbar. If a control matching this criteria is found, the aCtrl object variable will be assigned a reference to that control. If no visible custom controls exist on the
▲ Standard toolbar, the aCtrl object variable is assigned the value **Nothing**.

Putting It Together: A Menu-type Command Bar

You've learned a lot about menu-type command bars and command bar controls on menus in this lesson. Now you're ready to put all this new knowledge to work and create a working menu system. The menu system in Listing 17.5 doesn't do much in the way of real work, but it does demonstrate how to use all the important command bar and command bar control objects on a menu-type command bar.

The menu system created by Listing 17.5 also illustrates an important requirement for any menu system: making sure there is some kind of exit command available. If you don't include a way to exit from the menu system you activate, you won't ever be able to get the application's built-in menus back in the current work session—you'll have to exit the application and restart it to get the standard menus back.

The custom menu bar created by Listing 17.5 has only two choices on it: File and Demo. The File menu has only three menu items on it: two simulated commands (Open and Save) and the Exit command. Selecting File, Exit restores whatever menu bar the application would normally display and then deletes the menu bar.

The Demo menu has two menu items and one submenu on it. The submenu has four menu items on it. The first menu item demonstrates how to toggle a menu check mark on and off; the second menu item demonstrates toggling the button icon on a menu. The first two menu items also demonstrate changing a menu item's caption. All the menu items on the Demo menu and its submenu call the same dummy command procedure; in a real menu system, you'd have separate event procedures for each menu command. Figure 17.6 shows the custom menu bar created by Listing 17.5, with the Demo menu dropped down and the submenu expanded. As shown in Figure 17.6, the first submenu selection has its check mark turned on.

17

FIGURE 17.6

The menu bar created by DemoMenuSystem, *showing a menu with two levels of submenus.*

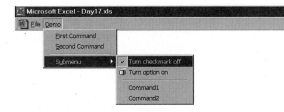

INPUT   **LISTING 17.5**   THE DemoMenuSystem PROCEDURE PRODUCES A MINIMAL MENU BAR

```
 1:  Option Explicit
 2:
 3:  Const MenuName = "Demo Menu"
 4:  Const OpenIcon = 23
 5:  Const SaveIcon = 3
 6:  Const MugIcon = 480
 7:
 8:
 9:  Sub DemoMenuSystem()
10:  'creates and installs a demonstration menu system.
11:
12:    Dim myMenuBar As CommandBar
13:    Dim aMenu As Object
14:
15:    'create the custom command bar
16:    Set myMenuBar = CommandBars.Add(Name:="Demo Menu", _
17:                                    MenuBar:=True, _
18:                                    temporary:=True)
19:
```

continues

LISTING 17.5   CONTINUED

```
20:     'add top-level menus to the menu-style command bar
21:     With myMenuBar.Controls
22:       'add the File menu
23:       Set aMenu = .Add(Type:=msoControlPopup, temporary:=True)
24:       aMenu.Caption = "&File"
25:
26:       'add the Demo menu
27:       Set aMenu = .Add(Type:=msoControlPopup, temporary:=True)
28:       aMenu.Caption = "&Demo"
29:     End With
30:
31:     'populate the File menu
32:     With myMenuBar.Controls("File").Controls
33:       'add the File | Open menu item
34:       Set aMenu = .Add(Type:=msoControlButton, temporary:=True)
35:       aMenu.Caption = "&Open"
36:       aMenu.FaceId = OpenIcon
37:       aMenu.OnAction = "DummyCommand"
38:       aMenu.Parameter = "File Open"
39:
40:       'add the File | Save menu item
41:       Set aMenu = .Add(Type:=msoControlButton, temporary:=True)
42:       aMenu.Caption = "&Save"
43:       aMenu.FaceId = SaveIcon
44:       aMenu.OnAction = "DummyCommand"
45:       aMenu.Parameter = "File Save"
46:
47:       'add the File | Exit menu item, starting a new group
48:       Set aMenu = .Add(Type:=msoControlButton, temporary:=True)
49:       aMenu.Caption = "E&xit"
50:       aMenu.OnAction = "ExitCommand"
51:       aMenu.Parameter = "File Exit"
52:       aMenu.BeginGroup = True   'adds separator in front of item
53:     End With
54:
55:     'populate the Demo menu
56:     With myMenuBar.Controls("Demo").Controls
57:       'add the first demo command
58:       Set aMenu = .Add(Type:=msoControlButton, temporary:=True)
59:       aMenu.Caption = "&First Command"
60:       aMenu.OnAction = "DummyCommand"
61:       aMenu.Parameter = "Demo First"
62:
63:       'add the second demo command
64:       Set aMenu = .Add(Type:=msoControlButton, temporary:=True)
65:       aMenu.Caption = "&Second Command"
66:       aMenu.OnAction = "DummyCommand"
67:       aMenu.Parameter = "Demo Second"
68:
```

```
 69:        'add a submenu to the command by adding a popup control
 70:        Set aMenu = .Add(Type:=msoControlPopup, temporary:=True)
 71:        aMenu.Caption = "S&ubmenu"
 72:        aMenu.BeginGroup = True    'adds separator in front of control
 73:     End With
 74:
 75:     'populate the Demo ¦ Submenu menu.
 76:     With myMenuBar.Controls("Demo").Controls("Submenu").Controls
 77:        'add a menu command to demonstrate a toggle with checkmark
 78:        Set aMenu = .Add(Type:=msoControlButton, temporary:=True)
 79:        aMenu.Caption = "Turn checkmark on"
 80:        aMenu.OnAction = "CheckToggle"
 81:
 82:        'add a menu command to demonstrate a toggle with button
 83:        Set aMenu = .Add(Type:=msoControlButton, temporary:=True)
 84:        aMenu.Caption = "Turn option on"
 85:        aMenu.FaceId = MugIcon
 86:        aMenu.OnAction = "ButtonToggle"
 87:
 88:        'add a menu command with a separator
 89:        Set aMenu = .Add(Type:=msoControlButton, temporary:=True)
 90:        aMenu.Caption = "Command1"
 91:        aMenu.OnAction = "DummyCommand"
 92:        aMenu.Parameter = aMenu.Caption
 93:        aMenu.BeginGroup = True
 94:
 95:        'add another dummy menu command
 96:        Set aMenu = .Add(Type:=msoControlButton, temporary:=True)
 97:        aMenu.Caption = "Command2"
 98:        aMenu.OnAction = "DummyCommand"
 99:        aMenu.Parameter = aMenu.Caption
100:     End With
101:
102:     myMenuBar.Visible = True    'activate the menu
103: End Sub
104:
105:
106: Sub CheckToggle()
107: 'toggles the checkmark, and changes caption
108:
109:     With CommandBars("Demo Menu").Controls("Demo")
110:        With .Controls("Submenu").Controls(1)
111:         If .State = msoButtonUp Then
112:            .State = msoButtonDown
113:            .Caption = "Turn checkmark off"
114:         Else
115:            .State = msoButtonUp
116:            .Caption = "Turn checkmark on"
117:         End If
118:        End With
```

17

continues

LISTING 17.5   CONTINUED

```
119:    End With
120: End Sub
121:
122:
123: Sub ButtonToggle()
124: 'toggles the button's state, and changes the menu caption
125:
126:    With CommandBars(MenuName).Controls("Demo")
127:      With .Controls("Submenu").Controls(2)
128:        If .State = msoButtonUp Then
129:          .State = msoButtonDown
130:          .Caption = "Turn option off"
131:        Else
132:          .State = msoButtonUp
133:          .Caption = "Turn option on"
134:        End If
135:      End With
136:    End With
137: End Sub
138:
139:
140: Sub DummyCommand()
141: 'displays a message dialog to simulate execution of a command
142:
143:    Dim CmdCtrl As Object
144:
145:    Set CmdCtrl = CommandBars.ActionControl
146:
147:    If CmdCtrl Is Nothing Then Exit Sub
148:
149:    MsgBox prompt:="Simulation of the " & _
150:                   CmdCtrl.Parameter & " command.", _
151:           Buttons:=vbInformation, _
152:           Title:="Menu System Demonstration"
153: End Sub
154:
155:
156: Sub ExitCommand()
157: 'removes the custom menu bar
158:    CommandBars(MenuName).Delete
159: End Sub
```

ANALYSIS   The DemoMenuSystem procedure (lines 9 through 103 in Listing 17.5) starts out by adding a custom command bar to the CommandBars collection with the statement in lines 16 through 18. For convenience, the result of the Add method (an object reference to the newly created command bar) is assigned to the myMenuBar object variable.

Notice that the MenuBar argument of the Add method is **True**; as a result, the new command bar is created as a menu-type command bar. In addition, the Temporary argument is also **True** so that this menu-type command bar will *not* be automatically saved.

> **Note**
>
> Enter all the code in Listing 17.5 before running the DemoMenuSystem procedure. After running the DemoMenuSystem procedure, notice that you can still edit your worksheet, choose buttons from onscreen toolbars, and perform other actions while your custom menu command bar is onscreen. You must choose the File, Exit command from the custom menu bar to restore access to Excel's built-in menu bars.

17

Lines 21 through 29 add the File and Demo menus to the menu command bar. Line 23 uses the Add method of the Controls collection to create a new command bar control for the File menu. Notice that the Type argument of the Add method uses the msoControlPopup constant to indicate that this control should be created as a pop-up menu control: this is how the File menu is created on the menu command bar. For convenience, the result of the Add method (an object reference to the new control) is assigned to the aMenu object variable. Line 28 sets the pop-up menu control's caption by assigning a string to the Caption property of the new control. Notice that the ampersand (&) is used to indicate that the "F" in "File" is to become the menu's hot-key. Similarly, lines 27 and 28 create another pop-up menu control and assign a value to its caption. These are the statements that create the File and Demo menus visible in Figure 17.6.

At this point, the menu command bar consists of the command bar, itself, and two empty menus. Lines 32 through 53 populate the File menu by adding controls to the command bar that is part of the pop-up menu control. Notice that line 32 starts a **With** statement that refers to the Controls collection belonging to the "File" control in the menu command bar's Controls collection.

Lines 34 through 38 add a control named Open to the File menu's command bar. Line 34 uses the Add method to create the control; notice that the Type argument in this case specifies that the control should be created as an msoControlButton control type. Adding control buttons to a menu creates menu items on that menu. Line 35 sets the caption for the menu control; this is the text that appears on the menu as the command choice. Line 36 assigns a value to the button control's FacID value; this specifies the graphic image displayed to the left of the menu item. Line 37 sets the button control's OnAction property to execute the DummyCommand procedure. (The DummyCommand procedure is used to simulate the actual command that might be carried out by this menu choice.) Finally, line 38 sets the button control's Parameter property. The DummyCommand procedure uses the value in the control's `Parameter` property to report on which menu command it is simulating.

Lines 40 through 45 add a Save command to the menu. As before, a control button is added to the File menu's command bar. Next, the command's name is assigned to the `Caption` property, a value is assigned to the `FaceId` property, an event procedure name is stored in the `OnAction` property, and the `Parameter` property is set so that the `DummyCommand` procedure can report on which command it is simulating.

Finally, lines 47 through 52 add the Exit command to the File menu. Again, the control type is specified as a control button in order to create a menu command. This time, no `FaceId` is set; as a result, the space to the left of the menu command will be blank. Notice also that the Exit control button's `OnAction` property is set to the `ExitCommand` procedure. This procedure removes this demonstration menu command bar.

Whenever the File, Exit menu command is chosen, VBA will execute the `ExitCommand` procedure (in lines 156 through 159 of Listing 17.5). Line 52 sets the `BeginGroup` property of the Exit control button so that a separator line is displayed on the menu in front of the Exit command.

Lines 56 through 73 add commands to the Demo menu by adding controls to the command bar inherent to the Demo pop-up control. Lines 58 through 61 add another dummy menu command, and lines 64 through 67 add a second dummy command. Pay attention, however, to lines 70 through 72: these statements create a submenu on the Demo menu. Notice that the `Type` argument of the `Add` method in line 70 creates a pop-up control; this pop-up control becomes a submenu on the Demo menu. Notice also that line 72 sets this control's `BeginGroup` property to **True** in order to display a separator in the menu in front of this control. The statement in line 72 is responsible for the presence of the separator bar visible on the Demo menu in Figure 17.6.

At this point, the submenu on the Demo menu doesn't contain any controls, so lines 76 through 100 add controls to the Demo, Submenu control. Notice that the first two control buttons on the submenu have special event procedures that are different from the `DummyCommand` procedure specified for all the other menu commands.

Finally, line 102 ensures that the custom menu command bar is displayed onscreen by setting its `Visible` property to **True**. The new menu command bar is displayed onscreen, replacing whatever menu bar was previously displayed.

Lines 106 through 120 contain the CheckToggle procedure. The CheckToggle procedure is executed whenever the Demo, Submenu, Turn Checkmark off (or Demo, Submenu, Turn Checkmark on) command is selected. The CheckToggle procedure adds or removes the check mark next to the first command on the Demo, Submenu menu item and changes the command's caption accordingly. When first created, the check mark is not on and the control's caption is Turn checkmark on.

The CheckToggle procedure begins by evaluating the current state of the button. If the control button's State property contains msoButtonUp, the button's state is changed to msoButtonDown and its caption is changed to Turn checkmark off. If the button's State property is msoButtonDown, a check mark appears next to the control button, as shown in Figure 17.6. If the button's state is already msoButtonDown, its state is changed to msoButtonUp and its caption is changed to Turn checkmark on.

Lines 123 through 137 contain the ButtonToggle procedure. This procedure executes whenever the Demo, Submenu, Turn option off (or Demo, Submenu, Turn option on) command is chosen. This procedure works essentially the same as the CheckToggle procedure just described. Because this control has a graphic image, no check mark appears when the button's state is "down," but the image to the left of the menu command takes on the appearance of a button pushed "down."

Lines 140 through 153 contain the DummyCommand procedure, which exists solely to simulate the event procedures that might be called by various menu commands. The DummyCommand procedure is executed whenever one of the File, Open; File, Save; Demo, First Command; Demo, Second Command; Demo, Submenu, Command1; or Demo, Submenu, Command2 menu items is selected.

Notice line 145: This line uses the ActionControl property of the CommandBars collection to return an object reference to the control object that resulted in the execution of this procedure. The Parameter property of the control is used in the message dialog displayed by the DummyCommand procedure to identify the control that called this procedure. This code is included in the DummyCommand procedure in order to demonstrate how you can find out which control resulted in the execution of a particular procedure and to demonstrate how you can use the Parameter property to provide data for an event procedure to use.

Finally, lines 156 through 159 contain the ExitCommand procedure. This procedure is executed whenever the File, Exit command is selected. Line 158 uses the Delete method to delete the custom command bar. As soon as the menu command bar is deleted, Excel displays its own menu bar once again.

17

Do

DO remember that you can create menu separators by assigning **True** to the `BeginGroup` property of the control in front of which you want the separator to appear.

DO remember to always provide a File menu with an Exit or Close command on it that will shut down your program and remove your custom menu bar.

Putting It Together: A Toolbar-type Command Bar

The `DemoToolbarSystem` procedure in Listing 17.6 creates a custom toolbar, populates it with a few buttons and other controls, and then displays it in a floating toolbar window. Although the custom toolbar created by `DemoToolbarSystem` doesn't do any real work, it demonstrates several of the command bar controls that are typically used on toolbars. Most important, Listing 17.6 demonstrates how you can construct your own working toolbars.

Figure 17.7 shows what the toolbar created by the `DemoToolbarSystem` looks like when it is displayed onscreen in a floating toolbar window. This toolbar is protected from being hidden, docked, resized, or customized. Clicking the white light-bulb button collapses the toolbar so that it contains only one button: a yellow light-bulb button, which expands the toolbar.

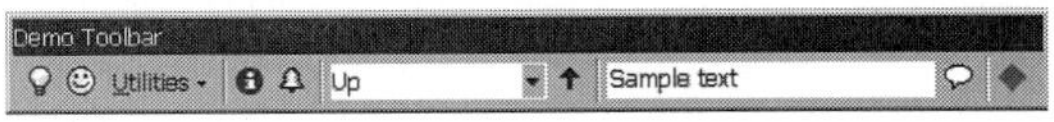

FIGURE 17.7

The DemoToolbarSystem *procedure in Listing 17.6 creates this custom toolbar.*

The happy-face button demonstrates how to make a toggle button work. Clicking the happy-face button disables all the other controls on the toolbar; the happy-face button stays in its down position and its face changes to a sad-face button. Clicking the sad-face button enables all the other controls on the toolbar, restores the button to its up position, and changes its face back to a happy-face button.

The Utilities button demonstrates how to use a pop-up control on a toolbar. Clicking the Utilities button displays a pop-up menu containing Disable Toolbar, Hide Toolbar, and Delete Toolbar commands. (Each of these commands performs the same action as other buttons on the toolbar; they are present for demonstration purposes only.)

Clicking the toolbar button with the Info symbol on it displays a message dialog with some information about VBA's current operating environment. Clicking the toolbar button with the bell symbol causes the system's default beep noise to sound.

The next control demonstrates a drop-down list on a toolbar. Because this is a drop-down list, the user can only select values that appear in the list. The selection in this control determines the face of the button to the right of the drop-down list control; choosing Up, Down, Left, and Right in the list causes the face of the button immediately to the right to change to match the list selection. Clicking the button to the right of the drop-down list echoes the value selected in the list. These controls were included to show how to add and populate a list control and how to retrieve a list control's value.

The next pair of controls consists of an edit box and a button that echoes the value in the edit box. You can type any text in the edit box; clicking the speech-balloon button at the right of the edit box displays a message dialog that displays the current value of the edit box. These controls were included to show how to add an edit box control and how to retrieve the edit box's value.

Clicking the button with the red diamond shape on it causes the custom toolbar to be removed from the onscreen display and deleted from the CommandBars collection.

After you execute the DemoToolbarSystem procedure to create the custom toolbar and display it onscreen, experiment with dragging the toolbar to different docking locations. Notice that you can't dock the toolbar, and that the custom toolbar doesn't show up in the list of toolbars displayed by the View, Toolbars command. This is because the DemoToolbarSystem procedure sets the Protection property of the custom command bar to prevent it from being docked, resized, or hidden.

Also notice the ScreenTips that appear when you position the mouse cursor over the toolbar's controls; the ScreenTip text is obtained from the button's TooltipText property. (ScreenTips is a switchable feature; if your ScreenTips don't appear, choose the View, Toolbars, Customize command and check the Show ScreenTips on Toolbars option on the Customize dialog's Options tab.)

INPUT **LISTING 17.6** CREATING A WORKING CUSTOM TOOLBAR

```
1:   Option Explicit
2:
3:   Private Const Demo_tbName = "Demo Toolbar"
4:   Private Const HappyButton = 59
5:   Private Const SadButton = 276
6:   Private Const WhiteBulbButton = 342
7:   Private Const YellowBulbButton = 343
```

continues

LISTING 17.6 CONTINUED

```
 8:    Private Const InfoButton = 487
 9:    Private Const BellButton = 273
10:    Private Const DmndButton = 482
11:    Private Const UpArrowIcon = 38
12:    Private Const RightArrowIcon = 39
13:    Private Const DownArrowIcon = 40
14:    Private Const LeftArrowIcon = 41
15:    Private Const SpeechIcon = 274
16:
17:
18:    Sub DemoToolbarSystem()
19:
20:      Dim myToolBar As CommandBar
21:      Dim aBtn As CommandBarControl
22:
23:      'create a new toolbar
24:      Set myToolBar = CommandBars.Add(Name:=Demo_tbName, _
25:                                       Position:=msoBarFloating, _
26:                                       MenuBar:=False, _
27:                                       temporary:=True)
28:      'populate the toolbar
29:      With myToolBar.Controls
30:        'create the collapse/expand button
31:        Set aBtn = .Add(Type:=msoControlButton, temporary:=True)
32:        aBtn.FaceId = WhiteBulbButton
33:        aBtn.OnAction = "ExpandButton_Click"
34:        aBtn.Caption = "ExpandButton"
35:        aBtn.TooltipText = "Collapse this toolbar"
36:        aBtn.Tag = True
37:
38:        'create the enable/disable toggle button
39:        Set aBtn = .Add(Type:=msoControlButton, temporary:=True)
40:        aBtn.FaceId = HappyButton
41:        aBtn.State = msoButtonUp
42:        aBtn.OnAction = "EnableButton_Click"
43:        aBtn.Caption = "EnableButton"
44:        aBtn.TooltipText = "Disable toolbar buttons"
45:
46:        'add an empty popup menu control
47:        Set aBtn = .Add(Type:=msoControlPopup, temporary:=True)
48:        aBtn.Caption = "&Utilities"
49:        aBtn.TooltipText = "Utility Commands"
50:
51:        'create the information button, starting a new control group
52:        Set aBtn = .Add(Type:=msoControlButton, temporary:=True)
53:        aBtn.FaceId = InfoButton
54:        aBtn.OnAction = "InfoButton_Click"
55:        aBtn.Caption = "InfoButton"
56:        aBtn.TooltipText = "VBA Information"
```

```
57:        aBtn.BeginGroup = True
58:
59:        'create the bell button, starting a new control group
60:        Set aBtn = .Add(Type:=msoControlButton, temporary:=True)
61:        aBtn.FaceId = BellButton
62:        aBtn.OnAction = "BellButton_Click"
63:        aBtn.Caption = "BellButton"
64:        aBtn.TooltipText = "Beep"
65:
66:        'create the arrow-icon selection drop-down list
67:        Set aBtn = .Add(Type:=msoControlDropdown, temporary:=True)
68:        aBtn.BeginGroup = True
69:        aBtn.Caption = "IconSelect"
70:        aBtn.Tag = aBtn.Caption
71:        aBtn.TooltipText = "Select the button icon"
72:        aBtn.OnAction = "IconSelect_Update"
73:        aBtn.AddItem "Up"
74:        aBtn.AddItem "Down"
75:        aBtn.AddItem "Left"
76:        aBtn.AddItem "Right"
77:        aBtn.ListIndex = 1
78:        aBtn.Width = 100
79:
80:        'create the icon-display button
81:        Set aBtn = .Add(Type:=msoControlButton, temporary:=True)
82:        aBtn.FaceId = UpArrowIcon
83:        aBtn.OnAction = "IconButton_Click"
84:        aBtn.Caption = "IconButton"
85:        aBtn.TooltipText = "Display list selection"
86:
87:        'create a text box for entering some text
88:        Set aBtn = .Add(Type:=msoControlEdit, temporary:=True)
89:        aBtn.BeginGroup = True
90:        aBtn.Caption = "AnyText"
91:        aBtn.TooltipText = "Enter some text"
92:        aBtn.Width = 150
93:        aBtn.Text = "Sample text"
94:
95:        'create a button to echo the entered text
96:        Set aBtn = .Add(Type:=msoControlButton, temporary:=True)
97:        aBtn.Caption = "EchoButton"
98:        aBtn.TooltipText = "Echoes the text box entry"
99:        aBtn.OnAction = "EchoButton_Click"
100:       aBtn.FaceId = SpeechIcon
101:
102:       'create the button that destroys this toolbar
103:       Set aBtn = .Add(Type:=msoControlButton, temporary:=True)
104:       aBtn.FaceId = DmndButton
105:       aBtn.OnAction = "RemoveDemoToolbar"
```

17

continues

LISTING 17.6 CONTINUED

```
106:      aBtn.Caption = "Remove the demo toolbar"
107:      aBtn.BeginGroup = True
108:    End With
109:
110:    'populate the Utilities menu popup control
111:    With myToolBar.Controls("Utilities").CommandBar.Controls
112:      Set aBtn = .Add(Type:=msoControlButton, temporary:=True)
113:      aBtn.Caption = "&Disable Toolbar"
114:      aBtn.OnAction = "EnableButton_Click"
115:      aBtn.FaceId = HappyButton
116:
117:      Set aBtn = .Add(Type:=msoControlButton, temporary:=True)
118:      aBtn.Caption = "&Hide Toolbar"
119:      aBtn.OnAction = "ExpandButton_Click"
120:      aBtn.FaceId = WhiteBulbButton
121:
122:      Set aBtn = .Add(Type:=msoControlButton, temporary:=True)
123:      aBtn.Caption = "Delete Toolbar"
124:      aBtn.OnAction = "RemoveDemoToolbar"
125:      aBtn.FaceId = DmndButton
126:    End With
127:
128:    'final toolbar configuration
129:    With myToolBar
130:      'set the toolbar's protection
131:      .Protection = msoBarNoCustomize + msoBarNoResize + _
132:                    msoBarNoChangeVisible + msoBarNoChangeDock
133:      .Left = 200
134:      .Top = 200                    'position the toolbar
135:      .Position = msoBarFloating    'floating by default
136:      .Visible = True               'make it visible
137:    End With
138: End Sub
139:
140:
141: Sub ExpandButton_Click()
142: 'expands or collapses the toolbar by changing the Visible properties
143: 'of the controls on the toolbar
144:    Dim k As Integer
145:    Dim aBtn As CommandBarControl
146:    Dim aCmdBar As CommandBar
147:
148:    Set aCmdBar = CommandBars(Demo_tbName)
149:    Set aBtn = aCmdBar.Controls("ExpandButton")
150:
151:    With aBtn
152:      If .Tag = True Then
153:        .Tag = False
```

```
154:          .FaceId = YellowBulbButton
155:          .TooltipText = "Expand this toolbar"
156:          For k = 2 To aCmdBar.Controls.Count
157:            aCmdBar.Controls(k).Visible = False
158:          Next k
159:        Else
160:          .Tag = True
161:          .FaceId = WhiteBulbButton
162:          .TooltipText = "Collapse this toolbar"
163:          For k = 2 To aCmdBar.Controls.Count
164:            aCmdBar.Controls(k).Visible = True
165:          Next k
166:        End If
167:      End With
168: End Sub
169:
170:
171: Sub EnableButton_Click()
172: 'enables or disables the toolbar buttons
173:    Dim aCmdBtn As CommandBarControl
174:    Dim aBtn As CommandBarControl
175:    Dim aCmdBar As CommandBar
176:
177:    Set aCmdBar = CommandBars(Demo_tbName)
178:    Set aBtn = aCmdBar.Controls("EnableButton")
179:
180:    With aBtn
181:      If .State = msoButtonUp Then
182:        .State = msoButtonDown
183:        .FaceId = SadButton
184:        .TooltipText = "Enable toolbar buttons"
185:        For Each aCmdBtn In aCmdBar.Controls
186:          If aCmdBtn.Caption <> "EnableButton" Then
187:            aCmdBtn.Enabled = False
188:          End If
189:        Next aCmdBtn
190:      Else
191:        .State = msoButtonUp
192:        .FaceId = HappyButton
193:        .TooltipText = "Disable toolbar buttons"
194:        For Each aCmdBtn In aCmdBar.Controls
195:          If aCmdBtn.Caption <> "EnableButton" Then
196:            aCmdBtn.Enabled = True
197:          End If
198:        Next aCmdBtn
199:      End If
200:    End With
201: End Sub
202:
```

17

continues

LISTING 17.6   CONTINUED

```
203:
204: Sub InfoButton_Click()
205: 'displays info about VBA's environment
206:
207:   Const aTitle = "Info - Toolbar Demo"
208:
209:   MsgBox Buttons:=vbInformation, _
210:          Title:="VBA " & aTitle, _
211:          prompt:="VBA is running in:" & vbCr & _
212:                    Application.Name & vbCr & _
213:                    "Build: " & Application.Build
214: End Sub
215:
216:
217: Sub IconButton_Click()
218: 'displays the current drop-down list selection
219:
220:   Dim tmp As String
221:   Dim aBtn As CommandBarControl
222:
223:   Set aBtn = CommandBars.FindControl(Tag:="IconSelect")
224:
225:   MsgBox prompt:="The current list selection is: " _
226:                  & aBtn.Text, _
227:          Buttons:=vbInformation, _
228:          Title:="Icon Selection"
229: End Sub
230:
231:
232: Sub IconSelect_Update()
233: 'updates the IconButton's FaceID whenever the list
234: 'selection changes
235:
236:   Dim IconButton As CommandBarControl
237:   Dim IconSelect As CommandBarControl
238:
239:   With CommandBars(Demo_tbName)
240:     Set IconButton = .Controls("IconButton")
241:     Set IconSelect = .Controls("IconSelect")
242:   End With
243:
244:   With IconButton
245:     Select Case Trim(IconSelect.Text)
246:       Case "Up"
247:         .FaceId = UpArrowIcon
248:       Case "Down"
249:         .FaceId = DownArrowIcon
250:       Case "Left"
```

```
251:           .FaceId = LeftArrowIcon
252:        Case "Right"
253:           .FaceId = RightArrowIcon
254:      End Select
255:   End With
256: End Sub
257:
258:
259: Sub EchoButton_Click()
260: 'echoes the text box entry
261:    With CommandBars(Demo_tbName).Controls("AnyText")
262:      MsgBox prompt:="The text box contains: " & vbCr & _
263:                     "'" & .Text & "'", _
264:             Buttons:=vbInformation, _
265:             Title:="Text Box Selection"
266:    End With
267: End Sub
268:
269:
270: Sub BellButton_Click()
271: 'sound system Beep tone; exact sound produced depends
272: 'on your hardware and Windows configuration
273:    Beep
274: End Sub
275:
276:
277: Sub RemoveDemoToolbar()
278: 'removes the demo toolbar
279:    With CommandBars(Demo_tbName)
280:      If .Visible Then .Visible = False
281:      .Delete
282:    End With
283: End Sub
```

ANALYSIS Lines 3 through 15 declare several private constants used to supply the face ID numbers for the toolbar's buttons. The values for these constants were obtained by executing the DisplayAllFaceIDs procedure in Listing 17.3 and then examining the resulting set of toolbars for the desired faces.

The DemoToolbarSystem procedure (lines 18 through 138 of Listing 17.6) starts out by creating a new toolbar object in line 24. Notice that the MenuBar argument is **False** so that the new command bar will be a toolbar. This statement assigns the result of the Add method and assigns it to the myToolBar object variable. An object variable is used to save some typing and to make the ensuing code more concise.

17

Lines 31 through 36 add the first control to the new toolbar. Line 31 uses the `Controls` collection's `Add` method to add an `msoControlButton` control to the toolbar. Line 32 assigns a face to the control button by setting its `FaceId` property. Line 33 sets the button's event procedure by assigning a value to the `OnAction` property; in this case, clicking the button will execute the "ExpandButton_Click" procedure. Line 34 names the button by setting its `Caption` property, and line 35 establishes the button's ScreenTip text by setting its `TooltipText` property.

Lines 39 through 44 add the second button to the toolbar. This control is also a button, and its face ID, caption, event procedure, and Tooltip text are all initialized. Notice that line 41 also initializes this button's `State` property. Because this control is used to implement a toggle button, it is important to initialize its status.

Next, lines 47 through 49 add a pop-up control to the toolbar: This pop-up control creates the Utilities button visible in Figure 17.7. After the pop-up control, lines 52 through 57 create the control button used as the Information command. Notice that line 57 sets the InfoButton's `BeginGroup` property to **True**, causing a separator line to appear in front of this control. Lines 60 through 64 create the Bell control button.

Lines 67 through 78 require some special attention. These statements create the drop-down list control and fill the list with selections. Line 67 uses the `Add` method to create a new control; the `Type` argument is used to specify that the new control should be a drop-down list control. This control also begins a new group, so line 68 sets the `BeginGroup` property accordingly. After setting the drop-down list control's `Caption`, `TooltipText`, `Tag`, and `OnAction` properties, lines 73 through 76 populate the list; each statement uses the `AddItem` method of the list control to add an item to the list. Line 77 sets the current list selection to the first item in the list by assigning 1 to the `ListIndex` property, and the width of the list control is set to 100 pixels. Lines 81 through 85 create the control button associated with the drop-down list control just created.

Lines 88 through 93 also require a bit of special attention. These statements create the edit box control. Notice the use of the `msoControlEdit` constant with the `Type` argument of the `Add` method. Notice also that line 93 sets the control's `Text` property, thereby assigning a default value to the edit box.

Lines 96 through 100 create the control button associated with the edit box, and lines 103 through 107 create the command button that is used to remove this toolbar.

At this point, the Utilities pop-up menu is still blank, so lines 111 through 126 populate the Utilities menu. Finally, lines 129 through 137 finalize the toolbar's property settings. Line 131 sets the toolbar's `Protection` property so that the toolbar is protected from customization, resizing, hiding, and docking. Notice that the protection constants are added together to combine their values and provide multiple forms of protection for the toolbar. Lines 133 through 136 set the toolbar's position onscreen and ensure that the toolbar is visible.

The remaining procedures in Listing 17.6 are the event procedures for the various toolbar buttons.

The ExpandButton_Click procedure (lines 141 through 168) is executed whenever the lightbulb button on the toolbar is clicked. This procedure examines the Tag property of the ExpandButton control; if this property is **True**, the toolbar is already expanded and should be collapsed. In this case, the statements in lines 153 through 158 are executed. These statements invert the value of the Tag property, change the button's face ID to a yellow light-bulb icon, and then loop through all the remaining controls in the toolbar's Controls collection, changing their Visible property to **False**. The result of this action is to cause the other controls to disappear from the toolbar, effectively collapsing the toolbar to a single button.

If the ExpandButton's Tag property is **False**, the toolbar is already collapsed and should be expanded. In this case, lines 160 through 166 are executed. These statements restore the remaining controls to visibility—expanding the toolbar—and change the button's face back to a white lightbulb. The ExpandButton_Click procedure demonstrates one way of implementing a toggle control.

Lines 171 through 201 contain the EnableButton_Click procedure. This procedure is executed whenever the happy-face (or sad-face) button is clicked. If the button is already up, its state is changed to msoButtonDown, its face is changed to a sad-face icon, and all controls except this one are disabled. If the button is already down, its state is changed to msoButtonUp, its face is changed to a happy-face icon, and all the toolbar's controls are enabled. The button's TooltipText property is also changed appropriately to reflect the button's action after being clicked.

Lines 204 through 229 contain the InfoButton_Click procedure, which is executed whenever the InfoButton control is clicked. This procedure simply displays a message dialog that contains some information about the environment in which VBA is currently executing.

Lines 217 through 229 contain the IconButton_Click procedure. This procedure is executed whenever the IconButton control is clicked. This procedure simply displays a message dialog that displays the current status of the IconSelect drop-down list control. Notice line 223, which assigns a reference to the IconSelect control to the aBtn object variable.

17

The `IconSelect_Update` procedure (lines 232 through 256) is executed whenever a selection is made in the IconSelect drop-down list. This procedure evaluates the list selection (contained in the list control's `Text` property) and selects an appropriate face for the IconButton control.

Lines 259 through 267 contain the `EchoButton_Click` procedure, which is executed whenever the EchoButton control is clicked. This procedure simply displays a message dialog that echoes the text currently entered in the `AnyText` edit box control.

The `BellButton_Click` procedure (lines 270 through 274) is executed whenever the BellButton control is clicked. This procedure uses the `Beep` statement to sound the Windows system's default sound. The exact sound produced depends on your computer's hardware and software configuration; on most systems it is a bell-like "ding" sound.

Finally, lines 277 through 283 contain the `RemoveDemoToolbar` procedure. This procedure uses the `Delete` method to remove the custom toolbar from the `CommandBars` collection.

Summary

This chapter taught you how to create and manipulate custom command bars by using VBA objects and their properties and methods. You learned about the various VBA objects that you can use to create menu-type command bars and toolbars, as well as to alter built-in menus and toolbars.

This lesson gave you details on creating, displaying, and deleting command bars. You also learned how to create submenus, buttons, and other controls on a command bar. You learned how to change control captions, and assign event procedures to controls. The material in this lesson concluded with a working example of a complete menu system as well as a working example of a toolbar.

Q&A

Q How can you tell if a command bar is built in?

A Use the `BuiltIn` property; if this property is **True**, the command bar is built in.

Q How can I pass information to a procedure's arguments if that procedure is an event procedure for a command bar control?

A You can't assign procedures that have arguments to the `OnAction` property of a menu item or toolbar button. Instead, use a procedure without arguments and make the needed information available to the event procedure through private module-level variables, the control's `Tag` property, or the control's `Parameter` property.

Q Do I have to always use Excel's built-in controls to perform their built-in tasks?

A No. You can add built-in controls to your own custom command bars. If you don't specify an OnAction event procedure, the control uses its built-in behavior. You can, however, assign a new action to the built-in control by specifying an event procedure. Make sure that the tasks you assign to built-in toolbar buttons are similar to their usual tasks, or you'll confuse your command bar's users.

Workshop

Answers to the quiz and exercises questions are in Appendix A.

Quiz

1. How do you add a submenu to a menu?

2. Why should you always include a File, Exit or similar command on your custom menu bars?

3. Do you have to specify an event procedure when you create a command bar control?

4. How do you specify the type of a command bar when you create it?

5. How do you specify the type of a command bar control when you create it?

6. Can you change the State property of a built-in command bar control?

Exercises

1. Modify the procedure in Listing 17.1 to create a procedure named ListAllCommandBars that will list *all* the command bars in an application, including custom command bars. Add an additional column to the list to indicate whether the command bar is a custom command bar or a built-in command bar.

2. Further modify the ListAllCommandBars procedure you just created in Exercise 1 to create a procedure named ListCommandBarTypes, which adds a third column to the list of command bars indicating the type of command bar (that is, whether the command bar is a menu, toolbar, or pop-up). (HINT: Use the command bar's Type property and compare its contents to the msoBarTypeMenuBar, msoBarTypeNormal, and msoBarTypePopup constants to determine the command bar's type.)

3. Write a procedure named AddMyMenu that adds a temporary menu to whatever menu bar is currently active in Excel. Your custom menu should contain one menu item: a control button. The event procedure for the control button should remove your temporary menu from the menu bar. (HINT: Use the ActiveMenuBar property

of the `Application.CommandBars` collection to return a reference to the active menu bar.)

4. Write a procedure named `AddVBA_ToolbarExtras` that creates and displays a custom toolbar (named "VBA Programmer") that contains three buttons. Separate each control button from the others with a separator line. The first control button should be the built-in New control, which creates a new workbook. The second control button should be a custom control button that executes the `ExcelVBAHelp` procedure. The third control button should also be a custom control; this control button should execute a procedure that deletes the custom toolbar. (HINTS: For the first control button, the control ID for the New built-in control is 2520 in Excel. For the second control button, use face ID 49; for the third control button, use face ID 478.)

Use this procedure as the event procedure for the second control button:

```
Sub ExcelVBAHelp()
  Application.Help "vbaxl9.chm"
End Sub
```

DAY 18

Error Handling

Your VBA procedures and programs, especially during the development stages, will often contain logical errors or fail to properly handle certain data values acquired from a user or read from a disk file. These logic errors and other failures produce runtime errors that bring your VBA programs to an abrupt end. By now, you've probably gotten a lot of experience with VBA's runtime error dialog; it's something that happens to all programmers because no one can write perfect code all the time.

In today's lesson, you learn about VBA's special error-handling mechanisms. These mechanisms enable you to write code that will gracefully handle various runtime errors, allowing your VBA program to either circumvent the error or to at least shut down in an orderly fashion. Error handling is an important feature of professional programs. Today's lesson covers the following topics:

- An overview of error-handling strategies.
- How to trap errors by using the **On Error GoTo** statement.
- How to handle errors by using the **Resume** statement.
- How to use the Err and Erl functions to find out the type of error and where it occurred.
- How to force a user-defined error condition by using the Error statement.

Strategies for Error Handling

Basically, there are two general error-handling strategies that you can adopt: defensive programming and error-trapping. In most programs, you'll use a combination of both strategies.

Defensive programming is a lot like defensive driving. When you drive defensively, you attempt to anticipate dangerous road situations and avoid them. In a defensive programming strategy, you attempt to anticipate conditions that will result in runtime errors and to write your code to detect and avoid those conditions.

Defensive programming can take many guises. You've already seen one example of defensive programming: screening a user's input to make sure that the values the user enters are the kind of values that your program expects. For example, if you display an InputBox dialog to get an integer value, and the user instead types in a string that can't be converted to a numeric value, you'll probably end up with a type-mismatch runtime error at some point in your program after the InputBox statement. To use defensive programming for this situation, you add code to your input procedure so that it checks the value that the user enters (by using the IsNumeric function, say) and repeats the input request until an appropriate value has been entered. By making sure that the input meets expectations, you defensively avoid possible runtime errors.

Another example of defensive programming is shown in the following code fragment. Because dividing a number by zero is mathematically impossible, VBA will always generate a runtime error if you attempt to divide a number by zero. You might, therefore, use an **If** statement to guard against division by zero:

```
X = Val(InputBox("Enter first number ", "Input", ""))
Y = Val(InputBox("Enter second number ", "Input", ""))
If Y <> 0 Then
  MsgBox Str(X) & "/" & Str(Y) & "=" & Str(X / Y)
Else
  MsgBox "Cannot divide by zero!"
End If
```

The preceding statements prevent a runtime error by checking the values in the division operation first, and only performing the division if the divisor isn't 0. Another way of handling this issue is to use a looping structure to get input from the user until a non-zero divisor is entered.

You've seen many examples of defensive programming throughout this book. By now, you should have a pretty good sense of how to use defensive programming techniques. It isn't always possible, however, to imagine all the possible situations that might produce a runtime error in your VBA programs. Frequently, runtime errors occur as the result of unexpected and unanticipated events. For example, your program might use a particular workbook to store data. If a user deletes or moves your program's workbook to another disk folder, your program is likely to produce a runtime error when it tries to open the missing workbook. There really isn't a way to anticipate this kind of problem or to write defensive code for it.

In an *error-trapping* strategy, you use special VBA commands to "trap" the error, which prevents VBA from generating the usual runtime error dialog. The VBA error-trapping statements tell VBA that you want to handle the runtime error yourself and specify which part of your code to execute when a runtime error occurs. You then write the code to gracefully handle runtime errors under your program's control.

To handle something like a missing workbook file, as an example, you could use error-trapping statements in the procedure that opens the file. Instead of getting a runtime error and having your program halt its execution because of the missing file, you could use the error-trapping feature to invoke a special error-handling procedure that informs the user about exactly what file is missing, gives advice on solving the problem, removes menu bars, and otherwise shuts your program down in an orderly fashion—instead of leaving a mess for your program's user to clean up as a result of your program's unexpected termination.

In some cases, you can even resolve runtime errors without halting your program. Using error trapping can also sometimes reduce the amount of defensive programming code that you have to write.

VBA uses an interdependent system of statements and functions for error trapping and error handling. The next few sections of this lesson first explain VBA's error-trapping statements and their syntax and then present several examples of putting these error-trapping and error-handling statements and functions to work.

The On Error GoTo Statement

Before you can handle an error, you must be able to trap it. The VBA runtime system always detects runtime errors whenever they occur. By trapping the error, you prevent the VBA runtime system from displaying the usual runtime error dialog as a result of detecting a runtime error. When you trap errors, you also must specify which statements VBA should execute to handle the error. You use the **On Error GoTo** statement to both trap runtime errors and to specify which part of your own code VBA should execute in order to handle the error. You can also use **On Error GoTo** to turn off error trapping.

18

The **On Error GoTo** statement has these two syntax forms:

```
On Error GoTo Label
```

```
On Error GoTo 0
```

In the first syntax form, *Label* represents either a line label or a line number. (You learned about line labels and numbers along with the unconditional **GoTo** statement in Day 8.) When VBA executes the **On Error GoTo** *Label* statement, it installs an error trap. If a runtime error occurs after VBA has executed the **On Error GoTo** *Label* statement, execution is passed to the source code line specified by *Label*, instead of producing a runtime error dialog. The *Label* must be in the same procedure as the **On Error GoTo** statement that refers to it or VBA will display a compiler error message. When the procedure that contains the **On Error GoTo** *Label* statement ends, VBA removes the error trap; error traps installed with **On Error GoTo** *Label* have the same persistence as local variables. If more than one procedure in the calling chain installs an error trap, VBA uses the error trap with the most local scope. If a procedure installs more than one error trap, VBA uses the most recently executed **On Error GoTo** *Label* statement to determine which error trap to use.

Using **On Error GoTo** 0, as shown in the second syntax form, causes VBA to remove any error trap you might have previously installed with the **On Error GoTo** *Label* form. Any runtime error that occurs after VBA executes an **On Error GoTo** 0 statement will again produce the usual runtime error dialog. Use the **On Error GoTo** 0 statement to clear any error handlers that you might have installed with **On Error GoTo** *Label*. For example, you might want to install an error handler for a particular segment of code within a procedure, and then want VBA to generate the standard runtime error dialog for any statements that occur after that particular code segment. In this case, you would set up the error handler with an **On Error GoTo** *Label* statement, followed by the VBA statements for which you want to handle the error yourself, which are then followed by the **On Error GoTo** 0 statement to clear the error-handling trap.

The following code fragment uses an **On Error GoTo** statement to trap a division-by-zero error and then clears the error handler after the critical statements have been executed:

```
X = Val(InputBox("Enter first number ", "Input", ""))
Y = Val(InputBox("Enter second number ", "Input", ""))
'set up the error trap
On Error GoTo DivideByZero
MsgBox Str(X) & "/" & Str(Y) & "=" & Str(X / Y)
Goto Skip1     'skip over the error-handling code
DivideByZero:
MsgBox "Cannot divide by zero"
Skip1:
On Error GoTo 0    'resume normal error-handling
```

The Resume Statement

The **On Error GoTo** *Label* statement directs VBA's execution of statements to a specific point in your procedure, specified by a line number or label, where your code to handle the error is located. If the error is not a fatal error, you can handle the error and then resume your procedure's execution at the point where the runtime error originally occurred or at some other specified point in your procedure's code. (A *fatal* error is any error from which you can't recover, such as a missing data file or insufficient memory; a *non-fatal* error is any error you can correct or recover from, such as bad user input.)

You use the **Resume** statement in your error-handling code to tell VBA when to resume program execution and where. Also, whenever VBA encounters a **Resume** statement, it considers the runtime error resolved and resets its internal runtime error-handling mechanisms for the next error.

The **Resume** statement has four different syntax forms:

▼ SYNTAX

```
Resume

Resume 0

Resume Next

Resume Label
```

The **Resume** and **Resume 0** syntax forms both have the same effect: They cause VBA to resume execution with the same statement that originally caused the runtime error. Essentially, **Resume** and **Resume 0** direct VBA to retry the statement that caused the error. Typically, you use **Resume** or **Resume 0** to retry a statement after attempting to correct the conditions that caused that statement to produce an error. Use one of these forms to resolve errors such as a failed attempt to open a disk file: Your error-handling code, for example, might get an alternate file location or perhaps even create the missing file, and then try the same file opening statement again by using the **Resume** or **Resume 0** statements.

The **Resume Next** syntax form causes VBA to resume execution with the first statement *after* the statement that originally caused the runtime error. Use this form of the **Resume** statement if the statement that caused the runtime error is one that can be successfully skipped. It's unusual to have a procedure whose correct operation won't be adversely affected by simply skipping over statements that cause runtime errors, so you probably won't use the **Resume Next** statement very often—unless, of course, you make certain that your error-handling code contains statements that accomplish the same (or a parallel)

▼ task as the statement that caused the runtime error.

18

▼ The final syntax form, **Resume** *Label*, causes VBA to resume execution with the first statement after the specified *Label*, which can be any line label or line number. Use the **Resume** *Label* statement if you need to resume execution at a point in your code before the statement that caused the runtime error or if you want to resume execution at a point several statements after the one that caused the runtime error.

> **Note**
>
> VBA considers a runtime error to be resolved whenever it executes a **Resume** statement (in any of its syntax forms). Until then, any additional runtime errors that occur *will not* be trapped and will result in a runtime error dialog, thus halting your procedure's execution. VBA must execute a **Resume** statement in order to reset its internal runtime error-handling mechanisms.

The following series of code fragments each shows an example of using one of the forms of the **Resume** statement:

```
' example 1
  X = Val(InputBox("Enter first number ", "Input", ""))
  Y = Val(InputBox("Enter second number ", "Input", ""))
  On Error GoTo DivideByZero
  Z = X / Y
  MsgBox Str(X) & "/" & Str(Y) & "=" & Str(Z)
  Goto Skip1     'skip over the error-handling code
DivideByZero:
  Do
    Y = Val(InputBox("Enter a non-zero second number "))
  Loop Until Y <> 0
  Resume 0          'try the offending statement again
Skip1:
  On Error GoTo 0   'restore normal error handling
```

The error-handling code in the preceding example executes a loop to get a non-zero number from the user and then resumes at the same statement that originally caused the runtime error: the division operation. An **On Error GoTo 0** statement is included after the error-handling code to remove the error-handling trap. Assuming that this is not the end of the procedure, it might no longer be appropriate for future runtime errors in this procedure to be handled by the error-handling code at the DivideByZero label.

```
' example 2
  X = Val(InputBox("Enter first number ", "Input", ""))
  Y = Val(InputBox("Enter second number ", "Input", ""))
  On Error Goto DivideByZero
  Z = X / Y
  MsgBox Str(X) & "/" & Str(Y) & "=" & Str(Z)
▼ Goto Skip2
```

▼
```
DivideByZero:
    Resume Next
Skip2:
    On Error GoTo 0      'restore normal error-handling
```

The preceding example essentially ignores the runtime error and resumes execution with the next statement after the one that caused the error: the `MsgBox` statement that displays the division result. An **On Error GoTo 0** statement is also included after the error-handling code in this example for the same reasons as in the preceding example.

```
' example 3
    X = Val(InputBox("Enter first number ", "Input", ""))
Retry:
    Y = Val(InputBox("Enter second number ", "Input", ""))
    On Error Goto DivideByZero
    Z = X / Y
    MsgBox Str(X) & "/" & Str(Y) & "=" & Str(Z)
    Goto Skip3
DivideByZero:
    MsgBox "Division by 0 not allowed. Try again."
    Resume Retry
Skip3:
    On Error GoTo 0      'restore normal error-handling
```

This final example uses a line label (`Retry:`) in front of the statement that gets the divisor from the user. If a division-by-zero runtime error occurs, the user sees a message explaining the problem and the **Resume** statement directs VBA to resume execution at the `Retry` label. The user is then prompted for another divisor and the division operation is
▲ repeated. This behavior will repeat itself until the user enters a non-zero divisor.

18

Do

DO make sure that you have somehow resolved the error before resuming code execution. In particular, if you use **Resume** or **Resume Next** to retry the offending statement without resolving the conditions responsible for the error, your procedure might end up looping infinitely; the runtime error will occur again, your procedure will execute the error-handling code, and then return to the error-causing statement, which starts the cycle over again.

DO remember to remove any custom menu bars, close workbooks and documents, and save data (if possible) before shutting down a program as a result of a fatal error.

Finding the Runtime Error's Type, Message, and Location

Frequently, you'll need to know the exact type of runtime error that occurred in order to successfully resolve a problem. It might also be useful for you to retrieve the error message text that corresponds to the runtime error that occurred. Less frequently, you'll need to know the exact location where a runtime error occurred. VBA provides the Err function to let you determine the exact runtime error that occurred, the Error function to determine what message text corresponds to a particular runtime error, and the Erl function to determine where in your code the runtime error occurred. In addition, VBA also provides you with the Err object, from which you can obtain the error number, error message text, and the specific object or module in which the error occurred.

To understand why you might need to know the exact type of a runtime error and the exact location of the offending statement, consider the following code fragment:

```
X = CDbl(InputBox("Enter first number ", "Input", ""))
Y = CDbl(InputBox("Enter second number ", "Input", ""))
MsgBox Str(X) & "/" & Str(Y) & "=" & Str(X / Y)
```

In the preceding code, the results of the InputBox functions in the first two lines are converted to double-precision numbers by the **CDbl** function. Not only is it possible for the user to enter 0 in the second input dialog (resulting in a divide-by-zero runtime error), but it is also possible for the user to enter a string that can't be converted to a number. With the **CDbl** function, this produces a runtime error. (The Val function was used in earlier examples because it returns 0 when it can't convert a string to a number.)

To know how to handle a runtime error in the preceding code fragment, you need to know whether the error stems from division-by-zero or a string value that can't be converted to a number. To know the most suitable point to resume program execution, you need to be able to determine which statement produced the error: one of the two input dialogs or the division operation.

The next few sections of this lesson show you how to retrieve the specific error type, the corresponding error message text, and the location of the error.

Determining the Runtime Error Type: Using the Err Function

To find out the specific runtime error that occurred, use the Err function, which returns an integer number code designating the specific runtime error.

SYNTAX ▼

The Err function has this syntax:

```
Err
```

The Err function has no arguments and simply returns an integer number that indicates the specific runtime error (this number is called an *error code*). Table 18.1 lists VBA's runtime error codes and briefly describes their meaning. (To find out more about these errors, search the online help system for the topic "Trappable Errors.") The Err function will always return one of these codes or a user-defined error code (creating user-defined error codes is described later in this lesson). The following code fragment shows an example of using the Err function to return the error code:

```
On Error Goto HaveError
   X = 1 / 0
   Goto Skip1
HaveError:
   MsgBox "Error number " & Str(Err)
▲ Skip1:
```

TABLE 18.1   VBA'S TRAPPABLE RUNTIME ERROR CODES

Error Code	Description
3	**Return** without **GoSub**
5	Invalid procedure call
6	Overflow
7	Out of memory
9	Subscript out of range
10	Fixed or temporarily locked array
11	Division by zero
13	Type mismatch
14	Out of string space
16	Expression too complex

continues

18

TABLE 18.1 CONTINUED

Error Code	Description
17	Can't perform requested operation
18	User interrupt occurred
20	Resume without error
28	Out of stack space
35	Sub, function or property not defined
47	Too many code resource or DLL application clients
48	Error in loading code resource or DLL
49	Bad code resource or DLL calling convention
51	Internal error
52	Bad filename or number
53	File not found
54	Bad file mode
55	File already open
57	Device I/O error
58	File already exists
59	Bad record length
61	Disk full
62	Input past end of file
63	Bad record number
67	Too many files
68	Device unavailable
70	Permission denied
71	Disk not ready
74	Can't rename with different drive
75	Path/file access error
76	Path not found
91	Object variable or `With` block variable not set
92	`For` loop not initialized
93	Invalid pattern string
94	Invalid use of `Null`
97	Can't call friend procedure on an object that is not an instance of the defining class

Error Code	Description
98	A property or method call cannot include reference to a private object either as an argument or return value
298	System resource or DLL could not be loaded
320	Can't use character device names in specified filenames
321	Invalid file format
322	Can't create necessary temporary file
325	Invalid format in resource file
327	Data value named not found
328	Illegal parameter; can't write arrays
335	Could not access system Registry
336	Component not correctly registered
337	Component not found
338	Component did not run correctly
360	Object already loaded
361	Can't load or unload this object
363	Control specified not found
364	Object was unloaded
365	Unable to unload within this context
368	The specified file is out of date. This program requires a later version
371	The specified object can't be used as an owner form for Show
380	Invalid property value
381	Invalid property-array index
382	**Property Set** can't be executed at run time
383	**Property Set** can't be used with a read-only property
385	Need property-array index
387	**Property Set** not permitted
393	**Property Get** can't be executed at run time
394	**Property Get** can't be executed on write-only property
400	Form already displayed; can't show modally
402	Code must close topmost modal form first
419	Permission to use object denied
422	Property not found

18

continues

TABLE 18.1   CONTINUED

Error Code	Description
423	Property or method not found
424	Object required
425	Invalid object use
429	Component can't create object or return reference to this object
430	Class does not support Automation
432	Filename or class name not found during Automation operation
438	Object doesn't support this property or method
440	Automation error
442	Connection to type library or object library for remote process has been lost
443	Automation object doesn't have a default value
445	Object doesn't support this action
446	Object doesn't support named arguments
447	Object doesn't support current locale setting
448	Named argument not found
449	Argument not optional or invalid property assignment
450	Wrong number of arguments or invalid property assignment
451	Object not a collection
452	Invalid ordinal
453	Specified code resource not found
454	Code resource not found
455	Code resource lock error
457	This key is already associated with an element of this collection
458	Variable uses a type not supported in Visual Basic
459	This component doesn't support the set of events
460	Invalid Clipboard format
461	Method or data member not found
462	Remote server machine does not exist or is unavailable
463	Class not registered on local machine
480	Can't create AutoRedraw image
481	Invalid picture
482	Printer error
483	Printer driver does not support specified property

Error Code	Description
484	Problem getting printer information from the system. Make sure the printer is set up correctly
485	Invalid picture type
486	Can't print form image to this type of printer
520	Can't empty Clipboard
521	Can't open Clipboard
735	Can't save file to TEMP directory
744	Search text not found
746	Replacements too long
31001	Out of memory
31004	No object
31018	Class is not set
31027	Unable to activate object
31032	Unable to create embedded object
31036	Error saving to file
31037	Error loading from file

18

Getting the Runtime Error Message Text: Using the Error Function

To find out what the text for a specific error code is, use the Error function, which returns a string containing the text that corresponds to a particular error code.

The Error function has this syntax:

▼ SYNTAX

```
Error([errorcode])
```

The optional *errorcode* argument can be any numeric expression that evaluates to one of the error codes listed in Table 18.1. If you omit the *errorcode* argument, Error returns the error message text corresponding to the last unresolved runtime error that occurred. If there is no unresolved runtime error, the Error function returns an empty string (""). As an example, the next code fragment displays a message dialog containing the error number and the string corresponding to that error:

```
On Error GoTo ShutDown
    X = 1 / 0   'illegal operation
▼   GoTo Skip1
```

```
▼  ShutDown:
     MsgBox Str(Err) & " means " & Error
     End  'halts all program execution
   Skip1:
```

This code fragment installs an error trap with the **On Error** statement and then executes
the illegal division-by-zero operation. The MsgBox statement displays the text 11 means
Division by zero by concatenating the error code number with its corresponding text
▲ message.

Determining the Runtime Error Location: Using the Erl Function

To find out where an error occurred, VBA provides the Erl function. This function
reports the line number closest to, but still preceding, the line that produced the runtime
error.

The general syntax for the Erl function is

```
Erl
```

The Erl function returns the last line number that appears before the line containing the
offending statement. Erl does *not* return line labels—only line numbers. In order to use
the Erl function, you need to add line numbers to some of the lines in your procedure, as
shown in the following code example. If the procedure does not contain any line numbers or no error has occurred, Erl returns 0.

> **Note**
>
> Line numbers are another historic legacy in VBA. In the original BASIC pro-
> gramming language, line numbers were required; each line of a program
> had a number in front of it, and execution proceeded from lower-numbered
> lines to higher-numbered lines. Except for special uses, such as the Erl func-
> tion, you don't need to use line numbers in VBA.
>
> To create a line number in your VBA code, simply make sure that the first
> character in a line is a number and that the VBA statements on the line are
> separated from the number by at least one space character; VBA assumes
> that the number at the beginning of the line is a line number.

In the following code fragment, the first three lines of code have line numbers (1 through
3). The MsgBox statement displays the message Runtime Error on line 2 by calling
the Erl function to get the last line number before the line containing the error—in this
▼ case, the same line as the line containing the error.

```
▼  1 On Error GoTo ShutDown
   2 X = 1 / 0  'illegal operation
   3 GoTo Skip1
   ShutDown:
     MsgBox "Runtime Error on line " & Str(Erl)
     End  'halts all program execution
▲  Skip1:
```

Do

DO use a **Select Case** statement when evaluating the Err function's result to identify the specific runtime error and the appropriate action to take.

DO use the Error function to get text corresponding to a specific error code.

DON'T

DON'T frustrate your procedure's end-user with cryptic error messages. Make your error messages as clear as possible and offer suggestions on correcting the problem as often as possible.

18

Forcing Runtime Errors and Creating User-Defined Error Codes: The Error Statement

VBA permits you to either artificially force a runtime error to occur or to create your own runtime error codes by using the Error statement. Use the Error statement to force runtime errors with a user-defined error code any time you want to handle a situation as if it were a runtime error.

Note

Don't confuse the Error *function* with the Error *statement*. The Error function returns a text message corresponding to a particular runtime error code. The Error statement enables you to create your own error codes.

Use the Error statement to force a runtime error with one of the error codes from Table 18.1 in situations where you want to handle an improper condition or value in your procedure as if it were a runtime error. For example, suppose you have a procedure that has an optional argument that must always contain an integer value or a value that can be converted to an integer. If your optional argument is a **Variant** data type, you can't rely on VBA to generate a type-mismatch runtime error to let you know you've made a pro-gramming mistake and are passing the wrong data type in that procedure's optional argu-ment. Instead, you might check the data type passed in the optional argument and then use the Error statement to force the production of a type-mismatch runtime error.

Whether you use the Error statement to force a runtime error with a predefined error code or with a user-defined error code, VBA behaves exactly the same as for any other runtime error. VBA will use any error trap that you install with an **On Error GoTo** state-ment; if there is no error trap, VBA displays a runtime error dialog, as usual.

The general syntax for the Error statement is

```
Error errorNumber
```

errorNumber represents any numeric expression that results in a number from 0 to 65,535. If the errorNumber argument is one of the error code numbers listed in Table 18.1, VBA behaves as if that runtime error had occurred; the Err function, Erl function, and Error functions will all return results corresponding to the runtime error code you specified in errorNumber.

If you use a number other than one of the error codes listed in Table 18.1, VBA sets the Err function to return that number and sets the Erl function to report on the last line number before the Error statement. The Error function will return the string Application-defined or object-defined error.

The following code fragment, for example, sets up an error trap and then uses the Error statement to generate a user-defined error whenever the value in A is zero.

```
' example 1
  Dim A As Double
  On Error Goto BadValue
Retry:
  A = Val(InputBox("Enter a non-zero number "))
  'create user defined error for zero-number input
  If A = 0 Then Error 65535
  MsgBox "1 /" & A & "=" & (1/A)
  Goto EndIt
BadValue:
  MsgBox "Non-zero numbers only! Try again."
  GoTo Retry
EndIt:
```

The next code fragment sets up an error trap and then uses the Error statement to gener-ate runtime error 11, division by zero, whenever the contents of A are zero.

```
' example 2
  Dim A As Double
▼ On Error Goto BadValue
```

```
▼ Retry:
    A = Val(InputBox("Enter a non-zero number "))
    'force divide-by-zero error BEFORE it actually occurs
    If A = 0 Then Error 11
    MsgBox "1 /" & A & "=" & (1/A)
    Goto EndIt
  BadValue:
    MsgBox "Cannot divide by zero"
    GoTo Retry
▲ EndIt:
```

> **Tip**
>
> To avoid any potential conflict with VBA's predefined runtime error codes, it's usually a good idea to start your custom error code numbering at 65,535 and work down.

Using the Err Object

It is important that you understand how to use the `Err` function, the `Erl` function, and the `Error` function and `Error` statement. You will see these functions used in error-handling code in other programmer's projects and in code that you might obtain from an online source. You'll also frequently see the error information functions described earlier in this chapter in VBA code developed for Excel 5, Excel 7, WordBASIC, and other implementations of BASIC. The error information functions discussed earlier in this chapter have been parts of the BASIC programming language since its inception.

Starting with VBA in Office 97, however, the preferred technique for obtaining information about an error, or to force the occurrence of an error, is to use the `Err` object. Any VBA error-handling code you write in any Office 2000 host application should use the `Err` object. All remaining error-handling examples in this and subsequent lessons use the `Err` object. The `Err` object has several properties that enable you to obtain the same information that you can get by using any one of the error information functions described previously, including additional information related to using external code resources such as DLL routines (the topic of Day 20). Table 18.2 lists the `Err` object's properties and gives a brief description of each property's purpose.

18

TABLE 18.2   THE Err OBJECT'S PROPERTIES

Property	Type	Description
Description	Read/write	A string expression that contains the error's description. The Description property provides the same information as the Error function.
HelpContext	Read/write	A string expression specifying the ID for a topic in a Microsoft Windows help file.
HelpFile	Read/write	A string expression giving the drive, folder path, and filename of a Microsoft Windows help file.
LastDLLError	Read-only	An error code corresponding to an error that occurred when calling a procedure in a DLL.
Number	Read/write	A VBA or user-defined error number; must be in the range 0 through 65,535. The Number property provides the same information as the Err function.
Source	Read/write	A string expression specifying the name of the object or application that originally generated the error.

The HelpContext and HelpFile properties might not be of much use to you. These properties are intended for use with a Microsoft Windows help file, which you must create with the Microsoft Windows help compiler (or a third-party help creation tool such as Blue Sky Software's RoboHelp or Wextech's Doc-To-Help). The Microsoft Windows help compiler isn't included with VBA (or Microsoft Office); you can obtain the help compiler separately from Microsoft, however.

In addition to the properties listed in Table 18.2, the Err object has two methods that you can use to either clear VBA's internal error-handling mechanism or to force the occurrence of a VBA or user-defined runtime error: Clear and Raise, respectively.

▼ SYNTAX

The syntax for the Clear method is

```
Err.Clear
```

The Clear method has no arguments. Calling the Clear method causes the Err object to clear any error information it might currently be storing. The Err object's properties are reset automatically whenever the VBA runtime system considers an error resolved, but

▼ you can use the Clear method to explicitly clear an error.

▼ You are more likely to use the `Raise` method to force a runtime error or to create a user-defined error. In particular, you should use the `Raise` method if you want to generate a user-defined error in one of your class modules.

The syntax for the `Raise` method is

```
Err.Raise number [, source, description, helpfile, helpcontext]
```

In the preceding syntax, *number* is the only required argument; *number* is a numeric expression that evaluates to an error code, either one of VBA's error-code numbers or a user-defined error code. (User-defined error codes were described in the preceding section of this chapter.)

source is any string expression and represents the source code location of the error. If you omit this argument when you use the `Raise` method, the `Err` object's default value is the name of the current VBA project. If you set this argument while raising an error in a class module, specify the source name in the form *project.class*, where *project* is the name of the VBA project and *class* is the class module's name.

description is a string expression describing the specific error. If you omit this argument and you raise a VBA error, the `Err` object automatically supplies the corresponding text description for the error you raise. If you omit this argument when raising a user-defined error, the `Err` object uses the default value `"Application-defined or object-defined error"`.

Helpfile represents a string expression giving the full drive, folder, and filename of a Microsoft Windows help file; *helpcontext* represents a string expression specifying the specific help topic associated with this error. If you omit these arguments when you raise a VBA error code, they are automatically filled in with the help topics related to the VBA ▲ error. As mentioned earlier in this section, you must use a help compiler to create help files; there is no help compiler included with VBA or Microsoft Office.

18

Do

DO make sure you use the `Err` object's `Raise` method if you want to create user-defined runtime error code in one of your class modules.

DO add the `vbObjectError` intrinsic constant to any user-defined error codes that you generate within a class module. For example, if you want to raise user-defined error 6010 in a class module, you would use the `Raise` method with an argument of `vbObjectError + 6010`. This enables the VBA runtime error system to accurately report the runtime error as being object-related.

Putting It Together: Examples of Error Handling

The remaining sections of this lesson show examples of the different ways you can use the error-handling techniques described in the first few sections of this lesson. All of the examples in the remainder of this lesson and throughout the rest of this book use the Err object as the preferred technique for obtaining error information or forcing runtime errors.

The first four listings are all variations on each other and show different ways of handling the same runtime error. The final example shows how to use forced runtime errors to help make your own procedures behave more like VBA's built-in procedures.

Handling Fatal Errors

The first error-handling example is Listing 18.1, which contains the DemoFatalError procedure. The basic task performed in this (and the next three listings) is to display a table of square roots from 5 to –2 in an Excel worksheet, which are computed by using VBA's Sqr function. The Sqr function, however, requires its argument to be a non-negative number and produces a runtime error anytime you pass a negative number to it: runtime error code 5, Invalid procedure call, to be precise. Listings 18.1 through 18.4 each demonstrate a different error-handling technique to resolve this problem.

> **Note**
>
> VBA's Sqr function produces a runtime error for negative numbers because negative numbers don't really have a square root. (Whenever you multiply two negative numbers together, the result is a positive number.) However, it doesn't seem to make sense that the number 4 has a square root and the number -4 doesn't. To resolve this apparent contradiction, mathematicians invented an imaginary number, represented by the symbol *i*, to represent the square root of -1. By using *i*, it becomes possible to represent the square roots of negative numbers. For example, although the square root of 4 is 2, the square root of -4 is *2i*, that is, 2 multiplied by the imaginary square root of -1.

The DemoFatalError procedure in Listing 18.1 treats the runtime error as being unresolvable, that is, as a fatal error. When the call to the Sqr function generates a runtime error, the error-handling code displays a message about the error and the procedure ends. DemoFatalError uses the Err object's properties to identify the error type and uses the Erl function to identify the line number that contains the offending statement.

Note   As you enter the code in Listing 18.1, pay special attention to lines 26 through 30 of the listing. The additional line numbers in the VBA statements really are part of the VBA code you should enter. These line numbers are included so that the Erl function will be able to report where the runtime error occurred.

LISTING 18.1   THE DemoFatalError PROCEDURE USES THE Err OBJECT AND THE Erl FUNCTION

INPUT

```
1:   Option Explicit
2:
3:   Sub DemoFatalError()
4:
5:       Const tblHead = "Table of Square Roots"
6:       Const FIRST As Integer = 5
7:       Const LAST As Integer = -2
8:       Const INCR As Integer = -1
9:
10:      Dim Count As Integer
11:      Dim cRow As Integer
12:      Dim oldSheet As String
13:
14:      oldSheet = ActiveSheet.Name  'preserve original sheet
15:      Worksheets("Sheet1").Select  'change to worksheet
16:
17:      On Error GoTo BadValue       'set error trap
18:
19:      Cells(1, 2).Value = tblHead      'set up table headings
20:      Cells(2, 1).Value = "   X"
21:      Cells(2, 2).Value = "  Sqr(X)"
22:      Cells(3, 1).Value = String(35, "-")
23:      Cells(3, 2).Value = String(35, "-")
24:
25:      cRow = 4
26:  1:  For Count = FIRST To LAST Step INCR
27:  2:      Cells(cRow, 1).Value = Count
28:  3:      Cells(cRow, 2).Value = CStr(Sqr(Count))
29:  4:      cRow = cRow + 1
30:  5:  Next Count
31:
32:      MsgBox Buttons:=vbInformation, Title:=tblHead, _
33:             prompt:="Square root table completed."
34:
35:      GoTo Ending  'skip over error handling code
36:
```

continues

LISTING 18.1 CONTINUED

```
37:  BadValue:
38:    MsgBox Buttons:=vbCritical, Title:=tblHead, _
39:         prompt:="Error! " & Err.Number & ": " & _
40:                Err.Description & " in line " & _
41:                Erl & " of " & Err.Source & vbCr & _
42:                "Bad value was: " & Count & vbCr & _
43:                "Procedure Terminating."
44:
45:  Ending:   'stuff that should be done regardless of error
46:    Sheets(oldSheet).Select
47:  End Sub
```

ANALYSIS If you enter Listing 18.1 exactly as shown, the `DemoFatalError` procedure will display the dialog shown in Figure 18.1 (assuming you rename your project to `Day18` from the default `VBAProject`).

FIGURE 18.1

The `DemoFatalError` procedure in Listing 18.1 displays this dialog describing the run-time error.

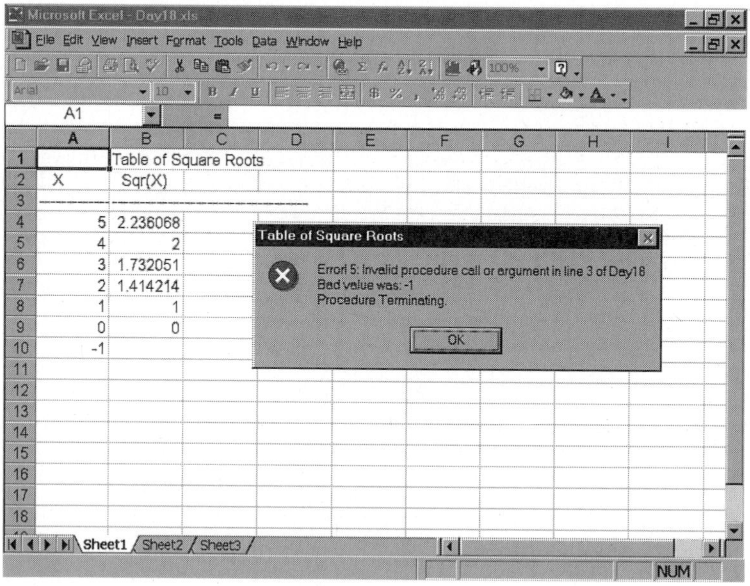

`DemoFatalError` is the only procedure in Listing 18.1. Lines 5 through 8 declare several constants used by this procedure: a title for the square root table and the dialogs displayed by this procedure, a starting value for the square root table, an ending value for the square root table, and an increment value for a **For** loop. Lines 10 through 12 declare the variables used by `DemoFatalError`: a counting variable, a variable for the current worksheet row, and a variable to store the name of the sheet that was active when this procedure started. Line 14 preserves the current worksheet's name and then line 15 switches to the worksheet named Sheet1.

Line 17 installs the error trap with an **On Error GoTo** statement, and lines 19 through 23 set up table and column headings on the worksheet for the square root table.

Pay special attention to lines 26 through 30. These statements contain a **For...Next** loop that builds the square root table. Each line in the loop has a line number in front of it: The statements are numbered 1 through 5. These line numbers make it possible for Erl to identify the line that generates the runtime error. Otherwise, Erl would return 0.

Lines 32 and 33 display a message dialog announcing that the square root table is complete. Actually, these lines never get executed in this procedure because it is written so that a runtime error always occurs. Because this procedure's error-handling code treats the error as a fatal error, execution never gets to this point. (As an experiment, change the LAST constant to 1, instead of -2, and then run the DemoFatalError procedure.)

Line 35 contains a **GoTo** statement that directs statement execution to the line indicated by the Ending line label in order to skip over the error handling code in lines 37 through 42. (**GoTo** statements were covered in Day 8.)

The actual error-handling code is in lines 37 through 43. Because the **On Error GoTo** statement specifies the BadValue line label when it installs the error trap, VBA begins executing statements in line 37 whenever a runtime error occurs in the DemoFatalError procedure. For this procedure, the error-handling code simply displays a message dialog stating what the error number and error text are, in what line the error occurred, and what the offending value was (refer to Figure 18.1).

18

> **Tip**
>
> You can sometimes use your own error-handling code to deliver more information about a runtime error than VBA can. Notice that the dialog produced by Listing 18.1 (shown in Figure 18.1) also reports what the offending value is—something that VBA isn't able to do.

Because the error-handling code is at the end of the procedure and because there is no **Resume** statement, VBA continues code execution with the first statement after line 43.

Notice the Ending line label in line 45 and the statement in line 46, which restores the sheet that was active at the time this procedure started. The statement in line 46 should be executed whether or not a runtime error occurs.

> **Note**
>
> When you install an error-handling trap in a procedure, it is only in effect for that particular procedure. As soon as that procedure stops executing, the error trap is no longer in effect. Each procedure must install its own error-handling trap and have its own error-handling code. Your error-handling code can, however, call other procedures or functions.

Do

DO always make sure that your procedure does whatever housekeeping is necessary—such as closing workbooks, removing menu bars, or saving data—before you end it due to a fatal error you have detected.

Don't

DON'T number all the lines in all of your VBA code. Just number lines that you think might cause problems.

Resolving Runtime Errors without Halting

The DemoFatalError procedure in Listing 18.1 simply halts after displaying the error number, message, and location. It makes no effort to resolve the error and resume execution of the procedure. The DemoResolveError procedure in Listing 18.2, however, resolves the error condition by entering a value for an imaginary number into the square root table (the square root of a negative number is an imaginary number). DemoResolveError deals with the runtime error internally and gives the user the impression that everything is working without problems by resolving the condition that produced the runtime error and using the **Resume Next** statement to continue program execution.

INPUT **LISTING 18.2** THE DemoResolveError PROCEDURE USES THE **Resume Next** STATEMENT

```
1:    Option Explicit
2:
3:    Sub DemoResolveError()
4:
5:        Const tblHead = "Table of Square Roots"
6:        Const FIRST As Integer = 5
```

```
 7:        Const LAST As Integer = -2
 8:        Const INCR As Integer = -1
 9:
10:        Dim Count As Integer
11:        Dim cRow As Integer
12:        Dim oldSheet As String
13:
14:        oldSheet = ActiveSheet.Name   'preserve original sheet
15:        Worksheets("Sheet1").Select   'change to worksheet
16:
17:        On Error GoTo BadValue        'set error trap
18:
19:        Cells(1, 2).Value = tblHead     'set up table headings
20:        Cells(2, 1).Value = "   X"
21:        Cells(2, 2).Value = "  Sqr(X)"
22:        Cells(3, 1).Value = String(35, "-")
23:        Cells(3, 2).Value = String(35, "-")
24:
25:        cRow = 4
26:        For Count = FIRST To LAST Step INCR
27:          Cells(cRow, 1).Value = Count
28:          Cells(cRow, 2).Value = Sqr(Count)
29:          cRow = cRow + 1
30:        Next Count
31:
32:        MsgBox Buttons:=vbInformation, TITLE:=tblHead, _
33:              prompt:="Square root table completed."
34:
35:        Sheets(oldSheet).Select
36:        Exit Sub  'no more work to do
37:
38:  BadValue:
39:        Cells(cRow, 2).Value = Sqr(Abs(Count)) & "i"
40:        Resume Next
41:
42:  End Sub
```

18

ANALYSIS The DemoResolveError procedure in Listing 18.2 displays the worksheet and dialog shown in Figure 18.2. Notice that this time the procedure is able to complete the square root table, even for the negative numbers.

DemoResolveError works exactly the same as the procedure from Listing 18.1, with the exception of how the runtime error is handled and the placement of the housekeeping code.

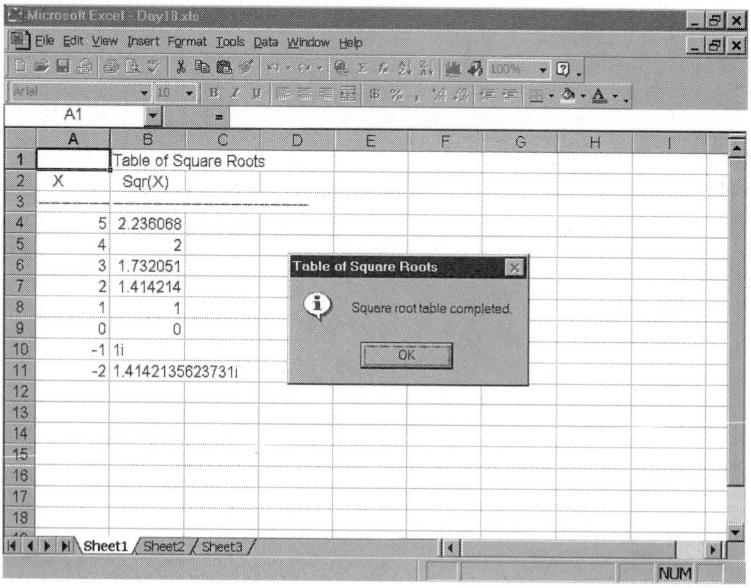

FIGURE 18.2

The DemoResolveError
*procedure can com-
plete the square root
table, even for negative
numbers.*

As before, the **On Error GoTo** statement in line 17 installs the error trap for this procedure. Lines 19 through 23 create the table's column headings and lines 25 through 30 fill
the table. Notice that this time, there are no line numbers in the VBA statements: This
procedure doesn't use the Erl function, so there is no reason to include line numbers.

When the inevitable runtime error occurs (passing a negative number to the Sqr function), the error trap causes execution to pass to the first statement after the BadValue line
label: in this case, line 39. Line 39 sidesteps the reason for the runtime error; it uses the
Abs function to get the absolute value of the Count variable and then finds the Sqr of
that. (The *absolute value* of a number is the number's value, regardless of its sign—the
absolute value of both 2 and -2 is 2, for example.) After computing the square root of the
absolute value, the statement in line 39 then concatenates the letter *i* to the end of the
number to show that it is an imaginary number.

Line 40 is important. After computing the imaginary square root of a negative number in
line 39, the **Resume Next** statement in line 40 causes VBA to resume execution at the
statement immediately after the statement that caused the runtime error: in this case, line
29 (inside the **For** loop). This has the effect of letting the procedure continue running as
if the runtime error had never occurred—in a sense, it never did.

Because this procedure resolves the runtime error caused by passing a negative number to the Sqr function, the procedure will actually finish executing the **For** loop in lines 26 through 30 and will then execute the statements in lines 32 through 36. Line 32 starts a MsgBox statement that lets the user know the square root table is finished, line 35 restores the sheet that was active when this procedure started, and line 36 exits the procedure. The only remaining statements in the procedure are the error-handling code, thus the procedure has accomplished its work, so it is safe and appropriate to exit the procedure.

Retrying the Error-Causing Statement

Listing 18.3 shows yet another way to resolve the runtime error that occurs while building the square root table. This solution uses the **Resume 0** statement to retry the statement that caused the runtime error after manipulating the offending values so that the runtime error no longer occurs.

LISTING 18.3 THE DemoRetryError PROCEDURE USES THE **Resume 0**
INPUT STATEMENT TO RETRY THE ERROR-CAUSING STATEMENT

```
1:   Option Explicit
2:
3:   Sub DemoRetryError()
4:
5:       Const tblHead = "Table of Square Roots"
6:       Const FIRST As Integer = 5
7:       Const LAST As Integer = -2
8:       Const INCR As Integer = -1
9:
10:      Dim Count As Integer
11:      Dim cRow As Integer
12:      Dim oldSheet As String
13:      Dim Temp As Integer
14:      Dim tStr As String
15:
16:      oldSheet = ActiveSheet.Name   'preserve original sheet
17:      Worksheets("Sheet1").Select   'change to worksheet
18:
19:      On Error GoTo BadValue        'set error trap
20:
21:      Cells(1, 2).Value = tblHead   'set up table headings
22:      Cells(2, 1).Value = "   X"
23:      Cells(2, 2).Value = "  Sqr(X)"
24:      Cells(3, 1).Value = String(35, "-")
25:      Cells(3, 2).Value = String(35, "-")
26:
27:      cRow = 4
```

continues

18

LISTING 18.3   CONTINUED

```
28:     For Count = FIRST To LAST Step INCR
29:        tStr = ""
30:        Temp = Count
31:        Cells(cRow, 1).Value = Temp
32:        Cells(cRow, 2).Value = CStr(Sqr(Temp)) & tStr
33:        cRow = cRow + 1
34:     Next Count
35:
36:     MsgBox Buttons:=vbInformation, TITLE:=tblHead, _
37:            prompt:="Square root table completed."
38:
39:     Sheets(oldSheet).Select
40:     Exit Sub     'no more work to do
41:
42:   BadValue:
43:      Temp = -Temp
44:      tStr = "i"
45:      Resume 0
46:   End Sub
```

ANALYSIS   The DemoRetryError procedure in Listing 18.3 produces the same worksheet and dialog as already shown in Figure 18.2; the technique for achieving those results is different, however.

Listing 18.3 is the same as Listing 18.2, with a few exceptions. First, notice the addition of two new variables declared in lines 13 and 14. The Temp variable is used to temporarily store and work with the loop counter's value. The tStr variable is used to add the designation for imaginary numbers, when necessary.

As before, the current sheet's name is preserved, Sheet1 is selected, the error trap is installed, and the column headings are written onto the worksheet.

The **For** loop in lines 28 through 34 has changed, however. Notice that line 29 sets the tStr variable to be an empty string and line 30 assigns the current Count value to the Temp variable. Lines 31 and 32, which fill in the current row of the square root table, now use the Temp variable instead of the loop counter variable. This is because the error-handling code (lines 42 through 45) changes the contents of the variable causing the runtime error. If this procedure actually changed the value of the Count variable, the **For** loop would not execute the correct number of times.

As soon as the loop counter becomes a negative number, the usual runtime error will occur. As before, VBA directs statement execution to the statements after the BadValue label because of the error trap installed in line 19. Line 43 simply inverts the sign of the number stored in Temp and assigns the result back into the Temp variable. Line 44 assigns the letter "i" to the tStr variable. Finally, line 45 uses the **Resume** 0 statement to cause VBA to resume execution with the *same* statement that originally caused the runtime error. The value in Temp is now a positive number (because its sign was inverted in line 43), so the Sqr function in line 32 won't cause a runtime error. Because the tStr variable contains the letter "i," the square root is entered into the worksheet with the appropriate suffix to indicate it is an imaginary number. (The next time through the loop, tStr will again be set to contain an empty string.)

DON'T

DON'T modify a **For** loop counter's variable unless you really want to change the number of times the loop executes.

Resuming Execution at a Specified Point

Another way to handle a runtime error is to ignore it or to skip over the operation that produces the runtime error. This technique can be particularly useful in looping situations: You can simply ignore the runtime error and assume that it will not occur in the next iteration of the loop. The example in Listing 18.4 uses exactly that technique to resolve its runtime error. When the runtime error occurs due to attempting to find the square root of a negative number, the DemoResumeError procedure ignores the runtime error and permits the loop to continue executing.

LISTING 18.4 THE DemoResumeError PROCEDURE USES THE **Resume** *label* STATEMENT

INPUT

```
1:   Option Explicit
2:
3:   Sub DemoResumeError()
4:
5:       Const tblHead = "Table of Square Roots"
6:       Const FIRST As Integer = 5
7:       Const LAST As Integer = -2
8:       Const INCR As Integer = -1
9:
10:      Dim Count As Integer
11:      Dim cRow As Integer
12:      Dim oldSheet As String
13:      Dim Temp As Double
14:
```

18

continues

LISTING 18.4 CONTINUED

```
15:     oldSheet = ActiveSheet.Name   'preserve original sheet
16:     Worksheets("Sheet1").Select   'change to worksheet
17:
18:     On Error GoTo BadValue        'set error trap
19:
20:     Cells(1, 2).Value = tblHead     'set up table headings
21:     Cells(2, 1).Value = "   X"
22:     Cells(2, 2).Value = "  Sqr(X)"
23:     Cells(3, 1).Value = String(35, "-")
24:     Cells(3, 2).Value = String(35, "-")
25:
26:     cRow = 4
27:     For Count = FIRST To LAST Step INCR
28:       Temp = Sqr(Count)
29:       Cells(cRow, 1).Value = Count
30:       Cells(cRow, 2).Value = CStr(Temp)
31:       cRow = cRow + 1
32:   ResumeLoop:
33:     Next Count
34:
35:     MsgBox Buttons:=vbInformation, TITLE:=tblHead, _
36:           prompt:="Square root table completed."
37:
38:     Sheets(oldSheet).Select
39:     Exit Sub     'no more work to do
40:
41:   BadValue:
42:     Resume ResumeLoop
43:   End Sub
```

ANALYSIS Figure 18.3 shows the worksheet and dialog displayed by the DemoResumeError procedure in Listing 18.4. Notice that the table of square roots stops with 0 and does *not* contain any negative numbers.

The DemoResumeError procedure works essentially the same as the procedures you've already seen in this lesson. Again, only the error-handling technique is different.

Notice that line 13 declares a Temp variable of type **Double**. This variable is used to temporarily store the computed square root value. In the **For** loop in lines 27 through 33, notice that the result of the Sqr function is assigned to the Temp variable. If the argument for the Sqr function is negative, line 28 is the statement that will cause a runtime error. Notice also the addition of the ResumeLoop line label in line 32. This is the point where the loop's execution will resume after the runtime error.

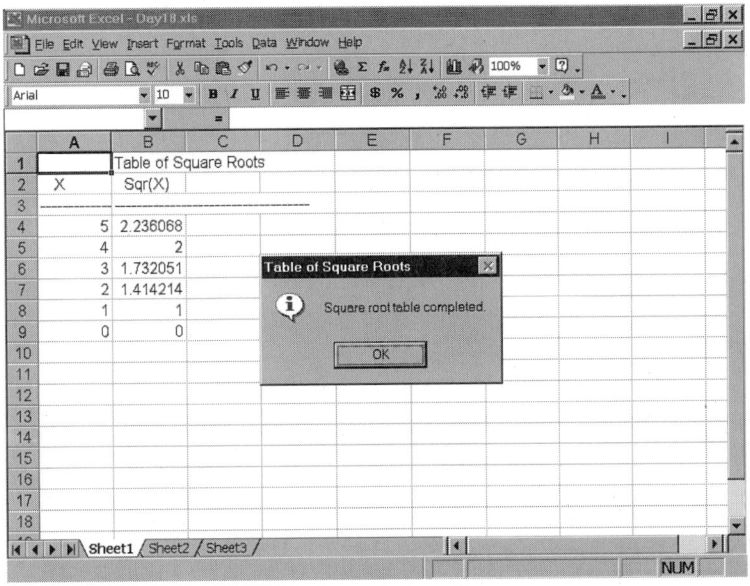

FIGURE 18.3

The DemoResumeError *procedure completes the square root table, but ignores negative numbers that cause runtime errors.*

When a runtime error occurs, VBA shifts execution to the first statement after the BadValue line label because of the error trap installed in line 18. The error-handling code in this procedure consists of the single **Resume** ResumeLoop statement in line 42. When VBA executes this statement, it shifts program execution to the first statement after the ResumeLoop line label: the **Next** statement in line 33. The **For...Next** loop then continues executing normally, as if no error had occurred. Handling the error this way has the effect of simply ignoring any negative numbers in the square root table, allowing the procedure to complete its operation without interruption.

Forcing a Runtime Error

This final example uses the Raise method of the Err object to generate the runtime error *before* it actually occurs in a call to the Sqr function. You can use a similar technique with user-defined error codes.

INPUT

LISTING 18.5 THE DemoForcedError PROCEDURE USES THE Raise METHOD OF THE Err OBJECT TO FORCE A RUNTIME ERROR

```
1:   Option Explicit
2:   Option Base 1
3:
```

continues

LISTING 18.5   CONTINUED

```
 4:   Const rtBadProcedureCall As Integer = 5
 5:   Const BINCOMP As Integer = 0
 6:   Const StrCmpLess As Integer = -1
 7:   Const StrCmpGreat As Integer = 1
 8:
 9:
10:   Sub DemoForcedError()
11:
12:      Const dTitle = "Forced Error"
13:
14:      Dim oldSheet As String
15:      Dim strArray(6) As String
16:      Dim tmpArray As Variant
17:      Dim intArray(6) As Integer
18:      Dim Count As Integer
19:      Dim Ans As Integer
20:      Dim ErrLine As Long
21:
22:      On Error GoTo rtError          'set error trap
23:
24:      oldSheet = ActiveSheet.Name    'preserve original sheet
25:      Worksheets("Sheet1").Select    'change to worksheet
26:
27:      Cells(1, 2).Value = dTitle
28:
29:      strArray(1) = "a": strArray(2) = "b": strArray(3) = "c"
30:      strArray(4) = "A": strArray(5) = "B": strArray(6) = "C"
31:
32:      intArray(1) = 2: intArray(2) = 6: intArray(3) = 4
33:      intArray(4) = 5: intArray(5) = 1: intArray(6) = 3
34:
35:   Test1:
36:      tmpArray = strArray
37:   1  SortStringList List:=tmpArray, Descending:=True
38:      For Count = 1 To UBound(tmpArray)
39:        Cells(Count + 1, 1).Value = tmpArray(Count)
40:      Next Count
41:
42:   Test2:
43:      tmpArray = strArray
44:   2  SortStringList List:=tmpArray
45:      For Count = 1 To UBound(tmpArray)
46:        Cells(Count + 1, 2).Value = tmpArray(Count)
47:      Next Count
48:
49:   Test3:
50:      Ans = MsgBox(Buttons:=vbQuestion + vbYesNo, _
51:                   Title:=dTitle, _
52:                   prompt:="Test invalid direction argument?")
```

```
53:     If Ans = vbYes Then
54:        tmpArray = strArray
55: 3    SortStringList List:=tmpArray, Descending:="True"
56:        For Count = 1 To UBound(tmpArray)
57:           Cells(Count + 1, 3).Value = tmpArray(Count)
58:        Next Count
59:     End If
60:
61: Test4:
62:     Ans = MsgBox(Buttons:=vbQuestion + vbYesNo, _
63:                  Title:=dTitle, _
64:                  prompt:="Test invalid array argument?")
65:     If Ans = vbYes Then
66:        tmpArray = intArray
67: 4    SortStringList List:=tmpArray
68:        For Count = 1 To UBound(tmpArray)
69:           Cells(Count + 1, 4).Value = tmpArray(Count)
70:        Next Count
71:     End If
72:
73: AfterTests:
74:     MsgBox Buttons:=vbInformation, Title:=dTitle, _
75:            prompt:="Sorting test completed."
76:     Sheets(oldSheet).Select
77:     Exit Sub    'no more work to do
78:
79: rtError:  'handles runtime error
80:     ErrLine = Erl
81:     MsgBox Buttons:=vbCritical, Title:=dTitle, _
82:            prompt:="Error! " & Err.Number & vbCr & _
83:                    Err.Description & " in " & _
84:                    Err.Source
85:     Select Case ErrLine
86:        Case Is = 3
87:           Resume Test4
88:        Case Is = 4
89:           Resume AfterTests
90:        Case Else
91:           MsgBox Buttons:=vbCritical, Title:=dTitle, _
92:                  prompt:="Unable to Continue!"
93:     End Select
94: End Sub
95:
96:
97: Sub SortStringList(ByRef List As Variant, _
98:                     Optional Descending)
99: 'sorts on ascending or descending order,
100: 'depending on value of Descending argument
101:
```

18

continues

LISTING 18.5   CONTINUED

```
102:   Dim uCount As Integer, dCount As Integer
103:   Dim CmpResult As Integer
104:
105:   If IsMissing(Descending) Then Descending = False
106:   If TypeName(Descending) <> "Boolean" Then
107:     Err.Raise Number:=rtBadProcedureCall, _
108:               Description:="Descending argument not Boolean", _
109:               Source:="SortStringList"
110:   End If
111:
112:   If TypeName(List) <> "String()" Then
113:     Err.Raise Number:=rtBadProcedureCall, _
114:               Description:="List array not a string array", _
115:               Source:="SortStringList"
116:   End If
117:
118:   For uCount = LBound(List) To UBound(List) - 1
119:     For dCount = uCount + 1 To UBound(List)
120:     CmpResult = StrComp(List(uCount), List(dCount), BINCOMP)
121:       If Descending Then
122:         If CmpResult = StrCmpLess Then _
123:           Swap List(uCount), List(dCount)
124:       Else
125:         If CmpResult = StrCmpGreat Then _
126:           Swap List(uCount), List(dCount)
127:       End If
128:     Next dCount
129:   Next uCount
130: End Sub
131:
132: Sub Swap(I1 As Variant, I2 As Variant)
133:   Dim Temp As Variant
134:   Temp = I1: I1 = I2: I2 = Temp
135: End Sub
```

ANALYSIS Listing 18.5 shows a practical way of using the Err object's Raise method to make your own procedures and functions behave more like VBA's built-in procedures and functions by forcing a runtime error. By now, you know that VBA's built-in procedures and functions generate a runtime error if you pass an argument of the wrong type or with an invalid value. These runtime errors can help you spot your programming mistakes. By adding similar behavior to your own procedures—especially if you intend to distribute them to other users—you can make them easier to use.

Listing 18.5 contains several procedures. The DemoForcedError procedure (lines 10 through 94) simply sets up the variables needed to test the SortStringList procedure and then calls that procedure several times with both valid and invalid arguments. Figure 18.4 shows the worksheet and dialog displayed by DemoForcedError after performing the third test of the SortStringList procedure.

FIGURE 18.4

The DemoForcedError *procedure displays this message dialog when it tries to test the* SortStringList *procedure with an invalid argument.*

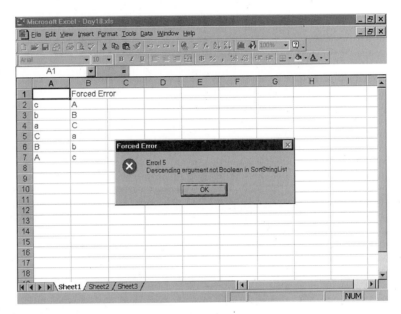

The SortStringList procedure (lines 97 through 130) is a version of the bubble-sort designed to sort arrays of strings in either ascending or descending order. SortStringList has two arguments. The first, required argument is a **Variant** type; SortStringList expects it to contain an array of strings. The second, optional argument is also a **Variant** type; SortStringList expects this argument to be a **Boolean** value indicating whether the list should be sorted in descending order. If either argument is *not* of the expected type, the SortStringList procedure uses the Err object's Raise method to force VBA to generate a runtime error. The next few paragraphs take a closer look at how the code in Listing 18.5 works.

Listing 18.5 contains an entire module. Notice the **Option Base** 1 directive in line 2, which forces all arrays in this module to have a starting subscript of 1. Lines 4 through 7 declare some module-level constants. Line 4 declares a constant for the runtime error value, line 5 declares a constant to specify the type of string comparison desired, and lines 6 and 7 declare constants representing some of the return values of the StrComp function.

The DemoForcedError procedure starts in line 10. Lines 12 through 20 declare constants and variables. Notice that line 15 declares a string array, line 16 declares a **Variant** type variable, and line 17 declares an integer array.

Line 22 installs an error-handling trap for the DemoForcedError procedure, lines 24 and 25 preserve the current sheet name and switch the active sheet to Sheet1, and line 27 enters a title on the worksheet. Lines 29 and 30 fill the string array with some test values and lines 32 and 33 fill the integer array with test values. Notice that these lines contain multiple statements separated with a colon (:).

Lines 35 through 40 form the first test of the SortStringList procedure. First, the string array is assigned to the tmpArray **Variant** variable. Because **Variant** type variables can store any data type, the result of the assignment operation in line 36 is to store a copy of the string array in the tmpArray variable.

Line 37 calls the SortStringList procedure, passing tmpArray as the array to be sorted and specifying a descending sort order. Notice that this line also has a line number: It is line number 1 (because this is the first line that tests the SortStringList procedure). After the array is sorted, lines 38 through 40 contain a **For** loop that displays the sorted array in the first column of the worksheet. Because both arguments are of the correct type, this test of the SortStringList procedure does not produce any runtime errors.

Lines 42 through 47 contain the second test of the SortStringList procedure. This test works exactly the same as the first test, except it calls the SortStringList procedure without the optional argument. The SortStringList procedure assumes that if the sort direction is not specified, the list should be sorted in ascending order. Because the second argument is optional (and can be omitted), and because the first argument is of the correct data type (an array of strings), this call to SortStringList does not produce any runtime errors. Notice that line 44, which calls the SortStringList procedure, has a line number: It is line 2 because this is the second call to SortStringList.

Lines 49 through 59 contain the third test of the SortStringList procedure. The user is first asked if she wants to perform this test; if the user clicks the Yes command button, the SortStringList procedure test is performed. Line 55 calls the SortStringList procedure, deliberately passing a string value for the optional Descending argument. Because this argument should be a **Boolean** value and not a string value, the SortStringList procedure generates a runtime error and the DemoForcedError procedure's error-handling code is invoked. (The exact operation of the SortStringList procedure is described later). Notice that line 55, which calls SortStringList, has line number 3 because this is the third line that calls SortStringList.

Lines 61 through 71 contain the fourth, and final, test of the SortStringList procedure. Again, the user is asked whether to perform the test. If so, the SortStringList procedure is called by the statement in line 67. Notice that the statement in line 66 assigns the integer array to the tmpArray variable. When SortStringList is called in line 67, the List argument is an integer array, not a string array. Because this argument has the wrong data type, SortStringList generates a runtime error.

Lines 73 through 77 of DemoForcedError display a message informing the user that testing is complete and restore the original sheet. Line 77 exits the procedure because there is no more work to be done and because the error-handling code at the end of the procedure needs to be skipped over; it's simplest to just end the procedure at this point.

Lines 79 through 93 contain the DemoForcedError procedure's error-handling statements. When a runtime error occurs, VBA shifts execution to the first statement after the rtError line label because of the error trap installed by the **On Error GoTo** statement in line 22. First, line 80 preserves the result of the Erl function in the ErrLine variable. Next, lines 81 through 84 contain a MsgBox statement that informs the user of the runtime error, reporting the precise error code number, its corresponding text, and the error line number. Now, lines 85 through 93 contain a **Select Case** statement that selects the appropriate point to resume the DemoForcedError procedure based on which line produced the runtime error. If the runtime error occurred in the third test, the procedure resumes with the fourth test; if the runtime error occurred in the fourth test, the procedure resumes at a point after all the tests.

Note

> As an experiment, replace the **Select Case** statement in lines 85 through 93 of Listing 18.5 with a single **Resume Next** statement and observe how the DemoForcedError procedure's behavior changes.

Lines 97 through 130 contain the SortStringList procedure. Lines 102 and 103 declare the variables used by SortStringList. Line 105 checks to see whether the optional Descending argument was included; if that argument is missing, it's set to a default value of **False** so that the list will be sorted in ascending order.

Line 106 tests to see what the data type of the Descending argument is by using the TypeName function. If the Descending argument doesn't have a **Boolean** type, line 10 uses the Err object's Raise method to force a runtime error: in this case, the runtime error specified by the rtBadProcedureCall constant (which stores the error code number for an Invalid Procedure Call error). The optional Description and Source arguments are used with the Raise method to make the resulting error message as explicit as possible: The Description argument is passed a string that describes the precise problem detected and the Source argument is passed a string that describes the precise procedure in which the error has occurred.

Because of the forced runtime error, VBA immediately stops executing the SortStringList procedure and returns to the DemoForcedError procedure. After returning to the DemoForcedError procedure, VBA sets its internal error mechanisms to indicate that an invalid procedure call has been made and also interrupts the execution of the DemoForcedError procedure. Because the DemoForcedError procedure has an error trap installed, it handles the runtime error itself.

Note

> As an experiment, remove the **On Error GoTo** statement from line 22 of Listing 18.5 and see what happens when the SortStringList procedure is called with invalid arguments.

If the Descending argument has the correct type, execution continues with line 112, which also uses the TypeName function to test the type of the List argument. If the List argument is an array of strings, the TypeName function returns String() as its result. If the List argument is *not* an array of strings, the Err.Raise method call in line 113 is executed, forcing a runtime error. This statement has the same effect as line 107: SortStringList terminates and the runtime error is reported in the context of the procedure that called SortStringList (DemoForcedError in this case). The remainder of the SortStringList procedure carries out the bubble-sort that you're already familiar with.

Lines 132 through 135 contain the Swap procedure used by SortStringList. You already know how this procedure works.

Summary

This lesson presented the mechanisms for trapping and handling errors in your VBA procedures. You learned that there are two basic error-handling strategies: defensive programming and error trapping. The first strategy detects conditions that will cause a runtime error and takes the necessary steps to avoid the error. Error trapping involves installing an error trap (by using the **On Error GoTo** statement) that causes VBA to automatically branch to a particular spot in your procedure, which usually contains code to handle the error without halting the procedure's execution.

This lesson showed you how to use the **On Error GoTo** statement to install an error trap. You learned that the **On Error GoTo** statement uses a line label to specify a location in your procedure to which VBA switches program execution if a runtime error occurs. You also learned how to use the **Resume** statement to determine where your procedure's code should resume execution. Typically, your error-handling code will end with a **Resume** statement of some kind after dealing with the runtime error.

This lesson also taught you how to use the Err, Erl, and Error functions to find out the specific runtime error code, the line number of the statement that caused the runtime error, and the corresponding text for the error message. You also learned how to use the Error statement to force a runtime error to occur with either a predefined VBA error code or an error code that you define.

Finally, you learned how to use the Err object's properties and methods to get information about runtime errors and to force the occurrence of a runtime error with either a predefined VBA error code or a user-defined error code.

This lesson concluded with several examples of putting error-handling statements and the Err object to work.

Q&A

Q At what point in my procedure should I install an error trap with the On Error GoTo **statement?**

A Usually, you should install the error trap at the beginning of your procedure, especially if it's intended to handle any runtime error that might occur while the procedure is executing. Alternatively, you can install the error trap immediately in front of any error-prone statement—your procedure can even contain more than one **On Error GoTo** statement, with each statement pointing to a different section of error-handling statements. In general, though, you should use only one **On Error GoTo** statement.

Q What happens if another runtime error occurs as a result of one of the statements in my procedure's error-handling code?

A VBA will stop executing your procedure's code and display a runtime error dialog for the additional runtime error because it can't deal with the new runtime error until you reset VBA's internal runtime error mechanisms with a **Resume** statement.

18

Q Can I use an `On Error GoTo` statement in my error-handling code to take care of any additional runtime errors that occur while my code resolves the first runtime error?

A Yes, but you must first use a **Resume** statement to clear VBA's internal runtime error-handling mechanisms or use the `Err` object's `Clear` method. Here is the general form for a nested error handler:

```
FirstError:
      'statements to record the error number, etc.
      Resume NextLine1
NextLine1:
      'install second error handler
      On Error GoTo SecondError
      'statements that handle first error
      GoTo ReturnLabel
SecondError:
      'statements to handle second error
      Resume ReturnLabel
```

Notice that the first **Resume** statement simply directs execution to resume at the label on the following line. This programming trick satisfies VBA's need to handle the first error. The **On Error GoTo** statement then sets the internal error handler.

Q What happens if I just use a `Resume 0` statement to handle an error?

A Your procedure will enter an infinite loop because the error isn't actually being resolved and the statement causing the error isn't being skipped over. A runtime error will occur, VBA will execute the **Resume 0** statement in your error-handling code, return to the offending statement, and the same runtime error will occur again. Only use the **Resume 0** statement after your error-handling code has resolved the conditions that produced the runtime error (by modifying variable values, changing to another worksheet or workbook, and so on).

Workshop

Answers are in Appendix A.

Quiz

1. What statement can you use to cause your procedure to resume execution at the statement immediately following the one that caused a runtime error?

2. What happens if a new runtime error occurs while your procedure is still handling a previous runtime error?

3. Can a procedure have multiple sets of error-handling statements?

4. Which statement can you use to cause your procedure to resume execution with the same statement that caused a runtime error?

5. How do you disable your error trap?

6. What statement clears VBA's internal runtime error handling mechanisms? What Err object method clears VBA's internal runtime error handling mechanisms?

7. What function returns the error message text corresponding to a particular runtime error code? What Err object property returns the error message text corresponding to a particular runtime error code?

8. What statement forces a runtime error to occur? Which Err object method forces a runtime error to occur?

Exercises

1. Write a procedure named MyErrorHandler that traps and handles the runtime error produced when you call the Mid function with invalid indices. (Mid returns a specified portion of a string.) Here is the pseudo-code for the MyErrorHandler procedure:

```
1. Install the error-trap.
2. Prompt the user to enter a string.
3. Prompt user to enter the starting index.
4. Prompt user to enter the number of characters to extract.
5. Call the Mid function, and assign its result to a variable.
6. Display the original string and the extracted string.
7. End the procedure.
```

The Mid function produces a runtime error any time its arguments are negative or zero. Your procedure should handle the error along the lines of the following pseudo-code:

```
1. Assign an empty string to the variable for the extracted string.
2. Display an error message.
3. Resume execution at the statement following the one that caused
   the runtime error.
```

2. What is displayed in the message dialog after the following statements are executed?

```
Dim S As String
Dim L As Integer
On Error GoTo RunTimeError
S = "Hello"
L = 0
Mid(S, L, 1) = "J"
MsgBox S
GoTo EndIt
RunTimeError:
```

18

```
    Resume Next
EndIt:
```

3. What is displayed in the message dialog after these statements execute?

```
Dim S As String
Dim L As Integer
  On Error GoTo RunTimeError
  S = "Hello"
  L = 0
  Mid(S, L, 1) = "J"
  MsgBox S
  GoTo EndIt
RunTimeError:
  L = 1
  Resume 0
EndIt:
```

4. What is displayed in the message dialog after the following statements are executed? What does it tell you about the number of times the macro calls the error-handling statements?

```
Dim S As String
Dim L As Integer
Dim Count As Integer
Count = 0
On Error GoTo RunTimeError
S = "Hello"
L = -10
Mid(S, L, 1) = "J"
MsgBox S & vbCr & vbCr & Count
GoTo EndIt
RunTimeError:
  Count = Count + 1
  L = L + 1
  Resume 0
EndIt:
```

5. What is displayed in the message dialog after the following statements are executed?

```
Dim S As String
Dim L As Integer
On Error GoTo RunTimeError
S = "Hello"
L = 0
Mid(S, L, 1) = "J"
MsgBox S
GoTo EndIt
RunTimeError:
  MsgBox "Runtime error number" & Err
EndIt:
```

DAY **19**

Controlling Excel with VBA

As you have already learned, Visual Basic for Applications is a programming language designed primarily to work with and enhance existing software programs. Excel makes many different objects available to VBA. These objects' properties and methods enable you to control almost every aspect of Excel through your VBA code. In today's lesson, you'll learn how to manipulate the most important and basic objects in Excel 97 and Excel 2000 (also known as Excel 8 and Excel 9, respectively); specifically:

- How to work with Excel Workbook and Worksheet objects.
- Use Excel object methods that return Range objects, including how to define and select ranges in a worksheet.
- How to enter values and formulas in Excel worksheet cells.
- How to insert, cut, copy, or paste data in Excel worksheets.

Working with Workbook Objects

Excel 97 introduced a new workbook format; this new format is an enhancement of the workbook format used previously in Excel 5 and Excel 7. Excel 97 and Excel 2000 use the same workbook format. The primary differences between the Excel 97/2000 workbook format and its two prior versions is the way your VBA projects are stored in the workbook file and the fact that events associated with a workbook or worksheet object are exposed to VBA; you can create procedures that Excel executes automatically whenever certain events occur, such as a workbook's opening, activation, closing, and so on. You'll learn more about workbook event procedures in Day 21; this lesson covers basic operations using Excel objects.

The Excel 97/2000 workbook format is a great way to make common spreadsheet tasks faster and easier. Excel makes a number of objects, methods, and properties available to VBA, enabling you to perform basic chores on your workbooks under programmatic control. The next few sections look at some of the most common objects, methods, and properties.

Returning a Workbook Object

In Excel, each workbook is a `Workbook` object, and `Workbooks` is the collection of all the open workbooks in the current Excel session. To refer to a specific workbook, use the `Application` object's `Workbooks` method:

SYNTAX ▼

`Workbooks(Index)`

`Index` can be either of the following:

- A numeric expression representing the workbook that you want to use. 1 signifies the first workbook opened in this session, 2 signifies the second workbook opened, and so on.

- A string expression representing the name of the open workbook that you want to use.

▲ The most common—and usually the most readable—way of using `Index` is as a text string. Listing 19.1 shows an example.

INPUT   **LISTING 19.1**   USING THE `Workbooks` COLLECTION TO RETURN A WORKBOOK

```
1:   Sub SetWorkbookProtection()
2:   'Activates workbook protection
3:
4:     Workbooks("DAY19.XLS").Protect Structure:=True, Windows:=True
7:     MsgBox "Workbook protection for DAY19.XLS activated."
8:   End Sub
```

ANALYSIS The expression in line 4, `Workbooks("DAY19.XLS")`, returns an object reference to the Day19.xls workbook object. The `Protect` method sets up protection for the workbook's structure and windows. The `MsgBox` statement in line 7 displays a message telling you that protection has been activated for this workbook. (This procedure assumes that a workbook named Day19.xls is currently open; if it isn't, you'll get a run-time error.)

Do

DO use `ActiveWorkbook` to refer to the active workbook.

DO use `ThisWorkbook` to refer to the workbook that contains the currently running procedure, especially if you intend to convert your program to an Excel add-in program.

DON'T

DON'T use numbers for the `Index` argument of the `Workbooks` method if you don't have to. The meaning of a statement such as `Workbooks("DAY19.XLS")` is much clearer than, say, `Workbooks(2)`. Using the text name of the workbook is also more accurate. Unless all the workbooks in the current Excel session are opened by your program, you cannot be sure that the Day19.xls workbook is, in fact, the second workbook.

Opening a Workbook

If the workbook that you need is not open, use the `Open` method to load the workbook into memory.

`Workbooks.Open(Filename)`

The `Filename` argument is a text string representing the full directory path of the workbook: drive, folder, and filename. If you don't specify the drive or folder name, Excel looks for the workbook file in the current drive or folder. Listing 19.2 shows the `Open` method in action.

INPUT **LISTING 19.2** USING THE `Open` METHOD TO OPEN A WORKBOOK

```
1:  Sub OpenWorkbook()
2:  'Prompts for, and then opens a workbook
3:
4:    Dim WorkbookName As String
5:
```

continues

LISTING 19.2   CONTINUED

```
 6:      WorkbookName = _
 7:          InputBox("Enter the full path name of the workbook to open:")
 8:      If WorkbookName <> "" Then
 9:          Workbooks.Open Filename:=WorkbookName
10:      End If
11:  End Sub
```

ANALYSIS   In this procedure, a variable called WorkbookName is declared as a **String** (line 4), and an InputBox function prompts the user for the name of a workbook file (lines 6 and 7). The **If...Then** statement in line 8 checks whether the user canceled the input dialog. If not—in other words, if WorkbookName isn't blank—the Open method uses WorkbookName to open the file (line 9).

Do

DO take advantage of Excel's built-in Open dialog if you need or want the user to select a file to open. You can use Excel's built-in Open dialog either by using the GetOpenFileName method (discussed in Day 12) or by using the Dialogs collection as shown here (the Dialogs collection contains all the dialogs built-in to Excel):

```
Application.Dialogs(xlDialogOpen).Show
```

DON'T

DON'T despair if you want to open a workbook as read-only or if you need to open a workbook with a password. The Open method has no less than 13 different arguments that cover situations like these. Use the Object Browser to see, paste, or get help on the various arguments for the Open method.

Creating a New Workbook

If your procedure needs to create a new workbook, use the Workbooks collection's Add method to get the job done.

▼ SYNTAX

```
Workbooks.Add([Template])
```

The optional *Template* argument determines the kind of workbook that Excel creates. If you omit *Template*, Excel creates a default workbook containing a number of blank worksheets; the number of blank worksheets in the new workbook is determined on the

▼ General tab of the Options dialog (accessed by choosing the Tools, Options command). You can also set the number of blank worksheets in a new workbook by setting the `Application.SheetsInNewWorkBook` property.

To create a new workbook based on an existing workbook template, supply a string expression specifying the name of the template as the *Template* argument. If the workbook template you want to use is not in Excel's startup or alternate startup directory, include the full path—drive, folder, and template filename—in the *Template* argument.

To create a workbook that contains only a single sheet, use one of the following intrinsic constants for the *Template* argument (these constants are defined in the `xlWBATemplate` class): `xlWBATWorksheet`, `xlWBATChart`, `xlWBATExcel4MacroSheet`, or `xlWBATExcel4IntlMacroSheet`.

▲ Listing 19.3 shows an example procedure that creates a new workbook.

INPUT   **LISTING 19.3**   USING THE Add METHOD TO CREATE A NEW WORKBOOK

```
 1:    Sub CreateMonthlyReport()
 2:    'Creates new workbook based on Excel's Invoice template
 3:
 4:        Dim dPath As String
 5:
 6:        dPath = "C:\Program Files\Microsoft Office"
 7:        dPath = dPath & "\Templates\"
 8:        Workbooks.Add Template:=dPath & "Expense Statement"
 9:        With ActiveWorkbook
10:            .Title = "Expenses for Joseph P. Doakes"
11:            .Subject = "Expenses for January 1999"
12:            .Author = "Lisa Simpson"
13:        End With
14:    End Sub
```

19

ANALYSIS   Listing 19.3 creates a new workbook from the `Expense Statement` template supplied with Excel and Microsoft Office 2000 (line 8). (The path to the workbook template used in this example is for Microsoft Office 2000 installed into its default folders—your template file might be in a different location.) Any new workbook automatically becomes the active workbook. Lines 9 through 13 use the `ActiveWorkbook` object to add some summary information for the new workbook file: `Title`, `Subject`, and `Author`.

Activating a Workbook

If your VBA program keeps several workbooks open at once, you might need to switch from one workbook to another to display, for example, a report or a data entry screen.

SYNTAX

Use the `Activate` method to make any open workbook the active workbook:

`Object.Activate`

Here, `Object` represents any valid object reference to the worksheet you want to activate. Listing 19.4 displays an example procedure that uses the `Activate` method.

INPUT **LISTING 19.4** USING THE `Activate` METHOD TO SWITCH TO A WORKBOOK

```
 1:  Sub ActivateTest()
 2:  'Activates two workbooks without changing the screen.
 3:
 4:    Dim SaveBook As String
 5:
 6:    SaveBook = ActiveWorkbook.Name
 7:
 8:    Application.ScreenUpdating = False
 9:    Workbooks("DATA.XLS").Activate
10:
11:    'Code that does stuff to DATA.XLS goes here
12:
13:    Workbooks(SaveBook).Activate
14:    Application.ScreenUpdating = True
15:  End Sub
```

ANALYSIS This simple procedure demonstrates two tenets of good programming.

- Whenever possible, hide your program's intermediate operations from the user. For example, if the procedure has a number of statements that format ranges and enter data, perform these tasks "behind the scenes." Present the user only with the finished screen. You do this by setting the `Application` object's `ScreenUpdating` property to **False**.

- If you're activating a workbook because your code needs to—and not because you want the user to see a different file—your procedure should always return the user to where she started. Especially for novice users, it is highly disconcerting to start a procedure and to end up suddenly in a different workbook for no obvious reason.

The purpose of the procedure in Listing 19.4 is to switch from the current workbook to another workbook (Data.xls) to make some modifications to it by means of code and then to return to the original workbook. First, in line 4, the name of the current active workbook is saved in the SaveBook string variable. Next, to keep the user from seeing the details of the procedure's action, line 8 sets the ScreenUpdating property to **False**. Line 9 activates the Data.xls workbook. The following lines would perform actions in the Data.xls workbook—the actual code that modifies Data.xls has been omitted from this example. To get the user back to the original workbook, line 13 reactivates the original workbook. Line 14 sets ScreenUpdating back to **True**.

Do

DO let the user know what's happening if you switch from one workbook to another. A simple MsgBox statement can tell the user where she is now and what she should expect.

DON'T

DON'T activate a workbook if you don't have to. You can almost always modify or get information about a workbook simply by referring to the appropriate Workbook object. For example, to find out the format of Data.xls by using the FileFormat property, you can use the following statement without activating the workbook:

```
FileFmt = Workbooks("Data.xls").FileFormat
```

Saving a Workbook

If your VBA program makes changes to a workbook, you should give the user an opportunity to save those changes or have your program save them outright. This is easily accomplished either by including Excel's built-in Save command in your program's menu or by adding the Save button to your program's toolbar if your program has menus or toolbars.

There might be times, though, when you need or want to save a workbook under the control of a procedure. For example, you might want to create your own version of the File, Save command. Likewise, you might be trying to protect a novice user from performing actions with unfortunate consequences, such as closing a workbook or exiting your program or Excel without saving her work.

To save a workbook, you use—appropriately enough—the Save method.

▼ SYNTAX

```
Object.Save
```

With this method, *Object* is an object reference to the open Workbook object you want to save.

19

▼   A slightly different, but handy, method is called SaveCopyAs. This method saves a copy
    of the specified workbook to disk without affecting the workbook in memory. This
    method is useful, for example, if you want to create a Revert command that returns a
    workbook to its original state. You use SaveCopyAs at the beginning of your program to
    make a copy of the workbook file to disk before any changes are made in the workbook.
    Then, you can revert to this saved copy by opening it and saving it again with its original
    filename. Here is the general form of the SaveCopyAs method:

    Object.SaveCopyAs(*Filename*)

    Object is an object reference to the Workbook to be saved and *Filename* is a string
    expression for the name you want to use for the saved workbook copy.

▲   Listing 19.5 shows an example procedure that uses both Save and SaveCopyAs.

INPUT   **LISTING 19.5**   USING THE Save AND SaveCopyAs METHODS

```
 1:   Sub BackUpToFloppy()
 2:   'Saves and backs up the active workbook to floppy A:
 3:
 4:      Const FloppyDrv = "A:"
 5:
 6:      With ActiveWorkbook
 7:          If Not .Saved Then .Save
 8:          .SaveCopyAs Filename:=FloppyDrv & .Name
 9:      End With
10:   End Sub
```

ANALYSIS   This procedure saves the active workbook and makes a backup copy on a floppy
               disk in drive A. The procedure begins by declaring a single constant for the flop-
py drive letter. The **With** statement processes several commands for the ActiveWorkbook
object.

An **If...Then** test (line 7) checks the workbook's Saved property. If this property is
False, the workbook has changes that haven't been saved yet, so the procedure calls the
Save method.

The name of the backup file is created by concatenating the FloppyDrv constant value
with the workbook's Name property. The result is used as the Name argument to the
SaveCopyAs method (line 8), which saves a copy of the workbook to the floppy drive.

Do
DO use the `Workbook` object's `Path` property to check whether a workbook has ever been saved. If `Path` returns an empty string (`""`), the workbook has never been saved before.

DON'T
DON'T use the `Save` method for a new workbook that has never been saved before. If you do, Excel saves the new workbook with its current name, for example, Book1.xls. Instead, use the `SaveAs` method to assign a name to the workbook the first time you save it: `Object.SaveAs(Filename)` The `SaveAs` method includes several other arguments that enable you, among other things, to specify a file format or assign a password to the file. Use the Object Browser to see, paste, or get help on all the `SaveAs` method arguments.

Closing a Workbook

When you're finished with a workbook, you should close it to save memory and to avoid cluttering the screen. You close a workbook by using one of the following forms of the `Close` method.

```
Workbooks.Close
```

```
Object.Close(SaveChanges)
```

The first syntax form simply closes every open workbook. Excel prompts you to save changes in the workbooks before closing them, if necessary. The second syntax form closes a specific workbook, denoted by `Object`. Use the `SaveChanges` argument as follows:

- If `SaveChanges` is **True**, Excel saves the workbook automatically before closing it.
- If `SaveChanges` is **False**, Excel closes the workbook without saving any changes.
- If you omit `SaveChanges`, Excel prompts you to save changes, if necessary.

Listing 19.6 demonstrates the `Close` method.

▼ SYNTAX

19

```
 1:    Sub CloseAll()
 2:    'Closes all open workbooks and prompts to save changes
 3:
 4:        Const qButtons = vbYesNo + vbQuestion
 5:
 6:        Dim Book As Workbook
 7:        Dim Ans As Integer
 8:        Dim MsgPrompt As String
 9:
10:        For Each Book In Workbooks
11:            If Not (Book.Name = ThisWorkbook.Name) Then
12:                If Not Book.Saved Then
13:                    MsgPrompt = "Save changes to " & Book.Name & "?"
14:                    Ans = MsgBox(prompt:=MsgPrompt, Buttons:=qButtons)
15:                    If Ans = vbYes Then
16:                        Book.Close SaveChanges:=True
17:                    Else
18:                        Book.Close SaveChanges:=False
19:                    End If
20:                Else
21:                    Book.Close
22:                End If
23:            End If
24:        Next Book
25:    End Sub
```

ANALYSIS   This procedure closes all the open workbooks (*except* the workbook containing this procedure) and prompts the user to save changes for each workbook with unsaved changes. Use a procedure like this one instead of the Workbooks.Close method when you need to prevent a user from canceling the operation; Excel's built-in Save prompts have a Cancel button. After declaring a constant and several variables (lines 4 through 8), the procedure starts a **For Each** loop to process all the workbooks in the Workbooks collection.

Because closing the workbook containing the currently executing procedure causes that procedure to stop executing, line 11 contains an **If...Then** statement that checks to see whether the workbook currently being processed has the same name as the workbook containing the CloseAll procedure. If so, the code that closes the workbook is skipped; lines 12 through 22 are executed only if the workbook does *not* contain the CloseAll procedure. (The ThisWorkBook property returns a reference to the workbook containing the currently executing VBA code.)

If the workbook has changes that haven't been saved (line 12), a `MsgBox` function (line 13) asks whether to save the changes. If the user chooses the Yes button (so that `vbYes` is returned in the `Ans` variable), the procedure runs the `Close` method with `SaveChanges` set to **True** (line 15 and 16). Otherwise, the procedure closes the workbook with `SaveChanges` set to **False** (line 18). If the workbook doesn't have unsaved changes, the procedure runs the `Close` method without arguments (line 21).

Do

DO investigate the full syntax of the `Close` method in the Object Browser or the VBA help system. This method includes two other arguments that enable you to specify a filename for a workbook that has never been saved and to route a workbook over a network.

DO use the `Application.ThisWorkbook` property whenever you want to reference the workbook that contains the currently executing procedure.

Working with Worksheet Objects

`Worksheet` objects contain a number of properties and methods that you can exploit in your VBA code. With these properties and methods, you can activate and hide worksheets; add new worksheets to a workbook; and move, copy, rename, or delete worksheets. The next sections discuss each of these worksheet operations.

Returning a Worksheet Object

Each worksheet is a `Worksheet` object, and `Worksheets` is the collection of all the worksheets in a given workbook. To refer to a specific worksheet, use the `Workbook` object's `Worksheets` collection:

▼ SYNTAX

Object.Worksheets(*Index*)

Object represents a reference to the `Workbook` object that contains the worksheet. *Index* can be either of the following:

- A number representing the worksheet that you want to use. 1 signifies the first worksheet in the workbook, 2 signifies the second worksheet, and so on.

- The name, as a string, of the worksheet you want to use. This is the name as it appears on the worksheet's tab.

▲

Listing 19.7 shows an example of the most common way of using the `Worksheets` method: using a text string to identify a worksheet.

19

INPUT   **LISTING 19.7**   USING THE Worksheets COLLECTION TO RETURN A WORKSHEET

```
1:   Sub SetWorksheetProtection()
2:   'Activates worksheet protection
3:
4:       Workbooks("DAY19.XLS").Worksheets("Sheet1").Protect _
5:                       Contents:=True, Scenarios:=True
6:       MsgBox "Protection for 'Sheet1' sheet now active."
7:   End Sub
```

ANALYSIS   Workbooks("DAY19.XLS").Worksheets("Sheet1") returns an object reference to
the sheet named Sheet1 in the Day19.xls workbook. The Protect method sets
up protection for the worksheet's contents and scenarios. The MsgBox statement tells the
user that worksheet protection has been activated.

Do

DO use the workbook's ActiveSheet property if you need to refer to the active worksheet.

DO use the Sheets collection, instead of the WorkSheets collection, when you need to
refer to *every* sheet in a workbook (or you're not sure what kind of sheet you're selecting). The Sheets collection contains not only worksheets, but also chart sheets.

DON'T

DON'T specify the Workbook object if the procedure and worksheet are in the same workbook.

DON'T use numbers for the Index argument if you don't have to. Something such as
Worksheets("June Sales") is clearer and easier to read than, say, Worksheets(6).

Activating a Worksheet

Most workbooks contain more than one worksheet, so your VBA program might need to
switch from one worksheet to another. For example, you might need to display one
worksheet for data entry and then switch to another worksheet to view a report or chart.
You can switch among worksheets by using the Activate method.

Object.Activate

Object represents a reference to the Worksheet object you want to activate. Listing 19.8
shows an example of the Activate method.

INPUT   **LISTING 19.8**   USING THE `Activate` METHOD TO SWITCH TO A WORKSHEET

```
 1:   Sub DisplayReport()
 2:   'Activates the "Sheet1" sheet if the user wants to see it
 3:
 4:      Dim Ans As Integer, qBtns As Integer
 5:      Dim mPrompt As String
 6:
 7:      mPrompt = "Do you want to view ""Sheet1""?"
 8:      qBtns = vbYesNo + vbQuestion + vbDefaultButton2
 9:      Ans = MsgBox(prompt:=mPrompt, Buttons:=qBtns)
10:      If Ans = vbYes Then
11:         Workbooks("DAY19.XLS").Worksheets("Sheet1").Activate
12:      End If
13:   End Sub
```

ANALYSIS   This procedure asks whether the user wants to see a particular worksheet, the default Sheet1, in this case (lines 7–9). If the user chooses the Yes button, the worksheet named Sheet1 is activated (line 11).

Do

DO use the `Select` method if you need to select a worksheet:

> `Object.Select`

This method is useful for creating three-dimensional references and for defining the sheets that you want to print. (A *three-dimensional reference* is a reference to a range of cells on more than one worksheet.)

DON'T

DON'T activate a worksheet if you don't have to. For most `Worksheet` object properties and methods, you can simply use the `Worksheets` method to refer to the worksheet that you want to use. The following statement, for example, returns the standard width of the `June Sales` worksheet without activating the sheet:

> `StdWidth = Worksheets("June Sales").StandardWidth`

19

Creating a New Worksheet

The Worksheets collection has an Add method that you can use to insert new worksheets into a workbook. The syntax for this method is

Object.Worksheets.Add([*Before*] [,*After*] [,*Count*] [,*Type*])

Object represents a reference to the Workbook object in which you want to add a new worksheet. The *Before* argument specifies the sheet before which the new sheet is added; the *After* argument specifies the sheet after which the new sheet is added. (You can't use the *Before* and *After* arguments together in the same statement.) If you omit both *Before* and *After*, VBA adds the new worksheet before the active sheet.

Count is the number of new worksheets to add. (The Add method adds one worksheet if you omit *Count*.) *Type* is the type of worksheet you want to add. You have three choices for the *Type* argument (defined in the XlSheetType class): xlWorksheet (which is the default), xlExcel4MacroSheet, or xlExcel4IntlMacroSheet. Listing 19.9 shows the Worksheets.Add method in action.

▲

LISTING 19.9   USING THE Add METHOD TO CREATE A NEW WORKSHEET

```
1:    Sub CreateTempWorksheet()
2:    'Creates a new, temporary, worksheet and then hides it
3:
4:       Application.ScreenUpdating = False
5:       Worksheets.Add
6:       With ActiveSheet
7:          .Name = "Temporary"
8:          .Visible = False
9:       End With
10:      Application.ScreenUpdating = True
11:   End Sub
```

This procedure is useful for creating a new worksheet that will hold intermediate results or other data that you don't want the user to see. After it turns off screen updates (line 4), the procedure adds a new worksheet (line 5). In the **With** statement (lines 6 through 9), two operations are performed on this new, active sheet. First, line 7 uses the Name property (described in the next section) to change the name of the new worksheet to Temporary. Second, line 8 hides the new worksheet by setting its Visible property to **False**.

Renaming a Worksheet

The name of a worksheet is the text that appears inside the sheet's tab. If you need to rename a worksheet, change the sheet's Name property:

Object.Name

Object is the worksheet you want to rename. Listing 19.9, which you've just seen, has an example procedure that changes a worksheet's Name property.

Copying and Moving a Worksheet

If you need to rearrange the sheets in a workbook, use the Copy and Move methods. For both methods, the syntax is identical.

▼ SYNTAX

Object.Copy([*Before*] [,*After*])

Object.Move([*Before*] [,*After*])

Object is an object reference to the worksheet you want to copy or move. *Before* specifies the worksheet before which the sheet is copied or moved; *After* specifies the worksheet after which the sheet is copied or moved. (You can't use the *Before* and *After* arguments together in the same statement.) If you omit both *Before* and *After*, VBA creates a new workbook for the copied or moved sheet. Listing 19.10 presents a procedure that uses the Move method.

▲

INPUT **LISTING 19.10** USING THE MOVE METHOD TO MOVE A WORKSHEET

19

```
 1:   Sub CreateWorksheetAtEnd()
 2:   'Creates a new worksheet at the end of the workbook
 3:
 4:      Dim NewSheet As String
 5:
 6:      Application.ScreenUpdating = False
 7:
 8:      Worksheets.Add before:=Worksheets(Worksheets.Count)
 9:      NewSheet = ActiveSheet.Name
10:      With Worksheets(NewSheet)
11:         .Move after:=Worksheets(Worksheets.Count)
12:         .Activate
13:      End With
14:
15:      Application.ScreenUpdating = True
16:   End Sub
```

ANALYSIS
After `CreateWorksheetAtEnd` declares a variable and turns off screen updating, it uses the `Add` method to add a worksheet (line 8). This call to the `Add` method uses the optional `before` argument to insert the new worksheet directly in front of the last worksheet already in the workbook. Line 8 determines the number of the last sheet in the workbook by using the `Count` property, which simply returns a count of the worksheets in the workbook. Then, the new worksheet's name is saved in the `NewSheet` variable.

Line 11 uses the `Move` method to move the new worksheet behind the last worksheet of the workbook. Again, the `Count` property is used to get the number of worksheets in the workbook. The new sheet is activated (line 12) and screen updates are turned on again (line 15).

Do

DO remember that you can also insert sheets after a specified sheet. The procedure in Listing 19.10 inserts a sheet before the last sheet and then moves it because Excel doesn't permit you to insert sheets at the end of a workbook. Use the `After` argument with the `Add` method to insert a worksheet anywhere except as the last sheet.

DON'T

DON'T forget to turn screen updating back on if your procedure turns it off.

Deleting a Worksheet

To keep your workbooks manageable and to save disk space, you should delete worksheets that you don't need. This is especially true if your application creates temporary sheets to hold intermediate results (as shown in Listing 19.9, earlier in this lesson). Use the `Delete` method to delete a worksheet.

`Object.Delete`

Object is a reference to the `Worksheet` you want to delete. Listing 19.11 shows an example of the `Delete` method.

INPUT **LISTING 19.11**   USING THE Delete METHOD TO DELETE A WORKSHEET

```
 1:   Sub DeleteTemporarySheets()
 2:   'Deletes all temporary worksheets
 3:
 4:      Dim Sheet As Worksheet
 5:
 6:      Application.DisplayAlerts = False
 7:
 8:      For Each Sheet In Workbooks("DAY19.XLS").Worksheets
 9:         If InStr(1, Sheet.Name, "Temporary") Then
10:            Sheet.Delete
11:         End If
12:      Next Sheet
13:
14:      Application.DisplayAlerts = True
15:   End Sub
```

ANALYSIS   This procedure cycles through every worksheet in a workbook and deletes all the temporary sheets that have been created. The procedure assumes that the temporary sheets have names such as Temporary1 and Temporary2.

The procedure declares a Worksheet object variable—Sheet—and sets the Application object's DisplayAlerts property to **False** (line 6). This suppresses Excel's normal confirmation dialog, which you see whenever you delete a worksheet. Line 8 starts a **For Each** loop to go through all the worksheets in the Day19.xls workbook. For each sheet, an InStr function tests whether the string Temporary is in the sheet name. If it is, line 10 deletes the sheet. When this process is complete, the DisplayAlerts property is set back to **True** (line 14).

19

Do

DO use the *compare* argument in the InStr function to make a text comparison for sheet names so that the comparison is not case sensitive. The procedure in Listing 19.11 assumes that **Option Compare Text** is the current global comparison setting.

Don't

DON'T forget to turn Excel's alerts back on if your procedure turns them off.

Methods That Return Range Objects

Most worksheet chores—whether entering information, cutting or copying data, or applying formatting options—involve cells, ranges, and range names. It should come as no surprise that many Excel object methods in VBA end up doing *something* to a range.

Just as you must select a worksheet range before you do anything to it, you must reference a worksheet range in a VBA procedure before you can do anything to it. To do that, you need to work with the most common of all Excel objects: the Range object. A Range object can be a single cell, a row or a column, a selection of cells, or even a three-dimensional range (that is, a range that includes selected cells on more than one worksheet). The following sections look at various methods and properties that return Range objects.

Using the Range Method

The easiest and most straightforward way of identifying a cell or range is with the Range method.

The Range method has this syntax

`Object.Range(Name)`

Object is a reference to the Worksheet object that contains the range. If you omit *Object*, VBA assumes that the method applies to the ActiveSheet object. The *Name* argument is a range reference or range name entered as text. The Range method also works with named ranges.

Listing 19.12 shows an example of the Range method.

INPUT   **LISTING 19.12**   USING THE Range METHOD TO WORK WITH A RANGE

```
1:  Sub FormatRangeFont()
2:  'Sets the font of a range using the Range method
3:
4:     With Worksheets("Sheet1")
5:        .Range("A1:L1").Font.Size = 24
6:        .Range("A1:L1").Font.Bold = True
7:        .Range("A1:L1").Font.Name = "Times New Roman"
8:     End With
9:  End Sub
```

ANALYSIS   In this example, all three statements (lines 5 through 7) return the range A1:L1 on the worksheet named Sheet1. (Notice that you must enclose the range coordinates in quotation marks.)

The procedure in Listing 19.12 sets several font attributes for the specified range. Font is a property of the Range object and returns a reference to the Font object associated with the specified range. A Font object's properties are the same as the font attributes that you assign with the Font dialog: bold, italic, underline, and so on. The following list provides a sample of Font object properties; in each case, *Object* is a Range object. Use the Object Browser to see a full list of Font properties.

- *Object*.Font.Bold: Turns the bold font style on (**True**) or off (**False**).

- *Object*.Font.Italic: Turns the italic font style on (**True**) or off (**False**).

- *Object*.Font.Underline: Turns the underline font effect on or off; the value of the Underline property can be any one of these intrinsic constants (defined in the XlUnderlineStyle class): xlUnderlineStyleNone, xlUnderlineStyleSingle, xlUnderlineStyleDouble, xlUnderlineStyleSingleAccounting, or xlUnderlineStyleDoubleAccounting.

- *Object*.Font.Name: Sets the name of the font's typeface. You specify the value of the Name property as a string, "Arial", for example.

- *Object*.Font.Size: Sets the size of the font in points.

Tip

Many objects in Excel have a Font property that returns a Font object you can use to format text in that object: Range, Characters, Style, and the Excel application itself are only a few of the objects that have a Font property. Use the Object Browser to determine whether a specific object has a Font property.

19

Do

DO take advantage of the alternative syntax for the Range method that requires two arguments:

```
Object.Range(Cell1, Cell2)
```

As before, *Object* is the Worksheet object that contains the range. The *Cell1* argument defines the upper-left corner of the range and *Cell2* defines the lower-right corner. Each argument can be a cell address as text, a Range object consisting of a single cell, or an entire column or row.

The advantage of this syntax is that it separates the range corners into separate arguments, which enables you to modify each corner under procedural control. For example, you could set up variables named, for example, UpperLeft and LowerRight and return Range objects of different sizes, as in

```
Range(UpperLeft, LowerRight)
```

Using the `Cells` Method

Although you can use the `Range` method to return a single cell, the `Cells` method also does the job and gives you much greater flexibility.

Object.Cells(*RowIndex*, *ColumnIndex*)

Object is a reference to either the `Worksheet` or the `Range` object that contains the cell with which you want to work. If you omit *Object*, the method applies to the `ActiveSheet` object.

RowIndex is the row number of the cell. If *Object* is a worksheet, a *RowIndex* of 1 refers to row 1 on the sheet. If *Object* is a range, a *RowIndex* of 1 refers to the first row of the range.

ColumnIndex is the column of the cell. You can enter either a letter (as a literal constant or as a string variable) or a number to specify the column. If *Object* is a worksheet, a *ColumnIndex* of "A" or 1 refers to column A on the worksheet. If *Object* is a range, a *ColumnIndex* of "A" or 1 refers to the first column of the range.

Listing 19.13 shows an example of the `Cells` method.

INPUT   **LISTING 19.13**   USING THE `Cells` METHOD TO RETURN A CELL

```
 1:  Sub WriteNewData()
 2:  'Enters data from a user form dialog into a worksheet
 3:
 4:     Dim I As Integer
 5:     Dim DBNewRow As Integer
 6:     Dim NewRange As String
 7:
 8:     With Range("Database")
 9:        'find the new data row
10:        DBNewRow = .Row + .Rows.Count
11:
12:        'Enter dialog box data into cells in new row
13:        For I = 1 To .Columns.Count
14:           Cells(DBNewRow, (I + .Column) - 1).Value = _
15:              Listing13Form.Controls("txt" & CStr(I)).Text
16:        Next I
```

```
17:
18:        'extend the Database range
19:        NewRange = "=" & .Parent.Name & "!"
20:        NewRange = NewRange & Cells(.Row, .Column).Address & ":"
21:        NewRange = NewRange & _
22:                    Cells(DBNewRow, (.Column + .Columns.Count) -
                 ➥1).Address
23:        Names("Database").RefersTo = NewRange
24:     End With
25:  End Sub
```

ANALYSIS   This procedure is part of a database maintenance application. The user enters the database information into a user form custom dialog (similar to the one shown in Figure 19.1). The WriteNewData procedure is called from the OnClick event procedure of the Write New Data button in the dialog. The WriteNewData procedure writes the new data into the worksheet at the bottom of the database range and increases the database range to include the new data rows.

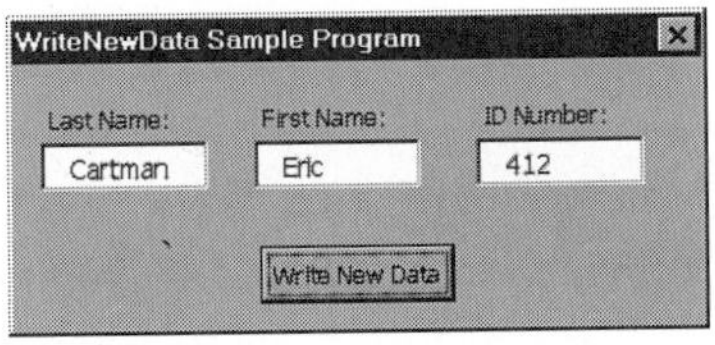

FIGURE 19.1

The WriteNewData *procedure in Listing 19.13 assumes you are entering data using a dialog like this one.*

Lines 4 through 6 declare the variables used in this procedure. Line 8 begins a **With** statement that specifies the range of cells currently referenced by the database name. Line 10 assigns the DBNewRow variable a value corresponding to the row immediately after the database range; this is the row where the new data should be stored.

The **For...Next** loop in lines 13 through 16 transfers values from the user form dialog to the worksheet. The loop counter (I) runs from 1 to the number of columns in the range, which is obtained by retrieving the Count property of the Columns collection of the Range object. (The Columns collection contains all the columns in the Range object, and its Count property returns the number of columns.)

Inside the loop, the Cells method (line 14) returns each cell in the new row and the cell's Value property is set to the appropriate edit box control's text. This code assumes each edit box control in the user form is named txt*N*, where *N* is the corresponding column number in the database range. Line 15 therefore assembles the name of the edit box control from which the data value is being transferred by concatenating the string equivalent of the current loop counter variable with the literal constant "txt". (The "Entering Values and Formulas" section later in this chapter has more information on the Value property.)

19

The definition of the database range now needs to be changed to include the new row. You can redefine the range referenced by a particular name by changing that name's RefersTo property. (Named ranges in a worksheet are Name objects and can be accessed through the Names collection of the worksheet.) The RefersTo property must contain a string in the form "=sheet!reference", where *sheet* is the name of the worksheet containing the named range and *reference* is an R1C1-style range address.

Lines 19 through 23 assemble a properly formatted string to specify the new database range: Line 19 adds the sheet name to the range address by using the Parent property of the Range object to obtain the name of the worksheet that contains that Range object. Next, line 20 adds the coordinates for the top left corner of the new range by using the Address property of the Cells object to return a string containing the address of the referenced cell: in this case, the same row and column currently referenced by the database range. Line 21 adds the coordinates for the bottom right corner of the new range by also using the Address property—this time for a cell referenced by the new row and the number of columns currently in the database range. Finally, line 23 assigns the new range definition to the RefersTo property of the database range—referenced through the Names collection.

Using the Offset Method

When you define your Range objects, you often don't know the specific range address to use. For example, you might need to refer to the cell that is two rows down from and one column to the right of the active cell. Although you could find the address of the active cell and calculate the address of the other cell, Excel VBA gives you an easier and more flexible way: the Offset method. Offset returns a Range object that is offset from a specified range by a certain number of rows and columns.

▼ SYNTAX

```
Object.Offset([RowOffset] [,ColumnOffset])
```

Object is a reference to the original Range object. *RowOffset* is the number of rows to offset *Object*. You can use a positive number (to move down), a negative number (to move up), or 0 (to use the same row). If you omit *RowOffset*, the default is 0.

ColumnOffset is the number of columns to offset *Object*. Again, you can use a positive number (to move right), a negative number (to move left), or 0 (to use the same column). If you omit *ColumnOffset*, the default is 0.

▲

Listing 19.14 shows a procedure that uses the Offset method.

INPUT **LISTING 19.14** USING THE Offset METHOD TO RETURN A RANGE

```
 1:   Sub SelectData()
 2:   'Selects the data area of a database range
 3:
 4:      Dim DBRows As Integer
 5:
 6:      Worksheets("Sheet1").Select
 7:      With Range("Database")
 8:         DBRows = .Rows.Count
 9:         .Offset(1, 0).Resize(DBRows - 1, .Columns.Count).Select
10:      End With
11:   End Sub
```

ANALYSIS This procedure selects the data area of a range named Database, that is, it selects a range presumed to include only data and to exclude column headings by omitting the first row of the named range from the selection. This is handy if you need to perform a global operation on the data, such as sorting or applying a format.

Line 6 selects the Sheet1 worksheet, and the **With** statement in line 7 specifies the Range object on that worksheet named Database. Line 8 obtains the number of rows in the range by using the Rows.Count property of the Range object, storing it in the DBRows variable.

In line 9, the Offset(1, 0) method returns a range that is offset from the Database range by one row down. Because this new range includes a (presumably) blank row below the Database range, you must eliminate this extra row. To do that, you can use the Resize property to change the size of the range:

Object.Resize([*RowSize*] [,*ColumnSize*])

Object is an object reference to the range you want to resize. *RowSize* is the number of rows in the returned range. *ColumnSize* is the number of columns in the returned range. In line 9, the Resize(DBRows - 1, .Columns.Count) expression removes the unneeded bottom row from the offset range.

The Select method in line 9 selects the new range. (The "Selecting a Range" section later in this chapter has more information on the Select method.)

19

Other Methods and Properties that Return Ranges

Range, Cells, and Offset are the most common methods for returning Range objects, but they are by no means the only ones. In Listing 19.14 you saw how the Resize method can return a range of a specific size. A few more methods and properties that return Range objects are

- [cellRef]. You can return a single cell by enclosing the cell reference in square brackets. For example, [A1].Font.Size = 16 sets the font in cell A1 to size 16. Notice that, in this case, no quotation marks are used around the cell reference (cellRef).

- Object.Rows(Index). This method returns a row in the worksheet or range specified by Object. If you omit Object, VBA uses ActiveSheet. Index is the row number. If Object is a worksheet, an Index of 1 refers to row 1 on the sheet. If Object is a range, an Index of 1 refers to the first row of the range.

- Object.EntireRow. This property returns the entire row or rows that contain the range specified by Object.

- Object.Columns(Index). This method returns a column in the worksheet or range specified by Object. If you omit Object, VBA uses ActiveSheet. Index is the column letter or number. If Object is a worksheet, an Index of "A" or 1 refers to column A on the sheet. If Object is a range, an Index of "A" or 1 refers to the first column of the range.

- Object.EntireColumn. This property returns the entire column or columns that contain the range specified by Object.

- Object.CurrentRegion. This property returns the *current region* of the range Object. The current region is defined as the area surrounding the current cell or range that is bounded by blank rows on the top and bottom, and blank columns on the left and right.

Working with Cells and Ranges

Now that you know how to return a Range object, you can take advantage of the long list of Range properties and methods. The next section examines a few of these properties and methods. Use the Object Browser to see all of the Range object's methods and properties and to access the online help text for the Range object.

Selecting a Cell or Range

To select a cell or range of cells, use the `Select` method:

`Object.Select`

`Object` is a reference to the `Range` object you want to select. Listing 19.15 shows an example.

INPUT **LISTING 19.15** USING THE `Select` METHOD TO SELECT A RANGE

```
1:   Sub CreateChart()
2:   'Creates a chart with data from the Sales range
3:
4:      With Workbooks("DAY19.XLS").Worksheets("Sheet2")
5:         .Activate
6:         .Range("Sales").Select
7:      End With
8:
9:      Charts.Add
10:  End Sub
```

ANALYSIS This procedure creates a new chart sheet from a selected range. Line 5 activates the `Workbooks("DAY19.XLS").Worksheets("Sheet2")` worksheet. Line 6 selects the range on the worksheet named `Sales`. Line 9 executes the `Charts` object's `Add` method to create the chart sheet.

Do
DO use the `Selection` property to return the `Range` object that is currently selected.

Don't
DON'T select a range if you don't have to. `Select` is one of the slowest of all VBA methods, so avoiding it wherever possible speeds up your code.

19

Working with Values and Formulas

Most of your VBA programs for Excel will utilize worksheet data in one form or another. For example, a procedure might need to read the contents of a cell to perform a data validation routine. Alternatively, your program might gather data by using a user form dialog, and you might need to transfer the data entered in the dialog's edit box controls into the appropriate worksheet cells. (See Listing 19.13 for an example of how to do this.)

If you need to get the contents of a cell or if you need to enter data into a range, VBA offers two Range object properties: Value and Formula. The syntax for each one is

```
Object.Value
```

```
Object.Formula
```

In both cases, Object represents an object reference to the Range object with which you want to work. To get the contents of a cell, follow these guidelines:

- If all you want is the cell's result, use the Value property. For example, if cell A1 contains the formula =2*2, Range("A1").Value returns 4.

- If you want the cell's formula, use the Formula property. For example, if Cell A1 contains the formula =2*2, Range("A1").Formula returns the text string =2*2.

To enter data in a cell or range, you can use Value or Formula interchangeably. Listing 19.16 shows several examples.

INPUT **LISTING 19.16** USING THE Value AND Formula METHODS TO ENTER DATA

```
1:   Sub CreateLoanPmtCalculator()
2:   'Creates a loan payment calculator on Sheet3
3:
4:      Worksheets("Sheet3").Select
5:
6:      With Range("A1")      'Enter labels
7:         .Value = "Loan Payment Calculator"
8:         .Font.Bold = True
9:         .Font.Italic = True
10:        .Font.Size = 18
11:        .Offset(1).Value = "Rate"
12:        .Offset(2).Value = "Period"
13:        .Offset(3).Value = "Amount"
14:        .Offset(5).Value = "Payment"
15:     End With
16:
17:     'Enter number formats and formula
18:     With Range("A1")
19:        .Offset(1, 1).NumberFormat = "0.00%"
20:        .Offset(3, 1).NumberFormat = "$#,##0_);[Red]($#,##0)"
21:        .Offset(5, 1).NumberFormat = "$#,##0.00_);[Red]($#,##0.00)"
22:        .Offset(5, 1).Formula = "=PMT($B$2/12, $B$3*12, $B$4)"
23:     End With
24:  End Sub
```

ANALYSIS   This procedure creates a simple loan payment calculator on `Sheet3` in the active workbook. The first **With** statement (line 6) uses cell A1 as a starting point. This cell's `Value` property is set to contain the text `"Loan Payment Calculator"` (line 7), and some font options are set in lines 8 through 10. The next four lines (11–14) use the `Value` property of cells A2, A3, A4, and A6 to enter the labels. Notice the use of the `Offset` method to work with these cells.

The second **With** statement (line 18) also uses cell A1. The actions in this procedure have been divided into two different **With** statements for extra clarity; there is no technical requirement that they be divided this way. The next three lines (19–21) set the numeric format of cells B2, B4, and B6. This is accomplished by using the `NumberFormat` property of the referenced range:

`Object.NumberFormat = FormatString`

`Object` is an object reference to the cell or range to format and `FormatString` is a text string that specifies the formatting.

Finally, line 22 uses the `Formula` property to enter the payment formula in cell B6.

Defining a Range Name

Range names in VBA are `Name` objects. To define them, you use the `Add` method for the `Names` collection, which usually is the collection of defined names in a workbook. Here is an abbreviated syntax for the `Names` collection's `Add` method. (This method has a total of nine arguments, so use the Object Browser to see all the available arguments and to access the online help for full details on the `Add` method.)

▼ SYNTAX

`Names.Add(Name, RefersTo, RefersToR1C1)`

The `Name` argument is any string expression specifying the name that you want to use for the new named range. The `RefersTo` and `RefersToR1C1` arguments describe the range to which the name refers. Use these arguments as follows:

- `RefersTo`: Use this argument to enter the range description in A1-style, for example, `"=Sales!$A$1:$C$6"`.
- `RefersToR1C1`: Use this argument when the range description either is in R1C1-style, for example, `"=Sales!R1C1:R6C3"`, or when the range description is a method or property that returns a range, for example, `Range("A1:C6")` or `Selection`.

▲

Listing 19.17 shows an example of the `Names` collection's `Add` method.

19

INPUT   **LISTING 19.17**   NAMING A RANGE USING THE NAMES OBJECT'S ADD METHOD

```
 1:  Sub CreateNamedRange()
 2:  'Creates a named range, using coordinates and name
 3:  'entered by the user
 4:
 5:    Const strTaskName = "Name a Range"
 6:
 7:    Dim strTopLeft As String
 8:    Dim strBottomRight As String
 9:    Dim RngName As String
10:
11:    Worksheets("Sheet1").Select
12:
13:    'get the range coordinates and name
14:    strTopLeft = InputBox(prompt:="Enter the top left corner " & _
15:                              "in R1C1 format:", _
16:                        Title:=strTaskName)
17:    strBottomRight = InputBox(prompt:="Enter the bottom right " & _
18:                                  "corner in R1C1 format:", _
19:                          Title:=strTaskName)
20:    RngName = InputBox(prompt:="Enter the name for the " & _
21:                            "new range: ", _
22:                      Title:=strTaskName)
23:
24:    'define new range name
25:    Names.Add Name:=RngName, RefersTo:="=Sheet1!" & _
26:                                  strTopLeft & ":" & _
27:                                  strBottomRight
28:    'select the new range
29:    Range(RngName).Select
30:  End Sub
```

ANALYSIS   This procedure isn't very sophisticated; it just uses several InputBox statements to get the coordinates of a range (upper-left corner and lower-right corner) and the name for the range. The procedure then creates a named range using the supplied coordinates and name.

Lines 5 through 9 declare the constants and variables used by the CreateNamedRange procedure. Line 11 selects a worksheet, and lines 14 through 22 contain the InputBox statements to get information from the user.

Line 25 is the important statement in this procedure; it uses the Add method of the Names collection to add a new named range. The range's new name is supplied by the RngName variable and the actual range of cells is supplied as a string in the RefersToR1C1 argument. When VBA executes this statement, a new named range is created for the specified cells and is added to the collection of names in the workbook. To highlight the newly created range, line 29 uses the Select method to select the new range.

Cutting, Copying, and Clearing Data

If your procedures must do some basic worksheet editing chores, the Cut, Copy, and Clear methods can handle the job.

The Cut and Copy methods use identical syntax:

Object.Cut([*Destination*])

Object.Copy([*Destination*])

Object is an object reference to the Range object you want to cut or copy. *Destination* is the cell or range where you want the cut or copied range to be pasted. If you omit the *Destination* argument, the data is cut or copied to the Windows Clipboard.

To remove data from a range, you can use the Cut method with or without the destination argument, or you can use any of the following methods:

Object.Clear

Object.ClearContents

Object.ClearFormats

Object.ClearNotes

In each case, *Object* is an object reference to the range you want to clear. The Clear method removes everything from the range: content, formatting, and notes. ClearContents clears the contents of *Object*. ClearFormats clears the formatting of *Object*. ClearNotes clears the notes from *Object*.

Listing 19.18 shows examples of the Cut, Copy, and Clear methods.

INPUT **LISTING 19.18** USING THE Cut, Copy, AND Clear METHODS

```
1:  Sub CopyToTempSheet()
2:  'Copies data to a temporary worksheet
3:
4:      Dim LastCell As Range
5:      Dim oldSheet As String
6:
7:      Application.ScreenUpdating = False
8:
9:      oldSheet = ActiveSheet.Name        'current sheet name
10:     Worksheets.Add                     'create temp worksheet
```

continues

LISTING **19.18**   CONTINUED

```
11:    ActiveSheet.Name = "Temporary"
12:    Worksheets("Sheet1").Select        'select Sheet1
13:
14:    Set LastCell = Range("A1").SpecialCells(xlLastCell)
15:    With Worksheets("Temporary")
16:       .Cells.Clear
17:       Range("A1", LastCell).Copy Destination:=.Range("A1")
18:    End With
19:
20:    Sheets(oldSheet).Select   'restore original sheet
21:    Application.ScreenUpdating = True
22: End Sub
23:
24:
25: Sub RestoreFromTempSheet()
26: 'Restores data from temporary worksheet
27:
28:    Dim LastCell As Range
29:    Dim oldSheet As String
30:
31:    Application.ScreenUpdating = False
32:    oldSheet = ActiveSheet.Name
33:
34:    Worksheets("Sheet1").Select
35:    With Worksheets("Temporary")
36:       Set LastCell = .Range("A1").SpecialCells(xlLastCell)
37:       .Range("A1", LastCell).Cut Destination:=Range("A1")
38:    End With
39:
40:    Sheets(oldSheet).Select
41:    Application.ScreenUpdating = True
42: End Sub
```

ANALYSIS   The first procedure, CopyToTempSheet, adds a worksheet named Temporary and selects the worksheet named Sheet1. Next, the procedure copies all the data from the active worksheet and stores it in the temporary worksheet. This procedure uses the SpecialCells(xlLastCell) method (line 14) to return the last cell in the active sheet and stores the resulting Range object reference in the LastCell variable. Then, inside a **With** statement, two actions are performed on the Temporary worksheet. Line 16 uses Clear to clear the entire sheet. (The Cells method without any arguments returns every cell in a sheet.) Line 17 uses Copy to copy the range defined by A1 in the upper-left corner and LastCell in the lower-right corner. The destination is cell A1 in the Temporary worksheet.

The second procedure, RestoreFromTempSheet, essentially reverses the process. This time, LastCell is set to the last cell in the Temporary worksheet (line 36). The range from A1 to LastCell is cut and pasted to cell A1 in the active worksheet (line 37). (The active worksheet is Sheet1, selected in line 34.)

Do

DO use the Paste or PasteSpecial methods with a Worksheet or Range object to paste data from the Clipboard to a worksheet. The syntax for the Paste method is

```
Object.Paste ([Destination], [Link])
```

Object is any valid object reference to a worksheet. The optional argument *Destination* is any range object. The data is pasted beginning at the top-left corner of the range. If you omit the *Destination* argument, the data is pasted to the current selection. You can specify the *Destination* argument only if the contents of the Clipboard can be pasted to a range; using the *Destination* argument is the same as using the Edit, Paste command. The optional *Link* argument, if **True**, indicates that a link should be established to the data source; using the *Link* argument is the same as using the Edit, Paste Special command and checking the Link check box. You cannot use the *Destination* and *Link* arguments together in the same statement.

DO remember that the various Clear methods delete the data outright; it is *not* preserved on the Clipboard. Use the Cut method with no arguments to remove data from the worksheet and place the data on the Clipboard for later use.

Summary

Today's lesson showed you how to use Visual Basic for Applications to control Excel objects. You learned basic techniques for working with Excel's Workbook, Worksheet, and Range objects. You learned that you use the Workbooks collection to return a specific open Workbook object. You learned how to use the Open method to open a workbook, the Workbooks.Add method to create a new workbook, the Save method to save a workbook, and the Close method to close a workbook.

To return a Worksheet object, you learned how to use the Worksheets collection along with several important Worksheet methods and properties: Activate (for activating a worksheet), Worksheets.Add (for creating a new worksheet), Name (for returning or setting a worksheet's name), and Delete (for deleting a worksheet).

You also learned that Excel provides a number of methods for returning a worksheet Range object. The most common is the Range method, but you can also use Cells (for returning a single cell) and Offset (for returning a range offset from a specified range). Worksheet Range objects have dozens of properties and methods, and you learned about

19

a few of them. These included `Select` (for selecting a range), `Value` and `Formula` (for returning cell contents and entering values and formulas), `Names.Add` (for defining range names), as well as `Cut`, `Copy`, and `Clear`.

Q&A

Q I want to create a new Excel workbook based on an Excel template, so I'm using the `Template` argument in the `Workbooks.Add` method. Unfortunately, Excel keeps giving me an error. What am I doing wrong?

A The likely problem is that your template isn't stored in Excel's XLStart folder. When you use the `Template` argument, Excel looks in the XLStart folder for the template file. If it doesn't find the file there, Excel then looks in the alternate start-up folder (if there is one); if Excel still can't find the specified template file, Excel displays an error message. You can solve the problem in one of two ways: You can change your VBA code to specify the full path for the template you want to use, or you can designate the folder that contains the template file as your alternate startup folder.

There are two techniques that you can use to create an alternate startup folder:

- Use the Tools, Options command, select the General tab in the Options dialog, and then enter the folder in the Alternate Startup File Location edit box.
- Set the `Application` object's `AltStartupPath` property equal to a text string that defines the folder.

Whichever technique you use to designate the alternate startup folder, you'll need to restart Excel to put the change into effect.

Q The `Workbook` objects' `Name` property returns the name of the workbook as it appears in the title bar. Is there any way to get the full pathname of the workbook, including the drive and folder where the file is stored?

A Yes. You just need to use the `FullName` property:

`Object.FullName`

Here, `Object` is a reference to the workbook for which you want the pathname. If all you want is the workbook's drive and folder, use the `Workbook` object's `Path` property instead.

Q How do I format the font size and typeface in a `Range` object?

A Use the `Range` object's `Font` property, which returns a `Font` object through which you can set the range's font characteristics. A `Font` object's properties are the same as the font attributes that you assign with the Font dialog: bold, italic, underline, and so on. Use the Object Browser to see a full list of `Font` properties.

Q **What if I want to print an Excel workbook or worksheet from a VBA procedure?**

A No problem. Just use the `PrintOut` method with the following syntax:

`Object.PrintOut([From] [,To] [,Copies] [,Preview])`

`Object` is a reference to any printable object, such as a `Workbook`, `Worksheet`, or `Range`. `From` is an optional argument that specifies the first page to print. `To` is also optional; it specifies the last page to print. `Copies` determines the number of copies you want. If you omit `Copies`, Excel prints one copy. `Preview` determines whether the print preview screen is displayed before printing. The screen is displayed if `Preview` is **True**; the screen is not displayed if `Preview` is **False** or is omitted. The `PrintOut` method also has arguments to specify the active printer and whether to print to a file. Refer to Excel VBA's online help for more information on the `PrintOut` method.

Workshop

Answers are in Appendix A.

Quiz

1. What is the difference between a `Workbook` object's `Save` method, the `SaveAs` method, and the `SaveCopyAs` method?

2. What happens if you use the `Save` method on a new, unsaved `Workbook` object?

3. When you use the `Copy` or `Move` methods on a worksheet, what happens if you omit both the `Before` and `After` arguments?

4. What is the difference between the `Worksheets` collection and the `Sheets` collection?

5. What are the three main methods for returning a worksheet range and how do they differ?

6. The following two procedures perform similar tasks. Can you figure out what they're doing?

```
Sub FillAcross()
  Dim SheetArray As Variant
  SheetArray = Array("Sheet1", "Sheet2", "Sheet3")
  Worksheets("Sheet1").Range("A1").Value = "Sheet Title"
  Worksheets(SheetArray).FillAcrossSheets _
    Range:=Worksheets("Sheet1").Range("A1")
End Sub
```

19

```
Sub SpearTest()
  Dim SheetArray As Variant
  SheetArray = Array("Sheet1", "Sheet2", "Sheet3")
  Worksheets(SheetArray).Select
  Worksheets("Sheet1").Range("A1").Activate
  Selection.Value = "Sheet Title"
End Sub
```

7. What is the difference between the `Value` and `Formula` properties for returning the contents of a cell?

8. Under which circumstances should you use the `RefersToR1C1` argument in the `Names.Add` method instead of `RefersTo`?

9. Name the five methods available that you can use to remove data from a range.

Exercises

1. Write a procedure that saves every open workbook. The code should check for new, unnamed workbooks. If the workbook is unnamed, the procedure should ask whether the workbook should be saved. If so, the procedure should display the Save As dialog to enable the user to supply a filename and storage location.

2. Excel doesn't enable you to cut or copy a *multiple selection*, that is, a selection that includes multiple, noncontiguous worksheet ranges. Write a procedure that enables you to cut or copy multiple selections to the same position in a different worksheet. (HINT: The `Areas` method returns a collection that consists of all the ranges in a multiple selection.)

3. **BUG BUSTER:** The following procedure executes three `Names.Add` methods. None of these statements causes an error, but each one creates unexpected results. Can you see why?

```
Sub NameTests()
  Names.Add Name:="Test1", RefersTo:="Sheet4!$A$1"
  Names.Add Name:="Test2",
RefersTo:=Worksheets("Sheet4").Range("A1:E10")
  Names.Add Name:="Test3", RefersTo:="='June Sales'!A1:A10"
End Sub
```

4. Listing 19.13 showed you how to enter the results of a custom user form dialog into a new row of a worksheet database. Write a procedure that performs the opposite function. It should load the contents of a database record—a row—into the edit boxes of a custom user form dialog. As in Listing 19.13, assume that there is a one-to-one correspondence between the database fields and the dialog's edit boxes; you don't have to create the dialog user form.

DAY 20

Working with Other Applications

This lesson shows you how to use Visual Basic for Applications to work with and control an application other than Excel. For example, you can use Excel VBA to control operations in Word, Access, Outlook, and other Microsoft Office components, as well as applications outside the Microsoft Office family. You can use Excel VBA to control any application that supports OLE or Automation. The final sections of today's lesson include information on how to control applications that don't support OLE or Automation. In today's lesson, you'll learn

- What OLE and Automation are and what you can do with them.
- How to link and embed objects in a worksheet.
- How to work with linked and embedded objects.
- How to use Automation to control other applications.
- How to start other applications from within a VBA procedure.
- How to send keystrokes to other running applications from Excel VBA.
- How to declare and use dynamic-link library (DLL) functions.

What Is Automation and OLE?

Before you learn how to use Visual Basic for Applications to work with Automation objects and OLE, you need to understand what Automation is, what OLE is, and what you can do with them.

A Brief History of OLE

Object linking and embedding—abbreviated OLE and pronounced *oh-lay*—enables users to create a *compound document*. A compound document is any file that contains data from more than one application. For example, you can create a worksheet in Excel that contains a Word document or pictures from a paint program in addition to its native numbers and formulas; such a worksheet is a compound document. OLE makes it easier and simpler for applications to interact with one another.

With early versions of Microsoft Windows, you could exchange data between applications only by using the Clipboard. You copied the data from one program to the Clipboard and then pasted it from the Clipboard into another application. If you needed to make changes to the data, you had to open the original application, open the appropriate file, make the changes, and then repeat the entire copying and pasting process.

Although using the Clipboard to transfer information between applications is better than not being able to transfer information at all, it still isn't the most efficient way to work. Microsoft introduced Dynamic Data Exchange (DDE) as a way of reducing the number of steps involved in transferring and updating information between two different applications. In a DDE exchange, the process begins by creating data in one application—the *server*—and then copying that data to the Clipboard. An application that supports DDE—the *client*—uses the Paste Link command to paste data from the Clipboard into another application. The Paste Link command establishes a communications link between the two applications. This communications link provides a means for the data to be subsequently updated from the DDE server to the DDE client, more or less automatically.

DON'T

DON'T confuse the terms *client* and *server*. These terms are used throughout this chapter, so it's important that you understand what they mean. The client is always the application that receives the data; the server is always the application that supplies the data. An analogy to keep in mind is the relationship between a customer and a business. The customer (that is, the client) requests goods and services (data) from the business that provides those goods and services (the server).

DDE was a significant improvement over the original copy-and-paste technique, but it still had deficiencies. First, data pasted from the Clipboard, regardless of whether it is pasted with a DDE link, is simply inserted into the client application with little or no formatting. Second, to make changes in DDE linked data, you must switch to or start the server application for the linked data. At best, this situation is inconvenient, but it poses special difficulties if you're not sure which application is the server for the DDE linked data or if you can't remember which server document contains the source data.

To address these issues, Microsoft took a new approach to sharing data: Object Linking and Embedding. With OLE, data pasted from the server application appears in the client document as an *object*. Each object can be pasted in one of two ways: *linked* or *embedded*. Both types of OLE objects store the OLE server's name and any information that the server needs. The features of the two types of OLE object are as follows:

- *Linked:* The object contains an image of the server data and maintains a link between the client and the server, much as DDE does. The original data remains in a separate file under the control of the server application. If the data changes, the link ensures that the client object is updated automatically. For example, if you link a Word document to a worksheet, Excel offers to update the link each time you open the workbook containing the link. Usually, OLE can maintain the link even if the server data file (such as a Word document) is renamed or moved to a different disk folder. If the server data file is deleted, Excel displays an error message if you try to edit the linked object, but otherwise displays the last image of the server data, without displaying an error message. In general, you should paste an object as linked when other applications might require access to the same data file.

- *Embedded:* The object contains a standalone version of the server data, essentially a copy of the server data. No link is established between the server and the client because none is needed. The client object contains not only the data but also all the underlying information associated with the server application, such as the name of the application, the file structure, and formatting codes. In general, you should paste an object as embedded when you'll be working with the data only from inside the client application.

20

Note You can manually manage the OLE links in a workbook by using the Edit, Links command to display the Links dialog. The Links dialog enables you to specify whether a link is updated automatically or manually, change the source of a link, update links immediately, and other actions related to managing linked data. Refer to Excel's online help for more information on the Links dialog.

Another advantage of OLE is that, in many cases, you don't need a server document. You can create the data by starting the server application within the client application and then inserting the data into the client document as an embedded object. This means, for example, you could insert an empty Word document into an Excel worksheet as an embedded OLE object and *then* type the letter, memo, note, or whatever.

Whether you link or embed data, an OLE object retains the original formatting of the data. This means that OLE objects appear in the client document exactly as they do in the server application. An OLE object stores the name of its server application and, if the OLE object is linked, the name of the server file the object came from. This means that you never need to know which application and which file are the source of the embedded data. You simply double-click the object: OLE loads the server application and, if necessary, opens the correct source data file.

OLE also gives you the following advantages:

- *Drag-and-drop data sharing.* You can move information between two open OLE applications simply by dragging selected data from one application and dropping it in the other. If you want to copy the data, hold down the Ctrl key while dragging.

- *In-place inserting.* If you insert an OLE object from within the client application, the client activates in-place inserting. With in-place inserting, certain features of the client window—for example, toolbars and menu commands—are temporarily replaced by the OLE server's features; the server application is not displayed in a separate window. In other words, the *document* stays the same and the surrounding application changes.

- *In-place editing.* With in-place editing, when you double-click an OLE object to edit it, the object remains in the document and the client window changes as it does with in-place inserting.

- *Automation.* For a VBA programmer, the most exciting development in OLE is Automation. (Automation was first known as *OLE Automation.*) With Automation, an application's objects (such as Workbook, Worksheet, Chart, and so on) are *exposed*—that is, made visible—to other Automation applications. In particular, an application's exposed objects are available to VBA. This makes it possible for you to write VBA procedures in one application that control objects in a different application. For example, a VBA procedure in Excel can use Automation to control application objects in another application, such as Microsoft Word, Microsoft Access, or Microsoft Project. Any application that supports Automation exposes some or all of its objects, whether or not it also supports VBA. This means that you can use your VBA programs to control objects in applications that do not have VBA, but *do* function as an OLE or Automation server.

How Does Visual Basic for Applications Fit In?

Microsoft designed Visual Basic for Applications with Automation and OLE in mind; in fact, many of the application objects that you work with in VBA are also Automation objects (known as Automation *components*). In particular, the host application—such as Excel—typically provides you with special objects and object collections that enable you to access OLE features in other applications. These objects and their related collections have many properties and methods that enable you to create and work with either linked or embedded data. In this lesson, you'll learn about the OLE-related objects and collections in Excel.

In addition, VBA can utilize objects in other applications that support Automation. This means that an Excel VBA procedure, for example, can access and manipulate objects created by another Automation application just as though the VBA procedure is working in the other application itself. VBA's Automation techniques are examined later in this lesson.

Looking Up an Object's Class Type

In Day 7, you learned that objects in a VBA host application are divided into various classes. The objects that applications expose for OLE and as Automation components are also divided into various classes.

Frequently, you'll need to specify an OLE object's or Automation component's class before you can invoke or use that object in your VBA code. By specifying the object class, you give VBA the information it needs to locate the object's definition and to execute the object's methods. In order to specify an object's class type—also called the *programmatic ID*—you first need to know what that object's class type is.

> **Note**
>
> An OLE object's or Automation component's class indicates exactly what kind of object it is: an Excel worksheet, a Word document, an Access database, and so on. Each class has a unique name and identifier code that designates its specific OLE or Automation object class. Windows uses the class type to determine which application is the server for a particular linked or embedded OLE object and to determine where the code resources for Automation objects can be found.

20

Windows maintains a *Registry database* that contains, among other things, information about the applications installed on your system, including specific information about the Automation components and OLE objects they expose. One of the secrets to how OLE and Automation work is the fact that the Windows Registry lists all the classes of objects exposed by various applications or libraries and keeps track of which executable files supply the resources for those object classes. When your VBA application needs the services of an Automation component, VBA asks the Windows operating system to execute the correct code for that object; Windows does so based on the object's class type.

To find out the programmatic ID of any Automation component or OLE object available on your system, you can look up the object's class type in the Windows Registry database. Alternatively, you can use the Microsoft System Information applet to get information about the programmatic ID of Automation components and OLE objects available on your computer system. The next few paragraphs explain how to use either technique to look up an object's class type.

Using the Windows Registry

The Windows Registry database contains complete information about your system's hardware and software configuration. The Registry database actually consists of several files: System.dat, User.dat, and Policy.pol. The Policy.pol file is an optional component used in Windows network configurations. Every Windows system will have the System.dat and User.dat files. The Windows Registry Editor reads the separate data files simultaneously and displays them as if they were a single database file.

Note

The Windows 95/98 Registry database replaces the WIN.INI, SYSTEM.INI, and REG.DAT files used by previous versions of Windows.

Starting the Registry Editor

To view the contents of the Registry database, you need to use the Registry Editor utility program provided with Windows 95/98. (The Registry Editor is typically installed in the Windows folder, but is not placed on the Windows Start menu.) To start the Registry Editor program, follow these steps:

1. From the Windows Start menu, choose the Run command.
2. In the Open edit box, type **C:\Windows\Regedit.exe** (assuming Windows is installed in the Windows folder on drive C) and then choose OK. Windows starts the Registry Editor, which displays the window shown in Figure 20.1. The exact appearance of the tree diagram on your system might be different depending on your specific system's configuration.

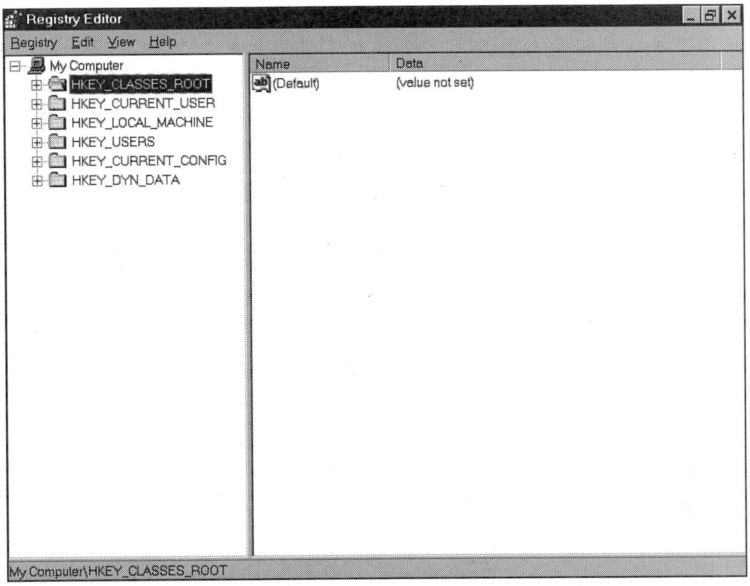

FIGURE 20.1

The Registry Editor window contains a tree diagram of the data about your computer's software and hardware.

The Registry Editor displays a tree diagram of the Registry database's contents in the left pane of the window and the specific data contained by the selected database entry in the right pane of the window. It is normal for many of the tree branches in the Registry database to show (value not set) in the Data column of the right window pane, as does the HKEY_CLASSES_ROOT branch in Figure 20.1. This doesn't mean that there is no data entered into that branch of the database; instead, it usually means that the selected branch of the Registry database tree leads to additional branches or entries in the Registry.

Finding Object Classes in the Registry Database

The Registry stores information about Automation components and OLE objects in the HKEY_CLASSES_ROOT branch of the database tree, which is shown selected in Figure 20.1. To view the registered OLE and Automation object classes on your system, follow these steps:

1. Click the square box to the left of the HKEY_CLASSES_ROOT branch of the tree diagram to expand that branch. The Registry Editor now displays a list of all the registered file types and OLE objects. (This list is usually *very* long.)

2. Scroll through the tree diagram in the left pane of the Registry Editor window until you find the names of the registered OLE object classes. (Because there are many different file extensions and because they alphabetize before most of the OLE object class names, you might need to scroll quite a bit before reaching the OLE object class names.)

20

You can recognize OLE object class types in the Registry because they usually begin with the name of the server application. Figure 20.2 shows the expanded HKEY_CLASS-ES_ROOT branch of the Registry database scrolled to the point where Excel OLE objects and Automation components appear in the list. The Excel.Application.9 object class is shown selected in Figure 20.2; this object class represents the Excel application, itself. (Excel 2000 is Excel version 9; Excel 97 is Excel version 8).

FIGURE 20.2

The
HKEY_CLASSES_ROOT
branch of the Registry database contains the registered OLE object classes for your system.

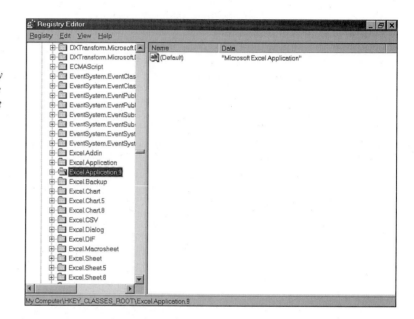

Notice that the data shown in the right pane of the Registry Editor window in Figure 20.2 gives the name of the selected object class: "Microsoft Excel Application". Notice also the other Excel OLE objects and Automation components visible in the left pane of the Registry Editor window: Excel.Addin, Excel.Chart.8, Excel.Sheet.8, Excel.Template, and so on. Each of these entries is the name of an OLE or Automation object; this is the name you should use when you need to specify the object's class type.

After you find the object class you want to use in the Registry database, make a note of the object's class name for future use. Table 20.1 lists the class types for a few common objects.

TABLE 20.1 CLASS TYPES FOR COMMON OBJECTS

Object	Class Type
Microsoft Access Application	Access.Application
Microsoft Excel Application	Excel.Application
Excel Chart	Excel.Chart
Excel Worksheet	Excel.Sheet
Microsoft Graph Chart	MSGraph.Chart
MS PowerPoint Presentation	PowerPoint.Show
MS PowerPoint Slide	PowerPoint.Slide
MS Project Project	MSProject.Project
Microsoft Word Application	Word.Application
MS Word Document	Word.Document
MS Word Picture	Word.Picture
MS WordArt	MSWordArt
Package (Object Packager)	Package
Paintbrush Picture	PBrush
Bitmap image (MS Paint Picture)	Paint.Picture
Wave Sound	SoundRec

Do

DO check an application's documentation or its developer's technical support department to find out whether that specific application supports OLE or is an Automation component.

Don't

DON'T edit, rename, or otherwise alter the contents of the Registry database unless you are a Windows expert. Incorrect or missing entries in the Registry database can prevent your computer from starting or operating correctly.

DON'T assume that every entry you see in the Registry database has full OLE or Automation capabilities. Some are only OLE servers, such as Microsoft Draw. Some are only OLE clients. Others don't do OLE at all.

20

Using the System Information Applet

Another way to get information about the Automation components and OLE objects installed on your computer system is to use the Microsoft System Information applet that is provided with Microsoft Office. (An *applet* is a small-scale application that performs a single task, such as the Windows Calculator utility.)

You can access the System Information applet in two ways:

- Through the Help, About command available in any Microsoft Office application.
- By running the Msinfo32.exe program stored in the \Program Files\Common Files\Microsoft Shared\MSInfo folder on your hard drive.

To start Microsoft System Information from the Help, About command, follow these steps:

1. In any MS Office application (such as Excel), choose the Help, About menu command. The application displays its About dialog, which shows the application's name and version and some copyright information about the application. The specific appearance of the About dialog varies from application to application, but each About dialog contains OK, System Info, and Tech Support buttons.

2. Click the System Info button in the About dialog. The application launches the Microsoft System Information applet, which displays a window similar to the one shown in Figure 20.3, which has been maximized to occupy the entire screen.

 Tip

> The Help, About command in the VB Editor also displays an About dialog that contains the System Info button to activate the System Information applet.

The System Information applet displays a tree diagram of some of your system's configuration information in the left pane of its window. The right pane of the System Information window displays the specific information for the category selected in the left pane. Clicking the square box at the left of entries in the tree diagram expands or collapses that branch of the tree.

Figure 20.3 shows the OLE Registration branch of the information tree expanded and the Registry Settings sub-branch selected. The right pane displays a list of all OLE objects that are installed in your system's Registry database. Notice that the class type ID for Excel worksheets (Excel.Sheet.8) and Word documents (Word.Document.8) is visible in the Object list of the System Information applet. The Excel and Word application objects, however, aren't listed.

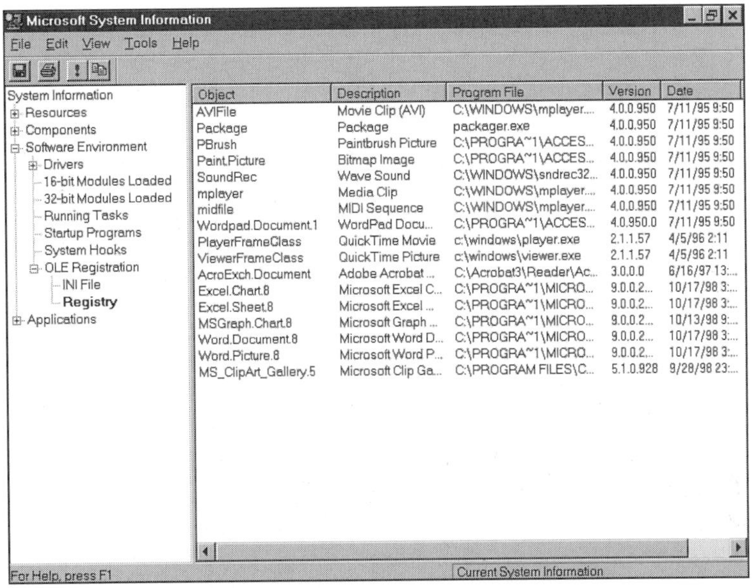

FIGURE 20.3

The Microsoft System Information applet enables you to view a list of installed OLE objects.

The information in the System Information window isn't as complete as the information you can obtain directly from the Registry database, but using the System Information applet is much simpler, and less risky, than using the Registry Editor. For many purposes, looking up an object's class type in the System Information applet is faster and easier than using the Registry database.

Adding Linked and Embedded Objects

OLE adds powerful features to your application. The price that end users pay for this advanced technology is added complexity. This is especially true for novice users, who might be uncomfortable with the various choices available in a typical OLE operation. For example, if you've copied data from an OLE server application, the client's Paste Special command gives you a number of choices: You can paste the information as an object or as a picture or text (depending on the data), you can paste the data linked or unlinked, and you can paste the data as an icon or in full view.

You can use VBA procedures that manipulate OLE objects to simplify tasks for your program's users because VBA gives you control over each of these decisions at the procedural level. For example, you can give your users a single command or toolbar button that creates a specified OLE object, but hides all the details and choices involved in creating that OLE object. The next sections show you how to create OLE objects with VBA.

20

Understanding the `Shape` and `OLEFormat` Objects

In Excel, `Shape` objects exist in a worksheet's *drawing layer*. The drawing layer is the portion of a worksheet that contains lines, rectangles, bitmap pictures, frames, and other drawing shapes. It is called a *layer* because it exists independently of the worksheet data, but is displayed on top of the worksheet in much the same way that architects and engineers use clear sheets to create overlapping layers on their plans and schematics. Objects in the drawing layer can be anchored or otherwise related to a particular location in the worksheet.

A `Shape` object can be an OLE object, a freeform drawing object, an Autoshape object, or a picture object. This lesson concentrates only on `Shape` objects used to store OLE objects.

Each `Shape` object has a property—`OLEFormat`—that returns an `OLEFormat` object. The `OLEFormat` object contains information about the OLE characteristics of the `Shape` object. The `OLEFormat` object has a `ProgId` property that stores the programmatic ID for that particular OLE object.

The next few sections of this lesson explain how to add OLE objects from varying sources to the `Shapes` collection.

Using the `AddOLEObject` Method of the `Shapes` Collection

To add an OLE object to Excel's `Shapes` collection, use the `AddOLEObject` method. You can use the `AddOLEObject` method to add either linked or embedded OLE objects to the `Shapes` collection. This section explains how to use the `AddOLEObject` method and how this method differs between Word and Excel.

Excel's `AddOLEObject` method has this syntax:

```
Object.AddOLEObject([ClassType], [FileName], [Link], [DisplayAsIcon],
                    [IconFileName], [IconIndex], [IconLabel], [Left],
                    [Top], [Width], [Height])
```

`Object` is any expression that provides a valid reference to a `Shapes` collection. Use the `Worksheet.Shapes` property to return a reference to a `Shapes` collection. The following list summarizes the `AddOLEObject` method's arguments:

- `ClassType`: This optional argument is a string expression specifying the class name of the object you want to insert. Use this argument when you want to insert a new (blank or empty) OLE object. For example, to insert an empty Word document into an Excel worksheet, use the string `Word.Document` for the `ClassType` argument.

▼

(The section "Looking Up an Object's Class Type" earlier in this lesson explains how to determine the class type of various OLE objects.) You must include either the *ClassType* argument or the *FileName* argument when you use the AddOLEObject method.

- *FileName*: This optional argument is a string expression specifying the filename of the object you want to insert; the filename must have an extension corresponding to a registered OLE server application. Use the *FileName* argument to insert an existing file as an OLE object. For example, if you want to insert an existing Word document file into an Excel worksheet, you might use a string such as C:\Accounts\MyWords.doc as the *FileName* argument (assuming the file you want to insert is named MyWords.doc and is located in a folder named Accounts). If you use the *ClassType* argument, the *FileName* argument is ignored.

- *Link*: This optional argument indicates whether the object created from *FileName* is linked or embedded. If **True**, the OLE object specified by *FileName* is linked. If **False** (the default), the OLE object specified by *FileName* is embedded. (Embedding an object creates an independent copy of the object.) If you specify the *ClassType*, the *Link/LinkToFile* argument must be **False** or omitted.

- *DisplayAsIcon*: This optional argument determines how the object is displayed. If **True**, the object is displayed onscreen as an icon. If **False** or omitted, the object is displayed in its normal form.

- *IconFileName*: Use this optional argument only if *DisplayAsIcon* is **True**. *IconFileName* is a string specifying the name of the file that contains the icon you want to display for the inserted OLE object. If you omit *IconFileName* or the specified file doesn't contain any icons, the default icon for the OLE class is used.

- *IconIndex*: Some files contain more than one icon; use the *IconIndex* argument to select which icon in the file you want to display. Icon numbering starts at 0: the first icon in a file is 0, the second is 1, and so on. Use *IconIndex* only if *DisplayAsIcon* is **True** and you've included the *IconFileName* argument. If you specify an icon number that doesn't exist, the icon numbered 1 (that is, the second icon in the file) is used. The default value for the *IconIndex* argument is 0.

- *IconLabel*: Use this optional argument (only if *DisplayAsIcon* is **True**) to customize the label for the OLE object's icon. The *IconLabel* argument can be any string expression.

- *Left* and *Top*: These optional arguments set the position of the object's top-left corner, in points, from the top-left edges of the worksheet, *not* the screen. The object in the Shapes collection is positioned using point measurements from the

▼

20

▼   left and top edges of the worksheet so that the object will both display and print in
      the same relative location. The default value for both *Left* and *Top* is 0, that is,
      flush with the left and top edges of the worksheet.

   • *Width* and *Height*: These optional arguments set the initial width and height of the
     OLE object, measured in points. Again, the object's size is measured in points so
     that it will both display and print with the same relative size. The default values for
     the *Width* and *Height* arguments are chosen depending on the object being inserted
     and whether you choose to display it as an icon.

▲   The next few sections show you how to use the AddOLEObject method.

Do

DO remember that only Excel's Worksheet and Chart objects can contain Shapes collections.

DON'T

DON'T forget that you use the Shapes property of the Worksheet and Chart objects to
return the Shapes collection belonging to that particular object.

Inserting a New Embedded Object

To insert a new embedded object into a worksheet, you must execute the AddOLEObject
method of the Shapes collection and use the ClassType argument. Listing 20.1 provides
one example by inserting a new WordPad document object into an Excel worksheet.

INPUT   **LISTING 20.1**   USING THE AddOLEObject METHOD TO EMBED A NEW OBJECT
             IN AN EXCEL WORKSHEET

```
 1:   Sub InsertNewWordPadDocument()
 2:   'Inserts new, embedded Wordpad document object into active cell
 3:
 4:      Dim Ans As Integer
 5:
 6:      Ans = MsgBox(Prompt:="Insert a new Wordpad document?", _
 7:                 Buttons:=vbOKCancel + vbQuestion, _
 8:                 Title:="Insert New Wordpad Document")
 9:      If Ans = vbOK Then
10:         Application.StatusBar = "Inserting Wordpad document..."
11:         Worksheets("Sheet1").Shapes.AddOLEObject _
```

```
12:                              ClassType:="Wordpad.Document.1"
13:      Application.StatusBar = False
14:    End If
15:  End Sub
```

ANALYSIS The InsertNewWordPadDocument procedure in Listing 20.1 is designed to insert a new Microsoft WordPad document object into an Excel worksheet. The procedure begins by displaying a message dialog to get the user's confirmation for inserting the object (lines 6 through 8). The If...Then statement in line 9 tests the user's response. If the user chooses the OK button, MsgBox returns the value vbOK and lines 10 through 13 are executed. Line 10 displays a message in the status bar to let the user know that the WordPad object is being inserted. Lines 11 and 12 contain the statement invoking the AddOLEObject method, inserting a new WordPad OLE object into the worksheet named Sheet1. Finally, line 13 gives control of the status bar back to Excel. Figure 20.4 shows the results of executing the InsertNewWordPadDocument procedure.

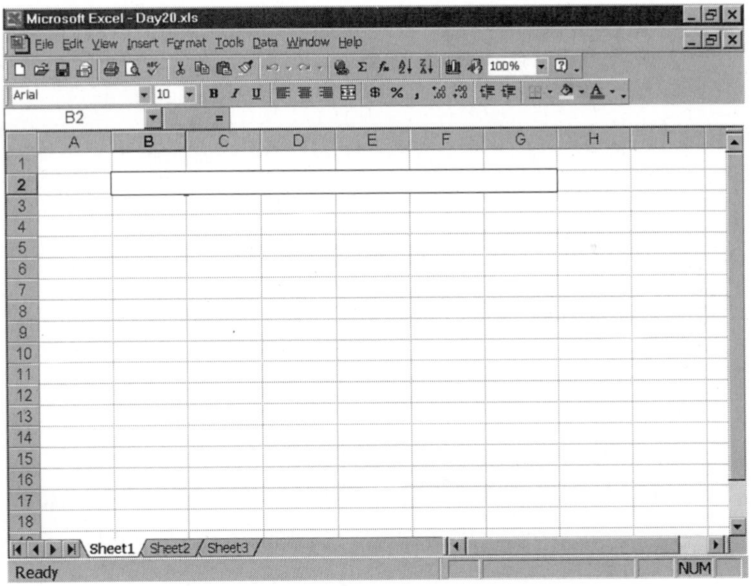

FIGURE 20.4

The InsertNewWordPad- Document procedure in Listing 20.1 inserts this empty WordPad document into the worksheet.

Unless you add the object as an icon, the appearance of the OLE object you insert depends largely on the server application. In some cases, the server application loads into memory and presents you a blank or empty object, as does WordPad in the example in Listing 20.1. Other server applications display a default object; for example, Microsoft Data Map displays a world map when you add a new object. In most cases, though, you just get a container—that is, a blank picture box—for the object, as shown in Figure 20.4.

In Excel, when the AddOLEObject method executes, the new object is inserted into the worksheet but is not activated.

Do

DO keep in mind that if you include parentheses around its argument list, the AddOLEObject method acts as a function, returning an object reference to the newly inserted Shape object. You can create a new object and assign a reference to an object variable simultaneously:

```
Set aShape = aSheet.Shapes.AddOLEObject(ClassType:="MSMap.8")
```

DO use the Activate method in Excel VBA if you want to make sure the new object is open for editing so that the user can immediately work with the new object. Activate is a method of the OLEFormat object contained in the new Shape object. The following statement shows an example of using the Activate method (aSheet is an object variable that references a Worksheet object):

```
aSheet.Shapes.AddOLEObject(ClassType:="MSMap.8").OLEFormat.Activate
```

DO remember that the length of time it takes to insert an object depends on whether the server application is already running. If it is, the insertion might take only a second or two. Otherwise, you must wait for the server application to load itself into memory.

Don't

DON'T forget that the new object's default position is determined by the currently active cell; Excel uses the active cell to position the top left corner of the object. Position the active cell where you want the OLE object to appear before you insert the new object.

Inserting an Existing File as an Embedded Object

To embed an OLE object from an existing file, you need to use the AddOLEObject method with the FileName argument. You must also either set the Link argument to **False** or omit it altogether. Listing 20.2 shows you how this is done in Excel.

INPUT   **LISTING 20.2**   USING THE AddOLEObject METHOD TO EMBED AN EXISTING FILE

```
1:    Sub EmbedPaintPicture()
2:    'Embeds an existing MSPaint file
3:
```

```
 4:     With Worksheets("Sheet1").Shapes
 5:         .AddOLEObject FileName:="C:\WINDOWS\BUBBLES.BMP", _
 6:                       DisplayAsIcon:=True, _
 7:                       IconFileName:="C:\Program Files" & _
 8:                                     "\Accessories\MSPaint.EXE", _
 9:                       IconIndex:=0, _
10:                       IconLabel:="Bubbles.bmp - Double-click to open"
11:     End With
12: End Sub
```

ANALYSIS The EmbedPaintPicture procedure embeds a Microsoft Paint bitmap picture into an Excel worksheet by specifying the filename in the AddOLEObject method (line 5) and by omitting the Link argument. (The Bubbles.bmp file is a wallpaper file provided with Windows; it is located in the folder in which you installed Windows—you might need to change the folder path in lines 5 and 7 for this procedure to work on your system. Alternatively, you can use any .bmp file you have available.) The procedure also displays the object as an icon by setting the DisplayAsIcon argument to **True** (line 6) and specifying an icon file (the MS Paint executable in lines 7 and 8), an icon index (line 9), and an icon label, which appears beneath the icon (line 10). Figure 20.5 shows the icon and label inserted by this procedure.

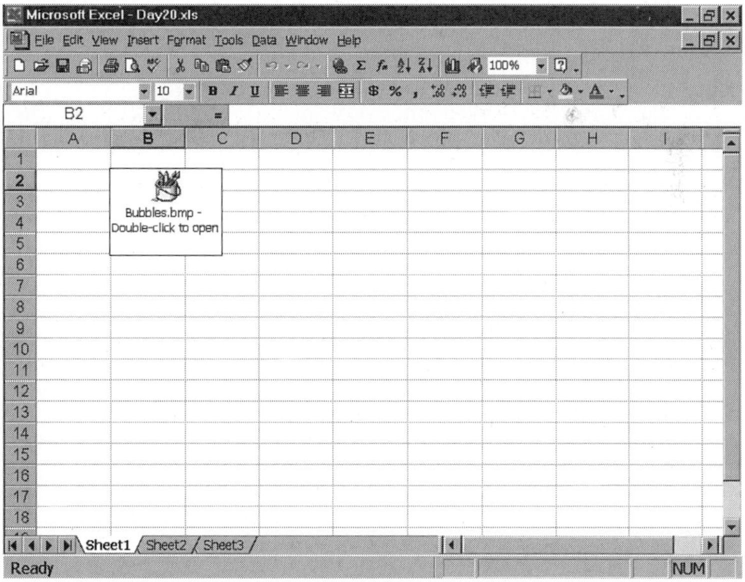

FIGURE 20.5

The EmbedPaintPicture procedure in Listing 20.2 embeds the Bubbles.bmp bitmap into the worksheet as an icon with a customized caption.

20

Inserting an Existing File as a Linked Object

If you would rather insert an existing file as linked instead of embedded, you need to set the AddOLEObject method's Link argument to **True**, as shown in Listing 20.3.

INPUT **LISTING 20.3** USING THE AddOLEObject METHOD TO INSERT AN EXISTING FILE AS A LINKED OBJECT

```
1:   Sub LinkPaintPicture()
2:   'Inserts a bitmap (BMP) file as a linked object
3:
4:       Application.ScreenUpdating = False
5:       With Worksheets("Sheet1")
6:         .Activate
7:         .Cells(2, 2).Select
8:         .Shapes.AddOLEObject FileName:="C:\Windows\Forest.bmp", _
9:                              Link:=True
10:      End With
11:      Application.ScreenUpdating = True
12:  End Sub
```

ANALYSIS The LinkPaintPicture procedure inserts a bitmap file into an Excel worksheet as a linked object. The first few statements turn off screen updating (line 4), activate the worksheet (line 6), and then select the cell where the upper-left corner of the object will appear (line 7).

Next, the AddOLEObject method is executed to insert the file (lines 8 and 9). The FileName argument specifies the bitmap file, and the Link argument is set to **True** to establish the link. (The Forest.bmp file is one of the wallpaper files supplied with Windows, and resides in the folder in which you installed Windows. You might need to change the drive or folder path for this procedure to work; alternatively, use any .bmp file you have available.) Figure 20.6 shows the linked bitmap object inserted by this procedure.

Do

DO link files if you want the data in the linked image to be updatable and if you're certain the linked file will always be available in the location from which it was linked.

DO embed files if you're not certain that the external file will always be available or if you don't want or don't need the data in the linked image to be updated.

FIGURE 20.6

The LinkPaintPicture *procedure of Listing 20.3 inserts this linked bitmap file onto the worksheet.*

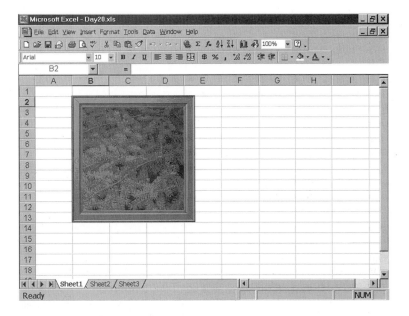

The OLEObjects Collection

In addition to the Shapes collection, Excel also supports the OLEObjects collection. OLEObjects is a collection of all linked or embedded OLE objects on a worksheet; each object in the OLEObjects collection is an OLEObject. Unlike the Shapes collection, which can contain lines, rectangles, and other elements of the drawing layer, the OLEObjects collection contains only linked or embedded OLE Objects. To add an OLEObject to the OLEObjects collection, use the Add method with this syntax:

▼ SYNTAX

```
Object.OLEObjects.Add([ClassType], [FileName], [Link], [DisplayAsIcon],
                      [IconFileName], [IconIndex], [IconLabel],
                      [Left], [Top], [Width], [Height])
```

For this method, *Object* represents any valid object reference to a Worksheet object. The OLEObjects.Add method's arguments are the same as those for the Shapes.AddOLEObject method. Refer to the syntax of the Shapes.AddOLEObject method presented earlier in this lesson for a description of the OLEObjects.Add methods' arguments. Listing 20.4 shows the procedure from Listing 20.2 modified to use the OLEObjects collection instead of the Shapes collection.

▲

20

Tip

> If you're trying to program OLE objects in a version of Excel prior to Excel 97, use the OLEObjects collection instead of the Shapes collection.

LISTING 20.4   USING OLEObjects.Add TO INSERT AN EMBEDDED BITMAP FILE INTO AN EXCEL WORKSHEET

```
 1:    Sub EmbedPaintPicture()
 2:    'Embeds an existing MSPaint file
 3:
 4:       With Worksheets("Sheet1")
 5:         .OLEObjects.Add FileName:="C:\WINDOWS\BUBBLES.BMP", _
 6:                         DisplayAsIcon:=True, _
 7:                         IconFileName:="C:\Program Files" & _
 8:                                       "\Accessories\MSPaint.EXE", _
 9:                         IconIndex:=0, _
10:                         IconLabel:="Bubbles.bmp - Double-click to open"
11:       End With
12:    End Sub
```

ANALYSIS   This procedure works exactly the same as the procedure presented in Listing 20.2, but uses the OLEObjects collection and its Add method to insert the embedded OLE object (line 5). Compare this procedure with the one shown in Listing 20.2 and notice that the FileName, DisplayAsIcon, IconFileName, IconIndex, and IconLabel arguments are identical: only the object collection and method used are different.

Do

DO keep in mind that the Shapes and OLEObjects collections overlap: Each object in the OLEObjects collection is also contained in the Shapes collection, and every OLE object in the Shapes collection is also contained in the OLEObjects collection. Use the OLEObjects collection if you want to refer only to the OLE objects in a worksheet, without having to screen out the other objects in the Shapes collection.

DON'T

DON'T forget that the OLEObjects collection contains OLEObject items. The OLEObject has slightly different properties than those available in the combination of Shape and OLEFormat objects.

Working with Linked and Embedded Objects

After you link or embed an OLE object into a worksheet, you can—among other things—change the object's size and formatting, update the OLE object's data, edit the object, and delete the object from the worksheet.

You manipulate linked or embedded OLE objects by using the properties and methods of the Shape object and the OLEFormat object contained within the Shape object. When working in Excel, you also have the option of manipulating linked or embedded OLE objects through the properties and methods of the OLEObject.

Accessing OLE Objects

Before you examine the techniques for manipulating OLE objects, though, you need to know how to refer to OLE objects after you add them to a worksheet. One way of doing this is to use the Shapes collection as the object accessor.

▼ SYNTAX

```
Object.Shapes(Index)
```

Object represents any valid reference to a Worksheet object containing the OLE object you want to work with. The *Index* argument can be either of the following:

- A number representing the object that you want to use. 1 signifies the first Shape object inserted into the worksheet, 2 signifies the second Shape object inserted, and so on.

- The name, as text, of the Shape object you want to use. Each OLE object added to the Shapes collection is assigned a name in the form *Object n*, where *n* is a number corresponding to the order in which the object was inserted into the worksheet. The first OLE object is *Object 1*, the second is *Object 2*, and so on.

▲ You'll see examples of accessing the Shapes collection in listings later in this lesson.

Excel VBA also gives you the option of accessing individual OLE objects through the OLEObjects collection. Use the same accessor syntax with the OLEObjects collection as you do in the Shapes collection, as shown in the following example (both expressions reference the same OLE object in the workbook):

```
ActiveWorkbook.Worksheets("Sheet1").OLEObjects(1)
ActiveWorkbook.Worksheets("Sheet1").OLEObjects("Object 1")
```

20

Tip   In Excel, you can find out the name of any OLE object by clicking it and looking in the formula bar's Name box.

Using OLE Object Properties

As you know by now, the Shapes collection contains Shape objects. Like every other object in VBA, the Shape object has a number of properties that you can use in your VBA code to change the Shape object's appearance or behavior.

One of the Shape object's properties is the OLEFormat property, which returns an OLEFormat object. The OLEFormat object is contained by the Shape object and stores additional information needed to completely represent an embedded OLE object. Another Shape object property is the LinkFormat property, which returns a LinkFormat object. The LinkFormat object is also contained by the Shape object and stores some of the additional information needed to represent a linked OLE object.

Table 20.2 summarizes the most commonly used properties related to OLE objects. In addition to briefly describing each property, the table indicates which object the property is available in.

TABLE 20.2 COMMONLY USED PROPERTIES RELATED TO OLE OBJECTS

Property	Object	Meaning/Purpose
AutoUpdate	LinkFormat	**True** if the linked OLE object is automatically updated when the server data changes.
BottomRightCell	Shape	Returns a Range object specifying the worksheet cell underneath the bottom right corner of the Shape object.
Height	Shape	Sets or returns the height of the Shape object in points.

Property	Object	Meaning/Purpose
Left	Shape	Sets or returns the position of the left edge of the object, in points, from the left edge of the worksheet.
Line	Shape	Returns a LineFormat object whose properties control the appearance of the OLE object's border.
LinkFormat	Shape	Returns a LinkFormat object whose properties store information about a linked OLE object.
Name	Shape	The name of the object. Use this property to retrieve or rename the OLE object.
Object	OLEFormat	Returns the Automation object associated with the object. Refer to "Using Automation" later in this lesson.
OLEFormat	Shape	Returns an OLEFormat object whose properties store information about both linked and embedded OLE objects.
OnAction	Shape	Use this property to set or retrieve the name of the event procedure for this Shape.
ProgId	OLEFormat	Returns a string containing the OLE object's class type.
Shadow	Shape	Returns a reference to a ShadowFormat object, which stores information about the drop-shadow displayed around the object: whether it is visible, its color, its off-set from the object, and so on.
Top	Shape	Sets or returns the position of the top edge of the object, in points, from the top edge of the worksheet.
TopLeftCell	Shape	Returns a Range object specifying the worksheet cell underneath the top left corner of the Shape. Use TopLeftCell and BottomRightCell to determine which worksheet cells are covered by the Shape.
Type	Shape	Returns a numeric value indicating the type of the Shape. Use the MsoShapeType intrinsic constants to determine the type of a Shape.
Visible	Shape	Set this property to **False** to hide an object; **True** to make it visible.
Width	Shape	Sets or returns the width of the Shape, in points.

20

Listing 20.5 demonstrates the use of some of these properties.

LISTING 20.5 AN EXCEL PROCEDURE THAT USES SEVERAL OLE OBJECT
INPUT PROPERTIES

```
 1:   Sub OLEObjectProperties()
 2:   'This procedure embeds a new object
 3:   'and then sets a few of its properties
 4:
 5:      Dim BMPObj As Shape
 6:
 7:      With Worksheets("Sheet1")
 8:         .Activate
 9:         .Cells(2, 2).Value = "Double-click to edit picture"
10:         .Cells(3, 2).Select
11:         Set BMPObj = .Shapes.AddOLEObject( _
12:                          FileName:="C:\Windows\Gold Weave.bmp")
13:      End With
14:
15:      With BMPObj
16:         .Line.Weight = xlThin
17:         .Name = "Gold Weave Bitmap"
18:         .Shadow.Visible = True
19:         .Shadow.OffsetX = 8
20:         .Shadow.OffsetY = 8
21:      End With
22:   End Sub
```

ANALYSIS   The OLEObjectProperties procedure inserts an embedded bitmap picture into
an Excel worksheet and then sets some properties for the new OLE object. The
procedure begins by declaring a Shape type variable named BMPObject to store a reference to the new object (line 5). Lines 8 through 10 set up the worksheet.

Like the Add methods of most object collections, you can use the AddOLEObject method
as a function, creating the new object and returning a reference to that object at the same
time. The statement in lines 11 and 12 does just that: It invokes the AddOLEObject
method to insert the Gold Weave.bmp file as an embedded OLE object on the worksheet
and assigns the resulting object reference to the BMPObject variable.

Lines 15 through 21 contain a **With** statement that uses the BMPObject variable to refer to
the newly inserted OLE object. Line 16 sets the thickness of the Shape object's border to
a thin line by assigning the xlThin constant to the Weight property of the LineFormat
object returned by the Shape object's Line property. Line 17 changes the name of the
inserted object by assigning the string "Gold Weave Bitmap" to the Name property. Lines

18 through 20 establish a shadow for the Shape object by assigning values to the properties of the ShadowFormat object returned by the Shape object's Shadow property. Line 18 ensures that the shadow is visible, and lines 19 and 20 establish how much of the shadow is visible around the Shape object. Figure 20.7 shows the resulting worksheet appearance after executing the OLEObjectProperties procedure.

FIGURE 20.7

The OLEObjectProperties procedure inserts the Gold Weave.bmp embedded object shown here, sets the border style, and adds a shadow to the image.

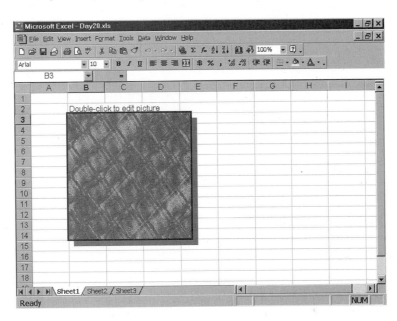

Do

DO remember that a linked OLE object's information is divided among the Shape, OLEFormat, and LinkFormat objects; an embedded OLE object's information is stored in only two objects: Shape and OLEFormat.

DO use the Application.InchesToPoints method to convert measurements in inches to measurements in points for the Top and Left properties. (The Application.CentimetersToPoints method is available to convert centimeters to points, as well.)

DO research the LineFormat and ShadowFormat objects in the Object Browser to learn more about the properties you can set through these objects.

DO use the Object Browser to check on the availability and type of specific properties in the Shape and OLEObject objects.

20

> **DON'T**
>
> **DON'T** forget that you can also use the OLEObjects collection in Excel to access OLE objects in a worksheet and to set those objects' properties. Some OLEObject properties are different from Shape object properties, however; the OLEObject.Shadow property, for example, is merely a **Boolean** value that indicates whether the shadow should be displayed, instead of the more complex ShadowFormat object returned by the Shape.Shadow property.

Using OLE Object Methods

Shape objects also come equipped with several methods that you can use to manipulate objects after you insert them. Many of these methods, such as Copy, Cut, Delete, Activate, and Select, are straightforward and operate in much the same way as the methods of the same name do for the Excel Worksheet objects described in Day 19. However, there are two methods—Update and Verb—that have special significance for OLE objects; these methods are accessed through the Shape.OLEFormat property. The next two sections take a closer look at these methods.

The Update Method

If you insert a Shape object that contains a linked OLE object, the link between the object and the server file is usually automatic. This means that whenever the server file changes, the client object is updated automatically. There are two circumstances where updating is *not* automatic:

- If you have changed the link to manual. (You can do this by choosing the Edit, Links command, selecting the source file in the Links dialog box, and then selecting the Manual update option.)
- If you closed and then reopened the client document and chose No when Excel asked whether you wanted to re-establish the links.

In these situations, you need to use the Update method to update the object:

Object.LinkFormat.Update

Here, *Object* is a reference to the Shape object that contains the linked OLE object you want to update. If you're working with OLEObject objects, use the following syntax for the Update method instead (where *Object* is a reference to an OLEObject in Excel):

Object.Update

▲ Listing 20.6 provides an example of how to use the Update method with Shape objects.

LISTING 20.6   USING THE Update METHOD TO UPDATE OLE OBJECTS IN AN
EXCEL WORKBOOK

```
1:   Sub UpdateAllObjects()
2:   'This procedure updates OLE objects
3:
4:      Dim aSheet As Worksheet
5:      Dim Obj As Object
6:
7:      For Each aSheet In ActiveWorkbook.Worksheets
8:        Application.StatusBar = "Now updating objects in " _
9:                             & aSheet.Name
10:         For Each Obj In aSheet.Shapes
11:            If Obj.Type = msoLinkedOLEObject Then
12:               Obj.LinkFormat.Update
13:            End If
15:         Next Obj
16:      Next aSheet
17:      Application.StatusBar = False
18:      MsgBox prompt:="Link update complete.", _
19:            Title:="Update All Objects"
20:   End Sub
```

This Excel VBA procedure updates all the linked OLE objects on each worksheet
in the active workbook. The first **For Each** loop (line 7) uses the aSheet variable
to loop through each worksheet in the active workbook. The StatusBar property displays
the name of each worksheet in the status bar so that the user can watch the progress of
the operation (lines 8 and 9). A nested **For Each** loop, starting in line 10, uses the Obj
variable to loop through every Shape object in the current worksheet. Line 11 checks to
see if the Shape object is a linked OLE object, that is, its Type property equals
msoLinkedOLEObject. If the Shape object does contain a linked OLE object, it gets
updated with the LinkFormat object's Update method (line 12). When both **For Each**
loops are complete, the procedure resets Excel's status bar (line 17) and displays a completion message (lines 18 and 19).

20

Do

DO use the OLEObject.Update method to update a linked OLE object in Excel's OLEObjects
collection.

The Verb Method

Each OLE object has one or more verbs that specify the actions that can be performed on it. Unlike methods, which tell you what actions you can perform on the object from VBA's point of view, verbs tell you what actions you can perform on the object *from the server's point of view*, in other words, actions performed on the OLE object by the application you used to create the object. For example, a typical verb is Edit: sending the Edit verb to the OLE object opens the server application so that you can edit the object.

To send a verb to an OLE object, use the Verb method. Before getting into the specific syntax for the Verb method, here are some facts to keep in mind as you deal with OLE object verbs:

- All OLE objects have a *primary* verb, which is the same as the action taken when you double-click the object.

- For most objects, the primary verb lets you edit the object. If you want to edit an object but you're not sure what its primary verb does, use the Open verb.

- If the object supports a secondary verb, you can specify this verb by using 2 as the value for the *Verb* or *VerbIndex* arguments (explained in the syntax discussions of the Verb method).

- For embedded objects that support OLE 2.0 or higher, the primary verb lets you edit the object in place and the secondary verb lets you open the object in a separate server window.

▼ SYNTAX

Excel's OLEFormat.Verb method has this syntax:

```
Object.Verb([Verb])
```

In this syntax, *Object* is a reference to any Excel OLEFormat object. The optional *Verb* argument is a numeric expression specifying the verb action that you want the OLE server to carry out. Excel defines the XlOLEVerb class of intrinsic constants to make it easier to specify a value for the *Verb* argument. Use xlOpen to send the open verb and xlPrimary to send the primary verb. If you omit the *Verb* argument, the default verb is sent to the OLE server.

▲ Listing 20.7 shows an example of using the Verb method in an Excel VBA procedure.

INPUT **LISTING 20.7** USING THE OLEFormat.Verb METHOD TO EDIT AN OLE OBJECT

```
1:    Sub InsertAndEditWordDoc()
2:    'This procedure adds and edits an OLE object
3:    'If user declines to edit in-place, then the
4:    'embedded document is edited in a separate window.
```

```
 5:    'If user cancels, embedded document is removed.
 6:
 7:       Dim WordDoc As Object
 8:       Dim Ans As Integer
 9:       Dim aSheet As Worksheet
10:
11:       Set aSheet = ActiveWorkbook.Worksheets("Sheet1")
12:       With aSheet
13:          .Activate
14:          .Cells(3, 1).Select
15:          Set WordDoc = .Shapes.AddOLEObject(ClassType:="Word.Document")
16:       End With
17:
18:       Ans = MsgBox(prompt:="Edit the document in-place?", _
19:                    Buttons:=vbYesNoCancel + vbQuestion, _
20:                    Title:="Insert and Edit Word Document")
21:       If Ans = vbYes Then
22:          WordDoc.OLEFormat.Verb xlPrimary
23:       Else
24:         If Ans = vbNo Then
25:            WordDoc.OLEFormat.Verb xlOpen
26:         Else
27:            WordDoc.Delete
28:         End If
29:       End If
30:    End Sub
```

ANALYSIS This procedure embeds a new MS Word document into an Excel worksheet. The procedure then asks the user if she wants to edit the document in-place; if the user answers No, the document is edited in a separate window. If the user cancels the procedure, the newly embedded document object is deleted.

Lines 7 through 9 declare the variables used by this procedure. The WordDoc variable is declared as a generic **Object** variable because the Document object type is unknown in Excel (unless you have a reference to the Word type library established for this workbook; references were discussed in Day 12).

Line 11 sets the aSheet variable to refer to a worksheet named Sheet1; the aSheet variable is used to make object references later in this procedure easier to write. Lines 13 and 14 set up the worksheet: the worksheet is activated and the cell in the first column of the third row is selected—this will be the location of the top-left corner of the new OLE object.

Line 15 inserts the embedded document; the statement in line 15 uses the AddOLEObject method as a function and the resulting object reference is stored in the WordDoc variable. Lines 18 through 20 use a MsgBox statement to display a message that asks the user how she wants to edit the document. The user's choice is stored in the Ans variable.

20

If Ans is vbYes—that is, the user wants to edit in-place—the Verb method is used with the xlPrimary constant (line 22). If Ans is vbNo—that is, the user doesn't want to edit in-place—the Verb method is used with the xlOpen constant (line 25). Finally, if Ans is vbCancel (the user chose to cancel the operation), line 27 calls the Shape object's Delete method to delete the unused OLE object.

> **Note**
>
> If you include parentheses around the *Verb* or *DoVerb* argument (as shown in the syntax samples for Excel and Word), the Verb/DoVerb method returns a **Boolean** result: **True** if the method completed successfully, **False** otherwise.

> **Note**
>
> You can determine which verbs are available for a particular OLE object by using the Windows Registry Editor to look up the available verbs in the Registry database. Start the Registry Editor as described earlier in this lesson for looking up an object's class type, and use the Registry Editor's Edit, Find command to search for the object's class type. Press the F3 key (or choose Edit, Find Next) until you reach the \HKEY_CLASSES_ROOT\<class type> branch in the Registry (where <class type> is the class type you were searching for). Expand the Registry branches under this entry until you can see the \HKEY_CLASSES_ROOT\<class type>\protocol\StdFileEditing\Verb branch—the list in the Verb entry lists the verbs that class type can understand. Figure 20.8 shows the Registry Editor window after searching for the Excel.Sheet.8 class type and then expanding the appropriate Registry database branches.
>
> Use the numeric value (0, 1, and so on) of the Verb branches in the Registry database as the argument value for the Verb method to specify a particular verb. Using the Registry information visible in Figure 20.8, you would use 0 as the argument for the Verb method to activate in-place editing of an Excel worksheet.

Using Automation

One of the advantages of OLE (especially OLE 2+) is the fact that you gain access to the OLE object's original tools. With a simple double-click or a Verb method, you can edit the OLE object with the full power of the server's menus and commands.

Until fairly recently, the one thing that had been missing is the capability to control an OLE server by means of programming. To edit or create an OLE object, whether it is in-place or in a separate window, you had to be at least familiar with the server application. Although *you* might be willing to spend time and effort learning a new program, the users of your VBA programs might not.

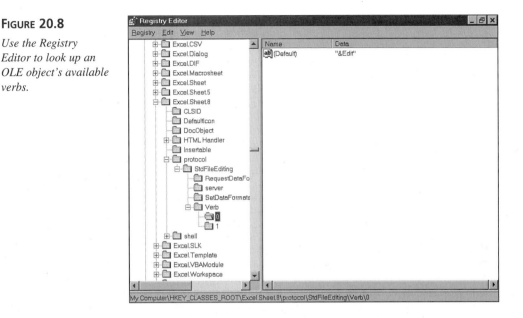

FIGURE 20.8

Use the Registry Editor to look up an OLE object's available verbs.

This situation changed with the introduction of OLE Automation in Microsoft Office 95. OLE Automation is now known simply as *Automation* with the advent of Office 97. Windows applications that support Automation expose their objects to VBA, as well as to any other applications and development tools that support the Automation standard.

Just as VBA can recognize and manipulate objects within the host application, VBA can also recognize and manipulate objects from other Automation applications. Microsoft Access, Visio, Microsoft Graph, Microsoft Word, and PowerPoint are a few of the applications that expose a number of objects to VBA. Visio 2.0, for example, exposes objects such as documents, pages, shapes, and windows; Microsoft Access exposes objects such as forms, reports, and modules. Each of these objects has its own collection of methods and properties that can be read or altered by a VBA program, just like Excel's methods and properties.

The number of Windows applications that currently support Automation is growing rapidly, although it is still relatively small. Many experts accept that Automation is becoming *the* standard for application interoperability in the near future. Certainly, any other applications that use Visual Basic for Applications will also support Automation. Indeed, Microsoft has already made Visual Basic for Applications a part of all its major Windows applications; the current roster of Microsoft applications that host VBA and Automation includes Excel, Word, Access, Outlook, Project, PowerPoint, and Visual Basic 6.

20

Accessing Automation Objects

How you access an Automation object from VBA depends on whether the object provides an object library file (.olb), a type library file (.tlb), or a dynamic link library (.dll) that contains the definitions of objects exposed by that library. Microsoft Access, for example, exposes its objects through the Msacc9.olb file; Office exposes objects through the Mso98.dll file; and Automation itself exposes objects through the Stdole.tlb file.

If the application provides an object library, you can refer to the objects from that library directly in your VBA code, just as you refer to objects native to Excel. To make the objects defined in an Automation library file available to a particular VBA project, use the VB Editor's Tools, References command and make sure that the object library's check box is selected in the References dialog.

Some applications don't have an object library, but do enable you to directly access some of their objects, anyway. If the application doesn't provide an object library and you want to access a new object, use the `CreateObject` function. If the application doesn't have a library and you want to access an existing object, use the `GetObject` function.

The next few sections discuss techniques for using Automation in more detail.

Accessing Objects Directly

Accessing objects directly is the easiest way to work with Automation. This section explains how to use VBA to directly control objects defined in another application.

Use this syntax to access an object defined by another application:

```
Application.ObjectName
```

Here, `Application` is the name of the application that contains the object you want to access and `ObjectName` is the name of the object. If you're not sure what to use for the application name, each `OLEFormat` object has an `Object` property that can supply you with the application name or a reference to the application:

```
Object.Object.Application
```

Here, `Object` is a reference to an `OLEFormat` object. (`OLEFormat` objects are contained within a `Shape` object.) The `Application` method, when applied in this manner, returns a string containing the name of the Automation application.

You can also use the `Application` method to return a reference to the object's original application. Suppose that you have embedded a Word document in an Excel worksheet and you have assigned the `WordDoc` object variable so that it stores a reference to the `Shape` object that contains the embedded Word document. You would use the following statement to display the name of the Word application's `ActivePrinter` property:

▼   MsgBox "Word's active printer is: " & _
          WordDoc.OLEFormat.Object.Application.ActivePrinter

Listing 20.8 shows an example of accessing an Automation object directly from Excel
▲   VBA.

```
 1:    Sub AutomateWordObject()
 2:    'This procedure embeds a new Word document and then
 3:    'works with the document using its own methods and application
 4:
 5:       Dim WdApp As Object
 6:       Dim WdDoc As Object
 7:       Dim aShape As Shape
 8:
 9:       Application.StatusBar = "Embedding & Editing document..."
10:       Application.ScreenUpdating = False
11:
12:       'Select the upper left cell
13:       With Worksheets("Sheet1")
14:          .Activate
15:          .Cells(2, 1).Select
16:          'create the new embedded document
17:          Set aShape = .Shapes.AddOLEObject(ClassType:="Word.Document")
18:       End With
19:
20:       'set references to Word application and embedded document
21:       Set WdApp = aShape.OLEFormat.Object.Object.Application
22:       Set WdDoc = aShape.OLEFormat.Object.Object
23:
24:       WdDoc.Activate        'activate the embedded document
25:
26:       'Access the Word application object directly
27:       With WdApp
28:          .Selection.TypeText Text:="I'm an Automation object!"
29:          .Selection.Expand Unit:=4  'expand the selection to a paragraph
30:          .Selection.Range.Bold = True
31:       End With
32:
33:       'make sure the object's representation is updated
34:       aShape.OLEFormat.Verb Verb:=xlVerbPrimary
35:       Cells(1, 1).Select
36:
37:       Application.ScreenUpdating = True
38:       Application.StatusBar = False
39:    End Sub
```

20

ANALYSIS The Excel VBA procedure in Listing 20.8 embeds a new Word document in a worksheet and then uses Word's (and the document's) methods and properties to edit the document. The procedure begins by declaring two **Object** type variables: WdDoc will store a reference to the embedded document object and WdApp will store a reference to the Word Application object. A third object variable, aShape, will store a reference to the Shape object created to hold the embedded document.

Because the tasks carried out by the AutomateWordObject procedure might take several seconds, line 9 displays a message in Excel's status bar. Line 10 turns Excel's screen updating off so that the user won't see the changes onscreen until the inserting and editing process is complete.

In the **With** statement in lines 13 through 18, a worksheet is activated (line 14), the first cell in the second row is selected (line 15), and a Word document is embedded, simultaneously setting the aShape variable to refer to the new document object (line 17).

Next, line 21 sets the WdApp variable to refer to the Word Application object. Line 22 sets the WdDoc variable to refer to the Document Automation object exposed by Word. Line 24 uses the Document object's Activate method so that the embedded document becomes the active document in Word. (Word is automatically loaded, if necessary, when the Automation objects are utilized.)

Note

> The double occurrence of the Object property in lines 21 and 22 of Listing 20.8 is *not* a misprint or typographical error! In Excel, you must use the Object method of the OLEFormat property twice in order to reference the Automation objects behind a linked or embedded OLE object. If you use the TypeName function to check the type of object returned by the *Shape*.OLEFormat.Object property, you'll find that this property actually returns an OLEObject type. (*Shape* is any shape object.) The expression *Shape*.OLEFormat.Object.Object, however, returns a reference to the actual Automation object.

The **With** statement in lines 27 through 31 contains statements that edit the embedded Word document object by using Word's Selection object. The Word application is accessed through the Automation object referenced by WdApp. Line 28 inserts some text, line 29 expands the selection to include the current paragraph, and line 30 makes the selected text in the document bold. Line 29 uses a literal numeric constant to specify a value equivalent to Word's wdParagraph constant value.

Tip

> You can find out the value of any intrinsic constant in any version of VBA by using the Object Browser: just select the desired constant in the Members of list and read the value from the window at the bottom of the Object Browser.

Line 34 uses the `Verb` method to activate the `Shape` object for in-place editing. Without this step, the embedded Word document's presentation isn't updated and the document—even though it now contains some text—will still appear onscreen as an empty box. By opening the embedded document for in-place editing, Excel is forced to update the object's presentation. Because it isn't really desired, in this procedure, to leave the embedded document in an editing mode, line 35 selects the first cell of the worksheet, which closes the embedded document. Figure 20.9 shows the results of executing this procedure.

FIGURE 20.9

The procedure in Listing 20.8 inserts this document embedded in an Excel worksheet.

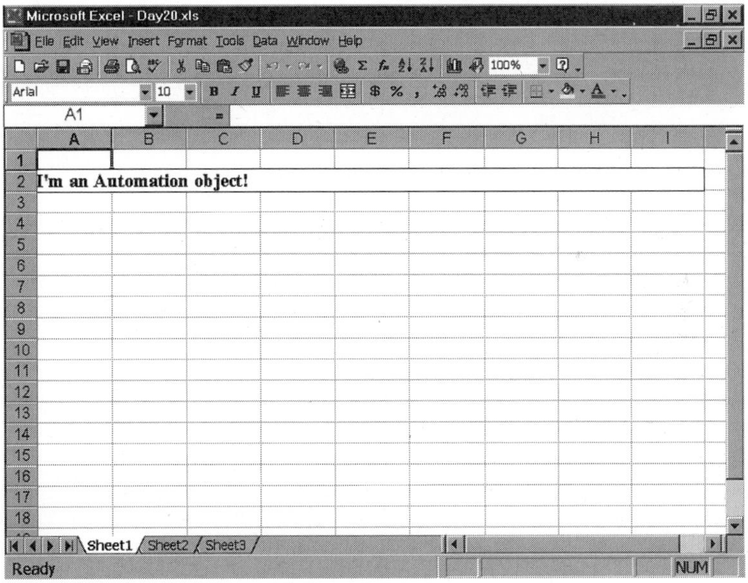

	A	B	C	D	E	F	G	H	I
1									
2	I'm an Automation object!								

Microsoft Excel - Day20.xls

20

Creating a New Automation Object

If an Automation application provides an object library, you can use the application's objects directly in your code by creating a reference in your VBA project to the Automation object's library. If the application does not have an object library, or you don't want to establish a reference to the object library, you can use VBA's

CreateObject function to create new Automation objects. This section discusses both techniques for creating new instances of Automation objects in your VBA code.

Using the CreateObject Function

The CreateObject function is one of VBA's Interaction class of functions, and has this syntax:

CreateObject(*Class*)

The *Class* argument is the *programmatic identifier*—in other words, the class type—that specifies the Automation application and the type of object you want to create. For example, the programmatic identifier for Word is Word.Application, for Excel it is Excel.Application. As other examples, you would use Visio.Application for the Visio application; for a Microsoft Access application you would use Access.Application. The CreateObject function returns an object reference to the newly created object. Listing 20.9 provides an example of using the CreateObject function.

INPUT   **LISTING 20.9**   USING CreateObject TO CREATE AN AUTOMATION OBJECT

```
1:    Sub CreateWordObject()
2:    'This procedure starts Word, creates a new document,
3:    'and then links the document in the worksheet
4:
5:       Dim WordApp As Object
6:       Dim WdDoc As Object
7:       Dim fName As String      'document name
8:       Dim iconfName As String   'icon file name
9:
10:
11:      'Create an instance of the Word application
12:      Set WordApp = CreateObject("Word.Application")
13:
14:      'set up a filename using the active workbook's folder
15:      fName = ActiveWorkbook.Path
16:      fName = fName & "\Document Created by Excel VBA.doc"
17:
18:      'create a new document and set an object reference to it
19:      Set WdDoc = WordApp.Documents.Add
20:
21:      'add some content to the new document
22:      With WordApp
23:        .Selection.TypeText Text:="This document was created by " & _
24:                                  "a VBA program executing in Excel."
25:        .Selection.TypeParagraph
26:      End With
27:
```

```
28:    With WdDoc
29:       'set some document properties
30:       .BuiltinDocumentProperties("Title") = "Test Document"
31:       .BuiltinDocumentProperties("Subject") = "Testing Automation"
32:
33:       'save the document and close it
34:       .SaveAs fName
35:       .Close
36:    End With
37:
38:    WordApp.Quit        'Quit Word
39:
40:    'Insert the linked document into Excel
41:    iconfName = "C:\Program Files\Microsoft Office\" & _
42:                "Office\WinWord.exe"
43:
44:    With ActiveSheet
45:       .Cells(2, 2).Activate
46:       .Shapes.AddOLEObject FileName:=fName, _
47:                            Link:=True, _
48:                            DisplayAsIcon:=True, _
49:                            IconFileName:=iconfName, _
50:                            IconIndex:=1, _
51:                            IconLabel:="Word Test Document"
52:    End With
53: End Sub
```

ANALYSIS   To start Word, the procedure uses the `CreateObject` function to create a
"Word.Application" object (line 12). This object is stored in the `WordApp` variable. Through the Word application object, you now have complete access to all of
Word's objects, methods, and properties.

For example, you can create a new Word document by using the `Documents.Add` method,
as shown in line 19. Next, lines 22 through 26 use Word's `Selection` object to insert
some text into the new document. Lines 28 through 36 set some of the document's properties (lines 30 and 31), save the document (line 34), and then close the document (line
35). Finally, line 38 uses the `Quit` method to terminate the Word working session that
was started by the `CreateObject` function call (back in line 12).

Lines 41 and 42 set up the `iconfName` variable to hold the full path and name of the
Word program file; this file will be used as the source of an icon for the linked OLE
object. (If your copy of Word is installed on a different drive or folder, you'll need to
change this line to match your system.) Line 45 selects the second cell in the second row
of the active worksheet (remember, the `AddOLEObject` method inserts the OLE object in
the current active worksheet cell). Lines 46 through 51 contain a single `AddOLEObject`

20

method statement, using several of its arguments. The document is inserted as a linked object from a filename (using the fName variable initialized at the beginning of the procedure in lines 15 and 16). The inserted object is displayed as an icon, using the second icon from the Word program file, and with a customized icon label. Figure 20.10 shows the resulting worksheet display.

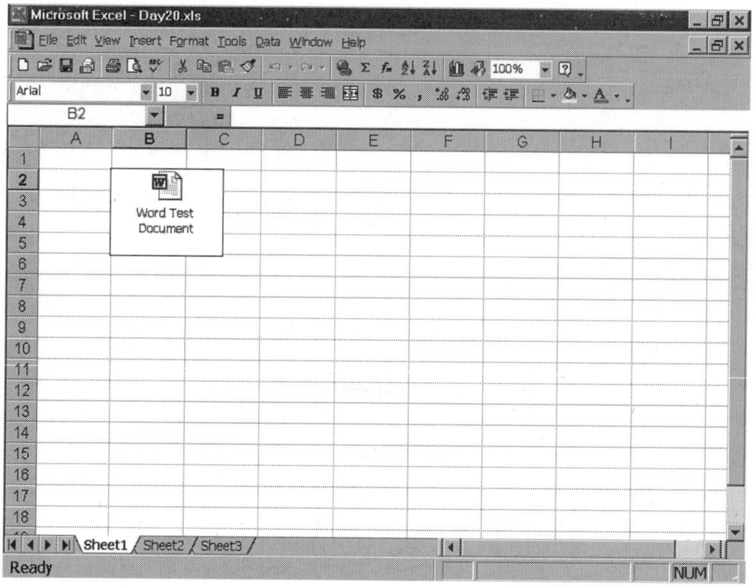

FIGURE 20.10

The CreateWordObject *procedure creates a new Word document by using the* CreateObject *function and then links it to the worksheet.*

Using Referenced Object Libraries

If you establish a reference to an object library for your VBA project, you can declare variables that have specific data types of objects from the library, and you can create new instances of objects in the library by using the **New** keyword (which was covered in Day 12). Listing 20.10 shows an example of using objects from a referenced library.

INPUT

LISTING 20.10 USING AUTOMATION OBJECTS FROM A REFERENCED OBJECT LIBRARY

```
1:    Sub CreateReferencedObject()
2:    'This procedure starts Word, creates a new document,
3:    'and then links the document into the worksheet
4:    'NOTE: This procedure won't compile unless the VBA project
5:    'has a reference to the Word object library.
6:
7:        Dim appWord As Object
8:        Dim WdDoc As Document
```

```
 9:     Dim fName As String        'document name
10:     Dim iconfName As String    'icon file name
11:
12:     'Create an instance of the Word application
13:     Set appWord = New Word.Application
14:
15:     'set up a filename using the active workbook's folder
16:     fName = ActiveWorkbook.Path
17:     fName = fName & "\Document Created With Referenced Objects.doc"
18:
19:     'create a new document and set an object reference to it
20:     Set WdDoc = appWord.Documents.Add
21:
22:     'add some content to the new document
23:     With appWord.Selection
24:         .TypeText Text:="This document was created by " & _
25:                         "a VBA program executing in Excel," & _
26:                         " using referenced Word objects."
27:         .TypeParagraph
28:     End With
29:
30:     With WdDoc
31:         'set some document properties
32:         .BuiltinDocumentProperties("Title") = "Test Document 2"
33:         .BuiltinDocumentProperties("Subject") = "Automation References"
34:
35:         'save the document and close it
36:         .SaveAs fName
37:         .Close
38:     End With
39:
40:     appWord.Quit      'Quit Word
41:     Set appWord = Nothing  'release the application instance
42:
43:     'Insert the linked document into Excel
44:     iconfName = "C:\Program Files\Microsoft Office\" & _
45:                 "Office\WinWord.exe"
46:     With ActiveSheet
47:         .Cells(2, 2).Activate
48:         .Shapes.AddOLEObject FileName:=fName, _
49:                              Link:=True, _
50:                              DisplayAsIcon:=True, _
51:                              IconFileName:=iconfName, _
52:                              IconIndex:=1, _
53:                              IconLabel:="Word Automation Test Document"
54:     End With
55: End Sub
```

ANALYSIS The CreateReferencedObject procedure in Listing 20.10 performs essentially the same functions as the procedure in Listing 20.9, but obtains access to Word

Automation objects through a reference to Word's object library. Lines 7 through 10 declare several object variables used by this procedure. Notice that, because there is a reference to the Word object library for this project, the declaration in line 8 uses a specific Word object type—a Document object—even though this procedure is in Excel VBA.

> **Note**
>
> For the procedure in Listing 20.10 to compile correctly, your Excel VBA project must have a reference to the Word 9.0 object library. To establish this reference, choose the Tools, References command in the VB Editor and then select the check box to the left of the Microsoft Word 9.0 Object Library choice in the Available References list. If this choice doesn't appear, Word is either not installed on your system or it was not installed correctly.

Next, lines 32 and 33 set some of the document's properties. The document is then saved (line 36) and the document is closed (line 37). Line 40 uses the Word application's Quit method to terminate the Word work session, and then line 41 assigns **Nothing** to the appWord object variable to ensure that the instance of the Word application is released.

Finally, lines 44 through 53 select the cell in the second column of the second row of whatever worksheet is currently active and then link the document into the workbook. Figure 20.11 shows the result of executing this procedure in a sample workbook.

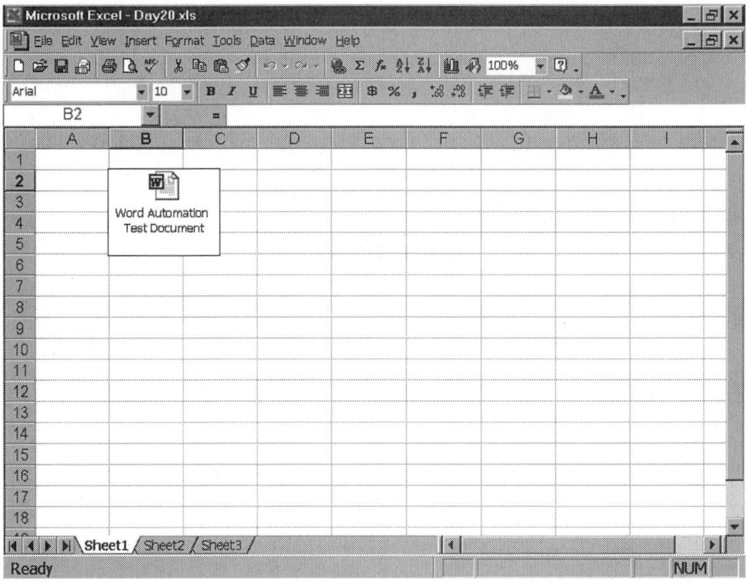

FIGURE 20.11

The CreateReferenced-Object *procedure creates a new Word document using referenced Automation objects and then links it to the worksheet.*

Accessing an Existing Automation Object

Instead of creating a new object instance, you might need to work with an existing object instance. If the server application is already running, use VBA's `GetObject` function to access an existing Automation object:

```
GetObject([pathname], [Class])
```

In this syntax, the optional *pathname* argument is a string specifying the full folder path and filename containing the object you want to retrieve. If you omit the *pathname* argument, the *Class* argument is required.

The optional *Class* argument is a string specifying the programmatic identifier of the object you want to work with. (Use the same syntax when supplying the *Class* argument for the `GetObject` function as you do when supplying the *Class* argument for the `CreateObject` function.) If you omit the *Class* argument, the *pathname* argument is required and the class of the object is determined by the file you have specified: the file's three-letter extension determines the file type, and VBA uses the Windows Registry to determine which Automation server is correct for that type of file.

Use the `GetObject` function to create an instance of an Automation object based on a particular file. The following code fragment shows an example of how this works:

```
Dim AppVisio As Object
Set AppVisio = GetObject(pathname:="C:\Visio\Drawing.vsd", _
                         Class:="Visio.Application")
```

In the preceding example, the `AppVisio` object variable is assigned a reference to an instance of the Visio application with the Drawing.vsd file loaded.

If the *pathname* argument is an empty string (`""`), `GetObject` creates a new instance of the specified Automation object, similar to the `CreateObject` function. The following code fragment, for example, creates a new instance of Word:

```
Dim AppWord As Object
Set AppWord = GetObject(pathname:="", _
                        Class:="Word.Application")
```

If you omit the *pathname* argument altogether, `GetObject` returns any currently active object of the specified type; if there is no existing instance of the specified object, VBA generates a runtime error. As an example, the following code fragment stores a reference to an existing instance of Word in the `AppWord` object variable:

```
Dim AppWord As Object
Set AppWord = GetObject(Class:="Word.Application")
```

In the preceding example, if there isn't at least one instance of Word running at the time these statements are executed, a runtime error occurs.

20

Do

DO use Automation objects referenced through an embedded object's `OLEFormat.Object` property as the best technique for manipulating embedded objects, whether or not you have a reference to the embedded object's Automation object library.

DO use Automation objects referenced through an object library, the `CreateObject` method, or the `GetObject` method as the best technique for manipulating linked objects.

DO use the `CreateObject` and `GetObject` methods to manipulate Automation objects in VBA projects that do *not* have a reference to the Automation object's library.

DO use `CreateObject` whenever you want to create a completely new instance of an Automation object.

DO use `GetObject` whenever you want to create an instance of an Automation object with a particular file already opened, or if there is already an instance of the Automation object running and you don't want to start another.

DO keep in mind that if an Automation server is registered in the Windows Registry as a single-instance object (that is, only one instance at a time can exist on your system), no matter how many times you call the `CreateObject` function, only one instance will be created. Similarly, the `GetObject` function will always return the same object instance for single-instance objects.

Accessing DLLs from Visual Basic for Applications

Another way to work with the resources provided by another application is to use utilize code directly from the other application's dynamic-link libraries. *Dynamic-link libraries* (DLLs) are collections of functions and procedures that are available to all Windows applications. Windows itself comes with a number of DLL files that provide developers with hundreds of specialized—and very fast—functions. Tapping into these procedures is an easy way to include powerful Windows functionality in your VBA programs. Taken together, the DLL libraries supplied with Windows form what is known as the Windows *Application Programming Interface* (API).

Although most of the Windows API functions are highly technical, you can take advantage of a few of them in your VBA procedures. The next sections show you how to access DLLs in your VBA code. You also get to see a few examples.

Declaring DLL Procedures

Before you can use a function from a DLL, you must tell VBA where to find the DLL file and what arguments the function needs. You do this by entering a **Declare** statement at the module level, that is, before any procedure declarations in the module. Depending on whether the procedure is a **Function** or **Sub** procedure, you use one of the following forms:

```
Declare Function Name Lib "LibName" [Alias AliasName] (Arguments)
➥[As Type]
Declare Sub Name Lib "LibName" [Alias AliasName] (Arguments) [As Type]
```

As with VBA variables and constants, you can declare DLL procedures to be either **Public** (to make the procedure available to all modules in all projects) or **Private** (to make the procedure available only in the module in which it is declared).

Name represents the name of the procedure and *LibName* is the name of the DLL file, for example, "USER32". If the procedure has the same name as a VBA keyword or a **Public** variable, you can't use the procedure's own original name in your code. Instead, use *AliasName* to specify a different name for the procedure.

Arguments is the list of arguments required by the procedure. This list uses the following syntax:

```
[Optional][ByVal¦ByRef][ParamArray] VarName [As Type]
```

Optional specifies that the argument isn't required. **ByVal** means that the argument is passed by value, as is the case with most DLL procedures. **ByRef** means that the argument is passed by reference. **ParamArray** is used with arrays of **Variant** type data. **ParamArray** must be the last argument in the argument list; you cannot use **ParamArray** in combination with **Optional**, **ByVal**, or **ByRef**. *VarName* is the name of the argument and *Type* specifies the data type of the argument.

The following statement, for example, declares a function named MessageBeep from the User32.exe DLL:

```
Declare Sub MessageBeep Lib "USER32" (ByVal BeepType As Integer)
```

After you declare the DLL procedure, you can use it in your VBA code just like any ▲ other **Sub** or **Function** procedure.

20

Note

When a DLL filename ends with the digits 32, it signifies that the DLL contains 32-bit code. Whenever you have a choice, you should use the 32-bit versions of any DLL in your VBA code.

Some DLL Examples

This section provides you with several examples of how to use DLL procedures in VBA code. To learn more about DLLs and the Windows API, you might want to get a copy of *Win32 API Desktop Reference* by James McCord. This book provides complete coverage of the subjects.

Beeping the Speaker

VBA provides you with a simple Beep statement that you can use to get the user's attention. Unfortunately, Beep produces only a single sound. This isn't a problem most of the time, but there are plenty of situations for which you'll want to do more. For example, you usually want to beep the speaker at the end of a long operation to bring the user's attention back to the screen. But what if an error occurs during the operation? It would be nice to have a different sound to go with your error message.

If different sounds are what you want, the DLL procedure MessageBeep gives you access to five individual sounds. To take advantage of MessageBeep, you or the users of your VBA program need a sound card supported by Windows.

Note

> The DLL that contains the MessageBeep procedure—User32—is stored in a disk file named User32.dll in your \Windows\System directory. It is supplied with Windows. User32.dll contains other useful functions and procedures in addition to MessageBeep, all of which are part of the standard 32-bit Windows API. To get full information on the functions and procedures in User32.dll, refer to the Win32 Software Developer's Kit documentation, available from Microsoft.

Here's the **Declare** statement to use with MessageBeep:

```
Declare Sub MessageBeep Lib "USER32" (ByVal BeepType As Long)
```

The *BeepType* argument takes one of five values, which are listed in Table 20.3.

TABLE 20.3   VALUES FOR THE BeepType ARGUMENT

BeepType *Value*	*Sound Produced*
0	Default beep
16	Critical stop
32	Question
48	Exclamation
64	Asterisk

These sounds are all defined in the Sounds icon of the Control Panel. Listing 20.11 displays a procedure that plays all five sounds.

INPUT **LISTING 20.11**   USING THE MessageBeep DLL PROCEDURE

```
 1:  Option Explicit
 2:
 3:  Declare Sub MessageBeep Lib "USER32" (ByVal BeepType As Long)
 4:
 5:  Sub BeepTest()
 6:  'This procedure plays all five MessageBeep sounds.
 7:
 8:     Dim I As Integer
 9:
10:     For I = 0 To 64 Step 16
11:        Select Case I
12:          Case 0
13:             Application.StatusBar = "Default Beep"
14:          Case 16
15:             Application.StatusBar = "Critical Stop"
16:          Case 32
17:             Application.StatusBar = "Question"
18:          Case 48
19:             Application.StatusBar = "Exclamation"
20:          Case 64
21:             Application.StatusBar = "Asterisk"
22:        End Select
23:        MessageBeep I
24:        WaitDelay DelaySeconds:=2
25:     Next I
26:
27:     Application.StatusBar = False
28:  End Sub
29:
30:
31:  Sub WaitDelay(DelaySeconds As Integer)
32:     Dim TimeNow As Date
33:     TimeNow = Timer
34:     Do
35:     Loop Until ((Timer - TimeNow) > DelaySeconds)
36:  End Sub
```

20

ANALYSIS   Listing 20.11 shows an entire module; this module contains two procedures. The BeepTest procedure (lines 5 through 28) simply runs through all the values accepted by MessageBeep and plays the associated sounds. The WaitDelay procedure (lines 31 through 36) simply delays a specified number of seconds.

Notice line 3 of this listing. Line 3 contains the **Declare** statement for the MessageBeep procedure; this is the statement that makes that routine in the User32.dll available to VBA in this module.

> **Note**
>
> The specific sounds played by the BeepTest procedure depend on your computer's configuration. Unless you installed all the sounds provided with Windows, you might hear only one or two different sounds for all the different sounds that BeepTest plays. You can change the sounds that Windows plays for specific events—such as the Asterisk, Question, and others—by using the Sounds applet in the Windows Control Panel.

The **For...Next** structure (lines 10 through 25) loops through values of the variable I from 0 to 64 in steps of 16. A **Select Case** statement (line 11) looks for each value of I and displays the sound name in the status bar. MessageBeep plays the sound (line 23) and then the procedure delays for two seconds (the call to WaitDelay in line 24) before it moves on to the next value.

Do

DO declare the MessageBeep arguments as constants if you'll be using them throughout a procedure or module. For example, the following statement declares the QuestionBeep constant as 32:

```
Const QuestionBeep = 32
```

DON'T

DON'T worry about running MessageBeep on a system without a sound card or sound driver. If the system can't play the sound, MessageBeep uses the computer's default beep.

Determining the Windows Folder

The GetWindowsDirectory DLL function determines the pathname of the Windows folder. This is handy if you need to find out which folder Windows is installed in or if you need to find out where one of Windows's accessory applets is located (such as the Phone Dialer applet used in Listing 20.15). You declare the GetWindowsDirectory function as follows (in this case, the **Alias** portion of the declaration is required):

```
Declare Function GetWindowsDirectory Lib "kernel32" _
              Alias "GetWindowsDirectoryA" _
                  (ByVal Buffer As String, _
                  ByVal Size As Long) As Long
```

The *Buffer* argument is a string variable into which GetWindowsDirectory places the Windows pathname. You must ensure that the string you pass is already long enough to hold the path name because DLLs can't increase the length of strings passed to them. If the string is not long enough to accommodate the folder path name, the string returned in the *Buffer* argument might overwrite memory locations not reserved for use by VBA, with disastrous consequences. Anything from General Protection Fault errors to an outright system crash is possible. The *Buffer* argument is an ideal use for a fixed-length string. The following declaration, for example, is an appropriate string to use as the *Buffer* argument:

```
Dim WinDir As String * 255
```

The *Size* argument is the maximum size of the buffer. You can use the Len function to determine the length of the buffer variable and use the result as the *Size* argument.

The GetWindowsDirectory function returns the length of the path name string copied into *Buffer*. Listing 20.12 shows an example.

INPUT   **LISTING 20.12**   USING THE GetWindowsDirectory DLL FUNCTION

```
1:   Option Explicit
2:
3:   Declare Function GetWindowsDirectory Lib "kernel32" _
4:                 Alias "GetWindowsDirectoryA" _
5:                     (ByVal Buffer As String, _
6:                     ByVal Size As Long) As Long
7:
8:   Sub LaunchWordPad()
9:   'Loads WordPad applet
10:
11:    Dim WinDir As String * 255
12:    Dim DirLength As Long
13:    Dim FullName As String
14:
15:    DirLength = GetWindowsDirectory(Buffer:=WinDir, _
16:                              Size:=Len(WinDir))
17:    If DirLength = 0 Then
18:      MsgBox "Unable to determine Windows directory!"
19:    Else
20:      FullName = Left(WinDir, DirLength) & "\WRITE.EXE"
21:      Shell PathName:=FullName, WindowStyle:=vbMaximizedFocus
22:    End If
23:  End Sub
```

20

ANALYSIS Listing 20.12 contains a complete module. The LaunchWordPad procedure uses the Shell function to load the WordPad applet provided with Windows and leaves it open, ready for editing. (The Shell function is explained in the next section of this lesson.)

Lines 3 through 6 of Listing 20.12 contain the **Declare** statement for the GetWindowsDirectory function. In this case, the **Alias** portion of the statement is required. The actual name of the DLL procedure is GetWindowsDirectoryA; without the **Alias** information, VBA can't find the function in the DLL.

The LaunchWordPad procedure begins by declaring the WinDir variable as a fixed-length string 255 characters long (line 11). WinDir is used as the buffer for the GetWindowsDirectory function (line 15). The size of the directory string copied to WinDir is stored in the DirLength variable. If DirLength is 0, it means that the function failed (line 17). In this case, a message to that effect is displayed (line 18). Otherwise, the full directory pathname for the Write.exe applet (which launches WordPad) is created by concatenating the Windows directory—as given by the Left(WinDir, DirLength) function—with "\WRITE.EXE" (line 20). The Shell statement runs WordPad in a maximized window with focus (line 21).

> **Note**
>
> The behavior of the LaunchWordPad procedure might seem a little confusing: It loads a program named Write.exe, instead of WordPad.exe, but WordPad is the program that appears onscreen. In versions of Microsoft Windows prior to Windows 95, the built-in word-processing program was called Write. Write was replaced by WordPad in Windows 95; the WordPad.exe file is actually stored in a folder other than the Windows folder. (WordPad is usually found in the \Program Files\Accessories folder). For backward compatibility, however, Windows still includes a Write program installed in the Windows folder. When the Windows Write.exe program is executed, it simply starts WordPad.exe. LaunchWordPad takes advantage of this by using the GetWindowsDirectory function to return the Windows folder and then execute the Write.exe program in the Windows folder.

Working with Applications that Don't Support Automation or OLE

Not all applications support Automation or OLE. In some cases the only way you can work with another application is to simply start it and either let your procedure's user work with the other application directly or (as explained later in this section) use the SendKeys method to send keystrokes to the application.

Starting Another Application

You use VBA's `Shell` function to start another application from a VBA procedure:

▼ SYNTAX

```
Shell(PathName [,WindowStyle])
```

PathName is a string expression for the name of the file that starts the application. To start Microsoft Access, for example, you would use the filename for the Access program: Msaccess.exe. You must include the drive and folder to ensure that VBA can find the file. You can also include any command-line switches or arguments for the application you're starting in the *PathName* argument's string. For example, to start Microsoft Access and open the MyData.mdb database, you would use a string such as this one for the *PathName* argument (assuming Access is installed on drive C in the \Program Files\Microsoft Office\Office folder):

```
C:\Program Files\Microsoft Office\Office\Msaccess.exe MyData.mdb
```

WindowStyle is a number that specifies how the application window will appear. VBA defines several intrinsic constants that make it easier to use the *WindowStyle* argument; these constants and their meanings are listed in Table 20.4. If you omit the *WindowStyle* argument, the application is started minimized, with focus.

If the `Shell` function is successful, it returns a numeric value: the *task identification number* for the application just started. (Windows internally identifies every currently running application with a unique task ID number; the task ID number for an application changes from work session to work session.) If `Shell` is unsuccessful, it generates an error. Listing 20.13 shows an example of the `Shell` function.

▲

TABLE 20.4 VBA's Intrinsic Constants for the `Shell` Function's WindowStyle Argument

WindowStyle	Window Appearance
vbHide	Hidden, with focus
vbNormalFocus	Normal size, with focus
vbMinimizedFocus	Minimized, with focus
vbMaximizeFocus	Maximized, with focus
vbNormalNoFocus	Normal size, without focus
vbMinizedNoFocus	Minimized, without focus

20

LISTING 20.13 USING THE Shell FUNCTION TO START AN APPLICATION

```
 1:   Option Explicit
 2:
 3:   Sub StartControlPanel(sIcon As String)
 4:   'Starts the Control Panel icon specified by sIcon argument.
 5:
 6:     On Error GoTo BadStart
 7:
 8:     Shell PathName:="CONTROL.EXE MAIN.CPL " & sIcon, _
 9:         WindowStyle:=vbNormalFocus
10:     Exit Sub
11:
12:   BadStart:
13:     MsgBox prompt:="Could not start Control Panel!", _
14:         Buttons:=vbOKOnly + vbExclamation, _
15:         Title:="Start Control Panel: " & sIcon
16:   End Sub
17:
18:
19:   Sub ChangePrinter()
20:   'Calls StartControlPanel to open Printers folder
21:     StartControlPanel ("PRINTERS")
22:   End Sub
```

ANALYSIS The Windows Control Panel, a frequently used applet, enables you to control many aspects of the Windows environment, including printer settings, fonts, and colors. The StartControlPanel procedure takes advantage of the fact that you can start many Control Panel icons directly by using the following command-line syntax:

CONTROL.EXE MAIN.CPL IconName

Here, Main.cpl is a .cpl—short for Control Panel Library—file of icons. IconName is the name of the Control Panel icon you want to run, for example, PRINTERS or FONTS.

The StartControlPanel procedure (lines 3 through 16) takes an sIcon argument that specifies the Control Panel icon with which you want to work. The procedure sets up an **On Error** handler (line 6) in case Control Panel doesn't start properly. Line 8 executes the Shell function (ignoring its result) to load Control Panel and run the module specified by sIcon. If all goes well, the procedure exits normally with **Exit Sub** (line 16). If an error occurs, the procedure jumps to the BadStart label (line 12) and a MsgBox statement displays the bad news (lines 13 through 15).

The ChangePrinter procedure (lines 19 through 22) is an example of how you would call StartControlPanel.

Do

DO save the result of the `Shell` function—the task identification number of the application you started—in a module-level or public scope variable if you intend to have your VBA program refer to this application again later in the procedure or program.

DO use the VBA `ChDir` statement if you need to change to an application's directory before starting the program (refer to Day 13).

Don't

DON'T enter statements after a `Shell` function if you want the statements to execute only when you've finished with the other application. The `Shell` statement runs an application *asynchronously*, which means that VBA starts the program and then immediately continues executing the rest of the procedure.

Activating a Running Application

After you have some other programs running, your application might need to switch among them. For example, you might want the user to switch between Excel and Control Panel to change various settings. To switch to any running application, use the `AppActivate` statement:

▼ SYNTAX

```
AppActivate(Title [,Wait])
```

Title can be either a numeric expression that evaluates to a valid task identification number (as returned by the `Shell` function) or a string expression containing the name of the application to which you want to switch. In this case, the name of the application is the text that appears in the application's title bar. For some applications, the title bar includes both the name of the application and the name of the active document. If *Title* doesn't match any application's title bar exactly, VBA tries to find a title bar that begins with the string passed in the *Title* argument. If *Title* matches the beginning of more than one running application's title bar, one of the applications is arbitrarily activated.

The optional *Wait* argument is a **Boolean** value that determines when VBA switches to the application. If *Wait* is **True**, `AppActivate` waits until the calling application is active before it switches to the other application; in VBA, this means `AppActivate` waits until the VBA host application (such as Excel) is activated before switching. If *Wait* is **False** or is omitted, `AppActivate` switches to the other application immediately. Set *Wait* to **True** whenever you want to ensure that your VBA program activates the other application *only* when the VBA host application is active and *not* when it is executing in the background. Listing 20.14 shows `AppActivate` in action.

20

INPUT   **LISTING 20.14**   USING THE AppActivate STATEMENT TO SWITCH TO A RUNNING
          APPLICATION

```
 1:   Option Explicit
 2:
 3:   Dim NPadID As Long
 4:
 5:   Sub LoadWinReadMe()
 6:   'Loads the Windows Read Me text file into Notepad
 7:
 8:      Const lTitle = "Load Windows Read Me File"
 9:      Const WinReadMe = "C:\Windows\ReadMe.txt"
10:
11:      If Dir(WinReadMe) <> "" Then
12:        NPadID = Shell(PathName:="C:\Windows\Notepad.exe " & _
13:                                  WinReadMe, _
14:                    WindowStyle:=vbNormalNoFocus)
15:        Application.OnKey Key:="^+E", _
16:                          Procedure:="ActivateNotePad"
17:        MsgBox prompt:="Windows Read Me loaded!" & vbCr & _
18:                       "Press Ctrl+Shift+E to activate.", _
19:              Buttons:=vbInformation, Title:=lTitle
20:      Else
21:        MsgBox prompt:="Can't find " & WinReadMe, _
22:              Buttons:=vbExclamation, Title:=lTitle
23:      End If
24:   End Sub
25:
26:
27:   Sub ActivateNotePad()
28:   'Activates Notepad when user presses Ctrl+Shift+E
29:
30:      On Error GoTo NotRunning
31:
32:      AppActivate Title:=NPadID, Wait:=True
33:      Exit Sub
34:
35:   NotRunning:
36:      MsgBox prompt:="Notepad isn't loaded!", _
37:             Buttons:=vbExclamation, _
38:             Title:="Hot Key Switch to Notepad"
39:   End Sub
```

ANALYSIS   The LoadWinReadMe procedure loads the file ReadMe.txt from the Windows folder into Notepad and sets up a shortcut key for activating Notepad in Excel. (The ReadMe.txt file in the Windows folder is supplied with Windows and is loaded onto your hard disk at the time Windows is installed on your computer; the ReadMe.txt file contains late-breaking news and information about the Windows operating system.)

Listing 20.14 is a complete module. Notice line 3, which declares a module-level variable, NPadID. NPadID is used to store the task identification number returned by the Shell function. Declaring this as a module-level variable ensures that the task identification number for the instance of NotePad launched by the LoadWinReadMe procedure will be available to all of the procedures in this module.

The LoadWin95ReadMe procedure starts in line 5. Lines 8 and 9 declare constants local to the procedure: a title for the message boxes displayed by this procedure and a constant for the name and folder path of the Windows ReadMe.txt file. (This file is installed with Windows in Window's installed folder; you might need to change this constant declaration if Windows is installed in a different drive or folder on your computer.)

Lines 11 through 23 perform the real work of this procedure. First, line 11 starts an **If...Then** statement that calls the Dir function (explained in Day 13) to ensure that the Windows ReadMe.txt file is in the specified folder. If it is, lines 12 through 19 are executed; otherwise, lines 21 and 22 display a message box announcing that the file can't be found.

Line 12 calls the Shell function to start the NotePad program. Notice that the PathName argument concatenates the name of the NotePad program with the WinReadMe constant; when NotePad starts, it will automatically load the specified file. The result of the Shell function—the task identification number for this instance of NotePad—is assigned to the NPadID variable for later use.

Next, line 15 creates an OnKey event that causes the ActivateNotePad procedure to be invoked whenever the user presses the Ctrl+Shift+E key combination. (Excel's OnKey events are described in more detail in Day 21.) Finally, lines 17 through 19 display a message dialog announcing the successful loading of the Windows Read Me text file into NotePad.

The ActivateNotepad procedure (lines 27 through 39) activates the NotePad application. Line 30 sets up an **On Error GoTo** handler in case the copy of NotePad started by the LoadWinReadMe procedure is no longer running. If all is well, the AppActivate statement in line 32 activates NotePad. If an error occurs, the code jumps to the NotRunning label (line 35) and an error message is displayed (lines 36 through 38).

Sending Keystrokes to Another Application

After you load an application with the Shell function or activate it with AppActivate, a user can work with that application directly. Frequently, though, this solution isn't satisfactory because the typical goal of a VBA program is to automate a task so that the user doesn't have to perform any actions herself.

20

You can control another application, even if it doesn't support Automation or OLE, by sending keystrokes to the other application with VBA's SendKeys statement. (The SendKeys statement is one of VBA's interaction procedures.) You can send any key or key combination—including those that use the Alt, Ctrl, and Shift keys—to an application. The result is exactly the same as if you typed those keystrokes directly in the application. Here is the syntax of the SendKeys statement:

▼ SYNTAX

SendKeys(*String* [,*Wait*])

String is the key or key combination you want to send to the active application. For letters, numbers, or punctuation marks, you simply enclose the character in quotes, as in "a". For other keys, use the strings listed in Table 20.5.

The optional *Wait* argument is a **Boolean** value indicating whether VBA waits for the keystrokes to be processed by the receiving application before VBA continues. If *Wait* is **True**, VBA waits for the application to finish processing the keys you send before moving on to the next statement in the procedure; otherwise, VBA continues executing your procedure without waiting.

To use SendKeys, all you have to do is activate a program with Shell or AppActivate. Then you can send whatever keystrokes you want. For example, you can close any active Windows application by sending the Alt+F4 key combination, as follows:

▲   SendKeys String:="%{F4}"

TABLE 20.5 STRINGS TO USE FOR THE SendKeys METHOD'S String ARGUMENT

For...	Use...
Backspace	{BACKSPACE} or {BS} or {BKSP}
Break	{BREAK}
Caps Lock	{CAPSLOCK}
Delete	{DELETE} or {DEL}
Down Arrow	{DOWN}
End	{END}
Enter (keypad)	{ENTER}
Enter	~ (tilde) or {ENTER}
Esc	{ESCAPE} or {ESC}
Help	{HELP}
Home	{HOME}
Insert	{INSERT} or {INS}
Left Arrow	{LEFT}

For...	Use...
Num Lock	{NUMLOCK}
Page Down	{PGDN}
Page Up	{PGUP}
Print Screen	{PRTSC}
Right Arrow	{RIGHT}
Scroll Lock	{SCROLLLOCK}
Tab	{TAB}
Up Arrow	{UP}
F1 through F12	{F1} through {F12}

By combining the keys from Table 20.5 with the Alt, Ctrl, and Shift keys, you can create any key combination. Just precede a string from Table 20.5 with one or more of the codes listed in Table 20.6.

TABLE 20.6 CODES FOR THE ALT, CTRL, AND SHIFT KEYS

For...	Use...
Alt	% (percent)
Ctrl	^ (caret)
Shift	+ (plus)

Listing 20.15 shows an example of sending keystrokes that uses the Windows Phone Dialer applet to dial a phone number from the current cell in a worksheet.

LISTING 20.15 CONTROLLING AN APPLICATION USING THE SendKeys STATEMENT

INPUT

```
1:  Sub XLDialIt()
2:  'Use the Phone dialer applet to dial a phone number
3:  'from the active worksheet cell.
4:
5:      Dim PhoneNumber As String
6:      Dim Ans As Integer
7:
8:      With ActiveCell
9:        Ans = MsgBox(prompt:="About to dial " & .Value & _
10:                    vbCr & "Make sure modem is on.", _
11:                    Buttons:=vbOKCancel + vbExclamation, _
```

20

continues

LISTING 20.15 CONTINUED

```
12:                      Title:="Invoking Phone Dialer")
13:      If Ans = vbCancel Then Exit Sub
14:       .Copy
15:    End With
16:
17:    Shell PathName:="C:\Windows\Dialer.exe", _
18:         WindowStyle:=vbNormalFocus    'Start Phone Dialer
19:    SendKeys String:="^v", Wait:=True   'Paste phone number
20:    SendKeys String:="%d", Wait:=True   'Start Dialing
21:
22:    Application.Wait Now + TimeValue("00:00:15")
23:
24:    SendKeys String:="~", Wait:=True
25:    SendKeys String:="%h", Wait:=True
26:    SendKeys String:="%{F4}", Wait:=True
27:
28:    Application.CutCopyMode = False
29:  End Sub
```

ANALYSIS The XLDialIt procedure uses the Windows Phone Dialer applet to dial a telephone number entered in the active worksheet cell. To execute this procedure, you need to first enter a phone number in any worksheet cell, make that cell active, and then execute the XLDialIt procedure with the Tools, Macro, Macros command.

Using ActiveCell in a **With** statement (lines 8 through 15), the procedure first displays a message dialog showing the phone number that will be dialed and warning the user to make sure that her modem is turned on. If the user chooses Cancel (or presses Esc), the procedure exits (line 13). Otherwise, the contents of the active cell are copied to the Clipboard (line 14).

Next, the procedure starts the Phone Dialer applet by using the Shell function (line 17). Two SendKeys statements send the following keys to the Phone Dialer (lines 19 and 20):

Ctrl+V—To paste the phone number from the Clipboard

Alt+D—To dial the number

At this point, Phone Dialer displays a "Pick up the phone" dialog. Go ahead and pick up the receiver, but don't press Enter to clear the dialog. The XLDialIt procedure waits 15 seconds to give your telephone time to dial (line 22) and then another group of SendKeys statements sends the following keys:

Enter—To remove the dialog box

Alt+H—To cause phone dialer to hang up

Alt+F4—To close the Phone Dialer applet

Finally, Excel's CutCopyMode property is set to **False** (line 28) to take Excel out of Copy mode.

Do

DO keep in mind that the SendKeys statement is case sensitive. For example, the strings "^P" and "^+p" both send the key combination Ctrl+Shift+P. If you want to send only Ctrl+P, use "^p".

DO include the following characters in braces—{}—if you want to send them in a SendKeys string:

```
~ % ^ ( ) + { } [ ]
```

For example, you send a percent sign as follows:

```
SendKeys "{%}"
```

Summary

This chapter showed you how to work with object linking and embedding (OLE) and Automation. The lesson began with a look at OLE's history. You learned that OLE works by inserting data from a server application into a client document. You can either link the object (in which case the data remains with the server application) or you can embed the object (in which case the data is stored entirely in the client document). OLE provides features such as in-place editing and Automation.

You learned how to use the AddOLEObject method of the Shape object to insert embedded or linked OLE objects into Excel worksheets. For new objects, you specify a class type; for existing objects, you specify a filename. You also learned how to use the OLEFormat and LinkFormat properties of the Shape object to work with an OLE object once you've linked or embedded it.

Next, this lesson looked at Automation features. Automation is a software standard that enables applications to expose their objects to languages such as VBA. Your procedure can work with these objects by executing their methods and reading or setting their properties. For applications with object libraries, you can refer to their objects directly. Otherwise, you use the CreateObject and GetObject functions.

20

To round out your knowledge of how to work with another application's resources, you also learned how to work with dynamic-link libraries (DLLs) in your VBA code. DLLs offer hundreds of specialized functions and procedures that enable you to perform tasks that are otherwise extremely difficult, if not impossible, with VBA alone.

Finally, this lesson walked you through a few techniques for working with applications that don't support Automation or OLE. You learned how to use the simple `Shell` function to start another application. You also learned that you can activate any running application by using the `AppActivate` statement. You learned that you can use the task ID returned by the `Shell` function to activate an application, or that you can specify the name of the application as it appears in the application's title bar in order to activate it. You learned that you can control applications that don't support either Automation or OLE by sending keystrokes. The `SendKeys` statement can send any key or key combination to an active Windows application. The results are the same as if you typed the keys yourself.

Q&A

Q How do the items in the Registry database get entered?

A Typically, entries in the Registry database are made automatically when you install new software, so you never need to worry about it. Although the Registry Editor does enable you to add, delete, or edit information in the Registry database, it is *highly recommended that you avoid altering the registration database*, unless you are instructed by a technical support engineer or by someone else who is extremely knowledgeable about the workings of the Registry database.

Q When I use the `AddOLEObject` method to insert a new embedded object, I get an error message telling me that Excel cannot insert object. What am I doing wrong?

A You're not doing anything wrong. It's just that some applications don't support embedding. Instead, you should try inserting these objects from existing files and linking them rather than embedding them. Refer to the listings in this lesson for examples of inserting linked OLE objects from existing files.

Q Besides using the Registry database, is there a way to find out what verbs exist for each OLE object?

A Yes, there is. Pull down the Edit menu and select the *<ObjectType>* Object command. (<ObjectType> is the type of object you've selected, such as Microsoft Graph.) This displays a cascade menu, the top half of which lists the object's verbs.

Q How do I know whether an Automation application provides an object library?

A In the VB Editor, select the Tools, References command. The References dialog shows you a list of all the object libraries on your system. If an object library appears in the list, and you select the library to add that reference to your VBA project, you can then see the Automation library's exposed objects in the Object Browser dialog.

Q When I try to run the `StartControlPanel` procedure in Listing 20.13 with the Password, Time and Date, International, Desktop, or other options, I get a display other than the one I expect, or nothing at all happens. Is something wrong with Control Panel?

A No, Control Panel is fine. The problem is that many of the Control Panel setting icons are actually located in different .cpl files. For example, the Password settings are in the Password.cpl file, the International settings are in the Intl.cpl file, and so on. To find out what .cpl files are available for you to use, use Windows' Start, Find, Files or Folders command and search for files named *.cpl.

Q Can I use the `Shell` function to run DOS commands or DOS programs?

A Sure. For external DOS commands—in other words, commands such as FORMAT, ATTRIB, or XCOPY32 that have their own executable files—just execute `Shell` with the name of the appropriate .exe or .com file, for example, FORMAT.COM or ATTRIB.EXE. For internal DOS commands, such as `DIR` and `COPY`, you can use the following syntax:

```
Shell "COMMAND.COM /C DOSCommand"
```

This statement creates a DOS box in Windows and issues a command to the DOS command interpreter, COMMAND.COM. The `/C` parameter tells DOS that this copy of COMMAND.COM in memory is temporary. *DOSCommand* is a string containing the internal command you want to execute and any additional switches or parameters. Use the exact syntax for the command that you would use at the DOS command line. For example, the following statement redirects the output of a `DIR` command to a file named DIR.TXT:

```
Shell "COMMAND.COM /C DIR /-P > DIR.TXT"
```

You should remember from Days 5 and 13, however, that VBA includes several functions and statements that can perform many of the duties for which you might use DOS commands.

20

Workshop

Answers are in Appendix A.

Quiz

1. In OLE terminology, what is a *server* and what is a *client*?

2. What is the difference between a linked object and an embedded object?

3. Name, and give a brief explanation of, the four main features found in OLE.

4. What is the purpose of the Windows Registry database?

5. What arguments would you use with the AddOLEObject method to perform the following tasks? Ignore the icon-related arguments.

   A. Insert a linked, existing word processing document.

   B. Insert a new presentation slide.

   C. Insert an embedded, existing bitmap image.

6. What is an OLE verb? What does the primary verb usually do?

7. What is Automation?

8. What are the three techniques that you can use to access Automation objects?

9. What does it mean to say that the Shell function executes applications asynchronously?

10. In a SendKeys statement, what does the Wait argument do?

11. What is a dynamic-link library?

12. What is the Windows API?

Exercises

1. Write a procedure that will cycle through the Shapes collection and report the name and programmatic identifier of each OLE object in the worksheet and also indicate whether the object is linked or embedded. To test your procedure, use the Insert, Object command to interactively insert a variety of linked or embedded OLE objects into a worksheet. (HINT: Trying to read the ProgID property of a linked OLEObject will cause a runtime error; test to see whether the object is linked or embedded by comparing the Type property to the msoEmbeddedOLEObject constant before checking the ProgID property.)

2. **BUG BUSTER:** The following procedure looks for a file named DirList.txt and deletes it if it exists. The first Shell function runs the DOS DIR command and redirects the output to DirList.txt. The second Shell statement is supposed to open

DirList.txt in NotePad, but—in most cases—an error occurs instead. Do you know why?

```
Sub GetDirListText()
  If Dir("c:\windows\dirlist.txt") <> "" Then _
    Kill "c:\windows\dirlist.txt"
  Shell "command.com /c dir ""c:\"" > c:\windows\dirlist.txt"
  Shell "notepad.exe c:\windows\dirlist.txt", vbNormalFocus
End Sub
```

DAY 21

Using Event Procedures and Add-Ins

As you've seen throughout this book, Visual Basic for Applications doesn't skimp on the number of ways in which you can run your procedures. You can start them by using the Macro dialog, a shortcut key, a customized menu command, or a customized toolbar button.

The common feature of these methods is that you have to do *something* to run the procedure: choose a menu command, press a key combination, or click a toolbar button. VBA also has several techniques that enable you to create procedures that run automatically when a certain event occurs, such as opening a workbook or selecting a worksheet. Your final lesson covers these automatic routines. You'll learn the following:

- How to run a procedure when you open, close, or save a workbook.
- How to run a procedure when you activate or deactivate an Excel worksheet, or when you activate a window that displays a particular worksheet.

- How to create procedures that run in response to specified keystrokes, key combinations, or mouse actions.
- How to run a procedure at a specific time.
- How to set up Excel VBA procedures that respond when the user enters data or when the worksheet recalculates.
- How to create and work with add-in applications in Excel.

What Are Events and Event Procedures?

You were introduced to the concept of event procedures and event-driven programming earlier in this book. In particular, in Day 16 you learned how to create event procedures for controls on a user form. In this lesson, you'll learn how to create event procedures for specific events associated with various objects in Excel. First, however, it might be helpful to you to review some facts about event-driven programs and event procedures.

An *event-driven* program is one that loops indefinitely, waiting for—and responding to—various events instead of simply following a linear path from beginning to end. An *event* is something that happens in the program, such as a particular keystroke, a mouse click, the activating or deactivating of a worksheet, or the opening or closing of a workbook. Because the specific events that occur while the program is executing guide the program's behavior, the program is said to be *driven* by those events, hence the term *event-driven*. When an event occurs, the program executes one or more procedures related to that event. These procedures are generally referred to as *event handlers* or *event procedures*.

You already know that objects within Excel make their properties and methods available to you for manipulation in your VBA code. A few objects also expose certain events, such as a mouse double-click or a file being opened or closed. You can create your own event-handling procedure for any event exposed by an object. Your event-handling procedures can—depending on the specific event—enhance, replace, or eliminate the object's built-in behavior for that event. For example, you can prevent a user from resizing a worksheet window by writing your own `WindowResize` event procedure.

Although Excel contains hundreds of objects, only a few of those objects expose events you can capture with your own event-handling procedures. Excel objects that expose events you can capture are limited to the `Application`, `Workbook`, `Worksheet`, and `Chart` objects.

In addition to the events exposed by objects, you can also create event-handling procedures that respond to the press of a specific key combination or that respond to the occurrence of a particular time of day. You can use the OnKey method to define which procedure Excel should execute in response to a particular keystroke. For example, you can use the Excel OnKey method to specify that a procedure named OpenComments is executed every time the Ctrl+Alt+N key combination is pressed.

Excel also provides an OnTime method that enables you to create events associated with a particular date and time of day. You'll learn how to create time-related and keystroke-related event procedures later in this lesson.

Do

DO use the Object Browser to find out what events are exposed by an object, if any. Events appear in the Members of *<class>* list and are designated with a lightning-bolt icon to their left.

DO keep in mind that the same event is often exposed at different levels in the object hierarchy. For example, Excel worksheets expose a SelectionChange event that occurs whenever the current selection on the worksheet changes. The same event is exposed at a workbook level through the SheetSelectionChange event, which occurs when the selection in any worksheet in the workbook changes.

Understanding Where Event Procedures Are Stored

Instead of storing an object's event-handling procedures in a standard module, you store them in the object's class module. Objects in Excel such as Workbook, Worksheet, and Chart each contain a class module in which you can store that object's event-handling procedures.

Figure 21.1 shows an open Code Window for the class module of a worksheet object in Excel VBA. Notice that the Worksheet object is selected in the Object list of the Code Window. The Procedure list of the Code Window (shown dropped down in Figure 21.1) contains a list of all the events for which you can create event-handling procedures. Selecting an event in the Procedure list of the Code Window causes the VB Editor to insert an empty procedure declaration for that event procedure if one doesn't exist already. In Figure 21.1, the empty event-handling procedure declaration for the worksheet's SelectionChange event is visible in the Code Window.

21

FIGURE 21.1

You create event-handling procedures in an object's class module.

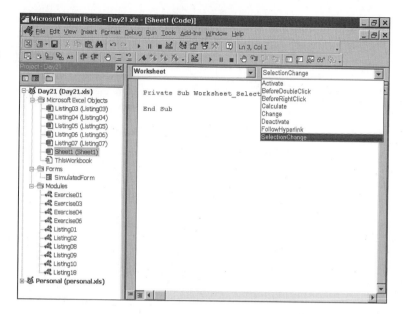

The exception to these rules about where and how event-handling procedures are stored is the `Application` object. The `Application` object does not have a class module in which to store its event-handling procedures. Instead, you store an `Application` object's event-handling procedures in a class module that you create. The section "Working with `Application` Object Events" later in this lesson describes the techniques for associating your event-handling procedures with an `Application` object's events.

To display or create an event-handling procedure for objects other than the `Application` object, follow these steps:

1. In the VB Editor, display the Project Explorer window if it isn't already displayed.

2. In the Project Explorer window, select the object for which you want to create (or modify) an event-handling procedure. Figure 21.1 shows the Sheet1 worksheet of an Excel workbook selected.

3. In the Project Explorer window, click the View Code button to display the selected object's class module in a Code Window (refer to Figure 21.1).

4. In the Code Window's Object list, select the object itself, that is, if you selected a `Worksheet` object in the Project Explorer window, you should select the `Worksheet` item in the Object list, as shown in Figure 21.1.

5. Select the event-handling procedure you want to create or modify in the Procedures list. The Procedures list will contain only entries corresponding to the events exposed by the object whose class module you have opened.

Event Procedure Names and Declarations

VBA associates a particular procedure in an object's class module with a specific event based on the procedure's name. For this reason, the event procedures you create must follow specific naming conventions, as well as a few other rules regarding how they are declared.

▼ SYNTAX

In general, event procedures must use this declaration syntax:

```
Private Sub Object_EventName(Arguments)
```

Event-handling procedures must be declared **Private** to the object's class module. In this syntax, *Object* represents the name of the object type to which the event-handling procedure belongs, such as App (for the Application object) or Workbook. *EventName* represents the name of the event to be handled, such as BeforeSave, BeforeDoubleClick, and so on. *Arguments* represents the event-handling procedure's argument list. Argument lists for event-handling procedures are discussed in the next section.

As an example, the following line declares a procedure for a Worksheet intended to handle the Activate event:

```
Private Sub Worksheet_Activate()
```

You'll see other examples of event-handling procedure declarations throughout this lesson.

▲

Do

DO use the event procedure declaration that the VB Editor inserts for you automatically. This declaration will have the correct name for the event and will also automatically include the event procedure's argument list.

Event Procedure Arguments

Some event-handling procedures have one or more arguments; others have none. Typically, an event procedure's arguments fulfill one of two purposes: to pass information to the event handler that you might need in order to handle the event and to provide a means for you to cancel the object's built-in response to the event.

As an example, consider the following event handler declaration:

```
Private Sub Workbook_BeforeClose(Cancel As Boolean)
```

21

The procedure created by this declaration will be invoked whenever the Workbook object is closed. The BeforeClose event occurs immediately before the workbook is closed, whether the workbook is closed by your VBA code or by an action performed interactively by the Excel user. The Workbook_BeforeClose event-handling procedure will, therefore, be executed immediately before the workbook is closed. The Workbook_BeforeClose procedure might contain code that validates new data entries or checks to see if data in the workbook has been saved. If there is invalid data or unsaved data, you might want to prevent the workbook from being closed. The Cancel argument enables you to do just that.

At the time the BeforeClose event triggers the execution of the Workbook_BeforeClose procedure, the Cancel argument is set to **False**. If you change the Cancel argument to **True** at some point in the Workbook_BeforeClose procedure, the actual closing of the workbook will be prevented. Not every event-handling procedure includes a Cancel argument.

As another example, look at the following event procedure declaration:

```
Private Sub Workbook_SheetActivate(ByVal Sh As Object)
```

This event-handling procedure declaration is for the SheetActivate event of a Workbook object. The SheetActivate event is triggered whenever any sheet in a workbook is activated. The Sh argument passes a reference to the activated sheet (either a worksheet or chart); because this event occurs within a workbook for any activated sheet, your event-handling procedure will need to be able to determine which sheet was activated. The Sh argument provides the means to do so.

Working with Application Object Events

The preceding section explained that event-handling procedures for individual objects within an application—Workbook, Worksheet, and so on—are stored in the class module that belongs to those objects. The Application object does not, however, have a class module. Creating event-handling procedures for the Application object in Excel is, therefore, slightly more complex. This section gives you an overview of how to create event-handling procedures for an Application object.

Creating an event-handling procedure for an Application object involves the following basic steps:

1. Create a new class module in a VBA project. You can give this class module any name you want.

2. Add the following declaration to the General section of the class module; the declaration must appear exactly as follows:

```
Public WithEvents App As Application
```

After you add the preceding declaration, the App object will appear in the class module's Object list (in the Code Window).

Note

You must use the name App in the **WithEvents** declaration or your application-level event-handling procedures won't work.

3. Write your event-handling procedures for the App object in the class module by selecting the desired event from the Procedures list in the Code Window.

4. Connect the event-handling procedures in the class module to the Application object by first declaring a module-level variable for your new class and then creating a procedure that sets the module-level variable to refer to the Application object. You can create this declaration and procedure in any module.

Assuming that your class module is named ApplicationEvents, you would use the following declaration and procedure to connect the event-handling procedures in the ApplicationEvents class module to the Application object:

```
Dim EventEnabledApp As New ApplicationEvents

Sub InitializeAppEvents()
  Set EventEnabledApp = Application
End Sub
```

Figure 21.2 shows the Code Window of an Excel class module named ApplicationEvents. Notice the **Public WithEvents** App **As** Application declaration visible in the General area of the class module (the declaration is partially obscured by the dropped-down Procedures list). As soon as you add the App object variable declaration to the General area of the class module, the App object choice appears in the Object list of the Code Window. In Figure 21.2, the App object has already been selected in the Object list and the Procedures list has been dropped down to show that the class module now automatically lists all of the events available for the Application object, just as for any other object. (Compare Figure 21.2 with Figure 21.1.)

21

FIGURE 21.2

*You create
application-level
event-handling proce-
dures by creating a
special class module
to store them.*

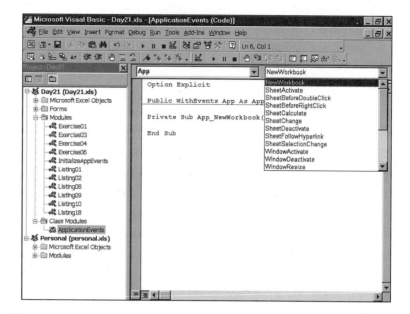

Do

DO consider creating the class module for an Application object's events in the Personal.xls workbook if you want your Application object event-handling procedures to be in effect at all times.

DO consider making the application-level event-handling initialization code a part of a workbook's Open event-handling code so that you can be sure the application-level events are initialized whenever your VBA project is loaded.

Don't

DON'T forget that your Application event-handling procedures will be in effect only if the workbook that contains the class module with the application's event-handling procedures is currently loaded.

DON'T load more than one workbook that contains application-level event-handling procedures; otherwise, you'll create an ambiguous situation in VBA, with unpredictable results.

DON'T forget that you must execute the initialization procedure that assigns a reference to the Application object to an instance of your new object class in order to complete the connection of your application-level event-handling procedures to the Application object.

Working with Excel Object Events

Even though the number of objects in Excel that expose events is fairly small, there are a total of 46 unique events available to you. Table 21.1 lists several of the most frequently used Excel object events, the objects they belong to, and a description of the events. The sections following Table 21.1 gives specific information on using the most important events listed in Table 21.1.

TABLE 21.1 FREQUENTLY USED EXCEL OBJECT EVENTS

Event	Belongs To	Occurs When
Activate	Chart, Workbook, Worksheet	Object is activated by VBA code or user interaction.
AddinInstall	Workbook	The workbook is installed as an add-in.
AddinUninstall	Workbook	The workbook is uninstalled as an add-in.
BeforeClose	Workbook	Before the workbook closes and before the user is asked to save changes.
BeforeDoubleClick	Chart, Worksheet	An embedded chart or worksheet is double-clicked but before the default double-click action.
BeforePrint	Workbook	Before the workbook or any part of its content is printed.
BeforeRightClick	Chart, Worksheet	An embedded chart or worksheet is double-clicked but before the default right-click action.
BeforeSave	Workbook	Before the workbook is saved.
Calculate	Chart, Worksheet	After the worksheet is recalculated or after a chart plots new or changed data.
Change	Worksheet	The Value property of a cell changes, whether changed by VBA or user interaction.
Deactivate	Chart, Workbook, Worksheet	The object is deactivated, whether by VBA code or user interaction.
NewSheet	Workbook	A new sheet (chart or worksheet) is created in the workbook.
NewWorkbook	Application	A new workbook is created.
Open	Workbook	A workbook is opened.

21

continues

TABLE 21.1 CONTINUED

Event	Belongs To	Occurs When
SelectionChange	Worksheet	The selection on a worksheet changes.
SheetActivate	Application, Workbook	Any sheet is activated.
SheetBeforeDoubleClick	Application, Workbook	A worksheet is double-clicked but before the default double-click action.
SheetBeforeRightClick	Application, Workbook	A worksheet is right-clicked but before the default right-click action.
SheetCalculate	Application, Workbook	A worksheet is recalculated or data on a chart is changed.
SheetChange	Application, Workbook	A cell in a worksheet is changed by the user or an external link.
SheetDeactivate	Application, Workbook	A sheet (worksheet or chart) is deactivated.
SheetSelectionChange	Application, Workbook	The worksheet selection changes.
WindowActivate	Application, Workbook	Any workbook window is activated.
WindowDeactivate	Application, Workbook	Any workbook window is deactivated.
WindowResize	Application, Workbook	Any workbook window is resized.
WorkbookActivate	Application	Any workbook is activated.
WorkbookAddinInstall	Application	Any workbook is installed as an add-in.
WorkbookAddinUninstall	Application	Any workbook is uninstalled as an add-in.
WorkbookBeforeClose	Application	Immediately before any workbook closes.
WorkbookBeforePrint	Application	Immediately before any workbook (or portion thereof) is printed.
WorkbookBeforeSave	Application	Immediately before any open workbook is saved.
WorkbookDeactivate	Application	Any open workbook is deactivated.
WorkbookNewSheet	Application	A new sheet (worksheet or chart) is created in any open workbook.
WorkbookOpen	Application	A workbook is opened.

> **Do**
>
> **DO** keep in mind that Table 21.1 lists only a little over 30 events of the available 46. Use the Object Browser to view all of the available Excel object events.

The Open Event

To function properly, most large-scale Excel VBA programs modify the host application's environment in some way. These modifications might involve adding custom menu commands, displaying a custom toolbar, or setting options for Excel. In most cases, these modifications must be made to Excel as soon as the user starts your VBA program so that your program's menu commands and toolbars are available from the start.

If you want your VBA program to be well received, you shouldn't impose the chore of adding menus and toolbars or changing option settings on the user. Instead, you should make these adjustments automatically at startup with an event-handling procedure for the workbook's Open event. The Open event is generated whenever a workbook is opened; the code in your Open event-handling procedure will, therefore, be executed each time the workbook is opened, providing an ideal opportunity to establish any special conditions needed by that workbook.

Some items you can include in an Open event-handling procedure are

- Code that installs or customizes command bars to create menus and toolbars for your VBA program.
- Program-wide settings, such as the calculation mode, the default file path, the standard font, and the objects displayed onscreen (including the status and formula bars).
- OnKey and OnTime event procedure assignments.
- A custom dialog of option settings for your program.

You can, of course, include any other action you need or want to have performed each and every time the workbook is opened.

Listing 21.1 shows an example of an Open event-handling procedure.

Note

For the Workbook_Open procedure in Listing 21.1 to work correctly, you must enter it into the class module of the ThisWorkbook object. In the VB Editor, open the Project Explorer window and expand the Microsoft Excel Objects folder list (if necessary) to see the ThisWorkbook object choice. Double-click

21

ThisWorkbook to display its class module's Code Window. Next, select Workbook in the Code Window's Object list and then select Open in the Procedures list. The VB Editor will automatically enter the Open event procedure's declaration; you can then enter the code from Listing 21.1.

INPUT **LISTING 21.1** USING A WORKBOOK'S Open EVENT

```
 1:   Private Sub Workbook_Open()
 2:   'Listing 21-1
 3:   'This procedure runs when workbook is opened
 4:
 5:      Application.StatusBar = "Loading VBA application..."
 6:
 7:      'Initialize environment
 8:      With Application
 9:        .AlertBeforeOverwriting = True
10:        .Calculation = xlManual
11:        .Caption = "VBA Rules!"
12:        .DisplayRecentFiles = False
13:        .MoveAfterReturn = False
14:        .PromptForSummaryInfo = False
15:        .SheetsInNewWorkbook = 8
16:        .UserName = InputBox(prompt:="Enter your name:", _
17:                             Title:="Open Event Procedure", _
18:                             Default:=.UserName)
19:      End With
20:
21:      'Display VB toolbar
22:      With Application.CommandBars("Visual Basic")
23:        .Visible = True
24:        .Position = msoBarFloating
25:        .Left = 400
26:        .Top = 200
27:      End With
28:      Application.StatusBar = False
29:   End Sub
```

The Workbook_Open event procedure begins by using the Application object's StatusBar property to display a message telling the user what's going on (line 5). (You can use the StatusBar property in any procedure. It's an easy way to keep the user informed, and it's less intrusive than the MsgBox function.)

Lines 8 through 19 contain a **With** statement, which sets several properties of the Excel `Application` object. Most of these properties are available in the Options dialog; you would use the Tools, Options command to set these properties manually. The `Caption` property (line 11), however, is different. This property controls the text that appears in the title of the host application's main window. In Excel, for example, this is normally Microsoft Excel, but you can change it to the name of your application, the name of your company, or whatever you like.

The next **With** statement (lines 21 through 27) displays and positions the Visual Basic toolbar. The procedure ends by setting the `StatusBar` property to `False` (line 28), which clears the message in the status bar and returns control of the status bar to Excel.

Do

DO hold down the Shift key while opening a workbook to prevent Excel from executing the `Workbook_Open` event procedure. Excel will open the workbook without executing the `Open` event and will enter design mode immediately after the workbook is opened.

DO remember that—except when you hold down the Shift key—Excel *always* executes the `Workbook_Open` event procedure, whether you open the workbook with your VBA code (by using the `Workbooks.Open` method) or use Excel's menu commands to open the workbook.

DO use the Object Browser to research the `WorkbookOpen` event of the `Application` object. You can use an event-handling procedure associated with the `WorkbookOpen` event to perform actions when *any* workbook in Excel is opened.

The `BeforeClose` Event

When you close a workbook, you might need to reset the Excel application's environment, especially if a `Workbook_Open` procedure has added menu commands or toolbars. To make this chore easier, you can create a `Workbook_BeforeClose` event-handling procedure. The `BeforeClose` event is executed immediately before the workbook is closed. Listing 21.2 shows an example of a `Workbook_BeforeClose` procedure.

INPUT   **LISTING 21.2**   USING A WORKBOOK'S BeforeClose EVENT

```
 1:  Private Sub Workbook_BeforeClose(Cancel As Boolean)
 2:  'Listing 21-2
 3:  'This procedure runs when the workbook closes
 4:
 5:      Application.StatusBar = "Closing VBA application..."
 6:
```

21

continues

LISTING 21.2 CONTINUED

```
 7:      'Reset environment
 8:      With Application
 9:        .Caption = Empty
10:        .DisplayRecentFiles = True
11:        .RecentFiles.Maximum = 5
12:        .Calculation = xlAutomatic
13:        .MoveAfterReturn = True
14:        .PromptForSummaryInfo = True
15:        .SheetsInNewWorkbook = 3
16:        .CommandBars("Visual Basic").Visible = False
17:      End With
18:
19:      'save the workbook's new settings
20:      ThisWorkbook.Save
21:      Application.StatusBar = False
22:    End Sub
```

ANALYSIS This procedure resets many of the environment options that were modified in the previous Workbook_Open event procedure (lines 8 through 17). Notice that the Caption property is assigned the value **Empty** in line 9. Assigning the special **Empty** value to the Caption property restores the original application's caption in the title bar of the main window. Because this procedure alters the workbook's settings (the options set by this code are stored with the workbook), line 20 saves the workbook before closing it; otherwise, Excel displays a message asking the user if she wants to save changes to the workbook.

Do

DO notice that the Workbook_BeforeClose event has a Cancel argument. You can cancel the workbook's closing by setting Cancel to **True**. This is particularly useful if you use the BeforeClose event procedure to validate data in the workbook; you can cancel the closing if you detect invalid data in the workbook.

DO remember that Excel *always* executes the Workbook_BeforeClose event procedure, whether you close the workbook with your VBA code or use Excel's menu commands to close the workbook.

DO use the Object Browser to research the WorkbookBeforeClose event of the Application object. You can use an event-handling procedure associated with the WorkbookBeforeClose event to perform actions when *any* workbook in Excel is closed.

The `Activate` Event

The `Workbook_Open` procedure demonstrated earlier in this lesson is useful for setting up menus, toolbars, and global settings used by every workbook and worksheet in a VBA program. Many programs that use multiple workbooks and multiple sheets in each workbook, however, require different settings as the user moves from sheet to sheet and book to book. For example, you might need to display a custom data entry dialog whenever the user selects a certain worksheet, or you might need to customize a menu or display a different toolbar when the user moves to another workbook.

In these cases, the user is activating different objects: worksheets and workbooks. Activating a specific object is an event, and you can trap these events by writing an event-handling procedure for the `Activate` event. The `Activate` event is available in the `Chart`, `Workbook`, and `Worksheet` objects and occurs whenever the object is activated, whether it is activated by VBA code or by a user's interaction with Excel. An object is activated when it is displayed in the active window.

Listing 21.3 shows an example of how to use the `Activate` event.

INPUT **LISTING 21.3** USING A WORKSHEET'S `Activate` EVENT

```
1:  Option Explicit
2:
3:  Private Sub ProcessData()
4:    MsgBox prompt:="Stand-in for a data-processing routine.", _
5:          Title:="Demo Activate Event Procedure"
6:  End Sub
7:
8:
9:  Private Sub Worksheet_Activate()
10: 'Executed whenever the worksheet is activated
11:
12:    Do While True
13:      SimulatedForm.Show
14:      If Not SimulatedForm.Canceled Then
15:        ProcessData
16:      Else
17:        Exit Do
18:      End If
19:    Loop
20: End Sub
```

21

ANALYSIS Listing 21.3 contains the entire class module of a worksheet. Lines 1 through 6 represent the code in the class module's General section; lines 9 through 20 contain the `Worksheet_Activate` event-handling procedure, which is contained in the Worksheet section of the class module. Whenever the worksheet that contains this class module is activated, the `Worksheet_Activate` event-handling procedure is executed.

The `Worksheet_Activate` procedure begins by starting a **Do While** loop that displays a user form dialog used for data entry on that worksheet (line 13). This procedure assumes that the user form's class module contains a `Canceled` variable that is **True** if the data entry dialog is canceled and **False** otherwise. Line 14 checks the status of the user form dialog's `Canceled` variable; if the user has not canceled the data entry dialog, line 15 executes a procedure named `ProcessData` (lines 3 through 6 of Listing 21.3). Otherwise, an **Exit Do** statement exits the loop (line 17). The `ProcessData` procedure in lines 3 through 6 is just a dummy procedure to represent whatever processing might be needed for the data entered into the user form dialog.

Do

DO consider using the other `Activate` events available to you. You can create `Workbook_Activate` and `Chart_Activate` event-handling procedures in addition to `Worksheet_Activate` event handlers.

DO keep in mind that the `Activate` event is exposed at several different object levels: You can use the `SheetActivate` event to handle the activation of any worksheet or chart sheet at a `Workbook` level or at the `Application` level.

DO use the `WorkbookActivate` event of the application object to create an event-handling procedure that is executed whenever any workbook is activated.

DO use the `WindowActivate` event of the `Workbook` object to create an event-handling procedure that is executed whenever a window displaying any portion of the workbook is activated. The `WindowActivate` event is also exposed at the `Application` level.

The `Deactivate` Event

As you saw earlier in this lesson, a `BeforeClose` event handler is useful for resetting any changes made to the Excel environment by an `Open` event handler. Similarly, you can use the `Deactivate` event to create an event handler that restores menus, validates data, or performs other tasks when a `Worksheet`, `Chart`, or `Workbook` object is deactivated. The `Deactivate` event occurs whenever the object ceases to be displayed in the active window.

Listing 21.4 shows an example of a `Deactivate` event-handling procedure.

LISTING 21.4   USING A WORKSHEET'S Deactivate EVENT

```
1:   Option Explicit
2:
3:   Private Sub Worksheet_Activate()
4:   'Prepares Budget sheet for use
5:     With Application.CommandBars("PivotTable")
6:        .Visible = True
7:        .Left = 100
8:        .Top = 200
9:     End With
10:  End Sub
11:
12:
13:  Private Sub Worksheet_Deactivate()
14:  'Removes Toolbars displayed for the Budget sheet
15:     With Application.CommandBars("PivotTable")
16:        .Visible = False
17:     End With
18:  End Sub
```

ANALYSIS Listing 21.4 contains the entire class module of a Worksheet object. The Worksheet_Activate procedure (lines 3 through 10) is the Activate event handler for the worksheet; it simulates setting up special conditions for a worksheet by displaying the Pivot Table toolbar.

Lines 13 through 18 contain the Worksheet_Deactivate procedure, which is the event-handling procedure for the worksheet's Deactivate event. The Worksheet_Deactivate procedure is intended to remove any special configuration applied by the Activate event-handling procedure. In this case, Worksheet_Deactivate merely hides the Pivot Table toolbar.

Do

DO consider using the other Deactivate events available to you. You can create Workbook_Deactivate and Chart_Deactivate event-handling procedures in addition to Worksheet_Deactivate event handlers.

DO keep in mind that the Deactivate event is exposed at several different object levels: You can use the SheetDeactivate event to handle the deactivation of any worksheet or chart sheet at a Workbook level or at the Application level.

DO use the WorkbookDeactivate event of the application object to create an event-handling procedure that is executed whenever any workbook is deactivated.

DO use the WindowDeactivate event of the Workbook object to create an event-handling procedure that is executed whenever a window displaying any portion of the workbook is deactivated. The WindowDeactivate event is also exposed at the Application level.

21

> **DON'T**
>
> **DON'T** use the `ActiveWorkbook` or `ActiveSheet` objects within the `Deactivate` event-handling procedure. Excel switches to the new workbook or sheet before it runs the event-handling procedure. Therefore, any code that references the active workbook or active sheet might not run properly.

The `BeforeDoubleClick` Event

Double-clicking the mouse in Excel produces different results depending on the object involved. For example, double-clicking a cell activates in-cell editing, whereas double-clicking a chart displays the Format Chart dialog. Either of these behaviors could be dangerous because they enable the user to edit cells or objects you might not want edited. You can use the `BeforeDoubleClick` event to trap double-clicks in `Worksheet` or `Chart` objects. The `BeforeDoubleClick` event occurs immediately before the object carries out its built-in response to the double-click event.

The `BeforeDoubleClick` event provides two arguments: `Target` and `Cancel`. Use the `Target` argument (a reference to an Excel `Range` object) to determine which worksheet cell the double-click occurred in. Use the `Cancel` argument to cancel the object's built-in response to a double-click event. Listing 21.5 shows an example of a `BeforeDoubleClick` event-handling procedure for a `Worksheet` object that uses both of the available arguments.

INPUT   **LISTING 21.5**   USING A WORKSHEET'S BeforeDoubleClick EVENT

```
 1:    Private Sub Worksheet_BeforeDoubleClick(ByVal Target As Excel.Range, _
 2:                                        Cancel As Boolean)
 3:    'Prevents editing of cells in odd-numbered columns and rows
 4:
 5:       With Target
 6:         If ((.Column Mod 2) <> 0) Or _
 7:           ((.Row Mod 2) <> 0) Then
 8:           MsgBox prompt:="You can't edit cells in " & _
 9:                       "odd-numbered columns or rows.", _
10:                 Title:="BeforeDoubleClick Event Demo"
11:           Cancel = True
12:         End If
13:       End With
14:    End Sub
```

ANALYSIS Listing 21.5 contains only one procedure, `Worksheet_BeforeDoubleClick`, which is the event-handling procedure for the workbook's `BeforeDoubleClick` procedure. This event-handling procedure is fairly simple and merely demonstrates how you might construct a `BeforeDoubleClick` procedure and use its arguments.

Lines 1 and 2 contain the declaration for the `Worksheet_BeforeDoubleClick` procedure (the declaration was reformatted with a line-continuation character to fit the margins of this book). Notice that the `Worksheet_BeforeDoubleClick` procedure has two arguments: `Target` and `Cancel`. These arguments are provided automatically by the `Worksheet` object when this event-handling procedure is executed. `Target` is a reference to the cell over which the mouse was double-clicked and `Cancel` stores a **Boolean** value indicating whether you want the `Worksheet` object to cancel its inherent double-click event-handling.

Line 5 starts a **With** statement that uses the `Target` object variable. Lines 6 and 7 contain a single **If** expression that checks whether the cell's row or column number is an odd number. (The **Mod** operator returns the remainder of an integer division operation; if there is a remainder after dividing a number by 2, that number is odd.) If either the cell's column or row is an odd number, lines 8 through 10 use a `MsgBox` statement to display a message explaining why in-cell editing won't occur.

Notice line 11. This statement sets the `BeforeDoubleClick` event's `Cancel` argument to **True**. The statement in line 11 cancels the `Workbook` object's built-in double-click event handler; the overall effect is to prohibit in-cell editing for any cell in an odd-numbered column or an odd-numbered row.

Do

DO keep in mind that using the `BeforeDoubleClick` event of a `Chart` sheet is an excellent way to create drill-down charts.

DO remember that the double-click event is also exposed at the `Application` and `Workbook` levels as the `SheetBeforeDoubleClick` event; this event is triggered when any sheet in a workbook is double-clicked (for `Workbook` objects) or when any sheet in any workbook is double-clicked (for the `Application` object).

Don't

DON'T forget about the `BeforeRightClick` and `SheetBeforeRightClick` events; you can use these events to display customized pop-up menus for worksheets and charts.

21

The Change Event

To ensure the accuracy of your worksheet data, it helps if you can verify each cell entry. For example, you might check to make sure that a date field entry is really a date or that an entered number satisfies a particular condition, such as being a positive number. You can do this by setting up a procedure to handle the Change event. The Change event provides one argument—Target—which is a reference to an Excel Range object.

Listing 21.6 shows an example of how to use the Change event for data verification.

INPUT   **LISTING 21.6**   USING A WORKSHEET'S Change EVENT

```
 1:    Option Explicit
 2:
 3:    Private Function VerifiedCellData(ByVal rngSource As Excel.Range)
 4:    'verifies that the data in the specified cell is valid
 5:    'column 1 should be a Date, column 2 should be a positive number
 6:
 7:       Const strTitle = "Verifying Cell Data"
 8:
 9:       VerifiedCellData = False   'assume failure
10:
11:       With rngSource
12:         Select Case .Column
13:           Case 1        'Date field
14:             If Not IsDate(.Value) Then
15:               MsgBox prompt:="Invalid entry in Date column.", _
16:                      Title:=strTitle
17:               Exit Function
18:             Else
19:               .NumberFormat = "mmmm d, yyyy"
20:             End If
21:           Case 2         'Amount field
22:             If IsNumeric(.Value) Then
23:               If .Value < 0 Then
24:                 MsgBox prompt:="Amount cannot be negative.", _
25:                        Title:=strTitle
26:                 Exit Function
27:               Else
28:                 .NumberFormat = "$#,##0.00_);($#,##0.00)"
29:               End If
30:             Else
31:               MsgBox prompt:="You must enter a numeric value.", _
32:                      Title:=strTitle
33:               Exit Function
34:             End If
35:         End Select
36:       End With
37:
```

```
38:    VerifiedCellData = True    'only a valid value if we get to here
39: End Function
40:
41:
42: Private Sub Worksheet_Change(ByVal Target As Excel.Range)
43: 'Uses the Change event to verify data entered in the worksheet
44:
45:    Static InError As Boolean
46:
47:    If InError Then
48:      InError = False
49:    Else
50:      If Not VerifiedCellData(Target) Then
51:         InError = True
52:         Target.Select
53:         Target.ClearContents
54:      End If
55:    End If
56: End Sub
```

ANALYSIS   Listing 21.6 contains the entire class module of a worksheet. Lines 1 through 39 represent the code in the General section of the class module; lines 42 through 56 contain the Worksheet_Change event-handling procedure from the Worksheet section of the class module. This analysis discusses the Worksheet_Change procedure first.

The Worksheet_Change event-handling procedure is executed whenever the Value property of any cell on the worksheet changes, whether the change is made by VBA code or by a user's entry at the keyboard. Notice the Target argument in line 42; this argument is automatically supplied by the Worksheet object whenever the Worksheet_Change event procedure is executed. Target contains a reference to the cell whose Value property has changed.

Notice the **Static** variable declaration in line 45. This **Boolean** variable is important in the operation of the Worksheet_Change event; InError is used to keep track of whether an error in the cell is currently being processed.

When any cell's Value property changes, the Worksheet_Change procedure is executed. Line 47 checks the value of the InError variable; if it is **False**, line 50 calls the VerifiedCellData function. VerifiedCellData returns **True** if the data in the cell referenced by Target is valid and returns **False** otherwise. If the VerifiedCellData returns **False**, line 51 sets InError to **True** to indicate that an error is now being processed. Next, line 52 selects the worksheet cell referenced by Target; this action returns the selection to the cell so that the user can easily re-enter the offending data value. Line 53 clears the erroneous value from the cell.

21

When line 53 is executed, the Worksheet_Change event-handling procedure is immediately called again because a cell on the worksheet has had its Value property changed; the Worksheet_Change procedure, therefore, executes recursively. Unless there is some way to halt the recursion, the Worksheet_Change event-handling procedure will continue to execute infinitely. The InError static variable is used to determine whether Worksheet_Change is in a recursive call. The first time an error is detected, InError is set to **True**. When Worksheet_Change executes recursively, InError is **True** and line 48 is executed, resetting the InError variable to **False**. The recursive call ends and the original call to Worksheet_Change also ends.

The effect of the Worksheet_Change event procedure, therefore, is to test the validity of the cell's value. If the cell contains invalid data, the selection is returned to the cell that contained the offending value, a message regarding the offending value is displayed, and the offending value is cleared from the cell.

The VerifiedCellData function (lines 3 through 36) accepts a single argument—rngSource—which is a reference to the cell being verified. When the Worksheet_Change procedure calls VerifiedCellData, it passes the Target range to VerifiedCellData through the rngSource argument. VerifiedCellData uses a **Case** statement (lines 12 through 35) to validate the cell's data based on which column the cell is in. Cells in the first column of the worksheet must contain **Date** type values; cells in the second column must contain positive numeric values. If a value isn't correct, VerifiedCellData displays a message describing what's wrong with the value and returns **False**; otherwise, VerifiedCellData returns **True**.

Do

DO use the Change event's Target argument to refer to the cell that has changed.

DO expect the Change event-handling procedure to run after the user uses the Cut, Paste, or Delete commands to change the contents of a cell. The Worksheet object triggers the Change event whenever a cell's Value property changes.

DON'T

DON'T forget that the Change event is also exposed at the Workbook and Application level through the SheetChange event. The SheetChange event is triggered for a Workbook object whenever any cell in any worksheet of the workbook changes. The SheetChange event is triggered in the Application object when any cell of any worksheet in any open workbook changes.

DON'T forget that if your Change event-handling procedure (or any procedure it calls) alters the contents of any cell, the Change event is again triggered, resulting in recursive execution of your event handler.

The `Calculate` Event

In a worksheet with a large and complex model, changing one variable can affect dozens of formulas. If you can't keep an eye on all these formulas—to check, for example, that a boundary condition is still being met—you can use the `Calculate` event to execute a procedure that will check for you. The `Calculate` event has no arguments. Listing 21.7 shows an example of putting the `Calculate` event to work.

INPUT   **LISTING 21.7**   USING A WORKSHEET'S `Calculate` EVENT

```
1:  Option Explicit
2:
3:  Private Sub Worksheet_Calculate()
4:  'Executes whenever the worksheet recalculates
5:    If Range("GrossMargin") < 0.2 Then
6:      MsgBox prompt:="Gross Margin has fallen below 20%", _
7:             Title:="Calculate Event Demo"
8:    End If
9:  End Sub
```

ANALYSIS   The `Worksheet_Calculate` event-handling procedure in Listing 21.7 is quite simple and demonstrates a simple use for the `Calculate` event. The `Worksheet_Calculate` procedure is executed whenever the worksheet is calculated, whether the calculation is made manually or automatically. The `Worksheet_Calculate` event procedure in Listing 21.7 assumes that there is a range on the worksheet named `GrossMargin` that displays the result of a formula that calculates a gross profit margin. When the worksheet is calculated, the `Worksheet_Calculate` procedure is executed and checks the value of the `GrossMargin` range; if this value is below 0.2 (that is, less than 20 percent), a message to that effect is displayed.

Do

DO keep in mind that the `Calculate` event is also exposed at the `Workbook` and `Application` level through the `SheetCalculate` event. The `SheetCalculate` event is triggered for a `Workbook` object whenever any sheet in the workbook is calculated. The `SheetCalculate` event is triggered in the `Application` object when any sheet in any open workbook calculates.

21

DON'T

DON'T forget that the `Calculate` event is also exposed for `Chart` sheets.

Other Events

As you can see from Table 21.1, there are many more events available than those discussed in the preceding sections; and Table 21.1 lists only a portion of the 46 unique events exposed by Excel objects! There are too many Excel events to provide examples of all of them in this book. There are a few other Excel object events that you should be aware of, however, because they can be quite useful. The following list summarizes these other events, grouping them by related function:

- *Printing.* The `Workbook` object exposes the `BeforePrint` event and the `Application` object exposes the `WorkbookBeforePrint` event. Use the `BeforePrint` event to handle any tasks you want performed before printing occurs. For example, you could use the `Workbook` object's `BeforePrint` event-handling procedure to ensure that all worksheets have been calculated, that a report is formatted, or to select specific views for printing. Using the `BeforePrint` event-handling procedure can help you automate the setup for complex reports: let the user choose the Print command and then let your `BeforePrint` event handler select the views or sheets to print.

- *Saving workbooks.* The `Workbook` object exposes the `BeforeSave` event and the `Application` object exposes the `WorkbookBeforeSave` event. These events occur immediately before a workbook is saved (or any workbook is saved, for the `Application` object). Use the `BeforeSave` event to perform data validation, to delete temporary worksheets, or to perform other tasks before a workbook is saved. The `BeforeSave` event provides two arguments. `SaveAsUi` is a **Boolean** value; if it is **True**, Excel will display the Save As dialog. The `Cancel` argument is another **Boolean** value; if you set this argument to **True**, the save operation is canceled after your event-handling procedure ends.

- *Creating new objects.* The `Workbook` object exposes the `NewSheet` event; this event occurs whenever a new chart or worksheet is added to the workbook. The `Application` object exposes the `WorkbookNewSheet` event and the `NewWorkbook` event. The `WorkbookNewSheet` event occurs whenever any open workbook has a new sheet added to it; the `NewWorkbook` event occurs whenever a new workbook is created. Use the `NewSheet` and `NewWorkbook` events to add predetermined elements—such as column headings, sheet names, named ranges, and so on—to a sheet or workbook as it is created.

- *Changing the selection.* The `Worksheet` object exposes the `SelectionChange` event, which occurs whenever the selection on the worksheet is changed. The `SheetSelectionChange` event is exposed by the `Workbook` and `Application` objects. Use the `SelectionChange` event to guide the user's selection choices through a series of predetermined points on a worksheet or to validate the contents of a cell as the selection is moved away from it.

Working with Excel's Event-Related Properties and Methods

In addition to the events exposed by objects, Excel also has a few event-related properties and methods. You can use these event-related properties and methods to establish event-handling procedures for events that aren't directly exposed by Excel's objects. For example, you can use the `OnKey` method to install your own special key commands; your key-command procedures will be invoked whenever a particular keystroke is entered at the keyboard. The `OnKey` method, therefore, provides you with a way to indirectly install procedures that respond to specific keyboard events. The next few sections of this lesson describe Excel's event-related properties and methods in more detail.

Excel's `OnWindow` Property

The `OnWindow` property fulfills a purpose similar to the `WindowActivate` event: `OnWindow` specifies an event procedure that runs whenever the user activates a particular window. Use the `OnWindow` property if you want to execute a particular procedure whenever any window on a particular worksheet becomes the active window. Another use for the `OnWindow` property is if you need to evaluate the contents of the current window and enable or disable menu commands or toolbars in your application depending on the window's specific contents. (Remember, you can have multiple windows open for the same worksheet.) The `OnWindow` property is found in the `Application` and `Window` objects. The syntax for setting the `OnWindow` property is

```
Object.OnWindow = "ProcedureName"
```

Here, *Object* is an object reference to either a `Window` object or the `Application` object. If *Object* references a `Window` object, the event procedure executes whenever the user switches to the specified window. If *Object* references the `Application` object, the event procedure executes whenever the user switches to any window.

To remove an event procedure associated with a window through the `OnWindow` property, assign a zero-length string to the `OnWindow` property:

```
Object.OnWindow = ""
```

Listing 21.8 shows an example of the `OnWindow` property.

21

INPUT **LISTING 21.8** USING THE OnWindow PROPERTY

```
 1:  Option Explicit
 2:
 3:  Sub SetWindowHandler()
 4:  'Sets up the event trapping for the OnWindow property
 5:
 6:      Windows("DAY21.XLS:2").OnWindow = "WindowHandler"
 7:  End Sub
 8:
 9:
10:  Sub WindowHandler()
11:  'Runs whenever the DAY21.XLS:2 window is activated
12:
13:      With Windows("DAY21.XLS:2")
14:          .SplitVertical = 150
15:          .DisplayFormulas = True
16:          .DisplayGridlines = False
17:          .DisplayZeros = False
18:          .FreezePanes = True
19:          .WindowState = xlMaximized
20:      End With
21:  End Sub
22:
23:
24:  Sub ClearWindowHandler()
25:  'Removes event trapping for the OnWindow property
26:
27:      Windows("DAY21.XLS:2").OnWindow = ""
28:  End Sub
```

ANALYSIS Listing 21.8 contains an entire standard module. In this example, a procedure named SetWindowHandler (lines 3 through 7) sets the OnWindow property for a window named Day21.xls:2 (line 6). The event procedure—WindowHandler—sets several of the window's properties inside a **With** statement (lines 13 through 20). The window is split vertically (line 14), formulas are displayed (line 15), gridlines are turned off (line 16), zeros are hidden (line 17), the panes are frozen (line 18), and the window is maximized (line 19). (The WindowHandler procedure works only if the sheet currently displayed in the window is a worksheet; otherwise, it will produce runtime errors.)

Tip

To create a new window for a workbook, first make sure that the workbook window is *not* maximized. Next, right-click on the workbook window's title bar and select the New Window command. Excel opens a new window to view the workbook.

For the `WindowHandler` procedure to work correctly, you must first execute the `SetWindowHandler` procedure *after* opening the second window on the Day21.xls workbook. To remove the `WindowHandler` event procedure, execute the `ClearWindowHandler` procedure.

Do

DO keep in mind that the event-handling procedures you create by assigning them to the `OnWindow` property can be stored in any module, unlike the event-handling procedures associated with an object's exposed events, which must be stored in a class module.

DO remember that event-handling procedures you create through the `OnWindow` property must be installed by a procedure that makes an assignment to the `OnWindow` property. Unlike object events, there is no way to automatically associate an `OnWindow` event-handling procedure with a particular window.

DO use the `WindowActivate` and `WindowDeactivate` object events instead of the `OnWindow` property if you want a particular series of steps to execute whenever any window displaying a particular worksheet or workbook is activated or deactivated. The `OnWindow` property creates an event-handling procedure for a specific window.

Excel's `OnKey` Method

As you know, you can assign shortcut key combinations to your Excel VBA procedures interactively by using the Tools, Macro, Macro command, selecting a procedure in the Macros dialog, and then clicking the Options command button. You can also install custom shortcut key combinations in your Excel VBA code by using the `OnKey` method. The keystroke shortcuts generally take the form Ctrl+*key*, where *key* is a letter of the alphabet. (Remember that Excel differentiates between uppercase and lowercase letters.) Although your choice of letters is limited—especially because Excel uses some letters for its built-in shortcut keys, such as Ctrl+C for the Edit, Copy command—this technique works fine in most applications.

The `OnKey` method is also useful if you want to disable specific keystrokes. For example, if you want to prevent a user from deleting anything, you would use your VBA code to remove the Cut button from the toolbar and the Cut and Clear commands from the menus, but then what about the Delete key? You can use the `OnKey` method to install your own event handler for the Delete key or any other keystroke:

21

▼ SYNTAX

```
Application.OnKey(Key, [Procedure])
```

The required *Key* argument is a string specifying the key or key combination you want to trap. For letters, numbers, or punctuation marks, simply enclose the character in quotes, for example, "a". For other keys, use the text strings outlined in Table 21.2. You can also create key combinations by combining a letter key or one of the keys from Table 21.2 with the Alt, Ctrl, and Shift keys by preceding the key letter or code with one or more of the codes listed in Table 21.3. (The key values shown in Tables 21.2 and 21.3 are the same as the key values you use with the SendKeys method described in Day 20.)

The optional *Procedure* argument is a string specifying the name of the procedure that is to be executed whenever the user presses the specified key. If you enter a zero-length string ("") for the *Procedure* argument, the key is disabled. If you omit the *Procedure* argument, Excel resets the key to its normal state.

TABLE 21.2   TEXT STRINGS TO USE FOR THE OnKey METHOD'S Key ARGUMENT

For...	Use...
Backspace	{BACKSPACE} or {BS}
Break	{BREAK}
Caps Lock	{CAPSLOCK}
Delete	{DELETE} or {DEL}
Down Arrow	{DOWN}
End	{END}
Enter (keypad)	{ENTER}
Enter	{~} (tilde)
Esc	{ESCAPE} or {ESC}
Home	{HOME}
Insert	{INSERT}
Left Arrow	{LEFT}
Num Lock	{NUMLOCK}
Page Down	{PGDN}
Page Up	{PGUP}
Right Arrow	{RIGHT}
Scroll Lock	{SCROLLLOCK}
Tab	{TAB}
Up Arrow	{UP}
F1 through F12	{F1} through {F12}

TABLE 21.3   CODES FOR THE ALT, CTRL, AND SHIFT KEYS

For...	Use...
Alt	% (percent)
Ctrl	^ (caret)
Shift	+ (plus)

Listing 21.9 shows you how to use the OnKey method.

INPUT   **LISTING 21.9**   USING THE OnKey METHOD

```
 1:   Option Explicit
 2:
 3:   Sub SetShortcutKeys()
 4:   'Sets the Ctrl+Shift+O and Ctrl+Shift+G shortcut keys
 5:     With Application
 6:        .OnKey Key:="^+O", Procedure:="DisplayGeneralOptions"
 7:        .OnKey Key:="^+G", Procedure:="ToggleGridlines"
 8:     End With
 9:   End Sub
10:
11:
12:   Sub DisplayGeneralOptions()
13:   'Displays the General tab of the Options dialog box
14:     Application.Dialogs(xlDialogOptionsGeneral).Show
15:   End Sub
16:
17:   Sub ToggleGridlines()
18:   'This procedure toggles gridlines on and off
19:     With ActiveWindow
20:        .DisplayGridlines = Not .DisplayGridlines
21:     End With
22:   End Sub
23:
24:   Sub ResetShortcutKeys()
25:   'Resets the Ctrl+Shift+O and Ctrl+Shift+G shortcut keys
26:     With Application
27:        .OnKey Key:="^+O"
28:        .OnKey Key:="^+G"
29:     End With
30:   End Sub
```

ANALYSIS   Listing 21.9 contains a complete module with four different procedures in it. The first procedure—SetShortcutKeys—uses two OnKey methods to define two shortcut keys. The first OnKey statement (line 6) assigns the procedure

21

`DisplayGeneralOptions` to be executed whenever the Ctrl+Shift+O key combination is pressed. The second `OnKey` statement (line 7) assigns the procedure `ToggleGridlines` to be executed whenever the Ctrl+Shift+G key combination is pressed.

The `DisplayGeneralOptions` procedure (lines 12 through 15) invokes the `Show` method (line 14) to display the General tab in the Options dialog box (specified by the `xlDialogOptionsGeneral` constant). The `ToggleGridlines` procedure (lines 17 through 22) simply toggles the `DisplayGridlines` property for the `ActiveWindow` (line 20).

The `ResetShortcutKeys` procedure (lines 24 through 30) restores the two shortcut key combinations (Ctrl+Shift+O and Ctrl+Shift+G) to their original actions—nothing, in the case of Ctrl+Shift+G—by using the `OnKey` method without the `Procedure` argument (lines 27 and 28).

Excel's `OnTime` Method

Excel's `OnTime` method enables you to execute a VBA procedure at a specific time, even on a specific day. The `OnTime` method is useful for setting time- and date-related event-handling procedures to carry out tasks such as the following:

- Executing timed backups of workbook data. Day 19 showed you a procedure that backs up a workbook to a floppy disk. You could set up `OnTime` to run this program at, say, 5:00 p.m. every day to back up workbooks to floppy disk, a file server, or some other location.

- If you're going to be away from your desk for a while, you could schedule a few time-consuming chores, such as recalculating a large worksheet or printing a report.

- You could have Excel display reminders about meetings, appointments, coffee breaks, and so on.

- You could run another program at a certain time to check your email or perform some other task.

The general syntax for the `OnTime` method is

▼ SYNTAX

`Application.OnTime(EarliestTime, Procedure, [LatestTime], [Schedule])`

The required `EarliestTime` argument is a number representing the time—and date, if desired—when you want the designated procedure to run. Use a serial date number for the `EarliestTime` argument. (Serial date numbers were described in Day 3.) The required `Procedure` argument is a string containing the name of the procedure you want executed when the time specified by `EarliestTime` arrives.

▼ If Excel isn't ready to execute the specified procedure at `EarliestTime`—that is, if Excel isn't in Ready, Cut, Copy, or Find mode—it will keep trying to execute the procedure

▼ until a time specified by the optional *LatestTime* argument. The *LatestTime* argument is also a serial date number. If you omit *LatestTime*, Excel executes the specified procedure as soon as possible after the *EarliestTime*.

The optional *Schedule* argument is a **Boolean** value that tells Excel whether to execute the designated procedure at the designated time. If the *Schedule* argument is **True** or omitted, Excel will execute the event procedure at the scheduled time. If the *Schedule* argument is **False**, Excel cancels the OnTime setting.

▲ Listing 21.10 shows an example of the OnTime method.

> **Tip**
>
> The easiest way to enter a serial date number to specify a time or date in the OnTime method arguments is to use VBA's TimeValue or DateValue functions. Use the TimeValue function to create a serial date number containing only a time value:
>
> TimeValue(*Time*)
>
> Here, *Time* is a string representing what time you want, for example, "5:00 PM" or "17:00". Similarly, if you want to obtain a date serial number with both date and time values, use the DateValue function:
>
> DateValue(*Date*)
>
> The *Date* argument is a string representing what date and time you want, for example, "3/15/94 5:00 PM".

INPUT   **LISTING 21.10**   USING EXCEL'S OnTime METHOD

```
1:  Sub SetReminder()
2:  'Installs an OnTime event
3:    Application.OnTime EarliestTime:=TimeValue("3:22 PM"), _
4:                      Procedure:="DAY21.XLS!RemindMe"
5:  End Sub
6:
7:
8:  Sub RemindMe()
9:  'This procedure displays a reminder message
10:    Beep
11:    MsgBox prompt:="The time is now " & _
12:                   Format(Time, "h:mm AM/PM") & "." & _
13:                   vbCr & _
14:                   "Don't forget your meeting with Simpson!"
15:  End Sub
```

21

ANALYSIS Listing 21.10 contains two procedures. The first procedure, `SetReminder` (lines 1 through 5), uses the `OnTime` method to install the `RemindMe` procedure to be executed at 3:22 p.m. (lines 3 and 4). The `RemindMe` procedure (lines 8 through 15) beeps the speaker (line 10) and displays a reminder message (lines 11 through 14). The `vbCr` constant in line 13 represents a carriage return character in the message. This is handy when you need to start a new line in a message box.

Do

DO remember that Excel runs an `OnTime` event procedure only once. If you run a procedure at noon today, the same procedure will not run again at noon tomorrow, even if you leave your computer on and keep Excel loaded.

DON'T

DON'T try to cancel an `OnTime` method that has already expired or Excel will generate an error message.

Working with Add-In Applications

If you've used any of Excel's add-in applications, you know how handy they are. They add extra functions and commands that look as though they were built into Excel. For your own VBA programs, you can convert your workbooks to add-ins and gain the following advantages:

- In Excel, your **Sub** procedures don't appear in the Macros dialog and your add-in's objects won't appear in the Object Browser. This means that users must access your add-in procedures with shortcut keys, menu commands, toolbar buttons, or other indirect means, such as event handlers.
- Add-ins execute somewhat faster than normal files.
- You can protect the source code in your add-in so that other users can't view or modify it.

It is important to keep in mind that add-in applications are *demand loaded*. This means that when you install your application, it gets read into memory in two stages:

1. The add-in application's shortcut keys are enabled, its command bars are installed, and (in Excel) the add-in application's functions are added to the Function Wizard.
2. The rest of the application is loaded into memory when the user either chooses one of the add-in functions, presses an add-in shortcut key, selects an add-in menu item, or clicks an add-in toolbar button.

The exception to the preceding demand-loading rules occurs when the add-in application has an Open event procedure. In this case, the entire add-in is loaded at the start.

Creating an Add-In Application

Creating an add-in is a fairly straightforward process. Add-ins you create are stored as Excel add-in files; Excel add-in files end with the .xla file extension.

> **Note**
>
> You might notice that some of the add-ins provided with Excel—or obtained from a third party—end with the file extension .xll. These add-ins aren't created with VBA; you can create only .xla add-in programs with VBA.

After you fully debug and test your code, you're ready to distribute it to your users. Follow these steps to convert a VBA project stored in a workbook into the add-in format:

1. Open the Excel workbook that contains the VBA application you want to convert to an add-in.

2. Hide any worksheets you want to be sure a user can't see and then use the Tools, Protection, Protect Workbook command to password-protect the workbook's structure.

3. Switch to the VB Editor.

4. In the VB Editor, display the Project Explorer window and select the VBA project you want to convert to an add-in.

5. Choose the Debug, Compile command to compile your VBA project; compiling your project immediately before converting it to an add-in ensures that all the code in the add-in is in a compiled state and that your add-in program will execute at its best speed.

6. Choose the Tools, <project> Properties command to display the Project Properties dialog and click the Protection tab to display the Protection properties sheet (if it isn't already displayed). Figure 21.3 shows the completed Project Properties dialog for an add-in based on a VBA project named Day21.

7. In the Protection sheet of the Project Properties dialog, select the Lock project for viewing option (refer to Figure 21.3).

8. Enter a password for your add-in program in the Password text box. After you save the add-in, the project's source code will only be editable if the user can supply the correct password.

21

9. Confirm your password by entering it a second time in the Confirm password text box. If the two passwords aren't the same, the VB Editor will display an error message when you click OK.

10. Click OK. The VB Editor protects your project. The project's components now cannot be viewed in the Project Explorer, and the source code cannot be displayed in a Code Window without supplying the correct password.

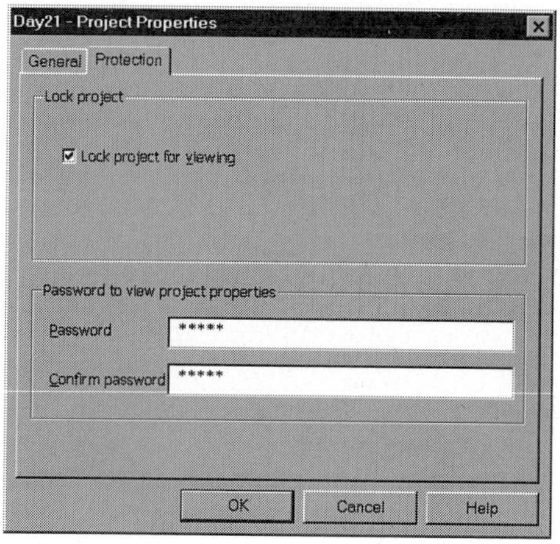

FIGURE 21.3

Use the Project Properties dialog to password protect your VBA project's source code.

Day21 - Project Properties	×
General Protection	

Lock project

☑ Lock project for viewing

Password to view project properties

Password   *****

Confirm password *****

[OK]   [Cancel]   [Help]

Caution

There is no way to recover or rediscover lost passwords for your add-in program. Make sure you don't forget the passwords you use to protect your workbooks and VBA projects.

11. Choose the File, Save As command.

12. Select Microsoft Excel Add-In (*.xla) in the Save As Type drop-down list of the Save As dialog.

13. Fill in the remaining Save As dialog options as you want; enter a filename and select a folder for the add-in.

14. Click Save to save the workbook; you have now created your new add-in application.

Do

DO keep in mind that if you don't add password protection to your project, the resulting add-in program's source code and objects can still be edited by a user. Adding password protection is the step that prevents the add-in's source code from being available to other users.

DO use the General tab of the Project Properties dialog to alter your project's name, to enter a description for your add-in, to specify a help file and help context for your add-in, or to specify conditional compilation arguments.

DO be sure to remove any debugging code from your procedures. Any `Stop` or `Debug.Print` statements remaining in your code will cause problems when the user runs the add-in.

DO fill in the Title and Comments boxes in the Summary tab of the workbook's properties sheet *before* you convert the workbook to an add-in. The Title text supplies the name of your add-in program in the Add-Ins dialog; the Comments appear as the add-in's description at the bottom of the Add-Ins dialog. Select the File, Properties command to display a file's properties sheet; click the Summary tab to display the Title and Comments text boxes.

DO use `ThisWorkbook` to refer to objects inside the add-in workbook.

Controlling Add-Ins with Visual Basic

VBA provides several methods and properties that enable you to control add-in applications at the procedural level. From a VBA point of view, an `AddIn` object is an individual add-in application, and `AddIns` is the collection of all the add-in applications available to the host application. The `AddIns` collection is identical with the list of add-ins you see when you display the Add-Ins dialog by selecting the Tools, Add-Ins command in Excel.

To refer to an `AddIn` object, use the `AddIns` method:

`AddIns(Index)`

The *Index* argument can be any of the following:

- A number representing the add-in you want to use. 1 signifies the first add-in that appears in the Add-Ins dialog, 2 signifies the second, and so on.

- The name, as text, of the add-in you want to use. For the add-ins that come with Excel, the name of the add-in is the name that appears in the Add-Ins dialog. For your own add-ins, the name is either the filename minus the extension or the text you entered in the Title text box of the Summary tab of the workbook's properties sheet (accessed through the File, Properties command).

For example, the following expression refers to Excel's Solver add-in application:

 `AddIns("Solver Add-In")`

21

Before you can work with your own add-ins, you must add them to the AddIns collection. To do that, use the Add method.

SYNTAX

The Add method in Excel has this syntax:

```
AddIns.Add(FileName, [CopyFile])
```

The required *FileName* argument is a string containing the full pathname of the add-in file. The optional *CopyFile* argument is a **Boolean** value used when the add-in file is stored on a floppy disk, CD-ROM, or network drive. If *CopyFile* is **True**, Excel copies the add-in file to your hard disk. If *CopyFile* is **False**, Excel leaves the file where it is. If you omit *CopyFile*, Excel displays a dialog that asks what you want to do. The *CopyFile* argument is ignored if *FileName* references a file on your hard disk.

Using the Add method merely makes the new AddIn object available. To actually *use* the add-in—that is, to make its commands and functions available to the user—you must install it by setting its Installed property to **True**. Setting an AddIn object's Installed property to **True** is the equivalent of activating the add-in's check box in the Add-Ins dialog and does two things:

- The first part of the demand-loading sequence is performed. The add-in's functions, shortcut keys, menus, and toolbars become available.

- The add-in's WorkbookAddInInstall event occurs and the event-handling procedure—if it has one—is executed. The AddInInstall event is similar to the Open event you learned about earlier in this lesson but is only generated when a workbook is installed as an add-in. The AddInInstall event-handling procedure is useful for things such as initializing the add-in and telling the user that the add-in is loaded.

Listing 21.11 shows you how to work with add-ins.

INPUT   **LISTING 21.11**   WORKING WITH ADD-IN APPLICATIONS

```
1:   Sub InstallBudgetTools()
2:   'Installs an add-in application
3:     Dim aAddIn As AddIn
4:
5:     Set aAddIn = AddIns.Add(FileName:="C:\VBA21\Budget Tools.XLA")
6:     With aAddIn
7:        .Installed = True
8:        MsgBox "The " & .Title & _
9:           " add-in is now installed.", _
10:          vbInformation
11:    End With
12:  End Sub
```

```
13:
14:
15:   Sub RemoveBudgetTools()
16:   'Removes an add-in application
17:     With AddIns("XL Add-In: Budget Tools")
18:         .Installed = False
19:         MsgBox "The " & .Title & _
20:             " add-in is now UNinstalled.", _
21:             vbInformation
22:     End With
23:   End Sub
```

ANALYSIS The InstallBudgetTools procedure adds and installs an add-in named Budget Tools. Line 5 uses the Add method to make the add-in available to Excel. Line 5 also sets the object variable aAddIn to refer to the newly added AddIn object. The With statement (line 6) installs the Budget Tools add-in (line 7) and displays a message telling the user that the add-in has been installed (lines 8 through 10).

Notice the use of the Title property in line 8. AddIn objects share many of the same properties found in Workbook objects. These properties include Author, Comments, FullName, Name, Path, Subject, and Title.

When you no longer need to work with an add-in, you can remove it by setting its Installed property to **False**, as shown in the RemoveBudgetTools procedure. Setting the Installed property to **False** also triggers the AddInUninstall event.

Do

DO use the AddinInstall and AddinUninstall events the same way you would use a workbook's Open and BeforeClose event, respectively.

DO use the WorkbookAddinInstall and WorkbookAddinUninstall events, exposed by Excel's Application object, to detect when any add-in is installed or uninstalled.

Summary

Excel offers a number of ways to execute your VBA procedures. They include the Macro dialog, shortcut keys, menu commands, and toolbar buttons. In each case, you or the user of your application has to do something to execute the procedure. This chapter showed you several ways to execute procedures automatically: through object events and through event-related methods and properties.

21

Objects expose certain events, such as closing or opening a workbook. You can write procedures associated with these events. Your event procedures run whenever the particular event occurs. This lesson showed examples of working with several different object events. You also learned that you can use Excel's OnKey method to install event procedures that respond to specific keystrokes.

Q&A

Q I have a workbook for which I've written several event-handling procedures. Can I create new workbooks that contain the same event-handling procedures by default?

A Yes. Just save a copy of your workbook as an Excel template file. Any workbooks you later create from the template file will contain event-handling code—and other code—just like the code stored in the workbook template.

Q I have a worksheet that I've created event-handling procedures for. I want to copy the event-handling code to another worksheet, but I don't want the worksheet's data or formulas copied. Is there any way to copy a worksheet's event-handling code without copying the entire worksheet?

A Yes, although somewhat indirectly. You can copy a workbook's or worksheet's event-handling procedures to another object of the same type by using the VB Editor's File, Export File command to export the object's class module. You can then import the class module into another project.

Q The `DoubleClick` event procedure is handy, but I want to run a procedure when the user clicks a picture. Is that possible?

A Yes. Use the `OnAction` property of the `Shape` object to assign a procedure to a shape object. (`OnAction` stores a string containing the name of the procedure you want executed.) After assigning a procedure to the `OnAction` property, you'll see the mouse pointer change to a hand with a pointing finger when it is over the `Shape` object. Click the `Shape` object to execute the procedure.

Q I have several event procedures I use every day—shortcut keys, `OnTime` events, and so on. Is there any way to install all of these event procedures automatically every time I start Excel?

A Absolutely. Unhide the Personal Macro Workbook (Personal.xls). In this workbook's class module, create an `Open` procedure and include in it all the statements that set up your `OnKey` and `OnTime` event procedures. In each of these statements, be sure to enter the procedure string as follows:

```
"PERSONAL.XLS!procedureName"
```

Here, *procedureName* is the name of the event procedure. This tells Excel where to find each procedure. Copy the event-handling procedures for your keystroke and time events to the Personal.xls module, as well, so that they are always available. After you save your changes, don't forget to hide Personal.xls again.

Q My `OnKey` event procedures don't seem to work while another procedure is running. Am I doing something wrong?

A Not at all. That's simply the default behavior of the `OnKey` property. Excel traps the key or key combination only when other procedures are not running.

Workshop

Answers are in Appendix A.

Quiz

1. What is an event-handling procedure?

2. Can you store an event-handling procedure in a standard module?

3. In Excel's `OnKey` method, what happens if you assign a zero-length string (`""`) to the `Procedure` argument? What happens if you leave out the `Procedure` argument altogether?

4. In Excel's `OnTime` method, what's the difference between the `EarliestTime` and `LatestTime` arguments?

5. What does it mean to say an add-in application is *demand loaded*?

6. Does the `Change` event-handling procedure execute when you paste data to a worksheet?

7. When does the Excel `Application` object's `SheetActivate` event occur?

Exercises

1. A well-designed VBA program always resets the environment when it exits. In Excel VBA, create an `Open` event-handling procedure that saves the current state of the Excel `Application` object's `DefaultFilePath`, `PromptForSummaryInfo`, and `SheetsInNewWorkbook` properties. Then write a `BeforeClose` event-handling procedure that resets each property to its original state.

2. **BUG BUSTER:** The `Worksheet_Deactivate` procedure shown here does not work correctly. Can you tell why?

```
Sub Worksheet_Deactivate()
  With ActiveSheet
    .UsedRange.Clear
```

21

```
        .Cells(1, 1).Value = "Sample Data"
      End With
    End Sub
```

3. Create procedures that test which Excel event procedure runs first: the `Worksheet_Activate` event-handling procedure or the event procedure set with the `OnWindow` method.

4. Pressing the Delete key normally wipes out only a cell's contents. Write the necessary procedures that set up (and later remove) the Ctrl+Delete key combination to delete everything in a cell: contents, formats, and notes.

5. It's possible to set up the `OnTime` method in Excel to run a procedure at regular intervals—say, every 60 minutes—instead of at a specific time. For example, if you have a procedure that backs up the active workbook to a network file server, you could have `OnTime` run this procedure every 5 or 10 minutes so that you don't have to worry about backing up your work manually. Write a procedure that sets up an `OnTime` event procedure to run at a regular interval specified by the user.

WEEK 3

In Review: Utilities Add-In Module and Customized Workbook Class

Congratulations! You have completed your third and final week of learning to program in VBA. This final week covered advanced VBA topics, including custom dialogs, error handling, customized command bars for menus and toolbars, and controlling other Windows applications from your VBA programs. This final week ended by showing you how to utilize the events exposed by objects in Excel, how to use various event-related properties and methods, and how to create add-in applications. The listings in this review put together several of the concepts you have learned, in particular, creating customized command bars and utilizing custom dialog boxes.

The following listings represent three complete Excel VBA modules. For all the code in these two modules to work, the third Excel VBA module from the Week 2 review must be in the same workbook (all four modules fit together).

The module in Listing R3.1 is a collection of useful utility procedures. As you study this listing, notice that some of the procedures use support routines from the support library module in Listing R2.3 (from the Week 2 review).

```
 1:   Option Explicit
 2:
 3:   'MessageBeep routine from Windows DLL
 4:   Declare Sub MessageBeep Lib "USER32" (ByVal BeepType As Long)
 5:
 6:   'MessageBeep constants
 7:   Const mBeepDefault = 0
 8:   Const mBeepCritical = 16
 9:   Const mBeepQuestion = 32
10:   Const mBeepExclamation = 48
11:   Const mBeepAsterisk = 64
12:
13:   Sub CopyFiles()
14:   'copies a file selected by the user to a new name, drive
15:   'or folder selected by the user.
16:
17:     Const msgTitle = "File Copy"
18:
19:     Dim sName As String    'source file name
20:     Dim dName As String    'destination file name
21:     Dim orgDrive As String  'original drive/folder
22:
23:     On Error GoTo BadNews    'set up error handler
24:
25:     orgDrive = CurDir()  'preserve logged drive/directory
26:
27:     With Application
28:       .StatusBar = "Select file to be copied."
29:       sName = .GetOpenFilename(Title:=msgTitle & " - Source")
30:       If sName = "False" Then GoTo CancelJob
31:       .StatusBar = "Select destination or new file name."
32:       dName = .GetSaveAsFilename( _
33:               Title:=msgTitle & " - Destination", _
34:               initialFilename:=FullName2BookName(sName))
35:       If dName = "False" Then GoTo CancelJob
36:       .StatusBar = "Copying " & sName & " to " & dName
37:       FileCopy Source:=sName, Destination:=dName
38:     End With
39:
40:   CancelJob:  'jump here if job is canceled
41:     ChDrive orgDrive   'restore original drive
42:     ChDir orgDrive     'restore original directory
43:     Application.StatusBar = False
44:     Exit Sub
45:
46:   BadNews:  'only executed if there's a runtime error
47:     MessageBeep mBeepCritical
48:     MsgBox Prompt:="Unable to complete File Copy." & _
```

```
49:                        vbCr & Err.Description, _
50:            Title:=msgTitle, _
51:            Buttons:=vbCritical
52:     ChDrive orgDrive
53:     ChDir orgDrive
54:     Application.StatusBar = False
55:  End Sub
56:
57:
58:  Sub Convert2Template()
59:  'saves the current workbook as a template file.
60:
61:     Const FilterList = "Templates (*.xlt),*.xlt"
62:     Const msgTitle = "Convert WorkBook to Template"
63:
64:     Dim dName As String         'destination filename
65:     Dim iName As String         'file name from user
66:     Dim orgDrive As String      'original drive/folder
67:
68:     On Error GoTo BadNews  'set error-handling
69:
70:     'ensure that it's safe to change workbook format
71:     With ActiveWorkbook
72:       If Not .Saved Then
73:         MessageBeep mBeepAsterisk
74:         MsgBox Prompt:=.Name & " has unsaved changes." & _
75:                        vbCr & "Save the workbook " & _
76:                        "before creating a template.", _
77:              Buttons:=vbInformation, _
78:              Title:=msgTitle
79:         Exit Sub
80:       End If
81:     End With
82:
83:     orgDrive = CurDir()      'preserve original drive/folder
84:
85:     'set up default destination filename
86:     dName = Left(ActiveWorkbook.Name, _
87:                  Len(ActiveWorkbook.Name) - 4)
88:
89:     With Application
90:       'change drive/directory to Excel's templates path
91:       ChDrive .TemplatesPath
92:       ChDir .TemplatesPath
93:       .StatusBar = "Select new template name."
94:
95:       'get the SaveAs filename from user
96:       iName = .GetSaveAsFilename(Title:=msgTitle, _
97:                                  initialFilename:=dName, _
98:                                  FileFilter:=FilterList)
```

continues

LISTING R3.1   CONTINUED

```
 99:    End With
100:
101:    If iName <> "False" Then
102:      Application.StatusBar = "Creating template..."
103:      ActiveWorkbook.SaveAs fileName:=iName, _
104:                            FileFormat:=xlTemplate
105:      MessageBeep mBeepAsterisk
106:      MsgBox Prompt:="Template created successfully.", _
107:            Buttons:=vbInformation, _
108:            Title:=msgTitle
109:    End If
110:
111:    'restore original logged drive/folder
112:    ChDrive orgDrive
113:    ChDir orgDrive
114:
115:    Application.StatusBar = False
116:    Exit Sub 'no more work to do
117:
118: BadNews:    'only get here if there's a runtime error
119:    MessageBeep mBeepCritical
120:    MsgBox Prompt:="Can't convert workbook to template" & _
121:                  vbCr & Err.Description, _
122:          Title:=msgTitle, _
123:          Buttons:=vbCritical
124:    Application.StatusBar = False
125:    ChDrive orgDrive
126:    ChDir orgDrive
127: End Sub
128:
129:
130: Sub Backup_ActiveBook()
131: 'Creates backup copy of active workbook under new filename
132: 'using the SaveCopyAs method. New name has "(backup)" appended
133:
134:    Dim FName As String
135:    Dim OldComment As String
136:
137:    With ActiveWorkbook
138:      'preserve original file comments
139:      OldComment = .Comments
140:
141:      'Add new comments for the backup copy
142:      .Comments = "Backup copy of " & .Name & _
143:                  ", made by backup procedure." & OldComment
144:
145:      'Make backup file name from original file name
146:      FName = Left(.Name, InStr(.Name, ".")) & "(backup).xls"
```

```
147:
148:      .SaveCopyAs fileName:=FName
149:      .Comments = OldComment      'restore comments
150:   End With
151: End Sub
```

ANALYSIS   Listing R3.1 is a complete module. Line 4 contains a declaration for the external DLL procedure, `MessageBeep` (Day 20), and lines 7 through 11 declare global constants for use in selecting the tone to be played by `MessageBeep`.

Lines 13 through 38 contain the `CopyFiles` procedure. This is a version of a procedure that appeared in Day 13. Notice the **On Error GoTo** statement (Day 18) in line 23. If any errors occur when this procedure executes—such as a full disk—the runtime error-handling code in lines 46 through 54 displays an error message and performs some housekeeping.

Lines 58 through 127 contain the `Convert2Template` procedure, which converts the active workbook to an Excel template file. This procedure also uses an **On Error GoTo** statement (line 68) to set up an error-handling routine.

Lines 130 through 151 contain the `Backup_ActiveBook` procedure, which makes a backup copy of the current workbook, giving the new file a name that contains the string `"(backup)"` to designate the backup file. This procedure is similar to one that appeared in Day 7, but is a somewhat more sophisticated version.

The next listing shows another complete module, this time a class module for a workbook. This class module contains `Open` and `BeforeClose` event procedures that customize Excel's menus whenever the workbook containing this module is opened. The class module also contains a procedure used to support the actions carried out by the workbook object's event-handling procedures.

Note   To enter code into the class module for a workbook, double-click the `ThisWorkbook` object in the Project Explorer window. The VB Editor will display the workbook's class module and you can then type in the event procedures and other code for that object.

INPUT

LISTING R3.2   THE WORKBOOK'S CLASS MODULE, CONTAINING EVENT
PROCEDURES AND THEIR SUPPORTING PROCEDURES

```
 1:  Option Explicit
 2:
 3:  Private Sub Create_UtilityMenu(cmdBar As CommandBar)
 4:  'adds Utility menu to specified command bar
 5:
 6:      Dim ctrlMenu As CommandBarPopup
 7:      Dim ctrlTemp As CommandBarButton
 8:
 9:      With cmdBar.Controls
10:        Set ctrlMenu = .Add(Type:=msoControlPopup, _
11:                            before:=.Count, _
12:                            temporary:=True)
13:        ctrlMenu.Caption = "&Utilities"
14:      End With
15:
16:      With ctrlMenu
17:        'add the Copy File menu choice
18:        Set ctrlTemp = .Controls.Add(Type:=msoControlButton)
19:        ctrlTemp.Caption = "&Copy File"
20:        ctrlTemp.OnAction = "CopyFiles"
21:        ctrlTemp.DescriptionText = "Copy any file"
22:
23:        'add the Backup menu choice
24:        Set ctrlTemp = .Controls.Add(Type:=msoControlButton)
25:        ctrlTemp.Caption = "&Backup Active Book"
26:        ctrlTemp.OnAction = "Backup_ActiveBook"
27:        ctrlTemp.DescriptionText = "Back up the active workbook"
28:        ctrlTemp.BeginGroup = True
29:
30:        'add the Convert to Template menu choice
31:        Set ctrlTemp = .Controls.Add(Type:=msoControlButton)
32:        ctrlTemp.Caption = "Convert To &Template"
33:        ctrlTemp.OnAction = "Convert2Template"
34:        ctrlTemp.DescriptionText = "Convert active workbook " & _
35:                                   "to an Excel template."
36:        ctrlTemp.BeginGroup = True
37:      End With
38:  End Sub
39:
40:
41:  Sub Workbook_Open()
42:  'creates the Utilities menu, and modifies the File Menu
43:
44:      Dim aMenu As CommandBar
45:      Dim ctrlMenu As CommandBarButton
46:
47:      For Each aMenu In Application.CommandBars
```

```
48:      If aMenu.BuiltIn Then    'only modify built-in menus
49:       If aMenu.Type = msoBarTypeMenuBar Then 'only modify menus
50:        Create_UtilityMenu cmdBar:=aMenu   'add Utilities menu
51:        With aMenu.Controls("File").Controls  'add to File menu
52:         Set ctrlMenu = .Add(Type:=msoControlButton, _
53:                                before:=2)
54:         ctrlMenu.Caption = "C&reate Named Workbook..."
55:         ctrlMenu.OnAction = "OpenNewBook"
56:         ctrlMenu.DescriptionText = "Create new workbook with " & _
57:                                "a specific name"
58:        End With
59:       End If
60:      End If
61:    Next aMenu
62: End Sub
63:
64:
65: Private Sub Workbook_BeforeClose(Cancel As Boolean)
66:
67:    Dim aMenu As CommandBar
68:
69:    For Each aMenu In Application.CommandBars
70:      With aMenu
71:       If .BuiltIn And (.Type = msoBarTypeMenuBar) Then
72:        aMenu.Controls("Utilities").Delete
73:        With aMenu.Controls("File")         'clean up File menu
74:          .Controls("Create Named Workbook...").Delete
75:        End With
76:       End If
77:      End With
78:    Next aMenu
79: End Sub
```

ANALYSIS First of all, notice that this class module contains three procedures: Create_UtilityMenu (lines 3 through 38), Workbook_Open (lines 41 through 62), and Workbook_BeforeClose (lines 65 through 79). Only two of the three procedures are event procedures for the workbook object; the Create_UtilityMenu procedure is a supporting procedure used by the Workbook_Open event-handling procedure and appears in the class module's General section. The remaining procedures appear in the Workbook section of the class module.

In Listing R3.2, notice also that *all* the procedures are declared with the **Private** keyword. The VB Editor automatically adds the **Private** keyword when it inserts the event procedure's declaration for you. Procedures in an object's class module are declared **Private** so that they won't be accessible outside of the class module and won't appear in the Macros dialog. The Create_UtilityMenu procedure is also declared **Private** because it is intended for use only by the `Workbook_Open` event-handling procedure; the **Private** declaration restricts the `Create_UtilityMenu` procedure's availability to the `Workbook` object's class module.

Lines 41 through 62 contain the `Workbook_Open` event-handling procedure. This procedure essentially consists of a single **For Each** loop (line 47) that loops through all of Excel's command bars and adds a Utilities menu to each built-in menu command bar. Only built-in command bars of the `msoBarTypeMenuBar` type are altered to avoid interfering with any other custom menu command bars that might have been installed by another VBA program or an add-in program.

To add the custom Utilities menu, the `Workbook_Open` procedure calls the `Create_UtilityMenu` procedure (line 50). Lines 51 through 58 of the `Workbook_Open` procedure add a single menu choice to the Excel File menu, creating the new custom File, Create Named Workbook command. Notice that this new menu command executes the `OpenNewBook` procedure in Listing R3.3 (the `OnAction` argument in line 55). Line 56 sets the `DescriptionText` property of the new menu item in order to provide a hint to the user about what this command does.

Lines 65 through 79 contain the `Workbook_BeforeClose` event-handling procedure, which removes all the custom menus and commands when the workbook is closed. The `Workbook_BeforeClose` procedure removes the custom Utilities menu and the custom File, Create Named Book command from each of Excel's built-in menu-type command bars.

Going back to the General section of the class module, lines 3 through 38 contain the `Create_UtilityMenu` procedure, which adds the custom Utility menu to the command bar specified by the `cmdBar` argument. Notice that this procedure is declared with the **Private** keyword so that it is not available outside of this particular module.

Lines 9 through 14 of `Create_UtilityMenu` contain the statements that add the Utilities menu choice, itself. Lines 18 through 21 add the Utilities, Copy File command (specifying that this menu item should execute the `CopyFiles` procedure) and set the new menu item's `DescriptionText` property. Lines 24 through 28 add the Utilities, Backup Active Book command (specifying that this menu item should execute the `Backup_ActiveBook` procedure) and also set this menu item's `DescriptionText` property. Notice that line 28 sets the `BeginGroup` property to **True** so that this command on the menu is separated from the preceding command by a line on the menu. Similarly, lines 31 through 35 add the Utilities, Convert To Template command with the `Convert2Template` procedure as its event procedure. This final menu command is also separated from the preceding commands with a separator line on the menu.

Listing R3.3 also contains an entire module. Listing R3.3 provides the code needed to carry out the bulk of the tasks required to create a new, named workbook with a specified number of worksheets, optionally named and sorted at the time the workbook is created. Listing R3.3 contains the OpenNewBook procedure called whenever the custom File, Create Named Workbook command is selected. The remaining procedures in Listing R3.3 are used by the OpenNewBook procedure as it carries out its task.

INPUT **LISTING R3.3** THE OpenNewBook PROCEDURE AND SUPPORTING ROUTINES

```
1:    Option Private Module
2:    Option Explicit
3:
4:    Public Const STREQUAL As Integer = 0 'StrComp: equality
5:    Public Const STRLESS As Integer = -1 'StrComp: less than
6:    Public Const STRGREAT As Integer = 1 'StrComp: greater than
7:
8:
9:    Sub OpenNewBook()
10:   'Creates a new workbook, ensuring that the chosen workbook
11:   'is not already open, and does not already exist in the
12:   'current disk folder. Optionally allows user to select the
13:   'number of worksheets and modules, and allows user to give
14:   'them specific names when creating the workbook.
15:
16:      Const nfTitle = "Open New Workbook"
17:
18:      Dim FName As String       'filename, including path
19:      Dim BName As String        'filename, without path
20:      Dim OKName As Boolean
21:      Dim Ans As Integer          'answers from MsgBox
22:      Dim mPrompt As String        'prompt for MsgBox
23:      Dim nBook As Workbook      'object for new workbook
24:
25:      'display status bar message
26:      Application.StatusBar = "Creating New Workbook..."
27:
28:      BName = "New Workbook"       'get new filename from user
29:      OKName = False
30:      Do
31:        FName = GetBookName(Dflt:=BName, Title:=nfTitle & _
32:                    " - Select Save As Name for New Workbook")
33:        If FName = "False" Then EndNewBook    'user canceled
34:
35:        BName = FullName2BookName(FName)
36:        If IsBookOpen(BName) Then
37:          mPrompt = BName & " is already open. " & _
38:                    "Would you like to switch to it?"
```

continues

LISTING R3.3   CONTINUED

```
39:          Ans = MsgBox(Prompt:=mPrompt, Title:=nfTitle, _
40:                       Buttons:=vbQuestion + vbYesNo)
41:        If Ans = vbYes Then
42:           Workbooks(BName).Activate
43:           EndNewBook
44:        End If
45:      ElseIf IsDiskFile(FName) Then
46:        mPrompt = FName & vbCr & _
47:            " already exists. Would you like to open it?"
48:          Ans = MsgBox(Prompt:=mPrompt, Title:=nfTitle, _
49:                       Buttons:=vbQuestion + vbYesNo)
50:        If Ans = vbYes Then
51:           Workbooks.Open FName
52:           EndNewBook
53:        End If
54:      Else
55:        OKName = True    'book is neither open nor exists
56:      End If
57:    Loop Until OKName
58:
59:    'load the form
60:    Load frmOpenNewBook
61:
62:    'set form caption
63:    frmOpenNewBook.Caption = "Set Options for " & BName
64:
65:    'show the form
66:    frmOpenNewBook.Show
67:    If frmOpenNewBook.Canceled Then EndNewBook
68:
69:    'create new workbook with one worksheet
70:    Set nBook = Workbooks.Add(xlWorksheet)
71:
72:    'set summary information
73:    With frmOpenNewBook     'fill in summary information
74:      nBook.Title = .txtTitle
75:      nBook.Subject = .txtSubject
76:      nBook.Author = .txtAuthor
77:    End With
78:
79:    If frmOpenNewBook.spnNumSheets.Value > 1 Then
80:      'adjust number of worksheets
81:      NewBook_Worksheets nBook, nfTitle
82:    End If
83:
84:    'Finally, save the new workbook file
85:    nBook.SaveAs fileName:=FName, _
86:                 FileFormat:=xlNormal, _
87:                 ReadOnlyRecommended:=False, _
```

```
88:                   CreateBackup:=False
89:     nBook.Activate
90:     nBook.Sheets(1).Activate
91:     EndNewBook 'do housekeeping
92:  End Sub
93:
94:  Sub EndNewBook()
95:  'ends OpenNewBook program, after cleaning up
96:     Application.StatusBar = False
97:     End
98:  End Sub
99:
100: Sub NewBook_Worksheets(ByRef Book As Workbook, _
101:                        ByVal Title As String)
102: 'Get and set number of worksheets for the new workbook
103:
104:    Dim shtNames() As String        'array for workbook names
105:    Dim numSheets As Integer   'number of worksheets from user
106:    Dim Ans As Integer         'MsgBox answers
107:    Dim k As Integer           'loop counter
108:    Dim Sht As Worksheet
109:    Dim Sht2 As Worksheet
110:
111:    Title = Title & " - Select Worksheets"
112:
113:    numSheets = frmOpenNewBook.spnNumSheets.Value
114:
115:    Ans = MsgBox(Title:=Title, _
116:                 Buttons:=vbQuestion + vbYesNo, _
117:                 Prompt:="Change default worksheet names?")
118:    If Ans = vbNo Then   'just add sheets
119:      For k = (Book.Worksheets.Count + 1) To numSheets
120:        Set Sht = Book.Worksheets(Book.Worksheets.Count)
121:        Set Sht2 = Book.Worksheets.Add
122:        Sht2.Move after:=Sht
123:      Next k
124:      Exit Sub 'no more work to do
125:    End If
126:
127:    ReDim shtNames(1 To numSheets)   'size the array of names
128:    For k = 1 To numSheets
129:      shtNames(k) = "Sheet" & k      'make default names
130:    Next k
131:
132:    'get names of worksheets from user
133:    Get_NameList Book:=Book, List:=shtNames, _
134:                 Prompt:="Enter a worksheet name:", _
135:                 Title:=Title
136:    Ans = MsgBox(Title:=Title, _
```

continues

LISTING R3.3 CONTINUED

```
137:                        Buttons:=vbQuestion + vbYesNo, _
138:               Prompt:="Sort worksheet names alphabetically?")
139:     If Ans = vbYes Then BubbleSortStrings shtNames
140:
141:     'create the worksheets with names
142:     With Book
143:        'start by just renaming the first sheet
144:        .Worksheets(1).Name = shtNames(1)
145:        For k = 2 To numSheets
146:           Set Sht = .Worksheets(.Worksheets.Count)
147:           Set Sht2 = .Worksheets.Add
148:           Sht2.Move after:=Sht
149:           Sht2.Name = shtNames(k)
150:        Next k
151:     End With
152: End Sub
153:
154: Sub Get_NameList(Book As Workbook, _
155:                  List() As String, _
156:                  Prompt As String, _
157:                  Title As String)
158: 'gets a list of worksheet names as strings
159:     Dim k As Long, tStr As String, GoodName As Boolean
160:
161:     For k = LBound(List) To UBound(List)
162:        Do 'ask for a unique name
163:           tStr = InputBox(Prompt:=Prompt, _
164:                        Title:=Title, _
165:                        Default:=List(k))
166:        If Trim(tStr) = "" Then
167:           Exit Sub  'user canceled, no more work
168:        Else
169:           If StrComp(tStr, List(k), vbTextCompare) = STREQUAL Then
170:              GoodName = True
171:           Else
172:              If InListSoFar(List, tStr, k - 1) Or _
173:                 SheetExists(Book, tStr) Then
174:                 MsgBox Prompt:="Use a different name. " & _
175:                        "This name already exists; " & _
176:                        "sheet names must be unique.", _
177:                        Title:="Sheet Name Error", _
178:                        Buttons:=vbExclamation
179:              GoodName = False
180:              Else
181:                 GoodName = True
182:                 List(k) = tStr
183:              End If
184:           End If
```

```
185:        End If
186:      Loop Until GoodName
187:   Next k
188: End Sub
189:
190: Sub BubbleSortStrings(Arr() As String)
191: 'sorts any string array in ascending order
192:   Dim I As Integer, J As Integer
193:   For I = LBound(Arr) To UBound(Arr) - 1
194:     For J = I + 1 To UBound(Arr)
195:       If StrComp(Arr(I), Arr(J), vbBinaryCompare) = STRGREAT Then
196:         Swap Arr(I), Arr(J)
197:       End If
198:     Next J
199:   Next I
200: End Sub
201:
202: Sub Swap(T1 As Variant, T2 As Variant)
203:   Dim tmp As Variant
204:     tmp = T1: T1 = T2: T2 = tmp
205: End Sub
```

ANALYSIS   Notice that this module is private (line 1). Lines 4 through 6 declare constants used when checking the result of a StrCompare test. Lines 9 through 92 contain the OpenNewBook procedure.

The OpenNewBook procedure is similar to the procedure of the same name presented in the Week 2 Review, but now uses a custom dialog box to obtain information from the user, making this procedure easier to use. Line 26 displays a message in the Excel status bar to help the user keep track of what is going on. Line 28 sets a default name for the new workbook and line 29 sets the sentinel value for the **Do** loop that begins in line 30 (and ends in line 57). In this loop, the GetBookName function (from Listing R2.3 of the Week 2 Review) is called to get a workbook name.

Assuming the user does not cancel the dialog asking for a filename, lines 36 through 56 check to make sure that creating a new workbook with the selected name is reasonable. Only if the new workbook name is not the same as an already open workbook and does not already exist on the disk in the same folder will a new workbook be created.

If the name selected by the user passes all its tests, line 60 loads the frmOpenNewBook user form into memory without displaying it. Next, line 63 sets the form's Caption property, which controls the contents of the forms title bar onscreen. Line 66 shows the frmOpenNewBook dialog. (Listing R3.4 contains the code for the frmOpenNewBook form's class module.) Figure R3.1 shows the frmOpenNewBook form in run mode and indicates the names of the controls on the form.

FIGURE R3.1

The frmOpenNewBook
user form's controls.

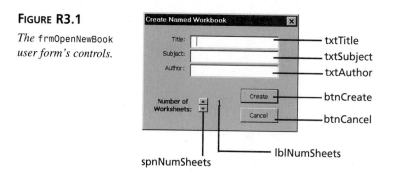

When the user clicks either the Create button or the Cancel button on the form, the form
is hidden and line 67 in the OpenNewBook procedure checks to see whether the user canceled the dialog. If so, the OpenNewBook procedure ends.

Line 70 creates the new workbook. Lines 73 through 77 transfer the workbook's summary information from the frmOpenNewBook form's controls to the workbook. If the user
elected to put more than one worksheet into the workbook, line 81 calls the
NewBook_Worksheets procedure to get add the worksheets to the workbook. After saving
the workbook (line 85), the new workbook is activated, the first worksheet in the workbook is activated, and the EndNewBook procedure is called to finish up the housekeeping.

The EndNewBook, Get_NameList, BubbleSortStrings, and Swap procedures work the
same as the procedures of the same name described in Listing R2.2 in Week 2 in Review.
The NewBook_Worksheets procedure also works essentially the same as described previously, but here it gets the value for the number of worksheets to add to the workbook
from the spnNumSheets control of the frmOpenNewBook form instead of using an
InputBox statement. Using a custom form in this version of the OpenNewBook procedure
eliminated five different input dialogs from the previous version.

Listing R3.4 contains the code for the frmOpenNewBook form's class module.

INPUT   **LISTING R3.4**   THE frmOpenNewBook CLASS MODULE

```
 1:    Option Explicit
 2:
 3:    Private fmCanceled As Boolean
 4:
 5:    Property Get Canceled() As Boolean
 6:       Canceled = fmCanceled
 7:    End Property
 8:
 9:    Private Sub btnCancel_Click()
10:       Me.Hide
```

```
11:     fmCanceled = True
12: End Sub
13:
14: Private Sub btnCreate_Click()
15: 'validate the data & hide the form
16:    With Me
17:      If (Trim(.txtAuthor) = "") Or _
18:         (Trim(.txtSubject) = "") Or _
19:         (Trim(.txtTitle) = "") Then
20:        MsgBox Prompt:="You must enter the Title, Subject," & _
21:                       " and Author.", _
22:               Buttons:=vbExclamation, _
23:               Title:=.Caption
24:      Else
25:        .Hide
26:        fmCanceled = False
27:      End If
28:    End With
29: End Sub
30:
31: Private Sub spnNumSheets_Change()
32: 'sync the spinner label
33:    With Me
34:       .lblNumSheets.Caption = .spnNumSheets.Value
35:    End With
36: End Sub
37:
38: Private Sub UserForm_Activate()
39: 'reset the canceled flag
40:    fmCanceled = False
41: End Sub
42:
43: Private Sub UserForm_Initialize()
44: 'sync the spinner and it's label
45:    With Me
46:       .spnNumSheets.Value = 1
47:       .lblNumSheets.Caption = .spnNumSheets.Value
48:       fmCanceled = False
49:    End With
50: End Sub
```

ANALYSIS Line 3 declares the fmCanceled variable, which is used to track whether the dialog was canceled. Lines 5 through 7 contain the **Property Get** Canceled procedure that enables other procedures to sample the status of the fmCanceled variable.

Lines 9 through 12 contain the btnCancel_Click event procedure. This procedure is executed whenever the btnCancel command button on the form is clicked. btnCancel_Click simply hides the form (line 10) and sets the fmCanceled variable **True** so that the form's Canceled property (lines 5-7) will correctly indicate that the dialog was canceled.

> **Note**
>
> Make sure you set the Cancel property of the btnCancel command button to **True** so that pressing Esc has the same effect as clicking the Cancel button.

Lines 14 through 29 contain the btnCreate_Click event procedure. This procedure executes whenever the Create button is clicked. This procedure first checks to ensure that a subject, title, and author have been entered (lines 17 through 19) and displays an error message if they have not (lines 20 through 23). If all required information is supplied, however, line 25 hides the form and line 26 ensures that the Canceled property will correctly reflect the fact that the dialog was *not* canceled.

Lines 31 through 36 contain the spnNumSheets_Change event procedure. This procedure executes whenever the value of the spnNumSheets spin button control changes. This procedure merely ensures that the lblNumSheets text label (which displays the spin button's current value) is correctly synchronized. Whenever the spin button is clicked, the label's caption is changed to reflect the new value.

Lines 38 through 41 contain the UserForm_Activate event procedure, and lines 43 through 50 contain the UserForm_Initialize event procedure. These two procedures ensure that when the form is first loaded in memory (that is, initialized) that the spin button control and its label are correctly synchronized and that the fmCanceled variable is **False**.

Appendix A

Answers

Day 1, "Getting Started"

Quiz

1. A plain, recorded macro is inflexible. It cannot efficiently repeat actions or make decisions based on conditions that occur while the macro is executing.

2. The core portions of Visual Basic for Applications and Visual Basic are identical. Visual Basic for Applications has these differences from Visual Basic:

   - VBA stores its macro source code in the application's files (for example, an Excel workbook) instead of separate text files.

   - Programs written in VBA must be started from inside the application in which the program was written. For example, a VBA program written inside Excel must always be executed from Excel. (You could, however, have another application use Automation to cause Excel to run a particular VBA macro program.)

- VBA contains many extensions to the core portion of Visual Basic; the specific extensions depend on the host application in which you use VBA. In Excel 2000, for example, VBA contains added features that relate to manipulating workbooks and worksheets, and to making financial and statistical calculations.

3. Three major benefits obtained by adding VBA program elements to a recorded macro:

   - Ability to repeat actions efficiently.
   - Ability to have a macro execute different instructions, depending on conditions that occur while the macro is operating or depending on choices that the macro's user makes.
   - Ability to connect several smaller macros into a large program in order to perform highly complex tasks.

4. No, you can't assign an Excel macro to a toolbar when you first record it, although you can assign an Excel macro to a shortcut key when you first record it. To assign an Excel macro to a toolbar, you must use the Tools, Customize command after you finish recording the macro.

5. Excel stores the macros you record in a workbook file. At the time you record an Excel macro, you can choose to store the macro in the current workbook, a new workbook, or in the Personal.xls workbook.

6. To execute a macro in Excel, choose the Tools, Macro, Macros command.

7. To start the macro recorder, choose the Tools, Macro, Record Macro command.

8. To make an Excel macro available to any open workbook during any work session, you would store it in the Personal.xls workbook.

9. The Excel Macro dialog lists *all* the macros in *all* the currently opened workbooks, whether or not the workbooks are hidden.

Exercises

1. If you record the Excel macro as described in the exercise instructions, you'll have a macro that creates a new workbook, and then saves and closes the workbook file.

2. Running your recorded Excel macro creates and saves another workbook in the same drive and folder, also named NewWorkbook.

3. Because the NewBook macro attempts to save the new workbook file to disk with a name that duplicates a file already on the disk, Excel displays a dialog asking whether you want to replace the existing file. This dialog contains four buttons:

Yes, No, Cancel, and Help. If you choose Yes, Excel replaces the existing work-book file (its contents, if any, are consequently lost) and the recorded macro com-pletes executing normally.

If you choose No (or Cancel), the file save operation is canceled. Because the can-celed operation causes an instruction in the recorded macro to fail, the macro is interrupted and doesn't continue running.

This exercise illustrates that, if an instruction in a recorded macro does not com-plete normally, the recorded macro does not continue executing. As you learn in later lessons, adding VBA program elements helps you control the behavior of a macro more closely. For example, it would be more desirable if the NewBook macro asked the user to enter a different filename and then attempted the save operation again, instead of failing with an error message.

Day 2, "Writing and Editing Simple Macros"

Quiz

1. A module stores your VBA source code. A module can contain none, one, or sever-al procedures up to the maximum of approximately 4,000 lines. Modules are stored in the files that the application normally stores information in—Excel workbooks, Word documents and templates, and so on.

2. You add comments to a recorded macro to document the use and purpose of the macro and to describe any special conditions that must exist before the macro will execute correctly. Adding comments to a recorded macro immediately after record-ing it can help you remember which parts of the recorded code are the result of specific actions that you performed and make it easier to change the macro later, if necessary. You should also add comments whenever you make changes in a macro; these comments make it easier to determine which parts of a macro you edited and what those changes accomplished.

   You should also add comments to procedures that you write yourself, for similar reasons.

3. A VBA keyword is any word or symbol that is part of the VBA programming lan-guage, as opposed to words (such as macro and procedure names) that you create.

4. To produce a syntactically correct procedure, you must define the macro with the keyword **Sub** followed by the procedure name and a pair of parentheses on the same line. End the macro with the keywords **End Sub** on a line by themselves (the VB Editor will add this statement for you). None, one, or many program state-ments can occur between the procedure declaration line and the line ending the

procedure. The following sample shows the required elements of a procedure:

```
Sub AnyMacro()
    'None, one, or any number of program statements
End Sub
```

5. A procedure declaration is the first line of a procedure (containing the **Sub** keyword) that indicates the name of the procedure.

6. The body of a procedure is the part of the procedure that contains the actual commands and program statements that the procedure executes. The body of the procedure is the part of a procedure between the line containing the procedure declaration and the **End Sub** line that ends the procedure.

7. The Object Browser enables you to view a list of all the currently available macros and procedures. The Object Browser lists all the modules and procedures in the project currently selected in the Project Explorer.

8. Recorded VBA source code is indented in order to make the code more readable by a human being. You should indent your source code as you write procedures for the same reason: to enhance the readability (and understandability) of your procedures.

9. The MsgBox procedure provides a simple way for your procedures to display messages to the user.

10. An argument is information passed to a VBA procedure for use by that procedure. Some procedures can use more than one argument—in this case, the arguments are written in a list and separated with commas, forming an argument list.

11. The line-continuation symbol consists of a space character followed by an underscore character (_). The line-continuation symbol is used to indicate to VBA that the following line should be joined with the current line to form a single VBA statement. By using the line-continuation symbol, you can divide VBA statements onto several lines in order to enhance the readability of your procedure's source code. The following source code fragment shows five lines containing line-continuation symbols. The result of these line-continuation symbols is to join all six of the physical lines in the code fragment into one logical line containing a single VBA statement.

```
ActiveWorkbook.SaveAs Filename:="NEWFILE.XLS", _
                      FileFormat:=xlNormal, _
                      Password:="", _
                      WriteResPassword:="", _
                      ReadOnlyRecommended:= False, _
                      CreateBackup:=False
```

12. Whenever you move the insertion point away from a line in your VBA code that you have just edited or typed, VBA first parses the line to ensure that it is syntactically correct and then compiles your code into a form that VBA can directly utilize without having to parse your source code a second time.

13. A syntax error is an error resulting from an improperly formed VBA program statement. Syntax errors usually result from such things as missing or improperly placed commas, parentheses, quotation marks, and so on. Syntax errors also frequently result from missing keywords, such as omitting the **Sub** keyword or deleting the **End Sub** keywords in a procedure definition.

    VBA usually notifies you of syntax errors as you write each line of code. If you do not correct syntax errors when they are first detected, VBA will again display an error message when you run the procedure.

14. A runtime error is an error that occurs while your procedure is executing. Runtime errors have many different causes; they result most frequently from statements that are syntactically correct but contain data of the wrong type, attempts to operate on files or parts of a file (such as a specific worksheet) that are not present at the time the procedure executes, and so on.

Exercises

1. The purpose of this exercise is to give you some practice entering code with the VB Editor and modules. This procedure uses a command—line 5 of the listing— that invokes Excel's (and hence Windows's) help system and specifies that the Excel VBA reference is the help file to open. (The help file for Excel VBA is separate from Excel's main help file; in Excel 2000, the VBA help file is named VBAXL9.CHM.)

    If this procedure does not execute, or does not display the Excel VBA reference opened at the Object Model topic, check to make sure you copied the listing exactly. Specifically, check to make sure that both the **Sub** and **End Sub** keywords are included, as well as the quote marks around the help filename in line 5. Also, make sure that you included the period (.) between the word Application and the word Help in line 5.

2. This one is just a little tricky. If you get syntax errors while writing the line that uses the MsgBox procedure, remember that you must include the placeholding comma for the missing second argument.

    Your procedure should appear similar to the following listing, although you probably chose a different name for your procedure:

```
Sub MyMessage()
'Exercise 2.3
'This macro displays a message.

    MsgBox "I am a Visual Basic message", , "VBA Message"
End Sub
```

3. Line 2 of the original procedure did not contain the quotation marks around the message text. As a result, VBA detected a syntax error. If you typed in this procedure as-is to see what VBA's error messages were, you might have noticed that the syntax error message did not directly relate to the actual problem. Instead, because VBA interpreted the unquoted text as variable names, you received error messages stating that a comma or parenthesis was expected.

This exercise illustrates the fact that VBA cannot always report the exactly correct syntax error. Sometimes, as with these missing quotation marks, the syntax error that VBA reports is actually caused by a different syntax error that occurred earlier in the program source code—perhaps earlier in the same line, perhaps one or more lines earlier. If you get syntax errors regarding missing commas or parentheses, and the syntax error does not seem appropriate, look for things such as missing quotation marks earlier in the line.

The corrected procedure is shown below:

```
Sub Broken()
'Exercise 2.4
'This macro was broken, but now it's fixed

    MsgBox "Yet Another Message"
End Sub
```

Day 3, "Understanding Data Types, Variables, and Constants"

Quiz

1. There are six numeric data types in VBA: **Byte**, **Integer**, **Long**, **Single**, **Double**, and **Currency**.

2. The primary difference between the **Integer** and **Single** data types is that an **Integer** data type can store only whole numbers (numbers with no decimal point), whereas the **Single** data type can store numbers with a decimal point; secondarily, the range of the **Single** data type is much greater than that of the **Integer**.

   Both the **Integer** and the **Long** data type can store whole numbers only; the only difference between an **Integer** and a **Long** is that the range of values that you can store in a **Long** is much greater than the range you can store in an **Integer**.

3. A type-definition character is a special symbol that, when added to the end of a variable or constant name, specifies the data type of that variable or constant.

4. You declare variables implicitly by simply using the variable. If the variable does not already exist, VBA understands that the variable needs to be created and does so. To explicitly declare a variable, you use the VBA **Dim** statement to specifically instruct VBA to create the variable.

5. Identifier names must begin with a letter of the alphabet, and can optionally be followed by any combination of letters or digits; although the underscore character (_) is permitted in an identifier, you cannot use spaces, a period (.), or any other symbols (except type-definition characters) in an identifier. When choosing identifier names, you should choose names that are descriptive and that reflect the use or purpose of the identifier—whether the identifier is a variable, constant, or procedure name. Finally, use capital letters and the underscore character to make long identifiers easier to read and understand.

6. The advantages of explicitly declaring variables include:
   - Speeding up execution of VBA code.
   - Helping avoid errors due to misspelling variable names.
   - Making your source code easier to read and understand.
   - Standardizing capitalization of every occurrence of a variable name to match the capitalization in the variable declaration.

7. The advantages of declaring a variable's type include:
   - Speeding up execution of VBA code.
   - Making your programs use memory more efficiently.
   - Making your source code easier to read and understand.
   - Helping prevent bugs in your program.

8. You should use named constants in your programs to make them easier to read and understand and easier to maintain. Use named constants for values that are used repeatedly or for values that are difficult to remember or whose meaning is not immediately clear.

9. The purpose of the InputBox function is to obtain input from the user for use by a procedure, such as filenames, numbers to use in calculations, and so on. The InputBox function displays a dialog containing text (which you supply) that prompts the user to enter some value and also contains a text box for the user to type the requested value in.

10. The first argument for the InputBox function—the string containing the text which prompts the user to enter a value—is required. All other arguments are optional.

11. The InputBox function always returns a **String** data type value.

Exercises

1. One of the keys in choosing whether to declare a data item as a variable or a constant is whether or not the value is computed by the program as it executes or the value is known ahead of time. The variable and constant names here were chosen to be as descriptive as possible. Notice that several of the variable names attempt to strike a balance between being easily understood and avoiding having to type very long words. Although you might have chosen different names for the various items, your declarations should look like this:

   (a) A computed count of columns in a worksheet must be a variable because the value it contains is determined after the program starts running. Because it is unlikely that there will be more than 32,767 columns in a worksheet, an **Integer** data type was chosen as the smallest and fastest numeric type capable of holding the anticipated data. The second line below shows the declaration using a type-definition character:

   ```
   Dim NumCols As Integer
   Dim NumCols%              'using Integer type-definition character
   ```

   (b) Because this is a value computed by the program, it must be stored in a variable. The **Currency** data type is specified because the numeric value to be stored represents a dollar value; the **Currency** data type is the fastest, most accurate data type for dollar values. The second line below shows the declaration using a type-definition character:

   ```
   Dim EastCoast_Sales As Currency
   Dim EastCoast_Sales@ 'using Currency type-definition character
   ```

   (c) This item is a little tricky. If the projected number of respondents from a marketing survey is computed by the procedure, this would be a variable. Usually, however, an item like this is a constant, representing a quantity known ahead of time. The constant declaration below assumes that the response from the marketing survey will be about 2 percent, and is declared as a **Double** in order to have the greatest accuracy in computations using this constant. The second line below shows the declaration using a type-definition character:

   ```
   Const ProjectedResp As Double = 2
   Const ProjectedResp# = 2       'Double type-definition character
   ```

   (d) Again, because this value is calculated by the procedure, a variable is chosen. Again, a **Double** data type is declared in order to have the greatest range and accuracy when calculating the cylinder's surface area.

   ```
   Dim CylinderArea As Double
   Dim CylinderArea#        'using Double type-definition character
   ```

A

(e) The multiplier to convert inches to centimeters is a constant. This is the kind of data that is ideal for a named constant. (Notice how the numeral 2 is included in the constant name as a sort of phonic synonym for the word *to*. This is a common practice among programmers to make identifiers expressive, but to avoid extra typing.)

```
Const Inch2Cm As Double = 0.3937
Const Inch2Cm# = 0.3937    'using Double type-definition
character
```

(f) Once again, a variable is declared because the value for the percent profit is calculated by the program. Notice how an underscore, numeral, and capitalization were used to make this variable name both expressive and still relatively short. A **Single** data type was chosen because percentage values are typically only worked out to two decimal places. If your program needs more accuracy, you might want to use a **Double**; if, on the other hand, you are more concerned about rounding errors, or if you expect to use the value in other computations involving money values, you might want to use a **Currency** data type instead.

```
Dim PcntProfit_1stQ As Single
Dim PcntProfit_1stQ!    'Single type-definition character
```

(g) A self-employment tax rate, of course, is a constant. This also is the ideal type of data for a named constant. Because this tax rate might change at some point in time, you make the program easy to update by using a named constant—you simply alter the constant declaration. A **Currency** data type was chosen for this value because it will be used in computations with values representing money.

```
Const SelfEmp_Tax As Currency = 12
Const SelfEmp_Tax@    'Currency type-definition character
```

2. Your procedure should look something like the following listing. Notice lines 7 and 8: these lines declare a constant for the dialog title bars and declare all the variables used in the procedure. Lines 9 and 10 do the work. Line 9 uses InputBox to get a string from the user, and line 10 uses MsgBox to display the string typed by the user.

```
1:  Sub EchoThis()
2:  'Exercise 3.2
3:  'Procedure:  EchoThis
4:  'takes a string from the user, and echoes it with MsgBox
5:  '
6:
7:    Const BoxTitle = "Echo"
8:    Dim User$
```

```
9:    User$ = InputBox("Type any text:", BoxTitle)
10:   MsgBox User$, , BoxTitle
11: End Sub
```

3. The listing below shows how the recorded Excel macro should appear before editing. (The filename you opened might be different, of course.) Because opening the workbook was the first action taken, and because the name of the open workbook is known (VBA_Sample.xls, in this case), it is fairly easy to determine that line 6 is the VBA statement that actually opens the workbook. Therefore, the InputBox statement to ask the user for the workbook filename should be inserted immediately before line 6.

```
1:    Sub OpenSheet3()
2:    '
3:    ' OpenSheet3 Macro -- Unedited version
4:    ' Opens the selected workbook to "Sheet3"
5:    '
6:        Workbooks.Open Filename:="C:\TVA-214\VBA_Sample.xls"
7:        Sheets("Sheet3").Select
8:    End Sub
```

The following listing shows the macro after adding InputBox. Line 7 declares a variable to store the string for the filename. Line 8 uses the InputBox function to ask the user for the filename and assigns the function result to the FName variable. Line 10 is the same VBA statement from line 6 in the unedited listing; here, the line has been changed so that the FName variable replaces the literal quoted string from before. Now, when the macro executes, whatever filename is stored in the FName variable is opened.

```
1:    Sub OpenSheet3()
2:    '
3:    ' OpenSheet3 Macro
4:    ' Opens a workbook and selects sheet named "Sheet3"
5:    ' Modified to ask user for file to open.
6:    '
7:        Dim FName As String
8:        FName = InputBox("Enter the name of the file to open:", _
9:                         "Open Sheet 3")
10:       Workbooks.Open Filename:=FName
11:       Sheets("Sheet3").Select
12: End Sub
```

4. The following listing shows how the Excel macro from Exercise 1 on Day 1 might be modified to ask the user for the filename to open. The changes made to this macro are similar to the changes made in the preceding exercise.

```
1:    Sub NewBook()
2:    '
3:    ' NewBook Macro
```

```
 4:    ' Creates and saves a new workbook.
 5:    ' Modified to ask user for name of the newly created file.
 6:
 7:    Dim FName As String
 8:
 9:    'Next line creates the workbook
10:    Workbooks.Add
11:
12:    'the next line gets the new file name from the user
13:    FName = InputBox("Enter a name for the new workbook:", _
14:                    "New Workbook")
15:
16:    'Next line saves the workbook
17:    ActiveWorkbook.SaveAs FileName:=FName, _
18:                         FileFormat:=xlNormal, _
19:                         Password:="", _
20:                         WriteResPassword:="", _
21:                         ReadOnlyRecommended:=False, _
22:                         CreateBackup:=False
23:
24:    'Next line closes the workbook
25:    ActiveWindow.Close
26:  End Sub
```

Day 4, "Operators and Expressions"

Quiz

1. An *expression* is a value or group of values representing a single quantity. An *expression result* is the value obtained when all operations specified in an expression have been carried out and the expression has been reduced to a single quantity.

2. An expression can contain one or more different values. Values in an expression are connected by operators.

3. Yes.

4. Expression results are assigned to variables or used as function or procedure arguments. The result of an expression must be used in some way.

5. The equals sign (=) is used to indicate both the assignment operation and the test for equality.

6. The / symbol indicates a floating-point division operation; the result of this division is always a floating-point number, usually a **Double** type. The \ symbol indicates integer division; the result of integer division is always an integer number, either an **Integer** or **Long** type.

7. The results of the expressions are

    (a) the Boolean value **False**

    (b) the number 40

    (c) the string 1723

    (d) the number 0

    (e) the string 23Skidoo

Exercises

1. The expressions, with parentheses added, are

    (a) 3 * (5 - 7)

    (b) (4.7 + 26) / 10

    (c) 312 / ((47 + 16) - 2)

    (d) ((17 - 5) - (44 / 2)) ^ 2

2. Your procedure, when finished, should look something like the following listing:

```
1:    Sub ThreeWords()
2:    'Exercise 4.2
3:    'Get three words from the user, assemble them into a single
4:    'string, and display that string on the screen
5:
6:        Const Title1 = "Input: "
7:        Const Title2 = " Word"
8:        Const Prmpt = "Enter a word:"      'prompt for InputBox
9:
10:       Dim strEcho As String          'assembled string for display
11:       Dim strWord As String          'temporarily store user word
12:
13:       strWord = InputBox(Prmpt, Title1 & "First" & Title2)
14:       strEcho = strWord
15:       strWord = InputBox(Prmpt, Title1 & "Second" & Title2)
16:       strEcho = strEcho & " " & strWord
17:       strWord = InputBox(Prmpt, Title1 & "Third" & Title2)
18:       strEcho = strEcho & " " & strWord
19:
20:       MsgBox strEcho, , "Three Words"
21:   End Sub
```

Lines 6 through 8 declare the necessary constants for this procedure. Notice that this procedure uses two separate named constants for the unchanging part of the title used for the InputBox dialogs. Lines 10 and 11 declare all the variables needed for this procedure. Lines 13 through 18 ask the user for a word and add each word to the strEcho string as it is entered. Line 20 displays the three words assembled into a single string.

Day 5, "Visual Basic and Excel Functions"

Quiz

1. Any three of the following:

   - Converting text strings to other data types.
   - Converting other data types to text strings or returning information about text strings.
   - Formatting numbers or other data types for display.
   - Manipulating or generating date values.
   - Performing trigonometric, logarithmic, statistical, financial, and other calculations.
   - Getting information about files, disk drives, or the environment in which VBA or your application is currently running.

2. You can use a function to supply a value anywhere in any VBA statement where you can legitimately use a constant or variable value (except at the left side of an assignment operation).

3. Omit the parentheses from the argument list of the function to tell VBA that you want to ignore the function's result. You cannot ignore the result of every VBA function, only those that carry out a specific task as well as returning a result.

4. The VBA functions are inherent to VBA, and are available in any version of VBA regardless of the host application (whether it is Microsoft Excel, Word, Access, Project, or some other application). The functions provided by Excel—or any other VBA host application—exist only in the host application. Although some or all of a host application's functions might be available to VBA, they are not part of VBA and might not be available in every host application.

5. You must include the `Application` keyword and a period (`.`) in front of the name of the host application function that you intend to use.

6. No.

7. The Object Browser enables you to determine which VBA and host application functions are available and provides easy access to the online help for these functions. You can also copy function names and argument lists from the Object Browser into the Windows Clipboard for later pasting into a module.

8. Manipulating string data is important because text string data is your program's primary means of exchanging information (displaying messages and receiving input) with your program's user. The more effectively you can manipulate string

data, the more likely you are to successfully display attractive, coherent messages for your program's user, or to be able to analyze the data that your program's user enters.

Exercises

1. The corrected expressions are:

   (a) `Sum$ = CStr(12 + 15)`

   (b) `Num% = CInt("47") + CInt("52")`

   (c) `Num@ = 12.98 * CCur("16")`

   (d) `Root! = Sqr(CSng(User_Input$))`

2. Your completed Excel procedure should look something like the following:

```
1:  Sub Demo_Min()
2:  'Exercise 5.2
3:      Const InPrompt = "Enter a number:"
4:      Const InTitle = "Number "
5:      Dim N1 As String, N2 As String, N3 As String
6:      Dim NMin As String
7:      N1 = InputBox(Prompt:=InPrompt, Title:=InTitle & "1")
8:      N2 = InputBox(Prompt:=InPrompt, Title:=InTitle & "2")
9:      N3 = InputBox(Prompt:=InPrompt, Title:=InTitle & "3")
10:      NMin = Application.Min(N1, N2, N3)
11:      MsgBox "The minimum of " & N1 & ", " & N2 & ", and " _
12:             & N3 & " is: " & Nmin
13: End Sub
```

Lines 7 through 9 use the `InputBox` function to get numbers from the user and assign them to variables. Line 10 calls the Excel `MIN` function and line 11 displays the results of the function to the user. You might have displayed the function result directly with the `MsgBox` function; this is perfectly acceptable.

Notice that this procedure attempts to produce the most complete, coherent, and cosmetically appealing messages for the user. In general, all of your procedures should do the same.

3. Your completed procedure should look something like the following:

```
1:  Sub Demo_Substrings()
2:  'Exercise 5.3
3:      Const InTitle = "Substring Extraction"
4:      Dim UserIn As String
5:      UserIn = InputBox(Prompt:="Enter some text:", _
6:                         Title:=InTitle, Default:="Suggested")
7:      MsgBox Left(UserIn, 3)
8:      MsgBox Right(UserIn, 4)
9:      MsgBox Mid(UserIn, 3, 4)
10:     End Sub
```

A

4. Your completed procedure should look something like the following:

```
1:  Sub SearchDemo()
2:  'Exercise 5.4
3:    Const BoxTitle = "Substring Search Demo"
4:    Dim UserIn As String, SrchFor As String
5:    UserIn = InputBox(Prompt:="Enter some text:", _
6:                Title:=BoxTitle, Default:="Default string")
7:    SrchFor = "L"
8:    MsgBox Prompt:=InStr(1, UserIn, SrchFor, vbTextCompare), _
9:          Title:=BoxTitle & ": Text Comparison"
10:   MsgBox Prompt:=InStr(1, UserIn, SrchFor, vbBinaryCompare), _
11:         Title:=BoxTitle & ": Binary Comparison"
12:   MsgBox Prompt:=InStr(UserIn, SrchFor), _
13:         Title:=BoxTitle & ": Using Option Compare Setting"
14: End Sub
```

In this procedure, lines 8 through 13 display the results of the InStr search using each of the possible comparison options (if you have only one of these in your procedure, that's fine). All three lines begin searching at the first character of the UserIn string. Line 8 performs a text comparison, line 10 performs a binary comparison, and line 9 uses whatever the current **Option Compare** setting is.

Try changing the case of SrchFor from "L" to "l" and see how the results returned by InStr change. Also try changing the **Option Compare** setting in the module and see how the result changes.

Day 6, "Creating and Using VBA Function Procedures and Excel User-Defined Functions"

Quiz

1. Function procedures are enclosed by the **Function** and **End Function** keywords instead of the **Sub** and **End Sub** keywords. A function returns a result; a procedure does not.

2. A user-defined function is the same thing as a function procedure, except that *user-defined function* is the term used for any function procedure that observes the restrictions against altering Excel's environment so that the function procedure can be used in worksheet cells. To create a user-defined function for use in Excel worksheets, you must ensure that your function doesn't alter Excel's operating environment in any way.

3. A user-defined function must not alter the host application's environment in any way. This means that a user-defined function cannot add, delete, edit, or format data in a host application such as Excel.

4. A function assignment is a statement in a function procedure that tells VBA what value the function returns. A function can have more than one function assignment statement. The function will return whatever value was specified by the last function assignment executed before the function stops executing.

5. Recursion is when a function (or other procedure) calls itself.

6. Sorry, this one is a bit of a trick question. Generally, you should never use recursive function procedures. Recursive procedures are often difficult to understand, and can consume a great deal of memory—sometimes too much for them to complete the computation or manipulation. The main reason this lesson explained recursion is so that you can understand what happens when you accidentally create a recursive function or procedure.

7. Use the IsMissing function to test whether a particular optional argument was present when a function (or other) procedure was called.

8. The IsMissing function only works with optional arguments that have the **Variant** data type. If the optional argument has any other data type, the IsMissing function always returns **False**.

9. The **StrComp** function was used in the FlipCase function because it compares two strings and enables you to specify the exact comparison method to use for that specific comparison. The entire operation of the FlipCase function centers around determining whether a particular letter is upper- or lowercase. If a plain relational operator is used, its action is affected by the **Option Compare** setting; if **Option Compare** is set to **Text**, a test with plain relational operators would not be able to tell the difference between the letter "A" and the letter "a". By using **StrComp**, the tests are guaranteed to use a binary comparison, regardless of the **Option Compare** setting.

10. You should specify that a function argument is passed by value whenever your function alters any of the values in its argument variables. Passing the argument by reference gives the function a copy of the original data in the argument so that the function can safely change the value without affecting the original data.

11. You would use the View, Object Browser command. Function procedures are not listed in the Macro dialog opened by the Tools, Macro command.

Exercises

1. Your equivalent functions should be similar to the following two listings.

   An Excel user-defined function equivalent for Visual Basic's **Eqv** operator:

   ```
   1:  Function uEQV(L1 As Boolean, L2 As Boolean) As Boolean
   2:      uEQV = L1 Eqv L2
   3:  End Function
   ```

   An Excel user-defined function equivalent for Visual Basic's **Imp** operator:

   ```
   1:  Function uIMP(L1 As Boolean, L2 As Boolean) As Boolean
   2:      uIMP = L1 Imp L2
   3:  End Function
   ```

2. If you carry out the steps described in this lesson correctly, you should see the description you enter in the Object Browser appear in Excel's Paste Function dialog.

3. Your function procedure should be similar to the one shown below:

   ```
   1:  Function Yds2Inch(yds As Double) As Double
   2:  'returns a measurement in inches equivalent to the number
   3:  'of yards in yds
   4:      Yds2Inch = yds * 36
   5:  End Function
   ```

   In this function, the **Double** data type was chosen for both the argument data type and the function result data type to offer the greatest possible range of values for both this function's input and its return value. An **Integer** or **Long** type is not suitable for either the function argument or the function result because you might have a fractional number of yards, resulting in an equivalent in inches, which also has a fractional part. If you used **Variant** or **Single** data types for this function, that's fine too.

   Your testing procedure should be similar to the following listing:

   ```
   1:  Sub Test_Yds2Inch()
   2:      Dim UserIn
   3:      UserIn = InputBox("Enter a measurement in yards:", _
   4:                        "Yds2Inch")
   5:      MsgBox UserIn & " yards is " & Yds2Inch(CDbl(UserIn)) _
   6:            & " inches"
   7:      MsgBox "The value of the user input after " & _
   8:            "Yds2Inch is called: " & UserIn
   9:  End Sub
   ```

   In this testing procedure, the test values are obtained by using the InputBox function. This is usually easier than using literal constants and editing the test program several times. Notice that the test procedure not only displays the result of calling the function, but also checks the original input value to the function argument to ensure that the function does not change its argument in any way. (In a function this simple, this last step is not really necessary, but it's a good idea to get into the habit of checking whether your functions modify their arguments.)

4. Your function procedure should be similar to the one shown in the following listing:

```
1:  Function Inch2Cm(inches As Double) As Double
2:  'returns a measurement in centimeters equivalent to the _
3:  'number of inches
4:      Inch2Cm = inches * 2.54
5:  End Function
```

The data types for the function arguments and function result are the same as in the function in Exercise 6.3, and for the same reasons.

Your testing procedure for this function should be similar to the following listing:

```
1:  Sub Test_Inch2Cm()
2:      Dim UserIn
3:      UserIn = InputBox("Enter a measurement in inches:", _
4:                        "Inch2Cm")
5:      MsgBox UserIn & " inches is " & Inch2Cm(CDbl(UserIn)) _
6:             & " centimeters"
7:      MsgBox "The value of the user input after Inch2Cm " & _
8:             "is called: " & UserIn
9:  End Sub
```

Notice that this test procedure also gets the test values from the user and tests to ensure that the function does not alter its arguments.

5. Your procedure to display a measurement in yards converted to centimeters should be similar to the following listing:

```
1:  Sub Yds2Cm()
2:      Dim UserIn As String
3:      UserIn = InputBox(prompt:="Enter a measurement in " & _
4:                        "yards:", _
5:                        Title:="Yards to Centimeters")
6:      MsgBox UserIn & " yards is " & _
7:             Inch2Cm(Yds2Inch(CDbl(UserIn))) & " centimeters."
8:  End Sub
```

Notice, in line 7 of the preceding listing, that the **CDbl** conversion function is used to explicitly convert the string entered by the user into a **Double** type number; because the function argument's data type is a **Double**, VBA requires that the data type passed to the function also be a **Double**.

Day 7, "Understanding Objects and Collections"

Quiz

1. The main idea behind object-oriented programming is that a software application, like the world around you, should consist of individual objects, each with its own properties and behaviors.

2. A program object consists of code and data bound together so that you can treat it as a single entity.

3. A property is an inherent quality of a program object, such as whether it is visible, its color, its filename, and so on. Properties control an object's appearance and behavior. You use object properties to alter an object's appearance or behavior, or to find out about an object's current appearance and behavior.

4. No. Some properties you can alter, others you cannot. Whether or not you can alter an object property, you can always retrieve its value.

5. No. Each object stores the data for its own properties separately. Although objects have properties with the same names, they do not share the values stored in the property.

6. A method is an inherent behavior of a program object, such as a workbook's capability to add a new worksheet to itself, a workbook's capability to save itself to a disk file, or the application's capability to open a workbook or to create a new workbook. You use an object's methods to perform actions on or with the properties and user data stored by an object.

7. (a) Examine current condition or status of an object by retrieving a property value.

   (b) Change the condition or status of an object by setting a property value.

   (c) Use a method to cause the object to carry out one of its built-in actions.

8. *Object.Identifier,* where *Object* is any valid object reference and *Identifier* is any property or method valid for the referenced object. The dot separator (.) between the object reference and the property or method identifier is required.

9. The dot separator (.) both separates and joins the identifiers that make up the object reference. You must write the object identifiers together, without spaces, to form a single identifier that VBA uses to determine which object you intend to reference. The dot separator lets you join the identifiers together, but also separates one identifier from another so that VBA can recognize each separate piece of the object reference.

10. An object expression is any VBA expression that specifies an object. Object expressions must evaluate to a single object reference; you use object expressions to create references to specific objects in your VBA programs.

11. Use object methods and properties (starting with the Application property, if necessary) that return object references; for ease of typing or conciseness in your program, you can also assign object references to a variable by using the **Set** command.

12. An object collection is a group of related objects, such as all the worksheets in a workbook or all the graphic objects in a worksheet. An element is a single object in the collection.

Exercises

1. The flaw in the NewBook procedure relates to the **With...End With** statement and the object references inside it.

   The problem is that the dot separator (.) in front of the property names for the active workbook have been omitted. As a result, VBA interprets the Title, Subject, Author, Keywords, and Comments properties as variable names, rather than references to the ActiveWorkbook's properties. This is why VBA complains that there are undefined variables if the **Option Explicit** statement is on.

   To correct the problem, add the dot separator (.) in front of each property name, as shown in the following listing:

```
 1:  Sub NewBook()
 2:  'Creates new workbook, and fills in the summary information
 3:  'for the new workbook with some information from the user,
 4:  'and some information from the Application object.
 5:
 6:     Const nbTitle = "New Book"
 7:
 8:     Workbooks.Add        'adds workbook to Workbooks collection
 9:     With ActiveWorkbook
10:       .Title = InputBox(prompt:= _
11:                         "Enter a title for this workbook:", _
12:                         Title:=nbTitle)
13:       .Subject = InputBox(prompt:= _
14:                         "Enter the subject of this workbook:", _
15:                         Title:=nbTitle)
16:       .Author = Application.OrganizationName
17:       .Keywords = ""
18:       .Comments = InputBox(prompt:= _
19:                         "Enter a comment regarding this workbook:", _
20:                         Title:=nbTitle)
21:     End With
22: End Sub
```

A

2. After rewriting the Show_SystemInfo procedure to use a **With...End With** statement, it should appear similar to the following:

```
1:   Sub Show_SystemInfo()
2:   'uses various host application properties to display
3:   'information about your computer system
4:
5:      With Application
6:        MsgBox "Host Application: " & vbCR & .Name & " v" _
7:                & .Version & ", Build " & .Build & vbCR & vbCR & _
8:                "Library Path: " & .LibraryPath & vbCR & vbCR & _
9:                "User: " & .UserName & vbCR & "            " & _
10:               .OrganizationName
11:        MsgBox "Operating System: " & .OperatingSystem & _
12:               vbCR & vbCR & "Mouse is Available: " & _
13:               .MouseAvailable & vbCR & vbCR & _
14:               "Total Memory: " & .MemoryTotal & vbCR & _
15:               "Used Memory: " & .MemoryUsed & vbCR & _
16:               "Free Memory: " & .MemoryFree
17:     End With
18: End Sub
```

Notice that the dot separator is included in front of each Application object property within the **With...End With** statement. Incidentally, notice how this procedure uses the vbCR intrinsic constant. The vbCR intrinsic constant represents a carriage-return character—this is how the MsgBox text is broken into several lines for display.

3. The problem with the GetNumber function is that it is supposed to use the Excel InputBox function, *not* the VBA InputBox function. Because both Excel *and* VBA have functions named InputBox, you must specify the Application object to use Excel's version of this function. Because GetNumber omitted the object reference to the Application object, VBA assumed that the VBA InputBox function is intended, which does not have the Type argument.

The corrected GetNumber function appears below; notice the change to line 5:

```
1:   Function GetNumber()
2:   'Uses the application's InputBox function to return
3:   'a number obtained from the user.
4:
5:     GetNumber = Application.InputBox(Prompt:="Enter a " & _
6:                                     "number:", Type:=1)
7:   End Function
8:
9:
10: Sub Test_GetNumber()
11:     MsgBox GetNumber
12: End Sub
```

Lines 10 through 12 are the same test procedure to test the GetNumber function.

You might want to use a function such as GetNumber in your Excel procedures to ensure that the user enters numeric data only. By using a function like this, you also avoid having to supply a prompt each time you use InputBox, which can help you make your code shorter and more concise.

4. Your completed procedure should be similar to the following:

```
1:  Sub SheetInsert()
2:  'Adds new worksheet to current workbook, then renames that
3:  'sheet, using a name supplied by the user.
4:
5:     Dim sName As String
6:     Dim oldSheet As Object
7:
8:     Set oldSheet = ActiveSheet
9:     sName = InputBox(Prompt:="Enter name for new " & _
10:                      "worksheet:", Title:="Add New Sheet")
11:    Worksheets.Add
12:    ActiveSheet.Name = sName
13:    oldSheet.Select
14: End Sub
```

Line 8 uses the **Set** statement to assign an object reference to the current active sheet to the oldSheet variable. Next, line 9 uses the InputBox function to get a name for the new worksheet from the user, storing it in the sName variable. Line 11 uses the Add method of the Worksheets collection to add a new worksheet to the active workbook. Excel adds a new worksheet and makes it the active sheet. Line 12 renames the new worksheet by assigning the string stored in sName to the Name property of the active sheet. Finally, line 13 switches back to the sheet that was active at the time this procedure began executing. The Select method causes an object to select itself; the oldSheet variable supplies the object reference to the original active sheet.

Day 8, "Making Decisions in Visual Basic for Applications"

Quiz

1. A conditional branching statement alters the flow of VBA's execution of statements in a procedure based on whether a particular condition is true or false. An unconditional branching statement redirects VBA's execution of statements without testing for any particular condition.

A

2. You use logical expressions to specify the condition under which VBA should or should not execute a particular program branch.

3. VBA's conditional branching statements are

   (a) **If...Then**

   (b) **If...Then...Else**

   (c) **If...Then...ElseIf**

   (d) **Select Case**

4. VBA has only one unconditional branching statement: the **GoTo** statement.

5. Nesting.

6. An **If...Then...ElseIf** statement can contain an unlimited number of **ElseIf** clauses. You can include *one* **Else** clause in an **If...Then...ElseIf** statement; the **Else** clause must come after all the **ElseIf** clauses and before the **End If** keywords.

7. You can include as many **Case** clauses in a **Select Case** statement as you want. You can specify a branch of statements for VBA to execute if none of the **Case** clauses is met by adding a **Case Else** clause to the **Select Case** statement. The **Case Else** clause must be the last clause in the **Select Case** statement, before the **End Select** keywords.

8. Use **Select Case** when you need to make more than three or four choices; using **Select Case** makes it easier to write, read, and understand your code when you need to make several choices.

9. You use **Exit Sub** to end a procedure early and **Exit Function** function to end a function early.

10. The **End** keyword on a line by itself ends all VBA statement execution, terminating your entire program. All variable values are lost.

11. You use the **Buttons** argument for **MsgBox** to

   (a) Specify how many and what type of buttons appear in the message dialog.

   (b) Specify which Windows's icon (Information, Query, Warning, or Critical) appears in the message dialog.

   (c) Specify which command button is the initial default command button in the message dialog.

   VBA provides several intrinsic constants (listed on the back cover of this book, and in the VBA online reference) to help you specify values for the **Buttons** argument.

12. The return value from the MsgBox function represents which button the user chose in the dialog. VBA provides you with several intrinsic constants (listed on the back cover of this book, and in the VBA online reference) to help you interpret the MsgBox function's return values.

Exercises

1. The corrected listing is shown below. The problem with the **Select Case** statement in this procedure involved the **Case** condition statements in lines 12 and 14.

In the original version of this procedure, the **Case** condition in line 12 checked to see whether Num was between 1 and 10, inclusive. This allowed any numbers with values between 0 and 1 to be missed; because they didn't match any of the **Case** conditions, they were handled by the **Case Else** statement. Line 12 in the corrected version correctly checks to see whether Num is between 0 and 10, eliminating the gap.

Similarly, the **Case** condition in line 14 checks to see whether Num is between 11 and 20, missing numbers between 10 and 11. Again, the corrected line 14 now checks to see whether the number is between 10 and 20.

```
1:  Sub Case_Demo()
2:
3:      Dim sNum As String
4:      Dim Num As Double
5:
6:      sNum = InputBox("enter a number:")
7:      Num = CDbl(sNum)
8:
9:      Select Case Num
10:         Case Is < 0
11:             MsgBox "Num is less than 0"
12:         Case 0 To 10
13:             MsgBox "Num is between 0 and 10"
14:         Case 10 To 20
15:             MsgBox "Num is between 10 and 20"
16:         Case Else
17:             MsgBox "Num is greater than 20"
18:     End Select
19: End Sub
```

2. One possible way of completing this exercise appears in the following listing:

```
1:  Sub TeleDigits()
2:  'displays the telephone number pad digit corresponding to
3:  'the alphabetic letter entered by the user.
4:
5:      Const tdTitle = "TeleDigits"
6:
```

```
 7:    Dim Letter As String
 8:    Dim Msg As String
 9:
10:
11:    Letter = InputBox(prompt:="Enter a single letter " & _
12:                      "of the alphabet:", Title:=tdTitle)
13:    If Len(Trim(Letter)) = 0 Then
14:      MsgBox prompt:="Entry operation canceled.", _
15:             Title:=tdTitle, _
16:             Buttons:=vbExclamation
17:      Exit Sub
18:    End If
19:
20:    If Len(Trim(Letter)) > 1 Then
21:      MsgBox prompt:="You must enter a single " & _
22:             "character - Canceled.", Title:=tdTitle, _
23:             Buttons:=vbExclamation
24:      Exit Sub
25:    End If
26:
27:    Letter = UCase(Letter)
28:
29:    Msg = "The telephone digit for " & Letter & " is: "
30:
31:    Select Case Letter
32:      Case "A" To "C"
33:        MsgBox prompt:=Msg & "2", _
34:               Title:=tdTitle, _
35:               Buttons:=vbInformation
36:      Case "D" To "F"
37:        MsgBox prompt:=Msg & "3", _
38:               Title:=tdTitle, _
39:               Buttons:=vbInformation
40:      Case "G" To "I"
41:        MsgBox prompt:=Msg & "4", _
42:               Title:=tdTitle, _
43:               Buttons:=vbInformation
44:      Case "J" To "L"
45:        MsgBox prompt:=Msg & "5", _
46:               Title:=tdTitle, _
47:               Buttons:=vbInformation
48:      Case "M" To "O"
49:        MsgBox prompt:=Msg & "6", _
50:               Title:=tdTitle, _
51:               Buttons:=vbInformation
52:      Case "P", "R", "S"
53:        MsgBox prompt:=Msg & "7", _
54:               Title:=tdTitle, _
55:               Buttons:=vbInformation
56:      Case "T" To "V"
57:        MsgBox prompt:=Msg & "8", _
```

```
58:                   Title:=tdTitle, _
59:                   Buttons:=vbInformation
60:      Case "W" To "Y"
61:        MsgBox prompt:=Msg & "9", _
62:                   Title:=tdTitle, _
63:                   Buttons:=vbInformation
64:      Case Else
65:        MsgBox prompt:="There is no telephone digit " & _
66:                   "match for " & Letter, Title:=tdTitle, _
67:                   Buttons:=vbExclamation
68:    End Select
69: End Sub
```

Line 27 converts the character in Letter to uppercase to simplify later tests. Line 29 assembles a standard string used by message boxes later in the procedure.

Finally, lines 31 through 68 contain a **Select Case** statement that evaluates the letter that the user entered. The first eight **Case** condition branches test the character in Letter to find out which range of characters it falls into and then displays the appropriate message for that digit. Notice that all but one of the **Case** condition expressions use the **To** keyword to set a range of characters, and that all the characters in the **Case** condition expressions are uppercase. Using all uppercase characters eliminates worrying about making lowercase comparisons, also.

Pay special attention to line 52, which is the only **Case** condition expression that lists the values to match. There is no digit match for the letter Q—the range "P" **To** "S" includes the letter Q, which is not desired, so this expression must list each of the letters individually.

If the character in Letter does not match any of the first eight **Case** expressions, VBA executes the **Case Else** clause in lines 64 through 67. These statements simply display a message dialog with the message that the character has no match.

Day 9, "Repeating Actions in Visual Basic: Loops"

Quiz

1. A fixed loop always repeats a fixed number of times. An indefinite loop repeats an indefinite number of times, depending on conditions that occur while the loop executes.

2. No. The **For...Next** loop is a fixed loop and always executes a set number of times, although you can end a **For** loop early with the **Exit For** statement.

3. If the logical expression for the determinant condition appears at the top of the loop, VBA tests the condition before executing the loop. If the logical expression for the determinant condition appears at the bottom of the loop, VBA tests the condition after executing the loop.

4. If you use the **While** keyword, VBA executes the loop as long as the determinant condition is **True** and stops executing the loop when the determinant condition becomes **False**. If you use the **Until** keyword, VBA executes the loop until the determinant condition becomes **True**, that is, VBA executes the loop as long as the determinant condition is **False** and stops executing the loop when the determinant becomes **True**.

5. A count-controlled loop is a **Do** loop that executes while a count is above or below a particular limit. A count-controlled **Do** loop is very similar in concept to a **For...Next** loop. You use a count-controlled **Do** loop, however, whenever the count is incremented at irregular intervals.

6. An event-controlled **Do** loop is a loop whose determinant condition becomes **True** or **False** depending on events that occur while the loop executes, such as the user entering a particular value.

7. A flag-controlled loop is a **Do** loop that uses a **Boolean** variable as the determinant condition. You use statements both before and within the loop to change the value of the flag variable, indicating whether or not the loop should continue to execute.

Exercises

1. The problem with this loop is that it is impossible for the user to enter the value that will end the loop! The Excel `Application.InputBox` function, when used with the optional `Type` argument to specify that the user should enter numeric-only data, prohibits the user from entering a string such as *exit*. Therefore, the determinant condition for the loop can never become **True** and the loop executes infinitely.

   There are two ways you can correct the loop in this procedure. In the first listing below, the determinant condition (line 9) was changed to end the loop any time the value 0 is entered. By experimenting with the `Application.InputBox` function a little, you can determine that it returns 0 if the user cancels the input dialog.

```
1:  Sub GetNumber()
2:  'loops indefinitely, getting numeric input from the user
3:
4:      Dim Num
5:
6:      Do
7:          Num = Application.InputBox(prompt:="Enter a number:", _
8:                                     Type:=1)
```

```
 9:    Loop Until Num = 0
10:
11:    MsgBox "Number entry ended."
12: End Sub
```

The second way to correct the problem with this loop is to use the VBA `InputBox` function instead of the Excel `Application.InputBox` function (line 7). This solution might not be as desirable as the first because it means giving up the number-only screening provided by the Excel `Application.InputBox` function's Type argument. (The next lesson describes how you can write your own data-screening code.)

```
 1: Sub GetNumber()
 2: 'loops indefinitely, getting numeric input from the user
 3:
 4:    Dim iNum
 5:
 6:    Do
 7:       iNum = InputBox(prompt:="Enter a number:")
 8:    Loop Until iNum = "exit"
 9:
10:    MsgBox "Number entry ended."
11: End Sub
```

2. There are several different solutions that will produce the desired results for this exercise. The following listing shows one of them:

```
 1: Sub Three_Words()
 2: 'gets three words from the user, and assembles them into
 3: 'a single sentence.
 4:
 5:    Const lTitle = "Three Words"
 6:
 7:    Dim uStr As String           'string for user input
 8:    Dim Sentence As String       'string for output sentence
 9:    Dim k As Integer             'loop counter
10:
11:    Sentence = ""
12:    For k = 1 To 3
13:       uStr = InputBox(prompt:="Enter a word:", Title:=lTitle)
14:       If Trim(uStr) = "" Then
15:          MsgBox prompt:="Word entry canceled.", Title:=lTitle
16:          Exit For
17:       Else
18:          Sentence = Sentence & " " & Trim(uStr)
19:       End If
20:    Next k
21:
22:    'if uStr empty, then last input was canceled
23:    If Trim(uStr) <> "" Then
```

A

```
24:     MsgBox prompt:="You entered the following sentence:" _
25:                 & Chr(13) & Chr(13) & Sentence, _
26:          Title:=lTitle
27:   End If
28: End Sub
```

Line 12 starts a **For...Next** loop set to execute three times. The statements to get a word from the user are in the body of this **For...Next** loop, so the loop will ask the user for a word three times.

Line 13 uses the InputBox function to assign the user's input to the uStr variable. Lines 14 through 19 contain an **If...Then...Else** statement to evaluate the user's input. If uStr is empty (or consists of only space characters), the statements in lines 15 and 16 display a message stating that word entry is canceled and then exit the **For** loop. If uStr is not empty, line 18 concatenates the user's string with the string in the Sentence variable, including a space between words. By cumulatively assembling the sentence inside the loop, you can avoid using more than two string variables. The Trim function is used several times to avoid unnecessary leading and trailing spaces.

Lines 23 through 27 contain an **If...Then** statement that checks to make sure that uStr is not empty. If uStr is not empty, the MsgBox statement in lines 24 through 26 displays the assembled sentence. If uStr is empty, it means that the user canceled the last input operation and the assembled sentence should not be displayed.

3. One possible solution is

```
1:  Sub GetSentence()
2:  'repeatedly gets words from the user, assembles them into
3:  'a single sentence. Stops collecting words from the user
4:  'when the user enters a period (.)
5:
6:     Const lTitle = "Build a Sentence"
7:
8:     Dim uStr As String          'string for user input
9:     Dim Sentence As String      'string for output sentence
10:
11:    Sentence = ""
12:    Do
13:      uStr = InputBox(prompt:="Enter a word ('.' to end):", _
14:                  Title:=lTitle)
15:      If Trim(uStr) = "" Then
16:        MsgBox prompt:="Word entry canceled.", Title:=lTitle
17:        Exit Do
18:      Else
19:        If Trim(uStr) = "." Then
20:          Sentence = Sentence & Trim(uStr)
21:        Else
22:          Sentence = Sentence & " " & Trim(uStr)
```

```
23:        End If
24:      End If
25:    Loop Until Trim(uStr) = "."
26:
27:      'if uStr is empty, then the last input was canceled
28:    If Trim(uStr) <> "" Then
29:      MsgBox prompt:="You entered the following sentence:" _
30:                    & Chr(13) & Chr(13) & Sentence, _
31:              Title:=lTitle
32:    End If
33: End Sub
```

Line 12 starts the **Do** loop. Because the determinant condition is at the end of the loop, VBA immediately begins to execute the loop's body starting in line 13.

Line 13 uses the `InputBox` function to assign the user's input to uStr. Lines 15 through 24 contain a pair of nested **If...Then** statements. The outer **If...Then** statement, like the one in the procedure from Exercise 9.2, evaluates the user's input. If uStr is empty (or consists only of space characters), VBA executes lines 16 and 17, which display a message stating that word entry was canceled and exits the loop, this time using an **Exit Do** statement because this is a **Do** loop.

If uStr is not empty, VBA executes the outer **If...Then** statement's **Else** clause in lines 19 through 23, which contains another **If...Then** statement. This inner **If...Then** statement was included mostly for cosmetic reasons. If the user's input is a period (.), it is concatenated to the string in Sentence without a space. If it is not a period, the uStr is concatenated to Sentence with a space between the two words.

As soon as the user enters a period (.) by itself, the loop determinant condition in line 25 becomes **True** and VBA stops executing the loop.

4. The completed IsBookOpen function and a testing procedure for it are shown below:

```
1:  Function IsBookOpen(bName As String) As Boolean
2:  'Returns True if workbook named by sName is currently open
3:
4:    Dim aBook As Object
5:
6:    IsBookOpen = False  'assume book won't be found
7:
8:      'cycle through all books, compare each book's name to
9:      'bName, as a text comparison.
10:   For Each aBook In Workbooks
11:     If (StrComp(aBook.Name, bName, 1) = 0) Then
12:       IsBookOpen = True   'if book names match, return true
13:       Exit For
14:     End If
```

A

```
15:    Next aBook
16: End Function
17:
18:
19: Sub Test_IsBookOpen()
20: 'tests the IsBookOpen function
21:
22:    Dim uStr As String
23:
24:    uStr = InputBox("Enter a workbook name (include " & _
25:                    "the .XLS extension):")
26:    If IsBookOpen(uStr) Then
27:       MsgBox "Book '" & uStr & "' IS open."
28:    Else
29:       MsgBox "Book '" & uStr & "' IS NOT open."
30:    End If
31: End Sub
```

This function and testing procedure work in exactly the same way as the
SheetExists function shown in Listing 9.9, except that it uses the Workbooks collection instead of the Sheets collection.

5. The SVal function and testing procedure shown below are one possible solution:

```
 1: Function SVal(ByVal iStr As String) As Double
 2: 'removes non-digit characters from iStr argument, and then
 3: 'returns the numeric equivalent of the string. Returns 0 if
 4: 'input string does not contain any digits, or has more than
 5: 'one decimal place
 6:    Dim oStr As String        'working string for output
 7:    Dim k As Long             'loop counter
 8:    Dim PCount As Long        'count for number of periods (.)
 9:
10:    iStr = Trim(iStr)     'remove spaces from the input string
11:    oStr = ""             'make sure working string is empty
12:    PCount = 0            'make sure period count starts at 0
13:
14:    For k = 1 To Len(iStr)
15:        'is the kth character a digit or decimal place?
16:      If (InStr(1, "0123456789.", Mid(iStr,k,1),1) <> 0) Then
17:        oStr = oStr & Mid(iStr, k, 1) 'copy the character
18:          'keep track of how many decimal places (.)
19:        If Mid(iStr, k, 1) = "." Then PCount = PCount + 1
20:      End If
21:    Next k
22:
23:    If (PCount > 1) Or (oStr = "") Then
24:      SVal = 0     'return zero as the result
25:    Else
26:      SVal = Val(oStr)
27:    End If
```

```
28: End Function
29:
30:
31: Sub Test_Sval()
32: 'this procedure tests the SVal function
33:
34:    Dim uStr As String
35:    Dim Num As Double
36:
37:    uStr = InputBox("Enter a string: ")
38:    Num = SVal(uStr)
39:    MsgBox "You entered: " & uStr & " which converted to: " _
40:      & Num
41: End Sub
```

Line 14 begins a **For...Next** loop that executes for as many characters as there are in iStr.

When the loop has finished executing, oStr contains a copy of iStr, excluding any non-digit characters. The **If...Then** statement in lines 23 through 28 evaluates both the PCount and the oStr variables. If PCount is greater than 1, the input string has too many decimal places. If oStr is still empty, the input string does not contain *any* digit characters. If either condition is **True**, the string cannot be converted to a number and the return result of SVal is assigned 0.

If neither of these conditions is **True**, VBA executes the **Else** clause in line 26, which assigns the SVal function result as the result of converting oStr to a number with the VBA Val function.

Lines 31 through 40 contain a procedure to test the SVal function.

Day 10, "Advanced Techniques for Using Data Types and Variables"

Quiz

1. The VBA information functions that begin with the word Is are all used to determine whether a variable has a particular data type.

2. You are most likely to use IsNumeric, IsDate, and IsObject.

3. The TypeName and VarType functions provide the most specific information about the data contained in a particular variable.

4. Use the TypeName function to return a string containing the specific name of the object; VarType can only tell you whether the object supports Automation.

5. IsMissing tells you whether a particular optional **Variant** argument was included at the time a function was called. IsMissing always returns **False** if the optional argument is any data type other than **Variant**.

6. The *Nothing* return means that the object variable you tested has not yet been set to refer to any object. The *Unknown* return means that TypeName was unable to determine the specific type of the referenced object.

7. The **Empty** value indicates that a **Variant** variable has not yet had a value assigned to it. VBA assigns this value to every **Variant** variable at the time it creates the variable.

8. The **Null** value indicates that a **Variant** variable does not contain valid data. VBA does not assign this value to any variables. The only way a **Variant** variable can end up containing the **Null** value is if you, the programmer, assign **Null** to a variable.

9. Defensive programming is just a name given to the techniques used to validate data values in a program in order to avoid runtime errors or to handle runtime errors more gracefully than VBA alone.

10. The purpose of the **Static** keyword is to indicate to VBA which variables in a function or procedure that you want to keep in between function or procedure calls. Unlike other procedure-level variables, VBA does *not* dispose of the contents of a static variable when a procedure or function ends. Instead, VBA preserves the variable's value.

11. You use the **Static** keyword instead of the **Dim** keyword to declare a static variable. If you want all of the variables in a procedure or function to be static, place the **Static** keyword at the beginning of the function or procedure's declaration.

Exercises

Starting with this chapter, the Exercise answers will no longer include an analysis of the programming solutions, except occasionally to point out a particularly useful or tricky part of the solution. Although this Appendix will continue to provide programming solutions to the Exercises, keep in mind that there are often many different solutions to a particular exercise, all of which might have equal merit. Don't be dismayed if your solutions differ from the ones shown here; these solutions are here to help you get going again if you're stumped by a particular exercise. Also, you might find it useful to see a solution besides the one you come up with.

1. Your function should look something like this:

```
1:  Function IsMasterCard(CardNum As String) As Boolean
2:  'evaluates the string in CardNum, and returns True if the
```

```
3:  'string represents a valid MasterCard number. Valid
4:  'MasterCard numbers always begin with the digit 5, and
5:  'consist of four groups of four digits, with each group
6:  'separated by a hyphen.
7:
8:  IsMasterCard = (CardNum Like "5###[-]####[-]####[-]####")
9:  End Function
10:
11:
12: Sub Test_IsMasterCard()
13: 'This procedure tests the IsMasterCard function.
14:
15:    Dim uStr As String
16:
17:    Do
18:      uStr = InputBox("Enter a MasterCard number " & _
19:                        "(include the hyphens):")
20:      MsgBox IsMasterCard(uStr)
21:    Loop Until Len(Trim(uStr)) = 0
22: End Sub
```

2. Your procedure should look something like this one:

```
1:  Sub Get_MasterCardNum()
2:  'gets a MasterCard credit card number from user, looping
3:  'repeatedly until user enters a valid MasterCard number.
4:
5:     Dim uStr As String
6:     Dim Ans As Integer
7:
8:     Do
9:       uStr = InputBox("Enter a MasterCard number " & _
10:          "(include the hyphens):", "Credit Card Data Entry")
11:      If Len(Trim(uStr)) = 0 Then
12:        Ans = MsgBox(prompt:="Cancel Card Number Entry?", _
13:                      Title:="Card Entry - Confirm Cancel", _
14:                      Buttons:=vbQuestion + vbYesNo)
15:        If Ans = vbYes Then Exit Sub
16:      ElseIf Not IsMasterCard(uStr) Then
17:            MsgBox prompt:="You entered an invalid " & _
18:                      "MasterCard number." & Chr(13) & _
19:                      "Please try again.", _
20:                      Title:="Error: Invalid Card Number", _
21:                      Buttons:=vbExclamation
22:      End If
23:    Loop Until IsMasterCard(uStr)
24:
25:    'code to store or use valid MasterCard number goes here.
26: End Sub
```

Day 11, "Creating Your Own Data Types and Object Classes"

Quiz

1. A user-defined type is a data type that you construct by combining elements based on VBA's fundamental data types. A user-defined data type binds together several different, but related, types of data.

2. The **Type** keyword begins a user-defined type definition.

3. You must place user-defined type definitions in the declarations area of a module at the module level—before any procedure or function declarations.

4. You create a user-defined class by adding a class module to your project and then writing the property and method procedures that define your class's properties and methods.

5. You define a class's properties by writing **Property Get** and **Property Let** procedures. Usually, you write property procedures in pairs: The **Get** procedure retrieves the property value and the **Let** procedure assigns a value to the property.

6. To create a read/write property for a user-defined object, you must write a pair of **Property** procedures: a **Property Get** procedure to retrieve the property's value and a **Property Let** procedure to assign a value to a property. Both property procedures must have the same name. In addition, the data type of the **Property Get** return value must match the data type of the **Property Let** argument.

7. You define a class's methods by writing **Sub** and **Function** procedures in the class module. Each **Sub** and **Function** procedure you write in the class module becomes a method of the object.

8. You should immediately rename a class module because the name of the class module is the name of your user-defined object class.

9. Only if the **Instancing** property of the class module is set to **PublicNoCreate**. Using this property setting, however, disables you from creating new instances of your custom object. Usually, you'll use the **Private** setting for the **Instancing** property, which does enable you to create as many instances of your custom object as you want, but limits the accessibility of the custom object to the workbook containing the class module that defines your object.

10. Yes. As you define each property and method for your object (by writing the appropriate VBA procedures and functions in the class module), each new property or method will appear in the Object Browser.

Exercises

1. Your user-defined type for the mailing list information should look something like this (the State and Zip elements are declared as fixed-length strings so that they will automatically get truncated to the correct length):

```
1:  Type MailAddress
2:      FName As String
3:      LName As String
4:      Company As String
5:      Street As String
6:      City As String
7:      State As String * 2
8:      Zip As String * 5
9:  End Type
```

2. Your function and procedure should look something like this (notice that the following listing contains a complete module):

```
1:  Option Explicit
2:
3:  Type MailAddress
4:      FName As String
5:      LName As String
6:      Company As String
7:      Street As String
8:      City As String
9:      State As String * 2
10:     Zip As String * 5
11: End Type
12:
13: Const MailTitle = "Mailing List Data Entry"
14:
15: Sub Enter_MailingData()
16: 'enters information for a mailing list. It calls
17: 'Get_MailAddress to get data for a single mailing address,
18: 'and then transfers the data to a worksheet, looping until
19: 'there is no more data.
20:
21:     Dim Person As MailAddress
22:     Dim Done As Boolean
23:     Dim RNum As Integer
24:
25:     Worksheets("Sheet2").Select      'put the data in Sheet2
26:
27:     RNum = 0
28:     Done = False
29:     Do Until Done
30:        Person = Get_MailAddress
31:        If Len(Trim(Person.LName)) = 0 Then  'no more data
32:           Done = True
```

A

```
33:    Else                        'store data in worksheet
34:      RNum = RNum + 1
35:      With Person
36:         Cells(RNum, 1).Value = .LName
37:         Cells(RNum, 2).Value = .FName
38:         Cells(RNum, 3).Value = .Company
39:         Cells(RNum, 4).Value = .Street
40:         Cells(RNum, 5).Value = .City
41:         Cells(RNum, 6).Value = .State
42:         Cells(RNum, 7).Value = .Zip
43:      End With
44:    End If
45:    Loop
46:    MsgBox prompt:="Data entry complete. " & RNum & _
47:            "records entered.", Title:=MailTitle
48: End Sub
49:
50:
51: Function Get_MailAddress() As MailAddress
52: 'gets all the data for a single mailing list entry, and
53: 'returns it in a MailAddress user type.
54:
55:    Dim Item As MailAddress
56:    Dim Tmp As Variant
57:
58:    With Item
59:      Do                'get the person's last name
60:        .LName = InputBox(prompt:="Enter person's LAST " & _
61:                             "name:", Title:=MailTitle)
62:        If Len(Trim(.LName)) = 0 Then        'cancel?
63:          Tmp = MsgBox(prompt:="End mail list data entry?", _
64:                       Title:=MailTitle, _
65:                       Buttons:=vbQuestion + vbYesNo)
66:        If Tmp = vbYes Then
67:          .LName = ""
68:          Get_MailAddress = Item
69:          Exit Function
70:        End If
71:      End If
72:      Loop While Len(Trim(.LName)) = 0
73:
74:      Do                'get the person's first name
75:        .FName = InputBox(prompt:="Enter person's FIRST " & _
76:                             "name:", Title:=MailTitle)
77:      Loop While Len(Trim(.FName)) = 0
78:
79:      Do                'get the company name
80:          .Company = InputBox(prompt:="Enter company " & _
81:                             "name:", Title:=MailTitle)
82:      Loop While Len(Trim(.Company)) = 0
83:
```

```
 84:      Do               'get street address
 85:        .Street = InputBox(prompt:="Enter street number " & _
 86:                            "and name:", Title:=MailTitle)
 87:      Loop While Len(Trim(.Street)) = 0
 88:
 89:      Do               'get city
 90:        .City = InputBox(prompt:="Enter the city name:", _
 91:                            Title:=MailTitle)
 92:      Loop While Len(Trim(.City)) = 0
 93:
 94:      Do               'get the state
 95:        .State = InputBox(prompt:="Enter 2 letter State " & _
 96:                            "name:", Title:=MailTitle)
 97:      Loop While Len(Trim(.State)) = 0
 98:
 99:      Do               'get zip code
100:        .Zip = InputBox(prompt:="Enter 5 digit zip code:", _
101:                            Title:=MailTitle)
102:      Loop While Len(Trim(.Zip)) = 0
103:    End With
104:    Get_MailAddress = Item       'return filled MailAddress
105: End Function
```

Day 12, "Creating Libraries and Whole Programs: Modular Programming Techniques"

Quiz

1. VBA first searches for the procedure in the current module and then searches the other modules in the current project. VBA then searches any projects referenced by the project calling the procedure.

2. Use the Object Browser. The Macro dialog lists procedures only.

3. Any project can be a library project. You create a library project by placing procedures and functions in the project and then making sure that the project is available.

4. You can either make sure that the project is always open by placing it in Excel's startup folder or you can create a reference to the library project.

5. Establish a reference to the project library to make the procedures and functions it contains available to the VBA code in your current project.

6. The StartupPath property returns the name of Excel's startup folder. This property is a read-only property, you cannot change it.

7. The `AltStartupPath` property returns the name of Excel's alternate startup directory. This is a read-write property; you *can* use this property to change Excel's alternate startup directory.

8. Use the VB Editor's Tools, References command to create a reference.

9. Private scope means that an item's availability is limited to the module in which it is declared. Public scope means that an item is available to any module.

10. `Option Private Module` limits the availability of items in the module that contains the directive to the project that contains that module.

11. The `Private` keyword causes an item—such as a procedure or function—that would normally have public scope to have private (module-level) scope, instead. The `Public` keyword causes an item—such as a module-level variable or constant—that would normally have private scope to have public scope, instead.

12. No. Local variables declared inside a procedure or function are never available outside the procedure or function in which you declare them. If you need to make the value in one procedure available to another procedure, pass it as an argument to the second procedure.

13. To pass information to a procedure, or to return a value from a procedure.

14. The Macro dialog does not list procedures if they have required arguments. If *all* of a procedure's arguments are optional, the Macro dialog will list that procedure. The Object Browser lists all available procedures, whether or not their arguments are optional or required.

15. By reference.

Exercises

1. The changed listing is

```
1:      Option Explicit
2:      Option Private Module
3:
4:      Private Type InvoiceHeader
5:          CustomerName As String
6:          CustomerNumber As Integer
7:          InvoiceNumber As Long
8:          InvoiceDate As Date
9:      End Type
10:
11:     Public Spinning As Boolean
12:     Public CurrentInvoice As Long
13:     Public InvoiceList() As InvoiceHeader
14:
```

```
15:
16:        Private Sub FetchInvoice()
17:            ' procedure body
18:        End Sub
19:
20:
21:        Private Sub ShutDown()
22:            ' procedure body
23:        End Sub
24:
25:
26:        Private Sub LocateInvoiceBody()
27:            ' procedure body
28:        End Sub
29:
30:
31:        Private Sub DisplayLineItems()
32:            ' procedure body
33:        End Sub
34:
35:        Private Function InvoiceTotal() As Currency
36:            ' procedure body
37:        End Function
```

All items that normally have private scope now have public scope, and all items that normally have public scope now have private scope.

2. No answer for this exercise is provided. Refer to the listing for Exercise 3 of Day 12 (following) for an example of the VBA code resulting from this design exercise.

3. Your completed program might look like the following (this listing contains one entire module):

```
1:     Option Explicit
2:
3:     Sub BalanceCheckBook()
4:
5:        Dim Balance As Currency          'the check book balance
6:        Dim Transaction As Currency      'the transaction amount
7:        Dim Done As Boolean              'flag to end transaction loop
8:
9:
10:       Get_StartBalance Amt:=Balance         'get starting balance
11:       MsgBox "Your Starting Balance is: $" & Balance
12:
13:       Do                              'get transactions
14:         Get_Transaction Amt:=Transaction, LastItem:=Done
15:         If Not Done Then
16:           Balance = Balance + Transaction
17:           Display_NewBal Bal:=Balance, Amt:=Transaction
18:         End If
```

```
19:   Loop Until Done
20:                                 'Display ending balance
21:   Display_NewBal Bal:=Balance
22: End Sub
23:
24:
25: Sub Get_StartBalance(Amt As Currency)
26: 'gets starting balance from user, and returns it in Amt
27:
28:   Dim iStr As String
29:
30:   Amt = 0
31:   Do
32:     iStr = InputBox("Enter the starting balance:")
33:     If Len(Trim(iStr)) = 0 Then    'canceled input?
34:       If ConfirmCancel("Do you want to stop program?") Then
35:         End   'stop entire program
36:       End If
37:     ElseIf Not IsNumeric(iStr) Then
38:       MsgBox prompt:="Please enter a number, only.", _
39:             Buttons:=vbExclamation
40:     End If
41:   Loop Until IsNumeric(iStr)
42:   Amt = CCur(iStr)
43: End Sub
44:
45:
46: Sub Get_Transaction(Amt As Currency, LastItem As Boolean)
47: 'gets a single transaction from user, and signals whether
48: 'or not it is last transaction by setting LastItem True.
49:
50:   Dim iStr As String
51:
52:   Amt = 0
53:   LastItem = False    'assume this is not the last item
54:   Do
55:     iStr = InputBox("Enter the transaction amount: ")
56:     If Len(Trim(iStr)) = 0 Then    'canceled?
57:       If ConfirmCancel("Stop entering transactions?") Then
58:         LastItem = True
59:         Exit Sub
60:       End If
61:     ElseIf Not IsNumeric(iStr) Then
62:       MsgBox prompt:="Please enter numbers only. " & _
63:               "Enter negative numbers for debits, " & _
64:               "positive numbers for credits.", _
65:               Buttons:=vbExclamation
66:     End If
67:   Loop Until IsNumeric(iStr)
68:   Amt = CCur(iStr)
69: End Sub
```

```
70:
71: Sub Display_NewBal(Bal As Currency, Optional Amt)
72: 'displays the balance. If the optional Amt argument is
73: 'included, it is assumed to be a transaction amount.
74:
75:    Dim Msg1 As String       'message to display, in two parts
76:    Dim Msg2 As String
77:    Dim Btns As Integer     'buttons options for message box
78:
79:    Msg1 = ""
80:    Msg2 = "Your "
81:    If IsMissing(Amt) Then     'is Amt present?
82:          Msg2 = Msg2 & "Ending "
83:       Else                    'is transaction a credit or debit?
84:          If Amt < 0 Then Msg1 = "Debit" Else Msg1 = "Credit"
85:          Msg1 = Msg1 & " amount is: $" & Abs(Amt) & _
86:                   vbCr & vbCr
87:    End If
88:    Msg2 = Msg2 & "Balance is: $" & Bal
89:
90:             'add warning, if necessary
91:    If Bal < 100 Then
92:      Btns = vbExclamation
93:      Msg2 = Msg2 & vbCr & vbCr & _
94:              "CAUTION, your balance is very low!"
95:    Else
96:      Btns = 0
97:    End If
98:    MsgBox prompt:=Msg1 & Msg2, Buttons:=Btns
99: End Sub
100:
101:
102: Function ConfirmCancel(pStr As String) As Boolean
103: 'returns true or false, depending on whether or not user
104: 'answers yes to the question poses in pStr.
105:
106:    Dim Ans As Integer
107:
108:    Ans = MsgBox(prompt:=pStr, _
109:                 Buttons:=vbQuestion + vbYesNo)
110:    If Ans = vbYes Then
111:       ConfirmCancel = True
112:    Else
113:       ConfirmCancel = False
114:    End If
115: End Function
```

Day 13, "Managing Files with Visual Basic for Applications"

A

Quiz

1. Archive, Directory, Hidden, Normal, Read-Only, System, Volume Label.

2. By adding them together. The file attribute code number for a file is the sum of all its attributes.

3. Use the `GetAttr` function to retrieve a file's attributes. The function returns a single number containing the sum of the file's attribute code numbers.

4. No. You cannot assign the Directory or Volume Label attributes to a file with `SetAttr`. To create a directory (folder), use the `MkDir` statement. VBA does not provide a way to create or remove disk Volume Labels.

5. `GetOpenFilename` displays a dialog that looks and behaves exactly like the Excel File Open dialog. `GetSaveAsFilename` displays a dialog that looks and behaves exactly like Excel's File Save As dialog.

6. You use the `Dir` function in two stages. First, you call it *with* arguments in order to find the first matching file. Then, you call `Dir` repeatedly *without* arguments to find any additional matching files. `Dir` returns an empty string when there are no more matching files.

7. Use the `CurDir` function, which returns a string containing the complete path of the current folder, including the drive letter.

8. The `FileCopy` statement.

9. Use the `Name` statement to move a file from one folder to another on the same disk. You cannot use `Name` to move a file to a different disk drive, you must use `FileCopy` to copy the file.

Exercises

1. In (A), the `Application` object reference is missing. In (B), the dot separator (.) in front of the `GetSaveAsFilename` method is missing. The corrected fragments are:

   (A):

   ```
   fName = Application.GetOpenFilename
   ```

   (B):
   ```
   With Application
     fName = .GetSaveAsFilename
   End With
   ```

2. The statement attempts to use `Name` to move a file to a different disk drive, which is not possible. Use the following code to move the file, instead:

```
FileCopy "C:\EXAMPLES\SALES.XLS", "A:\SALES.XLS"
Kill "C:\EXAMPLES\SALES.XLS"
```

3. Your `IsDiskFolder` function might look like this:

```
1:    Function IsDiskFolder(dirName As String) As Boolean
2:    'return True if dirName is found on disk
3:
4:        If (Dir(dirName, vbDirectory) <> "") Then
5:            IsDiskFolder = True
6:        Else
7:            IsDiskFolder = False
8:        End If
9:    End Function
```

4. Your procedure might look like this:

```
1:    Sub SwitchDir()
2:    'switches to a new subdirectory,
3:    'creating it if it does not already exist.
4:
5:        Const iTitle = "Switch Directory"
6:        Dim iName As String
7:        Dim Ans As Integer
8:
9:        iName = InputBox(prompt:="Enter a directory name: ", _
10:                         Title:=iTitle)
11:       If Trim(iName) = "" Then Exit Sub
12:
13:       If IsDiskFolder(iName) Then
14:          ChDrive iName
15:          ChDir iName
16:       Else
17:          Ans = MsgBox(prompt:=iName & " does not exist. " & _
18:                       vbCr & vbCr & "Create it?", _
19:                       Title:=iTitle, _
20:                       Buttons:=vbQuestion + vbYesNo)
21:         If Ans = vbYes Then
22:            MkDir iName
23:            ChDrive iName
24:            ChDir iName
25:         End If
26:       End If
27:    End Sub
```

A

Day 14, "Arrays"

Quiz

1. The `Lookup` array has 150 elements (5 times 3 times 10); the `Cube` array has 27 elements (3 times 3 times 3). You compute the number of elements in an array by multiplying the number of elements in each dimension together.

2. The values returned by the various function calls are

   (A)   1980
   (B)   1
   (C)   5
   (D)   1990
   (E)   10
   (F)   9

3. The **ReDim** statement in line 10 is incorrect. You cannot use **ReDim** to alter the data type of the array's elements.

4. No. Not even using the **Erase** statement will let you alter the data type of the array's elements.

5. Yes. VBA treats a single array element just like any simple variable.

6. Yes, a linear search will work correctly on both a sorted and unsorted array.

7. You should use a binary search on a sorted array because binary searches take advantage of the fact that the elements in the array are in order, resulting in a much faster and more efficient search. Binary searches only work on sorted arrays. Using a binary search on an unsorted array will produce incorrect results.

Exercises

1. Your procedure might look something like this (notice that the `BubbleSort` procedure in this module uses an optional argument to specify whether the sort is ascending or descending):

```
1:   Option Explicit
2:   Option Base 1
3:
4:   Private Const FORMATSTR As String = "####"
5:
6:   Sub Sorter2()
7:     Const NUM_ROWS As Integer = 15
8:     Const NUM_COLS As Integer = 4
9:     Const iTitle As String = "Sorter2 Information"
10:    Const SortCol As Integer = 2
11:
12:    Dim NumTable(NUM_ROWS, NUM_COLS) As Integer
```

```
13:    Dim I As Integer
14:    Dim J As Integer
15:    Dim oldSheet As String
16:
17:    oldSheet = ActiveSheet.Name   'preserve current sheet
18:    Sheets("Sheet1").Select        'switch to new sheet
19:
20:    Randomize Timer   'reseed random number generator
21:    For I = 1 To NUM_ROWS    'fill array w/random numbers
22:      For J = 1 To NUM_COLS
23:        NumTable(I, J) = Int(Rnd * 1000)
24:      Next J
25:    Next I
26:    DisplayArray NumTable          'display the array elements
27:    MsgBox prompt:="Ready to start sorting.", _
28:           Buttons:=vbInformation, _
29:           Title:=iTitle
30:
31:    'sort array ascending
32:    BubbleSort xArray:=NumTable, sCol:=SortCol, Ascend:=True
33:    DisplayArray NumTable  'display sorted array elements
34:    MsgBox prompt:="Array now sorted in ascending order.", _
35:           Buttons:=vbInformation, _
36:           Title:=iTitle
37:
38:    'sort array descending
39:    BubbleSort xArray:=NumTable, sCol:=SortCol, Ascend:=False
40:    DisplayArray NumTable  'display sorted array elements
41:    MsgBox prompt:="Array now sorted in descending order.", _
42:           Buttons:=vbInformation, _
43:           Title:=iTitle
44:    Sheets(oldSheet).Select    'restore worksheet
45: End Sub
46:
47: Sub BubbleSort(xArray() As Integer, _
48:               sCol As Integer, _
49:               Optional Ascend)
50: 'sorts on ascending or descending order,
51: 'depending on value of Ascend argument
52:    Dim I As Integer, J As Integer
53:
54:    If IsMissing(Ascend) Or _
55:       TypeName(Ascend) <> "Boolean" Then Ascend = True
56:    For I = LBound(xArray, 1) To UBound(xArray, 1) - 1
57:      For J = I + 1 To UBound(xArray, 1)
58:        If Ascend Then
59:          If xArray(I, sCol) > xArray(J, sCol) Then _
60:            SwapRow xArray, I, J
61:        Else
62:          If xArray(I, sCol) < xArray(J, sCol) Then _
63:            SwapRow xArray, I, J
```

```
64:        End If
65:      Next J
66:    Next I
67: End Sub
68:
69: Sub SwapRow(xArray() As Integer, _
70:              sRow1 As Integer, _
71:              sRow2 As Integer)
72: 'swap elements at rows sRow1 and sRow2
73:    Dim k As Integer
74:    For k = LBound(xArray, 2) To UBound(xArray, 2)
75:      Swap xArray(sRow1, k), xArray(sRow2, k)
76:    Next k
77: End Sub
78:
79: Sub Swap(I1 As Integer, I2 As Integer)
80:    Dim temp As Integer
81:    temp = I1
82:    I1 = I2
83:    I2 = temp
84: End Sub
85:
86: Sub DisplayArray(xArr() As Integer)
87:    Dim k1 As Integer, k2 As Integer
88:    For k1 = LBound(xArr, 1) To UBound(xArr, 1)
89:      For k2 = LBound(xArr, 2) To UBound(xArr, 2)
90:        Cells(k1, k2).Value = Format(xArr(k1, k2), FORMATSTR)
91:      Next k2
92:    Next k1
93: End Sub
```

2. The elements in array A have the following values:

```
A(1) contains 2
A(2) contains 3
A(3) contains 5
A(4) contains 9
A(5) contains 17
A(6) contains 33
A(7) contains 65
A(8) contains 129
A(9) contains 257
```

3. This listing actually has two problems. First, the **For...Next** loop in line 4 causes a runtime error because the element ProjIncome(I-1) is not valid when I equals 1995: 1995 minus 1 is 1994, which is below the lower limit of array subscripts. Second, the upper limit of the **For** loop will also produce a runtime error because 2000 is not a valid subscript to the ProjIncome array—this time it is past the upper limit of array subscripts.

4. The array X is declared as a static array in line 2; the **ReDim** statement in line 10 causes an error because you can't redimension a static array.

5. The **Option Base** statement in line 1 is at fault—you can only use 0 or 1 with the **Option Base** compiler directive.

6. The **Option Base** statement in line 3 is at fault—a module can contain only one **Option Base** directive.

7. The **Option Base** statement in line 2 is at fault—the **Option Base** directive must appear in a module before any arrays are declared.

Day 15, "Debugging and Testing VBA Code"

Quiz

1. You place a breakpoint before a statement that is causing a runtime error or that you suspect as being the cause of a logical error.

2. Place multiple breakpoints before several statements that are involved (or at least suspected of being involved) with a runtime error. When the procedure execution stops at each breakpoint, inspect the watched variables and then resume executing the procedure at normal speed until the next breakpoint is reached. This scheme enables you to quickly move between trouble spots.

3. No. You can only watch the value in an individual array element.

4. Use the **Print** command in the Immediate Window. The **Print** command enables you to supply various arguments to the function to determine whether or not it works correctly.

5. The Run, Reset command resets a macro.

Exercises

1. Changing the expression Lo > Hi to Lo >= Hi in line 58 of Listing 15.2 introduces a subtle defect into the binary search. After making this change, the binary search routine will fail to find some of the elements that are known to exist in the list. To prove this for yourself, make the suggested change and then search for whatever the first number in the list turns out to be—the binary search will erroneously report that the first element of the list is not to be found. Watch the code execute with the debugger to see why it is so important to end the loop *only* when the lower search boundary is *greater* than the upper search boundary.

A

2. Making this change causes the binary search routine to execute infinitely whenever it tries to change the search boundaries into the upper half of the current search region. If the new value of the lower search boundary isn't set correctly, the binary search routine won't search the correct segment of the array and becomes "stuck" searching the same area of the array over and over.

If you make this change and execute the DemoDebug2 procedure, you'll have to press Ctrl+Break to interrupt code execution. Look at the list of values generated in the Immediate Window by the **Debug.Print** statements—you'll see how the same segment of the array was searched repeatedly.

3. The **Do** loop does not increment the variable I, which enables the loop to examine the characters of string S. Consequently, the loop repeats indefinitely. Here is the corrected version of the loop:

```
11: Do While I < Len(S)
12:    If Mid(S, I, 1) = FindChar Then
13:       Mid(S, I, 1) = ReplChar
14:    Else
15:       I = I + 1
16:    End If
17: Loop
```

4. The condition of the **If** statement is never true (no number can be both less than 10 and greater than 100 at the same time). This error is a logical error.

5. The call to function InStr in line 10 has a logically incorrect first argument. The correct code is

```
1:  Dim S As String
2:  Dim SubStr As String
3:  Dim I As Integer
4:
5:  S = "The rain is Spain stays mainly in the plain"
6:  SubStr = "ain"
7:  I = InStr(S, SubStr)
8:  Do While I > 0
9:     Debug.Print "Match at "; I
10:    I = InStr(I + 1, S, SubStr)
11: Loop
```

Day 16, "Creating Custom Dialog Boxes"

Quiz

1. Design mode means working with a form in the VB Editor. In design mode, you can add or delete controls on a form, edit controls, and use the Properties Window to set the form and control properties.

2. The Show method displays a form onscreen, loading it into memory if it isn't already loaded.

3. The Hide method hides a form so that it is no longer visible and cannot receive the focus. When you use the Hide method, the form remains loaded in memory.

4. No. A form must be loaded into memory before you can access its properties, methods, or controls.

5. The Load statement loads a form into memory but does not display it. The Unload statement removes a form from memory; all of the form's internal values are lost when a form is unloaded.

6. You can create an instance of a form by referring to it directly:

```
frmInsertFigure.Show
```

You can also create an instance of a form by using the **Set** or **Dim** keywords in combination with the **New** keyword:

```
Dim FigDialog As New frmInsertFigure   'declares variable and creates
                                       'new instance

Dim FigDialog As Object
Set FigDialog = New frmInsertFigure    'creates a new instance
```

7. An event procedure is a procedure you write in a form's class module to handle a specific event (such as a mouse click or double-click, a change in a control's value, and so on).

8. You create event procedures by writing the procedure's code in the class module of a form. To create an event procedure for a specific event in a specific object, you select the object in the Code Window's Object list and then select the event in the Code Window's Procedure list. The VB Editor automatically creates the declaration for the event procedure.

9. Yes, you can create custom properties and methods for your form. You create custom properties by writing **Property Get** and **Property Let** procedures in the General area of the form's class module. You create custom methods by writing procedures and functions in the General area of the form's class module.

10. Tab order is the term used to describe the order in which controls on a form receive the focus when you press the Tab key (to move forward) or Shift+Tab (to move backward).

11. If you want to manipulate the controls of a form before displaying the form onscreen, you would first load the form using the Load statement:

```
Load frmInsertFigure
```

12. Yes. Each form you add to your project creates a new object class.

Exercises

1. No code is provided as a solution for this exercise. To complete this exercise, all you have to do is replace the ListBox control in the frmCityList form with a ComboBox control. Otherwise, you can use exactly the same code presented in Listing 16.5 for the form's class module and the same code as presented in Listing 16.6 to exercise the form. The only changes you might have to make in the project's code will be to accommodate any changes you might make in the names of the form or its controls.

2. Here is one possible version of the frmCOCA form's class module, plus a procedure in a standard module to display the frmCOCA form. Most of the work for this form is handled by the Click event procedure for the btnCalculate command button. The Change event procedures for the operand and operator text box controls simply clear the result text box so that no result is shown until the Calculate button has actually been clicked. Refer to Figure 16.18 for an illustration of the frmCOCA form's controls.

The frmCOCA class module:

```
1:  Option Explicit
2:
3:  Function ValidateSelf() As Boolean
4:
5:      ValidateSelf = False   'assume failure
6:
7:      With Me
8:        If (Not IsNumeric(.txtOperand1)) Or _
9:          (Not IsNumeric(.txtOperand2)) Then
10:         MsgBox prompt:="The operands must be numeric values.", _
11:               Title:=.Caption, _
12:               Buttons:=vbExclamation
13:         Exit Function
14:       End If
15:
16:       If Len(Trim(.cmbOperator.Value)) = 0 Then
17:         MsgBox prompt:="No operator/function specified", _
18:               Buttons:=vbExclamation, Title:=.Caption
19:         Exit Function
20:       End If
21:
22:     End With
23:
24:     ValidateSelf = True    'if we get here, data is OK
25:   End Function
26:
27:   Private Sub btnCalculate_Click()
28:     Dim Operand1 As Double
```

```
29:     Dim Operand2 As Double
30:     Dim Result As Double
31:     Dim OpStr As String
32:
33:     If Not ValidateSelf Then Exit Sub
34:
35:     With Me
36:       'get the operands and operator/function. Use Val to
37:       'convert strings to numbers so that blank strings
38:       'are converted as zero
39:       Operand1 = Val(.txtOperand1.Value)
40:       OpStr = UCase(Trim(.cmbOperator.Value))
41:       Operand2 = Val(.txtOperand2.Value)
42:
43:       Select Case OpStr
44:         Case Is = "+"
45:             Result = Operand1 + Operand2
46:         Case Is = "-"
47:             Result = Operand1 - Operand2
48:         Case Is = "*"
49:             Result = Operand1 * Operand2
50:         Case Is = "^"
51:             Result = Operand1 ^ Operand2
52:         Case Is = "/"
53:           If Operand2 <> 0 Then
54:             Result = Operand1 / Operand2
55:           Else
56:             MsgBox prompt:="Division-by-zero error", _
57:                     Buttons:=vbExclamation, Title:=.Caption
58:             Exit Sub
59:           End If
60:         Case Is = "SQR"
61:           If Operand1 > 0 Then
62:             Result = Sqr(Operand1)
63:           Else
64:             MsgBox prompt:="Bad function argument", _
65:                     Buttons:=vbExclamation, Title:=.Caption
66:             Exit Sub
67:           End If
68:         Case Else
69:           MsgBox prompt:="Unknown operator", _
70:                   Buttons:=vbExclamation, Title:=.Caption
71:           Exit Sub
72:       End Select
73:
74:       'display the result
75:       .txtResult.Value = CStr(Result)
76:     End With
77: End Sub
78:
79: Private Sub btnClose_Click()
```

```
80:    Me.Hide
81: End Sub
82:
83: Private Sub txtOperand1_Change()
84:    Me.txtResult = ""
85: End Sub
86:
87: Private Sub txtOperand2_Change()
88:    Me.txtResult = ""
89: End Sub
90:
91: Private Sub txtOperation_Change()
92:    Me.txtResult = ""
93: End Sub
94:
95: Private Sub UserForm_Initialize()
96: 'populate the operator list
97:    With Me.cmbOperator
98:       .AddItem "+"
99:       .AddItem "-"
100:      .AddItem "*"
101:      .AddItem "^"
102:      .AddItem "/"
103:      .AddItem "Sqr"
104:    End With
105: End Sub
```

A procedure in a standard module to display the frmCOCA form:

```
1:    Option Explicit
2:
3:    Sub DemoCOCA()
4:    'shows the frmCOCA form
5:       frmCOCA.Show
6:    End Sub
```

Day 17, "Menus and Toolbars"

Quiz

1. By using the Add method of the CommandBarControls collection for the pop-up menu to which you want to add the submenu.

2. It's important to make sure the user has a way to exit from your program or from the menu system that you've installed; otherwise, the user can never get back to the application's original menus.

3. No, you don't have to specify an event procedure when you create a command bar control. If you leave the `OnAction` property blank for a custom control, however, it won't perform any action when clicked. Setting the `OnAction` property for a built-in conrol overrides its inherent behavior.

4. You specify the type of a command bar when you create it by using the appropriate `MsoBarType` constant with the `Add` method's `Type` argument.

5. You specify the type of a command bar control when you create it by using the appropriate `MsoControlType` constant with the `Add` method's `Type` argument.

6. No. Excel determines a built-in control's `State` property.

Exercises

1. Your solution to this exercise should look something like this:

```
1:   Sub ListAllCommandBars()
2:   'creates an Excel worksheet listing all command bars
3:
4:       Dim CmdBar As CommandBar
5:       Dim RCount As Long
6:
7:       'display information in an Excel worksheet
8:       ActiveWorkbook.Sheets("sheet3").Activate
9:       ActiveSheet.Cells(1, 1).Value = "Type"
10:      ActiveSheet.Cells(1, 2).Value = "Command Bar Name"
11:
12:      RCount = 2
13:      For Each CmdBar In Application.CommandBars
14:        Application.StatusBar = "Listing " & CmdBar.Name
15:        If CmdBar.BuiltIn Then
16:          ActiveSheet.Cells(RCount, 1).Value = "Built-In"
17:        Else
18:          ActiveSheet.Cells(RCount, 1).Value = "Custom"
19:        End If
20:        ActiveSheet.Cells(RCount, 2).Value = CmdBar.Name
21:        RCount = RCount + 1
22:      Next CmdBar
23:
24:      Application.StatusBar = False
25:   End Sub
```

2. Your solution to this exercise should look something like this:

```
1:   Sub ListCommandBarTypes()
2:   'creates an Excel worksheet listing
3:   'all built-in command bars, their names, and their type
4:
5:       Dim CmdBar As CommandBar
6:       Dim RCount As Long
```

```
7:      Dim strType As String
8:
9:      'display information in an Excel worksheet
10:     ActiveWorkbook.Sheets("sheet3").Activate
11:     ActiveSheet.Cells(1, 1).Value = "Built-In"
12:     ActiveSheet.Cells(1, 2).Value = "Bar Type"
13:     ActiveSheet.Cells(1, 3).Value = "Command Bar Name"
14:
15:     RCount = 2
16:     For Each CmdBar In Application.CommandBars
17:       Application.StatusBar = "Listing " & CmdBar.Name
18:       If CmdBar.BuiltIn Then
19:         ActiveSheet.Cells(RCount, 1).Value = "Built-In"
20:       Else
21:         ActiveSheet.Cells(RCount, 1).Value = "Custom"
22:       End If
23:
24:       Select Case CmdBar.Type
25:         Case Is = msoBarTypeMenuBar
26:           strType = "Menu Bar"
27:         Case Is = msoBarTypeNormal
28:           strType = "Toolbar"
29:         Case Is = msoBarTypePopup
30:           strType = "Popup Menu"
31:         Case Else
32:           strType = "Unknown"
33:       End Select
34:
35:       ActiveSheet.Cells(RCount, 2).Value = strType
36:       ActiveSheet.Cells(RCount, 3).Value = CmdBar.Name
37:       RCount = RCount + 1
38:     Next CmdBar
39:
40:     Application.StatusBar = False
41: End Sub
```

3. Your solution to this exercise should look something like this:

```
1:  Sub AddMyMenu()
2:  'adds a menu to the currently active menu bar
3:
4:      Dim CmdBar As CommandBar
5:      Dim aBtn As CommandBarControl
6:
7:      'get a reference to the active menu bar
8:      Set CmdBar = CommandBars.ActiveMenuBar
9:
10:     Set aBtn = CmdBar.Controls.Add(Type:=msoControlPopup, _
11:                                    temporary:=True)
12:     aBtn.Caption = "MyMenu"
13:
```

```
14:    With CmdBar.Controls("MyMenu")
15:      Set aBtn = .Controls.Add(Type:=msoControlButton, _
16:                               temporary:=True)
17:    End With
18:
19:    aBtn.Caption = "Remove this menu"
20:    aBtn.OnAction = "RemoveMyMenu"
21: End Sub
22:
23: Sub RemoveMyMenu()
24: 'removes the custom menu from the menu bar
25:    CommandBars.ActiveMenuBar.Controls("MyMenu").Delete
26: End Sub
```

4. Your solution to this exercise should look something like this:

```
1:    Sub AddVBA_ToolbarExtras()
2:
3:       Dim CmdBar As CommandBar
4:       Dim aBtn As CommandBarControl
5:
6:       Set CmdBar = CommandBars.Add(Name:="VBA Programmer", _
7:                                    Position:=msoBarFloating, _
8:                                    MenuBar:=False, _
9:                                    temporary:=True)
10:      With CmdBar
11:        .Visible = True
12:
13:        'add the New built-in control
14:        .Controls.Add Type:=msoControlButton, _
15:                      ID:=2520, _
16:                      temporary:=True
17:
18:        'add the Help button
19:        Set aBtn = .Controls.Add(Type:=msoControlButton, _
20:                                 temporary:=True)
21:        aBtn.Caption = "VBA Help"
22:        aBtn.FaceId = 49
23:        aBtn.BeginGroup = True
24:        aBtn.OnAction = "ExcelVBAHelp"
25:
26:        'add the Delete button
27:        Set aBtn = .Controls.Add(Type:=msoControlButton, _
28:                                 temporary:=True)
29:        aBtn.Caption = "Delete toolbar"
30:        aBtn.FaceId = 478
31:        aBtn.BeginGroup = True
32:        aBtn.OnAction = "DeleteVBAExtras"
33:      End With
34:    End Sub
35:
```

A

```
36:
37:    Sub ExcelVBAHelp()
38:       Application.Help "vbaxl9.chm"
39:    End Sub
40:
41:
42:    Sub DeleteVBAExtras()
43:       CommandBars("VBA Programmer").Delete
44:    End Sub
```

Day 18, "Error Handling"

Quiz

1. The **On Error Resume Next** statement.

2. VBA stops code execution and displays a runtime error dialog.

3. Certainly! Each set of statements handles a specific kind of error.

4. The **Resume 0** statement, which is usually placed at the end of your error-handling statements.

5. Use the **On Error Goto 0** statement.

6. The **Resume** statement clears VBA's internal runtime error-handling mechanisms. The Err.Clear method also clears VBA's internal runtime error-handling mechanisms.

7. The Error function returns the error message text corresponding to a particular runtime error code. The Err.Description property also returns the error message text of the last error.

8. The Error statement forces a runtime error to occur. (Don't confuse the Error statement, which forces a runtime error, with the Error function, which returns the text of an error message.) The Err.Raise method is the preferred technique for forcing a runtime error.

Exercise

1. Your procedure might look something like this one:

```
1:    Sub MyErrorHandler()
2:
3:       'declare constants
4:       Const ERR_MSG = "Invalid indexes for Mid function"
5:       Const dTitle = "My Error Handler"
6:
7:       'declare variables
8:       Static iStr As String
```

```
9:     Dim eStr As String
10:    Dim pStr As String
11:    Dim Start As Integer
12:    Dim Count As Integer
13:
14:    On Error GoTo BadIndex   'install error trap
15:
16:    'get source string, start index, and number of chars
17:    iStr = InputBox(prompt:="Enter a string", _
18:                 Title:=dTitle, default:=iStr)
19:    pStr = "Enter the index for the first character " & _
20:          "to be extracted."
21:    Start = Val(InputBox(prompt:=pStr, Title:=dTitle))
22:    pStr = "Enter the number of characters to extract."
23:    Count = Val(InputBox(prompt:=pStr, Title:=dTitle))
24:
25:    eStr = Mid(iStr, Start, Count)
26:    MsgBox Buttons:=vbInformation, Title:=dTitle, _
27:          prompt:="'" & iStr & "'" & vbCr & _
28:                  "'" & eStr & "'"
29:    Exit Sub
30:
31: BadIndex:
32:    eStr = ""
33:    MsgBox Buttons:=vbCritical, Title:=dTitle, _
34:          prompt:=ERR_MSG
35:    Resume Next
36: End Sub
```

2. The statements display the string `Hello`.

3. The statements display the string `Jello`.

4. The statements display the following in a message dialog:
```
Jello
11
```

The number 11 indicates that the `Mid` statement caused a runtime error 11 times.

5. The statements display the following:
```
Runtime error number 5
```

Day 19, "Controlling Excel with VBA"

Quiz

1. The `Workbook` object's `Save` method saves the specified workbook to disk with the same filename it had before. The `SaveAs` method works like the File, Save As command, saving the workbook under a new name and also changing the open

workbook's name to the new name. The SaveCopyAs method, however, saves a *copy* of the specified workbook to a different file and leaves the original file unaltered, both on disk and in memory.

2. The workbook is saved using its current name. If the workbook is called Book1, Excel names the file Book1.xls.

   You should use the Workbook object's SaveAs method to assign a name to a new file. You can tell if a file has been saved before by checking whether the workbook's FullName property returns a zero-length string (" ").

3. Excel creates a new workbook to store the copied or moved worksheet.

4. The Worksheets collection contains only the worksheets in the current workbook, whereas the Sheets collection contains worksheets and chart sheets.

5. The three main methods used to return a worksheet range are Range, Cells, and Offset. Range uses either range coordinates or a range name to return a cell or range. Cells uses row and column numbers to return a single cell. Offset returns a range that is offset from another range by a specified number of rows and columns.

6. Both procedures create three-dimensional references across multiple Excel sheets and enter data into the same cell in each sheet. Both sheets use an array (SheetArray) to hold the names of three sheets (Sheet1, Sheet2, and Sheet3).

   In the first procedure (FillAcross), a label is entered in cell A1 of Sheet1 and the FillAcrossSheets method is applied to the Worksheets object. This method, which is the VBA equivalent of the Edit, Fill, Across Worksheets command, uses the following syntax:

   `Object.FillAcrossSheets(Range [,Type])`

   Object is an object reference to a Worksheets collection. *Range* is the range to fill across the worksheets; it must be from one of the sheets in *Object*. *Type* specifies how to copy the range: xlAll, xlContents, or xlFormulas.

   The second procedure uses Select to group the array of worksheets, activates cell A1 in Sheet1, and enters the label in the Selection. This is the equivalent of a technique known as *spearing,* where you select a group of sheets, type in a value, and press Ctrl+Enter.

   Of these two procedures, the first is probably better because you can fill a range—not just a single cell—across the sheets. Likewise, it doesn't use the slow Select and Activate methods.

7. Value always returns the value of a cell, that is, the data stored in the cell or the result of the cell's formula. Formula, on the other hand, either returns the cell's value (if the cell contains a constant) or the cell's formula as a string (if the cell contains a formula).

8. Use `RefersToR1C1` when your range description either is in R1C1-style or is a method or property that returns a range.

9. `Cut` without the `Destination` argument, `Clear`, `ClearContents`, `ClearFormats`, and `ClearNotes`.

Exercises

1. Your solution should look something like this:

```
1:   Option Explicit
2:
3:   Sub SaveAllWorkbooks()
4:   'saves all workbooks
5:
6:      Dim wBook As Workbook
7:      Dim Ans As Integer
8:      Dim mPrompt As String
9:      Dim qBtns As Integer
10:     Dim mTitle As String
11:     Dim NewName As Variant
12:
13:     For Each wBook In Workbooks
14:        'workbook has unsaved changes or a zero-length path?
15:        If (Not wBook.Saved) Or (wBook.Path = "") Then
16:           'If so, check for new, unnamed workbook
17:           If wBook.Path = "" Then
18:              'Ask user if they want to save it
19:              mPrompt = "Do you want to save " & wBook.Name & "?"
20:              qBtns = vbYesNoCancel + vbQuestion
21:              mTitle = "Save All Workbooks"
22:              Ans = MsgBox(Prompt:=mPrompt, Buttons:=qBtns, _
23:                           Title:=mTitle)
24:              Select Case Ans
25:                 Case vbYes  'display GetSaveAsFileName dialog
26:                    NewName = Application.GetSaveAsFilename( _
27:                           InitialFilename:=wBook.Name, _
28:                           FileFilter:="Excel Workbooks,*.xls", _
29:                           Title:=mTitle & " -Select Name")
30:                    If NewName <> False Then
31:                       wBook.SaveAs filename:=NewName
32:                    End If
33:                 Case vbCancel
34:                    Exit Sub    'canceled, bail out
35:              End Select
36:           Else  'Otherwise, just save it
37:              wBook.Save
38:           End If
39:        End If
40:     Next wBook
41:  End Sub
```

2. Here's the code for a multiple selection copy. To convert this procedure to a multiple selection cut, just change the Copy method to a Cut method.

```
1:   Option Explicit
2:
3:   Sub CopyMultipleSelection()
4:
5:      Dim R As Range
6:      Dim SheetStr As String
7:      Dim DestSheet As Worksheet
8:
9:      'Request the name of the sheet
10:     SheetStr = InputBox("Enter the destination sheet name:", _
11:                         "Multiple Selection Copy")
12:
13:     'Check to see if user pressed Cancel
14:     If SheetStr <> "" Then
15:        'If not, convert InputBox string to Worksheet object
16:        Set DestSheet = Worksheets(SheetStr)
17:        'Loop through each area in selection and copy
18:        'it to destination sheet
19:        For Each R In Selection.Areas
20:           R.Copy Destination:=DestSheet.Cells(R.Row, R.Column)
21:        Next R
22:     End If
23:  End Sub
```

3. The first Names.Add method defines the name Test1 to refer to the string constant Sheet1!$A$1. The problem is an incorrect range description in the RefersTo argument:

Names.Add Name:="Test1", RefersTo:="Sheet1!$A$1"

The argument should read RefersTo:="=Sheet1!$A$1".

The second Names.Add method defines Test2 to refer to the *contents* of the cell Sheet1!A1, instead of the cell itself. The problem is the use of the RefersTo argument instead of RefersToR1C1.

The third Names.Add method defines a range name, but the definition of the range changes depending on which cell is the active cell. The problem is that the RefersTo argument uses a relative range ('June Sales'!A1:A10). Unless you specifically need a relative range name, always use absolute references when you define range names.

4. Your procedure should look something like this:

```
1:   Sub EditData()
2:
3:      Dim I As Integer
4:      Dim CurrRow As Integer
```

```
5:        Dim DBColumns As Integer
6:        Dim DBColStart As Integer
7:
8:        'Get current row
9:        CurrRow = ActiveCell.Row
10:       'Get number of columns in Database range
11:       DBColumns = Range("Database").Columns.Count
12:       'Get leftmost column of Database range
13:       DBColStart = Range("Database").Column
14:
15:       'Load record data into dialog form
16:       For I = 1 To DBColumns
17:         Listing13Form.Controls("txt" & CStr(I)).Text = _
18:             Cells(CurrRow, (I + DBColStart) - 1).Value
19:       Next I
21:   End Sub
```

Day 20, "Working with Other Applications"

Quiz

1. The server is the application that supplies the OLE object and provides services for that object. The client is the application that contains the OLE object. Client applications are also sometimes called *container* applications.

2. A linked object contains an image of the server data and maintains a link between the client and server. An embedded object contains not only the server data but also all the underlying information associated with the server application, such as the name of the application, the file structure, and all the formatting codes.

3. The first advantage that you get with OLE is that you can drag and drop data between two open OLE applications. The second advantage is that you can insert objects in-place, that is, you can stay in the same document and the surrounding menus and toolbars change to that of the server application. The third advantage is that you can edit objects in-place, that is, when you double-click an object to edit it, the object remains in the document and the server's tools appear in place of the client's. The fourth advantage is that you can use Automation to control the exposed objects of another OLE application.

4. The Registry database contains information about the Windows applications installed on your computer. The database records data related to the OLE and Automation support of each application, such as the class type for the application's objects.

5. (A) Set `FileName` equal to the name of the document and set `Link` to **True**.

   (B) Set `ClassType` equal to the class type of the presentation graphics program.

   (C) Set `FileName` equal to the name of the bitmap file and either omit `Link` or set it to **False**.

6. A verb tells you what actions can be performed on an OLE object from the point of view of the object's native application.

   The primary verb is the default action that can be performed on an object, in other words, the action that occurs when you double-click the object. Typically, the primary verb will open or edit the OLE object.

7. Automation is a standard by which applications expose their objects to other applications running on the system. Languages such as Visual Basic for Applications can recognize and manipulate these objects by running methods and setting properties.

8. You can refer to the server application's objects directly. You can create new objects with the `CreateObject` function. You can access existing objects by using the `GetObject` function.

9. Executing an application asynchronously means that once VBA has started the application, it immediately returns to the procedure that contains the `Shell` function and continues executing the other statements in the procedure.

10. The `Wait` argument determines whether your procedure waits for the application to process the keystrokes before it continues. If you set `Wait` to **True**, the procedure waits for the application. If you set `Wait` to **False**, the procedure continues executing without waiting for the application.

11. Dynamic-link libraries are collections of functions and procedures that are available to all Windows applications. You can use DLL procedures in your VBA code by declaring the procedures at the module level.

12. The API is the Applications Programming Interface. It is the sum-total of the functions and procedures in the DLLs that come with Windows.

Exercises

1. Your procedure should be similar to the following:

```
1:   Sub EnumerateShapes()
2:       Dim aShape As Shape
3:       Dim aMsg As String
4:
5:       For Each aShape In ActiveSheet.Shapes
6:           With aShape
7:               aMsg = "Type: " & .Type & vbCr
```

```
 8:          aMsg = "Name: " & .Name & vbCr
 9:          If (.OLEFormat Is Nothing) Then
10:            aMsg = aMsg & "Not an OLE object" & vbCr
11:          Else
12:            aMsg = aMsg & "OLE object is "
13:            If .Type = msoEmbeddedOLEObject Then
14:              aMsg = aMsg & "embedded." & vbCr
15:              aMsg = aMsg & "ProgID: " & .OLEFormat.ProgId & vbCr
16:            Else
17:              aMsg = aMsg & "linked." & vbCr
18:            End If
19:          End If
20:        End With
21:        MsgBox prompt:=aMsg, Title:="Enumerate Shapes"
22:      Next aShape
23:    End Sub
```

2. Because Shell is asynchronous, the second Shell—the one that runs Notepad—
   might begin to execute *before* the first Shell (which creates DirList.txt) is finished.
   Therefore, Notepad can't find DirList.txt and it displays an error message.
   (Sometimes, Notepad will display DirList.txt as an empty file.) The solution is to
   insert a delay between the two Shell statements. For example, the following Excel
   VBA statement creates a three-second delay, which should be long enough in most
   cases:

```
Application.Wait Now + TimeValue("00:00:03")
```

Day 21, "Using Event Procedures and Add-Ins"

Quiz

1. An event-handling procedure is a Sub procedure associated with a specific event—
   such as opening or closing a workbook, selecting a worksheet, and so on—exposed
   by an object in Excel. The event-handling procedure is executed automatically
   when the event that it is associated with occurs.

2. Event-handling procedures for an object's events must be stored in that object's
   class module. Only event-handling procedures you install through an event-related
   property or method—such as OnWindow, OnKey, OnTime, and so on—can be stored
   in standard modules.

3. If you assign a zero-length string to the Procedure argument, Excel disables the
   key. If you omit the Procedure argument, the key reverts to its normal behavior,
   which might be nothing.

4. The `EarliestTime` argument is the time when you want the specified event procedure to run. `LatestTime` is the time until which Excel will wait in order to run the procedure if the program is not ready at `EarliestTime`.

5. *Demand-loaded* means that the add-in gets loaded into memory in two stages. First, the add-in's functions, menus, and toolbars are made available. Then, the entire add-in is loaded when the user selects one of the add-in functions, menu commands, or toolbar buttons.

6. Yes, it does. The `Change` event occurs whenever a worksheet cell's value changes, no matter what the source of that change is.

7. The Excel `Application` object's `SheetActivate` event occurs when any sheet in any open workbook is activated.

Exercises

1. As the code below shows, you first declare three variables to hold each of the original settings. You declare these variables at the module level—in other words, outside of any procedures in the module—so that they are available to each procedure. The workbook's `Open` event-handling procedure stores the current settings in the appropriate variable and changes the property to the new value. In the workbook's `BeforeClose` event-handling procedure, use the variables to reinstate the original value of each property.

```
1:   Dim OldDefaultFilePath As String
2:   Dim OldPromptForSummaryInfo As Boolean
3:   Dim OldSheetsInNewWorkbook As Integer
4:
5:   Private Sub Workbook_Open()
6:      With Application
7:         OldDefaultFilePath = .DefaultFilePath
8:         .DefaultFilePath = "C:\VBA21"
9:         OldPromptForSummaryInfo = .PromptForSummaryInfo
10:        .PromptForSummaryInfo = False
11:        OldSheetsInNewWorkbook = .SheetsInNewWorkbook
12:        .SheetsInNewWorkbook = 8
13:     End With
14:  End Sub
15:
16:
17:  Private Sub Workbook_BeforeClose(Cancel As Boolean)
18:     With Application
19:        .DefaultFilePath = OldDefaultFilePath
20:        .PromptForSummaryInfo = OldPromptForSummaryInfo
21:        .SheetsInNewWorkbook = OldSheetsInNewWorkbook
22:     End With
23:  End Sub
```

2. At first glance, it appears that the `Worksheet_Deactivate` event-handling procedure is trying to clean up the current worksheet before moving on to the next sheet. However, `Worksheet_Deactivate` uses the `ActiveSheet` object to perform its tasks. This is a no-no because Excel activates the sheet you're moving to before it generates the `Deactivate` event. This means that every statement inside the **With** affects the new sheet, not the sheet just left.

   If you want to perform tasks on the sheet you're leaving, you must spell out the appropriate `Worksheet` object, for example, `Worksheets("Scratch Pad")`. If you want to use the `Deactivate` event-handling procedure for multiple worksheets, you could declare a **Public** variable to hold the name of the current sheet. You could set this variable in the sheet's `Worksheet_Activate` event procedure and use it again in the `Worksheet_Deactivate` code.

3. Use the following procedures to demonstrate that Excel runs the `OnWindow` event procedure after it runs the `Workbook_Activate` event procedure (the first listing below should be stored in a standard module, the second listing should be stored in the workbook's class module):

```
1:  Sub SetHandlers()
2:      Windows(ThisWorkbook.Name).OnWindow = "OnWindowEventHandler"
3:  End Sub
4:
5:  Sub OnWindowEventHandler()
6:      MsgBox "This is the OnWindow procedure."
7:  End Sub
```

   Place this listing in the workbook's class module:

```
1:  Private Sub Workbook_Activate()
2:      MsgBox "This is the workbook's Activate event procedure."
3:  End Sub
```

4. Your solution might look something like this:

```
1:  Sub Set_CtrlDeleteHandler()
2:      Application.OnKey Key:="^{Del}", _
3:                        Procedure:="DeleteAll"
4:  End Sub
5:
6:  Sub DeleteAll()
7:      Selection.Clear
8:  End Sub
```

5. The `GetInterval` procedure uses `InputBox` to get the number of minutes between events. This is stored in a global variable named `Interval`. Then, `GetInterval` calls the `SetRegularInterval` procedure to initialize the `OnTime` property. `SetRegularInterval` converts the number of minutes in `Interval` to a day

fraction—**CInt**(Interval) / (60 * 24)—and adds this fraction to the Now function. This is stored in the nextTime variable. In the OnTime property, the
EarliestTime argument is set to nextTime and the Procedure argument is set to
SaveWorkbook. The IntervalProc procedure simulates whatever action you want
performed at a regular interval and runs the SetRegularInterval procedure again
to create the next OnTime event. The SetRegularInterval procedure will be called
for as long as the Continue variable remains **True**. The RemoveIntervalProc stops
the renewal of the OnTime event by setting Continue to **False**.

```
1:   Dim Interval As String
2:   Dim Continue As Boolean
3:
4:   Sub GetInterval()
5:     Interval = InputBox("Enter the interval, in minutes:")
6:     Continue = True
7:     SetRegularInterval
8:   End Sub
9:
10:  Sub SetRegularInterval()
11:    Dim nextTime As Date
12:
13:    If Interval <> "" Then
14:      nextTime = Now + CInt(Interval) / (60 * 24)
15:      Application.OnTime EarliestTime:=nextTime, _
16:                         Procedure:="IntervalProc"
17:    End If
18:  End Sub
19:
20:  Sub IntervalProc()
21:    Beep
22:    With Application
23:      .StatusBar = "Interval Procedure now executing."
24:      .Wait Now + TimeValue("00:00:07")
25:      .StatusBar = False
26:    End With
27:    If Continue Then SetRegularInterval
28:  End Sub
29:
30:  Sub RemoveIntervalProc()
31:    Continue = False
32:  End Sub
```

INDEX

Symbols

! (exclamation point)
  placeholder, 217
  Single type-definition
    character, 115
" (quotation marks)
  procedures, 77
  string constants, 121
 # (pound sign)
  date constants, 122
  Double type-definition
    character, 115
  Like operator pattern-
    matching character, 155
  placeholder, 216
**#VALUE! error (work-
    sheets), 248**
$ (dollar sign)
  placeholder, 216
  String type-definition
    character, 115

% (percent sign)
  Alt key code (OnKey
    method), 967
  Alt key code (SendKeys
    statement), 931
  Integer type-definition
    character, 115
  placeholder, 216
& (ampersand)
  command bar controls,
    776
  concatenation operator,
    138, 164, 170
    adding string charac-
      ters, 211
    syntax, 164
  Long type-definition char-
    acter, 115, 165
  placeholder, 217
**' (apostrophe), comments,
  62**

( ) parentheses
  array subscripts, 567-568
  ignoring values, 273
  operator precedence rules,
    167
  macro names, 61
  TypeName function, 409
; (colon)
  placeholder, 217
  same-line statements, 312
**>= (greater than equal to),
  150**
> (greater than)
  comparison operator, 150
  placeholder, 217
  sorting arrays, 597
<= (less than equal to), 150
< (less than)
  comparison operator, 150
  placeholder, 217
  sorting arrays, 597

Other Related Titles

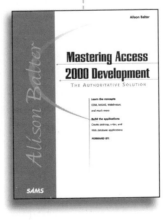